Germany

Hamburg &
the North
p152

Lower Saxony
& Bremen
p693

Berlin
p58
⭐

Around
Berlin
p136

Cologne &
Northern Rhineland
p628

Central
Germany
p221

Saxony
p291

Frankfurt &
Southern Rhineland
p533

Bavaria
p385

Stuttgart & the
Black Forest
p467

Munich
p338

Marc Di Duca, Anthony Ham, Catherine Le Nevez, Ali Lemer,
Andrea Schulte-Peevers, Benedict Walker, Kerry
Hugh McNaughtan, Leonid Ragozin

Mar 2019

Contents

ON THE ROAD

MPAYNE13/BUDGET TRAVEL©

Contents

EAST SIDE GALLERY P89

Welcome to Germany

Prepare for a roller-coaster ride of feasts, treats and temptations experiencing Germany's soul-stirring scenery, spirit-lifting culture, big-city beauties, romantic palaces and half-timbered towns.

Bewitching Scenery

There's something undeniably artistic in the way Germany's scenery unfolds; the corrugated, dune-fringed coasts of the north; the moody forests, romantic river valleys and vast vineyards of the centre; and the off-the-charts splendour of the Alps, carved into rugged glory by glaciers and the elements. All of these are integral parts of a magical natural matrix that's bound to give your camera batteries a good workout. Get off the highway and into the great outdoors to soak up the epic landscapes that make each delicious, slow, winding mile so precious.

Pleasures of Civilisation

You'll encounter history in towns where streets were laid out long before Columbus set sail, and in castles that loom above prim, half-timbered villages where flower boxes billow with crimson geraniums. The great cities – Berlin, Munich and Hamburg – come in more flavours than a jar of jelly beans but all will wow you with a cultural kaleidoscope that spans the arc from art museums and high-brow opera to naughty cabaret and underground clubs. And wherever you go, Romanesque, Gothic and baroque classics rub rafters with architectural creations from modern masters such as Daniel Libeskind, David Chipperfield and Frank Gehry.

Gastro Delights

Experiencing Germany through its food and drink will add a rich layer to your memories (and possibly to your belly!). You'll quickly discover that the local food is so much more than sausages and pretzels, schnitzel and roast pork accompanied by big mugs of foamy beer. Beyond the clichés awaits a cornucopia of regional and seasonal palate-teasers. Share the German people's obsession with white asparagus in springtime, chanterelle mushrooms in summer and game in autumn. Sample not only the famous beer but also world-class wines, most notably the noble Riesling.

High on History

Few countries have had as much impact on the world as Germany, which has given us the Hanseatic League, the Reformation and, yes, Hitler and the Holocaust, but also the printing press, the automobile, aspirin and MP3 technology. It's the birthplace of Martin Luther, Albert Einstein and Karl Marx, of Goethe, Beethoven, the Brothers Grimm and other heavyweights who have left their mark on human history. You can stand in a Roman amphitheatre, sleep in a medieval castle and walk along remnants of the Berlin Wall – in Germany the past is very much present wherever you go.

Why I Love Germany

By Kerry Christiani, Writer

My first trip to Germany some 20 years ago sparked a lifelong love affair. The snowbound spruce forests and castle-topped villages of Bavaria and the Black Forest were more ludicrously beautiful than my wildest childhood dreams. I was so smitten with the south of the country that I spent six years living in the depths of the Black Forest: hiking, cycling and berry picking in summer, mushrooming in the crisp days of autumn, and cross-country skiing in winters where the landscape was transformed into a Christmas card scene. Still today, when I return to the *Schwarzwald,* it's like coming home.

For more about our writers, see p848

Above: The Black Forest (p490)

Germany

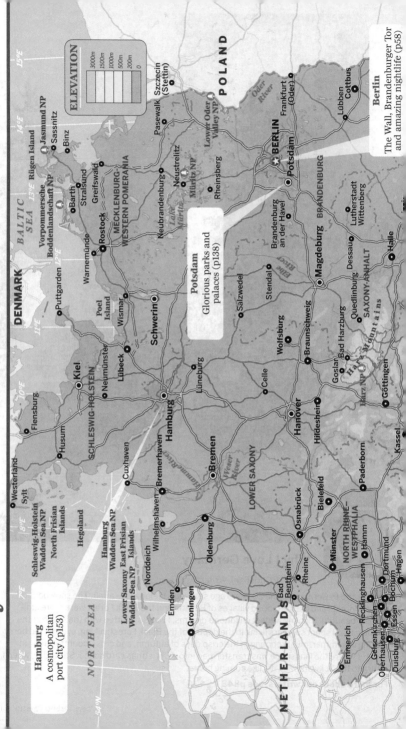

Hamburg
A cosmopolitan port city (p153)

Potsdam
Glorious parks and palaces (p138)

Berlin
The Wall, Brandenburger Tor and amazing nightlife (p58)

ELEVATION

3000m
1500m
1000m
500m
200m
0

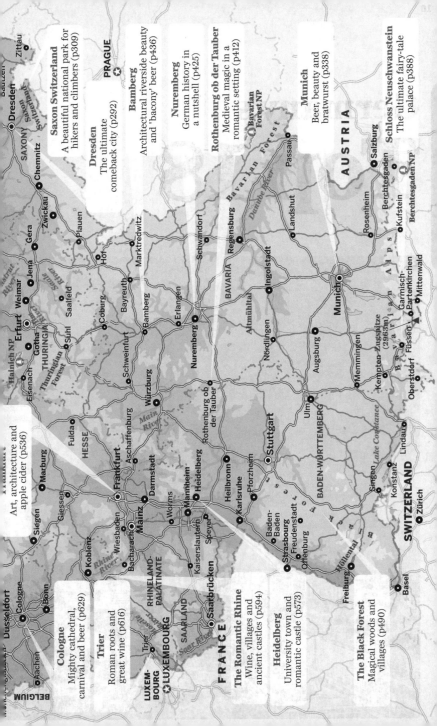

Saxon Switzerland
A beautiful national park for hikers and climbers (p309)

Dresden
The ultimate comeback city (p292)

Bamberg
Architectural riverside beauty and 'bacony' beer (p436)

Nuremberg
German history in a nutshell (p425)

Rothenburg ob der Tauber
Medieval magic in a romantic setting (p412)

Munich
Beer, beauty and bratwurst (p338)

Schloss Neuschwanstein
The ultimate fairy-tale palace (p388)

Art, architecture and apple cider (p536)

Cologne
Mighty cathedral, carnival and beer (p629)

Trier
Roman roots and great wine (p616)

The Romantic Rhine
Wine, villages and ancient castles (p594)

Heidelberg
University town and romantic castle (p573)

The Black Forest
Magical woods and villages (p490)

PRAGUE

SAXONY

Dresden

Zittau

Bautzen

Chemnitz

Zwickau

Gera

Plauen

Hof

Marktredwitz

Bayreuth

Bamberg

Erlangen

Nuremberg

Schwandorf

Regensburg

Bavarian Forest NP

Passau

AUSTRIA

Salzburg

Berchtesgaden

Kufstein

Berchtesgaden NP

Rosenheim

Landshut

Ingolstadt

Altmühl

Nördlingen

Augsburg

Munich

Memmingen

Kempten

Zugspitze (2963m)

Garmisch-Partenkirchen

Mittenwald

Oberstdorf

Füssen

B a v a r i a n   A l p s

BAVARIA

Danube River

Bavarian Forest

Schweinfurt

Würzburg

Rothenburg ob der Tauber

Ulm

Stuttgart

Heilbronn

Pforzheim

Karlsruhe

BADEN-WÜRTTEMBERG

Baden-Baden

Freudenstadt

Offenburg

Strasbourg

Freiburg

Höllental

Basel

SWITZERLAND

Zürich

Konstanz

Singen

Lindau

Lake Constance

B l a c k   F o r e s t

Coburg

Saalfeld

Suhl

Jena

Weimar

Erfurt

Gotha

Eisenach

THURINGIA

Thuringian Forest

Hainich NP

Marburg

Giessen

Siegen

Fulda

HESSE

Aschaffenburg

Frankfurt

Darmstadt

Mainz

Wiesbaden

Worms

Mannheim

Heidelberg

Speyer

Kaiserslautern

Saarbrücken

SAARLAND

RHINELAND-PALATINATE

Saar River

Trier

Mosel River

Bacharach

Koblenz

Rhine River

Bonn

Cologne

Düsseldorf

Aachen

BELGIUM

Nahe River

Saale River

Main River

Neckar River

LUXEMBOURG

FRANCE

Düsseldorf

Germany's
Top 18

Berlin

1 Berlin's (p58) alternative edge, exciting food scene, palpable history and urban glamour never fail to enthral and enchant. More than a quarter century after the Wall's collapse, the German capital has grown up without relinquishing its indie spirit and penchant for creative improvisation. There's haute cuisine in a former brewery, all-night parties in power stations and world-class art in a WWII bunker. Visit major historical sights – including the Reichstag, Brandenburger Tor and Checkpoint Charlie – then feast on a smorgasbord of culture in myriad museums. Below left: Fernsehturm (p72)

Munich

2 If you are looking for Alpine clichés, Munich (p338) will hand them to you in one chic and compact package. But the Bavarian capital also has plenty of unexpected trump cards under its often bright-blue skies. Here, folklore and age-old traditions exist side by side with sleek BMWs, designer boutiques and high-powered industry. The city's museums showcase everything from artistic masterpieces to technological treasures and Oktoberfest history, while its music and cultural scenes are second only to those found in Berlin. Below right: Museum Brandhorst (p351)

CANADASTOCK/SHUTTERSTOCK ©

CHRISTIAN BEIRLE GONZÁLEZ/GETTY IMAGES ©

Schloss Neuschwanstein

3 Commissioned by Bavaria's most celebrated 19th-century monarch, King Ludwig II, Schloss Neuschwanstein (p388) rises from the Alpine forests like a storybook illustration. Inside, the make-believe continues, with chambers reflecting Ludwig's obsession with the mythical Teutonic past – and his admiration of composer Wagner – in a confection that puts even the flashiest oligarch's *palazzo* in the shade. This folly is said to have inspired Walt's castle at Disney World; now it inspires travellers to make the pilgrimage along the Romantic Road, which culminates at its gates.

The Black Forest

4 Mist, snow or shine, the deep, dark Black Forest (p490) is just beautiful. If it's back-to-nature moments you're after, this sylvan slice of southwestern Germany is the place to linger. Every valley reveals new surprises: half-timbered villages looking every inch the fairy-tale fantasy, thunderous waterfalls, cuckoo clocks the size of houses. Breathe in the cold, sappy air, drive roller-coaster roads to middle-of-nowhere lakes, have your cake, walk it off on trail after trail, then hide away in a heavy-lidded farmhouse. Hear that? Silence. What a wonderful thing. Top right: Schiltach (p501)

3

The Romantic Rhine

5 As the mighty Rhine flows from Rüdesheim to Koblenz (p594), the landscape's unique face-off between rock and water creates a magical mix of the wild (churning whirlpools, dramatic cliffs), the agricultural (near-vertical vineyards), the medieval (hilltop castles, half-timbered hamlets), the legendary (Loreley) and the modern (in the 19th-century sense: barges, ferries, passenger steamers and trains). From every riverside village, trails take you through vineyards and forests, up to panoramic viewpoints and massive stone fortresses, and back to a romantic evening spent sampling the local wines.

Heidelberg

6 The 19th-century romantics found sublime beauty and spiritual inspiration in Germany's oldest university town (p573) and so, in his way, did Mark Twain, who was beguiled by the ruins of the hillside castle. Generations of students have attended lectures, sung lustily with beer steins in hand, carved their names into tavern tables and, occasionally, been sent to the student jail. All of this has left its mark on the modern-day city, where age-old traditions endure alongside world-class research, innovative cultural events and a sometimes raucous nightlife scene.
Universitätsbibliothek (p574)

Bamberg

7 Often overlooked by travellers but actually one of Germany's most attractive towns, Bamberg (p436) is a medieval and baroque masterwork chockfull of Unesco-listed townhouses that were mercifully spared the destruction of WWII. Half of the Altstadt's beauty comes from its location straddling two waterways, the River Regnitz and the Rhine-Main-Danube Canal. Away from the urban eye candy, lower-brow entertainment is provided by Bamberg's numerous brewpubs, which cook up the town's unique *Rauchbier* (smoked beer) – some say it tastes a bit like bacon.
Schlenkerla tavern (p440)

Trier

8 There was a time when Trier (p616) was the capital of Western Europe. That time was 2000 years ago, when Emperor Constantine ruled the fading Roman Empire from here. Nowhere else in Germany has the Roman legacy survived as beautifully and tangibly as in this charming town with its ancient amphitheatre, thermal baths and Porta Nigra city gate (p616; pictured above right) – Unesco noticed, designating nine World Heritage sites. Today, Germany's oldest city is as unhurried as the Moselle River it sits on, within a grape toss of the country's finest – and steepest – vineyards.

German Food & Drink

9 If you crave traditional German comfort food, you'll certainly find plenty of places to indulge in a meat-potato-cabbage diet. These days, though, 'typical' German fare (p44) is lighter, healthier, more creative and prepared with seasonal and locally sourced ingredients. The cities especially brim with organic eateries, gourmet kitchens, vegan bistros and a UN's worth of ethnic restaurants. Talented chefs have been racking up the Michelin stars, especially in the Black Forest. And then there's German beer and bread. Is there any other country that does either better?

MARK READ/LONELY PLANET ©

9

Potsdam

10 We can almost guarantee that your camera will have a love affair with Potsdam's (p138) marvellous palaces, idyllic parks, stunning views, inspired architecture and tantalising Cold War sites. Just across the Glienicke 'spy bridge' from Berlin, the state capital of Brandenburg was catapulted to prominence by King Frederick the Great. His giddily rococo Schloss Sanssouci (p138; pictured above top) is the glorious crown of this Unesco-recognised cultural tapestry that synthesises 18th-century artistic trends from around Europe in one stupendous masterpiece.

Rothenburg ob der Tauber

11 With its jumble of neatly restored half-timbered houses enclosed by sturdy ramparts, Rothenburg ob der Tauber (p412) lays on the medieval cuteness with a trowel. (One might even say it's too cute for its own good, if the deluges of day trippers are any indication.) The trick is to experience this historical wonderland at its most magical: early or late in the day, when the last coaches have hit the road and you can soak up the romance all by yourself on gentle strolls along moonlit cobbled lanes.

Hamburg

12 Anyone who thinks Germany doesn't have round-the-clock delights hasn't been to Hamburg (p153). This ancient, wealthy city on the Elbe traces it roots back to the Hanseatic League and beyond. By day you can tour its magnificent port, explore its history in restored quarters and discover shops selling goods you didn't think were sold. By night, some of Europe's best music clubs pull in the punters, and diversions for virtually every other taste are plentiful as well. And then, another Hamburg day begins. Top: HafenCity (p157)

Dresden

13 The apocalypse came on a February night in 1945 – hours of carpet-bombing reduced Germany's 'Florence on the Elbe' (p292) to a smouldering pile of bricks. The dead Dresden's comeback is nothing short of a miracle. Reconstructed architectural jewels pair with stunning art collections that justify the city's place in the pantheon of European cultural capitals. Add to that an energetic pub quarter, Daniel Libeskind's dramatically redesigned Military History Museum (p298; pictured above) and a tiara of villas and palaces lining up along the river and you've got one enticing package of discovery.

SEANPAVONEPHOTO/GETTY IMAGES /ISTOCKPHOTO ©

Nuremberg

14 Capital of Franco-
nia, an independ-
ent region until 1806,
Nuremberg (p425) may
conjure visions of Nazi
rallies and grisly war trials, but there's so much
more to this energetic
city. Dürer hailed from the
Altstadt, his house now
a museum. Germany's
first railway trundled
from here to neighbour-
ing Fürth, leaving a trail of
choo-choo heritage. And
Germany's toy capital has
heaps of things for kids to
enjoy. When you're done
with sightseeing, the local
beer is as dark as the coffee and best employed to
chase down Nuremberg's
delicious finger-sized
bratwurst.

Cologne Cathedral

15 At unexpected
moments you see
it: Cologne's cathedral
(p629), the city's twin-
towered icon, looming
over an urban vista and
the timeless course of the
Rhine. And why shouldn't
it? This perfectly formed
testament to faith and
conviction was started in
1248 and completed six
centuries later. You can
feel the echoes of the passage of time as you sit in
its soaring stained-glass-lit
and artwork-filled interior.
Climb the 95m-high tower
for views of the surrounding city that are like no
others.

Saxon Switzerland

16 Isn't nature incredible? This is the first
thought that springs to
mind when you clap eyes
on the sandstone won-
derland of the Sächsische
Schweiz (p309), just south
of Dresden. A bizarre
rockscape of pinnacles,
buttresses, mesas and
spires, this national park –
a favourite of 19th-century
Romantic artists – is ar-
restingly beautiful. And its
beauty, some say, is best
appreciated by hitting one
of the many hiking trails
leading deep into thick
forest or to medieval castle
ruins. Free climbers are in
their element in these
rugged heights.

Oktoberfest

17 Anyone with a taste for hops-scented froth knows that the daddy of all beer festivals, Oktoberfest (p360), takes place annually in Munich. The world's favourite suds-fest actually begins in mid-September and runs for 16 ethanol-fuelled days on the Theresienwiese (Theresa's Meadow), with troops of crimson-faced oompah bands entertaining revellers; armies of traditionally garbed locals and foreigners guzzling their way through seven million litres of lager; and entire farms of chickens hitting the grill. So find your favourite tent and raise your 1L stein. '*O'zapft is!*' (The tap is in!).

Frankfurt

18 Germany's financial capital, Frankfurt (p536) may first appear all buttoned up, but behind the corporate demeanour lurks a city brimming with cultural, culinary and shopping diversions. The best way to discover the city's soul is to head away from the high-rises. It's easy to join Frisbee-tossing locals in the grassy parkland along the Main River (pictured below), grab an espresso at an old-time cafe, go museum-hopping along the riverbank and sip tart *Ebbelwei* (apple cider) while tucking into hearty local fare at a wood-panelled tavern.

Need to Know

For more information, see Survival Guide (p801)

Currency
Euro (€)

Language
German

Visas
Generally not required for tourist stays up to 90 days (or at all for EU nationals); some nationalities need a Schengen Visa (p810).

Money
ATMs widely available in cities and towns, rarely in villages. Credit cards are not widely accepted.

Mobile Phones
Mobile phones operate on GSM 900/1800. If you have a European or Australian phone, save money by slipping in a German SIM card.

Time
Central European Time (GMT/UTC plus one hour).

When to Go

Warm to hot summers, mild winters
Warm to hot summers, cold winters
Mild summers, cold winters
Cold climate

Hamburg
GO May–Sep

Berlin
GO May, Jun, Sep & Oct

Frankfurt
GO May–Sep

Munich
GO Apr, May, Sep & Oct

Freiburg
GO Jun–Sep & Dec

High Season (Jul–Aug)

➡ Busy roads and long lines at key sights.

➡ Vacancies at a premium and higher prices in seaside and mountain resorts.

➡ Festivals celebrate everything from music to wine and sailing to samba.

Shoulder Season (Apr–Jun, Sep–Oct)

➡ Expect smaller crowds and lower prices, except on public holidays.

➡ Blooming, colourful flowers in spring and radiant foliage in autumn.

➡ Sunny, temperate weather that's ideal for outdoor pursuits and exploration.

Low Season (Nov–Mar)

➡ No queues but shorter hours at key sights, some of which may close for the season.

➡ Theatre, concert and opera season in full swing.

➡ Ski resorts busiest in January and February.

Useful Websites

Lonely Planet (www.lonely planet.com/germany) Destination information, hotel bookings, traveller forum and more.

German National Tourist Office (www.germany.travel) The low-down on every aspect of travel in Germany, with handy maps and a personal travel planner.

Deutsche Welle (www.dw.com) The latest news in English.

Facts About Germany (www. tatsachen-ueber-deutschland. de/en) Reference tool covering all aspects of German society.

Deutschland Online (www. magazine-deutschland.de) Insightful features on culture, business and politics.

Online German course (www. deutsch-lernen.com) Brush up on your *Deutsch* with free online lessons – from beginners to advanced.

Important Numbers

Germany's country code	☏49
International access code	☏00
Ambulance, fire brigade	☏112
Police	☏110

Exchange Rates

Australia	A$1	€0.62
Canada	C$1	€0.65
Japan	¥100	€0.75
New Zealand	NZ$1	€0.56
UK	UK£1	€1.12
US	US$1	€0.85

For current exchange rates see www.xe.com.

Daily Costs

Budget: Less than €120

➡ Hostel, camping or private room: €15–30

➡ Low-cost meal or self-catering: up to €8

➡ Day ticket on public transport: €5–7

Midrange: €120–200

➡ Private apartment or double room: €60–120

➡ Three-course dinner at a good restaurant: €30–40

➡ Couple of beers in a pub or beer garden: €8

Top end: More than €200

➡ Fancy loft apartment or double in top hotel: from €150

➡ Sit-down lunch or dinner at top-rated restaurant: €100

➡ Concert or opera tickets: €50–150

Opening Hours

The following are typical opening hours; these may vary seasonally and between cities and villages. We've provided those applicable in high season.

Banks 9am to 4pm Monday to Friday, extended hours usually Tuesday and Thursday, some open Saturday

Bars 6pm to 1am

Cafes 8am to 8pm

Clubs 11pm to early morning

Post offices 9am to 6pm Monday to Friday, 9am–1pm Saturday

Restaurants 11am to 11pm (food service often stops at 9pm in rural areas)

Major stores and supermarkets 9.30am to 8pm Monday to Saturday (shorter hours outside city centres)

Arriving in Germany

Frankfurt Airport *S-Bahn* train lines S8 and S9 link the airport with the city centre several times hourly for €4.90 (11 minutes). Taxis make the trip in 20 to 30 minutes and average €30.

Munich Airport The S1 and S8 trains link the airport with the city centre in 40 minutes (€10.80). The Lufthansa Airport Bus (€10.50) departs every 20 minutes and takes about the same time as the train. A taxi costs about €60.

Getting Around

Germans are whizzes at moving people around, and the public transport network is one of the best in Europe. The best ways of getting around the country are by car and by train.

Train Extensive network of long-distance and regional trains with frequent departures; fairly expensive but numerous deals available.

Car Useful for travelling at your own pace or for visiting regions with no or minimal public transport. Cars can be hired in every town and city. Drive on the right.

Bus Cheaper and slower than trains and with a growing long-haul network. Regional bus services fill the gaps in areas not served by rail.

Air Only useful for longer distances, eg Hamburg to Munich or Berlin to Munich.

For much more on **getting around**, see p815

First Time Germany

For more information, see Survival Guide (p801)

Checklist

➡ Make sure your passport is valid for at least four months

➡ Make advance bookings for events, travel, accommodation and sights

➡ Check the airline baggage restrictions

➡ Alert your credit-/debit-card company

➡ Organise travel insurance (p806)

➡ Check your mobile/cell phone (p809) restrictions

➡ Find out what you need to hire (p817) a car

What to Pack

➡ Good walking shoes and a daypack for mountain and forest trails

➡ Travel adapter plug

➡ Umbrella/raincoat

➡ Bathing suit

➡ Sunhat and sunglasses

➡ Ski gear and multiple layers (in winter)

➡ Pocket knife

➡ Curiosity and a sense of humour

Top Tips for Your Trip

➡ As much fun as it is to tear up the rubber on the autobahn, make sure you get onto some country roads to sample the sublime scenery.

➡ Go local. A destination's spirit best reveals itself to those leaving the main sights and walking around a neighbourhood.

➡ Don't be shy about chatting to strangers. Most Germans speak at least a few words of English. Ask locals for recommendations.

➡ Make the most of local money-saving guest cards; look out for the *Sparpreis* (saver fare) when you book with Deutsche Bahn in advance.

What to Wear

Anything goes, but if you want to blend in, remember that Hamburg, Stuttgart, Frankfurt and Munich are considerably more fashion-conscious than Berlin, Cologne or Dresden. Since the weather is unpredictable, even in summer, bring layers of clothing. A waterproof coat and sturdy shoes are a good idea. Winters can get fiercely cold, so pack gloves, a hat, and a heavy coat and boots. For evening wear, smart casual is the norm, but upmarket places may insist on shoes (not trainers) and trousers or dresses instead of jeans. Jackets and ties are only required in casinos and at the most formal establishments.

Sleeping

Outside of high season, around holidays and during major trade shows it's generally not necessary to book accommodation in advance.

Hotels Range from mom-and-pop joints to restored castles and international chains.

Hostels Both indie hostels and those belonging to Hostelling International are plentiful.

Ferienwohnungen Furnished flats and holiday homes, particularly prevalent in rural areas. Inexpensive option for families and groups.

Gasthäuser/Gasthöfe Country inns, often in lovely locations, offer cultural immersion and a restaurant.

Pensionen The German version of B&Bs is prevalent in rural areas and offers good value.

Money

Germany is still largely a cash-based society and credit card use is not common. International hotel chains, high-end restaurants, department stores and fancy boutiques usually accept credit cards, but enquire first. Mastercard and Visa are more widely accepted than American Express and Diners Club. ATMs are ubiquitous in towns and cities but not usually in rural areas. ATMs do not recognise PINs with more than four digits.

For more information, see p807.

Bargaining

Gentle haggling is common at flea markets; in all other instances you're expected to pay the stated price. In hotels, you may get a better rate if you're staying more than one night.

Tipping

Hotels €1 per bag is standard. It's nice to leave a little cash for the room cleaners (€1 or €2 per day).

Restaurants Bills always include *Bedienung* (service charge); most people add 5% or 10% unless service was truly abhorrent.

Bars About 5%, rounded to nearest euro. For drinks brought to your table, tip as for restaurants.

Taxis Tip about 10%, rounded to the nearest euro.

Toilet attendants Loose change.

Language

In all but the most off-the-radar places, it is perfectly possible to travel in Germany without speaking a word of German, but life gets easier – and more enjoyable – if you master a few basic phrases. People are more likely to speak English in big cities, the western part of the country and in tourist hot-spots. Things get a little trickier in rural areas, especially in the former East Germany.

1 **Do you accept credit cards?**
Nehmen Sie Kreditkarten?
nay·men zee kre·deet·kar·ten

Cash is still king in Germany, so don't assume you'll be able to pay by credit card – it's best to enquire first.

2 **Which beer would you recommend?**
Welches Bier empfehlen Sie?
vel·khes beer emp·fay·len zee

Who better to ask for advice on beer than the Germans, whether at a beer garden, hall, cellar or on a brewery tour?

3 **Can I get this without meat?**
Kann ich das ohne Fleisch bekommen?
kan ikh das aw·ne flaish be·ko·men

In the land of *Wurst* and *Schnitzel* it may be difficult to find a variety of vegetarian meals, especially in smaller towns.

4 **Do you speak English?**
Sprechen Sie Englisch?
shpre·khen zee eng·lish

Given Berlin's cosmopolitan tapestry, the answer will most likely be 'yes' but it's still polite not to assume and to ask first.

5 **Do you run original versions?**
Spielen auch Originalversionen?
shpee·len owkh o·ri·gi·nahl·fer·zi·aw·nen

German cinemas usually run movies dubbed into German – look for a cinema that runs subtitled original versions.

Etiquette

Germany is a fairly formal society; the following tips will help you avoid faux pas.

Greetings Shake hands and say 'Guten Morgen' (before noon), 'Guten Tag' (between noon and 6pm) or 'Guten Abend' (after 6pm). Use the formal 'Sie' (you) with strangers and only switch to the informal 'du' and first names if invited to do so. With friends and children, use first names and 'du'.

Asking for Help Germans use the same word, 'Entschuldigung', to say 'excuse me' (to attract attention) and 'sorry' (to apologise).

Eating & Drinking At the table, say 'Guten Appetit' before digging in. Germans hold the fork in the left hand and the knife in the right hand. To signal that you have finished eating, lay your knife and fork parallel across your plate. If drinking wine, the proper toast is 'Zum Wohl', with beer it's 'Prost'.

What's New

Elbphilharmonie

The icing on the cake of Hamburg's re-vamped HafenCity waterfront district is this architecturally striking concert hall and performance space, courtesy of Pritz-ker Prize winning architects Herzog & de Meuron. (p157)

Swabian Alps

Cue prehistory: the cave-riddled Swabian Alps are having a moment after snap-ping up Unesco World Heritage status in 2017 for their peerless stash of ice age art, dating from 43,000 to 33,000 years ago. (p479)

Urban Nation

Click into Berlin's ever-evolving street art scene at this museum bringing urban artists with attitude and edge to the fore. Even the facade itself is a giant canvas. (p100)

Bauhaus Museum

Weimar's new Bauhaus Museum is set to open just in time for the seminal artistic movement's centenary in 2019. (p794)

Weissenhof Estate

The clean-lined aesthetic of Le Corbusier's modernist residential buildings shine at the newly reopened Weissenhof Estate in Stuttgart. Unesco approved. (p470)

Pergamon Panorama

Unveiled in summer 2018 in a space oppo-site the Pergamonmuseum, Yadegar Asisi's mind-blowing 360-degree panorama wings you back to Ancient Greece. (p79)

Dresden's Zwinger

Dresden's number one baroque palace is undergoing a major revamp and is set to shine again in all its lavish glory when it reopens in 2019. (p293)

Gin Monkey

The global thirst for quality craft gins shows no sign of waning, and Monkey 47 (p501) is swinging with its Black Forest botanicals and distillery tours (free but make sure you book well ahead).

Testturm

Going up... Rottweil's futuristic, 246m-high Testturm, open to the public since late 2017, has Germany's highest lookout platform and ravishing views of the Black Forest. (p519)

Hochmoselbrücke

Straddling the Moselle Valley, this 1.7km new road bridge is slated to open in late 2018, linking Ürzig and Zeltingen-Rachtig and providing speedy links to the Frank-furt area and beyond. (p609)

Museum Barberini

Opened in 2017, this outstanding Potsdam museum lodges in a replica baroque Ro-man palazzo. The collection of old and modern masters was bankrolled by bil-lionaire software magnate Hasso Plattner. (p141)

For more recommendations and reviews, see lonelyplanet.com/germany

If You Like...

Castles & Palaces

Over centuries, Germany has collected castles and palaces the way some people collect stamps – a legacy of the feudal system that saw the country divided into hundreds of fiefdoms until its 1871 unification.

Schloss Neuschwanstein Germany's most famous palace was the inspiration for Disney's *Sleeping Beauty* castle. (p388)

Wartburg Martin Luther translated the New Testament into German while hiding at this Eisenach medieval castle. (p254)

Schloss Heidelberg Destroyed repeatedly throughout the centuries, there's still a majesty surrounding this red-sandstone hilltop Gothic pile. (p573)

Burg Hohenzollern Every inch the fairy-tale dream, this castle's the ancestral seat of the Prussian ruling family. (p482)

Romantic Rhine Castles More than a dozen medieval robber-baron hang-outs straddle craggy hilltops along this fabled river stretch. (p594)

Schloss Sanssouci Frederick the Great sought solace amid the intimate splendour of his Potsdam summer palace. (p138)

Churches & Cathedrals

More than places of worship, Germany's churches and cathedrals are also great architectural monuments often filled with priceless treasures reflecting artistic acumen through the ages.

Kölner Dom The riverside twin spires of the Germany's largest cathedral dominate Cologne's skyline. (p629)

Aachener Dom Some 30 German kings were crowned where Charlemagne lies buried in an elaborate gilded shrine. (p655)

Schlosskirche Martin Luther is buried inside the church where he pinned his 95 theses in 1517. (p285)

Wieskirche Rococo church rising from an Alpine meadow where a miracle-working Jesus statue was found. (p423)

Frauenkirche Dresden's harmoniously proportioned church rose from the ashes of WWII with this spitting-image replica. (p293)

Ulmer Münster The world's tallest steeple tops this Goliath of cathedrals, which took 500 years to build. (p484)

Enchanting Villages

There's no simpler pleasure than strolling around a charismatic village laced with time-worn lanes, peppered with ancient churches and anchored by a fountain-studded square.

Quedlinburg Drift around this medieval warren of cobbled lanes lined by more than 1400 half-timbered houses. (p268)

Lindau Pastel-painted Lindau has a 9th-century pedigree and a to-die-for location on a Lake Constance island. (p530)

Bacharach Pint-sized medieval Moselle town flanked by vineyards and lorded over by a mighty castle. (p599)

Schiltach In the Kinzig Valley, this romantic Black Forest town oozes history from every flower-festooned facade. (p501)

Görlitz Germany's easternmost town is so pristinely preserved that it's often used as a film location. (p331)

Celle A radiant old-world gem with colourfully painted and ornately carved half-timbered buildings. (p706)

Cochem Petite, pretty Moselle town with a hilltop castle and pastel houses. (p610)

WWII Sites

Shudder at the atrocities committed by the Nazis, then honour those who gave their lives to rid the world of the Third Reich at these original sites.

Berchtesgaden Alpine town home to Hitler's southern headquarters at the Dokumentation Obersalzberg, and the 'Eagle's Nest'. (p404)

Concentration Camps WWII's darkest side is commemorated at Bergen-Belsen (p709), Buchenwald (p244), Dachau (p382), Mittelbau Dora (p262), Sachsenhausen (p144) and Neuengamme (p180) camps.

Haus der Wannsee-Konferenz Nazis plotted the 'Final Solution' – the systematic deportation and murder of Jews – at this villa. (p103)

Historisch-Technisches Museum The deadly V2 rocket was developed in a Usedom Island research facility, now this museum. (p219)

Nuremberg See the site of Nazi mass rallies at the Reichsparteitagsgelände, then visit the Nuremberg Trials courtroom. (p425)

Laboe Clamber around WWII-era U-Boat 995 in this town on Kiel Firth. (p189)

Denkort Bunker Valentin This former submarine factory, built with slave labour, was one of Nazi Germany's largest military projects. (p722)

Topographie des Terrors The site where the Gestapo headquarters and SS central command once stood. (p77)

Hamburg A window into Nazi horrors at Bullenhuser Damm Schule and former concentration camp Gedenkstätte Neuengamme. (p180)

Top: A replica of Martin Luther's desk at Wartburg (p254)

Bottom: The entrance to the Gedenkstätte Buchenwald (p244) outside Weimar

Jewish Sites

Jewish history in Germany is often equated with the Holocaust, but not even the Nazis could wipe out 1600 years of Jewish life and cultural contributions to this country.

Holocaust Memorial Peter Eisenman poignantly captures the Holocaust's horror with this vast undulating maze of tomb-like plinths. (p71)

Jüdisches Museum Extraordinary zinc-clad building that's a powerful metaphor for Berlin's chronicle of Jewish life in Germany. (p85)

Ulmer Synagogue Ulm's architectural showstopper sits near where the former synagogue was destroyed during Kristallnacht in 1938. (p485)

Judenhof The oldest, largest and best preserved *Mikwe* (ritual bath) north of the Alps. (p581)

Museum Judengasse This recently revamped museum traces Jewish life, with remains of Frankfurt's former ghetto. (p539)

Stolpersteine Blocks embedded in pavements throughout Germany marking the last residences of Jews deported by Nazis. (p77)

Alte Synagoge Dating partly to the 11th century, this synagogue in Erfurt is one of Europe's oldest. (p240)

Train Journeys

Slow travel was never more fun than aboard Germany's historical trains, some of them more than 100 years old and pulled by steam locomotives.

Zugspitzbahn Have your breath literally taken away on this pulse-quickening journey up Germany's tallest mountain. (p394)

Molli Schmalspurbahn This pint-sized train has shuttled through gorgeous scenery from Bad Doberan to Heiligendamm since 1886. (p207)

Harzer Schmalspurbahnen The mother lode for narrow-gauge train fans traverses the Harz Mountains on three scenic routes. (p273)

Lössnitzgrundbahn The most scenic approach to Moritzburg Castle near Dresden is aboard this historical steam train. (p307)

Chiemseebahn Dating from 1887, this is the world's oldest narrow-gauge steam train. (p403)

Schwarzaldbahn The Black Forest opens up like a kids' picture book on this scenic ride between Konstanz and Offenburg. (p526)

Breweries & Distilleries

Beer is as popular as ever, *natürlich,* but muscling in on the action are craft microbreweries and distilleries quenching the thirst for small-batch spirits.

Monkey 47 For German craft gin, this Black Forest distillery is at the top of the tree. (p501)

BRLO One of Berlin's foremost craft breweries – head straight for the beer garden in summer. (p116)

Zum Uerige Pull up a chair in this old-world Düsseldorf boozer for hoppy, malty *Altbier* brews. (p666)

Jägermeister Factory Tour Learn all about the famous green herbal liqueur at the HQ in Wolfenbüttel. (p717)

Brauerei zur Malzmühle A Cologne brewpub classic, where you can quaff malty *Mühlen Kölsch.* (p641)

Beck's Brewery Factory Tour Tours and tastings at one of Germany's most internationally famous breweries. (p722)

Staatsbrauerei Weihenstephan The world's oldest operating brewery, rolling out the barrel in Bavaria since 1040. (p458)

Wine Tasting

Estate tastings, vineyard hikes, cellar tours or wine festivals; an immersion in German wine culture should be part of every itinerary.

Rüdesheim Sample the renowned Rieslings of the celebrated Rheingau region. (p595)

Kaiserstuhl Sun and fertile soil create ideal conditions for *Spätburger* (Pinot Noir) and *Grauburgunder* (Pinot gris). (p512)

Deutsche Weinstrasse The bucolic German Wine Route is famous for muscular Rieslings and robust Dornfelder reds. (p588)

Moselle This meandering region grows light-bodied whites and has a wine-growing tradition rooted in Roman times. (p607)

Mittelrhein Wine tasting here is as much about the romantic Rhine Gorge setting as the wonderful vintages. (p594)

Freyburg This lovely riverside town is the home of the Rotkäppchen, Germany's largest producer of sparkling wine. (p275)

Harzer Schmalspurbahnen (p273)

Historisches Museum der Pfalz The world's oldest wine is among the fascinating exhibits at this well-curated museum in Speyer. (p581)

Great Outdoors

Germany is an all-seasons outdoor playground – whatever your adrenaline fix, you'll find it here.

Black Forest Fir-cloaked hills, steep gorges, misty waterfalls and sweeping viewpoints await in this fabled region. (p490)

Spreewald Dip your paddles into this timeless warren of gentle waterways near Berlin. (p145)

Altmühltal Radweg Stop at a pebbled beach after pedalling past rock formations carved by this Bavarian river. (p446)

Saxon Switzerland Rock hounds can choose from hundreds of climbs on soul-stirring cliffs and rockscapes. (p309)

Zugspitze Only seasoned mountaineers should make the breathtaking ascent to the 'roof' of Germany. (p394)

Oberstdorf Downhill, cross-country or boarding: this pretty region has a piste with your name on it. (p398)

Kellerwald-Edersee Immerse yourself in the ethereal wilderness of ancient beech forests in this national park. (p229)

Islands

For an authentic experience off the usual tourist track, catch a boat to these off-shore escapes.

Rügen Germany's largest island has sandy beaches, white chalk cliffs and historical resorts. (p214)

East Frisian Islands There are more seals than people on these flat-as-a-pancake islets in the North Sea. (p736)

Mainau This garden island has an enchanting profusion of tulips, dahlias, roses and orchids. (p523)

Sylt Big wind and waves translate into world-class windsurfing on this North Sea island. (p195)

Hiddensee For a genuine sense of happy isolation, visit this car-free Baltic island in the winter. (p219)

Herreninsel This island in the Chiemsee is home to Ludwig's II grandest palace, Schloss Herrenchiemsee. (p402)

Norderney The most accessible of the East Frisian Islands has enough soft white sand for everyone. (p740)

Month by Month

TOP EVENTS
Berlin Film Festival
February

Karneval/Fasching
February

Kieler Woche June

Oktoberfest
September

Christmas Markets
December

January

Except in the ski resorts, the Germans have the country pretty much to themselves this month. The short and cold days make this a good time to make in-depth explorations of museums and churches.

🏃 Mountain Madness

Grab your skis or snowboard and hit the slopes in top resorts that range from glam (Garmisch-Partenkirchen; p393) to family-friendly (Bavarian Forest; p464). No matter whether you're a black diamond daredevil or Sesame Street novice, there's a piste for you.

February

It's not as sweltering as Rio, but the German Carnival is still a good excuse for a party. Ski resorts are busiest thanks to school holidays; make reservations.

☆ Berlin Film Festival

Stars, directors and critics sashay down the red carpet for two weeks of screenings and glamour parties at the Berlinale, one of Europe's most prestigious celluloid festivals. (p105)

🎭 Karneval (Fasching)

The pre-Lenten season is celebrated with costumed street partying, parades, satirical shows and general revelry. The biggest parties are along the Rhine in Düsseldorf, Cologne and Mainz, but the Black Forest, Munich and samba-crazy Bremen also have their own traditions.

March

Days start getting longer and the first inkling of spring is in the air. Fresh herring hits the menus, especially along the coastal regions, and dishes prepared with *Bärlauch* (wild garlic) are all the rage.

🎭 Cebit

Geeks, suits and the merely tech-curious all converge en masse on Hanover's fairground for the world's largest digital trade fair. (p700)

April

Come April, there's no escaping the Easter Bunny in Germany. Meanwhile, nothing epitomises the arrival of spring more than the first crop of white asparagus. Germans go nuts for it.

◉ Maifest

Villagers celebrate the end of winter on 30 April by chopping down a tree for a maypole (*Maibaum*), painting, carving and decorating it, and staging a merry revelry with traditional costumes, singing and dancing.

◉ Walpurgisnacht

The pagan Witches' Sabbath festival on 30 April

sees Harz villages roaring to life as young and old dress up as witches and warlocks and parade through the streets singing and dancing.

May

One of the loveliest months, often surprisingly warm and sunny, perfect for ringing in beer garden season. Plenty of public holidays, which Germans turn into extended weekends or miniholidays, meaning busy roads and lodging shortages.

☉ Labour Day

Some cities host political demonstrations for workers' rights on 1 May, a public holiday in Germany. In Berlin, protests have taken on a violent nature in the past, although now it's mostly a big street fair.

✸ Hafengeburtstag

Hamburg lets its hair down in early May at this raucous three-day harbourside festival with a fun fair, music and merriment. (p165)

☉ Vatertag

Father's Day, now also known as *Männertag* (Men's Day), is essentially an excuse for men to get liquored up with the blessing of the missus. It's always on Ascension Day.

☆ International Händel Festival

Göttingen rocks with baroque at its International Händel Festival in mid-May, with a formidable line-up of opera, oratorios and concerts. (p234)

☉ Muttertag

Mothers are honoured on the second Sunday of May, much to the delight of florists, sweet shops and greeting-card companies. Make restaurant reservations far in advance.

✸ Karneval der Kulturen

Hundreds of thousands of revellers celebrate Berlin's multicultural tapestry with parties, exotic nosh and a fun parade of flamboyantly dressed dancers, DJs, artists and musicians shimmying through the streets of Kreuzberg. (p105)

✸ Wave-Gotik-Treffen

Thousands of Goths paint the town black as they descend upon Leipzig during the long Whitsuntide/Pentecost weekend, in what is billed as the world's largest Goth gathering. (p319)

✸ Stocherkahnrennen

Tübingen's traditional punting boat race pits rivalling student fraternities against each other in a hilarious and wacky costumed spectacle on the Neckar River. (p481)

June

Germany's festival pace quickens, while gourmets can rejoice in the bounty of fresh, local produce in the markets. Life moves outdoors as the summer solstice means the sun doesn't set until around 9.30pm.

✸ Africa-Festival

Europe's largest festival of African music and culture attracts an estimated 100,000 people to Würzburg with concerts, foods and crafts. (p410)

✸ Kieler Woche

Around half a million salty types flock to the Baltic Sea each summer when Kiel hosts the world's biggest boat party, with hundreds of regattas, ship parades, historical vessels and non-stop week-long partying. (p189)

☆ Bachfest

This nine-day music festival in Leipzig celebrates not only the work of Johann Sebastian Bach but also of other major composers. (p319)

✸ Christopher Street Day

No matter your sexual persuasion, come out and paint the town pink at major gay-pride celebrations in Berlin, Cologne and Hamburg. (p124)

July

School's out for the summer and peak travelling season begins. Pre-book accommodation whether you're headed to the mountains or the coast. Swimming is now possible in lakes, rivers, and the Baltic and North seas.

☆ Samba Festival

This orgy of song and dance in Coburg attracts around 100 bands and 3000 performers from a dozen nations, and up to 200,000 visitors. (p445)

⭐ Schlagermove

Hamburg's St Pauli quarter reverberates with 1970s disco-pop fun and fashion at this flamboyant street parade reaching from the port area to the Reeperbahn. (p165)

⭐ Schleswig-Holstein Musik Festival

Leading international musicians and promising young artists perform during this festival, in castles, churches, warehouses and animal barns throughout Germany's northernmost state. Held from mid-July until August. (p183)

August

August tends to be Germany's hottest month but days are often cooled by afternoon thunderstorms. It's the season for *Pfifferlinge* (chanterelle mushrooms) and fresh berries, which you can pick in the forests.

✨ Stuttgarter Sommerfest

More than half a million people come out to Stuttgart's Schlossplatz and Eckensee Lake for this chic four-day festival with open-air concerts, entertainment and culinary treats. (p469)

⊙ Kinderzeche

Dinkelsbühl, on the Romantic Road, hosts this 10-day festival featuring children performing in historical re-enactments,

along with a pageant and the usual merriment. (p416)

⭐ MS Dockville

This happening music festival hits the south bank of the Elbe in Hamburg in mid-August, with established and up-and-coming musicians in the mix. (p165)

⭐ Wagner Festival

German high society descends upon Bayreuth to practise the art of listening at epic productions of Wagner operas staged in a custom-built festival hall. Mere mortals must hope to score tickets via a lottery system. (p441)

⊙ Museumsuferfest

Some 2.5 million culture vultures descend upon Frankfurt's Museum Embankment in late August to nose around museums, shop for global crafts and enjoy concerts and dance performances along the Main River. (p545)

⊙ Shooting Festivals

More than a million Germans (mostly men) belong to shooting clubs and show off their skills at marksmen's festivals. The biggest one is in Hanover; the oldest, in Düsseldorf.

🍷 Wine Festivals

Grapes ripen to a plump sweetness, and the wine festival season starts, with tastings, folkloric parades, fireworks and the election of local and regional wine queens. The Dürkheimer Wurstmarkt is one of the biggest and most famous of these festivals. (p593)

September

Often sunny but not too hot. The main travel season is over but September is busy thanks to lots of wine and autumn festivals. Trees may start changing colour towards the end of the month.

⊙ Erntedankfest

Rural German towns celebrate the annual harvest with decorated church altars, *Erntedankzug* (processions) and villagers dressed up in folkloric garments.

🏃 Berlin Marathon

Sweat it out with more than 40,000 runners or just cheer 'em on during Germany's biggest street race, which has seen nine world records set since 1977. (p106)

🍺 Oktoberfest

Dust off your Dirndl or squeeze into a strapping pair of Lederhosen for Munich's legendary beer-swilling, stein-swinging party. There's no beer fest bigger than this one. (p360)

🍺 Cannstatter Volksfest

Stuttgart's answer to Oktoberfest, this beer-guzzling bash, held over three consecutive weekends, lifts spirits with oompah bands, carnival rides and fireworks. (p473)

⭐ Reeperbahn Festival

Live music of every imaginable genre cranks up at St Pauli's venues – from nightclubs to churches – at Hamburg's biggest bash. (p165)

October

Trade-fair season kicks into high gear, affecting lodging prices and availability in cities including Frankfurt, Cologne, Berlin and Hamburg. Tourist offices, museums and attractions start keeping shorter hours. Some close for the winter.

🔒 Frankfurt Book Fair

Bookworms invade Frankfurt for the world's largest book fair, held over five days and featuring 7300 exhibitors from more than a hundred countries. (p546)

November

This can be a dreary month mainly spent indoors. However, queues at tourist sights are short and theatre, concert, opera and other cultural events are plentiful. Bring warm clothes and rain gear.

◉ St Martinstag

This festival (10–11 November) honours the 4th-century St Martin, known for his humility and generosity, with a lantern procession and re-enactment of the famous scene where he cut his coat in half to share with a beggar. It's followed by a stuffed roast-goose feast.

December

Cold, sun-deprived days are brightened by Advent, four weeks of festivities preceding Christmas celebrated with enchanting markets, illuminated streets, Advent calendars, candle-festooned wreaths, home-baked cookies and more. Ski resorts usually get their first snow dusting.

◉ Nikolaustag

On the eve of 5 December, German children put their boots outside the door

hoping that St Nick will fill them with sweets and small toys overnight. Ill-behaved children, though, may find only a prickly rod left behind by St Nick's helper, Knecht Ruprecht.

🔒 Christmas Markets

Glühwein (mulled wine), spicy gingerbread biscuits, shimmering ornaments and decorations – these and lots more are typical features of German Christmas markets, held from late November until late December. Nuremberg's Christkindlesmarkt (p431) is especially famous.

✨ Silvester

New Year's Eve is called 'Silvester' in honour of the 4th-century pope under whom the Romans adopted Christianity as their official religion. The new year is greeted with fireworks launched by many thousands of amateur pyromaniacs.

Itineraries

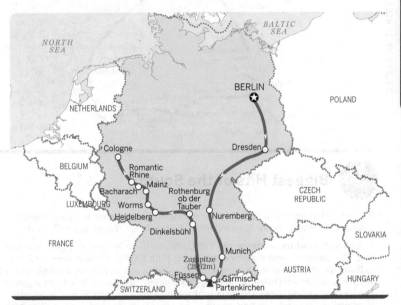

Top of the Pops

Bookended by great cities, this road trip is a fine introduction for first-timers that lets you sample the best of German culture, character, architecture and landscapes.

Kick off in **Berlin** to sample its top-notch museums, old and bold architecture and nice-to-naughty nightlife. Next, drive to showstopping **Dresden**, sitting proud and pretty in its baroque splendour on the Elbe River. Push south to **Nuremberg**, with its evocative walled medieval centre, and on to **Munich** to wrap up a day of palace- and museum-hopping with an evening in a beer garden. Head to **Garmisch-Partenkirchen** to breathe the fresh Alpine air on an exhilarating train-and-cable-car trip up the **Zugspitze**, then get up early the next day to beat the crowds swarming 'Mad' King Ludwig II's Schloss Neuschwanstein in **Füssen**. In the afternoon, point the compass north for the Romantic Road, possibly overnighting in **Dinkelsbühl** or **Rothenburg ob der Tauber**. Next, cut west to historical **Heidelberg**, with its romantically ruined fortress, then north to **Worms** and **Mainz** with their majestic Romanesque cathedrals. After a night in enchanting **Bacharach**, follow the **Romantic Rhine** through fairy-tale scenery before winding up in cosmopolitan **Cologne** for church-hopping, great art and rustic beer halls.

2 WEEKS Biggest Hits of the South

Follow this driving route linking the most storied stops in the south, including majestic mountains, legendary rivers, historical towns, half-timbered villages and lordly castles.

Start in **Frankfurt**, where you can soak up culture in world-class museums, apple wine in traditional taverns and skyline views from the Main River promenade. Steer northwest to **Koblenz**, the gateway to the Romantic Rhine, a scene-stealing combo of steeply terraced vineyards, lordly medieval castles and higgledy-piggledy villages. Say hello to the legendary Loreley as you follow the western river bank south, perhaps stopping in postcard-pretty **Boppard** and fairy-tale-like **Bacharach**, or fancying yourself knight or damsel for a night in a luxurious castle hotel. The next morning, make a quick stop in **Mainz**, where Johannes Gutenberg ushered in the information age by inventing moveable printing type.

Next, follow in the footsteps of Mark Twain in bewitching **Heidelberg**, Germany's oldest university town, with its imposing hilltop castle. Take a day's break from culture in **Baden-Baden**, the legendary spa resort where royals, celebrities, politicians and mere mortals have for centuries frolicked in elegant bathing temples. From here, go cuckoo for the Black Forest, an intoxicating mosaic of forest-cloaked hills, glacial lakes, snug valleys and half-timbered villages such as **Gengenbach**, **Schiltach** and **Triberg**. Build in at least a half-day in student-flavoured **Freiburg**, with its imposing minster; it's the place to enjoy crisp local wine al fresco amid tangled cobbled lanes.

From here, cut east to **Lake Constance** and follow its scenic northern shore, perhaps stopping in pretty **Meersburg**, at the prehistoric Pfahlbauten (pile dwellings) or in **Friedrichshafen**, the birthplace of the Zeppelin airship. Overnight in lovely **Lindau**, a teensy, alley-laced island. You're now in Bavaria, en route to the fabled Schloss Neuschwanstein in **Füssen** and on to **Garmisch-Partenkirchen**, where a train-and-cable-car combo delivers you to the top of the Zugspitze, Germany's highest Alpine peak. Come back down to earth in a beer hall in **Munich** before wrapping up your journey with a couple of days of oohing and aahing your way up the Romantic Road. Essential stops include **Rothenburg ob der Tauber** and **Würzburg**, from where it's a quick drive back to Frankfurt.

 Tour de Germany

4 WEEKS

With a month at your disposal, this epic trip offers the mother lode of soul-stirring land-scapes and villages but also lets you experience urban edginess in Germany's top cities. It's best done by car but a train-and-bus combo is also an option.

Base yourself in **Berlin** for a few days and add a one-day excursion to park-and-palace-filled **Potsdam**. Putter around, preferably in a kayak or canoe, the canal-laced **Spreewald** before embarking on a quick detour to **Görlitz** on the Polish border, one of Germany's best-preserved small towns. Set aside two days to get properly acquainted with the cultural riches of **Dresden**, then continue on to **Weimar** and **Erfurt** to walk in the footsteps of Germany's greatest intellects – from Luther and Goethe to Gropius.

Spend the next three days exploring a trio of evocative medieval gems: compact **Bamberg** with its romantic old town; the powerhouse of **Nuremberg** that is also (in)famous for its Third Reich legacy; and **Regensburg**, a lively university town studded with medieval townhouses overlooking the coursing Danube. Wend your way towards Munich via the enchanting **Altmühltal Nature Park**, best savoured slowly, on foot, by bike or by boat.

Make a study of **Munich** for a few days, with day trips up the **Zugspitze** and to King Ludwig II's **Schloss Neuschwanstein**. Continue west to Lake Constance, where stops should include enchanting **Lindau** and picture-perfect **Meersburg**. Revel in the youthful university spirit of ancient **Freiburg** for a day, then steer north for scenic drives through the Black Forest, ending in **Baden-Baden** for the night. Relax in the town's thermal spas before moving on to **Heidelberg**, with its ancient student taverns and charismatic ruined castle. Cut across the Rhine to **Speyer** for a spin around its Romanesque cathedral, then compare it to its upriver cousins in **Worms** and **Mainz**.

You're in the heart of wine country now, so sample the local tipple in idyllic villages such as **Bacharach** or **Boppard** as you follow the Romantic Rhine north through dramatic castle-studded scenery. Your grand tour culminates in **Cologne**; its magnificent cathedral will come into view long before you've reached town. Its great museums, Romanesque churches and Rhenish *joie de vivre* will easily keep you entertained for a day or two.

Top: Bacharach (p599)

Left: Zugspitze (p394)

MILDAX/SHUTTERSTOCK ©

Hanseatic Highlights

1 WEEK

This itinerary hops around northern Germany to delightful cities shaped by the sea and a long mercantile tradition rooted in the medieval Hanseatic League. You can drive it, but it's just as easily done by train.

Kick off in cosmopolitan **Hamburg**, a maritime city that cradles an elegant historic centre, a converted docklands quarter, the red-brick Speicherstadt (warehouse district) and a gloriously seedy party and red-light district under its self-confident mantle. Venture on to enchanting **Lübeck**, where the landmark Holsten Gate is a shutterbug's favourite. Try the delicious local marzipan before heading to pastoral **Schwerin**, a cultural hub hemmed in by crystalline lakes; sitting pretty on an island in one of them is the much-photographed, golden-domed Schloss Schwerin. Carry on to **Bremen**, the northern terminus of the 'Fairy-Tale Road'. After greeting the statue of the Town Musicians, check out expressionist architecture, mummified corpses and the Beck's brewery before partying until dawn in Das Viertel. Steer north to **Bremerhaven**, the port of dreams for millions hoping for a better life in the New World. The superb German Emigration Centre tells their story.

Romans, Rivers & Rieslings

1 WEEK

This scenic journey folds grand architecture, absorbing history, world-class art and fine wine into once enticing package.

Start in **Cologne**, where you can stand in awe of the twin-spired Kölner Dom, explore museums dedicated to chocolate, contemporary art or sports, and guzzle *Kölsch* beer in a Rhenish tavern. Head to **Aachen** to walk in the footsteps of Charlemagne and to munch on a *Printen* cookie, then travel back in time another few centuries in storied **Trier**. More than 2000 years old, it's home to some of the finest Roman monuments north of the Alps. The following day, mosey along the Moselle River, which runs its serene, serpentine course past steep vineyards to meet the Rhine at Koblenz. En route, swoon over crisp Riesling in half-timbered **Bernkastel-Kues** or fairy-tale **Beilstein**, then compare it with wines grown in the slate-rich Rhine soil. Follow the Rhine south from **Koblenz** as it carves past picture-postcard villages including **Boppard** and **Bacharach**, craggy cliffs crowned by medieval castles and near-vertical vineyards. Wrap up in **Mainz** with its grand cathedral and fabulous museum dedicated to moveable type inventor and local boy Johannes Gutenberg.

Hiking in the Black Forest (p490)

Plan Your Trip

Germany Outdoors

Rain or shine, Germany's outdoors is nothing short of extraordinary – whether you're hiking in dark forests ripe for a Brothers Grimm fairy tale, diving into a gem-coloured Alpine lake, cycling along mighty rivers and lake shores, or schussing down slopes backed by mountains of myth.

JÜRGEN WACKENHUT/SHUTTERSTOCK ©

Best of the Outdoors

Best Skiing

Bavarian Alps (p388) A holy grail for downhill and cross-country skiers, with titanic peaks, groomed slopes and an impeccable snow record.

Best Hiking

Black Forest (p490) Mile after pine-scented mile of trails weaving through forests, mist-enshrouded valleys and half-timbered villages, freshly minted for a fairy tale.

Best Climbing

Saxon Switzerland (p309) Sandstone wonderland with an exhilarating 1100 peaks and scenery that moves the soul.

Best Canoeing

Lake Constance (p520) Kayak over to Switzerland or Austria and glimpse the Alps on the horizon as you paddle.

Best Cycling

Altmühltal Radweg (p446) A 'Best of Bavaria' bike ride, taking in river bends and dense forests, ragged limestone cliffs and castle-topped villages.

Hiking & Mountaineering

Wanderlust? Germans coined the word. And their passion for *Wandern* (walking) is unrivalled. High-altitude treks in the Bavarian Alps, Black Forest hikes over wooded hill and dale, Rhineland vineyard strolls – this country will soon have you itching to grab your boots and stride its 200,000km of well-signposted trails, some traversing national and nature parks or biosphere reserves.

Local tourist offices can help you find a route to match your fitness and time frame, and can supply you with maps and tips. Many offer multiday 'hiking without luggage' packages that include accommodation and luggage transfers between hotels.

The Bavarian Alps are Germany's mountaineering and rock-climbing heartland, whether for challenging ascents, day treks or multiday hut-to-hut hikes. Before heading out, seek local advice and instruction on routes, equipment and weather, as trails can be narrow, steep and have icy patches, even in summer.

The Deutscher Alpenverein (DAV; www.alpenverein.de) climbing association is a goldmine of information and maintains hundreds of Alpine huts, where you can spend the night and get a meal. Local DAV chapters also organise courses and guided treks. Membership can yield a 30% to 50% discount on huts, and other benefits.

Rock Climbing

Clambering around steep rock faces is popular in the crag-riddled heights of central and southern Germany. Rock hounds test their mettle on limestone cliffs in Bavaria's Altmühltal Nature Park (p446), with climbs from grades 1 to 10. Another *klettern* (climbing) hotspot, particularly among free climbers, is Saxon Switzerland (p309), with 1100 climbing peaks, routes graded 1 to 12, and exhilarating views over bizarre sandstone rock formations. Most towns have climbing walls where you can limber up. For information see www.dav-felsinfo.de, www.klettern.de or www.climbing.de.

Best Walks for...

Alpine trekkers

Colossal mountains and jewel-coloured lakes in the Berchtesgaden National Park (p404); a summit ascent to Zugspitze (p394; 2962m).

Family ramblers

Red squirrel-spotting on the trail shadowing Triberger Wasserfälle (p516; 163m), Germany's highest waterfall.

Beachcombers

Bracing sea air atop the wild limestone cliffs of Rügen's Stubbenkammer (p217); dune walking on Sylt (p195); walking across mudflats to the East Frisian Islands (p736).

Culture cravers

The 410km Lutherweg (p259) pilgrimage trail hits major Reformation sites in Thuringia, Hesse, Saxony and Bavaria.

Long-distance hikers

The wild and woody 169km Rennsteig (p256); the 280km Westweg (www.black forest-tourism.com), the ultimate Black Forest walk.

Wine lovers

Vine-strewn hills in the Rhine Valley (p594); sipping Pinots along the Kaiserstuhl's 15km Winzerweg (p514).

Birdwatchers

Ospreys, white-tailed eagles and kingfishers in the Müritz National Park (p203).

Escapists

The fir-cloaked hills of the Black Forest and the Bavarian Forest National Park (p464).

Rock fans

The rockscapes of Saxon Switzerland (p309); limestone cliffs in Naturpark Obere Donau (p518).

Rock climbing, Saxon Switzerland (p309)

Cycling

Strap on your helmet! Germany is superb cycling territory, whether you're off on a leisurely spin along the beach, a downhill ride in the Alps or a multiday freewheeling adventure. In East Frisia, there are 'Paddle & Pedal' stations, allowing you to canoe along canals before cycling back. Local tourist offices can give you advice on day trips and you can rent city, mountain and electro-bikes in most towns. Ever the eco-exponent, Germany is making tracks at the moment with a growing network of bike-sharing schemes, including those run by VRNnextbike (p584).

The country is criss-crossed by more than 200 well-signposted long-distance trails covering 70,000km – ideal for *Radwandern* (bike touring). Routes combine lightly travelled back roads, forestry tracks and paved highways with dedicated bike lanes. Many traverse nature reserves, meander along rivers or venture into steep mountain terrain.

The national cycling organisation Allgemeiner Deutscher Fahrrad Club (www.adfc.de) produces the best maps for on-the-road navigation. These indicate inclines, track conditions, repair shops and UTM grid coordinates for GPS users. The ADFC also offers a useful directory called *Bett & Bike* (www.bettundbike.de; available online or in bookshops) that lists bicycle-friendly hotels, inns and hostels.

RESPONSIBLE HIKING

➡ Stick to existing tracks and avoid short cuts that bypass a switchback. If you blaze a new trail straight down a slope, it will turn into a watercourse with the next heavy rainfall.

➡ Avoid removing the plant life that keeps topsoil in place.

➡ Make an effort to use toilets in huts and refuges where provided.

➡ Where there is none, bury your waste. Dig a small hole 15cm deep and at least 100m from any watercourse. Cover the waste with soil and a rock. Use toilet paper sparingly and bury that, too. In snow, dig down beneath the soil.

Skiing, Berchtesgaden National Park (p404)

Top Long-Distance Cycling Routes

Altmühltal Radweg

Rothenburg ob der Tauber (p412) to Beilngries; follows the river through the Altmühltal Nature Park (p446); easy to moderate (160km)

Elberadweg

Elbe River from Saxon Switzerland (p309) to Hamburg (p153); rolling through wine country, heath and marshland, past Dresden (p292), Dessau and Wittenberg; easy to moderate (860km)

Donauradweg

Neu-Ulm to Passau (p460); a delightful riverside trip; easy to moderate (434km)

Bodensee–Königssee Radweg

Lindau (p530) to Berchtesgaden (p404); route running along the foot of the Alps with magnificent views; moderate (418km)

Romantische Strasse

Würzburg (p407) to Füssen (p388); though busy during summer, it's one of the nicest ways to explore this famous holiday route; easy to moderate (359km)

Water Sports & Riverboats

Germany's lakes, rivers, canals and coasts offer plenty of water-based action, though the swimming season is relatively short (June to September) and water temperatures rarely climb above 21°C.

Slip into a canoe or kayak to absorb the natural rhythm of the waterways threading through the lushly wooded Spreewald (p145) and Bavaria's Altmühltal Nature Park (p446). The lake-dotted wilderness of the Müritz National Park (p203) is great for paddle-and-camp trips. Or paddle across Lake Constance (p520) to Switzerland and Austria with the Alps on the horizon. The season runs from around April to October and a one-/two-person canoe or kayak costs around €25/30 per day.

Stiff breezes and big waves draw sailors, surfers, windsurfers and kitesurfers to the North Sea and Baltic coasts. Sylt (p195) on the North Sea and Rügen (p214) on the Baltic have some of the country's top conditions and schools for water-based activities.

Kayaking, Spreewald (p145)

Surfing

Surf is up on the wavy North Sea island of Sylt (p195), where you can hire a board or take lessons.

Romantic river cruising

Take in scenic and historical views on a cruise along the Romantic Rhine (p594).

Kayaking and mountain-gazing

Hire a kayak on Lake Constance (p520) and paddle over to Switzerland and Austria, with the Alps looming on the horizon.

Windsurfing and kitesurfing

Try your hand at windsurfing and kitesurfing by harnessing the fabulous breezes on the Baltic island of Rügen (p214).

Boat trips and wine tasting

Enjoy wine tasting on board a mini-cruise along the Moselle between Koblenz (p605) and Trier (p616).

If you'd rather let someone else do the hard work, put your feet up and watch the great outdoors drift past on a riverboat cruise along some of Germany's greatest rivers (from Easter to October).

High on the list is the Romantic Rhine (p594), where boats drift past vine-covered hills, cliffs crowned with robber-knight castles and picturesque villages. Or combine wine-tasting with a mini-cruise along the Moselle between Koblenz and Trier, each bend in the river revealing vine-draped loveliness.

In Berlin you can mix sightseeing with a meander along the Spree, in Hamburg the Elbe, in Passau the Danube, and in Stuttgart the Neckar. For a taste of history, hop aboard a paddle-wheel steam boat in Dresden (p299) or a punt in Tübingen (p482).

Best Water Activities

Canoeing and camping

Take to the glorious forest-rimmed lakes of the Müritz National Park (p203), where you can canoe, camp and enjoy the off-the-radar silence and birdwatching.

Winter Sports

Modern lifts, primed ski runs from easy-peasy blues to death-wish blacks, cross-country trails through untouched nature, log huts, steaming mulled wine, hearty dinners by crackling fires: these are the hallmarks of a German skiing holiday.

The Bavarian Alps (p388), only an hour's drive south of Munich, offer the best downhill slopes and most reliable snow conditions. The most famous and ritzy resort is Garmisch-Partenkirchen (p393), which hosted the FIS Alpine Skiing World Championships in 2011 and is just a snowball's throw from Zugspitze (p394). It has 60km of slopes, mostly geared towards intermediates. Picture-book-pretty Oberstdorf (p398) in the Allgäu Alps forms the heart of the Oberstdorf-Kleinwalsertal ski region, which has 130km of slopes. It's good for boarders, with snow parks and a half-pipe to play on, and cross-country skiers come to glide along 75km of classic tracks and 55km of skating tracks. For low-key skiing and stunning scenery, there is Berchtesgaden (p404) and Mittenwald (p397), presided over by the jagged Karwendel range. Can't or won't ski? All resorts offer snowy fun from tobogganing and ice skating to snowshoeing and winter walking.

Elsewhere in the country, the mountains may not soar as high, but prices are cheaper and the atmosphere is less frenetic. The Bavarian Forest (p463) and the Black Forest (p490) have the most reliable snow levels, with moderate downhill action on the Grosser Arber and Feldberg mountains, as well as abundant *Langlaufloipen* (cross-country trails) where you can shuffle through frozen woods in quiet exhilaration.

At higher elevations, the season generally runs from late November or early December to March. Rates for skis, boots and poles cost around €25/15 for downhill/cross-country gear hire and group ski/snowboard lessons cost around €45 per day.

Best Snow Sports For...

Cross-country enthusiasts

It's as much about the uphill climb as the downhill buzz with *Langlauf* (cross-country skiing). Give it a go in the Black Forest (p490) or Oberstdorf (p398).

Families

Berchtesgaden (p404) and Mittenwald (p397) in the Bavarian Alps come up trumps for family fun from tobogganing right through to ice skating and snowshoeing.

High-altitude thrill seekers

Peaks don't come any higher in Germany than the 2962m Zugspitze (p394), with its glacier, tremendous views and well-groomed runs that are easy-to-moderate in difficulty.

RESOURCES

German National Tourist Office (www.germany.travel) Inspiration on walking and cycling throughout Germany.

Kompass (www.kompass.de) A reliable series of 1:25,000 scale walking maps and information on trails.

Tourentipp (www.tourentipp.de) Weather forecasts, hut info and walks organised by region.

Wanderbares Deutschland (www.wanderbares-deutschland.de) Dozens of walking trails, with a handy interactive map.

Wandern ohne Gepäck (www.wandern-ohne-gepaeck-deutschland.de) The 'hiking without luggage' specialists.

Downhill skiers

Garmisch-Partenkirchen (p393) is intermediate heaven, with 60km of cruisy downhill slopes to whizz down.

Snowboarders

Glide on over to Oberstdorf (p398) in the Allgäu Alps for snow parks, a half-pipe and 130km of slopes.

Spargel (asparagus) on sale at a mark

Plan Your Trip

Eat & Drink Like a Local

'Keep it simple, local and seasonal' is the ethos in Germany, a rising star in Europe's kitchen. Food will play a big part in your travels – you'll never forget that first creamy forkful of real Black Forest gateau, tangy Rieslings sipped in Rhineland wineries and seafood savoured on Baltic beaches.

The Year in Food

JUERGEN FAELCHLE/SHUTTERSTOCK ©

Spring (Mar–May)

Germans go nuts for asparagus during *Spargelzeit* (asparagus season). *Bärlauch* (wild garlic) is bountiful and Baltic towns celebrate the humble herring.

Summer (Jun–Aug)

Pfifferlinge (chanterelle mushrooms) and a feast of forest berries trumpet summer's arrival. Beer gardens brim with people lapping up the warm weather, and folksy wine festivals are in full swing.

Autumn (Sep–Oct)

Autumn days are rich and earthy, with game, wild mushrooms and pumpkins aplenty. At Oktoberfest in September, 6.9 million partygoers wash down entire farms of pigs, oxen and chickens with *Mass* (litres) of beer.

Winter (Nov–Feb)

'Tis the season for gingerbread and mulled wine at Christmas. Later, Munich throws festivals for pre-Lenten *Starkbier* (strong beer), the malty 7.5% brews monks once dubbed *flüssiges Brot* (liquid bread).

Food Experiences

Cheap Treats

Some of your best German food experiences are likely to be the snack-on-the-hoof variety. At street stalls you'll get versed in German *Wurst* (sausage) and chomp your way around the globe, often with change from a €5 note. In Berlin and other cities, street food includes Greek, Italian, Mexican, Middle Eastern and Chinese bites. The *Imbiss* fast-food stall is a ubiquitous phenomenon, allowing you to eat on the run.

Germany's Turkish population invented the modern doner kebab *(Döner)*. Most kebab joints also do vegetarian versions. In the briny north, snack on fish (usually herring) sandwiches.

Going Gourmet

Germany has been redeeming itself gastronomically over the past decade, notching up a whopping 300 Michelin-starred restaurants in 2018, including 11 with the holy grail of three stars. In top kitchens across the country, chefs are putting an imaginative spin on regional, seasonal ingredients big on integral flavours.

To see Germany's meteoric rise in the Michelin world, look no further than the Black Forest village of Baiersbronn, where master chefs Torsten Michel, of Schwarzwaldstube (p500), and Peter Lumpp, from Restaurant Bareiss (p500), have both been awarded the coveted three Michelin stars. They are no exception: Berlin alone has 21 Michelin-starred restaurants, including seven with two stars in 2018 – and other cities are swiftly following suit.

Besides Michelin and Gault Millau, Germany has its own ratings and guides, including Der Feinschmecker (www.der-feinschmecker.de), Aral's Schlemmer Atlas (www.schlemmer-atlas.de) and Marcellino's Restaurant Report (www.marcellinos.de).

Dare to Try

Feeling daring? Why not give some of Germany's more unusual dishes a whirl.

Sauere Kuttlen/Nierle/Lüngerl (sour tripe/kidneys/lung) No Baden-Württemberg beer fest would be complete without these offal faves, simmered in vinegar or wine, bay, laurel, juniper and spices.

Handkäs mit Musik (hand cheese with music) Hesse's pongy sour-milk cheese, rolled by hand and marinated in oil and vinegar with onions. A sure-fire recipe for flatulence – hence the music!

Saumagen Rhineland-Palatinate brings you stuffed pig stomach (reminiscent of haggis). Eat it with sauerkraut and sautéed potatoes.

Labskaus Every Hamburg seafarer worth his salt adores this mishmash of corned beef, beetroot, potatoes, onions and occasionally herring, topped with a fried egg and served with gherkins.

Bubespitzle Otherwise known as *Schupfnudeln*, this Swabian dish's ingredients are innocuous: potato noodles tossed in butter, served with sauerkraut and speck (cured ham). But the name (literally, 'little boys' penises') certainly isn't.

Local Specialities

Drift to the Baltic and North Sea coasts for pickled herrings with oomph and the sweet-sour *Mecklenburger Rippenbraten* (rolled pork stuffed with lemons, apples, plums and raisins). Hamburg locals love their eels and *Labskaus* (minced corned beef, potato and beetroot, served with a fried egg and gherkins), while Bavarians match excellent beer with gut-busting platters of pork knuckles and *Klösse* (dumplings). Then there's Saxony and Thuringia for lentil and potato soups, the Black Forest for its trout, ham and famous gateau, and rural Swabia for culinary one-offs such as *Spätzle* (noodle-dumpling hybrids) and *Maultaschen* (ravioli's Teutonic relative). Traditional fare such as *Eisbein* (salt-cured ham hock with sauerkraut) and *Bouletten* (meatballs) never goes out of fashion in Berlin.

Almost every town in Germany has a weekly *Bauernmarkt* (farmers market). This is the place to bag local fruit and veg, cheese, wurst, fish, preserves, herbs

Bratwurst with sauerkraut

and sometimes home-grown wine and schnapps. *Biomärkte* (organic markets and supermarkets) can also be found in most towns and cities.

MENU DECODER

Abendessen Dinner

Degustationsmenü Tasting menu

Frühstück Breakfast

Gefroren Frozen

Hauptspeise Main course

Hausgemacht Homemade

Kaffee und Kuchen Afternoon coffee and cake

Mittagsmenü/Tagesmenü Fixed-price lunch menu

Nachspeise Dessert

Schnellimbiss Fast food

Tagesteller Dish of the day

Vesper/Imbiss Snack

Vorspeise Starter

How to Eat & Drink

When to Eat

Though city folk might just grab a coffee en route to the office, *Frühstück* (breakfast) is traditionally a sweet and savoury smorgasbord of bread, cheese, salami, wurst, preserves, yoghurt and muesli. At weekends, it's a more leisurely, family-oriented affair. Many cafes have embraced the brunch trend, serving all-you-can eat buffets with fresh rolls, eggs, smoked fish, fruit salad and even Prosecco.

While the older generation may still sit down for *Mittagessen* at noon sharp, the focus on lunch as the main meal of the day is waning thanks to a shift in work patterns. Many restaurants still tout a fixed lunch menu (*Mittagsmenü* or *Tagesmenü*), which can be an affordable way of dining at upscale restaurants.

Traditional Christmas biscuits

Dinner is served in homes at around 7pm. For those who have already eaten heartily at midday, there is *Abendbrot,* bread with cold cuts. At home, meals are relaxed and require few airs and graces beyond the obligatory '*Guten Appetit*' (good appetite) salutation, exchanged before eating. Outside the cities, with their late-night dining scenes, Germans head to restaurants earlier than elsewhere in Europe, and many kitchens in rural areas stop serving at around 9pm.

Where to Eat

Gaststätten & Gasthöfe Rural inns with a laid-back feel, local crowd and solid menu of *gutbürgerliche Küche* (home cooking).

Eiscafé Italian-style cafes, where you can grab an ice cream or cappuccino and head outside to slurp and sip.

Stehcafé A stand-up cafe for coffee and snacks at speed and on the cheap.

Cafe-Konditorei A traditional cake shop and cafe.

Ratskeller Atmospheric town-hall basement restaurant, generally frequented more by tourists than locals nowadays.

Bierkeller & Weinkeller The emphasis is on beer and wine respectively, with a little food (sausages, pretzels, cold cuts) on the side.

Imbiss Handy speed-feed stops for savoury fodder, such as wurst-in-a-bun, kebabs or pizza.

Apfelweinwirtschaft Frankfurt's historical *Ebbelwei* (apple wine) taverns. Warm, woody and serving good honest regional fare.

Biergarten Beer garden – often with tree shade and a meaty menu.

Dining Tips

One early-20th-century German book of manners that we have seen exhorts dinner guests not to use their knives to carve their initials into the table of their hosts. Things have moved on somewhat since those days. With good manners now automatic, there's little need to panic at the dinner table, although a few tips might come in handy for first-time visitors.

On the menu English menus are prevalent in big cities, but the more rural and remote you travel, the less common they become. Most places will have a waiter or waitress who can translate, but it helps to learn a few phrases of German.

MEALS OF A LIFETIME

From fine dining to hearty German grub served with a dollop of history, whet your appetite with our pick of the best.

Söl'ring Hof (p196) In a dune setting in Sylt, with crashing surf as the backbeat, Johannes King's kitchen wows with stunning renditions of seasonal produce and seafood.

Schwarzwaldstube (p500) Torsten Michel cooks with precision and panache at this triple-Michelin-starred Black Forest hideaway in Baiersbronn.

Zur Herrenmühle (p577) Dine under 300-year-old wooden beams at this 1690 flour mill turned elegant country-style restaurant in Heidelberg.

Esszimmer (p371) Bobby Bräuer helms this Michelin-starred Mediterranean number at BMW World. It's Munich's finest.

Tulus Lotrek (p113) This Michelin-starred Kreuzberg number has flavours as bright and original as Toulouse-Lautrec's impressionist fantasies.

Paying the bill Sometimes the person who invites will pay, but generally Germans go Dutch and split the bill evenly. This might mean everyone chipping in at the end of a meal or asking to pay separately (*getrennte Rechnung*). Buying rounds in bars British-style is not usually the done thing, though Germans might buy each other the odd drink. In bars and beer halls, table service is still quite common and waiting staff often come around to *abkassieren* (cash up).

Table reservations If you want to dine at trendy or Michelin-starred restaurants, it is wise to make reservations at least a week in advance. Most

Gasthöfe and *Gaststätten* (inns), cafes and beer halls should be able to squeeze you in at a moment's notice.

Tipping Service charge is not included in the bill. Tipping is quite an individual matter, but most Germans will tip between 5% and 10% in restaurants, and simply round to the nearest euro in cafes and bars. Do whatever you're comfortable with, given the service and setting. Give any tip directly to the server when paying your bill. Say either the amount you want to pay, or '*Stimmt so*' if you don't want change.

Dresden's Striezelmarkt Christmas market (p300)

Plan Your Trip

Travel with Children

Travelling to Germany with tots can be child's play, especially if you keep a light schedule and involve them in trip planning. Plus, kids are a great excuse if you secretly yearn to ride roller coasters or dip into the fairy-tale landscapes of the Brothers Grimm.

Best Regions for Kids

Stuttgart & the Black Forest

Fairy-tale forest trails, farmstays and outdoor activities galore. Zip across to Lake Constance (p520) for kayaking, swimming and cycling, Triberg (p516) for its whopping cuckoo clocks and Europa-Park (p510) to race around Europe in miniature.

Munich & Bavaria

Storybook Germany, with its Christmas-card mountain scenery and high-on-a-hill Schloss Neuschwanstein (p388), the blueprint for Disney's *Sleeping Beauty* castle. Find diversions aplenty in Munich (p338) and sight-packed Nuremberg (p425) – one of Germany's most engaging cities for kiddies.

Central Germany

Hike in the mythical Harz Mountains (p260) and the Thuringian Forest (p253) and enjoy happy-ever-after moments along the 600km Fairy-Tale Road (p224), taking in castles, hamlets and other stops that inspired the tales of Brothers Grimm.

Northern Germany

Go for the puppet theatre (p187) in Lübeck (p182), pearly white beaches and candy-striped lighthouses on the Baltic and North Sea coasts. Müritz National Park (p203) is fabulous for paddle-and-camp trips, and Sylt (p195) for boat trips to seal colonies.

Germany for Kids

Travelling to Germany with kids in tow? You're in for a treat. Kids will already have seen in bedtime picture books many of the things that make the country so special: enchanting palaces and legend-shrouded castles lifted high by mountaintops; medieval towns and half-timbered villages that take you back several centuries; islands and meandering rivers; and deep, dark forests that fire little imaginations. This is the birthplace of the Brothers Grimm and their unforgettable fairy tales. Follow the Fairy-Tale Road (p224) to see Sleeping Beauty's castle (p388) and dance to

the tune of the Pied Piper in the town of Hamelin (p235).

Cities also have much to keep the little ones amused, with interactive museums, imaginative playgrounds, puppet shows, outdoor pools and zoos.

Tourist offices can point you to children's attractions, child-care facilities and English-speaking paediatricians. If you need a babysitter, ask staff at your hotel for a referral.

Breastfeeding in public is practised, although most women are discreet about it. Restaurants are rarely equipped with nappy-change facilities, but some fast-food places have a fold-down change table in the women's toilet.

Outdoor Activities

Germany's great outdoors yields an endless variety of activities. Tourist offices can recommend well-marked walking trails suitable for families, including those pushing strollers, or hook you up with a local guide. Ask about kid-geared activities such as geocaching, animal-spotting safaris and nature walks.

Water babies will love frolicking on Germany's beaches, which are clean and usually devoid of big surf and dangerous undercurrents. Water temperatures rarely exceed 21°C (70°F), though lakes tend to be a bit warmer. Many have an inexpensive *Strandbad* (lido) with change rooms, playgrounds, splash zones, slides, ping-pong tables, restaurants or boat rentals. Kayaking is active fun for children from the age of seven, and short excursions or multiday paddle-and-camp trips are available.

Cycling is big in Germany, with safe, well-signposted routes running along lakes and coastlines, through forests and up into the hills. The vast majority of bike rental outlets have children's bikes and can recommend kid-friendly tours.

All ski resorts have ski schools with English-speaking instructors that initiate kids in the art of the snow plough in group or private lessons. Families with kids under 10 years may find smaller resorts in the Bavarian Forest (p463) or Black Forest (p490) easier to navigate and better value than bigger Alpine resorts such as Garmisch-Partenkirchen (p393). All of them, of course, have plenty of off-piste fun as well: snowshoeing, sledding, walking and ice skating.

Museums

Germany is full of child-friendly museums that play to young imaginations or impart knowledge in interactive and engaging ways. Kid-oriented audioguides (in German and English) are becoming more widely available. Staff also run tot-geared activities, although these are usually in German.

Dining Out

As long as they're not running wild, children are generally welcome in German restaurants, especially in informal cafes, bistros, pizzerias or *Gaststätten* (inns). High chairs are common and the server may even bring a damp cloth at the end of your meal to wipe sticky little fingers.

Many less formal restaurants offer a limited *Kindermenü* (children's menu) or *Kinderteller* (children's meals). Dishes generally loved by children include *Schnitzel mit Pommes* (schnitzel with fries), *Bratwurst* (sausage), *Nudeln mit Tomatensosse* (pasta with tomato sauce), *Spätzle* (egg-based mini-dumpling-like noodles) or the German version of mac 'n' cheese, *Käsespätzle. Maultaschen,* a spin on ravioli, may also go down well. Pizzerias are cheap, ubiquitous and most will be happy to customise pizzas.

Germany is fabulous snack territory. Larger malls have food courts, while self-service cafeterias are often found in department stores; farmers markets also have food stalls. The most popular snacks on the run are bratwurst-in-a-bun and doner kebabs (sliced meat in a pita pocket with salad and sauce). And there's no shortage of international fast food chains. Note that you have to pay extra for ketchup.

Baby food, infant formulas, soy and cow's milk and nappies (diapers) are widely available in supermarkets and chemists (drugstores).

GE VISION/SHUTTERSTOCK ©

Europa-Park (p510)

Märchengarten (p479) Low-key fairy-tale-themed park for tots in Ludwigsburg.

Steinwasen Park (www.steinwasen-park.de; Steinwasen 1, L126; adult/concession €23/19; ☉9am-6pm Jul-early Sep, 10am-5pm early Sep-early Nov & late Mar-Jun) Forest park near Freiburg with rides, Alpine animals and a hanging bridge.

Ravensburger Spieleland (p529) Board-game-inspired park with giant rubber-duck races and speed cow milking.

Children's Highlights

Amusement Parks

Europa-Park (p510) Huge Europe-themed amusement park with whizzy rides and a mouse mascot.

PLAN YOUR TRIP TRAVEL WITH CHILDREN

USEFUL WEBSITES

German National Tourist Office (www.germany.travel) Popular family sights and destinations.

Familotel (www.familotel.com) Family-friendly hotels that are sure-fire kid-pleasers.

Urlaub auf dem Bauernhof (www.bauernhofurlaub.de) More than 5000 farmstay properties throughout Germany.

Deutsches Technikmuseum (p88), Berlin

Feenweltchen (Fairy Grottoes; ☎03671-550 40; www.feengrotten.de; Feengrottenweg 2; adult/child €12/7.90, with Grottoneum & Fairy World €15/9.90; ⏰9.30am-5pm May-Nov, 10.30am-3.30pm Nov-Apr; 🅿🚼) A magical world of elves, fairies and sprites attached to a colourful grotto in Saalfeld.

Playmobil (p433) Tots love the life-sized versions of these famous German toys in Nurmeberg.

Energy Burners

Black Forest (p12) Go down to these seemingly never-ending woods for hiking, cycling, skiing, sledding and snowshoeing.

Spreewald (p145) Navigate the channels and canals of this Unesco Biosphere Reserve by canoe, kayak or punt.

Sylt (p195) This wave-lashed island in the North Sea is ideal for surfing, windsurfing or horse riding.

Bavarian Alps (p388) Strike out on foot for those Heidi moments, or take to the slopes in winter.

Lake Constance (p520) A family magnet, where you can walk, pedal, kayak or boat it over to Switzerland and Austria.

Rügen (p214) Sheltered Baltic Sea beaches and family rambles along limestone cliffs and through enchanting beech forests.

Planes, Trains & Automobiles

Also see If You Like… Train Journeys (p27) for fun narrow-gauge train rides.

Nürburgring (p653) Legendary car racing track.

Technik Museum (p581) A Boeing 747, 1960s U-boat and Soviet space shuttle await inspection in Speyer.

Deutsches Technikmuseum (p88) Giant shrine to technology in Berlin.

Phaeno (☎05361-890 100; www.phaeno.de; Willy-Brandt-Platz 1; adult/child €14/9; ⏰9am-5pm Tue-Fri, 10am-6pm Sat & Sun) Scientific exhibits and experiments in Wolfsburg's cutting-edge building by Zaha Hadid.

Miniatur Wunderland (p157) In Hamburg, one of the world's largest model railways.

Deutsche Bahn Museum (p425) Choo-choo themed attractions including Children's Railway World; in Nuremberg.

Königssee (p404)

have more of a party vibe and don't always welcome children.

Getting Around

Children under 12 years or smaller than 1.5m (59 inches) must ride in the back seat in cars (taxis included) and use a car seat or booster that's appropriate for their weight. Only children older than 12 years and over 1.5m tall may ride in front. Car seats are occasionally provided free by rental companies but must be reserved.

The train is a great way to get around Germany. Children under 15 years travel free if accompanied by at least one parent or grandparent. The only proviso is that names of children aged between six and 14 must be registered on your ticket at the time of purchase. Children under six always travel free and without a ticket.

The superfast ICE trains have compartments for families with small children (*Kleinkindabteil*) that are equipped with tables, stroller storage, an electrical outlet (for warming bottles) and, sometimes, a change table. Book these early.

Seat reservations for families (*Familienreservierung*) cost a flat €9 for two adults and up to three children.

Planning

For all-round information and advice, check out Lonely Planet's *Travel with Children*.

Accommodation

Many hotels have family rooms with three or four beds, large doubles with a sofa-bed or adjoining rooms with a connecting door. Practically all can provide cots, though sometimes a small extra charge applies. In some properties, smaller children (generally those under 12 years) stay free or are given a discount.

Farmstays (*Urlaub auf dem Bauernhof*) are popular with families and offer a low-key, inexpensive experience. Meanwhile, *Heuhotels* (hay hotels) offer the option of literally sleeping in a barn on a bed of hay: see www.heuhotels.de for details. Camping is also huge; in summer the most popular sites book out far in advance.

Hostelling International–affiliated hostels (DJH hostels) have family rooms and activities, but independent hostels tend to

CHILDREN'S DISCOUNTS

Many museums, monuments and attractions are free to anyone under 18 years, but the cut-off age varies. In general, you can assume kids under five don't pay at all. Most places also offer family tickets.

Children qualify for discounts on public transport and tours, where they usually pay half price, sometimes less. Some hotels, including many international chains, have discounted rates for kids or don't charge extra if they're under a certain age (varying from three to 16) and stay in their parents' room without extra bedding. The *Kurtaxe* (tourist tax) you pay in most resorts gets you a *Gästekarte* (guest card) for free local transport and entry to museums, pools and attractions.

Regions at a Glance

Berlin

Museums & Palaces
From art deco to agriculture, sex to sugar, and diamonds to dinosaurs, there is hardly a theme not covered in Berlin's nearly 200 museums, most famously in the tantalising treasures of Museum Island.

All-Night Parties
Berlin is the spiritual home of the 'lost weekend'. Kick off a night on the razzle in a bar or pub, catch tomorrow's headline acts in an indie-music venue, then dance till dawn or beyond in clubs helmed by DJ royalty.

Historic Sights
In Berlin the past is always present. Its legendary sights take you back to the era of Prussian glory, the dark ages of the Third Reich, the tense period of the Cold War and the euphoria of reunification.

p58

Around Berlin

Palaces
Water Fun
History

A Taste of Royalty
Schloss Sanssouci is the jewel among Potsdam's palaces, but the nearby Neues Palais, Marmorpalais and Schloss Cecilienhof are other fabled and fanciful addresses.

Aquatic Adventures
Tour Potsdam's palaces by boat, take a punt to a Sorb village in the emerald-green Spreewald or kayak around Brandenburg an der Havel. This region is best experienced from the water.

Momentous Moments
Visit seminal sites of the 20th century, such as one of Germany's first concentration camps, the palace where Allied leaders decided the country's post–WWII fate, and a sinister KGB prison.

p136

Hamburg & the North

Coast
History
City Life

Island Escapes
There's something almost otherworldly about Germany's islands, from the glamorous Sylt to the family-friendly Usedom. Hit the surf, cycle among the dunes or relax on a white sandy beach.

Hanseatic League
Savour the red-brick splendour of charismatic Lübeck, Wismar, Stralsund and Greifswald; all are Baltic towns with pedigrees going right back to the Hanseatic League.

Hamburg Past to Present
In the 'gateway to the world', you can discover the newly minted (Elbphilharmonie), the naughty (the Reeperbahn red-light district), the historic (St Nikolai), the futuristic (HafenCity), the posh (Alster Lakes) and the raucous (Fischmarkt).

p152

Central Germany

Drives
History
Outdoors

Fairy-Tale Drives

Look out for witches, goblins and 'sleeping beauties' as you follow in the footsteps of the Brothers Grimm along the Fairy-Tale Road.

Reformation & Bauhaus

A keystone of German culture, this region gave birth to Martin Luther and the Reformation, inspired dramatists Goethe and Schiller, launched the Bauhaus design movement and pioneered optical precision technology.

Mountains & Mines

Forest trails beckon in the Harz Mountains, including the trek up myth-laden Mt Brocken. Stop also in half-timbered Quedlinburg, explore medieval mining history in Goslar, and hurtle along on an old narrow-gauge steam train.

p221

Saxony

Museums
Heritage
Art & Culture

Classical & Baroque Treasures

Dresden's wealth of paintings, porcelain, armour, sculptures and other priceless collections is truly stunning. If time is tight, focus on the whimsical objects in the unmissable Green Vault.

Opulent Palaces

Style, grandeur and artistry combine in grand palaces, such as the Elbe-fronting Schloss Pillnitz, the moated Moritzburg and the hulking Albrechtsburg.

Great Painters & Composers

Saxony's landscapes have long tugged at the hearts of artists such as Canaletto and Caspar David Friedrich, while Bach, Schumann and Wagner have shaped its musical heritage. Walk in their footsteps in Leipzig, Zwickau and Dresden.

p291

Munich

History
Museums
Beer

Historic Sights

Losing yourself in the House of Wittelsbach's Residenz, taking a tour of Nazi-related sites or discovering the city's sporting past at the Olympiapark are just some of the experiences on offer.

Well-Rounded Culture

From the hands-on fun of the Deutsches Museum to the masterpieces of the Alte Pinakothek, and the pop art of the Museum Brandhorst to the waxed classics of the BMW Museum, Munich has a repository of the past for every rainy day.

Ale Capital

Mammoth beer halls swaying to the oompah beat; chestnut-canopied beer gardens and Oktoberfest; proud breweries striving to out-brew their rivals and breakfasts of *Weissbier* and *Weisswurst* – Munich is the beer capital of the world.

p338

Bavaria

Castles
Romance
Mountains

Fairy-Tale Palaces

From spectacular hilltop follies such as Neuschwanstein to medieval strongholds like Nuremberg's Kaiserburg, visits to palaces provide some of Bavaria's most memorable days out.

Romantic Scenery

Whether it be the panorama from an Alpine peak or a cruise along the Danube, Bavaria packs in a lot of dreamy encounters. The biggest chunk of romance comes in the form of the Romantic Road, a route meandering from one medieval town to the next.

Alpine Magic

Bavaria possesses but a scant sliver of the Alps, but there's still bags of dramatic scenery out there to enjoy. Winter skiing and summer hiking are the main draws.

p385

Stuttgart & the Black Forest

Food
Nature
Cities

Gateau & Gourmet

Black Forest gateau, brook trout, smoked ham, *Maultaschen*, *Spätzle* – foodies, eat your hearts out in this culinary paradise with Germany's greatest density of Michelin-starred chefs.

Forest Hikes

No matter whether it's a short woodland ramble to a waterfall or a multiday trek from village to village, in the Black Forest you'll discover natural beauty combined with timeless traditions.

Urban Highs

Stuttgart tunes into the zeitgeist, with craft beer bars and the futuristic Mercedes-Benz and Porsche museums. Find Roman roots in lakeside Konstanz, Einstein in cathedral-topped Ulm and medieval splendour in forest-backed Freiburg.

p467

Frankfurt & Southern Rhineland

Wine
History & Heritage
City Life

Pinot & Riesling Tasting

Nope, Germany is not all about beer. Put some zing in your step sampling crisp whites and velvety reds in the top wine-growing areas that hug the Moselle River and Rhine.

Medieval Castles

Few buildings speak more to the imagination than craggy medieval stone castles. From Heidelberg and the Romantic Rhine to the Palatinate, this region delivers them in abundance.

Urban Cool

The business of Frankfurt may be business, but this 'Mainhattan' is no buttoned-up metropolis, as you'll quickly discover in its apple-wine taverns, fine museums and fashionable shopping areas.

p533

Cologne & Northern Rhineland

History
City Life
Offbeat Heritage

Romans & Charlemagne

Hunt for history and connect with the Romans in Xanten and Cologne, pay your respects to Charlemagne in Aachen, and applaud Münster and Osnabrück where the epic Thirty Years' War ended.

Mighty Cathedrals & Rivers

Break for *a Kölsch* between marvelling at Cologne's magnificent cathedral, sampling the city's portfolio of museums or taking a cruise on the Rhine.

Post-Industrial Culture

It takes ingenuity to recycle dormant industrial sites into something exciting. In the Ruhrgebiet you can see art in a gas tank, sip martinis in a boiler house or listen to Mozart in a compressor hall.

p628

Lower Saxony & Bremen

Outdoors
City Life
Gardens

Island Walks

Sure, you can walk around an island, but have you ever walked *to* an island? You can do so across the tidal flats in the Wadden Sea National Park in East Frisia.

Medieval Ports

A major trading town since the Middle Ages, Bremen now wows with a charming historical centre, a hip nightlife quarter, a vast container port and a poignant emigration museum.

Landscaped Wonders

A touch of Versailles is what you'll find at Hanover's Herrenhäuser Gärten, a manicured jumble of gardens accented with whimsical art by Niki de Saint Phalle.

p693

On the Road

Berlin

🎵 030 / POP 3.71 MILLION

Best Places to Eat

➡ Restaurant Tim Raue (p110)

➡ Einsunternull (p111)

➡ Restaurant Faubourg (p117)

➡ Katz Orange (p111)

➡ Restaurant am Steinplatz (p109)

Best Places to Stay

➡ Orania Hotel (p108)

➡ Capri by Fraser (p106)

➡ Michelberger Hotel (p108)

➡ Das Stue (p107)

➡ EastSeven Berlin Hostel (p108)

Why Go?

Berlin is a bon vivant, passionately feasting on the smorgasbord of life, never taking things – or itself – too seriously. Its unique blend of glamour and grit is bound to mesmerise anyone keen to connect with its vibrant culture, superb museums, fabulous food, intense parties and tangible history. When it comes to creativity, the sky's the limit in Berlin. Since the fall of the Wall, the city has become a giant lab of cultural experimentation thanks to an abundance of space, cheap rent and a free-wheeling spirit that nurtures and encourages new ideas. Must-sees or aimless explorations – this city delivers it all in one exciting and memorable package.

When to Go

Spring and autumn are generally best for visiting Berlin as the weather is the most stable and cultural events of all stripes are in full swing.

Summer essentially brings a population exchange as locals leave town for hotter climes and tourists, especially from southern Europe, flock to Berlin to escape the heat. This is the time of outdoor anything: concerts, festivals, beer gardens, parties, beach bars, cinema.

Winter is cold and dark, and life moves indoors, except during Christmas market season in December.

History

Berlin has long been in the cross-hairs of history: it staged a revolution, was headquartered by fascists, bombed to bits, ripped in half and finally reunited – all just in the 20th century! An accidental capital whose medieval birth was a mere blip on the map of history, Berlin puttered along in relative obscurity until becoming the royal capital of Prussia in 1701. It was only in fairly recent times that it significantly impacted on world history.

◉ Sights

Berlin is split into 12 official *Bezirke* (districts; for example, Mitte, Prenzlauer Berg, Kreuzberg), which are subdivided into individual *Kieze* (neighbourhoods). Key sights such as the Brandenburger Tor and Museumsinsel cluster in the walkable historic city centre – Mitte – which also cradles the fashion-centric Scheunenviertel around Hackescher Markt.

North of Mitte, residential Prenzlauer Berg has almost Parisian flair (especially around Kollwitzplatz) and brims with boutiques, cafes and a fun flea market. South of Mitte loom the contemporary high-rises of Potsdamer Platz and the Kulturforum museum and music hub. Further south, Kreuzberg and Neukölln are party central, as is student-flavoured Friedrichshain east across the Spree River.

Mitte is linked to Charlottenburg, the main western district, via the vast Tiergarten park. Its commercial hub, in turn, is the City West around Zoo station and along the Kurfürstendamm shopping strips. The sightseeing highlight here is Schloss Charlottenburg, about 3.5km northwest of the City West.

◉ Historic Mitte

★ Gendarmenmarkt   SQUARE
(Map p66; Ⓤ Französische Strasse, Stadtmitte) This graceful square is bookended by the domed German and French cathedrals and punctuated by a grandly porticoed concert hall, the Konzerthaus (Map p66; ☏ 030-203 092 333; www.konzerthaus.de; Gendarmenmarkt 2). It was named for the Gens d'Armes, an 18th-century Prussian regiment consisting of French Huguenot refugees.

The area shows Berlin at its ritziest, dappled with luxury hotels, fancy restaurants and bars.

★ Deutsches Historisches Museum   MUSEUM
(German Historical Museum; Map p66; ☏ 030-203 040; www.dhm.de; Unter den Linden 2; adult/concession/child under 18 incl IM Pei Bau €8/4/free; ⊙ 10am-6pm; ☐ 100, 200, Ⓤ Hausvogteiplatz, Ⓢ Hackescher Markt) If you're wondering what the Germans have been up to for the past 1500 years, take a spin around the baroque Zeughaus, formerly the Prussian arsenal and now home of the German Historical Museum. Upstairs, displays concentrate on the period from the 6th century AD to the end of WWI in 1918, while the ground floor tracks the 20th century all the way through to the early years after German reunification.

The adjacent modern annexe (IM Pei Exhibition Hall; Map p66; Hinter dem Giesshaus 3; adult/concession/child under 18 incl Deutsches Historisches Museum €8/4/free), designed by Chinese-American architect IM Pei, presents high-calibre changing exhibitions.

Pariser Platz   SQUARE
(Map p66; Pariser Platz; Ⓢ Brandenburger Tor, Ⓤ Brandenburger Tor) Lorded over by the landmark Brandenburg Gate (p70), this elegant square was completely flattened in WWII, then spent the Cold War trapped just east of the Berlin Wall. Look around now: the US, French and British embassies, banks and a luxury hotel have returned to their original sites and once again frame the bustling plaza, just as they did during its 19th century heyday.

★ Checkpoint Charlie   HISTORIC SITE
(Map p66; cnr Zimmerstrasse & Friedrichstrasse; ⊙ 24hr; Ⓤ Kochstrasse) **FREE** Checkpoint Charlie was the principal gateway for foreigners and diplomats between the two Berlins from 1961 to 1990. Unfortunately, this potent symbol of the Cold War has degenerated into a tacky tourist trap, though a free open-air exhibit that illustrates milestones in Cold War history is one redeeming aspect.

★ Hamburger Bahnhof – Museum für Gegenwart   MUSEUM
(Contemporary Art Museum; Map p66; ☏ 030-266 424 242; www.smb.museum; Invalidenstrasse 50-51; adult/concession €10/5, free 4-8pm 1st Thu of the month; ⊙ 10am-6pm Tue, Wed & Fri, to 8pm Thu, 11am-6pm Sat & Sun; ☐ M5, M8, M10, Ⓢ Hauptbahnhof, Ⓤ Hauptbahnhof) Berlin's contemporary art showcase opened in 1996 in an old

BERLIN HISTORY

Berlin Highlights

1 Brandenburger Tor (p70) Snapping selfies with this elegant symbol of reunited Germany.

2 Reichstag (p74) Getting giddy from the knock-out views from the rooftop glass dome.

3 Gedenkstätte Berliner Mauer (p96) Peeling back the curtain on the Berlin Wall.

4 Museumsinsel (p78) Feasting eyes and soul on 6000 years of art and cultural treasures.

5 Nightlife (p117) Losing your weekend in Berlin's hedonistic playgrounds.

6 Potsdamer Platz (p77) Marvelling at this showcase of architecture built in the 1990s.

7 Holocaust Memorial (p71) Feeling the presence of uncounted souls at this haunting site.

8 Street Art (p101) Finding out why Berlin is the world's most 'bombed' city.

9 Schloss Charlottenburg (p98) Connecting with the rich and royal at this lavish palace.

10 Kulturforum (p77) Gobbling up canvas candy in this cluster of art museums.

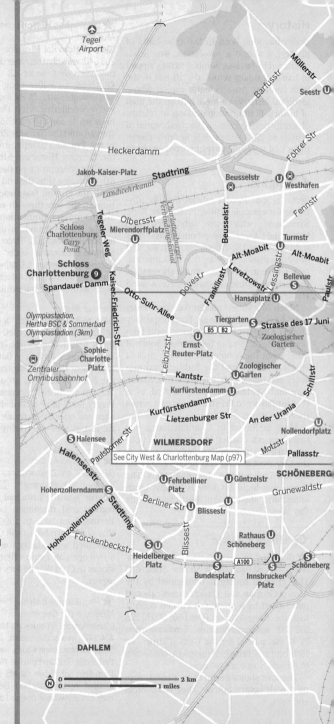

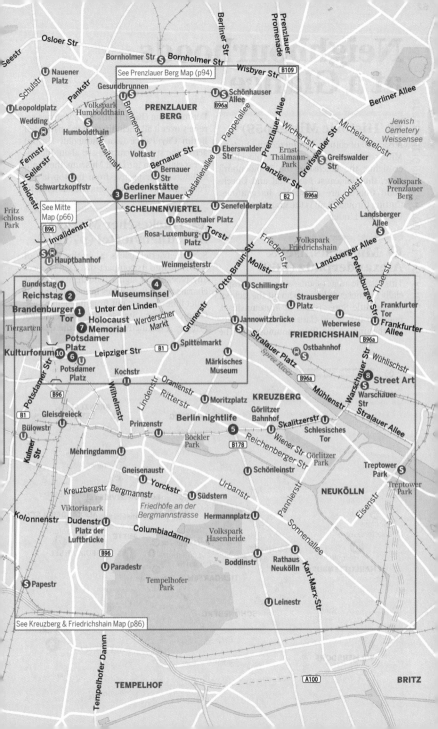

Neighbourhoods at a Glance

❶ Historic Mitte (p59)

A cocktail of culture, commerce and history, Mitte packs it in when it comes to blockbuster sights: the Reichstag, the Brandenburg Gate, the Holocaust Memorial and Checkpoint Charlie are all within its confines. Cutting through it all is the grand boulevard Unter den Linden.

❷ Museumsinsel & Alexanderplatz (p69)

This historic area is sightseeing central, especially for museum lovers who hit the jackpot on the little Spree island of Museumsinsel, home to five world-class museums, including the unmissable Pergamonmuseum. The

Berliner Dom (Berlin cathedral) watches serenely over it all, including the reconstructed Berlin City Palace (aka Humboldt Forum) across the street. Nearby, learn about life under socialism in the DDR Museum, then gain a different perspective from the top of the Fernsehturm on socialist-era Alexanderplatz.

❸ Hackescher Markt & Scheunenviertel (p73)

Scheunenviertel packs a mother lode of charisma into its compact size. Don't expect any blockbuster sights though: its greatest charms reveal themselves in the labyrinth of quiet lanes fanning out from its main drags, Oranienburger Strasse and Rosenthaler Strasse. A distinctive feature of the quarter

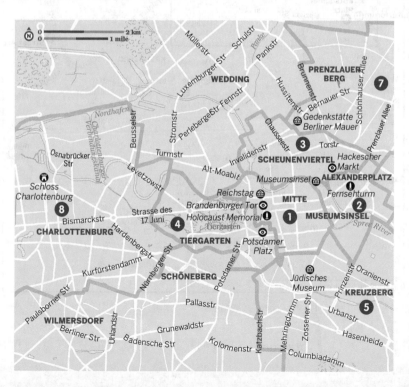

is its *Höfe* – interlinked courtyards filled with cafes, shops and drinking temples.

❹ Potsdamer Platz & Tiergarten (p77)

This new quarter, forged from ground once bisected by the Berlin Wall, is a showcase of fabulous contemporary architecture and home to big cinemas and shopping. Culture lovers should not skip the Kulturforum museums, especially the Gemäldegalerie, which sits right next to the world-class Berliner Philharmonie. The leafy Tiergarten makes for a perfect sightseeing break.

❺ Kreuzberg & Neukölln (p85)

Kreuzberg and Neukölln across the canal are Berlin's most dynamic and cool neighbourhoods. With the Jewish Museum and the German Museum of Technology, the area offers a couple of blockbuster sights, but its main

draw is its global village atmosphere, accompanied by a burgeoning roster of eclectic eateries, bars, nightlife and indie shopping.

❻ Friedrichshain (p89)

The former East Berlin district of Friedrichshain is famous for high-profile GDR-era relics such as the longest surviving stretch of the Berlin Wall (the East Side Gallery), the socialist boulevard Karl-Marx-Allee and the former Stasi headquarters. But the area also stakes its reputation on having Berlin's most rambunctious nightlife scene, with a glut of clubs and bars holding forth along Revaler Strasse and around the Ostkreuz train station.

❼ Prenzlauer Berg (p92)

Splendidly well-groomed Prenzlauer Berg is one of Berlin's most charismatic residential neighbourhoods, filled with cafes, historic buildings and indie boutiques. It's a joy to explore on foot. On Sundays, the world descends on its Mauerpark for flea marketeering, summertime karaoke and chilling in the sun. It's easily combined with a visit to the quarter's main sightseeing attraction, the Gedenkstätte Berliner Mauer.

❽ City West & Charlottenburg (p95)

The glittering heart of West Berlin during the Cold War, Charlottenburg is a big draw for shopaholics, royal groupies and art lovers. Its main sightseeing attraction is Schloss Charlottenburg, with its park and adjacent art museums. About 3.5km southeast of here, the City West area, around Zoologischer Garten (Zoo Station), is characterised by Berlin's biggest shopping boulevard, the Kurfürstendamm.

❾ Schöneberg (p100)

Largely residential Schöneberg's leafy side streets are lined with stately 19th-century town houses and teem with charming cafes and indie boutiques. The area is also home to Berlin's traditional gay quarter and red-light district, although the latter is gradually being displaced by an influx of galleries and cool bars and restaurants on Potsdamer Strasse.

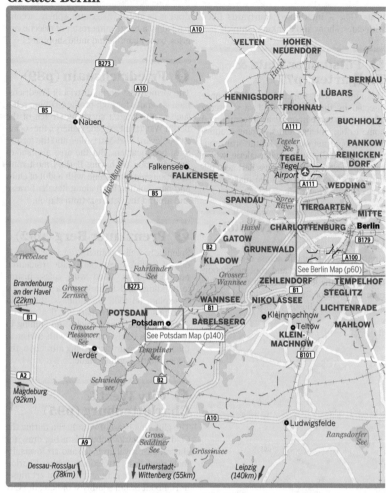

railway station, whose grandeur is a great backdrop for this Aladdin's cave of paintings, installations, sculptures and video art. Changing exhibits span the arc of post-1950 artistic movements – from conceptual art and pop art to minimal art and Fluxus – and include seminal works by such major players as Andy Warhol, Cy Twombly, Joseph Beuys and Robert Rauschenberg.

★**Sammlung Boros**   GALLERY
(Boros Collection; Map p66; ☑030-2759 4065; www.sammlung-boros.de; Reinhardtstrasse 20; adult/concession €12/6; ☺tours 3-6.30pm Thu,

10.30am-6.30pm Fri, 10am-6.30pm Sat & Sun; ☒M1, ⓢFriedrichstrasse, ⓤOranienburger Tor, Friedrichstrasse) This Nazi-era bunker presents one of Berlin's finest private contemporary art collections, amassed by advertising guru Christian Boros who acquired the behemoth in 2003. A third selection of works went live in May 2017 and includes installations by Katja Novitskova, digital paintings by Avery Singer and photo series by Peter Piller. Book online (weeks, if not months, ahead) to join a guided tour (also in English) and to pick up fascinating nuggets about the building's surprising other peacetime incarnations.

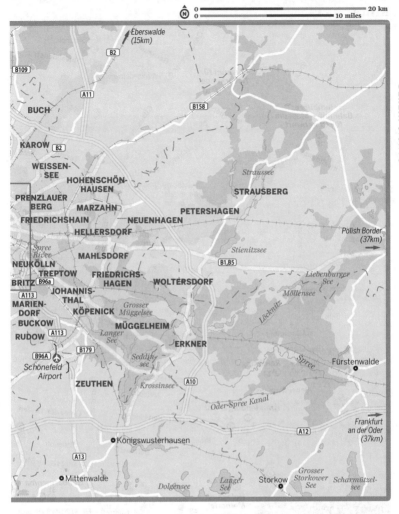

0 _____ 20 km
0 _____ 10 miles

Éberswalde (15km)

B2

B109

A11

BUCH

B158

KAROW B2

WEISSEN-SEE

HOHENSCHÖN-HAUSEN

Straussee

PRENZLAUER BERG

STRAUSBERG

MARZAHN

FRIEDRICHSHAIN

NEUENHAGEN

PETERSHAGEN

HELLERSDORF

Polish Border (37km)

Spree River

MAHLSDORF

Stienitzsee

B1,B5

NEUKÖLLN

TREPTOW

FRIEDRICHS-HAGEN

WOLTERSDORF

Liebenburger See

BRITZ B96a

Möllensee

A113

JOHANNIS-THAL

Grosser Müggelsee

Löcknitz

MARIEN-DORF

KÖPENICK

BUCKOW

MÜGGELHEIM

Langer See

RUDOW A113

ERKNER

Spree

B96A

B179

Fürstenwalde

Schönefeld Airport

Seddin-see

ZEUTHEN

Krossinsee

A10

Oder-Spree Kanal

Frankfurt an der Oder (37km)

A12

Königswusterhausen

A13

Grosser Storkower See

Mittenwalde

Dolgensee

Langer See

Storkow

Scharmützel-see

★ **Museum für Naturkunde**   MUSEUM
(Museum of Natural History; Map p66; ☏030-2093 8591; www.naturkundemuseum.berlin; Invalidenstrasse 43; adult/concession incl audioguide €8/5; ⊙9.30am-6pm Tue-Fri, 10am-6pm Sat & Sun; ♿; ▣M5, M8, M10, 12, ⓤNaturkundemuseum) Fossils and minerals don't quicken your pulse? Well, how about Tristan, the T-Rex? His skeleton is among the best-preserved in the world and, along with the 12m-high *Brachiosaurus branchai*, part of the Jurassic superstar line-up at this highly engaging museum. Elsewhere you can wave at Knut, the world's most famous dead polar bear;

marvel at the fragile bones of an ultrarare *Archaeopteryx* protobird, and find out why zebras are striped.

There are lots of unexpected highlights, including the massively magnified insect models and a creepy but artistically illuminated gallery of ethanol-preserved creatures used for research. In the miniplanetarium you can journey deep into space and learn what the big bang was all about and how the planets were formed. The Evolution in Action hall clears up some age-old mysteries such as why peacocks have such beautiful feathers.

Mitte

BERLIN

Scharnhorststr

Habersaathstr

Chausseestr

Bernauer Str

Nordbahnhof

Invalidenstr

Museum für Naturkunde
10

Naturkundemuseum

Chausseestr

Tieckstr

Gartenstr

Novalisstr

Torstr

74

Tucholskystr

Hamburger Bahnhof – Museum für Gegenwart
8

Heidestr

Invalidenstr

Invalidenstr

57

Charité - Universitätsmedizin Berlin

Luisenstr

Hannoversche Str

66

Linienstr

Oranienburger Tor

Oranienburger Str

Oranienburger Str

72

Europaplatz
111

Hauptbahnhof

Humboldt-Universität zu Berlin

78

80

99

Oranienburger Str

Johannisstr

Heckmann Höfe

Washington-platz

Alexanderufer

Kapelleufer

Charité-Platz

Kammerspiele

Schumannstr

Sammlung Boros
15

Friedrichstr

94

Ziegelstr

Rahel-Hirsch-Str

Spree River

Spreebogenpark

Moltkebrücke

Otto-von-Bismarck-Allee

Reinhardtstr

Karlplatz

Marienstr

Albrechtstr

Schiffbauerdamm

Am Weidendamm

Planckstr

Geschwister-Scholl-Str

Luisenstr

Friedrichstr
50

Bahnhof Friedrichstr

Friedrichstr

Georgenstr

Hegelplatz

Heinrich-Von-Gagern-Str

Bundestag

Paul-Löbe-Allee

Platz der Republik

Reichstag
14

Reichstagufer

Dorotheenstr

101

Charlottenstr

Yitzhak-Rabin-Str

Scheidemannstr

Mittelstr

Friedrichstr

Strasse des 17 Juni

Brandenburger Tor
1 44

110

Unter den Linden

Unter den Linden

20

Brandenburger Tor

95

63

Behrenstr

Behrenstr

68

25

9 42

Holocaust Memorial

48

Französische Str

Französische Str

108

Gendarmenmarkt

60 31 6

Tiergarten

In den Ministergärten

An der Kolonnade

Wilhelmstr

Taubenstr

Friedrichstadtpassagen

Stadtmitte

107

Mohrenstr

Mohrenstr

Glinkastr

Jägerstr

Mohrenstr

Kronenstr

Tiergartenstr

Lennéstr

Am Park

Vossstr

Bellevuestr

Ben-Gurion-Str

22

93 16

33

38

Auguste-Hauschner-Str

58

Leipziger Platz

105

Leipziger Str

Leipziger Str

Wilhelmstr

Friedrichstr

Charlottenstr

Markgrafenstr

Ebertstr

Sony Center

Potsdamer Str

56

43

24

Potsdamer Platz
26

Potsdamer Platz

Erna-Berger-Str

Potsdamer Str

Alte Potsdamer Str

62

106

Köthener Str

Linkstr

Stresemannstr

Niederkirchner Str

Checkpoint Charlie

51 Niederkirchner Str

2 73

102

36

Rudi-Dutschke-Str

35

17

Topographie des Terrors

Kochstr

Kochstr

Mauerstr

KREUZBERG

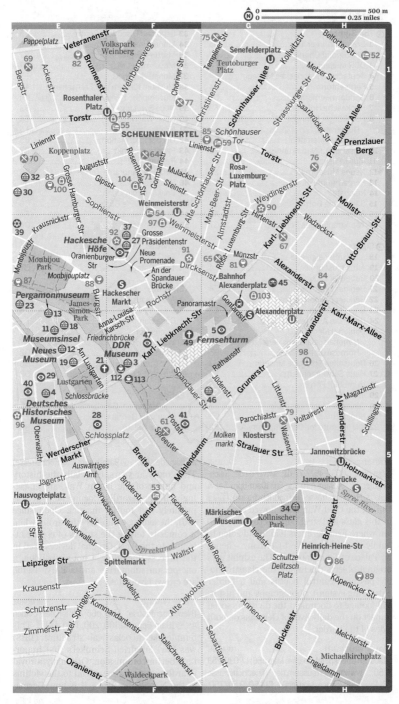

Mitte

Tränenpalast   MUSEUM

(Map p66; ☑ 030-4677 77911; www.hdg.de; Reichstagufer 17; ⊘ 9am-7pm Tue-Fri, 10am-6pm Sat & Sun; ⑤ Friedrichstrasse, Ⓤ Friedrichstrasse) **FREE** During the Cold War, tears flowed copiously in this glass-and-steel border-crossing pavilion where East Berliners had to bid adieu to family visiting from West Germany – hence its 'Palace of Tears' moniker. The exhibit uses original objects (including the claustrophobic passport control booths and a border auto-firing system), photographs and historical footage to document the division's social impact on the daily lives of Germans on both sides of the border.

Mauermuseum   MUSEUM

(Haus am Checkpoint Charlie; Map p66; ☑ 030-253 7250; www.mauermuseum.de; Friedrichstrasse 43-45; adult/concession/child €14.50/9.50/7.50,

audioguide €5; ⊘ 9am-10pm; Ⓤ Kochstrasse) The Cold War years, especially the history and horror of the Berlin Wall, are engagingly, if haphazardly, documented in this privately run tourist magnet. Open since 1961, the ageing exhibit is still strong when it comes to telling the stories of escape attempts to the West. Original devices used in the process, including a hot-air balloon, a one-person submarine and a BMW Isetta, are crowd favourites.

Neue Wache   MEMORIAL

(New Guardhouse; Map p66; Unter den Linden 4; ⊘ 10am-6pm; ⧠ 100, 200, TXL) **FREE** This temple-like neoclassical structure (1818) was Karl Friedrich Schinkel's first important Berlin commission. Originally a royal guardhouse and a memorial to the victims of the Napoleonic Wars, it is now Germany's central memorial for the victims of war and dictatorship. Its sombre and austere interior is dominated by Käthe Kollwitz' heart-wrenching Pietà-style sculpture of a mother helplessly cradling her dead soldier son.

Bebelplatz SQUARE
(Map p66; Bebelplatz; ☐100, 200, TXL, ⓊHausvogteiplatz) The heart of a cultural centre envisioned by King Frederick the Great, austere Bebelplatz is infamous as the site of the first full-blown public book burning in Nazi Germany. Members of the Nazi German Students' League cheered as works by Brecht, Mann, Marx and others deemed 'subversive' went up in flames on 10 May 1933. Originally called Opernplatz, it was renamed for August Bebel, the co-founder of Germany's Social Democratic Party (SPD), in 1947.

Site of Hitler's Bunker HISTORIC SITE
(Map p66; cnr In den Ministergärten & Gertrud-Kolmar-Strasse; ⊘24hr; ⓈBrandenburger Tor, ⓊBrandenburger Tor) Berlin was burning and Soviet tanks advancing relentlessly when Adolf Hitler killed himself on 30 April 1945, alongside Eva Braun, his long-time female companion, hours after their marriage. Today, a parking lot covers the site, revealing its dark history only via an information panel with a diagram of the vast bunker network, construction data and the site's post-WWII history.

◉ Museumsinsel & Alexanderplatz

Berliner Dom CHURCH
(Berlin Cathedral; Map p66; ☑ticket office 030-2026 9136; www.berlinerdom.de; Am Lustgarten; adult/concession €7/5; ⊘9am-8pm Apr-Sep, to 7pm

BY MARTIN DEJA/GETTY IMAGES ©

TOP SIGHT
BRANDENBURGER TOR

The Brandenburg Gate is Berlin's most famous – and most photographed – landmark. Trapped right behind the Berlin Wall during the Cold War, it went from symbol of division to epitomising German reunification when the hated barrier fell in 1989. It now serves as a photogenic backdrop for raucous New Years' Eve parties, concerts, festivals and mega-events including FIFA World Cup finals.

Commissioned by Prussian king Friedrich Wilhelm II, the gate was completed in 1791 as a symbol of peace and a suitably impressive entrance to the grand boulevard Unter den Linden. Architect Carl Gotthard Langhans looked to the Acropolis in Athens for inspiration for this elegant triumphal arch, which is the only surviving one of 18 city gates that once ringed historic Berlin.

Standing 26m high, 65.5m wide and 11m deep, the neoclassical sandstone structure punctuates Pariser Platz (p59), a harmoniously proportioned square framed by banks, a luxury hotel and the US, British and French embassies. The gate is fronted by 12 Doric columns and divided into five passageways. The wider central passage was reserved for the king and his entourage; common folk had to use the four narrower ones.

Crowning the Brandenburg Gate is the *Quadriga,* Johann Gottfried Schadow's famous sculpture of a winged goddess piloting a chariot drawn by four horses. After trouncing Prussia in 1806, Napoleon kidnapped the lady and held her hostage in Paris until she was freed by a gallant Prussian general in 1815. Afterwards, the goddess, who originally represented Eirene (the goddess of peace), was promoted to Victoria (the goddess of victory) and equipped with a new trophy designed by Karl Friedrich Schinkel: an iron cross wrapped into an oak wreath and topped with a Prussian eagle.

DON'T MISS
➡ Quadriga
➡ View from Pariser Platz at sunset

PRACTICALITIES
➡ Brandenburg Gate
➡ Map p66
➡ Pariser Platz
➡ S Brandenburger Tor, U Brandenburger Tor

PHOTO:REO MICHAL BEDNAREK/SHUTTERSTOCK ©

HOLOCAUST MEMORIAL

The **Denkmal für die ermordeten Juden Europas (Memorial to the Murdered Jews of Europe)** was officially dedicated in 2005. Colloquially known as the Holocaust Memorial, it's Germany's central memorial to the Nazi-planned genocide during the Third Reich. For the football-field-sized space, New York architect Peter Eisenman created 2711 sarcophagi-like concrete stelae (slabs) of equal size but various heights, rising in sombre silence from undulating ground.

You're free to access this massive concrete maze at any point and make your individual journey through it. At first it may seem austere, even sterile. But take time to feel the coolness of the stone and contemplate the interplay of light and shadow, then stumble aimlessly among the narrow passageways, and you'll soon connect with a metaphorical sense of disorientation, confusion and claustrophobia.

For context, visit the subterranean **Ort der Information** (Information Centre; Map p66; ☑ 030-7407 2929; www.holocaust-mahnmal.de; audio guide €3; ☺10am-8pm Tue-Sun Apr-Sep, to 7pm Oct-Mar, last admission 45min before closing) **FREE**, which movingly lifts the veil of anonymity from the six million Holocaust victims. A graphic timeline of Jewish persecution during the Third Reich is followed by a series of rooms documenting the fates of individuals and families. The most visceral is the darkened Room of Names, where the names and years of birth and death of Jewish victims are projected onto all four walls while a solemn voice reads their short biographies. Poignant and heart-wrenching, these exhibits leave no one untouched. Not recommended for children under 14.

DON'T MISS

➡ Field of stelae

➡ Ort der Information

➡ Room of Names

PRACTICALITIES

➡ Memorial to the Murdered Jews of Europe

➡ Map p66

➡ ☑ 030-2639 4336

➡ www.stiftung-denkmal.de

➡ Cora-Berliner-Strasse 1

➡ audioguide €3

➡ ☺24hr

➡ ⑤ Brandenburger Tor, ⓤ Brandenburger Tor

HUMBOLDT FORUM: BERLIN'S NEW CULTURAL HUB

In the heart of Berlin, across from the Berlin Dom and the famous museums of Museumsinsel, looms the **Humboldt Forum im Berliner Schloss** (Map p66; www.humboldt forum.com; Schlossplatz; 📮100, 200, TXL, U Klosterstrasse), a cultural hub built to look like an exact replica of the baroque Berlin City Palace, but with a modern interior.

Although barely damaged in WWII, the grand palace where Prussian rulers had made their home since 1443 was blown up by East Germany's government in 1950 to drop the final curtain on Prussian and Nazi rule. To emphasise the point, the new communist rulers built their own modernist parliament – called Palast der Repubilk (Palace of the Republic) – on top of the ruins 26 years later. Riddled with asbestos, it too had a date with the wrecking ball in 2006.

After two decades of debate and bickering, construction of the replica finally kicked off in July 2013. The building itself is said to be on schedule for completion by early 2019. If all then continues to go according to plan, the Humboldt Forum could open to the public – at least partly – by the end of that year.

When it does, it will not only be the new home of the Museum of Ethnology and the Museum of Asian Art but will also host films and lectures that explore topical issues in science, art, religion, politics and business. The Berlin Ausstellung (Berlin Exhibit) will focus on the links between Berlin and the world and examine such issues as migration, war, fashion, revolution, free spaces, borders and entertainment. Also on the 1st floor will be the university-run Humboldt Laboratory, an interdisciplinary exhibition and cultural space that unravels the processes that result in the creation of new knowledge and shows how science is relevant to all of us. Admission to all permanent exhibits is expected to be free for the first three years.

The Schloss 2.0 comes with a projected price tag of €590 million for the building alone, with most of the bill having been footed by the federal government. The design by Italian architect Franco Stella has three sides of the facade looking like a baroque blast from the past, thus visually restoring the historic ensemble of Museumsinsel, Berliner Dom and the Neuer Marstall (New Royal Stables). Only the facade facing the Spree River will be without baroque adornments. A cupola graces the western end.

Oct-Mar; 📮100, 200, TXL, S Hackescher Markt) Pompous yet majestic, the Italian Renaissance–style former royal court church (1905) does triple duty as house of worship, museum and concert hall. Inside it's gilt to the hilt and outfitted with a lavish marble-and-onyx altar, a 7269-pipe Sauer organ and elaborate royal sarcophagi. Climb up the 267 steps to the gallery for glorious city views.

★ DDR Museum
MUSEUM

(GDR (East Germany) Museum; Map p66; 📲030-847 123 731; www.ddr-museum.de; Karl-Liebknecht-Strasse 1; adult/concession €9.80/6; ⊗10am-8pm Sun-Fri, to 10pm Sat; 📮100, 200, TXL, S Hackescher Markt) This touchy-feely museum does an insightful and entertaining job of pulling back the iron curtain on daily life in socialist East Germany. You'll learn how kids were put through collective potty training, engineers earned little more than farmers, and everyone, it seems, went on nudist holidays. A perennial crowd-pleaser among the historic objects on display is a Trabi, the tinny East German standard car – sit in it to take a virtual spin around an East Berlin neighbourhood.

The more sinister sides of daily life, including the chronic supply shortages and surveillance by the Stasi (secret police), are also addressed.

★ Fernsehturm
LANDMARK

(Map p66; 📲030-247 575 875; www.tv-turm.de; Panoramastrasse 1a; adult/child €15.50/9.50, fast track online ticket €19.50/12; ⊗9am-midnight Mar-Oct, 10am-midnight Nov-Feb, last ascent 11.30pm; 📮100, 200, TXL, U Alexanderplatz, S Alexanderplatz) Germany's tallest structure, the TV Tower has been soaring 368m high since 1969 and is as iconic to Berlin as the Eiffel Tower is to Paris. On clear days, views are stunning from the observation deck (with bar) at 203m or from the upstairs **Sphere restaurant** (Map p66; mains lunch €10.50-18, dinner €12.50-28; ⊗10am-11pm; 📶), which makes one revolution per hour.

Built in 1969, the tower was supposed to demonstrate the GDR's engineering prowess, but ended up being a bit of a laughing stock when it turned out that, when hit by the sun, the steel sphere below the antenna produced the reflection of a giant cross. West Berliners gleefully dubbed the phenomenon 'the Pope's revenge'.

St Marienkirche
CHURCH

(St Mary's Church; Map p66; www.marienkirche-berlin.de; Karl-Liebknecht-Strasse 8; ⏰10am-6pm Apr-Dec, to 4pm Jan-Mar; 🚌100, 200, TXL, Ⓢ Hackescher Markt, Alexanderplatz, Ⓤ Alexanderplatz) This Gothic brick gem has welcomed worshippers since the early 14th century, making it one of Berlin's oldest surviving churches. A 22m-long *Dance of Death* fresco in the vestibule inspired by a 15th-century plague leads to a relatively plain interior enlivened by numerous other art treasures. The oldest is the 1437 bronze baptismal font buttressed by a trio of dragons. The baroque alabaster pulpit by Andreas Schlüter from 1703 is equally eye-catching.

Rotes Rathaus
HISTORIC BUILDING

(Berlin Town Hall; Map p66; 📞030-9026 2032; www.berlin.de/berliner-rathaus; Rathausstrasse 15; ⏰9am-6pm Mon-Fri; Ⓢ Alexanderplatz, Ⓤ Alexanderplatz, Klosterstrasse) FREE The Rotes Rathaus (Red Town Hall) is the seat of Berlin's governing mayor and a red-brick neo-Renaissance pile completed in 1869. Outside, note the terracotta frieze that illustrates Berlin milestones until 1871. Except during special events, much of the town hall is open to the public – pick up a brochure with a self-guided tour in the foyer and also check out the free special exhibits.

The moniker 'red', by the way, was inspired by the red brick facade and not (necessarily) the political leanings of its occupants.

Nikolaiviertel
AREA

(Map p66; btwn Rathausstrasse, Breite Strasse, Spandauer Strasse & Mühlendamm; Ⓤ Klosterstrasse) FREE Commissioned by the East German government to celebrate Berlin's 750th birthday, the twee Nicholas Quarter is a half-hearted attempt at recreating the city's medieval birthplace around its oldest surviving building, the 1230 Nikolaikirche. The maze of cobbled lanes is worth a quick stroll, while several olde-worlde-style restaurants provide sustenance.

Märkisches Museum
MUSEUM

(Map p66; 📞030-2400 2162; www.stadt museum.de; Am Köllnischen Park 5; adult/concession/under 18 €7/4/free; ⏰10am-6pm Tue-Sun; Ⓤ Märkisches Museum) Compact, engaging and interactive, the permanent exhibit at this local history museum zeroes in on historic milestones and key protagonists that shaped Berlin's evolution from the medieval trading village of Berlin-Cölln into today's European metropolis. Displays tackle questions such as what gives Berlin its special character and how its residents impact the city and vice versa. Period rooms like the Gothic Hall with its displays of medieval religious art, the Guild Hall and the Weapons Hall provide atmospheric eye candy.

Curators also mount changing exhibits on the ground floor that shine the spotlight on specific themes of Berlin's often turbulent past. The museum itself is housed in an imposing mash-up of parts of historic buildings from the surrounding region, including a bishop's palace tower and the Gothic gables of a church. A copy of the Roland statue, a medieval symbol of civic liberty and freedom, stands guard at the entrance. Note that the museum is set to close for an extended restoration in 2021.

Sealife Berlin
AQUARIUM

(Map p66; 📞0180-666 690 101; www.visitsealife.com; Spandauer Strasse 3; adult/child €18/14.50, cheaper online; ⏰10am-7pm, last admission 6pm; 🚌100, 200, TXL, Ⓢ Hackescher Markt, Alexanderplatz) Smile-inducing seahorses, ethereal jellyfish, Ophira the octopus and a marine dinosaur skeleton that can be 'reanimated' are some of the crowd favourites among the 5000 denizens of this rambling aquarium, where visits conclude with a slow lift ride through the Aquadom, a 25m-high cylindrical tropical fish tank.

Also popular are the feeding sessions of rays, sharks, catfish and other creatures that take place between 11.30am and 3.30pm.

◉ Hackescher Markt & Scheunenviertel

★ Hackesche Höfe
HISTORIC SITE

(Hackesche Courtyards; Map p66; 📞030-2809 8010; www.hackesche-hoefe.com; enter from Rosenthaler Strasse 40/41 or Sophienstrasse 6; 🚋M1, Ⓢ Hackescher Markt, Ⓤ Weinmeisterstrasse) The Hackesche Höfe is the largest and most famous of the courtyard ensembles peppered throughout the Scheunenviertel. Built in 1907, the eight interlinked *Höfe* reopened in 1996 with a congenial mix of cafes, galleries, shops and entertainment venues. The main entrance on Rosenthaler Strasse

MBBIRDY/GETTY IMAGES ©

TOP SIGHT
REICHSTAG

It's been burned, bombed, rebuilt, buttressed by the Berlin Wall, wrapped in fabric and finally turned into the modern home of the German parliament by Norman Foster: the Reichstag is one of Berlin's most iconic buildings. Its most eye-catching feature is the glistening glass dome, which draws more than three million visitors each year.

Dome

Resembling a giant glass beehive, the sparkling cupola is open at the top and bottom and sits right above the plenary chamber as a visual metaphor for transparency and openness in politics. A lift whisks you to the rooftop terrace, from where you can easily pinpoint such sights as the curvaceous House of World Cultures and the majestic Berliner Dom (Berlin Cathedral) or marvel at the enormous dimensions of Tiergarten park. To learn more about these and other landmarks, the Reichstag building and the workings of parliament, pick up a free multilingual audioguide as you exit the lift. The commentary starts automatically as you mosey up the dome's 230m-long ramp, which spirals around a mirror-clad cone that deflects daylight down into the plenary chamber.

Home of the Bundestag

Today, the Reichstag is the historic anchor of the new federal government quarter built after reunification. The Bundestag, Germany's parliament, has hammered out its policies here since moving from the former German capital of Bonn to Berlin in 1999. The parliament's arrival followed a complete architectural revamp masterminded

DON'T MISS

→ Views from the rooftop

→ The facade

→ Audioguide tour of the dome

PRACTICALITIES

→ Map p66

→ www.bundestag.de

→ Platz der Republik 1, Visitors Centre, Scheidemannstrasse

→ ⊙ lift 8am–midnight, last entry 9.45pm, Visitors Centre 8am–8pm Apr–Oct, to 6pm Nov–Mar

→ ♿

→ 🚌 100, S Brandenburger Tor, Hauptbahnhof, U Brandenburger Tor, Bundestag

by Lord Norman Foster, who preserved only the building's 19th-century shell and added the landmark glass dome.

Main Facade

Stylistically, the monumental west-facing main facade borrows heavily from the Italian Renaissance, with a few neo-baroque elements thrown into the mix. A massive staircase leads up to a portico curtained by six Corinthian columns and topped by the dedication 'Dem Deutschen Volke' (To the German People), which wasn't added until 1916. The bronze letters were designed by Peter Behrens, one of the fathers of modern architecture, and cast from two French cannons captured during the Napoleonic Wars of 1813–15. The original dome, made of steel and glass and considered a high-tech marvel at the time, was destroyed during the Reichstag fire in 1933.

Historic Milestones

The grand old structure was designed by Paul Wallot and completed in 1894, when Germany was still a constitutional monarchy known as the Deutsches Reich (German Empire) – hence the building's name. Home of the German parliament from 1894 to 1933 and again from 1999, the hulking building will likely give you more flashbacks to high-school history than any other Berlin landmark. On 9 November 1919, parliament member Philipp Scheidemann proclaimed the German republic from one of its windows. In 1933, the Nazis used a mysterious fire as a pretext to seize dictatorial powers. A dozen years later, victorious Red Army troops raised the Soviet flag on the bombed-out building, which stood damaged and empty on the western side of the Berlin Wall throughout the Cold War. In the late 1980s, megastars including David Bowie, Pink Floyd and Michael Jackson performed concerts on the lawn in front of the building.

The Wall collapsed soon thereafter, paving the way to German reunification, which was enacted here in 1990. Five years later, the Reichstag made headlines once again when the artist couple Christo and Jeanne-Claude wrapped the massive structure in silvery fabric. It had taken an act of the German parliament to approve the project, which was intended to mark the end of the Cold War and the beginning of a new era. For two weeks starting in late June 1995, visitors from around the world flocked to Berlin to admire this unique sight. Shortly after the fabric came down, Lord Norman Foster set to work.

An extensive photographic exhibit at the bottom of the dome captures many of these historic moments.

VISITING THE DOME

Free reservations for visiting the Reichstag dome must be made at www.bundestag.de. Book early, especially in summer, and prepare to show picture ID, pass through a metal detector and have your belongings X-rayed. Guided tours and lectures can also be booked via the website. If you haven't prebooked, swing by the Visitors' Centre near the Reichstag to enquire about remaining tickets for that day or the next two. You can also reach the rooftop by making reservations at the Dachgartenrestaurant Käfer.

It was the night of 27 February 1933: the Reichstag was ablaze. In the aftermath, a Dutch anarchist named Marinus van der Lubbe was arrested for arson without conclusive proof. Historians regard the incident as a pivotal moment in Hitler's power grab. Claiming that the fire was part of a large-scale Communist conspiracy, the Nazis pushed through the 'Reichstag Fire Decree', quashing civil rights and triggering the persecution of political opponents. The true events of that night remain a mystery. Its impact on history does not.

LOCAL KNOWLEDGE

EYE-POPPING VIEWS ON A BUDGET

Heading up the Fernsehturm (p72) may give you bragging rights for having been atop Germany's tallest structure, but those wonderful vistas come at a price (and with long lines unless you prebook). Here are a couple of nearby alternatives that will leave less of a dent in your wallet, while having the added benefit of featuring the photogenic TV tower itself in your snapshots.

Park Inn Panorama Terrasse (Map p66; ☑ 030-238 90; www.parkinn-berlin.de/en/panorama-terrace; Alexanderplatz 7; €4; ☉ noon-10pm Apr-Oct, to 6pm Nov-Mar, weather permitting; U Alexanderplatz, S Alexanderplatz) At 150m above the ground, the Panorama Terrasse atop the Park Inn Hotel on Alexanderplatz puts you 53m lower than the viewing platform of the Fernsehturm, but lets you relax with a cold drink while draped over a sunlounger or marvelling at gutsy base-flyers leaping off the edge of the building (Friday to Sunday only). Attached to a special winch rappel system usually used by stunt performers, these daredevils plunge towards the ground in a controlled fall, reaching near free-fall speeds.

House of Weekend (p117) On a hot summer night, the absolute high point for party people is the rooftop garden of this club atop the GDR-era Haus des Reisens (House of Travel). Aside from picture-postcard views, you can look forward to a fun crowd and cool cocktails. After 11pm, the action moves down to the 15th floor for some quality dancing until the wee hours.

leads to Court I, prettily festooned with art nouveau tiles, while Court VII segues to the romantic Rosenhöfe with a sunken rose garden and tendril-like balustrades.

Neue Synagoge
SYNAGOGUE

(Map p66; ☑ 030-8802 8300; www.centrumjudaicum.de; Oranienburger Strasse 28-30; adult/concession €5/4, audioguide €3; ☉ 10am-6pm Mon-Fri, to 7pm Sun, closes 3pm Fri & 6pm Sun Oct-Mar; ☒ M1, U Oranienburger Tor, S Oranienburger Strasse) The gleaming gold dome of the Neue Synagoge is the most visible symbol of Berlin's revitalised Jewish community. The 1866 original was Germany's largest synagogue but its modern incarnation is not so much a house of worship (although prayer services do take place), as a museum and place of remembrance called Centrum Judaicum. The dome can be climbed from April to September (adult/concession €3/2.50).

Haus Schwarzenberg
HISTORIC BUILDING

(Map p66; www.haus-schwarzenberg.org; Rosenthaler Strasse 39; ☉ courtyard 24hr; ☒ M1, S Hackescher Markt) **FREE** Haus Schwarzenberg is the last holdout in the heavily gentrified area around the Hackescher Markt. Run by a nonprofit organisation, it's an unpretentious space where art and creativity are allowed to flourish beyond the mainstream and commerce. Festooned with street art and bizarre metal sculptures, the courtyards lead to studios, offices, the underground 'amusement park' Monsterkabinett (Map p66; ☑ 0152 1259

8687; www.monsterkabinett.de; tours adult/concession €8/5; ☉ tours 6-10pm Wed & Thu, 4-10pm Fri & Sat), the edgy-arty **Eschschloraque Rümschrümp** (Map p66; www.eschschloraque.de; ☉ from 2pm) bar, an art-house **cinema** (Map p66; ☑ 030-2859 9973; www.kino-central.de; tickets €8.50) – outdoors in summer – and a couple of small museums dealing with Jewish persecution during the Third Reich.

KW Institute for Contemporary Art
GALLERY

(Map p66; ☑ 030-243 4590; www.kw-berlin.de; Auguststrasse 69; adult/concession €8/6, free 6-9pm Thu; ☉ 11am-7pm Wed-Mon, to 9pm Thu; ☒ M1, S Oranienburger Strasse, U Oranienburger Tor) Founded in the early 1990s in an old margarine factory, nonprofit KW played a key role in turning the Scheunenviertel into Berlin's first major post-Wall art district. It continues to stage boundary-pushing exhibits that reflect the latest – and often radical – trends in contemporary art.

Jüdische Mädchenschule
HISTORIC BUILDING

(Jewish Girls' School; Map p66; www.maedchenschule.org; Auguststrasse 11-13; ☉ hours vary; ☒ M1, S Oranienburger Strasse, U Oranienburger Tor) **FREE** This 1920s former Jewish girls' school, which was forcibly closed by the Nazis in 1942, was injected with new life as a cultural and culinary hub in 2012. Three galleries and the Museum the Kennedys have set up shop in the former classrooms, while the former gym now houses a Michelin-starred restaurant. The structure was built in the austere New Objectivity style by the renowned Jewish architect Alexander Beer, who perished at Theresienstadt concentration camp.

Plenty of original design features have survived, including the tiles in the entrance and the classroom lights.

Museum the Kennedys   MUSEUM
(Map p66; ☑030-2065 3570; www.the kennedys.de; Auguststrasse 11-13; adult/concession €5/2.50; ☉10am-6pm Tue-Fri, 11am-6pm Sat & Sun; ⓖM1, ⓢOranienburger Strasse, ⓤOranienburger Tor) US president John F Kennedy has held a special place in German hearts since his defiant *'Ich bin ein Berliner!'* ('I am a Berliner') solidarity speech in 1963. This private exhibit addresses the president's continued mystique as well as such topics as the Berlin visit and his assassination in Dallas through photographs, documents, video footage and memorabilia.

Among the standout relics are JFK's reading glasses and crocodile-leather briefcase, Jackie's Persian-lamb pillbox hat and a hilarious Superman comic book starring the president. Temporary presentations, including an inaugural photo exhibit of former President Obama, supplement the permanent galleries.

◉ Potsdamer Platz & Tiergarten

★ Sony Center   NOTABLE BUILDING
(Map p66; www.potsdamer-platz.net; Potsdamer Strasse; ⓖ200, ⓤPotsdamer Platz, ⓢPotsdamer Platz) Designed by Helmut Jahn, the visually dramatic Sony Center is fronted by a 26-floor, glass-and-steel tower and integrates rare relics from the prewar era of Potsdamer Platz (Alte Potsdamer Strasse), such as the opulent Kaisersaal. The heart of the Sony Center, though, is a central plaza canopied by a tentlike glass roof with supporting beams radiating like bicycle spokes. The plaza and its many cafes are popular places to hang out and people-watch.

★ Gemäldegalerie   GALLERY
(Gallery of Old Masters; Map p86; ☑030-266 424 242; www.smb.museum/gg; Matthäikirchplatz; adult/concession/under 18 €10/5/free; ☉10am-6pm Tue, Wed & Fri, to 8pm Thu, 11am-6pm Sat & Sun; ♿; ⓖM29, M48, M85, 200, ⓢPotsdamer Platz, ⓤPotsdamer Platz) This museum ranks among the world's finest and most comprehensive collections of European art with about 1500 paintings spanning the arc of artistic vision from the 13th to the 18th century. Wear comfy

shoes when exploring the 72 galleries: a walk past masterpieces by Titian, Dürer, Hals, Vermeer, Gainsborough and many more Old Masters covers almost 2km. Don't miss the Rembrandt Room (Room X).

German, Dutch and Flemish masters dominate the east wing where highlights include the *Fountain of Youth* by Lucas Cranach the Elder in Room III and Pieter Bruegel the Elder's *Dutch Proverbs* in Room 7. The West Wing is dedicated to the Italians with such top canvasses as Caravaggio's *Amor Victorius* and Boticelli's *Madonna with Child and Singing Angels*. The excellent free audioguide has the low-down on these and other selected works. Note that the room numbering system is quite confusing as both Latin (I, II, III) and Arabic numbers (1, 2, 3) are used.

★ Topographie des Terrors   MUSEUM
(Topography of Terror; Map p66; ☑030-2545 0950; www.topographie.de; Niederkirchner Strasse 8; ☉10am-8pm, grounds close at dusk or 8pm at the latest; ⓖM41, ⓢPotsdamer Platz, ⓤPotsdamer Platz) FREE In the spot where the most feared institutions of Nazi Germany (including the Gestapo headquarters and the SS central command) once stood, this compelling exhibit chronicles the stages of terror and persecution, puts a face on the perpetrators and details the impact these brutal institutions had on all of Europe. A second exhibit outside zeroes in on how life changed for Berlin and its people after the Nazis made it their capital.

(Continued on page 84)

STUMBLING UPON HISTORY

If you lower your gaze, you'll see them all over town but nowhere are they more concentrated than in the Scheunenviertel: small brass paving stones in front of house entrances. Called Stolpersteine (stumbling blocks), they are part of a nationwide project by Berlin-born artist Gunter Demnig and are essentially mini-memorials honouring the people (usually Jews) who lived in the respective houses before being killed by the Nazis. The engravings indicate the person's name, birth year, year of deportation, the name of the concentration camp where they were taken and the date they perished.

CLAUDIO DIVIZIA/SHUTTERSTOCK © · AUTHORIZED BY BPK-BILDAGENTUR

TOP SIGHT
MUSEUMSINSEL

Walk through ancient Babylon, meet an Egyptian queen or be mesmerised by Monet's landscapes. Welcome to Museumsinsel, Berlin's famous treasure trove of 6000 years' worth of art, artefacts, sculpture and architecture from Europe and beyond. Spread across five grand museums built between 1830 and 1930, the complex covers the northern half of the Spree Island where Berlin's settlement began in the 13th century.

Berlin's Louvre

The first repository to open was the Altes Museum (Old Museum), completed in 1830 next to the Berlin Cathedral and the Lustgarten park. Today it presents Greek, Etruscan and Roman antiquities. Behind it, the Neues Museum (New Museum; pictured above) showcases the Egyptian collection, most famously the bust of Queen Nefertiti, and also houses the Museum of Pre- and Early History. The temple-like Alte Nationalgalerie (Old National Gallery) trains the focus on 19th-century European art. The island's top draw is the Pergamonmuseum, with its monumental architecture from ancient worlds, including the namesake Pergamon Altar. The Bode-Museum, at the island's northern tip, is famous for its medieval sculptures.

Museumsinsel Master Plan

In 1999 the Museumsinsel repositories collectively became a Unesco World Heritage Site. The distinction was at least partly achieved because of a master plan for the renovation

DON'T MISS

➡ Ishtar Gate

➡ Bust of Nefertiti

➡ Berliner Goldhut

➡ *Praying Boy*

➡ Sculpture by Tilman Riemenschneider

➡ Paintings by Caspar David Friedrich

PRACTICALITIES

➡ Map p66

➡ ☏ 030-266 424 242

➡ www.smb.museum

➡ day tickets for all 5 museums adult/concession/under 18 €18/9/free

➡ ⊘ varies by museum

➡ 🚌 100, 200, TXL, Ⓢ Hackescher Markt, Friedrichstrasse, Ⓤ Friedrichstrasse

and modernisation of the complex, which is expected to be completed in 2026 under the aegis of British architect David Chipperfield. Except for the Pergamon, whose exhibits are currently being reorganised, the restoration of the museums themselves has been completed. Construction is also well under way on the colonnaded James-Simon-Galerie, the new entrance building named for an early-20th-century German-Jewish patron and philanthropist. Expected to open in 2019, the building will serve as the central visitors centre with ticket desks, a cafe, a shop and direct access to the Pergamonmuseum and the Neues Museum. It will also lead to the 'Archaeological Promenade', a subterranean walkway set to link the Altes Museum with the Bode-Museum in the north. For more details see www.museumsinsel-berlin.de.

Pergamonmuseum

The Pergamonmuseum (Map p66; Bodestrasse 1-3; adult/concession/under 18yr €12/6/free; ⊙10am-6pm Fri-Wed, to 8pm Thu) opens a fascinating window on to the ancient world. Completed in 1930, the palatial three-wing complex presents a rich feast of classical sculpture and monumental architecture from Greece, Rome, Babylon and the Middle East in three collections: the Collection of Classical Antiquities, the Museum of the Ancient Near East and the Museum of Islamic Art. Most of the pieces were excavated and spirited to Berlin by German archaeologists around the turn of the 20th century.

The Pergamonmuseum is the fourth treasure chest on Museumsinsel to undergo extensive, gradual restoration work that will leave some sections closed for years. The north wing and the hall containing the namesake Pergamon Altar will be off limits until 2023. During the second phase, the south wing will be closed and a fourth wing facing the Spree River will be constructed so that in future all parts of the museum can be experienced on a continuous walk, possibly by 2026.

During the revamp, the museum entrance is off Bodestrasse, behind the Neues Museum.

Neues Museum

David Chipperfield's reconstruction of the bombed-out Neues Museum (New Museum; Map p66; Bodestrasse 1-3; adult/concession/under 18yr €12/6/free; ⊙10am-6pm Fri-Wed, to 8pm Thu) is now the residence of Queen Nefertiti, the showstopper of the Egyptian Museum, which also features mummies, sculptures and sarcophagi. Pride of place at the Museum of Pre- and Early History (in the same building) goes to Trojan antiquities, a Neanderthal skull and the

TOP TIPS

➡ Avoid culture fatigue by focusing on just two of the five museums in a single day.

➡ If you plan on visiting more than one museum, save by buying the Museumsinsel ticket (€18, concession €9), good for one-day admission to all five museums.

➡ Admission is free for those under 18.

➡ Arrive early or late on weekdays, or skip the queues by purchasing your ticket online.

➡ Make use of the excellent multilanguage audioguides included in the admission price.

➡ In good weather, the lawns of the Lustgarten, outside the Altes Museum, are an inviting spot to chill.

Pergamon was the capital of the Kingdom of Pergamon, which reigned over vast stretches of the eastern Mediterranean in the 3rd and 2nd centuries BC. Inspired by Athens, its rulers, the Attalids, turned their royal residence into a major cultural and intellectual centre. Draped over a 330m-high ridge were grand palaces, a library, a theatre and glorious temples dedicated to Trajan, Dionysus and Athena.

3000-year-old 'Berliner Goldhut', a golden conical hat. Skip the queue by buying your timed ticket online.

Nefertiti's bust was part of the treasure trove unearthed by a Berlin expedition of archaeologists around 1912 while sifting through the sands of Armana, the royal city built by Nefertiti's husband, Akhenaten (r 1353–1336 BC). A key item from the Late Egyptian Period (around 400 BC), which shows Greek influence, is the sculpture of a priest's head carved from smooth green stone and hence called 'Berlin Green Head'. Until the opening of the Humboldt Forum cultural centre, which is under construction nearby, the galleries will also be temporary host of selected highlights from the Museum of Asian Art and the Museum of Ethnology.

Competing with the exhibits is the building itself. Like a giant jigsaw puzzle, Chipperfield's design incorporates every original shard, scrap and brick he could find into this dynamic space, which juxtaposes massive stairwells, intimate domed rooms, mural walls and airy, high-ceilinged halls.

Altes Museum

Architect Karl Friedrich Schinkel pulled out all the stops for the grand neoclassical Altes Museum (Old Museum; Map p66; Am Lustgarten; adult/concession/under 18 €10/5/ free; ⊙10am-6pm Tue, Wed & Fri-Sun, to 8pm Thu), which was the first exhibition space to open on Museumsinsel in 1830. A curtain of fluted columns gives way to a Pantheon-inspired rotunda that's the focal point of a prized antiquities collection. In the downstairs galleries, sculptures, vases, tomb reliefs and jewellery shed light on various facets of life in ancient Greece, while upstairs the focus is on the Etruscans and Romans. Top draws include the *Praying Boy* bronze sculpture, Roman silver vessels and portraits of Caesar and Cleopatra.

Bode-Museum

On the northern tip of Museumsinsel, the palatial Bode-Museum (Map p66; cnr Am Kupfergraben & Monbijoubrücke; adult/concession/under 18 €12/6/free; ⊙10am-6pm Tue, Wed & Fri-Sun, to 8pm Thu) houses a comprehensive collection of European sculpture from the early Middle Ages to the 18th century, including priceless masterpieces by Tilman Riemenschneider, Donatello and Giovanni Pisano. Other rooms harbour a precious coin collection and a smattering of Byzantine art, including sarcophagi and ivory carvings.

The building, designed by Ernst von Ihne, was originally named Kaiser-Friedrich-Museum before being renamed for its first director, Wilhelm von Bode, in 1956. It's a beautifully proportioned architectural composition built around a central axis. Sweeping staircases, interior courtyards, frescoed ceilings and marble floors give the museum the grandeur of a palace.

The tone is set in the grand domed entrance hall where visitors are greeted by Andreas Schlüter's monumental sculpture of Great Elector Friedrich Wilhelm on horseback. From here head straight to the central Italian Renaissance–style

ASISI PANORAMA

While the Pergamon Altar will be closed for restoration until at least 2023, visitors will still be able to grasp its impressive beauty in a temporary exhibit that will present masterpieces excavated at Pergamon with a 360° panorama by Iranian artist and architect Yadegar Asisi. Doors to a purpose-built rotunda opposite the Bode-Museum will be open to the public from summer 2018. The panorama is an updated version of a similar project erected outside the Pergamonmuseum in 2011/12 and presents a vision of the city in AD 129. On display will be 80 original sculptures from the site, including a colossal head of Heracles and a big piece from the famous Telephos frieze.

Bode-Museum

A HOME FOR DUG-UP TREASURE

The Pergamonmuseum was purpose-built between 1910 and 1930 to house the massive volume of ancient art and scientists treasure excavated by German scientists at such sites as Babylon, Assur, Uruk and Miletus. Designed by Alfred Messel, the building was constructed by his close friend Ludwig Hoffmann following Messel's death, and was later badly pummelled in WWII. Lots of objects were whisked to the Soviet Union as war booty but many were returned in 1958.

basilica, where all eyes are on a colourfully glazed terracotta sculpture by Luca della Robbia. This leads to a smaller domed, rococo-style hall with marble statues of Frederick the Great and his generals. The galleries radiate from both sides of this axis and continue upstairs.

Alte Nationalgalerie

The Greek temple–style Alte Nationalgalerie (Old National Gallery; Map p66; Bodestrasse 1-3; adult/concession €10/5; ☉10am-6pm Tue, Wed & Fri-Sun, to 8pm Thu), open since 1876, is a three-storey showcase of first-rate 19th-century European art.

On the 1st floor, Johann Gottfried Schadow's *Statue of Two Princesses* and a bust of Johann Wolfgang von Goethe are standout sculptures. The painter Adolph Menzel also gets the star treatment – look for his famous *A Flute Concert of Frederick the Great at Sanssouci*, showing the king playing the flute at his Potsdam palace.

The 2nd floor shows impressionist paintings by famous French artists including Monet, Degas, Cézanne, Renoir and Manet, the last of whose *In the Conservatory* is considered a masterpiece. Among the Germans, there's Arnold Böcklin's *Isle of Death* and several canvases by Max Liebermann.

Romantics rule the top floor where all eyes are on Caspar David Friedrich's mystical landscapes and the Gothic fantasies of Karl Friedrich Schinkel. Also look for key works by Carl Blechen and portraits by Philipp Otto Runge and Carl Spitzweg.

Looking like a baptismal font for giants, the massive granite basin outside the Altes Museum was designed by Karl Friedrich Schinkel and carved from a single slab by Christian Gottlieb Cantian. It was considered an artistic and technical feat back in the 1820s. The original plan to install it in the museum's rotunda had to be ditched when the bowl ended up being too massive to fit into the site allocated for it. Almost 7m in diameter, it was carved in situ from a massive boulder in Brandenburg and transported via a custom-built wooden railway to the Spree and from there by barge to Berlin.

Museumsinsel

A HALF-DAY TOUR

Navigating around this five-museum treasure repository can be daunting, so we've created this itinerary to help you find the must-see highlights while maximising your time and energy. You'll need at least four hours and a Museumsinsel ticket for entry to all museums.

Start in the Altes Museum where you can admire the roll call of antique gods guarded by a perky bronze statue called the ❶ **Praying Boy**, the poster child of a prized collection of antiquities. Next up, head to the Neues Museum for your audience with ❷ **Queen Nefertiti**, the star of the Egyptian collection atop the grand central staircase.

One more floor up, don't miss the dazzling Bronze Age ❸ **Berliner Goldhut** (room 305). Leaving the Neues Museum, turn left for the Pergamonmuseum. With the namesake altar off limits until at least 2023, the first major sight you'll see is the ❹ **Ishtar Gate**. Upstairs, pick your way through the Islamic collection, past carpets, prayer niches and a caliph's palace facade to the intricately painted ❺ **Aleppo Room**.

Jump ahead to the 19th century at the Alte Nationalgalerie to zero in on paintings by ❻ **Caspar David Friedrich** on the 3rd floor and precious sculptures such as Schadow's ❼ **Statue of Two Princesses** on the first floor. Wrap up your explorations at the Bode-Museum, reached in a five-minute walk. Admire the foyer with its equestrian statue of Friedrich Wilhelm, then feast your eyes on European sculpture without missing masterpieces by ❽ **Tilman Riemenschneider**.

FAST FACTS

Oldest object 700,000-year-old Paleolithic hand axe at Neues Museum

Newest object A piece of barbed wire from the Berlin Wall at Neues Museum

Oldest museum Altes Museum, 1830

Most popular museum on Museumsinsel Neues Museum (777,000 visitors)

Total Museumsinsel visitors (2017) 2.33 million

Sculptures by Tilman Riemenschneider (Bode-Museum)

Dazzling detail and great emotional expressiveness characterise the wooden sculptures by late-Gothic master carver Tilman Riemenschneider, as in his portrayal of *St Anne and Her Three Husbands* from around 1510.

Bust of Queen Nefertiti (Room 210, Neues Museum)

In the north dome, fall in love with Berlin's most beautiful woman – the 3330-year-old Egyptian queen Nefertiti, she of the long graceful neck and timeless good looks – despite the odd wrinkle and a missing eye.

VLADIMIR WRANGEL/SHUTTERSTOCK ©
AUTHORIZED BY BPK-BILDAGENTUR ©

Aleppo Room (Room 16, Pergamonmuseum)

A highlight of the Museum of Islamic Art, this richly painted, wood-panelled reception room from a 17th-century Aleppo, Syria, combines Islamic floral and geometric motifs with courtly scenes and Christian themes.

Ishtar Gate (Room 9, Pergamonmuseum)

Draw breath as you enter the 2600-year-old city gate to Babylon, which has soaring walls sheathed in radiant blue-glazed bricks and adorned with ochre reliefs of strutting lions, bulls and dragons representing Babylonian gods.

Pergamonmuseum

Spree River

5
4
6
Alte Nationalgalerie
7

Entrance

2

Entrance

Entrance

Neues Museum

Paintings by Caspar David Friedrich (Top Floor, Alte Nationalgalerie)

A key artist of the romantic period, Caspar David Friedrich put his own stamp on landscape painting with his dark, moody and subtly dramatic meditations on the boundaries of human life versus the infinity of nature.

Statue of Two Princesses (1st Floor, Alte Nationalgalerie)

Johann Gottfried Schadow captures Prussian princesses (and sisters) Luise and Friederike in a moment of intimacy and thoughtfulness in this double marble statue created in 1795 at the height of the neoclassical period.

Bodestrasse

3

1

Altes Museum

Entrance

Berliner Dom

Lustgarten

Berliner Goldhut (Room 305, Neues Museum)

Marvel at the Bronze Age artistry of the Berlin Gold Hat, a ceremonial gold cone embossed with ornamental bands believed to have been used in predicting the best times for planting and harvesting.

Praying Boy (Room 5, Altes Museum)

The top draw at the Old Museum is the *Praying Boy*, ancient Greece's 'Next Top Model'. The life-size bronze statue of a young male nude is the epitome of physical perfection and was cast around 300 BC in Rhodes.

RADIOOKKA/SHUTTERSTOCK © - AUTHORIZED BY BPK-BILDAGENTUR

PI03/SHUTTERSTOCK © - AUTHORIZED BY BPK-BILDAGENTUR

JAROSLAV MORAVCIK/SHUTTERSTOCK © - AUTHORIZED BY BPK-BILDAGENTUR

VIEW FROM THE TOP

Europe's fastest lift, **Panoramapunkt** (Map p66; ☑ 030-2593 7080; www.pano ramapunkt.de; Potsdamer Platz 1; adult/ concession €7.50/6, without wait €11.50/9; ☺ 10am-8pm Apr-Oct, to 6pm Nov-Mar; ☐ M41, 200, Ⓢ Potsdamer Platz, Ⓤ Potsdamer Platz) yo-yos up and down the red-brick postmodern Kollhoff Tower in 20 seconds. From the bilevel viewing platform at a lofty 100m, you can pinpoint the sights, make a java stop in the 1930s-style cafe, enjoy sunset from the terrace and check out the exhibit that peels back the layers of the square's history.

(Continued from page 77)

To complement the exhibits, a self-guided tour of the historic grounds takes you past 15 information stations with photos, documents and 3D graphics, as well as a 200m stretch of the Berlin Wall.

Martin-Gropius-Bau GALLERY

(Map p66; ☑ 030-254 860; www.gropiusbau.de; Niederkirchner Strasse 7; cost varies, usually €10-12, under 16 free; ☺ 10am-7pm Wed-Mon; ☐ M41, Ⓢ Potsdamer Platz, Ⓤ Potsdamer Platz) With its mosaics, terracotta reliefs and airy atrium, this Italian Renaissance–style exhibit space named for its architect (Bauhaus founder Walter Gropius' great-uncle) is a celebrated venue for high-calibre art and cultural exhibits. Whether it's a David Bowie retrospective or an ethnological exhibit on the mysteries of Angkor Wat, it's bound to be well curated and utterly fascinating.

Museum für Film und Fernsehen MUSEUM

(Map p66; ☑ 030-300 9030; www.deutsche-kinemathek.de; Potsdamer Strasse 2; adult/concession €8/5, free 4-8pm Thu; ☺ 10am-6pm Wed & Fri-Mon, to 8pm Thu; ☐ 200, Ⓢ Potsdamer Platz, Ⓤ Potsdamer Platz) Germany's film history gets the star treatment at this engaging museum. Explore galleries dedicated to pioneers like Fritz Lang, ground-breaking movies like Leni Riefenstahl's Nazi-era *Olympia* and legendary divas like Marlene Dietrich. The TV exhibit has more niche appeal but is still fun if you want to know what *Star Trek* sounds like in German.

Legoland Discovery Centre AMUSEMENT PARK

(Map p66; ☑ 01806-6669 0110; www.legoland discoverycentre.de/berlin; Potsdamer Strasse 4; €19.50; ☺ 10am-7pm, last admission 5pm; ☐ 200, Ⓢ Potsdamer Platz, Ⓤ Potsdamer Platz) Geared towards the primary school set, this cute indoor amusement park counts a 4D cinema, a Lego space station and a slow-mo ride through the Dragon Castle among its attractions. Check online for discounts and combination tickets with other attractions.

In the Ninjago City Adventure, kids can train as a ninja and then test their courage by battling snakes and braving a laser labyrinth in the Ninjago Temple. Grown-ups can marvel at a mini-Berlin with landmarks recreated entirely from those tiny plastic bricks.

Kunstgewerbemuseum MUSEUM

(Museum of Decorative Arts; Map p86; ☑ 030-266 424 242; www.smb.museum; Matthäikirchplatz; adult/concession/under 18 €8/4/free; ☺ 10am-6pm Tue-Fri, 11am-6pm Sat & Sun; ☐ M29, M48, M85, 200, Ⓢ Potsdamer Platz, Ⓤ Potsdamer Platz) This prized collection of European design, fashion and decorative arts from the Middle Ages to today is part of the Kulturforum museum cluster. You can feast your eyes on exquisitely ornate medieval reliquaries and portable altars or compare Bauhaus classics to contemporary designs by Philippe Starck and Ettore Sottsass. Pride of place goes to the Fashion Gallery with classic designer outfits and accessories from the past 150 years.

Berliner Philharmonie ARCHITECTURE, CONCERT HALL

(Map p66; ☑ 030-2548 8156; www.berliner-philharmoniker.de; Herbert-von-Karajan-Strasse 1; tours adult/concession €5/3; ☺ tours 1.30pm Sep-Jun; ☐ M29, M48, M85, 200, Ⓢ Potsdamer Platz, Ⓤ Potsdamer Platz) A masterpiece of organic architecture, Hans Scharoun's 1963 iconic, honey-coloured concert venue is the home base of the prestigious Berliner Philharmoniker (p127). The auditorium feels like the inside of a finely crafted instrument and boasts supreme acoustics and excellent sight lines from every seat.

Gedenkstätte Deutscher Widerstand MEMORIAL

(German Resistance Memorial Centre; Map p86; ☑ 030-2699 5000; www.gdw-berlin.de; Stauffenbergstrasse 13-14, enter via courtyard; ☺ 9am-6pm Mon-Wed & Fri, to 8pm Thu, 10am-6pm Sat & Sun; ☐ M29, M48, Ⓢ Potsdamer Platz, Ⓤ Potsdamer Platz, Kurfürstenstrasse) **FREE** This memorial exhibit on German Nazi resistance occupies the very rooms where high-ranking officers led by Claus Schenk Graf von Stauffenberg plotted the assassination attempt on Hitler on 20 July 1944. There's a memorial in the courtyard where the main conspirators were shot right after the failed coup, a story poignantly retold in the 2008 movie *Valkyrie*.

Aside from detailing the Stauffenberg-led coup, the centre also documents the efforts of many other Germans who risked their lives opposing the Third Reich for ideological, religious or military reasons.

Dalí – Die Ausstellung
GALLERY

(Map p66; www.daliberlin.de; Leipziger Platz 7; adult/concession €12.50/9.50, with tour €19.50/14; ☉10am-8pm Jul & Aug, noon-8pm Sep-Jun; 📧200, M41, M48, M85, Ⓢ Potsdamer Platz, Ⓤ Potsdamer Platz) If you only know Salvador Dalí as the painter of melting watches, burning giraffes and other surrealist imagery, this private collection will likely open new perspectives on the man and his work. Here, the focus is on his graphics, illustrations, sculptures, drawings and films, with highlights including etchings on the theme of Tristan and Isolde and epic sculptures like *Surrealist Angel*, as well as the *Don Quixote* lithographs.

Deutsches Spionage Museum
MUSEUM

(German Spy Museum; Map p66; ☑030-398 200 451; www.deutsches-spionagemuseum.de; Leipziger Platz 9; adult/concession €12/8; ☉10am-8pm, last entry 7pm; 📧200, Ⓢ Potsdamer Platz, Ⓤ Potsdamer Platz) High-tech and interactive, this private museum not only documents the evolution of spying from ancient Egypt to the 20th century, it also displays hundreds of ingenious tools of the trade, including a lipstick pistol, shoe bugs and an ultra-rare Enigma cipher machine. You learn about famous spies, get to encrypt a message, and discover your digital transparency in the Facebook puzzle. A hit with kids of all ages is the wicked laser labyrinth.

◉ Kreuzberg & Neukölln

★ Jüdisches Museum
MUSEUM

(Jewish Museum; Map p86; ☑030-2599 3300; www.jmberlin.de; Lindenstrasse 9-14; adult/concession €8/3, audioguide €3; ☉10am-8pm; Ⓤ Hallesches Tor, Kochstrasse) In a landmark building by American-Polish architect Daniel Libeskind, Berlin's Jewish Museum offers a chronicle of the trials and triumphs in 2000 years of Jewish life in Germany. The exhibit smoothly navigates all major periods, from the Middle Ages via the Enlightenment to the community's post-1990 renaissance. Find out about Jewish cultural

BERLIN SIGHTS

TEMPELHOFER FELD: AIRPORT TURNS URBAN PLAYGROUND

In Berlin history, Tempelhof Airport is a site of legend. It was here in 1909 that aviation pioneer Orville Wright ran his first flight experiments, managing to keep his homemade flying machine in the air for a full minute. The first Zeppelin landed the same year and in 1926 Lufthansa's first scheduled flight took off for Zurich. The Nazis held massive rallies on the airfield and enlarged the smallish terminal into a massive semicircular compound measuring 1.23km from one end to the other. Designed by Ernst Sagebiel, it was constructed in only two years and is still one of the world's largest freestanding buildings. Despite its monumentalism, Sagebiel managed to inject some pleasing design features, especially in the grand art deco–style departure hall.

After the war, the US Armed Forces took over the airport and expanded its facilities, installing a powerplant, bowling alley and basketball court. In 1948–49, the airport saw its finest hours during the Berlin Airlift. After Tegel Airport opened in 1975, passenger volume declined, and flight operations stopped in 2008 following much brouhaha and (initially) against the wishes of many Berliners. That sentiment changed dramatically when the airfield opened as a public **park** (Map p86; www.gruen-berlin.de/tempelhofer-feld; enter via Oderstrasse, Tempelhofer Damm or Columbiadamm; ☉sunrise to sunset; 🚲; Ⓤ Paradestrasse, Boddinstrasse, Leinestrasse, Tempelhof, Ⓢ Tempelhof) 🅿️ FREE, a wonderfully non-commercial and creative open-sky space, where cyclists, bladers and kite-surfers whisk along the tarmac. Fun zones include a **beer garden** (Map p86; ☑0152 2255 9174; www.luftgarten-berlin.de; Tempelhofer Feld, enter Columbiadamm; ☉11am-midnight or later Apr-Oct, weather permitting; Ⓤ Boddinstrasse) barbecue areas, an artsy minigolf course, art installations, abandoned aeroplanes and an urban gardening project.

English-language **tours** (Map p86; ☑030-200 037 441; www.thf-berlin.de; Tempelhofer Damm 1-7; tours adult/concession €15/10; ☉English tours 1.30pm Wed & Fri-Sun; Ⓤ Platz der Luftbrücke) of both airport and airfield are available.

Kreuzberg & Friedrichshain

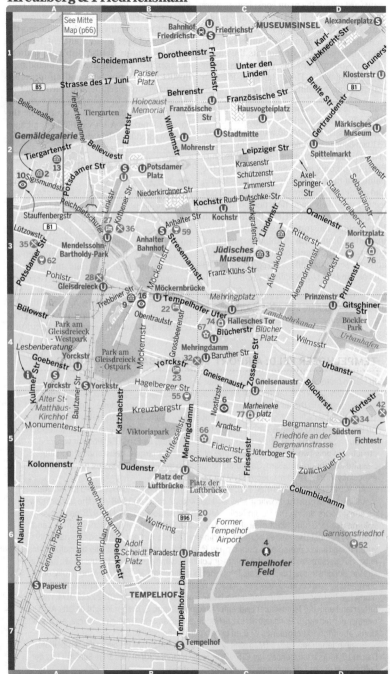

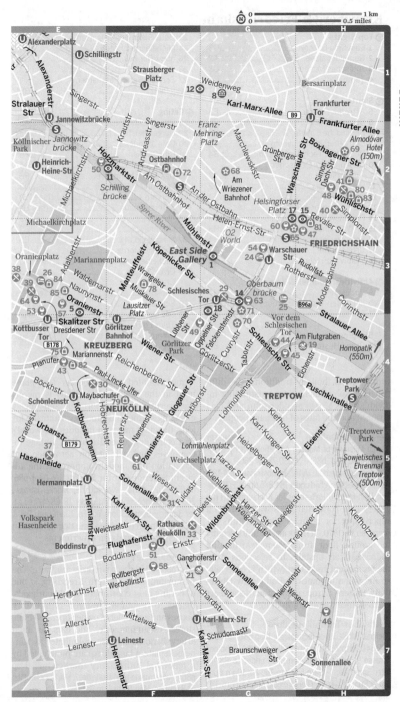

Kreuzberg & Friedrichshain

contributions, holiday traditions, the difficult road to emancipation, outstanding individuals (eg Moses Mendelssohn and Levi Strauss) and the fates of ordinary people.

Berlinische Galerie   GALLERY
(Berlin Museum of Modern Art, Photography & Architecture; Map p86; ☏ 030-7890 2600; www.berlinischegalerie.de; Alte Jakobstrasse 124-128; adult/concession/child under 18 €8/5/free; ☺ 10am-6pm Wed-Mon; Ⓤ Hallesches Tor, Kochstrasse) This gallery in a converted glass warehouse is a superb spot for taking stock of Berlin's art scene since 1870. Temporary exhibits occupy the ground floor, from where two floating staircases lead upstairs to selections from the permanent collection, which is especially strong when it comes to Dada, New Objectivity, Eastern European avant-garde, and art created since reunification in 1990.

Deutsches Technikmuseum   MUSEUM
(German Museum of Technology; Map p86; ☏ 030-902 540; http://sdtb.de/technikmuseum; Trebbiner Strasse 9; adult/concession/child under 18 €8/4/ after 3pm free; ☺ 9am-5.30pm Tue-Fri, 10am-6pm Sat & Sun; Ⓟ ♿; Ⓤ Gleisdreieck, Möckernbrücke) A roof-mounted 'candy bomber' (the plane used in the 1948 Berlin Airlift) is merely the overture to this enormous and hugely engaging shrine to technology. Fantastic for kids, the giant museum includes the world's first computer, an entire hall of vintage locomotives and exhibits on aerospace and navigation in a modern annexe. At the adjacent **Science Center Spectrum** (Map p86; ☏ 030-9025 4284; www.sdtb.de; Möckernstrasse 26; adult/concession/child under 18 €8/4/free after 3pm; ☺ 9am-5.30pm Tue-Fri, 10am-6pm Sat & Sun; Ⓟ), entered on the same ticket, kids can participate in hands-on experiments.

Bergmannkiez   AREA
(Map p86; Ⓤ Mehringdamm, Gneisenaustrasse) The Bergmannkiez in western Kreuzberg is one of Berlin's most charismatic neighbourhoods, thanks to beautifully restored 19th-century houses and a number of owner-operated indie stores, restaurants, cafes and bars. Its main artery, Bergmannstrasse, culminates in Marheinekeplatz, a historic square punctuated by a renovated 19th-century market hall (Map p86; www.meine-markthalle.de; Marheinekeplatz; ☺ 8am-8pm Mon-Fri, to 6pm Sat).

Drinking & Nightlife

Entertainment

Shopping

Friedrichshain

★East Side Gallery LANDMARK

(Map p86; www.eastsidegallery-berlin.de; Mühlenstrasse btwn Oberbaumbrücke & Ostbahnhof; 24hr; U Warschauer Strasse, S Ostbahnhof, Warschauer Strasse) FREE In 1989, after 28 years, the Berlin Wall, that grim and grey divider of humanity, was finally torn down. Most of it was quickly dismantled, but along Mühlenstrasse, paralleling the Spree, a 1.3km stretch became the East Side Gallery, the world's largest open-air mural collection. In more than 100 paintings, dozens of international artists translated the era's global euphoria and optimism into a mix of political statements, drug-induced musings and truly artistic visions.

★Volkspark Friedrichshain PARK

(Map p94; bounded by Am Friedrichshain, Friedenstrasse, Danziger Strasse & Landsberger Allee; 24hr; 142, 200, 21, M4, M5, M6, M8, M10, U Schillingstrasse) Berlin's oldest public park has provided relief from urbanity since 1840, but has been hilly only since the late 1940s, when wartime debris was piled up here to create two 'mountains' – the taller one, **Mont Klamott** (Map p94) FREE, rises 78m high. Diversions include expansive lawns for lazing, tennis courts, a half-pipe for skaters, a couple of handily placed beer gardens and an outdoor cinema.

Karl-Marx-Allee STREET

(Map p86; U Strausberger Platz, Weberwiese, Frankfurter Tor) FREE It's easy to feel like Gulliver in the Land of Brobdingnag when walking down monumental Karl-Marx-Allee, one of Berlin's most impressive GDR-era relics. Built between 1952 and 1960, the 90m-wide boulevard runs for 2.3km between Alexanderplatz and Frankfurter Tor and is a fabulous showcase of East German architecture. A considerable source of national pride back then, it provided modern flats for comrades and served as a backdrop for military parades.

RAW Gelände CULTURAL CENTRE

(Map p86; along Revaler Strasse; S Warschauer Strasse, Ostkreuz, U Warschauer Strasse) This jumble of derelict buildings is one of the last subcultural compounds in central Berlin. Founded in 1867 as a train repair station ('Reichsbahn-Ausbesserungs-Werk', aka RAW), it remained in operation until 1994. Since 1999 the graffiti-slathered grounds

(Continued on page 92)

The Berlin Wall

The construction of the Berlin Wall was a unique event in human history, not only for physically bisecting a city but by becoming a dividing line between competing ideologies and political systems. It's this global impact and universal legacy that continues to fascinate people decades after its triumphant tear-down. Fortunately, plenty of original Wall segments and other vestiges remain, along with museums and memorials, to help fathom the realities and challenges of daily life in Berlin during the Cold War.

Our illustration points out the top highlights you can visit to learn about different aspects of these often tense decades. The best place to start is the ❶ **Gedenkstätte Berliner Mauer**, for an excellent introduction to what the inner-city border really looked liked and what it meant to live in its shadow. Reflect upon what you've learned while relaxing along the former death strip, now the ❷ **Mauerpark**, before heading to the emotionally charged exhibit at the ❸ **Tränenpalast**, an actual border-crossing pavilion. Relive the euphoria of the

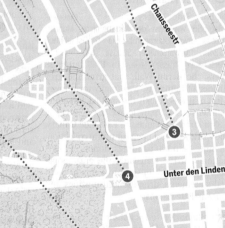

Tränenpalast
This modernist 1962 glass-and-steel border pavilion was dubbed 'Palace of Tears' because of the many tearful farewells that took place outside the building as East Germans and their western visitors had to say goodbye.

CANADASTOCK/SHUTTERSTOCK ©

Brandenburger Tor
People around the world cheered as East and West Berliners partied together atop the Berlin Wall in front of the iconic city gate, which today is a photogenic symbol of united Germany.

TAKASHI IMAGES/SHUTTERSTOCK ©

Potsdamer Platz
Nowhere was the death strip as wide as on the former no-man's-land around Potsdamer Platz from which sprouted a new postmodern city quarter in the 1990s. A tiny section of the Berlin Wall serves as a reminder.

ANDERSPHOTO/SHUTTERSTOCK ©

Checkpoint Charlie
Only diplomats and foreigners were allowed to use this border crossing. Weeks after the Wall was built, US and Soviet tanks faced off here in one of the hottest moments of the Cold War.

Bernauer Strasse

Chausseestr

Unter den Linden

Leipziger Str

Wall's demise at the **❹ Brandenburger Tor**, then marvel at the revival of **❺ Potsdamer Platz**, which was nothing but death-strip wasteland until the 1990s. The Wall's geopolitical significance is the focus at **❻ Checkpoint Charlie**, which saw some of the tensest moments of the Cold War. Wrap up with finding your favourite mural motif at the **❼ East Side Gallery**.

It's possible to explore these sights by using a combination of walking and public transport, but a bike ride is the best method for gaining a sense of the former Wall's erratic flow through the central city.

FAST FACTS

Beginning of construction 13 August 1961

Fall of the Wall 9 November 1989

Total length 155km

Height 3.6m

Weight of each segment 2.6 tonnes

Number of watchtowers 300

Remnants of the Wall →

Gedenkstätte Berliner Mauer
Germany's central memorial to the Berlin Wall and its victims exposes the complexity and barbaric nature of the border installation along a 1.4km stretch of the barrier's course.

Mauerpark
Famous for its flea market and karaoke, this popular park actually occupies a converted section of the death strip. A 30m segment of surviving Wall is now an official practice ground for budding graffiti artists.

Alexanderplatz

Alexanderstr

East Side Gallery
Paralleling the Spree for 1.3km, this is the longest Wall vestige. After its collapse, more than a hundred international artists expressed their feelings about this historic moment in a series of colourful murals.

DON'T MISS

TOP FIVE EAST SIDE GALLERY MURALS

You'll find your own favourite among the 100 or so murals, but here's our take:

It Happened in November (Kani Alavi) A wave of people being squeezed through a breached Wall in a metaphorical rebirth reflects Alavi's recollection of the events of 9 November 1989. Note the different expressions on the faces, ranging from hope, joy and euphoria to disbelief and fear.

Test the Rest (Birgit Kinder) Another shutterbug favourite is Kinder's painting of a GDR-era Trabant car (known as a Trabi) bursting through the Wall with the licence plate reading 'November 9, 1989'. Originally called *Test the Best,* the artist renamed her work after the image's 2009 restoration.

Homage to the Young Generation (Thierry Noir) This Berlin-based French artist has done work for Wim Wenders and U2, but he's most famous for these cartoon-like heads. Naive, simple and boldly coloured, they symbolise the new-found freedom that followed the Wall's collapse. Noir was one of the few artists who had painted the western side of the Wall before its demise.

Detour to the Japanese Sector (Thomas Klingenstein) Born in East Berlin, Klingenstein spent time in a Stasi prison for dissent before being extradited to West Germany in 1980. This mural was inspired by his childhood love for Japan, where he ended up living from 1984 to the mid-'90s.

My God, Help Me To Survive This Deadly Love (Dmitri Vrubel) The gallery's best-known painting – showing Soviet and GDR leaders Leonid Brezhnev and Erich Honecker locking lips with eyes closed – is based on an actual photograph taken by French journalist Remy Bossu during Brezhnev's 1979 Berlin visit. This kind of fraternal kiss was an expression of great respect in socialist countries.

(Continued from page 89)

have been a thriving offbeat sociocultural centre for creatives of all stripes. They also harbour clubs, bars, an indoor skate park, a bunker-turned-climbing-wall, a swimming pool club and a Sunday flea market.

Computerspielemuseum　　MUSEUM
(Computer Games Museum; Map p86; ☑ 030-6098 8577; www.computerspielemuseum.de; Karl-Marx-Allee 93a; adult/concession €9/6, after 6pm €7/5; ☺ 10am-8pm; ☒ 240, 347, ⓤ Weberwiese) No matter if you grew up with Nimrod, Pac-Man, World of Warcraft or no games at all, this well-curated museum takes you on a fascinating trip down computer-game memory lane while putting the industry's evolution into historical and cultural context. Colourful and engaging, it features interactive stations amid hundreds of original exhibits, including an ultra-rare 1972 Pong arcade machine and its twisted modern cousin, the 'PainStation' (must be over 18 to play...).

Holzmarkt　　AREA
(Map p86; www.holzmarkt.com; Holzmarktstrasse 25; ⓤ Jannowitzbrücke) The Holzmarkt urban village on the Spree is a perpetually evolving cultural open playground – and

a nose-thumbing at the luxury lofts, hotels and office buildings that continue to gobble up the riverside real estate.

Grab a pizza and a beer and count the boats passing by while chilling in the Mörchenpark, or treat yourself to a fine meal at Katerschmaus (p114) and dance through the night at Kater Blau (Map p86; www.katerblau.de; Holzmarktstrasse 25; ☺ Fri-Mon).

◎ Prenzlauer Berg

Mauerpark　　PARK
(Map p94; www.mauerpark.info; btwn Bernauer Strasse, Schwedter Strasse & Gleimstrasse; ☒ M1, M10, 12, ⓤ Eberswalder Strasse) With its wimpy trees and anaemic lawn, Mauerpark is hardly your typical leafy oasis, especially given that it was forged from a section of Cold War–era death strip (a short stretch of Berlin Wall survives). It's this mystique combined with an unassuming vibe and a hugely popular Sunday flea market and karaoke show that has endeared the place to locals and visitors alike.

Behind the Wall segment – now an officially sanctioned practice ground for graffiti artists – loom the floodlights of the Friedrich-Ludwig-Jahn-Sportpark (Map p94; Jahnsportpark@seninnDS.berlin.de; Cantianstrasse 24; ⓟ), the stadium where Stasi chief Erich Mielke used to cheer on his beloved Dynamo Berlin football (soccer) team. Just north of here is the **Max-Schmeling-Halle** (Map p94; ☑030-4430 4430; www.max-schmeling-halle.de; Falkplatz 1), a venue for concerts, competitions and sports events.

★ **Zeiss Grossplanetarium**   PLANETARIUM
(Map p94; ☑030-4218 4510; www.planetarium. berlin; Prenzlauer Allee 80; adult €8-9.50, concession €6-7.50; 🚇M2, Ⓢ Prenzlauer Allee) It was the most advanced planetarium in East Germany at its opening in 1987 and after the recent renovation it has upped the scientific, tech-

nology and comfort factor ante once again to become one of the most modern in Europe. It's a beautiful space to delve into the mysteries not only of the cosmos but of science in general. Many programs are in English, some are set to music, others are geared to children. Tickets are available online.

Kulturbrauerei   CULTURAL CENTRE
(Map p94; ☑030-4435 2170; www.kulturbrauerei. de; btwn Schönhauser Allee, Knaackstrasse, Eberswalder Strasse & Sredzskistrasse; Ⓟ; Ⓤ Eberswalder Strasse, 🚇M1) The red-and-yellow brick buildings of this 19th-century brewery have been upcycled into a cultural powerhouse

---

WORTH A TRIP

THE STASI: FEAR & LOATHING IN EAST BERLIN

In East Germany, the walls had ears. Modelled after the Soviet KGB, the GDR's Ministerium für Staatssicherheit (Ministry for State Security, 'Stasi' for short) was founded in 1950. It was secret police, central intelligence agency and bureau of criminal investigation all rolled into one. Called the 'shield and sword' of the SED (the sole East German party), it put millions of GDR citizens under surveillance in order to suppress internal opposition. The Stasi grew steadily in power and size and, by the end, had 91,000 official full-time employees and 189,000 IMs (*inoffizielle Mitarbeiter,* unofficial informants). The latter were regular folks recruited to spy on their coworkers, friends, family and neighbours. There were also 3000 IMs based in West Germany.

When the Wall fell, the Stasi fell with it. Thousands of citizens stormed the organisation's headquarters in January 1990, thus preventing the shredding of documents that reveal the full extent of institutionalised surveillance and repression through wire-tapping, videotape observation, opening private mail and other methods. The often cunningly low-tech surveillance devices (hidden in watering cans, rocks, even neckties) are among the more intriguing exhibits in the **Stasimuseum** (☑030-553 6854; www.stasimuseum.de; Haus 1, Ruschestrasse 103; adult/concession €6/4.50; ⊙10am-6pm Mon-Fri, 11am-6pm Sat & Sun, English tour 3pm Sat-Mon; Ⓤ Magdalenenstrasse), which occupies several floors of the fortress-like former ministry. At its peak, more than 8000 people worked in this compound alone; the scale model in the entrance foyer will help you grasp its vast dimensions.

Another museum highlight is the 'lion's den' itself, the stuffy offices, private quarters and conference rooms of Erich Mielke, head of the Stasi for an incredible 32 years, from 1957 until the bitter end. Other rooms introduce the ideology, rituals and institutions of East German society. Information panels are partly in English.

Few words are needed to understand the purpose of the van in the foyer. Outfitted with five tiny, lightless cells, it was used to transport suspects to the **Stasi prison** (Gedenkstätte Berlin-Hohenschönhausen; ☑030-9860 8230; www.stiftung-hsh.de; Genslerstrasse 66; tours adult/concession €6/3, exhibit free; ⊙tours in English 10.30am, 12.30pm & 2.30pm Mar-Oct, 11.30am & 2.30pm Nov-Feb, exhibit 9am-6pm, German tours more frequent; Ⓟ; 🚇M5) a few kilometres from the ministry. The prison, too, is a memorial site today – officially called Gedenkstätte Berlin-Hohenschönhausen – and is, if anything, even more creepy than the Stasi Museum.

Tours, sometimes led by former prisoners, reveal the full extent of the terror and cruelty perpetrated upon thousands of suspected political opponents, many utterly innocent. If you've seen the Academy Award–winning film *The Lives of Others,* you may recognise many of the original settings. An exhibit uses photographs, objects and a free audioguide to document daily life behind bars and also allows for a look at the offices of the former prison administration.

Prenzlauer Berg

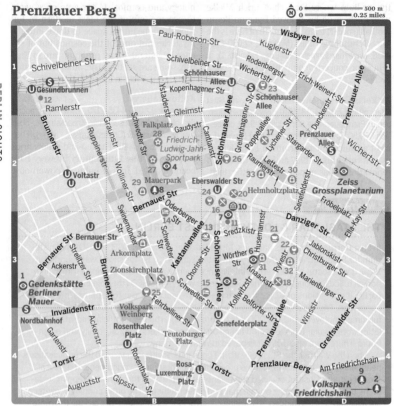

BERLIN SIGHTS

with a small village's worth of venues, from concert and theatre halls to nightclubs, dance studios, a multiplex cinema and a free GDR history museum. The main entrances are on Knaackstrasse and Sredzkistrasse.

On Sundays, foodies fill up on global treats at the street-food market, while in December, the old buildings make a lovely backdrop for a Swedish-style Lucia Christmas market.

Museum in der Kulturbrauerei MUSEUM
(Map p94; ☎030-467 777 911; www.hdg.de; Knaackstrasse 97; ☉10am-6pm Tue, Wed & Fri-Sun, to 8pm Thu; ℗; ⓗM1, 12, ⓤEberswalder Strasse) FREE Original documents, historical footage and objects (including a camper-style Trabi car) bring daily life under socialism in East Germany to life in this government-sponsored exhibit. As you wander the halls, you'll realise the stark contrast between the lofty aspirations of the socialist state and the sobering realities of material shortages, surveillance and oppression its people had to endure.

Kollwitzplatz SQUARE
(Map p94; ⓗ; ⓤSenefelderplatz) Triangular Kollwitzplatz was ground zero of Prenzlauer Berg gentrification. To pick up on the local vibe, linger with macchiato mamas and media daddies in a street cafe or join them at the twice-weekly farmers market (p131). The park in the square's centre is tot heaven with three playgrounds plus a bronze sculpture of the artist Käthe Kollwitz for clambering on.

Jüdischer Friedhof
Schönhauser Allee CEMETERY
(Map p94; ☎030-441 9824; www.jg-berlin.org; Schönhauser Allee 23-25; ☉8am-4pm Mon-Thu, 7.30am-2.30pm Fri; ⓤSenefelderplatz) Berlin's second Jewish cemetery opened in 1827 and hosts many well-known dearly departed, such as the artist Max Liebermann and the composer Giacomo Meyerbeer. It's a pretty place with dappled light filtering through big old chestnuts and linden trees and a sense of melancholy emanating from

Prenzlauer Berg

BERLIN SIGHTS

ivy-draped graves and toppled tombstones. The nicest and oldest have been moved to the Lapidarium by the main entrance.

Liebermann's tomb is next to his family's crypt roughly in the centre along the back wall. Men must cover their heads; pick up a free skullcap by the entrance.

⊙ City West & Charlottenburg

Kurfürstendamm   AREA
(Map p97; Kurfürstendamm; ⓤ Kurfürstendamm, Uhlandstrasse) The 3.5km Kurfürstendamm is a ribbon of commerce that began as a bridle path to the royal hunting lodge in the Grunewald forest. In the early 1870s, Otto von Bismarck, the Iron Chancellor, decided that the capital of the newly founded German Reich needed its own representative boulevard, which he envisioned as even bigger and better than Paris' Champs-Élysées. Today it is Berlin's busiest shopping strip, especially towards its eastern end.

Kaiser-Wilhelm-Gedächtniskirche   CHURCH
(Kaiser Wilhelm Memorial Church; Map p97; ☏ 030-218 5023; www.gedaechtniskirche.com; Breitscheidplatz; ⊙ church 9am-7pm, memorial hall 10am-6pm Mon-Sat, noon-5.30pm Sun; ⓖ 100, 200, ⓤ Zoologischer Garten, Kurfürstendamm,

ⓢ Zoologischer Garten) FREE Allied bombing in 1943 left only the husk of the west tower of this once magnificent neo-Romanesque church standing. Now an antiwar memorial, it stands quiet and dignified amid the roaring traffic. Historic photographs displayed in the Gedenkhalle (Hall of Remembrance), at the bottom of the tower, help you visualise the former grandeur of this 1895 church. The adjacent octagonal hall of worship, added in 1961, has glowing midnight-blue glass walls and a giant 'floating' Jesus.

The Hall of Remembrance also contains remnants of the elaborate mosaics that once swathed the original church, depicting heroic moments from Kaiser Wilhelm I's life, among other scenes. Note the marble reliefs, liturgical objects and two symbols of reconciliation: an icon cross donated by the Russian Orthodox church and a copy of the Cross of Nails from Coventry Cathedral, which was destroyed by Luftwaffe bombers in 1940.

The bell tower and new octagonal church were designed by Egon Eiermann, one of Germany's most prominent post-WWII architects. The huge golden statue of the resurrected Christ above the altar is made of tombac, a type of brass with a high copper

GEDENKSTÄTTE BERLINER MAUER

For an insightful primer on the Berlin Wall, visit this 1.4km-long **outdoor memorial** (Berlin Wall Memorial; Map p94; ☎030-467 986 666; www.berliner-mauer-gedenkstaette.de; Bernauer Strasse btwn Schwedter Strasse & Gartenstrasse; ⊘visitor & documentation centre 10am-6pm Tue-Sun, open-air exhibit 8am-10pm daily; ⑤Nordbahnhof, Bernauer Strasse, Eberswalder Strasse) **FREE** north of the Scheunenviertel. It explains the physical layout of the barrier and the death strip, how the border fortifications were enlarged and perfected over time and what impact they had on the daily lives of people on both sides of the Wall.

The memorial exhibit extends along Bernauer Strasse, one of the streets that played a pivotal role in Cold War history. The Berlin Wall ran along its entire length, with one side of the street located in West Berlin and the other in East Berlin. The exhibit is divided into four sections with overarching themes. Integrated within are an original section of the Wall, vestiges of the border installations and escape tunnels, a chapel and a monument. Multimedia stations, 'archaeological windows' and markers provide context and details about events that took place along here.

content, and weighs 300kg. Also note the *Stalingrad Madonna* (a charcoal drawing) against the north wall.

Story of Berlin
MUSEUM

(Map p97; ☎030-8872 0100; www.story-of-berlin.de; Kurfürstendamm 207-208, enter via Ku'damm Karree mall; adult/concession/child €12/9/5; ⊘10am-8pm, last admission 6pm; ☐X9, X10, 109, 110, M19, M29, TXL, ⓤUhlandstrasse) This engaging museum breaks 800 years of Berlin history into bite-size chunks that are easy to swallow but substantial enough to be satisfying. Each of the 23 rooms uses sound, light, technology and original objects to zero in on a specific theme or epoch in the city's history, from its founding in 1237 to the fall of the Berlin Wall. Tickets include a 45-minute tour (in English) of a still-functional 1970s atomic bomb shelter beneath the building.

Museum Berggruen
MUSEUM

(☎030-266 424 242; www.smb.museum/mb; Schlossstrasse 1; adult/concession incl Sammlung Scharf-Gerstenberg €10/5; ⊘10am-6pm Tue-Fri, from 11am Sat & Sun; Ⓟ; ☐M45, 109, 309, ⓤRichard-Wagner-Platz, Sophie-Charlotte-Platz, ⑤Westend) Classic modern art is the ammo of this delightful museum where Picasso is especially well represented, with paintings, drawings and sculptures from all his major creative phases. Elsewhere it's off to Paul Klee's emotional world, Henri Matisse's paper cut-outs, Alberto Giacometti's elongated sculptures and a sprinkling of African art that inspired both Klee and Picasso.

Standouts by Picasso include the *Seated Harlequin* from the early blue and rose periods, bold cubist canvases such as his portrait

of Georges Braque, and the mellower paintings of his later years, including *The Yellow Pullover* from 1939. The stately neoclassical building that houses the collection started life as the officer barracks for the Prussian king's personal bodyguards.

Sammlung Scharf-Gerstenberg
GALLERY

(☎030-266 424 242; www.smb.museum; Schlossstrasse 70; adult/concession incl Museum Berggruen €10/5; ⊘10am-6pm Tue-Fri, from 11am Sat & Sun; ☐M45, 109, 309, ⓤSophie-Charlotte-Platz, Richard-Wagner-Platz, ⑤Westend) This smart gallery is a treasure trove for aficionados of surrealism, a fantastical art form that peaked in the 1920s. It introduces works by the main protagonists – Max Ernst, René Magritte and Salvador Dalí, among others – and provides context by examining surreal aspects introduced by earlier artists. These include Goya's spooky etchings and the creepy dungeon scenes by Italian engraver Giovanni Battista Piranesi. Post-WWII surrealist interpretations are represented by Jean Dubuffet.

The collection is housed in the 19th-century barracks of the Gardes du Corps, the officers who served as the personal bodyguards of the Prussian king.

Bröhan Museum
MUSEUM

(☎030-3269 0600; www.broehan-museum.de; Schlossstrasse 1a; adult/concession/child under 18 €8/5/free; ⊘10am-6pm Tue-Sun; ☐M45, 109, 309, ⓤSophie-Charlotte-Platz, Richard-Wagner-Platz) This lovely museum trains the spotlight on applied arts from the late 19th century until the outbreak of WWII. Pride of place goes to the art nouveau collection, with period

(Continued on page 100)

City West & Charlottenburg

City West & Charlottenburg

◎ Top Sights
1 Zoo Berlin C2

◎ Sights
2 Akademie der Künste D1
3 Berlin Aquarium C2
4 C/O Berlin C2
5 Kaiser-Wilhelm-Gedächtniskirche........ C2
6 Kurfürstendamm B2
7 Museum für Fotografie C2
8 Schloss Bellevue D1
9 Schwules Museum D2
10 Siegessäule D1
11 Story of Berlin B3
12 Urban Nation D3

⊜ Sleeping
13 25hours Hotel Bikini Berlin C2
14 Das Stue D2
15 Hotel am Steinplatz B2
16 Hotel Henri B3
17 Sir Savigny B2

⊗ Eating
18 Ali Baba B2
19 Dicke Wirtin B2
20 Good Friends B2
    Kantini ....(see 13)
21 Kuchenladen B2
    Mine Restaurant ....(see 16)
    Neni ....(see 13)

22 Restaurant am Steinplatz............(see 15)
22 Restaurant Faubourg C2
23 Schleusenkrug C1
24 Schwein B2
25 Teehaus im Englischen Garten.............. D1

◎ Drinking & Nightlife
    Bar am Steinplatz ....(see 15)
26 Café am Neuen See D2
27 Connection Club C3
28 Diener Tattersall B2
29 Heile Welt D3
    Monkey Bar ....(see 13)
    Stue Bar ....(see 14)

◎ Entertainment
30 Bar Jeder Vernunft B3
31 Deutsche Oper Berlin A1
32 Schaubühne A3

◎ Shopping
33 Bikini Berlin C2
34 KaDeWe C2
35 Käthe Wohlfahrt C2
36 Manufactum B1
37 Stilwerk B2

◉ Information
38 Berlin Tourist Info – Europa-Center..... C2
39 Mann-O-Meter.. D3

DANIEL LINDNER/STIFTUNG PREUSSISCHE SCHLÖSSER UND GÄRTEN BERLIN-BRANDENBURG ©

TOP SIGHT
SCHLOSS CHARLOTTENBURG

Schloss Charlottenburg is an exquisite baroque palace and the best place in Berlin to soak up the one-time grandeur of the royal Hohenzollern clan. A visit is especially pleasant in summer, when you can fold a stroll around the palace garden into a day of peeking at royal treasures and lavishly furnished period rooms reflecting centuries of royal tastes and lifestyles.

Altes Schloss

Also known as the Nering-Eosander Building after its two architects, the Altes Schloss (Old Palace; adult/concession €10/7; ⊙10am-5.30pm Tue-Sun Apr-Oct, to 5pm Tue-Sun Nov & Dec, to 4.30pm Tue-Sun Jan-Mar) is the central, and oldest, section of the palace, and is fronted by Andreas Schlüter's grand equestrian statue of the Great Elector (1699). Inside, the baroque living quarters of Friedrich I and Sophie-Charlotte are an extravaganza in stucco, brocade and overall opulence. After a comprehensive restoration, you can now again ooh and aah over the Oak Gallery, a wood-panelled festival hall draped in family portraits; the charming Oval Hall overlooking the park; Friedrich I's bedchamber, with its grand bed and the first-ever bathroom in a baroque palace; and the Eosander Chapel, with its trompe l'œil arches. The king's passion for precious china is reflected in the dazzling Porcelain Chamber, which is smothered in nearly 3000 pieces of Chinese and Japanese blue ware.

DON'T MISS

➡ Frederick the Great's apartments in the Neuer Flügel

➡ Schlossgarten Charlottenburg

➡ Neuer Flügel's paintings by French masters

➡ Picasso & Co in Museum Berggruen

PRACTICALITIES

➡ Charlottenburg Palace

➡ ☎ 030-320 910

➡ www.spsg.de

➡ Spandauer Damm 10-22

➡ day pass to all 4 bldgs adult/concession €17/13

➡ ⊙ hours vary by bldg

➡ 🚌 M45, 109, 309, Ⓤ Richard-Wagner-Platz, Sophie-Charlotte-Platz

Neuer Flügel

The palace's most beautiful rooms are the flamboyant private quarters of Frederick the Great in the Neuer Flügel (New Wing; adult/concession incl audio guide €10/7; ☉10am-5.30pm Tue-Sun Apr-Oct, to 5pm Tue-Sun Nov & Dec, to 4.30pm Tue-Sun Jan-Mar) extension, designed in 1746 by royal buddy and star architect of the period Georg Wenzeslaus von Knobelsdorff. The confection-like White Hall banquet room and the Golden Gallery, a rococo fantasy of mirrors and gilding, are both standouts. Fans of 18th-century French masters such as Watteau and Pesne will also get an eyeful. Frederick the Great's nephew and successor added a summer residence with Chinese and Etruscan design elements as well as the more sombre Winter Chambers. These rooms were mostly used by his daughter-in-law Luise (1776–1810; a popular queen and wife of King Friedrich Wilhelm III), for whom Karl Friedrich Schinkel designed a stunning bedroom.

Neuer Pavillion

Returning from a trip to Italy, Friedrich Wilhelm III (r 1797–1848) commissioned Karl Friedrich Schinkel to design the Neuer Pavillon (New Pavilion; adult/concession €4/3; ☉10am-5.30pm Tue-Sun Apr-Oct, noon-4pm Tue-Sun Nov-Mar) as a summer retreat modelled on neoclassical Italian villas. Today, the minipalace shows off Schinkel's many talents as architect, painter and designer, while also presenting sculpture by Christian Daniel Rauch and master paintings by such Schinkel contemporaries as Caspar David Friedrich and Eduard Gaertner.

Belvedere

The late-rococo Belvedere (Spandauer Damm 20-24; adult/concession €4/3; ☉10am-5.30pm Tue-Sun Apr-Oct) palace, with its distinctive cupola, got its start in 1788 as a private sanctuary for Friedrich Wilhelm II. These days it houses porcelain masterpieces by the royal manufacturer KPM, which was established in 1763 by Frederick the Great. Among the exhibit highlights are the dainty teacups painted with cheeky cherubs.

Mausoleum

The 1810 temple-shaped Mausoleum (€3; ☉10am-5.30pm Tue-Sun Apr-Oct) was conceived as the final resting place of Queen Luise, and was twice expanded to make room for other royals, including Kaiser Wilhelm I and his wife Augusta. Their marble sarcophagi are exquisitely sculpted works of art. More royals are buried in the crypt (closed to the public).

TOP TIPS

➡ The 'Charlottenburg+' ticket (adult/concession €17/13) is a day pass valid for one-day admission to every open building within the palace gardens (special exhibits excepted).

➡ Avoid weekends, especially in summer, as queues can be long.

➡ Skip the queue by buying timed tickets at http://tickets.spsg.de (€2 service fee).

➡ A palace visit is easily combined with a spin around the trio of adjacent art museums.

➡ A Sammlung Scharf-Gerstenberg ticket will also get you into the Museum Berggruen and vice versa.

➡ Luggage can be checked for free in the cloakroom in the Altes Schloss.

Feel like a member of the Prussian court during the Berliner Residenz Konzerte (www.residenzkonzerte.berlin; concert only €34–55, with dinner €71–116; ☉dinner 6pm, concert 8pm), a concert series held by candlelight with musicians dressed in powdered wigs and historical costumes playing works by baroque and early classical composers. Various packages are available, including one featuring a pre-concert dinner.

(Continued from page 96)

rooms, porcelain and glass art from England, France, Germany, Scandinavia and Austria. A secondary focus is on art deco and functionalism, both styles of the 1920s and '30s. A picture gallery with works by Berlin Secession artists complements the exhibits.

Tickets include an audioguide in English and German. The museum is named for its founder Karl H Bröhan, who donated his private collection to the city in 1981.

C/O Berlin
GALLERY

(Map p97; 030-284 441 662; www.co-berlin.org; Hardenbergstrasse 22-24; adult/concession/child under 18 €10/5/free; 11am-8pm; S Zoologischer Garten, U Zoologischer Garten) Founded in 2000, C/O Berlin is the capital's most respected private, nonprofit exhibition centre for international photography and is based at the iconic Amerika Haus, which served as a United States cultural and information centre from 1957 until 2006. C/O's roster of highbrow exhibits has featured many members of the shutterbug elite, including Annie Leibovitz, Stephen Shore, Nan Goldin and Anton Corbijn.

Museum für Fotografie
MUSEUM

(Map p97; 030-266 424 242; www.smb.museum/mf; Jebensstrasse 2; adult/concession €10/5; 11am-7pm Tue, Wed & Fri-Sun, to 8pm Thu; S Zoologischer Garten, U Zoologischer Garten) A former Prussian officers' casino now showcases the artistic legacy of Helmut Newton (1920–2004), the Berlin-born *enfant terrible* of fashion and lifestyle photography, with the two lower floors dedicated to his life and work. On the top floor, the gloriously restored barrel-vaulted Kaisersaal (Emperor's Hall) forms a grand backdrop for changing international photography exhibits.

Before his fatal car crash, Newton donated 1500 images along with personal effects to the city in which he was born. He had studied photography here with famed fashion photographer Yva before fleeing Nazi Germany in 1938. His work reflects a lifelong obsession with the female body, which he often portrayed in controversial, quasi-pornographic poses. The ground-floor exhibit, entitled 'Helmut Newton's Private Property', provides a personal look at the man. On view are his partially recreated Monte Carlo office, his first camera (an Agfa Box he bought aged 12) and his customised Jeep (dubbed the Newton-Mobile). The galleries on the 1st floor showcase changing exhibitions of Newton's work, as well as that of his wife Alice Springs and

other contemporaries such as James Nachtwey and David LaChapelle.

★ Zoo Berlin
ZOO

(Map p97; 030-254 010; www.zoo-berlin.de; Hardenbergplatz 8; adult/child €15.50/8, with aquarium €21/10.50; 9am-6.30pm Apr-Sep, to 6pm Mar & Oct, to 4.30pm Nov-Feb; 100, 200, S Zoologischer Garten, U Zoologischer Garten, Kurfürstendamm) Berlin's zoo holds a triple record as Germany's oldest (since 1844), most species-rich and most popular animal park. Top billing at the moment goes to a pair of bamboo-devouring pandas on loan from China. The menagerie includes nearly 20,000 critters representing 1500 species, including orangutans, koalas, rhinos, giraffes and penguins. Public feeding sessions take place throughout the day – check the schedule online and by the ticket counter.

Berlin Aquarium
AQUARIUM

(Map p97; 030-254 010; www.aquarium-berlin.de; Budapester Strasse 32; adult/child €15.50/8, with zoo €21/10.50; 9am-6pm; ; S Zoologischer Garten, U Zoologischer Garten) Three whole floors of exotic fish, amphibians and reptiles await at this endearingly old-fashioned aquarium with its darkened halls and glowing tanks. Some of the denizens of the famous Crocodile Hall could be the stuff of nightmares, but dancing jellyfish, iridescent poison frogs and a real-life 'Nemo' bring smiles to young and old.

◉ Schöneberg

Urban Nation
MUSEUM

(Map p97; www.urban-nation.com; Bülowstrasse 7; 10am-6pm Tue-Sun; U Nollendorfplatz) FREE Creating a museum for street art may be akin to caging a wild animal. Yet, this showcase of works by top urban artists pulls the genre out from the underpasses and abandoned buildings and makes them accessible to an entirely new audience. From Alias to Zezao, the beautiful bi-level space designed by Graft architects is a handy introduction to the various players and the style they employ – stencils to paste-up to sculpture. Even the facade doubles as an everchanging canvas.

Schwules Museum
MUSEUM

(Gay Museum; Map p97; 030-6959 9050; www.schwulesmuseum.de; Lützowstrasse 73; adult/concession €7.50/4; 2-6pm Mon, Wed, Fri & Sun, to 8pm Thu, to 7pm Sat; M29, U Nollendorfplatz, Kurfürstenstrasse) In a former print shop, this nonprofit museum is one of the largest and most important cultural institutions documenting LGBTIQ culture around the world, albeit with a special focus on Berlin and Germany. It presents changing exhibits on gay icons, artists, gender issues and historical themes and also hosts film screenings and discussions to keep things dynamic.

Ask about guided English-language tours.

◉ Southwestern Berlin

Pfaueninsel PARK

(Peacock Island; ☑ 030-8058 6830; www.spsg.de; Nikolskoer Weg; adult/concession ferry return €4/3, Meierei €3/2; ☺ ferry 9am-8pm May-Aug, shorter hours Sep-Apr, Meierei 10am-5.30pm Sat & Sun Apr-Oct; ⓢ Wannsee, then bus 218) 'Back to nature' was the dictum in the 18th century, so Friedrich Wilhelm II had this little Havel island turned into an idyllic playground, perfect for retreating from state affairs and for frolicking with his mistress in a snowy-white fairy-tale palace (closed for renovation). For

added romance, he brought in a flock of peacocks that gave the island its name; you'll find the eponymous birds strutting their stuff to this day.

Even with the palace closed, Pfaueninsel makes for a lovely excursion. A standout among the smattering of other buildings is the Meierei, a dairy farm in the shape of a ruined Gothic monastery at the island's northern end.

The island is a nature preserve, so no smoking, cycling or swimming. There are no cafes or restaurants but picnicking is allowed. The island is about 4km northwest of the Wannsee S-Bahn station, from where bus 218 goes to the ferry dock several times hourly.

Brücke-Museum GALLERY

(☑ 030-831 2029; www.bruecke-museum.de; Bussardsteig 9; adult/concession €6/4; ☺11am-5pm Wed-Mon; ⓟ; ⓤ Oskar-Helene-Heim, then bus 115 to Pücklerstrasse) In 1905 Karl Schmidt-Rottluff, Erich Heckel and Ernst Ludwig Kirchner

---

❶ STREET ART & WHERE TO FIND IT
....

Stencils, paste-ups, throw-ups, burners and bombings. These are some of the magic words in street art and graffiti, the edgy art forms that have helped shape the aesthetic of contemporary Berlin. A capital of street art, the city is now home to the world's first urban art museum, the Urban Nation (p100) in Schöneberg. Out in the field, Berlin is the canvas of such international heavyweights as Blu, JR, Os Gemeos, Romero, Shepard Fairey and ROA, along with local talent like Alias, El Bocho and XOOOOX. Every night, hundreds of hopeful next-gen artists haunt the streets, staying one step ahead of the police as they aerosol their screaming visions, often within seconds.

There's street art pretty much everywhere, and the area around U-Bahn station Schlesisches Tor in Kreuzberg has some house-wall-size classics, including **Pink Man** (Map p86; Falckensteinstrasse 48) by Blu and **Yellow Man** (Map p86; Oppelner Strasse 3) by the Brazilian twins Os Gemeos. Skalitzer Strasse is also a fertile hunting ground with Victor Ash's **Astronaut** (Map p86; Mariannenstrasse; ⓤ Kottbusser Tor) and ROA's **Nature Morte** being highlights (you can even spot them on the northern side of the tracks when riding the above-ground U1). There's a work by street-art superstar Shepard Fairey called **Make Art Not War** on Mehringplatz.

Across the Spree River in Friedrichshain, the RAW Gelände (p89) is a constantly evolving canvas and even has a dedicated street art gallery, the **Urban Spree** (Map p86; ☑ 030-740 7597; www.urbanspree.com; Revaler Strasse 99; ☺ noon-11pm; ⓤ Warschauer Strasse, ⓢ Warschauer Strasse). Around Boxhagener Platz you'll find works by Boxi, Alias and El Bocho. The facade of the **Kino Intimes** (Map p86; ☑ 030-2977 7640; www.kino-intimes.de; Boxhagener Strasse 107; adult/concession €6.90/4.90; 🚊21, ⓤ Frankfurter Tor) is also worth checking out. In Mitte, there's plenty of art underneath the S-Bahn arches, although the undisputed hub is the courtyard of Haus Schwarzenberg (p76). Prenzlauer Berg has the Mauerpark (p92), where budding artists may legally hone their skills along a section of the Berlin Wall. In the entryway of the dilapidated building at Kastanienallee 86 are works by Alias and El Bocho. You'll also pass by plenty of graffiti when riding the circle S41/S42.

Several walking tour companies offer street-art tours, including Alternative Berlin Tours (p104) whose four-hour tours are artist-led and end with a hands-on street-art workshop. A good book on the subject is *Street Art in Berlin* by Kai Jakob (2015).

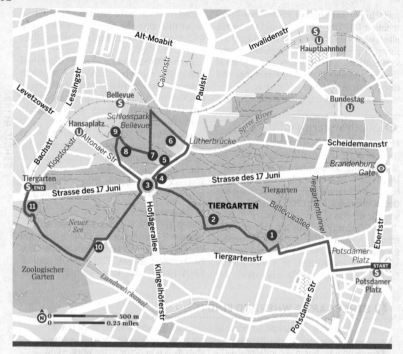

🏃 City Walk
A Leisurely Tiergarten Meander

START POTSDAMER PLATZ
END TIERGARTEN S-BAHN STATION
LENGTH 5KM; TWO HOURS

A ramble around Tiergarten delivers a relaxing respite from sightseeing. From Potsdamer Platz, head to **1 Luiseninsel**, an enchanting gated garden dotted with statues and seasonal flower beds. Not far away is **2 Rousseauinsel**, a memorial to 18th-century French philosopher Jean-Jacques ('Back to Nature') Rousseau. It was modelled after his actual burial site near Paris and placed on a teensy island in a sweet little pond.

At the heart of the park, engulfed by traffic, the imposing **3 Siegessäule** is crowned by a gilded statue of the goddess Victoria and commemorates Prussian military triumphs enforced by Iron Chancellor Otto von Bismarck. Nearby, the colossal **4 Bismarck Denkmal**, a monument to the man, shows him flanked by statues of Atlas (with the world on his back), Siegfried (wielding a sword) and Germania (stomping a panther).

Following Spreeweg north takes you past the oval **5 Bundespräsidialamt**, the offices of the German president, to the presidential residence in **6 Schloss Bellevue**, a neoclassical royal palace built for the younger brother of Frederick the Great in 1785.

Follow the path along the Spree, then turn left into the **7 Englischer Garten** (English Garden) created in the '50s to commemorate the 1948 Berlin Airlift. Overlooking a pond, the thatched-roof **8 Teehaus im Englischen Garten** hosts free summer concerts in its beer garden. Afterwards, check out the latest art exhibit at the nearby **9 Akademie der Künste**, on the edge of the Hansaviertel, a modernist quarter that emerged from a 1957 international building exhibition.

Walk south back through the park, crossing Altonaer Strasse and Strasse des 17 Juni, to arrive at the Neuer See with **10 Café am Neuen See** (p120) at its south end. Stroll north along the Landwehrkanal via the **11 Gaslaternenmuseum**, an open-air collection of 90 historic gas lanterns, and wrap up your tour at Tiergarten S-Bahn station.

founded Germany's first modern-artist group, called Die Brücke (The Bridge). Rejecting traditional techniques taught in the academies, they experimented with bright, emotional colours and warped perspectives that paved the way for German expressionism and modern art in general. Schmidt-Rottluff's personal collection forms the core of this lovely presentation of expressionist art.

A visit here is easily combined with the nearby Kunsthaus Dahlem (combination tickets adult/concession €8/5).

Kunsthaus Dahlem   GALLERY

(☑ 030-832 227 258; www.kunsthaus-dahlem.de; Käuzchensteig 8; adult/concession/under 19 €6/4/free, with Brücke-Museum adult/concession €8/5; ◷ 11am-5pm Wed-Mon; P; U Oskar-Helene-Heim, then bus 115 or X10) This private art museum in the monumental studio of Nazi-era sculptor Arno Breker presents modernist works created in Germany in the years between WWII and the construction of the Berlin Wall in 1961. While artists in West Germany embraced abstraction, in the East social realism emerged as the guiding principle. Although sculpture is the primary focus, photographs, paintings and drawings provide additional dimensions, as do four temporary exhibits per year mounted in the upstairs galleries.

AlliiertenMuseum Berlin   MUSEUM

(Allied Museum; ☑ 030-818 1990; www.alliierten-museum.de; Clayallee 135; ◷ 10am-6pm Tue-Sun; P; U Oskar-Helene-Heim) FREE The original Checkpoint Charlie guard cabin, a Berlin Airlift plane and a reconstructed spy tunnel are among the dramatic exhibits at the Allied Museum, which documents historic milestones and the challenges faced by the Western Allies during the Cold War. There's also a survey of events leading to the collapse of communism and the fall of the Berlin Wall. An original piece of the Wall sits in the yard.

There are plans to move the museum to Tempelhof Airport, although no specific date has been set.

Haus der Wannsee-Konferenz   MEMORIAL

(☑ 030-805 0010; www.ghwk.de; Am Grossen Wannsee 56-58; ◷ 10am-6pm; S Wannsee, then bus 114) FREE In January 1942 a group of 15 high-ranking Nazi officials met in a stately villa near Lake Wannsee to hammer out details of the 'Final Solution', the systematic deportation and murder of European Jews. The 13-room exhibit (in German and English) in the very rooms where discussions took place illustrates the sinister meeting; it also examines

the racial policies and persecution leading up to it and such issues as how aware ordinary Germans were of the genocidal actions.

You can study the actual minutes of the meeting (taken by Adolf Eichmann) and look at photographs of those involved, many of whom lived to a ripe old age. The site is about 2.5km northwest of Wannsee S-Bahn station and served from there by bus 114 several times hourly.

Liebermann-Villa am Wannsee   MUSEUM

(☑ 030-8058 5900; www.liebermann-villa.de; Colomierstrasse 3; adult/concession/under 14 €8/5/free, multimedia guide €4.50; ◷ 10am-6pm Wed-Mon Apr-Sep, 11am-5pm Wed-Mon Oct-Mar; S Wannsee, then bus 114) This lovely villa was the summer retreat of German impressionist painter and Berliner Secession founder Max Liebermann from 1909 until his death in 1935. Liebermann loved the lyricism of nature and often painted the gardens as seen through the window of his barrel-vaulted upstairs studio. A selection of these works is on permanent display along with a timeline of the artist's life and impact.

The beautifully restored gardens consist of three hedge gardens – shaped like a circle, a square and an oval – and are flanked by beech trees. Drink in the glorious views over coffee and cake from the terrace of the villa's Wannsee-facing Cafe Max. Bus 114 makes the trip to the villa several times hourly from the S-Bahn station Wannsee.

Tours

Bus

You'll see them everywhere around town: colourful buses (in summer, often open-top double-deckers) that tick off all the key sights on two-hour loops with basic taped commentary in multiple languages. You're free to get off and back on at any of the stops. Buses depart roughly every 15 or 30 minutes between 10am and 5pm or 6pm daily; tickets cost from €10 to €20 (half-price for teens, free for children). Look for flyers in hotel lobbies or in tourist offices.

Bicycle

Fat Tire Tours Berlin   CYCLING

(Map p66; ☑ 030-2404 7991; www.fattiretours.com/berlin; Panoramastrasse 1a; adult/concession/under 12 incl bicycle from €28/26/14; S Alexanderplatz, U Alexanderplatz) This top-rated outfit runs English-language tours by bike, e-bike and Segway. Options include a classic city spin; tours with a focus on Nazi Germany,

WORTH A TRIP

TREPTOWER PARK & THE SOVIET WAR MEMORIAL

Southeast of Kreuzberg, Treptower Park is an easy escape from the urban bustle with a patchwork of forest, lawns, a lake, an observatory and beer gardens. The park's main sight is the gargantuan Soviet War Memorial (⏲24hr; ⓡTreptower Park) FREE (1949), which looms above the graves of 5000 Soviet soldiers killed in the Battle of Berlin, a bombastic but sobering testament to the immensity of the country's wartime losses. To reach the memorial from the S-Bahn station, head southeast for 750m on Puschkinallee, then enter the park through the stone gate and walk past the statue of Mother Russia grieving for her dead children.

Beyond here, flanking the gateway, two mighty walls are fronted by soldiers kneeling in sorrow; the red marble used here was supposedly scavenged from Hitler's ruined chancellery. This gives way to a massive sunken lawn lined by sarcophagi representing the then 16 Soviet republics, each decorated with war scenes and Stalin quotes. The epic dramaturgy reaches a crescendo at the mausoleum, topped by a 13m statue of a Russian soldier clutching a child, his sword resting melodramatically on a shattered swastika. The socialist-realism mosaic inside the plinth shows grateful Soviets honouring the fallen.

the Cold War or 'Modern Berlin'; a trip to Potsdam; and an evening food tour. Tours leave from the Fernsehturm (TV Tower) main entrance. Reservations advised.

Berlin on Bike CYCLING
(Map p94; ☎030-4373 9999; www.berlinon bike.de; Knaackstrasse 97, Kulturbrauerei, Court 4; tours incl bike adult/concession €24/20, bike rental per 24hr €10; ⏲8am-8pm mid-Mar–mid-Nov, 10am-4pm Mon-Sat mid-Nov–mid-Mar; ⓜM1, ⓤEberswalder Strasse) This well-established company has a busy schedule of insightful and fun bike tours led by locals. There are daily English-language city tours (Berlin's Best) and Berlin Wall tours as well as an Alternative Berlin tour thrice weekly and a Street-Art tour on Fridays. Other tours (eg night tours) are available on request. Reservations recommended for all tours.

Also rents bicycles for €10 per 24 hours or €50 per week.

Walking

Alternative Berlin Tours WALKING
(☎0162 819 8264; www.alternativeberlin.com; tours €12-35) Not your run-of-the-mill tour company, this outfit runs subculture tours that get beneath the skin of the city, including an excellent street-art tour and workshop, an alternative pub crawl and a craft beer tour. For a primer on the city, join the tip-based 'Free Tour' offered twice daily in season. The website has all the details and a booking function.

Original Berlin Walks WALKING
(☎030-301 9194; www.berlinwalks.de; adult/concession from €14/12) Berlin's longest-running

English-language walking tour company has a general city tour plus a roster of themed tours (eg Hitler's Germany, East Berlin, Queer Berlin), as well as a food crawl, a craft beer tour and trips out to Sachsenhausen concentration camp and Potsdam. The website has details on timings and meeting points.

Brewer's Berlin Tours WALKING
(☎0177 388 1537; www.brewersberlintours.com; adult/concession €15/12) Local experts run an epic six-hour Best of Berlin tour (€25) and a shorter donation-based Berlin Free Tour, as well as a Craft Beer & Breweries tour with tastings (€39), a street-art tour (€12) and a food crawl (€29). Details and booking online.

Insider Tour Berlin WALKING
(☎030-692 3149; www.insidertour.com; adult/concession €14/12) This well-established company offers an insightful general city tour plus themed tours (eg Cold War, Third Reich, Jewish Berlin) and trips to Sachsenhausen concentration camp, Potsdam and Dresden. No prebooking required. Check the website for timings and meeting points.

New Berlin Tours WALKING
(www.newberlintours.com; tours adult/concession from €14/12; ⏲free tour 10am, 11am, noon, 2pm & 4pm) Entertaining and informative city spins by the pioneers of the donation-based 'free tour' and the pub crawl (€12). Also offers tours to Sachsenhausen concentration camp, themed tours (Red Berlin, Third Reich, Alternative Berlin) as well as a beer tour and a trip to Potsdam. Check the website for timings, prices and meeting points.

Special Interest

Berliner Unterwelten
TOURS

(Map p94; ☑030-4991 0517; www.berliner-unterwelten.de; Brunnenstrasse 105; adult/concession €12/10; ☺Dark Worlds tours in English 11am Wed-Sun, 11am & 1pm Mon year-round, 3pm Mon, Wed-Sun, 1pm & 3pm Wed-Sun Apr-Oct; ⑤Gesundbrunnen, ⓤGesundbrunnen) After you've checked off the Brandenburg Gate and the TV Tower, why not explore Berlin's dark and dank underbelly? Join Berliner Unterwelten on its 1½-hour 'Dark Worlds' tour of a WWII underground bunker and pick your way through a warren of claustrophobic rooms, past heavy steel doors, hospital beds, helmets, guns, boots and lots of other wartime artefacts.

Trabi Safari
DRIVING

(Map p66; ☑030-3020 1030; www.trabi-safari.de; Zimmerstrasse 97; adult/child under 17 from €49/free; ⓤKochstrasse) Catch the *Good Bye, Lenin!* vibe on daily tours of Berlin with you driving or riding as a passenger in a convoy of GDR-made Trabant (Trabi) cars, with live commentary (in English by prior arrangement) piped into your vehicle. The 'compact' tour lasts 1¼ hours, the 'XXL' tour 2¼ hours; both travel to both eastern and western Berlin.

Berlin Music Tours
BUS, WALKING

(☑0172 424 2037; www.musictours-berlin.com; Bowie walk €19; ☺noon Sat & Sun Apr-Oct, 11.30am Nov-Mar) Berlin's music history – Bowie to U2 and Rammstein, cult clubs to the Love Parade – comes to life during expertly guided bus and walking tours run by this well-respected outfit. There is a regularly scheduled walk in Bowie's footsteps, but other options such as a multimedia bus tour and U2 and Depeche Mode tours run by request only. Some even get you inside the fabled Hansa Studios.

Green Me Berlin Tours
WALKING TOUR

(www.greenmeberlin.com; public tours per person €30-50, private tours on request) 🌿 Making the world a better place one footstep at a time, Green Me's walking tours show visitors Berlin's sustainable side. Its small-size tours pop by off-grid organic cafes, urban gardens, ethical stores and backyard workshops, introducing you to the passionate people behind the concepts. Most include a small tasting, such as vegan ice cream or *kombucha*.

✪ Festivals & Events

Berlin Fashion Week
FASHION

(www.fashion-week-berlin.com; various locations; ☺Jan & Jul) Twice a year, in January and in July, international fashion folk descend on the city for chic shows, presentations and conferences showcasing the latest threads by both emerging and established German designers and brands.

See the website for events that are open to the public.

Berlinale
FILM

(www.berlinale.de; ☺Feb) The world's stars and starlets, directors and critics invade in February for Berlin's glamorous 10-day international film festival. Tickets for public screenings are available online, at sales offices and at the festival offices. The website has details.

Karneval der Kulturen
FAIR

(www.karneval-berlin.de; ☺May) This exuberant four-day festival in the streets of Kreuzberg celebrates the city's global population and culminates in a parade of costumed dancers,

---

BERLIN FOR CHILDREN

There's plenty to do to keep youngsters occupied in Berlin, from zoos to kid-oriented museums. Parks and imaginative playgrounds abound in all neighbourhoods, as do public pools.

If the 20,000 furry, feathered and finned friends at the Zoo Berlin (p100) fail to enchant the little ones, there's always the enormous adventure playground or the crocodiles and jellyfish next door at the Berlin Aquarium (p100). Finny friends take centre stage at SeaLife Berlin (p73) – its smaller size makes it suitable for the kindergarten set, as does the Legoland Discovery Centre (p84).

Kid-friendly museums include the Museum für Naturkunde (p65), with its giant dinosaur skeletons, and the Deutsches Technikmuseum (p88), with its planes, trains and automobiles and hands-on science centre.

Older kids might get a kick out of the interactive computer games at the Computerspielemuseum (p92) or the Cold War spy exhibits at the Deutsches Spionage Museum (p85).

singers, DJs and musicians. It's held during Pentecost (Whitsuntide) weekend in May.

Internationales Berliner Bierfestival BEER
(www.bierfestival-berlin.de; Karl-Marx-Allee; ☉early Aug; Ⓤ Schillingstrasse) Who needs Oktoberfest when you can hang out in the world's longest beer garden? As the bands play on, pick your poison from some 350 breweries representing 90 countries with over 2400 beers along 2.2km of Karl-Marx-Allee.

Berlin Marathon SPORTS
(www.berlin-marathon.com; ☉Sep) Sweat it out with over 40,000 other runners or just cheer 'em on during one of the world's biggest and most prestigious street races. Related events include an in-line skating marathon, a wheelchair race and kids' races.

Jazzfest Berlin MUSIC
(www.jazzfest-berlin.de; various locations; ☉early Nov) This top-rated jazz festival has doo-wopped in Berlin since 1964 with performances by fresh and big-time international talent held around town.

Christmas Markets CHRISTMAS MARKET
(www.weihnachteninberlin.de; ☉late Nov-late Dec) Pick up shimmering ornaments or indulge in potent *Glühwein* (mulled wine) at dozens of Yuletide markets held throughout the city in the lead-up to Christmas.

🛏 Sleeping

Berlin offers the gamut of places to unpack your suitcase. Just about every internation-al chain now has an offering in the German capital, but more interesting options that better reflect the city's verve and spirit abound.

🛏 Historic Mitte & Around

⭐**Wombat's Berlin** HOSTEL €
(Map p66; ☎030-8471 0820; www.wombats-hostels.com/berlin; Alte Schönhauser Strasse 2; dm/d from €17/60; ☯@🖤; Ⓤ Rosa-Luxemburg-Platz) Sociable and central, Wombat's gets hostelling right. From backpack-sized in-room lockers to individual reading lamps and a guest kitchen with dishwasher, the attention to detail here is impressive. Spacious and clean en-suite dorms are as much part of the deal as free linen and a welcome drink, best enjoyed with fellow party pilgrims at sunset in the rooftop bar.

⭐**Miniloft Berlin** APARTMENT €€
(Map p66; ☎030-847 1090; www.miniloft.com; Hessische Strasse 5; apt €135-185, 2 night minimum; P☯🖤; Ⓤ Naturkundemuseum) 🍃 These stunning lofts close to the main train station spread across an historic building and an adjoining modern annexe and were created by their architect-owners with lots of energy-saving features. Units are light-flooded and come with stylishly minimalist furnishings and petite but functional kitchenettes. Those in the old wing are quieter but not accessible by lift.

⭐**Capri by Fraser** APARTMENT €€
(Map p66; ☎030-20 07 70 1888; https://berlin.capribyfraser.com; Scharrenstrasse 22; r from €150; P☯✳🖤🖤; Ⓤ Spittelmarkt) These 143 self-catering studios and one-bedroom apartments on Museumsinsel (Museum Island) are a sweet fusion of substance and style. Smartly laid-out rooms come with plenty of closet space, device docks and kitchenettes, and there's a guest laundry, bar and restaurant on-site. In the lobby, a glass floor covers medieval foundations unearthed during construction.

Circus Hotel HOTEL €€
(Map p66; ☎030-2000 3939; www.circus-berlin.de; Rosenthaler Strasse 1; d/apt from €89/120; P☯@🖤; Ⓤ Rosenthaler Platz) At this supercentral budget boutique hotel, none of the compact, mod rooms are alike, but all feature upbeat colours, thoughtful design touches, a tea station and organic bath products. Unexpected perks include a

---

BERLIN BY BOAT

A lovely way to experience Berlin from April to October – and take a break from museum-hopping – is on the open-air deck of a river cruiser. Several companies run relaxing Spree spins through the city centre from landing docks on the eastern side of Museumsinsel, for example outside the **DDR Museum** (Map p66; Ⓢ Alexanderplatz, Hackescher Markt, Ⓤ Alexanderplatz) and from the **Nikolaiviertel** (Map p66; 🚌100, 200, TXL, Ⓤ Alexanderplatz, Ⓢ Alexanderplatz). Sip refreshments while a guide showers you with anecdotes (in English and German) as you glide past grand old buildings and museums, beer gardens and the government quarter. Expect the one-hour tour to cost between €12 and €14.

SPLISH-SPLASH: GETTING WET IN BERLIN

On a hot summer day, do as Berliners do and keep cool by getting wet. If you're fitness-inclined, there are lots of public pools for swimming laps.

Badeschiff (Map p86; ☑0162 545 1374; www.arena-berlin.de; Eichenstrasse 4; adult/concession €5.50/3; ⊙8am-varies (weather dependent) May-early Sep; ☑265, ☑Treptower Park, Ⓤ Schlesisches Tor) Take an old river barge, fill it with water, moor it in the Spree and – voila! – you get an artist-designed urban lifestyle pool that is a popular swim-and-chill spot. With music blaring, a sandy beach, wooden decks, lots of hot bods and a bar to fuel the fun, the vibe is distinctly 'Ibiza on the Spree'. Come early on scorching days as it's often filled to capacity (1500 people max) by noon.

Haubentaucher (Map p86; www.haubentaucher.berlin; Revaler Strasse 99, Gate 1; admission varies, usually €6; ⊙noon-late Mon-Fri, from 11am Sat & Sun May-Sep, weather permitting; ☎; ☑M10, M13, Ⓤ Warschauer Strasse, Ⓢ Warschauer Strasse) Behind the brick walls of the graffiti-festooned RAW Gelände (p89) hides this ingenious urban beach club with industrial charm and Med flair. At its heart is a good-size heated outdoor swimming pool wrapped in a sun deck of white stone and wooden planks; shade is provided by a vine-festooned garden lounge.

Stadtbad Oderberger Strasse (Map p94; ☑030-780 089 760; www.hotel-oderberger. berlin/bad; Oderberger Strasse 57; adult/concession €6/4; ☑12, M1, Ⓤ Eberswalder Strasse) These historic baths that kept locals clean from 1902 until 1986 have been meticulously restored. Since 2016 you can once again swim laps in the 20m-long pool canopied by a lofty arched ceiling and flanked by arcades with neo-Renaissance flourishes. It's inside the Oderberger Hotel but open to the public unless used for special events – check ahead.

Stadtbad Neukölln (Map p86; ☑030-2219 0011; www.berlinerbaeder.de; Ganghoferstrasse 3; adult €3.50-5.50, concession €2-3.50; ⊙hours vary; Ⓤ Rathaus Neukölln, Karl-Marx-Strasse) This gorgeous bathing temple from 1914 wows swimmers with mosaics, frescos, marble and brass. There are two pools (19m and 25m) and a Russian-Roman bath with sauna (€16). Check the schedule for timings; Mondays are reserved for women only, Sunday nights are nude swimming.

roof terrace (with yoga classes), bike rentals and a fabulous breakfast buffet (€9) served in the hugely popular Commonground cafe. Need more space? Go for an apartment.

★**Casa Camper**   DESIGN HOTEL €€€
(Map p66; ☑030-2000 3410; www.casacamper. com; Weinmeisterstrasse 1; r/ste incl breakfast €165-250; P❄❈☎; Ⓤ Weinmeisterstrasse) Catalan shoemaker Camper has translated its concept of chic yet sensible footwear into this style-pit for trend-conscious global nomads. Minimalist-mod rooms come with day-lit bathrooms with natural amenities, and beds that invite hitting the snooze button. Minibars are eschewed for a top-floor lounge with stellar views and free 24/7 hot and cold snacks and drinks.

🛏 Potsdamer Platz & Tiergarten

Scandic Berlin Potsdamer Platz   HOTEL €€
(Map p86; ☑030-700 7790; www.scandichotels. com; Gabriele-Tegirt-Promenade 19; d from €130; P❄❈☎❋; Ⓤ Mendelssohn-Bartholdy-Park) 🍃

This Scandinavian import gets kudos for its central location and spacious blond-wood rooms with box-spring beds, panoramic windows with blackout curtains and for going the extra mile when it comes to being green. Distinctive features include the good-sized 8th-floor gym-with-a-view, honey from the rooftop beehive and free bikes. Optional (partly organic) breakfast is €14.

Kids under 13 stay free.

★**Das Stue**   BOUTIQUE HOTEL €€€
(Map p97; ☑030-311 7220; www.das-stue.com; Drakestrasse 1; d from €300; P❄❈@☎❋❋; ☑100, 106, 200) This charismatic refuge in a 1930s Danish diplomatic outpost flaunts understated grandeur and has the Tiergarten park as a front yard. A crocodile sculpture flanked by sweeping staircases fluidly leads the way to a cool **bar** (Map p97; ⊙noon-1am Sun-Thu, to 2am Fri & Sat), a Michelin-starred restaurant and sleekly furnished and oversized rooms (some with terrace or balcony). The elegant spa has a pool, a sauna and top-notch massages.

Optional breakfast is €35. Guests have free admission to the Berlin Zoo.

🛏 Kreuzberg & Neukölln

★ Grand Hostel Berlin Classic   HOSTEL €
(Map p86; ☑ 030-2009 5450; www.grandhostel-berlin.de; Tempelhofer Ufer 14; dm €10-44, tw €75-150, tw without bathroom €50-110; ⊖ @ 🛜; Ⓤ Möckernbrücke) Cocktails in the library bar? Check. Free German lessons? Got 'em. Canal views? Yep. Ensconced in a fully renovated 1870s building, the Grand Hostel is one of Berlin's most supremely comfortable, convivial and atmospheric hostels. Breakfast is €7.50.

★ Orania Hotel   HOTEL €€
(Map p86; ☑ 030-6953 9680; www.orania.berlin; Oranienstrasse 40; d from €150; ⊖ ❄ 🛜 🏊; Ⓤ Moritzplatz) This gorgeous hotel in a sensitively restored 1913 building wraps everything that makes Berlin special – culture, class and culinary acumen, infused with a freewheeling cosmopolitan spirit – into one tidy package. Great warmth radiates from the open lobby bar, whose stylish furniture, sultry lighting and open fireplace exude living-room flair. Catch shuteye in 41 comfy rooms that mix retro and modern touches.

Hotel Riehmers Hofgarten   HOTEL €€
(Map p86; ☑ 030-7809 8800; www.riehmers-hofgarten.de; Yorckstrasse 83; d €112-156, ste €147-175; Ⓟ ⊖ @ 🛜 🏊; Ⓤ Mehringdamm) Take a romantic 19th-century building, add contemporary art, stir in a few zeitgeist touches and you'll get one winning cocktail of a hotel. Riehmers' high-ceilinged rooms are modern but not stark; if you're noise-sensitive, get a (slightly pricier) courtyard-facing room. Assets include in-room tea and coffee facilities, a gourmet restaurant and free laptop rental. Breakfast buffet is €10.

🛏 Friedrichshain

★ Michelberger Hotel   HOTEL €€
(Map p86; ☑ 030-2977 8590; www.michelbergerhotel.com; Warschauer Strasse 39; d €95-190; Ⓟ ⊖ 🛜; Ⓤ Warschauer Strasse, Ⓢ Warschauer Strasse) Offering the ultimate in creative crash pads, Michelberger perfectly encapsulates Berlin's offbeat DIY spirit without being self-consciously cool. Rooms don't hide their factory pedigree, but are comfortable and come in sizes suitable for lovebirds, families or rock bands. Staff are friendly and clued-up, and the restaurant (p114) is popular with both guests and locals. Breakfast is €16.

Almodóvar Hotel   HOTEL €€
(☑ 030-692 097 080; www.almodovarhotel.de; Boxhagener Strasse 83; d €99-162; Ⓟ ⊖ 🛜; 🚌 240, 🚌 M10, M13, Ⓢ Ostkreuz, Ⓤ Samariterstrasse) 🌿 A certified organic hotel, Almodóvar is perfect for keeping your healthy ways while travelling. A yoga mat is a standard amenity in the 60 rooms with modern-rustic natural wood furniture and sky-blue accent walls. The upbeat deli serves meat-free tapas, salads and light meals, while the rooftop sauna will heat you up on cold days. Breakfast is €16.50.

nhow Berlin   DESIGN HOTEL €€
(Map p86; ☑ 030-290 2990; www.nhow-hotels.com; Stralauer Allee 3; d €114-164; Ⓟ ⊖ ❄ 🛜 🏊; Ⓢ Warschauer Strasse, Ⓤ Warschauer Strasse) This riverside behemoth bills itself as a 'music and lifestyle' hotel and underscores the point by offering two recording studios and e-guitar rentals. The look is definitely dynamic, with a sideways tower jutting out over the Spree and Karim Rashid's digi-pop-pink design. Kudos to the restaurant with riverside terrace and the party-people-friendly late Sunday checkout. Massive breakfast buffet is €24 (served till 3pm).

🛏 Prenzlauer Berg

★ EastSeven Berlin Hostel   HOSTEL €
(Map p94; ☑ 030-9362 2240; www.eastseven.de; Schwedter Strasse 7; dm/d from €25/65; ⊖ @ 🛜; Ⓤ Senefelderplatz) An excellent choice for solo travellers, this small indie hostel has personable staff who go out of their way to make all feel welcome. Make new friends while chilling in the lounge or garden (hammocks!), firing up the BBQ or hanging out in the 24-hour kitchen. Brightly painted dorms feature comfy pine beds and lockers. Linen is free, breakfast €3.

★ Brilliant Apartments   APARTMENT €€
(Map p94; ☑ 030-8061 4796; www.brilliant-apartments.de; Oderberger Strasse 38; apt from €93; ⊖ 🛜 🏊; Ⓤ Eberswalder Strasse) These 11 stylish and modern self-catering studios, two- and three-bed apartments have full kitchens, plenty of design cache and neat historic touches such as exposed red-brick walls and wooden floors. Four have balconies, one a little garden. The location puts you in the middle of a neighbourhood filled with cafes, restaurants and boutiques and close to the Mauerpark.

Apartments facing out back are quieter. Three-night minimum stay most times. The cleaning fee is €35.

★ **Ackselhaus & Blue Home** BOUTIQUE HOTEL €€€

(Map p66; 📞030-4433 7633; www.ackselhaus.de; Belforter Strasse 21; ste incl breakfast €130-180, apt €150-340; ⊕@🖤; 🚇M10, Ⓤ Senefelderplatz) At this charismatic refuge in a 19th-century building you'll sleep in spacious, classily themed rooms (eg Africa, Rome, Maritime), each sporting hand-picked features reflecting the owner's penchant for art, vintage furniture and travel: a free-standing tub, perhaps, a four-poster bed or Chinese antiques. Many units face the enchanting courtyard garden.

The breakfast buffet (€19) is served until 11am (until 12.30pm at weekends).

🛏 City West & Charlottenburg

★ **25hours Hotel Bikini Berlin** DESIGN HOTEL €€

(Map p97; 📞030-120 2210; www.25hours-hotels.com; Budapester Strasse 40; r €110-250; 🅿⊕🖤@🖤; 🚇100, 200, Ⓢ Zoologischer Garten, Ⓤ Zoologischer Garten) The 'urban jungle' theme of this lifestyle outpost in the iconic 1950s Bikini Haus plays on its location between the zoo and main shopping district. Rooms are cool, and drip with clever design touches; the best face the animal park. Quirks include an on-site bakery, hammocks in the public areas and the 'jungle-sauna' with zoo view. The rooftop **Monkey Bar** (Map p97; 📞030-120 221 210; www.monkeybarberlin.de; ⊗noon-2am; 🖤) and **Neni** (Map p97; 📞030-120 221 200; www.neniberlin.de; mains €13-23; ⊗12.30-11pm) restaurant draw a good local crowd as well.

★ **Sir Savigny** BOUTIQUE HOTEL €€

(Map p97; 📞030-323 015 600; www.hotel-sir-savigny.de; Kantstrasse 144; r from €130; ⊕🖤🖤; Ⓢ Savignyplatz) Global nomads with a hankering for style would be well advised to point their compass to this cosmopolitan crash pad. Each of the 44 rooms exudes delightfully risqué glamour and teems with mod cons and clever design touches. And yes, the beds are fab. If you're feeling social, report to the book-filled 'kitchen' lounge or the cool bar and burger joint. Breakfast is €18.

Hotel Henri BOUTIQUE HOTEL €€

(Map p97; 📞030-884 430; www.henri-berlin.com; Meinekestrasse 9; r €108-215; 🅿⊕@; Ⓤ Kurfürstendamm) This newcomer takes you through a belle-époque time warp while delivering personal flair, modern comforts and an urban setting close to top restaurants and shopping. Rooms come in three categories:

petite Kabinett, classical Les Chambres and the ritzy Salon. Rates include a German-style cold supper buffet, set up in the retro kitchen. Full breakfast is €16, coffee and croissants €4.50.

★ **Hotel am Steinplatz** HOTEL €€€

(Map p97; 📞030-554 4440; www.hotelsteinplatz.com; Steinplatz 4; r €100-290; 🅿⊕❄@🖤🖤; 🚇M45, 245, Ⓤ Ernst-Reuter-Platz) Vladimir Nabokov and Romy Schneider were among the guests of the original Hotel am Steinplatz, which got a second lease of life in 2013, a century after it first opened. Rooms in this elegant art deco jewel reinterpret the 1920s in contemporary style with fantastic lamps, ultra-comfy beds and device docking stations. Classy bar (p123) and **restaurant** (Map p97; 2-/3-course lunch €19/23, dinner mains €23-30; ⊗noon-2.30pm & 6-10pm Mon-Fri, 6-10pm Sat & Sun), too. The optional breakfast costs €35.

🍴 Eating

Berlin's food scene is growing in leaps and bounds and maturing as beautifully as a fine Barolo. Sure, you can still get your fill of traditional German comfort staples, from sausage to roast pork knuckle, but it's the influx of experimental chefs from around the globe that makes eating in the capital such a delicious and exciting experience.

🍴 Historic Mitte

★ **India Club** NORTH INDIAN €€

(Map p66; 📞030-2062 8610; www.india-club-berlin.com; Behrenstrasse 72; mains €16-27; ⊗6-10.30pm; 🖤; Ⓢ Brandenburger Tor) No need to book a flight to Mumbai or London: authentic Indian cuisine has finally landed in Berlin. Thanks to top toque Manish Bahukhandi, these curries are like culinary poetry, the chicken tikka perfectly succulent and the stuffed cauliflower an inspiration. The dark mahogany furniture is enlivened by splashes of colour in the plates, the chandeliers and the servers' uniforms.

Augustiner am Gendarmenmarkt GERMAN €€

(Map p66; 📞030-2045 4020; www.augustiner-braeu-berlin.de; Charlottenstrasse 55; mains €7.50-30, lunch special €5.90; ⊗10am-2am; Ⓤ Französische Strasse) Tourists, concertgoers and heartyfood lovers rub shoulders at rustic tables in this authentic Bavarian beer hall. Soak up the down-to-earth vibe right along with a mug of full-bodied Augustiner brew straight from

Munich. Sausages, roast pork and pretzels provide rib-sticking sustenance with only a token salad offered for non-carnivores. Good-value weekday lunch specials.

★ Cookies Cream VEGETARIAN €€€

(Map p66; ☑ 030-2749 2940; www.cookies cream.com; Behrenstrasse 55; mains €25, 3-/4-course menu €49/59; ⏲ 6pm-midnight Tue-Sat; ☑; Ⓤ Französische Strasse) In 2017, this perennial local favourite became Berlin's first flesh-free restaurant to enter the Michelin pantheon, on its 10th anniversary no less. Its industrial look and clandestine location are as unorthodox as the compositions of head chef Stephan Hentschel. The entrance is off the service alley of the Westin Grand Hotel (past the chandelier, ring the bell).

★ Restaurant Tim Raue ASIAN €€€

(Map p66; ☑ 030-2593 7930; www.tim-raue.com; Rudi-Dutschke-Strasse 26; 3-/4-course lunch €58/68, 8-course dinner €198, mains €48-66; ⏲ noon-3pm & 7pm-midnight Wed-Sat; Ⓤ Kochstrasse) Now here's a double-Michelin-starred restaurant we can get our mind around. Unstuffy ambience and a stylishly reduced design with walnut and Vitra chairs perfectly juxtapose with Berliner Tim Raue's brilliant Asian-inspired plates, which each shine the spotlight on a few choice ingredients. His interpretation of Peking duck is a perennial bestseller.

In 2017, the restaurant came in at 34 on the top 50 list of the world's best restaurants. The same year, Raue was featured in an episode of *Chef's Table*. The kitchen closes at 1.30pm for lunch service and 9pm for dinner. Book at least a couple of weeks in advance for dinner.

✖ Museumsinsel & Alexanderplatz

Dolores CALIFORNIAN €

(Map p66; ☑ 030-2809 9597; www.dolores-online.de; Rosa-Luxemburg-Strasse 7; burritos from €4.50; ⏲ 11.30am-10pm Mon-Sat, 1-10pm Sun; ☑; ☐ 100, 200, Ⓢ Alexanderplatz, Ⓤ Alexanderplatz) Dolores hasn't lost a step since introducing the California-style burrito to Berlin. Pick your favourites from among the marinated meats (or tofu), rice, beans, veggies, cheeses and homemade salsas, and the cheerful staff will build it on the spot. Goes perfectly with an *agua fresca* (Mexican-style lemonade).

Brauhaus Georgbräu GERMAN €€

(Map p66; ☑ 030-242 4244; www.brauhaus-georgbraeu.de; Spreeufer 4; mains €6-15;

⏲ noon-midnight; Ⓤ Klosterstrasse) Solidly on the tourist track, this old-style gastropub churns out its own light and dark Georg-Bräu, which can even be ordered by the metre (12 glasses at 0.2L). In winter, the woodsy beer hall is perfect for tucking into hearty Berlin-style fare, while in summer tables in the riverside beer garden are golden.

Zur Letzten Instanz GERMAN €€

(Map p66; ☑ 030-242 5528; www.zurletzten instanz.de; Waisenstrasse 14-16; mains €13-23; ⏲ noon-1am Tue-Sat, noon-10pm Sun; Ⓤ Klosterstrasse) With its folksy Old Berlin charm, this rustic eatery has been an enduring hit since 1621 and has fed everyone from Napoleon to Beethoven to Angela Merkel. Although the restaurant is now tourist-geared, the food quality is reassuringly high when it comes to such local rib-stickers as grilled pork knuckle or meatballs in caper sauce.

Hofbräuhaus Berlin GERMAN €€

(Map p66; ☑ 030-679 665 520; www.hof braeu-wirtshaus.de/berlin; Karl-Liebknecht-Strasse 30; sausages €6-9, mains €11-20; ⏲ 10am-1am Sun-Thu, to 2am Fri & Sat; ☑; Ⓢ Alexanderplatz, Ⓤ Alexanderplatz) Popular with coach tourists and field-tripping teens, this giant beer hall with 2km of wooden benches does not have the patina of the Munich original but at least it serves the same litre-size mugs of beer and big plates piled high with gut-busting German fare.

✖ Hackescher Markt & Scheunenviertel

House of Small Wonder INTERNATIONAL €

(Map p66; ☑ 030-2758 2877; www.houseofsmall wonder.de; Johannisstrasse 20; dishes €8-13; ⏲ 9am-5pm; ☑; Ⓤ Oranienburger Tor, Ⓢ Oranienburger Strasse, Friedrichstrasse) A wrought-iron staircase spirals up to this brunch and lunch oasis where potted plants and whimsical decor create a relaxed backyard garden feel. The global comfort is just as beautiful, no matter if you go for eggs Benedict with homemade yoghurt scones, Okinawan Taco Rice or zoodles with cashew miso pesto. Also a good spot just for coffee and pastries.

Store Kitchen INTERNATIONAL €

(Map p66; ☑ 030-405 044 550; www.thestores. com; Torstrasse 1; dishes €6-12; ⏲ 10am-7pm Mon-Sat; ☑; Ⓤ Rosa-Luxemburg-Platz) This is the kind of impossibly trendy yet welcoming place that had food fanciers excited the moment it opened inside hipper-than-thou lifestyle and fashion temple the Store, on the ground floor of Soho House. Head here if you crave breakfast, salads, sandwiches and light meals that capture the latest global food trends while using local suppliers.

★ **Katz Orange**   INTERNATIONAL €€
(Map p66; ☑ 030-983 208 430; www.katzorange. com; Bergstrasse 22; mains €17-24; ☺ 6-11pm; ☑ M8, ☑ Rosenthaler Platz) 🗷 With its holistic farm-to-table menu, stylish country flair and top-notch cocktails, the 'Orange Cat' hits a gastro grand slam. It will have you purring for such perennial favourites as Duroc pork that's been slow-roasted for 12 hours (nicknamed 'candy on bone'). The setting in a castle-like former brewery is stunning, especially in summer when the patio opens.

Muret La Barba   ITALIAN €€
(Map p66; ☑ 030-2809 7212; www.muretlabarba. de; Rosenthaler Strasse 61; mains €14.50-27; ☺ 10am-midnight Mon-Fri, noon-midnight Sat & Sun; ☑ M1, ☑ Rosenthaler Platz) This wine shop-bar-restaurant combo exudes the kind of rustic authenticity that instantly transports cognoscenti to Italy. The food is hearty, inventive and made with top ingredients imported from the motherland. All wine is available by the glass or by the bottle (corkage fee €10).

Night Kitchen   INTERNATIONAL €€
(Map p66; ☑ 030-2357 5075; www.nightkitchen berlin.com; Oranienburger Strasse 32; dishes €4-19, Dinner with Friends per person €36; ☺ 5pm-midnight daily, 11am-4pm Sun; 🕿 🗷; ☑ M1, ☑ Oranienburger Strasse, ☑ Oranienburger Tor) This smartly seductive courtyard bistro is often packed to capacity with punters hungry for modern Med spins inspired by the mothership in Tel Aviv. You're free to order à la carte but the guiding concept here is 'Dinner with Friends', a chef-collated meal designed for sharing. Sit inside at high tables or at the bar, or in the candlelit courtyard.

District Môt   VIETNAMESE €€
(Map p66; ☑ 030-2008 9284; www.district mot.com; Rosenthaler Strasse 62; dishes €7-19; ☺ noon-midnight; 🕿; ☑ M1, ☑ Rosenthaler Platz) At this colourful mock-Saigon street-food parlour, patrons squat on tiny plastic stools around wooden tables where rolls of toilet paper irreverently stand in for paper napkins. The small-plate menu mixes the familiar (steamy *pho* noodle soup, papaya salad) with the adventurous (stewed eel, deep-fried silk) but it's their De La Sauce *bao* burger that has collected the accolades.

Schwarzwaldstuben   GERMAN €€
(Map p66; ☑ 030-2809 8084; www.schwarz waldstuben-berlin.com; Tucholskystrasse 48; mains €7-16.50; ☺ 9am-midnight; ☑ M1, ☑ Oranienburger Strasse) In the mood for a Hansel and Gretel moment? Then join the other 'lost kids' for satisfying slow food from the southwest German regions of Baden and Swabia. Tuck into gut-filling platters of *spaetzle* (mac 'n' cheese), *Maultaschen* (ravioli-like pasta) or giant schnitzel with fried potatoes. Dine amid rustic and tongue-in-cheek forest decor or grab a table on the pavement.

★ **Zenkichi**   JAPANESE €€€
(Map p66; ☑ 030-2463 0810; www.zenkichi.de; Johannisstrasse 20; 4-/8-course tasting menu €45/65, small plates €4.50-26; ☺ 6pm-midnight; 🗷; ☑ Oranienburger Tor, Friedrichstrasse, ☑ Friedrichstrasse) Romance runs high at this lantern-lit basement *izakaya*, which serves faithfully executed gourmet Japanese fare and premium sake in cosy alcoves with black-lacquer tables shielded by bamboo blinds for privacy. Expect your tastebuds to do cartwheels, no matter if you treat yourself to the seasonal *omakase* (chef's) dinner or compose your own culinary symphony from the small-plate menu.

★ **Einsunternull**   INTERNATIONAL €€€
(Map p66; ☑ 030-2757 7810; www.einsunternull. com; Hannoversche Strasse 1; 4-/5-course lunch menus €59/69, 6-course dinner menus €99, additional courses €10; ☺ noon-2pm Tue-Sat, 7-11pm Mon-Sat; 🗷; ☑ M1, ☑ Oranienburger Tor) 🗷 The name means 'one below zero' but the food at Michelin-starred Einsunternull is actually happening hot. Adventurous palates get to embark on a radically regional, product-focused journey that draws upon such time-tested techniques as preservation and fermentation. Lunches are served amid Scandinavian-type airyness next to the glass-fronted kitchen while dinners unfold in the cosy cellar.

Lokal   GERMAN €€€
(Map p66; ☑ 030-2844 9500; www.lokal-berlin. blogspot.de; Linienstrasse 160; mains €15-29; ☺ 5.30-11pm; 🗷; ☑ Rosenthaler Platz, ☑ Oranienburger Strasse) The stripped down Nordic aesthetic of this locally adored joint is a perfect foil for the kitchen's inspired farm-to-table riffs on German fare, including meat-free options. It's food that is at once comforting and exciting with awesome bread to boot. Reservations are a must.

✘ Potsdamer Platz & Tiergarten

Mabuhay
INDONESIAN €

(Map p86; ☎030-265 1867; www.mabuhay.juisy food.com; Köthener Strasse 28; mains €6-13; ☺noon-3pm Mon-Fri, 5-9.30pm Mon-Sat; ☑; ☑Mendelssohn-Bartholdy-Park) Tucked into a concrete courtyard, this hole-in-the-wall scores a one for looks and a 10 for the food. Usually packed (especially at lunchtime), it delivers Indonesian food with as much authenticity as possible. The heat meter has been adjusted for German tastes, but the spicing of such dishes as gado gado or curry rendang is still feisty and satisfying.

Caffe e Gelato
ICE CREAM €

(Map p66; ☎030-2529 7832; www.caffe-e-gelato.de; Alte Potsdamer Strasse 7, Potsdamer Platz Arkaden; scoops €1.60-2.20; ☺10am-10.30pm Mon-Thu, to 11pm Fri, to 11.30pm Sat, 10.30am-10.30pm Sun; ☑Potsdamer Platz, Ⓢ Potsdamer Platz) Traditional Italian-style ice cream gets a 21st-century twist at this huge cafe on the upper floor of the Potsdamer Platz Arkaden (p130) mall. Among the homemade creamy concoctions are organic and gluten-, lactose- and sugar-free varieties in unusual flavours, including yoghurt-walnut-fig and almond crunch.

★ Ki-Nova
INTERNATIONAL €€

(Map p66; ☎030-2546 4860; www.ki-nova.de; Potsdamer Strasse 2; mains €9-17; ☺11.30am-11pm Mon-Fri, 1-11pm Sat, 1-9pm Sun; ☎☑; ☑200, ☑Potsdamer Platz, Ⓢ Potsdamer Platz) ∅ The name of this lunchtime favourite hints at the concept: 'ki' is Japanese for energy and 'nova' Latin for new. 'New energy' in this case translates into health-focused yet comforting bites starring global and regional superfoods from kale to cranberries. The contempo interior radiates urban warmth with heavy plank tables, black tiled bar, movie stills and floor-to-ceiling windows.

Qiu
INTERNATIONAL €€

(Map p66; ☎030-590 051 230; www.qiu.de; Potsdamer Strasse 3, Mandala Hotel; 2-course lunches €16-25; ☺noon-1am Sun-Wed, to 3am Thu-Sat; ☑; ☑200, Ⓢ Potsdamer Platz, ☑Potsdamer Platz) The weekly changing business lunch (noon to 3pm Monday to Friday) at this stylish bar-lounge at the Mandala Hotel (Map p66; ☎030-590 051 221; www.themandala.de; ste from €180; ☑☺☻☎) also includes soup or salad, a non-alcoholic beverage, and coffee or tea. That's a steal. It's also a nice spot for cocktails with a view of the golden Bisazza mosaic water wall.

✘ Kreuzberg & Neukölln

★ Burgermeister
BURGERS €

(Map p86; ☎030-2388 3840; www.burger-meister. de; Oberbaumstrasse 8; burgers €3.50-4.80; ☺11am-3am Mon-Thu, 11am-4am Fri, noon-4am Sat, noon-3am Sun; ☑Schlesisches Tor) It's green, ornate, a century old and...it used to be a toilet. Now it's a burger joint beneath the elevated U-Bahn tracks. Get in line for the plump all-beef patties (try the Meisterburger with fried onions, bacon and barbecue sauce) tucked between a brioche bun and paired with thickly cut cheese fries. Fast-food heaven!

Masaniello
ITALIAN €

(Map p86; ☎030-692 6657; www.masaniello.de; Hasenheide 20; pizza €6.50-11; ☺noon-midnight; ☑Hermannplatz) The tables are almost too small for the wagon-wheel-sized certified Neapolitan pizzas tickled by wood fire at Luigi and Pascale's old-school but much-adored pizzeria. The crust is crispy, the tomato sauce has just the right amount of tang, and the toppings are piled on generously.

Fresh fish is served on Friday and Saturday.

City Chicken
MIDDLE EASTERN €

(Map p86; ☎030-624 8600; www.facebook.com/citychickenberlin; Sonnenallee 59; half-chicken plate €7.50; ☺11am-2am; ☑Rathaus Neukölln) There's chicken and then there's City Chicken, an absolute cult destination when it comes to juicy birds sent through the rotisserie for the perfect tan. All birds are served with creamy hummus, vampire-repelling garlic sauce and salad. Sit outside for the full-on Neukölln street-life immersion.

There's also a full menu of other Middle Eastern dishes.

Damaskus Konditorei
MIDDLE EASTERN €

(Map p86; ☎030-7037 0711; www.facebook.com/Konditorei.Damaskus; Sonnenallee 93; snacks from €2; ☺9am-9pm Mon-Sat, 11.30am-8pm Sun; ☑M41, ☑Rathaus Neukölln) Of all the baklava shops in Neukölln, Damaskus stands out for its truly artistic and rave-worthy pastries. The shop is run by a Syrian family who had to leave behind their thriving bakery and resettle in Germany. Stop counting calories and try their divine *kanafeh* (cheese-filled pastry drenched in syrup) or their signature *halawat al jubn* (rosewater cheese pockets).

Curry 36
GERMAN €

(Map p86; ☎030-2580 088 336; www.curry36. de; Mehringdamm 36; snacks €2-6; ☺9am-5am;

U Mehringdamm) Day after day, night after night, a motley crowd – cops, cabbies, queens, office jockeys, tourists etc – wait their turn at this popular *Currywurst* snack shop that's been frying 'em up since 1981.

Other sausage varieties – bratwurst, wiener and bockwurst – are also available, along with traditional potato and noodle salads.

★ Fes Turkish Barbecue   TURKISH €€

(Map p86; ☑ 030-2391 7778; http://fes-turkish bbq.de; Hasenheide 58; meze €4-10, meat from €15; ☺ 5-10pm Tue-Sun; U Südstern) If you like a DIY approach to dining, give this innovative Turkish restaurant a try. Perhaps borrowing a page from the Koreans, it requires you to cook your own slabs of marinated chicken, beef fillet and tender lamb on a grill sunk right into your table.

Book a few days ahead on weekends.

★ Cafe Jacques   MEDITERRANEAN €€

(Map p86; ☑ 030-694 1048; http://cafejacques. de; Maybachufer 14; mains €12.50-19; ☺ 6pm-late; U Schönleinstrasse) Like a fine wine, this darling French-Mediterranean lair keeps improving with age. Candlelit wooden tables and art-festooned brick walls feel as warm and welcoming as an old friend's embrace. And indeed, a welcoming embrace from charismatic owner-host Ahmad may well await you. The blackboard menu is a rotating festival of flavours, including mouth-watering meze, homemade pasta and fresh fish.

Reservations advised.

Max und Moritz   GERMAN €€

(Map p86; ☑ 030-6951 5911; www.maxundmoritz berlin.de; Oranienstrasse 162; mains €11.50-17; ☺ 5pm-midnight; ☎; U Moritzplatz) The patina of yesteryear hangs over this ode-to-old-school gastropub, named for the cheeky Wilhelm Busch cartoon characters. Since 1902, it has packed hungry diners and thirsty drinkers into its rustic tile-and stucco-ornamented rooms for sudsy homebrews and granny-style Berlin fare. A menu favourite is the *Königsberger Klopse* (veal meatballs in caper sauce).

Ora   INTERNATIONAL €€

(Map p86; http://ora-berlin.de; Oranienplatz 14; mains €8-15; ☺ noon-1am Mon-Fri, from 9.30am Sat & Sun; U Kottbusser Tor) A 19th-century pharmacy has been splendidly rebooted as this stylishly casual cafe-bar-restaurant. The antique wooden medicine cabinets are now the back bar, where craft beer and cocktails are dispensed to a down-to-earth crowd with an appreciation for the finer things in life. The menu is modern brasserie food and makes deft use of seasonal and local ingredients.

★ Orania   GERMAN €€€

(Map p86; ☑ 030-6953 9680; https://orania. berlin/restaurant; Oranienstrasse 40; mains €30-36; ☺ 6-11pm; U Moritzplatz) Punctilious artisanship meets boundless creativity at Orania, where a small army of chefs fusses around culinary wunderkind Philipp Vogel in the shiny open kitchen. The flair is cosmo-chic with food and cocktails to match. Only three ingredients find a spot in each product-focused dish, inspired by global flavours rather than the latest trends and often served with live music in the background.

★ Tulus Lotrek   INTERNATIONAL €€€

(Map p86; ☑ 030-4195 6687; www.tulus lotrek.de; Fichtestrasse 24; 6-/7-/8-course dinner €99/110/119; ☺ 7pm-midnight Fri-Tue; U Südstern) Artist Henri de Toulouse-Lautrec was a bon vivant who embraced good food and wine, which is exactly what owner-chef Maximilian Strohe and owner-mâitre Ilona Scholl want their guests to do. With several awards and a Michelin star under their belts, the charismatic couple dishes up intellectually ambitious food with soul.

★ Horváth   AUSTRIAN €€€

(Map p86; ☑ 030-6128 9992; www.restaurant-horvath.de; Paul-Lincke-Ufer 44a; 5-/7-/9-course menu €100/120/140; ☺ 6-11pm Wed-Sun; U Kottbusser Tor) At his canal-side restaurant, Sebastian Frank performs culinary alchemy with Austrian classics, fearlessly combining products, textures and flavours. The stunning results have earned him two Michelin stars and the title of Best Chef of Europe 2018. Wines are fabulous, of course, but Frank is also proud of his food-matching nonalcoholic beverage line-up, including tea infusions, vegetable juices and reductions.

✗ Friedrichshain

Silo Coffee   CAFE €

(Map p86; www.facebook.com/silocoffee; Gabriel-Max-Strasse 4; dishes €6-12; ☺ 8.30am-5pm Mon-Fri, 9.30am-6pm Sat & Sun; ☎ ☑; ☐ M10, M13, U Warschauer Strasse, S Warschauer Strasse) If you've greeted the day with bloodshot eyes, get back in gear at this Aussie-run coffee and breakfast joint favoured by Friedrichshain's hip and expat. Beans from Fjord coffee roasters ensure possibly the best flat white in town, while bread from Sironi (Markthalle

GLOBAL BITES

Street Food Thursday (www.markthalleneun.de; Eisenbahnstrasse 42-43; ⊘5-10pm Thu; Ⓤ Görlitzer Bahnhof) has taken place every Thursday evening since 2013. A couple of dozen aspiring chefs set up their food stalls in Markthalle Neun (p130), a historic market hall in Kreuzberg, and serve up delicious global street food. Order your favourites, lug them to a communal table and gobble them up with a glass of Heidenpeters, a craft beer brewed right on the premises.

Some of the original food purveyors have enjoyed such roaring success that they have opened brick-and-mortar restaurants around the city.

As its name implies, Markthalle Neun was the ninth (of a total of 14) market halls built in Berlin in the late 19th century. It did a roaring trade for decades, but over time succumbed to competition from supermarkets, eventually becoming the haunt of tacky discount stores. Aside from this weekly street-food event, it also hosts a regular farmers market on Tuesday, Friday and Saturday.

Neun) adds scrumptiousness to the poached-egg avo toast.

Vöner
VEGAN €

(☑0176 9651 3869; www.facebook.com/Voener; Boxhagener Strasse 56; dishes €3.50-6.50; ⊘noon-11pm; ☑; Ⓢ Ostkreuz) Vöner stands for 'vegan doner kebab' and is a spit-roasted blend of wheat protein, vegetables and herbs. It was dreamed up more than a 20 years ago by Holger Frerichs, a one-time resident of a so-called *Wagenburg*, a countercultural commune made up of old vans, buses and caravans. The alt-spirit lives on in his original Vöner outlet.

Michelberger
INTERNATIONAL €€

(Map p86; ☑030-2977 8590; www.michelbergerhotel.com; Warschauer Strasse 39; 3-course lunch €12, dinner dishes €8-15; ⊘7-11am, noon-2.30pm & 6.30-11pm; ☜☑; Ⓢ Warschauer Strasse, Ⓤ Warschauer Strasse) 🖉 Ensconced in one of Berlin's coolest hotels (p108), Michelberger makes creative dishes that often combine unusual organic ingredients (eg wild boar with miso, scallops, cabbage and gooseberry). Sit inside the lofty, white-tiled restaurant or in the breezy courtyard.

Schalander
GERMAN €€

(☑030-8961 7073; www.schalander-berlin.de; Bänschstrasse 91; mains €8.50-17.50; ⊘5pm-late Tue-Sat, noon-midnight Sun; ☜☝; ☒21, Ⓢ Frankfurter Allee, Ⓤ Samariterstrasse) The full-bodied pilsner, *Dunkel* (dark) and *Weizen* (wheat) beers are now brewed offsite but this charismatic gastropub is still worth a detour from the tourist track. The menu features crispy *Flammkuchen* (Alsatian pizza) alongside beer-hall-type meaty mains such as pork roast and schnitzel. For an unusual finish, order the wheat-beer crème brûlée.

Schneeweiss
EUROPEAN €€

(Map p86; ☑030-2904 9704; www.schneeweiss-berlin.de; Simplonstrasse 16; mains €13-25, Sun brunch €15; ⊘10am-3pm & 6pm-1am Mon-Fri, 10am-1am Sat & Sun; ☝; ☒M13, Ⓤ Warschauer Strasse, Ⓢ Warschauer Strasse) The chilly-chic snowy white decor, with an eye-catching 'ice' chandelier, complements the Alpine menu at this fine-dining pioneer in Friedrichshain. Although the emphasis is on such classics as schnitzel, goulash and *spaetzle* (mac 'n' cheese), the chef's talents also shine through with seasonal specials. Reservations essential for weekend brunch.

Katerschmaus
INTERNATIONAL €€€

(Map p86; ☑0152 2941 3262; www.katerschmaus.de; Holzmarktstrasse 25; multicourse dinners €50-80; ⊘noon-4pm & 7-10.30pm Tue-Sat; ☜; Ⓤ Jannowitzbrücke, Ⓢ Jannowitzbrücke) From the homemade bread to the wicked crème brûlée, dining at this carefully designed ramshackle space under the U-Bahn tracks is very much a Berlin experience. The kitchen embraces the regional-seasonal credo and presents meaty, fishy or vegetarian multicourse dinners as well as à la carte dining. Reservations essential.

🍴 Prenzlauer Berg

Yafo
ISRAELI €

(Map p66; ☑030-9235 0250; www.yafoberlin.com; Gormannstrasse 17; dishes €6-13; ⊘noon-3am; ☜☑; ☒M8, M10, Ⓤ Rosenthaler Platz, Rosa-Luxemburg-Platz) This charming resto-bar combo transplants Tel Aviv's palpable energy, sensuous food and convivial vibes to a quiet corner in Berlin. Drop by for a refreshing Aracboy (a cocktail made with Arac, cucumber, lemon and ginger beer) in the buzzy bar or plunge into the eclectically furnished dining room for tahini-drizzled baked cauliflower and other tantalising treats.

Umami
VIETNAMESE €

(Map p94; ☑ 030-2886 0626; www.umami-restaurant.de; Knaackstrasse 16; most mains €7.80; ◷ noon-11pm; ☎ ⚐; ☒ M2, ⓤ Senefelderplatz) A mellow 1950s lounge vibe and an inspired menu of Indochine home cooking divided into 'regular' and 'vegetarian' choices are the main draws of this restaurant with a large sidewalk terrace. Leave room for the cupcake riff (called 'popcake'). The six-course family meal is a steal at €23 (€10 per additional person).

There are two other branches in Kreuzberg, including one in the **Bergmannkiez** (Map p86; ☑ 030-6832 5085; Bergmannstrasse 97; mains €8-19; ◷ noon-10pm; ⓤ Gneisenaustrasse, Mehringdamm) and a third at Schlesische Strasse 5.

W-Der Imbiss
FUSION €

(Map p94; ☑ 030-4435 2206; www.w-derimbiss.de; Kastanienallee 49; dishes €5-13.50; ◷ noon-10pm Sun-Thu, to 11pm Fri & Sat; ⚐; ☒ M1, ⓤ Rosenthaler Platz) The self-described home of 'indo-mexical-ital' fusion, W is always busy as a beehive with fans of its signature naan pizza freshly baked in the tandoor oven and decorated with anything from avocado to smoked salmon. Other standouts are the fish tacos, the thali curry spread and the tandoori salmon.

Enjoy it all amid cheerful tiki decor alongside a healthy spirulina-laced apple juice. There's a second branch in Schöneberg at Nollendorf Strasse 10.

Konnopke's Imbiss
GERMAN €

(Map p94; ☑ 030-442 7765; www.konnopke-imbiss.de; Schönhauser Allee 44a; sausages €1.60-2.90; ◷ 10am-8pm Mon-Fri, 11.30am-8pm Sat; ☒ M1, M10, M13, ⓤ Eberswalder Strasse) Brave the inevitable queue at this famous sausage kitchen, ensconced in the same spot below the elevated U-Bahn tracks since 1930, but now equipped with a heated pavilion and an English menu. The 'secret' sauce topping is classic *Currywurst* and comes in a four-tier heat scale from mild to wild.

★ Mrs Robinson's
INTERNATIONAL €€

(Map p94; ☑ 030-5462 2839, 01520 518 8946; www.mrsrobinsons.de; Pappelallee 29; mains €16-20; ◷ 6-11pm Thu-Mon; ☎ ⚐; ☒ 12, ⓤ Schön-

hauser Allee, Ⓢ Schönhauser Allee) When Israel transplant Ben Zviel and his partner Samina Raza launched their minimalist parlour (white-brick walls, polished wooden tables) in 2016, they added another notch to Berlin's food ladder. The menu is constantly in flux, but by turning carefully edited ingredients into shareable small and big plates, Ben fearlessly captures the city's adventurous and uninhibited spirit. Casual fine dining at its best.

Zum Schusterjungen
GERMAN €€

(Map p94; ☑ 030-442 7654; www.zumschusterjungen.com; Danziger Strasse 9; mains €7.50-17; ◷ 11am-midnight; ⓤ Eberswalder Strasse) Tourists, expats and locals descend upon this old-school gastropub where rustic Berlin charm is doled out with as much abandon as the delish home cooking. Big platters of goulash, roast pork and *sauerbraten* feed both tummy and soul, as do the regionally brewed Berliner Schusterjunge pilsner and Märkischer Landmann black beer.

Standard – Serious Pizza
ITALIAN €€

(Map p66; ☑ 030-4862 5614; www.standard-berlin.de; Templiner Strasse 7; pizza €8.50-17.50; ◷ 6pm-midnight Tue-Fri, 1pm-midnight Sat & Sun; ☎; ⓤ Senefelderplatz) The name is the game: serious Neapolitan-style pizza *truly* is the standard at this modern parlour where the dough is kneaded daily and the bases are topped with such quality ingredients as San Marzano tomatoes from the heel of Vesuvius. Best of all, they're tickled to perfection in a ferociously hot cupola furnace.

Restaurant Oderberger
GERMAN €€€

(Map p94; ☑ 030-7800 8976 811; www.restaurant-oderberger.de; Oderberger Strasse 57; mains €18-28, 3-course menu €39; ◷ 6pm-midnight Tue-Sat; ☎; ☒ M1, 12, ⓤ Eberswalder Strasse) ⌀ This exciting newcomer spreads across three open levels in an industrial-chic ex-boiler room of a public swimming pool. The chef's orchestrations are just as upbeat and tantalising as the decor. The 'Dit is Berlin' menu stars riffs on local classics like bacon-wrapped perch and veal dumplings in caper sauce while the seasonal menu comes alive with freshly gathered ingredients from regional farmers.

✕ Charlottenburg & Schöneberg

★ Kuchenladen
CAFE €

(Map p97; ☑ 030-3101 8424; www.derkuchenladen.de; Kantstrasse 138; cakes €2.50-4.50; ◷ 10am-8pm; Ⓢ Savignyplatz) Even size-0 locals can't resist the siren call of this classic cafe whose homemade cakes are like works of art wrought from flour, sugar and cream. From cheesecake to carrot cake to the ridiculously rich Sacher Torte, it's all delicious down to the last crumb.

Kantini
INTERNATIONAL €

(Map p97; Budapester Strasse, Bikini Berlin; ⊗10am-8pm Mon-Sat; 🅿️🚻; U Zoologischer Garten, S Zoologischer Garten) This next-gen food court at the stylish Bikini Berlin shopping mall has Instaworthy looks thanks to its mash-up of industrial edge and playful design touches, including potted plants, candy-coloured furniture and Berlin Zoo views. The 13 eateries pick up on tradition and trends – from Berlin *Currywurst* to Hawaiian *poké* bowls – often with high quality.

Ali Baba
ITALIAN €

(Map p97; ☑030-881 1350; www.alibaba-berlin. de; Bleibtreustrasse 45; dishes €4-12; ⊗11am-1am Sun-Thu, to 2am Fri & Sat; 🍴; S Savignyplatz) In business for more years than there are robbers in the eponymous fairy tale, Ali Baba is a bustling port-of-call with cult status among local shoppers, students, cabbies and party people. They come for its delicious thin-crust pizza and heaps of pasta paired with crusty homemade bread for sopping up the juices.

★ BRLO Brwhouse
INTERNATIONAL €€

(Map p86; ☑0151 7437 4235; www.brlo-brwhouse. de; Schöneberger Strasse 16; mains from €18; ⊗restaurant 5pm-midnight Tue-Fri, noon-midnight Sat & Sun, beer garden noon-midnight Apr-Sep; 🍴🚻; U Gleisdreieck) The house-crafted suds flow freely at this shooting star among Berlin's craft breweries. Production, taproom and restaurant are all housed in 38 shipping containers fronted by a big beer garden with sand box and views of Gleisdreieckpark. Shareable dishes are mostly vegetable-centric, although missing out on the meat prepared to succulent perfection in a smoker would be a shame.

Dicke Wirtin
GERMAN €€

(Map p97; ☑030-312 4952; www.dicke-wirtin. de; Carmerstrasse 9; mains €11-18; ⊗11am-late; S Savignyplatz) Old Berlin charm is in every nook and cranny of this been-here-forever pub, which pours eight draught beers (including the superb Kloster Andechs) and nearly three dozen homemade schnapps varieties. Hearty local and German fare, such as meatballs in caper sauce, beef liver and pork roast, keeps brains balanced. Bargain lunches, too.

Good Friends
CHINESE €€

(Map p97; ☑030-313 2659; www.goodfriends-berlin.de; Kantstrasse 30; 2-course weekday lunch €7-7.70, dinner mains €8-21; ⊗noon-1am; S Savignyplatz) Good Friends is widely considered Berlin's best Cantonese restaurant. The ducks dangling in the window are merely an overture to a menu long enough to confuse Confucius, including plenty of authentic homestyle dishes (on a separate menu). If steamed chicken feet prove too challenging, you can always fall back on sweet-and-sour pork or fried rice with shrimp.

Schleusenkrug
GERMAN €€

(Map p97; ☑030-313 9909; www.schleusen krug.de; Müller-Breslau-Strasse; mains €6-16; ⊗10am-midnight May-Sep, 11am-6pm Oct-Apr; S Zoologischer Garten, U Zoologischer Garten) Sitting pretty on the edge of the Tiergarten park, next to a canal lock, Schleusenkrug truly comes into its own during beer-garden season. People from all walks of life hunker over big mugs and comfort food – from grilled sausages to *Flammkuchen* (Alsatian pizza) and weekly specials. Breakfast is served until 2pm.

★ Kin Dee
THAI €€€

(Map p86; ☑030-215 5294; www.kindeeberlin. com; Lützowstrasse 81; tasting menu €45; ⊗6-10pm Tue-Sat; 🍴; U Kurfürstenstrasse) One of most buzzed-about new restaurants on Potsdamer Strasse is Dalad Kambhu's lair Kin Dee, where she fearlessly catapults classic Thai dishes into the 21st century, and even adapts them by using locally grown ingredients. One constant is her signature homemade spice pastes that beautifully underline the aromatic dimensions of each dish.

★ Schwein
INTERNATIONAL €€€

(Map p97; ☑030-2435 6282; www.schwein.online; Mommsenstrasse 63; dishes €13-37, 4-/5-course menu €65/75; ⊗6pm-midnight Mon-Fri, to 2am Sat; 🍴🍴; S Savignyplatz) This casual fine-dining lair delivers the perfect trifecta – fabulous food, wine and long drinks. Order the multicourse menu to truly experience the genius of kitchen champion Christopher Kümper, who creates globally inspired and regionally sourced symphonies of taste and textures. Or keep it 'casual' with just a bite and a gin and tonic.

★ Mine Restaurant
ITALIAN €€€

(Map p97; ☑030-8892 6363; www.mineres taurant.de; Meinekestrasse 10; mains €15-29; ⊗5.30pm-midnight; B Uhlandstrasse) Italian restaurants may be a dime a dozen but Mine's decor, menu and service all blend together as perfectly as a Sicilian stew. The Berlin outpost of Russian TV celebrity chef Aram Mnatsakanov, it presents feistily flavoured next-gen fare from around the Boot by riffing on traditional recipes in innovative ways. The wine list should make even demanding oenophiles swoon.

★ **Restaurant Faubourg** FRENCH €€€
(Map p97; ☑030-800 999 7700; www.sofitel-berlin-kurfurstendamm.com; Augsburger Strasse 41; 2-/3-course lunch €19/23, dinner appetisers €14, mains €25-38; ☺noon-11pm; ☎; Ⓤ Kurfürstendamm) At this Sofitel hotel's château-worthy French restaurant, head chef Felix Mielke applies punctilious artisanship to top-notch regional ingredients, creating intensely flavoured and beautifully plated dishes. For maximum palate exposure, put together a meal from the appetiser menu, although the mains – prepared either in classic or contemporary fashion – also command attention, as does the wine list. The gorgeous Bauhaus-inspired decor completes the experience.

🍸 Drinking & Nightlife

As one of Europe's primo party playgrounds, Berlin offers a thousand and one scenarios for getting your cocktails and kicks (or wine or beer, for that matter). From cocktail lairs and concept bars, craft beer pubs to rooftop lounge, the next thirst parlour is usually within stumbling distance.

🍸 Museumsinsel & Alexanderplatz

Braufactum Berlin CRAFT BEER
(Map p66; ☑030-8471 2959; www.braufactum.de; Memhardstrasse 1; ☺noon-midnight Sun-Thu, to 2am Fri & Sat; ☐100, Ⓤ Alexanderplatz, Ⓢ Alexanderplatz) With its urban-contempo looks and big terrace, this concept-driven craft beer outpost shakes up the gastro wasteland of Alexanderplatz. Aside from the dozen house brews like the subtly sweet-bitter India Pale Ale Progusta and the whisky-barrel-matured Barrel 1, the blackboard menu also features suds from other breweries like Mikkeler and Firestone Walker. Elevated pub grub helps keep brains in balance.

House of Weekend CLUB
(Map p66; ☑reservations 0152 2429 3140; www.houseofweekend.berlin; Am Alexanderplatz 5; ☺11pm-6am Fri & Sat, roof garden from 7pm, weath-

BERLIN'S LITTLE ASIA

It's not quite Chinatown, but if you're in the mood for Asian food, head to Kantstrasse between Savignyplatz and Wilmersdorfer Strasse to find the city's densest concentration of authentic Chinese, Vietnamese and Thai restaurants, including the perennially popular Good Friends (p116). At lunchtime most offer value-priced specials, perfect for filling up on the cheap.

er permitting; Ⓢ Alexanderplatz, Ⓤ Alexanderplatz) This veteran electro club has a high-flying location on the 15th floor of a socialist-era office building and often has big-name local and international DJs helming its decks. In summer, the action expands to the rooftop terrace for sundowners, private cabanas and 360° views.

🍸 Hackescher Markt & Scheunenviertel

★ **Clärchens Ballhaus** CLUB
(Map p66; ☑030-282 9295; www.ballhaus.de; Auguststrasse 24; Sun-Thu free, Fri & Sat €5; ☺11am-late; ☐M1, Ⓢ Oranienburger Strasse) Yesteryear is now at this early-20th-century dance hall where groovers and grannies hoof it across the parquet without even a touch of irony. There are different sounds nightly – salsa to swing, tango to disco – and a live band on Saturday. Dancing kicks off from 9pm or 9.30pm. Ask about dance lessons. Tables can only be reserved if you plan on eating.

Pizza and German staples provide sustenance all day long, in summer in the pretty garden, in winter in the upstairs Spiegesaal (Mirror Hall; pizza €6.60 to €14, mains €6.50 to €20). Minimum spend of €25 for groups of 10 or more.

★ **Buck & Breck** COCKTAIL BAR
(Map p66; www.buckandbreck.com; Brunnenstrasse 177; ☺7pm-late Apr-Oct, 8pm-late Nov-Mar; ☐M1, Ⓤ Rosenthaler Platz) Liquid maestro Gonçalo de Sousa Monteiro and his baseball-cap wearing team treat grown-up patrons to libational flights of fancy in their clandestine cocktail salon with classic yet friendly flair. Historical short drinks are a strength, including the eponymous bubbly-based cocktail Buck and Breck, named for mid-19th-century US president James Buchanan and his VP John Breckinridge.

(Continued on page 120)

BERLIN DRINKING & NIGHTLIFE

Berlin Art Scene

Art aficionados will find their compass on perpetual spin in Berlin. With hundreds of galleries, scores of world-class collections and some 33,000 international artists, the city has assumed a pole position on the global artistic circuit. Perpetual energy, restlessness and experimental spirit combined and infused with an undercurrent of grit are what give this 'eternally unfinished' city its art cred.

IAIN MASTERTON/GETTY IMAGES © – AUTHORISED BY BPK-BILDAGENTUR

1. Sammlung Boros (p64)
An edgy private art collection housed in a WWII bunker.

2. Gemäldegalerie (p77)
One of the world's finest collections of European art.

3. Alte Nationalgalerie (p81)
An art temple packed with Neoclassical, Romantic, impressionist and early modernist art.

4. Street art (p101)
Astronaut Mural by Victor Ash.

5. East Side Gallery (p89)
Erich Honecker and Leonid Brezhnev lock lips in Dmitri Vrubel's *My God, Help Me To Survive This Deadly Love*.

CAROL ANNE/SHUTTERSTOCK ©

TAKASHI IMAGES/SHUTTERSTOCK © – AUTHORISED BY BPK-BILDAGENTUR

(Continued from page 117)

It's often packed to capacity, but you can leave your number and someone will call you when space opens up.

★**Strandbar Mitte** BAR
(Map p66; ☎030-2838 5588; www.strandbar-mitte.de; Monbijoustrasse 3; dancing €4; ⏰10am-late May-Sep; M1, Oranienburger Strasse) A full-on view of the Spree River and the majestic Bode-Museum combines with a relaxed ambience at Germany's first beach bar (since 2002). A stint here is great for balancing a surfeit of sightseeing stimulus with a reviving drink and pizza. At night, there's dancing under the stars with tango, cha-cha, swing and salsa, often preceded by dance lessons.

Aufsturz PUB
(Map p66; ☎030-2804 7407; www.aufsturz.de; Oranienburger Strasse 67; ⏰noon-late; ; M1, M5, U Oranienburger Tor, S Oranienburger Strasse) Mingle in the warm glow of this old-school German pub teeming with global DNA and serving some 100 beers on tap and in the bottle, alongside a line-up of belly-filling pub grub. There's local art on the wall and changing gigs in the basement club to boot.

Kaffee Burger CLUB
(Map p66; www.kaffeeburger.de; Torstrasse 60; ⏰9pm-4am; U Rosa-Luxemburg-Platz) Nothing to do with either coffee or meat patties, this sweaty cult club with lovingly faded retro decor is a fun-for-all concert and party pen. The sound policy swings from indie and electro to klezmer punk without missing a beat.

Potsdamer Platz & Tiergarten

Fragrances COCKTAIL BAR
(Map p66; ☎030-337 775 403; www.ritzcarlton.com; Potsdamer Platz 3, Ritz-Carlton; ⏰from 7pm Wed-Sat; ; 200, S Potsdamer Platz, U Potsdamer Platz) Another baby by Berlin cocktail maven Arnd Heissen, Fragrances claims to be the world's first 'perfume bar', a libation station where Heissen mixes potions mimicking famous scents. The black-mirrored space in the **Ritz-Carlton** (Map p66; ☎030-337 777; d €150-450; P) is like a 3D menu where adventurous drinkers sniff out their favourite from among a row of perfume bottles, then settle back into flocked couches for stylish imbibing.

Solar Lounge BAR
(Map p86; ☎0163 765 2700; www.solar-berlin.de; Stresemannstrasse 76; ⏰6pm-2am Sun-Thu, to 3am Fri & Sat; S Anhalter Bahnhof) Watch the city light up from this 17th-floor glass-walled sky lounge above a posh restaurant. With its dim lighting, soft black leather couches and breathtaking panorama, it's a great spot for sunset drinks or a date night. Getting there aboard an exterior glass lift is half the fun. The entrance is behind the Pit Stop auto shop.

Café am Neuen See BEER GARDEN
(Map p97; ☎030-254 4930; www.cafeamneuensee.de; Lichtensteinallee 2; ⏰restaurant 9am-11pm, beer garden noon-late Mon-Fri, 11am-late Sat & Sun; ; 200, U Zoologischer Garten, S Zoologischer Garten, Tiergarten) Next to an idyllic lake in Tiergarten, this restaurant gets jammed year-round for its sumptuous breakfast and seasonal fare, but it really comes into its own during beer garden season. Enjoy a microvacation over a cold one and a pretzel or pizza, then take your sweetie for a spin in a rowing boat. Children's playground, too.

Kreuzberg & Neukölln

Ritter Butzke CLUB
(Map p86; www.ritterbutzke.de; Ritterstrasse 24; ⏰midnight-late Thu-Sat; U Moritzplatz) Ritter Butzke has origins as an illegal club but is now a Kreuzberg party circuit fixture. Wrinkle-free folk hit the four floors in a former bathroom-fittings factory for high-quality music, courtesy of both DJ legends and the latest sound spinners of the house and techno scenes. It also hosts concerts and there's a courtyard in summer.

Griessmühle CLUB
(Map p86; www.griessmuehle.de; Sonnenallee 221; ⏰club from 10pm Fri & Sat; S Sonnenallee) Hugging an idyllic canal in Neukölln, Griessmühle is a sprawling indoor-outdoor space with a funky garden strewn with tree houses, Trabis (GDR-era cars) and flower beds. The project by the ZMF artist collective woos attitude-free electro lovers with an events roster that includes not only parties and concerts but also a monthly flea market, movie nights and ping-pong parties.

Club der Visionäre CLUB
(Map p86; ☎030-6951 8942; www.clubdervisionaere.com; Am Flutgraben 1; ⏰2pm-late Mon-Fri, from noon Sat & Sun; S Treptower Park, U Schlesisches Tor) It's cold beer, crispy pizza and fine electro at this summertime day-to-night-and-back-to-day chill and party playground in an old canal-side boat shed. Park yourself beneath the weeping willows, stake out some

turf on the upstairs deck or hit the tiny dance floor. Alternatively, head to the sun deck of CDV's nearby second venue, the Hoppetoose boat, which doubles as a winter location.

Birgit&Bier · CLUB
(Map p86; ☑ 030-618 7240; www.facebook.com/birgitundbier; Schleusenufer 3; ☺ 2pm-5am Mon-Wed, to 6am Thu, to noon Fri & Sat, to 6am Sun; 🚌 165, 265, N65, 🚊 Treptower Park, Ⓤ Schlesisches Tor) Enter through the iron gate and embark on a magical mystery tour that'll have you chilling in the beer garden, taking selfies with wacky art, dancing under the disco ball and lounging in a retired carousel. An eclectic roster of events, including outdoor cinema, deep-flow music yoga and magical party nights, pretty much guarantees a good time.

★Thelonius · COCKTAIL BAR
(Map p86; ☑ 030-5561 8232; www.facebook.com/theloniousbarberlin; Weserstrasse 202; ☺ 7pm-1am or later; Ⓤ Hermannplatz) Embraced by a mellow soundscape and complexion-friendly lighting, well-mannered patrons pack this narrow burrow named for American jazz giant Thelonius Monk. Owner Laura Maria, who travelled the world before returning to her Neukölln roots, is the consummate host and creator of the drinks menu that ticks all the boxes, from classics to the adventurous.

Roses · BAR
(Map p86; ☑ 030-615 6570; Oranienstrasse 187; ☺ 10pm-6am; Ⓤ Kottbusser Tor) A palace of camp and kitsch with pink furry walls that Barbie would love, Roses has been a glittery fixture on the LGBT-and-friends Kreuzberg booze circuit for over 25 years. Drinks are cheap and the bartenders pour with a generous elbow, making this a packed – and polysexual – pit stop during hard-party nights. Not for the fainthearted.

Würgeengel · BAR
(Map p86; ☑ 030-615 5560; www.wuergeengel.de; Dresdener Strasse 122; ☺ 7pm-2am or later; Ⓤ Kottbusser Tor) For a swish night out, point your compass to this stylish art deco–style bar with lots of chandeliers and shiny black surfaces. It's always busy but especially so after the final credits roll at the adjacent Babylon cinema. Transcendent cocktails, fine nibbles.

Klunkerkranich · BAR
(Map p86; www.klunkerkranich.de; Karl-Marx-Strasse 66; ☺ 4pm-2am; 🐾; Ⓤ Rathaus Neukölln) In the warmer months, vibes, views and sounds are the ammo of this club-garden-bar combo on the rooftop parking deck of the Neukölln Arcaden shopping mall. It's a great place for day-to-night drinking and chilling to local DJs or bands. Sustenance is provided. Check the website – these folks come up with new ideas all the time (gardening workshops anyone?).

To get up here, take the lifts just inside the 'Bibliothek/Post' entrance on Karl-Marx-Strasse to the 5th floor.

Tresor · CLUB
(Map p66; www.tresorberlin.com; Köpenicker Strasse 70; ☺ midnight-10am or noon Mon, Wed, Fri & Sat; Ⓤ Heinrich-Heine-Strasse) One of Berlin's original techno labels and dance temples, Tresor has not only the pedigree but all the right ingredients for success: the industrial maze of a derelict power station, awesome sound and a great DJ line-up. Look for the namesake vault in the basement at the end of a 30m-long tunnel. The door is relatively easy.

Watergate · CLUB
(Map p86; ☑ 030-6128 0394; www.water-gate.de; Falckensteinstrasse 49a; ☺ midnight-5am or later Wed-Sat; Ⓤ Schlesisches Tor) For a short night's journey into day, check into this high-octane riverside club with two floors, panoramic windows and a floating terrace overlooking the Oberbaumbrücke and Universal Music. Top DJs keep electro-hungry hipsters hot and sweaty till way past sunrise. Long queues, tight door.

Möbel Olfe · PUB
(Map p86; ☑ 030-2327 4690; www.moebel-olfe.de; Reichenberger Strasse 177; ☺ 6pm-3am or later Tue-Sun; Ⓤ Kottbusser Tor) An old furniture store has been recast as this pleasantly trashy and always-busy drinking den with cheap Polish beer and a friendly crowd, which is usually mixed but goes predominantly boy on Thursday and girl on Tuesday. Enter via Dresdener Strasse.

SO36 · CLUB
(Map p86; ☑ 030-6140 1306; www.so36.de; Oranienstrasse 190; ☺ Mon-Sun; Ⓤ Kottbusser Tor) This legendary club began as an artist squat in the early 1970s and soon evolved into Berlin's seminal punk venue, known for wild concerts by the Dead Kennedys, Die Ärzte and Einstürzende Neubauten. Today the crowd depends on the night's program: electro party, punk concert, lesbigay tea dance, night flea market, '80s, 'Bad Taste' – pretty much anything goes. Easy door.

Ankerklause
PUB

(Map p86; ☑ 030-693 5649; www.ankerklause. de; Kottbusser Damm 104; ⊙ 4pm-late Mon, from 10am Tue-Sun; Ⓤ Schönleinstrasse) Ahoy there! Drop anchor at this nautical-kitsch tavern in an old harbour master's shack and enjoy the arse-kicking jukebox, cold beers and surprisingly good German pub fare. The best seats are on the geranium-festooned terrace, where you can wave at the tourist boats puttering along the canal. A cult pit stop from breakfast until the wee hours.

SchwuZ
GAY

(Map p86; ☑ 030-5770 2270; www.schwuz.de; Rollbergstrasse 26; ⊙ 11pm-late Thu-Sat; 🚌 104, 167, Ⓤ Rathaus Neukölln) This long-running queer party institution is the go-to spot for high-energy flirting and dancing. Different parties draw different punters to the three floors, lovingly nicknamed 'cathedral', 'bunker' and 'salon' and ringing with the entire sound spectrum from pop to techno, depending on the night. A great spot for easing into Berlin's LGBTIQ party scene.

Friedrichshain

★ Berghain/Panorama Bar
CLUB

(Map p86; www.berghain.de; Am Wriezener Bahnhof; ⊙ Fri-Mon; Ⓢ Ostbahnhof) Only world-class spin-masters heat up this hedonistic bass-junkie hellhole inside a labyrinthine ex-powerplant. Hard-edged minimal techno dominates the ex-turbine hall (Berghain) while house dominates at Panorama Bar, one floor up. Long lines, strict door, no cameras. Check the website for midweek concerts and record-release parties at the main venue and the adjacent Kantine am Berghain (p126).

★ ://about blank
CLUB

(www.aboutparty.net; Markgrafendamm 24c; ⊙ hours vary, always Fri & Sat; Ⓢ Ostkreuz) At this gritty multifloor party pen with lots of nooks and crannies, a steady line-up of top DJs feeds a diverse bunch of revellers dance-worthy electronic gruel. Intense club nights usually segue into the morning and beyond. Run by a collective, the venue also hosts cultural, political and gender events.

Suicide Circus
CLUB

(Map p86; http://suicide-berlin.com; Revaler Strasse 99; ⊙ hours vary, often from midnight Tue-Sun; Ⓢ Warschauer Strasse, Ⓤ Warschauer Strasse) Residents and visitors hungry for an eclectic techno shower invade this midsize dancing den with its industrial warehouse feel, top-notch sound system and consistently capable DJs. In summer, watch the stars fade from the open-air floor and garden. It's still a great spot to connect with the earthy Berlin club flair.

Chapel Bar
COCKTAIL BAR

(☑ 0157 3200 0032; Sonntagstrasse 30; ⊙ 6pm-1am Tue & Wed, to 2am Thu, to 3.30am Fri & Sat; Ⓢ Ostkreuz) A star in the Friedrichshain

---

MAIN PARTY STRIPS

RAW Gelände & Revaler Strasse The skinny-jeanster set invades the gritty clubs and bars along the 'techno strip' sprawling out over a former train repair station. Live concerts at Astra Kulturhaus, techno-electro at Suicide Circus, eclectic sounds at Cassiopeia and various off-kilter bars in between.

Ostkreuz Draw a bead on this party zone by staggering through the dark trying to find the entrance to Salon zur Wilden Renate or ://about blank.

Ostbahnhof Hardcore partying at Berghain/Panorama Bar and mellow chilling at Yaam.

Simon-Dach-Strasse If you need a cheap buzz, head to this well-trodden booze strip popular with field-tripping school groups and stag parties.

Weserstrasse & Around The main party drag in the hyped hood of Neukölln is packed with an eclectic mix of pubs and bars, from trashy to stylish.

Kottbusser Tor & Oranienstrasse Grunge-tastic area perfect for dedicated drink-a-thons with a punky-funky flair.

Schlesische Strasse Freestyle strip with a potpourri of party stations from beer gardens to concert venues, techno temples to daytime outdoor chill zones.

Skalitzer Strasse Eclectic drag with small clubs and some quality cocktail bars just off it.

Torstrasse A globe-spanning roster of monied creatives populates the chic drinking dens with their well-thought-out bar concepts and drinks made with top-shelf spirits.

cocktail firmament, the Chapel Bar has a delightfully cluttered living-room look and a convivial vibe, thanks to a crowd more interested in good drinks than looking good. The folks behind the bar wield the shaker with confidence, be it to create classics or their own 'liquid dreams' such as the whisky-based Köppernickel.

Hops & Barley
MICROBREWERY

(Map p86; ☑030-2936 7534; www.hopsandbarley-berlin.de; Wühlischstrasse 22/23; ⊙5pm-late Mon-Fri, from 3pm Sat & Sun; ☒M13, ⓤWarschauer Strasse, ⓢWarschauer Strasse) Conversation flows as freely as the unfiltered pilsner, malty *Dunkel* (dark) and fruity *Weizen* (wheat) produced right here at one of Berlin's oldest craft breweries (since 2008). The pub is inside a former butcher's shop and still has the tiled walls to prove it. Two beamers project football (soccer) games.

Monster Ronson's
Ichiban Karaoke
KARAOKE

(Map p86; ☑030-8975 1327; www.karaokemonster.de; Warschauer Strasse 34; ⊙7pm-4am; ⓢWarschauer Strasse, ⓤWarschauer Strasse) Knock back a couple of brewskis if you need to loosen your nerves before belting out your best Adele or Lady Gaga at this mad, great karaoke joint, which went through a major rejuvenation in early 2018. Shy types can book a private booth for music and mischief. It also has gay-themed nights and drag queen shows on Tuesdays.

Sisyphos
CLUB

(☑030-9836 6839; www.sisyphos-berlin.net; Hauptstrasse 15; ⊙hours vary, usually midnight Fri-10am Mon May-Aug; ☒21, ⓢOstkreuz) On summer weekends, an old dog-food factory about 2km southeast of S-Bahn station Ostkreuz turns into a hedonistic indoor-outdoor party village that proves that Berlin can still 'do underground'. Techno dominates the turntables on the main floor with its great sound system, while a second floor is more house oriented. Take tram 21 to Gustav-Holzmann-Strasse.

Prenzlauer Berg

★Prater Garten
BEER GARDEN

(Map p94; ☑030-448 5688; www.pratergarten.de; Kastanienallee 7-9; snacks €2.50-7.50; ⊙noon-late Apr-Sep, weather permitting; ☚; ☒M1, 12, ⓤEberswalder Strasse) Berlin's oldest beer garden has seen beer-soaked days and nights since 1837 and is still a charismatic spot for guzzling a custom-brewed Prater pilsner

(self-service) beneath the ancient chestnut trees. Kids can enjoy the small play area.

★Weinerei Forum
WINE BAR

(Map p94; ☑030-440 6983; www.weinerei.com; Fehrbelliner Strasse 57; ⊙10am-midnight; ☜; ☒M1, ⓤRosenthaler Platz) After 8pm, this living-room-style cafe turns into a wine bar that works on the honour principle: you 'rent' a wine glass for €2, then help yourself to as much vino as you like and in the end decide what you want to pay. Please be fair to keep this fantastic concept going.

Bryk Bar
COCKTAIL BAR

(Map p94; ☑030-3810 0165; www.bryk-bar.com; Rykestrasse 18; ⊙7pm-late; ☒M2, M10, ⓢPrenzlauer Allee) Both vintage and industrial elements contribute to the unhurried, dapper ambience at this darkly lit cocktail lab. Bar chef Frank Grosser whips unusual ingredients into such experimental liquid teasers as the rum-based Kamasutra with a Hangover topped with white chocolate–horseradish foam. The free dill popcorn is positively addictive.

Zum Starken August
PUB

(Map p94; ☑030-2520 9020; www.zumstarkenaugust.de; Schönhauser Allee 56; ⊙3pm-2.30am Mon-Thu, to 5am Fri, 2pm-5am Sat, 2pm-2.30am Sun; ☒M1, M10, ⓤEberswalder Strasse) Part circus, part burlesque bar, this vibrant venue dressed in Victorian-era exuberance is a fun and friendly addition to the Prenzlauer Berg pub culture. Join the unpretentious, international crowd over cocktails and craft beers while being entertained with drag-hosted bingo, burlesque divas or wicked cabaret.

Anna Blume
CAFE

(Map p94; ☑030-4404 8749; www.cafe-anna-blume.de; Kollwitzstrasse 83; breakfast €3.50-12.50, mains €9-13; ⊙8am-midnight; ☒M2, M10, ⓤEberswalder Strasse) Potent java, home-made cakes, and flowers from the attached shop perfume the art nouveau interior of this cafe named for a 1919 Dadaist poem by German artist Kurt Schwitters. In fine weather the outdoor terrace offers primo people-watching. Great for breakfast (served any time), especially if you order the tiered tray for two.

Charlottenburg & Schöneberg

★Bar am Steinplatz
COCKTAIL BAR

(Map p97; ☑030-554 4440; www.hotelsteinplatz.com; Steinplatz 4; ⊙4pm-late; ⓤErnst-Reuter-Platz) Christian Gentemann's liquid

LGBTIQ+ BERLIN

Berlin's legendary liberalism has spawned one of the world's biggest, most divine and diverse LGBT+ playgrounds. Anything goes in 'Homopolis' (and we do mean anything!), from the highbrow to the hands-on, the bourgeois to the bizarre, the mainstream to the flamboyant. Except for the most hard-core places, gay spots get their share of opposite-sex and straight patrons.

Resources

Mann-O-Meter (Map p97; ☑ 030-216 8008; www.mann-o-meter.de; Bülowstrasse 106; ☺ 5-10pm Mon-Fri, 4-8pm Sat; Ⓤ Nollendorfplatz) Gay men's information centre.

Maneo (☑ 030-216 3336; www.maneo.de; ☺ assault line 5-7pm) Gay victim support centre and gay-attack hotline.

Lesbenberatung (Lesbian Counselling Centre; Map p86; ☑ 030-215 2000; www.lesben beratung-berlin.de; Kulmer Strasse 20a; ☺ 2-5pm Mon, Wed & Fri, 10am-4pm Tue, 3-6.30 Thu; Ⓤ Yorckstrasse, Ⓢ Yorckstrasse) Lesbian resource centre.

Gay Berlin4u (www.gayberlin4u.com) Covers all aspects of Berlin's gay scene, in English.

GayCities Berlin (https://berlin.gaycities.com) Berlin edition of the worldwide guide offers a basic overview of the scene, in English.

Patroc Gay Guide (www.patroc.de/berlin) Focuses on events but also has some info on venues; in German.

Festivals

Christopher Street Day (www.csd-berlin.de; various locations; ☺ Jun or Jul) People of every sexual orientation paint the town pink at one of Europe's biggest gay-pride demonstration, parade and party series.

Lesbisch-Schwules Stadtfest (Lesbigay Street Festival; www.stadtfest.berlin; ☺ Jul; Ⓤ Nollendorfplatz) The enormous Lesbigay Street Festival draws up to 350,000 revellers to the Schöneberg rainbow village around Nollendorfplatz for one long weekend of bands, food, info booths and partying.

Sights

Schwules Museum (p100) Gay Museum.

Memorial to the Homosexuals Persecuted under the Nazi Regime (Memorial to the Homosexuals Persecuted under the Nazi Regime; Map p66; www.stiftung-denkmal.de; Ebertstrasse; ☺ 24hr; Ⓢ Brandenburger Tor, Potsdamer Platz, Ⓤ Brandenburger Tor, Potsdamer Platz) FREE

Bars

Möbel Olfe (p121) Relaxed Kreuzberg joint goes into gay turbodrive on Thursdays; women dominate on Tuesdays.

Heile Welt (Map p97; ☑ 030-2191 7507; Motzstrasse 5; ☺ 7pm-3am; Ⓤ Nollendorfplatz) Stylish lounge good for chatting and mingling over cocktails.

Himmelreich (Map p86; ☑ 030-2936 9292; www.himmelreich-berlin.de; Simon-Dach-Strasse 36; ☺ 6pm-2am or later Mon-Sat, 4pm-1am or later Sun; ᰥ M13, M10, Ⓢ Warschauer Strasse, Ⓤ Warschauer Strasse) This '50s retro lounge is a lesbigay-scene stalwart in Friedrichshain.

Coven (Map p66; ☑ 01511 498 2524; www.thecovenberlin.com; Kleine Präsidentenstrasse 3; ☺ 8pm-2am Sun-Thu, 9pm-3am Fri & Sat; ☏; ᰥ M1, M4, M5, Ⓢ Hackescher Markt) Stylish Mitte bar with industrial decor and strong drinks.

Rauschgold (Map p86; ☑ 030-9227 4178; www.rauschgold.berlin; Mehringdamm 62; ☺ 8pm-late; ☏; Ⓤ Mehringdamm) Small glitter-glam bar for all-night fun with pop, karaoke and drag shows.

Roses (p121) This pink-fur-walled kitsch institution is an unmissable late-night fuelling stop.

Zum Schmutzigen Hobby (Map p86; ☎030-3646 8446; www.facebook.com/zumschmut zigenhobby; Revaler Strasse 99, RAW Gelände, Gate 2; ⊙7.30pm-late; ⬚M10, M13, ⬚Warschauer Strasse, ⬚Warschauer Strasse) Fabulously wacky party pen in a former fire station.

Parties & Clubbing

Berlin's scene is especially fickle and venues and dates may change at any time, so make sure you always check the websites or the listings magazines for the latest scoop. A selection of regular parties follows. Unless noted, all are geared towards men.

B:East Party (http://beastparty.com) Monthly party for gays and friends with techno, house and disco, now at Polygon (www.polygon-club.com; Wiesenweg 1-4; ⊙11.45pm-10am Fri & Sat; ⬚Frankfurter Allee, ⬚Frankfurter Allee, Ostkreuz). Last Saturday of the month.

Cafe Fatal All comers descend on SO36 (p121) for the ultimate rainbow Sunday tea dance, which goes from 'strictly ballroom' to 'dirty dancing' in a flash.

Chantals House of Shame (www.facebook.com/ChantalsHouseofShame) Trash diva Chantal's louche lair at Suicide Circus (p122) is a beloved institution, not so much for the glam factor as for the over-the-top drag shows and the hotties who love 'em. Thursdays.

Gayhane Geared towards gay and lesbian Muslims, but everyone's welcome to rock the kasbah when this 'homoriental' party takes over SO36 (p121) with Middle Eastern beats and belly dancing. Last Saturday of the month.

Gegen (www.gegenberlin.com) Countercultural party at KitKatClub (p127) brings in anti-trendy types for crazy electro and wacky art performances. First Friday, alternate months.

Girls Town (www.girlstown-berlin.de) Suse and Zoe's buzzy girl-fest takes over Gretchen (p126) in Kreuzberg with down-and-dirty pop, electro, indie and rock. Second Saturday, alternate months, September to May.

GMF (www.gmf-berlin.de) Berlin's premier techno-house Sunday club, currently at House of Weekend (p117), is known for excessive SM (standing and modelling) with lots of smooth surfaces. Predominantly boyz, but girls are welcome.

Irrenhouse The name means 'insane asylum', and that's no joke. Party hostess with the mostest, trash queen Nina Queer puts on nutty, naughty shows at Kreuzberg's Musik & Frieden (Map p86; ☎030-2391 9994; www.musikundfrieden.de; Falckensteinstrasse 48; ⊙hours vary; ⬚Schlesisches Tor), which are not for the faint-of-heart. Expect the best. Fear the worst. Third Saturday of the month.

Revolver (www.facebook.com/RevolverPartyGlobal) This London export hosted by Oliver and Gary is a sizzling and sexy party at the KitKatClub (p127) with no special dress code required. Second Friday of the month.

Sex Clubs & Darkrooms

Lab.oratory (Map p86; www.lab-oratory.de; Am Wriezener Bahnhof; ⊙Thu-Sun; ⬚Ostbahnhof) Fetish-oriented experimental play zone in industrial setting below Berghain.

Greifbar (Map p94; ☎030-8975 1498; www.greifbar.com; Wichertstrasse 10; ⊙10pm-6am; ⬚Schönhauser Allee, ⬚Schönhauser Allee) Friendly cruising bar in Prenzlauer Berg with video, darkroom and private areas.

Connection Club (Map p97; ☎030-218 1432; www.connectionclub.de; Fuggerstrasse 33; ⊙11pm-6am Fri & Sat; ⬚Wittenbergplatz) Legendary dance club in Schöneberg with Berlin's largest cruising labyrinth.

playground at the art deco Hotel am Steinplatz (p109) was crowned 'Hotel Bar of the Year' in 2016 and 2017, and for good reason The drinks are simply sensational and the ambience a perfect blend of hip and grown-up. The illustrated cocktail menu teases the imagination by listing ingredients and tastes for each drink instead of just an abstract name.

Diener Tattersall
PUB

(Map p97; ☑030-881 5329; www.diener-berlin.de; Grolmanstrasse 47; ⊙6pm-2am; ⑤Savignyplatz) In business for over a century, this Old Berlin haunt was taken over by German heavyweight champion Franz Diener in the 1950s and became one of West Berlin's iconic artist pubs. From Billy Wilder to Harry Belafonte, they all came for beer and *Bulette* (meat patties) and left behind signed black-and-white photographs that grace Diener's walls to this day.

Tiger Bar
BAR

(Map p86; ☑030-983 208 435; www.oh-panama.com/en/tigerbar; Potsdamer Strasse 191; ⊙8pm-midnight or later Tue-Sat; ⑤Kurfürstenstrasse) Tiger Bar is a stylish and slightly trippy jewel for curious imbibers. Sustainability is key for bar manager Phum Sila-Trakoon, which is why discarded banana peels from the affiliated Panama (Map p86; Potsdamer Strasse 91; dishes €9-19; ⊙6-11pm Wed-Sat; ☎) restaurant kitchen may well end up as syrup in his bar. Cocktails range from classic to 'outthere' like Paloma's Fall, a tequila-based potion with grapefruit, buttermilk and sea salt.

☆ Entertainment

Berlin's cultural scene is lively, edgy and the richest and most varied in all of the German-speaking world. With three state-supported opera houses, five major orchestras – including the world-class Berliner Philharmoniker – scores of theatres, cinemas, cabarets and concert venues, Berlin is spoiled for entertainment options.

Babylon
CINEMA

(Map p66; ☑030-242 5969; www.babylonberlin.de; Rosa-Luxemburg-Strasse 30; tickets €7-10; ⑤Rosa-Luxemburg-Platz) This top-rated indie screens a smart line-up of cinematic expression, from new German films and international arthouse flicks to themed retrospectives and other stuff you'd never catch at the multiplex. For silent movies, the original theatre organ is put through its paces. Also hosts occasional readings and concerts.

Arsenal
CINEMA

(Map p66; ☑030-2695 5100; www.arsenal-berlin.de; Potsdamer Strasse 2, Sony Center; tickets €8; ☐200, ⑤Potsdamer Platz, ⑤Potsdamer Platz) The antithesis of popcorn culture, this arty twin-screen cinema features a bold global flick schedule that hopscotches from Japanese satire to Brazilian comedy and German road movies. Many films have English subtitles.

Cinestar Original im Sony Center
CINEMA

(Map p66; www.cinestar.de; Potsdamer Strasse 4, Sony Center; tickets 2D €6.50-8.80, 3D €9.50-11.80, glasses €1; ☐200, ⑤Potsdamer Platz, ⑤Potsdamer Platz) This state-of-the-art cinema with nine screens, comfy seats and top technology shows the latest Hollywood blockbusters in 2D and 3D, all in English, all the time. Buy tickets online to skip the queue.

Astra Kulturhaus
LIVE MUSIC

(Map p86; ☑030-2005 6767; www.astra-berlin.de; Revaler Strasse 99, RAW Gelände; ⊙hours vary, always Thu-Sat; ☐M13, ⑤Warschauer Strasse, ⑤Warschauer Strasse) With space for 1500 in the former cultural hall of a Cold War–era train repair station, Astra is one of Berlin's bigger indie concert venues, yet it often fills up easily, and not just when international headliners hit the stage. In addition, parties lure punters with danceable tunes across the sound spectrum.

Lido
LIVE MUSIC

(Map p86; ☑030-6956 6840; www.lido-berlin.de; Cuvrystrasse 7; ⑤Schlesisches Tor) A 1950s cinema has been recycled into a rock-indie-electro-pop hub with mosh-pit electricity and a crowd that cares more about the music than about looking good. Global DJs and talented upwardly mobile live noisemakers pull in the punters. Its monthly Balkanbeats party is legendary.

Kantine am Berghain
LIVE MUSIC

(Map p86; www.berghain.de; Am Wriezener Bahnhof; admission varies; ⊙hours vary; ⑤Ostbahnhof) Big bad Berghain (p122)'s little sister has taken over the former staff canteen of the giant ex-power station. The space holds up to 200 people and mostly puts on concerts starting around 9pm. In summer, the attached beer garden (Bierhof Rüdersdorf) with outdoor fireplace is an ideal chill zone. Easy door.

Gretchen
LIVE MUSIC

(Map p86; ☑030-2592 2702; www.gretchen-club.de; Obentrautstrasse 19-21; ⊙hours vary, always Fri & Sat; ⑤Mehringdamm, Hallesches Tor)

One of Berlin's finest music venues has set up in the gorgeous slender-columned and brick-vaulted stables of a 19th-century Prussian regiment. The low-key crowd defines the word eclectic, as does the music, which hops around contemporary trends from electro to dubstep, indie to hip-hop, funk to house. Hosts concerts and DJ sets.

b-Flat   LIVE MUSIC
(Map p66; ☑ 030-283 3123; www.b-flat-berlin.de; Dircksenstrasse 40; tickets €14-16; ☺8pm-late; Ⓤ Weinmeisterstrasse, Alexanderplatz, Ⓢ Hackescher Markt) Cool cats of all ages come out to this jazz and acoustic music venue, where the audience sits within spitting distance of the performers. Big names like Mal Waldron, Randy Brecker and Mikis Theodorakis have all graced its stage, but mostly the focus is on top homegrown talent. Wednesday's free jam session often brings down the house.

Waldbühne Berlin   LIVE MUSIC
(☑ tickets 01806 570 070; www.waldbuehne-berlin. de; Glockenturmstrasse 1; ☺May-Sep; Ⓢ Pichelsberg) Summers in Berlin just wouldn't be the same without this chilled spot for big-name rock, jazz and comedy acts as well as symphonies under the stars. The 22,000-seat open-air amphitheatre in the woods has been around since 1936 and has exceptional acoustics.

The venue is located just west of the Olympiastadion and 550m north of S-Bahn station Pichelsberg via Schirwindter Allee and Passenheimer Strasse.

Berliner Philharmoniker   CLASSICAL MUSIC
(Map p66; ☑ tickets 030-2548 8999; www.berliner-philharmoniker.de; Herbert-von-Karajan-Strasse 1; tickets €21-290; ☐M29, M48, M85, 200, ⓈPotsdamer Platz, Ⓤ Potsdamer Platz) One of the world's most famous orchestras, the Berliner Philharmoniker, is based at the tent-like Philharmonie (p84), designed by Hans Scharoun in the 1950s and built in the 1960s. In 2019, Sir Simon Rattle, who's been chief conductor since 2002, will pass on the baton to the Russia-born Kirill Petrenko. Tickets can be booked online.

Konzerthaus Berlin   CLASSICAL MUSIC
(Map p66; ☑ tickets 030-203 092 101; www.konzerthaus.de; Gendarmenmarkt 2; tickets €15-85; Ⓤ Stadtmitte, Französische Strasse) This lovely classical music venue – a Schinkel design

---

SEX & THE CITY

The decadence of the Weimar years is alive and kicking in this city long known for its libertine leanings. While full-on sex clubs are most common in the gay scene (eg Lab. oratory; p125),the following places allow straights, gays, lesbians, the bi-curious and polysexuals to live out their fantasies in a safe if public setting.

Surprisingly, there's nothing seedy about this, but you do need to check your inhibitions – and much of your clothing – at the door. If fetish gear doesn't do it for you, wear something sexy or glamorous; men can usually get away with tight pants and an open (or no) shirt. No normal street clothes, no tighty-whities. As elsewhere, couples and girl groups get in more easily than all-guy crews. And don't forget Mum's 'safe sex only' speech (condoms are usually provided).

KitKatClub (Map p66; www.kitkatclub.de; Köpenicker Strasse 76; ☺11pm-late Fri, Sat & Mon, from 8am Sun; Ⓤ Heinrich-Heine-Strasse) This 'kitty' is naughty, sexy and decadent, listens to electro of all stripes and fancies extravagant get-ups (or nothing at all). Berlin's most (in) famous erotic nightclub hides out at Sage Club with its four dance floors, shimmering pool and fire-breathing dragon. The Saturday-night CareBall Bizarre party is a classic among Berlin's hedonistic havens. The website has dress-code tips. Enter via Brückenstrasse.

Insomnia (www.insomnia-berlin.de; Alt-Tempelhof 17-19; ☺Tue-Sun; Ⓤ Alt-Tempelhof) Expect a wild night of erotic partying in this 19th-century ballroom-turned-deliciously decadent Berlin nightlife fixture. With its international DJs, performances from bondage to burlesque and various playrooms, Insomnia draws an all-ages crowd of hedonists to live out their fantasies during Saturday's tech-house parties or Friday's theme party from Master & Servant (Depeche Mode) to Infame Royale (1920s).

The vibe is easygoing, nobody forces you to do anything, but unbridled voyeurism is discouraged. Dress code: sexy, fetish, elegant. During the week, more advanced players invade for special-themed sex and swinger parties that often require preregistration. Check the website for full details.

from 1821 – counts the top-ranked Konzerthausorchester Berlin as its 'house band', but also hosts visiting soloists and orchestras in three venues. For a sightseeing break, check the schedule for weekly one-hour lunchtime 'Espresso Concerts' costing a mere €8.

Staatsoper Berlin
OPERA
(Map p66; ☑030-2035 4554; www.staatsoper-berlin.de; Unter den Linden 7; tickets €12-250; ⬛100, 200, TXL, Ⓤ Französische Strasse) After a seven-year exile, Berlin's most famous opera company once again performs at the venerable neoclassical Staatsoper Unter den Linden, which emerged from a massive refurbishment in 2017. Its repertory includes works from four centuries along with concerts and classical and modern ballet, all under the musical leadership of Daniel Barenboim.

Komische Oper
OPERA
(Comic Opera; Map p66; ☑tickets 030-4799 7400; www.komische-oper-berlin.de; Behrenstrasse 55-57; tickets €12-90; ☺box office 11am-7pm Mon-Sat, 1-4pm Sun; ⬛100, 200, TXL, Ⓤ Französische Strasse) The smallest among Berlin's trio of opera houses is also its least stuffy, even if its flashy neo-baroque auditorium might suggest otherwise. Productions are innovative and unconventional – yet top quality – and often reinterpret classic (and sometimes obscure) pieces in zeitgeist-capturing ways.

THE MYSTIQUE OF BERLIN'S OLYMPIC STADIUM

Built for the 1936 Olympic Games, Berlin's coliseum-style Olympiastadion (☑030-2500 2322; https://olympiastadion. berlin; Olympischer Platz 3; adult/concession self-guided tour €8/5.50, highlights tour €11/9.50; ☺9am-7pm Apr-Jul, Sep & Oct, to 8pm Aug, 10am-4pm Nov-Mar; Ⓢ Olympiastadion, Ⓤ Olympiastadion) was completely revamped for the 2006 FIFA World Cup and now sports a spidery oval roof, snazzy VIP boxes and top-notch sound, lighting and projection systems. On nonevent days (check the website) you can explore the stadium on your own (multimedia guide €2) or join a guided tour for access to the locker rooms, warm-up areas and VIP areas. The Hertha BSC Tour (☑030-300 928 1892; https://olympiastadion. berlin/en/guided-tours; adult/student/child €12/10.50/9; ☺select dates) must be prebooked online.

Seats feature an ingenious subtitling system in English, Turkish and other languages.

Deutsche Oper Berlin
OPERA
(German Opera Berlin; Map p97; ☑030-3438 4343; www.deutscheoperberlin.de; Bismarckstrasse 35; tickets €22-128; Ⓤ Deutsche Oper) Founded by Berliners in 1912 as a counterpoint to the royal opera on Unter den Linden, the Deutsche Oper presents a classic 19th-century opera repertory from Verdi and Puccini to Wagner and Strauss, all sung in their original languages. If you like your opera more experimental, check out the Tischlerei (joinery), a studio space for boundary-pushing (and more budget-friendly) musical interpretations.

Schaubühne
THEATRE
(Map p97; ☑030-890 023; www.schaubuehne.de; Kurfürstendamm 153; tickets €7-48; Ⓤ Adenauerplatz) In a converted 1920s expressionist cinema by Erich Mendelsohn, Schaubühne is western Berlin's main stage for experimental, contemporary theatre, usually with a critical and analytical look at current social and political issues. The ensemble is directed by Thomas Ostermeier and includes many top names from German film and TV. Some performances feature English or French surtitles.

Bar Jeder Vernunft
CABARET
(Map p97; ☑030-883 1582; www.bar-jeder-vernunft.de; Schaperstrasse 24; admission varies; Ⓤ Spichernstrasse) Life's still a cabaret at this intimate 1912 mirrored art nouveau tent theatre, one of Berlin's most beloved venues for sophisticated song-and-dance shows, comedy and *chansons* (songs). Sip a glass of bubbly while relaxing at a candlelit cafe table or in a curvy red-velvet booth bathed in flickering candlelight reflected in the mirrors. Many shows do not require any German-language skills.

English Theatre Berlin
THEATRE
(Map p86; ☑030-691 1211; www.etberlin.de; Fidicinstrasse 40; ⬛M19, Ⓤ Platz der Luftbrücke) Berlin's oldest English-language theatre puts on an engaging roster of in-house productions, plays by international visiting troupes, concerts, comedy, dance and cabaret by local performers. Quality is often high and the cast international. Tickets usually cost around €15.

Chamäleon Theatre
CABARET
(Map p66; ☑030-400 0590; www.chamaeleonberlin.com; Rosenthaler Strasse 40/41; tickets €37-59; ⬛M1, Ⓢ Hackescher Markt) A marriage of art

nouveau charms and high-tech theatre trappings, this intimate venue in a 1920s-style old ballroom hosts 'contemporary circus' shows that blend comedy, acrobatics, music, juggling and dance – often in sassy, sexy and unconventional fashion. Sit at the bar, at bistro tables or in comfy armchairs.

Friedrichstadt-Palast Berlin   PERFORMING ARTS
(Map p66; ☎030-2326 2326; www.palast.berlin; Friedrichstrasse 107; tickets €20-130; ⬚M1, ⓊOranienburger Tor, ⓈFriedrichstrasse, Oranienburger Strasse) Europe's largest revue theatre puts on innovative, high-tech and visually stunning shows that are an artistic amalgam of music, dance, costumes, acrobatics and stage wizardry. Most have a two-year run; the latest, called *Vivid*, opened in September 2018. German language skills not required.

Hertha BSC   SPECTATOR SPORT
(www.herthabsc.de; Olympischer Platz 3; tickets €15-96; ⓈOlympiastadion, ⓊOlympiastadion) Many Berliners live and die by the fortunes of the local soccer team, Hertha BSC, which has seen its shares of ups and downs in recent years, but has mostly managed to stay in the Bundesliga (German national football league). Home games are played at the Olympiastadion. Tickets are usually still available on game day at the stadium and online.

🔓 Shopping

🔓 Historic Mitte

⭐**Frau Tonis Parfum**   PERFUME
(Map p66; ☎030-2021 5310; www.frau-tonisparfum.com; Zimmerstrasse 13; ⊙10am-6pm Mon-Sat; ⓊKochstrasse) Follow your nose to this scent-sational made-in-Berlin perfume boutique, where a 'scent test' reveals if you're the floral, fruity, woody or oriental type to help you choose a matching fragrance. Bestsellers include the fresh and light 'Berlin Summer'. Individualists can have their own customised blend created in a one-hour session (€125, including 50ml eau de parfum; reservations advised).

⭐**Dussmann –
Das Kulturkaufhaus**   BOOKS
(Map p66; ☎030-2025 1111; www.kulturkaufhaus.de; Friedrichstrasse 90; ⊙9am-11.30pm Mon-Sat; 🛜; ⓈFriedrichstrasse, ⓊFriedrichstrasse) It's easy to lose track of time in this cultural playground with wall-to-wall books (including an extensive English section), DVDs and

DON'T MISS

BEARPIT KARAOKE

On most summer Sundays, Berlin's best free entertainment kicks off around 3pm when Joe Hatchiban sets up his custom-made mobile **karaoke** (Map p94; www.bearpitkaraoke.com; Amphitheatre Mauerpark; ⊙around 3-8pm Sun spring-autumn; ⬚M1, M10, 12, ⓊEberswalder Strasse) unit in the Mauerpark's amphitheatre. As many as 2000 people cram on to the stone bleachers to cheer and clap for eager crooners ranging from giggling kids to Broadway-calibre belters. Check www.facebook.com/bearpitkaraoke for exact dates.

CDs, leaving no genre unaccounted for. Bonus points for the downstairs cafe, the vertical garden, and the performance space used for free concerts, political discussions and high-profile book readings and signings.

Rausch Schokoladenhaus   CHOCOLATE
(Map p66; ☎030-757 880; www.rausch.de; Charlottenstrasse 60; ⊙10am-8pm Mon-Sat, from 11am Sun; ⓊStadtmitte) If the Aztecs regarded chocolate as the elixir of the gods, then this emporium of truffles and pralines must be heaven. The shop features Instaworthy replicas of Berlin landmarks such as the Brandenburg Gate and the Fernsehturm (TV Tower), while the upstairs cafe-restaurant delivers views of Gendarmenmarkt along with sinful drinking chocolates and artsy handmade cakes and *tartes*.

Ritter Sport Bunte Schokowelt   CHOCOLATE
(Map p66; ☎030-2009 5080; www.ritter-sport.de; Französische Strasse 24; ⊙10am-7pm Mon-Wed, to 8pm Thu-Sat, to 6pm Sun; 📶; ⓊFranzösische Strasse) Fans of Ritter Sport's colourful square chocolate bars can pick up limited edition, organic, vegan and diet varieties in addition to all the classics at this flagship store. Upstairs, a free exhibit explains the journey from cocoa bean to finished product, but kids are more enchanted by the chocolate kitchen, where staff create your own personalised bars.

🔓 Museumsinsel &
Alexanderplatz

Alexa   MALL
(Map p66; ☎030-269 3400; www.alexacentre.com; Grunerstrasse 20; ⊙10am-9pm Mon-Sat; ⓈAlexanderplatz, ⓊAlexanderplatz) Power shoppers

love this XXL mall, which cuts a rose-hued presence near Alexanderplatz and features the predictable range of high-street retailers. Good food court for a bite on the run.

Galeria Kaufhof DEPARTMENT STORE
(Map p66; ☑030-247 430; www.galeria-kaufhof. de; Alexanderplatz 9; ⊙9.30am-8pm Mon-Wed, to 10pm Thu-Sat; Ⓢ Alexanderplatz, Ⓤ Alexanderplatz) A full makeover by the late Josef Paul Kleihues turned this former GDR-era department store into a glitzy retail cube, complete with a glass-domed light court and a sleek travertine skin that glows green at night. There's little you won't find on the five football-field-size floors, including a gourmet supermarket on the ground floor.

🄰 Hackescher Markt & Scheunenviertel

⭐**Bonbonmacherei** FOOD
(Map p66; ☑030-4405 5243; www.bonbon macherei.de; Oranienburger Strasse 32, Heckmann Höfe; ⊙noon-7pm Wed-Sat Sep-Jun; ☒M1, Ⓢ Oranienburger Strasse) The aroma of peppermint and liquorice wafts through this old-fashioned basement candy kitchen whose owners use antique equipment and time-tested and modern recipes to churn out such souvenir-worthy treats as their signature leaf-shaped Berliner Maiblätter made with woodruff. Mix and match your own bag.

Kauf Dich Glücklich FASHION & ACCESSORIES
(Map p66; ☑030-2887 8817; www.kaufdich gluecklich-shop.de; Rosenthaler Strasse 17; ⊙11am-8pm Mon-Sat; Ⓤ Weinmeisterstrasse, Rosenthaler Platz) What began as a waffle cafe and vintage shop has turned into a small emporium of indie concept boutiques with this branch being the flagship. It's a prettily arranged and eclectic mix of reasonably priced on-trend clothing, accessories and jewellery from the own-brand KDG-collection and other hand-picked labels, mostly from Scandinavia.

Do You Read Me?! BOOKS
(Map p66; ☑030-6954 9695; www.doyouread me.de; Auguststrasse 28; ⊙10am-7.30pm Mon-Sat; Ⓢ Oranienburger Strasse, Ⓤ Rosenthaler Platz) Trend chasers could probably spend hours flicking through this gallery-style assortment of cool, obscure and small-print magazines from around the world. There's a distinct focus on fashion, design, architecture, music, art and contemporary trends, and knowledgeable staff to help you navigate, if needed.

1. Absinth Depot Berlin FOOD & DRINKS
(Map p66; ☑030-281 6789; www.erstesabsinth depotberlin.de; Weinmeisterstrasse 4; ⊙2pm-midnight Mon-Fri, 1pm-midnight Sat; Ⓤ Weinmeisterstrasse) Van Gogh, Toulouse-Lautrec and Oscar Wilde are among the fin-de-siècle artists who drew inspiration from the 'green fairy', as absinthe is also known. This quaint little shop has over 100 varieties of the potent stuff and an expert owner who'll happily help you pick out the perfect bottle for your mind-altering rendezvous.

🄰 Potsdamer Platz & Tiergarten

LP12 Mall of Berlin MALL
(Map p66; www.mallofberlin.de; Leipziger Platz 12; ⊙10am-9pm Mon-Sat; ☎; ☒200, Ⓤ Potsdamer Platz, Ⓢ Potsdamer Platz) This sparkling retail quarter is tailor-made for black-belt mall rats. More than 270 shops vie for your shopping euros, including flagship stores by Karl Lagerfeld, Hugo Boss, Liebeskind, Marc Cain, Muji and other international high-end brands alongside the usual high-street chains.

Potsdamer Platz Arkaden MALL
(Map p66; ☑030-255 9270; www.potsdamer platz.de/potsdamer-platz-arkaden; Alte Potsdamer Strasse 7; ⊙10am-9pm Mon-Sat; ☎; Ⓢ Potsdamer Platz, Ⓤ Potsdamer Platz) All your basic shopping cravings will be met at this attractive indoor mall with 130 shops spread over three floors. The basement has supermarkets, a chemist and numerous fast-food outlets. Ice-cream fans flock to Caffe e Gelato (p112) on the 1st floor.

🄰 Kreuzberg & Neukölln

⭐**Markthalle Neun** MARKET
(Map p86; ☑030-6107 3473; www.markthalle neun.de; Eisenbahnstrasse 42-43; ⊙noon-6pm Mon-Wed & Fri, noon-10pm Thu, 10am-6pm Sat; Ⓤ Görlitzer Bahnhof) This delightful 1891 market hall with its iron-beam-supported ceiling was saved by dedicated locals in 2009. On market days, local and regional producers present their wares, while on Street Food Thursday (p114), a couple of dozen international amateur or semipro chefs set up their stalls to serve delicious snacks from around the world. There's even an on-site craft brewery, Heidenpeters.

⭐**VooStore** FASHION & ACCESSORIES
(Map p86; ☑030-6165 1112; www.vooberlin. com; Oranienstrasse 24; ⊙10am-8pm Mon-Sat;

Ⓤ Kottbusser Tor) Kreuzberg's first concept store opened in an old backyard locksmith shop off gritty Oranienstrasse, stocking style-forward designer threads and accessories by a changing roster of crave-worthy brands, along with a tightly curated spread of books, gadgets, mags and spirits. The in-house Companion Cafe serves specialty coffees and tea from micro farms.

★ **Türkischer Markt**   MARKET
(Turkish Market; Map p86; www.tuerkenmarkt.de; Maybachufer; ☺ 11am-6.30pm Tue & Fri; Ⓤ Schönleinstrasse) At this lively canal-side market, thrifty kids mix it up with Turkish-Germans and pram-pushing mums. Stock up on olives, creamy cheese spreads, crusty flatbreads and mountains of fruit and vegetables, all at bargain prices. In good weather, market-goers gather for impromptu concerts towards the eastern end of the strip.

Kreuzboerg Flowmarkt   MARKET
(Map p86; www.kreuzboerg.de; Moritzplatz; ☺ 10am-5pm alternate Sun Apr-Oct; Ⓤ Moritzplatz) This small and relaxed flea market sets up in the leafy Prinzessinnengärten urban garden project and is a good place to source preloved clothing, music, art and local designs. Double-check dates on the website.

Hard Wax   MUSIC
(Map p86; ☎ 030-6113 0111; www.hardwax.com; Paul-Lincke-Ufer 44a, 3rd fl, door A, 2nd courtyard; ☺ noon-8pm Mon-Sat; Ⓤ Kottbusser Tor) This well-hidden outpost has been on the cutting edge of electronic music for about two decades and is a must-stop for fans of techno, house, minimal, dubstep and whatever permutation comes along next.

★ **Hallesches Haus**   HOMEWARES
(Map p86; www.hallescheshaus.com; Tempelhofer Ufer 1; ☺ 10am-7pm Mon-Fri, to 6pm Sat, to 5pm Sun; ☏; Ⓤ Hallesches Tor) 🖉 IKEA fans with a mod penchant will go ga-ga at this pretty pad packed with stylish whimsies for the home. Even day-to-day items get a zany twist in this airy space converted from an old post office. The in-store cafe serves locally roasted coffee, baked goods and light meals at lunchtime, much of it organic and local.

UVR Connected   FASHION & ACCESSORIES
(Map p86; ☎ 030-6981 4350; www.uvr-connected.de; Oranienstrasse 36; ☺ 11am-8pm Mon-Sat; Ⓤ Kottbusser Tor, Moritzplatz) The Berlin-based UVR label designs urban fashions for grown-up women with a penchant for classic cuts

and styles and subdued colours. All clothing is produced in Germany, Poland or Italy. Stores also stock other 'it' brands such as Bench, Dept and Freesoul, plus plenty of accessories.

There are also branches in Mitte (Map p66; ☎ 030-2809 6157; Rosenthaler Strasse 1; ☺ 11am-8pm Mon-Sat; 🚇 M1, Ⓤ Rosenthaler Platz), Schöneberg (☎ 030-2196 2284; Goltzstrasse 40a; ☺ 11am-7pm Tue-Fri, 10am-6pm Sat; Ⓤ Eisenacher Strasse) and Friedrichshain (Map p86; Gärtnerstrasse 5; ☺ 11am-8pm Mon-Sat; 🚇 M10, M13, Ⓤ Samariterstrasse, Warschauer Strasse, Ⓢ Warschauer Strasse).

🏛 Friedrichshain

Antikmarkt am Ostbahnhof   ANTIQUES
(Map p86; Erich-Steinfurth-Strasse; ☺ 9am-5pm Sun; Ⓢ Ostbahnhof) If you're after antiques and collectables, head to this sprawling market outside the Ostbahnhof station's north exit. The Grosser Antikmarkt (large antiques market) is more professional and brims with old coins, Iron Curtain–era relics, gramophone records, books, stamps, jewellery, etc. It segues neatly into the Kleiner Antikmarkt (small antiques market), which has more bric-a-brac and lower prices.

Wochenmarkt Boxhagener Platz   MARKET
(Map p86; http://boxhagenerplatz.org; ☺ 9am-3.30pm Sat; 🚇 M10, M13, Ⓤ Samariterstrasse, Frankfurter Tor) This popular farmers market brings out the entire neighbourhood for fresh fare along with homemade liqueurs, a global cheese selection, exotic spices, smoked fish, hemp muesli, purple potatoes and other unusual culinary delights. There are plenty of snack stands along with crafts and gift items, many of them handmade.

Prachtmädchen   FASHION & ACCESSORIES
(Map p86; ☎ 030-9700 2780; www.prachtmaedchen.de; Wühlischstrasse 28; ☺ 11am-8pm Mon-Fri, to 4pm Sat; 🚇 M13, Ⓢ Warschauer Strasse, Ⓤ Warschauer Strasse) Low-key and friendly, this pioneer on Wühlischstrasse (aka Friedrichshain's 'fashion mile') is great for kitting yourself out head to toe with affordable threads and accessories by such grown-up streetwear labels as Blutsgeschwister, Skunkfunk and Tokyo Jane.

🏛 Prenzlauer Berg

Kollwitzplatzmarkt   MARKET
(Map p94; Kollwitzstrasse & Wörhter Strasse; ☺ noon-7pm Thu Apr-Dec, to 6pm Thu Jan-Mar, 9am-4pm Sat; Ⓤ Senefelderplatz) On the edge

of lovely and leafy Kollwitzplatz square, this posh farmers market has everything you need to put together a gourmet picnic or meal. Velvety gorgonzola, juniper-berry smoked ham, crusty sourdough bread and homemade pesto are among the exquisite morsels scooped up by well-heeled locals.

The Thursday edition is all-organic, while the Saturday market features handicrafts.

Trödelmarkt Arkonaplatz   MARKET
(Map p94; www.troedelmarkt-arkonaplatz.de; Arkonaplatz; ⊙10am-4pm Sun; 🚆M1, M10, Ⓤ Bernauer Strasse) Surrounded by cafes perfect for carbo-loading, this smallish flea market on a leafy square lets you ride the retro frenzy with plenty of groovy furniture, accessories, clothing, vinyl and books, including some East German vintage items. It's easily combined with a visit to the famous Flohmarkt im am Mauerpark (p133).

Saint Georges   BOOKS
(Map p94; 🕿030-8179 8333; www.saintgeorges bookshop.com; Wörther Strasse 27; ⊙11am-8pm Mon-Fri, to 7pm Sat; 🕿; 🚆M2, Ⓤ Senefelderplatz) Laid-back and low-key, Saint Georges bookshop is a sterling spot to track down new and used English-language fiction and nonfiction. The selection includes plenty of rare and out-of-print books as well as a big shelf of literature by German and international authors translated into English.

When you're done, you can even return the book for 50% store credit on the purchase price.

Ta(u)sche   FASHION & ACCESSORIES
(Map p94; 🕿030-4030 1770; www.tausche.de; Raumerstrasse 8; ⊙11am-7pm Mon-Fri, to 6pm Sat; 🚆12, Ⓤ Eberswalder Strasse) Heike Braun and Antje Strubels now sell their ingenious messenger-style bags around the world, but this is the shop where it all began. Bags come in 12 models, 10 colours, three types of material and your choice of exchangeable flaps that zip off and on in seconds.

Goldhahn und Sampson   FOOD
(Map p94; 🕿030-4119 8366; www.goldhahn undsampson.de; Dunckerstrasse 9; ⊙8am-8pm Mon-Fri, 9am-8pm Sat; 🚆12, Ⓤ Eberswalder Strasse) Pink Himalaya salt, Moroccan argan oil and crusty German bread are among the global pantry stockers tastefully displayed at this stylish gourmet gallery. Owners Sascha and Andreas hand-source all items, most of them rare, organic and from small artisanal suppliers. For inspiration, nose around the cookbook library or join up for a class at the on-site cooking school.

Ratzekatz   TOYS
(Map p94; 🕿030-681 9564; www.ratzekatz.de; Raumerstrasse 7; ⊙10am-7pm Mon-Sat; 🚆12, Ⓤ Eberswalder Strasse) Packed with quality playthings, this adorable shop made headlines a few years ago when Angelina Jolie and son Maddox picked out a Jurassic Park's worth of dinosaurs. Even without the celeb glow, it's a fine place to source toys for all age groups – from babies to teens.

🏛 Charlottenburg & Schöneberg

⭐ Manufactum   HOMEWARES
(Map p97; 🕿030-2403 3844; www.manufact um.de; Hardenbergstrasse 4-5; ⊙10am-8pm Mon-Fri, to 6pm Sat; Ⓤ Ernst-Reuter-Platz) 🍴 Long before sustainable became a buzzword, this shop (the brainchild of a German Green Party member) stocked traditionally made quality products from around the world, many of which have stood the test of time. Cool finds include hand-forged iron pans by Turk, lavender soap from a French monastery and Japanese knives by Kenyo.

⭐ KaDeWe   DEPARTMENT STORE
(Map p97; 🕿030-212 10; www.kadewe.de; Tauentzienstrasse 21-24; ⊙10am-8pm Mon-Thu, to 9pm Fri, 9.30am-8pm Sat; Ⓤ Wittenbergplatz) Continental Europe's largest department store has been going strong since 1907 and boasts an assortment so vast that a pirate-style campaign is the best way to plunder its bounty. If pushed for time, at least hurry up to the legendary 6th-floor gourmet food hall. The name, by the way, stands for *Kaufhaus des Westens* (department store of the West).

Stilwerk   HOMEWARES
(Map p97; 🕿030-315 150; www.stilwerk.de/ berlin; Kantstrasse 17; ⊙10am-7pm Mon-Sat; Ⓢ Savignyplatz) This four-storey temple of good taste will have devotees of the finer things itching to redecorate. Everything you could possibly want for home and hearth is here – from key rings to grand pianos and vintage lamps – representing over 500 brands in 55 stores.

Bikini Berlin   MALL
(Map p97; 🕿030-5549 6455; www.bikiniberlin.de; Budapester Strasse 38-50; ⊙shops 10am-8pm Mon-Sat, Bldg 9am-8.30pm Mon-Sat, noon-6pm Sun; 🕿; 🚆100, 200, Ⓤ Zoologischer Garten, Ⓢ Zoologischer Garten) Germany's first concept mall opened in 2014 in a smoothly rehabil-

BERLIN'S BEST FLEA MARKETS

Flohmarkt am Mauerpark (Map p94; www.flohmarktimmauerpark.de; Bernauer Strasse 63-64; ⊙9am-6pm Sun; 🚌M1, M10, 12, Ⓤ Eberswalder Strasse) The mother of all markets is overrun but still a good show.

Nowkoelln Flowmarkt (Map p86; www.nowkoelln.de; Maybachufer; ⊙10am-6pm 2nd & 4th Sun of month Mar-Oct or later; Ⓤ Kottbusser Tor, Schönleinstrasse) This internationally flavoured market is also a showcase of local creativity.

Flohmarkt am Boxhagener Platz (Map p86; Boxhagener Platz; ⊙10am-6pm Sun; 🚌M13, Ⓢ Warschauer Strasse, Ⓤ Warschauer Strasse, Samariterstrasse) Fun finds abound at this charmer on a leafy square.

RAW Flohmarkt (Map p86; www.raw-flohmarkt-berlin.de; Revaler Strasse 99, RAW Gelände; ⊙9am-5pm Sun; 🚌M10, M13, Ⓢ Warschauer Strasse, Ⓤ Warschauer Strasse) Bargains can still be had at this little market on the grounds of a railway repair station turned party zone.

itated 1950s architectural icon nicknamed 'Bikini' because of its design: 200m-long upper and lower sections separated by an open floor, now chastely covered by a glass facade. Inside are three floors of urban indie boutiques, short-lease pop-up 'boxes' for up-and-comers, and an international streetfood court.

Käthe Wohlfahrt ARTS & CRAFTS
(Map p97; 🎫09861-4090; www.wohlfahrt.com; Kurfürstendamm 225-226; ⊙10am-6pm Mon-Fri, to 6.30pm Sat; Ⓤ Kurfürstendamm) With its mind-boggling assortment of traditional German Yuletide decorations and ornaments, this shop lets you celebrate Christmas year-round. It's accessed via a ramp that spirals around an 8m-high ornament-laden Christmas tree.

ℹ Information

DANGERS & ANNOYANCES

Berlin is one of the safest capital cities in the world, but that doesn't mean you should let your guard down.

➡ Pickpocketing has dramatically increased, so watch your belongings, especially in tourist-heavy areas, in crowds and at events.

➡ Crime levels have risen notably around Kottbusser Tor in Kreuzberg and the RAW Gelände in Friedrichshain. This includes drug dealing, pickpocketing, assault and sexual assault. Exercise caution.

➡ Carry enough cash for a cab ride back to wherever you're staying.

➡ On the U-Bahn or S-Bahn, and increasingly at outdoor cafes, you'll encounter homeless folks begging or selling street newspapers (called *Motz* or *Strassenfeger*). Buskers are also quite common. You're free to give or not.

MEDICAL SERVICES

The most central hospital with a 24-hour emergency room is the renowned **Charité Mitte** (🎫030-450 50; www.charite.de; Luisenstrasse 65; ⊙24hr; 🚌147, Ⓤ Oranienburger Tor).

TOURIST INFORMATION

Visit Berlin (www.visitberlin.de), the Berlin tourist board, operates five walk-in offices, info desks at the airports, and a **call centre** (🎫030-2500 2333; ⊙9am-6pm Mon-Fri) whose multi lingual staff field general questions and make hotel and ticket bookings.

Alexanderplatz (Map p66; 🎫030-250 025; www.visitberlin.de; lobby Park Inn, Alexanderplatz 7; ⊙7am-9pm Mon-Sat, 8am-6pm Sun; 🚌100, 200, TXL, Ⓤ Alexanderplatz, Ⓢ Alexanderplatz)

Brandenburger Tor (Map p66; 🎫030-250 023; www.visitberlin.de; Pariser Platz, Brandenburger Tor, south wing; ⊙9.30am-7pm Apr-Oct, to 6pm Nov-Mar; Ⓢ Brandenburger Tor, Ⓤ Brandenburger Tor)

Central Bus Station (ZOB; www.visitberlin.de; Masurenallee 4-6; ⊙8am-8pm Mon, Fri & Sat, to 4pm Tue-Thu & Sun; Ⓢ Messe Nord/ICC)

Europa-Center (Map p97; 🎫030-2500 2333; www.visitberlin.de; Tauentzienstrasse 9, Europa-Center, ground fl; ⊙10am-8pm Mon-Sat; 🚌100, 200, Ⓤ Kurfürstendamm, Zoologischer Garten, Ⓢ Zoologischer Garten)

Hauptbahnhof (Map p66; 🎫030-250 025; www.visitberlin.de; Hauptbahnhof, Europaplatz entrance, ground fl; ⊙8am-10pm; Ⓢ Hauptbahnhof, 🚈Hauptbahnhof)

ℹ Getting There & Away

AIR

Most visitors arrive in Berlin by air. Until the opening of the new Berlin Brandenburg Airport, flights continue to land at the city's Tegel and Schönefeld airports.

BUS

→ The upgraded **Zentraler Omnibusbahnhof** (ZOB, Central Bus Station; ☎ 030-3010 0175; www.zob-berlin.de; Messedamm 8; ⑤ Messe/ICC Nord, Ⓤ Kaiserdamm) is near the trade fairgrounds on the western city edge. Flixbus also stops at a dozen other points in town, including the airports and Alexanderplatz.

→ The closest U-Bahn station to ZOB is Kaiserdamm, about 400m north and served by the U2 line, which travels to Zoologischer Garten in about eight minutes and to Alexanderplatz in 28 minutes. Tickets cost €2.80 (Tariff AB).

→ The nearest S-Bahn station is Messe Süd/ICC, about 200m east of ZOB. It is served by the Ringbahn (circle line) S41/S42 and handy for such districts as Prenzlauer Berg, Friedrichshain and Neukölln. You need an AB ticket (€2.80).

→ Budget about €14 for a taxi ride to the western city centre around Zoo station and €24 to the eastern city centre around Alexanderplatz.

CAR & MOTORCYCLE

Berlin is served by the A2 autobahn from points west, the A24 from Hamburg, the A11 from the north, the A9 from the south and the A12 from the east. All roads link with the Berliner Ring (A10), a ring road around the city.

TRAIN

→ Berlin's **Hauptbahnhof** (Main Train Station; Europaplatz, Washingtonplatz; ⑤ Hauptbahnhof, Ⓤ Hauptbahnhof) is in the heart of the city, just north of the Reichstag and Brandenburg Gate. From the station, the U-Bahn, the S-Bahn, trams and buses provide links to all parts of town. Taxi ranks are located outside the north exit (Europaplatz) and the south exit (Washingtonplatz).

→ Buy tickets in the Reisezentrum (travel centre) between tracks 14 and 15 on the first upper level (OG1), online at www.bahn.de or, for shorter distances, at station vending machines.

→ The left-luggage office (€5 per piece, per 24 hours) is behind the Reisebank currency exchange on level OG1, opposite the Reisezentrum.

ℹ Getting Around

TO/FROM THE AIRPORTS

Tegel Airport

Bus The bus stop is outside the main entrance to Terminal A. The TXL express bus connects Tegel to Alexanderplatz (€2.80, AB ticket; 40 minutes) via Hauptbahnhof (central train station) and Unter den Linden every 10 minutes. For City West around Zoologischer Garten take bus X9 (€2.80, AB ticket; 20 minutes), which also runs at 10-minute intervals. Bus 109 heads

to U-/S-Bahn station Zoologischer Garten every 10 minutes; it's slower and useful only if you're headed somewhere along Kurfürstendamm (€2.80, AB ticket; 20 to 30 minutes).

U-Bahn The U-Bahn station closest to the airport is Jakob-Kaiser-Platz, which is connected by bus 109 and X9 to the airport. From Jakob-Kaiser-Platz, the U7 takes you directly to Schöneberg, Kreuzberg and Neukölln. Trips cost €2.80 (Tariff AB).

S-Bahn The closest S-Bahn station is Jungfernheide, which is a stop on the S41/S42 (the Ringbahn, or circle line). It is linked to the airport by bus X9. Another Ringbahn station, Beusselstrasse, links up with the TXL bus route. Trips, including bus and train, cost €2.80 (Tariff AB).

Taxi Taxi rides cost about €25 to Zoologischer Garten and €28 to Alexanderplatz and take 30 to 45 minutes. There's a €0.50 surcharge for trips originating at this airport.

Schönefeld Airport

Regional Trains This is the fastest way to get into town. The airport train station is 400m from the terminals; free shuttle buses run every 10 minutes. Airport-Express trains make the trip to central Berlin twice hourly. Note: these are regular Deutsche Bahn regional trains denoted as RE7 and RB14 in timetables. The journey takes 20 minutes to Alexanderplatz and 30 minutes to Zoologischer Garten.

S-Bahn The S-Bahn S9 runs every 20 minutes and is slower, but useful if you're headed to Friedrichshain (eg Ostkreuz, 30 minutes) or Prenzlauer Berg (eg Schönhauser Allee, 45 minutes). For the Messe (trade fairgrounds), take the S45 to Südkreuz and change to the S41 to Messe Nord/ICC. Trains run every 20 minutes and the journey takes 55 minutes. All journeys cost €3.40.

U-Bahn Schönefeld is not served by the U-Bahn. The nearest station, Rudow, is about a 10-minute ride on bus X7 or bus 171 from the airport. From Rudow, the U7 takes you straight into town. This connection is useful if you're headed for Neukölln or Kreuzberg. You will need an ABC transport ticket (€3.40).

Taxi Budget about €45 to €50 and 45 minutes to an hour for the cab ride to central Berlin.

BICYCLE

→ Bikes are handy both for in-depth explorations of local neighbourhoods and for getting across town. More than 650km of dedicated bike paths make getting around less intimidating even for riders who are not experienced or confident.

→ Having said that, always be aware of dangers caused by aggressive or inattentive drivers. Watch out for car doors opening and for cars

TICKETS & PASSES

➡ One ticket is valid for all forms of public transport.

➡ The network comprises fare zones A, B and C with tickets available for zones AB, BC or ABC.

➡ AB tickets, valid for two hours, cover most city trips (interruptions and transfers allowed, but round-trips are not). Exceptions: Potsdam and Schönefeld Airport (ABC tariff).

➡ Children aged six to 14 qualify for reduced (ermässigt) rates; kids under six travel free.

➡ Buy tickets from bus drivers, vending machines at U- or S-Bahn stations, and aboard trams, station offices and news kiosks sporting the yellow BVG logo. Some vending machines accept debit cards. Bus drivers and tram vending machines only take cash.

➡ Single tickets, except those bought from bus drivers and in trams, must be validated at station platform entrances.

➡ On-the-spot fine for travelling without a valid ticket: €60.

➡ A range of travel passes offer better value than single tickets.

turning right in front of you at intersections. Getting caught in tram tracks is another potential problem.

➡ Bicycles may be taken aboard designated U-Bahn and S-Bahn carriages (look for the bicycle logo) as well as on night buses (Sunday to Thursday only) and trams. You need a separate bicycle ticket called a Fahrradkarte (€1.90). Taking a bike on regional trains (RE, RB) costs €3.30 per trip or €6 per day.

➡ The websites www.bbbike.de and www.vmz-info.de are handy for route planning.

PUBLIC TRANSPORT

Berlin's extensive and efficient public transport system is operated by BVG (☑ hotline 030-194 49; www.bvg.de) and consists of the U-Bahn (underground, or subway), the S-Bahn (light rail), buses and trams. For trip planning and general information, call the 24-hour hotline or check the website.

Bus

➡ Buses are slow but useful for sightseeing on the cheap (especially routes 100 and 200). They run frequently between 4.30am and 12.30am. Night buses (N19, N23 etc) take over after 12.30am.

➡ MetroBuses, designated M19, M41 etc, operate 24/7.

➡ Tickets bought from bus drivers (cash only) don't need to be validated.

U-Bahn

➡ The U-Bahn is the quickest way of getting around Berlin. Lines (referred to as U1, U2 etc) operate from 4am until about 12.30am and throughout the night on Friday, Saturday and public holidays (all lines except the U4 and U55). From Sunday to Thursday, night buses take over in the interim.

➡ Tickets are available from vending machines (no credit cards) in stations or on platforms and must be validated before boarding.

S-Bahn

➡ S-Bahn trains (S1, S2 etc) don't run as frequently as the U-Bahn, but they make fewer stops and are useful for covering longer distances. Trains operate from 4am to 12.30am and all night on Friday, Saturday and public holidays.

➡ Destinations further afield are served by RB and RE trains. You'll need an ABC or **Deutsche Bahn** (☑ 01806 99 66 33; www.bahn.de) ticket to use these trains.

➡ Tickets are available from vending machines (no credit cards) in stations or on platforms and must be validated before boarding.

Tram

➡ Trams (Strassenbahn) operate almost exclusively in the eastern districts.

➡ Those designated M1, M2 etc run 24/7.

➡ A useful line is the M1, which links Prenzlauer Berg with Museum Island via Hackescher Markt.

➡ Tickets are available from in-tram vending machines (cash only) and don't need to be validated.

TAXI

You can order a **taxi** (☑ 030-210 202, 030-443 322, 030-210 101; www.taxi-in-berlin.de) by phone, flag one down or pick one up at a rank. At night, cars often wait outside theatres, clubs and other venues. Flag fall is €3.90, then it's €2 per kilometre up to 7km and €1.50 for each additional kilometre. There's a surcharge of €1.50 if paying by credit or debit card, but none for night trips. Bulky luggage is charged at €1 per piece. Best avoided during daytime rush hour. Tip about 10%.

Around Berlin

Best Places to Eat

➡ Maison Charlotte (p143)

➡ Schlossrestaurant Linari (p148)

➡ Restaurant Altes Gärtnerhaus (p146)

➡ Restaurant an der Dominsel (p149)

Best Places to Stay

➡ Hotel Villa Monte Vino (p142)

➡ Schlosshotel Lübbenau (p147)

➡ Sorat Hotel Brandenburg (p149)

➡ Hotel am Grossen Waisenhaus (p142)

Why Go?

Berlin is fabulous, and you'll certainly want to spend quite a bit of time there, but don't forget to earmark a day (or two or three) for the surrounding state of Brandenburg. A land shaped by lakes, canals and waterways, large swathes of it are protected as biosphere preserves and nature parks, creating a delightful escape from the urban hustle for Berliners and visitors.

Culture lovers, too, will be rewarded. Headlining the list of discoveries is the drop-dead-gorgeous park and palace of Sanssouci (the 'German Versailles') in Potsdam, a mere half-hour train ride from central Berlin. The Spreewald, one of Germany's most unique landscapes, is home to the indigenous Sorb ethnic minority, who cling to ancient customs and traditions in handsome remote hamlets. A sobering antidote to all that splendour – and no less important or memorable – is the Nazi-era concentration camp at Sachsenhausen, north of Berlin.

When to Go

Water characterises much of the countryside around Berlin, meaning that a visit between spring and autumn is when you can experience the region at its best by taking a boat trip or hiring a kayak.

Crowds can get heavy on blue-sky weekends, during the summer school holidays and around public holidays.

Potsdam is best visited midweek during summer, but its palaces and museum make it a fine destination year-round.

Sachsenhausen concentration camp is worth a visit any time of year.

Come in December to experience Christmas markets in enchanting locations, including the Spreewald.

Around Berlin Highlights

1 **Schloss Sanssouci**
(p138) Connecting with your inner prince or princess while exploring this most enchanting of the Potsdam palaces, embedded within a sprawling and lusciously landscaped park.

2 **Spreewald** (p145)
Communing with nature while punting around this forested web of incredible waterways that's also home to the Sorbs, one of Germany's ethnic minorities.

3 **Park & Schloss Branitz**
(p149) Getting into the mind of an eccentric aristocratic garden artist at this rambling estate in Cottbus.

4 **Sachsenhausen** (p144)
Confronting the ghosts of history and the many who died in this concentration camp.

5 **Schiffshebewerk Niederfinow** (p151) Rubbing your eyes in disbelief as huge barges are hoisted or lowered 36m in this massive ship's lift.

Potsdam

📱 0331 / POP 175,700

Potsdam, on the Havel River just 25km southwest of central Berlin, is the capital and crown jewel of the federal state of Brandenburg. Easily reached by S-Bahn, the former Prussian royal seat is the most popular day trip from Berlin, luring visitors with its splendid gardens and palaces, which garnered Unesco World Heritage status in 1990.

Headlining the roll-call of royal pads is Schloss Sanssouci, the private retreat of King Friedrich II (Frederick the Great), who was also the mastermind behind many of Potsdam's other fabulous parks and palaces. Miraculously, most survived WWII with nary a shrapnel wound. When the shooting stopped, the Allies chose Schloss Cecilienhof (p142) to host the Potsdam Conference of 1945 to lay the groundwork for Germany's post-war fate.

◉ Sights

◉ Schloss & Park Sanssouci

This glorious park and palace ensemble is what happens when a king has good taste, plenty of cash and access to the finest architects and artists of the day. Sanssouci was dreamed up by Frederick the Great (1712–86) and is anchored by the eponymous palace, his favourite summer retreat, a place where he could be *'sans souci'* (without cares).

★ **Schloss Sanssouci**   PALACE
(📱0331-969 4200; www.spsg.de; Maulbeerallee; adult/concession incl tour or audioguide €12/8; ◷10am-5.30pm Tue-Sun Apr-Oct, to 5pm Nov & Dec, to 4.30pm Jan-Mar; 🚌614, 650, 695) Frederick the Great's famous summer palace, this rococo gem was designed by Georg Wenzeslaus von Knobelsdorff in 1747 and sits daintily above vine-draped terraces with the king's grave nearby. Admission is limited and by timed ticket only; book online to avoid wait times and/or disappointment. Otherwise, only city tours booked through the tourist office guarantee entry to the Schloss.

★ **Chinesisches Haus**   HISTORIC BUILDING
(Chinese House; Am Grünen Gitter; adult/concession €4/3; ◷10am-5.30pm Tue-Sun May-Oct; 🚌605, 606, 🚋91) The 18th-century fad for the Far East is strongly reflected in the adorable Chinese House. The cloverleaf-shaped pavilion is among the park's most photographed buildings thanks to its enchanting exterior of exotically dressed, gilded figures shown sipping tea, dancing and playing musical instruments amid palm-shaped pillars. Inside is a precious collection of Chinese and Meissen porcelain.

Neues Palais   PALACE
(New Palace; Am Neuen Palais; adult/concession incl tour or audioguide €8/6; ◷10am-5.30pm Mon & Wed-Sun Apr-Oct, to 5pm Nov-Dec, to 4.30pm Jan-Mar; 🚌605, 606, 695, 🚊Potsdam Charlottenhof) The final palace commissioned by Frederick the Great, the Neues Palais has made-to-

---

ℹ️ **TOP TIPS FOR VISITING SANSSOUCI**

➡ Book your timed ticket to Schloss Sanssouci online to avoid wait times and/or disappointment.

➡ Avoid visiting on Monday when most palaces are closed.

➡ The sanssouci+ ticket, a one-day pass to palaces in Potsdam, costs €19 (concession €14) and is sold online and at each building.

➡ Picnicking is permitted throughout the park, but cycling is limited to Ökonomieweg and Maulbeerallee.

➡ There's a fee (€3 per day) for taking pictures (*Fotoerlaubnis*) inside the palaces.

➡ Palaces are fairly well spaced – it's almost 2km between the Neues Palais and Schloss Sanssouci.

➡ There are two visitors centres at either end of Park Sanssouci: the **Besucherzentrum an der Historischen Mühle** (📱0331-969 4200; www.spsg.de; An der Orangerie 1; ◷8.30am-5.30pm Tue-Sun Apr-Oct, to 4.30pm Nov-Mar; 🚌614, 650, 695) near Schloss Sanssouci and the **Besucherzentrum im Neuen Palais** (📱0331-969 4200; www.spsg. de; Am Neuen Palais; ◷9am-5.30pm Wed-Mon Apr-Oct, to 4.30pm Nov-Mar; 🚌605, 606, 695).

impress dimensions, a central dome and a lavish exterior capped with a parade of sandstone figures. The interior attests to the high level of artistry and craftwork of the 18th century. It's an opulent symphony of ceiling frescoes, gilded stucco ornamentation, ornately carved wainscoting and fanciful wall coverings alongside paintings (by Antoine Pesne, for example) and elaborately crafted furniture.

Bildergalerie
GALLERY

(Gallery of Old Masters; Im Park Sanssouci 4; adult/concession €6/5; ⊘10am-5.30pm Tue-Sun May-Oct; 🚌650, 695) The Picture Gallery shelters Frederick the Great's prized collection of Old Masters, including such pearls as Caravaggio's *Doubting Thomas*, Anthony van Dyck's *Pentecost* and several works by Peter Paul Rubens.

Neue Kammern
PALACE

(New Chambers; Park Sanssouci; adult/concession incl tour or audioguide €6/5; ⊘10am-5.30pm Tue-Sun Apr-Oct; 🚌614, 650, 695) The New Chambers, built by Knobelsdorff in 1748, were originally an orangery and later converted into a guest palace. The interior drips with rococo opulence, most notably the square Jasper Hall, which is drenched in precious stones and lidded by a Venus fresco, and the Ovidsaal, a grand ballroom with gilded wall reliefs depicting scenes from Ovid's *Metamorphosis*.

Orangerieschloss
PALACE

(Orangery Palace; An der Orangerie 3-5; adult/concession €6/5, tower €3/2; ⊘10am-5.30pm Tue-Sun May-Oct, 10am-5.30pm Sat & Sun Apr; 🚌695) Modelled after an Italian Renaissance villa, the 300m-long Orangery Palace (1864) was the favourite building project of Friedrich Wilhelm IV – a passionate Italophile. Its highlight is the Raffaelsaal (Raphael Hall), which brims with 19th-century copies of the famous painter's masterpieces. The greenhouses are still used for storing potted plants in winter. Views from the tower are quite nice as well.

Belvedere auf dem Klausberg
HISTORIC BUILDING

(☑0331-969 4200; www.spsg.de; An der Orangerie 1; ⊘open for special events only; 🚌695) Frederick the Great's final building project was this temple-like belvedere, modelled on Nero's palace in Rome. The panorama of park, lakes and Potsdam is predictably fabulous from up here.

TAKING A BREAK

Right in the park, **Drachenhaus** (☑0331-505 3808; www.drachenhaus.de; Maulbeerallee 4; mains €10-25; ⊘11am-7pm daily Apr-Oct, noon-6pm Tue-Sun Nov, Dec & Mar, noon-6pm Sat & Sun Jan & Feb; 🚲; 🚌695) is a pagoda-style miniature palace serving coffee, cakes and seasonal cuisine.

For international favourites, head to **Potsdam Zur Historischen Mühle** (☑0331-281 493; www.moevenpick-restaurants.com; Zur Historischen Mühle 2; mains €11-20; ⊘8am-10pm; 🅿🚲; 🚌614, 650, 695); it has a beer garden and children's playground.

Park Charlottenhof
PARK

(Geschwister-Scholl-Strasse 34a; Ⓢ Potsdam Charlottenhof Bahnhof) FREE Laid out by Peter Lenné for Friedrich Wilhelm IV, Park Charlottenhof segues imperceptibly from **Park Sanssouci** (⊘8am-dusk; 🅿; 🚌614, 650, 695) FREE but gets far fewer visitors. Buildings here reflect the king's passion for Italy. The small neoclassical **Schloss Charlottenhof** (Charlottenhof Palace; ☑0331-969 4200; tours adult/concession €6/5; ⊘tours 10am-5.30pm Tue-Sun May-Oct), for instance, was modelled after a Roman villa. It was designed by Karl Friedrich Schinkel.

◉ Altstadt

Although much of Potsdam's historic town centre fell victim to WWII bombing and socialist town planning, it's been nicely restored and is worth exploring on foot. A landmark is the baroque **Brandenburger Tor** (Brandenburg Gate; Luisenplatz; 🚌606, 631, 🚲91), a triumphal arch built to commemorate Frederick the Great's 1763 victory in the Seven Years' War. It's the gateway to pedestrianised Brandenburger Strasse, the main commercial drag, which links with the scenic Holländisches Viertel (Dutch Quarter).

Holländisches Viertel
AREA

(Dutch Quarter; www.hollaendisches-viertel.net; Mittelstrasse; 🚌606, 631) This picturesque cluster of 134 gabled red-brick houses was built around 1730 for Dutch workers invited to Potsdam by Friedrich Wilhelm I. The entire district has been done up beautifully and brims with galleries, boutiques, cafes

Potsdam

0 — 500 m
0 — 0.25 miles

Wannsee S (7km);
Berlin (24km)

Neuer Garten 10

Schloss Cecilienhof (850m)
Am Neuen Garten

Heiliger See

Seestr

Berliner Str

Lotte-
Pulewka-Str

Humboldtring

Babelsberger Str

Potsdam Tourist
Office – Hauptbahnhof
19

Potsdam
Hauptbahnhof

Lange
Brücke

Museum
Barberini

Joliot-
Curie-Str

Burgstr

18

16 2
4
20
8
Am Alten
Markt

Platz der
Einheit

Am Kanal

Charlottenstr

Yorckstr

29

Dortustr

Leiblstr

Kurfürstenstr

Gutenbergstr

Benkertstr

27

9

Mittelstr

26

Jägerstr

24

Gutenbergstr

Brandenburger Str

Friedrich-Ebert-Str

Hebbelstr

Alleestr

Am Schragen

Voltaireweg

Pappelallee

Jägerallee

Hegelallee

Gregor-Mendel-Str

Weinbergstr

23

22

Schopenhauerstr

Bornstedter Str

Schloss
Sanssouci
28

An der
Mühle

11

Sizilianischer
Garten

6

3

Besucherzentrum an der
Historischen Mühle

13

An der
Orangerie

Ribbeckstr

Bornstedter See

Ökonomieweg

Chinesisches
Haus
1

Brandenburger Tor

Luisenplatz
7

Zimmerstr

Lindenstr

21

Feuerbachstr

Breite Str

Zeppelinstr

Auf dem Kiewitt

Neustädter
Havelbucht

Potsdam
Charlottenhof
Bahnhof

Geschwister-Scholl-Str

Schafgraben

Lennéstr

15

Hauptallee

Park
Sanssouci

25

5

Maulbeerallee

Park
Charlottenhof

14

Maschinenteich

17

Besucherzentrum
im Neuen Palais
12

Am Neuen Palais

Potsdam;
Park
Sanssouci
Bahnhof

Potsdam

AROUND BERLIN POTSDAM

and restaurants; Mittelstrasse is especially scenic. Further up Friedrich-Ebert-Strasse is the Nauener Tor (Nauen Gate, 1755), a fanciful city gate.

★**Museum Barberini** MUSEUM
(www.museum-barberini.com; Alter Markt, Humboldtstrasse 5-6; adult/concession/under 18 €14/10/free; ⊙10am-7pm Wed-Mon, 1st Thu of month to 9pm; ⊠91, 92, 93, 96, 99 Alter Markt/Landtag) The original Barberini Palace was a baroque Roman palazzo commissioned by Frederick the Great and bombed to bits in World War II. Since January 2017, a majestic replica has added a new jewel to Potsdam's already bursting cultural landscape. It houses a private art museum, funded by German software impresario Hasso Plattner, and mounts three high-calibre exhibits per year with an artistic arc that spans East German works, Old Masters and modern greats such as Gerhard Richter.

Potsdamer Stadtschloss HISTORIC BUILDING
(Landtag Brandenburg, Potsdam City Palace; ☑0331-966 1260; www.stadtschloss-potsdam. org; Alter Markt; ⊙usually 8am-5pm Mon-Fri; ⊠631, ⊠93, 98) FREE One of Potsdam's newest landmarks is this replica of the 18th-century Prussian City Palace that was partly destroyed in WWII and completely removed by East German town planners in 1960. It reopened in 2014 as the new home of the Brandenburg state parliament. Of the original building, only the ornate Fortuna Portal remains; it now forms the

main entrance to the compound, sections of which (including the rooftop terrace and the staircase designed by Knobelsdorff) are open to the public.

St Nikolai-Kirche CHURCH
(☑0331-270 8602; www.nikolai-potsdam.de; Alter Markt 1; ⊙9am-7pm Mon-Sat, 11.30am-7pm Sun Apr-Oct, to 5pm Nov-Mar; ⊠631, ⊠93, 98) In Potsdam's historic centre, around the **Alter Markt** (Old Market; ⊠91, 92, 93, 96, 99 Alter Markt/Landtag), the great patina-green dome of Karl Friedrich Schinkel's neoclassical Nikolaikirche (1850) is complemented by a 16m-high obelisk festooned with imagery of famous local architects, including Schinkel.

⊙ Neuer Garten & Around

North of the Potsdam old town, the winding lakeside Neuer Garten (New Garden) is laid out in natural English style on the western shore of the Heiliger See. It gets a lot less busy than Park Sanssouci and is a fine place in which to relax. A couple of palaces provide cultural diversions.

Marmorpalais PALACE
(Marble Palace; ☑0331-969 4550; www.spsg. de; Im Neuen Garten 10; tours adult/concession €6/5; ⊙10am-5.30pm Tue-Sun May-Oct & Sat & Sun Apr, to 4pm Sat & Sun Jan-Mar; ⊠603) As the name suggests, the early-neoclassical Marmorpalais is a symphony in colourful marble on floors, walls, ceilings and fireplaces. The palace was built in 1792 as a

summer retreat for Friedrich Wilhelm II by Carl von Gontard and overlooks the Heiliger See. The most fanciful rooms are the Konzertsaal (concert hall), designed to resemble an antique temple, and the Turkish-tent-style Orientalisches Kabinett (Oriental Cabinet) upstairs.

Combination tickets with nearby Schloss Cecilienhof cost €10 (concession €7).

Schloss Cecilienhof PALACE

(☑ 0331-969 4200; www.spsg.de; Im Neuen Garten 11; conference room adult/concession €8/6, royal quarters €6/5; ☉ 10am-5.30pm Tue-Sun Apr-Oct, to 5pm Nov-Dec, to 4.30pm Tue Jan-Mar; ☒ 603) This English-style country palace, completed in 1917 for Crown Prince Wilhelm and his wife Cecilie, was the last residence built by the Hohenzollern clan. Their private quarters can be seen on a tour, but the site is mostly famous for hosting the 1945 Potsdam Conference where Stalin, Truman and Churchill (and later his successor Clement Attlee) hammered out Germany's post-war fate and incidentally laid the foundation for the Cold War.

☞ Tours

Schiffahrt in Potsdam BOATING

(☑ 0331-275 9210; www.schiffahrt-in-potsdam.de; Lange Brücke 6; ☉ Apr-Oct; ☒ 605, 610, 631, 694, ☒ 91, 92, 93, 98) A relaxing way to enjoy Potsdam is from the deck of a cruise boat. The most popular trip is the 90-minute *Schlösse rundfahrt* palace cruise (€16); there's also a two-hour tour to Lake Wannsee (€17) and a three-hour trip around several Havel lakes (€18). Boats depart from the docks below the Mercure Hotel. English commentary available.

🛏 Sleeping

Most people visit Potsdam on a day trip from Berlin, but there are actually some extremely charming historical private hotels that would make an overnight stay quite enjoyable. All room rates are subject to a 5% tourist tax in addition to VAT (business travellers are exempt).

★ Hotel Villa Monte Vino HOTEL €€

(☑ 0331-201 3339; www.hotelvillamontevino.de; Gregor-Mendel-Strasse 27; d €110-190; 🅿 ⊜ @ 🛜; ☒ 612, 614, 650, 695) This romantic 1890 villa, complete with dreamy garden and Rapunzel tower, is a superb find tucked into the leafy hillside above Schloss Sanssouci (p138). Run by passionate owners, it's in top shape and

harmoniously blends historical and modern touches; it even has a small sauna. Rooms don't skimp on space and are sheathed in soothing earth tones.

Snacks available in the evening. Optional breakfast is €11.

Hotel am Grossen Waisenhaus HOTEL €€

(☑ 0331-601 0780; www.hotelwaisenhaus.de; Lindenstrasse 28/29; d incl breakfast €95-165; 🅿 ⊜ 🛜; ☒ 605, 606, 610, 631, ☒ 91,94, 98) This classy entry occupies 18th-century baroque barracks for married soldiers, which also went through a stint as an orphanage hospital (as reflected in the name). Historical quirks combine with carefully designed contemporary features in four room categories, all with sparkling plank floors. Generous breakfast.

Remise Blumberg PENSION €€

(☑ 0331-280 3231; http://remise-blumberg.de; Weinbergstrasse 26; d incl breakfast €90-100; 🅿 ⊜ 🛜; ☒ 612, 614, 650) In this quiet eight-room historical gem, you'll have plenty of space to stretch out in elegantly furnished units with cooking facilities. Greet the day with an excellent breakfast (complete with sparkling wine), which, in fine weather, is served in the secluded courtyard. Rates include free public transport passes.

🍴 Eating

Potsdam's Altstadt brims with atmospheric eating options, especially in the Holländisches Viertel (p139). For cafes and fast food, head to the pedestrianised Brandenburger Strasse. However, even the centre gets very quiet at night.

Hafthorn PUB FOOD €

(☑ 0331-280 0820; www.hafthorn.de; Friedrich-Ebert-Strasse 90; dishes €6-10; ☉ 6pm-midnight or later Mon-Fri, from 1pm Sat & Sun; 🛜; ☒ 604, 609, 638, ☒ 92, 96) Check your pretensions at the door of this cheerful, charming pub, the home of quirky metal lamps, big burgers and cold beer. An all-ages crowd shares laughter inside this former bakery and, in summer, along benches in the beer garden. Occasional live music.

Brasserie zu Gutenberg FRENCH €€

(☑ 0331-7403 6878; www.brasserie-zu-gutenberg. de; Jägerstrasse 10; mains €9-28; ☉ noon-midnight; ☒ 604, 609, 638, ☒ 92, 96) This charming little brasserie with dark tables and chocolate-brown banquettes is great for a hearty meal, perhaps featuring a steak cooked on the lava grill, or the signature coq au vin with a glass of fine Bordeaux. If you just need a little sustenance, order a *Flammkuchen* (tarte flambée), crêpes or *croque-monsieur* (fried ham and cheese sandwich).

Schmiede 9 — GERMAN €€

(☑ 0331-200 6887; www.kutschstall.de; Am Neuen Markt 9a; mains €11.50-22; ⊗ 10am-5pm; ☎; 🚌 603, 605, 631, 650, 695, 🚊 91, 92, 93) A restored smithy in a half-timbered house forms the backdrop for this trend-conscious cafe and restaurant where a small army of chefs prepares modern regional fare in a show kitchen. Also has a lunch buffet from 11.30am to 2pm.

Meierei Brauhaus — GASTROPUB €€

(☑ 0331-704 3211; www.meierei-potsdam.de; Im Neuen Garten 10; mains €9-15; ⊗ noon-9pm Tue-Sat, to 7pm Sun; 🚌 603 to Höhenstrasse) The Berlin Wall once ran right past this brewpub, where the beer garden invites you to count the boats sailing on the Jungfernsee in summer. The hearty German dishes are a perfect match for the delicious craft beers, including the classic *Helles* (pale lager) and seasonal suds brewed on the premises.

Maison Charlotte — FRENCH €€€

(☑ 0331-280 5450; www.maison-charlotte.de; Mittelstrasse 20; Flammkuchen €8.50-14.50, mains €24.50-25.50, 3-/4-course menus €44/53; ⊗ noon-11pm; 🚌 604, 609, 638, 🚊 92, 96) There's a rustic lyricism to the French country cuisine in this darling Dutch Quarter bistro, no matter whether your appetite runs towards a simple *Flammkuchen* (Alsatian pizza), Breton fish soup or a multicourse menu. Bon vivants on a budget come for the daily lunch special (€7.50), which includes a glass of wine; it's best enjoyed on the patio in summer.

ℹ Information

Potsdam Tourist Office – Hauptbahnhof
(☑ 0331-2755 8899; www.potsdam-tourism.com; Potsdam Hauptbahnhof; ⊗ 9.30am-6pm Mon-Sat; 🚇 Potsdam Hauptbahnhof) Inside the main train station.

ℹ Getting There & Away

CAR

Drivers coming from Berlin should take the A100 to the A115.

TRAIN

Regional trains leaving from the Berlin Hauptbahnhof and Zoologischer Garten take about 25 minutes to reach **Potsdam Hauptbahnhof** (www.bahnhof.de/bahnhof-de/Potsdam_Hbf-1037224; Friedrich-Engels-Strasse 99); some continue on to Potsdam Charlottenhof and Potsdam Sanssouci, which are actually closer to Park Sanssouci (p139). The S7 from central Berlin makes the trip in about 40 minutes. You need a ticket covering zones ABC (€3.40) for either service.

POTSDAM'S CELLULOID LEGACY

Film buffs will know that Potsdam is famous not merely for its palaces but also for being the birthplace of European film production. For it was here, in the suburb of Babelsberg, about 4km west of the city centre, that the venerable UFA Studio was founded in 1912. A few years later, it was already producing such seminal flicks as Metropolis and Blue Angel. Continuing as DEFA (Deutsche Filmakademie) in GDR times, the dream factory was resurrected as Studio Babelsberg after reunification and has since produced or coproduced such international blockbusters as *Inglourious Basterds*, *The Grand Budapest Hotel* and *The Hunger Games*.

There are two ways to plug into the Potsdam film experience. In town, handsome baroque royal stables now house the **Filmmuseum Potsdam** (☑ 0331-271 8112; www.filmmuseum-potsdam.de; Breite Strasse 1a; adult/concession €5/4; ⊗ 10am-6pm Tue-Sun; 🚌 631, 🚊 93, 98), which presents an engaging romp through German movie history with an emphasis on the DEFA period. In Babelsberg, next to the actual film studios, **Filmpark Babelsberg** (☑ 0331-721 2750; www.filmpark-babelsberg.de; Grossbeerenstrasse 200; adult/concession/child €22/18/15; ⊗ 10am-6pm Apr-Sep, to 5pm Oct; 🅿; 🚌 601, 690, 🚇 Potsdam Hauptbahnhof, Babelsberg) is a movie-themed amusement park with plenty of shows and behind-the-scenes tours.

❶ Getting Around

BICYCLE

If the weather cooperates, a bicycle is a great way to explore Potsdam. **Potsdam per Pedales** (☑ 0331-8871 9917; www.potsdam-per-pedales. de; Babelsberger Strasse 10; adult/concession per day from €11/9, e-bike €25/20; ☺ 7am-7pm Mon-Fri, 9.30am-7pm Sat & Sun Apr-Oct, 8am-7pm Mon-Fri, 9.30am-7pm Sun Nov-Mar; Ⓢ Potsdam Hauptbahnhof) rents bikes outside the train station.

PUBLIC TRANSPORT

Buses and trams operate throughout Potsdam. Buses for Sanssouci (lines 614 and 695) leave from right outside Potsdam Hauptbahnhof (p143).

Sachsenhausen Concentration Camp

★ **Gedenkstätte und Museum Sachsenhausen**   MEMORIAL
(Memorial & Museum Sachsenhausen; ☑ 03301-200 200; www.stiftung-bg.de; Strasse der Nationen 22, Oranienburg; ☺ 8.30am-6pm mid-Mar–mid-Oct, to 4.30pm mid-Oct–mid-Mar, museums closed Mon mid-Oct–mid-Mar; Ⓟ; Ⓢ Oranienburg) FREE About 35km north of Berlin, Sachsenhausen was built by prisoners and opened in 1936 as a prototype for other camps. By 1945, some 200,000 people had passed through its sinister gates, most of them political opponents, Jews, Roma people and, after 1939, POWs. Tens of thousands died here from hunger, exhaustion, illness, exposure, medical experiments and executions. A tour of the memorial site with its remaining buildings and exhibits will leave no one untouched.

Thousands more succumbed during the death march of April 1945, when the Nazis evacuated the camp in advance of the Red Army. Note the memorial plaque to these victims as you walk towards the camp from S-Bahn station Oranienburg (at the corner of Strasse der Einheit and Strasse der Nationen).

Unless you're on a guided tour, pick up a leaflet (€0.50) or, better yet, an audio guide (€3, including leaflet) at the visitor centre to get a better grasp of this huge site. Between mid-October and mid-March, avoid visiting on a Monday when all indoor exhibits are closed.

The approach to the camp takes you past photographs taken during the death march and the camp's liberation in April 1945. Just beyond the perimeter, the Neues Museum (New Museum) has exhibits on Sachsen-hausen's precursor, the nearby Oranienburg concentration camp, in a repurposed brewery, and on the history of the memorial site during the GDR-era (1950 to 1990).

Proceed to Tower A, the entrance gate, cynically labelled, as at Auschwitz, *Arbeit Macht Frei* (Work Sets You Free). It houses an exhibit on the organisation of the concentration camp and its architectural layout. Beyond here is the roll-call area, with barracks and other buildings fanning out beyond. Off to the right, two restored barracks illustrate the abysmal living conditions prisoners endured. Barrack 38 has an exhibit on Jewish inmates, while Barrack 39 graphically portrays daily life at the camp. The prison next door was an especially sinister place of torture and murder. Famous inmates included Hitler's would-be assassin Georg Elser and the anti-Nazi minister Martin Niemöller, author of the *First They Came...* poem.

Moving towards the centre, the Prisoners' Kitchen chronicles key moments in the camp's history. Exhibits include instruments of torture, the original gallows that stood in the roll-call area and, in the cellar, heart-wrenching artwork scratched into the wall by prisoners.

The most sickening displays, though, are about the extermination area called Station Z, which was separated from the rest of the grounds and consisted of an execution trench, a crematorium and a gas chamber. The most notorious mass executions took place in autumn 1941 when more than 10,000 Soviet POWs were executed here in the course of four weeks.

In the far right corner, a modern building and two original barracks house the Soviet Special Camp exhibit, which documents Sachsenhausen's stint as Speciallager No 7, a German POW camp run by the Soviets from 1945 until 1950. About 60,000 people were held here; some 12,000 of them died, mostly of malnutrition and disease. After 1950, Soviet and East German military used the grounds for another decade until the camp became a memorial site in 1961.

Exhibits in the original infirmary barracks on the other side of the roll-call area illustrate the camp's poor medical care and the horrific medical experiments performed on prisoners. One section focuses on the men and women incarcerated in Sachsenhausen after the failed assassination attempt on Hitler on 20 July 1944.

Note that no food is available at the memorial site, although a vending machine in the Neues Museum dispenses hot drinks. You're allowed to bring food and drink with you. There are cafes, bakeries and small markets outside Oranienburg train station.

Tours

Friends of Sachsenhausen   WALKING
(www.stiftung-bg.de/foerderverein; adult/concession €14/12; ☺English tours 10.20am Tue, Thu & Sun year-round, 2.30pm Tue, Thu & Sun Apr-Oct) The nonprofit Friends of Sachsenhausen runs guided four-hour tours to the memorial from the historic traffic light on Potsdamer Platz in central Berlin. No registration is required. If you prefer, you can also make your own way to the memorial and join the tour at the visitors centre at 11.45am year-round and also at 2.30pm from April to October.

Getting There & Away

The S1 makes the trip thrice hourly from central Berlin (eg Friedrichstrasse station) to Oranienburg (ABC ticket €3.40, 45 minutes). Hourly regional RE5 and RB12 trains leaving from Hauptbahnhof are faster (ABC ticket €3.40, 30 minutes). The camp is about 2km from the Oranienburg train station. Turn right onto Stralsunder Strasse, right on Bernauer Strasse, left on Strasse der Einheit and right on Strasse der Nationen. Alternatively, bus 804 makes hourly trips from the station straight to the site (use same ticket, seven minutes).

Spreewald

The Spreewald, a unique lacework of channels and canals hemmed in by forest, is the closest thing Berlin has to a backyard garden. Visitors come to this Unesco Biosphere Reserve in droves to hike, fish and punt, canoe or kayak on its extensive network of waterways. Lübben and Lübbenau, the main tourist towns, often drown beneath the tides of visitors vying for rides aboard a *Kahn* (shallow punt boat) steered by ferrymen in traditional garb and once the only way of getting around in these parts. To truly appreciate the Spreewald's many charms, hire your own canoe or kayak or get yourself onto a walking trail.

The Spreewald is also famous for being the home of the Sorb ethnic minority and for producing more than 40,000 tonnes of gherkins every year.

Lübben

☑ 03546 / POP 13,860
Tidy Lübben has a history going back to the 12th century. Activity centres on the Schloss and the adjacent harbour area, both about 1.5km east of the train station. En route to the Schloss, you'll pass the Paul-Gerhardt-Kirche, where 17th-century poet and hymn writer Paul Gerhardt is buried.

Sights & Activities

Museum Schloss Lübben   MUSEUM
(☑03546-187 478; www.museum-luebben.de; Ernst-von-Houwald-Damm 14; adult/concession €4.50/2.50; ☺10am-5pm Wed-Sun) The prettiest building in town is the petite Schloss, now home to a nicely curated regional history museum. Exhibit highlights include an interactive town model and a 2m-long medieval executioner's sword. Follow up with a (free) wander around the Schlossinsel, an artificial archipelago with gardens, a leafy maze, playgrounds, cafes and a harbour area where you can board punts for leisurely tours.

Bootsverleih Gebauer   BOATING
(☑03546-7194; www.spreewald-bootsverleih.de; Lindenstrasse 18; s kayak 2hr/day €9/19, bicycle per day €14) Rents canoes, kayaks and row boats for one to four people, as well as bicycles.

Sleeping & Eating

Hotel Lindengarten   HOTEL €€
(☑03546-4172; www.spreewald-luebben.de; Treppendorfer Dorfstrasse 15; d incl breakfast €83-90; ℗) This family-run hotel has bright and airy rooms, an upbeat feel and a nice restaurant serving local dishes. Free pickups from the station can be arranged.

> ### SPENDING THE NIGHT
> The Spreewald is a hugely popular getaway and has plenty of lodging options to meet demand. In summer and around the holidays, the better places book up early. Hotels, B&Bs, holiday flats and houses and camping are all enticing options.
>
> Many places impose minimum stays or charge extra if you're only staying one night. A daily resort tax (*Kurtaxe*) of €2 for everyone over 18 is added to overnight stays. In exchange you get a *Gästecard* that grants various discounts throughout the Spreewald.

AROUND BERLIN SPREEWALD

SPREEWALD PICKLES

The Spreewald is world renowned for its pickled cucumbers, cherished by connoisseurs for their low acidity, crunchy texture and delicate spicing. The official name, *Spreewälder Gurke*, is even an EU-certified Protected Geographical Indication, just like champagne and cognac. Flemish clothmakers introduced the pickle seeds that thrive in the region's watery and humus-rich soil. Only about 20 companies, each using their own 'secret' family recipe, are allowed to produce the vegetable. Discover more pickle secrets on the 260km-long Gurkenradweg (Gherkin Cycle Path) or at the Gurkenmuseum in Lehde.

Restaurant Altes
Gärtnerhaus   MEDITERRANEAN €€
(☑ 03546-186 956; www.altes-gärtnerhaus-lübben. de; Ernst-von-Houwald-Damm 6; mains €7-14; ◷ 2-10pm Tue-Fri, noon-10pm Sat & Sun) This lovingly decorated little cottage with living-room charm and a small beer garden is a popular stop, be it just for coffee and a slice of homemade cake or for a full meal of tasty Mediterranean or regional dishes, including fish. It's in the former palace gardener's house.

Goldener Löwe   GERMAN €€
(☑ 03546-7309; www.goldenerloewe-luebben.de; Hauptstrasse 14; mains €7.50-13; ◷ 11am-10pm) Lübben's oldest restaurant is an atmospheric purveyor of German and Spreewald dishes, including a fish platter featuring local eel, perch and carp. In summer, enjoy your meal in the beer garden. It also has a few rooms for rent (doubles €70), in case you feel like dawdling.

❶ Information

Lübben Tourist Office (☑ 03546-3090; www. luebben.de; Ernst-von-Houwald-Damm 15; ◷10am-6pm Mon-Fri, to 4pm Sat & Sun May-Sep, 10am-6pm Mon-Fri, to 4pm Sat Apr-Oct, 10am-12.30pm & 1-4pm Mon, Tue, Thu, Fri Nov-Mar)

❶ Getting There & Around

Hourly regional trains take about an hour from central Berlin (eg Hauptbahnhof, Alexanderplatz) to Lübben (€10).

At the station, **Spreewaldradler/Vitalpunkt** (☑ 035603-158 790; Lübben train station; bikes per day €8-17; ◷ call ahead) rents bikes; call ahead to reserve.

Lübbenau

☑ 03542 / POP 16,100

Poet Theodor Fontane called Lübbenau the 'secret capital' of the Spreewald and, indeed, it is a pretty little town, even when deluged by day trippers. Its entire economy seems

built on tourism and no matter where you go, a forest of signs points to hotels, restaurants and other businesses, making navigating a snap. Wander away from the harbour and main street to escape the crowds.

◉ Sights & Activities

★ Freilandmuseum Lehde   MUSEUM
(Open-Air Museum Lehde; ☑ Apr-Oct 03542-871 508, Nov-Mar 03542-2472; www.museum-osl.de; An der Giglitza 1a; adult/concession €5/3.50; ◷10am-6pm Apr-Sep, to 5pm Oct) In the protected village of Lehde, this cluster of historical Sorb farm buildings gives you a good sense of what rural life in the Spreewald was like a century ago. Wander among the reed-covered buildings, stop at a punt-builder's workshop, meet local folk dressed in colourful Sorb costumes and discover the secrets of the famous Spreewald gherkin.

A popular two-hour boat tour (€10) goes out to Lehde from Lübbenau, but you can escape the crowds by walking the 2km instead. The route through the forest follows the Leiper Weg, which was the first road built in the Spreewald in 1935–6.

Spreewald-Museum Lübbenau   MUSEUM
(☑ 03542-2472; www.museum-osl.de; Topfmarkt 12; adult/concession €5/3.50; ◷10am-6pm Tue-Sun Apr-Oct, noon-4pm Tue-Sun Nov-Mar) Take a trip down the Spreewald memory lane at this regional history museum imaginatively set up like a historical department store. Stops include a grocery, a bakery, a furrier and a shoemaker as well as a clothing store featuring traditional Sorb garb. A modern annexe houses the locomotive and a passenger car of the *Spreewaldbahn*, a narrow-gauge train that connected local villages from 1898 until 1970.

Gurkenmuseum Lehde   MUSEUM
(Gherkin Museum; ☑ 03542-899 960; www.spree wald-starick.de; An der Dolzke 6; ◷9am-6pm Apr-Oct & by appointment) **FREE** This little private

museum reveals the secrets behind the famous Spreewald pickles and lets you sample different varieties. It also crowns the *Gurkenkönigin* (Pickle Queen) every year in July.

Haus für Mensch und Natur
MUSEUM

(📞 03542-892 10; Schulstrasse 9; ⊘10am-5pm Tue-Sun Apr-Oct, to 3pm Tue-Fri Nov-Mar) FREE An old school building now houses the Spreewald Biosphere Reserve information centre where you can learn all about the region's natural development, marvel at its incredible plant and animal diversity and test your eco-IQ at a computer game. It's right next to the tourist office (p148).

Bootsverleih Richter
BOATING

(📞 03542-3764; www.bootsverleih-richter.de; Dammstrasse 75; kayak per person 2hr/day €11/16-19; ⊘9am-6pm late-Mar–mid-Oct) Several outfits hire out canoes and kayaks, including this dynamic operation with a huge fleet of well-maintained boats. Staff can help you put together tours of various lengths.

🕝 Tours

Grosser Hafen Lübbenau
BOATING

(📞 03542-2225; www.grosser-kahnhafen.de; Dammstrasse 77a; boat tours €12-28; ⊘8.30am-7pm Mon-Thu, 9am-5pm Fri-Sun May-Sep, shorter hours Oct-Apr) To truly understand the spirit of the Spreewald you need to get out on a boat. In season, punt boats depart continu-

ously from this little harbour. The shortest tour is a two-hour trip to Lehde (includes 30 minutes in Lehde, no reservations necessary), the longest a nine-hour tour through the entire area. Children get a 50% discount.

🛏 Sleeping & Eating

Brauhaus & Pension Babben
PENSION €

(📞 03542-2126; www.babben-bier.de; Brauhausgasse 2; d incl breakfast €70-75; 🅿😊🐱) This family-owned brewery has made a mean Pilsner and seasonal beers since 1928. Upstairs is a handful of cosy rooms that will do nicely if you've had one beer too many. There's also a few holiday apartments here and across the street that sleep up to four but come with a five-day minimum rental.

Pension am Alten Bauernhafen
PENSION €

(📞 03542-2930; www.am-alten-bauernhafen.de; Stottoff 5; d incl breakfast from €59; 🅿😊) This family-run pension is in a quiet side street in the heart of the historical centre and right by the water. Rooms are simply furnished but clean and proper. Many of the breakfast items are sourced from the owner couple's organic garden.

Schlosshotel Lübbenau
HOTEL €€

(📞 03542-8730; www.schloss-luebbenau.de; Schlossbezirk 6; d €100-180; 🅿🐱) Lübbenau's poshest digs occupy the local palace, idyllically surrounded by a tranquil park. Rooms

AROUND BERLIN SPREEWALD

THE SORBS

The Spreewald is part of the area inhabited by the Sorbs, one of four officially recognised German national minorities (the others being Danes, Frisians and Roma/Sinti); they have their own language, customs and traditions. This intriguing group, numbering around 60,000, descends from the Slavic Wends, who settled between the Elbe and Oder rivers in the 5th century in an area called Lusatia (Luzia in Sorbian).

After Lusatia was conquered by the German King Heinrich I in 929, the Sorbs lost their political independence and, for centuries, were subjected to relentless Christianisation and Germanisation. In 1815, their land was partitioned into Lower Sorbia – centred on the Spreewald and Cottbus (Chośebuz), which went to Prussia – and Upper Sorbia, around Bautzen (Budyšin), which went to Saxony. The Upper Sorbian dialect, closely related to Czech, enjoyed a certain prestige in Saxony, but the Kingdom of Prussia tried to suppress Lower Sorbian, which is similar to Polish.

Sorbian groups banded together under an organisation called Domowina in 1912 in order to fight for the group's rights and interests. The Nazis outlawed the organisation and banned their culture and language. In GDR times, Sorbs enjoyed protected status but were also forced to vacate large parts of their land to make room for coal mining operations. In reunited Germany, Sorbs receive subsidies from state and federal governments (around €17 million in 2015) to keep their culture alive. Colourful Sorbian festivals such as the *Vogelhochzeit* (Birds' Wedding) on 25 January and a symbolic witch-burning on 30 April attract great media attention and huge numbers of tourists.

For further information, contact the Sorbisches Institut (www.serbski-institut.de).

don't skimp on space, are warmly furnished in natural colours and come with sitting areas and parquet floors. After a day in nature, unwind with a steam or massage in the vaulted spa decorated with hand-painted tiles before reporting to dinner at the elegant restaurant.

Hotel Nordic Spreewald
HOTEL €€

(☑ 03542-424 41; www.nordic-spreewald.de; Hauptstrasse 33, Ortsteil Zerkwitz; d incl breakfast €72-109; P ⊜ ⊚) The charming owner-hosts of this adorable oasis, about 2km west of the train station, often go the extra mile to make their guests happy. A small breakfast is included in the room rate but it's well worth the extra €10 per person for the big buffet spread.

★ Schlossrestaurant Linari
INTERNATIONAL €€€

(☑ 03542-8730; www.schloss-luebbenau.de; Schlossbezirk 6; mains €17.50-29, 3-course menu from €28; ⊙ 11.30am-10.30pm; P) This delightful restaurant in the Lübbenau Palace is elegant without being stuffy, and the chef keeps the innovative menu in flux with seasonal and regionally hunted-and-gathered ingredients. In summer, the terrace with a full-on view of the gardens is the place to sit, while in winter the Sunday roast and goose feasts make reservations de rigueur.

ⓘ Information

Lübbenau Tourist Office (☑ 03542-887 040; www.luebbenau-spreewald.com; Ehm-Welk-Strasse 15; ⊙ 10am-6pm Mon-Fri, to 4pm Sat & Sun)

ⓘ Getting There & Away

Regional trains from central Berlin make the trip to Lübbenau in just over one hour (€11.70).

Brandenburg an der Havel

☑ 03381 / POP 72,150

The pretty town of Brandenburg an der Havel, some 50km west of Berlin, was shaped by water. Set amid a pastoral landscape of lakes, rivers and canals, its historical centre is peppered with stately examples of medieval Gothic red-brick architecture. First settled by Slavs in the 6th century, Brandenburg was a bishopric in the early Middle Ages and the regional capital until the 15th century. Today it's an easy day trip from Berlin or a lovely base for exploring the region by bicycle or boat.

⊙ Sights

Brandenburg is split into three sections – the Neustadt, the Altstadt and the Dominsel – each on its own island in the Havel River.

Dom zu Brandenburg & Museum
CHURCH

(☑ 03381-211 2223; www.dom-brandenburg.de; Burghof 10; ⊙ 10am-5pm Mon-Sat, noon-5pm Sun Apr-Oct, 11am-4pm Mon-Sat, noon-4pm Sun Nov-Mar) FREE On an island in the middle of town, the Dom was founded more than 850 years ago and is predominantly Gothic in style. It's filled with a bevy of treasures, most notably the carved 14th-century Bohemian altar in the south transept, the vaulted painted *Bunte Kapelle* (Coloured Chapel) in the north transept and the medieval stained glass in the choir. The museum has outstanding medieval vestments and a so-called *Hungertuch* (hunger blanket, 1290) with embroidered medallions depicting Jesus' life.

Archäologisches Landesmuseum Brandenburg
MUSEUM

(☑ 03381-410 4112; www.landesmuseum-branden burg.de; Neustädtische Heidestrasse 28; adult/concession €5/3.50; ⊙ 10am-5pm Tue-Sun; P; ⊠ Brandenburg an der Havel) The beautiful Gothic red-brick St Pauli monastery has risen from ruins and now forms an atmospheric backdrop for nine rooms brimming with Brandenburg's archaeological treasures, including rare Stone Age textiles, Bronze Age gold rings, Germanic tools and medieval coins.

⊙ Tours

Fahrgastschiff Havelfee
BOATING

(☑ 03381-522 331; www.fgs-havelfee.de; Heinrich-Heine-Ufer; tours €10-16; ⊙ Apr-Oct) On a sunny day, a lovely way to appreciate Brandenburg's medieval landmarks and watery layout is on a boat tour around the Altstadt or to adjacent lakes.

Boats depart from the Heinrich-Heine-Ufer, just southwest of the Jahrtausendbrücke, in the town centre.

Nordstern Reederei
BOATING

(☑ 017 2311 7868, 03381-226 960; www.nordstern reederei.de; Salzhofufer; tours €10-16; ⊙ Apr-Oct) Nordstern operates one- to 2½-hour boat tours around Brandenburg an der Havel

PARK & SCHLOSS BRANITZ

A highlight of a visit to Cottbus is the Park & Schloss Branitz (☑ 0355-751 50; www.pueckler-museum.de; Robinienweg 5; park free, Schloss adult/concession €6.50/4.50; ☉ 10am-6pm daily Apr-Oct, 11am-4pm Tue-Sun Nov-Mar; ℗; ☐ 10 to Branitz Schloss), which stems from the feverish brow of Prince Hermann von Pückler-Muskau (1785–1871) – aristocrat, writer, ladies' man, eccentric and one of Germany's most formidable garden architects. From 1845 until his death, he turned his bleak ancestral family estate into an arcadian English-style park – shaping hills, moving trees, digging canals and lakes, and building pyramid-shaped tumuli, one of which serves as his burial place.

For an introduction to this brilliant, if kooky, man, swing by the visitors centre in the Gutshof (adult/concession €4.50/3.50; 10am-5pm Apr-Oct), then see how his fascination for the exotic translated into his living space on a spin around the Schloss itself. While the private salons on the ground floor have been restored to their former glory, the Schloss' main draw – the exotic oriental rooms upstairs – will be undergoing a facelift until at least 2019. Once completed they will have exhibits about Pückler's life and achievements as well as a gallery covering the history of the palace. Meanwhile, temporary exhibits are housed in the Marstall (adult/concession €3.50/2.50; 11am-5pm Apr-Sep).

Bus 10 makes the 4km trip from Cottbus train station to the park at least hourly (€1.50, 25 minutes).

from landing docks at Am Salzufer, near the Jahrtausendbrücke (bridge).

🛏 Sleeping

Brandenburg is easily explored on a day trip from Berlin but also has a good assortment of lodging options, from private rooms to fancy hotels with fine-dining restaurants.

Pension zum Birnbaum PENSION €
(☑ 03381-527 50; www.pension-zum-birnbaum.de; Mittelstrasse 1; d incl breakfast €65-70; ℗ ☻ ☎ ☀) A singing host, breakfast under a pear tree and modern, if snug, rooms recommend this little 19th-century inn that places you close to the train station and the Neustadt.

Sorat Hotel Brandenburg HOTEL €€
(☑ 03381-5970; www.sorat-hotels.com/brandenburg; Altstädtischer Markt 1; d from €80; ℗ ☻ ☎ ☀) You'll sleep well in these bright, modern rooms rendered in cheerful reds and yellows and in pretty surrounds right by the town hall. Facilities include bike rentals and a small gym for keeping fit, a pretty good restaurant and a sauna for winding down at the end of the day. Breakfast is €11.

🍴 Eating

With all that water around, fish naturally features big on Brandenburg's menus, especially locally caught pike-perch and trout. Best enjoyed at a lakeside restaurant.

Cafébar im Brückenhäuschen CAFE €
(☑ 03381-229 048; www.cafebar-kanu.de; Ritterstrasse 76; snacks €2.20-6.50; ☉ 8.30am-6.30pm Mon-Fri, from 9.30am Sat & Sun) This kiosk right by the Jahrtausendbrücke is a top address for coffee and homemade cake. In fine weather you can relax canal-side in beach chairs or rent a canoe (per two hours €10, per day €28).

Fisch am Mühlendamm SEAFOOD €
(☑ 03381-211 724; Mühlendamm 1; snacks from €2.20; ☉ 9am-8pm Mon-Fri, 8am-noon Sat) For a quick fish snack, pop into this little shack along Mühlendamm overlooking the water.

Restaurant an der Dominsel GERMAN €€
(☑ 03381-891 807; www.restaurant-dominsel.de; Neustädtische Fischerstrasse 14; mains €15-24; ☉ 11am-midnight) Built around vestiges of the medieval town wall, this restaurant specialises in regional food, especially fish dishes. But what you'll probably remember most are the fabulous Dom views, preferably from the waterfront terrace. It's right by the Mühlentorturm, a handsome red-brick tower that was once part of the medieval fortifications.

ℹ Information

Brandenburg an der Havel Tourist Office
(☑ 03381-796 360; www.stg-brandenburg.de; Neustädtischer Markt 3, St Annen Galerie; ☉ 9am-8pm Mon-Sat year-round, 10am-3pm

Sun May-Sep) Staff can help with maps, information and hotel rooms. It's in the St Annen Galerie shopping centre.

❶ Getting There & Around

Regional trains link Brandenburg twice hourly with all major stations in central Berlin, including the Hauptbahnhof (€6.90, 45 minutes), and with Potsdam (€5.70, 30 minutes).

From the Bahnhof (train station), it's about a 1.2km walk via Geschwister-Scholl-Strasse and St-Annen-Strasse to the Neustädtischer Markt. Trams 2 and 6 will get you there as well in about five minutes.

Free parking is available at the corner of Grillendamm and Krakauer Strasse, just north of the Dom.

Frankfurt (Oder)

📋 0335 / POP 58,000

Germany's 'other' Frankfurt, on the Oder River 90km east of Berlin, was practically wiped off the map in the final days of WWII. It never recovered its one-time grandeur as a medieval trading centre and university town. It didn't help that the city was split in two after the war, with the eastern suburb across the river becoming the Polish town of Słubice. The post-war years produced a decidedly unflattering Stalinist look, but its scenic river setting, a few architectural gems and its proximity to Poland (cheaper vodka and cigarettes, for all you hedonists) make fairly compelling excuses to pop by.

◉ Sights

St Marienkirche   CHURCH
(📋 0335-224 42; www.st-marien-ffo.de; Oberkirchplatz; ☺10am-6pm May-Sep, to 4pm Oct-Apr) Looming above Marktplatz is the crenellated tower of the Church of St Mary, a huge red-brick Gothic hall church. Ruined by war and socialist-era disregard, it now has a proud new roof and fantastic medieval stained-glass windows, some of which have been squirrelled to Russia as war booty after 1945; they were returned to Frankfurt (Oder) in 2002. Today the church building hosts events, concerts and exhibitions.

Kleist-Museum   MUSEUM
(📋 0335-387 2210; www.kleist-museum.de; Faberstrasse 6-7; adult/concession €5/3; ☺10am-6pm Tue-Sun) Heinrich von Kleist, one of Germany's key poets and dramatists of the Romantic Age, was born in Frankfurt (Oder) in 1777. A pilgrimage stop for literature fans, this sensitively curated exhibit in an old garrison school on the river walk chronicles the life, works and importance of the man who committed suicide, along with his lover, at age 34.

For a self-guided walking tour in the footsteps of Kleist, pick up the free *Kleist-Route* pamphlet at the museum or the tourist office, or download it at: www.frankfurt-oder.de/Tourismus/Sehenswürdigkeiten/Kleist-Route.

Brandenburgisches Landesmuseum
für Moderne Kunst   MUSEUM
(📋 0335-2839 6183; www.blmk.de; Marktplatz 1; adult/concession €6/4.20; ☺11am-5pm Tue-Sun) This fusion of two art museums from Frankfurt and Cottbus resulted in this vastly expanded and complementary collection of art created in East Germany, including paintings by Werner Tübke, sculpture by Gustav Seitz and installations by Via Lewandowsky. In Frankfurt, exhibits are presented in two locations: the entrance hall of the Rathaus at Marktplatz 1, and the Packhof at Carl-Philipp-Emanuel-Bach-Strasse 11, about 250m northwest.

🛏️ Sleeping & Eating

Hotel zur Alten Oder   HOTEL €
(📋 0335-556 220; www.zuraltenoder.de; Fischerstrasse 32; d from €59; 🅿🌐🛜; 🚆1 Stadion) No two rooms are exactly alike in this little hotel in a historical building, but all have coral-coloured carpet, tasteful art and big windows. Breakfast costs €9.50 but is a lavish affair that should tide you over until the early afternoon. It's about 1.5km south of the city centre.

Restaurant Turm 24   GERMAN €€
(📋 0335-2301 0024; http://turm24.business.site; Logenstrasse 8; mains €5-30; ☺7am-10pm Mon-Fri, 10am-11pm Sat & Sun) Some locals joke that the best thing about this smart restaurant on the 24th floor of the Oderturm is that you can't see the Oderturm, Frankfurt's tallest building. Perhaps. But the panoramic views from up here are indeed fabulous and the German-Polish food is solid. It's also a good spot for breakfast.

❶ Information

The local **tourist office** (📋 0335-610 0800; www.tourismus-ffo.de; Grosse Oderstrasse 29; ☺10am-6pm Mon-Fri, to 2pm Sat) can provide information about both Frankfurt and Słubice, on the Polish side of the Oder.

ℹ Getting There & Around

Regional trains leave Berlin Hauptbahnhof half-hourly (€10, 1¼ hours). The central Markt-platz is about 1km northeast of the train station.

Chorin & Niederfinow

About 60km northeast of Berlin, the Bio-sphere Reserve Schorfheide-Chorin is one of the largest forest areas in Germany and makes for a peaceful getaway for city dwellers. But the area also delivers a couple of blockbuster attractions worthy of the attention of visitors from further afield: an impressive 1934 ship's lift in Niederfinow and, about a 20km drive northwest, the medieval Chorin monastery that hosts a popular summertime concert series (p118). Seeing the monastery in the morning, then cycling the 8km route over to the ship's lift and back, makes for a nice day trip.

◉ Sights & Activities

Kloster Chorin   HISTORIC SITE
(Chorin Monastery; ☑ 033366-703 77; www.kloster-chorin.org; Amt Chorin 11a; adult/concession €6/3.50; ⊙9am-6pm Apr-Oct, 10am-4pm Nov-Mar; ℙ) A popular day trip from Berlin, this romantically ruined monastery near a little lake and surrounded by a lush park was built by Cistercian monks in the 13th century. It is widely considered one of the finest red-brick Gothic structures in northern Germany. The monastery was secularised in 1542 and fell into disrepair after the Thirty Years' War (1618–48). Today it hosts concerts, theatre performances and festivals.

Schiffshebewerk Niederfinow   MONUMENT
(Ship's Lift; ☑ 033362-215; www.schiffshebewerk-niederfinow.info; Hebewerkstrasse 52; adult/concession €3/2; ⊙9.30am-5.30pm late Apr-Oct, to 4pm Nov, Dec & Mar, closed Jan & Feb) Tiny Niederfinow would be a mere blip on the map were it not for this spectacular historical ship's lift, which links the Oder River and the Oder-Havel Canal. This remarkable feat of engineering was completed in 1934 and measures 60m high, 27m wide and 94m long. Cargo barges (and tourist boats) sail into a sort of giant bath-tub, which is then raised or lowered 36m, water and all.

To accommodate larger and multiple boats, an even more massive modern ship's lift has been taking shape adjacent to the historical one. Operation might start in 2019. The old lift will remain operational for the time being.

Fahrgastschifffahrt Neumann   BOATING
(☑ 03334-244 05; www.schiffshebewerk-niederfinow.info/neumann; Hebewerkstrasse; adult/child €7/4; ⊙11am, 1pm & 3pm late Mar-Oct) This boat company takes passengers 36m up and down the 1934 Niederfinow ship's lift, a technological marvel built to enable cargo boats to travel from the Oder River to the Oder-Havel Canal and vice versa.

🛏 Sleeping & Eating

You'll find a few country inns, pensions and holiday apartments in and around Chorin and Niederfinow. The next sizeable town is Eberswalde. The local tourist office in the Chorin train station can help.

There are adequate restaurants at the Kloster and at the ship's lift. Alternatively, bring a picnic. There's a small shop in the Chorin train station.

ℹ Information

Chorin Tourist Office (☑ 033366-530 053; www.schorfheidechorin.info; Bahnhofstrasse 2)

ℹ Getting There & Around

CHORIN
By train, take the RE3 from Berlin Hauptbahnhof to Bahnhof Chorin (€8.50, 1¼ hours) from where it's a 2km walk along a signed path to the Kloster.

If you're driving, the fastest route from Berlin is via the A11.

Bikes (☑ 033366-537 00; www.fahrradverleih-chorin.de; Bahnhofstrasse 2; 8hrs €9.80; ⊙10am-5pm Mon-Thu, 9am-6pm Fri-Sun Apr-Oct) can be rented at the station.

NIEDERFINOW
To get to the Schiffshebewerk by car, follow the B158 for about 60km. By train, hop on the RE3 (for instance at Berlin Hauptbahnhof), get off at Eberswalde and continue on bus 916. The entire trip takes approximately 90 mintues and costs €6.90.

Hamburg & the North

POP 6.5 MILLION

Best Places to Eat

➡ Das Dorf (p170)

➡ Deichgraf (p169)

➡ Die Bank (p170)

➡ Alt Hamburger Aalspeicher (p169)

➡ Altes Mädchen (p172)

Best Places to Stay

➡ The Westin Hamburg (p167)

➡ Renaissance Hamburg Hotel (p166)

➡ Fairmont Vier Jahrseiten Hamburg (p166)

➡ Hotel Wedina (p167)

➡ Henri Hotel (p166)

Why Go?

Head to Germany's north because you love the water. From the posh pleasures of Sylt in the west, to the fabled Baltic heritage of historic towns like Lübeck, Wismar, Stralsund and Greifswald, you can sense the legacy of the Hanseatic League in beautiful old quarters created with iconic black and red bricks.

Even inland there is water. Mecklenburg's lakes are a maze of places to paddle. But really, most visitors will be happiest right at the edge of the sea. There are beaches everywhere, and while the temperatures aren't tropical, the drama of the sea crashing onto the white sand is irresistible.

Then there's Hamburg, a city with a love of life that ignites its fabled clubs, where proximity to the water has brought the city both wealth and vigour through the centuries. It's well on its way to being one of Europe's coolest cities.

When to Go

Summer seems the obvious time to hit northern Germany but let's be honest, just because it's August it doesn't mean you won't be wrapped up in a blanket on a Baltic beach. So free yourself from bikini-clad fantasies and go to the coast any time to enjoy its beauty.

The best reason to go in summer is for the days that go on and on and on. Sitting outside a Hamburg cafe and enjoying the passing pedestrian parade in daylight at 10pm is one of life's great pleasures.

HAMBURG

040 / POP 1.8 MILLION

When all's said and done, Hamburg's appeal can be narrowed down to one simple calling card: Welcome to one of the coolest cities on earth.

Hamburg's historic label, 'The gateway to the world', might be a bold claim, but Germany's second-largest city and biggest port has never been shy. Hamburg has engaged in business with the world ever since it joined the Hanseatic League back in the Middle Ages. Its role as a centre of international trade in the late 19th and early 20th centuries brought it great wealth (and Unesco World Heritage recognition in 2015), a legacy that continues today: it's one of Germany's wealthiest cities.

Hamburg's maritime spirit infuses the entire city; from architecture to menus to the cry of gulls, you always know you're near the water. The city has given rise to vibrant neighbourhoods awash with multicultural eateries, as well as the gloriously seedy Reeperbahn red-light district. Hamburg nurtured the early promise of the Beatles, and today its distinctive live-music scene thrives in unique harbourside venues.

History

Hamburg's commercial character was forged in 1189, when local noble Count Adolf III persuaded Emperor Friedrich I (Barbarossa) to grant the city free trading rights and an exemption from customs duties. This transformed the former missionary settlement and 9th-century moated fortress of Hammaburg into an important port and member of the Hanseatic League.

The city prospered until 1842, when the Great Fire destroyed a third of its buildings. It joined the German Reich in 1871, but the city was then involved in two devastating world wars. After WWI, most of Hamburg's merchant fleet (almost 1500 ships) was forfeited to the Allies. WWII saw more than half of Hamburg's housing, 80% of its port and 40% of its industry reduced to rubble; tens of thousands of civilians were killed.

In the post-war years, Hamburg harnessed its resilience to participate in Germany's economic miracle *(Wirtschaftswunder)*. Its harbour and media industries are now the backbone of its wealth. The majority of Germany's largest publications are produced here, including news magazines *Stern* and *Der Spiegel*.

Sights

To really see and explore Hamburg, count on spending at least three days prowling its neighbourhoods, waterfront, museums, shops and more.

Altstadt

The centre of old Hamburg is also the hub of the modern city. Largely reconstructed after WWII, the city's ages-old wealth is apparent as you stroll among its most important civic and commercial institutions. In Hanseatic times, this was where you found the rich merchants and their businesses along the canals.

★**Rathaus** HISTORIC BUILDING

(Map p158; 040-428 3124; Rathausmarkt 1; tours adult/under 14yr €5/free; ⊙ tours half-hourly 11am-4pm Mon-Fri, 10am-5pm Sat, to 4pm Sun, English tours depend on demand; Rathausmarkt, Jungfernstieg, Jungfernstieg) With its spectacular coffered ceiling, Hamburg's baroque Rathaus is one of Europe's most opulent, and is renowned for its Emperor's Hall and Great Hall. The 40-minute tours take in only a fraction of this beehive of 647 rooms. A good secret to know about is the inner courtyard, where you can take a break from exploring the Rathaus on comfy chairs with tables.

★**Hamburger Kunsthalle** MUSEUM

(Map p164; 040-428 131 200; www.hamburger-kunsthalle.de; Glockengiesserwall; adult/child €14/free, Thu evening €8/free; ⊙10am-6pm Tue, Wed & Fri-Sun, to 9pm Thu; Hauptbahnhof-Nord) A treasure trove of art from the Renaissance to the present day, the Kunsthalle spans two buildings linked by an underground passage. The main building houses works ranging from medieval portraiture to 20th-century classics, such as Klee and Kokoschka. There's also a memorable room of 19th-century landscapes by Caspar David Friedrich. Its stark white modern cube, the Galerie der Gegenwart, showcases contemporary German artists.

★**Chilehaus** HISTORIC BUILDING

(Map p164; 040-349 194 247; www.chilehaus.de; Fischertwiete 2; Messberg) One of Hamburg's most beautiful buildings is the crowning gem of the new Unesco-anointed Kontorhaus District. The brown-brick 1924 Chilehaus is shaped like an ocean liner, with remarkable curved walls meeting in the shape of a ship's bow and staggered balconies that look

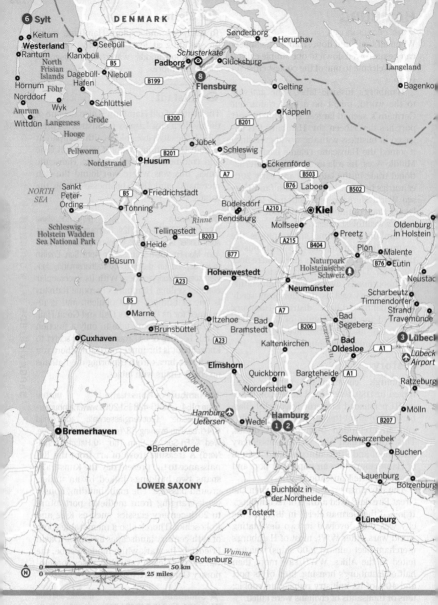

Hamburg & the North

1 **St Pauli** (p173) Having a hard day's night – like the Beatles – no matter what your taste.

2 **Hamburg harbour tour** (p161) Discovering a world of enormous ships and fab city views.

3 **Lübeck** (p182) Wandering through one of Germany's prettiest town centres.

4 **Schwerin** (p197) Cycling past Schwerin's palace and half-timbered buildings, then out around the lakes.

5 **Stralsund** (p211) Climbing to the summit of Marienkirche, marvelling at the Nikolaikirche

then watching penguins at the Ozeaneum.

6 **Sylt** (p195) Finding your own perfect beach, then dining like royalty.

7 **Jasmund National Park** (p217) Gazing out to sea from the dramatic clifftops on Rugen Island.

8 **Flensburg** (p191) Catching the buzz of this city with pretty architecture and rum-soaked history.

9 **Wismar** (p207) Letting your feet decide which way to go amid the highlight-speckled streets.

like decks. It was designed by architect Fritz Höger for a merchant who derived his wealth from trading with Chile. Casual visitors are not really welcome inside, but it's the exterior that you come here to see.

★ Mahnmal St-Nikolai — MEMORIAL

(Memorial St Nicholas; Map p158; ✆040-371 125; www.mahnmal-st-nikolai.de; Willy-Brandt-Strasse 60; adult/child €5/3; ⊙10am-6pm May-Sep, to 5pm Oct-Apr; ⓤRödingsmarkt) St Nikolai church was the world's tallest building from 1874 to 1876, and it remains Hamburg's second-tallest structure (after the TV tower). Mostly destroyed in WWII, it is now called Mahnmal St-Nikolai. You can take a glass lift up to a 76.3m-high viewing platform inside the surviving spire for views of Hamburg's centre, put into context of the wartime destruction. The crypt houses an unflinching underground exhibit on the horrors of war.

Deichstrasse — STREET

(Map p158; ⓤRödingsmarkt) Hamburg's Great Fire of 1842 broke out in Deichstrasse, which features a few restored 18th-century homes, most now housing restaurants. You can get a feel for the old canal and merchants' quarter here, thanks to their mostly historic appearance.

⊙ Neustadt

The Neustadt blends seamlessly with the Altstadt in the posh surrounds of the Binnenalster. The mood is set by the elegant Renaissance-style arcades of the Alsterark-aden (Map p158; off Poststrasse; Ⓢ Jungfernstieg), which shelter upscale shops and cafes alongside the Alsterfleet canal. Further south, the district blends into the heart of the port area.

★ St Michaelis Kirche — CHURCH

(Church of St Michael; Map p158; ✆040-376 780; www.st-michaelis.de; Englische Planke 1; tower adult/child €5/3.50, crypt €4/2.50, combo ticket €7/4, church only €2; ⊙9am-7.30pm May-Oct, 10am-5.30pm Nov-Apr, last entry 30min before closing; ⓤRödingsmarkt) 'Der Michel', as it is affectionately called, is one of Hamburg's most recognisable landmarks and northern Germany's largest Protestant baroque church. Ascending the tower (by steps or lift) rewards visitors with great panoramas across the city and canals. The crypt has an engaging multimedia exhibit on the city's history.

Johannes Brahms Museum — MUSEUM

(Map p158; ✆040-4191 3086; www.brahms-hamburg.de; Peterstrasse 39; adult/child €5/free, combined ticket with Komponisten-Quartier €7; ⊙10am-5pm Tue-Sun; ⓤSt Pauli, Ⓢ Stadthausbrücke) Master composer Johannes Brahms (1833-1897) was born in Hamburg. Although the house where he was born was destroyed in 1943, this fine 18th-century building is an excellent substitute. All manner of original Brahms memorabilia is on display and there's a CD library with all of Brahms' works.

Krameramtswohnungen — HISTORIC BUILDING

(Map p158; Krayenkamp 10; Ⓢ Stadthausbrücke) In an alley off Krayenkamp 10 are the

---

ℹ DISCOUNT HAMBURG

There are a handful of programs that allow you to cut costs while in Hamburg, although as always with such schemes you need to visit lots of places in a short time to make them worthwhile. Options include:

Hamburg Card (www.hamburg-travel.com/search-book/hamburg-card; 1 day €10.50) Offers discounts on entry to museums, theatre tickets and harbour tours, and free public transport (including harbour ferries). You'll need to plan well and read what's covered carefully to make it worthwhile. Purchase online or at any tourist office.

Hamburg City Pass (✆040-8788 098 50; www.turbopass.de; 1 day €39.90) Includes entry to most Hamburg museums and covers free public transport, a free harbour tour and free bus sightseeing. You'll need to keep moving to make it worthwhile, but it's generally a good deal. The pass can be bought online.

Kunstmeile Hamburg (Museum Mile; ✆040-428 134 110; www.kunstmeile-hamburg. de; 3-day pass adult/child €25/free, 1-year pass €36/free) Five of Hamburg's art museums offer a joint admission ticket that can provide great savings. Buy it at the museums. The standard version lasts for 12 months, but the cheaper three-day version is great value; the latter must be used over consecutive days.

Krameramtswohnungen, a row of tiny half-timbered houses from the 17th century that, for nearly 200 years, were almshouses for the widows of members of the Guild of Small Shopkeepers. Today they house shops and restaurants, plus a little summer-only museum relating to the buildings.

◉ St Georg

St Georg, with all its character and contradictions, is Hamburg in microcosm. Along its main thoroughfare, Lange Reihe, you'll find fab restaurants, bars and a real buzz, much of which comes from the city's vibrant gay community which loves St Georg. In the neighbourhood's southern end, it's notably seedier. And everywhere you look, Hamburg's increasingly multicultural population is changing the face of St Georg. There aren't that many static attractions to bring you here, but it's an essential place to come if you want to understand the city.

Museum für Kunst und Gewerbe   MUSEUM
(Museum for Art & Trade; Map p164; ☏040-428 542 732; www.mkg-hamburg.de; Steintorplatz 1; adult/child €12/free, after 5pm Thu €10; ☉10am-6pm Tue-Sun, to 9pm Thu; Ⓤ Hauptbahnhof-Süd) The Museum für Kunst und Gewerbe is lots of fun. Its vast collection of sculpture, furniture, fashion, jewellery, posters, porcelain, musical instruments and household objects runs the gamut from Italian to Islamic, Japanese to Viennese and medieval to pop art, and includes an art-nouveau salon from the 1900 Paris World Fair. The museum cafe is part of the exhibition space.

◉ Speicherstadt & HafenCity

Welcome to Hamburg's waterfront. The seven-storey red-brick warehouses lining the Speicherstadt archipelago are a famous Hamburg symbol and they're increasingly filled with fine museums. HafenCity, crowned by the superlative Elbphilharmonie, is Hamburg's most architecturally dynamic corner, with a world seemingly being created before your eyes. This vast new quarter, when fully completed, will transform the city. Then again, it already has.

★ Elbphilharmonie   ARTS CENTRE
(Elbe Philharmonic Hall; Map p158; ☏040-3576 6666; www.elbphilharmonie.de; Platz der Deutschen Einheit 4; ☉9am-11.30pm; Ⓢ Baumwall) FREE Welcome to one of the most Europe's most

SIGHTSEEING LIKE A REAL HAMBURGER

This maritime city offers a bewildering array of boat trips, but locals will tell you that you don't have to book a cruise to see the port – the city's harbour ferries will take you up the river on a regular public transport ticket, and you can avoid hokey narration!

One recommended route is to catch ferry route 62 from Landungsbrücken to Finkenwerder, then change for the 64 to Teufelsbrücke. From Teufelsbrücke, you can wander along the Elbe eastwards to Neumühlen, from where you can catch bus 112 back to the Altona S-Bahn station or ferry 62 back to Landungsbrücken.

On land, the U3 U-Bahn line is particularly scenic, especially the elevated track between the St Pauli and Rathaus U-Bahn stations.

exciting recent architectural creations. A squat brown-brick former warehouse at the far west of HafenCity was the base for the architecturally bold Elbphilharmonie, a major concert hall and performance space, not to mention architectural icon. Pritzker Prize-winning Swiss architects Herzog & de Meuron were responsible for the design, which captivates with details like 1096 individually curved glass panes.

Enter via Europe's longest (and really rather beautiful) escalator up to the Plaza, from where you can emerge onto the wrap-around balcony for terrific city and harbour views in all directions. And make sure you return for a live performance (p175).

★ Miniatur Wunderland   MUSEUM
(Map p158; ☏040-300 6800; www.miniatur-wunderland.de; Kehrwieder 2; adult/child €15/7.50; ☉hours vary; Ⓤ Baumwall) Even the worst cynics are quickly transformed into fans of this vast miniature world that goes on and on. The model trains wending their way through the Alps are impressive, but slightly predictable. But when you see a model A380 swoop out of the sky and land at the fully functional model of Hamburg's airport, you can't help but gasp! On weekends and in summer holidays, pre-purchase your ticket online to skip the queues.

Central Hamburg

Langenfelder Str

Sternschanze

Sternschanzenpark

Sternschanze

Altonaer Str

32

Sternschanze

41

Max-Brauer-Allee

58

Lagerstr

Rentzelstr

Susannenstr

Bartelsstr

Kampstr

Schanzenstr

Schulterblatt

SCHANZENVIERTEL

Stresemannstr

36

Lippmannstr

Bernstorffstr

Vorwerkstr

Grabenstr

Wohlers Allee

Sternstr

Beckstr

SCHANZENVIERTEL

Marktstr

Glashüttenstr

Karolinenstr

Marktstr

Messehallen

Neuer
Pferdemarkt

72

Intervention

Thadenstr

Neuer Kamp

Feldstrasse

Feldstr

Neuer
Pferdemarkt

20

HEILIGENGEISTFELD

51

Gilbertstr

67

Grosse
Wallanlagen

Paul-Roosen-Str

Holstenstr

54

Annenstr

Budapester Str

Clemens-Schultz-Str

Louise-
Schroeder-Str

17

65

70

Glacischaussee

Peterstr

57

Rendsburgerstr

Talstr

Simon-von-Utrecht-Str

66

Grosse Freiheit

29

Millerntorplatz

St Pauli

Holstenwall

33

Hütten

14

Seilerstr

St Pauli
Nachtmarkt

22

Reeperbahn

61

26

63

7

16

Helgoländer Allee

Reeperbahn

Hans-
Albers-
Platz

62

Gerhardstr

Davidstr

Spielbudenplatz

9

Reeperbahn

ST PAULI

28

Zirkusweg

Hein
Köllisch
Platz

Baldunstr

Erichstr

59

Kastanienallee

Hopfenstr

Böhmkenstr

Friedrichstr

30

Seewartenstr

Elbpark

34

Venusberg

Bernhard-Nocht-Str

St-Pauli-Hafenstr

Port
Area

Landungsbrücken

46

55

St-Pauli-Fischmarkt

45

Tourist
Information
am Hafen

18

Ditmar-Koel-Str

2

Fischmarkt

24

Rambachstr

Elbe
River

St Pauli
Harbour

Johannisbollwerk

Vorsetzen

St Pauli Elbtunnel

Norderelbstr

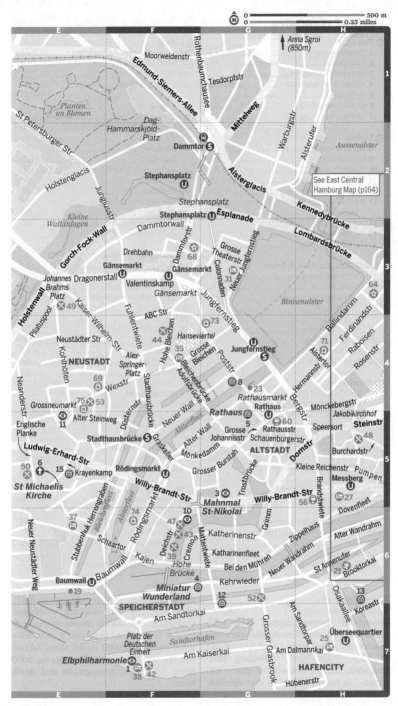

N 0 _____ 500 m
0 _____ 0.25 miles

↑ Anna Sgroi (850m)

Moorweidenstr
Rothenbaumchaussee
Tesdorpfstr
Edmund-Siemers-Allee
Mittelweg
Warburgstr
Alsteruferstr

Planten un Blomen

St Petersburger Str

Dag-Hammarskjöld-Platz
Dammtor S
Aussenalster

Holstenglacis
Jungiusstr
Stephansplatz U
Alsterglacis
Kennedybrücke

See East Central Hamburg Map (p164)

Kleine Wallanlagen
Stephansplatz
Stephansplatz U
Esplanade
Lombardsbrücke

Gorch-Fock-Wall
Dammtorwall
Grosse Theaterstr
Neuer Jungfernstieg

Drehbahn
Dammtorstr
68
Colonnaden
Binnenalster
64

Johannes Dragonerstall
Gänsemarkt U
Gänsemarkt
Valentinskamp
Gänsemarkt
Jungfernstieg
Holstenwall
Brahms Platz
Kaiser-Wilhelm-Str
ABC Str
73
Neuer Jungfernstieg
Ballindamm
Ferdinandstr

49
Fuhlentwiete
Hanseviertel
44
Hohe Bleichen
35
Grosse Bleichen
Poststr
Jungfernstieg U S
71
Alstertor
Hermannstr
Raboisen
Rosenstr

Neustädter Str
NEUSTADT
Alex-Springer-Platz
Bleichenbrücke
Adolfsbrücke
8
23
Hermannstr
Mönckebergstr
Jakobikirchhof
Steinstr

Kohlhöfen
69
Wexstr
Stadthausbrücke
Alsterfleet
Rathausmarkt
Rathaus
Rathaus
60
Speersort
48

Grossneumarkt
75
53
Neuer Wall
5
Rathausstr
Bergstr
Burchardstr

11
Alter Steinweg
Düsternstr
Alter Wall
Grosse Johannisstr
Schauenburgerstr
ALTSTADT
Domstr
Kleine Reichenstr
Pumpen

Englische Planke
Stadthausbrücke S
Mönkedamm
Messberg U
27
Dovenfleet

Ludwig-Erhard-Str
Rödingsmarkt U
Grosser Burstah
Trostbrücke
Willy-Brandt-Str
56
Brandstwiete
Alter Wandrahm

50
6
15
Krayenkamp
Willy-Brandt-Str
3
10
Mahnmal St-Nikolai
Grimm
Zippelhaus
Neuer Wandrahm
St Annenufer
21
Brooktorkai

St Michaelis Kirche
37
Stubbenhuk Herrengraben
74
47
43
Katherinenstr
Katharinenfleet
Bei den Mühren

Neuer Neustädter Weg
Schaartor
Deichstr
39
Hohe Brücke
4
Kehrwieder
13
Koreastr

Baumwall U
Baumwall
Kajen
Cremon
Mattentwiete
12
52
Miniatur Wunderland
SPEICHERSTADT
Am Sandtorkai
Osakaallee

19
Am Sandtorpark
25
Überseequartier U

Platz der Deutschen Einheit
Sandtorhafen
Am Kaiserkai
Grosser Grasbrook
Am Dalmannkai
HAFENCITY

Elbphilharmonie
1
38
42
Hübenerstr

Central Hamburg

Internationales Maritimes Museum MUSEUM
(International Maritime Museum; Map p158; ☎040-428 1310; www.internationales-maritimes-museum.de; Koreastrasse 1; adult/concession €13/9.50; ☉10am-6pm; ⓤMessberg, Überseequartier) Hamburg's maritime past – and future – is fully explored in this excellent private museum that sprawls over 10 floors of a revamped brick shipping warehouse. Considered the world's largest private collection of maritime treasures, it includes a mind-boggling 26,000 model ships, 50,000 construction plans, 5000 illustrations, 2000 films, 1.5 million photographs and much more.

HafenCity InfoCenter | MUSEUM

(Map p158; ☑040-3690 1799; www.hafencity.com; Am Sandtorkai 30; ⏰10am-6pm Tue-Sun; ⓊMessberg, Baumwall, Überseequartier) 🆓You can pick up brochures and check out detailed architectural models and installations that give a sense of the immensity of the project; there's a scale model of the whole city. The centre offers a program of free guided tours through the evolving district; check the website for more information and timings.

◉ St Pauli & Reeperbahn

St Pauli has soul. Without it, Hamburg would be just another beautiful European city. But the energy, creativity and, yes, even the vices of this perennial *enfant terrible* transform Hamburg daily into one of the continent's coolest cities. On a wet weekday morning, St Pauli is like a sad, ageing burlesque dancer with her make-up running after a hard night. When a party or market takes over Spielbundenplatz on a sunny day, however, there are few finer places to be. And explore St Pauli at night and you may never want to leave.

★**Fischmarkt** | MARKET

(Map p158; Grosse Elbstrasse 9; ⏰5am-9.30am Sun Apr-Oct, from 7am Nov-Mar; 🚌112 to Fischmarkt, ⑤Reeperbahn) Here's the perfect excuse to stay up all Saturday night. Every Sunday in the wee hours, some 70,000 locals and visitors descend upon the famous Fischmarkt in St Pauli. The market has been running since 1703, and its undisputed stars are the boisterous *Marktschreier* (market criers) who hawk their wares at full volume. Live bands also entertainingly crank out cover versions of ancient German pop songs in the adjoining Fischauktionshalle (Fish Auction Hall).

Davidwache | NOTABLE BUILDING

(Map p158; Spielbudenplatz 31, cnr Davidstrasse; ⑤Reeperbahn, ⓊSt Pauli) South of the Reeperbahn stands the star of many a German crime film and TV show, the Davidwache. This brick police station, festooned with ornate ceramic tiles, is the base for 150 officers, who keep the lurid surrounds reasonably tame. Its presence here is a reminder that while St Pauli loves to thumb its nose at authority, it needs that authority to define itself...

★**St Pauli Nachtmarkt** | MARKET

(Map p158; Spielbudenplatz; ⏰4-11pm Wed Apr-Sep, to 10pm Oct-Mar) Wednesday late afternoon and evening is a terrific time to be in St Pauli when the weekly night market takes over Spielbudenplatz with food stalls, live bands (usually around 6pm or 7pm) and plenty of comfy chairs to knock back a beer.

◉ Altona & Elbmeile

Definitely one of the coolest corners of in the city, Altona is many visitors' favourite neighbourhood. Its gentrified village-like feel in places is endlessly appealing, a quiet world of stylish, sometimes quirky, attractions that include terrific restaurants, drinking holes and all kinds of shops. It's at its best west of the S-Bahn and train stations. Down the hill and down by the water, a string of restaurants stretch along the Elbmeile, along with bars, cafes and a modern architectural icon.

★**Altonaer Balkon** | VIEWPOINT

(Altona Balcony; Map p162; off Klopstockstrasse; ⑤Königstrasse) Thrill to some of Hamburg's best harbour views from this accurately named and quite pretty park.

Dockland | ARCHITECTURE

(Map p162; Van-der-Smissen-Strasse 9; 🚌112, ⑤Königstrasse) One of Hamburg's more striking waterfront structures and right on the water, Dockland was finished in 2006; it has wonderfully sharp angles and terrific views from the rooftop terrace. At first glance, it resembles a cruise ship moored at the docks.

☞ Tours

Boat Tours

For port tours, it's easiest to just go to Landungsbrücken and pick a boat that's leaving when you want. You can also float past elegant buildings aboard an Alster Lakes cruise. Possibilities include:

Abicht | BOATING

(Map p158; ☑040-317 8220; www.abicht.de; Brücke 1; 1hr tour adult/child €20/10; ⏰noon Apr-Oct; ⓊLandungsbrücken, ⑤Landungsbrücken) This company's harbour tours are rightly popular; it also offers Saturday-evening tours taking you past the illuminated warehouses (departure times vary according to tides).

Western Hamburg

Western Hamburg

Barkassen-Centrale Ehlers   BOATING
(Map p158; ☎ 040-319 916 170; www.barkassen-centrale.de; Vorsetzen-Angleger; tours from adult/child €20/10; Ⓤ Baumwall) Offers the usual one-hour harbour tour, but also runs a fascinating two-hour tour of the harbour, as well as canal tours and specialised trips in historic boats.

Hadag   BOATING
(Map p158; ☎ 040-311 7070; www.hadag.de; Brücke 2; 1hr harbour tour adult/child from €18/9; ☺ daily Apr-Sep, Sat & Sun Oct-Mar; Ⓤ Landungsbrücken, Ⓢ Landungsbrücken) Harbour tours plus more adventuresome trips to the Lower Elbe (April to September). Also offers a hop-on, hop-off service along the Elbe.

Maritime Circle Line   BOATING
(Map p158; ☎ 040-2849 3963; www.maritime-circle-line.de; Landungsbrücken 10, Jetty 10; adult/child €16/8; Ⓤ Landungsbrücken, Ⓢ Landungsbrücken) Harbour shuttle service connecting

Hamburg's maritime cultural attractions, including the **Auswanderermuseum Ballin Stadt** (Emigration Museum; ☎040-3197 9160; www.ballinstadt.de; Veddeler Bogen 2; adult/child €13/7; ◷10am-6pm Apr-Oct, to 4.30pm Nov-Mar; ⓇVeddel) and Miniatur Wunderland (p157). The entire loop takes around 95 minutes; you can hop on or off at any of its stops.

HafenCity Riverbus   BOATING
(Map p158; ☎040-7675 7500; www.hafencity riverbus.de; Brooktorkai 16, Block 5; adult/child €29.50/20.50; ◷every 90 min from 10am Feb-Dec, last departures vary; ⓊMessberg) Now here's something a little different – a 70-minute tour of the city in an amphibious bus, with 40 minutes spent on land and 30 minutes on the Elbe river. Commentary is German only.

Bus Tours
Hamburg's numerous bus tour companies offer identical fixed prices and at times mediocre service.

There are four tour routes:

Route A The most popular, it gives a good overview of Hamburg. You can hop on and hop off the buses of the various companies using the same ticket.

Route B This tour visits far-flung maritime sights, but uses motorways for part of the route and interesting vistas can fly past.

Routes C & D Variations on Route A.

On the tours:

➡ On sunny days, look for buses with open tops. Some drivers refuse to open the tops, creating rolling saunas.

➡ English narration *may* be provided, despite promises otherwise. Check before you board.

➡ Don't expect route maps.

➡ Complete route loops take about 90 minutes.

➡ Most tours stop at both Landungsbrücken and the Hauptbahnhof (Kirchenallee exit).

➡ Buy tickets on board.

Walking Tours
Dozens of walking tours operate throughout the city, many with specific themes, such as culinary tours, red-light district tours and more. Tourist offices have full details.

Abenteuer Hamburg   WALKING
(Map p158; ☎040-7566 3399; www.abenteuer-hamburg.com; Simon-von-Utrecht-Strasse 1; ⓈReeperbahn) A number of tours are on offer here, but the one that really gets under the surface of St Pauli is the adults-only 'Sex & Crime' tour (€23), which takes you through the sex and sleaze of the neighbourhood with plenty of humour and anecdotes along the way.

HAMBURG'S NEIGHBOURHOODS

Hamburg is as watery as Venice and Amsterdam. Set around two lakes, the Binnenalster and Aussenalster (Inner and Outer Alster Lakes), in the city centre, it's also traversed by three rivers – the Elbe, the Alster and the Bille – and a grid of narrow canals called *Fleete*.

The half-moon-shaped city centre arches north of the Elbe and is bisected diagonally by the Alsterfleet, the canal that once separated the now almost-seamless Altstadt (old town) and Neustadt (new town).

Within the sprawling city are distinct neighbourhoods, which include:

Altstadt The biggest churches, museums and department stores.

Neustadt Leafier and less office-filled than the Altstadt, although still very much part of the centre.

St Georg East of the Hauptbahnhof; gentrified in parts and also accented with Balkan, Middle Eastern and African flavours, it's the hub of Hamburg's gay scene.

Speicherstadt & HafenCity The former is an atmospheric restored warehouse district with interesting attractions, the latter is a new city being built from scratch.

St Pauli & Reeperbahn Includes the notorious Reeperbahn strip of sin and frolic, plus leafier quarters and port area views. In the north, it includes Schanzenviertel and Karolinenviertel, home to old hippies, young goths and Hamburg's most creative and alternative scene.

Altona & Elbmeile The former is gentrified and merges with the waterfront of the latter. The family-filled neighbourhood of Ottensen abuts on the west.

Beatles Tour
WALKING

(Map p158; ☎040-3003 3790; www.hempels-musictour.com; tour €28; ⊗6pm Sat Apr-Nov; ⓤFeldstrasse) For an entertaining look at the Beatles in Hamburg, try this Beatles tour offered by the fun-filled and engaging Stephanie Hempel. It starts from the Subway Station Feldstrasse and includes museum entry and a small concert.

Hamburg Touren
WALKING

(Map p158; ☎040-3863 3997; www.hamburg-erlebniswelt.de; tours €15-30; ⓤSt Pauli) This dynamic company organises tours to the Elbphilharmonie, but it's like a decoy for their mischievous side, namely their 'St Pauli by Night' (€24.90) and 'Sex, Drugs & Currywurst' (€29.90) tours. The latter tours last two hours and leave at 8pm from the entrance to the St Pauli U-Bahn station. Advance bookings recommended.

Hamburg Walks
WALKING

(Map p158; www.hamburgwalks.de; Schleusen-brücke 1; adult/concession €14/12; ⊗10.30am Mon, Wed & Fri-Sun; ⓢRathaus, Jungfernstieg) These well-run tours cover most of the city centre in three hours, with plenty of historical detail and local stories.

East Central Hamburg

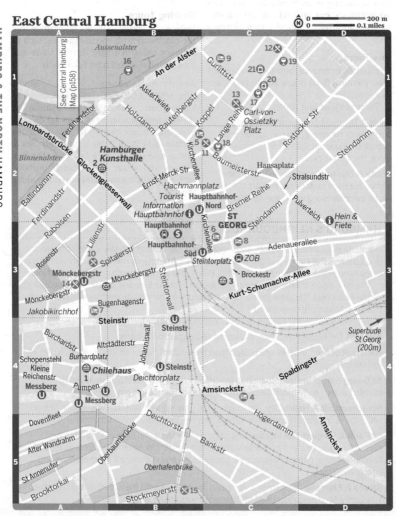

Robin & the Tour Guides   WALKING
(☑040-2320 5049; www.robinandthetourguides.
de; €0-36) Free, two-hour tours covering the
'Historic City Centre' run daily at 11am (a tip
is expected) in English, German and Spanish. They also have a 'Hamburg Craft Beer
Tasting Tour' and a 'St Pauli, Reeperbahn
and Harbour Tour'.

**Sandemans
New Hamburg**   WALKING
(www.neweuropetours.eu; by donation up to €12;
⊙11am & 2pm daily) These highly regarded
free city tours begin at Rathausplatz and
explore most of downtown Hamburg's attractions over the course of three hours.
These guides work hard and if you enjoy
the tour, a tip is expected. They also run
tours of St Pauli (€12, 7pm) that leave from
the Clock Tower, and a popular Hamburg
Pub Crawl (€12, 9.30pm) that starts in Beatles Platz, Reeperbahn.

🎎 Festivals & Events

Hafengeburtstag   CULTURAL
(Harbour Birthday; www.hamburg.de/hafengeburts
tag; ⊙early May) The city's biggest annual
event is this three-day gala. It commemorates Emperor Barbarossa granting Hamburg customs exemption and is energetically
celebrated with harbourside concerts, funfairs and gallons of beer. Lots of fun.

Schlagermove   PARADE
(www.schlagermove.de; ⊙mid-Jul) St Pauli is
taken over by a typically extravagant street
parade. Everyone dresses up in a rather fun
1970s fashion to celebrate German-language
disco pop songs. It takes places across the

neighbourhood from the port area to the
Reeperbahn. As you can imagine, the party
spills over into the bars and nightclubs...

Reeperbahn Festival   MUSIC
(www.reeperbahnfestival.com; ⊙Sep) This happening live-music celebration covers every
musical genre imaginable and fills St Pauli's
venues (from seedy nightclubs to churches!) with crowds and quality performances. In 2018, some events were even held in
the newly minted Elbphilharmonie (p157).
Download the festival app to help make
sense of it all.

Hamburger Dom   CARNIVAL
(www.hamburg.de/dom; Heiligengeistfeld; ⊙Mar,
Jul & Nov; Ⓤ Feldstrasse) Established in 1329,
the month-long Hamburger Dom is held
three times a year and is one of Europe's
largest and oldest funfairs. This colourful
carnival takes place on Heiligengeistfeld,
between St Pauli and Schanzenviertel.

MS Dockville   MUSIC
(www.msdockville.de/festival; ⊙mid-Aug) This
wild music festival takes over Wilhelmsburg on the south bank of the Elbe in
with a heady mix of more than a hundred
well-known and up-and-coming musicians
from Germany and further afield. Works by
emerging artists are also exhibited.

Christmas Markets   CHRISTMAS MARKET
From late November, numerous Christmas
markets spring up all over the city. It's difficult to miss them, with examples on the
Jungfernstieg waterfront, Altstadt, Hamburg and St Pauli.

HAMBURG & THE NORTH HAMBURG

East Central Hamburg

🛏 Sleeping

Hamburg has excellent hotels, and standards are generally high across all budgets; even basic accommodation will likely be clean and comfortable. Reservations are a good idea between June and September, and around major public holidays and festivals. The city is big, and although it's easy to get from one area to another, consider where you'll be spending most of your time before you decide where to stay.

🛏 Altstadt

There are better places to stay in Hamburg than in the Altstadt. That's not because of the location – you couldn't be more central. Rather, although there are two notable exceptions, you'll generally pay above the odds for being in the centre, and the ratio of price to quality is not as good as you'll find elsewhere.

★ Adina Apartment
Hotel Speicherstadt　　　APARTMENT €€
(Map p158; ☑040-334 6080; www.adinahotels. com/hotel/hamburg-speicherstadt; Willy-Brandt-Strasse 25; r from €144; P ❄ 🐶 🏊; ⓤ Messberg) An excellent addition to the Adina portfolio, this sophisticated place ticks all the boxes when it comes to location (within easy walking distance to most attractions), price (much more reasonable than many Hamburg apartment hotels) and comfort (the studio rooms are large, stylish and exceptionally soundproof). The swimming pool, gym and sauna are all nice touches. Multinight stays attract discounts.

★ Henri Hotel　　　　　　　HOTEL €€
(Map p164; ☑040-554 357 557; www.henri-hotel. com; Bugenhagenstrasse 21; s/d from €98/118; 🐶; ⓢ Mönckebergstrasse) Kidney-shaped tables, plush armchairs, vintage typewriters – the Henri channels the 1950s so successfully that you half expect to run into Don Draper. Its 65 rooms and studios are a good fit for urban lifestyle junkies who like the alchemy of modern comforts and retro design. For more elbow room get an L-sized room with a king-size bed.

🛏 Neustadt

In keeping with its upscale atmosphere, distinguished architecture and high-end shops, Neustadt is very much a magnet for top-end travellers – the neighbourhood is home to some of the city's most luxurious hotels. Midrange options are limited, and what's here tends to be in Neustadt's outer reaches, away from the water and high-end shopping district. Budget options are non-existent.

★ Hotel Motel One
Hamburg am Michel　　　　HOTEL €€
(Map p158; ☑040-3571 8900; www.motel-one. com; Ludwig-Erhard-Strasse 26; r from €79; 🐶; ⓤ St Pauli) Part of an excellent chain of 'Budget Design' hotels, the Hamburg Am Michel is proof that you don't need to pay over the odds to appreciate style and comfort. The rooms and public areas put many much pricier hotels to shame and the ambience is casual but professional.

★ Renaissance
Hamburg Hotel　　　　　　HOTEL €€€
(Map p158; ☑040-349 180; www.marriott.com; Grosse Bleichen; s/d from €159/179; ❄ 🐶 🏊; ⓤ Jungfernstieg, ⓢ Jungfernstieg) Part of the upscale Marriott chain, and very much in keeping with Neustadt's refined sense of sophistication, the Renaissance is a terrific deal. It inhabits an early-20th-century building, but the rooms are at once supremely comfortable and stylish, with a cool and contemporary colour scheme. Service is impeccable.

★ The Madison Hotel　　　　HOTEL €€€
(Map p158; ☑040-376 660; www.madison hotel.de; Schaarsteinweg 4; s/d €159/179; ❄ @ 🐶; ⓤ Baumwall) The handsome four-star Madison is wonderfully located close to the water, and the spacious rooms, which range from studios to suites and apartments, sparkle with style and high levels of comfort. A more personal touch also makes this place stand out.

★ Fairmont Vier
Jahrseiten Hamburg　　HISTORIC HOTEL €€€
(Map p158; ☑040-3494 3151; www.hvj.de; Neuer Jungfernstieg 9-14; r from €285; ❄ 🐶 🏊; ⓤ Stephansplatz) This five-star hotel overlooking the waters of Binnenalster opened in 1897 and retains an air of the grand old European hotels of the past. Rooms are gorgeous and stately, furnished in a classic style but with a pervasive sense of light and space. Rooms overlooking the water are magnificent, and there's an on-site spa and fitness centre.

🛏 St Georg

Convenient to the Hauptbahnhof, St Georg is ripe with midrange hotels as well as a few budget choices, some much better than others. Without a booking, be ready to leave your bag in a locker and compare a few. Note that the area around the Steindamm and Hansaplatz can be seedy, but it's also close to the Hauptbahnhof. Further north, closer to the water and Lange Reihe, it all goes a little upmarket, both in price and atmosphere. There are also a couple of hostels just outside the neighbourhood boundary worth considering: **A&O Hamburg Hauptbahnhof** (Map p164; ☑030-809 475 110; www. aohostels.com; Amsinckstrasse 10; dm/s/d from €23/60/70; P ⊖ @ ☎; U Steinstrasse) and Superbude St Georg.

Alpha Hotel-Pension   PENSION €
(Mapp164;☑040-245365;www.alphahotel.biz;Koppel 4-6; s/d from €44/55; ⊖ ☎; U Hauptbahnhof-Nord) An excellent choice only 300m from the Hauptbahnhof. The 21 rooms here are basic but comfortable. The reception staff are especially warm and helpful. If it's your first visit to Hamburg, your every question will be answered with aplomb. Some rooms share baths, others have access to a tiny rooftop playground.

Superbude St Georg   HOSTEL €
(☑040-380 8780; www.superbude.de/hostel-hamburg/st-georg; Spaldingstrasse 152; r from €68; ☎) A short walk southwest of St Georg, this fun, colourful hostel has hotel-standard rooms with splashes of colour; it's worth paying a little extra for the more spacious 'Plus' rooms. Staff are plugged in to Hamburg's multifarious attractions.

Generator Hostels   HOSTEL €
(Map p164; ☑040-226 358 460; www.generator hostels.com; Steintorplatz 3; dm/d from €16/64; ☎; U Hauptbahnhof-Süd) One of Hamburg's best hostels, the Generator has modern rooms within sight of the Hauptbahnhof. With parquetry floors, a commitment to cleanliness and savvy staff, it's a great deal and easily the best for budget travellers in this part of town.

Hotel Village   HOTEL €€
(Map p164; ☑040-480 6490; www.hotel-village.de; Steindamm 4; r from €50-195; @ ☎; U Hauptbahnhof-Süd) You can tell this edgy gem was once a bordello: the 20 boudoirs feature various kitsch mixes of red velvet, gold flock wallpaper and leopard prints, and several have huge mirrors above the bed. It attracts a mix of gay and straight guests. Economy rooms have bathrooms outside the room.

★ Hotel Wedina   HOTEL €€€
(Map p164; ☑040-280 8900; www.hotelwedina. de; Gurlittstrasse 23; r €125-275; P @ ☎; S Hauptbahnhof) Margaret Atwood, Jonathan Franzen and Martin Walser are among the literary greats who've stayed at this loveable lair. Rooms are spread over five brightly pigmented buildings that in different ways express the owners' love for literature, architecture and art. It's close to the train station and the Alster lakes. The breakfasts are especially good.

🛏 Speicherstadt & HafenCity

There still aren't that many hotels in this corner of Hamburg, and there's nothing for budget travellers. As HafenCity's development continues apace, expect more hotels, especially in the top-end category, to arrive. The three hotels that have already set up shop are excellent.

25hours Hotel HafenCity   HOTEL €€
(Map p158; ☑040-257 7770; www.25hours-hotel. de; Überseeallee 5; r €100-225; P ⊖ ☎; U Überseequartier) Offbeat decor, an infectious irreverence and postmodern vintage flair make this pad a top choice among global nomads. Sporting maritime flourishes, the decor channels an old-timey seaman's club in the lobby, the excellent restaurant and the 170 cabin-style rooms. Enjoy views of the emerging HafenCity neighbourhood from the rooftop sauna.

★ The Westin Hamburg   HOTEL €€€
(Map p158; ☑040-800 0100; www.westin hamburg.com; Platz der Deutschen Einheit 2; r with atrium/city view from €225/275; P ☎ ≋; U Baumwall) This has to be Hamburg's premier address, inside the lower half of the daring new Elbphilharmonie. It's *definitely* worth paying extra for a room with a city or harbour view, especially one on the upper floor (ask when you book) – if you do, you may never wish to leave your room. Rooms are stylish, minimalist and the service is professional.

🛏 St Pauli & Reeperbahn

St Pauli offers greatly divergent accommodation: wild near the Reeperbahn, leafy in its genteel neighbourhoods and flashy on its knoll overlooking the bright lights of the city and harbour. Edgy neighbourhoods deserve edgy – yet restful – rooms, which you'll find here. There are also some good hostels serving budget travellers.

Jugendherberge Hamburg HOSTEL €

(Map p158; ☑ 040-570 1590; www.jugendher berge.de; Alfred-Wegener-Weg 5; dm €22-28, d/tr €79/99; ☎; S Landungsbrücken, U Landungs-brücken) This busy and well-run youth hostel is a terrific deal, with tidy rooms (some of the dorms have harbour views!) and a hand-ful of bars where you can hook up with other travellers.

A&O Hamburg Reeperbahn HOSTEL €

(Map p158; ☑ 040-3176 9994 600; www.aohostels. com; Reeperbahn 154; dm/s/d from €18/49/61; ☎; S Reeperbahn) In the heart of Reeperbahn, with all its clamour, energy and sleaze, A&O Hamburg Reeperbahn is something of an oasis – clean, modern and quieter than you might expect given the location.

Arcotel Onyx Hamburg HOTEL €€

(Map p158; ☑ 040-209 4090; www.arcotelhotels. com; Reeperbahn 1a; r/ste €152/242; ✳@☎; U St Pauli) Rooms here are zany (some suites have circular beds) and contemporary, with bright colours and high levels of comfort. There's a restaurant on site, and you're on the cusp of the Reeperbahn with none of the sleaziness.

East HOTEL €€

(Map p158; ☑ 040-309 933; www.east-hamburg.de; Simon-von-Utrecht-Strasse 31; r €100-225; ✳@☎; U St Pauli) In an old iron foundry, East's bold and dramatic design never fails to impress. The walls, lamps and huge pillars of this hotel's public areas emulate organic forms – droplets, flowers, trees – giving it a warm, rich and enveloping feel. Rooms come with handmade furniture and are accented with tactile fabrics and leather. It's on a cool St Pauli street.

Empire Riverside HOTEL €€€

(Map p158; ☑ 040-311 190; www.empire-river side.de; Bernhard-Nocht-Strasse 97; r €130-210, ste from €239; P✳☎; U St Pauli) Sparing splashes of colour brighten the restaurant, bars and 327 streamlined rooms with floor-to-ceiling windows, most with harbour views. Those on the higher of the 20 floors may not wish to leave their rooms as they'll be captivated by the goings-on of all Ham-burg around them. There's a good spa and exercise room.

🛏 Altona & Elbmeile

Altona is a lovely part of Hamburg to wake up in. The less-than-clamorous night-time streets, the residential feel and a real ab-sence of tourists, not to mention great places to eat at any time of the day, all make Altona a good place to get a feel for what it must be like to live in Hamburg – and the charms of the city are only a short S-Bahn ride away. There are some good choices, although none that sparkle.

⭐ Superbude St Pauli HOTEL €

(Map p158; ☑ 040-807 915 820; www.super bude.de; Juliusstrasse 1-7; r from €65; @☎; U Sternschanze, S Sternschanze) The young and forever-young mix and mingle without a shred of prejudice at this rocking design hotel-hostel combo that's all about living, laughing, partying and, yes, even sleeping well. All rooms have comfy beds and sleek private baths, breakfast is served until noon and there's even a 'rock star suite' with an Astra beer as a pillow treat.

Meininger Hotel Hamburg City Center HOSTEL €

(Map p162; ☑ 040-2846 4388; www.meininger-hotels.com; Goetheallee 11; dm €15-30, s/d from €75/90; P@☎; S Altona) The Hamburg branch of this upscale chain of hostel-hotels is convenient to Altona train station and the many enticements of the neighbourhood. The 116 rooms are colourful, with hardwood floors, and are set in a modern six-storey building with a lift. There's a laundry, stor-age lockers, games room, bar and more.

⭐ Fritz im Pyjama Hotel BOUTIQUE HOTEL €€

(Map p158; ☑ 040-314 838; www.fritz-im-pyjama. de; Schanzenstrasse 101-103; s/d from €82/129; ☎; S Sternschanze) This stylish townhouse hotel sits smack dab in the heart of the Schanzenviertel party zone. Rooms are smallish, with wooden floors, angular furni-ture and large windows; seven of the 17 have a balcony. Those without are quieter as they face the courtyard.

Stadthaushotel Hamburg HOTEL €€

(☑ 040-389 9200; www.stadthaushotel.com; Hol-stenstrasse 118; s/d €98/135; P☎; S Altona, Sternschanze) Going by the motto 'different and good', this decent midrange hotel in Altona's north is staffed almost entirely by people with a disability. The rooms are large, nicely turned out and, as you'd expect, are accessible and adapted for those with a disability; rooms are also allergy-friendly.

🍴 Eating

Virtually every part of Hamburg has good dining options ranging from humble to fine. Unsurprisingly, seafood is a favourite in this port city, with everything from traditional regional specialities to sushi on offer. You'll also find a truly global variety of foods reflecting this city's international links and traditions, but don't neglect the widely available local specialties.

🍴 Altstadt

Many of the restaurants in the Altstadt cater to bankers and other office workers. There are alternatives, including Deichstrasse, which is lined with atmospheric old buildings – a rarity in this area despite the neighbourhood's name.

Local specialties are something of a recurring theme, making Altstadt a terrific place to try regional cooking. There are also a handful of high-class restaurants where tourists rub shoulders with local gastronomes.

★ Mö-Grill   GERMAN €
(Map p164; Mönckebergstrasse 11; mains from €4; ⊙10am-7pm; Ⓤ Mönckebergstrasse) You can smell the curry and see the crowds from two streets away at this very popular venue for that beloved German fast food, the *Currywurst*. Locals agree that the versions here (and at a second stand across the street) are about the best anywhere.

★ Laufauf   GERMAN €€
(Map p158; ☑040-326 626; www.laufauf.de; Kattrepel 2; mains €10.50-16; ⊙noon-10pm Mon-Sat; Ⓤ Mönckebergstrasse) A bastion for northern German and Hamburg cooking, Laufauf is something of a Hamburg institution. The *Hamburger Pannfisch* (locally fried fish), *Bratheringe* (fried herring), *Labskaus* (a meat, fish and potato stew with beetroot) or *Matjesfilet* (Herring fillet) are particularly good. It's a pretty casual place, which gets a mostly local crowd.

★ Ahoi by Steffen Henssler   INTERNATIONAL €€
(Map p164; ☑040-6466 0560; www.ahoiby steffenhenssler.de; Spitalerstrasse 12; mains from €9.50; ⊙noon-9pm Mon-Sat; Ⓤ Mönckeberg-

WORTH A TRIP

ANNA SGROI
....
Lauded chef **Anna Sgroi** (☑040-2800 3930; www.annasgroi.de; Milchstrasse 7; set menu from €75, mains €25-39; ⊙noon-2.30pm & 7-10.30pm Tue-Fri, 7-10.30pm Sat; Ⓤ Hallerstrasse) has taken the foods of her southern Italian childhood and elevated them to culinary heights. A seemingly mundane dish like stuffed artichokes is sublime, and that's just to start. While never the same, expect dishes with bold flavours, the finest ingredients and flawless execution. Service is smooth and unfussy.

strasse) German-born but always with his eye on the horizon, celebrated local chef Steffen Henssler has made a name for himself as a sushi chef. He also does burgers, salads and even a *Currywurst*. Downstairs at street level you can also get a mean fish and chips (€5.90).

Kartoffelkeller   GERMAN €€
(Map p158; ☑040-365 585; www.kartoffel keller-hamburg.de; Deichstrasse 21; mains €6-16; ⊙noon-10pm Thu-Tue; Ⓤ Rödingsmarkt) One of numerous good choices along pretty Deichstrasse, Kartoffelkeller is true to its name and lives for the potato – *Kartoffelsalate* (potato salad), *Kartoffelpuffer* (potato pancakes), *Kartoffelsuppe* (potato soup), *Pellkartoffel* (jacket potatoes), *Kartoffelknödel* (potato dumplings)... It's all good, although you may wish to not see a potato again for a while.

★ Deichgraf   GERMAN €€€
(Map p158; ☑040-364 208; www.deichgraf-hamburg.de; Deichstrasse 23; mains €15-26; ⊙noon-3pm & 5.30-10pm Mon-Fri, 5.30-10pm Sat; Ⓤ Rödingsmarkt) In a prime setting, with the water on one side and long street-side tables on the other, Deichgraf excels in Hamburg specialities cooked to a high standard. The menu changes seasonally and much of the food is sourced from the region. Their *Labskaus* is especially good, and, unusually, they offer a smaller portion for those wanting a taste.

★ Alt Hamburger Aalspeicher   GERMAN €€€
(Map p158; ☑040-362 990; www.aalspeicher.de; Deichstrasse 43; mains €13-27; ⊙noon-11pm Wed-Sun; Ⓤ Rödingsmarkt) Despite its tourist-friendly location, the knick-knack-filled

dining room and warm service at this restaurant, in a 400-year-old canalside building, make you feel like you're dining in your *Oma's* (grandma's) house – it's a real slice of old Hamburg where you'd least expect it. Smoked eel from its own smokehouse is a speciality.

✘ Neustadt

True to its refined personality, Neustadt is dominated by high-end restaurants, including some of the city's most celebrated tables. Look for luxe cafes under the beautiful columned arcades of the Alsterarkaden (p156) and the appropriately named Colonnaden.

But away from the waterfront, there are plenty of more reasonably priced options, with particularly rich pickings along Colonnaden (west of Binnenalster) and, even more so, along Wexstrasse, out in Neustadt's far west; the latter has some stunning little options that are utterly unpretentious. Food trucks are feature of the Wednesday market at **Grossneumarkt** (Map p158; ☺ market 8.30am-2am Wed & Sat; Ⓢ Stadthausbrücke).

★ Zum Spätzle   GERMAN €
(Map p158; ☑ 040-357 395 16; www.zumspaetzle. de; Wexstrasse 31; mains from €8.90; ☺ noon-10pm; Ⓢ Stadthausbrücke) Specialising in *Spätzle* (a pasta-like dish from Schwabia) and *Maultaschen* (a filled pasta, also from further south), Zum Spätzle is a terrific place to sample German regional cuisine. But we also love it for its love of home cooking and the calm intimacy of its small dining room.

Old Commercial Room   GERMAN €€
(Map p158; ☑ 040-366 319; www.oldcommercial room.de; Englische Planke 10; mains €13-35; ☺ noon-midnight; Ⓤ Rödingsmarkt) Around since 1795 and opposite the entrance to St Michaelis Kirche, this fine old bastion of tradition has long been serving some of Hamburg's best *labskaus* (a meat, fish and potato stew). Yes, it's touristy and they certainly don't mind name-dropping of all the international celebrities that have visited here. But the food is excellent.

★ Die Bank   BRASSERIE €€€
(Map p158; ☑ 040-0238 0030; www.diebank-brasserie.de; Hohe Bleichen 17; mains €19-35, set menus from €39; ☺ noon-4.30pm & 5.30-10.30pm Mon-Sat; Ⓤ Jungfernstieg, Gänsemarkt, Ⓢ Jungfernstieg) Inhabiting the glorious *Jugendstil* (art-nouveau) interior of an 1897 bank, Die Bank is one of Hamburg's most respected kitchens and draws the great and good of the city. Head chef Thomas Fischer has won a Michelin star elsewhere, and his cooking is light, assured and creative. The menu changes with the seasons.

Marblau   MEDITERRANEAN €€€
(Map p158; ☑ 040-226 161 555; www.marblau. de; Poolstrasse 21; mains €12-26; ☺ noon-3pm & 5pm-midnight Mon-Fri, 5-11pm Sat, 12.30-3pm & 5-11pm Sun; Ⓤ Gänsemarkt) You could order a pizza here, but Marblau is known for its creative Med fusion dishes, with subtle riffs on pastas and grills. The decor is a mix of retro and contemporary, which kind of suits the whole outlook here – faithful to tradition but with one eye on the future.

✘ St Georg

St Georg is one of Hamburg's culinary hotspots to watch. All along Lange Reihe, old-school German eating houses rub shoulders with cool cafes, French and Italian bistros, and some of Hamburg's best burgers.

★ Café Gnosa   CAFE €
(Map p164; ☑ 040-243 034; www.gnosa.de; Lange Reihe 93; mains €7-14; ☺ 10am-1am; Ⓤ Hauptbahnhof-Nord) With its abstract art and in-house bakery, Café Gnosa draws an affable gay and straight crowd in St Georg. The curved glass windows give it an art deco vibe. There are outside tables, and serving breakfast until 4pm daily is precisely the kind of understanding that Hamburg's nightlife deserves. It's always busy, and deservedly so.

Das Dorf   GERMAN €€€
(Map p164; ☑ 040-458 119; www.restaurant-dorf. de; Lange Reihe 39; mains €20-24; ☺ noon-11pm Mon-Fri, from 5pm Sat; Ⓤ Hauptbahnhof-Nord) There are lots of reasons to visit this wonderfully traditional restaurant with its wood-panelled dining room. But we love it especially for its homemade bread and *Labskaus*. It's not always on the menu in summer, but when it is, it consistently ranks among the best in Hamburg.

✘ Speicherstadt & HafenCity

For our money, the culinary offering in Speicherstadt and HafenCity is lagging a little behind the rest of the development. There are plenty of places to eat, but there are few that stand out. We expect that to change over the coming years.

Speicherstadt has a couple of excellent traditional restaurants amid its old restored warehouses. HafenCity has a few newish eateries but until the area gets more built up, they have a slightly soulless feel among the never-ending construction.

Carls Brasserie

BISTRO €€

(Map p158; ☑ 040-300 322 400; www.carls-brasserie.de; Am Kaiserkai 69; bistro mains €9-13, brasserie mains €15-34; ⊙ noon-11pm; Ⓤ Baumwall) Facing the Elbphilharmonie, this casual place offers predominantly French cuisine, such as *croque monsieur* and other toasts in the bistro, with a little more sophistication in the brasserie. The bistro offers better value.

★ Vlet in der Speicherstadt

GERMAN €€€

(Map p158; ☑ 040-334 753 750; www.vlet.de; Am Sandtorkai 23-24; mains €23-38; ⊙ 5pm-midnight Mon-Sat; Ⓤ Messberg) Right by the pedestrian bridge, Vlet has three different menus (plus a children's version) and the recurring theme is the intersection between contemporary flair and German traditional dishes – options include *Labskaus*, *Pannfisch* (fried Arctic char), and steak tartare (with truffle paste). There are also some weird and wonderful starters.

Oberhafen Kantine

GERMAN €€€

(Map p164; ☑ 040-3280 9984; www.oberhafen kantine-hamburg.de; Stockmeyerstrasse 39; mains €10-28; ⊙ noon-10pm Tue-Sat, noon-5.30pm Sun; Ⓤ Steinstrasse) Since 1925, this slightly tilted brick restaurant has served up the most traditional Hamburg fare. Here you can order a 'Hamburger' and you get the real thing: a patty made with various seasonings and onions. Roast beef and fish round out a trip back to the days when the surrounding piers echoed to the shouts of seafarers.

✖ St Pauli & Reeperbahn

Note that it's easy to escape the clamour of St Pauli's manufactured sleaze by getting just a few streets off the Reeperbahn, especially to the north where you can find quiet squares and cool cafes. In fact, the further you get from the Reeperbahn, the better your odds of having something tasty to eat (unless it's 4am, in which case the gaggle of fast-food spots along this notorious street will do just fine).

Right on the water you'll find a plethora of ice-cream stands, fried-fish stalls and other victuals-pushers for the strolling masses.

★ Fischbrötchenbude Brücke 10

SEAFOOD €

(Map p158; ☑ 040-3339 9339; www.bruecke-10.de; Landungsbrücken, Pier 10; sandwiches €3-9.50; ⊙ 10am-10pm; Ⓢ Landungsbrücken, Ⓤ Landungsbrücken) There are a gazillion fish sandwich vendors in Hamburg, but we're going to stick our neck out and say that this vibrant, clean and contemporary outpost makes the best. Try a classic *Bismarck* (pickled herring) or *Matjes* (brined herring), or treat yourself to a bulging shrimp sandwich. Lovely tables outside.

Kleine Haie Grosse Fische

SANDWICHES €

(Map p158; ☑ 0176-1033 7847; www.kleinehaie-grossefische.de; Querstrasse 4; mains from €4; ⊙ 6pm-midnight Wed & Thu, 2pm-4am Fri & Sat; Ⓢ Reeperbahn) St Pauli's version of the late-night kebab stop is this timeless place serving fish sandwiches, as well as smoked fish and meats. There's nothing quite like a herring sandwich at 3am.

Kiez Curry

FAST FOOD €

(Map p158; ☑ 040-6367 3829; www.kiezcurry.de; Querstrasse 2; mains from €3; ⊙ 5pm-midnight Tue-Thu, to 5am Fri & Sat; Ⓢ Reeperbahn) All manner of *Currywurst* (there's even a vegan version) have made this an icon of St Pauli's nights – a *Currywurst* at 4am after a hard night of partying just feels right in Hamburg. If you're really hungry, add the potato salad to your order. They operate slightly shorter hours in winter.

Pauline

CAFE €

(Map p158; ☑ 040-4135 9964; www.pauline-hamburg.de; Neuer Pferdemarkt 3; mains €3-10, Sun brunch €18.70; ⊙ 8.30am-4pm Mon-Fri, 9am-6pm Sat, 10am-6pm Sun; Ⓤ Feldstrasse) Tucked away on a residential street and as good for breakfast as for lunch, this classy cafe is enduringly popular with locals, but they can't keep it all to themselves. The small but thoughtfully chosen lunch menu includes quiche, salad or pasta, while the breakfasts are excellent. The Sunday brunch (10am to 3.30pm, with sittings at 10am and 12.30pm) is excellent.

Fischerhaus

SEAFOOD €€

(Map p158; ☑ 040-314 053; www.restaurant-fischerhaus.de; St Pauli Fischmarkt 14; mains €9-25; ⊙ 11.30am-10.30pm; Ⓤ Reeperbahn) Arguably the pick of the sit-down fish restaurants down in the Fischmarkt, Fischerhaus has three different dining spaces – the views are better from the Hafenblick room, but it's more casual and kid-friendly at Rustikal, where prices also tend to be slightly lower. Fried fish is a specialty, but you could pick anything here and leave satisfied.

★**Clouds** INTERNATIONAL €€€
(Map p158; ☑040 309 932 80; www.clouds-hamburg.de; Reeperbahn 1, Tanzende Türme; mains €29-54; ☉11.30am-2pm & 5-11pm Mon-Fri, 5-11pm Sat & Sun; ⓤSt Pauli) Arguably St Pauli's most prestigious table, Clouds, on the 23rd floor of the **Tanzende Türme** (Map p158), is an elegant space with marvellous views out over the city. The menu is dominated by steaks and a few French touches; you'll need to book ahead at all times and dress nicely. After your meal, head upstairs to Heaven's Nest.

✖ Altona & Elbmeile

In the village-like area around Altona train station, you'll find dozens of casual and ethnic eateries, especially in the gentrified climes of Ottensen to the west. These streets are among our favourite places for a meal in Hamburg.

The city's western riverfront, from Altona to Övelgönne, known as the Elbmeile (Elbe Mile), has a dense concentration of popular and trendy restaurants – many drawing menu inspiration from the waterfront location.

★**GaumenGanoven** INTERNATIONAL €
(Map p162; ☑0176-329 351 79; www.gaumengan oven.de; Friedensallee 7-9; mains from €5; ☉noon-3pm & 6-10pm Tue & Wed, noon-3pm & 6pm-11pm Thu, to 1am Fri; ⑤Altona) We *love* this place. A fun, brick-lined setting is the backdrop for little morsels – rather like tapas or antipasto (here they're called '*Dinger*') – that you take, eat and then tally up when you're done. It works on the honour system, and boy does it work. Tastes often come in surprising combinations like prawns with mango-chilli and sesame, or octopus with hummus.

★**Mikkels** CAFE €
(Map p162; ☑040-7699 5072; www.mikkels.de; Kleine Rainstrasse 10; mains from €4.50; ☉9am-6pm Mon-Sat, 10am-6pm Sun; ⑤Altona) Even if you miss the morning at this cheery spot which mixes affability with pastel style, you can still sit outside and catch the afternoon sun. Baked goods are fabulous, and egg dishes are all-organic. The coffee? Good as you'd expect.

★**Altes Mädchen** EUROPEAN €€
(Map p158; ☑040-800 077 750; www.altes-maedchen.com; Lagerstrasse 28b; mains €6-29; ☉noon-late Mon-Sat, 10am-late Sun; ⑤Sternschanze, ⓤSternschanze) The lofty red-brick halls of a 19th-century animal market have been upcycled into a hip culinary destination that includes a coffee roastery, a celebrity chef restaurant, and this beguiling brewpub with a central bar, in-house bakery and garden.

★**Bullerei** INTERNATIONAL €€
(Map p158; ☑040-3344 2110; www.bullerei.com; Lagerstrasse 34b; mains €10-25; ☉11am-11pm; ⑤Sternschanze) One of the coolest dining spaces in the city, Bullerei inhabits a converted former slaughterhouse with lovely high ceilings and a real buzz that bounces off the walls – don't come here for a quiet romantic dinner. Service is cool and attentive, and the menu revolves around steak dishes and Italian-inflected choices.

Von Der Motte FAST FOOD €€
(Map p162; ☑040-8470 3618; www.vonder motte.de; Mottenburger Twiete 14; mains €8-12; ☉10am-9pm Tue-Fri, to 6pm Sat & Sun; ⑤Altona) In a tiny little pedestrian street, Von Der Motte does soups, sandwiches and salads, or what they refer to as 'fast slow food' – service is rapid, but the food slow-cooked and tasty. The breakfast menu is long, the sandwiches excellent, and we enjoyed the grilled vegetables with warm goat cheese.

⊘ Drinking & Nightlife

Hamburg's nightlife is legendary, and rightly so. Elite cocktail bars, nonstop nightclubs and world-class DJs are all part of a mix that rocks and rolls with energy and innovation. Hamburg is renowned for its electro-punk sound, which started in the 1980s and has evolved and morphed endlessly. Clubkombinat (www.clubkombinat.de) has club listings.

⊘ Altstadt

★**Le Lion** COCKTAIL BAR
(Map p158; ☑040-334 753 780; www.lelion.net; Rathausstrasse 3; ☉6pm-3am Mon-Sat, to 1am Sun; ⓤRathaus) Easily the classiest, most exclusive bar (by virtue of size) you'll find in Hamburg. If there's space and you're nicely dressed, they'll let you into this little lair of serious cocktails – their signature is the gin basil smash.

Gröninger Privatbrauerei BREWERY

(Map p158; ☑040-570 105 100; www.groeninger-hamburg.de; Willy Brandt Strasse 47; ⊙11am-midnight Mon-Fri, 5pm-midnight Sat, 3-10pm Sun; Ⓤ Messberg) Drink in the cellar in one of Hamburg's oldest breweries, where they serve Gröninger Pils from old oak barrels. If you get the munchies, their pork knuckles served with crackling is *the* order.

🍴 St Georg

a.mora BAR

(Map p164; ☑040-2805 6735; www.a-mora.com; An der Alster 72; ⊙10am-late; Ⓤ Hauptbahnhof-Nord) Perched on the jetty overlooking Aussenalster, this suave bar is as good for breakfast or a coffee as it is for a late-night cocktail. It attracts a fairly stylish crowd, and the reclining day beds right by the water are rarely relinquished on a summer's day. It's not the most adventurous cocktail list, but why mess with the classics?

★Bacaro Wine Bar WINE BAR

(Map p164; ☑040-3570 6829; www.bacaro-winebar.de; Lange Reihe 68-70; ⊙noon-3pm & 5.30-11pm Mon-Thu, to midnight Fri, 5pm-midnight Sat, 5-11pm Sun; Ⓤ Hauptbahnhof-Nord) This classy little wine bar has a contemporary feel and is ideal for an evening spent in serious conversation over Italian wine. The food, too, is excellent, making it an great place to start the night.

Kyti Voo BAR

(Map p164; ☑040-2805 5565; www.kytivoo.com; Lange Reihe 82; ⊙5pm-late Mon-Sat, from 2pm Sun; Ⓤ Hauptbahnhof-Nord) A mixed crowd mixes it up with an especially rewarding menu of craft beer and cocktails until *very*

late. At sunnier (or less dark) times, grab a table on the outdoor terrace. Cocktail happy hour is a particularly generous 5pm to 8pm daily.

Bar M & V BAR

(Map p164; ☑040-2800 6973; www.mvbar.de; Lange Reihe 22; ⊙5pm-2am; Ⓤ Hauptbahnhof-Nord) The drinks menu is like a designer catalogue at this grand old St Georg bar, which has been beautifully restored. Settle into one of the wooden booths, smell the freesias and enjoy the merry, mixed crowd.

🍴 St Pauli & Reeperbahn

★Café du Port CAFE

(Map p158; ☑040-6483 3238; www.cafe-du-port.de; Hein-Hoyer-Strasse 56; pastries from €3; ⊙9am-7pm Sun-Tue & Thu, to 8pm Fri & Sat; Ⓤ St Pauli, Ⓢ Reeperbahn) One of our favourite little perches in St Pauli, this gorgeous cafe does buttery croissants, cakes and other pastries, with fine coffee to nurse as you look for an excuse to linger in this intimate space.

★Golden Pudel Club BAR, LIVE MUSIC

(Map p158; ☑040-3197 9930; www.pudel.com; St-Pauli-Fischmarkt 27; ⊙11pm-6am; Ⓢ Reeperbahn) In a 19th-century bootleggers' jail, this tiny bar-club is run by members of the legendary ex-punk band Die Goldenen Zitronen and is an essential stop on the St Pauli party circuit. Night after night it gets packed to the rafters for its countercultural vibe, quality bands and DJs, and relaxed crowd.

Clouds Bar COCKTAIL BAR

(Heaven's Nest; Map p158; ☑040-3099 3280; www.clouds-hamburg.de/bar; Reeperbahn 1, Tanzende Türme; ⊙11.30am-late Mon-Fri, from noon

---

GAY & LESBIAN HAMBURG

Hamburg is popular with *Schwule* (gay) and *Lesbische* (lesbian) travellers, with the rainbow flag flying especially proudly in St Georg, particularly along Lange Reihe and surrounding streets. It's fine to be openly gay in much of Hamburg, but public displays of affection may attract unwanted attention in areas with high immigrant populations; this includes the Steindamm and Hansaplatz areas of St Georg.

Throughout the year, **Hein & Fiete** (Map p164; ☑040-240 333; www.heinfiete.de; Pulverteich 21; ⊙4-9pm Mon-Fri, to 7pm Sat; Ⓤ Hauptbahnhof-Süd) is an excellent information centre devoted to Hamburg's gay scene. Lesbians can contact the **Intervention** (Map p158; ☑040-245 002; www.intervention-hamburg.de; Glashüttenstrasse 2; ⊙hours vary; Ⓤ Feldstrasse) for more information on Hamburg's lesbian scene.

Hamburg's pride shindig, **Hamburg Pride** (Christopher Street Day; www.hamburg-pride.de), runs over a week in late July and/or early August, with plenty of musical events, parades and a festive sense of celebration in St Georg.

Homosexuality has been legal since the late 1960s. Same-sex marriage is legal.

SPIELBUDENPLATZ

There always seems to be something going on in Spielbudenplatz. Wednesdays is the St Pauli Nachtmarkt (p161), but other semi-regular occurrences include:

➡ Live music and container bars nightly from 4pm from April to September.

➡ Street-food trucks turn up on Thursdays from 5pm to 11pm from April to October, and 6pm to 9pm from January to March.

➡ Twice a year, a flea market takes over the *platz*, usually on the first Sunday in June and September.

➡ Also twice a year, in May and September, the **St Pauli Food Truck Festival** (www. spielbudenplatz.eu) arrives.

➡ St Pauli's Christmas Market (from late November to 23 December) is a typically irreverent affair.

For more information on what's going on, visit www.spielbudenplatz.eu.

Sat & Sun; Ⓤ St Pauli) This elegant bar, above Clouds Restaurant (p172) at the eastern entrance to St Pauli, is popular with an upmarket crowd who come here for the highballs (of course!) and perfectly mixed cocktails. When the weather is fine and clear, head to the lounge chairs at the open-air Heaven's Nest right on the summit. The dress code is 'casual elegant'.

Komet Musik Bar   BAR
(Map p158; ☏ 040-2786 8686; www.komet-st-pauli.de; Erichstrasse 11; ⏰ 9pm-late; Ⓤ St Pauli) Vinyl and only vinyl spins at this treasure of a music bar. Nightly themes range from ska and rocksteady to '60s garage punk and hip hop. Order a Helga, a sweetish house drink that will have everything sounding dreamy in no time.

★ Zum Silbersack   PUB
(Map p158; ☏ 040-314 589; www.facebook.com/zumsilbersack1949; Silbersackstrasse 9; ⏰ 5pm-1am Sun, to 3am Mon-Wed, to 4am Thu, 3pm-5am Fri & Sat; Ⓢ Reeperbahn) A real St Pauli icon, Zum Silbersack is one of our favourites in the area. It's the sort of place where you'll find students, junkies, executives, greenies, millionaires and prostitutes. Anything seems possible and it can be a little rough around the edges, but it's *very* St Pauli.

Indra Club   CLUB
(Map p158; www.indramusikclub.com; 64 Grosse Freiheit; ⏰ 9pm-late Wed-Sun; Ⓢ Reeperbahn) The Beatles' small first venue is open again and has live acts some nights. The interior is vastly different from the 1960s and there is a fine beer garden.

★ Zur Ritze   BAR
(Map p158; www.zurritze.com; Reeperbahn 140; ⏰ 5pm-6am Mon-Thu, from 2pm Fri-Sun; Ⓢ Reeperbahn) The uniqueness of this Reeperbahn classic begins from the moment you pass through the long laneway and between the legs of the large 'receptionist' painted over the door. Inside, it's a serious drinking den, that even draws a few local celebrities. Down in the basement is a boxing gym. It's very eclectic in the finest St Pauli tradition.

Molotow   CLUB
(Map p158; ☏ 040-310 845; www.molotowclub.com; Nobistor 14; ⏰ 6pm-late; Ⓢ Reeperbahn) This legendary indie club still rocks on as hot 'n heavy as ever after moving to new digs when its old location was torn down.

📍 Altona & Elbmeile

★ Katze   COCKTAIL BAR
(Map p158; ☏ 040-5577 5910; Schulterblatt 88; ⏰ 1pm-3am Mon-Sat, to midnight Sun; Ⓢ Sternschanze) Small and sleek, this 'kitty' (*Katze* = cat) gets the crowd purring for well-priced cocktails (the best caipirinhas in town) and great music (there's dancing on weekends). It's one of the most popular amongst the watering holes on this main Schanzenviertel booze strip.

Reh Bar   BAR
(Map p162; ☏ 040-3990 6363; Ottenser Hauptstrasse 52; ⏰ 10am-midnight Sun-Wed, to 2am Thu, to 4am Fri & Sat; Ⓢ Altona) If you could somehow bottle the Altona spirit and turn it into a bar, Reh Bar would go close. Cosy and welcoming, as good for a morning coffee as for

a late-night cocktail, Reh Bar draws a young crowd of local professionals every night.

☆ Entertainment

Gruenspan
LIVE MUSIC

(Map p158; ☑040-313 616; www.gruenspan.de; Grosse Freiheit 58; ⊗6pm-late; ⑤Reeperbahn) Around since the 1960s, Gruenspan has evolved since its time as a notorious drug den into one of St Pauli's best live music venues. Just about any musical genre can take to the stage here, but they seem to have a particular fondness for singer-songwriters – check the website to see if what's on suits your mood.

★ Mojo Club
JAZZ

(Map p158; ☑040-319 1999; www.mojo.de; Reeperbahn 1, Tanzende Türme; from €17; ⊗7pm-late; ⑪St Pauli) This legendary Hamburg jazz club inhabits the fab basement of the Tanzende Türme (p172) office towers. Stellar local and international acts take to the stage here and it's always worth checking what's on. Great atmosphere, great acoustics, knowledgeable jazz crowd – it's one of Hamburg's best nights out. Opening hours vary, but most acts take to the stage around 8pm.

Kaiserkeller
LIVE MUSIC

(Map p158; Grosse Freiheit 36; ⑤Reeperbahn) One of the more respectable clubs today on the Grosse Freiheit, this second venue for the Beatles survives in a much-altered form with regular live acts.

Cascadas
LIVE MUSIC

(Map p158; www.cascadas.club; Ferdinandstrasse 12; €0-10; ⊗7pm-late) One of the better live music venues outside of St Pauli, Cascadas offers up a nightly program that ranges across soul, jazz, Latin, funk, Caribbean and blues. Things usually get going around 8pm, but check the website for upcoming gigs and times.

Fabrik
LIVE PERFORMANCE

(Map p162; ☑040-391 070; www.fabrik.de; Barnerstrasse 36; ⑤Altona) They're making beautiful music in this former factory that's an iconic Altona venue, where the music ranges from classical to club and the program spans theatre to film.

Elbphilharmonie
CLASSICAL MUSIC

(Map p158; ☑040-3576 6666; www.elbphilharmonie.de; Platz der Deutschen Einheit 4; tickets €10-75; ⊗box office 11am-8pm; ⑪Baumwall) Coming to a concert here is an essential part of Hamburg's most exciting architec-

tural icon. With a full program, a number of different performance spaces and world-leading acoustics, it's a terrific experience, whatever you see. Advance bookings are always recommended.

Staatsoper
OPERA

(Map p158; ☑040-356 868; www.hamburgische-staatsoper.de; Grosse Theaterstrasse 25; ⊗box office 10am-6pm Mon-Sat, plus 90min prior to performances; ⑪Stephansplatz) Among the world's most respected opera houses, the Staatsoper has been directed by the likes of Gustav Mahler and Karl Böhm during its 325-year-plus history.

Millerntor-Stadion
STADIUM

(Map p158; ☑040-3178 7451; www.fcstpauli.com; Heiligengeistfeld; ⑪Feldstrasse) Favourite local football team FC St Pauli plays at home in the multi-use Millerntor stadium.

Barclaycard Arena
STADIUM

(☑040-806 020 80; www.barclaycard-arena.de; Sylvesterallee 7; ⊗ticket office 11am-6pm Mon-Fri, 9am-2pm Sat, plus two hours before games) Hamburg's huge Barclaycard Arena (previously sponsored by O2) was extensively refurbished for the 2006 football World Cup, and is home to Bundesliga club Hamburger SV (www.hsv.de). Take S-Bahn 21 or 3 to 'Stellingen', which is linked by free shuttle buses to the stadium. For tickets, ring the ticket hotline, or visit the ticket office next to the E2 gate.

🛍 Shopping

Hamburg's shopping may not rival its nightlife in profile, but there are numerous interesting finds – from mainstream to offbeat – as you explore the city. As a general rule, shopping possibilities reflect the neighbourhoods they inhabit – Neustadt and Altstadt are refined and upmarket, while St Pauli, Altona and St Georg are more about smaller boutiques and artsy corner shops.

🛍 Altstadt

Sleeping Dogs
HOMEWARES

(Map p158; ☑040-3861 4044; www.sleepingdogs.de; Rödingsmarkt 20; ⊗11am-7pm Mon-Fri, to 4pm Sat; ⑪Rödingsmarkt) This stunning concept store is partly about homeware brands, from local designers to international stars. But just as much thought has gone into the display – it's like an art gallery in here. The look ranges from clean-lined Scandinavian minimalism to vintage classics.

Dr Götze Land & Karte BOOKS
(Map p158; ☑040-357 4630; www.landundkarte.
de; Alstertor 14-18; ☺10am-7pm Mon-Fri, to 6pm
Sat, 1-6pm Sun; Ⓤ Mönckebergstrasse, Jungfernstieg, Ⓢ Jungfernstieg) Enormous range of
guidebooks and maps. Browse the world.

Neustadt

⭐**Mutterland** FOOD & DRINKS
(Map p158; ☑040-3500 4360; www.mutterland.
de; Poststrasse 14-16; ☺8am-8pm Mon-Fri, from
9am Sat; Ⓤ Jungfernstieg, Ⓢ Jungfernstieg) This
'Made in Germany' delicatessen has beautifully packaged and utterly tempting foods
(jams, chocolates etc) and drinks (try the
Monkey 47 Schwarzwald Dry Gin, from the
Black Forest). It's a stunning collection and
it's very difficult to leave without spending
large amounts of money.

⭐**Anne Zimmer** JEWELLERY
(Map p158; ☑040-557 754 47; www.annezimmer.
de; Wexstrasse 28; ☺11am-7pm Tue-Fri, to 4pm
Sat; Ⓢ Stadthausbrücke) This gorgeous little
boutique selling handmade gold and other jewellery is a lovely counterpoint to the
luxury international brands that dominate
Neustadt elsewhere. Beautiful homewares
also inhabit the light and airy space.

Tobias Strauch Weinkontor WINE
(Map p158; ☑040-226 161 544; www.tobias-
strauch.de; Wexstrasse 35; ☺noon-8pm Mon-Fri,
11am-6pm Sat; Ⓢ Stadthausbrücke) Well-known
Hamburg culinary celebrity Tobias Strauch
knows what he's talking about when it
comes to wine. His carefully chosen selection of mostly European wines is one of the
best you'll find.

St Georg

⭐**Koppel 66** ARTS & CRAFTS
(Map p164; ☑040-386 419 30; www.koppel66.
de; Koppel 66; ☺11am-6pm Mon-Fri, to 4pm Sat;
Ⓤ Hauptbahnhof-Nord) Arguably Hamburg's
premier collection of art-and-craft stores,
the arcade at Koppel 66 has some intriguing
options – from hat-makers and handmade
soaps, to purveyors of handmade pens and
artisan jewellers. Break up your visit with a
meal at **Café Koppel** (☑040-249 235; www.
cafe-koppel.de; Lange Reihe 66; mains €5-10;
☺10am-11pm; ☑; Ⓤ Hauptbahnhof-Nord).

Kaufhaus Hamburg GIFTS & SOUVENIRS
(Map p164; ☑040-2281 5669; www.kaufhaus-
hamburg.de; Lange Reihe 70; ☺11am-7pm Mon-Fri,

from 10am Sat; Ⓤ Hauptbahnhof-Nord) Fun Ham-
burg-themed souvenirs make shopping for
a gift back home rather enjoyable. There's
everything from stationery and homewares to
games and food.

St Pauli & Reeperbahn

Flohschanze MARKET
(Map p158; Neuer Kamp 30; ☺8am-4pm Sat;
Ⓤ Feldstrasse) Flohschanze, Hamburg's best
flea market, is nirvana for thrifty trinket
hunters and vintage junkies, with hundreds
of vendors holding forth outdoors in the hip
Karolinenviertel.

Ars Japonica ARTS & CRAFTS
(Map p158; ☑040-319 3875; www.arsjaponica.
de; Hein-Hoyer-Strasse 48; ☺1-5pm Tue-Fri,
10.30am-2pm Sat; Ⓢ Reeperbahn, Ⓤ St Pauli)
Exquisite Japanese works of miniature and
other art, as well as some homewares in
the same vein; pieces adorned with Japanese calligraphy are a recurring theme. It's
only small, but everything here is in perfect
taste.

Altona & Elbmeile

⭐**Atelier Nigoh** ARTS & CRAFTS
(Map p162; ☑040-657 969 95; www.nigoh.de;
Eulenstrasse 62; ☺11am-12.30pm & 1.30-7pm Tue-
Fri, 11am-4pm Sat) Original prints and postcards, many of which are pop-art originals
and signed by the artist, Nina Hasselluhn
herself, are worth browsing through at this
lovely small studio. We especially like the
silhouette pieces of Hamburg port, which
make a terrific souvenir of your visit, but
there's so much to turn the head here. Nina
also runs painting courses.

❶ Information

DANGERS & ANNOYANCES
Hamburg is generally a safe city and most visitors visit without encountering any problems.
That said, Hamburg is also undeniably sleazy
in parts.
➡ Red-light districts are found around the
Hauptbahnhof and the Reeperbahn.
➡ Petty crime is rare but does occur in major
tourist areas. Keep a careful eye on your belongings anywhere where there are crowds and
large numbers of tourists.
➡ In St Georg, Steindamm and Hansaplatz can
be dicey, both day and night.
➡ In areas where crime can be an issue, there's
usually a strong police presence.

EMERGENCY

Germany's country code	☎ 49
International access code	☎ 00
Ambulance	☎ 112
Fire	☎ 110
Police	☎ 110

INTERNET ACCESS

➡ You can find free wi-fi around the city.

➡ Some cafes and bars have wi-fi hot spots that let laptop-toting customers hook up for free, although you usually need to ask for a password.

➡ Many hotels have an internet corner for their guests, often at no charge.

➡ Note that in some properties wi-fi access may be limited to some rooms and/or public areas, so if you need in-room access be sure to specify at the time of booking.

➡ Hamburg's Hauptbahnhof offers 30 minutes free wi-fi with registration via Deutsche Telekom.

➡ Use www.hotspot-locations.com to locate wi-fi hot spots.

POST

Post Office (Map p164; ☎ 01802-3333; www.deutschepost.de; Mönckeberg-strasse 7; ⊙ 9am-7pm Mon-Fri, to 3pm Sat; Ⓤ Mönckebergstrasse) The post office near the Hauptbahnhof is often the most convenient.

TOURIST INFORMATION

Hamburg's tourist information offices are friendly and helpful, with a range of brochures on offer. Ask for the monthly *Hamburg Guide*, which is not always on display. Useful offices include:

Tourist Information Airport (Terminals 1 & 2; ⊙ 6am-11pm) On the arrival level, next to the baggage collection belts.

Tourist Information am Hafen (Map p158; ☎ 040-3005 1701; www.hamburg-travel.com; btwn piers 4 & 5, St Pauli Landungsbrücken; ⊙ 9am-6pm Sun-Wed, to 7pm Thu-Sat; Ⓢ Landungsbrücken) No hotel bookings.

Tourist Information Hauptbahnhof (Map p164; ☎ 040-3005 1701; www.hamburg-travel.com; Hauptbahnhof, near Kirchenallee exit; ⊙ 9am-7pm Mon-Sat, 10am-6pm Sun; Ⓡ Hauptbahnhof, Ⓤ Hauptbahnhof) Busy all the time and with plenty of brochures and booking information.

❶ Getting There & Away

AIR

Hamburg Airport (Flughafen Hamburg Helmut Schmidt; HAM; ☎ 040-507 50; www.hamburg-airport.de; Flughafenstrasse; Ⓡ Hamburg Airport) has frequent flights to domestic and European cities with Lufthansa and most other major European carriers.

Low-cost carriers include Ryan Air, Air Berlin, EasyJet and Eurowings. There are also a handful of intercontinental flights, such as to New York and Dubai.

BOAT

There are no international ferry services from Hamburg; the nearest departures are from Kiel.

Hamburg is a popular port of call for cruise ships. There are two main places they dock:

Hamburg Cruise Center Altona (www.hamburgcruisecenter.eu; Van-der-Smissen-Strasse 5; ⊠ 112) A popular dock for large cruise ships.

Hamburg Cruise Center HafenCity (www.hamburgcruisecenter.eu; Grosser Grasbrook;

TICKETS

The city is divided into zones. Ring A covers the city centre, inner suburbs and airport.

Day passes cover travel for one adult and up to three children aged six to 14. Kids under six travel free.

Train tickets must be purchased from machines at stations; bus tickets are available from the driver. Ticket types include the following:

TICKET GROSSBEREICH/RING A & B REGION	PRICE
Short journey/*Kurzstrecke* (only two to three stops)	€1.60
Single/*Einzelkarte*	€3.30
9-hour day pass/*9-Uhr-Tageskarte* (after 9am)	€6.40
Day pass/*Ganztageskarte* (valid from 6am to 6am the next day)	€7.70
Group day pass/*Gruppenkarte* (after 9am, up to five people of any age)	€12.00

If you catch an express bus (*Schnellbus*), it costs an extra €2.20. Please note that there are no barriers at S-Bahn and U-Bahn stations. Random ticket checks are conducted on board.

ℹ️ ARRIVING IN HAMBURG

Hamburg Airport The S1 S-Bahn connects the airport directly with the city centre. The journey takes 25 minutes and costs €3.30. Taxis cost €20 to €30 and take around 30 minutes, longer during peak hour.

Hamburg Hauptbahnhof The main train station is in the heart of the city and within walking distance of many hotels. Otherwise take the subway, for which a single ticket costs €3.30.

Ⓢ Überseequartier) Many large cruise ships dock here, close to HafenCity.

BUS

The **ZOB** (Zentraler Omnibusbahnhof, Central Bus Station; Map p164; ☎ 040-247 576; www. zob-hamburg.de; Adenauerallee 78; Ⓡ Hauptbahnhof, Ⓤ Hauptbahnhof-Süd) is southeast of the Hauptbahnhof. Domestic and international buses arrive and depart around the clock.

Buses from Hamburg

Flixbus (www.flixbus.com) is usually the cheapest of the companies serving domestic destinations. Services include:

DESTINATION	HOURS	COST	FREQUENCY
Berlin	3¼	from €10	half-hourly
Bremen	1½	from €5	half-hourly
Cologne	7-11	from €18	12 daily
Flensburg	2-3	from €8	up to 11 daily
Frankfurt	7-10	from €19	hourly
Hannover	2¼	from €8	hourly
Lübeck	1	from €5	two daily
Stralsund	4½	from €20	two daily

TRAIN

Frequent trains serve regional and long-distance destinations from Hamburg. There are two main-line stations worth noting:

Hamburg Hauptbahnhof (Main Train Station; www.hamburger-hbf.de; Ⓡ Hauptbahnhof) The main rail hub for northern Germany. In addition to domestic services, there are several trains daily to Copenhagen (from €80, five to six hours).

Hamburg Altona (Ⓢ Altona) Many Hamburg trains, including some long-distance services, begin or end their journeys at this medium-sized station in the heart of its namesake neighbourhood.

Direct domestic services include:

DESTINATION	DURATION (HOURS)	COST
Berlin	1¾	from €30
Bremen	1	from €20
Cologne	4	from €36
Flensburg	2½	from €20
Frankfurt	3½	from €34
Kiel	1¼	from €20
Lübeck	¾	from €14.50
Munich	5¾-7	from €68
Schwerin	1	from €20
Stralsund	4-5	from €30

ℹ️ Getting Around

CAR & MOTORCYCLE

Driving around town is easy: thoroughfares are well signposted (watch for one-way streets in the city centre), and parking stations plentiful. Most inner-city parking stations charge around €4 per hour or €28 per day. Ask if your hotel has private or discounted parking when making your reservation.

For on-street parking, you'll need to pay between 9am and 8pm and there's often a two-hour limit. It usually costs €0.50 per 10 minutes, or €6 for two hours.

PUBLIC TRANSPORT
Ferry

The ferry system is an excellent way to get around, and a much cheaper alternative to the tourist-oriented harbour ferries. Ferries operate all along the Elbe and between HafenCity and Teufelsbrück.

Ferries run between 5.30am and 11.15pm; for most of that time, there are departures every 15 minutes.

Tickets are the same as those for bus and U-/S-Bahn services and can be purchased at vending machines at most stops.

Train

Easily the best way to get around the city, the U-Bahn (four lines) and S-Bahn (six lines) trains are easy to work out; maps of the system are found on all city maps and inside the stations.

There is little difference between the two types of service, although U-Bahn trains generally pass by more frequently (every two to 10 minutes) when compared to S-Bahn trains (every 10 to 20 minutes). U-Bahn and S-Bahn lines frequently intersect.

TAXI & UBER

Hamburg's cream-coloured taxis are easy to find – either flag down a passing taxi, catch one from a designated rank, or phone to have one pick you up. If doing the latter, **Taxi Hamburg** (☑ 040-666 666; www.taxihamburg.de) is one of the better companies.

Flagfall ranges between €3.50 and €4.20, depending on the time of day, with each kilometre charged at €1.50 to €2.50; the further you travel, the lower the per-kilometre tariff.

Uber (www.uber.com) is not widely used after a court ruled in May 2015 that traditional Uber services violated German transportation laws. Uber reacted by creating UberX, which uses only professionally licensed drivers. Trip costs tend to be between 3% and 12% less than regular taxi fares.

AROUND HAMBURG

Although dominated by its namesake city, Hamburg State does encompass part of the Altes Land, a fertile area reclaimed from marshy ground by Dutch experts in the Middle Ages. Flatness as a terrain feature here takes on its own certain stark beauty. The towns in this region are more than mere Hamburg shadows, with both Stade and Lüneburg retaining charming and architecturally rich medieval cores. Stade is the prettier of the two, but Lüneburg is quietly earning plaudits as a culinary superstar in the making. More sobering is KZ-Gedenkstätte Neuengamme, Hamburg's little-known concentration camp. It is a haunting, silent place.

Germany's excellent train system and great-value day passes make most destinations in this region easy to visit on a day trip from Hamburg.

Stade

☑ 04141 / POP 47,600

You half expect some Pied Piper-type character to come tooting around a corner as you wander the ancient lanes of Stade, a stand-in for everybody's idea of a perfectly clichéd old German village.

Easily reached in an hour by public transit from Hamburg, Stade makes an ideal escape from the urban hustle and is a great daytrip. First mentioned in historical records in the 10th century, Stade has half-timbered buildings, a series of little canals and some moody old churches.

◉ Sights

St Wilhadi Kirche   CHURCH

(off Flutstrasse; ◷ 11am-4pm Mon-Sat Apr-Oct, 11.30am-1.30pm Nov-Mar) Stade's oldest building is this hulking church, which has parts dating to the 14th century. Keeping the building standing to the present day has been the stuff of drama, what with wars, lightning and water-logged ground. Note the heavy buttresses on the exterior and the bands of iron around the pillars in the detail-packed interior. The small history brochure is a good read.

🛏 Sleeping & Eating

★ Störtebeker   GUESTHOUSE €

(☑ 04141-690 420; Salzstrasse 15; s/d from €47/64; [P][🛜]) Central old-town location, excellent modern rooms at reasonable prices, and friendly guesthouse feel – what more could you want? The only drawback is the single rooms can be a little poky. There's a small but pretty garden, and local artefacts inhabit the public areas. Ask for a room with balcony. A great deal all round.

Ratskeller Stade   GERMAN €€

(☑ 04141-787 228; www.ratskeller-stade.de; Hökerstrasse 10; mains €10-20; ◷ noon-3pm & 5-10pm Mon-Fri, noon-11pm Sat & Sun) A cut above your average *Ratskeller*, Stade's is on a shady back lane near St Wilhadi. It has its own brewery, fine hearty, meaty fare and plenty of outdoor tables.

❶ Getting There & Away

From Hamburg, the S3 line, as well as hourly express trains from the Hauptbahnhof, reach Stade in one hour. Tickets cost €8.75 one way, so buy the day pass '9-Uhr Tageskarte Ring ABCDE' for €16.50.

Lüneburg

☑ 04131 / POP 75,000

An off-kilter church steeple, buildings leaning on each other and houses with swollen 'beer-belly' facades: in parts it looks like the charming town of Lüneburg has drunk too much of the Pilsner lager it used to brew. Of course, the city's wobbly angles and uneven pavements have a more prosaic cause. For centuries until 1980, Lüneburg was a salt-mining town, and as this 'white gold' was extracted from the earth, shifting ground and subsidence caused many buildings to tilt sideways.

Its wobbly comic-book streets aside, Lüneburg is a lovely town with attractive stepped-gable facades and Hanseatic architecture. It has a lively student population.

Sights & Activities

★ Rathaus
HISTORIC BUILDING
(☑04131-207 6620; Markt; tours adult/child €6/3.50; ⊗tours 11am & 2pm Tue-Sun Jan-Mar, noon & 3pm Tue-Sat, 11am & 2pm Sun Apr-Dec) The medieval Rathaus has a spectacular baroque facade, added in 1720 and decorated with coats of arms and three tiers of statues. The top row represents (from left to right): strength, trade, peace (the one with the staff), justice and moderation. The steeple, topped with 41 Meissen china bells, was installed on the city's 1000th birthday in 1956. Tours cover the lavishly restored interior.

★ Am Sande
STREET
The cobbled, slightly wobbly street and square Am Sande is full of red-brick buildings with typically Hanseatic stepped gables. Even among these striking buildings, the black-and-white Industrie und Handelskammer (Trade and Industry Chamber, 1548) at the far western end stands out.

Markt
SQUARE
(Markt) Besides the Rathaus, notable buildings around the large Markt include the Court of Justice, the little gated-in, grotto-like area with paintings depicting scenes of justice being carried out throughout the centuries; and the former Ducal Palace, now a courthouse.

Auf dem Meere
STREET
If you continue west along Waagestrasse from the Markt and veer left, you'll come to Auf dem Meere, a particularly striking Lüneburg street. Here the wavy pavements have pushed facades sideways or made buildings buckle in the middle. The street feels wonky all the way to St Michaeliskirche. Look at the steps leading to the church!

St Johanniskirche
CHURCH
(☑04131-445 42; www.st-johanniskirche.de; Am Sande; ⊗10am-5pm Mon-Sat, 11am-4pm Sun Mar-Oct, shorter hours Nov-Feb) At the eastern edge of Am Sande stands the 14th-century St Johanniskirche, whose 108m-high spire leans 2.2m off centre. Local legend has it that the architect was so upset by this crooked steeple that he tried to do himself in by jumping off it. He fell into a hay cart and was saved, but, celebrating his escape later in the pub, drank himself into a stupor, fell over, hit his head and died after all.

SaLü Salztherme
SPA
(Spa Baths; ☑04131-723 110; www.kurzentrum. de; Uelzener Strasse 1-5; adult/child from €8/3; ⊗10am-11pm Mon-Sat, 8am-9pm Sun) With Lüneburg having made its fortune from salt, where better to try the mineral's therapeutic properties than at the town's salt baths? You can bathe in saltwater at 36°C and try out

---

HAMBURG'S CONCENTRATION CAMP

In the 1938, the Nazis converted an old brick factory 25km southeast of Hamburg into a concentration camp: **KZ-Gedenkstätte Neuengamme** (Neuengamme Concentration Camp; ☑040-428 131 500; www.kz-gedenkstaette-neuengamme.de; Jean-Dolidier-Weg 75; ⊗9.30am-4pm Mon-Fri, noon-7pm Sat & Sun Apr-Sep, to 5pm Sat & Sun Oct-Mar). Over the next seven years, countless numbers of people were imprisoned here. At least 42,900 were killed, either murdered directly, or indirectly due to the horrible living conditions.

Exhibits recount the Holocaust, both locally and nationally. Only a few historic buildings remain, but the general layout of the huge camp is shown. Take the S-Bahn to Bergedorf, then bus 227 or 327 (about one hour, €8.10).

Much less known than other camps such as Sachsenhausen near Berlin, Neuengamme was only fully opened as a memorial in 2005, after prisons on the site had been closed. Its setting amid vast expanses of flat farmland adds a mundane horror.

You can spend a couple of hours wandering the site, reading the plaques that explain what happened where and going inside surviving buildings for the many exhibits. Combine your time here with a visit to **Bullenhuser Damm Schule** (Bullenhuser Damm School; ☑040-428 1310; www.kz-gedenkstaette-neuengamme.de; Bullenhuser Damm 92-94; ⊗10am-5pm Sun; Ⓢ Rothenburgsort) in Hamburg for a gruelling window into the horrors of 75 years ago.

HAMBURG & THE NORTH LÜNEBURG

the single-sex or mixed sauna area, water fountains and whirlpool.

🛏 Sleeping

DJH Hostel   HOSTEL €
(☑04131-418 64; www.lueneburg.jugendherberge. de; Soltauer Strasse 133; dm €28-31; P🚭@🛜) After sundown, the lights glow a warm welcome from the glass-walled stairwell of this spacious and relatively luxurious 148-bed hostel. It's 4km southwest of the Markt, right near the university. Bus services – 5011 or 5012 from the train station to Scharnhorstrasse/DJH – don't run late.

★ Hotel Scheffler   HOTEL €€
(☑04131-200 80; www.hotel-scheffler.de; Bardowicker Strasse 7; s/d from €76/98; P🚭🛜) The hotel most in keeping with Lüneburg's quirky character, this 16-room place just off the Markt greets you with brickwork, stained glass, carved wooden stair-rails, animal trophies and indoor plants. The bright rooms are less idiosyncratic; there's a restaurant on-site.

Hotel Bremer Hof   HOTEL €€
(☑04131-2240; www.bremer-hof.de; Lüner Strasse 12-13; s/d from €66/86; P🚭🛜) This ivy-covered 54-room hotel offers rooms across a range of budgets, from plain and inexpensive in a modern annex to historic rooms with beamed ceilings in the main building. It has been in the same family since 1889 and is just northeast of the Markt.

🍴 Eating & Drinking

Bell & Beans   CAFE €
(☑04131-864 7120; www.bellandbeans.de; Glockenstrasse 6; mains from €5; ☺8am-6pm Mon-Fri, from 9am Sat, from 10am Sun) Our favourite breakfast spot in the city, Bell & Beans has a cool Berlinesque sensibility with terrific breakfasts and coffee. Locals love it too, so it can be hard to get a table.

Anders Restaurant   CAFE, GERMAN €€
(☑04131-400 4240; www.anders-lueneberg.de; Friedrich-Penseler-Strasse 9b; mains €8-17; ☺8am-6pm Mon-Wed, to 10pm Thu & Fri, 5-10pm Sat) You'll need a vehicle to get here and it's a bit out on a limb, but it is worth the effort. The cafe dishes here are much-loved classics – Wiener schnitzel, *Currywurst* and *Pannfisch* – but they're perfectly prepared and filled with flavour. Then again, you could abandon all sense of tradition and try the excellent brioche burger.

Viscvle Kitchen & Bar   INTERNATIONAL €€
(☑04131-284 0395; www.viscvle.de; Salzstrasse Am Wasser 3-5; mains €12-22; ☺11am-midnight Mon-Sat) With an atmosphere as fresh as the tastes they prepare in the kitchen, Viscvle is fun and ranges from veggie flatbread or bruschetta up to steaks.

Zum Alten Brauhaus   GERMAN €€€
(☑04131-721 277; www.brauhaus-lueneburg.de; Grapengiesserstrasse 11; mains €17-28; ☺noon-11pm Tue-Sat) This old-style *Brauhaus* (brewery) has been around in some form since the 16th century. Dishes flit effortlessly between tradition and a few outside influences – the dry-aged steak or wiener schnitzel are assuring, while Italian pasta makes an appearance as well. It's right in the centre, just off the western end of Am Sande.

★ Sa Bacca   BAR
(☑04131-390 405; www.sabacca.com; Am Markt 4; ☺7pm-midnight Mon-Sat) Fronting onto Marktplatz, Sa Bacca couldn't be a more central pit stop as you explore town. The vaulted brick cellar and extravagantly tiled bar are the perfect backdrop to enjoying the city's best cocktails.

Gasthausbrauerei und
Brennerei Nolte   BREWERY
(☑04131-522 32; www.gasthausbrauereinolte.de; Dahlenburger Landstrasse 102; ☺4-11pm Wed-Sat, 11am-10pm Sun) They've been brewing here since 1906; the dark beer is especially good out in the garden. Unlike many beer-centric places, food is taken seriously at this local legend; fish is house-smoked, the menu lists the provenance of the dishes and you can enjoy regional specialities like sour pork in aspic. It's about 500m east of the train station.

ℹ Information

Lüneburg Tourist-Information Office
(☑04131-207 6620; www.lueneburg.de; Am Markt; ☺9.30am-4pm May-Oct, closed Sun Nov-Apr) Offers city tours and has info on trips to the surrounding Lüneburger Heide.

ℹ Getting There & Away

There are frequent IC train services to Hamburg (€13.50, 30 minutes) and Hanover (€29.50, one hour). A web of cheaper regional trains also service these destinations and more from the station, which is 300m east of the centre.

SCHLESWIG-HOLSTEIN

Sandy beaches, jaunty red-and-white striped lighthouses, deep fjords carved by glaciers, sandpipers and seals have made this sweeping peninsula between the North and Baltic Seas Germany's most elite summer retreat.

Much of the peninsula's interior is made up of of seemingly never-ending expanses of flat, green farmland interrupted only by wind farms and grazing black-and-white-splotched cows. But its coastline – and especially the North Frisian Islands off Schleswig-Holstein's western coast – remains the country's answer to the Côte d'Azur. Of course, the fickle northern European climate makes it a funny sort of answer, as cold winds and dark clouds periodically drive even the hardiest holidaymakers from their *Strandkörbe* (sheltered straw 'beach basket' seats).

Don't miss Lübeck, the magnificently preserved medieval headquarters of the Hanseatic League. Flensburg, too, is a lively harbour town

Schleswig-Holstein belonged to neighbouring Denmark until 1864 and you'll find Scandinavian overtones throughout the region, particularly in Flensburg and Schleswig.

Lübeck

📞 0451 / POP 218,523

A 12th-century gem boasting more than a thousand historic buildings, Lübeck's picture-book appearance is an enduring reminder of its role as one of the founding cities of the mighty Hanseatic League and its moniker 'Queen of the Hanse'. Behind its landmark Holstentor, you'll find streets lined with medieval merchants' homes and spired churches forming Lübeck's 'crown'.

Recognised by Unesco as a World Heritage Site in 1987, today this thriving provincial city retains many enchanting corners to explore, including a fab museum that tells the Lübeck story.

⊙ Sights

★ **Europäisches Hansemuseum** MUSEUM
(European Hanseatic Museum; 📞 0451-809 0990; www.hansemuseum.eu; An der Untertrave 1; adult/child €12.50/7.50; ⊗ 10am-6pm) Opened in 2015, this brilliant museum tells the remarkable story of the Hanseatic League, Lübeck and the region. For 600 years, city

states in northern Europe and along the Baltic discovered that shared interests in trade made everybody's life better than war. Transfixing exhibits use every modern technology to tell a story as dramatic as any thing on *Game of Thrones*. The complex includes the beautifully restored medieval **Castle Friary.**

★ **Holstentor** LANDMARK
(Holsten Gate) Built in 1464 and looking so settled-in that it appears to sag, Lübeck's charming red-brick city gate is a national icon. Its twin pointed cylindrical towers, leaning together across the stepped gable that joins them, captivated Andy Warhol (his print is in the St Annen Museum), and have graced postcards, paintings, posters and marzipan souvenirs. Discover this and more inside the **Museum Holstentor** (📞 0451-122 4129; www.museum-holstentor.de; adult/child €7/2.50; ⊗ 10am-6pm Apr-Dec, 11am-5pm Tue-Sun Jan-Mar), which sheds light on the history of the gate and on Lübeck's medieval mercantile glory days.

★ **Museumsquartier St Annen** MUSEUM
(Museum Quarter St Annen; 📞 0451-122 4137; www.museumsquartier-st-annen.de; St-Annen-Strasse; adult/child €12/6; ⊗ 10am-5pm Tue-Sun Apr-Dec, from 11am Jan-Mar) This museum quarter includes an old synagogue, church and medieval buildings along its uneven streets. The namesake St Annen Museum details the diverse history of the neighbourhood as it traces 700 years of art and culture. The adjoining St Annen Kunstalle has ecclesiastical art (including Hans Memling's 1491 Passion Altar) and contemporary art, including Andy Warhol's print of Lübeck's Holstentor. There's a chic little **cafe** in the courtyard.

Rathaus HISTORIC BUILDING
(Town Hall; 📞 0451-122 1005; Breite Strasse 62; adult/concession €4/2; ⊗ tours 11am, noon & 3pm Mon-Fri, 1.30pm Sat & Sun) Sometimes described as a 'fairy tale in stone', Lübeck's 13th- to 15th-century Rathaus is widely regarded as one of the most beautiful in Germany. Inside, a highlight is the *Audienzsaal* (audience hall), a light-flooded hall decked out in festive rococo.

Günter Grass-Haus MUSEUM
(📞 0451-122 4230; www.grass-haus.de; Glockengiesserstrasse 21; adult/child €7/2.50; ⊗ 10am-5pm Apr-Dec, from 11am Jan-Mar) Born

in Danzig (now Gdańsk), Poland, Günter Grass had been living just outside Lübeck for 13 years when he collected his Nobel Prize in 1999. But this post-war literary colossus initially trained as an artist, and he always continued to draw and sculpt. The Günter Grass-Haus is filled with the author's leitmotifs – flounders, rats, snails and eels – brought to life in bronze and charcoal, as well as in prose. The small bookshop is excellent.

You can view a copy of the first typewritten page of *Die Blechtrommel* (The Tin Drum; 1959). Grass died in Lübeck in 2015.

Buddenbrookhaus   MUSEUM
(📞 0451-122 4190; www.buddenbrookhaus.de; Mengstrasse 4; adult/child €7/2.50; ⊙ 10am-6pm Apr-Dec, 11am-5pm Feb & Mar, 11am-5pm Tue-Sun Jan) Thomas Mann, winner of the 1929 Nobel Prize for Literature, was born in Lübeck in 1875, and his family's former home is now the Buddenbrookhaus. Named after Mann's novel about a wealthy Lübeck family in decline, *The Buddenbrooks* (1901), this museum is a monument to the author of such classics as *Der Tod in Venedig* (Death in Venice) and *Der Zauberberg* (The Magic Mountain).

Willy Brandt House   MUSEUM
(📞 0451-122 4250; www.willy-brandt.de; Königstrasse 21; ⊙ 11am-6pm) **FREE** Besides Gunther Grass, Lübeck's other big Nobel Prize winner was chancellor of West Germany (1969–74) and was honoured for his efforts to reconcile with East Germany. Exhibits capture the tense times of the Cold War and Willy Brandt's role at this pivotal time. He was born in this house in 1913.

Dom   CATHEDRAL
(📞 0451-747 04; www.domzuluebeck.de; Domkirchhof; ⊙ 10am-6pm Apr-Sep, to 5pm Oct, to 4pm Nov-Mar) The Dom was founded in 1173 by Heinrich der Löwe when he took over Lübeck. Locals like to joke that if you approach the Dom from the northeast, you have to go through *Hölle* (hell) and *Fegefeuer* (purgatory) – the actual names of streets – to see *Paradies* (paradise), the lavish vestibule to the Dom. Although spartan, the interior has good displays showing reconstruction after the 1942 bombing raid.

Theater Figuren Museum   MUSEUM
(Museum of Theatre Puppets; 📞 0451-786 26; www.theaterfigurenmuseum.de; Am Kolk 14; 🖭) Even if

DON'T MISS

SCHLESWIG-HOLSTEIN MUSIK FESTIVAL

Leading international musicians and promising young artists perform during this festival (www.shmf.de), in castles, churches, warehouses and animal barns throughout Germany's northernmost state. Held from mid-July until August.

you think you don't like puppets, don't miss this wondrous collection of some 1200 puppets, props, posters and more from Europe, Asia and Africa. The artistry is amazing, as is the ancient alley where it's located; try to catch a performance at its theatre (p187). The museum was closed for renovations at the time of writing.

Marienkirche   CHURCH
(St Mary's Church; 📞 0451-397 700; www.st-marien-luebeck.com; Marienkirchhof 1; adult/child €2/free; ⊙ 10am-6pm Apr-Sep, to 4pm Nov-Mar) This fine Gothic church boasts the world's highest brick-vaulted roof and was the model for dozens of churches in northern Germany. Crane your neck to take in the painted cross-vaulted ceilings supported by slender, ribbed pillars. A WWII bombing raid brought down the church's bells, which have been left where they fell in 1942 and have become a famous symbol of the city.

Katharinenkirche   CHURCH
(www.museumskirche.de; cnr Glockengiesserstrasse & Königstrasse; adult/child €2/free; ⊙ noon-4pm) Art lovers will enjoy the Katharinenkirche for its sculptures by Ernst Barlach and Gerhard Marcks, plus *The Resurrection of Lazarus* by Tintoretto. It has no tower, owing to the rules of the Cistercian order that built it in the 14th century. It's worth wandering the arched hallway beneath the balcony and sitting to appreciate the rich decoration, some of it recently restored.

Salzspeicher   HISTORIC BUILDING
(off Holstenbrücke) Just behind the Holstentor (to the east) stand the Salzspeicher: six gabled brick shop-filled buildings once used to store salt transported from Lüneburg. The stuff was then bartered for furs from Scandinavia and used to preserve the herrings

Lübeck

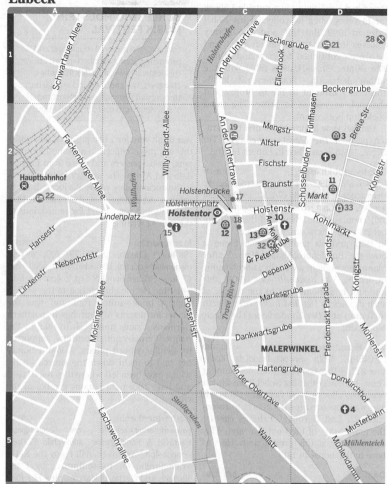

that formed a substantial chunk of Lübeck's Hanseatic trade.

Petrikirche CHURCH
(Church of St Peter; ☎ 0451-397 730; www.st-petri-luebeck.de; Petrikirchhof 1; tower adult/child €4/2.50; ⏰ church 10am-4pm, tower 9am-8pm Mar-Sep, 10am-7pm Oct-Dec, 10am-6pm Jan & Feb) Thanks to a lift, even the fitness-phobic get to enjoy panoramic views from the 50m-high platform in the tower of the 13th-century Petrikirche. No longer an active parish, the starkly whitewashed interior hosts exhibits and events.

🏃 Activities

Mietrad Mielke CYCLING
(☎ 0176 2728 0353; An der Mauer; rental per day from €9; ⏰ 10am-6pm Mon-Sat) This cheery English-speaking shop rents a huge range of bikes, including electric models.

Guided Tours

The Trave River forms a moat around the Altstadt, and cruising it aboard a boat is a fine way to get a feel for the city. The tourist office has a list of options. There are also bus and walking tours.

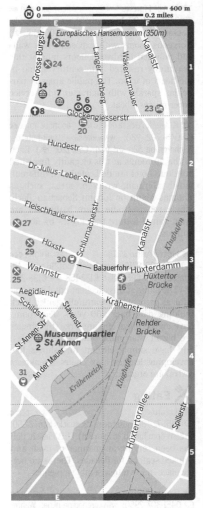

Lübeck

◎ Top Sights
1	Holstentor	C3
2	Museumsquartier St Annen	E4

◎ Sights
3	Buddenbrookhaus	D2
4	Dom	D5
5	Füchtingshof	E1
6	Glandorps Gang	E1
7	Günter Grass-Haus	E1
8	Katharinenkirche	E1
9	Marienkirche	D2
	Museum Holstentor	(see 1)
10	Petrikirche	C3
11	Rathaus	D2
12	Salzspeicher	C3
13	Theater Figuren Museum	C3
14	Willy Brandt House	E1

⊕ Activities, Courses & Tours
15	Lübecker Verkehrsverein	B3
16	Mietrad Mielke	F3
17	Open-Air City Tour	C2
18	Quandt-Linie	C3

⊜ Sleeping
19	Hotel Anno 1216	C2
20	Hotel Haase	E2
21	Klassik Altstadt Hotel	D1
22	niu Rig	A2
23	Rucksackhotel	F1

⊗ Eating
	Café Niederegger	(see 33)
24	Die Zimberei	E1
25	Grenadine	E3
26	Kartoffel Keller	E1
27	Krützfeld	E3
28	Schiffergesellschaft	D1
29	Vai	E3

⊕ Drinking & Nightlife
30	CafeBar	E3
31	Im Alten Zolln	E4

⊕ Entertainment
32	Figurentheater	C3

⊕ Shopping
33	Niederegger	D3

Lübecker Verkehrsverein TOURS
(☑ 0451-764 60; www.verkehrsverein-luebeck.de; per person €10; ⊙ 11am & 2pm Mon-Sat, 11am Sun May-Oct, shorter hours Nov-Apr) These two-hour walking tours of the old city are a good way to get to know Lübeck. Tours leave from outside the tourist office.

Quandt-Linie BOATING
(☑ 0451-777 99; www.quandt-linie.de; Holstentor-terrassen; adult/child from €14/7; ⊙ half-hourly 10am-6pm May-Oct) One-hour city tours leave from next to the Holstentor. Also on offer are

tours to the seaside resort of Travemünde. Tours are less frequent November to April.

Open-Air City Tour BUS
(www.sv-luebeck.de/de/freizeit/open-air-bus; An der Untertrave; adult/child €10/6; ⊙ hourly 10am-4pm May-Oct, Sat & Sun only Mar & Apr) Open-top buses make 50-minute circuits of the historic

city. Ask at the tourist office for departure points.

🎊 Festivals & Events

Brahms Festival
MUSIC

(www.brahms-festival.de) In early May, Lübeck celebrates Hamburg-born composer Johannes Brahms with concerts in various venues across the city.

🛏 Sleeping

Rucksackhotel
HOSTEL €

(☑ 0451-706 892; www.rucksackhotel-luebeck. com; Kanalstrasse 70; dm/s/d from €17/29/40; P @ ☎) This 30-bed family-run hostel has a relaxed atmosphere and good facilities, including a well-equipped kitchen and round-the-clock access. The decor is colourful, with the odd tropical touch.

Campingplatz Schönböcken
CAMPGROUND €

(☑ 0451-893 090; www.camping-luebeck.de; Steinrader Damm 12; per tent €4-6, adult/child €6/2) This modern camping ground is a good bet for its grassy sites, kiosk, restaurant, entertainment room and children's playground. It's a 10-minute bus ride west of the city centre (take bus 2).

★ niu Rig
HOTEL €€

(☑ 0201-649 780; www.niu.de; Am Bahnhof 17-19; r from €69) Due to open in late 2018, this stunning new hotel opposite the train station may even have us doubting that the best hotels in town are in the old city. Sleek, ultra-modern rooms come with all the latest gadgets. Expect prices to rise once its reputation is established.

GÄNGE & HÖFE

In the Middle Ages, Lübeck was home to numerous craftspeople and artisans. Their presence caused demand for housing to outgrow the available space, so tiny single-storey homes were built in courtyards behind existing rows of houses. These were then made accessible via little walkways from the street.

Almost 90 such *Gänge* (walkways) and *Höfe* (courtyards) still exist. The most famous include the **Füchtingshof** (Glockengiessserstrasse 25), with its beautiful carvings, and the 1612 **Glandorps Gang** (Glockengiessserstrasse 41-51), which you can usually peer into.

★ Hotel Haase
BOUTIQUE HOTEL €€

(☑ 0451-7074 90 1; www.hotel-haase-luebeck.de; Glockengießerstrasse 24; s/d from €100/116; ☎) Gorgeous rooms with exposed brick walls and polished hardwood floors inhabit this beautifully restored 14th-century home in the heart of town. The public areas in particular sparkle with character, and service never misses a beat.

★ Klassik Altstadt Hotel
BOUTIQUE HOTEL €€

(☑ 0451-702 980; www.klassik-altstadt-hotel.de; Fischergrube 52; s/d from €55/120; ☎) Each of the 29 rooms at this elegantly furnished boutique hotel are dedicated to a different, mostly German, writer or artist, such as Thomas Mann or Johann Sebastian Bach. Single rooms (some share baths and are great value) feature travelogues by famous authors.

★ Hotel Anno 1216
DESIGN HOTEL €€€

(☑ 0451-400 8210; www.hotelanno1216.com; Alfstrasse 38; s €98-138, d €132-168, ste €198-258; ☎) The name at this excellent hotel isn't fanciful, as parts of this beautifully gabled brick building date back 800 years. The rooms have high ceilings and are large (the singles are bigger than most other hotel doubles) and have simply elegant furnishings like enveloping leather easy chairs. Breakfasts (extra) are organic.

🍴 Eating

Krützfeld
DELI €

(☑ 0451-728 32; Hüxstrasse 23; snacks from €2.50; ⊙ 8am-6pm Tue-Fri, to 2pm Sat) This classic deli has been serving all manner of fresh and smoked seafood for decades. There's no better place in town to assemble a picnic.

★ Grenadine
BISTRO €€

(☑ 0451-307 2950; www.grenadine-hl.de; Wahmstrasse 40; mains €10-23; ⊙ 9am-4pm Mon, to 10pm Tue-Thu, to midnight Fri & Sat, to 3pm Sun; ☎) This narrow, elongated bar leads through to a garden out the back. Enjoy bistro fare amid chic, retro-minimalist style. The long drinks menu goes well with tapas choices. Sandwiches, salads and pasta, plus a gorgeous breakfast buffet (€14.50 to €17.50), are served.

Kartoffel Keller
GERMAN €€

(☑ 0451-762 154; www.kartoffel-keller.de; Koberg 8; mains €10-14; ⊙ 11.30am-10.30pm Sun-Thu, to 11pm Fri & Sat) One of the oldest traditional cellars in the city still open to the public,

Kartoffel Keller has a lovely vaulted ceiling as well as some appealing outdoor tables in summer. It does get a bit touristy and it does love potatoes (baked, pancakes etc), but there's also a mean rare roast beef and some stews, and it's a good deal.

Vai
EUROPEAN €€€

(☑0451-400 8083; www.restaurant-vai.de; Hüxstrasse 42; mains lunch €11, dinner €16-39; ☺11am-10pm Mon-Sat) Glossy, richly grained timber lines the walls, tables and even the alfresco courtyard of this sleek, stylish restaurant. The good-value top-end lunches are popular and feature pasta, seafood and salads. The menu is more complex at night with steaks and lobster appearing. Great wine list; book ahead.

Schiffergesellschaft
GERMAN €€€

(☑0451-767 76; www.schiffergesellschaft.de; Breite Strasse 2; mains €15-31; ☺kitchen 11.30am-11pm, bar 10am-1am) In the historic seafarers' guild hall (1535), Lübeck's most atmospheric – if not best – restaurant is a veritable museum. Ships' lanterns, old model ships and revolving Chinese-style silhouette lamps dangle from the beamed ceiling of the wood-lined dining room. White-aproned waitstaff deliver regional specialities to tables here or in the hidden garden out back. Book ahead for dinner.

Die Zimberei
EUROPEAN €€€

(☑0451-738 12; www.zimberei.de; Königstrasse 5-7; mains €29-38, 3-/4-course set menus €46/53; ☺5-9.30pm Tue-Sat) Take one historic Hanseatic merchant's house, mix in three beautifully restored ballrooms and season with restored elegant gardens. The result is this excellent restaurant which serves modern takes on local meats and seafood.

Drinking & Entertainment

★Im Alten Zolln
PUB

(☑0451-723 95; www.alter-zolln.de; Mühlenstrasse 93-95; ☺11am-late; 🖥) This classic pub inhabits a 16th-century customs post. There's an excellent beer selection. Patrons people-watch from terrace and sidewalk tables in summer and watch bands (rock and jazz) inside in winter. Fortify yourself with schnitzel and Lübeck's best roast potatoes.

CafeBar
BAR

(☑0451-4893 8679; Hüxstrasse 94; ☺11am-late) Cafe by day, bar by... you get it. During daylight hours savour coffee drinks while grazing fresh and tasty casual fare. But the real appeal here are the night-time smokin' hot DJs who mix techno, R&B and groovy sounds.

Figurentheater
THEATRE

(☑0451-700 60; www.figurentheater-luebeck.de; Am Kolk 20-22; tickets €6-20; ☺Tue-Sun; 🖥) This adorable puppet theatre, which is part of the Theater Figuren Museum (p183), puts on a children's show at 3pm, and another for adults on some evenings at 7.30pm, as well as occasional performances in English.

🛍 Shopping

Hüxstraase is one of Germany's best shopping streets. It's lined with an array of creative and interesting boutiques, clothing stores, bookshops, cafes and much more. Nearby Schlumacherstrasse is also good.

★Niederegger
FOOD

(☑0451-530 1126; www.niederegger.de; Breite Strasse 89; ☺9am-7pm Mon-Fri, 9am-6pm Sat, 10am-6pm Sun) Lübeck's mecca for marzipan lovers, the almond confectionery from Arabia, which has been made locally for centuries. Even if you're not buying, the shop's elaborate seasonal displays are a feast for the eyes. In its small museum, Marzipan-Salon, you'll learn that in medieval Europe marzipan was considered medicine, not a treat. At the back there's an elegant cafe (mains €4-15; ☺9am-7pm Mon-Fri, to 6pm Sat, 10am-6pm Sun).

ℹ Information

Tourist Office (☑0451-889 9700; www.luebeck-tourismus.de; Holstentorplatz 1; ☺9am-7pm Mon-Fri, 10am-4pm Sat, 10am-3pm Sun Jun-Aug, shorter hours Sep-Apr) One of Schleswig-Holstein's better tourist offices, with a cafe and internet terminals.

ℹ Getting There & Away

BUS

Regional and local buses use the central bus station near the Hauptbahnhof. Two daily buses operated by Flixbus (www.flixbus.com) go to/from Hamburg (€5, one hour).

TRAIN

Lübeck has connections every hour to Hamburg (€14.50, 45 minutes) and Kiel (from €18.70, 1¼ hours).

ℹ Getting Around

Lübeck's Altstadt (old town) is on an island encircled by the canalised Trave River. The

Hauptbahnhof and central bus station are 500m west of the **Holstentor** (p182).

Lübeck's centre is easily walked. Many streets are pedestrianised and off limits to all but hotel guests' vehicles. Bus tickets cost €2; day cards cost €5.50.

Hourly trains connect Lübeck to Travemünde (€3.50, 22 minutes); there are also boats between the two.

Travemünde

📞 04502 / POP 14,200

Writer Thomas Mann declared that he spent his happiest days in Travemünde, just outside Lübeck (which bought it in 1329 to control the shipping coming into its harbour). Located at the point where the Trave River flows into the Baltic Sea, its 4.5km of sandy beaches have held long appeal, drawing everyone from Dostoyevsky to northern Europe's elite. The town was, for a time in the 19th century, known as the German St Tropez. That may be overstating things a little, but there is an unmistakeable sense of sophistication and nostalgia here. Water sports are now the main draw, along with a colourful sailing regatta (www.travemuender-woche.com) in the last week of July.

The town is all wide streets and has a certain 1960s feel. Vorderreihe, on the waterfront, is lined with pricey shops and cafes.

The town takes great pride in its historic four-masted sailing ship-turned-museum, Passat (📞 04502-122 5202; www.rettetdiepassat.de; Am Priwallhafen 16a; adult/child €5/2.50; ☑10am-5pm Apr-Oct) , which used to do the run around South America's Cape Horn in the early to mid-20th century. A regular passenger ferry (€1) crosses the river to the ship.

❶ Getting There & Away

Travemünde is a gateway to Scandinavia, with major ferry lines sailing from its Skandinavienkai.

Hourly trains connect Lübeck to Travemünde (€3.50, 22 minutes), which has several train stations, including Skandinavienkai (for international ferries) and Strandbahnhof (for the beach and tourist office).

Könemann Schiffahrt (📞 0451-280 1635; www.koenemannschiffahrt.de; adult one-way/return €14/20.50, child €6.50/11; ☑twice daily Apr-mid-Oct) runs scenic ferries to/from Lübeck (1¾ hours). You can sail one way and take the train the other.

Kiel

📞 0431 / POP 249,023

Some locals admit that Kiel, the capital of Schleswig-Holstein, has a city centre that's *grottenhässlich* (ugly as sin). And unfortunately it is true; it was obliterated during WWII by bombing raids on its U-boat pens and then rapidly rebuilt. Today, it is a series of charmless indoor malls linked by pedestrian bridges.

However, Kiel's grand harbour continues on as it has for centuries and this, along with the city's museums, should be the focus of your visit. Huge ferries transport millions of passengers to and from Scandinavia, while summer sees locals strolling the long waterfront promenade.

⊙ Sights

Kiellinie   WATERFRONT

The splendid waterfront promenade known as the Kiellinie begins northeast of the Schlossgarten. Sailing clubs, a tiny **aquarium** (📞 0431-600 1637; www.aquarium-geomar.de; Düsternbrooker Weg 20; adult/child €3/2; ☑9am-6pm), cafes and restaurants line the way, and there is an ever-changing series of vistas of the harbour and huge ships. Eventually the 3.5km-promenade becomes the Hindenburgufer. About 2km from the start, at Reventloubrücke, you can get hourly ferries back to near the train station or on to Laboe.

Nord-Ostsee-Kanal   CANAL

(viewing platform adult/child €2/1) The 99km-long Nord-Ostsee-Kanal reaches the Baltic Sea from the North Sea at Kiel, with some 60,000 ships passing through every year. It's easy to view the Schleusen (locks) at Holtenau, 7km north of Kiel. The viewing platform here is open from sunrise to sunset. There's a museum on the southern side of the canal. To get to the locks, take bus 11 to Wik, Kanal. A free ferry shuttles back and forth between the southern and northern banks.

Inaugurated in 1895, the canal is now the third-most trafficked in the world, after the Suez and Panama canals.

☞ Tours

Adler-Schiffe   BOATING

(📞 01805 123 344; www.adler-schiffe.de; Bahnhofskai; adult/child from €52/26; ☑Jun-Sep) Experience the full engineering glory of the Nord-Ostsee-Kanal and take in the passing ship traffic on an eight-hour journey with the *Raddampfer Freya*. The best way to appreciate the canal, this historic steamship sails to Rendsburg and back from Bahnhofskai in Kiel (some services are aboard regular boats).

 Festivals & Events

★ **Kieler Woche** SAILING

(Kiel Week; www.kieler-woche.de; ⊗ late Jun) Kiel's biggest annual event is the giant week-long Kieler Woche. Revolving around a series of yachting regattas, it's attended by more than 4000 of the world's sailing elite and half a million spectators. Even if you're not into boats, it's one nonstop party and easily the best time to be in town.

🛏 **Sleeping**

Atlantic Hotel HOTEL €€

(✆ 0431-374 990; www.atlantic-hotels.de/en/hotel-kiel; Raiffeisenstrasse 2; s/d from €129/169) This large harbourside hotel is as good as things get in Kiel – it's a comfortable, modern four-star place aimed at business travellers, with perfectly adequate rooms and a rooftop terrace with sweeping downtown views.

 Drinking & Nightlife

Kieler Brauerei BREWERY

(✆ 0431-906 290; www.kieler-brauerei.de; Alter Markt 9; ⊗ 10am-11pm) This city-centre micro brewery produces a very fine unfiltered beer that's redolent with herbs and hops. The menu is casual and has German standards (yes, schnitzel) and locally caught seafood.

ℹ **Information**

Tourist Information Kiel (✆ 0431-679 100; www.kiel-sailing-city.de; Andreas-Gayk-Strasse 31; ⊗ 9.30am-6pm Mon-Fri, 10am-3pm Sat May-Sep, to 2pm Sat Oct-Apr) About 300m north of the train station, next to the library.

ℹ **Getting There & Away**

Ferry services run between Kiel and Gothenburg, Oslo and Lithuania.

Numerous trains run between Kiel and Hamburg (from €19.90, 1¼ hours). Trains to Lübeck leave hourly (from €18.70, 1¼ hours). There are regular local connections to Schleswig, Husum, Schwerin and Flensburg.

WORTH A TRIP

SCHLESWIG-HOLSTEINISCHES FREILICHTMUSEUM

Beekeepers, bakers, potters and many more traditional craftspeople ply their trade in Molfsee, 6km south of Kiel. This excellent **museum** (Schleswig-Holstein Open-Air Museum; ✆ 0431-659 660; www.freilichtmuseum-sh.de; Alte Hamburger Landstrasse 97; adult/child €8/2; ⊗ 9am-6pm Apr-Oct, 11am-4pm Sun Nov-Mar) features some 70 traditional houses typical of the region, relocated from around the state.

To get to Molfsee from Kiel (€2.80, 30 minutes, hourly), take bus 501 from the latter's central bus station.

Laboe

✆ 04343 / POP 5475

At the mouth of the Kiel firth, on its eastern bank, the village of Laboe is home to some surprising reminders of WWII as well as decent beaches, cheap and somewhat cheerful waterfront cafes, and stirring views of the ceaseless water traffic of ships great and small.

◉ **Sights**

Marine Ehrenmal MEMORIAL

(Naval Memorial; ✆ 04343-4948 4962; Strandstrasse 92; adult/child €6/4, combined ticket with U-Boat 995 €9.50/6.50; ⊗ 9.30am-6pm) Nearly 100m tall, this memorial was opened in 1936 to commemorate German seamen killed during WWI. After WWII it became a memorial for sailors killed in both world wars. In one room you can see every ship lost during the conflicts. It's often striking, and you'll see that efforts to literally whitewash its Nazi past have been only partially successful.

U-Boat 995 HISTORIC SITE

(✆ 04343-427 062; www.deutscher-marinebund.de; Strandstrasse 92; combined ticket with Marine Ehrenmal adult/child €9.50/6.50; ⊗ 9.30am-6pm Apr-Oct, to 4pm Nov-Mar) Hundreds of subs like this one once called Kiel home; Wolfgang Petersen's seminal film *Das Boot* (1981) was set on a similar U-boat. You can climb through its claustrophobic interior.

WORTH A TRIP

NATURPARK HOLSTEINISCHE SCHWEIZ

Sprawling over 753 sq km between Lübeck to the south and Kiel to the north, the Naturpark Holsteinische Schweiz (www.naturpark-holsteinische-schweiz.de) is the region's largest outdoor playground. Germany's propensity to label its most scenic areas 'Swiss' (the name translates as 'Holstein Switzerland') reflects the park's undulating green hills, wildflower-strewn meadows and golden fields. This verdant landscape is interspersed with a string of some 200 lakes, of which 70 are over one hectare in size.

ⓘ Getting There & Away

From Kiel, the best option is to take the ferry (adult/child €3.60/2, 1¼ hours, up to 12 daily), or bus 100 or 102 (€3.20, 35 minutes, half-hourly). It's about 18km by bike.

Schleswig

📞 04621 / POP 23,471

Neat red-brick houses and manicured lawns conceal the Viking past of this tidy town on the Baltic Sea's longest fjord. Although Schleswig is sleepy today, the tall cathedral spire rising proudly above the water hints at a more active past.

Founded in 804, after a major Viking community put down roots across the Schlei fjord, the town was the continent's economic hub for some 200 years. Later the Dukes of Gottorf made Schleswig their power base from the 16th to 18th centuries. And countless generations of fisherfolk and their families have left their marks.

You can enjoy the long local heritage at excellent museums and along the pretty waterfront.

◉ Sights & Activities

★ Dom St Petri   CATHEDRAL

(📞 04621-989 585; Süderholmstrasse 2; ⊙ 9am-5pm Mon-Sat, from 1.30pm Sun May-Sep, 10am-4pm Mon-Sat, from 1.30pm Sun Oct-Apr) With its steeple towering above the Altstadt (old town), the Dom St Petri provides an excellent point of orientation. It's also home to the intricate Bordesholmer Altar (1521), a carving by Hans Brüggemann. The 12.6m by 7.14m altar, on the wall furthest from the entrance, shows more than 400 figures in 24 scenes relating the story of the Passion of Christ – the result of extraordinary artistry and patience.

Schleswig-Holstein Landesmuseum   MUSEUM

(Schleswig-Holstein State Museum; www.schloss-gottorf.de; Schlossinsel 1, Schloss Gottorf; adult/child €10/6; ⊙ 10am-5pm Mon-Fri, to 6pm Sat & Sun Apr-Oct, 10am-4pm Tue-Fri, to 5pm Sat & Sun Nov-Mar) The Schleswig-Holstein Landesmuseum, in Schloss Gottorf, is filled with art treasures. A roomful of paintings by Lucas Cranach the Elder and a wood-panelled 17th-century wine tavern from Lübeck create a memorable first impression. There's also the rococo Plöner Saal, with faïence from the Baltic region; the artistic beauty and lavish detail of the stunning Schlosskapelle; and the elegant Hirschsaal, the former banquet hall named for the bas-reliefs of deer on the walls.

★ Wikinger Museum   MUSEUM

(Viking Museum; 📞 04621-813 222; www.haithabu.de; Haddebyer Noor 5, Haddeby; adult/child €7/5, audioguide €2/1; ⊙ 9am-5pm Apr-Oct, 10am-4pm Tue-Sun Nov-Mar; ♿) Vikings ruled from their base here at Haithabu, across the Schlei from Schleswig, some 1000 to 1200 years ago. Located just outside the historic settlement (now an archaeological site), this child-friendly museum features replica huts and actors showing how Viking families lived their daily lives (but without the smell), and has halls filled with displays.

The museum lies east of the B76 that runs between Schleswig and Kiel, about 3km from Schleswig's Bahnhof. Otherwise, take bus 4810 and alight at Haddeby.

Kappeln   VILLAGE

(B199) This tiny fishing village is near the mouth of the Schlei. It makes for a good stroll, with some historic buildings and old boats. You can cycle here (about 32km), but the best way to arrive is on a tour boat from Schleswig.

Gottorfer Globus   SCULPTURE

(Gottorf Globe; Schloss Gottorf; adult/child €8/5.50; ⊙ 10am-5pm Mon-Fri, to 6pm Sat & Sun Apr-Oct) View a reconstruction of the famous Gottorfer Globus, which has been placed in its own house, a five-minute walk through the castle's lovely formal gardens. The exterior of the 3m-diameter globe shows how the continents and seas were thought to look in the 17th century. The real magic is inside, however. Several people can fit on a bench inside the globe and watch the Renaissance night sky change as the globe spins around them; eight minutes equals one day.

Fahrradverleigh Röhling   CYCLING
(☑04621-993 030; www.fahrradverleih-schleswig.de; Knud-Laward-Strasse 30, Holm; per day from €7.50; ⊘9.30am-6pm Mon-Fri, to 12.30pm Sat) Choose from a range of bikes in old Holm, 500m east of the Altstadt.

⌖ Tours

Schleischifffahrt A Bischoff   BOATING
(☑04621-233 19; www.schleischifffahrt.de; Gottorfer Damm 1; ⊘Apr–mid-Sep) Located near the Schloss, offers journeys to various destinations including Kappeln (one-way/return €14/21).

⊨ Sleeping & Eating

Zollhaus   HOTEL €€
(☑04621-290 340; www.zollhaus-zu-gottorf.de; Lollfuss 110; s €79-95, d €102-125, ste €139-159; ℗⊖☎) After a day sightseeing, you'll enjoy the refined yet relaxed atmosphere and comfortable rooms at this 200-year-old customs house. The 10 rooms have a pastel-accented decor, and many look out to the terrace overlooking the grassy grounds. A cafe provides tasty refreshments. The waterfront and Schloss are both close by.

Hotel Alter Kreisbahnhof   HOTEL €€
(☑04621-302 00; www.hotel-alter-kreisbahnhof.de; Königstrasse 9; s €74-88, d from €104; ⊘restaurant 7am-9.30pm; ℗⊖☎) Some of the spacious rooms at this hotel-restaurant, based in a turreted former railway station, have water views. All have a modern decor that's literally peachy (portholes, anyone?). The restaurant (mains €10 to €15) serves creative regional cuisine. It's nicely located in the Altstadt, 100m from the Dom.

Olschewski's   SEAFOOD €€
(☑04621-255 77; www.hotelolschewski.de; Hafenstrasse 40; mains €9-19; ⊘11am-9pm Wed-Mon May-Sep, Wed-Sun Oct-Apr) Right across from the harbour on the edge of the Altstadt, Olschewski's is a local icon. The large and sunny terrace fills up fast on weekends when you can hear the clanking masts of nearby boats. Seafood is a speciality, especially the *Holmer-pot,* a rich combo of whitefish and wine. Good, creative specials.

ⓘ SCHLESWIG-HOLSTEIN TOURIST INFORMATION

Schleswig-Holstein's tourism website (www.sh-tourismus.de) is an excellent resource, especially for activities.

An annex has basic rooms (single/double from €55/80).

Esch am Hafen   SEAFOOD €€
(☑04621-290 207; Hafengang 2; mains €6-21; ⊘10am-9pm Apr-Oct, shorter hours Nov-Mar) Like a cod in a school, this one-storey modern restaurant right on the waterfront looks, at best, unassuming. And the menu certainly doesn't stand out: there's fish and chips, prawns in many forms and even *Currywurst*. But the service is quick, the prices are good and all the fish dishes are excellent.

ⓘ Information

Tourist Office (☑04621-850 056; www.schleswig.de; Plessenstrasse 7; ⊘10am-6pm Mon-Fri, to 2pm Sat & Sun Jun-Sep, 10am-4pm Mon-Fri, to 2pm Sat Apr-May & Oct, shorter hours rest of year) Very helpful; in the Altstadt near the Dom. City maps and hotel brochures are available outside after hours.

ⓘ Getting There & Away

Hourly trains go to Hamburg (from €25.40, 1½ hours), Flensburg (from €8.55, 25 minutes), Kiel (from €12.40, 50 minutes) and Husum (from €8.55, 35 minutes).

Flensburg
☑0461 / POP 87,600

Situated on a busy industrial firth just 7km south of the Danish border, Flensburg is sometimes still dubbed 'Rumstadt' for its prosperous 18th-century trade in liquor with the Caribbean. Reminders of its seafaring, rum-trading days echo across the port area. The old town and the harbour are lovely and lively, making this one of our favourite towns in northern Germany.

⊙ Sights

★**Oluf-Samson-Gang**   STREET
Once a notorious thoroughfare known by sailors for its brothels, cobblestoned Oluf-Samson-Gang has been transformed into one of the prettiest streets in town. Its colourful

facades have been repainted and a number of artist and craft studios have moved in. It's a gorgeous spot.

★ **Braasch** HISTORIC BUILDING
(📞 0461-141 600; www.braasch-rum.de; Rote Strasse 26-28; ⊙ 10am-6.30pm Mon-Fri, to 4pm Sat) Some of the prettiest *Kaufmannshöfe* (merchants' courtyards) can be found off the very picturesque Rote Strasse, which is up from the harbour by the Rathaus. While here, you can buy rum in drinkable and edible forms at this lavish shop, which has a small museum. There's also a smaller shop further north.

Museumsberg Flensburg MUSEUM
(Municipal Museum; 📞 0461-852 956; www.museumsberg.flensburg.de; Museumsberg 1; adult/child €6/3, combined ticket incl Schiffahrtsmuseum €8/4; ⊙ 10am-5pm Tue-Sun) This hilltop museum features two wings: one contains a collection of rooms and furniture from Schleswig-Holstein history, including a remarkably painted cembalo (early piano covered in murals). The second has excellent art nouveau works by Flensburg-born painter Hans Christiansen, as well as an Emil Nolde room.

Schiffahrtsmuseum MUSEUM
(Maritime Museum; 📞 0461-852 970; www.schiffahrtsmuseum.flensburg.de; Schiffbrücke 39; adult/child €6/3, combined ticket incl Museumsberg Flensburg €8/4; ⊙ 10am-5pm Tue-Sun) An engrossing museum right on the old harbour. Displays here give the history of rum and the seafarers who shipped and drank it. Cool models show how ships were built before power tools. On the water, workshops demonstrate how old ships are restored.

☞ Tours

MS Viking BOATING
(📞 0461-255 20; www.viking-schifffahrt.de; Augastrasse 9; adult/child return €12/5; ⊙ Tue-Sun Apr-May & Sep, daily Jun-Aug) The *MS Viking* operates scenic cruises to Glücksburg (one hour each way; four or five times a day), departing from where Norderhofenden meets Schiffbrücke. If you're lucky, you'll stray into Denmark en route.

🛏 Sleeping

★ **Hotel Hafen Flensburg** BOUTIQUE HOTEL €€
(📞 0461-160 680; www.hotel-hafen-flensburg.de; Schiffbrücke 33; r €95-175; 🅿 🛜) Now here's something special. The main heritage waterfront building has been painstakingly and artfully restored with stunning, light-filled rooms which are large and supremely comfortable. Nice touches, such as the use of driftwood in some of the installations, adds to a sense of style. Even the rooms in the annex are superb, with hardwood floors.

Hotel Alte Post HOTEL €€
(📞 0461-807 0810; www.ap-hotel-flensburg.de; Rathausstrasse 2; s €85-125, d €115-145; 🅿 🛜) An excellent place in the town centre, the Alte Post has slick new rooms with a white-and-wood look, as well as a handful of original themed rooms that evoke the building's old brewing days.

SMOKIN' FISH

The smooth, oily fillets of northern fish are smoked for hours until they have a tangy, buttery softness that melts in your mouth. No wonder people love it. Here are some good places to try it:

Hamburg There's smoked fish by the tonne at Hamburg's Sunday Fischmarkt (p161) or order some house-smoked eel at Alt Hamburger Aalspeicher (p169).

Sylt Just saying 'Gosch (p196)' brings knowing nods of satisfaction from those who've had this seafood legend's smoked fish in its many varieties.

Wismar Ancient techniques dating to Hanseatic times make the young smoked eel at Kaminstube Wismar (p211) especially succulent.

Binz Just follow your nose to the glorified beach hut, Fischräucherei Kuse (p216).

Stralsund The harbour is ringed with stands selling smoked fish; Fischhalle (p213) is the pick.

Wieck Right at the sea, this tiny town has some excellent smoked fish stands, while Fischer-Hütte (p219) specialises in smoked herring.

Hotel Dittmer's Gasthof   HOTEL €€

(🖉0461-240 52; www.dittmersgasthof.de; Neumarkt 2; s/d from €85/125; [P]🛜) This flower-festooned historic inn spans two buildings and is between the train station and the harbour, close to the Rathaus. Run by the same family for more than 100 years, the rooms are basic and tidy.

✗ Eating

★ **Migge's Danish Bakery**   BAKERY €

(🖉0461-430 917 85; www.facebook.com/migges danishbakery; Norderstrasse 9; pastries from €1.10; ⊙7am-6pm Mon-Fri, 7.30am-4pm Sat, 8am-2pm Sun) Flensburg's best bakery serves up flaky Danish pastries straight out of the oven. The *Wienerbrot* with cinnamon is delicious, but then so is everything here. They've a few tables outside if you want to make a breakfast out of it.

★ **Weinstube im Krusehof**   GERMAN €€

(🖉0461-128 76; www.weinstube-flensburg.de; Rote Strasse 24; mains €11.50-16.50; ⊙11.30am-10.30pm Mon-Sat) Wander through the covered passage built from old ship timbers into a courtyard of goodness at this wine restaurant in the old town. Greeted by the irrepressible Steffi, loyal regulars enjoy a fine selection of German wines, along with *Flammenkuchen* – Alsatian 'pizzas' with cracker-crisp thin crusts and a variety of toppings.

Gosch Sylt   SEAFOOD €€

(🖉0461-1828 5330; www.gosch.de/standorte/gosch-an-land/flensburg; Am Kanalschuppen 4; fish sandwiches €3-6.50, mains €8-20; ⊙11am-10pm) Part of a nationwide chain with its origins on the chichi island of Sylt, this wildly popular place is loved as much for its location (right by the water) as for the fishy pasta dishes and grilled fish. We also love it for its *Fischbrötchen* (fish sandwiches) sold at a stand just by the entrance until around late afternoon.

🍺 Drinking & Nightlife

Beach Club Flensburg   BEER GARDEN

(🖉01575 819 0720; www.facebook.com/Beach clubFlensburg; Am Kanalschuppen 5; ⊙5-9pm Tue-Thu, 1pm-1am Fri & Sat, 1-8pm Sun May-Sep) Flensburg may not have a beach worthy of the name, but this cutesy outdoor bar has lounge chairs and even a handful of classically German *Strandkorb* (roofed wicker beach chairs). Beer, wine, cocktails and fine weather – it's a wonderful mix, and they're not averse to lengthening the opening hours when it's warm (or closing altogether when the weather's bad).

Porticus   BAR

(🖉0461-1468 1438; Marienstrasse 1; ⊙7pm-2am Mon-Wed, from 6pm Thu, 7am-4am Fri & Sat, 8pm-midnight Sun) In a ramshackle old half-timbered house, the enduringly popular Porticus has been around forever, and locals assure us that it hasn't changed at all in decades. A Flensburg classic.

Gaststätte Bärenhöhle   PUB

(🖉0461-238 50; Norderhofenden Altstadt 17; ⊙8pm-1am Tue-Thu, 1pm-5am Fri & Sat) This smoky old sailors' pub is a bit rough around the edges, but it's a real slice of local life that draws old sea dogs, students and a broad cross-section of Flensburg life.

🛍 Shopping

Braasch   DRINKS

(www.braasch.sh; Grosse Strasse 24; ⊙10am-6.30pm Mon-Fri, 10am-4pm Sat) Rum sold from the Braasch distillery, one of few still operating in town, can be tasted and bought at this tiny store on the main pedestrian thoroughfare.

ℹ Information

Flensburg Tourist Office (🖉0461-909 0920; www.flensburg-tourismus.de; Nikolaistrasse 8; ⊙9am-6pm Mon-Fri, 10am-2pm Sat) In the old town, with plenty of useful information.

ℹ Getting There & Away

Flensburg has hourly trains to Schleswig (€8.55, 30 minutes), Kiel (from €18.70, 1¼ hours) and Hamburg (from €29, two hours).

Glücksburg

🖉04631 / POP 6130

This small spa town is a timeless, upscale retreat overlooking the often-chilly Baltic waters, 10km northeast of Flensburg. It's a pleasant stroll around the lake up to the beach.

◉ Sights

Schloss Glücksburg   PALACE

(🖉04631-442 330; www.schloss-gluecksburg.de; off Schlossallee; adult/child/family €8/3/16; ⊙10am-6pm May-Oct, 11am-4pm Sat & Sun Nov-Apr) Glücksburg is renowned for this horse-shoe-shaped, blindingly white Renaissance palace, which appears to float in the middle of a large lake. Brooding when overcast, dazzling in the northern sunshine, it's a pretty place with a pleasing warren of period rooms to explore.

🛌 Sleeping

Strandhotel Glücksburg
HOTEL €€

(📞 04631-614 10; www.strandhotel-gluecksburg.de; Kirstenstrasse 6; s/d from €89/149; 🅿 😊 @ 🛜) The fabled 'white castle by the sea' counts Thomas Mann among its former guests. Rooms at this resplendent and sprawling beachfront villa (which dates to 1872) are now decked out in a cool, beachy pastel style. Decadences include a spa and restaurant serving a seasonal menu utilising local produce.

❶ Getting There & Away

Buses run hourly between Glücksburg and Flensburg's central bus station (€3.40, 45 minutes) or you can take the scenic route aboard the MS Viking (p192).

Husum

📞 04841 / POPULATION 23,400

Warmly toned buildings huddle around Husum's photogenic *Binnenhafen* (inner harbour), colourful gabled houses line its narrow, cobbled lanes, and in late March and early April millions of purple crocuses bloom in the **Schlosspark**. You can easily while away a couple hours here.

◉ Sights

Emil Nolde Stiftung
GALLERY

(📞 04664-983 930; www.nolde-stiftung.de; Neukirchen bei Seebüll; adult/child €8/free; ⊙ 10am-6pm Mar-Nov) By far the biggest and most impressive collection of Emil Nolde's work is in his architecturally arresting former atelier at Seebüll. The exhibition is worth a half-day's excursion, which is just as well because it's fairly remote – you'll need your own wheels to visit the location, which is almost on the Danish border. There's a suitably arty cafe.

Theodor-Storm-Haus
MUSEUM

(Theodor Storm House; 📞 04841-803 8630; www.storm-gesellschaft.de; Wasserreihe 31-35; adult/child €3.50/2.50; ⊙ 10am-5pm Tue-Fri, 11am-5pm Sat, 2-5pm Sun-Mon Apr-Oct, 2-5pm Tue, Sat & Sun Nov-Mar) Even if you're not familiar with the

19th-century author Theodor Storm, his tidy wooden house will whet your appetite. Well-placed biographical titbits fill in the life of this novelist, poet and proud Schleswig-Holstein citizen in the small, intimate rooms where he lived and wrote works such as his seminal North Frisian novella *Der Schimmelreiter* (The Rider on the White Horse).

Poppenspäler Museum
MUSEUM

(📞 04841-632 42; www.pole-poppenspaeler.de; König-Friedrich V-Allee 2; adult/child/family €2/1/5; ⊙ 11am-5pm Tue-Sun Mar-Oct, Sat & Sun Nov-Feb) Kids – and kids at heart – will be enchanted by the puppets on display at the Poppenspäler Museum, in Husum's Schloss. In summer, it presents a series of outdoor shows from its century-old 'puppet wagon'. Check with the museum for annual schedules.

🛌 Sleeping & Eating

Thomas Hotel
HOTEL €€

(📞 04841-662 00; www.thomas-hotel.de; Zingel 7-9; s €79-109, d €99-179; @ 🛜) Muted colours and supremely comfortable beds are the calling cards at this cool and contemporary hotel right next to Husum's inner harbour. The rooms with North Sea views are pricey but the views are cinematic in scope and service is professional. There's an on-site spa & sauna.

Best Western Theodor Storm Hotel
HOTEL €€

(📞 04841-896 60; www.bw-theodor-storm-hotel.de; Neustadt 60-68; s/d from €94-129; @ 🛜) In a prime location in the heart of town, the Theodor Storm won't win any style awards, but the rooms are bright, modern and spacious. It all adds up to an excellent price-to-quality ratio in the town centre.

Husums Brauhaus
GERMAN €€

(📞 04841-896 60; www.husums-brauhaus.de; Neustadt 60-68; mains €8-27; ⊙ 5pm-late) The in-house microbrewery at Theodor Storm Hotel has a good range of brews, a beer garden and casual German fare – everything from steaks to light meals.

Ratskeller
GERMAN €€€

(📞 04841-658 58; www.ratskellerhusum.com; Grossstrasse 27; mains €17-24; ⊙ noon-2pm & 6pm-midnight Tue-Sat) One of Husum's more upmarket dining experiences, Ratskeller serves up expertly prepared meat and fish dishes in slightly formal surrounds. Service is attentive and the wine list extensive.

ℹ Information

Husum Tourist Office (☏ 04841-898 70; www.
husum-tourismus.de; Grossstrasse 27; ⊙9am-
6pm Mon-Fri, 10am-4pm Sat Apr-Oct, 9am-5pm
Mon-Fri Nov-Mar) Can book rooms and offers
plenty of town info.

ℹ Getting There & Away

There are regular direct train connections
to Hamburg (€29, two hours) and Schleswig
(€8.55, 30 minutes), plus several links daily to
Westerland on Sylt (€16.60, 1¼ hours).

Husum is walkably compact and extremely
well signposted. The Bahnhof lies 700m south of
the city centre.

Sylt

☏ 04651 / POP 15,200

The star of Germany's North Frisian Islands,
glamorous Sylt (38.5km long and only 700m
wide at its narrowest point) has designer
boutiques housed in reed-thatched cottages,
luxury cars jamming the car parks, luxurious accommodation and some of northern
Germany's most acclaimed restaurants.

This anchor-shaped island is attached to
the mainland by a narrow causeway. On its
west coast, the North Sea's fierce surf and
strong winds gnaw at Sylt's shoreline, even
as the eastern Wadden Sea shore is tranquil.

Elsewhere, Sylt's candy-striped lighthouses rise above wide expanses of shifting
dunes, fields of gleaming yellow-gold rape
flower and tracts of heath. Along the beaches are saunas, where the idea is to heat up
and then run naked into the North Sea.

For some visitors (and many Germans),
Sylt is too much of a scene. But the mix of
glamour and North Sea beauty is an intoxicating mix. Come and see for yourself.

⊙ Sights

★ **Uwe Dune**   VIEWPOINT

Stunning Uwe Dune, at 52.5m, is Sylt's highest natural elevation. You can climb the
wooden steps to the top for a 360-degree view
over Sylt and, on a good day, to neighbouring Amrum and Föhr islands. It's signposted
along the main road the village of Kampen.

★ **Erlebniszentrum
Naturgewalten**   MUSEUM

(Forces of Nature Centre; ☏ 04651-836 190; www.
naturgewalten-sylt.de; Hafenstrasse 37; adult/child
€14.50/9; ⊙10am-7pm Jul & Aug, to 6pm Sep-Jun)

Dedicated to the North Sea, this state-of-
the-art ecological museum has multimedia
exhibits that keep both kids and adults
entertained (especially on rainy days). It's
housed in a vivid blue wave-like building
powered by renewable energy. Everyone enjoys the *Seehund* (seal) webcam.

Denghoog   ARCHAEOLOGICAL SITE

(☏ 04651-328 05; www.soelring-foriining.de; Am
Denghoog; adult/child €5/2.50; ⊙10am-5pm
Mon-Fri, from 11am Sat & Sun May-Sep, 10am-4pm
Mon-Fri, from 11am Sat & Sun Oct) Enter the
5000-year-old Denghoog, next to the town
church, which measures 3m by 5m and is
nearly 2m tall in parts. The outer walls con-
sist of 12 stones weighing around 40 tonnes.
How Stone Age builders moved these is a
Stonehenge-esque mystery.

Altfriesisches Haus   HISTORIC BUILDING

(Old Frisian House; ☏ 04651-311 01; www.soel
ring-foriining.de; Am Kliff 13; adult/child €6/3;
⊙10am-5pm Mon-Fri, from 11am Sat & Sun May-
Oct, 10am-5pm Mon-Fri, 11am-5pm Sat & Sun Oct,
noon-4pm Wed-Sat Nov-Apr) The days before
tourism are recalled in this 1739 house made
from brick and thatch.

☞ Tours

★ **Wattwandern Tour**   TOURS

(Tideland Tour; ☏ 01805 123 344; www.adler-
schiffe.de; Hörnum; adult/child €34/22.50; ⊙late
May-early Oct) See the Unesco-recognised
Wadden Sea up close – up really close. Take
a boat from Hörnum to the nearby islands of
either Amrum or Föhr (depending on tides)
then walk across the mud for 8km to the
other and take the boat back to Sylt. You will
be amazed at how the seemingly desolate
expanses come to life up close.

★ **Seal Colonies Boat Tour**   BOATING

(☏ 01805 123 344; www.adler-schiffe.de; Hörnum;
adult/child from €19/15; ⊙Apr-Oct) See seals
basking on the sandbanks on this 1½-hour
boat tour from Hörnum, one of the most
popular tours.

🛏 Sleeping

Campingplatz Rantum   CAMPGROUND €

(☏ 04651-807 55; www.camping-rantum.de; Hörnumer Strasse 3, Rantum; per adult/child €5/3, tent
€7-13, car €2.50; ⊙Apr-Oct; [P][🐾][📶]) In a natural
area of rolling dunes south of Westerland;
great facilities include a bakery, restaurant
and sauna.

Kamps
GUESTHOUSE €€

(☑04651-983 90; www.kamps-sylt.de; Gurtstich 41, Keitum; r/apt from €175/195; ℗⊜) Inside a traditional thatched-roof house in oh-so-quaint Keitum, this eight-room guesthouse plus apartments surprises with colours as bold as a Sylt sunrise on a clear day. And you'll probably catch the sunrise as you'll be esger for the fab breakfasts that include the family's homemade jams, waffles, luscious breads and more.

★ Bundersand
RESORT €€€

(☑04651-460 70; www.budersand.de; Am Kai 3, Hörnum; s/d from €270/335; ℗@⊜🏊) The 21st-century architecture is almost as stunning as the views at Sylt's most luxurious hotel. Many rooms have terraces with their own gardens where you can tickle your toes on grass while looking far out to the North Sea. The spa is legendary; use it to work out kinks generated on the beautiful private golf course.

Village
BOUTIQUE HOTEL €€€

(☑04651-469 70; www.village-kampen.de; Alte Dorfstrasse 7, Kampen; r from €299-355, ste €359-885; ℗⊜🏊) A thatched fantasy of a boutique hotel with a mere 15 rooms but service standards worthy of a palace. Discretion is the rule here, whether it's at the indoor pool or out in the lovely gardens. Strolling the town starts outside the gate. Food, including breakfast, is superb.

✖ Eating & Drinking

Gosch
SEAFOOD €€

(☑04651-870 383; www.gosch.de; Hafenstrasse 16, List; mains €4-24; ⊙11.30am-9pm) The site of Gosch's original kiosk in List harbour is now this nationwide chain's maritime-themed flagship, Alte Bootshalle. But across the island you'll find branches offering its delicious fish sandwiches, seafood pasta, smoked fish and *Rösti* (potato cakes), lobster and caviar.

★ Söl'ring Hof
EUROPEAN €€€

(☑04651-836 200; www.soelring-hof.de; Am Sandwall 1, Rantum; mains from €44, 6-/8-course tasting menu €174/194; ⊙6.30-9.30pm May-Oct, shorter hours rest of year) You'd come here just for the location set among dunes. From the terrace you can hear the crash of the surf, muted by blowing grasses. But chef Johannes King's kitchen is the draw, with breathtaking takes on local, seasonal produce and seafood. Think caviar, oysters and pure indulgence.

Alte Friesenstube
GERMAN €€€

(☑04651-1228; www.altefriesenstube.de; Gaadt 4; mains €23-37; ⊙5.30-10pm Tue-Sun) One of Sylt's best restaurants, Alte Friesenstube does fab fish and meat dishes – we've never had North Sea *Pannfisch* quite this nice. The setting is superb, rising above Westerland's general mediocrity with a lovely traditional building and a fresh-linen look in the interior.

Sansibar
LOUNGE

(☑04651-964 646; www.sansibar.de; Hörnumer Strasse 80, Rantum; ⊙10.30am-late, shorter hours in winter) Drink among the dunes in this large grass-roofed beach shack for the elite. Yes there's a fine restaurant, but the real reason to come is for that selfie which looks stolen from the pages of *Hello!* Sunset drinks on the terrace is the classic Sylt high-season extravagance.

ℹ Information

Westerland has the main tourist office, convenient for when you arrive on the island. Other towns have offices but they're usually only open a few hours on weekdays. A great source of info is www.sylt.de.

Tourist Information Desk (www.westerland. de; Bahnhofplatz, Westerland; ⊙9am-6pm) Inside the train station. A good first stop.

ℹ Getting There & Away

There is no direct land access to Sylt, although you can bring your car by ferry or train.

AIR

Flughafen Sylt (GWT, Sylt Airport; ☑04651-920 612; www.flughafen-sylt.de; Westerland) Sylt's airport is served by Air Berlin and Lufthansa, which have flights to major German cities, although mostly only around summer weekends.

TRAIN

Sylt is connected to the mainland by a causeway used exclusively by trains.

➡ IC trains serve Hamburg Hauptbahnhof (€53, 3¼ hours) a few times a day, while regional trains have hourly services to Hamburg Altona (€32, 3½ hours) via Husum. Make sure you're sitting in the correct part of the train, as they sometimes split en route.

➡ Vehicles use the **Sylt Shuttle** (www.sylt shuttle.de; one-way/return Fri-Mon €54/96, return Tue-Thu €83) from Niebüll. There are crossings every half-hour in both directions; it doesn't take reservations, and foot and bicycle passengers aren't allowed. With loading and unloading, expect the journey to take about an hour and be prepared to queue at busy times.

❶ Getting Around

Sylt is well covered by **buses** (www.svg-bus reisen.de; fares €2.50-8), which run at around 20-minute intervals on the main routes. Some buses have bike racks.

Regional trains to/from Westerland stop in Keitum.

Helgoland

Helgoland's former rulers, the British, really got the better deal in 1891 when they swapped it for then German-ruled Zanzibar. But Germans today are very fond of this lonesome North Sea outcrop of red sandstone rock with its fresh air and relatively warm weather, courtesy of the Gulf Stream.

The 80m-tall Lange Anna (Long Anna) rock on the island's southwest edge is a compelling sight, standing alone in the ocean. There are also WWII bunkers and ruins to explore, and resurgent numbers of Atlantic grey seals. Cycling is not permitted on the tiny 4.2-sq-km island.

Helgoland is not part of the EU's VAT area, so many of the 1150 residents make their living selling duty-free cigarettes, booze and perfume to day-trippers who prowl the main drag, Lung Wai (long way), with its colourful houses. To swim, head to neighbouring Düne, a blip in the ocean popular with nudists.

🛏 Sleeping

Helgoland makes an easy day-trip from several points, but if you want to stay overnight, there are more than 1000 hotel beds. Get more information at www.helgoland.de.

Haus Marinas   APARTMENT €€
(☑ 04725-800 425; www.marinas.de; Nordkaje; apt €85-145; 🛜) These appealing A-frame, two- to four-person apartments down by the harbour have a lovely whitewashed, contemporary look about them. Everything feels new and there's a wonderful sense of light and space. The only drawback is that the harbour it overlooks is not Helgoland's busiest – you'll need to walk to get to the prettier and busier corners of the island.

❶ Getting There & Away

Ferries here take up to four hours. Return trips are timed to allow three to four hours on the island. Services include:

Helgoline (☑ 0180-522 1445; www.helgo line.de; from Hamburg adult/child from €72.30/36.20, from Cuxhaven €58.70/29.40; ☺ from Hamburg 9am, Cuxhaven 11.30am Apr-Oct) Fast ferries run from Hamburg and Cuxhaven; there are also cheaper, slower boats.

Reederei Rahder (☑ 04834-3612; www. rahder.de; Büsum; day return from adult/child €39/22; ☺ Apr-Oct) Boats run from Büsum, which is on the rail network.

SCHWERIN & THE MECKLENBURG LAKE PLAINS

At the doorstep of the appealing state capital, Schwerin, the wilderness area of the Mecklenburg Lake Plains spreads across the centre of the state, and shelters the pristine Müritz National Park. Meandering through charming little villages and hamlets, many roads in the area are canopied by trees that were planted by medieval fish merchants to shield wagons from the heat of the summer sun. It's a beguiling, often overlooked corner of the north, which is all the more reason to visit.

Schwerin

☑ 0385 / POP 98,000

Picturesquely sited around seven lakes (or possibly more depending on how you tally them), the centrepiece of this engaging city is its Schloss (castle), built in the 14th century during the city's six centuries as the former seat of the Grand Duchy of Mecklenburg.

Schwerin has an upbeat, vibrant energy on its restored streets that befits its role as the capital of Mecklenburg-Western Pomerania. Cafes, interesting shops and flashes of the area's regal past make wandering a delight. Put simply, it's one of the loveliest cities in Germany's north.

◉ Sights

★ **Schloss & Gardens**   PALACE
(☑ 0385-525 2920; www.schloss-schwerin.de; Burg Island; adult/child €8.50/free; ☺ 10am-6pm Tue-Sun mid-Apr–mid-Oct, to 5pm mid-Oct–mid-Apr) Gothic and Renaissance turrets, Slavic

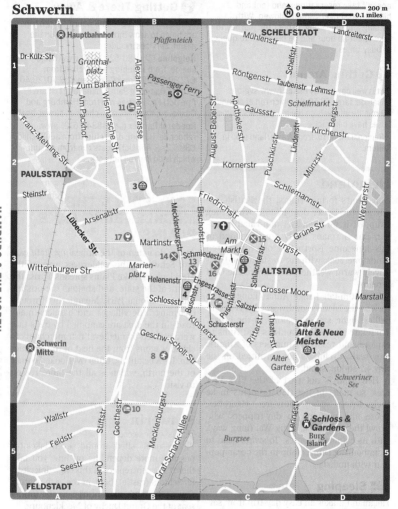

Schwerin

onion domes, Ottoman features and terracotta Hanseatic step gables are among the mishmash of architectural styles that make up Schwerin's inimitable Schloss, which is crowned by a gleaming golden dome. Nowadays the Schloss earns its keep as the state's parliament building.

Crossing the causeway south from the palace-surrounding Burggarten brings you to the baroque Schlossgarten (palace garden), intersected by several canals.

★ **Galerie Alte & Neue Meister**   MUSEUM
(Gallery of Old & New Masters; ☑ 0385-595 80; www.museum-schwerin.de; Alter Garten 3; adult/child €8.50/free; ⊙ 11am-6pm Tue-Sun Apr-Oct, to 5pm Nov-Mar) Revel in the Flemish masterpieces collected by the Mecklenburg dukes during the 17th and 18th centuries at this impressive museum with wide-ranging collections. Works include oils by Lucas Cranach the Elder, as well as paintings by Brueghel, Rembrandt and Rubens. The 15 statues in the Ernst Barlach room provide a small taste of the sculptor's work. There's a typically amusing and irreverent Marcel Duchamp collection.

Pfaffenteich   LAKE
Schwerin's central lake was created by a dam in the 12th century. Through the centuries it was surrounded by some of the city's most elegant buildings. At the southwest corner, the vividly orange **Arsenal** (Alexandrinenstrasse 1) dates from 1840. You can cross the waters on a small **ferry** (adult/child €2/1; ⊙ 10am-6pm Tue-Sun Apr-Sep) that makes four stops.

Half-Timbered House   HISTORIC BUILDING
(Buschstrasse 15) A walk southwest of the Rathaus to the appropriately named Engestrasse (Narrow Street) brings you past a lovely example of the city's earliest half-timbered house, which dates back to 1698.

Rathaus   HISTORIC BUILDING
(Am Markt) The bustling Markt is home to the Rathaus. It's quite a sober affair, something that the castle-like crenellations do little to alter.

Schwerin Dom   CHURCH
(☑ 0385-565 014; www.dom-schwerin.de; Am Dom 4; tower adult/child €3/1.50; ⊙ 11am-5pm Mon-Sat, from noon Sun) Above the Markt, the soaring Gothic Dom is a superb example of north German red-brick architecture. You can climb up to the viewing platform of its

19th-century cathedral tower (118m), which is a mere 50cm taller than Rostock's Petrikirche (p205). Down on earth, check out the elaborately carved pews. Construction lasted from 1270 to 1892.

🏃 Activities

Fahrrad Rachow   CYCLING
(☑ 0385-565 795; www.fahrradrachow.de; Mecklenburgstrasse 59; per day from €8; ⊙ 9am-6pm Mon-Fri, 10am-1pm Sat) Excellent long-running shop with a big selection of rental bikes. Usually has a summer location in the train station with longer hours.

Weisse Flotte   BOATING
(☑ 0385-557 770; www.weisseflotteschwerin. de; Werderstrasse; adult/child from €14.50/7.50; ⊙ Apr-Oct) Choose from three different 90-minute tours of Schwerin's lakes and waterways. It's all very picturesque, and personally we'd pick the one that leaves next as they're all similar.

🎭 Festivals & Events

Schlossfestspiele   THEATRE
(www.mecklenburgisches-staatstheater.de; ⊙ Jul) The highlight of Schwerin's cultural calendar is the Schlossfestspiele, when open-air opera concerts are performed on a stage near the Burggarten.

🛏 Sleeping

★ **Hotel Niederländischer Hof**   HOTEL €€
(☑ 0385-591 100; www.niederlaendischer-hof.de; Karl-Marx-Strasse 12-13; s €89-134, d €135-190; 🅿 🛜) Overlooking the Pfaffenteich, this regal 1901-established hotel has 33 elegant rooms with black marble bathrooms, a library warmed by an open fire, and a lauded restaurant. The decor is plushly period with whimsical touches.

Hotel Am Schloss   PENSION €€
(☑ 0385-593 230; www.hotel-am-schloss-schwerin. de; Heinrich-Mann-Strasse 3; s/d from €68/90; 🅿 🛜) This basic but comfortable pension has 25 modern rooms spread across seven floors, served by a lift. It is located in an old commercial bakery and warehouse. Some rooms have lovely wooden beams; all have questionable taste in curtains and upholstery. Take tram 3, 5, 7 or 19 from the train station to Schlossblick.

Zur guten Quelle   HOTEL €€
(☑ 0385-565 985; www.gasthof-schwerin.de; Schusterstrasse 12; s/d from €59/82; 🅿 🛜) One

of Schwerin's prettiest half-timbered houses, bang in the heart of the Altstadt, Zur guten Quelle is known for its cosy traditional restaurant and beer garden, but it also has six simple but comfortable rooms. Many have ancient timbers running right through the rooms.

✕ Eating

★ Rösterei Fuchs
CAFE €

(📞 0385-593 8444; www.roesterei-fuchs.de; Am Markt 4; mains €7-12; ⊙ 9am-8pm Mon-Fri, to 6pm Sat & Sun) The aroma of fresh coffee fills this chic cafe, which roasts its own coffee in-house and also sells beans, as well as gourmet chocolates. Drop by for an espresso or other warming drink. Breakfasts are fresh and healthy, while sandwiches, quiches and beautiful baked goods fill out the day. Outside tables peek at the Rathaus.

Der Käseladen Mühlenberg
DELI €

(📞 0385-568 328; Mecklenburgstrasse 37; snacks from €2; ⊙ 9am-7pm Mon-Fri, to 2.30pm Sat) A beautiful cheese store. The engaging owner will help you assemble a fabulous picnic to enjoy in the Schlossgarten.

Die Suppenstube
CAFE €

(📞 0172-382 5038; www.suppenstube.de; Puschkinstrasse 55; mains €4-6; ⊙ 10.30am-4.30pm Mon-Fri; 🍴) Light fittings made from cutlery, stripped floorboards and bare tables provide a minimalist contrast with the historic half-timbered walls of this house on the edge of the Markt. The soups here are tops, as are the desserts. Hide out in the small beer garden out back.

★ Buschérie
EUROPEAN €€

(📞 0385-923 6066; www.buscherie.de; Buschstrasse 9; mains €13-22; ⊙ 11.30am-11pm, kitchen to 9.30pm) Although historic and half-timbered, Buschstrasse is very much the modern bistro. Enjoy seasonal foods of the region with a few French inflections at an outdoor table with the Dom seeming to loom overhead. From mains to small plates, everything is well priced. Stop in for a glass of wine from the long list and listen to live jazz some nights.

🍷 Drinking & Nightlife

★ Zum Stadtkrug
BREWERY

(📞 0385-593 6693; www.altstadtbrauhaus.de; Wismarsche Strasse 126; ⊙ 11am-11pm) The dark beer brewery at this 1936-established pub consistently rates among the best in Germany. It's full of antique brewing equipment, and it opens to an inviting beer garden. The menu features a familiar – albeit well-prepared – assortment of schnitzels and porky mains.

ℹ Information

Tourist Office (📞 0385-592 5212; www.schwerin.com; Rathaus, Am Markt 14; ⊙ 9am-6pm Mon-Fri, from 10am Sat & Sun) Offers a good overview of the city's charms and attractions.

ℹ Getting There & Away

Hourly train links from Schwerin's **Hauptbahnhof** (📞 0381-240 1055; Grunthalplatz) include Hamburg (from €19.90, 1½ hours), Rostock (from €23, 1½ hours) and Berlin (from €27, three hours). Services to Stralsund (from €23, three hours) usually require a change or two. For Wismar, you'll need to take the bus (from €8.50, one hour).

Güstrow

📞 03843 / POP 31,750

Best known for its stately Renaissance Schloss, charming 775-plus-year-old Güstrow is also the place where famed 20th-century sculptor Ernst Barlach spent most of his working life. You can view his deeply felt, humanist works at several of the town's galleries. When combined with the fine architecture, it adds up to one of loveliest towns in this part of the country.

⊙ Sights

★ Schloss Güstrow
PALACE

(📞 03843-7520; www.schloss-guestrow.de; Franz-Parr-Platz 1; adult/child €6.50/4.50; ⊙ 11am-5pm Tue-Sun mid-Apr–mid-Oct, to 4pm mid-Oct–mid-Apr) Güstrow's fabulous Renaissance 16th-century Schloss is home to a historical museum as well as a cultural centre, period art exhibitions and occasional concerts. You can tour rooms that recall the luxe excesses of its royal residents. The formal gardens are an exercise in orderly flora.

Atelierhaus
GALLERY

(📞 03843-822 99; www.ernst-barlach-stiftung.de; Heidberg 15; adult/child/family €6/4/15; ⊙ 10am-5pm Tue-Sun Apr-Oct, 11am-4pm Tue-Sun Nov-Mar) Based on sketches he made in Russia, Ernst Barlach's squarish sculptures began bearing the same expressive gestures and hunched-over, wind-blown postures of the impoverished people he encountered. Banned by the Nazis, he died in 1938; after the war his works gained full appreciation. Many of his bronze and wood carvings are housed here, along with a biographical exhibition, at his former studio, the Atelierhaus. It's 4km south of the city at Inselsee; take bus 204 or 205.

Gertrudenkapelle   GALLERY

(☑ 03843-844 000; Gertrudenplatz 1; adult/child €5/3; ◷ 10am-5pm Tue-Sun Apr-Oct, 11am-4pm Tue-Sun Nov-Mar) The Ernst Barlach memorial in the Gertrudenkapelle displays many of his original works. It is about 300m west of the Pferdemarkt fountain in a large grassy park surrounded by housing.

🛏 Sleeping & Eating

Kurhaus am Inselsee   HOTEL €€

(☑ 03843-8500; www.kurhaus-guestrow.de; Heidberg 1; s €79-109, d €129-149, ste €149-219; 🅿 @ 🛜) South of town in the midst of lakeside woodlands, the Kurhaus am Inselsee has large, light-filled rooms in soothing tones (with balconies), although they're not averse to the occasional floral prints. There's a good restaurant and an on-site wellness centre.

Gästehaus Am Schlosspark   HOTEL €€

(☑ 03843-245 990; www.gaestehaus-guestrow. de; Neuwieder Weg; s/d €80/90; 🅿 @ 🛜) This great-value hotel overlooks the Schloss and its gardens. Most of the 100 modern rooms have views and some have small kitchen facilities. You can rent bikes (from €10 per day) to explore the area.

Cafe Küpper   CAFE €

(☑ 03843-682 485; Domstrasse 15; cakes from €4; ◷ 9am-6pm) The perfect pause for your Güstrow visit. This cafe has been creating luscious cakes in the shadow of the Dom since 1852.

Wunderbar   CAFE €€

(☑ 0384-776 927; www.wunderbar-guestrow.de; Krönchenhagen 10; mains from €8; ◷ 11am-10pm) Much loved by locals for its rare combination of cool, classy and warmth, Wunderbar is part cafe, part bar (great cocktails!) and very much a hub of local life. The cooking consists of light meals (usually with a veg or vegan option) and the cooking is assured.

ℹ Information

Güstrow Information (☑ 03843-681 023; www.guestrow-tourismus.de; Franz-Parr-Platz 10; ◷ 9am-7pm Mon-Fri, 10am-5pm Sat, 11am-5pm Sun May-Sep, shorter hours Oct-Apr) A

OFF THE BEATEN TRACK

THE HALLIGEN

The 10 low-lying islands, some of them little more than outcrops, known as the Halligen are a wonderfully windswept experience. Ranging in size from 7 hectares to 956 hectares, some of the islands were formerly attached to the mainland, but millennia of storm surges and erosion have washed away the land bridges. They also flood regularly in winter, meaning that most structures are built atop man-made mounds to avoid the rising waters.

Ferries connect the Halligen (especially Langeness) with the larger North Frisian island of Amrum on a semi-regular basis; there's a timetable of sorts available on www.langeness. de under 'Schiffsabfahrten'. Check also with Adler-Schiffe (www.adler-schiffe. de) who operate the ferries.

---

good info source; there is a small free museum covering Güstrow's history. Tours are offered.

ℹ Getting There & Away

Trains leave for Güstrow once or twice an hour from Rostock's Hauptbahnhof (€8.50, 25 minutes). Services to/from Schwerin require a change in Bad Kleinen. The station is 700m northwest of the Pferdemarkt fountain.

Neubrandenburg

☑ 0395 / POP 66,950

Neubrandenburg has few pretensions. It bills itself as 'the city of four gates on the Tollensesee Lake', and that's pretty well what it is. A largely intact medieval wall, with those gates, encircles the 13th-century Altstadt (bustling with shoppers, who ignore some harsh GDR architecture). It is an interesting stop.

◎ Sights

City Wall   HISTORIC SITE

Neubrandenburg was founded in 1248 by Herbord von Raven, a Mecklenburg knight granted the land by Brandenburg Margrave Johann I, and building progressed in the usual order: defence system, church, town hall, pub. The security system was the 2.3km-long, 7.5m-high stone wall that survives today, with four city gates and 56 sentry posts built into it.

🛏 Sleeping & Eating

Parkhotel Neubrendenburg HOTEL €€
(☑0395-559 00; www.parkhotel-nb.de; Windbergsweg 4; s €59-65, d €85-95, f €150-180; 🅿🛜) This centrally located, well-priced hotel has good, if unexciting rooms – ask for one with a balcony overlooking the surrounding parkland and you've made an excellent choice; doubles with balcony only cost €10 extra. As is often the case, some of the singles are rather small, but otherwise it's a welcoming, well-run place.

Landhotel Broda HOTEL €€
(☑0395-569 170; www.landhotel-broda.de; Oelmühlenstrasse 29; s/d from €59/89; 🛜) One of the most modern places in town, the Broda has a vaguely minimalist look to its rooms, with contemporary splashes of colour and character, as well as soothing clean lines. The breakfast is one of the best in town and it's an easy walk to the water's edge.

★ Wiekhaus 45 GERMAN €€
(☑0395-566 7762; www.wiekhaus45.de; 4th Ringstrasse 44; mains €13-18; ⊙11am-11.30pm) Easily the most appealing place to eat in Neubrandenburg is this renovated guardhouse set into the wall. Waiters zip up and down the narrow stairwell carrying huge portions of Mecklenburg specialities (start with the tasty onion soup served with fresh bread; look for fresh herring in season). There are outside tables in summer.

ℹ Information

Stadt Info (☑0395-194 33; www.neubrandenburg-touristinfo.de; Marktplatz 1; ⊙10am-7pm Mon-Fri, to 4pm Sat) In the centre of the old town in the newly renovated Haus der Kultur und Bildung.

ℹ Getting There & Away

Trains runs at two-hour intervals to/from Berlin (€27, 1¾ hours) and Stralsund (€20.90, 1¼ hours).

Ludwigslust

☑03874 / POP 12,306

Handsome Ludwigslust is a lovely little place, a planned baroque town with a neat, orderly layout that is an attraction in itself. Its castle, once described as the 'Versailles of the North', is the main attraction, but the town itself is a lovely spot to spend a few hours, either as a destination in its own right or on a day excursion from Schwerin.

◉ Sights

★ Schloss Ludwigslust PALACE
(☑03874-571 90; www.schloss-ludwigslust.de; Schloss Strasse; adult/child €6.50/free; ⊙10am-6pm Tue-Sun mid-Apr–mid-Oct, to 5pm mid-Oct–mid-Apr) Such was the allure of this palace that when the ducal seat moved 36km north to Schwerin in 1837, some family members continued living here until 1945. Now part of the Schwerin State Museum, its high point is the stately, gilt-columned, high-ceilinged Golden Hall. After lavish renovations, the East Wing has reopened; the royal bedrooms and living quarters are a gilded highlight.

Stadtkirche CHURCH
(An der Stadtkirche; €2; ⊙11am-5pm Tue-Sat, from noon Sun May-Sep, shorter hours rest of year) The striking Stadtkirche, built in the 18th century in a neoclassical style, is utterly unlike most churches in this part of Germany. Its grand Doric columns evoke a Greek temple, and within, the dual staircase that leads up behind the altar draws the eyes to a splendid fresco depicting the birth of Christ; it was only painted three decades ago.

🛏 Sleeping & Eating

★ Hotel Schloss
Neustadt-Glewe HISTORIC HOTEL €€
(☑038757-5320; www.hotel-schloss-neustadt-glewe.de; Schlossfreiheit 1, Neustadt-Glewe; r/ste from €70/108; 🅿🛜) If you have your own wheels and don't mind being 8km northeast of Ludwigslust, this castle-hotel is easily the most romantic choice in the area. The baroque castle dates back 400 years, and rooms in the main building and most of the public areas capture the spirit of the age, with stucco ceilings and period touches; other rooms are disappointingly modern.

Hotel Erbprinz HOTEL €€
(☑03874-250 40; www.erbprinz-ludwigslust.de; Schwerinerstrasse 38; r from €89; 🅿🛜) The large rooms here are either stylish and minimalist or a little stark and empty, depending on your perspective. We prefer the former, and there are hints at grandeur with some mock-period furnishings. Overall, it's a comfortable choice within walking distance of the town centre.

Schlosscafé Ludwigslust CAFE €
(☑03874-620 919; Schloss Strasse; cakes from €4; ⊙10am-5pm Tue-Sun) Given that this place is

part of the castle itself, there's no finer place in Ludwigslust for *Kaffee und Kuchen*.

★ **Alte Wache** GERMAN, INTERNATIONAL **€€**
(☑ 03874-570 353; www.altewache-ludwigslust.de; Schlossfreiheit 8; mains €10-20; ◷ noon-10pm Tue-Sat, 11am-6pm Sun) With outdoor tables that face the castle, the location here is the best in town. The food, too, is excellent, ranging from soups and risotto to steaks and grilled fish. There's also a kids menu.

❶ Information

Tourist Office (☑ 03874-526 251; www.stadtludwigslust.de/kultur-und-tourismus; Schlossstrasse 36; ◷ 10am-1pm & 2-5pm Mon & Thu, to 6pm Tue & Fri, 10am-1pm Wed, 10am-3pm Sat & Sun May–mid-Sep, shorter hours rest of year) Seasonal office with some useful info on the town.

❶ Getting There & Away

Trains run from Schwerin every two hours (from €9.30, 45 minutes).

If you're driving, Ludwigslust is signposted south off the A24; take the A14 exit.

Müritz National Park

Müritz National Park (☑ 039824-2520; www.mueritz-nationalpark.de) is an oasis of green and blue, a land of lakes and forests in the heart of otherwise unrelenting farm country midway between Berlin and Rostock. Müritz is commonly known as the land of a thousand lakes. While that's an exaggeration, there are well over 100 lakes here, as well as countless ponds, streams and rivers. This serene park consists of bog and wetlands, and is home to a wide range of waterfowl, including ospreys, white-tailed eagles and cranes.

The park's two main sections sprawl over 300 sq km to the east and (mainly) west of Neustrelitz, where the park's waterway begins on the Zierker See. Boardwalks and other features let you get close to nature.

The country road between Neustrelitz and Waren to the west cuts through the heart of the park and offers plenty of places to stop and admire the beech forests, which have been recognised by Unesco.

❶ Information

National Park Office (☑ 03981-253 106; www.mueritz-nationalpark.de/erleben-und-erholen/Infostellen; Strelitzerstrasse 1; ◷ 9am-6pm Mon-Fri, 9.30am-1pm Sat & Sun May-Sep, 9am-noon & 1-4pm Mon-Thu, 9am-noon Fri Oct, shorter hours rest of year) There are seven different park information offices scattered around the access roads to the park, but this one in Neustrelitz is the most useful. It has maps, information on walks and wildlife, and there's usually a ranger on duty.

❶ Getting There & Away

You'll need your own wheels to explore the park. The nearest town is Neustrelitz.

Neustrelitz

☑ 03981 / POP 20,426

One of the most elegant small towns in Western Pomerania, Neustrelitz has a stately collection of baroque buildings around its town centre. Neustrelitz is also a terrific base for exploring nearby Müritz National Park and it has its own pretty frontage onto the Zierker See. There's even a zoo.

◉ Sights

Begin your exploration of town in the central Markt, an expansive, octagonal space surrounded by some pretty buildings. On the north side, the 18th-century Stadtkirche is a fine example of Neustrelitz baroque, with a distinctive, four-sided bell tower. Watching it from across the square from the east is the muted Rathaus (1841).

Beyond the town centre to the west and southwest are the vast and lovely Schlossgarten – the palace may have disappeared but the gardens remain. They are worth wandering in their own right, and the **Schlosskirche** (Palace Church; Hertelstrasse 2; ◷ hours vary) and the **Luisentempel Neustrelitz** (Useriner Strasse 3) are both worth seeking out.

Just northeast of the centre, the smaller Glambecker See is a serene and attractive corner of town. Locals go swimming here in summer.

⬚ Sleeping & Eating

★ **Alter Kornspeicher** HOTEL **€€**
(☑ 03981-262 9646; www.alterkornspeicher.de; Am Stadthafen 5; s/d/ste from €78/90/140; ☏) Down by the water, with rooms that range from small singles to doubles and suites with exposed wooden beams and hints at period furnishings, this wonderful old warehouse is easily the best place to stay in town. Some bathrooms even have bathtubs!

HAMBURG & THE NORTH MÜRITZ NATIONAL PARK

Hotel Schlossgarten HOTEL €€
(☎03981-245 00; www.hotel-schlossgarten.de; Tiergartenstrasse 15; s €51-73, d €72-109; P ☜) Within walking distance of everywhere that's worth seeing in town, Hotel Schlossgarten has large, prim rooms (we prefer those with wooden floorboards) just across the road from the park.

Alter Kornspeicher GERMAN €€
(☎03981-262 9648; www.alterkornspeicher.de; Am Stadthafen 5; mains €11-22; ⏲8am-10pm Apr-Sep, 8am-2.30pm & 5-10pm Mon-Fri, 8am-10pm Sat & Sun Oct-Mar) Not just the best place to stay in Neustrelitz, Alter Kornspeicher is also the best restaurant, with assured cooking and a seasonal menu in a range of dining spaces. They even have their own roastery, so come for a coffee in the cafe even if you're not having a meal.

Fürstenhof GERMAN €€
(☎03981-204 774; www.ideenreich-grafikmanufaktur.de; Markt 3; mains €13-20; ⏲5.30-10pm Tue-Thu, noon-2.30pm & 5.30-10pm Fri & Sat, noon-2.30pm Sun) Fronting onto the historic Markt, Fürstenhof prides itself on local dishes and fresh local ingredients that change with the seasons. They also have a kids menu and excellent service.

ℹ Information

Tourist office (☎03981-253 119; www.neustrelitz.de/erleben/touristinfo; Strelitzer Strasse 1; ⏲9am-6pm Mon-Fri, 9.30am-1pm Sat & Sun May-Sep, 9am-noon & 1-4pm Mon-Thu, 9am-noon Fri Oct, shorter hours rest of year)

ℹ Getting There & Away

Trains run hourly between Neustrelitz and Berlin (from €26, 1¼ hours) or Neubrandenburg (from €9, 30 minutes).

There's surprisingly little public transport to/from Neustrelitz from elsewhere in the north. Bus and train services to Schwerin, Hamburg or Stralsund, for example, require a couple of changes and can take half a day.

COASTAL MECKLENBURG – WESTERN POMERANIA

This spectacular stretch of the Baltic coast is certainly one of Europe's better-kept secrets. But Germans know better and flock in summer to its dazzling clean white sand and glittering seas.

Hot spots during the brief beach-going season include three leafy resort islands: sprawling, villa-lined Rügen; car-free Hiddensee; and Usedom (which Germany shares with Poland). Warnemünde, the seaside resort near Rostock, is another sandy hot spot – when it's hot. For natural drama, the cliffs of Jasmund National Park are stunning.

Stralsund is the prize town of the region, combining seaside charms with beautiful old architecture. Other highlights include the gracious university town of Greifswald, which retains some exquisite medieval architecture, as does Wismar.

Rostock

☎0381 / POP 203,400

The large port city of Rostock will never win a beauty contest and for good reason – the town was devastated in WWII and later pummelled by socialist architectural 'ideals'. Its biggest drawcard – Warnemünde, which has one of Germany's most appealing beaches – is 13km northwest, where the Warnow River flows into the Baltic Sea.

Rostock *does* have small but attractive historic enclaves – but you generally have to wade past a landscape of concrete eyesores to reach them. Perhaps its best feature is the vibrant energy provided by the 11,000 university students.

◉ Sights

★**Marienkirche** CHURCH
(☎0381-453 325; www.marienkirche-rostock.de; Am Ziegenmarkt; requested donation €2; ⏲10am-6pm Mon-Sat, 11.15am-5pm Sun May-Sep, 10am-4pm Mon-Sat, 11.15am-12.15pm Sun Oct-Apr) Central Rostock's pride and joy is the 13th-century Marienkirche, the only main Rostock church to survive WWII unscathed (although restorations are ongoing). Behind the main altar, the church's 12m-high astrological clock was built in 1472 by Hans Düringer. At the very top of the clock is a series of doors. At noon and midnight the innermost right door opens and six of the 12 apostles march out to parade around Jesus (Judas is locked out).

Alter Markt SQUARE
Red-brick and pastel-coloured buildings on this large market square hark back to the 14th- and 15th-century Hanseatic era.

Neuer Markt SQUARE

Rostock's large, somewhat bland central square is dominated by the splendid 13th-century Rathaus. The building's baroque facade was added in 1727 after the original brick Gothic structure collapsed.

Opposite the Rathaus is a series of restored gabled houses and a stylised, sea-themed fountain, the Möwenbrunnen (2001), by artist Waldemar Otto. The explanatory plaque says the four figures are Neptune and his sons, although many believe they represent the four elements.

Petrikirche CHURCH

(📞0381-211 01; www.petrikirche-rostock.de; Alter Markt; tower adult/child €4/2.50; ⏰10am-6pm May-Sep, 10am-4pm Oct-Apr) The Gothic Petrikirche has a 117m-high steeple – a mariner's landmark for centuries – that was restored in 1994, having been missing since WWII. There's a lift up to the 45m-high viewing platform.

🛏 Sleeping

Blue Doors Hostel HOSTEL €

(📞0381-2529 9980; www.bluedoorshostel.de; Doberaner Strasse 136; dm €14-26, r with private bathroom €35-86; ❄@🌐) On the edge of the KTV, Rostock's trendy bar district, is this well-run operation with great facilities and plenty of in-the-know advice to animate your Rostock stay. From the Hauptbahnhof, take tram 4 or 5 to the Kabutzenhof stop.

★Hotel Motel One Rostock HOTEL €€

(📞0381-666 9190; www.motel-one.com/en/hotels/rostock/hotel-rostock; Schröderplatz 2; s/d €69/84; 🌐) Part of an excellent new chain which punches well above its weight when it comes to price-quality ratio, the Motel One has four-star rooms at three-star prices. Slick contemporary decor makes it feel like a boutique experience, and it's even better if you get a room overlooking the parkland.

Hotel Verdi HOTEL €€

(📞0381-252 240; www.hotel-verdi.de; Wollenweberstrasse 28; s/d/apt €69/89/99; 🌐) Opening to an umbrella-shaded, timber-decked terrace is this sparkling little hotel near the Petrikirche and Alter Markt, with a handful of attractively decorated rooms (some with kitchenettes), and two apartments with views.

✖ Eating & Drinking

Ursprung GERMAN €€

(📞0381-459 1983; www.ursprung-rostock.de; Alter Markt 16; mains €12-23; ⏰5pm-late Mon-Sat, from 10am Sun) You can let the hours slip past from one of the terrace tables here overlooking the historic square. The German food is typically hearty and well-priced, but they also do some tempting Indian dishes, as well as lighter salads. On many nights, the interior rocks to live bands.

Zur Kogge GERMAN €€

(📞0381-493 4493; www.zur-kogge.de; Wokrenterstrasse 27; mains €9-23; ⏰11.30am-11pm Mon-Sat; 👶) At this Rostock institution, cosy wooden booths are lined with stained-glass Hanseatic coats of armour and monster fish threatening sailing ships, while life preservers hang from the walls, and ships' lanterns are suspended from the ceiling. Local fish dishes dominate the menu.

★Studentenkeller Rostock BAR

(📞0381-455 928; www.studentenkeller.de; Universitätsplatz 5; ⏰5pm-late Tue-Sat) This cellar and garden joint has been rocking Rostock's learned youth for years. Check the website for parties, DJ sets and other events. There's a well-priced happy hour on Wednesdays from 9pm to 11pm.

M.A.U. Club CLUB

(📞0381-202 3576; www.mauclub.de; Warnowufer 56; ⏰hours vary) Everything from indie to punk to house infuses M.A.U Club, a former storage hall. It's well known for up-and-coming acts.

Café Central CAFE

(📞0381-490 4648; www.cafecentral-rostock.de; Leonhardstrasse 20; mains €5-16; ⏰9am-10pm Sun-Thu, to 11pm Fri & Sat) In the heart of the KTV bar scene, Café Central has cult status among Rostock locals. Students, artists, hipsters and suited-up professionals all loll around sipping long drinks on the banquettes or at tables out the front. It's 500m northwest of the Kröpeliner Tor.

ℹ Information

DISCOUNT CARDS

The **Rostock Card** (www.rostock.de/en/rostockcard/) covers 120 attractions in Rostock and surrounding areas. It starts from €12/16 for 24/48 hours and can be purchased at the tourist office.

TOURIST INFORMATION

Tourist Information Rostock (☑ 0381-381 2222; www.rostock.de; Universitätsplatz 6; ⊙10am-6pm Mon-Fri, 10am-3pm Sat & Sun May-Oct, 10am-5pm Mon-Fri, 10am-3pm Sat Nov-Apr) Sells the Rostock Card, which is good for public transport and discounts to some attractions.

❶ Getting There & Away

AIR

Rostock's airport, **Rostock-Laage** (☑ 038454-321 390; www.rostock-airport.de; Flughafenstrasse 1), is 26km south of the city and has scheduled services to Cologne-Bonn, Munich, Stuttgart and Zürich, plus seasonal charter flights to holiday resorts in Bulgaria, Greece, Spain, Tunisia and Turkey, among others.

BOAT

Ferries sail to/from Denmark, Sweden, Latvia and Finland. Boats depart from the Überseehafen (overseas seaport), which is on the east side of the Warnow. Take tram 3 or 4 from the Hauptbahnhof, then change for bus 49 to Seehafen. There's an S-Bahn stop at Seehafen, but it's a 20-minute walk from the station to the piers.

TRAIN

There are frequent direct trains to Berlin (from €27, 2½ hours) and Hamburg (from €19.90, 2¼ hours), and hourly services to Stralsund (€16.20, one hour) and Schwerin (€20.70, one hour).

❶ Getting Around

Journeys within Rostock cost €2.50/5.50 for a single/day pass. The Hauptbahnhof is about 1.5km south of the Altstadt.

Trams 5 and 6 travel from the Hauptbahnhof up Steinstrasse, around the very central Marienkirche and down Lange Strasse to the university.

Warnemünde

☑ 0381 / POP 8500

Warnemünde is all about promenading, eating fish, sipping cocktails, and lazing in a *Strandkorb* (sheltered straw 'beach basket' seat) on its long, wide and startlingly white beach.

Walking from Warnemünde's train station along Alter Strom, the boat-lined main canal, you'll pass a row of quaint cottages housing restaurants. Then you turn the corner into Am Leuchtturm and Seestrasse and see the sand.

For a fabulous view from above, climb the spiralling 135-step wrought-iron and granite staircase of the 1898-built lighthouse.

🛏 Sleeping & Eating

Hotel-Pension Zum Kater   GUESTHOUSE €€
(☑ 0381-548 210; www.pension-zum-kater.de; Alexandrinenstrasse 115; s €60-79, d €82-144; P 🕏) The beach is less than 10 minutes' stroll from this handsome 19-room guesthouse – rooms are large and light-filled. There's a supplement if you stay less than three nights on high-season weekends. Get a room with a roof terrace.

★**Yachthafenresidenz Hohe Düne**   HOTEL €€€
(☑ 0381-504 00; www.hohe-duene.de; Am Yacht hafen 1; s/d €265/385; P 🕏) Wonderfully atmospheric rooms and suites overlooking the yacht harbour are decorated with maritime nostalgia and high levels of comfort. It's an expensive place, but filled with character and worth every euro.

Fischerklause   SEAFOOD €€
(☑ 0381-525 16; www.fischer-klause.de; Am Strom 123; mains €7-15; ⊙11.30am-10pm Apr-Oct, Tue-Sat Nov-Mar; 🕏) Fischerklause is one of the atmospheric salty seadog joints lining the western bank of Alter Strom, and attracts plenty of tourists (as does all of Warnemünde). Still, its ship's cabin decor (think topless mermaid statues) and its tasty seafood make it worth seeking out.

Brasserie   EUROPEAN €€€
(☑ 0381-504 00; www.hohe-duene.de; Am Yacht hafen 1, Hohe Düne; mains €17.50-35; ⊙noon-10pm Mon-Fri, from 12.30pm Sat & Sun; P) The views from the terrace are worth it alone, but the food at this creative restaurant is excellent. Seasonal produce goes into menus that feature locally caught seafood. Long lunches with wine are a good time to survey the yacht harbour. It's on the east side of the channel in the Hohe Düne resort. Book in season.

❶ Getting There & Away

There are frequent S-Bahn trains between Rostock and Warnemünde (single/day pass €2.50/5.50, 22 minutes).

There are also boats from Rostock with **Reederei Schütt** (☑ 0381-637 2654; www.hafenrundfahrten-in-rostock.de; Stadthafen; ferry to Warnemünde adult/child €12/6, harbour cruise €18/9; ⊙May-Oct).

Bad Doberan

📞 038203 / POP 11,427

The former summer ducal residence of Bad Doberan, about 15km west of Rostock, was once the site of a powerful Cistercian monastery. Today, it boasts its fabulous, mighty and ever-so-slightly over-restored Münster. It's worth a quick detour if you're in the Rostock area.

◉ Sights

Münster Bad Doberan　　　　　CATHEDRAL
(📞 038203-627 16; www.muenster-doberan.de; Klosterstrasse 2; adult/child €3/free; ⊙9am-6pm Mon-Sat, from 11am Sun May-Sep, 10am-5pm Mon-Sat, 11am-6pm Sun Mar, Apr & Oct, 10am-4pm Mon-Sat, from 11am Sun Nov-Feb) Construction of this magnificent Gothic church started in 1280 but it wasn't consecrated until 1368. Treasures include an intricate high altar and an ornate pulpit. A massive restoration has made every one of the cathedral's 1.2 million bricks look like new – almost too new. Organ recitals are held May to September, usually on Friday evenings at 7.30pm.

ℹ Getting There & Away

Trains connect Bad Doberan with Rostock Hauptbahnhof (€9, 25 minutes) and Wismar (€9, 45 minutes) roughly hourly. The train station is 1km south of the Münster. If you're continuing on to the coastal resorts just to the north, the **Molli** is a wonderfully atmospheric rail journey.

Baltic Coastal Resorts

Heiligendamm and Kühlungsborn are among the atmospheric beach resorts dotted along the starkly beautiful coast west of Rostock.

A popular tourist train known as Molli travels along the coast from Bad Doberan. Alternate between taking the train and walking between stops for a gorgeous day out along the often wild Baltic shore.

◉ Sights

Heiligendamm　　　　　BEACH
The 'white town on the sea' is Germany's oldest seaside resort, founded in 1793 by Mecklenburg duke Friedrich Franz I, and was fashionable throughout the 19th century as a playground of the nobility. You can't miss the five gleaming white, heritage-listed buildings of the Grand Hotel Heiligendamm perched nearly on the beach. Sunshine is possible; warm weather is rare.

Kühlungsborn　　　　　BEACH
Kühlungsborn, the biggest Baltic Sea resort, with some 7500 inhabitants, has some lovely art deco buildings backing the long beach and adjoining a dense 130-hectare forest. The east and west ends of the sand are linked by the Ostseeallee promenade, lined with hotels and restaurants.

🏃 Activities

★ Molli　　　　　RAIL
(Mecklenburger Bäderbahn Molli; 📞 038293-431 331; www.molli-bahn.de; Bad Doberan Bahnhof; return adult/child €15/10; 🚻) This historic steam train departs Bad Doberan's train station (where it links to the rail network) on average 11 times a day. With a maximum speed of 45km/h, the train takes 15 minutes to reach the coast at Heiligendamm and 45 minutes in total to Kühlungsborn/West, with interim stops in Steilküste, Kühlungsborn/East and Kühlungsborn/Mitte.

🛏 Sleeping

**★ Grand Hotel
Heiligendamm**　　　　　HISTORIC HOTEL €€€
(📞 038203-7400; www.grandhotel-heiligendamm. de; Prof.-Dr.-Vogel-Strasse 6; r from €215; 🅿🛜🌊) This grand old dame of the Baltic Coast wears lightly its long history as one of northern Germany's most distinguished hotels. The public areas are rich in period touches, but the rooms are white and classy, ensuring the old-world charm rarely overwhelms. There are sea views from some rooms and suites, and there's a high-class restaurant; dress for dinner.

ℹ Getting There & Away

The Molli steam train links Bad Doberan with the coastal resorts.

Wismar

📞 03841 / POP 42,200

One of the prettiest towns along Germany's Baltic Coast, its gabled facades and cobbled streets make this small, photogenic city look essentially Hanseatic. But although it joined the Hanseatic trading league in the 13th century, it spent most of the 16th and 17th centuries as part of Sweden. There are

(Continued on page 210)

HAMBURG & THE NORTH BAD DOBERAN

DUGDAX/SHUTTERSTOCK ©

LAMIAFOTOGRAFIA/SHUTTERSTOCK ©

1. Jasmund National Park (p217)
Jagged white-chalk cliffs plunge into the sea at Germany's smallest national park, on Rügen Island.

2. Flensburg (p191)
Flensburg's port area is full of reminders of its seafaring, rum-trading days.

3. Travemünde (p188)
Sandy beaches are dotted with classic German *Strandkörbe* (sheltered straw 'beach basket' seats).

4. Warnemünde (p206)
Warnemünde seaside resort is a sandy spot on the Baltic coast.

LAMIAFOTOGRAFIA/SHUTTERSTOCK ©

(Continued from page 207)

numerous reminders of this era all over town. The entire Altstadt was Unesco-listed in 2002.

Wismar has been long popular with film-makers and its picturesque Alter Hafen (old harbour) starred in the 1922 Dracula movie *Nosferatu*.

Sights

★ St-Nikolai-Kirche   CHURCH
(St-Nikolai-Kirchhof; www.kirchen-in-wismar. de; St-Nikolai-Kirkhof; €2; ⊙8am-8pm Mon-Sat, from 11.30am Sun May-Sep, 10am-6pm Mon-Sat, from 11.30am Sun Apr & Oct, 11am-4pm Mon-Sat & from 11.30am Sun Nov-Mar) Of the three great red-brick churches that once rose above the rooftops of Wismar before WWII, only the sober St-Nikolai-Kirche, the largest of its kind in Europe, was left intact. It has elaborate carvings and a font from its older sister church, the St-Marien-Kirche. The linden-tree-shaded churchyard is next to a small canal and is by far Wismar's loveliest spot.

Markt   SQUARE
The centrepiece of Old Wismar, the Markt is an attractive square, dominated by the 1602-built **Wasserkunst** (waterworks), an ornate, 12-sided well that supplied Wismar's drinking water until 1897 and is the town's landmark. Behind it stands the red-brick Alter Schwede, which dates from 1380 and features a striking step buttress gable facade. It houses a restaurant and guesthouse, as well as a copy of one of the so-called Swedish Heads (two baroque busts of Hercules, which once stood on mooring posts at the harbour entrance).

Fürstenhof   HISTORIC BUILDING
(Vor dem Fürstenhof) Between the St-Marien and St-Georgen churches lies the restored Italian Renaissance Fürstenhof, now the city courthouse. The facades are slathered in terracotta reliefs depicting episodes from folklore and Wismar's history.

St-Georgen-Kirche   CHURCH
(St-Georgen-Kirchhof; tower adult/child €4/2.50; ⊙9am-5pm Apr-Oct, 10am-4pm Nov-Mar) The massive red shell of the St-Georgen-Kirche has been extensively reconstructed and while work continues, the intention is to use it for cultural (Abba cover bands!) and religious purposes. In 1945 a freezing populace was driven to burn what was left of the church's beautiful wooden statue of St George and the dragon. It was bombed only three weeks before the war ended. The tower can be climbed.

Rathaus   MUSEUM
(Markt; exhibition adult/child €4/2.50; ⊙exhibition 9am-5pm Apr-Sep, 10am-4pm Oct-Mar) The large Rathaus at the Markt's northern end was built between 1817 and 1819 and is home to the excellent Rathaus Historical Exhibition in its basement. Displays include an original 15th-century *Wandmalerei* (mural) uncovered by archaeologists in 1985, a glass-covered medieval well, and the Wrangel tomb – the coffin of influential Swedish General Helmut V Wrangel and his wife, with outsized wooden figures carved on top.

Schabbellhaus   MUSEUM
(Stadtgeschichtliches Museum; ☏03841-252 2870; Schweinsbrücke 8; adult/child €8/free; ⊙10am-6pm Jul & Aug, 10am-6pm Tue-Sun Apr-Jun, Sep & Oct, to 4pm Nov-Mar) The town's historical museum is in the Renaissance Schabbellhaus in a former brewery (1571), just south of St-Nikolai-Kirche across the canal. It reopened in December 2017 after undergoing massive reconstruction. It's an excellent collection, which is particularly strong on the Swedish and Hanseatic eras.

St-Marien-Kirche Steeple   TOWER
(St-Marien-Kirchof; tower adult/child €4/2.50; ⊙9am-5pm Apr-Oct, 10am-4pm Nov-Mar, tower 11am-3pm) All that remains of 13th-century St-Marien-Kirche is its great brick steeple (1339), which rises above the city. A multimedia exhibit on medieval church-building techniques is housed in the tower's base. The tower can be climbed.

Activities

Buddha Bikes   CYCLING
(☏03841-473 6202; www.buddha-bikes.de; Dankwartstrasse 49; per day from €8; ⊙9.30am-1pm & 3-6.30pm Mon-Fri, 10am-2pm Sat) Rents a variety of bikes and has route info; one street south of the Markt.

Sleeping

Pension Chez Fasan   PENSION €
(☏03841-213 425; www.unterkunft-pension-wismar.de; Bademutterstrasse 20a; s/d from €30/55; ⊙reception 2-8pm; ☎) The 25 simple but perfectly comfortable rooms in these three linked houses, just one block north

of the Markt, are fantastic value. Call ahead to make sure there's someone around to let you in.

★ **Hotel Reingard** HOTEL €€
(☑ 03841-284 972; www.hotel-reingard.de; Weberstrasse 18; s/d from €72/87; P 🌐) ✒ Wismar's most charming hotel has a dozen artistic rooms, a little garden and wonderfully idiosyncratic touches such as a light show to classical music that plays across the facade daily at 8.30pm. The breakfast includes apples from the owners' trees and eggs from their chickens.

Hotel Willert HOTEL €€
(☑ 0177 272 9813; www.hotelwillert.de; Schweriner Strasse 9; s/d from €44/70; P 🌐) This small, friendly hotel not far south of the old town is excellent value. Rooms are a real mix, some older with wooden floors, others far more stylish that we've come to expect for the price, with bold colours and artsy wallpaper.

✖ Eating

★ **Café Glücklich** CAFE €
(☑ 03841-796 9377; www.facebook.com/cafe.gluecklich; Schweinsbrücke 7; mains €3-9; ☉ 9am-6pm) Amid a few galleries, this artful cafe serves Wismar's finest coffees. Breakfasts are as beautiful as they are delicious, while the meat and cheese platters are a treat. Cakes, crumbles and more demand that you to save room for dessert.

Kaminstube Wismar GERMAN €€€
(☑ 03841-328 8340; www.kaminstube-wismar.de; Bademutterstrasse 19; mains €23-29; ☉ 5.30-10pm Mon-Sat) This warm and inviting traditional restaurant has friendly old-style service and gets consistently good reviews from travellers for the dry-aged beef, fish dishes, and the disconcerting but delicious *Schwarzwurzelsuppe* (black noodle soup). There's a good mix of German and Italian wines.

Restaurant Alter Schwede GERMAN €€€
(☑ 03841-283 552; www.alter-schwede-wismar.de; Am Markt 22; mains €12-26; ☉ 11.30am-10pm) Steaks, herring and other fish dishes dominate this central restaurant. Add to it good service and the fine backdrop of a historic brick-and-half-timber building, and it's a good all-round choice, if a little pricey.

🍷 Drinking & Nightlife

Brauhaus am Lohberg BREWERY
(☑ 03841-250 238; www.brauhaus-wismar.de; Kleine Hohe Strasse 15; ☉ 11am-late) This imposing brick half-timbered building was once home to the town's first brewery, which opened in 1452. After a long pause, beer is brewing again in enormous copper vats. Enjoy local classics like *Sauerfleisch* (sour-spiced pork) and seafood; live music cranks up throughout summer.

ℹ Information

Tourist Information (☑ 03841-194 33; www.wismar.de; Lübsche Strasse 23a, Welt Erbe Haus; ☉ 9am-5pm Apr-Sep, 10am-4pm Oct-Mar) Provides regional information as well as details on Wismar's Unesco-recognised heritage.

ℹ Getting There & Away

Trains travel every hour to/from Rostock (from €13.50, 1½ hours) and Schwerin (from €8.50, 45 minutes). Change at Schwerin for Hamburg and Rostock for Stralsund.

The train station is 400m north of the Markt near the Alter Hafen.

Stralsund

☑ 03831 / POP 58,756

Stralsund was once the second-most important member of the Hanseatic League, after Lübeck, and its square gables interspersed with turrets, ornate portals and vaulted arches make it one of the leading examples of *Backsteingotik* (classic red-brick Gothic gabled architecture) in northern Germany.

This vibrant city's historic cobbled streets and many attractions make it an unmissable stop in the region. Since 1990, Stralsund's elected representative in parliament has been Chancellor Angela Merkel.

◉ Sights

★ **Nikolaikirche** CHURCH
(☑ 03831-299 799; www.hst-nikolai.de; Alter Markt; adult/child €3/free; ☉ 9am-7pm Mon-Sat, noon-5pm Sun May-Sep, 10am-6pm Mon-Sat, noon-4pm Sun Oct-Apr) This masterpiece of medieval architecture dates to 1270 and is modelled on Lübeck's Marienkirche. Its interior is awash with colour and is filled with art treasures. The main altar (1708), designed by the baroque master Andreas Schlüter, shows the

HAMBURG & THE NORTH STRALSUND

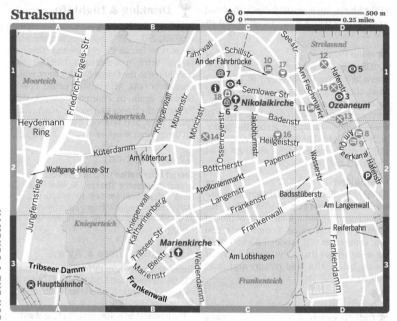

Stralsund

⊙ Top Sights
1 Marienkirche	B3
2 Nikolaikirche	C1
3 Ozeaneum	D1

⊙ Sights
4 Alter Markt	C1
5 Gorch Fock 1	D1
6 Rathaus	C1
7 Wulflamhaus	C1

⊜ Sleeping
8 Hafenspeicher	D2
9 Hotel Kontorhaus	D2
10 Hotel Scheelehof	C1

11 Pension am Ozeaneum	D1

⊗ Eating
12 Fischermann's	D1
13 Fischhalle	D1
14 Nur Fisch	C2
15 Speicher 8	D1

⊝ Drinking & Nightlife
16 T1	C2
17 Zur Fähre	C1

⊝ Shopping
18 Shokoladerie de Prie	C1

eye of God flanked by cherubs and capped by a depiction of the Last Supper. The main portal of is reached via an entrance off the Alter Markt.

★ **Marienkirche** CHURCH
(☎03831-298 965; www.st-mariengemeinde-stralsund.de; Marienstrasse 16, off Neuer Markt; church by donation, tower adult/child €4/2; ⊙9.30am-5.30pm) You will need divine inspiration to guess the number of bricks used to build the massive 14th-century Marienkirche, a superb example of north German

red-brick construction. We can however confirm that there are 206 stone or brick stairs and 143 wooden stairs up the tower for a sweeping view of the town, with its lovely red-tiled roofs, and Rügen Island. The ornate 17th-century organ is a stunner.

★ **Ozeaneum** AQUARIUM
(☎03831-265 0610; www.ozeaneum.de; Hafenstrasse 11; adult/child €17/8, combined ticket incl Meeresmuseum €23/12; ⊙9.30am-8pm Jun-Sep, to 6pm Oct-May) In an arctic-white wave-like building that leaps out from the surround-

ing red-brick warehouses, the state-of-the-art Ozeaneum takes you into an underwater world of creatures from the Baltic and North Seas and the Atlantic Ocean up to the polar latitudes. In a huge tank you can see what thousands of herring do before they end up dropping down northerner gullets. The Humboldt penguins are a highlight.

Alter Markt　　　　　　　　　　　　SQUARE
(Old Market) Stralsund's main square is a hub of its architectural treasures.

Gorch Fock 1　　　　　　　　　　　　SHIP
(☑ 03831-666 520; www.gorchfock1.de; Hafen; adult/child €5/2.50; ⊙10am-6pm Apr-Sep, to 4pm Oct-Mar) Built as a training ship by the German navy in 1933, the *Gorch Fock 1* is a large (82m-long) steel three-masted barque with quite a history. The Russians took her as war booty and from there she went to the Ukraine and the UK before ending up back in Stralsund, her original home port. There are long-standing plans for the ship to again sail the Baltic.

Rathaus　　　　　　　　　HISTORIC BUILDING
(Alter Markt) Seven copper turrets and six triangular gables grace the red-brick Gothic facade of the splendid 1370 Rathaus. The upper portion of the northern facade, or *Schauwand* (show wall), has openings to prevent strong winds from knocking it over. Inside, the sky-lit colonnade boasts shiny black pillars on carved and painted bases; on the western side of the building is an ornate portal.

Wulflamhaus　　　　　　　HISTORIC BUILDING
(Alter Markt 5) A beautiful 15th-century town house named after an old mayor, the turreted step gable imitates the Rathaus facade across the square.

★★ Festivals & Events

Wallensteintage　　　　　　　　　　CULTURAL
(☑ 03831-299 138; www.wallensteintage.de; ⊙3rd week of Jul) Stralsund celebrates repelling an enemy invasion in 1628 with merriment and fireworks.

⌁ Sleeping

Pension am Ozeaneum　　　　　　PENSION €
(☑ 03831-666 831; www.pension-ozeaneum.com; Am Fischmarkt 2; s €50-60, d €65-90; ⊛) There's nothing fancy about this basic 10-room place, but the location is unbeatable. Rooms have a maroon and beige details plus small fridges.

★**Hotel Kontorhaus**　　　　　　　　HOTEL €€
(☑ 03831-289 800; www.hotel-kontorhaus-stralsund.de; Am Querkanal 1; s €75-125, d €99-135, ste €120-155; ⊛) Modern views with large windows, harbour views and fresh maritime colours make this a fantastic choice. The rooftop panoramic suite is stunning in summer, and filled with the drama (with none of the discomfort) of the sea during a storm. Friendly service, good breakfasts and everything within walking distance round out a terrific package.

★**Hotel Scheelehof**　　　　BOUTIQUE HOTEL €€
(☑ 03831-283 300; www.hotel-stralsund-scheele hof.de; Fährstrasse 23-25; r €105-210; ⊛) One of Stralsund's most appealing places to stay, the Scheelehof's 94 rooms are all individually decorated and scattered about several adjoining historic buildings. Furnishings have a luxurious period feel (although we also like those with a more contemporary feel and exposed brick walls) and there is a small spa. The hotel is noted for its bars and restaurants.

Hafenspeicher　　　　　　　　APARTMENT €€
(☑ 03831-703 676, 0176 2210 9004; www.hafen speicher-stralsund.de; Am Querkanal 3a; r €70-165; ⊛) One of Stralsund's oldest brick waterfront warehouses has been converted into an appealing apartment-hotel. The design takes full advantage of the existing materials in the building. Rooms range from spacious doubles to rather large apartments; most have views over the water towards Rügen Island. All five floors are served by an elevator.

✕ Eating

★**Fischhalle**　　　　　　　　　　　SEAFOOD €
(☑ 03831-278 366; Neue Badenstrasse 2; mains €2.80-15; ⊙9am-8pm May-Oct, to 6pm Nov-Apr) Choose your pleasure (smoked fish for a picnic, or a sit-down meal) from the glass-fronted counters, order up, get a beer and wait for your meal's arrival at a picnic table inside or out. This uber-casual fish bar has the best of the Baltic and beyond and the *Fischbrötchen* (fish sandwiches) here are the biggest and best we tasted in town.

★**Speicher 8**　　　　　　　　　　GERMAN €€
(☑ 03831-288 2898; www.speicher8.de; Hafen-strasse 8; mains €10-23; ⊙10am-10pm) Simply roasted fish is one of the stars of this excellent casual restaurant in an old turreted

building right on the waterfront. There are great tables out front; inside it's all glass and exposed wood. Celebrate your love by ordering a meat or fish platter for two. Both are beautifully presented. Sushi and veggie fare are also on offer.

Fischermann's   SEAFOOD €€
(☏ 03831-292 322; www.fischermanns-restaurant. de; An der Fährbrücke 3; mains €9-18; ☺ 11.30am-10pm Mar-Oct, Tue-Sun Nov-Dec & Feb; ☏) Don't be dissuaded by Fischermann's touristy location in a tall red-brick warehouse on the waterfront. Diners pack its elevated terrace on sunny days; the views across to Rügen are just the bonus. Its broad appeal is summed up by the variety of its menu: terrific fish dishes but also simpler fish and chips or schnitzel. Has the full range of Störtebeker beers.

Nur Fisch   SEAFOOD €€
(☏ 03831-306 609; www.facebook.com/nurfisch; Heilgeiststrasse 92; mains €5-15; ☺ 10am-4pm Mon-Sat) Simple canteen-style bistro dedicated to marine delight, from fish sandwiches to sumptuous platters of local seafood. Dishes include pasta, salads, smoked fish and seasonal specials.

⚓ Drinking & Nightlife

★ **Zur Fähre**   BAR
(☏ 03831-297 196; www.zurfaehre-kneipe.de; Fährstrasse 17; ☺ 6pm-1am) They claim to be one of the oldest harbour bars in Europe, and the first historical record of a bar on this site dates back to 1332. The interior is dark wood and filled with all manner of memorabilia – it's beautifully done and the proprietor Hanni makes sure her guests are looked after.

T1   COCKTAIL BAR
(☏ 03831-282 8111; www.t1-stralsund.de; Heilgeiststrasse 64; ☺ 8pm-late Fri-Wed, from 6pm Thu) This hip yet refined cocktail lounge caters to an upscale crowd inside a central, step-gabled town house. They claim to open 365 days of the year, but we didn't stop by on Christmas night to check.

🛍 Shopping

Shokoladerie de Prie   CHOCOLATE
(☏ 03831-667 6991; www.schokoladerie.com; Alter Markt 10; ☺ 10am-6pm Mon-Sat) Beneath the arches behind the Rathaus facade, this divine shop sells chocolates from across the coastal region.

ℹ Information

Tourist Office (☏ 03831-252 340; www. stralsundtourismus.de; Alter Markt 9; ☺ 10am-6pm Mon-Fri, 11am-4pm Sat, 10am-2pm Sun May-Oct, 10am-5pm Mon-Fri, 10am-2pm Sat Nov-Apr) Tourist information and room bookings.

ℹ Getting There & Away

Regional trains travel to/from Rostock (€16.20, one hour), Berlin Hauptbahnhof (from €27, 3¼ hours) and most major towns in the region at least every two hours.

Rügen Island

With its white-sand beaches, canopies of chestnut, oak, elm and poplar trees, charming architecture and even its own national park, Rügen offers numerous ways to enjoy nature. Although summer draws thousands of visitors to its shores, Rügen's lush 1000-sq-km surface area fringed by 574km of coastline means there are still plenty of quiet corners to escape the crowds. You can appreciate Rügen on a day-trip from Stralsund.

Frequented in the late 19th and early 20th centuries by luminaries including Otto von Bismarck, Thomas Mann and Albert Einstein; its chalk coastline was also immortalised by Romantic artist Caspar David Friedrich in 1818.

◉ Sights & Activities

★ **Aussichtsturm Adlerhorst**   VIEWPOINT
(www.nezr.de; adult/child/family €11/8.50/23; ☺ 9.30am-7.30pm May-Sep, to 5.30pm Apr & Oct, to 4pm Nov-Mar) Northwest of Binz, in a lovely Rügen forest, the extraordinary spiral Aussichtsturm Adlerhorst rises 30m above the forest floor – the spiral ramp goes round and around for 600m. It's a wonderful experience and the views out over the treetops are stunning.

Ostsee-Flug-Rügen   SCENIC FLIGHTS
(OFR; ☏ 038306-1289; www.ostseeflugruegen.de; Flugplatz Rügen, Dreschvitz; 20/30/45/60 minutes per person €64/93/133/168) Scenic flights in a light plane are a wonderful way to see this spectacular coastline in all its glory. The 20-minute version will take you as far as Binz, Stralsund or Kap Arkona, while you'll need 60 minutes in the air to cover the whole island.

ℹ Information

Every town has at least one tourist office dispensing local information. **Tourismuszentrale Rügen** (www.ruegen.de) provides island-wide information.

ℹ Getting There & Away

BOAT

Adler-Schiffe (☑ 01805-123 344; www.adler-schiffe.de; adult/child €17/8.50; ☺ Apr-Oct) connects Peenemünde on Usedom Island with Göhren, Sellin and Binz once daily.

International ferries to Trelleborg (Sweden) and Rønne (Denmark) sail from Sassnitz Mukran, about 7km south of Sassnitz' Bahnhof (linked by buses 18 and 20).

CAR & MOTORCYCLE

The toll-free Rügenbrücke and neighbouring Rügendamm bridges cross the Strelasund channel from Stralsund.

TRAIN

Direct IC trains connect Binz with Hamburg (from €23, four hours) and beyond. There is an hourly Stralsund service (from €12.70, 50 minutes). To get to Putbus, change RE trains in Bergen.

ℹ Getting Around

BOAT

Adler-Schiffe (p217) will carry you around the coast from Göhren to Sassnitz, via Sellin and Binz between April and October. Most legs cost €10 each.

BUS

RPNV Buses (☑ 03838-822 90; www.rpnv. de) link practically all communities, though service can be sporadic. Fares are according to distance: Binz to Göhren, for example, costs €5.50. It is possible to purchase tickets on board.

CAR & MOTORCYCLE

If you don't have much time, a car is the most convenient (if not the most environmentally friendly) mode of transport on Rügen Island. The main artery is the B96.

TRAIN

More than just a tourist attraction, the **Rügensche Bäderbahn** (RBB; www.ruegensche-baederbahn.de) steam train serves as a handy mode of transport as it chuffs between Putbus and Göhren. En route, it stops in Binz, Jagdschloss Granitz, Sellin and Baabe. Much of the narrow track passes through sun-dappled forest. It's nickname is the ironic 'Rasender Roland' (Rushing Roland).

OFF THE BEATEN TRACK

DARSS-ZINGST PENINSULA

Nature lovers and artists will be captivated by the Darss-Zingst Peninsula. This far-flung splinter of land is home to 60,000 migratory cranes every spring and autumn.

The area is picturesque, so not surprisingly it's the location of an artists' colony in Ahrenshoop (www.ostsee-bad-ahrenshoop.de), which has an especially wild and windswept beach. The tiny town of Prerow is renowned for its model-ship-filled seafarers' church and lighthouse.

Public transport is infrequent in these parts, so you're best to explore with your own wheels – follow the signs to Ahrenshoop north off the B105 between Stralsund and Rostock.

The main interchange with the regular rail network is at Putbus. In Binz, the DB and RBB stations are 2km apart.

The route is divided into five zones, each costing €2.20. There are family discounts and a range of passes available.

Binz

☑ 038393 / POP 5700

Rügen's largest and most celebrated seaside resort, *Ostseebad* (Baltic Sea spa) Binz is an alluring confection of ornate, white Victorian-era villas, pale sand and blue water. Its roads are signed in Gothic script and lined with coastal pines and chestnut trees. Even if all the signs of 21st-century capitalism abound, especially along jam-packed Hauptstrasse, you can still feel the pull of history amid the modern-day crowds and therein lies its appeal – a stately resort with faint echoes of another age.

◉ Sights

★ **Dokumentationszentrum Prora**   MUSEUM

(Prora Documentation Centre; ☑ 038393-139 91; www.proradok.de; Strandstrasse 74; adult/child €6/free; ☺ 9.30am-7pm May-Aug, 10am-6pm Mar, Apr, Sep & Oct, to 5pm Feb, to 4pm Nov-Jan; ☐ 20, 23, ☑ Prora Nord) *Macht Urlaub* (Power Vacation) is a well-done exhibition on the Nazis and the role the workers' resort Prora played in their 'strength through joy' schemes. You can easily spend an hour or more fully engrossed in the exhibits. There are free German-language guided tours at 11.15am and 2pm from April to October, while the video that runs throughout the day all year has English subtitles. Use the Prora Nord stop on local trains or bus line 20 or 23.

Prora
HISTORIC SITE

The beach just north of Binz still bears testament to Nazi plans to create the world's largest resort: six hideous six-storey buildings, each 500m long, lining the sand. Begun in 1936, Prora was intended as a *Kraft-durch-Freude* (strength through joy) escape for 20,000 workers. The outbreak of WWII stopped its completion; no one has known what to do with it since. Much of it is a moody partial-ruin, with the echos of jackboots not far off.

Strandpromenade
STREET

A highlight of Binz is simply strolling its 4km-long north–south beach promenade, lined with elegant villas. At the southern end of the built-up area, you'll find the palatial Kurhaus, a lovely 1908 building housing a luxury hotel. In front of it is the long pier. Strandpromenade continues further south from here, and becomes markedly less busy.

Jagdschloss Granitz
PALACE

(☑038393-667 10; www.jagdschloss-granitz.de; Tempelberg; adult/child €6/free; ⓧ10am-6pm May-Sep, to 5pm Apr & Oct, to 4pm Tue-Sun Nov-Mar) A grandiose hunting palace built in 1723 on top of the 107m-high Tempelberg, Jagdschloss Granitz was significantly enlarged and altered by Wilhelm Malte I in 1837. The results will remind you of salt and pepper shakers or a phallic fantasy, depending on your outlook. Malte's flights of fancy also gave Rügen the grandiose Putbus. The RBB steam train (p215) stops at Jagdschloss and Garftitz, which serve the palace. Get off at one, enjoy some lovely hiking, and reboard at the other.

The Jagdschlossexpress (adult/child €8/4) is a fake 'train' that trundles from Binz to the palace. If driving, the parking areas (per hour €2) are a 2km walk to the palace.

🏃 Activities

Zweiradhandel Deutschmann
CYCLING

(☑038393-324 20; www.zweirad-deutschmann.de; Dollahnerstrasse 17, Ostseebad Binz Bahnhof; per day from €10; ⓧ9am-6pm Mon-Fri, 9am-noon &

5-6pm Sat & Sun) Has a huge selection of bikes right in the main train station.

Sail & Surf Rügen
WATER SPORTS

(☑038306-232 53; www.segelschule-ruegen.de; Am Fährberg 8, Altefähr) Sail & Surf Rügen rents SUPs (per day €38) as well as catamarans and windsurfing gear. It offers lessons for a variety of water sports and has locations across the island. The main office is in Altefähr, close to the Stralsund bridge.

🛏 Sleeping & Eating

★Pension Haus Colmsee
PENSION €€

(☑038393-325 56; www.hauscolmsee.de; Strandpromenade 8; r €75-109; 🅿🖨🛜) Relax in the leafy, quieter and altogether more pleasant eastern edge of town at this historic 1902 villa. Still family-run after many years, some of the comfy but unadorned rooms have sea views.

Hotel Imperial
HISTORIC HOTEL €€

(☑038393-1380; www.karin-loew-hotellerie.de/en/hotel-imperial; Strandpromenade 20; s €50-90, d €90-155; 🛜) A classic survivor from the glory days of Binz, this 1903 hotel has a romantic turret and several rooms with balconies and sea views. Rooms are warmly decorated and well-sized. Otherwise, it's as unadorned as the beach out front and offers a care-free escape in the centre of the action.

★Fischräucherei Kuse
SEAFOOD €€

(☑038393-2970; www.fischraeucherei-kuse.de; Strandpromenade 3; mains from €10; ⓧ9am-8pm Mar-Dec) For some of the most delicious and certainly the cheapest fish on Rügen, follow your nose – literally – to the far southeast end of the Strandpromenade, where fish has been freshly smoked since 1900. Choose from fish sandwiches and meals; dine at its indoor tables with lovely exposed brick as a backdrop, or out on the terrace.

★Freustil
GERMAN €€€

(☑038393-504 44; www.freustil.de; Zeppelinstrasse 8; 6-course set menu €60; ⓧnoon-3pm & 6pm-midnight Tue-Sun May-Oct, shorter hours Nov-Apr) One of the region's top restaurants has value to match its relaxed vibe. Exquisitely prepared seasonal dishes, sourced locally, are combined in set menus (one veggie) that delight with their creativity. Why moan about autumn, when your mushrooms will star here? Tables outside let you revel in the long summer nights.

ℹ Information

Tourist Office (☑ 038393-148 148; www. ostseebad-binz.de; Heinrich-Heine-Strasse 7; ⊙ 9am-6pm Mon-Fri, from 10am Sat & Sun Feb-Oct, 9am-4pm Mon-Fri, from 10am Sat & Sun Nov-Jan) Staff here provide visitors with lots of maps, island guides and booking services.

ℹ Getting There & Away

Binz has two train stations: the main Ostseebad Binz Bahnhof, serving DB, RE and IC trains, and Binz LB, 2km southeast, serving the RBB steam train.

A daytime shuttle bus circles the Binz environs (adult/child €2.75/free).

Sellin

☑ 038303 / POP 2650

The symbol of Ostseebad (Baltic Sea spa) Sellin is its Seebrücke (Pier). The pier lies at the end of gently sloping Wilhelmstrasse, Rügen's most attractive main drag. It is lined with elegant villas, hotels and cafes and un-like so many local towns, didn't get a cheesy early-1990s makeover in the heady postre-unification days. The pier is at the northwest end of Sellin's lovely white-sand beach and is 1.3km from the RBB train stop, Sellin Ost.

The easiest way to get here is by car, but don't forget the Rügensche Bäderbahn steam train (p215) stops in Sellin on its way between Putbus and Göhren.

Göhren

☑ 038308 / POP 1350

On the Nordperd spit, Göhren's stunning 7km-long beach – divided into the sleepier Südstrand and the more developed Nord-strand – lives up to its hype as Rügen's best resort beach. It looks a treat but tempera-tures are usually brisk at best.

Göhren is the eastern terminus of the RBB steam train; the stop is a mere 200m from the sand. In summer, parking is awful; take the train.

Putbus

☑ 038301 / POP 2825

Putbus appears like a mirage from the mid-dle of modest farming villages. At its heart lies a gigantic circular 19th-century plaza, known as the **Circus**, which has a 21m **ob-elisk** at the centre. Sixteen large, white neo-classical buildings surround it. You can still get a whiff of the GDR here. Some buildings are in better shape than others.

Nearby, the 75-hectare English park is filled with exotic botanical species. After you've soaked up the atmosphere (15 min-utes should do it), head for a beach.

This is the hub for the RBB steam train (p215). Interchange with Germany's main rail network here by catching a train to Ber-gen auf Rügen (€2, nine minutes, hourly), from where there are onward connections to Stralsund and beyond.

Jasmund National Park

The rugged beauty of Jasmund National Park (www.nationalpark-jasmund.de), Ger-many's smallest, first came to national atten-tion thanks to the romanticised paintings of Caspar David Friedrich in the early 19th century. His favourite spot was the Stubben-kammer, an area at the northern edge of the park, where jagged white-chalk cliffs plunge into the jade-coloured sea – it's one of the most dramatic corners of the Baltic Coast. Otherwise, the 30-sq-km park is dominated by pretty beech forests.

◎ Sights

Nationalpark-Zentrum Königsstuhl PARK
(☑ 38392-661 766; www.koenigsstuhl.com; Sassnitz; adult/child €9.50/4.50; ⊙ 9am-7pm Easter-Oct, 10am-5pm Nov-Easter) Admission to Jasmund National Park is through the Nationalpark-Zentrum Königsstuhl, which has multimedia displays on environmental themes, a 'climbing forest' and a cafe.

☞ Tours

★ **Adler-Schiffe** BOATING
(☑ 038392-3150; www.adler-schiffe.de; adult/child from €14/7.50; ⊙ Apr-Oct) Operates daily trips around the chalk cliffs from Sellin, Binz and Sassnitz.

ℹ Getting There & Away

Buses 20 and 23 go right to the Nationalpark-Zentrum Königsstuhl from the coastal towns. A Königsstuhlticket (adult/family €20/40) includes bus travel and park entry. Drivers must leave vehicles in the (paid) parking lot in Hagen, then either catch the shuttle bus or walk 2.5km past the Herthasee lake through the forest.

Kap Arkona

Rügen ends at the rugged cliffs of Kap Arkona, with its famous pair of lighthouses: the square, squat Schinkel-Leuchtturm, completed in 1827, and the cylindrical Neuer Leuchtturm, in business since 1902.

A few metres east of the lighthouses is the Burgwall, a complex that harbours the remains of the Tempelburg, a Slavic temple and fortress. The castle was taken over by the Danes in 1168, paving the way for the Christianisation of Rügen.

Most people sail around the cape (without landing) on boat tours operated by Adler-Schiffe (p217).

Cars must be parked in the gateway village of Putgarten. You can take the **Kap Arkona Bahn** (☑ 038391-132 13; www.kap-arkona-bahn.de; one-way adult/child €2.50/0.50) 'train' or make the 1.5km journey by foot.

Sassnitz

☑ 038392 / POP 10,600

While most people only pass through Sassnitz, at the southern end of the national park, the town has been redeveloping its Altstadt and harbour. The latter is reached from the town bluff by a dramatic pedestrian bridge and is home to cafes and maritime museums. It's worth a leisurely wander if you're in the area.

Infrequent buses connect Sassnitz to Rügen's other population centres, but you'll reach here more easily with your own wheels.

Greifswald

☑ 03834 / POP 56,400

The old university town of Greifswald, south of Stralsund, was largely unscathed by WWII thanks to a courageous German colonel who surrendered to Soviet troops.

The skyline of this former Hanseatic city – as once perfectly captured by native son Caspar David Friedrich – is defined by three churches: the 'Langer Nikolas' ('Long Nicholas'), 'Dicke Marie' ('Fat Mary') and 'Kleine Jakob' ('Small Jacob').

Greifswald has a pretty harbour in the charming district of Wieck; the entire area is worth a stop.

◉ Sights

Markt   SQUARE

The richly ornamented buildings ringing the Markt hint at Greifswald's stature in the Middle Ages. The Rathaus, at the western end, started life as some 14th-century shops. Among the red-brick gabled houses on the eastern side, the Coffee House (No 11) is gorgeous and a good example of a combined living and storage house owned by Hanseatic merchants.

Wieck   VILLAGE

The photogenic centre of this fishing village is a Dutch-style wooden drawbridge. The small harbour is often alive with fishing boats landing – and selling – their catch. There's a good hike through a large park to the ruins of the 12th-century Eldena Abbey and the beach. It's an easy 5km bike ride east of Greifswald's Markt.

**Pommersches
Landesmuseum**   MUSEUM

(☑ 03834-831 20; www.pommersches-landes museum.de; Rakower Strasse 9; adult/child €6.50/4.50; ⊙ 10am-6pm Tue-Sun May-Oct, to 5pm Nov-Apr) The outstanding Pommersches Landesmuseum links three Franciscan monastery buildings via a 73m-long, glassed-in hall. There's a major gallery of paintings, including half a dozen by Caspar David Friedrich, as well as history and natural history exhibits.

Marienkirche   CHURCH

(☑ 03834-2263; www.marien-greifswald.de; Brüggstrasse; ⊙ 10am-6pm Mon-Fri, 11am-3pm Sat, 11am-1pm Sun Jun-Sep, shorter hours rest of year) The 12th-century red-brick Marienkirche is a square three-nave tower trimmed with turrets. It's easy to see why it's called 'Fat Mary'. Look for the 16th-century elaborately carved pulpit and frescos.

🛏 Sleeping & Eating

Hanse-City-Boardinghouse   APARTMENT €€

(☑ 03834-884 5619; www.hanse-city.de; Pestalozzistrasse 26; apt €89-110; 🅿 🛜) Despite the slightly off-putting name, and the fact that it's little beyond the city centre, this place has gorgeous modern apartments, at once functional and stylish, with a fully equipped kitchen and plenty of space. Excellent prices, too.

Hotel Galerie   HOTEL €€

(☑ 03834-773 7830; www.hotelgalerie.de; Mühlenstrasse 10; s/d €80/95; 🅿 ♿ 🛜) The 13 rooms in this sparkling modern property are filled with a changing collection of works by contemporary artists. Room design is a cut above the usual hotel standard.

HAMBURG & THE NORTH GREIFSWALD

★ Fischer-Hütte
SEAFOOD €€

(☑ 03834-839 654; www.fischer-huette.de; An der Mühle 12, Wieck; mains €8-22; ☺ 11.30am-11pm; ♿) An exquisitely presented meal at the 'fisher's house' might start with Wieck-style fish soup and move onto the house speciality – smoked herring. You know everything is fresh as you can see the boats pulling up to the dock right outside.

Fritz Braugasthaus
PUB FOOD €€

(☑ 03834-578 30; www.fritz-braugasthaus.de; Am Markt 13a; mains €8-18; ☺ 11am-11pm) One of the most striking step-gabled red-brick buildings on the Markt is also a brewery. Besides German classics like schnitzels, there are good burgers on the menu. Ingredients are sourced locally; there's outdoor seating.

🛈 Getting There & Away

There are regular train services to Stralsund (from €8.30, 21 minutes) and Berlin Hauptbahnhof (from €27, 2½ to 3 hours).

Usedom Island

Nicknamed Badewanne Berlins (Berlin's Bathtub) in the pre-war period, Usedom Island is a sought-after holiday spot for its 42km stretch of beautiful beach. Its average of 1906 annual hours of sunshine makes it the sunniest place in Germany.

Usedom (Uznam in Polish) lies in the delta of the Oder River about 30km east of Greifswald; the island's eastern tip sits across the border in Poland. Although the German side accounts for 373 sq km of the island's total 445 sq km, the population of the Polish side is larger (45,000, compared with 31,500 on the German side).

Woodsy bike and hiking trails abound. Elegant 1920s villas with wrought-iron balconies grace many traditional resorts along its northern spine, including Zinnowitz, Ückeritz, Bansin, Heringsdorf and Ahlbeck.

◉ Sights

Historisch-Technisches Museum
MUSEUM

(Historical & Technological Museum; ☑ 038371-5050; www.peenemuende.de; Im Kraftwerk; adult/concession €8/5; ☺ 10am-6pm Apr-Sep, 10am-4pm Tue-Sun Oct-Mar) Peenemünde is immodestly billed as 'the birthplace of space travel' here. Displays – some in surviving buildings – do a good job of showing how the rockets were developed and the destruction they caused.

🛏 Sleeping

Hotel Asgard's Meereswarte
HOTEL €€

(☑ 038377-4670; www.hotelasgard.de/meereswarte; Dünenstrasse 20, Zinnowitz; r €76-187; 🅿 🛜 🏊) The fabulous location, just back from the beach in Zinnowitz, and the sense of another age in northern European coastal resorts don't quite penetrate the four-star rooms, which are modern and a touch sterile but extremely comfortable nonetheless. Prices rise in summer and rooms can be booked out months in advance; longer stays are usually rewarded with discounts.

Aparthotel Seeschlösschen
APARTMENT €€

(☑ 038377-4800; www.hotelasgard.de/seeschloesschen; Dünenstrasse 15, Zinnowitz; r €68-165; 🅿 🛜) The building here dates back to 1890, but the spacious studios and apartments sport a largely (and some might say disappointing) modern aesthetic.

🛈 Getting There & Away

Direct **UBB** (www.ubb-online.com) trains from Stralsund (and Greifswald) stop at coastal resorts before terminating in Świnoujście (Swinemünde in German), just over the Polish border. Peenemünde is on a branch line; change in Züssow (from Stralsund, two hours). A day ticket costs €16.50.

Ferries run between Peenemünde and Rügen Island.

Look for **Usedom Rad** (www.usedomrad.de) stations all over the island and Greifswald. You can rent bikes from machines for €9 per day.

Hiddensee Island

POP 1100

'Dat söte Länneken' (the sweet little land) is much mythologised in the German national imagination. This tiny patch off Rügen's western coast measures 18km long and just 1.8km across at its widest point. What makes Hiddensee so sweet is its breathtaking, remote landscape. The heath and meadows of the Dornbush area, with the island's landmark lighthouse and wind-buckled trees, extend north of the village of Kloster, while dunes wend their way south from the main village of Vitte to Neuendorf. In the 19th and early 20th centuries, Hiddensee bewitched artists and writers including Thomas Mann and Bertolt Brecht, as well Gerhart Hauptmann, who is buried here.

Cars are banned on Hiddensee but bikehire places are everywhere. Alternatively, you can see the island at a gentle pace aboard clip-clopping horse-drawn carriages. Horses appear well looked after.

🛏 Sleeping & Eating

Hotelanlage Heiderose   HOTEL €€
(☑038300-630; www.hiddensee-heiderose.de; In den Dünen 127, Vitte; s €64-79, d €79-115, apt €75-145; 🛜) Set amid expansive grounds and with lovely rooms that are both intimate and classy, this fine place is an excellent Hiddensee base. There's a good restaurant, and an on-site sauna.

Hotel Godewind   HOTEL €€
(☑038300-6600; www.hotelgodewind.de; Süderende, Vitte; s €49-95, d €59-135; 🛜) This warmly inviting place in Vitte has attractive rooms with homely decor (sometimes floral prints, sometimes more muted, with wooden beams) and an excellent on-site restaurant. Prices plummet in winter.

ℹ Information

Tourist office (☑038300-608685; www.seebad-hiddensee.de; Achtern Diek 18a; ⊗9am-3.30pm Mon-Fri, to 12.30pm Sat Apr-Sep) Operates a summer branch at Kloster harbour.

ℹ Getting There & Away

Reederei Hiddensee (☑0180-321 2150; www.reederei-hiddensee.de; return day tickets from Schaprode adult/child €15.70/9.10, from Stralsund €19.30/9.40) Ferries leave Schaprode, on Rügen's western shore, up to 12 times daily year-round and run to Neuendorf, Kloster and Vitte. Services from Stralsund run up to three times daily between April and October.

Central Germany

Best Places to Eat

➡ Renthof (p232)

➡ Weinrestaurant Turmschänke (p255)

➡ Zum Wenigemarkt 13 (p242)

➡ Landgrafen Jena (p258)

Best Places to Stay

➡ Hardenberg Burghotel (p234)

➡ Romantik Hotel auf der Wartburg (p255)

➡ Hotel am Hoken (p270)

➡ Design Apartments Weimar (p248)

➡ Scala Turm Hotel (p258)

Why Go?

Crucial to its culture, science, industry and history, Mittel-deutschland is Germany's beating heart. It is studded with cities whose historical importance matches their modern vitality (Weimar, Erfurt and Kassel are just the first names on this list); ridged by low, forested mountains that loom large in German mythology; and edified by museums, cathedrals and castles without number, so it's puzzling that such a rich destination is routinely overlooked by international visitors.

Goethe, Cranach, Schiller, Bach, Grimm, Gropius: the roll-call of German cultural giants nurtured by this region is truly astounding. And it's easy to trace their footsteps, whether you're wending your way along the Fairy-Tale Road, or exploring Wittenberg, where Luther lit the touchpaper to the Protestant Reformation. Add baroque palaces, strikingly preserved towns such as Goslar, Wernigerode and Quedlinburg, the wines of Saale-Unstrut and the ancient beech forests of the Kellerwald to the mix, and you have something like the ideal German destination.

When to Go

The warmer months from April to October are the best time to visit, when museums and sights emerge from hibernation or extend their opening hours, leafless landscapes burst back to life, and the region's wonderful hiking and cycling is at its finest.

As the days grow shorter, the Saale-Unstrut wine region, the Harz and Kyffhäuser Mountains and the Kellerwald and Thuringian Forests are all picturesque autumn destinations, though the weather can be fickle.

In winter, cross-country ski-hikes are popular in the Harz. Central Germany's many historic cities also do cold weather well, with cosy *Gastubes* (pubs) providing warmth and respite.

Central Germany Highlights

1 Kassel (p229)
Delighting in the baroque paradise of the Bergpark Wilhelmshöhe or invoking your inner child at Grimmwelt.

2 Erfurt (p238)
Climbing up to the Zitadelle Petersberg to gaze out over the this beautifully preserved city.

3 Lutherstadt Wittenberg (p284)
Walking in Luther's footsteps in this historic university town, and in nearby Lutherstadt Eisleben.

4 Weimar (p244)
Chasing the ghosts of Goethe and Schiller through baroque streets, then remembering the victims of Nazism at the haunting Gedenkstätte Buchenwald.

5 Dessau -Rosslau (p277) Locating the origins of modernist architecture and design in the city's many Bauhaus gems.

6 Quedlinburg (p268) Wandering Unesco-listed medieval streets past half-timbered houses.

7 Goslar (p264)
Exploring the fascinating history at the Rammelsberg mines and Kaiserpfalz residence.

8 Dornburger Schlösser (p256)
Sampling three palaces and eras iat once at this magnificent hill-top ensemble, overlooking the Saale River.

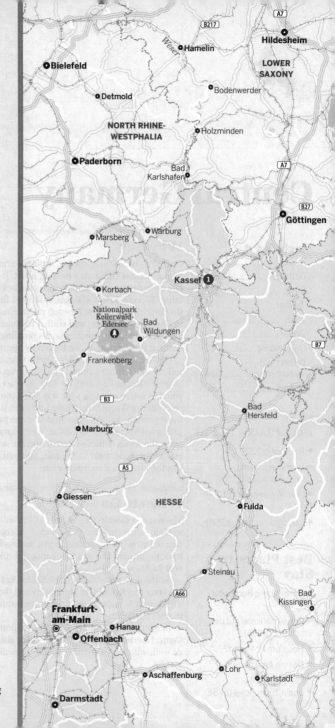

History

Humans have lived in the hilly Thuringian forests and on the fertile plains of Saxony-Anhalt for tens of thousands of years. Historical artefacts from as far back as the late Stone Age have been uncovered here, and the cities of Halle and Magdeburg are among Germany's oldest, dating well beyond 1200 years. Fulda owes its existence to an 8th-century monastery, and Weimar is mentioned as far back as 899.

In more recent times, many of the larger cities across the region suffered heavy allied bombing in WWII. Kassel was one of the most targeted, where over 10,000 civilians were killed and the city was razed. Magdeburg, Dessau and Jena also all suffered heavy losses, although Erfurt got off comparatively lightly. From 1949 to 1990 much of what is now known as Central Germany belonged to the former German Democratic Republic (GDR; East Germany). Although it's increasingly difficult to find signs of the former border today, there's still a discernible difference between what was 'West' and what was 'East', particularly in terms of architecture.

❶ Getting There & Around

Central Germany is, unsurprisingly, well connected to the rest of the country, and internationally. While it has no major international hub of its own, it sits close to the gateway airports of Frankfurt and Hanover, and is criss-crossed by the national autobahn, IC/ICE (Intercity Express) and bus networks, allowing easy overland access to other major centres such as Munich and Berlin.

FAIRY-TALE ROAD

The 600km Märchenstrasse (Fairy-Tale Road) is one of Germany's most popular tourist routes. It's made up of cities, towns and hamlets in four states (Hesse, Lower Saxony, North Rhine–Westphalia and Bremen), and isn't actually a single road: all its sites are connected by association with the works of Jakob (1785–1863) and Wilhelm (1786–1859) Grimm.

There are over 60 stops on the Märchenstrasse. Major ones include (from south to north): Hanau, the birthplace of Jakob and Wilhelm; Steinau, where the brothers spent their youth; Marburg, in the university in which they studied for a short time; Kassel, with a world-class museum dedicated to the Grimms; Göttingen, where they served as professors in the university before being expelled in 1837 for their liberal views; Bodenwerd-

er, made (in)famous by the 'Liar Baron' von Münchhausen; and Hamelin (Hameln), forever associated with the legend of the Pied Piper.

❶ Getting There & Around

The Fairy-Tale Road is more of a road trip than a route to be followed by public transport, but catching trains and buses is easy if you want to take in the main highlights. Take day trips from Frankfurt to Hanau and Steinau, or take a train further afield to Marburg, Kassel or Göttingen.

From the Hauptbahnhof at Hamelin, bus 520 follows the Weser to/from Holzminden (€17, 1½ hours) via Bodenwerder (€13) hourly on weekdays and every couple of hours on weekends. From Holzminden at least five trains leave daily for Bad Karlshafen (€12, 50 minutes), with a change at Ottbergen. Direct trains run every two hours from Bad Karlshafen to Göttingen (€13, one hour).

The Märchenstrasse (www.deutsche-maer chenstrasse.com) website has a downloadable map that provides an overview of the routes and towns; a good German road map is also useful, as it will illustrate minor roads through the countryside. Factor in time to stop, walk around and explore the countryside along the way.

Visit www.weser-radweg.de for details of the much-loved riverside Weser Radweg (Weser Cycle Path), which also connects with some Fairy-Tale Road villages.

Hanau & Steinau

POP HANAU: 95,370; STEINAU: 10,563

The towns of Hanau and Steinau are located so close to Frankfurt am Main that it is easy to visit them on day trips. Lying at the strategically important junction of the Main and Kinzig Rivers, Hanau is the birthplace of the Brothers Grimm and site of an important Napoleonic battle in 1813. Closer to Fulda than Frankfurt, Steinau (an der Strasse) is situated on the historic trade road between Frankfurt am Main and Leipzig. The historical importance of neither town is reflected in a wealth of antique attractions (Hanau was almost obliterated in WWII), but both have one or two attractions to repay a visit.

◉ Sights

Schloss Steinau CASTLE

(☑ 06663-6843; www.schloesser-hessen.de/steinau. html; Im Schloß 3; adult/concession €4/3.50; ◷ 10am-5pm Tue-Sun Mar-Nov) One of the most complete surviving early-modern castles in Europe, Steinau Castle is well worth a visit. Built for the Count of Hanau in the mid-16th century, its dry moat, flagged courtyard and pleasing jumble of towers and sloping roofs creates the very picture of a stern Germanic fortress. Access to the highest tower is an additional €1.

Brüder Grimm-Haus and Museum Steinau
MUSEUM

(☑ 06663-7605; www.brueder-grimm-haus.de; Brüder Grimm-Strasse 80, Steinau; adult/concession €6/3.50; ☉10am-5pm) The famous German folklorists, born in nearby Hanau, lived in this handsome Renaissance stone house as children, from 1791 to 1796. It now houses exhibits on the life and times of the brothers, their work, and the history of Steinau. Hourly regional trains run to Steinau from Frankfurt am Main; the house is a 20-minute walk from the train station.

Historisches Museum Schloss Philippsruhe
MUSEUM

(☑ 06181-295 564; www.hanau.de/kultur/museen/hanau; Philippsruher Allee 45, Hanau; adult/concession €4/3; ☉11am-6pm Tue-Sun; P) Located within the early-18th-century Philippsruhe Palace, this museum displays 17th- to 20th-century art and crafts (faience, silverwork and the like), with a special focus on Hanau and famous locals such as the Brothers Grimm. The parks and gardens (free to visit) are a beautiful place to stroll in snow or the warmth of May and June (when its 1300-seat amphitheatre comes alive for the Fairytale Festival) .

❶ Getting There & Away

Hanau and Steinau are each a short drive from Frankfurt am Main. The road route is marked with signs along the way. From Hanau, take the A66 to Steinau, north of which the route leaves the autobahn and travels along minor roads. Following the B83 along the Weser River is a highlight.

Frequent regional trains from Frankfurt stop at Hanau (€9, 20 minutes), a short walk from the Schloss Philippsruhe. Frankfurt–Steinau services (€15, 50 minutes) are also plentiful.

Fulda

☑ 0661 / POP 67,466

Although it's not officially on the Fairy-Tale Road, photogenic Fulda, a short distance northeast of Steinau (by car or train), is well worth a side trip for those interested in sumptuous baroque architecture, historic churches and religious relics. A Benedictine monastery was founded here in 744, and today Fulda remains a bishopric. In the Altstadt (old town), shutterbugs will find plenty of opportunities for happy snapping and

there's a handful of top spots to pause for a meal or a glass of wine.

◉ Sights

★ **Michaelskirche**
CHURCH

(St Michael's Church; ☑ 0661-102 1813; Michaelsberg 1; ☉10am-6pm Apr-Oct, 10am-noon & 2-5pm Nov-Mar) **FREE** A living kernel of Fulda's long history, this early-9th-century church was once the cemetery chapel for the Benedictine monastery around which the town grew. Considered one of the most important early-medieval churches in Germany, it's a truly beautiful building, with classic witch's-hat towers, a Carolingian rotunda, an 8th-century crypt that pre-dates the church and 11th-century paintings on the interior walls.

★ **Stadtschloss**
CASTLE

(☑ 0661-102 1814; adult/concession €3.50/2.50; ☉10am-5pm Tue-Sun) Fulda's spectacular Stadtschloss (town castle) was built from 1706 to 1721 as the prince-abbots' residence. Designed by famed baroque architect Johann Dientzenhofer (also responsible for the nearby cathedral), it now houses the city administration, but visitors can enter the reconstructed *Historiche Räume* (historic rooms) including the grandiose banquet hall, the octagonal *Schlossturm* (palace tower; open April to October only) for great views of the town, and the magnificent *Schlossgarten* (palace gardens) where locals play *pétanque* (boules) and sunbathe amid baroque and English-style landscapes.

Vonderau Museum
MUSEUM

(☑ 0661-102 3210; www.museum-fulda.de; Jesuitenplatz 2; adult/concession €3.50/2.30; ☉10am-5pm Tue-Sun) Named for an amateur archaeologist who discovered Stone, Bronze and Iron Age relics in the area (the seeds of the current collection), the Vonderau has permanent exhibits on cultural history, natural history and fine art. The focus remains local – human development since the Stone Age, painters and sculptors of note, and even the dinosaurs that roamed here countless aeons ago. There's also a 35-seat planetarium and examples of the much-lamented Fuldamobil, a GDR-era three-wheeler made here between 1950 and 1969.

Dom zu Fulda
CATHEDRAL

(☑ 0661-874 57; www.bistum-fulda.de; Domplatz 1; ☉10am-6pm Mon-Fri, to 3pm Sat, 1-6pm Sun Apr-Oct, to 5pm Mon-Fri Nov-Mar) Inside the baroque Dom (cathedral), built from 1704 to 1712, you'll find gilded furnishings, plenty of *putti* (figures of infant boys), some dramatic statues (such as those to the left of the altar) and the tomb of St Boniface, who died a martyr in 754. Recitals by visiting German and international organists (adult/child €4/3) are held here at noon every Saturday during May, June, July, September, October and December.

Dommuseum MUSEUM

(☑ 0661-872 07; www.bistum-fulda.de; Domplatz 2; adult/concession €2.10/1.30; ☺10am-5.30pm Tue-Sat, from 12.30pm Sun Apr-Oct, 10.30am-12.30pm & 1.30-4pm Tue-Sat, 12.30-4pm Nov–mid-Jan & mid-Feb–Mar) Reached through a delightful garden strewn with stone carvings, the Domdechaneigarten, this museum occupies the cathedral's former seminary chapel. Relics tell the story of the abbey church and cathedral back to Carolingian times – be sure to catch the spectacular Silver Altar and a spooky object reputed to be part of the skull of St Boniface.

🛏 Sleeping

Some of central Fulda's nicer options are quite modern, although there are enough old-fashioned (and long-established) hotels and guesthouses to keep vintage fans happy.

Romantik Hotel
Goldener Karpfen HISTORIC HOTEL €€€

(☑ 0661-868 00; www.hotel-goldener-karpfen.de; Simpliziusbrunnen 1; s/d €125/165; P ❄ @ 🛜) Family-run since 1904, the 'Golden Carp' is an elegant historic hotel offering both traditional and designer rooms in a handsome 18th-century townhouse. Equally worthy is the on-site restaurant of the same name, offering Teutonic staples such as *Tafelspitz* (boiled beef) alongside more adventurous fare such as lemongrass risotto with pankocrumbed zucchini (mains €22 to 26).

Arte Altstadt Hotel HOTEL €€€

(☑ 0661-2502 9880; www.altstadthotel-arte.de; Doll 2-4; s/d from €90/120; P ❄ @ 🛜) In a great spot on the fringe of the Altstadt, this modern hotel has fresh, bright rooms in a variety of sizes and configurations and an on-site brewpub-restaurant, Hohmanns Brauhaus. Parking is available beneath the hotel, for €10 per night.

🍴 Eating & Drinking

Wirtshaus Schwarzer Hahn GERMAN €€

(☑ 0661-240 312; www.schwarzerhahn-fulda.de; Friedrichstrasse 18; mains €17-19; ☺11.30am-

10.30pm) The walls of 'Black Hen Tavern' are plastered with photographs of local and family history and ring to the chatter of happy locals; it's a great spot to dine if you're seeking that authentic small-town German experience. It features a hearty menu of soups, dumplings, pork, fish and schnitzels. Vegetarians have three cheesy, carby options available to them.

Vini & Panini ITALIAN €€

(☑ 0661-774 93; www.vini-panini.de; Steinweg 2; pasta €13-15, mains €22; ☺10am-9pm Mon-Sat) Stop by this popular Italian eatery in the heart of the Altstadt for handmade pasta (perhaps ravioli of salmon and prawns in a pink-peppercorn and brandy sauce), a plate of antipasti and an aperitif, or even breakfast, with ciabatta and Italian small goods in abundance. Dine inside or alfresco in the square, and choose from a good selection of Italian wines.

Viva Havanna BAR

(☑ 0661-227 11; www.vivahavanna-fulda.de; Bonifatiusplatz 2; ☺11am-1am Sun-Thu, to 3am Fri & Sat; 🛜) Come for a Cuba Libra, a beer or a wine, if only to sit on the wonderful terrace with its unbeatable views of the palace. Decent tapas, *Flammkuchen* (Alsatian pizza) and pan-Latin American food is available to those who plan to linger.

ℹ Information

Fulda Tourist Office (☑ 0661-102 1814; www.tourismus-fulda.de; Bonifatiusplatz 1; ☺8.30am-6pm Mon-Fri, 9.30am-4pm Sat & Sun) This efficient, multilingual tourist office has English-language maps and brochures on Fulda and the Fairy-Tale Road. If you're planning to wander the Altstadt (old town) and see the Stadtschloss, consider hiring an English-language audioguide (€11/7 for both tours).

ℹ Getting There & Around

The Hauptbahnhof is about 600m east of the main sights, at the northeastern end of Bahnhofstrasse. Frequent InterCity Express (ICE) trains connect Fulda with Frankfurt (€20, one hour), Kassel (€20, 30 minutes) and Erfurt (€20, 1¼ hours). Regional trains connect Fulda with Steinau (€9, 30 minutes).

Good-quality bikes can be rented from **Hahner Zweiradtechnik** (☑ 0661-933 9944; www.hahner-zweirad.de; Beethovenstrasse 3; bikes per day from €13; ☺9am-6pm Mon-Fri, to 1pm Sat). Bike-path options are signposted down by the river.

Marburg

📞 06421 / POP 74,675

Hilly and historic, the university town of Marburg is situated 90km north of Frankfurt. It's a delight to wander around the narrow lanes of the town's vibrant Oberstadt (Upper Town; the old part), sandwiched between a palace (above) and a spectacular Gothic church (below).

Marburg's precipitous streets are thronged more by students than tourists, with well over a third of the term-time population studying or working at the University of Marburg (founded in 1527). Overall, this is a blessing – bars, restaurants and clubs are cheaper, and more plentiful, and the cultural scene is vibrant. It's easily reached on a day trip from Frankfurt, but also worth spending a night or two in.

◎ Sights & Activities

Most of Marburg's sights are concentrated in the medieval *Oberstadt* (Upper Town), which will present some challenges to the mobility-impaired. Steep, cobbled streets are everywhere.

★ Altstadt
AREA

(Old Town) One of the joys of Marburg is simply strolling around its steeply winding medieval core. Its focal point is the Marktplatz; on the southern side is the historic Rathaus (1512). From there it's a steep climb to the Lutheran St-Marien-Kirche, an imposing red-brick church with great views over the lower town. The terrace on the southern side is the place to watch the sunrise, particularly on weekends, and often in the company of students, revellers, dog walkers and rough sleepers.

Elisabethkirche
CHURCH

(📞 06421-655 73; www.elisabethkirche.de; Elisabethstrasse; adult/concession €2.70/1.70; ⊙ 9am-6pm Apr-Sep, to 5pm Oct, 10am-4pm Nov-Mar) Built by the knights of the Teutonic Order between 1235 and 1283 (its two high spires were added later), the Protestant Elisabethkirche is Germany's earliest purely Gothic hall church. The highlight inside is the *Hohe Chor* (high choir), where you can see beautiful Gothic stained glass behind an astounding stone *Hochaltar* (high altar). The cathedral also houses the golden *Elisabeth-Schrein* (Elisabeth Shrine), dedicated to St Elisabeth, whose burial here made the church a site of pilgrimage in the Middle Ages.

Landgrafenschloss
CASTLE

(📞 06421-282 5871; www.uni-marburg.de/uni-museum; Schloss 1; museum adult/concession €5/3; ⊙ museum 10am-6pm Apr-Oct, to 4pm Nov-Mar; 🚗) Perched at the highest point in Marburg is the massive Landgrave Castle, built between 1248 and 1300 by the first Hessian Landgrave, Heinrich I, on the site of a previous stronghold. It offers panoramic views of bucolic hills, jumbled Marburg rooftops and the Schlosspark, the amphitheatre of which hosts concerts and open-air films in summer. Five floors are given over to the University Museum for Cultural History, with exhibits on cultural history from prehistoric to modern times.

From April to October, tours of the castle leave from the courtyard on Saturday at 3.15pm and Sunday at 3pm (€4 plus entrance fee).

Velociped
CYCLING

(📞 06421-886 890; www.velociped.de; Alte Kasseler Strasse 43; ⊙ 9am-5.30pm Mon-Fri) Everything you ever wanted to know about cycling around Germany, either on your own bike, or one hired from Velociped. A huge range of tours and hire options are available – check the website for pricing details, or drop in to the store, located 400m north of the station.

Bootsverleih Marburg
BOATING, BICYCLE RENTAL

(📞 06421-804 8467; Auf dem Wehr 1a; e-bike/pedal boat per hour €4.50/10; ⊙ 9am-9pm) E-bikes, row-boats and pedal-boats can be hired on the eastern bank of the Lahn, just south of Weidenhäuser Brücke.

🛏 Sleeping & Eating

You've got a choice of more old-fashioned digs uphill in the Oberstadt, or more convenient and modern options down below. There's good value to be found in both.

DJH Hostel
HOSTEL €

(📞 06421-234 61; https://marburg.jugendherberge.de; Jahnstrasse 1; dm/s/d incl breakfast €23/32/58; @ 🐾) This clean, well-run youth hostel is located 500m south of the centre on the river and the Lahntal Radweg (Lahntal Bike Route). Staff can help plan outings, rent canoes and arrange bike hire, and there are 12 rooms well suited to families. Linen is included but you'll pay a surcharge of €4.50 per night if you're over 27.

Hostaria Del Castello
HOTEL €€

(📞 06421-243 02; www.del-castello.de; Marktplatz 19; s/d from €55/80; 🐾) Right in the thick of things, 50m up the hill from the Markt, this Italian-run establishment has seven rooms and a downstairs restaurant in a handsome old *fachwerk* (half-timbered) building. The rooms are basic but clean: try for one overlooking the historic Markt.

★ **Café Barfuss** CAFÉ €
(☑06421-253 49; www.cafebarfuss.de; Barfüsserstrasse 33; meals €8-14; ☻10am-1am Mon-Thu, to 2am Fri-Sun; 🕾🖉) A local institution, humble Barfuss is a no-fuss, offbeat place with walls covered in coffee-sacks and an eclectic clientele of students, elderly couples and sociable drinkers. The diverse menu offers hearty, healthy plates, including great cheap breakfasts and plenty of vegetarian and pasta options.

Bückingsgarten GERMAN €€€
(☑06421-165 7771; www.bueckingsgarten-marburg. de; Landgraf-Philipp-Strasse 6; mains €22-24; ☻noon-10pm) Choose from two separate menus at this venerable restaurant, opened by G Dietrich Bücking in 1807 and now offering German standards alongside lesser-spotted international classics such as bouillabaisse. Dine inside for the upscale experience, or enjoy a stein and schnitzel in the beer garden: both offer spectacular views from a hilltop position adjacent to the castle.

 Drinking & Entertainment

For listings, look no further than the free *Marburger Magazin Express* (www.marbuchverlag.de).

Trauma im G-Werk CLUB
(☑06421-889 772; www.cafetrauma.de; Afföllerwiesen 3a; ☻event hours vary) This versatile, uber-cool space, a self-proclaimed 'socio-cultural centre', hosts semi-regular parties, DJs, art shows, installations, live music, cinema and other cultural events. In keeping with its democratic, inclusive spirit, most events are free or under €4. Check the website for what's on and when.

Delirium mit Frazzkeller PUB
(☑06421-649 19; Steinweg 3; ☻8pm-3am) Delirium is upstairs, Frazzkeller is downstairs, and both of these student hang-outs scream 1970s and have great views over the Unterstadt (yes, even from the cellar). The house drink is Roter Korn, a redcurrant liqueur.

Jazzclub Cavete JAZZ
(☑06421-661 57; Steinweg 12; ☻9pm-2am Mon & Tue, to 3am Wed, to 4am Thu, to 5am Fri & Sat)

Look for the stone wall on Steinweg studded with cow-, horse- and goat-busts to find this prime port of call for jazz and blues lovers. Monday is open-stage night (no cover charge), established acts strut their stuff on Tuesday (€10) and frequent concerts and DJ nights (embracing even minimal techno) are programmed for the other nights.

❶ Information

Marburg Tourist Office (☑06421-991 20; www.marburg-tourismus.de; Biegenstrasse 15, Erwin Piscator Haus; ☻9am-6pm Mon-Fri, 10am-2pm Sat) Books inexpensive private rooms, has free maps of town and is the place to book English-language tours of the Altstadt between April and October (€4/3 adult/concession). Tours depart from Marktplatz at 5pm on the first Friday of every month.

❶ Getting There & Away

BICYCLE
The 245km Lahntal Radweg (Lahn Valley Bike Route) runs along the Lahn all the way to the Rhine, looping around Marburg's Oberstadt.

CAR
Follow the B3 north out of town for Bad Wildungen and the Nationalpark Kellerwald-Edersee, taking the B485 at Bad Zwesten. To go straight to Kassel, follow the B3 beyond this junction and join the A49 heading north.

TRAIN
There are frequent regional and InterCity (IC) connections with Frankfurt (from €20, one to 1¼ hours) and Kassel (from €20, one to 1½ hours).

❶ Getting Around

BUS
The Hauptbahnhof is linked to Rudolphsplatz (where Pilgrimstein meets Universitätsstrasse) by buses 2, 3 and 7. Bus 10 connects the Hauptbahnhof with the Elisabethkirche and Landgrafenschloss.

LIFT
About 100m north of the tourist office, free **public elevators** (Pilgrimstein; ☻7am-1.30am) whisk you up to Wettergasse in the Altstadt. A thigh-toughening alternative is nearby Enge Gasse, a monstrously steep stone staircase that was once a sewage sluice.

Nationalpark Kellerwald-Edersee

Established in 2004, the 57-sq-km National park Kellerwald-Edersee, Hesse's first national park, encompasses one of the largest extant red beech forests in Central Europe, the Kellerwald. There's also, the Edersee, a serpentine reservoir formed through the damming of the Eder, and now a beloved recreation spot. Fifty-five kilometres northeast of Marburg (and about the same distance southwest of Kassel), this national park, along with Hainich National Park in Thuringia and a cluster of other parks or reserves with large beech forests, became a Unesco World Cultural Heritage site in 2011.

◉ Sights

★ Nationalpark
Kellerwald-Edersee   NATIONAL PARK
(www.nationalpark-kellerwald-edersee.de) Hesse's first national park encompasses the Kellerwald, one of the largest extant red-beech forests in Central Europe and a rare survivor of the last Ice Age, and the Edersee, a serpentine artificial reservoir 55km northeast of Marburg. Animals such as red deer, lynx, honey buzzards, eagles, bats and fire salamanders live wild in the park, while some can be seen in protective custody at the Wildtierpark in Edertal. E-bikes and information aplenty are available at the NationalparkZentrum in Vöhl-Herzhausen.

WildtierPark Edersee   WILDLIFE RESERVE
(Wild Animal Park Edersee; ☏ 5623-973 030; www.wildtierpark-edersee.eu; Am Bericher Holz 1, Edertal; adult/concession €6/4; ☺ 9am-6pm May-Oct, 11am-4pm Nov-Feb, 10am-6pm Mar & Apr; 🅿 🖱) Species native (and often those that have been reintroduced) to the Kellerwald-Edersee National Park, including wolves, red deer, eagle owls, lynx, bison, wildcats, ibex and mouflon, can be seen up close at this 80-acre wildlife park on the northeastern corner of the lake in Edertal. An adventure playground, a petting zoo, an educational exhibition and an on-site restaurant make it a great bet for families.

🍴 Sleeping & Eating

Plenty of campgrounds spring to life along the shores of the Edersee around April, usually shutting down again before October.

Edertal, on the eastern edge of the Edersee, has the greatest range of eating options, especially in winter.

Camping & Ferienpark
Teichmann   CAMPGROUND €
(www.camping-teichmann.de; Zum Träumen 1a, Vöhl-Herzhausen; small tent site, 2 adults & 1 car €28.20, holiday house €80; ☺ mid-Apr–late Nov; 🅿) Right on the cusp of the Kellerwald-Edersee

National Park, this family-oriented campground comes alive in summer, with water sports aplenty alongside mini-golf, trampolines, a playground and all manner of other diversions. Fishing licences are sold here (€8/25 per day/week to match wits with the local carp, tench, trout, pike and other fish) and you're ideally based to explore the area.

❶ Information

NationalparkZentrum (☏ 05635-992 781; www.nationalparkzentrum-kellerwald.de; Weg zur Wildnis 1, Vöhl-Herzhausen, off B252; exhibition entry €6.50/4; ☺ 10am-6pm Apr-Oct, to 4.30pm Tue-Sun Nov-Mar; 🖱) For information and insights into the area's ecosystems, head to this striking visitors centre at the western end of the Edersee. There's literature on the park, a kids' wilderness adventure area, a cafe and shop, and the 'BaumTraum' exhibition, which includes interactive exhibits and a 4D cinema.

❶ Getting There & Around

Nordhessische Verkehrsbund (NVV; ☏ 0800-939 0800; www.nvv.de) runs buses into the national park during the 'season' (roughly April to October). Bus 510 goes from Korbach or Bad Wildungen to the Edertal-Hemfurth on the eastern side of the Edersee. From there, bus 503 runs from Edertal to Vöhl-Herzhausen, where the NationalparkZentrum is located.

Ultimately, it's much easier to enjoy the park with your own wheels.

Kassel
☏ 0561 / POP 199,062

Although wartime bombing and postwar reconstruction left Kassel looking undeniably utilitarian, you'd hardly know it today. Visitors to this culture-rich, sprawling hub on the Fulda River will discover a pleasant, modern city with a number of interesting and unusual museums and a one-of-a-kind baroque park Bergpark Wilhelmshöhe, that boasts a handsome palace with a priceless art collection and the gargantuan Herkules statue and Wasserspiel (water feature).

Kassel is a university town, attracting a vibrant young population that keeps the nightlife and culture vital. Invest in the time to explore its widely dispersed attractions, and you won't be disappointed.

◉ Sights

Kassel's sights are spread out – or, rather, they're concentrated in two nuclei: downtown Mitte, and the Bergpark Wilhelmshöhe,

5km to the west along Wilhelmshöhe Allee. If you're not driving, it's worth investing in a Kassel Card, giving you free use of the efficient tram system that carries you easily between the two areas (as well as providing discounts to the sights). Allow a full day to explore the Bad Wilhelmshöhe attractions.

★ **Grimmwelt** MUSEUM

(☑ 0561-598 6190; www.grimmwelt.de; Weinbergstrasse 21; adult/concession €8/6; ⊙ 10am-6pm Tue-Sun, to 8pm Fri; ☒) Occupying a prime position atop the Weinberg bunker in the scenic Weinbergpark, the fabulous Grimmwelt could be described as an architect-designed walk-in sculpture housing the most significant collection of Brothers Grimm memorabilia on the planet. Visitors are guided around original exhibits, state-of-the-art installations, and fun, hands-on activities, aided by entries from the Grimms' German Dictionary: there was more to these famous folklorists and linguists than just fairy tales, didn't you know?

★ **Bergpark Wilhelmshöhe** PARK

(☑ 0561-3168 0751; www.museum-kassel.de; Wilhelmshöher Allee 380, visitor centre; ⊙ 9am-sunset, visitor centre 10am-5pm May-Sep, to 4pm Sat & Sun Oct-Apr; P☒) FREE Situated 6.5km west of Kassel Hauptbahnhof, and 3km west of Kassel-Wilhelmshöhe station, in the enchanting Habichtswald nature park, this spectacular 560-hectare, Unesco-listed baroque parkland takes its name from Schloss Wilhelmshöhe, the late 18th-century palace situated within. You can spend an entire day here, walking through the forest, enjoying a romantic picnic and exploring the castles, fountains, grottoes, statues and water features. The *Herkules* statue and water feature and faux-medieval castle Löwenburg are also here.

★ **Herkules** STATUE

(☑ visitor centre 0561-3168 0781; www.museum-kassel.de; Schlosspark Wilhelmshöhe 26, Herkules-Terrassen; adult/concession €3/2; ⊙ 10am-5pm Tue-Sun mid-Mar–mid-Nov, daily May-Sep; P☒) Erected between 1707 and 1717 by Landgrave Karl and declared a Unesco World Heritage site in 2013, the 8.25m-high copper *Herkules* statue stands atop a towering stone pyramid, atop an octagonal amphitheatre, atop an imposing hill at the western end of Bergpark Wilhelmshöhe – altogether some 600m above sea level. Perhaps more phenomenal than the statue itself is the engineering ge-

nius behind its 2.3km Wasserspiele cascade, which takes place every Wednesday, Sunday and public holiday from 1 May to 3 October.

★ **Schloss Wilhelmshöhe** PALACE

(☑ 0561-316 800; www.museum-kassel.de; Schlosspark 1; adult/concession €6/4, Weissenstein wing incl tour €4/3, audioguide €3; ⊙ 10am-5pm Tue-Sun, to 8pm Wed; P) Erstwhile home to Kaiser Wilhelm II, Wilhelmshöhe Palace (1786–98) at the foot of Bergpark Wilhelmshöhe, today houses one of Germany's greatest art collections, especially of Flemish and Dutch baroque painting. The Gemäldegalerie Alte Meiste (Old Masters Gallery) features over 500 works by Rembrandt, Rubens, Jordaens, Cranach, Dürer, Van Dyck and many others. The 23 rooms of the Weissenstein wing comprise the oldest part of the palace, dating from 1790, undamaged in WWII and filled with original furnishings and paintings.

Fridericianum MUSEUM

(☑ 0561-707 2720; www.fridericianum.org; Friedrichsplatz 18; adult/concession €5/3, Wed free; ⊙ 11am-6pm Tue-Sun) This excellent contemporary art museum hosts temporary exhibitions and symposia exploring relevant, topical themes such as the re-emergence of fascism in Europe. Dating to 1779, it is thought to be the world's first purpose-built public museum, and briefly housed the parliament of Kassel during the reign of Jérôme Bonaparte, made King of Westphalia by his brother Napoléon in 1807. The building's historical value contrasts starkly with the innovative nature of the works on display.

Löwenburg CASTLE

(☑ 0561-3168 0244; www.museum-kassel.de; Schlosspark 9; adult/concession €4/3; ⊙ tours hourly 10am-4pm Tue-Sun Mar-mid-Nov; 10am-3pm Fri-Sun mid-Nov-Feb; ☒) Situated within Bergpark Wilhelmshöhe, the faux-ruined 'Lion's Castle' was built between 1793 and 1801 in a 'medieval' style so ornately romantic it's almost comical. Tours take in the Rüstkammer (Museum of Armaments) and Ritterzeitsmuseum (Museum of Chivalry). The castle is undergoing a long restoration process aimed at resurrecting the original vision of creator Landgrave Wilhelm IX, including medieval gardens and a tilt-yard, but most parts remain accessible.

Museum für Sepulkralkultur MUSEUM

(Museum for Sepulchral Culture; ☑ 0561-918 930; www.sepulkralmuseum.de; Weinbergstrasse 25-27; adult/concession €6/4; ⊙ 10am-5pm Tue-Sun, to

LOCAL KNOWLEDGE

WHERE TO WATCH THE WASSERSPIELE

If you're coming to see the Herkules's Wasserspiele (and if you have the time, you should – it's a remarkable feat of 18th-century hydraulic engineering), the burning question is: where's the best vantage point? We suggest it's a good idea to head to the top nice and early, so you can take a look around the Herkules statue itself and admire the views. Around 2pm, walk down to the base of the statue and get a good spot for the release of the water, at 2.30pm; you can watch it cascade down the hill, then follow the other pilgrims through the park to see the full show. Patience is a virtue, as the full cascade takes 1¼ hours, and is very popular. Bring a tripod if you plan to shoot some video.

8pm Wed) Billed as 'a meditative space for funerary art', this atypical museum examines attitudes to death and burial practices, and challenges western reluctance to discuss it. The permanent collection includes headstones, hearses, dancing-skeleton bookends and sculptures depicting death. There are also temporary exhibitions drawing from the museum's larger collection. Take trams 1 or 3 to Weigelstrasse, or 1, 3, 4, 5, 6 or 8 to Rathaus.

Documenta Halle GALLERY
(☑ 0561-707 270; www.documentahalle.de; Du-Ry-Strasse 1) Built expressly to augment the Museum Fridericianum as the primary exhibition space for Kassel's quinquennial art extravaganza Documenta, the Halle hosts changing exhibitions on modern art, plus readings, screenings and other events. See the website for event times and prices.

Neue Galerie GALLERY
(☑ 0561-3168 0400; www.museum-kassel.de; Schöne Aussicht 1; adult/concession €6/4; ⊗ 10am-5pm Tue-Sun, to 8pm Thu) The restored Neue Galerie, once the town residence of Napoleon's little brother Jérôme but sadly damaged in WWII, showcases paintings and sculptures by German artists from 1750 to the present, as well as pieces from past exhibitions.

🛏 Sleeping

Being a large university town with plenty of attractions, there's a huge range of sleeping options in Kassel. Be aware that it's a sprawling place, and you may end up a decent distance from things you want to see and do.

Pentahotel Kassel BOUTIQUE HOTEL €
(☑ 0561-933 9100; www.pentahotels.com; Bertha-von-Suttner Strasse 15; r from €80; P ✳ 🕾) Spread over six floors, this slick hotel has 137 compact, stylish rooms with ambient lighting, arty design elements and free high-speed wi-fi. There's a bar and restaurant on-site, and you're nice and close to the wonders

of Bergpark Wilhelmshöhe and the convenience of Kassel-Wilhelmshöhe station.

Tryp by Wyndham HOTEL €€
(☑ 0561-703 330; www.trypkassel.com; Erzbergerstrasse 1-5; s/d €63/77; P @ 🕾) This quality hotel with 56 bright, modern rooms is situated just northeast of Kassel Hauptbahnhof, or 600m north of Scheidemannplatz. There's an evening buffet in the restaurant, and a billiard room for after-dinner diversion, should you feel the urge. Take tram 7 to Scheidemannplatz.

★**Schlosshotel Bad Wilhelmshöhe** HOTEL €€€
(☑ 0561-308 80; www.schlosshotel-kassel.de; Schlosspark 8; s/d from €110/130; P 🕾) You can't stay closer to Schloss Wilhelmshöhe and the other delights of Bergpark Wilhelmshöhe than this luxurious spa-hotel, set in an idyllic garden. Built in the Bauhaus style by Kassel native Paul Bode, it boasts stylish and comfortable rooms with large windows allowing maximum perspective on the beauties without. Drop some cash in the day spa if you fancy pampering.

🍴 Eating

★**Pho Vang** VIETNAMESE €
(☑ 0561-937 1536; www.pho-vang.de; Garde-du-Corps Strasse 1; mains €7-10; ⊗ 11.30am-3pm & 5-10pm Mon-Fri, noon-10pm Sat; ☑) Spotless Pho Vang is a great alternative to heavy German fare, delivering authentic Vietnamese *pho* (noodle soup) and other traditional dishes that aren't altered too drastically to suit the European palate (excepting perhaps a popular crumbed chicken dish that's probably not often seen on the streets of Hanoi). It's cheap and delicious, with plenty of options for vegetarians.

Lohmann GERMAN €
(☑ 0561-701 6875; www.lohmann-kassel.de; Königstor 8; mains €9-11, steaks €21-22; ⊗ 11.30am-2.30pm Mon-Fri, 5-10pm Mon-Thu, 5-11pm Fri & Sat,

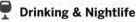

SOME ROCOCO WITH YOUR BAROQUE?

About 15km northwest of Kassel you'll find one of Germany's best-preserved and most beautiful rococo palaces, **Schloss Wilhelmsthal** (☑05674-6898; www.museum-kassel.de; Calden; adult/concession €4/3; ☺hourly tours 10am-4pm Tue-Sun Mar–mid-Nov, 10am-3pm Fri-Sun mid-Nov–Feb; ☐), built by Landgrave Wilhelm VIII as a leisure palace between 1747 and 1761. The magnificent baroque Schlosspark Wilhelmstahl is free to explore, while the palace itself can be visited only on an hourly guided tour. Among the many delightful rooms, visitors love the 'Gallery of Beauties' (paintings of court ladies) and the master kitchen, where the *Bratenwendemaschine* (roast turning machine) still functions.

To get here from Kassel, take the B7 north to Calden and follow the signs, or from Wilhelmshöhe, take the L3217 north and follow the signs.

11.30am-3pm & 4-10pm Sun) With roots that go back to 1888, this popular, family-run *Kneipe* (pub) has an old-style birch-and-maple-shaded beer garden with an outdoor grill, while indoors is all beery chatter and the happy tinkling of knives and forks. Schnitzel (always pork) features heavily on the menu.

★**Renthof** EUROPEAN €€
(☑0561-506 680; www.renthof-kassel.de; Renthof 3; mains €19-23; ☺noon-2.30pm & 5.30-10.30pm Mon-Fri, noon-10pm Sat & Sun; ☎☑) The classy in-house restaurant of the stylish Renthof hotel (single/double €7/115) manages the balancing act of satisfying both those seeking something hearty and traditional (Wiener schnitzel, naturally) and those with a lighter or more adventurous meal in mind (perhaps smoked tofu on a vegan chickpea and sweet-pepper ragu). Vegetarians will be happier here than most places in Kassel.

Matterhorn Stübli SWISS €€
(☑0561-399 33; www.matterhornstuebli.de; Wilhelmshöher Allee 326; mains €16-20; ☺5.30-11pm Tue-Sat, noon-2pm & 5.30-10pm Sun; ☑) If you love cheese, fondue, schnitzel, or all three, you're well advised to hotfoot it to this quaint Swiss restaurant. If you like mushrooms as well, try

the 'Original Züri Geschnätzläts': veal escalopes served with mushrooms and crispy rösti.

🍷 Drinking & Nightlife

Kassel's youthful population, including many students, guarantees a good selection of watering holes. The free monthly *Frizz* (www.frizz-kassel.de) has nightlife and entertainment listings.

Shamrock IRISH PUB
(☑0561-202 8630; www.irishpubkassel.com; Bürgermeister Brunner Strasse 19; ☺5pm-2am; ☎) This sprawling, low-ceilinged Irish bar, lined with 'authentic' Hibernian timber, leather and books, is popular with locals and travellers alike. It's a jovial haunt that brings together lovers of Guinness, Irish music and football, and even has an English-language pub quiz each Monday. It opens earlier when the football is on.

Bolero BAR
(☑0561-4501 0632; www.bolerobar.de; Schöne Aussicht 1a; ☺4am-2am Mon-Fri, from 11am Sat & 10am Sun; ☎) The best reason to visit this sleek, modern chain restaurant, with its crowd-pleasing Tex-Mex menu, is to sip a cocktail and enjoy the wonderful views over Karlsraue Park from one of two terraces. The daily happy hour (€5.50 cocktails from 5pm to 7pm) is dangerously followed by the daily jumbo hour (€9.90 jumbo cocktails 7pm to 9pm).

❶ Information

The great-value Kassel Card (1 or 2 people per 24/72hr €9/12) gets you discounts on a bunch of attractions and free use of public transport. It's sold at tourist offices and some hotels.

Kassel Marketing runs two tourist offices. **Innenstadt Tourist Office** (☑0561-707 707; www.kassel-marketing.de; Wilhelmsstrasse 23; ☺10am-6pm Mon-Sat) This well-resourced office in Mitte can advise on attractions, transport and accommodation in the city, and sells the Kassel Card.

Kassel-Wilhelmshöhe Tourist Office (☑0561-340 54; www.kassel-tourist.de; Willy-Brandt-Platz 1, Kassel-Wilhelmshöhe Train Station; ☺10am-1pm & 2-6pm Mon-Fri, 10am-2pm Sat) This offshoot is useful if you're connecting through Kassel-Wilhelmshöhe station. It's located at the end of Tram 1.

❶ Getting There & Away

Kassel has two main train stations. Kassel Hauptbahnhof, in the centre of town, is served by regional (RE) trains, but it's more likely that you'll be arriving into Kassel-Wilhelmshöhe

(Fernbahnhof) station, 3.5km to the west, which handles both regional and InterCity (IC) and InterCity Express (ICE) trains.

Direct ICE or IC connections from Kassel-Wilhelmshöhe include Fulda (from €20, 30 minutes), Marburg (€20, one hour), Göttingen (€20, 18 minutes) and Frankfurt (from €26, 1½ to two hours).

🛈 Getting Around

BICYCLE

Kassel's sprawling layout makes cycling an attractive option. **Heinrich Muller** (📞 0561-941 5909; www.hm-ebike.de; Baumgartenstraße 8a; 24hr hire €28) rents e-bikes and has discounts for multiday hire.

TRAM

Tram 1 runs the length of Wilhelmshöher Allee, linking the city centre with Wilhelmshöhe. Trams 1, 3 and 4 go from Kassel-Wilhelmshöhe train station to the centre. Almost all the city's tram lines run through Königsplatz. A short-distance single ride is €1.70.

Göttingen

📞 0551 / POP 118,914

Göttingen is a city of extraordinary intellectual accomplishment. Since 1734, the Georg-August Universität has sent more than 40 Nobel Prize winners into the world and alumni includes the fairy-tale-writing Brothers Grimm (as German linguistic teachers) and Prussian chancellor Otto von Bismarck (as a student). With over 30,000 students, this historic town nestled in a corner of Lower Saxony near the Hesse border still offers a good taste of university-town life in Germany's north.

Be sure to stroll around the pleasant Markt and nearby Barfüsserstrasse to admire the *fachwerk* houses.

◎ Sights & Activities

The Tourist Office (p235) runs a variety of interesting themed tours, including those delving into Göttingen's underworld. General Altstadt walking tours (adult/child €7.50/3.75) take place every Saturday, leaving from the old town hall at 11.30am.

Göttinger Wald   FOREST

(Göttingen Forest) Göttinger Wald is one of the best mixed forest stands of predominantly beech and oak in the region. It's easily reached by following Herzberger Landstrasse east from the centre of town to the point near where it forms a hairpin bend, and turning

into Borheckstrasse. From there, a bitumen track open to hikers and cyclists winds toward Am Kehr, 45 minutes away, where there's a small Bavarian-style beer garden.

Altes Rathaus   HISTORIC BUILDING

(Old Town Hall; Markt 9; ◎ 9.30am-6pm Mon-Sat, 10am-4pm Sun) FREE Built in 1270, the Old Town Hall once housed the merchants' guild. Inside, later decorations added to its Great Hall include frescos of the coats of arms of the Hanseatic cities and local bigwigs, grafted onto historic scenes. It's particularly lovely at dusk, and during special events and exhibitions (which may alter its opening hours).

Städtisches Museum   MUSEUM

(City Museum; 📞 0551-400 2843; www.museum. goettingen.de; Ritterplan 7-8; adult/concession €4/2; ◎ 10am-5pm Tue-Fri, from 11am Sat & Sun) This lovely four-storey *fachwerk* house, where Johannes Brahms stayed in the summer of 1853, is home to an interesting series of exhibits on Göttingen's long and lofty history. Special exhibitions on subjects such as the Reformation riots that shook the city in 1529 augment permanent displays on Jewish Göttingen, the University and more. The museum was undergoing renovations at the time of research and some (but not all) rooms and exhibits weren't accessible.

Gänseliesel   MONUMENT

(Markt) The *Gänseliesel* (little goose girl) statue, the symbol of the city, is hailed locally as the most kissed woman in the world – after graduating, doctoral students climb up to peck her on the cheek. The original statue, subject to vandalism, is kept in the Städtisches Museum.

Bismarckturm   TOWER

(Klepersteig; adult/concession €3/1; ◎ 11am-6pm Sat, Sun & holidays Apr-Sep) Set amid parkland southeast of the centre, Göttingen's 1898 Bismarck Tower has a 31m viewing platform from which you can see as far as the Göttingen Forest to the east, the Werra mountains to the south and the Weser mountains to the west.

Stadtwall   WALKING

(City Wall) Strolling along the 18th-century former city wall, now an attractive, raised and tree-lined path, is one of the best ways to introduce yourself to this historic, pedestrian-friendly town. The Stadtwall path runs inside the B27, looping around old Göttingen from Kurze-Geismar-Strasse in the south to Theaterplatz in the east.

✦ Festivals & Events

International Händel Festival · MUSIC
(☎ 0551-384 8130; www.haendel-festspiele.de) Lovers of baroque music, in particular that of adopted Briton George Friedric Händel, flock to Göttingen for this extravaganza, held in mid-May. Running since 1920, it's grown to incorporate a kids' festival and a program of talks, recitals, exhibitions of antique instruments (at Göttingen University) and other events.

🛏 Sleeping

If you're prepared to bus it into town, some of Göttingen's best-value and quietest hotels are on the fringes. Central options are expensive but plentiful.

Hostel 37 · HOSTEL €
(☎ 0551-6344 5177; www.hostel37.de; Groner Landstrasse 7; dm/s/d from €20/42/56; ⊙ office 3-9pm; @ 🛜) This modern hostel has four- and six-bed dorms, inexpensive private rooms, communal kitchen, lounge and games, and a brilliant downtown location.

Hotel Stadt Hannover · HOTEL €€
(☎ 0551-547 960; www.hotelstadthannover.de; Goetheallee 21; s/d from €85/120; P @ 🛜) Run by four generations of the same family, this charmer advertises its class with an art-nouveau etched-glass door and quaint entrance hall. Beyond, you'll find modern, comfortable rooms with a choice of bathtub or shower, and a lovely dining room, site of each morning's lavish breakfast buffet. Parking is €7 per night.

★ Hardenberg Burghotel · BOUTIQUE HOTEL €€€
(☎ 05503-9810; www.burghotel-hardenberg.de; Hinterhaus 11a, Nörten-Hardenberg; s/d incl breakfast from €135/180; P ✷ 🛜) This lovely Relais & Chateaux hotel, 13km north of Göttingen, sits on Count von Hardenberg's estate, beneath the ruins of Hardenberg castle. The spacious rooms are elegantly furnished, service is top-notch, the grounds and golf links are delightfully manicured, and there are two restaurants: the upmarket Novalis, and the more rustic KeilerSchänke.

✕ Eating & Drinking

Göttingen's large student population guarantees that good-value global cuisine augments the traditional fare on offer. It's easy to wander around the centre of town and find something to your budget and liking.

Zum Szultenburger · GERMAN €
(☎ 0551-431 33; Prinzenstrasse 7; mains €10-13; ⊙ 11am-3pm & 5-10pm Mon-Sat) This traditional German pub does things to the humble schnitzel that will make your mouth water, while the *Rindergulasch mit Spätzle* (beef goulash with hand-dropped noodles) is just the ticket in cold weather. It's cosy and cheap, the food is delicious, and the staff seem happy to be here, which makes all the difference. Cash only.

Cron & Lanz · CAFE €
(☎ 0551-5008 8710; www.cronundlanz.de; Weender Strasse 25; cakes €4-5; ⊙ 8.30am-6.30pm Mon-Sat, 1-6.30pm Sun) This ornate Viennese-style cafe is Göttingen's dignified haunt for connoisseurs of *Sahnetorten* (cream cakes), *Obsttorten* (fruit tarts) and other calorie bombs. It's also a good bet for breakfast (until 2pm), offering an international *Karte* (menu) to suit all appetites: from the hearty full English (eggs, bacon, marmalade etc) to a dainty French (a croissant with butter and jam).

Nudelhaus · GERMAN, EUROPEAN €
(☎ 0551-442 63; www.nudelhaus-goettingen.de; Rote Strasse 13; mains €8-11; ⊙ 11.30am-11.30pm) Carb-lovers are spoiled for choice at this ever-popular eatery, which specialises in house-made pasta, often sauced with slightly wacky creations (such as green tagliatelle with chicken and coconut curry). There's also a range of European dishes (such as delicious garlic mushrooms), as well as more traditional Italian pastas, and decent vegetarian options. The smoky central beer garden is often packed.

🍸 Drinking & Entertainment

Savoy · CLUB
(☎ 0551-531 4145; www.club-savoy.de; Berliner Strasse 5; cover €6.50-9.50; ⊙ 11pm-5am Wed, Fri & Sat, 7pm-12.30am Thu) Spread over several levels, this former bank just outside Göttingen's Innerstadt (inner city) changes its spots each night. Wednesday night is student night (naturally), while the 'after-work party' kicks off on Thursday and you're most likely to hear something banging on Friday too.

Apex · LIVE PERFORMANCE
(☎ 0551-468 86; www.apex-goe.de; Burgstrasse 46; ⊙ 5.30pm-midnight Mon-Sat) Started as a cabaret and culture venue in 1971, Apex offers the perfect combination of art gallery, performance

venue and restaurant. The food (served 6pm to 10.30pm Monday to Saturday) is better than ever here, since Jacqueline Amirfallah and Wolfgang Nisch, formerly of Göttingen gourmet destination Gauss, took over.

❶ Information

Göttingen Tourist Office (☎ 0551-499 800; www.goettingen-tourismus.de; Markt 9, Altes Rathaus; ◷ 9.30am-6pm Mon-Sat, plus 10am-2pm Sun Apr-Nov) Housed in Göttingen's beautiful Old Town Hall, this office offers free English-German brochures and walking maps, and can help you with just about everything.

❶ Getting There & Away

Göttingen is on the A7 autobahn, running north–south. The most convenient exit is 73, 3km southwest of the centre along Kasseler Land-strasse (an extension of Groner Landstrasse). Pick up the B27 south to the Weser River and northeast to the Harz Mountains for Fairy-Tale Road towns.

There are frequent direct InterCity Express (ICE) services to Hanover (from €20, 35 minutes), Hamburg (from €25, two hours), Frankfurt (from €30, two hours), Munich (from €48, 3¾ hours) and Berlin-Hauptbahnhof (from €36, 2½ hours). Regular, direct regional services go to Kassel (€16, one hour), Weimar (€22, two hours) and Erfurt (€22, 1¾ hours).

❶ Getting Around

Single tickets for Göttingen's extensive bus network cost €2.30; 24-hour tickets €5.60; see www.goevb.de for lines and details. For a taxi, call 0551-69300 or 0551-65000.

Bad Karlshafen

☎ 05672 / POP 3823

Bad Karlshafen's orderly streets and white-washed baroque buildings were built by French Huguenot refugees in the 18th century for Landgrave Karl von Hessen-Kassel. The town was planned with an impressive harbour and a canal connecting the Weser with the Rhine to attract trade, but the Landgrave died before his designs were completed. The only reminder of his grand plans is a tiny *Hafenbecken* (harbour basin) trafficked by white swans.

Although its original 18th-century grandeur has faded over the centuries, Bad Karlshafen remains a popular summer destination, with motorhomes and tents lining up along the northern banks of the Weser. Take a stroll around the compact town centre on the river's southern bank, with the *Hafenbecken* and its surrounding square, Hafenplatz, at its western end. The *Hafen* (harbour) is being restored to its original impressive condition.

There's no shortage of accommodation in this sweet, sleepy spa town. To complete the baroque-era experience, stay in an 18th-century guesthouse in the handsomely planned centre. Or, in the warmer months, camp by the Weser.

◉ Sights

Deutsches Hugenotten Museum   MUSEUM
(German Huguenot Museum; ☎ 05672-1410; www.huguenot-museum-germany.com; Hafenplatz 9a; adult/concession €4/2; ◷ 10am-5pm Tue-Fri, 11am-6pm Sat & Sun mid-Mar–Oct, 10am-noon Mon-Fri Nov–mid-Mar) Over three floors of a former tobacco warehouse, this interesting museum traces the history of the French Huguenot refugees in Germany. The exhibits illuminate the lives and persecution of these Protestant dissenters (tens of thousands of whom died in the St Bartholomew's Day massacre of 1572) in France, and their integration into life in Germany.

❶ Information

Bad Karlshafen Tourist Office (☎ 05672-922 6140; www.bad-karlshafen-tourismus.de; Weserstrasse 19; ◷ 10am-5pm Mon-Fri, to 1pm Sat May-Sep, 10am-1pm Mon-Fri & 2-5pm Mon-Thu Oct-Apr) Has local maps and guides to the area.

❶ Getting There & Away

Bad Karlshafen's train station is a 1km walk from the centre of town, across the Weser. It has regular connections to Göttingen (€13, one hour), with space for bikes in the carriages. Bus 180 runs from Hofgeismar to Bad Karlshafen (€5.70, 30 minutes), while R22 runs between Höxter and Bad Karlshafen (€6.90, 50 minutes).

For self-drivers, it's where B83 (towards Kassel) and B80 (towards Witzenhausen) meet.

Hamelin

☎ 05151 / POP 56,756

If you have a phobia about rats, you might give this picturesque town on the Weser River a wide berth. According to the tale of *The Pied Piper of Hamelin,* in the 13th century the Pied Piper *(Der Rattenfänger)* was employed by Hamelin's townsfolk to lure its nibbling rodents into the river. When they refused to pay him for his services, he picked up his flute and lured their children away.

Rats aside, Hamelin (Hameln, in German) is a pleasant town with half-timbered houses and opportunities for cycling along the Weser River, on the eastern bank of which lies Hamelin's circular Altstadt. The main streets are Osterstrasse, which runs east–west, and Bäckerstrasse, running north–south. Hamelin's heart is its Markt, the northern continuation of which, Pferdemarkt, is home to an interesting sculpture by artist Wolfgang Dreysse, dealing with the collapse of the East German border.

◉ Sights & Activities

Today rats are welcome in Hamelin – cute, fluffy stuffed rats, wooden rats, and tiny rats adorning the sights around town. Look for the rat symbols throughout the streets, along with information posts offering a glimpse into Hamelin's history and its restored 16th- to 18th-century architecture.

Schloss Hämelschenburg CASTLE
(☑05155-951 690; www.schloss-haemelschen burg.de; Schlossstrasse 1, Emmerthal; tours adult/concession €7.50/4.50; ☉tours 10am, 11am, noon, 2pm, 3pm, 4pm & 5pm Tue-Sun Apr-Oct, 10am & 5pm tours May-Sep only) Some 11km southwest of Hamelin, in pretty parkland near the Emmer River, sits this stunning palace, built in the Italianate Weser Renaissance style between 1588 and 1613. Among the finest of its kind in Germany, the schloss lies on a former pilgrimage road that eventually led to Santiago de Compostella in Spain. Tours take you through rooms decked out with original Renaissance furnishings and paintings, with the south wing especially preserved in its original layout.

Museum Hamelin MUSEUM
(☑05151-202 1217; www.museum-hameln.de; Osterstrasse 8-9; adult/concession €5/4; ☉11am-6pm Tue-Fri, from 10am Sat & Sun; 👶) Many of Hamelin's finest buildings were constructed in the Weser Renaissance style, which has strong Italian influences. Since 1912, two of the best have housed the town's museum, which has an excellent permanent exhibition of 1300 artefacts on regional history, rotating special exhibitions and a Pied Piper Theatre. The Leisthaus at No 9 was built for a patrician grain trader during 1585–89, while the Stiftsherrenhaus (1558) is Hamelin's only surviving building decorated with human (biblical and zodiacal) figures.

Flotte Weser CRUISE
(☑05151-939 999; www.flotte-weser.de; Am Stockhof 2; from €15; ☉8am-5pm Mon-Fri, to 4pm Sat) From April to October, boats operated by Flotte Weser travel from Hamelin to Bodenwerder on Wednesday, Saturday and Sunday (€14.50, 3½ hours). A range of themed cruises and packages are also available. The outfit has a second office in Nienburg.

🛏 Sleeping & Eating

Plenty of the Altstadt's historic houses have been sensitively resurrected as comfortable modern hotels. More accessible options are immediately outside the historic heart.

★Schlosshotel Münchhausen LUXURY HOTEL €€€
(☑05154-706 00; www.schlosshotel-muenchhau sen.com; Schwöbber 9, Aerzen; s/d tithe barn from €140/170, castle from €205/235, apt €170; P👹❄️🐾) Palatial Schlosshotel Münchhausen, 12km southwest of Hamelin, occupies a baronial castle built in 1570. Stylish, contemporary rooms in the main wing have historic touches, the suites have tasteful period furnishings and rooms in the tithe barn are entirely modern. Two restaurants, lavish spa facilities and two golf courses set in 8 hectares of gorgeous parkland round out the luxury.

★Komfort-Hotel Garni Christinenhof BOUTIQUE HOTEL €€€
(☑05151-950 80; https://christinenhof.de; Alte Marktstrasse 18; s/d incl breakfast €95/130; P🐾🏊) Historic outside, modern within, this super-welcoming hotel has a tiny swimming pool in the vaulted cellar, a sauna, and compact (but pleasant and uncluttered) rooms. The owners take particular care with the generous buffet breakfast (entirely homemade) and parking is free of charge. Spread over two buildings, this is a great option in central Hamelin.

Mexcal TEX-MEX €
(☑05151-428 06; http://mexcal-hameln.de; Osterstrasse 15; mains €9-13; ☉noon-11pm Sun-Thu, to midnight Fri & Sat) You don't expect to find delicious Tex-Mex food in a cellar on Hamelin's historic Osterstrasse, but this bustling brick-vaulted restaurant is a winner. Locals avoiding tourist-centred German restaurants pile into chimichangas, fajitas and other corny, cheesy delights, all washed down with margaritas and Coronas. Daily happy hours run from 3pm to 6pm and 10pm to 11pm, when all cocktails are €5.60.

★Rattenfängerhaus GERMAN €€
(☑05151-3888; www.rattenfaengerhaus.de; Osterstrasse 28; mains €15-18; ☉11.30am-2.30pm & 6.30-9.30pm Mon-Thu, 11.30am-9.30pm Fri-Sun;

🏠) One of Hamelin's finest ornamental Weser Renaissance–style buildings, the Rattenfängerhaus (Pied Piper House) has a facade dating to 1602, with older sections within. It's now home to an unashamedly tourist-centric restaurant, which has been serving 'rats' tails' flambéed at your table since 1966 (don't worry – it's all a pork-based ruse).

Aside from the novelty dishes, standard schnitzels, herrings, veggie dishes and 'rat killer' herb liquor are also offered.

ℹ Information

Hamelin Tourist Office (📞 05151-957 823; www.hameln.de; Diesterallee 1; ⊙9am-6pm Mon-Fri, 9.30am-3pm Sat, 9.30am-1pm Sun Apr-Oct, 9am-5pm Mon-Fri, 9.30am-1pm Sat Nov-Mar) Just outside the old town, this well-resourced office is great for literature and advice on Hamelin and the Weserbergland (Weser Uplands) – and of course the Pied Piper.

ℹ Getting There & Away

Take the B217 to/from Hanover.

Frequent S-Bahn trains (S5) head to Hamelin from Hanover's Hauptbahnhof (€13, 45 minutes). Regular direct trains connect Hanover's airport with Hamelin (€16, one hour).

ℹ Getting Around

Hamelin is compact and easily explored on foot.

If you'd like to ride around town, or by the Weser, **Troches Fahrradshop** (📞 05151-136 70; http://troche.graviton-audio.org; Kreuzstrasse 7; bike/e-bike, per day €10/25; ⊙9.30am-12.30pm & 2.30-6pm Mon-Fri, to 1pm Sat) near the train station rents city and touring bikes, plus e-bikes.

Buses 1 to 7 are just some of the bus routes that will take you into town from the Hauptbahnhof.

Bodenwerder

📞 05533 / POP 5957

Bodenwerder's most famous son is the Baron Hieronymous von Münchhausen (1720–97), one of history's most shameless liars. He gave his name to a psychological condition – Münchhausen's syndrome, or compulsive exaggeration of physical illness – and inspired both German author Rudolf Erich Raspe's 'account' of his 'adventures' and Terry Gilliam's cult film *The Adventures of Baron Munchausen* (1988). It's all perhaps a little unfair, as the real Baron, perhaps given to stretching the truth, wasn't quite the outrageous liar literature and film have made him out to be. But why let the truth get in the way?

WORTH A TRIP

BURGRUINE POLLE

Sitting on a crag in a loop of the Weser River in the little village of Polle, 15km from Bodenwerder, this wonderfully accessible castle ruin (c 1200; (📞05535-411; www.weserbergland-tourismus.de; Amtsstrasse 4a, Polle; adult/concession €2/1; ⊙10am-7pm May-Oct, Sat & Sun only Apr; 🅿) , affords beautiful views over the river valley below. You can climb to the top of the tower or just admire the views from the quirky sculpture garden within the garden walls. This is an offbeat, special spot.

In front of the town church of St Nicolai (dated to 1476) is the historical heart of this little town: Münchhausen's former manor house, remnants of fortifications, and the museum. Plenty of *fachwerk* (half-timbered) houses in the area complete the picture of antiquity.

Münchhausen Museum   MUSEUM
(📞05533-409 147; www.muenchhausenland. de; Münchhausenplatz 5; adult/child €2.50/1.50; ⊙10am-5pm Apr-Oct; 🅿) Bodenwerder's principal attraction struggles a little with the difficult task of conveying the chaos and fun associated with the 'liar baron' – a man who liked to regale dinner guests with his Crimean adventures, claiming he had, for example, tied his horse to a church steeple during a snow drift and ridden around a dining table without breaking one teacup. Among personal effects and other artefacts, there are paintings and displays of Münchhausen books in many languages.

ℹ Information

Bodenwerder Tourist office (📞05533-405 41; www.muenchhausenland.de; Münchhausenplatz 1; ⊙9am-noon & 2-5pm Mon-Fri, 10am-12.30pm Sat late Mar–mid-Oct, 9am-noon Mon-Fri mid-Oct–late Mar) An understandably Münchhausen-focused but generally useful office near the museum. Has information on canoe and bicycle hire in town, arranges accommodation and can answer other queries.

ℹ Getting There & Away

Bodenwerder straddles a broad loop of the Weser, where the B83 (to Hamelin) and B240 intersect. Buses 40 and 51 run between the two towns every hour or so (€6, 45 minutes).

THURINGIA

A land of forested hills, fertile plains and fabled fortresses, Thuringia sits at Germany's geographic heart. With cities of genuine historical heft sitting alongside World Heritage Sites like the unforgettable Wartburg fortress, it's a famous destination for domestic travellers. And no wonder: forever associated with immortal names such as Luther, Bach, Goethe, Schiller, Cranach, Wagner and Gropius, it can seriously claim to be one of Germany's most fertile cultural cradles.

Weimar – engine room of the German Enlightenment and the birthplace of the ill-fated Weimar Republic – and nearby Erfurt, Thuringia's lively, historic and attractive capital, are must-sees on any comprehensive German itinerary, while nearby Jena has a long history of scientific and technological achievement, and remains a vibrant university town. Mühlhausen has a wonderfully preserved medieval heart, and wilderness areas such as the Hainich National Park, sprawling Thuringian Forest and the much-mythologised Kyffhäuser Mountains give this region a deserved reputation as 'the green heart of Germany'.

❶ Information

The **ThüringenCard** (€18/13 for a one-day adult/concession pass, or €38/25 for three days, usable non-consecutively within a year) is available at tourist offices across Thuringia and offers considerable savings, especially if you plan to explore the region for a few days. Benefits include free admission to over 200 attractions and free or discounted public transport. Visit www.visit-thuringia.com for more information.

❶ Getting There & Around

Thuringia is well serviced by rail and bus networks, but hiring a car will afford you the freedom to explore the miles of quiet mountain and country roads and the innumerable quaint villages they serve.

Erfurt has ICE (Intercity Express) train connections to Frankfurt, Nuremberg, Leipzig and Berlin, while nearby Weimar is similarly connected to the latter two.

The A4 autobahn courses east–west across the region, running just south of Jena, Weimar, Erfurt and Goth, and looping north of Eisenach, making it particularly convenient for drivers. Without your own wheels you'll be dependent on buses to get to Hainich National Park or the Kyffhäuser Mountains.

Erfurt

🖉 0361 / POP 211,113

Erfurt, Thuringia's capital, is one of central Germany's most beguiling and significant cities. Holding its head as high as the former capital to the east, Weimar, it's a wonderfully preserved medieval city of grandiose churches, cobbled market squares, captivating museums and miraculously preserved architecture. And, as a university town, its contemporary culture is anything but backward-looking.

Straddling the Gera River, Erfurt was founded by St Boniface as a bishopric in 742, then propelled to prosperity in the Middle Ages as a major centre of the woad trade. In 1392 rich merchants founded the university, allowing students to study common law, rather than religious law. It was here that Martin Luther studied philosophy before taking holy orders.

With most of its historical centre spared destruction in WWII, today's Erfurt proves that modernity and history can coexist gracefully. The city's appearance honours its medieval roots, while adding often classy, sometimes quirky, contemporary flourishes.

◎ Sights

Erfurt has a number of lovely squares to stroll between: Domplatz, the largest and setting for the cathedral; Anger, a transport and shopping hub where old meets new; Wenigemarkt, a tiny old market square that's perfect for a casual meal; and Fischmarkt, the city's central square, where you'll find the neo-Gothic Rathaus and a collection of spectacular historical buildings, including the Renaissance Haus zum Breiten Herd and the Gildehaus with its facade depicting the four virtues.

★**Erfurter Dom**   CATHEDRAL
(Mariendom; 🖉 0361-646 1265; www.dom-erfurt.de; Domplatz; ⊙ 9.30am-6pm Mon-Sat, 1-6pm Sun May-Oct, to 5pm Nov-Apr) FREE Erfurt's cathedral, where Martin Luther was ordained a priest, grew over the centuries from a simple 8th-century chapel into the stately Gothic pile of today. Standouts in its treasure-filled interior include the stained-glass windows; the 'Wolfram' (an 850-year-old bronze candelabrum in the shape of a man); the 'Gloriosa' (the world's largest free-swinging medieval bell); a Romanesque stucco Madonna; Cranach's 'The Mystic Marriage of St Catherine'; and the intricately carved choir stalls. Group tours start at €4.50 per person.

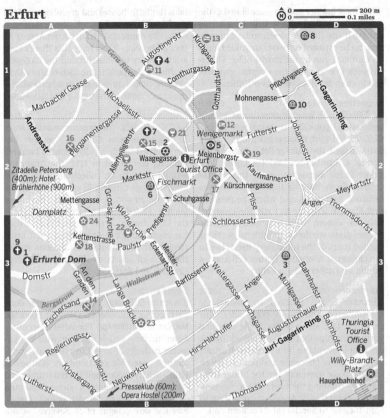

Erfurt

⊙ Top Sights

⊙ Sights

⊜ Sleeping

⊗ Eating

⊝ Drinking & Nightlife

⊙ Entertainment

★ **Zitadelle Petersberg**   FORTRESS
(☏0361-664 00; Petersberg 3; tour adult/concession
€8/4; ⊙7pm Fri & Sat May-Oct) Situated on the

Petersberg hill northwest of Domplatz, this
36-hectare citadel ranks among Europe's largest and best-preserved baroque fortresses.

While most interior buildings are closed to the public (and daubed with stencils by guerrilla artists), it sits above a honeycomb of tunnels that can be explored on two-hour guided tours (in German), run by the tourist office. Otherwise, it's free to roam the external grounds, and to enjoy fabulous views over Erfurt.

Augustinerkloster
CHURCH

(🖉 0361-576 600; www.augustinerkloster.de; Auginerstrasse 10; public German-language/group tour €7.50/25; ⊙ English-language group tours 9.30am-5pm Mon-Sat & 11am Sun Apr-Oct, 9.30am-3.30pm Mon-Sat & 11am Sun Nov-Mar) It's Luther lore galore at the monastery where the reformer lived from 1505 to 1511, where he was ordained as a monk and where he read his first Mass. You're free to roam the grounds, visit the church with its ethereal Gothic stained-glass windows and attend services. Guided tours of the monastery itself take in the cloister, a re-created Luther cell and an exhibit on Luther's life in Erfurt.

Krämerbrücke
BRIDGE

(Merchants' Bridge) Flanked by photogenic half-timbered houses on both sides, this charming 1325 stone bridge is the only one north of the Alps that's still inhabited. To this day people live above little shops with attractive displays of chocolate and pottery, jewellery and basic souvenirs. See the bridge from above by climbing the tower of the Ägidienkirche (Church of St Aegidius; open 11am to 5pm Tuesday to Sunday) at its eastern end.

Alte Synagoge
SYNAGOGUE

(🖉 0361-655 1520; www.juedisches-leben.erfurt. de; Waagegasse 8; adult/concession €8/5; ⊙ 10am-6pm Tue-Sun) This is one of Europe's oldest Jewish houses of worship, dating in part to the 11th century. Following the 'Black Death' pogrom of 1349 it was used as an inn and store, thus escaping destruction at the hands of the Nazis, ignorant of its true nature. Exhibits document the history of the building and showcase the 'Erfurt Treasure', unearthed during excavations nearby and including brooches, cutlery and, most famously, a very rare golden Jewish marriage ring from the early 14th century.

Egapark Erfurt
GARDENS

(Erfurter Gartenausstellung; 🖉 564 3737; www. egapark-erfurt.de; Gothaer Strasse 38; adult/concession €8/6.50 Apr-Oct, €6/4.80 Nov-Mar; ⊙ 9am-6pm mid-Mar–Oct, 10am-4pm Nov–mid-Mar) It's easy to spend hours amid the riotous flower beds, Japanese rock garden, Schmetterling-

haus (butterfly house) and greenhouses of the rambling GDR-era Egapark, about 4km west of the city centre (take tram 2 from Anger). At over 36 hectares it's so huge that there's even a little trolley to whisk around the foot-weary. Part of the park is the 15th-century Cyriaksburg citadel, now home to a horticultural museum – climb to the top for fantastic views.

Angermuseum
MUSEUM

(🖉 0361-655 1651; www.angermuseum.de; Anger 18; adult/concession €6/4; ⊙ 10am-6pm Tue-Sun) Housed inside a fully restored baroque building completed in 1712, the Angermuseum has a strong collection of medieval art, paintings ranging from the 17th century to contemporary times, and Thuringian faience (glazed earthenware). A highlight is the Heckelraum on the ground floor, which has expressionist frescos by the artist Erich Heckel, while temporary exhibitions attract the work of artists as significant as Lucas Cranach and Franz Markau.

Severikirche
CHURCH

(Church of St Severus; 🖉 0361-646 1265; Domplatz; tour €2; ⊙ 9.30am-6pm Mon-Sat, 1-6pm Sun May-Oct, to 5pm Nov-Apr) The late-13th-century Severikirche – which together with the adjacent cathedral forms Efrurt's iconic architectural ensemble on Domberg (Cathedral Hill) – is a five-aisled hall church with prized treasures that include a stone Madonna (1345), a 15m-high sandstonefont (1467), and the sarcophagus of St Severus, whose remains were brought to Germany from Ravenna in the 9th century.

Museum für Thüringer Volkskunde
MUSEUM

(Museum of Thuringian Folklore; 🖉 0361-655 5607; www.volkskundemuseum-erfurt.de; Juri-Gagarin-Ring 140a; adult/concession €6/4; ⊙ 10am-6pm Tue-Sun) This folklore museum is one of the largest of its kind in Germany, with an interesting collection focused on the applied arts, with household objects, furnishings and tools of all sorts. Its centrepiece is an exhibit on 19th-century village life, and there's a program of special exhibitions on subjects such as printing and photography in Thuringia.

Stadtmuseum
MUSEUM

(🖉 0361-655 5651; www.stadtmuseum-erfurt. de; Johannesstrasse 169; adult/concession €6/4; ⊙ 10am-6pm Tue-Sun) Behind the magnificent chequerboard facade of the late-Renaissance Haus am Stockfisch ('House of Stockfish', or dried cod) lies a fascinating exploration of Erfurt's long history. From material artefacts

THE DREI GLEICHEN

Marooned in central Thuringia, south of Gotha and Erfurt, is a trio of castles that still sit proudly upon the *Bergs* (hills) from which they once commanded the surrounding country. Known as the Drei Gleichen ('Thee Like') castles, they actually have quite distinct histories and profiles, with the earliest, **Mühlburg** (☑0160-225 0918; www.drei-gleichen. de; Mühlberg; adult/concession €2/1.50; ☉10am-5pm Mon-Fri, to 6pm Sat & Sun Mar-Oct), dating possibly to the 4th century (although nothing of that vintage remains) and the most recent, **Burg Gleichen** (☑036202-824 40; www.drei-gleichen.de; Wandersleben; €3; ☉10am-6pm Apr-Oct), to the 11th century. **Veste Wachsenburg** (☑03628-742 40; www.wachsen burg.com; Amt Wachsenburg; ☉restaurant 11am-8pm Tue-Sat, to 5pm Sun), dating to the 10th century, is the only one of the three that isn't ruinous; it was restored in more recent times, and now houses a hotel and restaurant. All three are striking, can be visited and explored to some extent, and are linked by an easy 12km walking trail, the Burgenroute.

such as a medieval bone-carver's tools to informative displays on everyday life under Nazism and Socialism, the museum illuminates facets of the city that might otherwise go unnoticed.

Kunsthalle Erfurt
GALLERY
(☑0361-655 5660; http://kunstmuseen.erfurt.de; Fischmarkt 7; adult/concession €6/4; ☉11am-6pm Mon-Sat, to 10pm Sun) Erfurt's most experimental art space offers a rigorously curated program of exhibitions, incorporating graphic art, audiovisual art and installations.

Michaeliskirche
CHURCH
(cnr Michaelisstrasse & Allerheiligenstrasse; photography €1; ☉11am-4pm Mon-Sat) Dating to the late 12th century, the old university church boasts a magnificent organ (1652), made by local master Ludwig Compenius, and was a key gathering place for 16th-century Protestants, and (centuries later) local dissidents in the final days of the GDR. The organ is fired up for 25-minute recitals every Wednesday at noon, and for frequent special performances.

✦✦ Festivals & Events

Güldener Herbst
MUSIC
(Güldener Autumn; ☑0361-227 5227; www.gueldener-herbst.de; ☉Sep & Oct) Lovers of obscure old music flock to Erfurt for this autumnal feast, in which forgotten operas, cantatas and other compositions are lovingly resurrected across Erfurt's many sacred and secular venues.

Domstufen-Festspiele
MUSIC
(www.domstufen-festspiele.de; ☉Aug) The summer music festival is held every August in the open air beneath the gothic extravagance of Erfurt Cathedral. Evenings are usually given over to iconic operas such as *Carmen* or *The Magic Flute,* but the days promise children's musicals and other diversions.

🛏 Sleeping

The Erfurt tourist office has access to a large contingent of private rooms and apartments starting at €25 per person. Visitors pay a 5% tax on accommodation to fund cultural upkeep.

★ Rad-Hof
PENSION €
(☑0361-602 7761; www.rad-hof.de; Kirchgasse 1b; s/d/tr incl breakfast from €50/60/70; @ 🖀) Sigrid and Dieter, the owners of this cyclist-friendly guesthouse next to the Augustinian monastery, have gone the extra mile in renovating the building with natural materials, such as wood and mud. No two rooms are alike, and the modest gardens are pleasantly leafy in the warmer months. Take tram 1 or 5 to Augustinerstrasse.

Opera Hostel
HOSTEL €
(☑0361-6013 1360; www.opera-hostel.de; Walkmühlstrasse 13; dm €15-22, s/d/tr €50/60/80, linen €2.50; @ 🖀) This upmarket hostel in an 18th-century hotel scores big with wallet-watching global nomads, especially as reception's open around the clock and there's no lockout or curfew. Rooms are bright and spacious, many with sofas. Make friends in the communal kitchen and on-site lounge-bar, or pedal around the city on one of the hostel's bikes (€10 per day).

From the train station, take bus 51 (direction Hochheim) to 'Alte Oper'.

★ Hotel Brühlerhöhe
BOUTIQUE HOTEL €€
(☑0361-241 4990; www.hotel-bruehlerhoehe-erfurt.de; Rudolfstrasse 48; s/d from €80/95; 🅿 🖀) This Prussian officers' casino turned chic city hotel gets high marks for its opulent breakfast spread (€12.50) and smiling,

quick-on-their-feet staff. Rooms are cosy and modern with chocolate-brown furniture, solid timberwork, thick carpets and sparkling baths. It's a short ride on tram 4 (from the Justizzentrum stop) into central Erfurt.

Hotel Krämerbrücke
BOUTIQUE HOTEL **€€**

(☑0361-674 00; www.ibbhotelerfurt.com; Gotthardtstrasse 27; s/d €85/115; P ❈ @ 🛜) This bright hotel, in a brilliant spot near a willow-fringed arm of the Gera River, gets a thumbs-up from design-minded travellers impressed by a thorough refurbishment in 2018. Eighty-five rooms of varying sizes are spread over two buildings, one an annexe on the historic Krämerbrücke. Limited parking is available, at €15 per night.

Evangelisches Augustinerkloster zu Erfurt
GUESTHOUSE **€€**

(☑0361-576 600; www.augustinerkloster.de; Augustinerstrasse 10; s/tw €65/100; P 🛜) Erfurt's venerable Augustinian monastery offers an unusual retreat from the rat race of everyday life – a bible, but no television, telephones or internet, in rooms barely larger than a monk's cell. It's undeniably a special and tranquil place, where you can allow your social networking accounts to digitally rust. Take tram 1 or 5 to Augustinerstrasse.

Eating

Traditional Thuringian *Gastubes* (pubs) and restaurants trading on the established tastes of the German tourist market are plentiful in the old parts of Erfurt. There are alternatives, however – principally Italian and fast-food restaurants. Outdoor dining, especially in places with frontage on the branches of the Gera that flow through town, comes into its own in summer.

Faustfood
BARBECUE **€**

(☑0361-6443 6300; www.faustfood.de; Waagegasse 1; mains €10; ⊘11am-11pm Wed-Sat, to 7pm Sun) Despite its casual, student-y vibe, this rambunctious grill house is a great place for traditional Thuringian grills (*Rostbrätel* and bratwurst), plus more international meaty treats such as spare ribs, steak and cheeseburgers. Dine in (under the canopy of grill-smoke that hangs below the rafters of what was a medieval barn) or take away, but head elsewhere if you're vegetarian!

Altstadt Cafe
CAFE **€**

(☑0361-562 6473; www.erfurt-altstadtcafe.de; Fischersand 1; mains €10; ⊘11.30am-11pm Mon-Fri, noon-10pm Sat, 2-7pm Sun) Chatty mothers, foot-weary sightseers and solo bookworms gather at this cheerful cafe in the former 14th-century fishmonger's house known as Kleiner Elephant ('Little Elephant'). Inside it's all bentwood chairs and photos of old Erfurt, while the terrace overlooking the Gera is an enchanting spot in fine weather.

★ Ginkgo
JAPANESE **€€**

(☑0361-601 5415; www.ginkgo-menu.de; Pergamentergasse 6; mains €20; ⊘5-11pm Tue, 11am-2pm & 5-11pm Wed-Sat, 1-10pm Sun) Behind an unassuming storefront down a side street off Domplatz, you'll find this purveyor of authentic Japanese sushi, run by the engaging Mr and Mrs Saburi. Their story is a fascinating one: be sure to enquire if you have the chance. You won't find real-deal sushi and sashimi like this anywhere else in Thuringia – prepared to order, and priced accordingly.

★ Zum Wenigemarkt 13
GERMAN **€€**

(☑0361-642 2379; www.wenigemarkt-13.de; Wenigemarkt 13; mains €13-18; ⊘11.30am-11pm) This upbeat restaurant in a delightful spot (an 18th-century house on the small marketplace at the eastern end of the Krämerbrücke) serves traditional and updated takes on Thuringian cuisine, starring regionally hunted and gathered ingredients where possible. Tender neck fillets of pork with sauerkraut and Thuringian dumplings and roasted char with potato-coconut purée are both menu stars. The three-course menu (€28) is great value.

Schnitzler
GERMAN **€€**

(☑0361-644 7557; www.schnitzler-restaurant.de; Domplatz 32; mains €12-15; ⊘11am-11pm; 🅿) It might be difficult for any self-proclaimed schnitzel lover to pass by a restaurant that pays such unabashed homage to the crumbed cutlet. There's an enormous variety to choose from (some using seasonal specialities such as wild garlic, mushrooms and asparagus), the prices are reasonable, and service comes with a smile.

La Gondola
ITALIAN **€€**

(☑0361-660 3920; Kürschnergasse 1/2; pizza €8-10, mains €18-22; ⊘11am-11pm) What's so great about this ostensibly run-of-the-mill Italian joint where nary a word of English is spoken and the meals are tasty and reasonably priced, but nothing out of the ordinary? Well, you won't find a lovelier spot in Erfurt than La Gondola's terrace – overlooking a little tributary of the Gera, as if in Venice.

🍷 Drinking & Nightlife

Erfurt's former university quarter to the north and east of Fischmarkt is a hub of nightspots, pubs and bars. Much of the action can be found along Michaelisstrasse and Futterstrasse.

Weinatelier Rue   WINE BAR
(📞 0361-4303 9105; www.weinatelier-rue.de; Kleine Arche 1; ⊙7pm-3am Tue-Sat, to 10.30pm Sun) This classy, art-bedizened wine shop and bar offers a fantastic introduction to local drops, including some hard-to-get bottles from the nearby Saale-Unstrut region. As many as 50 wines by the glass (and from around the world) are chalked up on the blackboard behind the sturdy wooden bar, and there are enough secluded alcoves and eating options to sustain the happy conversations.

Engelsburg   CLUB
(📞 0361-3025 9910; http://engelsburg.club; Allerheiligenstrasse 20/21; ⊙noon-2am) Good times are pretty much guaranteed at this student-focused 'Kulturzentrum' (cultural centre), whether you hunker down for beer and a chat in the Steinhaus pub (also does food), dance to local DJs and touring Berlin bands in the medieval cellar labyrinth, or go highbrow at the upstairs Café DuckDich, which programs theatre, film nights and poetry readings.

Hemingway   BAR
(📞 0361-551 9944; www.hemingway-erfurt.de; Michaelisstrasse 45; ⊙6pm-1am Sun-Mon, to 2am Fri & Sat) Everything the macho scribe loved is here in abundance, from dead animals to cigar humidors with personal drawers and a ridiculous variety of rum and daiquiris. Try the Hemingway Special, with Anejo rum, Bols and citrus.

Presseklub   CLUB
(📞 0361-789 4565; www.presseklub.net; Dalbergsweg 1; ⊙7pm-1am Wed, 9pm-4am Fri, 8pm-4.30am Sat) A former gathering spot for media types, this club is now a glittery cocktail lounge and dance venue. Nights range from 'Salsavanza' (celebrating the music of the Latin Caribbean) to more regulation '70s, '80s and electro-pop parties. Things usually kick off around 9pm, and there's sometimes a €5 cover charge.

☆ Entertainment

Consult the free zines *Dates, Takt* (www.takt-magazin.de) and *Blitz* (www.blitzworld.de) for event listings. Organ concerts are held year-round in the Predigerkirche and Michaeliskirche (Wednesday at noon), and in the Dom (Saturday).

Theater Waidspeicher   THEATRE
(📞 0361-598 2924; www.waidspeicher.de; Domplatz 18; adult/concession €13/10; ⊙box office 10am-2pm & 3-5.30pm Tue-Fri, to 1pm Sat; 🖐) Not only children will be enchanted by the adorable marionettes and puppets that perform at this cute theatre in a historic woad storehouse (reached via Mettengasse). Seven puppeteer-actors bring classics such as *King Lear* to life, alongside pieces developed especially for the theatre.

DasDie Brettl   PERFORMING ARTS
(📞 0361-551 166; www.dasdielive.de; Lange Brücke 29; ⊙box office 10am-6pm Mon-Fri, to 1pm Sat Sep-May; 11am-6pm Mon-Fri Jul & Aug) Drag shows, musicals and even dinner and theatre nights take centre stage in this cultural centre, which seats, feeds and waters up to 500 at its cabaret-style tables. Tickets are usually in the €20 to €40 range and there are smaller stages for music, comedy and other performances.

ℹ Information

Erfurt Tourist Office (📞 0361-664 00; www.erfurt-tourismus.de; Benediktsplatz 1; ⊙10am-6pm Mon-Sat, to 3pm Sun) Next to the central Fischmarkt. Sells the ErfurtCard, hires multimedia guides to the city (with/without ErfurtCard per day €10/6.50), which take you on a walking tour of 37 historic sites, and organises group tours in English (€105 for up to 35 people).

Thuringia Tourist Office (📞 0361-374 20; www.thuringia-tourism.com; Willy-Brandt-Platz 1; ⊙9am-7pm Mon-Fri, 10am-4pm Sat & Sun; 🖐) Opposite the Hauptbahnhof, this office covers the entire state as well as Erfurt.

ℹ Getting There & Away

AIR

The tiny **Erfurt-Weimar Flughafen** (📞 0361-656 2200; www.flughafen-erfurt-weimar.de; Binderlebener Landstrasse 100), about 6km west of the city centre, handles limited scheduled flights to Greece, Turkey, Spain, Bulgaria and Egypt.

CAR

Erfurt is just north of the A4 and is crossed by the B4 (Hamburg to Bamberg) and the B7 (Kassel to Jena). The A71 autobahn runs south to Schweinfurt via Ilmenau, and Oberhof.

TRAIN

Direct IC/ICE trains connect Erfurt with Berlin (from €40, two hours), Dresden (from €25, two hours) and Frankfurt (from €30, 2½ hours). Direct regional trains also run regularly to Mühlhausen (€14, 50 minutes), Weimar (€5.80, 15 minutes) and Eisenach (€14, 45 minutes).

ⓘ Getting Around

BICYCLE

Erfurt is an ideal city for two-wheeled exploration.

Radhaus Am Dom (☑ 0361-602 0640; www.radhaus-erfurt.de; Andreasstrasse 28; bikes per 24hr from €12; ⊙10am-6pm Mon-Fri, to 2pm Sat) Bike hire right among old Erfurt's attractions.

Radstation (☑ 0361-644 1506; www.radstation-erfurt.de; Bahnhofstrasse 22; bike/e-bike per 24hr €15/25; ⊙ 9am-6pm Mon-Fri, plus 9am-1pm Sat Jul & Aug) Bike hire at Erfurt's Hauptbahnhof. Per day prices drop sharply for longer rentals.

BUS & TRAM

Tram 4 directly links the airport with Anger in the city centre (€1.90, 25 minutes). Trams 3, 4 and 6 run from Hauptbahnhof via Anger and Fischmarkt to Domplatz. Tickets for trams and buses in the central (yellow) zone cost €2, or €5.10 for a day pass.

TAXI

Call ☑ 0361-5111 or ☑ 0361-666 666, or check www.bettertaxi.de.

Weimar

☑ 03643 / POP 64,131

The historical epicentre of Germany's 18th-century Enlightenment, Weimar is an essential stop for anyone with a passion for the country's history and culture. A pantheon of intellectual and creative giants lived and worked here: Goethe, Schiller, Bach, Cranach, Liszt, Nietzsche, Gropius, Herder, Feininger, Kandinsky – and the list goes on. You'll see them memorialised on the streets, in museums and in reverently preserved houses across town. In summer, Weimar's many parks and gardens lend themselves to quiet contemplation of all this intellectual and cultural gravity (or allow you to take a break from it).

Weimar is also the place where, post-WWI, the constitution of the German Reich, known by historians as the Weimar Republic (1919–33), was drafted, though there are strangely few reminders of this historical moment. Nearby, the unadorned, unaltered remains of the Buchenwald concentration camp provide sobering testament to the crimes of the subsequent Nazi regime.

◉ Sights

It's a 20-minute walk south of Weimar station to Goetheplatz, from where the historic centre unfolds its delights. Most of Weimar's attractions are easily covered on foot, although the moving Buchenwald Memorial requires a bus or car to reach.

★**Gedenkstätte Buchenwald** MEMORIAL
(☑ 03463-4300; www.buchenwald.de; Buchenwald; ⊙9am-6pm Apr-Oct, to 4pm Nov-Mar; Ⓟ) Between 1937 and 1945, hidden from Weimarers and surrounding villagers, 250,000 men, women and children were incarcerated here, some 56,500 of whom were murdered. Buchenwald ('Beech Forest') has been preserved almost untouched as a memorial, with visitors encouraged to wander quietly and freely around the numerous structures, including the crematorium. Tours, pamphlets and books in English are available, as are excellent multi-language audio guides (€3, or €5 with images). Last admission is 30 minutes before closing.

★**Goethe-Nationalmuseum** MUSEUM
(☑ 03643-545 400; www.klassik-stiftung.de; Frauenplan 1; adult/concession €12.50/9; ⊙9.30am-6pm Tue-Sun Apr-Oct, to 4pm Nov-Mar) This is the world's leading museum on Johann Wolfgang von Goethe, Germany's literary colossus. It incorporates his home of 50 years, gifted by Duke Carl August to keep him in Weimar, and left largely as it was upon his death in 1832. This is where Goethe worked, studied, researched, and penned *Faust* and other immortal works. In a modern annexe, documents and objects shed light on the man and his achievements in literature, art, science and politics.

★**Herzogin Anna Amalia Bibliothek** LIBRARY
(☑ 03643-545 400; www.klassik-stiftung.de; Platz der Demokratie 1; adult/concession €8/6.50; ⊙9.30am-2.30pm Tue-Sun) Assembled by Duchess Anna Amalia (1739–1807), the power (and purse) behind Weimar's classical florescence, this Unesco-listed library has been beautifully reconstructed after a fire in 2004 destroyed much of the building and its priceless contents. Some of the most precious tomes are housed in the magnificent Rokokosaal (Rococo Hall), and were once used by Goethe, Schiller, Christoph Wieland, Johann Herder and other Weimar hot shots, whose various busts and paintings still keep watch over the collection.

Schloss Tiefurt
PALACE

(☏ 03643-545 400; www.klassik-stiftung.de; Hauptstrasse 14; adult/concession €6.50/5; ⊙ 11am-5pm Tue-Sun Apr-Oct) Built in 1765 and developed by the younger brother of Duke Carl August, this Unesco-listed country house flowered under the ownership of Duchess Anna Amalia, who turned it into her 'temple of the muses'. The period rooms allow you to imagine intellectual salons attended by giants such as Goethe, Schiller and Herder and much of the art was collected by the Duchess on her Italian travels. The 23-hectare garden, skirted by the Ilm, is delightful. Take Bus 3 from Goetheplatz.

Thuriningian Museum of Pre- & Ancient History
MUSEUM

(☏ 03643-818 331; http://alt-thueringen.com; Humboldtstrasse 11; adult/concession €3.50/2.50; ⊙ 9am-6pm Tue, to 5pm Wed-Fri, 10am-5pm Sat & Sun; ⊕) Four-hundred-thousand years of Thurinigian history and prehistory are entertainingly charted in this multistorey museum, including remains of proto-humans, Palaeolithic and neolithic cultures, Roman imperial artefacts, art and material remains from the Kingdom of Thuringia and gold jewellery from the grave of the 'Lady of Ossmannstedt'.

Stadtmuseum Weimar
MUSEUM

(City Museum; ☏ 03643-826 00; http://stadtmuseum.weimar.de; Karl-Liebknecht-Strasse 5-9; adult/concession €3/1.50; ⊙ 10am-5pm Tue-Sun) Weimar's expertly curated city museum occupies the handsome late 18th-century Bertuchaus, named for the publisher and entrepreneur who built it. The story of the city from the time of Goethe, told through artefacts, documents, clothing and informative panels, starts on the 1st floor. A long-term exhibition on the period from the Weimar Republic (1919) to the reunification of Germany occupies the second.

Park an der Ilm
PARK

(www.klassik-stiftung.de) Following the Ilm, this Unesco-listed, 58-hectare park was landscaped between 1778 and 1828, and continues to provide a bucolic backdrop to old Weimar. Combining classical and romantic garden design, it's a lovely space to roam and explore three historic houses: the Goethe Gartenhaus (p247), where the writer lived from 1776 to 1782; the Römisches Haus (p247), the local duke's summer retreat, with period rooms and an exhibit on the park; and the Liszt-Haus, where the composer resided from 1869 to 1886.

Haus Hohe Pappeln
HISTORIC BUILDING

(☏ 03643-545 400; www.klassik-stiftung.de; Belvederer Allee 58; adult/concession €3.50/2.50; ⊙ 11am-5pm Tue-Sun Apr-Oct) This unusual house was designed by its first occupant, Belgian art-nouveau architect-designer Henry van de Velde. In 1902 van de Velde founded the arts and crafts seminar in Weimar, later developed into the Bauhaus by Walter Gropius. Built as an 'organism' in which interior, exterior and surroundings work harmoniously, it was home to his family from 1908 to 1917. Looking like an overturned ship, it features natural stone, stylised chimneys, loggias and oversized windows. Take bus 1 or 12 to Papiergraben.

Wittumspalais
MUSEUM

(☏ 03643-545 400; www.klassik-stiftung. de; Theaterplatz; adult/concession €6.50/5; ⊙ 10am-6pm Tue-Sun Apr-Oct, to 4pm Nov-Mar) This handsome neoclassical palace was home to the Duchess Anna Amalia from 1774, after the residential palace (today the Schlossmuseum) burned. Visitors proceed through a series of handsome rooms graced by period furniture and paintings and culminating in the fresco-ceilinged ballroom and the Green Salon, the living room of the Duchess.

Schillers Wohnhaus & Museum
HISTORIC BUILDING

(☏ 03643-545 400; www.klassik-stiftung.de; Schillerstrasse 12; adult/concession €8/6.50; ⊙ 9.30am-6pm Tue-Sun Apr-Oct, to 4pm Nov-Mar) The poet and dramatist Friedrich von Schiller (a close friend of Goethe) lived here from 1802 until his early death, in 1805. Study up on the man, his life and work in the modern Schiller Museum, before ducking through the low doors of his family home, which has been preserved in memoriam since 1847. Highlights include the study, with his deathbed and writing desk, Anton Graff's portrait of the writer, and poignant drawings made by the Schiller children.

Liszt-Haus
HISTORIC BUILDING

(Liszt House; ☏ 03643-545 400; www.klassikstiftung.de; Marienstrasse 17; adult/concession €4.50/3.50; ⊙ 10am-6pm Wed-Mon Apr-Oct, to 4pm Nov-Mar) At the western edge of Park an der Ilm, this is the house where Franz Liszt lived during his second stint in Weimar, from 1869 to his death in 1886. Opened to the public as a memorial shortly afterwards, its rooms, artworks, fittings and pianos are all much as they would have been when the

Weimar

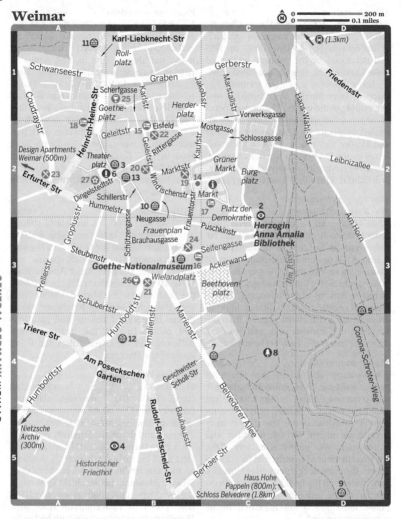

composer and pianist lived here. There's also an audiovisual exhibition to help visitors better appreciate his music.

Schloss Belvedere
PALACE

(☎03643-545 400; www.klassik-stiftung.de; Schloss und Park Weimar-Belvedere; adult/concession €6.50/5; ☺11am-5pm Tue-Sun Apr-Oct; P) Set amid Belvedere Park's lovely 43 hectares, this early-18th-century palace was once the hunting lodge of Duke Ernst August of Saxe-Weimar-Eisenach. Outside, the formal gardens and orangery have been carefully restored; inside there's an 18th-century craft museum displaying glass,

porcelain, faience and furniture in gorgeously decorated apartments. The easiest way to reach it is by bus 1 from Goetheplatz.

Nietzsche Archiv
HISTORIC BUILDING

(☎03643-545 400; www.klassik-stiftung.de; Humboldtstrasse 36; adult/concession €3.50/2.50; ☺11am-5pm Tue-Sun Apr-Oct) Belgian architect, designer and painter, Henry van de Velde added some art-nouveau touches to this house, where the philosopher Friedrich Nietzsche spent his final years in illness. No longer the actual site of the Nietzsche Archive, it's considered one of van de Velde's most beautiful interiors.

Weimar

Goethe Gartenhaus HISTORIC BUILDING
(☏03643-545 400; www.klassik-stiftung.de; Park an der Ilm; adult/concession €6.50/5; ☺10am-6pm Tue-Sun Apr-Oct, to 4pm Nov-Mar) From 1776 to 1782 Goethe lived in this house, a cottage given to him by Carl August in order to lure him to Weimar. It's spare in style externally, cosy within, and still has the three-part garden laid out by Goethe, including an orchard, ornamental plantings and vegetable beds. Audioguides are included with entry.

Fürstengruft TOMB
(Ducal Vault; ☏03643-545 400; www.klassik-stiftung.de; Am Poseckschen Garten; adult/concession €4.50/3.50; ☺10am-6pm Wed-Sun & Mon Apr-Oct, to 4pm Nov-Mar) Goethe and what was thought to be Schiller are interred at the Historischer Friedhof (Historical Cemetery) in this neoclassical mausoleum, along with Duke Carl August and other noble cadavers rescued from a 1774 fire in Weimar's castle. The mausoleum dates from 1828 and houses almost 50 sarcophagi of the House of Saxe-Weimar-Eisenach. Schiller's, however, is now empty, after tests showed that the remains originated from several different people (initially buried in a common grave, 'his' remains were chosen by guesswork).

Römisches Haus HISTORIC BUILDING
(www.klassik-stiftung.de; Park an der Ilm; adult/concession €4.50/3.50; ☺10am-6pm Wed-Mon Apr-Oct) Perched atop an artificial bluff in Park an der Ilm, the 'Roman House' was Weimar's first neoclassical dwelling, built under Goethe's supervision between 1791 and 1797. It was originally Duke Carl August's summer retreat; today it contains restored period rooms and an exhibit on the park's development.

☞ Tours

Belvedere Express BUS
(☏0178-887 7080; www.belvedere-express.de; Markt 2; adult/concession €19/17; ☺10.30am, 1pm, 3pm & 5pm Mon-Sat, 11am & 2pm Sun Apr-Oct, fewer tours Nov-Mar; 🚌) Aimed at the German market and making use of a handsome vintage bus, Weimar's classy city tour is a little pricey, but does provide a good low-down on all the sights, with a video commentary. Make sure you ask for the English headphones.

🛏 Sleeping

Weimar's accommodation ranges from bohemian hostels to cosy guesthouses and historic hotels, all of which are found in abundance. Visitors pay a supplement of €0.75 to €2 per person per night for the upkeep of cultural sites.

★**Labyrinth Hostel** HOSTEL €
(☏03643-811 822; www.weimar-hostel.com; Goetheplatz 6; dm/d €18/48, linen €2; @🖘) This super-friendly, professionally run hostel offers imaginative, artist-designed rooms. In one double the bed perches on stacks of books, while the 'purple room' features a wooden platform bed. There are en suites and shared bathrooms, plus a communal kitchen and lovely rooftop terrace. Breakfast costs €4, and

the hostel will buy ingredients for guests to cook shared meals from their home countries.

One dorm is reserved exclusively for female guests (the unfortunately-named and quite pink 'princess room').

★**Design**

Apartments Weimar APARTMENT €€

(☏017 2356 2210; www.hier-war-goethe-nie.de; Fuldaer Strasse 85; 1-/2-/3-bedroom apt from €60/95/95; ☎) Get in quick to snap up one of these enormous, self-contained, fully renovated heritage apartments, run by charming and generous hosts. The three apartments (with one, two or three bedrooms) are designed by Bauhaus University graduates: if you like their choice in fittings, they're available from the online shop. The ideal base from which to explore the delights of Weimar.

★**Casa dei Colori** PENSION €€

(☏03643-489 640; www.casa-colori.de; Eisfeld 1a; d incl breakfast from €100; ℗☎) Possibly Weimar's most charming boutique *Pension,* the 'House of Colours' convincingly imports Mediterranean style to central Europe. Run by an Italophile and decorated with framed testaments from delighted former guests, it offers 10 good-sized rooms dressed in bold colours and kitted out with small desks, comfy armchairs and stylish bathrooms.

Familienhotel HOTEL €€

(☏03643-457 9888; http://familienhotel-weimar. de; Seifengasse 8; apt from €95; ☎) This timber-fronted, multistoried hotel in Weimar's historical centre has won awards for its ecological principles and family-friendly attitude (kids are welcome, and given space to play). There are 11 apartments, and the equally agreeable Gretchen's Cafe is downstairs. Parking nearby is €6 per night.

Hotel Elephant LUXURY HOTEL €€

(☏03643-8020; www.luxurycollection.com/ elephant; Markt 19; s/d from €115/130, ste €220-600; ℗✳@☎) From the elegant art-deco lobby of this charmer, it's luxury all the way from here to the top. For over 300 years, this classic hotel has wooed statesmen, artists, scholars and the merely rich with first-class service and amenities. Prices vary by demand and day; check the website. The Elephant is being extensively renovated ahead of an expected reopening in autumn 2018.

✖ **Eating**

Weimar has some of the best eating in Thuringia: aside from the inevitable *Rostbratwurst* carts and *Bierstubes* selling traditional fare, there are some seriously upmarket options, and decent representations of Italian, French and Asian cuisine.

36 Pho Co VIETNAMESE €

(☏03643-468 4899; www.pho-co-weimar.de; Kaufstrasse 5; mains €8-10; ⊙10am-8pm Mon-Thu, 11am-9pm Fri & Sat) When you just can't face another *Thüringer Kloss* (potato dump-

---

GOETHE: THE LITERARY LION

Johann Wolfgang von Goethe (1749–1832) is the preeminent figure of German literature and philosophy. He lived to be 82, spending those decades in prolific production of novels, essays, treatises, scientific articles, travelogues, plays and poetry. A consummate politician, Goethe was also a classic 'Renaissance man', capable in many disciplines: during his life he served as town planner, architect, social reformer and scientist.

Born in Frankfurt am Main and trained as a lawyer, Goethe is most closely associated with this city, where he lived from 1775 until his death. He overcame the disadvantages of a wealthy background and a happy childhood to become the driving force of the 1770s *Sturm und Drang* (Storm and Stress) literary movement. Though he worked and experimented in various styles throughout his life, his work with Friedrich Schiller fostered the theatrical style known as Weimar classicism. Goethe himself once described his work as 'fragments of a great confession'.

Faust, his defining play in two parts, is a lyrical but highly charged retelling of the classic legend of a man selling his soul for knowledge. It's still regularly performed throughout Germany today. The beloved **Goethe-Schiller Denkmal** (Goethe-Schiller Monument; Theaterplatz), a statue of the two Weimar literary colossi rising directly in front of Weimar's **Deutsches Nationaltheater** (German National Theatre; ☏box office 0643-755 334; www.nationaltheater-weimar.de; Theaterplatz 2; adult/concession tickets from €14/9; ⊙box office 10am-6pm Mon-Sat, to 1pm Sun), where you may see his drama in production, still pulls a crowd.

ling), this slick two-floored modern Vietnamese feels like a godsend. Get your hit of fresh herbs with grilled pork and shredded veggies on rice noodles, or go for one of their boundary-busting 'bao burgers' – a mash-up between a burger and a Vietnamese baguette.

San
KOREAN €
(☑03643-258 942; http://sanrestaurant.de; Eisfeld 4; mains €8-9; ☉noon-4pm & 5-10pm Tue-Sun) If you find yourself inconveniently craving *kimchi* in Thuringia, this cosy little Korean has you covered. The *bibimbap* comes in hot stoneware, with sesame-scented rice, shiitake mushrooms, various veggies, beef (optional) and a fried egg. Slather it in *gochujang* (chilli paste), dip in to the accompanying pickles and *kimchi,* and warm your Seoul.

Gasthof Luise
GERMAN €
(☑03643-905 819; www.gasthof-luise-weimar.de; Wielandplatz 3, cnr Steubenstraße & Humboldtstraße; mains €8-10; ☉5pm-midnight) There's nothing fancy about this traditional Thuringian diner, which exudes a dark woodsy atmosphere. Offering seven beers on tap, it's cosy, comfortable and appreciated equally by local students and workers. Hearty eats include fries (great for soaking up the beer), bratwurst and local speciality *Thüringer Rostbrätel* (chargrilled marinated pork neck).

Crêperie du Palais
CRÊPES €
(☑03643-401 581; www.creperie-weimar.de; Am Palais 1; mains €7-8; ☉11.30am-11pm; ☑) Cosily tucked away among Weimar's old town, this bustling little cafe does a good line in crêpes, Breton galettes and *Flammkuchen* (Alsatian pizza). Sweet or savoury, there's plenty for all tastes, plus soups and salads for those seeking something vegetarian or just lighter fare.

★Gretchen's Cafe & Restaurant
CAFE €€
(☑03643-457 9877; http://gretchens-weimar.de; Seifengasse 8; mains €19-20; ☉9am-11pm; ☑) ☑ Located on the ground floor of the Familienhotel, and thus family-friendly, this passionately locavore cafe offers great alternatives to the Thuringian standards available across Weimar. For those intent only on snacking and chatting, it serves great cakes, tea and coffee, but the meals (including great value €7.50 midday specials such as salmon en papillote, with abundant salad) are wholesome and delightful.

If the weather's fine, take your tea on the wonderful rooftop terrace.

Tara Indian Dhaba
VEGETARIAN €€
(☑03643-900 0744; www.tara-weimar.de; Erfurter Strasse 4; mains €12-16; ☉11.30am-2.30pm & 5.30-10.30pm; ☑) Vegetarians rejoice! In the heart of meat-loving Thuringia, vegetarians (and even vegans) can choose from a decent and delicious selection at this friendly Indian *dhaba* (low-key restaurant). With dark timber tables and restrained decor, Tara offers dishes such as paneer in chilli-tomato sauce and bindi masala (okra in mixed spices) alongside fish, chicken and lamb curries.

Zum Weissen Schwan
GERMAN €€
(☑03643-908 751; www.hotelelephantweimar.com; Frauentorstrasse 23; mains €14-18; ☉noon-10pm Tue-Sat) At the White Swan, a venerable inn dating to the 16th century and numbering Cranach and Goethe among its erstwhile clientele, you can fill your boots with uncomplicated (and satisfying) Thuringian dishes in atmospherically vintage surrounds. Try the fried dumplings with mushrooms, or the schnitzel with cucumber salad and dill. The kitchen stops taking orders at 9pm.

🍷 Drinking & Nightlife

The presence of the Bauhaus University and constant stream of cultural sightseers means there are plenty of drinking options in Weimar – from tourist-focused terraced cafes setting out tables on the cobbles to subterranean student bars.

★Kasseturm
CLUB
(☑03643-851 670; www.kasseturm.de; Goetheplatz 10; ☉6pm-1am Tue-Sun) The circular Kasseturm took on a new identity in 1962, when students of the Bauhaus University converted this stout survivor of Weimar's 16th-century defences into a cultural venue. To this day it hosts an assortment of live acts, parties, jazz sessions, techno nights, and whatever else gets people off the couch. There are three floors of action, for young and old.

Weinbar Weimar
WINE BAR
(☑03643-469 9533; www.weinbar-weimar.de; Humboldtstrasse 2; ☉6pm-midnight Tue-Sat) Stylish and welcoming, with a veritable cornucopia of Thuringian, German and international wines to keep adventurous oenophiles occupied, this is a lovely little spot for sitting back and chatting over a glass, especially when the weather makes the vine-clad outdoor terrace feasible. Small plates of cured meats, cheese and other comestibles fortify extended adventures into the *Karte.*

ⓘ Information

Weimar Tourist Office (☑ 03643-7450; www.
weimar.de; Markt 10; ⊙ 9.30am-6pm Mon-Sat,
to 2pm Sun Apr-Oct, 9.30am-5pm Mon-Fri, to
2pm Sat & Sun Nov-Mar) Pick up a great-value
WeimarCard (€29.90 for two days) for free
admission to most museums, free iGuides, free
travel on city buses and discounted tours. The
office itself is very well resourced.

ⓘ Getting There & Away

Weimar is situated on the A4 autobahn, which
connects Eisenach and Erfurt in the west with
Dresden in the east. There's little parking in the
historical centre, but plenty of options immediately outside it.

Frequent regional trains go from Weimar
Hauptbahnhof, located 1km north of Goetheplatz, to Erfurt (€5.80, 15 minutes), Jena
(€5.80, 15 minutes), Gotha (€10, 40 minutes)
and Eisenach (€16, one hour). From Erfurt, direct ICE trains take you to Frankfurt (from €30,
2¼ hours), Munich (from €30, 2½ hours), Leipzig
(from €20, 45 minutes), Dresden (from €25, two
hours) and Berlin (from €34, two hours).

ⓘ Getting Around

BICYCLE

Grüne Liga (☑ 03643-492 796; www.gruene
liga-thueringen.de; Goetheplatz 9b; city bikes
per 24hr from €8; ⊙ 9am-3pm Mon-Fri, to noon
Sat) rents bikes to explore this cycle-friendly
town. Call ahead for rentals from November to
March.

BUS

Buses 1, 4, 5 and 6 run straight from Goetheplatz to Hauptbahnhof. A single ride/day pass
costs €2/5.10.

CAR

Driving in the Altstadt is severely restricted; it's
best to park outside the centre and walk around
this compact town. There's a free car park at
Hermann-Brill-Platz, about a 10-minute walk
northwest from the Weimar Altstadt, and paid parking
under the Weimar Atrium, about as far directly
north of the centre.

TAXI

Call ☑ 03643-903 600 or try www.bettertaxi.de.

Gotha

☑ 03621 / POP 45,172

With a pedigree stretching back to Charlemagne, and once famed as Thuringia's
wealthiest and most beautiful city, Gotha
has seen better days. The historical heart
of this former capital of the Saxe-Coburg-
Gotha Duchy retains much to fascinate, but

its outskirts struggle to cast off a grim GDR
heritage, and consequently its treasures remain under-appreciated.

Dominated by the grand Schloss Friedenstein, it is well worth a visit, if you're in the
area. Friedenstein, an almost-overwhelmingly
grand early-baroque palace, was built by Duke
Ernst I (1601–75), the founder of the House of
Saxe-Coburg-Gotha, whose descendants reinvented themselves as the House of Windsor
after WWI and today occupy the British royal
throne.

⊙ Sights & Activities

★ **Schloss Friedenstein**   PALACE
(☑ 03621-823 40; www.stiftungfriedenstein.
de; adult/concession €10/4, audioguide €2.50;
⊙ 10am-5pm Tue-Sun Apr-Oct, to 4pm Nov-Mar;
🅿 ♿) This horseshoe-shaped palace, surviving in exemplary condition as the largest
early baroque palace in Germany, is a lavish,
creaky-floored delight. Much of it comprises
the *Schlossmuseum* (Palace Museum), a glorious procession of 38 baroque, rococo and
neoclassical apartments, preserved much
as they were in the heyday of the Dukes of
Saxe-Gotha. Highlights include the exu-
berantly-stuccoed Festsaal (Ballroom), the
neoclassical wing, the Kunstkammer (a cu-
rio cabinet jammed with exotica) and the
Schlosskirche (Palace Church) in the northeast wing.

Herzogliches Museum   MUSEUM
(Ducal Museum; ☑ 03621-823 40; www.stiftung
friedenstein.de; Schlossplatz 1; adult/concession
€5/2.50; audioguide €2.50; ⊙ 10am-5pm Apr-
Oct, to 4pm Nov-Mar; 🅿) The handsome neo-
Renaissance building to the south of the
Schloss Friedenstein now houses many of
the artistic and historical treasures amassed
by the Dukes of Saxe-Gotha over the centuries. You'll find scant competition for a
good view of priceless works by Old Masters
including Rubens, Van Goyen and Cranach
the Elder, while the anonymously painted
Gothaer Liebespaar ('Gotha lovers', 1480)
is a luminous treasure that shouldn't be
missed. The outstanding sculpture collection includes works by Houdon and de Vries.

Rathaus   HISTORIC BUILDING
(Hauptmarkt; tower €1; ⊙ 11am-6pm Apr-Oct, to
4pm Nov-Mar) Hauptmarkt is dominated by
the picturesque Rathaus, with its colourful
Renaissance facade and 35m-tall tower. It
started out as a storage house in 1567, later
served as ducal pad of Ernst I while Schloss

Friedenstein was under construction, and only became a town hall in 1665. The 14th-century *Wasserkunst* (cascading fountain) originally supplied the city with water, but is now purely decorative.

Thüringerwaldbahn   TRAM
(www.waldbahn-gotha.de; per zone €1.50, day ticket €9.10) Gotha's city tram 4 curves around the ring road, crawls through some unlovely suburbs and then just keeps on going – like a local version of the Hogwarts Express – straight into the fairy-tale world of the Thuringian Forest, winding for about 45 minutes to Friedrichroda (three zones), a town of some 7400 people located 20km south of Gotha, and then on to Tabarz (four zones).

The tram departs Gotha every 30 to 60 minutes and takes one hour; take the tram in reverse to return to Gotha.

🎎 Festivals & Events

Ekhof Festival   PERFORMING ARTS
(☑ 03621-823 40; www.ekhof-festival.de; Schloss Friedenstein; tickets from €15; ☉ Jul & Aug) This popular festival re-animates the private theatre built for the Dukes of Saxe-Gotha in their monumental baroque Schloss Friedenstein. For two months in summer the public gets the chance to test its acoustics during classical recitals, and to see the original stage machinery (perhaps the oldest of its type surviving in working order) come to life during theatrical productions.

🛏 Sleeping & Eating

Aside from a few pensions, most of Gotha's hotels are found just outside the Altstadt. The streets around Hauptmarkt and Marktstrasse have the highest concentration of *Bierstubes* and restaurants – mainly German, with a few Italian and Asian options too.

❶ Information

Gotha Tourist Office (☑ 03621-510 450; www.kultourstadt.de; Hauptmarkt 33; ☉10am-6pm Mon-Fri, to 3pm Sat Oct-Apr, plus 10am-2pm Sun May-Sep) Friendly staff are happy to help with inquiries on Gotha's attractions, accommodation and transport. The office is prominently located in the Hauptmarkt.

❶ Getting There & Away

Gotha is just north of the A4 and is crossed by the B247 and B7.

Direct trains connect Gotha to Eisenach (€7.10, 25 minutes), Erfurt (€9, 20 minutes),

Weimar (€10, 40 minutes) and Mühlhausen (€9.70, 22 minutes).

Kyffhäuser Mountains

Though not particularly mighty or tall, there's an undeniable mystique to the low and densely forested uplands of the Kyffhäuser range, site of a bloody battle in the Peasants' War of 1525 that left at least 6000 dead and resulted in the capture and execution of their leader, the radical reformer Thomas Müntzer. The Kyffhäuser are also the reputed resting place of the Emperor Barbarossa ('Redbeard'), a legendary figure in German national mythology.

◉ Sights

Kyffhäuser Denkmal   MONUMENT
(☑ 034651-2780; www.kyffhaeuser-denkmal.de; Steinthaleben; adult/concession €7.50/4; ☉9.30am-6pm Apr-Oct, 10am-5pm Nov-Mar, to 7pm Fri, Sat & Sun Jul & Aug; ℗) The Kyffhäuser mountains were once home to one of Germany's largest castles, the Reichsburg, built in the 12th century by Emperor Friedrich Barbarossa (who, according to legend, lies in eternal sleep in the belly of the mountain). In the 19th century, Emperor Wilhelm I was seen as Barbarossa's spiritual successor, and in 1896, this statue, showing the emperor on horseback beneath a 60m-high tower on which Barbarossa sits enthroned, was erected atop the Reichsburg ruins.

At the foot of the monument, dining and accommodation options open in season. To get there, follow the B85 north from Bad Frankenhausen for about 9km, then turn east at the sign and continue for another 2km.

Panorama Museum   MUSEUM
(☑ 034671-6190; www.panorama-museum.de; Am Schlachtberg 9, Bad Frankenhausen; adult/concession €7/3; ☉10am-6pm Tue-Sun Apr-Oct, to 5pm Nov-Mar; ℗) This museum of visual arts sits just above Bad Frankenhausen, on the site where thousands died during the 1525 Peasants' War. One literally unmissable piece, playfully named *Frühbürgerliche Revolution in Deutschland* (Early Civil Revolution in Germany), by Werner Tübke, traces epochal change in Germany from the late Middle Ages to modernity. Fourteen metres high and 123m long and encircling the interior of the museum, it's literally monumental in scope and detail, taking from 1976 to 1987 to plan and complete.

Barbarossahöhle   CAVE
(☑ 034671-5450; www.hoehle.de; Mühlen 6, Rottleben; adult/child €7.50/4; ⊘ 10am-5pm Apr-Oct, to 4pm Nov-Mar; 🅿 ♿; 🚇) Accidentally uncovered by copper-shale miners in 1865, this anhydrite cave is one of the largest of its type in Europe. Fifty-minute tours through the 13,000-sq-metre cavern are conducted hourly, taking in shimmering underground lakes, bizarre gypsum ceilings and stone slabs mythically revered as the table and chair of the Emperor Barbarossa, supposedly buried in these hills. Outside, children can let off steam in a 'geo-adventure landscape' while learning about the area's geology.

The caves are 7km west of Bad Frankenhausen, north of Rottleben. Bus 451 runs regularly between thre two towns.

🛏 Sleeping & Eating

Bad Frankenhausen has the widest choice of accommodation in the Kyffhäusers and is the best place to stop for a meal. Dining options at the Kyffhäuser Denkmal are only open in summer. Some hotels close over winter.

ℹ Information

Bad Frankenhausen Tourist Office
(☑ 034671-717 17; www.bad-frankenhausen.de; Anger 14, Bad Frankenhausen; ⊘ 9.30am-6pm Mon-Fri, to 2pm Sat & Sun Apr-Oct, 9am-5pm Mon-Fri, to noon Sat & Sun Nov-Mar) Bad Frankenhausen's tourist office, in the central square, is good for information on the whole Kyffhäuser Mountains area. Can help with maps, directions and general info about Bad Frankenhausen and surrounds.

ℹ Getting There & Around

Bad Frankenhausen is 60km north of Erfurt via the A71 and B85. As the town is no longer served by train, it's a hassle to get here without two or four wheels. If you're determined, get yourself to nearby Sonderhausen from where you can catch bus 530 to Bad Frankenhausen (€3.70, 30 minutes).

There is little public transport in this sparsely populated area, but bike trails and roads are well signposted. The main town is Bad Frankenhausen.

Mühlhausen

☑ 03601 / POP 35,300
You can't get much more *Mitteldeutsch* than Mühlhausen, a handsome medieval town that sits at the country's geographical heart. Encircled by nearly intact fortifications, its historic centre is a warren of cobbled alleyways linking proud churches

(some desanctified and now housing museums) and half-timbered houses. In the early 16th century, the town became a focal point of the Reformation and a launch pad for the Peasants' War of 1525, led by local preacher Thomas Müntzer. The decisive battle took place on the Schlachtberg in nearby Bad Frankenhausen, where the rebellion was quickly crushed. Müntzer was decapitated outside the Mühlhausen town gates.

The GDR regime hailed the reformer as a great hero and an early social revolutionary. Numerous sites remain around town that uphold his memory. With reunification, Mühlhausen became united Germany's most central town, located a mere 5km north of the country's precise geographical centre in Niederdorla.

◉ Sights & Activities

Town Fortification   TOWER
(Am Frauentor; adult/concession €3/2; ⊘ 10am-5pm mid-Apr–Oct; ♿) One of the best places to admire the beauty of Mühlhausen's Altstadt is from the 370m section of the town fortification accessible through Inneres Frauentor. The original 12th-century fortification ran for 2.8km around the town, of which a remarkable 2km remain today. Plan the remainder of your city tour from the viewing platform in the Rabenturm (Raven's Tower).

Marienkirche   CHURCH
(St Mary's Church; ☑ 03601-856 60; Bei der Marienkirche; adult/concession €4/3; ⊘ 10am-5pm Tue-Sun) Thuringia's second-largest church (after the Dom in Erfurt, also dedicated to Mary), the striking, five-naved, 14th-century Gothic Marienkirche was desanctified in 1975. It's now used as a memorial museum to Thomas Müntzer, who preached here to his rebel followers before the disastrous Schlachtberg battle of the 1524–25 Peasants' War.

Rathaus   HISTORIC BUILDING
(City Hall; ☑ 03601-4520; Ratsstrasse 19; ⊘ 9am-noon Mon, Tue, Thu & Fri, plus 1-6pm Tue & Thu) Dating in parts to the early 14th century, Mühlhausen's Rathaus is an architecturally intriguing hotchpotch of Gothic, Renaissance and baroque styles. Inside, pay special attention to the Great Hall, the Gothic paintings on the walls of the salon and the Councillors' Chamber.

★ **Baumkronenpfad**   WALKING
(Tree Top Trail; www.baumkronen-pfad.de; Thiemsburg 1, Schönstedt; adult/concession/family

€11/9/24; ⊘10am-7pm Apr-Oct, reduced hours Nov-Mar) The Unesco World Heritage Hainich National Park (www.nationalpark-hainich.de), 15km southwest of Mühlhausen, protects Germany's largest coherent deciduous forest. There's hiking and cycling, of course, but the park's key draw is this elevated trail, meandering through the treetops at a vertiginous 44m above the forest floor. Enjoy magnificent views over the park, and observe its flora and fauna from this unique perspective.

From April to October, the Wunderbare Wanderbus (line 27a) runs between Wartburg (Eisenach) and Bad Langensalza, which is accessible by train from Mühlhausen (15 minutes) and Erfurt (45 minutes). It stops at the Baumkronenpfad.

Sleeping & Eating

There are good-value pensions, hotels and apartments dotted around the old town. Visit the Tourist Office if you hit town without a booking.

There are some very pleasant *Bierstubes* and hotel-restaurants in Mühlhausen's historic heart, and some unexpected options a little further out.

An Der Stadtmauer HOTEL €
(☑03601-465 00; www.muehlhausen-hotel.de; Breitenstrasse 15; s/d from €40/60; P🖥) The tasteful fittings, comfort and old-town location make this 19-room hotel an excellent choice. Some rooms open onto a courtyard and there's a small bar and beer garden.

Brauhaus zum Löwen HOTEL €€
(☑03601-4710; www.brauhaus-zum-loewen.de; Felchtaer Strasse 2-4; s/d €65/75; P🖥) Conversation flows as freely as the beer at this classic brewpub, where you can get fed and fuelled among the copper vats before retiring to boldly pigmented, country-style rooms. Adjacent you'll find the Leo disco, a focal point for Mühlhausen nightlife.

Landhaus Frank Zum Nachbarn GERMAN €€
(☑03601-812 513; www.landhaus-frank.de; Eisenacher Landstrasse 34; mains €15-18; ⊘11.30am-10pm, snack menu only 2.30-5.30pm) This 'Country Restaurant' on the outskirts of town serves very good German and international dishes in a homey dining room with exposed stonework and yolk-yellow walls. Fish is a highlight, as in the fried halibut with mustard sauce. Take bus 151, 152 or 153 to the *Friedhof* (cemetery) if you haven't got your own wheels.

❶ Information

Mühlhausen Tourist Office (☑03601-404 770; www.muehlhausen.de; Ratsstrasse 20; ⊘9am-5pm Mon-Fri, 10am-4pm Sat & Sun; 🖥) Get cycle and walking maps and general advice at this friendly little office between Obermarkt and Untermarkt, near the Rathaus (town hall).

❶ Getting There & Away

Mühlhausen is at the crossroads of the B249 from Sondershausen and the B247 from Gotha. Regional trains link Mühlhausen with Erfurt (€14, 50 minutes), Kassel (€25, 1½ hours) and Gotha (€9.70, 22 minutes).

THURINGIAN FOREST & THE SAALE VALLEY

If most of the larger towns of Thuringia are about culture, the Thuringian Forest (Thüringer Wald in German) and the Saale Valley are about tradition, scenic landscapes, and winegrowing. These regions take in Eisenach, known for the Wartburg, the spectacular castle that has played such a central role in German history, and where Luther sought protection after being excommunicated, the Saale-Unstrut wineland, as well as a cluster of small, historic towns dotting the countryside. Hiking, especially along the Rennsteig, is excellent here. Follow it far enough south and you will end up on the border of Bavaria.

❶ Getting There & Away

Jena, the second-largest city in Thuringia, is the main transport hub. It's well served for local connections, but has limited connection to the InterCity Express (ICE) network. To take advantage of that, you may need to head to Erfurt (€10, 30 minutes).

The A4 runs east–west across the north of the region, with various lesser roads (the B85 to Saalfeld and the B19 east of Schmalkalden) taking you to destinations further south.

Eisenach

☑03691 / POP 42,588
Approaching Eisenach, a small town on the edge of the Thuringian Forest, it might be easy to underestimate its historical gravity. Most significantly, it's inextricably linked to two German cultural immortals: Johann Sebastian Bach and Martin Luther. Luther went to school here and later returned to protective custody in the Wartburg, now one of Germany's most famous castles and a

Unesco World Heritage Site. A century later, Bach, the grandest of all baroque musicians, was born in a wattle-and-daub home and attended the same school as Luther had. Eisenach also has a century-old automotive tradition – the first car rolled off the assembly line in 1896, to be followed later (in 1929) by the world's first BMW. And when it's time to shake off culture and civilisation, remember that the famous Rennsteig hiking trail is only a hop, skip and jump away.

◉ Sights

★ Wartburg
CASTLE

(☑03691-2500; www.wartburg-eisenach.de; Auf der Wartburg 1; tour adult/concession €9/5, museum & Luther study only €5/3; ☺tours 8.30am-5pm Apr-Oct, 9am-3.30pm Nov-Mar, English tour 1.30pm) When it comes to medieval castles and their importance in German history, Eisenach's Unesco-listed Wartburg dominates the landscape. This huge medieval castle, 40,000 tonnes of sandstone on a craggy hill, has featured in a millennium of German history, and is where Martin Luther, excommunicated and under papal ban, translated the New Testament, in the process codifying the written German language. Allow at least two hours: one for the guided tour, and the remainder for the museum, Luther's rooms and the views.

Bachhaus
MUSEUM

(☑03691-793 40; www.bachhaus.de; Frauenplan 21; adult/concession €9.50/5; ☺10am-6pm) Comprising two 15th-century houses knocked together in the early 17th century, this is Johann Sebastian Bach's actual birthplace, and an international site of pilgrimage for music lovers. Founded in 1907 and still one of Germany's best biographical museums, the Bachhaus traces his professional and private life through exhibits with bilingual panelling, culminating in the modern annexe, where you can hover in bubble chairs listening to his sublime compositions. Admission includes a 20-minute concert on baroque keyboards, played on the hour.

Lutherhaus
HISTORIC BUILDING

(☑03691-298 30; www.lutherhaus-eisenach.com; Lutherplatz 8; permanent & special collections adult/concession €8/6; ☺10am-5pm, closed Mon Nov-Mar) The religious reformer Martin Luther lived here as a schoolboy from 1498 to 1501, in one of Thuringia's oldest and most handsome half-timbered houses. Now including a modern annexe, the museum's permanent collection focuses on his life and translation of the Bible, an essential step in unifying and codifying the German language. Special exhibitions (on subjects such as Catholic views on Luther's heresy) are intriguing, although you can opt out for a lower entrance price (€6/4).

Automobile Welt Eisenach
MUSEUM

(☑03691-772 12; www.awe-stiftung.de; Friedrich-Naumann-Strasse 10; adult/concession €6/3.50; ☺10am-6pm Apr-Oct, 11am-5pm Nov-Mar, closed Mon) Housed in the 1936 Automobilwerk Eisenach (AWE) factory, this museum celebrates a history of auto-manufacture dating to 1896, when the first 'Wartburg' (based on the French Decauville) was produced. There are plenty of gems for rare-car enthusiasts, including an 1899 Wartburg Dixi, a 1936 BMW 328 sports model and other vintage vehicles and memorabilia, much from the GDR era.

Stadtschloss
PALACE

(City Palace; ☑03691-670 450; Markt 24; adult/concession €4/3; ☺10am-5pm Wed-Sun) Dominating the northern side of Markt is the baroque facade of this former ducal residence, now housing tourist and municipal offices and the Thuringian Museum. Within, a series of restored rooms display Thuringian porcelain, clothing, faience, wrought iron, graphic art and other artefacts. While years of careful renovation were, at the time of research, nearly complete, the Rococo Hall and parts of the north wing remain inaccessible.

Georgenkirche
CHURCH

(Markt; ☺10am-noon & 2-4pm) Dominating Eisenach's central square, this is the baptismal church of St Elizabeth and Johann Sebastian Bach. It's also where Martin Luther sang as a boy soprano, and later preached his reforming doctrine while under papal ban. At 11am, Monday to Saturday from June to September, there are free 30-minute organ recitals; drop in to appreciate the same acoustics as the Bach family, various members of which played here for over 130 years.

Reuter-Wagner Museum
MUSEUM

(☑03691-743 293; Reuterweg 2; adult/concession €4/2; ☺2-5pm Wed-Sun) This museum, housed in the 1866 villa once owned by writer Fritz Reuter, hosts the most extensive collection on the composer Richard Wagner's life and times outside Bayreuth, with over 200,000 items. Located at the foot of the Wartburg, the inspiration for Wagner's *Tannhäuser*, it's like stepping back in time.

🛏 Sleeping

Hotel Villa Anna   BOUTIQUE HOTEL €€

(☎03691-239 50; www.hotel-villa-anna.de; Fritz-Koch-Strasse 12; s/d €80/120; 🅿🌀🛜) In a handsome three-storey townhouse built in 1907, this fantastic boutique hotel, at the foot of the Wartburg, has 15 classy, spacious rooms that design heads will love. The beds are ultra comfy, most rooms feature a decent desk and the breakfast buffet is more than generous. Take bus 3 or 10 to Prinzenteich.

Hotel Kaiserhof   HISTORIC HOTEL €€

(☎03691-888 90; www.kaiserhof-eisenach.de; Wartburgallee 2; s/d €75/105; 🅿🛜) A classic faded dame of a grand hotel, the Kaiserhof's former glories are evident in its plum position (where the Wartburgallee begins its climb from the old town to the castle) and bombastic architecture. Despite a founding date of 1897, standards are still being maintained, with super-welcoming staff, spotless rooms and a genuinely inviting front bar.

★Romantik Hotel auf der Wartburg   HOTEL €€€

(☎03691-7970; www.wartburghotel.de; Auf der Wartburg 2; s/d €170/250; 🅿🛜) Built in 1914 in a 'medieval' style, to complement the glowering Wartburg beneath which it sits, this luxury hotel allows you the fantasy of staying 'in' the historic fortress. 'Luther' rooms are cosy and have alcove beds, while 'Romantik' rooms amp up the space and luxury. The views are stunning and the Landgrafenstube, the on-site restaurant, is one of Eisenach's best.

🍴 Eating

Classic German and more-than-acceptable Italian are the best bets in old Eisenach.

Villa Antik Rinascita   ITALIAN €€

(☎03691-882 2382; http://villa-antik-rinascita.de; Wartburgallee 55; pasta €12-13, mains €20-23; ⊗5.30-10pm Tue-Sun, plus 11.30am-2.30pm Sat & Sun; 🅿) A little removed from the Old Town action, this free-standing villa on the road to the Wartburg shows some serious Italian flair in the kitchen. Vegetarians will need to stick to the pasta menu, but carnivores will enjoy the translucent beef carpaccio with rocket and parmesan, the *vitello tonnato* (veal in tuna mayonnaise) and the rack-of-lamb in balsamic vinegar.

La Grappa Pasquale Esposito   ITALIAN €€

(☎03691-733 860; www.lagrappa-eisenach.de; Frauenberg 8; pasta €9-10, mains €16-20; ⊗11.30am-2.30pm & 5.30-11.30pm Tue-Sun, no midday closure Apr-Sep; 🍴) The sunny terracotta terrace of this local favourite takes you straight back to the homeland. Heavier meat dishes such as pork fillet baked with cream, spinach and mozzarella are balanced by a broad choice of fish, soups and salads. Vegetarians have decent options on the antipasti, pizza and pasta menus.

Brunnenkeller   GERMAN €€

(☎03691-212 358; www.brunnenkeller-eisenach.de; Am Markt 10; mains €14-17; ⊗11am-11pm Apr-Oct, 5.30-10pm Mon-Sat, 11am-3pm Sun Nov-Mar) Linen-draped tables beneath an ancient vaulted brick ceiling (a cellar left over from the long-departed 12th-century castle) set the tone of this traditional chow house. Predictably, meals are honest-to-goodness German and regional classics such as *Thüringer Rostbrätel* (marinated pork neck) with rösti and salad. Tables spill out onto the Markt square in fine weather.

★Weinrestaurant Turmschänke   GERMAN €€€

(☎03691-213 533; www.turmschaenke-eisenach.de; Karlsplatz 28; mains €22-24, 3-/4-course menu €37/45; ⊗6-11pm Mon-Sat) Going strong since 1910 – when the hotelier of the Kaiserhof connected his premises to the 11th-century defensive tower next door – and persisting through the GDR years, this hushed hideaway scores a perfect 10 on the 'romance metre'. Walls of polished oak, beautiful table settings and immaculate service complement Ulrich Rösch's flavour-packed concoctions, which finely balance the trendy and the traditional.

ℹ Information

Eisenach Tourist Office (☎03691-792 30; www.eisenach.info; Markt 24; ⊗10am-6pm Mon-Fri, to 5pm Sat & Sun) On the ground floor of the Stadtschloss, the Eisenach tourist office has Rennsteig cycling and hiking brochures and maps, and sells the Thuringia Card and the Kombikarte.

ℹ Getting There & Away

Eisenach is on the A4 autobahn and is crossed by the B7, B19 and B84.

Buses to Kassel, Berlin, Prague, Cologne and other European destinations leave from the

RENNSTEIG RAMBLE

Germany's oldest and most popular long-distance trail, the 169km Rennsteig, is a back-woodsy hike along forested mountain ridges from Hörschel (near Eisenach) to Blankenstein on the Saale River. It's one place you can pack away the guidebook and just explore the villages you ramble by. If you press ahead as far as the Bavarian border region, the local dialect becomes incomprehensible even to many Germans.

The trail is marked by signposts reading 'R', and is best hiked in May/June and September/October. You should be moderately fit, with good shoes, a set of strong thighs and an indomitable spirit, to carry you for six or seven days. Day hikes offer a taste of the trail with lodging options aplenty in the villages below. The Rennsteig bike trail also begins in Hörschel and travels over asphalt, soft forest soil and gravel, mostly paralleling the hiking trail.

A time-honoured tradition for Rennsteig ramblers is to pick up a pebble from the Werra River at the beginning of your hike, carry it with you and throw it back into the Saale River upon completing the trail.

The Eisenach Tourist Office (p255) has hiking and cycling brochures and maps. From the office, bus 11 or regional bus 31 will drop you at the Hohe Sonne trail head, right on the Rennsteig hiking trail, although you could also hike the 6km there (or back) via the craggily romantic Drachenschlucht gorge.

Busbahnhof Eisenach (☑ 03 691 22 88 44; Wartburgallee).

Direct regional trains run frequently to Erfurt (€14, 45 minutes), Gotha (€7.10, 25 minutes) and Weimar (€15, one hour). There are also direct InterCity Express (ICE) trains to Erfurt (€20, 30 minutes), Gotha (€14,12 minutes) and Frankfurt (from €20, 1¾ hours).

ⓘ Getting Around

Zweirad Henning (☑ 03691-784 738; www.fahrrad-eisenach.de; Schmelzerstrasse 4-6; bikes per day €12; ☺9am-6pm Mon-Fri, to 1pm Sat) rents out bikes, but you may need to book two hours in advance.

Buses 1, 2, 7 and 12 run from the bus station opposite Hauptbahnhof to Markt; a single fare is €1.50.

Jena

☑ 03641 / POP 109,527

With almost one of every five residents a student, the second-largest city in Thuringia exudes a youthful, bohemian buzz, for all the lingering GDR aesthetics outside its historical centre. It's less touristy than nearby Weimar and Erfurt: you'll find lovely art nouveau neighbourhoods and challenging trails leading to glorious viewpoints outside the city centre.

Straddling the Saale River and flanked by limestone hills, Jena is a pleasant town blessed with a climate mild enough for grape vines. Although it's also an old university town (since 1558), and Goethe and Schiller were here, too, Jena has an entirely different feel to Weimar, some 20km to the west. The birthplace of precision optics – pioneered here by Carl Zeiss, Ernst Abbe and Otto Schott – it is Jena's pedigree as a city of science that justifies the moniker Lichtstadt ('City of Light'). Today several museums and the world's oldest public planetarium attest to this legacy.

◉ Sights

★**Dornburger Schlösser**　　　PALACE
(☑036497-222 91; www.dornburg-schloesser.de; Max-Krehan-Strasse 2, Dornburg; adult/concession combination ticket €4/3) About 15km north of Jena, you'll find this hillside trilogy of magnificently restored palaces in medieval, Renaissance and rococo styles, with stunning views and immaculate gardens. The Altes Schloss, the oldest, blends Romanesque, late-Gothic and baroque elements, but can only be viewed from the outside. You can enter both the 1539 Renaissance Palace (where Goethe sought solitude after the death of his patron, Duke Carl August) and the youngest, most beautiful Rococo Palace, used for temporary exhibitions, concerts and weddings.

It won't cost you a cent to stroll around the beautiful landscaped gardens and baroque park, enjoying wonderful views over vineyards to the Saale valley and admiring the palace exteriors. Trains travel frequently from Jena-Paradies to Dornburg (€2.80, 11 minutes), from where it's a steep 20- to 30-minute climb.

Zeiss Planetarium
PLANETARIUM

(☑03641-885 488; www.planetarium-jena.de; Am Planetarium 5; adult/concession €10/8.50; ☺box office 10.30am-1.30pm & 7-8pm Tue-Thu, 11am-noon & 7-8pm Fri, 2-8pm Sat, 1-6pm Sun) The world's oldest public planetarium (1926) has a state-of-the-art dome projection system, making it a heavenly setting for cosmic laser shows paying tribute to music legends such as Pink Floyd and Queen, or sending the kids deep into outer space. Show times and pricing varies by program; check the website for details.

Stadtmuseum & Kunstsammlung Jena
MUSEUM, GALLERY

(City Museum & Art Collection; ☑03641-498261; www.stadtmuseum-jena.de; Markt 7; adult/concession Stadtmuseum €4/3, Kunstsammlung €6/5; ☺10am-5pm Tue, Wed & Fri, 3-10pm Thu, 11am-6pm Sat & Sun) This handsome *fachwerk* town-house at the northern end of the market square dates in part to the 13th century. It now houses the Stadtmuseum (city museum) where you can learn how Jena evolved into a centre of philosophy and science and also the city's Kunstsammlung (art collection) with changing exhibitions on themes such as Marx's 200th birthday, augmenting a permanent collection of mostly 20th-century works.

Botanischer Garten
GARDENS

(☑03641-949 274; www.spezbot.uni-jena.de/botanischer-garten; Fürstengraben 26; adult/concession €4/2.50; ☺10am-7pm Apr-Oct, to 6pm Nov-Mar) Goethe himself planted the ginkgo tree in these wonderful botanic gardens, which have grown since their inception in 1794 to a collection of more than 12,000 plants from every climatic zone on earth. Naturally, some of those need the protection of a greenhouse, of which there are five.

Optisches Museum
MUSEUM

(Optical Museum; ☑03641-443165; www.optischesmuseum.de; Carl-Zeiss-Platz 12; adult/concession €5/4, combination ticket with Zeiss Planetarium €13.50/11; ☺10am-4.30pm Tue-Fri, 11am-5pm Sat) Carl Zeiss began building rudimentary microscopes in 1846 and, with Ernst Abbe's help, developed the first scientific microscope in 1857. Together with Otto Schott, the founder of Jenaer Glaswerke (glass works), they pioneered the production of optical precision instruments, which propelled Jena to prominence in the early 20th century. Founded in 1922, this museum now tells the connected stories of their lives and the evolution of optical technology through interactive exhibits featuring 3D holograms. Tours take in Zeiss's 1866 workshop.

Schillers Gartenhaus
HISTORIC BUILDING

(Schiller's Garden House; ☑03641-931 188; www.uni-jena.de; Schillergässchen 2; adult/concession €3.50/2; ☺11am-5pm Tue-Sun, closed Sun Nov-Mar) Goethe is credited with recruiting Schiller to Jena University in 1789. The poet, playwright and philosopher enjoyed Jena so much that he stayed for 10 years, longer than anywhere else, spending summers in what is now known as Schillers Gartenhaus. He wrote *Wallenstein* in the little wooden shack in the garden, while the oval stone table where he and Goethe liked to wax philosophical remains in place.

Stadtkirche St Michael
CHURCH

(Parish Church; www.stadtkirche-jena.de; Kirchplatz; ☺10am-5pm Tue-Sat, from 12.30pm Mon May-Oct) This late-Gothic church, one of the largest in Thuringia, is famous for having Martin Luther's original bronze gravestone, modelled on a portrait by Lucas Cranach the Elder (there's another in the Schloss-kirche of Wittenberg that is actually a 19th-century replica). Begun in 1380, St Michael's assumed something like its present form in 1506.

JenTower
TOWER

(☑03641-208 000; www.jentower.de; Leutragraben 1; viewing platforms €3.50; ☺viewing platforms 10am-11pm) Built in 1972, but deceptively modern in appearance, the 128m-tall cylindrical JenTower was intended to be a Zeiss research facility, but proved unsuitable. There's a shopping mall at ground level and two open-air observation decks at the top, offering sensational views from 125m above the city.

✯ Festivals & Events

Kulturarena Jena
MUSIC

(☑tickets 03641-498 060; www.kulturarena.com; ☺Jul & Aug) This eclectic international music festival – featuring everything from blues to rock, classical and jazz – gets the town rocking. Tickets can be bought online, over the phone, or from the Jena Tourist Office (p260).

🛏 Sleeping

There's quite a lot of variance in Jena's accommodation options, from sky-high boutique hotels to chain operations and old-school hostels.

Alpha One Hostel Jena
HOSTEL €

(☑ 03641-597 897; www.hostel-jena.de; Lassallestrasse 8; dm/s/d from €18/35/55; P @ ⛔) Jena's indie hostel is in a quiet street within staggering distance of the Wagnergasse pubs. The rooms, none bigger than a six-bed dorm, are splashed in bright colour, and those on the 3rd floor have great views (room 16 even has a balcony). Linen is €3, breakfast is €6 and dinner can be arranged, for groups, at €8.50 per person.

The closest bus stop is Ernst-Abbe-Platz (buses 16, 280, 424 and 425) and there's storage for bikes.

Hotel Rasenmühle
BOUTIQUE HOTEL €€

(☑ 03641-534 2130; www.hotel-rasenmuehle.de; Burgauer Weg 1a; s/d €60/95; P ⛔) While the rooms are smartly decorated and comfortable, the best thing about this little hotel is its leafy location in the midst of Paradies park. Most of the 11 rooms have views over the Saale River or parklands, there's free wi-fi and parking, and a communal kitchen is available to guests. At these prices, it's a winner.

Hotel VielHarmonie
HOTEL €€

(☑ 03641-796 2171; www.hotel-vielharmonie.de; Bachstrasse 14; s/d €75/100; P ⛔) Run by Brigitte and Thomas, two passionate natives of Jena, this stylish, culturally focused hotel spread over two buildings is one of the best the city has to offer. Among the 19 options are some cute attic rooms with small terraces and/or kitchenettes. Parking is €8 per night.

★ Scala Turm Hotel
BOUTIQUE HOTEL €€€

(☑ 03641-311 3888; www.scala-jena.de; Leutragraben 1, JenTower; s/d from €129/149; P ❀ ✳ ⛔) This circular hotel atop the iconic JenTower (at 120m, Germany's second-highest) boasts 17 oversized rooms and amazing views of the town and countryside. Super-stylish, slick, modern and minimalist, Scala Turm has all the right ingredients to make your night something special. The hotel's eponymous restaurant is equally impressive, so you won't have to wander far to dine.

✗ Eating

For a student town, there are perhaps not the cosmopolitan eating options you'd expect to find. The traditional German options, however, are more than fine.

Café Immergrün
CAFE €

(☑ 03641-447 313; www.cafe-immergruen.com; Jenergasse 6; mains €4-5; ⊙ 11am-1am Mon-Sat, from 10am Sun) Students of this university town make up much of the clientele and workforce of the 'Cafe Evergreen', a self-service bistro-pub long popular with the locals. With its plump, intimate sofas, leafy garden and (most of all) cheap baguettes, pasta and salads, it's not hard to see why. Board games and a play area also keep kids (and thus parents) happy.

Weekly specials, fresh cakes and live music complete a well-rounded picture.

Fuchsturm Berggaststätte
GERMAN €€

(☑ 03641-360 606; www.fuchsturmgaststaette. de; Turmgasse 26; mains €13-15; ⊙ 11.30am-9pm Tue-Fri, 11am-11pm Sat, 10am-8pm Sun; P ⛔) Beneath the ancient Fuchsturm, the solitary tower that is all that remains intact of the levelled Schloss Kirchberg, you'll find this atmospheric dining hall that has been serving hearty traditional fare to go with stunning views since 1868. Surprisingly, alongside the roast wild boar, Wiener schnitzel and goulash, there are a few thoughtful vegetarian options – salads and mains.

Stilbruch
INTERNATIONAL €€

(☑ 03641-827 171; www.stilbruch-jena.de; Wagnergasse 2; pasta €8-9, mains €14, steak €24-26; ⊙ 8.30am-1am Mon-Thu, 9am-3am Fri & Sat, to 2am Sun; ⛔) The competition is great on Wagnergasse, Jena's pub mile, but this multilevel contender is a worthy stop for drinks, with a menu that has something for everybody (even vegetarians). It's especially good for weekend brunch, although you might have to fight for a seat. For privacy, snag the table atop the spiral staircase; for people-watching, sit outside.

Schnitzelparadies
GERMAN €€

(☑ 03641-628 724; www.schnitzelparadies-jena. de; Grietgasse 2; schnitzel €13-16; ⊙ 11am-3pm & 5-11pm Wed-Fri, noon-11pm Sat & Sun) The name says it all: get ready for schnitzels galore. This popular downtown joint serves up more variations of the humble cutlet than you can begin to imagine, has an extensive beer menu for you to pair them with, and presents them to you with a smile. Fun and tasty.

★ Landgrafen Jena
MODERN EUROPEAN €€€

(☑ 03641-507 071; www.landgrafen.com; Landgrafenstieg 25; mains €18-21; ⊙ 3-11pm Tue-Thu, 11.30am-11pm Fri & Sat, 11.30am-8pm Sun; P) High in the hills, with stunning views over Jena, this smart multi-purpose restaurant serves genuinely interesting food such as

SCHMALKALDEN

Schmalkalden's old town groans and creaks under the sheer weight of its half-timbered houses and is crowned by a handsome hilltop castle, **Schloss Wilhelmsburg** (☑03683-403 186; www.museumwilhelmsburg.de; Schlossberg 9; adult/concession €6/4; ⊙10am-6pm Apr-Oct, to 4pm Tue-Sun Nov-Mar; ⓟ). About 40km south of Eisenach, the little town (pop. 19,149) played a big role during the Reformation. It was here in 1531 that the Protestant princes established the Schmalkaldic League to counter the central powers of Catholic emperor Charles V. Although they suffered a daunting military defeat in 1546, they managed to regroup and eventually got the emperor to sign the Peace of Augsburg in 1555, which allowed each of the German states to choose between Lutheranism and Catholicism.

The Altmarkt features a handsome Rathaus (1419), which once functioned as the meeting place of the Schmalkaldic League. The incongruous towers of the late-Gothic Stadtkirche St Georg (1437–1509) overlook the square.

The town is also the western terminus of a 16km easy-to-moderate leg of the much larger Lutherweg (www.lutherweg.de) hiking trail that winds across Thuringia, Hesse, Bavaria and Saxony.

Schmalkalden's well-resourced and cheerfully helpful **tourist office** (☑06383-609 7580; www.schmalkalden.com; Auer Gasse 6-8; ⊙10am-6pm Mon-Fri, to 3pm Sat & Sun Apr-Oct, 10am-5pm Mon-Fri, to 1pm Sat Nov-Mar; ⓢ) can advise on local hikes, and lodgings and even rents e-bikes.

Bahnhof Schmalkalden (☑03 69 35 08 60; www.sued-thueringen-bahn.de; Am Bahnhof 1) is served by the private Süd-Thüringen-Bahn (South-Thuringia Railway). Going to Erfurt (€20, two hours) requires a change in Zella-Mehlis; for Eisenach (€12, one hour), change in Wernshausen.

potato-wasabi soup with 'river-crab tails.' There's a summer garden with bratwursts, beers and a kids' playground, but the real appeal lies with the stylish terrace (for casual eats) or the dressy, upmarket dining room. Wines from the Saale-Unstrut region are featured.

🍷 Drinking & Nightlife

Jena has some nightlife gems – charismatic student-driven watering holes that welcome all-comers, provided they're friendly. The most obvious place to head out on the tiles is Wagnergasse, the pedestrianised 'pub mile.'

★ Rosenkeller　　　　　　CLUB
(☑03641-931 190; www.rosenkeller.org; Johannisstrasse 13; ⊙8pm-2am Fri-Sun) The network of historic wine cellars of this iconic club, resurrected by students in the 1960s, now echo to DJs, live acts, readings and other cultural events. it's kept vibrant by each new generation of Jena students, so you can expect reggae, no-wave, electro, drag and other themed nights, plus a genuinely welcoming vibe.

Gaststätte Grünowski　　　　PUB
(☑03641-446 620; www.gruenowski.de; Schillergässchen 5; ⊙noon-1am) Jena's students and bohos are naturally drawn to Grünowksi's uberchilled vibe and the soul-warming food that issues from its kitchen. Inside it's full of art, bentwood chairs and casual nooks and crannies to command; outside there's a rambling beer garden for the warmer months.

☆ Entertainment

Volksbad Jena　　　　LIVE PERFORMANCE
(☑03641-498 300; www.volksbad-jena.de; Knebelstrasse 10; ⊙10am-6pm) You can't swim in the 'People's Baths' (a heritage-listed public pool from the early-20th-century) any longer; instead you'll be showered with theatre, recitals and other cultural events, from the mainstream to the offbeat. It's opposite Jena-Paradies station. Check the website for event details.

Kassablanca Gleis 1　　　LIVE PERFORMANCE
(☑03641-282 60; www.kassablanca.de; Felsenkellerstrasse 13a) In a converted shed near Jena-West train station, this joint feeds the cultural cravings of the indie crowd with a potpourri of live concerts, dance parties, readings, experimental theatre, movies and even dance and DJ workshops. Cheap drinks fuel the fun. Prices and times depend on the event program: check the website.

ⓘ Information

Jena Tourist Office (☏ 03641-498 050; www.visit-jena.de; Markt 16; ⊙10am-7pm Mon-Fri, to 4pm Sat & Sun Apr-Dec, 10am-6pm Mon-Fri, to 3pm Sat Jan-Mar) Purchase the JenaCard (€11.90) here for 48 hours of discounted tours and admissions and free public transport. Guided tours of Jena leave from here (2pm Monday, Wednesday, Thursday and Saturday and 11pm Sunday between April and October; 2pm Monday, Wednesday and Saturday between November and March). Self-guided walking and cycling tours are also available.

ⓘ Getting There & Away

Jena is just north of the A4 from Dresden to Frankfurt, and west of the A9 from Berlin to Munich. The B7 links it with nearby Weimar, while the B88 goes south to Rudolstadt and Saalfeld.

Direct trains depart from Jena-West to Weimar (€5.80, 15 minutes) and Erfurt (€10, 30 minutes); change at either station for Eisenach, and at Erfurt for Berlin, Frankfurt or Munich. There's also a direct service to Saalfeld (€12, 40 minutes).

ⓘ Getting Around

BICYCLE

Flat (at least in the centre) and reasonably spread out, Jena's not a bad town to explore on two wheels. Try **Fahrrad Kirscht** (☏ 03641-441 539; www.fahrrad-kirscht.de; Löbdergraben 8; bike hire 24hr €15, extra day €10; ⊙ 9.30am-7pm Mon-Fri, to 4pm Sat) for quality rentals.

BUS

Bus 15 runs several times per hour from Jena-West to Holzmarkt, 150m south of Markt along Löbderstrasse. Single/daily bus or tram tickets cost €2/5.30.

TRAIN

Jena has two train stations. Long-distance trains arrive at Jena-Paradies, a 10-minute walk south of Markt. Regional trains from Erfurt or Weimar stop at the tiny Jena-West station, a 20-minute walk from Markt. To get to Markt from Jena-West, turn left onto Westbahnhofstrasse, follow it as it bends right and becomes Schillerstrasse, then turn right onto Kollegienstrasse. Alternatively, take bus 15.

TRAM

Jena has a tram network with five lines running by day, and three by night. A single trip within the central zone costs €2. All lines pass through the Paradies- and Bus-Bahnhof hub. Consult www.nahverkehr-jena.de for timetables and routes.

HARZ MOUNTAINS

What the Harz Mountains lack in alpine dramatics, they make up for in atmosphere and accessibility. Some of Germany's oldest, most endearing villages are tucked away in this broad region shared by three states: Lower Saxony, Saxony-Anhalt and Thuringia. Gorgeous Goslar's crumbling city walls, medieval cobbled streets and teeny-tiny miners' houses complement Quedlinburg's crooked, couldn't-be-cuter, half-timbered architecture. Both towns' welcoming vibes beckon you to linger. But the region's robust all-rounder is shutterbug's-delight Wernigerode, where you can visit a dazzling Disney-esque castle and catch a steam train to the top of the Brocken, the highest peak (1142m) in the Harz.

Come winter, a web of hiking and biking trails transforms into a serious network of cross-country ski routes come winter, though downhill powder-hounds generally go elsewhere. Whatever the season, keep an eye out for witches – especially on Walpurgisnacht (p264) when anything goes as the masses ascend the Brocken...as they've done for centuries.

ⓘ Information

The main information centre for the Harz Mountains is the Harzer Verkehrsverband (p268) in Goslar, but information on the Eastern Harz is best picked up in towns located there, particularly in Wernigerode. Tourism is everything to the Harz, so even in the smallest towns, you'll usually be able to find some kind of assistance.

ⓘ Getting There & Away

Deutsche Bahn (www.bahn.com) and FlixBus (www.meinfernbus.de) operate low-cost services between Berlin and Quedlinburg, Wernigerode and Goslar. Most services also stop at Magdeburg. Fares fluctuate; check the websites for details.

The area's main towns of Goslar, Wernigerode and Quedlinburg are serviced by frequent trains; visit the website of Deutsche Bahn (www.bahn.com) for details.

If you're driving, the area's main arteries are the east–west B6 and the north–south B4, which are accessed via the A7 (skirting the western edge of the Harz on its way south from Hanover) and the A2 (running north of the Harz between Hanover and Berlin).

ⓘ Getting Around

The Harz is one part of Germany where you'll rely on buses more than trains, and the various local

HARZ MOUNTAINS IN FOUR DAYS

This driving itinerary takes in the best of the Harz Mountains and assumes you're setting out from Hannover or cities to the west or south. If you're starting in Berlin, or cities east, follow the same route in reverse.

Arriving in Goslar (p264) mid-morning, wander the streets around the town's Markt-platz, perhaps visiting the Musikinstrumenten- und Puppenmuseum (p266) or the Zinnfiguren-Museum (p266) before lunch. Then head out to the World Heritage listed Rammelsberg Museum & Besucherbergwerk (p266), at the site of the only precious-metals mine to have operated for over 1000 years.

On day two, walk the wonderful treetop Baumwipfelpfad in Bad Harzburg, then soak in the healing waters of Sole Therme (p262) spa before taking a scenic drive over the mountains to Wernigerode via Torfhaus (p263) and Schierke (p272).

Waking in Wernigerode on the third day, decide whether you want to catch the Harzer Schmalspurbahnen (p273) to the top of the Brocken (p263), northern Germany's high-est peak, or step back in time at the magnificent Schloss Wernigerode (p272).

Your last day takes you through Thale (p271), where you can soak in more ther-mal waters, or ride a cable car to a peak steeped in legend, before arriving in magical Quedlinburg (p268) where you just might want to linger a little longer.

---

networks are fast and reliable. Narrow-gauge steam trains run to the Brocken and link major towns in the Eastern Harz.

Having your own wheels makes exploring this pretty area that much more enjoyable.

Bad Harzburg

☑ 05322 / POP 22,187

Nestled between low ridges just east of Go-slar, Bad Harzburg remains a popular spot for those who favour the healing properties of its thermal waters and the tranquility of its position outside the western boundary of the Harz National Park (☑ 03943-550 20; www.nationalpark-harz.de/en), whose many well-groomed trails offer excellent access to the picturesque vistas for which the Harz are famed.

Once a top holiday destination of the former GDR, parts of this quiet spa town straddling the main road into the moun-tains could use some TLC, but recent revital-isation of existing infrastructure, some new construction and tourist attractions, par-ticularly the uberpopular Baumwipfelpfad forest-canopy walk, continue to breathe new life into this fading former beauty.

Unless you're wanting to escape the sum-mer crowds drawn to the region's historical villages, most will elect to overnight in near-by Goslar, but be sure to pass through for a few daylight hours, if you're able to.

◎ Sights & Activities

Marked hiking trails lead into the Harz National Park from Berliner Platz. Popular trails include those to Sennhütte (1.3km), Molkenhaus (3km) and scenic Rabenklippe (7km), overlooking the Ecker Valley. Molk-enhaus and Rabenklippe have restaurants.

Grosser Burgberg RUINS
(⊙9am-5pm) It takes just over half an hour to walk from town, or a zippy three-minute ride on the Burgberg-Seilbahn, to reach the top of this humble peak (483m), which boasts the ruins of an 11th-century fortress built by Heinrich IV. Once at the top you can stroll around the fortress ruins or set out on longer hikes or mountain-bike rides.

★ **Baumwipfelpfad** WALKING
(☑ 05322-877 7920; www.baumwipfelpfad-harz.de; Nordhäuser Strasse 2d; adult/concession €8/7.50, incl one-way cable car €10/9.50; ⊙10am-4pm) 🌿 Comprising 18 platforms suspended above the ancient treetops of the Kalten Valley, the Harz's Baumwipfelpfad (treetop walkway) is sprinkled with scenic viewpoints and information stations, culminating (or orig-inating, depending on your approach) in a bubble-like observation dome.

Burgberg-Seilbahn CABLE CAR
(☑ 05322-753 70; Nordhäuser Strasse 2e; adult/ concession one way €3/1.50; ⊙9.30am-6pm Apr-Oct, 10am-5pm Nov-Mar) Since opening in 1929, this little cable car has whisked over 25 million visitors to the top of 483m high Grosser Burgberg, in around 3 minutes. Riding it to the top and walking down is a popular approach to the award-winning Baumwipfelpad elevated forest walk.

CENTRAL GERMANY BAD HARZBURG

KZ-GEDENKSTÄTTE MITTELBAU DORA

During the final stages of WWII, when Hitler's grand plan turned to conducting war from underground bunkers, **Mittelbau Dora** (☑ 03631-495 820; www.buchenwald.de/en/29; Kohnsteinweg 20, Nordhausen; ☺ 10am-6pm Tue-Sun Mar-Sep, to 4pm Oct-Feb) **FREE** was established as a satellite of the Buchenwald concentration camp, after British bombers destroyed missile plants in Peenemünde. At least 20,000 prisoners were worked to their deaths here. After years of decay under the GDR, the memorial today gives an insight into the horrors that unfolded here, and includes a modern museum that explains the background of the camp and the experiences of the prisoners.

From late 1943, thousands of mostly Russian, French and Polish POWs (many who had survived Auschwitz) toiled under horrific conditions digging a 20km labyrinth of tunnels in the chalk hills north of Nordhausen, within which were built the V1 and V2 rockets that rained destruction on London, Antwerp and other cities during the final stages of the war. The US army reached the gates in April 1945, cared for survivors and removed all missile equipment before turning the area over to Russia.

Visitors are free to roam the grounds, crematorium and museum. The tunnels (whose diameters match those of aircraft hangars) are only accessible on free 90-minute guided tours, which run at 11am and 2pm Tuesday to Friday and at 11am, 1pm and 3pm on weekends. Within the dank walls you can see partially assembled rockets that have lain untouched for over 70 years.

The easiest way to get to this isolated and moving place is by private vehicle. The nearest station (tram 10 and Harzquerbahn from Nordhausen) is Nordhausen-Krimderode, from where it's a 20-minute walk.

Sole Therme　　　　SPA
(☑ 05322-753 30; www.sole-therme-bad-harzburg. de; Nordhäuser Strasse 2a; adult/concession baths only €8.30/5.70, incl sauna €13.90/9; ☺ 8am-9pm Mon-Sat, to 7pm Sun) The reputedly healing waters of this thermal mega-spa spring from 840m beneath the ground into a handful of lukewarm indoor and outdoor pools. Most visitors come for the assorted saunas which vary in temperature and humidity and include a salt grotto: rub a handful onto your skin, let it do the trick, then wash it off in the water cascade.

Remember: wear swimming costumes in the pool, but not in the sauna.

🛏 Sleeping

This quiet, sprawling, low-mountain town depends on tourism for its survival. It's evident that the owners of Bad Harzburg's score of pleasant small hotels and inns take pride in their establishments, but the town itself lacks the historic appeal and range of services (though also the crowds) of nearby Goslar (14km). If you're looking to relax and get back to nature, overnighting in Bad Harzburg is a good bet.

★**Plumbohms Bio Suiten Hotel**　HOTEL €€
(☑ 05322-3277; www.plumbohms.de; Herzog-Wilhelm-Strasse 97; s/d/apt from €95/109/130;

P ⊜ ⓢ ⊠) Pretty Plumbohms is a smart, family-owned affair offering a selection of classy, eco-chic guest rooms and recently renovated apartments decorated to a high standard in earthy tones and fabrics and located in a great spot, close to Bad Harzburg's main attractions. Most of the light-filled, airy rooms feature balconies and/or fireplaces and represent the town's best quality-value proposition.

Vitalhotel am Stadtpark　HOTEL €€
(☑ 05322-780 90; www.vitalhotel-am-stadtpark. de; Am Stadtpark 2; s/d from €69/98; P ⊜ ⓢ) Located in a lovely, elevated spot just above the town centre by the city park, this pleasant, well-managed, private hotel occupies a handsome, historic building and features simple, spotless rooms with neutral, '90s decor that will neither offend nor break the bank. It's a short walk from Bad Harzburg's attractions.

Hotel Tannenhof-Solehotel　HOTEL €€€
(☑ 05322-968 80; www.solehotels.de; Nordhäuser Strasse 6; s/d from €94/144; P ⓢ) If you're coming to town to soak in the waters or bake in the sauna, this is the only hotel with direct access to the town's famed pools. Rooms vary in size and decor. Top floor 'suites' were refurbished in recent years and offer a little more space and comfort than standard rooms.

Eating

You're not spoiled for choice in terms of dining in Bad Harzburg, but the good news is that the selection you do have tends to be pretty reliable and not overpriced.

Golden Palast   CHINESE €

(☑ 05322-54 103; www.goldenpalast-badharzburg.com; Herzog-Wilhelm-Strasse 74; buffet lunch/dinner €8.90/13.90; ☉ 11am-3pm & 5-10.30pm) There are two reasons you'll want to dine at Bad Harzburg's best Chinese joint: the gorgeously retro, shabby-chic decor and the can't-be-beat, all-you-can-eat no-frills buffet. An á la carte menu is also available.

★ Braunschweiger Hof   MODERN EUROPEAN €€

(☑ 05322-7880; www.hotel-braunschweiger-hof.de; Herzog-Wilhelm-Strasse 54; mains €10-24; ☉ noon-2.30pm & 5-10pm; P�ⓡ) You'll find Bad Harzburg's fanciest feed in the Braunschweiger Hof hotel. A diverse menu of beautifully presented German and modern European cuisine and the town's most substantial wine list does an admirable job catering to even the most discerning of palates. Affable, attentive service and reasonable prices seal the deal.

Albert's Corner   GERMAN €€

(☑ 05322-516 98; www.alberts-corner.de; Herzog-Wilhelm-Strasse 118; mains €8-19) There's something about humble Albert's that just beckons you enter; you'll be greeted warmly and can relax while sipping on a hot drink or cold beer and soaking up the woodsy mountain atmosphere. When it's time to eat, tuck into fish, schnitzel or a good-value steak.

ⓘ Information

Haus der Natur (☑ 05322-784 337; www.haus-der-natur-harz.de; Nordhäuser Strasse 2e; ☉ 10am-5pm Tue-Sun)

Bad Harzburg Tourist Office (☑ 05322-753 30; www.bad-harzburg.de; Nordhäuser Strasse 4; ☉ 9am-6pm Mon-Fri, 10am-4pm Sat & Sun)

ⓘ Getting There & Around

BUS

KVG Braunschweig (☑ 05341-409 90; www.kvg-braunschweig.de) bus 810 departs Bad Harzburg for Goslar (€4, 20 minutes) at regular intervals, via the cable-car station; bus 871 heads for Wernigerode (€4.60, one hour). Bus 820 shuttles almost hourly to Torfhaus (€4, 25 minutes).

CAR

Bad Harzburg is on the A395 to Braunschweig; the B4 and B6 lead to Torfhaus and Wernigerode, respectively.

TRAIN

Bad Harzburg station is located about 1km from the town centre and 2km from the main attractions. Frequent train services link Bad Harzburg with Goslar (€4.20, 12 minutes), Hannover (€22.30, 1¼ hours), Braunschweig (€14.20, 45 minutes) and Wernigerode (€13.30, 30 minutes).

BICYCLE

Bike House Harz (☑ 05322-987 0623; www.bike-house-harz.de; Ilsenburger Strasse 112; bikes per day from €20)

Brocken & Torfhaus

There are prettier landscapes and hikes in the Harz National Park (p261), but the modest Brocken (1142m), northern Germany's highest peak, is what draws the crowds. On a sunny summer day, as many as 50,000 folks have been known to take the trek to the top, on foot or by steam train.

On 30 April, for the popular celebration of Walpurgisnacht (p264), people come from far and wide dressed as witches, or in their wackiest gear, to hike to the summit as

---

BROCKEN: NORTHERN GERMANY'S HIGHEST PEAK

From 1945 to 1989 the Harz region was a frontline in the Cold War, and the Brocken was used by the Soviets as a military base. During those years, you couldn't get anywhere near the top without the highest of security clearances.

Today, the mountain has been returned to the people, and hiking the Brocken, or riding a Harzer Schmalspurbahnen (p273) steam train to the summit, has become a popular day trip or weekend jaunt from Berlin or Hanover. The Goetheweg (p264) walking trail hugs the train line and ascends above soggy moorland to reach the open, windy summit for expansive views onto the valley below.

Once you arrive, the obligatory Brockenhaus sells tourist-priced treats and eats, street vendors hawk wurst and local wares and you can even get your Goethe on at a performance of *Faust*...as a rock opera (p264)!

they've done for centuries...only these days they've swapped broomsticks for beer and Bluetooth speakers.

◉ Sights & Activities

There are several ways to get to the top of the mountain, but the 8.8km Goetheweg trail, beginning in Torfhaus, is the main and most popular approach from the Western Harz.

Brockenhaus LANDMARK
(☑039455-500 05; www.nationalpark-brocken-haus.de; adult/concession €5/4; ⊙9.30am-5pm) The Brockenhaus, at the summit of the Brocken, has a cafe, interactive displays and a viewing platform. From May to October, rangers conduct one-hour tours of the Brocken plateau, departing from here and including the Brockengarten alpine garden, which contains around 1500 specimens of high-altitude plant species from around the world.

Goetheweg WALKING
The 8.8km Goetheweg trail is the easiest, most popular approach to the summit of the Brocken from the Western Harz. It begins in Torfhaus, hiking through bog before following a historic aqueduct, then crossing the Kaiserweg, a sweaty 11km trail from Bad Harzburg. Things get steep as you walk the former border between East and West Germany.

Bus 820 stops at Torfhaus (€3.90, 20 minutes) on the well-served Bad Harzburg–Braunlage route.

Kristall 'Heisser Brocken' Therme SPA
(☑05328-911 570; www.kristalltherme-altenau.de; Karl-Reinecke-Weg 35, Altenau; 3hr bathing pass adult/concession €13.50/8.60) This is the better of the two thermal spa complexes in the Harz. Located in the village of Altenau, it has warmer water, more modern facilities, larger outdoor pools and a higher elevation than its rival, Sole Therme (p262), a few minutes' drive down the hill in Bad Harzburg.

⚡ Festivals & Events

Hexennacht/Walpurgisnacht CULTURAL
(⊙30 Apr) Witches, warlocks, ghouls, goblins and goths of all sizes, young and old alike, descend upon Goetheweg and ascend the Brocken in the pagan tradition of Hexennacht (Witches' Night) and the Christian celebration of the canonisation of St Walpurgia – a heavyweight in the anti-witch brigade. Expect bonfires, booze, singing, dancing,

spell-casting, beer-spilling and general silliness...with an edge.

🛏 Sleeping & Eating

Accommodation in the tiny village of Torfhaus is limited to a handful of options catering mainly to hikers and cross-country skiers. There is no accommodation on the mountain itself.

You'll find a small selection of tourist-priced dining at the summit of the Brocken and there's a vendor or two in Torfhaus, otherwise, plan to dine in Goslar or one of the nearby villages.

DJH Jugendherberge Torfhaus HOSTEL €
(☑05320-242; www.jugendherberge.de/jugend herbergen/torfhaus-318/portraet; Torfhaus 3; dm from €26; 🛜) This no-frills official DJH youth hostel is open year-round and is located a few minutes' walk from the start of the Goetheweg trail for hikes to the top of the Brocken. It's a great place to meet other hikers and skiers of all ages and nationalities.

☆ Entertainment

Faust I & II THEATRE
(☑03943-558 145; www.hsb-wr.de; Friedrichstrasse 151, Wernigerode; tickets from €90) For something a little different and as German as the great writer Goethe himself, catch a steam train to the top of the Brocken for limited-date summer performances of the classicc play *Faust*...as a rock opera! The box office is located in Wernigerode.

ⓘ Getting There & Around

There is limited road access by private car to the summit of the Brocken, and in winter, heavy snow can mean even that's not an option. Plan to hike with everybody else or take the rickety, slow steam train for a dose of nostalgia along with your nature.

Bus 820, on the well-served Bad Harzburg–Braunlage route operated by KVG Braunschweig (p263), stops at Torfhaus (€4, 20 minutes), where you can pick up the Goetheweg trail.

Goslar

☑05321 / POP 41,785

This pretty town, one of the most popular places to visit in the Harz, is famed for its beautiful Altstadt (old town), with significant sections of its medieval wall and gates still intact, and the Unesco World Heritage-listed Rammelsberg mine, just outside town.

Founded by Heinrich I in 922, Goslar's early importance centred on mining silver.

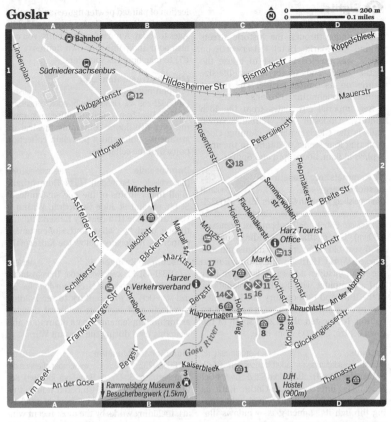

Goslar

◎ Sights
1 Domvorhalle	C4
2 Goslarer Museum	C4
3 Kaiserpfalz	B4
4 Mönchehaus Museum	B3
5 Museum im Zwinger	D4
6 Musikinstrumenten- und Puppenmuseum	C3
7 Rathaus	C3
8 Zinnfiguren-Museum	C4

⊜ Sleeping
9 Altstadt Apartments	B3
10 Hotel Alte Münze	C3
11 Hotel Kaiserworth	C3
12 Niedersächsischer Hof	B1
13 Schiefer	C3

✖ Eating
14 Barock-Café Anders	C3
15 Brauhaus	C3
16 Die Butterhanne	C3
17 Restaurant Aubergine	C3
18 Soup & Soul Kitchen	C2

Its Kaiserpfalz (imperial palace) was the seat of the Saxon kings from 1005 to 1219. Goslar fell into decline after a second period of prosperity in the 14th and 15th centuries, relinquishing its mine to Braunschweig in 1552 and then its soul to Prussia in 1802. Post-WWII, it was the most important town west of the former border between the Western and Eastern Harz.

Today, Goslar attracts visitors by the busload, especially in the mountain-fresh summer months, when you might miss out on both beds and dinner tables if you don't book ahead.

◉ Sights

One of the nicest things to do in Goslar is to wander through the historic streets around the Markt. Hotel Kaiserworth on Markt was erected in 1494 to house the textile guild, and sports almost life-size figures on its orange facade. The market fountain, celebrating Goslar's status as a free imperial city, dates from the 13th century. Opposite the Rathaus (town hall) is the Glockenspiel, a chiming clock depicting four scenes of mining in the area. It plays at 9am, noon, 3pm and 6pm.

★Rammelsberg Museum & Besucherbergwerk   MUSEUM

(Rammelsberg Museum & Visitors' Mine; ☑ 05321-7500; www.rammelsberg.de; Bergtal 19; adult/concession €14/9; ⊙ 9am-6pm, last admission 4.30pm) The shafts and buildings of this 1000-year-old mine are now a museum and Unesco World Heritage Site. Admission to the mine includes a German-language tour and a pamphlet with English explanations of the 18th- and 19th-century Roeder Shafts, the mine railway and the ore-processing section. It's located about 2km south of the town centre; bus 803 stops here.

Rathaus   HISTORIC BUILDING

(Markt; Huldigungssaal adult/concession €4/2; ⊙ 11am-3pm Mon-Fri, 10am-4pm Sat & Sun Apr-Oct & Dec) The impressive late-Gothic Rathaus is most beautiful at night, when light shining through its stained-glass windows illuminates the stone-patterned town square. Inside the highlight is a beautiful cycle of 16th-century religious paintings in the Huldigungssaal (Hall of Homage).

Kaiserpfalz   CASTLE

(☑ 05321-311 9693; Kaiserbleek 6; adult/concession €8/5; ⊙ 10am-4pm) This reconstructed 11th-century Romanesque palace is Goslar's pride and joy. After centuries of decay, the building was resurrected in the 19th century and adorned with interior frescos of idealised historical scenes. On the southern side is St Ulrich Chapel, housing a sarcophagus containing the heart of Heinrich III. Behind the palace, in pleasant gardens, is an excellent sculpture by Henry Moore called the *Goslarer Krieger* (Goslar Warrior).

Zinnfiguren-Museum   MUSEUM

(☑ 05321-258 89; www.zinnfigurenmuseum-goslar.de; Klapperhagen 1; adult/concession €4/2; ⊙ 10am-4pm Tue-Sun) This beautifully presented little museum boasts a colourful collection of painted pewter figures and depicts scenes of daily life in Goslar from the Middle Ages to today. A must for craft buffs, you can also pour and paint your own figures (€3 to €7) to take home as souvenirs.

Musikinstrumenten- und Puppenmuseum   MUSEUM

(☑ 05321-269 45; Hoher Weg 5; adult/concession €4/2; ⊙ 11am-5pm) A private museum sprawling over five floors, containing musical instruments, dolls and a porcelain collection housed in the cellar.

Domvorhalle   HISTORIC BUILDING

(Kaiserbleek; ⊙ 9am-5pm) FREE Domvorhalle is all that remains of the once-magnificent St Simon and St Jude Cathedral. Within it you can see the 11th-century Kaiserstuhl, the throne used by Salian and Hohenstaufen emperors. It's located below the Kaiserpfalz.

Museum im Zwinger   MUSEUM

(☑ 05321-431 40; www.zwinger.de; Thomasstrasse 2; adult/concession €6/3; ⊙ 11am-4pm Tue-Sat mid-Mar–Oct) A 16th-century tower holding a collection of such late-medieval delights as torture implements, coats of armour and weapons used during the Peasant Wars.

Mönchehaus Museum   GALLERY

(☑ 05321-295 70; www.moenchehaus.de; Mönchestrasse 3; €6; ⊙ 11am-5pm Tue-Sun) Set in a 16th-century half-timbered house, this museum has changing exhibits of modern art, including works by the most recent winner of the prestigious Kaiserring art prize; past winners include Henry Moore, Joseph Beuys and Rebecca Horn. Look for the interesting sculptures in the peaceful garden.

Goslarer Museum   MUSEUM

(☑ 05321-433 94; Königstrasse 1; adult/concession €4/2; ⊙ 10am-5pm Tue-Sun) This museum offers a good overview of the natural and cultural history of Goslar and the Harz. One room contains the treasures from the former Goslar Dom (cathedral), and there's also a cabinet with coins dating from the 10th century.

🛌 Sleeping

Goslar has a great little selection of private hotels ranging in style from traditional to boutique, and a wide array of individually owned and managed holiday-flat, *Fereinwohnung*-type accommodations. Rates go up and rooms fill fast in the spring and summer, while in the winter, things can get quite chilly and bargains can be found.

HALBERSTADT: JOHN CAGE ORGEL KUNST PROJECT

Although Halberstadt is the largest city in the Harz Mountains (population 48,258) there's no compelling reason to visit it save for one very special attraction. By that we mean, entirely unique in a global sense: the world's longest performance of a piece of music – a work by the famous American avant-garde composer and sound theorist John Cage (johncage.org). He is best known for his influential work *4'33"*, which has no notes for the duration of the piece (four minutes, 33 seconds). But few people are aware of Cage's other, more enchanting offering for the organ, composed in 1987, *Organ²/ASLSP (As slow as possible)*, in which each note is held for an unfathomably long time by an automated pipe organ.

More a music-art installation than a recital of a piece of music, the current **performance** (☏ 03941-621 620; www.aslsp.org/de; Am Kloster 1, Halberstadt; ⊙ 11am-5pm Tue-Sun) **FREE** of *Organ²/ASLSP* in the shell of Halberstadt's ages-old Kirche St Burchardi began in 2001 and is scheduled to have a duration of 639 years, ending in 2640!

One for lovers of art, music and thinking outside the box, visits here have quite an ethereal feel and you'll find yourself contemplating the preciousness of life and time when you realise that the piece will still be playing long after you've shuffled off this mortal coil.

Halberstadt is located 16km north of Quedlinburg and 25km east of Wernigerode. The site is a little out of the way and will be best enjoyed by self-drivers.

DJH Hostel HOSTEL €

(☏ 05321-222 40; www.djh-niedersachsen.de/jh/goslar; Rammelsberger Strasse 25; dm incl breakfast from €24.50; P @ 🖥) This pretty hostel on the road to the Rammelsberg Museum & Besucherbergwerk has excellent facilities, with single and twin rooms and six- to eight-bed dorms, as well as barbecue and sports areas. Take bus 803 to Theresienhof to reach it.

★ Hotel Alte Münze BOUTIQUE HOTEL €€

(☏ 05321-225 46; www.hotel-muenze.de; Münzstrasse 10-11; s/d from €79/109; P 🖥) There's very little not to like about this boutique hotel in the heart of the Altstadt, parts of which are over 500 years old. Operating as a mint in a previous incarnation, the hotel's hotchpotch of rooms have been beautifully brought up to date with spotless new bathrooms, flat-screen TVs and wi-fi to complement the antique-y, creaky, medieval vibe.

★ Altstadt Apartments APARTMENT €€€

(☏ 05321-302 508; www.altstadt-appartements-goslar.de; Frankenberger Strasse 3; apt from €160; P 🖥) If staying in quaint-but-quirky antique houses isn't your thing, these six smart, modern, fully self-contained apartments come highly recommended. There's private parking out back (a boon in Goslar) and an excellent location a short stroll from the centre of town.

Schiefer BOUTIQUE HOTEL €€€

(☏ 05321-382 270; www.schiefer-erleben.de; Markt 6; d incl breakfast from €129; P ❄ 🖥) Schief-er brings a touch of the modern to ancient Goslar, in a prime Markt location. Its air-conditioned rooms and maisonette apartments are tastefully furnished and spotlessly clean. There's on-site parking at the rear of the hotel (a blessing in largely pedestrian-only Goslar) and breakfast is served in your room. Highly recommended.

Niedersächsischer Hof HOTEL €€€

(☏ 05321-3160; www.niedersaechsicherhof-goslar.de; Klubgartenstrasse 1; s/d from €89/119; P 🖥) The 'Hof' toys with the idea of being an art hotel (kids will love the piece near the foyer with the cindered toy cars), and has bright rooms that are well-insulated against the bustle outside. Prices fluctuate according to the date, so call ahead. It's located opposite the train station.

Hotel Kaiserworth HOTEL €€€

(☏ 05321-7090; www.kaiserworth.de; Markt 3; s/d from €89/139; P ⊖ 🖥) This magnificent 500-year-old former merchant-guild building has tasteful rooms and a good restaurant open daily from 6am to 11pm. Insomniacs should head for the hotel's Café Nouvelle, which is open until 2am or when the last customer leaves.

✖ Eating & Drinking

There are plenty of great restaurants in Goslar, most of which are of the German or European ilk.

While Goslar is far from party central, its popularity as a tourist destination means you'll have no trouble finding a cosy pub or cocktail bar for a quiet beverage or two.

Soup & Soul Kitchen
VEGETARIAN €

(☑ 05321-756 3341; www.soulkitchen.house; Petersilienstrasse 5-7; mains €6-14; ☺ noon-8pm Tue-Sun; ☑) ✈ Locally sourced organic and biodynamic fruit and vegetables are used to create the hearty and delicious vegan and vegetarian soups, salads and pastas at Goslar's hippest healthy hang-out.

Barock-Café Anders
BAKERY €

(☑ 05321-238 14; www.barockcafe-anders.de; Hoher Weg 4; cakes from €4; ☺ 8.30am-6pm) Breathe in the smell of fresh baking as soon as you walk through the door; it's unlikely you'll be able to leave without a pastry for the road.

Die Butterhanne
GERMAN €€

(☑ 05321-228 86; www.butterhanne.de; Marktkirchhof 3; mains €9-17; ☺ 8.30am-midnight) The fare is traditional, the outdoor seating is nice and on the first Saturday of the month the tables are cleared and the place morphs into a throbbing nightspot from 10pm. The name refers to a famous local frieze showing a milkmaid churning butter while clutching her buttock to insult her employer – don't try it on disco night.

Brauhaus
GERMAN €€

(☑ 05321-685 804; www.brauhaus-goslar.de; Marktkirchhof 2; mains €9-22; ☺ 11am-11pm) A newcomer to Goslar's gastronomic and drinking scene, this gastropub brews four types of beer in its copper vats beyond the bar and serves meals focusing mostly on steaks and other meats, some of them organic and locally produced.

Restaurant Aubergine
MEDITERRANEAN €€

(☑ 05321-421 36; www.aubergine-goslar.de; Marktstrasse 4; mains €9-20; ☺ noon-2.30pm & 6-11.30pm) This neat little restaurant doesn't only serve dishes that include its namesake vegetable, but rather, artfully presented Mediterranean cuisine, in a classy, upbeat environment with crisp white linens, shiny silverware and attentive staff.

❶ Information

Harz Tourist Office (☑ 05321-780 60; www.goslar.de; Markt 7; ☺ 9.15am-6pm Mon-Fri, to 4pm Sat, to 2pm Sun)

Harzer Verkehrsverband (☑ 05321-340 40; www.harzinfo.de; Marktstrasse 45, Bäckergildehaus; ☺ 8am-5pm Mon-Thu, to 2pm Fri)

❶ Getting There & Away

BUS

Deutsche Bahn (www.bahn.com) and FlixBus (www.meinfernbus.de) each operate daily services to Berlin via Magdeburg. Prices fluctuate and schedules change, with FlixBus often having the cheapest fares and some direct services; check the websites for details.

Südniedersachsenbus (☑ 05321-194 49; www.rbb-bus.de; Hildesheimer Strasse 6; formerly Regionalbus Braunschweig and managed by Deutsche Bahn, just to confuse) operates services throughout the Harz region; use the easy online route planner for fare and timetable searches.

CAR & MOTORCYCLE

The B6 runs north to Hildesheim and east to Bad Harzburg, Wernigerode and Quedlinburg. The north–south A7 is reached via the B82. For Hahnenklee, take the B241.

TRAIN

Bad Harzburg–Hanover trains stop in Goslar, as do most trains on the Braunschweig–Göttingen line. There are direct trains to Wernigerode (€11, 40 minutes, every two hours) but services to most other destinations require changing trains in Vienenburg.

❶ Getting Around

It's easy to get around the Altstadt on foot, but Goslar is bigger than it first appears: tickets on local buses cost €2.50 per ride.

To book a taxi, ring ☑ 1313 or try www.better taxi.de.

Quedlinburg

☑ 03946 / POP 25,100

World Heritage–listed Quedlinburg is the must-visit village of the region, situated on a fertile plain at the northern cusp of the Harz Mountains. With its 1400-strong centuries-old half-timbered houses, an intact Altstadt (old town) of cobblestone streets and beautifully preserved Marktplatz, it also boasts a wonderful mix of original options for wining, dining and resting your head.

In the 10th century the Reich was briefly ruled from here by two women, Theophano and Adelheid, successive guardians of the child-king Otto III. Quedlinburg itself is closely associated with the *Frauenstift*, a medieval foundation for widows and daughters of the nobility that enjoyed the direct protection of the Kaiser.

Although this little gem of a town can get quite crowded on weekends and in summer,

Quedlinburg is almost always worth a visit, especially on quieter weekdays and in the cooler months, when it's the perfect spot to linger a little longer.

◉ Sights

With so many historic buildings, Quedlinburg is one town in which it's nice just to stroll the streets and soak up the atmosphere. The Rathaus (1320) dominates Markt, and in front of this is a Roland statue from 1426. Just behind the Rathaus is the Marktkirche St Benedikti (1233), and nearby is the Gildehaus zur Rose (1612) at Breite Strasse 39. Running off Markt is the tiny Schuhhof, a shoemakers' courtyard, with shutters and stable-like 'gossip doors'. Alter Klopstock (1580), which is found at Stieg 28, has scrolled beams typical of Quedlinburg's 16th-century half-timbered houses.

From Stieg 28 (just north of Schuhhof), it's a short walk north along Pölle to Zwischen den Städten, a historic bridge connecting the old town and Neustadt (new town), which developed alongside the town wall around 1200 when peasants fled a feudal power struggle on the land. Behind the Renaissance facade, tower and stone gables of the Hagensches Freihaus (1558) is now the Hotel Quedlinburger Stadtschloss. Many houses in this part of town have high archways and courtyards dotted with pigeon towers. A couple of other places of special note are the Hotel zur Goldenen Sonne building (1671) at Steinweg 11 and Zur Börse (1683) at No 23.

A program of classical music is held in the Stiftskirche St Servatius every year from June to September. For tickets and information, contact the tourist office.

Schlossmuseum   MUSEUM
(☑03946-905 681; Schlossberg 1; adult/concession €4.50/3.50; ⊙10am-5pm) The Schlossberg, on a 25m-high plateau above Quedlinburg, was initially graced with a church and residence under King Heinrich I (Henry the Fowler), credited with founding the first German empire. The present-day Renaissance-era Schloss (palace) contains the Schlossmuseum, with fascinating Ottonian-period exhibits dating from 919 to 1056 and displays recounting how the Nazi party used the site for propaganda by staging a series of events to celebrate Heinrich – whose life they skewed to justify their own ideology and crimes.

The museum is under ongoing restoration: ticket prices are discounted by €1 during periods of significant construction.

Stiftskirche St Cyriakus   CHURCH
(☑03948-5275; Burgstrasse 3, Gernrode; guided tour €4; ⊙9am-5pm Mon-Sat, from noon Sun Apr-Oct, tours 3pm daily year-round) One of the purest examples of Romanesque architecture from the Ottonian period is this church in Gernrode (p271), 8km south of Quedlinburg. Construction of the basilica, which is based on the form of a cross, was begun in 959. Especially noteworthy is the early use of alternating columns and pillars, later a common Romanesque feature. The octagonal *Taufstein* (christening stone), whose religious motifs culminate in the Ascension, dates from 1150.

Stiftskirche St Servatius   CHURCH
(☑03946-2730; Schlossberg 1; adult/concession €4.50/3.50; ⊙10am-6pm Tue-Sat) This 12th-century church is one of Germany's most significant from the Romanesque period. Its treasury contains valuable reliquaries and early Bibles. The crypt has some early religious frescos and contains the graves of King Heinrich I and his widow, Mathilde, along with those of the abbesses. From 1938, the church was occupied by the SS, under Heinrich Himmler, Hitler's right-hand man.

Klopstockhaus   MUSEUM
(☑905 691; Schlossberg 12; adult/concession €3.50/2.60; ⊙10am-5pm Wed-Sun) The early classicist poet Friedrich Gottlieb Klopstock (1724–1803) is one of Quedlinburg's most celebrated sons. He was born in this 16th-century house, which is now a museum containing some interesting exhibits on Klopstock himself and on Dorothea Erxleben (1715–62), Germany's first female doctor.

Lyonel Feininger Galerie   GALLERY
(☑03946-689 5930; www.feininger-galerie.de; Finkenherd 5a; adult/concession €6/4; ⊙10am-5pm Wed-Mon) This purpose-built gallery exhibits the work of influential Bauhaus artist Lyonel Feininger (1871–1956), who was born in New York and came to Germany at the age of 16, later fleeing the Nazis and returning to the US in 1937. The original graphics, drawings, watercolours and sketches on display are from the period 1906 to 1936.

Fachwerkmuseum im Ständerbau   MUSEUM
(☑03946-3828; Wordgasse 3; adult/concession €3/2; ⊙10am-5pm Fri-Wed) Germany's earliest

half-timbered houses were built using high perpendicular struts known as *Ständerbau*. The building dating to 1310 that now houses Quedlinburg's Fachwerkmusem is one of Germany's best-preserved examples of this technique. Inside, you'll find exhibits on the style itself and the physics behind this ancient method of construction.

🛌 Sleeping

Quedlinburg has a wide range of accommodation options, most of which are well priced and of a comfortable standard, styled to line up with the town's historic appeal.

DJH Hostel
HOSTEL €

(☑ 03946-811 703; www.jugendherberge-quedlinburg.de; Neuendorf 28; dm €20-23, linen €3.50) This excellent DJH hostel offers four- and 10-bed dorms in a quiet and very central location. It's relatively small and fills quickly in summer.

★ Hotel am Hoken
HOTEL €€

(☑ 03946-525 40; www.hotel-am-hoken.de; Hoken 3; s/d from €69/89; P ⊜ 🛜) This wonderfully romantic hotel off the Markt exemplifies traditional style and elegance, and has warm, accommodating staff, but it's not for everyone. The floors and furnishings are in attractive timber, which means everything creaks a little, and due to the building's age, there's only a narrow winding staircase to reach the rooms.

Wyndam Garden Quedlinburger Stadtschloss
HOTEL €€

(☑ 03946-526 00; www.wyndhamhotels.com; Bockstrasse 6/Klink 11; d from €98; P 🛜) Tasteful features and the wellness area (including a Finnish sauna, steam bath and whirlpool) of this hotel in a restored Renaissance-era residence make it worth considering.

Romantik Hotel am Brühl
BOUTIQUE HOTEL €€€

(☑ 03946-961 80; www.hotelambruehl.de; Billungstrasse 11; s/d/apt from €86/119/188; P ❄ 🛜) Well-appointed, spacious rooms and suites are individually and classically styled in this impressive boutique hotel on the outskirts of the Altstadt. The apartments are delightful and an excellent option for those travelling with children or in a small group. A plentiful breakfast buffet is included.

🍴 Eating

Its popularity with day-trippers and weekenders has meant that Quedlinburg's dining scene has upped its game compared to other towns in the reason. You'll have no trouble finding a good meal here, but it's always smart to make dinner reservations if you have the opportunity.

Any of the restaurants and bars opening onto the Markt make the perfect spot to enjoy an afternoon vino as you look out and appreciate the aesthetic beauty of times past.

Heilemann's FachwerQ
ITALIAN €

(☑ 03946-519 8051; www.fachwerq-quedlinburg.de; Markstrasse 10; bruschettas €6-13; ⊙ 10am-8pm Wed-Mon; 🖋) This awesome little bruschetteria (yes, there is such a thing) overlooking the Marktkirche St Benedikti doles out a clever selection of delicious bruschetta on freshly baked bread, with local tomatoes and other goodies. Pasta, wine, coffee and beer are also served.

Mom's Burgers
BURGERS €

(☑ 03946-528 2415; www.momsburger.de; Markstrasse 15; burgers €6-11; ⊙ noon-7pm) The name says it all: if you're craving a burger without the fast-food feel, this cute little hole-in-the-wall will likely satisfy. It's sweet and squeaky clean, and the burgers are pretty darn good, made from fresh, locally sourced ingredients.

Brauhaus Lüdde
GERMAN €€

(☑ 03946-705 206; www.hotel-brauhaus-luedde.de; Blasiistrasse 14; mains €9-21; ⊙ 11am-midnight Mon-Sat, to 10pm Sun) Decent food and good boutique beer (despite some rather flatulent names for the local drop) are the order of the day in this lively microbrewery. After the arrival of a coach group, the average age can soar to 70 years, decreasing slowly as the night grinds on.

Hössler
SEAFOOD €€

(☑ 915 255; www.fischgenuss-qlb.de; Steinbrücke 21; mains €8-18; ⊙ 8am-7.30pm Mon-Fri, 9am-8pm Sat, 2-7pm Sun) An excellent fish cafeteria, with a restaurant through the passage. The same meals are cheaper in the front section. It doesn't look like much from the outside, but the fish is delish and the portions are generous.

Münzenberger Klause
GERMAN €€

(☑ 03946-2928; www.muenzenberger-klause.de; Pölle 22; mains €9-20; ⊙ 11am-11pm Tue-Sat) Serving traditional German fare with flair, this atmospheric restaurant is loved by locals and visitors alike. If you're seeking hearty comfort food, look no further.

GERNRODE

An easy 8km south of Quedlinburg, Gernrode is well worth a few hours of your day. Its magnificent Romanesque Stiftskirche St Cyriakus (p269) has existed in some form on this site for over 1000 years. Other drawcards are quirkier and more inexplicable, including the world's largest wooden thermometer and the world's largest Skat table. Skat is a card game, but you knew that...didn't you?

Gernrode is a pretty place for picnicking, popular with hikers and steam-train enthusiasts. It's a great place to pick up the Selketalbahn line of the Harzer Schmalspurbahnen (p273) narrow-gauge railway if you plan to travel deeper into the mountains.

Regular bus services for Thale (€5.10, 35 minutes), and Quedlinburg-bound train (€5.10, 10 minutes) and bus (€5.10, 30 minutes) services, depart from Gernrode train station, where you can also buy tickets for trips on the Selketalbahn steam trains to/from Quedlinburg.

Zum Goldenen Drachen   CHINESE €€
(☑ 03946-700 386; Schmale Strasse 1a; mains €7-18; ⊙ noon-9pm; 🖉) There's nothing mind-blowing about this Chinese restaurant, but it's not disappointing either. Meals are tasty and good value, with lots of vegetarian options if you're needing a break from all the meat and cheese. Convenient and inexpensive.

ℹ Information

Quedlinburg Tourist Office (☑ 905 625; www.quedlinburg.de; Markt 2; ⊙ 9.30am-6pm Mon-Fri, to 3pm Sat, to 2pm Sun)

ℹ Getting There & Away

The Strasse der Romanik (Romanesque Road; not to be confused with the Romantic Road in Bavaria) theme road follows the L239 south to Gernrode and connects towns that have significant Romanesque architecture. The B6 runs west to Wernigerode, Goslar, the A395 (for Braunschweig) and the A7 between Kassel and Hanover. For Halle take the B6 east, and for Halberstadt the B79 north.

Frequent services operate between Quedlinburg and Thale (€2.80, 12 minutes). For trains to Wernigerode (€10.70, 40 minutes), you'll need to change at Halberstadt. The narrow-gauge *Selketalbahn* runs to Gernrode (€6, 15 minutes) and beyond.

ℹ Getting Around

It's easy to wander around the Aldstadt, indeed, there are many sections where motorised vehicles are not permitted. **2Rad Pavillon** (☑ 03946-709 507; www.zweiradpavillon.com; Bahnhofstrasse 1b; bikes per day from €6; ⊙ 9am-6pm Mon-Fri, 9.30am-noon Sat) hires out bicycles.

You'll find information on local and regional buses inside Quedlinburg train station and online at www.rbb-bus.de. Almost all buses through town stop here.

Thale

☑ 03947 / POP 17,014

Seated beneath the northern slopes of the Harz Mountains, once-industrial Thale has turned to tourism for its future. Its main attraction is the sensational landscape of rugged cliffs flanking the Bode River, and a lush valley ideal for hiking.

The two cliffs at the head of the valley are known as Hexentanzplatz and Rosstrappe. These once boasted Celtic fortresses and were used by Germanic tribes for occult rituals and sacrifices.

Postmodern pagans gather here in grand style and numbers each year on 30 April to celebrate Walpurgisnacht (p264).

⊙ Sights & Activities

Rosstrappe   VIEWPOINT
(☑ 03947-77 68 00; www.bodetal.de; chairlift return €6; ⊙ 9.30am-6pm Easter-Sep, 10am-4.30pm Oct-Easter) Lovely views await at the top of Rosstrappe peak, which takes its name from what is supposedly a horse's hoof print, visible in stone on the cliff, left by the mythical Brunhilde when she sprang over the gorge on horseback to avoid marrying the giant Bodo. He leapt after her, landing in a watery grave, horse and all. Access is by chairlift or a short but strenuous hiking trail. Go early or late in the day to avoid crowds.

Hexentanzplatz   VIEWPOINT
(☑ 03947-776 8000; www.bodetal.de; cable car return €8; ⊙ 9.30am-6pm) Of the two rocky bluffs flanking the Bode Valley, Hexentanzplatz is the most developed and popular.

CENTRAL GERMANY THALE

Take the cable car to the top for spectacular views and crisp, fresh air.

DDR Museum
MUSEUM

(☑03947-656 33; www.ddr-museum-thale.de; Steinbachstrasse 5a; ⊙10am-6pm Mon-Fri, to 4pm Sat) Step back into a time and a country gone forever in this interesting little museum remembering the not-so-good ol' days (depending on who you talk to) of the German Democratic Republic. Kitsch-city!

Therme Bodetal
SPA

(☑03947-778 450; www.therme-bodetal.de; Parkstrasse 4; ⊙10am-8pm) Thale's mineral spa is a treat for feet sore from hiking through the Harz; it's also very popular.

Harzer-Hexen-Stieg
WALKING

(www.hexenstieg.de) The Harzer-Hexen-Stieg walking trail (blue triangle, 10km) between Thale and Treseburg is highly recommended. If you take the bus from Thale to Treseburg, you can walk downstream and enjoy the most spectacular scenery· at the end. WVB bus 264 does the trip from April to early November, and QBus 18 runs via Hexentanzplatz from April to October.

🛏 Sleeping & Eating

Thale is a nice place to visit but with so many other noteworthy towns in the region, it really doesn't rate as the best place to overnight. If you do decide to linger, there are a handful of basic options but you're best advised to stay in one of Quedlinburg's many cheerful offerings, just 11km to the northeast.

There are more than a few places to dine after dark, but once-industrial Thale can still have a gloomy evening vibe, depending on the weather and your own melancholy. Head to nearby Quedlinburg to lift your spirits and whet your appetite.

ℹ Information

Thale Tourist Office (☑03947-776 8000; www.bodetal.de; Bahnhofstrasse 1; ⊙8am-6pm Mon-Fri, 9am-3pm Sat & Sun)

ℹ Getting There & Around

Frequent trains travel to Quedlinburg (€3, 12 minutes) and Wernigerode (change in Halberstadt; €12.30, one hour).

The bus station is located alongside the train station. For Wernigerode, take bus 253.

Karl-Marx-Strasse leads to the main junction for roads to Quedlinburg and Wernigerode.

For taxis, call ☑2505 or ☑2435 or try www.bettertaxi.de.

Wernigerode

☑03943 / POP 35,041

A bustling, attractive town on the northern edge of the Harz Mountains, Wernigerode is an excellent starting point for journeys into the eastern fringe of the Harz National Park (p261). Stay a day or a night if you can.

The winding streets of its Altstadt (old town) are flanked by prettily coloured half-timbered houses, presided over by a romantic 12th-century ducal castle nestled high above town. Folks also flock here to ride the steam-powered narrow-gauge *Harzquerbahn*, which has chugged its way around the region for almost a century; the line to the summit of the Brocken (1142m), northern Germany's highest peak, originates here.

Most of the Central Harz was, for a time, part of the GDR and Wernigerode was the major hub in this neck of the woods, although you'll be hard-pressed to find many relics of that period in history, architecturally or otherwise, unless you look very carefully.

◎ Sights

★ **Schloss Wernigerode**
CASTLE

(☑03943-553 040; www.schloss-wernigerode.de; Am Schloss 1; adult/concession €7/6, tower tour €2; ⊙10am-5pm, closed Mon Nov-Apr) Originally built in the 12th century to protect German Kaisers on hunting expeditions, Schloss Wernigerode was enlarged over the years to reflect late-Gothic and Renaissance tastes. The castle's fairy-tale facade came courtesy of Count Otto of Stolberg-Wernigerode in the 19th century. The museum inside includes portraits of Kaisers, beautiful panelled rooms with original furnishings, the opulent *Festsaal* (banquet hall) and stunning *Schlosskirche* (1880), with its altar and pulpit made of French marble.

You can walk (1.5km) or take a Bimmelbahn wagon ride (return adult/concession €5/2) from Marktstrasse. In summer, horse-drawn carts make the trek from Marktplatz.

Rathaus
HISTORIC BUILDING

(☑03943-6540; Marktplatz 1) Wernigerode's spectacular towered Rathaus (town hall) began life as a theatre around 1277, only to be given its mostly late-Gothic features, which loom over the town square, in the 16th century. The artisan who carved its 33 wooden figures is said to have fallen foul of the authorities. If you peer closely you can see a few of his mocking touches (hint: look for the positioning of the hands).

Marktplatz   SQUARE

Wernigerode's magnificent Marktplatz is presided over by its towering Rathaus. In the middle of the square, a neo-Gothic fountain (1848) was dedicated to charitable nobles, whose names and coats of arms are immortalised upon it.

Breite Strasse   STREET

Wernigerode's main thoroughfare, Breite Strasse, accommodates the pretty Cafe Wien building (1583) at No. 4, today a dignified cafe and worthwhile stopover for both architectural and gastronomic reasons. It's almost impossible to miss the carved facade of the Krummelsches Haus at number 72, as it depicts various countries symbolically; America is portrayed, strangely enough, as a naked woman riding an armadillo.

Oberpfarrkirchhof   AREA

Oberpfarrkirchhof surrounds the Gothic- and later, neo-Gothic–styled Sylvestrikirche. Here you'll also find the Gadenstedtsches Haus (1582) with its Renaissance oriel on the south side of the neighbourhood. To get here, follow the small Klint south from Marktplatz

(the street on the right-hand side if you face the town hall) past some historic buildings.

Harzmuseum Wernigerode   MUSEUM

(☏03943-654 454; www.harzmuseum.de; Klint 10; €2; ⊙10am-5pm Mon-Sat) This delightfully crooked little local-history museum has a neat collection of exhibits on geology, town history and half-timbered houses.

🛌 Sleeping

Wernigerode has a wide range of accommodation options to suit most tastes and budgets.

DJH Hostel Wernigerode   HOSTEL €

(☏03943-606 176; www.jugendherberge.de/jh/wernigerode; Am Eichberg 5; dm €21-24, linen €3.50; ☏) This hostel has two-, three- and four-bed dorms with bathrooms, as well as a sauna and solarium. The large Brockenbad swimming complex is nearby. It's located on the edge of the forest about 2.5km west of town in Hasserode; take bus 1 or 4 to Hochschule Harz and follow the signs for 500m.

Schlossidyll   PENSION €€

(☏0162-925 7515; www.schlossidyll.net; Freilandstieg 14; d/apt from €59/89; 🅿⚕☏) This six-room boutique *Pension* in the hills above Wernigerode could be one of the town's

---

HARZ NARROW-GUAGE RAILWAYS

Fans of old-time trains will be in their element on any of the three narrow-gauge railways crossing the Harz. This 140km integrated network – the largest in Europe – is served by 25 steam and 10 diesel locomotives, which tackle gradients of up to 1:25 (40%) and curves as tight as 60m in radius. Most locomotives date from the 1950s, but eight historic models, some from as early as 1897, are proudly rolled out for special occasions.

The network, a legacy of the GDR, consists of three lines.

The Harzquerbahn runs 60km on a north–south route between Wernigerode and Nordhausen. The serpentine 14km between Wernigerode and Drei Annen Hohne includes 72 bends; you'll get dropped off on the edge of Harz National Park.

From the junction at Drei Annen Hohne, the Brockenbahn begins the steep climb to Schierke and the Brocken. Trains to the Brocken (via Drei Annen Hohne) can be picked up from Wernigerode and Nordhausen; single/return tickets cost €24/12 from all stations. Many visitors take the train to Schierke and then follow a trail on foot to the Brocken summit (1142m).

The third service is the Selketalbahn, which begins in Quedlinburg and runs to Eisfelder Talmühle or Hasselfelde. At Eisfelder Tal, you can change trains for other lines. The picturesque Selketalbahn crosses the plain to Gernrode and follows Wellbach, a creek with a couple of good swimming holes, through deciduous forest to Mägdesprung, before joining the Selke Valley and climbing past Alexisbad to high plains around Friedrichshöhe, Stiege and beyond.

Passes for three/five days on all three lines cost €86/129 per adult (children half-price). Check in with the folks at Harzer Schmalspurbahnen (☏03943-5580; www.hsb-wr.de; Bahnhofsplatz 6, Wernigerode) for timetables, or hit the website.

best-kept secrets. A short walk from the Altstadt, it has views to the castle and spacious guest rooms and apartments that boast stylish, quality furnishings and clever design. Breakfast is available and there's a jacuzzi and sauna on-site. Excellent value.

HKK Hotel Wernigerode HOTEL €€
(☑ 03943-9410; www.hkk-wr.de; Pfarrstrasse 41; s/d incl breakfast from €82/112; P ❄ 🐾 🛜) This modern 258-room conference hotel is popular with bus and tour groups. It has spacious rooms, fast free wi-fi, and a convenient location a few minutes' walk from the Altstadt and station.

★ Hotel Gothisches Haus LUXURY HOTEL €€€
(☑ 03943-6750; www.travelcharme.com/en/hotels/gothisches-haus-wernigerode; Am Markt 1; s/d from €99/129, ste from €275; P ❄ 🛜) The warm Tuscan colours and thoughtful design of this luxury hotel make it literally a very attractive option, and the wellness area is hard to beat, with three saunas and a 'beach' with real sand. One suite has a waterbed.

🍴 Eating & Drinking

There's no shortage of restaurants and cafes in town, including some chain take-away joints (you know who we mean) that you won't find in most of the smaller towns in the Harz.

It's unlikely that you'll be having the time of your life, *Dirty Dancing*–style, but there are a few decent bars and pubs to be found around the Marktplatz area.

Harzer Baumkuchen BAKERY €
(☑ 03943-632 726; www.harzer-baumkuchen.de; Neustadter Ring 17; baumkuchen from €3.50; ⊗ 10am-6pm Mon-Sat, from noon Sun) Sample delicious German *baumkuchen* at this cake-shaped bakery.

Orchidea Huong SOUTHEAST ASIAN €€
(☑ 03943-625 162; www.orchidea-huong.de; Klintgasse 1; mains €9-24; ⊗ 5-10pm Mon & Wed-Fri, noon-3pm & 5-10pm Sat & Sun) If you need a break from heavy German food, you'll find this interesting establishment, incorporating restaurants Lan (Vietnamese) and Hanazono (Japanese), a pleasant surprise. For authenticity, err on the Vietnamese side, though the Japanese menu is also well executed.

Casa Vita MEDITERRANEAN €€
(☑ 03943-945 754; www.casa-vita-wr.de; Marktstrasse 35; mains €8-19; ⊗ 5-10pm; 🛜) This bistro and bar has an attractive, spacious

interior, a courtyard and a beer garden – all rounded off with a homely Mediterranean ambience. There's a diverse menu including a number of pizzas, many under €10, and a range of vegetarian options.

Bodega SPANISH €€
(☑ 03943-9492 6330; www.bodega-wernigerode.de; Marktstrasse 12; tapas from €4, mains €9-19; ⊗ 5-10pm Tue-Fri & Sun, from noon Sat) For authentic Spanish flavours and ambience, look no further than this popular, atmospheric hang-out, with tapas to share, vegetarian options and plenty of seafood and meat on the menu.

Restaurant Weisser Hirsch GERMAN €€
(☑ 03943-602 020; www.hotel-weisser-hirsch.de; Marktplatz 5; mains €11-26; ⊗ 11am-10pm) Crisp white tablecloths, glistening cutlery and wild hare on the menu underscore the traditional but enticing culinary approach at the 'White Stag'. Four- and five-course menus are also available (from €24.50 to €50). It's popular with travel groups, so it can be hit and miss with timing, and you may have to wait. Reservations advised.

ℹ️ Information

Wernigerode Tourist Office (☑ 03943-553 7835; www.wernigerode-tourismus.com; Marktplatz 10; ⊗ 9am-7pm Mon-Fri, 10am-4pm Sat, to 3pm Sun)

ℹ️ Getting There & Around

Bus 253 runs to Blankenburg and Thale, while bus 257 serves Drei Annen Hohne and Schierke.

In town, buses 1 and 2 run from the bus station to the Rendezvous bus stop just north of the Markt, connecting with bus 3.

Single rides cost €1.50, but if you're overnighting here, ask your hotel for a free Wernigerode pass, which lets you ride local transport for free, for the duration of your stay.

There are frequent trains to Goslar (€11, 40 minutes) and Halle (€23.20, 1¼ hours). Change at Halberstadt for Quedlinburg (€10.70, 40 minutes) and Thale (€12.30, one hour).

For bike hire, try **BadBikes** (☑ 03943-626 868; www.badbikes-online.de; Breite Strasse 48a; bikes per day from €20; ⊗ 9am-6pm Mon-Sat, from noon Sun).

SAALE-UNSTRUT REGION

The wine-growing region along the rivers Saale and Unstrut provides a wonderfully rural summer retreat. Europe's most northerly wine district produces crisp whites and fairly sharp reds, which you can enjoy at wine tastings, sometimes right at the estates. The 60km bicycle-friendly Weinstrasse (Wine Road) meanders through the region, past steeply terraced vineyards, castle-topped hills and small family-owned farms. Local tourist offices can help with information and maps.

❶ Getting There & Around

Freyburg and Naumburg are well serviced by rail, but renting a car will give you the freedom to explore the quaint little villages and vineyards of the valley.

Freyburg

📞 034464 / POP 3645

With its cobblestone streets and medieval castle clinging to vine-covered slopes, the little village of Freyburg has a rustic, vaguely French atmosphere. Sparkling-wine production has been the main source of income here since the middle of the 19th century, and to this day Freyburg is home to Germany's most famous bubbly brand, Rotkäppchen Sekt (named for the Little Red Riding Hood from the Grimm brothers' fairy tale).

The town seriously comes alive for its wine festival, the Freyburger Winzerfest, in the second week of September.

⦿ Sights

★ Schloss Neuenburg   CASTLE
(📞355 30; www.schloss-neuenburg.de; Schloss 25; adult/concession €6/3.50, with tour €8/6.50, tower €1.50/1; ⊙10am-6pm daily, tower Tue-Sun) This large medieval castle on the hill above town is one of Freyburg's highlights. It houses an excellent museum that illuminates various aspects of medieval life. The complex includes a rare Romanesque two-storey (or 'double') chapel and a free-standing tower, the Dicker Wilhelm, which has further historical exhibitions and splendid views.

Rotkäppchen Sektkellerei   WINERY
(📞034464-340; www.rotkaeppchen.de; Sektkellereistrasse 5; 45 min tour €5; ⊙tours 11am & 2pm daily, also 12.30pm & 3.30pm Sat & Sun) The biggest sparkling-wine producer in Germany, the Rotkäppchen Sektkellerei was established in 1856. It is one of the few companies that survived the GDR and, since reunification, has acquired enough muscle to buy other brands, including Mumm. Tours include the historic cellars and the production facilities. Between 10am and 5pm, you can also taste and buy a whole range of Sekt at the shop out front.

★ Festivals & Events

Freyburger Winzerfest   WINE
(⊙2nd week of Sep) The largest annual wine festival in Central Germany takes place here in the second week of September every year, when the streets around the Markt transform into one big outdoor wine bar.

🛏 Sleeping & Eating

There aren't many places to stay in town but if you decide you'd like to, check with the Freyburg Tourist Office (📞03445-272 60; www.freyburg-info.de; Markt 2; ⊙9am-5pm Mon-Thu, to 6pm Fri, 8am-2pm Sat) for a list of all your options.

Aside from a handful of rustic restaurants and irregularly open cellar doors, there's little by way of dining in the town.

❶ Getting There & Around

Freyburg lies about 9km north of Naumburg.

The towns are connected by trains (€3.80, eight minutes) and buses (€2.50, 23 minutes).

The B180 to Naumburg follows the river.

The well-marked bicycle route between Naumburg and Freyburg makes for a wonderful ride.

Naumburg

📞 03445 / POP 23,978

Naumburg has a handsome Altstadt (old town) with a striking Renaissance Rathaus (town hall) and an enormous cathedral of early Gothic styling as well as a museum or two. Located at the confluence of the Saale and Unstrut Rivers, it also has a downright pretty position on the water, great for a picnic lunch.

⦿ Sights

Naumberger Dom   CHURCH
(Cathedral of Sts Peter and Paul; 📞03445-230 1133; www.naumburger-dom.de; Domplatz 16-17; adult/concession €6.50/4.50; ⊙9am-6pm Mon-Sat, from noon Sun) The enormous Cathedral of Sts Peter and Paul is a masterpiece of medieval architecture. While the crypt and the east choir feature elements of the Romanesque, the famous west choir is a prime example of early Gothic design. Here you'll find a dozen monumental statues of the cathedral founders, the work of the so-called Master of Naumburg. Medieval stained-glass windows

are augmented by ruby-red modern panes by Neo Rauch, one of the premier artists of the New Leipzig School.

Nietzsche Haus — MUSEUM

(☑03445-201 638; www.mv-naumburg.de/nietzschehaus; Weingarten 18; adult/concession €3/2; ⊙2-5pm Tue-Fri, from 10am Sat & Sun) The exhibits here consist mostly of photos, documents and reams of biographical text about one of Germany's greatest philosophers. Friedrich Nietzsche (1844–1900) spent most of his childhood in this modest home, acquired by his mother after the death of her husband. In 1890 she brought her son back here to nurse him as he was going slowly mad, allegedly as a result of syphilis.

🛏 Sleeping & Eating

Accommodation options are limited to small private hotels and B&Bs.

There are a few restaurants and food outlets here, but you wouldn't say that the town caters to wide range of tastes.

As this is the largest of the Saale-Unstrut towns, at the heart of Central Germany's most productive wine-growing region, you won't have any trouble finding somewhere to sample the local nectar... but you won't find any banging nightlife here, either.

DJH Hostel — HOSTEL €

(☑03445-703 422; www.jugendherberge.de/jh/naumburg; Am Tennisplatz 9; dm incl breakfast €23-26.50, linen €3.50; 🅿🛜) Naumburg's large and well-equipped hostel is 1.5km south of the town centre and features simple dorm rooms, friendly staff and a pretty, quiet location.

Hotel Stadt Aachen — HOTEL €€

(☑03445-2470; www.hotel-stadt-aachen.de; Markt 11; s/d from €67/89) This comfortable traditional hotel on the bustling main square is a good choice for clean, central lodgings, with a standard array of offerings and friendly staff.

Bocks — INTERNATIONAL €€

(☑03445-261 5110; Steinweg 6; mains €10.50-24; ⊙10am-9pm; 🍴) Naumburg's top eatery boasts charming decor in its two rooms, a cafe area and excellent meat dishes, pasta and other fare.

ℹ Information

Naumberg Tourist Office (☑03445-273 125; www.naumburg.de; Markt 12; ⊙9am-6pm Mon-Fri, to 4pm Sat, 10am-1pm Sun)

ℹ Getting There & Around

From Halle or Leipzig, take the A9 to either the B87 or the B180 and head west; the B87 is less direct and more scenic, though it's the first exit from the A9.

Regional trains chug to Naumburg from Halle (€8.60, 45 minutes), Jena (€8.70, 45 minutes) and Weimar (€10.70, 35 minutes). A local line runs to Freyburg (€3.10, eight minutes). Direct ICE services operate to Leipzig (€21, 40 minutes).

Departing from in front of the station, the Naumburger Strassenbahn, a GDR-era tram (€2), will drop you at Theaterplatz, near Markt. If you're on foot, walk along Rossbacher Strasse (keep bearing left and uphill) past the cathedral.

Radhaus Steinmeyer (☑03445-203 119; www.radhaus-naumburg.de; Bahnhofstrasse 46; bikes per day from €10) rents bikes in the summer.

SAXONY-ANHALT

The region's standout destinations, especially for lovers of architecture, art and design, are Dessau-Rosslau, birthplace of the Bauhaus movement, and the stunning manicured pleasure gardens of Gartenreich Dessau-Wörlitz.

This otherwise unassuming region in the heart of the former German Democratic Republic is best known today for Lutherstadt Eisleben and Lutherstadt Wittenberg, two towns so inextricably linked to religious reformer Martin Luther that the townsfolk decided to tack on the 'Lutherstadt' to their town names. The 500th anniversary of the Reformation in 2017 was a very big deal in these parts and gave both towns a healthy economic boost and a restorative facelift, which has left each looking better than ever before.

History buffs could head also to Magdeburg, the state capital, and Halle, birthplace of heavyweight baroque composer Georg Händel. Both cities celebrated their 1200th birthdays in recent years and have also made efforts to improve their visual appeal.

ℹ Getting There & Away

The region is intersected by the A9 autobahn connecting Berlin to Leipzig and the A14, which runs from Leipzig to Halle and onwards to Magdeburg.

Saxony-Anhalt is well serviced by the Deutsche Bahn rail network with frequent trains allowing connections to most of Germany.

Dessau-Rosslau

☑ 0340 / POP 88,693

This little town was the birthplace of the most influential design school of the 20th century – Bauhaus. A mecca for architecture and design students, there's nowhere else you'll find a greater concentration of structures from Bauhaus' most creative period: 1925 to 1932.

Officially known as Dessau-Rosslau since a 2007 merger with its neighbour across the Elbe, the town is an easy day trip from Berlin. Spending a night in the area will, however, allow more time to contemplate the beauty of the stark, utilitarian Bauhaus sites in contrast to the opulent splendour of the numerous palaces of the surrounding Garden Realm.

The Bauhaus mainstay is an easy walk west of the Hauptbahnhof. The town centre is southeast, about 15 minutes away. Pedestrianised Zerbster Strasse is the main drag, leading to the Markt, town hall and the Rathaus-Center shopping mall.

◉ Sights & Activities

There are three main Bauhaus locations in Dessau-Rosslau: the Bauhausgebäude, where it all started, the Meisterhäuser (Masters' Houses) and the Törten Estate.

Exemplifying the Bauhaus credo of 'design for living', four of the original seven Meisterhäuser, where the Bauhaus' leading lights lived as neighbours, have been reconstructed after years of decay: Gropiushaus, Haus Feininger, Haus Muche/Schlemmer and Haus Kandinsky/Klee. They can all be found on leafy Ebertallee, a 15-minute walk west of the Hauptbahnhof.

★ **Bauhausgebäude**   ARCHITECTURE
(Bauhaus Building; ☑ 0340-650 8250; www.bauhaus-dessau.de; Gropiusallee 38; exhibition adult/concession €7.50/4.50, tour €6.50; ⊙ 10am-6pm, tours 11am & 2pm, also noon & 4pm Sat & Sun) It's almost impossible to overstate the significance of this building, erected in 1925–26, as a school of Bauhaus art, design and architecture. Today a smattering of lucky students from an urban studies program use some of the building, but much of it is open to the public. An audioguide is included with the admission fee, so you can tour the building and exhibition by yourself, although certain rooms are only revealed on a guided tour.

★ **Meisterhäuser**   ARCHITECTURE
(Masters' Houses; www.meisterhaeuser.de; Ebertallee; combined ticket adult/concession €7.50/5.50, tour €12/9; ⊙ 11am-6pm Tue-Sun, tours 12.30pm & 3.30pm daily, also 1.30pm Sat & Sun) You'll find the four surviving Meisterhäuser – Gropiushaus, Haus Feininger, Haus Muche/Schlemmer and Haus Kandinsky/Klee – on leafy Ebertallee. The leading lights of the Bauhaus movement lived together as neighbours in these white cubist structures that exemplify the Bauhaus aim of 'design for living' in a modern industrial world. The ticket price grants entry into all four buildings.

Kurt Weill Zentrum in Haus Feininger   ARCHITECTURE
(☑ 0340-619 595; www.meisterhaeuser.de; Ebertallee 63; combined ticket adult/concession €7/5.50; ⊙ 11am-5pm) Haus Feininger, former home of artist Lyonel Feininger, now pays homage to Dessau-born Kurt Weill (p279), who later became playwright Bertolt Brecht's musical collaborator in Berlin, and composed *The Threepenny Opera* and its hit 'Mack the Knife' (immortalised by a rasping Louis Armstrong).

The ticket price grants entry into all four buildings.

Gropiushaus   ARCHITECTURE
(☑ 0340-3406 5080; www.meisterhaeuser.de; Ebertallee 59; combined ticket adult/concession €7/5.50; ⊙ 11am-5pm) Walter Gropius' house is the most recently reconstructed of the Masters' Houses, opened to the public in 2014. It contains the ticket office for the remaining three Meisterhäuser, and is also used for special events.

Törten Estate   ARCHITECTURE
(Am Dreieck 1; tour €4; ⊙ tours 3pm Tue-Sun) The leafy Törten Estate, built in Dessau's south in the 1920s, is a prototype of the modern working-class estate. Although many of the 300-plus homes have been altered in ways that would have outraged their purist creator Walter Gropius (patios and rustic German doors added to a minimalist facade?), others retain their initial symmetry. To reach Törten, take tram 1 towards Dessau Süd, get off at Damaschkestrasse and follow the signs saying 'Bauhaus Architektur'.

You're free to roam the streets, but remember to be aware that this is a residential area. To have a peek inside the buildings, head to Konsumgebäude and Moses-Mendelssohn-Zentrum (☑ 0340-850 1199;

www.mendelssohn-dessau.de; Mittelring 38; €2; ⊙noon-4pm Tue-Sun).

Haus Muche/Schlemmer ARCHITECTURE

(☑0340-882 2138; www.meisterhaeuser.de; Ebertallee 65/67; combined ticket adult/concession €7/5.50; ⊙11am-5pm) Haus Muche/Schlemmer makes it apparent that the room proportions used by Bauhaus architects, and some of their design experiments, such as low balcony rails, don't really cut it in the modern world. At the same time, other features are startlingly innovative. The partially black bedroom here is intriguing; look out for the leaflet explaining the amusing story behind it – Marcel Breuer apparently burst in to paint it while reluctant owner Georg Muche was away on business.

Haus Kandinsky/Klee ARCHITECTURE

(☑0340-661 0934; www.meisterhaeuser.de; Ebertallee 69/71; combined ticket adult/concession €7/5.50; ⊙11am-5pm) Closed for renovation in 2018, Haus Kandinsky/Klee is scheduled to reopen in 2019 and is most notable for the varying pastel shades in which Wassily Kandinsky and Paul Klee painted their walls

(re-created today). There's also biographical information about the two artists and special exhibitions about their work.

Konsumgebäude HISTORIC BUILDING

(Co-op Building; ☑0340-650 8251; www.bauhaus-dessau.de; Am Dreieck 1; €2; ⊙11am-3.30pm Tue-Sun) The former Konsumgebäude building, once the centre for trade and cooperative living on the Törten Estate, today houses an information centre and a small permanent local-history exhibition.

Technikmuseum Hugo Junkers MUSEUM

(☑0340-661 1982; www.technikmuseum-dessau.de; Kühnauer Strasse 161a; adult/concession €6/3; ⊙10am-4pm Tue-Sun) Aviation fans will be wowed by the vintage aircraft on display at the Technikmuseum Hugo Junkers. Tram 1 goes straight to the museum (get off at Junkerspark) from the Hauptbahnhof.

Elberadweg CYCLING

(Elbe River Bike Trail; www.elberadweg.de) Dessau-Rosslau is an ideal hub for cycling part of the Elbe River Bike Trail, one of Germany's top three cycling routes. The trail wends its way some 860km west alongside the Elbe

---

BAUHAUS: DESIGN FOR LIFE

'Less is more' said the third and final Bauhaus director, Ludwig Mies van der Rohe. Given that this school survived fewer than 15 years, yet exerted more influence on modern design than any other, Mies was probably right. As Frank Whitford put it in *Bauhaus: World of Art* (1984): 'Everyone sitting on a chair with a tubular steel frame, using an adjustable reading lamp or living in a house partly or entirely constructed from prefabricated elements is benefiting from a revolution...largely brought about by the Bauhaus.'

Founded in Weimar in 1919 by Berlin architect Walter Gropius, this multidisciplinary school aimed to abolish the distinction between 'fine' and 'applied' arts, and to unite the artistic with daily life. Gropius reiterated that form follows function and exhorted his students to craft items with an eye towards mass production. Consequently, Bauhaus products stripped away decoration and ornamentation and returned to the fundamentals of design, with strong, clean lines.

From the very beginning, the movement attracted a roll call of the era's greatest talents, including Lyonel Feininger, Wassily Kandinsky, Paul Klee, László Moholy-Nagy and Oskar Schlemmer, plus now-legendary product designers Marianne Brandt, Marcel Breuer and Wilhelm Wagenfeld. After conservative politicians closed the Weimar school in 1925, the Bauhaus crew found a more welcoming reception in industrial Dessau.

Even here, though, right-wing political pressure continued against what was seen as the Bauhaus' undermining of traditional values, and Gropius resigned as director in 1928. He was succeeded by Swiss-born Hannes Meyer, whose Marxist sympathies meant that he, in turn, was soon replaced by Mies. The latter was at the helm when the school moved to Berlin in 1932 to escape Nazi oppression, but to no avail. Just one year later, the Nazis dissolved the school and its leading lights fled the country.

But the movement never quite died. After WWII, Gropius took over as director of Harvard's architecture school, while Mies (the architect of New York's Seagram Building) held the same post at the Illinois Institute of Technology in Chicago. Both men found long-lasting global fame as purveyors of Bauhaus' successor, the so-called International Style.

River, from the Czech border to Cuxhaven. The scenic 360km stretch in Saxony-Anhalt is particularly popular.

✯ Festivals & Events

Kurt Weill Festival   MUSIC
(www.kurt-weill.de) Although more closely associated with Berlin, and later New York, the composer Kurt Weill was born in Dessau. Every March the city hosts a Kurt Weill Festival, reprising and updating his collaborations with Bertolt Brecht, such as *The Threepenny Opera*. Performances take place in Dessau and surrounds.

🛏 Sleeping

Other than sleeping in the Bauhaus dorms (awesome) there's not much reason to overnight here, with Berlin and Leipzig so close. If you do stay, your options are relatively bland but good for the budget.

★ Bauhaus 'Prellerhaus'   HOSTEL €€
(☑ 0340-650 8318; www.bauhaus-dessau.de; Gropiusallee 38; s/d from €40/60; ℗) One for the architecture and design purists, who'll first need to come to terms with the fact that all rooms share showers and toilets. If you can swallow that, you'll be able to channel your modernist dream into something highly functional by staying in these minimally super-cool former students' quarters.

Radisson Blu Hotel
Fürst Leopold   HOTEL €€
(☑ 0340-251 50; www.hotel-dessau-city.de; Friedensplatz 1; r from €88; ℗ ❄ 🛜) Dessau-Rosslau's grandest hotel offers excellent facilities and value, with a bar, restaurant, fitness area and beauty spa. Prices vary by demand, but range mostly between €75 and €110. Take tram 1, 2 or 3 one stop from the train station to Theater or follow Fritz-Hesse-Strasse.

Hotel-Pension An den 7 Säulen   HOTEL €€
(☑ 0340-619 620; www.hotel-7-saeulen.de; Ebertallee 66; s/d incl breakfast from €65/85; ℗) Rooms at this small *Pension* are clean and nicely renovated; the owners are friendly, the garden is pleasant and the breakfast room overlooks the Meisterhäuser across the leafy street. Take bus 11 to Kornerhaus from Hauptbahnhof and walk back to Ebertallee.

🍴 Eating & Drinking

There's lots of fast food and cheap-and-cheery restaurants in this former GDR city,

but a distinct lack of world flavours or high-end cuisine.

Historically a centre for the study of art and architecture, it fits that you'll find a handful of good bars and watering holes where you can talk Kafka with the hipsters while you contemplate the colours of the Kandinksy (a copy) behind the bar.

★ Kornhaus   CAFE €€
(☑ 0340-6501 9963; www.kornhaus-dessau.de; Kornhausstrasse 146; mains €10-21) This striking Bauhaus riverside beer-and-dance hall was designed by Carl Flieger, an assistant to the school's founder, Walter Gropius. Apart from being a piece of modern architectural history, it offers the perfect spot to sit and enjoy a beer and some refreshingly light, modern German fare in the sun.

Ratskeller   GERMAN €€
(☑ 0340-221 5283; www.ratskeller-dessau.de; Zerbsterstrasse 4a; mains €8-22; ⊙ 11am-10pm) There's one in almost every town in Germany, a bar-restaurant located in the cellar of the town hall. This Ratskeller is uncharacteristically open and airy with tables outside to enjoy the view of the square. Standard German fare, including a wide range of schnitzels, and plenty of good beer, is on offer.

Brauhaus Zum alten Dessauer   PUB FOOD €€
(☑ 0340-220 5909; www.alter-dessauer.de; Lange Gasse 16; mains €9-22; ⊙ 11am-midnight) This fun, friendly, lively brewhouse serves excellent modern and traditional German food, including all the staples and, of course, a wide range of house-brewed beers. What more could you ask for at the end of a long day of sightseeing?

ℹ Information

For info on, and tours of, Bauhaus buildings (also available in English) check in with the folks operating **Bauhaus Stiftung** (Bauhaus Foundation; ☑ 0340-650 8250; www.bauhaus-dessau.de; Gropiusallee 38; ⊙ 10am-6pm) or stop by the **Dessau-Rosslau Tourist Office** (☑ 0340-204 1442; https://tourismus.dessau-rosslau.de; Zerbster Strasse 2c; ⊙ 10am-6pm Mon-Fri, to 1pm Sat; 🛈).

ℹ Getting There & Around

The A9 autobahn connects Dessau with Berlin to the northeast and Leipzig, onwards to Munich, to the south.

Direct regional services connect Dessau Rosslau to Berlin (€26.70, 1½ hours), Lutherstadt

Wittenberg (€9.30, 30 minutes), Leipzig (€14.10, 45 minutes), Halle (€17, 55 minutes) and Magdeburg (€14.30, 50 minutes).

Bus and tram tickets for a single/day pass cost €1.80/4.90.

For bicycle rentals, try **Beckers Radhaus** (☑ 0340-216 8989; www.beckers-radhaus. de; Kavalierstrasse 82; bikes per day from €15; ⊙ 9am-6pm Mon-Fri, 10am-3pm Sat) and **Mobilitätszentrale** (☑ 0340-213 366; Hauptbahnhof; bikes per 2hr from €5; ⊙ 7am-5pm Mon-Fri, 9am-1pm Sat).

Gartenreich Dessau-Wörlitz

The Gartenreich (Garden Realm) Dessau-Wörlitz is one of the finest garden ensembles in Germany. Its parks reflect the vision of Prince Leopold III Friedrich Franz von Anhalt-Dessau (1740–1817). A highly educated man, Leopold travelled to Holland, Italy, France and Switzerland for inspiration on how to apply the philosophy of the Enlightenment to the design of a landscape that would harmoniously combine nature, architecture and art.

Each of the six English-style gardens comes with its own palace and other buildings, in styles ranging from neoclassical to baroque to neo-Gothic. They were added to Unesco's World Heritage list in 2000 and are also protected under the Biosphärenreservat Mittelelbe (www.mittelelbe.com).

All parks are free and can be roamed during daylight hours (most aren't fenced off), but the palaces charge admission and have their own opening hours.

⊙ Sights

★ **Wörlitz Park & Schloss Wörlitz** PALACE
(☑ 039404-310 09; www.woerlitz-information.de; Förstergasse 26, Wörlitz; palace tour €5; ⊙ 10am-6pm Apr-Oct, to 4pm Mon-Fri Nov-Mar) With peacocks feeding on the lawn before a neo-Gothic house, a tree-lined stream flowing towards a Grecian-style temple and a gap in a hedge framing a distant villa, the 112-hectare English-style Wörlitz Park is the pinnacle of Prince Leopold's garden region. Take your sweet time to saunter amid this mosaic of paths, hedges and follies, but don't even think about picnicking on the sprawling lawns: even walking on them is very much verboten, as is bicycling within park grounds.

On the edge of the park nearest the town lies Prince Leopold's former country house, the neoclassical Schloss Wörlitz, which is still filled with original late-18th-century furniture and decorations.

Bus 334 does the 30-minute trip from Dessau-Rosslau to Wörlitz roughly every two hours between 6am and 5.30pm. From late March to early October, there's also a 35-minute train service on Wednesday, Saturday and Sunday. Check the timetable carefully before heading out or, better yet, check with the information kiosk Mobilitätszentrale outside the train station. By road from Dessau-Rosslau, take the B185 east to the B107 north, which brings you right into town.

Schloss & Park Grosskühnau GARDENS
(www.gartenreich.com; Ebenhanstrasse 8, Grosskühnau; ⊙ 11am-6pm Tue-Sun) Visitors are free to roam the delightful gardens, which include vineyards and partially restored fruit plantations. The neoclassical Schloss Grosskühnau, completed in 1780, currently houses the administrative offices of Kulturstiftung DessauWörlitz and is not open to the public. The palace is situated at the edge of Lake Grosskühnau, about 4km west of Dessau-Rosslau.

Schloss & Park Georgium PALACE
(☑ 039404-613 874; www.gartenreich.com; Puschkinallee 100, Dessau-Rosslau; palace adult/concession €3/2; ⊙ 10am-5pm Tue-Sun) The sprawling 18th-century Park Georgium is anchored by its neoclassical palace, now a picture gallery showcasing German and Dutch old masters such as Rubens and Lucas Cranach. The leafy grounds are also dotted with ponds and fake Roman ruins, including a triumphal arch and a round temple. The park is just a five-minute walk from Dessau-Rosslau Hauptbahnhof. Restoration of the palace was underway at the time of writing.

Schloss & Park Oranienbaum PALACE
(☑ 039404-202 59; www.gartenreich.com; Schlosstrasse 9a, Oranienbaum-Wörlitz; palace €7.50; ⊙ 10am-5pm Tue-Sun May-Sep) Ongoing restoration is underway at this delightful Dutch-inspired baroque ensemble, south of Wörlitz, but visitors can access most of the rooms and in some cases, take part in the restoration process. Oranienbaum is 14km southeast of Dessau or 6km south of Wörlitz. To get here, take bus 331.

Schloss & Park Mosigkau PALACE
(☑ 039404-521 139; www.gartenreich.com; Knobelsdorffallee 3, Dessau-Rosslau; palace €7.50; ⊙ 11am-6pm Wed-Sun May-Sep, to 7pm Sat & Sun Apr & Oct) Schloss Mosigkau is a petite rococo palace that's been called a 'miniature Sanssouci'. Many of its 17 rooms retain their original furnishings, although the highlight is the Galleriesaal, with paintings by Rubens and van Dyck. In summer, play hide-and-seek in the leafy labyrinth. It's located about 7km southwest of central Dessau. To get here, take bus 16 to Schloss.

Schloss & Park Luisium PALACE
(☑ 039404-218 3711; www.gartenreich.com; Schloss Luisium, Dessau-Rosslau; palace €7.50; ⊙ 11am-5pm Sat & Sun Apr-Nov) Schloss Luisium is an intimate neoclassical refuge framed by an idyllic English garden scattered with neo-Gothic and classical follies. East of central Dessau, about 4km towards Wörlitz, it is reached via bus 13 to Vogelherd.

ⓘ Information

The Dessau-Rosslau Tourist Office (p279) has details and information on the Garden Realm, or stop by **Wörlitz-Information** (☑ 034905-310 09; www.woerlitz.de; Förstergasse 26; ⊙ 9am-6pm).

There's also the nature-oriented **Biosphärenreservat Mittelelbe Info** (☑ 034904-4060; www.mittelelbe.com; Am Kapenschlösschen 3, Oranienbaum) en route to Schloss Oranienbaum. If you ask nicely, the staff can direct you to a nearby beaver compound, where you can observe the clever critters through a screen.

ⓘ Getting There & Around

The six parks are scattered over 142 sq km, with the town of Dessau-Rosslau loosely at the heart of the Garden Realm.

Direct regional train services connect Dessau-Rosslau to Berlin (€26.70, 1½ hours), Lutherstadt Wittenberg (€9.30, 30 minutes), Leipzig (€14.10, 45 minutes), Halle (€17, 55 minutes) and Magdeburg (€14.30, 50 minutes). Although there is imited access to the parks by public transport, this really is a region that is best explored by car.

The A9 autobahn connects Dessau with Berlin to the northeast and Leipzig, onwards to Munich, to the south, but if you're arriving by train, a number of car-rental agencies have offices near Dessau-Rosslau station. If you're unable to drive, be sure to check in with the local tourist offices for up-to-date public-transport information on the parks you wish to visit.

The most central park is Georgium, just five minutes' walk from Dessau-Rosslau train station. The most impressive, Wörlitz, is situated about 18km east of Dessau-Rosslau, making it also the furthest afield.

Halle

☑ 0345 / POP 231,600

Saxony-Anhalt's largest city, Halle has a handful of impressive museums spanning themes as diverse as art, archaeology and the Beatles. It's most famous for being the birthplace of Georg Friedrich Händel.

Halle was once a hotbed for the GDR's chemical industry. When the GDR collapsed, the chemical factories gradually disappeared and the smoke began to clear. Change was slow, but some intelligent planning and major projects leading up to Halle's 1200th birthday in 2006, combined with the presence of some 25,000 students attending the Martin Luther University, injected some life into this very old town.

Once more, though, Halle has seen better days: its beautiful bits are beautiful indeed, but if you look closely into its darker corners, you might make out the hairline cracks that are beginning to appear on the facade of unified Germany.

⊙ Sights

★ **Landesmuseum für Vorgeschichte** MUSEUM
(State Museum of Pre-History; ☑ 0345-524 7363; www.lda-lsa.de/en/state_museum_of_prehistory; Richard Wagner Strasse 9; adult/concession €6/4; ⊙ 9am-5pm Tue-Fri, 10am-6pm Sat & Sun) This phenomenal collection of major archaeological finds is one of the most significant in Europe. Priceless permanent exhibits shed light on the early to late Stone Age and early Bronze Age. Highlights include the famous bronze Nebra Sky Disk (the oldest known concrete depiction of astronomical phenomena), the oldest known recorded fingerprint, and displays on the discovery of the uniquely preserved 4600-year-old graves of Eulau. There's usually a special visiting exhibition, and audioguides are available.

Kunstmuseum Moritzburg GALLERY
(Moritzburg Art Gallery; ☑ 0345-212 5911; www.kunstmuseum-moritzburg.de; Friedemann-Bach-Platz 5; adult/concession €8/6; ⊙ 10am-6pm Thu-Tue) The late-Gothic Moritzburg castle forms a fantastic setting for this superb permanent collection of art. The addition of a glass and aluminium roof over the north and west wings, which had been ruined since the

Thirty Years' War (1618–48), nearly doubled the exhibition area. Airy and sky-lit, the new space is entirely dedicated to modern art. Older parts of the castle showcase works from medieval times to the 19th century.

Marktkirche Unser Lieben Frauen CHURCH
(Marktplatz 12; Luther exhibit €2; ⊙10am-5pm Mon-Sat, from 3pm Sun) Halle's central square has no fewer than five towers. One of these is the freestanding bell tower known as Roter Turm, but the other four rise up from the bulky late-Gothic Marktkirche. Inside is its prized possession, Luther's original death mask of wax (ask the attendant to take you into the separate room to see it). It also has a Renaissance pulpit from which he preached.

Beatles Museum MUSEUM
(☑0345-290 3900; www.beatlesmuseum.net; Alter Markt 12; adult/concession €6/4; ⊙10am-6pm Tue-Sun) Take a 'magical mystery tour' through the life and music of the Fab Four at the only year-round, though overly commercial, dedicated Beatles Museum on the European continent. Hard-core fan Rainer Moers has amassed enough knick-knacks to cram three floors with baby photos, birth certificates, album covers, film posters, wigs, jigsaws and even talcum powder – nothing is too trivial to be displayed.

Händel-Haus MUSEUM
(☑0345-500 900; www.handel-house.com; Grosse Nikolaistrasse 5; adult/concession €5/3.50; ⊙10am-6pm Tue-Sun) The house in which Georg Friedrich Händel (1685–1759) was born is now the Händel-Haus. An exhibit inside charts the composer's life, achievements and impact on the evolution of classical music, with an emphasis on his wider European career. Descriptions are in German and English, and the free audioguide is also useful.

🛏 Sleeping

Halle has plenty of budget hotels, but there are not too many reasons to stay overnight, with Leipzig a short distance away.

Dormero Rotes Ross HOTEL €€
(☑0345-233 430; www.dormero-hotel-rotes-ross. de; Leipziger Strasse 76; d from €74; P❄🛜) This four-star hotel boasts lots of marble, dark woods, heavy curtains and old-world-style furnishings. It has excellent amenities, including a sauna and wellness area with whirlpools, and benefits from a central location. Online discounts are available.

Ankerhotel Halle HOTEL €€
(☑0345-232 3200; www.ankerhof.de; Ankerstrasse 2a; s/d/ste from €79/108/160; P❄@) Walls clad in local stone and ceilings supported by heavy wooden beams hark back to the 19th century, when this was the Royal Customs Office. Completely modernised, it's now one of Halle's most charming hotels, with stylish, good-sized rooms; the nicest have river views. There's even a gym and sauna for sweating it out.

Take tram 2, 5, 10 or 11 to Ankerstrasse.

🍴 Eating

Dining options are standard for a city of this size, with plenty of fast food and takeaway counters around the Markt and a handful of above-average restaurants dotted about the city.

Ökoase VEGETARIAN €
(☑0345-290 1604; www.oekoase-halle.de; Kleine Ulrichstrasse 2; mains €6-14; ⊙8.30am-4.30pm Mon-Sat; 🥄) Vegetarian eatery featuring soups, salads and main dishes with curry and other infusions, changing on a weekly basis.

⭐**Schnitzelwirtin** GERMAN €€
(☑0345-2029938; www.schnitzelwirtin.de; Grosse Märkerstraße 18; mains €12-24; ⊙noon-10pm Mon-Sat, to 3pm Sun) If you're a fan of the breaded cutlets you must hurry to this fabulous *schnitzel-haus* which fries up more versions of the humble schnitzel than you can imagine. Dishes come in small and large sizes, but you really need two stomachs to get through a large! In summer, enjoy the lovely beer garden out back. Friendly staff.

⭐**Immergrün** INTERNATIONAL €€
(☑0345-521 6056; www.restaurant-immergruen.de; Kleine Klausstrasse 2; mains €13-24; ⊙5pm-midnight Tue-Sat) Clever, creatively prepared seasonal fish, poultry and meat dishes are served from a small menu that changes monthly and usually features a 'green' theme. Multicourse menus are available. You're strongly advised to make advance reservations for a table at this highly lauded establishment.

Hallesches Brauhaus GERMAN €€
(☑0345-212 570; www.halleschesbrauhaus.de; Grosse Nikolaistrasse 2; mains €9-15; ⊙4pm-midnight Mon-Fri, from 11am Sat, noon-9pm Sun) This brewhouse is a local institution, known for its crisp light beers and heavy dark ones, its lively atmosphere and its hearty pub fare, including *Flammkuchen*.

🍷 Drinking & Entertainment

Finding a party pen to match your mood is easy in Halle's trifecta of fun strips: Kleine Ulrichstrasse, Sternstrasse and the Bermudadreieck (around Seebener Strasse and Burgstrasse near Burg Giebichstein). Also consult the free magazines *Blitz* or *Frizz*.

Turm CLUB
(📞548 4686; www.turm-halle.de; Friedemann-Bach-Platz 5; ☺Wed, Fri & Sat) This old student club in the Moritzburg (p281) has DJs pressing out the latest sounds and hosts various events, including poetry slams some Sundays; check the website for event times.

Objekt 5 LIVE MUSIC
(📞4782 3360; www.objekt5.de; Seebener Strasse 5) This classic venue hosts folk, rock and occasional avant-garde concerts and regular DJs. Check the program for times. Take tram 8 to Burg Giebichenstein, the castle ruin nearby.

🛈 Information

Halle Tourist Office (📞122 9984; www.stadt marketing-halle.de; Marktplatz 13; ☺9am-7pm Mon-Fri, 10am-4pm Sat)

🛈 Getting There & Away

AIR
Leipzig-Halle Airport (LEJ; 📞0341-2240; www.leipzig-halle-airport.de) lies midway between both cities, and is served by domestic and international flights. The airport is linked with Halle Hauptbahnhof by frequent rail services (€6, 11 minutes).

CAR
From Leipzig, take the A14 west to the B100. The A14 connects Halle and Magdeburg in about one hour. The B91 runs south from Halle and links up with the A9 autobahn, which connects Munich and Berlin.

TRAIN
Leipzig and Halle are linked by frequent IC (€12, 25 minutes) and cheaper regional trains. IC and ICE trains also service Magdeburg (€22.50, 50 minutes) and Berlin (€48.50, 1¼ hours), respectively. Local trains connect Halle with Lutherstadt Eisleben (€9.50, 40 minutes) and Lutherstadt Wittenberg (€15.40, one hour).

🛈 Getting Around

Trams 2, 5, 7 and 9 run from the train station to the Marktplatz. Rides cost €2.10 (€1.50 for up to four stops) or €5 for day cards. Buy tickets from machines at many stops.

Lutherstadt Eisleben

📞03475 / POP 26,190

The former mining town of Lutherstadt Eisleben focuses almost exclusively on its native son Martin Luther (1483–1546). It may seem odd for a well-travelled man whose ideas revolutionised Europe to have died in the town where he was born. However, as Luther himself put it before his death, *'Mein Vaterland war Eisleben'* ('Eisleben was my fatherland').

👁 Sights

Most sights are knotted together around the Markt, just north of Hallesche Strasse, the main thoroughfare. To get there from the station, it's a 15-minute walk via Bahnhofsring (turn left on leaving the station) and Bahnhofstrasse. Buses going past Markt usually meet the trains.

Luther's Sterbehaus MUSEUM
(Luther's Death House; 📞714 7840; www.martin luther.de; Andreaskirchplatz 7; adult/concession €5/2.50; ☺10am-5pm, closed Mon Nov-Apr) This museum, expanded and updated in 2013, focuses on three themes: how the culture of death has evolved over the centuries; Eisleben native son Martin Luther's thoughts about death; and the last 24 hours of the religious reformer's life. The museum's prize literary exhibit is a Bible from 1541 – the last Luther worked on before his death here in 1546.

Luther's Geburtshaus MUSEUM
(Luther's Birthplace Museum; 📞03475-714 7814; www.martinluther.de; Lutherstrasse 15; adult/concession €5/2.50; ☺10am-5pm, closed Mon Nov-Apr) This house where the famous religious reformer Martin Luther was born has been a memorial site since 1693, though it has been updated since then. The original house is furnished in period style, while annex-wing exhibits focus on Luther's family and aspects of the society in which he grew up.

St Annenkirche CHURCH
(Annenkircheplatz; ☺10am-4pm Mon-Sat, from noon Sun May-Oct) This church features a stunning *Steinbilder-Bibel* (stone-picture Bible; 1585), the only one of its kind in Europe, and a wittily decorated pulpit. While district vicar, Martin Luther stayed in the apartments of the St Annenkirche, 10 minutes west of the Markt in the hills above Eisleben.

St Petri Pauli Kirche
CHURCH

(Petrikirchplatz; €1; ⊙10am-4pm Mon-Sat, from 11am Sun May-Oct) Notable for being the church where Martin Luther was baptised.

St Andreaskirche
CHURCH

(Andreaskirchplatz; €1; ⊙10am-4pm Mon-Sat, from 11am Sun May-Oct) Martin Luther delivered his last sermons in the St Andreaskirche, a late-Gothic hall church on the hill behind the central Markt.

🛏 Sleeping & Eating

There are a few good accommodation choices for such a little town, courtesy of the work done around the 500th anniversary of the Reformation in 2017.

⭐Hotel Graf von Mansfeld
HOTEL €€

(⏹663 00; www.hotel-eisleben.de; Markt 56; s/d/ste from €68/79/129; P@🛜) Eisleben's premier in-town hotel is a classic outpost of charm and tradition. Although over 500 years old, it has seriously slicked-up rooms with four-poster beds, and bright and airy flair. No two rooms are alike. The partner-run wellness area has three saunas for an extra fee.

Deckert's Hotel am Katherinsift
HOTEL €€

(⏹03475-632 670; www.deckerts-hotel.de; Sängerhauser Strasse 12/13; s/d incl breakfast from €65/85; P🛜) This small hotel in a historic building offers a great location a few minutes' walk from the Markt, and spotless, light-filled rooms with neutral furnishings and modern conveniences. Recommended.

Fellini
ITALIAN €€

(⏹03475-748 015; Sangerhäuser Strasse 10; mains €8-24; ⊙11am-2.30pm & 5.30-11pm) Friendly, efficient table service, a busy atmosphere, tasty authentic pizza and pasta (the carbonara is just right – not too creamy), reasonable prices and a nice ambience both indoors and al-fresco, earn Fellini our warm recommendation.

Plan B
BAR

(⏹03475-711 788; Markt 33; ⊙10am-6pm Mon-Fri, from noon Sat) This sleek, modern cafe-bar offers a contrast to the historic aspects of Eisleben. As well as serving wine and cocktails (in broad daylight), it does *Flammkuchen*, antipasti and salads.

ℹ Information

Lutherstadt Eisleben Tourist Office
(⏹03475-602 124; www.lutherstaedte-eisle-ben-mansfeld.de; Hallesche Strasse 4; ⊙10am-5pm Mon & Wed-Fri, to 6pm Tue, to 1pm Sat)

ℹ Getting There & Away

Eisleben is a 30 minute west of Halle on the B80.

There are frequent trains to Halle (€9.50, 40 minutes), where you can change for Lutherstadt Wittenberg (€23.90, 1¾ hours) and Leipzig (€17, 70 minutes).

Lutherstadt Wittenberg

📞 03491 / POP 50,408

As its full name suggests, Wittenberg is first and foremost about Martin Luther (1483–1546), the monk who triggered the German Reformation by publishing his 95 theses against church corruption in 1517, as the story goes, by provocatively nailing it to the door of the Schlosskirche in this very town.

Today, Wittenberg retains its significance for the world's 340 million Protestants, including 66 million Lutherans, and for those who simply admire Luther for his principled stand against authority. Sometimes called the 'Rome of the Protestants', its many Reformation-related sites garnered the city World Heritage status in 1996. If you're not into history or religion, it's still an interesting, if unremarkable, place to visit.

A university town since 1502, the Wittenberg of Luther's era was a hotbed of progressive thinking that also saw priests get married and educators such as Luther's friend Philipp Melanchthon argue for schools to accept female pupils.

◎ Sights

⭐Lutherhaus
MUSEUM

(⏹03491-420 3118; www.martinluther.de; Collegienstrasse 54; adult/concession €8/6; ⊙9am-6pm) Even those with no previous interest in the Reformation will likely be fascinated by the state-of-the-art exhibits in the Lutherhaus, the former monastery turned Luther family home, operated as a museum since 1883. Through an engaging mix of accessible narrative, artefacts, famous oil paintings and interactive multimedia stations, you'll learn about the man, his times and his impact on world history. Highlights include Cranach's *Ten Commandments* in the refectory and an original room furnished by Luther in 1535.

Cranach-Höfe
GALLERY

(⏹03491-420 1911; Markt 4; adult/concession €4/3; ⊙10am-5pm Mon-Sat, from 1pm Sun) The

Lutherstadt Wittenberg

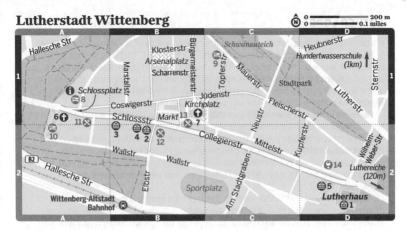

Lutherstadt Wittenberg

former residence and workplace of Lucas Cranach, considered to be among the most prolific German painters and printmakers of the Reformation, have been rebooted as a beautifully restored cultural complex built around two courtyards that often echo with music and readings. There's a permanent exhibit on the man, his life and his contemporaries.

Schlosskirche CHURCH
(Castle Church; ☎03491-402 585; www.schloss kirche-wittenberg.de; Schlossplatz; ⊙10am-6pm Mon-Sat, from 11.30am Sun) Did he or didn't he nail those 95 theses (p286) to the door of the Schlosskirche? We'll never know for sure, since the original portal was destroyed by fire in 1760 and replaced in 1858 with a massive bronze version inscribed with Martin Luther's theses in Latin. Luther himself is buried inside the church below the pulpit, opposite his friend and fellow reformer Philipp Melanchthon.

Haus der Geschichte MUSEUM
(House of History; ☎03491-409 004; www.pflug ev.de; Schlossstrasse 6; adult/concession €6/4.50; ⊙10am-6pm Tue-Sun) If you want to catch a glimpse of daily life in the region, especially life beyond the former Iron Curtain, pop by the Haus der Geschichte. The ground floor has a long-running special exhibition on German–Russian relations (many Russian soldiers were stationed in Lutherstadt Wittenberg during the GDR era), and other sections contain living rooms, kids' rooms and kitchens from the GDR era and before. The top floor is dedicated to children's toys from this same 60-year period.

Melanchthon Haus MUSEUM
(☎03491-420 3110; www.martinluther.de; Collegienstrasse 60; adult/concession €5/2.50; ⊙10am-6pm) This museum, expanded in 2013, occupies the former quarters of Philipp Melanchthon, an expert in ancient languages who helped Martin Luther translate the Bible into German from Greek and

LUTHER LORE

It's been so often repeated that Martin Luther nailed a copy of his revolutionary theses to the door of Wittenberg's Schlosskirche on 31 October 1517 that only serious scholars continue to argue to the contrary. Certainly, Luther did write 95 theses challenging some of the Catholic practices of the time, especially the selling of 'indulgences' to forgive sins and reduce the buyer's time in purgatory. However, it's another question entirely as to whether he publicised them in the way popular legend suggests.

Believers in the tale point to the fact that the Schlosskirche's door was used as a bulletin board of sorts by the university, that the alleged posting took place the day before the affluent congregation poured into the church on All Saints' Day (1 November), and the fact that at Luther's funeral, his influential friend Philipp Melanchthon said he witnessed Luther's deed. But Melanchthon didn't arrive in town until 1518 – the year after the supposed event. It's also odd that Luther's writings never once mentioned such a highly radical act.

While it is known that Luther sent his theses to the local archbishop to provoke discussion, some locals think it would have been out of character for a devout monk, interested mainly in an honest debate, to challenge the system so flagrantly without first exhausting all other options. In any event, nailed to the church door or not, the net effect of Luther's theses was the same. They triggered the Reformation and Protestantism, altering the way that large sections of the world's Christian population worship to this day.

Hebrew, becoming the preacher's friend and most eloquent advocate. The historic wing authentically re-creates the atmosphere in which Melanchthon lived. The modern annex houses an exhibition on Melanchthon's life, work and influence.

Historische Druckerstube GALLERY
(Historical Print Shop; Schlossstrasse 1; tour €3; ⊙9am-noon & 1-5pm Mon-Fri, 10am-1.30pm Sat) This gallery sells ancient-looking black-and-white sketches of Martin Luther, both typeset and printed by hand. Take a tour to hear the owner explain the sketches and early printing techniques. It's part of the Cranach-Höfe complex of courtyards (accessed separately from the main courtyards).

Luthereiche LANDMARK
(Luther Oak; cnr Lutherstrasse & Am Bahnhof) This oak tree marks the spot where, on 10 December 1520, Luther burned the papal bull (a treatise issued by then-Pope Leo X ordering his excommunication) and a number of other books on church law; the tree itself was only planted around 1830.

Stadtkirche Wittenberg CHURCH
(✆03491-628 30; www.stadtkirchengemeinde-wittenberg.de; Jüdenstrasse 35; ⊙10am-6pm Mon-Sat, from 11.30am Sun) The Stadt- und Pfarrkirche St Marien (Stadtkirche Wittenberg) was where Martin Luther's ecumeni-

cal revolution began, with the world's first Protestant worship services in 1521. It was also here that Luther preached his famous Lectern sermons in 1522, and where he married ex-nun Katharina von Bora three years later. Ongoing renovations continue.

Hundertwasserschule ARCHITECTURE
(Hundertwasser School; ✆03491-877 780; www.hundertwasserschule.de; Strasse der Völkerfreundschaft 130; tour adult/concession €2/1; ⊙1.30-4pm Tue-Fri, from 10am Sat & Sun) How would you like to study grammar and algebra in a building where trees sprout from the windows and gilded onion domes balance above a rooftop garden? This fantastical environment is everyday reality for the lucky pupils of Wittenberg's Hundertwasserschule. It's the penultimate work of eccentric Viennese artist, architect and eco-visionary Friedensreich Hundertwasser, who was famous for quite literally thinking 'outside the box'. In Wittenberg, he transformed a boxy GDR-era concrete monstrosity into this colourful and curvy dreamscape.

⭐ Festivals & Events

Wittenberger Reformationsfest RELIGIOUS
(www.wittenberger-reformationsfest.de) This annual festival, which begins on 31 October and runs into November, celebrates and commemorates the start of the Reformation.

Christians from around the world flock to town for a changing program of talks, religious events, performances and workshops.

Luthers Hochzeit
RELIGIOUS

(www.lutherhochzeit.de) Wittenberg is busiest during Luther's Wedding Festival, held in early or mid-June, when folks from all around Germany come to celebrate this nuptial re-enactment with much feasting, merriment and seemingly everyone in town dressed in period costume.

🛏 Sleeping

The tourist office operates a free room reservation service. Private rooms start at €19 per person.

DJH Hostel
HOSTEL €

(☑ 03491-505 205; www.jugendherberge-wittenberg.de; Schlossstrasse 14/15; dm €23-26; P @ ⊙) Wittenberg's excellent youth hostel has 40 bright rooms sleeping up to six people. Each are equipped with bathrooms, bedside reading lamps and private cabinets. Linen is included.

Alte Canzley
HOTEL €€

(☑ 03491-429 190; www.alte-canzley.de; Schlossplatz 3-5; s/d from €79/94; P @ ⊙) This lovely boutique hotel is located in a 14th-century building opposite the Schlosskirche. Each of the eight spacious units is furnished in dark woods and natural hues, named for a major historical figure and equipped with a kitchenette.

Am Schwanenteich
PENSION €€

(☑ 03491-402 807; www.wittenberg-schwanen teich.de; Töpferstrasse 1; s/d from €48/89; P ❋ ⊙) If it's friendly, familiar ambience and pleasant, comfortable, spotlessly clean rooms you seek, this humble *Pension* fits the bill. Great value.

🍴 Eating & Drinking

There's a handful of good restaurants in town, which upped its game in preparation for the millions of visitors who stopped by to celebrate the 500th anniversary of the Reformation in 2017.

Bittersüss
CAFE €

(☑ 03491-876 4030; www.meinbittersuess.de; Schlossstrasse 22; sweets from €4; ⊙ noon-6pm Mon & Sun, to 10pm Tue-Sat; ⊙) There's not a lot of bitter but a whole lot of sweet to this handsome, family-run cafe-by-day (serving delicious cakes, waffles, coffee and ice

cream) and bar-by-night (with some easy libations for the grown-ups). There's free wi-fi, too.

Tante Emmas Bier- & Caféhaus
GERMAN €€

(☑ 03491-419 757; www.tante-emma-wittenberg. de; Markt 9; mains €9-18; ⊙ 9am-5pm Mon, to midnight Tue-Sun) Take a step back to the 'good old times' in this German country kitchen, serving stodgy, traditional homestyle German fare...and beer! Servers wear frilly white aprons and the room is chock-full of bric-a-brac – from dolls and books to irons and a gramophone.

Brauhaus Wittenberg
GERMAN €€

(☑ 03491-433 130; www.brauhaus-wittenberg.de; Markt 6, Im Beyerhof; mains €8-18; ⊙ 11am-11pm) Wittenberg's brewhouse, with its cobbled courtyard, indoor brewery and shiny copper vats, thrums with the noise of people having a good time. The menu is hearty, but also features smaller dishes for waist-watchers. Oh, and there's beer also. This is a very fun spot.

Independent
BAR

(☑ 03491-413 257; Collegienstrasse 44; ⊙ 11am-2am Mon-Sat, from 5pm Sun) This popular bar is fresh from a facelift and it stands out from the crowd among the several other interesting bar/eateries you'll find all along Collegienstrasse.

❶ Information

Lutherstadt Wittenberg Tourist Office
(☑ 03491-498 610; www.lutherstadt-witten berg.de/en/service/tourist-information; Schlossplatz 2; ⊙ 9am-6pm Mon-Fri, 10am-4pm Sat & Sun)

❶ Getting There & Around

Wittenberg is connected to Leipzig and Halle (both €21.50, both one hour), and to Berlin by high-speed ICE trains (€34, 45 minutes) and regional services (€26, 1¼ hours). When coming from Berlin, be sure to board for 'Lutherstadt Wittenberg', as there's also a Wittenberge west of the capital.

The town is easily explored on foot or by bicycle. Parking enforcement is quite stringent, so use the car parks on the fringes of the Altstadt (such as near Elbtor and along Fleischerstrasse).

For bike rental, try **Fahrradhaus Kralisch** (☑ 03941-403 703; www.fahrradhaus-kralisch. de; Jüdenstrasse 11; bikes per 24hr €9; ⊙ 9am-6pm Mon-Fri, to noon Sat).

Magdeburg

☎0391 / POP 232,400

The capital of Saxony-Anhalt is one of the country's oldest cities, founded some 1200 years ago and home to the first Gothic cathedral on German soil. Magdeburg's newest architectural attraction, meanwhile, is the whimsical Grüne Zitadelle (Green Citadel), the last building of eccentric artist-architect Friedensreich Hundertwasser.

Few people could deny that Magdeburg is aesthetically challenged, thanks to WWII bombs and socialist city planners in love with wide boulevards and prefab concrete apartment blocks, the so-called *Plattenbauten*. But the Elbe River – demoted to industrial waterway in GDR times – is again a vital part of the city's green side, lined with beer gardens, beach bars, a promenade and a paved bikeway. The most historic parts of town are Hegelstrasse and nearby Hasselbachplatz.

Sights

Wasserstrassenkreuz BRIDGE

(www.wasserstrassenkreuz-magdeburg.de) You'll rub your eyes in disbelief when you first see it: a massive, water-filled bridge straddling the Elbe River. The Wasserstrassenkreuz is Europe's longest canal bridge and a miracle of modern engineering. The 918m-long 'bathtub' links two major shipping canals and has made life a lot easier for barge captains navigating between Berlin and western Germany.

It's about 15km northeast of central Magdeburg. Take the Magdeburg-Rothensee exit off the A2 or rent a bicycle and pedal along the scenic Elberadweg (p278).

Dom CHURCH

(www.magdeburgerdom.de; Am Dom 1; tour adult/concession €4/2; ⏲10am-5pm) Magdeburg's main historical landmark traces its roots back to 937 when Otto I founded a Benedictine monastery and built it into a fully fledged cathedral within two decades. The burial place of the king and his English wife Editha, it's packed with numerous artistic highlights ranging from the delicate 13th-century Magdeburg Virgins sculptures to a haunting anti-war memorial by Ernst Barlach. The original building was destroyed by a fire, then rebuilt as a Gothic three-aisled basilica with transept, choir and pointed windows.

Kunstmuseum Kloster Unser Lieben Frauen GALLERY

(☎0391-565 020; www.kunstmuseum-magdeburg.de; Regierungsstrasse 4-6; adult/concession €5/3; ⏲10am-5pm Tue-Sun, to 6pm Sat & Sun) Magdeburg's oldest building, a decommissioned medieval monastery, is now a museum presenting regional sculptures and contemporary art from Saxony-Anhalt. The front door, designed by popular local artist Heinrich Apel (b 1935), is fun: knock with the woman's necklace and push down on the man's hat to enter. Admission to the cloister is free.

Elbauenpark PARK

(www.elbauenpark.de; adult/concession €3/2; ⏲park 9am-8pm, butterfly house & Jahrtausenturm 10am-6pm Tue-Sun Apr-Oct) The Elbauenpark was carved out of the landscape for a 1999 garden exhibition, and has rose, sculpture and other gardens along with a butterfly house. Its most unusual attraction, though, is the conical, 60m-high *Jahrtausendturm* (Millennial Tower), which bills itself as the world's tallest wooden tower. Inside is a display on history from ancient times to the present, including a Foucault pendulum. Take tram 5 to Herrenkrug or tram 6 to Messegelände.

Grüne Zitadelle ARCHITECTURE

(Green Citadel; ☎0391-620 8655; www.gruene-zitadelle.de; Breiter Weg 9; tour adult/concession €6/5; ⏲information office 9am-2pm) This piglet-pink building with trees growing from its facade and meadows sprouting on its rooftops was the final design of Viennese artist Friedensreich Hundertwasser. Completed in 2005, it reflects his philosophy of creating unique spaces in harmony with nature, an 'oasis for humanity'. Inside are offices, flats and shops, as well as a small hotel and a cafe. If you understand German, join the one-hour guided tours to learn more about the man and his intriguing vision.

Sleeping

Magdeburg has two interesting hotels that might be enough for some folks to consider overnighting here. Most tourists choose to stay in Berlin or Leipzig.

DJH Hostel HOSTEL €

(☎0391-532 1010; www.jugendherberge.de/jh/magdeburg; Leiterstrasse 10; dm €23-26; P@🛜) Rooms in this large, modern hostel have

Magdeburg

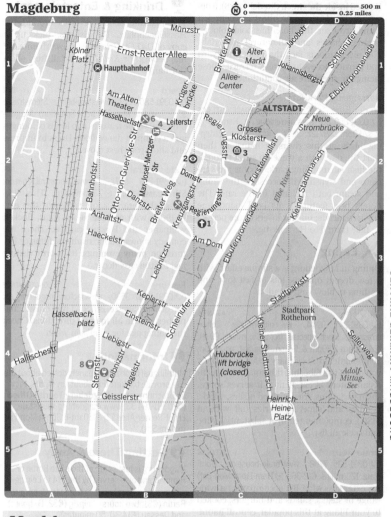

Magdeburg

◎ Sights

1 Dom	C3
2 Grüne Zitadelle	B2
3 Kunstmuseum Kloster Unser Lieben Frauen	C2

⌂ Sleeping

4 DJH Hostel	B2
Grüne Zitadelle	(see 2)

⊗ Eating

5 Bralo House	B2
6 Qilin	B2

⊙ Drinking & Nightlife

7 Café Central	B4
8 Stern	A4

shower and toilet attached and there's a family floor with a kiddie romper room. Linen is included.

★ **Grüne Zitadelle** BOUTIQUE HOTEL €€
(☎0391-620 780; www.arthotel-magdeburg.de; Breiter Weg 9; s/d from €98/104; P❋☎)

Housed inside the Green Citadel (p288), a design by the Austrian architect Friedenreich Hundertwasser, this hotel has bold colours, organic shapes and all-natural materials. The nicest rooms face the inner courtyard and provide access to a grassy terrace. Those facing the street are air-conditioned.

Herrenkrug Parkhotel
an der Elbe   HERITAGE HOTEL €€€
(☑0391-850 80; www.herrenkrug.de; Herrenkrug 3; s/d from €89/128; P@🅿🛜🐾) Rise to chirping birds at this riverside mansion, then start the day with a wake-up stroll through the lush surrounding park. Rooms are spacious and stylish, with access to the sauna and steam bath included in the rate. The hotel's best feature is its bold, handsome art-deco facade: one for lovers of the period.

Take tram 6 to Herrenkrug.

✗ Eating

Dining in Magdeburg is a simple affair, with a few decent options, lots of fast food and nothing to blow your mind.

★Qilin   ASIAN €€
(☑0391-243 9944; www.qilin-md.de; Leiterstrasse 1; lunch specials from €6, mains €9-21; ☺11.30am-2.30pm & 5-11pm Mon-Sat, noon-9pm Sun) Magdeburg's culinary scene won't blow you out of the Elbe, but this small, sleek pan-Asian eatery is excellent – it serves soups, sushi variations, fried seafood dishes, salads, noodles and superb stir-fries (all without MSG), complemented by a substantial wine and cocktail list.

Bralo House   STEAK €€
(☑0391-535 7708; www.bralo-house.de; Domplatz 12; mains €12-36; ☺11am-11pm Mon-Sat) An extensive wine list accompanies a wide range of steaks, salads and burgers, cooked to your liking at this popular, central haunt. There's not a lot for either vegetarians or pescatarians.

Die Saison   INTERNATIONAL €€€
(☑0391-850 80; www.herrenkrug.de; Herrenkrug Parkhotel an der Elbe, Herrenkrug 3; mains €20-36; ☺noon-3pm & 5-11pm) Classic German cuisine gets a modern international twist within the ornately detailed dark-green walls of the stylish art-deco dining room at this robust hotel.

🍷 Drinking & Entertainment

The nightlife action revolves around the Hasselbachplatz. For listings, pick up a copy of *DATEs, Urbanite* (www.urbanite.de/magdeburg) or *Kulturfalter* (all free, all in German).

Stern   BAR
(☑0391-580 2219; www.stern-bar.de; Sternstrasse 9; ☺7pm-late Mon-Sat, from 8pm Sun) Magdeburg's 'it' venue features two levels of lounges and a compact dance floor. Dress to impress and show your best moves.

Café Central   BAR
(☑0391-239 5671; www.cafecentral.k-n-o.de; Sternstrasse 30; ☺7.30pm-2am) This hip bar-slash-literary salon recreates the early 1900s with antique velvet sofas, flocked wallpaper and Persian carpets. There are comedy shows, public readings, films or lectures on many evenings. It's worth visiting just for the cosy decor.

Factory   CONCERT VENUE
(☑0391-5907 9530; www.factory-magdeburg.de; Karl-Schmidt-Strasse 26-29) Live music and parties here in all musical directions. Check the homepage for what's on when.

❶ Information

Multilingual information panels dotted about the city provide background about key sights. Pick up brochures at the **Magdeburg Tourist Office** (☑0391-194 33; www.magdeburg-tourist.de; Ernst-Reuter-Allee 12; ☺10am-6.30pm Mon-Fri, to 4pm Sat).

❶ Getting There & Away

Magdeburg is just south of the A2 to Berlin or Hanover and also served by the A14 to Leipzig.

There are direct services from Magdeburg to Berlin (€31, two hours), Leipzig (€32, 1¼ hours) and Dessau (€14.30, 50 minutes).

❶ Getting Around

Single/daily tickets cost €2/5. Buy them from vending machines at each stop and punch when you get on-board.

Little John Bikes (☑0391-733 0334; www.littlejohnbikes.de; Alter Markt 13-14; bikes per day from €12; ☺10am-7pm Mon-Fri, to 4pm Sat) can get you two-wheeling in no time.

Saxony

POP 4 MILLION

Best Places to Eat

➡ Restaurant Genuss-Atelier (p304)

➡ Restaurant Vincenz Richter (p309)

➡ Stadtpfeiffer (p323)

➡ Ouzeri Was Kost Das (p321)

➡ Stadtwirtschaft (p330)

Best Places to Stay

➡ Hotel Börse (p332)

➡ Steigenberger Grandhotel Handelshof (p321)

➡ Hotel Schloss Eckberg (p300)

➡ Burg Altrathen (p310)

➡ Ferdinands Homestay (p311)

Why Go?

Placed where northern plains abut mountain ranges and German efficiency meets Slavic flamboyance, packed with elegant hilltop castles and lavish baroque palaces, Saxony is the definition of Central Europe. It was also at the centre of events during the most decisive points in European history, such as the Reformation, Napoleonic Wars, and velvet revolutions that dismantled Communist regimes in the late 1980s.

It's likely you've seen some of Saxony's most striking sights on classical paintings, be it Canaletto's views of Dresden's captivating baroque cityscape or Friedrich's depictions of Saxon Switzerland, a breathtakingly beautiful passage cut through the mountains by the Elbe River. You've most definitely heard musical masterpieces written in Leipzig by Johann Sebastian Bach and Richard Wagner.

But there is more to discover – from quaint baroque towns to centuries-old industrial heritage. Halfway between Berlin and Prague, Saxony is a perfect introduction to what awaits you east of Germany.

When to Go

The Easter egg market draws crowds to Bautzen as the Sorbian minority braces for the annual equestrian parade through nearby villages.

The cities are fun in the summer when life moves outdoors, festivals are in full swing and you can boat or cycle along the Elbe River.

Consider visiting in September, when the bulk of summertime visitors has gone and the cooler weather is ideal for hiking through Saxon Switzerland, with mountains dressed in opulent autumn garbs.

In December, you will find mulled wine and hearty street food at Christmas markets in every hamlet, plus Dresden and Leipzig's concert seasons in full swing and miners parading through Freiberg.

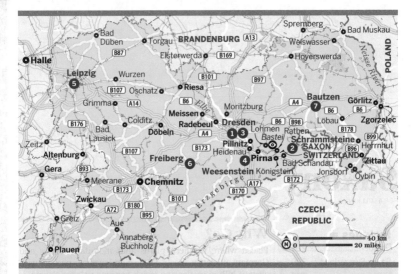

Saxony Highlights

❶ Residenzschloss
(p293) Taking in the
stunning baroque silhouette
of Dresden's Altstadt (old
town) and the elegant curve
of the Elbe.

❷ Schrammsteine (p312)
Clambering up a steep
slope for gob-smacking
panoramas of Saxon
Switzerland and the Elbe.

❸ Grünes Gewölbe
(p293) Getting blinded by
the dazzle of Saxon rulers'
treasures.

❹ Schloss Weesenstein
(p307) Playing games of
thrones in one of Saxony's
many stunning castles and
its interactive museum.

❺ Gewandhausorchester
(p324) Treating your ears to
a concert at Leipzig's storied
concert hall.

❻ Terra Mineralia (p327)
Submerging into a surreally
beautiful universe of shining
gems from all around the
world in Freiburg.

❼ Sorbian Easter (p336)
Watching horses and riders
don their 19th-century best
as Germany's Slavic minority
in Bautzer stages its annual
equestrian parade.

DRESDEN

📞 0351 / POP 563,000

There are few city silhouettes more striking
than Dresden's. The classic view from the
Elbe's northern bank takes in spires, towers
and domes belonging to palaces, churches
and stately buildings, and indeed it's hard to
believe that the city was all but wiped off the
map by Allied bombings in 1945.

Dresden's cultural heyday came during the 18th-century reigns of Augustus
the Strong (August der Starke) and his
son Augustus III, who sponsored many of
Dresden's iconic buildings, including the
Zwinger and the Frauenkirche. While the
devastating 1945 Allied firestorm levelled
most of these treasures, their contents were
safely removed before the bombings and

now take pride of place in Dresden's rebuilt
museums.

Across the river from this treasure trove
of classic art and architecture, Dresden's
Neustadt has dozens of funky restaurants,
shops and one of the liveliest nightlife
scenes in Germany's east.

◎ Sights

Key sights cluster in the compact Altstadt on
the Elbe's south bank, about 1km from the
Hauptbahnhof via Prager Strasse, the main
pedestrianised shopping strip. From here,
Augustusbrücke leads across the river to the
Neustadt, with its own major train station
(Dresden-Neustadt) and the main pub and
party quarter in the Äussere Neustadt (Outer Neustadt).

⊙ Altstadt

★ Zwinger   PALACE
(📞 0351-4914 2000; www.der-dresdner-zwinger.de; Theaterplatz 1; ticket for all museums adult/concession €12/9, courtyard free; ⊙ 6am-10pm Apr-Oct, to 8pm Nov-Mar) A collaboration between the architect Matthäus Pöppelmann and the sculptor Balthasar Permoser, the Zwinger was built between 1710 and 1728 on the orders of Augustus the Strong, who, having returned from seeing Louis XIV's palace at Versailles, wanted something similar for himself. Primarily a party palace for royals, the Zwinger has ornate portals that lead into the vast fountain-studded courtyard, which is framed by buildings lavishly festooned with evocative sculpture. Today it houses three superb museums within its baroque walls.

Atop the western pavilion stands a tense-looking Atlas. Opposite him is a cutesy carillon of 40 Meissen porcelain bells, which emit a tinkle every 15 minutes. Entry to the magnificent courtyard is free, but all three museums are ticketed. The Gemäldegalerie Alte Meister (p297; Old Masters Gallery) and Porzellansammlung (p297; Porcelain Collection) are unmissable, while the historic scientific instruments (globes, clocks, telescopes etc) at the Mathematisch-Physikalischer Salon (p297) are perhaps more for the scientifically minded.

★ Residenzschloss   PALACE
(📞 0351-4914 2000; www.skd.museum; Schlossplatz; adult/child under 17yr €12/free, incl Historisches Grünes Gewölbe €21/free; ⊙ 10am-6pm Wed-Mon) Dresden's extraordinary Renaissance city palace, home to its Saxon rulers from 1485 to 1918, now shelters multiple precious collections – including the unmissable Grünes Gewölbe (Green Vault), a real-life Aladdin's Cave spilling over with precious objects wrought from gold, ivory, silver, diamonds and jewels. The palace itself was bombed out in 1945, and though reconstruction began in the 1960s, it wasn't completed until 2013. The entire building, including its unique murals and baroque towers, is quite simply spectacular.

There's so much on display here that two separate treasure chambers – the Historisches Grünes Gewölbe and the Neues Grünes Gewölbe (p296) – are needed to display the extraordinary wealth of the Saxon rulers' private collections. Also housed here is the Kupferstich-Kabinett, which counts around half a million prints and drawings by 20,000 artists (including Dürer, Rembrandt and Michelangelo) in its possession. Numismatists might want to drop by the Münzkabinett (Coin Cabinet) in the palace tower for a small array of historic coins and medals.

The Türckische Cammer (Turkish Chamber), one of the richest collections of Ottoman art outside Turkey, is also here. A huge three-mast tent made of gold and silk is one standout among many. The new Riesensaal (Giant's Hall) houses a spectacular collection of armour, including including a recreation of several jousting tournaments.

You can easily spend several hours exploring the various collections here. On top of the combination ticket that includes everything Residenzschloss has on display, cheaper tickets can be bought separately for Historisches Grünes Gewölbe and for all other exhibitions excluding the former. One- and two-day cards, which allow you to enter exhibitions multiple times, are also available at €19 and €27 respectively.

★ Historisches Grünes Gewölbe   MUSEUM
(Historic Green Vault; 📞 0351-4914 2000; www.skd.museum; Residenzschloss; €12; ⊙ 10am-6pm Wed-Mon) The Historic Green Vault displays some 3000 precious items in the same fashion as during the time of August der Starke, namely on shelves and tables without glass protection in a series of increasingly lavish rooms. Admission is by timed ticket only, and only a limited number of visitors per hour may pass through the 'dust lock'. Get advance tickets online or by phone, since only 40% are sold at the palace box office for same-day admission.

Frauenkirche   CHURCH
(📞 0351-6560 6100; www.frauenkirche-dresden.de; Neumarkt; audioguide €2.50, cupola adult/student €8/5; ⊙ 10am-noon & 1-6pm Mon-Fri, weekend hours vary) The domed Frauenkirche – Dresden's most beloved symbol – has literally risen from the city's ashes. The original church graced the skyline for two centuries before collapsing after the February 1945 bombing, and was rebuilt from a pile of rubble between 1994 and 2005. A spitting image of the original, today's structure may not bear the gravitas of age but that only slightly detracts from its beauty, inside and out. The altar, reassembled from nearly 2000 fragments, is especially striking.

The cupola can be climbed, and the galleried interior is a wonderful place for concerts, meditations and services. Check the website

Dresden

SAXONY

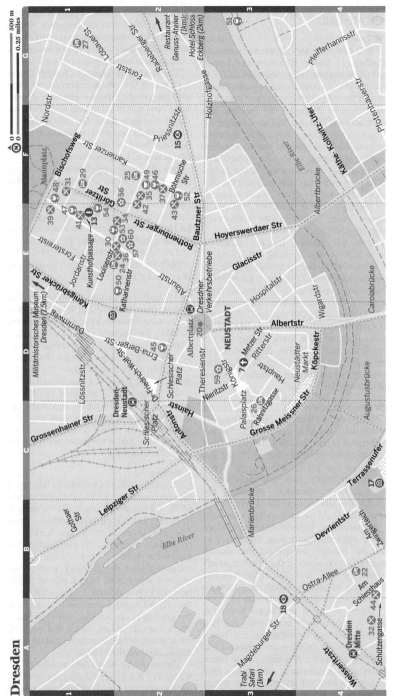

500 m
0.25 miles

Restaurant
Genuss-Atelier (1km);
Hotel Schloss
Eckberg (2km)

Löbauer St

27

Forststr

Radeberger Str

Nordstr

Kamenzer Str

Priesnitzstr

15

Bischofsweg

Maxinplatz

48
31

29

Görlitzer Str

25

49
46

56

Böhmische Str

Bautzner Str

39

47

Rothenburger Str

35
37

42

52

43

Forststr

41

13

54

Kunsthofpassage

53
34

60

Hoyerswerdaer Str

Jordanstr

30

24
36

57

Glacisstr

Louisenstr

50

Katharinenstr

Alaunstr

Hospitalstr

Wigardstr

Käthe-Kollwitz-Ufer

Pfefferhannstr

Prohlishauerstr

Albertbrücke

Carolabrücke

Dammweg

Königsbrücker Str

Militärhistorisches Museum
Dresden (1.5km)

Dresden
Verkehrsbetriebe

Albertplatz

20

NEUSTADT

Metzer Str

Ritterstr

Albertstr

Köpckestr

Lössnitzstr

Dr-Friedrich-Wolf-Str

Erna-Berger-Str

45

Schlesischer
Platz

Theresienstr

Nieritzstr

Königstr

Hauptstr

Neustädter
Markt

Augustusbrücke

Grossenhainer Str

Dresden
Neustadt

Schlesischer
Platz

59

Palaisplatz

Rähnitzgasse

26

Grosse Meissner Str

Antonstr

Hainstr

Leipziger Str

Marienbrücke

Elbe River

Devrientstr

Terrassenufer

17

Ostra-Allee

Am
Schiesshaus

22

44

32

Dresden
Mitte

Magdeburger Str

18

Trabi
Safari
(1km)

Schützengasse

Weisseritzstr

Gothaer
Str

SAXONY

Dresden

for the current schedule or stop by the Frauenkirche Visitors Centre, which screens a documentary about the church's history.

Neues Grünes Gewölbe　　　　MUSEUM
(New Green Vault; ☎0351-4914 2000; www.skd.museum; Residenzschloss; adult/child under 17yr incl audioguide €12/free; ⊙10am-6pm Wed-Mon) The New Green Vault presents some 1000 objects in 10 modern rooms. Key sights include a frigate fashioned from ivory with wafer-thin sails, a cherry pit with 185 faces carved into it, and an exotic ensemble of 132 gem-studded figurines representing a royal court in India. The artistry of each item is

dazzling. To avoid the worst crush of people, visit during lunchtime.

Katholische Hofkirche　　　　CHURCH
(Schlossplatz; ⊙9am-5pm Mon-Thu, 1-5pm Fri, 10am-5pm Sat, noon-4pm Sun) The Katholische Hofkirche (also called Dresden Cathedral) makes up an integral part of the baroque ensemble crowning the Altstadt, and is one of Dresden's most dazzling buildings. Built between 1739 and 1751 by Gaetano Chiaveri as a Catholic rival to the Protestant Frauenkirche, its detailed and exuberant exterior is extraordinarily impressive, while its rather bare interior is enlivened by the gilded altar,

pulpit and organ. Destroyed in WWII, it was rebuilt in the 1980s.

★ Gemäldegalerie Alte Meister   MUSEUM
(Old Masters Gallery; www.skd.museum; Zwinger, Theaterplatz 1; adult/concession €12/9, audio guide €3; ⊙10am-6pm Tue-Sun) This astounding collection of European art from the 16th to 18th centuries houses an incredible number of masterpieces, including Raphael's famous *Sistine Madonna* (1513), which dominates the enormous main hall on the ground floor, as well as works by Titian, Tintoretto, Holbein, Dürer, and Cranach, whose *Paradise* (1530) is particularly arresting. Upstairs you'll find an exquisite display of Rembrandt, Botticelli, Veronese, Van Dyck, Vermeer, Brueghel and Poussin. Finally, don't miss Canaletto's sumptuous portrayals of 18th-century Dresden on the top floor.

★ Albertinum   GALLERY
(Galerie Neue Meister; ☑0351-4914 2000; www.skd.museum; enter from Brühlsche Terrasse or Georg-Treu-Platz 2; adult/concession/child under 17yr €10/7.50/free; ⊙10am-6pm Tue-Sun) The Renaissance-era former arsenal is the stunning home of the Galerie Neue Meister (New Masters Gallery), which displays an array of paintings by some of the great names in art from the 18th century onwards. Caspar David Friedrich and Claude Monet's landscapes compete with the abstract visions of Marc Chagall and Gerhard Richter, all in gorgeous rooms orbiting a light-filled courtyard. There's also a superb sculpture collection spread over the lower floors.

Porzellansammlung   MUSEUM
(Porcelain Collection; www.skd.museum; Zwinger, Theaterplatz 1; adult/student €6/4.50) Housed in two gorgeously converted curving galleries, this extraordinary collection ranges from 17th- and 18th-century Chinese porcelain to that produced in Meissen, as the European art of making 'white gold' was perfected under August the Strong. The fabulous Tiersaal (animal hall) is the ultimate highlight, showing hundreds of animals rendered in porcelain – although the full-on crucifixion scene is quite a showstopper as well.

Mathematisch-Physikalischer Salon   MUSEUM
(www.skd.museum; Zwinger, Theaterplatz 1; adult/student/child under 17yr €6/4.50/free; ⊙10am-6pm Tue-Sun) This wonderful collection of scientific implements, dating from the early 16th century onwards, will delight anyone interested in the history of science and the Enlightenment, with its telescopes, barometers and dozens of other early instruments. A free audioguide puts the collection into context.

Semperoper   HISTORIC BUILDING, OPERA
(☑0351-320 7360; www.semperoper-erleben.de; Theaterplatz 2; tour adult/concession €11/7; ⊙hours vary) One of Germany's most famous opera houses, the Semperoper opened in 1841 and has hosted premieres of famous works by Richard Strauss, Carl Maria von Weber and Richard Wagner. Guided 45-minute tours operate almost daily (the 3pm tour is in English); exact times depend on rehearsal and performance schedules. Buy advance tickets online to skip the queue.

The original Semperoper burned down a mere three decades after its inauguration. After reopening in 1878, the neo-Renaissance jewel entered its most dazzling period. Alas, the building was destroyed during WWII and it wasn't until 1985 that music again filled the grand hall.

Kraftwerk Mitte   CULTURAL CENTRE
(☑0351-860 4679; www.kraftwerk-mitte-dresden.de; Kraftwerk Mitte 1; ⊙24hr) **FREE** If you are interested in urbanism and the redevelopment of industrial facilities, check out this giant 19th-century red-brick powerplant reborn as a cultural venue, housing a namesake nightclub, two theatres (including Staatsoperette; p305), two music schools and the Energy Museum. In summer, there are a few open-air cafes scattered around the vast premises.

Yenidze   ARCHITECTURE
(☑0351-490 5990; www.kuppelrestaurant.de; Weisseritzstrasse 3; ⊙noon-11pm) The huge mosque-like Yenidze began life in 1909 as a cigarette factory with a chimney disguised as a minaret and a stained-glass dome. Today, it's home to offices, a ho-hum restaurant and Dresden's highest beer garden (beneath the dome).

⊙ Neustadt

Despite its name, Neustadt (new town) is actually an older part of Dresden that was considerably less damaged in WWII than the Altstadt (old town). It consists of the gentrified Innere Neustadt, with Hauptstrasse as its main artery, and the still delightfully wacky Äussere (Outer) Neustadt pub district north of Albertplatz.

SAXONY DRESDEN

DRESDEN & WWII

Between 13 and 15 February 1945, British and American planes unleashed 3900 tonnes of explosives on Dresden in four huge air raids. Bombs and incendiary shells whipped up a mammoth firestorm, and ashes rained down on villages 35km away. When the blazes had died down and the dust settled, tens of thousands of Dresdners had lost their lives and 20 sq km of this once-elegant baroque city lay in smouldering ruins.

Historians still argue over whether this constituted a war crime committed by the Allies on an innocent civilian population. Some claim that with the Red Army at the gates of Berlin, the war was effectively won, and the Allies gained little military advantage from the destruction of Dresden. Others have said that, as the last urban centre in the east of the country left intact, Dresden could have provided shelter for German troops returning from the east and was a viable target.

★ **Militärhistorisches**
Museum Dresden MUSEUM
(☑0351-823 2803; www.mhmbw.de; Olbrichtplatz 2; adult/concession €5/3; ☉10am-6pm Thu-Sun & Tue, to 9pm Mon; 🚌7 or 8 to Stauffenbergallee) Even devout pacifists will be awed by this engaging museum, housed in a 19th-century arsenal bisected by a bold glass-and-steel wedge designed by Daniel Libeskind. Exhibits have been updated for the 21st century, so don't expect a rollcall of military victories or a parade of weapons. Instead, you'll find a progressive – and often artistic – look at the roots and ramifications of war and aggression.

Exhibits in the Libeskind wedge zero in on such sociocultural aspects as women in the war, animals in the war, war-themed toys, the economy of war and the suffering brought on by war. The historical wing presents a chronology of German wars from the Middle Ages to the 20th century. Standouts among the countless intriguing objects are a 1975 Soyuz landing capsule, a V2 rocket, and personal items of concentration camp victims. Allow at least two hours to do this amazing museum justice.

Kunsthofpassage PUBLIC ART
(enter from Alaunstrasse 70 or Görlitzer Strasse 23; ☉24hr) FREE Take a web of grimy courtyards, a load of paint and a bunch of visionary Dresden artists and out comes the Kunsthofpassage, one of the most refreshingly artistic spaces in the Neustadt. Each courtyard has its own charm, but favourites include the Court of the Elements, where 'music' is created by water running down interlinked rain pipes affixed to a turquoise facade, and the Court of the Animals, where monkeys leap above the head of a giant giraffe.

Pfunds Molkerei ARCHITECTURE
(☑0351-808 080; www.pfunds.de; Bautzner Strasse 79; ☉10am-6pm Mon-Sat, to 3pm Sun) FREE The Guinness-certified 'world's most beautiful dairy shop', founded in 1880, is a riot of hand-painted tiles and enamelled sculpture, all handmade by Villeroy & Boch. The shop sells replica tiles, wines, cheeses and other milk products. Not surprisingly, the upstairs cafe-restaurant has a strong lactose theme. Slip in between coach tours for a less shuffling look around.

Dreikönigskirche CHURCH
(☑0351-812 4102; www.hdk-dkk.de; Hauptstrasse 23; tower adult/concession €3/2; ☉9am-6pm Mon-Fri, 11am-5pm Sat, during service Sun) Designed by Zwinger architect Mätthaus Pöppelmann, the most eye-catching feature of the Dreikönigskirche is the baroque altar that was ruined in 1945 and left as a memorial. Also note the 12m-long Renaissance-era Dance of Death sandstone relief opposite the altar, beneath the organ. The 88m-high tower can be scaled for panoramic views (it's open from 11.30am to 4pm Tuesday, and 11am to 5pm Wednesday to Sunday).

◎ Grosser Garten & Around

Grosser Garten GARDENS
(www.grosser-garten-dresden.de; Hauptallee 5; ☉24hr) FREE The aptly named Grosser Garten (Great Garden) is a relaxing refuge during the warmer months. A visitor magnet here is the modernised **Zoo Dresden** (☑0351-478 060; www.zoo-dresden.de; Tiergartenstrasse 1; adult/child under 17yr €12/4; ☉8.30am-6.30pm Apr-Oct, to 4.30pm Nov-Mar) in the southwest corner, where crowds gravitate towards the Africa Hall and the lion enclosure. In the northwest corner is the architecturally distinguished transparent

Gläserne Manufaktur (Transparent Factory; ☏ 0351-420 4411; www.glaesernemanufaktur.de; cnr Lennéstrasse & Stübelallee; building free, tour adult/concession €7/4.50; ⊗ 8.30am-7pm Mon-Fri, 9am-6pm Sat & Sun, English-language tours 10am, noon, 3pm Mon-Fri, noon, 3pm, 5pm Sat, 3pm Sun), where you can observe how the Volkswagen luxury model 'Phaeton' is being constructed. Right next to it is the free *Botanischer Garten* (Botanical Garden).

Deutsches Hygiene-Museum   MUSEUM
(German Hygiene Museum; ☏ 0351-484 6400; www.dhmd.de; Lingnerplatz 1; adult/student/child under 16yr €8/4/free, valid on 2 consecutive days; ⊗ 10am-6pm Tue-Sun; ⊕) Not an institution dedicated to the history of cleaning products, the German Hygiene Museum is, in fact, all about human beings. The permanent exhibit uses intriguing objects, interpretive panelling, installations and interactive stations to examine the human body in its social, cultural, historical and scientific contexts. Living and dying, eating and drinking, sex and beauty are all addressed. The Children's Museum in the basement takes four- to 12-year-olds on an interactive romp through the mysteries of the five senses.

Asisi Panometer   GALLERY
(☏ 0341-355 5340; www.panometer.de/en; Gasanstaltstrasse 8b; adult/child €11.50/6; ⊗ 10am-5pm Mon-Fri, to 6pm Sat & Sun) Like its siblings in Leipzig and elsewhere in Germany, this old gasometer – a huge round-shaped building – has been transformed into a venue for German artist Yadegar Asisi's grandiose and seemingly three-dimensional panoramas dedicated to historical events or epochs. Themes change every year, with the inaugural panorama dedicated to the Dresden bombardment of 1945.

To get there, take the S1 train from Dresden Hauptbahnhof to Dresden-Reick, then walk 600m along Gasanstaltstrasse.

🕝 Tours

NightWalk Dresden   WALKING
(☏ 0172 781 5007; www.nightwalk-dresden.de; Albertplatz; €17; ⊗ 9pm) See street art, learn what life was like in East Germany and visit fun pubs and bars in the Outer Neustadt on this super-fun tour. NightWalk also has the exclusive rights to take visitors to the slaughterhouse where Kurt Vonnegut Jr survived the bombing of Dresden in 1945, and which he later immortalised in *Slaughterhouse-Five*.

Sächsische Dampfschiffahrt   BOATING
(☏ 0351-866 090; www.saechsische-dampf schiffahrt.de; Terrassenufer; adult/concession €18.50/11) Ninety-minute Elbe tours leave from the Terrassenufer dock several times daily in summer, aboard the world's oldest fleet of paddle-wheel steamers. There are also services to Saxon Switzerland and castles along the river.

Trabi Safari   DRIVING
(☏ 0351-8990 0110; www.trabi-safari.de; Bremer Strasse 35; adult/child under 17 €49/free) Get behind the wheel of the ultimate GDR-mobile for this 1½-hour guided drive around the city, taking in sights from all eras. The price depends on the number of people in the car; four people to a car is the best value.

🎭 Festivals & Events

Internationales Dixieland Festival   MUSIC
(www.dixieland.de; ⊗ May) Dixieland and jazz bands from around the world descend on Dresden for one week

Dresdner Musikfestspiele   MUSIC
(Dresden Music Festival; www.musikfestspiele.com) Held mid-May to June, with mostly classical music.

AND SO IT GOES: KURT VONNEGUT IN DRESDEN

Kurt Vonnegut Jr (1922–2007), one of America's most influential 20th-century writers, spent the end of WWII as a POW in Dresden and later based his famous 1969 novel, *Slaughterhouse-Five*, on his observations and experiences. Thanks to Danilo Hommel, owner of NightWalk Dresden, you can now walk in Vonnegut's footsteps, while being peppered with intriguing stories about why the writer ended up in Dresden, how he managed to survive the February 1945 bombing, and what he saw and suffered through in the aftermath. The highlight is a visit to the slaughterhouse meat locker where Vonnegut and his fellow POWs survived the fateful bombing. Tours run for two hours and start at 11am each weekday from the König Johann monument on Theaterplatz. Even if you don't do the tour, *Slaughterhouse-Five* is essential reading for anyone wanting to understand the horrific 20th-century fate of this city.

Bunte Republik Neustadt STREET CARNIVAL
(www.brn-dresden.de; ⊙ Jun) The city's Outer Neustadt district celebrates its alternative roots on the third weekend in June, with lots of music, food and wacky merriment.

Striezelmarkt CHRISTMAS MARKET
(Altmarkt; ⊙ Dec) During December, sample the famous Dresdner Stollen (fruit cake) at one of Germany's oldest and best Christmas markets.

🛏 Sleeping

Dresden's centrally located hotels can be both bland and horrendously expensive, with rates among the highest in Germany. Thankfully there are plenty of cheap beds available at the city's superb hostels. Given the efficient tram system, it's also worth looking into cheaper – and often better – hotel options in outlying districts.

🛏 Altstadt

Hotel Bülow Residenz HOTEL €€
(✆ 0351-800 3291; www.buelow-residenz.de; Rähnitzgasse 19; d from €89; P ❀ 🕸 🛜) This place occupying one of Dresden's oldest townhouses is a class act, from the welcome drink to the spacious gold-and-crimson-hued rooms cloaked in antiques, paintings and porcelain. Days get off to a breezy start with a lavish breakfast in the glass-covered courtyard atrium. You can get excellent deals by booking ahead online: walk-ins are far pricier.

Aparthotel am Zwinger APARTMENT €€
(✆ 0351-8990 0100; www.aparthotel-zwinger.de; Maxstrasse 3; apt from €60; P 🛜) This excellent option has bright, functional and spacious apartments with kitchens that even come equipped with Nespresso machines. Units are spread over several buildings, but all are supercentral and quiet. Access to the buffet breakfast costs €12.90, and it's a good option unless you're self-catering, as the neighbourhood is pretty low on breakfast options.

★ Gewandhaus Hotel BOUTIQUE HOTEL €€€
(✆ 0351-494 90; www.gewandhaus-hotel.de; Ringstrasse 1; d from €157; P ❀ @ 🛜 🛜) Revamped as a boutique hotel a few years ago, the stunning Gewandhaus, an 18th-century trading house of tailors and fabric merchants that burned down in 1945, boasts sleek public areas, beautiful and bright rooms, and a breakfast that sets a high bar for the city.

Hotel Taschenbergpalais Kempinski HOTEL €€€
(✆ 0351-491 20; www.kempinski-dresden.de; Taschenberg 3; r from €139; ❀ @ 🛜 🛜) You might never be get around to sightseeing when staying at this swanky 18th-century mansion, where luxury is taken very seriously. Checking in here buys views over the Zwinger from rakishly handsome rooms that beautifully bridge the traditional and the contemporary, with rich royal-blue colours and marble bathrooms with Bulgari toiletries. In winter, the courtyard turns into an ice rink.

🛏 Neustadt

Hostel Louise 20 HOSTEL €
(✆ 0351-889 4894; www.louise20.de; Louisenstrasse 20; dm/s/d/apt from €16/32/42/106; ⊜ @ 🛜) In the heart of the Outer Neustadt, this friendly and well-run hostel is an obvious choice for travellers wanting to hang out and take in the spirit of alternative Dresden. Dorms are simple, but clean and comfortable, each with lockers for security and shared bathrooms. Larger apartments are great for groups (up to eight people).

Lollis Homestay HOSTEL €
(✆ 0351-810 8458; www.lollishome.de; Görlitzer Strasse 34; dm/s/d from €13/30/40, linen €2, breakfast €5; @ 🛜) This is a textbook backpacker hostel: friendly, communicative, casual and with neatly designed themed rooms (Cinema, Desert, Giants), including a rather gimmicky double where you live out that *Good Bye, Lenin!* vibe by bedding down in a real GDR-era Trabi car. Bikes, tea and coffee are welcome freebies, and the communal room and kitchen are conducive to meeting fellow travellers.

Hostel Mondpalast HOSTEL €
(✆ 0351-563 4050; www.mondpalast.de; Louisenstrasse 77; dm/s/d from €14/29/37, linen €2.50; @ 🛜) A funky location in the thick of the Äussere Neustadt is the main draw of this out-of-this-world hostel-bar-cafe (with cheap drinks). Each playful room is designed to reflect a sign of the zodiac. Bonus points for the bike rentals and the well-equipped kitchen. Breakfast is €7.

★ Hotel Schloss Eckberg HOTEL €€
(✆ 0351-809 90; www.schloss-eckberg.de; Bautzner Strasse 134; d Kavaliershaus/Schloss from €99/134; P ❀ 🛜) This romantic castle set in its own riverside park east of the Neustadt is a breathtaking place to stay. Rooms in

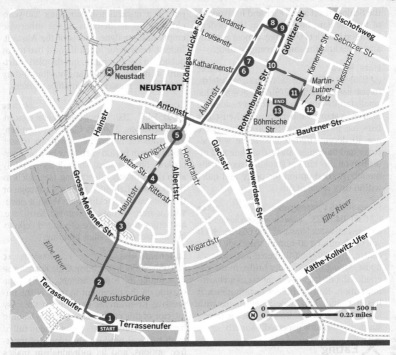

🏃 City Walk
From Baroque to Alt-Rock

START BRÜLSCHE TERRACE
END BÖHMISCHE STRASSE
LENGTH 3.5KM; TWO HOURS

Central Dresden's two parts couldn't be less alike: the baroque Altstadt is visually stunning, but real life is centred on the grittier but livelier and more welcoming Neustadt.

Start your tour on **1 Brülsche Terrace**, Dresden's prime lookout point, also dubbed the Balcony of Europe. Admire the views of Dresden's Neustadt before descending to **2 Augustusbrücke** – a bridge named after Augustus the Strong – and crossing the Elbe. You'll find yourself face to face with Augustus in the form of a gilded equestrian statue, known as **3 Golden Rider**, welcoming visitors to Neustadt, Dresden's alternative city within a city.

Check out **4 Dreikönigskirche** (p298) on your left before reaching **5 Albertplatz**, a plaza with two fountains representing turbulent and still waters. Now plunge into the depth of the the colourful, alt-flavoured

Äussere (Outer) Neustadt via Alaunstrasse. Soon on your right is **6 Die Scheune** (p305), Dresden's oldest youth club, which has been going strong since 1951, and made a decisive turn to alternative music when the Wall fell. Stop to admire the latest artistic outpourings on the officially designated **7 Graffiti Wall** just before Katy's Garage music venue. Keep going on Alaunstrasse to the whimsical **8 Kunsthofpassage** (p298), a cluster of five interlinked artist-designed courtyards. Grab an ice cream at **9 Neumanns Tiki** (p305), family-owned since 1966, then turn right onto Görlitzer Strasse.

Make a note to come back in the evening for the **10 Bermuda Triangle** of densely clustered bars and pubs around Louisenstrasse, then head down gritty Martin-Luther-Strasse, home to some especially fine **11 street art**. Note the imposing 19th-century **12 Martin Luther Church** on your left, then turn into one of Outer Neustadt's cutest lanes, Böhmische Strasse, home to art-squat-turned-gastro-pub **13 Raskolnikoff** (p304).

the Schloss itself are pricier and have oodles of historic flair, but staying in the modern Kavaliershaus lets you enjoy almost as many amenities and the same dreamy setting.

Hotel Privat
HOTEL €€

(🖉0351-811 770; www.das-nichtraucher-hotel.de; Forststrasse 22; s/d/tr €72/91/109; 🅿 😀 🛜) This small, family-run hotel in a quiet residential district, a short wander from the Neustadt's bars, has plenty of easy Saxon charm. There are 30 decent-sized rooms, some with alcoves and balconies, and a complete and utter ban on any kind of smoking (see website name!). A good option for peace and quiet within easy reach of fun.

Pensione la Campagnola
B&B €€

(🖉0351-314 1023; www.la-campagnola-dresden. de; Friedrich-Wieck-Strasse 45; s/d €69/95; 🛜) If you don't mind a 20-minute tram ride to the centre, this 1697 half-timbered ferrymaster's house, facing Blue Wonder bridge in the riverside villa district of Loschwitz, is a charming option. Run by Italian restaurateurs, it has eight individually designed rooms with lots of retro touches. Breakfast at the downstairs restaurant is expectedly superb.

Eating

Altstadt

Zum Schiesshaus
SAXON €€

(🖉0351-484 5990; www.zum-schiesshaus.de; Am Schiesshaus 19; mains €10-25; ⊙11am-1am) If you're yearning for something traditional, meaty and quintessentially Saxon, this is the place for you. Oozing old-world atmosphere, despite having been destroyed in both the Thirty Year War and WWII, this reconstructed former medieval shooting range offers hearty meals washed down with plenty of local beer.

Cafe Alte Meister
INTERNATIONAL €€

(🖉0351-481 0426; www.altemeister.net; Theaterplatz 1a; mains €18-25; ⊙11am-midnight) If you've worked up an appetite from museum-hopping or need a break from cultural overload, retreat to this elegant filling station for creative and seasonal bistro fare in its artsy interior or on the terrace. At night, the ambience is a bit more formal.

brennNessel
VEGETARIAN €€

(🖉0351-494 3319; www.brennnessel-dresden.de; Schützengasse 18; mains €13-16; ⊙11am-midnight; 🖉) This popular, largely vegetarian gastro-

pub in a miraculously surviving 350-year-old building is an oasis in the otherwise empty and anodyne streets of the Altstadt. Indeed, reserve for lunch if you'd like to eat outside in the charming, sun-dappled courtyard, as it's a favourite hang-out for off-duty Semperoper musicians and office workers.

Sophienkeller
SAXON €€

(🖉0351-497 260; www.sophienkeller-dresden. de; Taschenberg 3; mains €12-20; ⊙11am-1am) The 1730s theme, complete with waitresses trussed up in period garb, may be a bit overcooked, but the local specialities certainly aren't. It's mostly rib-sticking fare, such as the boneless half-duck with red cabbage or the spit-roasted suckling pig. Wash it down with a mug of dark Bohemian Krušovice, and enjoy the ambience of vaulted ceilings in the Taschenbergpalais building.

Ladencafé Aha
INTERNATIONAL €€

(🖉0351-496 0673; www.ladencafe.de; Kreuzstrasse 7; mains €8-16; ⊙9am-midnight; 🖉🖈) Dine outside on the pavement in front of the impressive Kreuzkirche, or retire to the cosy interior of this charming vegetarian-leaning health food cafe. There's a great menu full of fresh regional produce and plenty of meat-free options, and its individualism makes it a far cry from the other identikit Altstadt eating options. There's a kids' play area.

Grand Café
SAXON €€

(🖉0351-496 2444; www.coselpalais-dresden.de; An der Frauenkirche 12; mains €15-20; ⊙11am-11pm) The imaginative mains (try roasted pike-perch on crispy Dijon mustard rösti with lemon and vegetables) and sumptuous cakes are good, but they act more as appetisers for the gold-trimmed baroque Coselpalais, which houses the cafe and makes for a stylish (if slightly formal) refuelling stop.

Neustadt

Anamit
VIETNAMESE €

(🖉0351-6567 7999; http://anamit.de; Louisenstrasse 30; mains €6.50-14; ⊙11.30am-3pm, 5-11pm Mon-Fri, 11.30am-11pm Sat & Sun) Not your typical Vietnamese three-table eatery (a ubiquitous feature of any east German urban landscape), this is a large and atmospheric establishment with stylishly subdued decor. The menu reads like a jungle-trail description, with exotic ingredients such as lotus roots, mango and sugarcane featuring in the mouthwatering spring rolls, noodle soups and curries.

Dampfschwein
INTERNATIONAL €

(www.dampfschwein.de; Louisenstrasse 26; mains €3.50-7.50; ⊗11.30am-10pm Mon-Thu, to midnight Fri & Sat, 1-10pm Sun) Of course that favourite, pulled pork (slow-cooked pork so soft it can be easily torn into shreds), features prominently on Dresden's it-street. Fill freshly baked buns with delicious stacks of pork, add some barbecue or apple sauce and some spicy cheese and bam! – one of Dresden's best fast-food options.

England, England
BRITISH €

(www.englandengland.de; Martin-Luther-Strasse 25; snacks €2.50-5; ⊗noon-6pm Tue-Sat, from 10am Sun) In this tiny England away from England, the tea is milky, the breakfast (on Sundays only) is calorific, and the treats (do not miss the courgette and lemon cream cake) are as sugary as you'll find in Albion.

Curry & Co
GERMAN €

(☑0351-209 3154; www.curryundco.com; Louisenstrasse 62; sausages €2.60-3.60; ⊗11am-10pm Sun-Wed, to midnight Thu, to 2am Fri & Sat) This upbeat outfit has elevated the lowly *Currywurst* to an art form and is busy day and night. Choose from smoked, all-beef, chicken or vegan varieties, and pair your pick with your favourite homemade sauce, from mild curry to hot chilli-onion. Don't skip the fries.

Kochbox
BURGERS €

(☑0351-796 7138; Görlitzer Strasse 3; dishes €3-6; ⊗5pm-3am) This little joint gets howling in the wee hours, when starving nightowls invade in hopes of restoring balance to the brain with fist-sized burgers made from fresh (not frozen) meat.

★ Little India
INDIAN €€

(☑0351-3232 6400; www.littleindia-dresden.de; Louisenstrasse 48; mains €10-15; ⊗11am-2.30pm & 5-11pm Tue-Sat, to 10pm Sun; ☑) Bright, minimalist and informal, this fantastic Indian restaurant is a world away from most in Dresden, and its popularity is obvious (be prepared to wait for a table when it's busy). The large menu (available in English) includes superb tandoori dishes and an entire vegetarian section, as well as standard chicken, lamb and pork mains. The naan is heavenly.

Böhme
GERMAN €€

(☑0351-8894 8354; www.boehme-restaurant.de; Sebnitzer Strasse 11; mains €12-20; ⊗6-11pm) The menu at this easygoing but quietly elegant place, with bare-brick walls and interwar period furniture, celebrates the produce of the Free State's fertile lands, turning traditional staples, such as red cabbage, into contemporary masterpieces. Changing daily, the German-language menu is written in barely decipherable handwriting on a large blackboard, so consult English-speaking waiters.

Lila Sosse
GERMAN €€

(☑0351-803 6723; www.lilasosse.de; Alaunstrasse 70, Kunsthofpassage; appetisers €3.50-9.50, mains €13-15; ⊗4pm-late Mon-Fri, from noon Sat & Sun) This jumping joint puts a new spin on modern German cooking by serving intriguing appetisers in glass preserve jars. You're free to order just a couple (the fennel-orange salad and carp with capers are recommended) or, if your tummy needs silencing, pair them with a meaty main and dessert. Reservations essential. It's part of the charming Kunsthofpassage courtyard complex (p298).

mahl2
FUSION €€

(☑0351-4086 4241; www.mahl2.de; Görlitzer Strasse 23; mains €17-28; ⊗6-11.30pm) At the entrance to Kunsthofpassage (p298), this modern restaurant allows you to build your own meal out of five meat and fish options and a selection of sides. All of these are mouth-watering, but the four vegetarian mains, including the outstanding beetroot Knödel (dumplings), are arguably even better.

Cafe Continental
INTERNATIONAL €€

(☑0351-272 1722; www.cafe-continental-dresden.de; Görlitzer Strasse 1; dishes €6-20; ⊗9am-1am Sun-Thu, to 3am Fri & Sat; ☎) If the greenly lit openings behind the bar remind you of aquariums, you've hit the nail on the head, for buzzy 'Conti' was a pet store back in GDR days. Today, it's a great place to hit no matter the hour, for anything from cappucino or cocktails to homemade cakes or a full meal.

La Casina Rosa
ITALIAN €€

(☑0351-801 4848; www.la-casina-rosa.de; Alaunstrasse 93; mains €12-22; ⊗5.30-11.30pm Mon-Sat) Everybody feels like family at this neighbourhood-adored trattoria with its warren of cosy rooms (plus small summer garden out the back) and feisty pasta and pizza, plus seasonally inspired specials. Menu stars include the richly flavoured tagliatelle with porcini, veal, cherry tomatoes and thyme, and the 'piccola Capri' pizza topped with shrimp, zucchini and *rúcula*. Reservations are a good idea.

SAXONY DRESDEN

Raskolnikoff INTERNATIONAL €€
(☑0351-804 5706; www.raskolnikoff.de; Böhmische Strasse 34; mains €10-15; ☺11am-10.30pm Mon-Sat, from 9am Sun) An artist squat in the 1980s, Raskolnikoff now brims with grown-up artsy-bohemian flair, especially in the sweet little garden at the back, complete with a bizarre water feature. The seasonally calibrated menu showcases the fruits of the surrounding land in globally inspired dishes, including a variety of *pelmeni* (Russian dumplings), which proudly represent the Dostoyevsky character the establishment is named after.

PlanWirtschaft INTERNATIONAL €€
(☑0351-801 3187; Louisenstrasse 20; mains €9-17; ☺7.30am-1am) The winning formula has stayed the same at this long-time favourite: fresh ingredients sourced from local suppliers; a menu that dazzles with inventiveness; and smiley staff who make even first-timers feel at home. Sit inside the cafe, the romantic garden or the cosy brick cellar. Brunch is a definite highlight.

★ **Restaurant Genuss-Atelier** GERMAN €€€
(☑0351-2502 8337; www.genuss-atelier.net; Bautzner Strasse 149; mains €15-27; ☺5-11pm Wed-Fri, noon-3.30pm & 5-11pm Sat & Sun; ▣11 to Waldschlösschen) Lighting up Dresden's culinary scene is this fantastic place that's well worth the trip on the 11 tram. The creative menu is streets ahead of most offerings elsewhere, although the best way to experience the 'Pleasure-Atelier' is to book a surprise menu (three/four/five courses €39/49/59) and let the chefs show off their craft. Reservations essential.

Drinking & Nightlife

Altstadt

Karl May Bar BAR
(☑0351-491 20; www.kempinski.com; Taschenberg 3; ☺6pm-2am) Cocktail connoisseurs gravitate to this sophisticated old-school bar inside the Taschenbergpalais (p300) hotel. Sink into a heavy burgundy-coloured leather chair to sip tried-and-true classics, or sample one of 100 whiskies at the curved, dark wood bar. Live music Friday and Saturday; happy hour 6pm to 8pm.

Fährgarten Johannstadt BEER GARDEN
(☑0351-459 6262; www.faehrgarten.de; Käthe-Kollwitz-Ufer 23b; ☺10am-1am Apr-Oct) One of Dresden's most popular drinking spots, this idyllic riverfront beer garden has superb Elbe views, pulls great ales and does a mean barbecue.

Twist Sky Bar BAR
(☑0351-795 150; Salzgasse 4; ☺8pm-2am) Yes, it may be inside the rather faceless Hotel Innside, part of the Melia chain, but its 6th-floor cocktail lounge gives you incredible views of the next-door Frauenkirche dome, while the classic and contemporary cocktails are no let-down. Expect a rather staid crowd of business types and visitors.

Neustadt

Every other door leads into a bar in the centre of Outer Neustadt, at the crossing of Görlitzer Strasse and Louisenstrasse. Some people just plonk themselves down on the pavement come late afternoon and drink in big seated groups...who needs bars?

Bottoms Up BAR
(☑0351-802 0158; Martin-Luther-Strasse 31; ☺5pm-5am Mon-Fri, from 10am Sat & Sun) This is one of Neustadt's most popular and happening bars. There's an outside beer garden, cider on tap, choices of beers ranging from fancy Belgian to local German, and a cosy interior that gets packed at night. The weekend brunch is excellent.

Altes Wettbüro CLUB
(www.altes-wettbuero.de; Antonstrasse 8; ☺4pm-late Tue-Sat) Once a casino (its name means 'the old betting office'), this place is today better employed as a place for the Neustadt's young, mixed and alternative crowd to dance to a varied music selection, including live acts; there are even film showings. There's a beer garden with great food as well.

Lloyd's BAR
(☑0351-501 8775; www.lloyds-cafe-bar.de; Martin-Luther-Strasse 17; ☺8am-1am) In a quiet corner of the Neustadt, Lloyd's oozes grown-up flair thanks to stylish cream-coloured leather furniture, huge mirrors and fanciful chandeliers. It's a solid pit stop from breakfast to that last expertly poured cocktail; it even does a respectable afternoon tea and cake by the fireplace.

Louisengarten BEER GARDEN
(www.biergarten-dresden.de; Louisenstrasse 43; ☺4pm-1am Sun-Thu, 3pm-2am Fri & Sat) This boho-flavoured beer garden takes the go-local concept to the limit. Wind down the day with beer (Lenin's Hanf, aka Lenin's

Hemp) supplied by the nearby Neustädter Hausbrauerei and grilled meats courtesy of the butcher down the street.

Combo
CAFE

(Louisenstrasse 66; ⊙8am-2am) Laidback to the point of toppling, this '70s-retro cafe has enormous windows that fold back when the heat is on, as well as 1960s airport furniture and great coffee served with a side of water and two gummy bears.

Downtown
CLUB

(☑0351-811 5592; www.downtown-dresden.de; Katharinenstrasse 11-13; ⊙10pm-late Fri & Sat) This iconic old factory is home to one of Dresden's most popular clubs, a mainstream affair that packs in a young and up-for-it crowd with three floors of dance action. There's a main floor with hits of the '80s and '90s (you have been warned), an electro lounge and a loft floor with R'n'B sounds.

Café 100
PUB

(☑0351-273 5010; www.diehundert.org; Alaunstrasse 100; ⊙8pm-late) One of the oldest drinking dens in the Neustadt, Café 100 does double duty as a studenty pub on the ground floor and a candle-lit wine bar in the cavernous cellar. Jazz fans invade during the twice-monthly jam sessions.

Neumanns Tiki
BAR

(☑0351-810 3837; Görlitzer Strasse 21; ⊙11am-1am) This legendary Polynesian-style parlour has been plying locals with divine homemade ice cream since 1966, but is also a go-to place for colourful, umbrella-crowned cocktails.

Boys
GAY

(☑0351-563 3630; www.boys-dresden.de; Alaunstrasse 80; ⊙8pm-3am Sun-Thu, to 5am Fri & Sat) This is Dresden's standard-issue gay bar, and it's a lively place that draws a mixed-age crowd and hosts busy parties on Friday and Saturday.

Lebowski Bar
BAR

(www.dudes-bar.de; Görlitzer Strasse 5; ⊙7pm-5am Sun-Thu, to 7am Fri & Sat) When everything else is closed, 'dudes' can still toast the sunrise with a White Russian while the eponymous cult movie reels off in the background. It's nearly always busy with a welcoming local crowd.

☆ Entertainment

The finest all-round listings guide to Dresden is *SAX* (www.cybersax.de), sold at newsstands. Regular freebies include *Blitz* (www.blitzworld.de) and *Kneipensurfer* (www.kneipen-surfer.de). Each has an extensive internet presence, while print versions can be picked up at tourist offices, cafes, pubs and hostels.

★ Die Scheune
LIVE MUSIC

(☑0351-3235 5640; www.scheune.org; Alaunstrasse 36-40) Generations of young folks have memories of the 'Barn', which started out as a mainstream GDR-era youth club before turning into an offbeat culture centre with almost daily concerts, cabaret, parties or performances. The cafe serves Indian food, there's a beer garden and the weekend brunch is epic.

Semperoper Dresden
OPERA

(☑0351-491 1705; www.semperoper.de; Theaterplatz 2; ⊙ticket office 10am-6pm Mon-Fri, to 5pm Sat & Sun) Dresden's famous opera house is the home of the Sächsische Staatsoper Dresden, which puts on brilliant performances that usually sell out.

Katy's Garage
LIVE MUSIC

(www.katysgarage.de; Alaunstrasse 48; ⊙8pm-5am Mon-Sat) This institution can be found at the junction of the Neustadt's two most happening streets. As its name suggests, this cavernous party pit is set in a former tyre shop, with matching decor and even drinks named after car parts. It's part beer garden, part restaurant, part bar, part cinema, part live music venue and all Dresden.

Staatsoperette
THEATRE

(www.staatsoperette.de; Kraftwerk Mitte) An old-school musical theatre reinventing itself in the ultramodern premises of the converted Kraftwerk Mitte (p297) powerplant.

Kraftwerk Mitte
LIVE MUSIC

(☑0351-4188 4699; www.kraftwerk-club.de; Wettiner Platz 7) This large venue inside a redeveloped 19th-century powerplant holds weekly raves and live concerts.

Blue Note
JAZZ

(☑0351-801 4275; www.jazzdepartment.com; Görlitzer Strasse 2b; ⊙8pm-5am) Small, smoky and smooth, this converted space has concerts featuring regional talent almost nightly (usually jazz, but also blues and rock), then turns into a night-owl magnet until the wee hours. Many concerts are free. The drinks menu features beer from around the world and a mind-boggling selection of single-malt whiskies.

Dresdner Philharmonie
CLASSICAL MUSIC

(☑0351-486 6866; www.dresdnerphilharmonie.de) Fresh from a thorough reconstruction, this

ⓘ DRESDEN CARD

The excellent Dresden Card (www. dresden.de/dresdencard) provides free public transport as well as sweeping sightseeing discounts. Various cards are available from the Tourist Office. The one-day Dresden-City-Card (single/family €12/15) is good for transport and discounts to 90 sights, attractions, tours and other participating venues. The two-day version (€37/66) delivers free admission to all state museums with the exception of the Historisches Grünes Gewölbe, and discounts on many others.The Dresden-Regio-Card (from €20/30) includes all this plus discounts to 40 additional sights. All in all, they're excellent value and guarantee big savings if you plan to visit several museums in Dresden.

mammoth-sized GDR-era parallelepiped decorated with Communist-themed murals is home to a renowned orchestra.

Jazzclub Tonne LIVE MUSIC
(☑0351-802 6017; www.jazzclubtonne.de; Königstrasse 15; ⊙8pm-2am) Cool cats of all ages come out to this legendary Dresden jazz joint for good music from local and international talent.

🛍 Shopping

Globetrotter SPORTS & OUTDOORS
(www.globetrotter.de; Prager Str 10; ⊙10am-8pm Mon-Sat) You can fully prepare yourself for a hike in Saxon Switzerland, as well as for an expedition to the Amazon jungle or arctic tundra, in this giant store dedicated to travellers' needs, complete with a pool where you can try a new canoe. Maps and travel guides, including Lonely Planet, are sold on the ground floor.

ⓘ Information

EMERGENCY

Krankenhaus Dresden-Friedrichstadt
(☑0351-4800; www.khdf.de; Friedrichstrasse 41; ⊙24hr) Central hospital with 24-hour emergency room.

POST

Post Office Altmarkt Galerie (Altmarkt Galerie; ⊙9.30am-9pm Mon-Sat) Enter from Wallstrasse.
Post Office Neustadt (Königsbrücker Strasse 21-29; ⊙9am-7pm Mon-Fri, 10am-1pm Sat) The main post office in the Neustadt.

TOURIST INFORMATION

The following book rooms and tours, rent out audioguides and sell the excellent-value Dresden discount cards.
Tourist Office – Frauenkirche (☑0351-501 501; www.dresden.de; QF Passage, Neumarkt 2; ⊙10am-7pm Mon-Fri, to 6pm Sat, to 3pm Sun) Go to the basement of the shopping mall to find the city's most central tourist office, with helpful English-speaking staff.
Tourist Office – Hauptbahnhof (☑0351-501 501; www.dresden.de; Wiener Platz; ⊙8am-8pm) Small office inside the main train station.

ⓘ Getting There & Away

AIR

Dresden International Airport (DRS; ☑0351-881 3360; www.dresden-airport.de; Flughafenstrasse) has flights to many German cities and international destinations including Amsterdam, Zurich, Dubai and Moscow.

CAR & MOTORCYCLE

Dresden is connected to Chemnitz in the west and Poland in the east via the A4, to Leipzig via the A14, to Berlin via the A13/A113, and to Saxon Switzerland and the Czech Republic via the B172 south. All major international car rental companies have outlets at the airport.

TRAIN

Fast trains make the trip to Dresden from Berlin-Hauptbahnhof in two hours (€40) and Leipzig in 1¼ hours (€19.90). The S1 local train runs half-hourly to Meissen (€6.20, 40 minutes) and Bad Schandau in Saxon Switzerland (€6.20, 45 minutes). RE trains connect Dresden with Chemnitz (€16, one hour) via Freiberg (€9.70, 30 to 45 minutes).

ⓘ Getting Around

TO/FROM THE AIRPORT

Dresden airport is about 9km north of the city centre. The S2 train links the airport with the city centre several times hourly (€2.30, 20 minutes). Taxis are about €20.

BICYCLE

A flat and spacious city, Dresden is perfect for cycling. Ask at your hotel or hostel about bike rentals or try **Roll On** (☑0152 2267 3460; www.rollondresden.de; Königsbrücker Strasse 4a; bike/scooter per day from €10/23; ⊙9am-1pm & 5-7pm Mon-Fri, 9am-1pm & 6-7pm Sat & Sun), which also rents out motorised scooters.

PUBLIC TRANSPORT

Buses and trams are run by **Dresdner Verkehrsbetriebe** (DVB; ☑0351-857 1011; www.dvb.de/en). Fares within town cost €2.30, and a day pass €6, valid until 4am the following morning. Buy tickets from vending machines at stops or aboard trams, and remember to validate them in the machines provided.

TAXI

There are taxi ranks at the Hauptbahnhof and Neustadt station, or ring ☑ 0351-211 211.

AROUND DRESDEN

Dresden is surrounded by a trio of fabulous castles as well as the porcelain town of Meissen. If you only have time for one castle, then Schloss Pillnitz has the best garden, Schloss Moritzburg has the most interesting interiors and Schloss Weesenstein the most romantic location. Alternatively, Meissen offers a castle, a cathedral and its immense porcelain heritage. For a time-trip to the DDR era, head to the excellent museum in Pirna. The museum and castles are all easily reached by public transport.

◎ Sights

Schloss & Park Pillnitz   PALACE

(☑ 0351-261 3260; www.schlosspillnitz.de; Aug-Böckstiegel-Strasse 2; park btwn 9am & 6pm adult/concession €3/2.50, park, museums & greenhouses €8/6; ☺ park 6am-dusk, museums 10am-6pm Tue-Sun May-Oct) Baroque has gone exotic at Schloss Pillnitz, a delightful pleasure palace, festooned with fanciful Chinese flourishes. This is where the Saxon rulers once lived it up during long hot Dresden summers. Explore the wonderful gardens, then study the history of the palace and life at court in the Schlossmuseum. Two other buildings, the Wasserpalais and the Bergpalais, house the Kunstgewerbemuseum, which is filled with fancy furniture and knick-knacks from the Saxon court, including Augustus the Strong's throne.

Tickets are also good for the two greenhouses (February to April only). Pillnitz is dreamily wedged between vineyards and the Elbe, some 14km upriver from central Dresden. Drivers should take the B6 (Bautzner Landstrasse) to Pillnitzer Landstrasse. Otherwise, take tram 6 from Dresden-Neustadt, then catch bus 63 at Schillerplatz to Pillnitzer Platz. The loveliest approach is by steamer operated by Sächsische Dampfschiffahrt (p299), which makes the trip from Dresden's Terrassenufer in 90 minutes.

Schloss Weesenstein   PALACE

(☑ 035027-6260; www.schloss-weesenstein.de; Am Schlossberg 1, Müglitztal; adult/concession €7.50/6, audioguide €2; ☺ 10am-6pm Apr-Oct, to 4pm Tue-Sun Feb, Mar, Nov & Dec, to 5pm Sat & Sun Jan) A magnificent sight on a rocky crag high above the Müglitz River, Schloss Weesenstein is an amazing alchemy of styles, blending medieval roots with Renaissance and baroque embellishments. This has resulted in an architectural curiosity where the banquet halls ended up beneath the roof, the horse stables on the 5th floor, and the residential quarters in the cellar.

The palace owes its distinctive looks to the noble Bünau family who dabbled with it for 12 generations from 1406 until 1772. In the 19th century, it became the private retreat of King Johann of Saxony, who distinguished himself not only as a ruler but also as a philosopher and translator of Dante into German. Lavishly furnished and decorated period rooms on the ground floor contain an exhibit about the man and life at court. In keeping with the topsy-turvy architecture, the permanent exhibit takes you on a reverse journey through Saxon history, ending with the Middle Ages.

There are restaurants in the former palace prison, with a cafe, traditional brewpub and the upmarket Königliche Schlossküche. After filling your belly, you can take a digestive saunter in the lovely baroque park.

Schloss Weesenstein is about 16km southeast of Dresden. From Dresden Hauptbahnhof, take the S1 and change to the SB72 in Heidenau (€6, 25 minutes). Weesenstein train station is about 500m south of the castle – follow the road up the hill. By car, take the A17 to Pirna, then head towards Glashütte and follow the signs to the Schloss.

Schloss Moritzburg   PALACE

(☑ 035207-8730; www.schloss-moritzburg.de; Schlossallee; adult/concession €8/6; ☺ 10am-6pm, to 5pm Sat & Sun Mar) An impossibly romantic vision in yellow and white surrounded by an enormous moat-like lake and a park that is at turns wild and formal, baroque Schloss Moritzburg was the preferred hunting palace of the Saxon rulers – and the site of some lavish post-hunting parties under August the Strong. It's no surprise then that antlers are the main decorative feature in these halls sheathed in rich leather wall covering, some painted with mythological scenes.

Prized trophies include the antlers of an extinct species of giant stag, and bizarrely misshapen ones in the Hall of Monstrosities. Considerably prettier is the legendary Federzimmer (Feather Room) downstairs, the centrepiece of which is a bed made from over a million colourful duck, pheasant and peacock feathers.

SAXONY AROUND DRESDEN

Moritzburg is about 14km north of Dresden. Buses 326 and 457 make regular trips from Dresden-Neustadt train station (€4.10, 30 minutes). For a more atmospheric approach, take the S1 train to Radebeul-Ost (€4.10, 15 minutes) and from there the 1884 narrow-gauge **Lössnitzgrundbahn** (www.loessnitzgrundbahn.de; €7.30 minutes) to the palace.

DDR Museum Pirna MUSEUM

(☑ 03501-774 842; www.ddr-museum-pirna.de; Rottwerndorferstrasse 45; adult/child €8/6; ⊙ 10am-5pm Tue-Sun Apr-Oct, 10am-5pm Tue-Thu, Sat & Sun Nov-Mar) In a former army barracks, you can snoop around a furnished apartment, sit in a classroom with a portrait of GDR leader Walter Ulbricht glowering down at you, or find out how much a Junge Pioniere youth organisation uniform costs. Thousands of objects are creatively arranged and, while most are self-explanatory, others would benefit from informative text.

To get here, take the S1 from Dresden's Hauptbahnhof to Pirna, walk five minutes to the central bus station (ZOB) and hop on local bus N for 'Geibeltbad/Freizeitzentrum' (€4, 35 minutes). Note that there is no entry after 3.30pm.

ℹ Getting There & Away

All sights in the area can be easily reached by either train or bus from central Dresden, and all are located within the Dresden tariff zone. Sächsische Dampfschiffahrt (p299) boats come in handy for sights along the Elbe River.

ℹ GETTING AROUND SAXONY

Saxony has excellent public transport, and if you plan to travel all over the state, the **Sachsen-Ticket** is valid for unlimited 2nd-class travel on any regional Deutsche Bahn and many privately run trains. The cost is €24 for the first person, and €7 each for up to four additional people travelling together. There is no charge for bicycles.

You can buy tickets online and in stations from vending machines or ticket counters. Buses supplement train routes, and provision for cyclists is excellent across the state. Longer train journeys can often be purchased online with big discounts, if you book at least a few days beforehand and are flexible with travel times.

Meissen

☑ 03521 / POP 27,700

Straddling the Elbe around 25km northwest of Dresden, Meissen is the cradle of European porcelain manufacturing and still hitches its tourism appeal to the world-famous china first cooked up in its imposing castle in 1710. But even those left unmoved by August the Strong's 'white gold' will find the impressive position of the town compelling, with its soaring Gothic cathedral, fairy-tale castle and wonderful Elbe Valley views.

◉ Sights

★ **Erlebniswelt Haus Meissen** MUSEUM

(☑ 03521-468 208; www.meissen.com; Talstrasse 9; adult/concession €10/6; ⊙ 9am-6pm May-Oct, to 5pm Nov-Apr) Next to the historic porcelain factory south of the Altstadt, this museum is *the* place to witness the astonishing artistry and artisanship that makes Meissen porcelain unique. Visits start with a 30-minute group tour (with English audioguide) of four studios, where artists demonstrate vase throwing, plate painting, figure moulding and glazing. This gives you a better appreciation for the ensuing collections of historic and contemporary porcelain, which can be enjoyed at your own speed.

The museum is hugely popular and often totally overrun by coach tours. As entry is timed and only in groups, you may have to wait a while during high season.

Albrechtsburg CASTLE

(☑ 03521-470 70; www.albrechtsburg-meissen.de; Domplatz 1; adult/concession incl audioguide €8/6.50, with Dom €11/8; ⊙ 10am-6pm Mar-Oct, to 5pm Nov-Feb) Lording it over Meissen, the 15th-century Albrechtsburg was the first German castle constructed for residential purposes, but is more famous as the birthplace of European porcelain. An exhibit on the 2nd floor chronicles how it all began; a nifty touch terminal even lets you 'invent' your own porcelain.

It took a group of scientists led by Walther von Tschirnhaus and Johann Friedrich Böttger three years to discover the secret formula of the 'white gold', a feat achieved by the Chinese thousands of years earlier. Production began in the castle in 1710 and only moved to a custom-built factory in 1863. The invention's importance for Saxony is hard to overstate, bringing enormous wealth and prestige to the Saxon electors (princes).

The palace is distinguished by several architectural innovations, most notably a curvilinear staircase and an eye-catching cell vaulting in the Great Hall, swathed in epic murals depicting scenes from the history of the palace and its builders, Elector Ernst of Saxony and his brother Albrecht.

Dom
CATHEDRAL

(📞 03521-452 490; www.dom-zu-meissen.de; Domplatz 7; adult/concession €4.50/3, with Albrechtsburg €11/8; ☺ 9am-6pm Apr-Oct, 10am-4pm Nov-Mar) Meissen's dome, a high-Gothic masterpiece begun in 1250, does not impress as much by its size as by the wealth of its interior decorations. Stained-glass windows showing scenes from the Old and New Testaments create an ethereal backdrop for the delicately carved statues in the choir, presumed to be the work of the famous Master of Naumburg, a medieval stone sculptor whose name is now lost. The altar triptych is attributed to Lucas Cranach the Elder. Tower tours (adult/concession €6/4.50) are offered several times daily from April to October.

Markt
SQUARE

The handsome Markt is flanked by colourfully painted historic townhouses along with the **Rathaus** (1472) and the Gothic Frauenkirche.

Frauenkirche
CHURCH

(📞 03521-453 832; Markt; tower adult/concession €2/1; ☺ 10am-5pm Apr-Oct) The Gothic Frauenkirche's carillon, the world's oldest made from porcelain, chimes a different ditty six times daily. Climb the tower for fine red-roof views of the Altstadt.

🛏 Sleeping & Eating

Herberge Orange
HOSTEL €

(📞 03521-454 334; www.herberge-orange.de; Siebeneichener Strasse 34; dm/s/d incl breakfast €23.50/33.50/52; 🅿 🛜) This friendly, family-run riverside hostel is 1.5km south of the Markt, and is the best budget accommodation in Meissen. Add €2 per day for bed sheets and towel.

Hotel Goldener Löwe
HOTEL €€

(📞 03521-411 10; www.goldener-loewe-meissen.com; Heinrichsplatz 6; s/d €65/115, breakfast €14; 🅿 @ 🛜) Everything works like a well-oiled machine behind the cheerful yellow facade of this 17th-century inn near the Markt. Rooms are a harmonious blend of antique-style furnishings and modern touches. Wind down the day at the restaurant or enjoy a glass of local wine in the tavern.

★ Restaurant Vincenz Richter
GERMAN €€

(📞 03521-453 285; www.vincenz-richter.de; An der Frauenkirche 12; mains €12-24; ☺ noon-11pm Mon-Sat, to 6pm Sun; 🎦) Despite the historic guns and armour, the romance factor is high at this 16th-century inn thanks to attentive service, classy interpretations of classic Saxon dishes, and crisp whites from the Richters' own wine estate. Terrace tables have a view of the Markt.

Domkeller
GERMAN €€

(📞 03521-457 676; www.domkeller-meissen.com; Domplatz 9; mains €13-20; ☺ 11.30am-11pm) High above Meissen, this atmospheric tavern outside the cathedral has been in the hearty food and drink business since 1470. Standouts on the Saxon menu include a beer goulash served in a hollowed-out bread bowl and the meat skewer that's flambéed at the table. The terrace has staggering views – get here early at lunchtime to secure a place.

🛈 Information

Tourist Office (📞 03521-419 40; www.touristinfo-meissen.de; Markt 3; ☺ 10am-6pm Mon-Fri, to 4pm Sat & Sun Apr-Oct, to 5pm Mon-Fri, to 3pm Sat Nov, Dec, Feb & Mar)

🛈 Getting There & Around

BOAT

Sächsische Dampfschiffart (p299) steamboats depart from the Terrassenufer in Dresden. Boats return upstream to Dresden at 2.45pm, but take over three hours to make the trip. Many people opt to travel from Dresden by boat and return by train.

BUS

The **Stadtrundfahrt Meissen** (📞 03521-741 631; www.vg-meissen.de; day pass adult/concession €5/3.50; ☺ 9.30am-6pm Apr-Oct) hop-on, hop-off minibus links all the major sights along two intersecting routes.

TRAIN

From Dresden, take the half-hourly S1 train (€6, 20 minutes) to Meissen. For the porcelain factory, get off at Meissen-Triebischtal.

SAXON SWITZERLAND

About 40km south of Dresden, Saxon Switzerland (Sächsische Schweiz, aka Elbsandsteingebirge or Elbe Sandstone Mountains) embraces a unique and evocative landscape. This is wonderfully rugged country where nature has chiselled porous rock into bizarre columns, battered cliffs, tabletop mountains and deep valleys. The Elbe courses through thick forest, past villages and mighty hilltop castles. No wonder such fabled beauty was a big hit with 19th-century Romantic artists, including the painter Caspar David Friedrich. In 1990, about a third of the area became Saxony's only national park, Saxon Switzerland National Park (Nationalpark Sächsische Schweiz).

You could tick off the area's highlights on a long daytrip from Dresden, but to truly experience the magic of Saxon Switzerland, stay overnight and enjoy a couple of good walks. In addition to hiking, this is one of Germany's premier rock-climbing destinations, offering over 15,000 routes. Cyclists can follow the lovely Elberadweg.

🛏 Sleeping

Bad Schandau has the main cluster of hotels, but there are hotels and guesthouses pretty much everywhere in the Elbe Valley, including Königstein and Kurort Rathen.

❶ Getting There & Around

BOAT

From April to October, steamers operated by **Sächsische Dampfschiffahrt** (☑ 0331-866 090; www.saechsische-dampfschiffahrt.de) plough up the Elbe several times daily between Dresden and Bad Schandau, stopping in Rathen, Königstein and other towns. The entire one-way trip takes 5½ hours and costs €25 (concession €18). You can do the entire trip or hop aboard along the way.

Passenger ferries (bicycles allowed) cross the Elbe in Stadt Wehlen, Rathen and Königstein, though only the ferry in Rathen is very regular.

BUS

From mid-April to October, a bus service operated by **Frank Nuhn Freizeit und Tourismus** (☑ 035021-990 80; www.frank-nuhn-freizeit-und-tourismus.de) shuttles between Königstein, Bad Schandau and Mezni Louka in the Czech Republic three times daily (full trip €6). Buy tickets from the driver.

CAR & MOTORCYCLE

Towns are linked to Dresden and each other by the B172; coming from Dresden, it's faster to take the A17 and pick up the B172 in Pirna. There are only three bridges across the Elbe: two in Pirna and one in Bad Schandau.

TRAIN

The Dresden S1 S-Bahn line connects Bad Schandau, Königstein and Rathen with Dresden, Pirna, Radebeul and Meissen every 30 minutes. Bad Schandau is also a stop on long-distance EC trains travelling between Hamburg and Vienna.

Bastei

The Bastei is a stunning rock formation nearly 200m above the Elbe and the village of Rathen. It's a wonderland of fluted pinnacles and offers panoramic views of the surrounding forests, cliffs and the Elbe River below. The much-photographed Basteibrücke, a sandstone bridge built in 1851, leads through the rocks to the remnants of a partly reconstructed medieval castle, the **Felsenburg Neurathen** (adult/concession €2/1; ⊙ 9am-6pm), which is open for touring.

The Bastei is the most popular spot in Saxon Switzerland National Park (Nationalpark Sächsische Schweiz), so crowds are guaranteed unless you get here before 10am or after 4pm. Weekends and any day in summer will be busy, and an easy way to escape the crowds is by hitting the hiking trail. A 5km loop leads from the car park to the Schwedenlöcher, a hideout where local troops dodged the advancing Swedes during the Thirty Years' War (1618–48).

🛏 Sleeping & Eating

There are a few restaurants and food stands on both sides of the river in Kurort Rathen. A cafe also awaits you at the top of Bastei.

Villa Zeissig   GUESTHOUSE €
(☑ 035024-702 05; www.villa-zeissig.de; Zum Grünbach 3-4; d from €52; 🅿🕸) On the hillside above Rathen's main street, this charming alpine-style chalet has several modern and spacious rooms with balconies. It's a short clamber up a staircase from the road.

⭐**Burg Altrathen**   HOTEL €€
(☑ 035024-7600; www.burg-altrathen.de; Am Grünbach 10-11; d €80-130; ➾🕸) This charmingly located hotel occupies an impressive mock castle on a hilltop above Rathen. There are romantically decked-out rooms, a great restaurant and a terrace with stellar Elbe views. The welcome is warm, and if the hotel is booked up, there are more rooms in sister establishments scattered around town.

❶ Getting There & Away

The nearest train station is in Rathen, where you need to catch the ferry across the Elbe (€2), then follow a sweat-raising 30-minute trail to the top of the Bastei. Drivers can use the big car park near the train station. There's more parking available on the Bastei side of the Elbe; drive to Pirna and follow the Basteistrasse (S167/164) to Lohmen, then the S165 (direction Hohenstein) and follow the signs. If you arrive early (before 10am), you should be able to snag a spot in the inner Bastei car park, from where it's only a 10-minute walk to the viewpoints. Otherwise, you need to use the outer car park, about 3km away, and either catch a shuttle bus or walk.

Königstein

📱 035021 / POP 16,000

The charming village of Königstein has a cutesy town centre, a gorgeous location on the banks of the Elbe and is crowned by a massive citadel built on a tabletop mountain some 260m above. It's an excellent base for walkers, with most of the best walking in Saxon Switzerland National Park (Nationalpark Sächsische Schweiz) within easy striking distance.

⊙ Sights

Festung Königstein   FORTRESS
(📱 035021-646 07; www.festung-koenigstein.de; adult/concession Apr-Oct €10/7, Nov-Mar €8/6, audioguide €3; ⊙ 9am-6pm Apr-Oct, to 5pm Nov-Mar; 🚼) Festung Königstein is the largest intact fortress in Germany, and so imposing and formidable that noone in history has ever even bothered to attack it, let alone conquered it. Begun in the 13th century, it was repeatedly enlarged and is now a veritable textbook of military architecture, with 30 buildings spread across 9.5 hectares.

Inside, the main highlight is the In Lapide Regis, a superb permanent exhibition that tells the dramatic story of the fortress in an engaging and interactive way. Elsewhere within the sprawling fortress complex you can visit the Brunnenhaus, with its seemingly bottomless well, see an array of German weaponry, and enter the Georgenburg, once Saxony's most feared prison, whose famous inmates included Meissen porcelain inventor Johann Friedrich Böttger.

During WWII, the fortress served as a POW camp and a refuge for priceless art treasures from Dresden. Another draw is the widescreen view deep into the national park and across to the Lilienstein tabletop mountain.

From April to October, the **Festungsexpress** (📱 035021-990 80; www.frank-nuhn-freizeit-und-tourismus.de; Reissiger Platz; one-way/return €3/5; ⊙ 9am-4pm May-Oct, from 10am Apr) tourist train makes the steep climb half-hourly from Königstein to the fortress. Alternatively it's a strenuous 30- to 45-minute climb from the bottom. The nearest car park is off the B172 (exit Festung), from where it's a 10-minute walk to the fortress.

WHAT'S IN A NAME?

With its highest peak rising to just 723m, Saxon Switzerland ain't exactly the Alps. So how did the region get its name? Credit belongs to the Swiss. During the 18th century, the area's romantic scenery, with its needle-nose pinnacles and craggy cliffs, lured countless artists from around the world. Among them were the Swiss landscape artist Adrian Zingg and his friend, the portraitist Anton Graff, who had been hired to teach at Dresden's prestigious art academy. Both felt that the landscape very much resembled their homeland (the Swiss Jura) and voila, the phrase 'Saxon Switzerland' was born. Travel writers picked it up and so it remains to this day.

🍽 Sleeping & Eating

⭐**Ferdinands Homestay**   HOSTEL €
(📱 035022-547 75; www.ferdinandshomestay.de; Halbestadt 51; dm €14, s/d €30/40, campsite €2.50-5.50, campsite per person €6, breakfast €7; ⊙ Apr-Oct; 🅿🐾) Ferdinands Homestay is a small and friendly riverside hostel and camping ground in a secluded, remote spot on the northern bank of the Elbe, with some lovely river views. Booking ahead at weekends and during the summer months is always a good idea, as it's by far the best value in town.

Kleine Einkehr   SAXON €
(📱 035021-675 39; www.kleine-einkehr.de; Elbhäuserweg 23; mains €8-14; ⊙ noon-8pm Fri-Wed May-Oct, noon-8pm Sat & Sun Nov-Apr) A wonderful 2km riverside walk from Königstein proper (cross under the railway line and then hook a left onto the river embankment) takes you to this popular family-run Saxon restaurant with outdoor tables and hearty traditional fare.

ⓘ Information

The **tourist office** (📱 035021-682 61; www.koenigstein-sachsen.de; Pirnaer Strasse 2; ⊙ 9am-9pm May-Sep, to 6pm Apr & Oct, to 6pm Mon-Fri, to 1pm Sat & Sun Nov-Mar) is on the town's main square. The English-speaking staff can help with accommodation, tours and hiking maps.

ⓘ Getting There & Away

There's no bridge across the Elbe here, but there is a ferry that goes back and forth until 11pm.

Bad Schandau

☑ 035022 / POP 2920

The little spa town of Bad Schandau sits right on the Elbe and is the unofficial capital of Saxon Switzerland. Most of the region's hotels, supermarkets and restaurants are here, and it's also a central base for hiking.

◉ Sights & Activities

Personenaufzug　　　　　　　　　　　TOWER
(Rudolf-Sendig Str; adult/concession return €2.80/2.20; ☺ 9am-6pm Apr & Oct, to 8pm May-Sep) This old lift, which dates from 1905, whisks you up a 50m-high tower for views and access to a footbridge linking to a pretty forest path that runs into the national park. It's on the road out of town, towards the Czech border.

Nationalparkzentrum　　　　　　　　MUSEUM
(☑ 035022-502 40; www.lanu.de; Dresdner Strasse 2b; adult/concession €4/3; ☺ 9am-6pm, closed Jan & Mon Nov-Mar) The National Park Centre has ho-hum exhibitions on local flora, fauna and how the sandstone formations were shaped, but the evocative visuals of the 17-minute introductory movie almost justify the admission price, if you're not planning to explore the mountains yourself.

Schrammsteinaussicht　　　　　　　HIKING
(Nationalpark Sächsische Schweiz) The rugged Schrammsteine is the densest rock labyrinth in the Saxon Switzerland National Park. A moderate to strenuous trail leads to a fantastic viewpoint of the rocks, the Elbe Valley and the national park. The first 20 minutes up the steep Obrigensteig are tough, but then the trail levels out and leads through fabulous rock formations.

No technical skills are required, although you should be fairly surefooted. On your descent, follow the Mittelweg to the Elbleitenweg back to the Obrigensteig.

Toskana Therme　　　　　　　　　　SPA
(☑ 35022-546 10; www.toskanaworld.net; Rudolf-Sendig-Strasse 8a; 2 hr/4 hr/day card €17/21/27; ☺ 10am-10pm Sun-Thu, to midnight Fri & Sat) After a day of strenuous hiking, hardly anything is better that descending into a hot-water pool or sweating your fatigue off in a sauna. With an open-air pool coming face to face with the Elbe, this is a perfect place to do so. As ever in Germany, the sauna section is mixed gender and nude only.

Kirnitzschtalbahn　　　　　　　　　RAIL
(www.ovps.de; Kurpark; adult/concession €5/2.50, day pass €8/4; ☺ 9.30am-7.30pm Apr-Oct) This solar-powered tram quaintly trundles 7km northeast along the Kirnitzsch River to Beuthenfall. The Lichtenhainer Waterfall is just a 500m walk away and a good spot to begin a hike among the sandstone cliffs.

🍴 Sleeping & Eating

Bad Schandau has a lovely food scene, which includes a good number of kiosks and trailers peddling wurst (sausages) and other fast food.

Lindenhof　　　　　　　　　　　HOTEL €€
(☑ 035022-4890; www.lindenhof-bad-schandau.de; Rudolf-Sendig-Strasse 11; s/d €60/89; 🅿🛜) The Lindenhof, in the centre of Bad Schandau, is a popular choice for weekenders wanting urban comfort within easy reach of the mountains. There's also a good traditional restaurant on site.

ℹ Information

Tourist Office (☑ 035022-900 30; www.bad-schandau.de; Marktplatz 12; ☺ 9am-9pm May-Sep, to 6pm Apr & Oct, to 6pm Mon-Fri, to 1pm Sat & Sun Nov-Mar, closed Wed Jan & Feb; 🖳) Located on the town's main square, it has lots of information and interactive displays, and can help with booking accommodation and hiking trips.

ℹ Getting There & Away

S1 trains from Dresden Hauptbahnhof to Bad Schandau depart every 30 minutes (€6.20, 45 minutes).

LEIPZIG & WESTERN SAXONY

The more industrialised western part of Saxony centres on Leipzig, a green, hip and vibrant city with many stories to tell and places to enjoy. Hugely important in the history of music, it was home to Johann Sebastian Bach and Richard Wagner. To the south, Chemnitz is still full of vestiges of GDR-era Soviet influence, including a huge head of Karl Marx in the central square, but is now home to several exciting museums, including the newly opened state-of-the art SMAC museum of archaeology and prehistory. The lovely university town of Freiberg boasts a fantastic collection of minerals and a visitable ore mine, while Zwickau's former Audi factory has been turned into

ESCAPE TO COLDITZ

The very name Colditz is enough to send goosebumps down many people's spines, and so it might come as a surprise that the famous WWII-era high security prison for Allied officers is not as instantaneously recognisable to most Germans, who grew up without the string of books and films this iconic prison has inspired. A Renaissance castle straddling a crag above sleepy Colditz, **Schloss Colditz** (☑034381-437 77; www.schloss-colditz.com; Schlossgasse 1; adult/concession museum €4/3, tour €8.50/7; ☺museum 10am-5pm Apr-Oct, to 4pm Nov-Mar, tours 10.30am, 1pm & 3pm) has seen stints as a hunting lodge, a poorhouse and even a psychiatric hospital.

But its notoriety stems from its years as Oflag IVC, where the Nazis imprisoned officers who had already escaped from less secure camps and been recaptured, including a nephew of Winston Churchill.

As you would expect, some 300 prisoners here made further attempts to escape and 31 actually managed to flee. The would-be escapees were often aided by ingenious self-made gadgetry, including a glider fashioned from wood and bed sheets, and a homemade sewing machine for making fake German uniforms. Most astounding, perhaps, is a 44m-long tunnel below the chapel that French officers dug in 1941–42, before the Germans caught them. You can see some of these contraptions, along with lots of photographs, in the small but fascinating Fluchtmuseum (Escape Museum) within the castle.

On weekdays, bus 690 makes the trip from Leipzig Hauptbahnhof to Colditz, some 46km southeast of Leipzig, and back several times daily (€7, two hours). For timetables, see www.mdv.de.

---

an outstanding museum presenting Germany's complicated 20th-century history as a succession of gleaming retro cars, including the inevitable Trabbies in all shapes and forms.

Leipzig

☑0341 / POP 590,300

'Hypezig!' cry the papers, 'the New Berlin', says just about everybody. Yes, Leipzig is Saxony's coolest city, a playground for nomadic young creatives who have been displaced by the fast-gentrifying German capital, but it's also a city of enormous history, a trade-fair centre and solidly in the sights of music lovers due to its intrinsic connection to the lives and work of Bach, Mendelssohn and Wagner.

To this day, one of the world's top classical bands (the Gewandhausorchester) and oldest and finest boys' choirs (the 800-year-old Thomanerchor) continue to delight audiences. When it comes to art, the neo-realistic New Leipzig School has stirred up the international art world post-reunification with such protagonists as Neo Rauch and Tilo Baumgärtel.

Leipzig is known as the *Stadt der Helden* (City of Heroes) for its leading role in the 1989 'Peaceful Revolution' that led to the reunification of Germany.

◉ Sights

★**Museum der Bildenden Künste** MUSEUM
(Map p318; ☑0341-216 990; www.mdbk.de; Katharinenstrasse 10; adult/concession €10/7, audioguide €2; ☺10am-6pm Tue & Thu-Sun, noon-8pm Wed) This imposing modernist glass cube is the home of Leipzig's fine art museum and its world-class collection of paintings from the 15th century to today, including works by Caspar David Friedrich, Cranach, Munch and Monet. Highlights include rooms dedicated to native sons Max Beckmann, Max Klinger and Neo Rauch. Exhibits are playfully juxtaposed and include sculpture, installation and religious art. The collection is enormous, so set aside at least two hours to do it justice.

★**Museen im Grassi** MUSEUM
(Map p314; www.grassimuseum.de; Johannisplatz 5-11; combined ticket adult/concession €15/12; ☺10am-6pm Tue-Sun) The university-run Museen im Grassi harbours three fantastic collections that are often overlooked, despite being a five-minute walk from Augustusplatz. At the stellar **Musikinstrumenten-Museum** (Map p314; ☑0341-973 0750; http://mfm.uni-leipzig.de; adult/concession €6/3, audioguide €1; ☺10am-6pm Tue-Sun) you can discover music from five centuries in rarity-filled exhibits and an interactive sound laboratory. The **Museum für Völkerkunde** (Ethnological Museum; Map p314; ☑0341-973 1900; adult/

Greater Leipzig

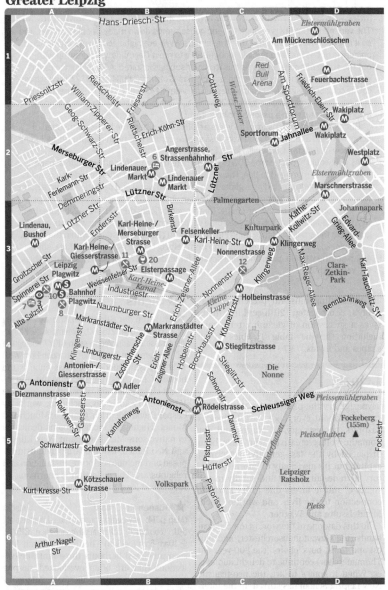

SAXONY LEIPZIG

concession €8/6) takes you on an eye-opening journey through the cultures of the world. The **Museum für Angewandte Kunst** (Museum of Applied Arts; Map p314; ☎ 0341-222 9100; adult/concession €8/5.50; ⊙10am-6pm Tue-Sun) has an excellent art nouveau and art deco

furniture, porcelain, glass and ceramics collection.

Asisi Panometer GALLERY
(Map p314; ☎ 0341-355 5340; www.asisi.de; Richard-Lehmann-Strasse 114; adult/concession

SAXONY LEIPZIG

gar Asisi, who uses paper and pencil and computer technology to create bafflingly detailed monumental scenes drawn from nature or history. Each work is about 100m long and 30m high.

Südfriedhof CEMETERY
(☎0341-123 5700; Prager Strasse; ☺grounds 8am-6pm, info centre 11am-4pm Mon-Thu) Leipzig's largest cemetery is a vast and beautiful park, filled with rosebay shrubs, populated by squirrels, rabbits and foxes and centred on a building that looks like a Disneyland castle, but is in fact a purpose-built crematorium. A monument to antifascists who died at the hands of the Nazis can be found in front of the building. The cemetery is a last resting place of Leipzig's many celebrities, including artist Max Klinger and the Baedeker family of travel guide fame.

The cemetery surrounds Völkerschlachtdenkmal, so plan your visit to see both in one go.

€11.50/10; ☺10am-5pm Mon-Fri, to 6pm Sat & Sun; ▣16 to Richard-Lehmann/Zwickauer Strasse) The happy marriage of a *pano*rama (a giant 360° painting) and a gaso*meter* (a giant gas tank) is a panometer. The unusual concept is the brainchild of Berlin-based artist Yade-

SAXONY LEIPZIG

DON'T MISS

CHURCH OF PEACE

This **church** (Church of St Nicholas; Map p318; www.nikolaikirche.de; Nikolaikirchhof 3; ⊙10am-6pm Mon-Sat, to 4pm Sun) has Romanesque and Gothic roots but since 1797 has sported a striking neoclassical interior with palm-like pillars and cream-coloured pews. While the design is certainly gorgeous, the church is most famous for playing a key role in the nonviolent movement that led to the downfall of the East German government. As early as 1982 it hosted 'peace prayers' every Monday at 5pm (still held today), which over time inspired and empowered local citizens to confront the injustices plaguing their country.

Starting in September 1989, the prayers were followed by candlelight demonstrations, which reached their peak on 9 October when 70,000 citizens took to the streets. The military, police and secret police stood ready to suppress the protests, as they had so violently done only two days earlier. But the order never came. The GDR leadership had capitulated. A singular palm-topped column outside the church commemorates this peaceful revolution.

Zeitgeschichtliches Forum   MUSEUM
(Forum of Contemporary History; Map p318; ☑0341-222 0400; www.hdg.de/leipzig; Grimmaische Strasse 6; ⊙9am-6pm Tue-Fri, from 10am Sat & Sun) FREE This fascinating, enormous and well-curated exhibit covers the political history of the GDR, from division and dictatorship to fall-of-the-Wall ecstasy and post-Wende blues. It's essential viewing for anyone seeking to understand the late country's political power apparatus, the systematic oppression of regime critics, milestones in inter-German and international relations, and the opposition movement that led to its downfall.

Zoo Leipzig   ZOO
(Map p314; ☑0341-593 3385; www.zoo-leipzig.de; Pfaffendorfer Strasse 29; adult/concession €21/17; ⊙9am-7pm May-Sep, to 6pm Apr & Oct, to 5pm Nov-Mar; 🚌12 to Zoo) The standout attraction at Leipzig Zoo, one of Germany's most progressive, is Gondwanaland, a jungly wonderland of 17,000 plants and 300 exotic animals. Rare and endangered species, such as komodo dragons and pygmy hippos, roam around spacious enclosures in a climate-controlled hall amid fragrant tropical plants. Explore by following a jungle path, a treetop trail or by drifting along in a boat.

Stasi Museum   MUSEUM
(Map p318; ☑0341-961 2443; www.runde-ecke-leipzig.de; Dittrichring 24; ⊙10am-6pm) FREE In the GDR the walls had ears, as is chillingly documented in this exhibit in the former Leipzig headquarters of the East German secret police (the Stasi), a building known as the Runde Ecke (Round Corner). English-language audioguides (€4) aid in understanding the all-German displays on propaganda, preposterous disguises, cunning surveillance devices, recruitment (even among children), scent storage and other chilling machinations.

Stadtgeschichtliches Museum   MUSEUM
(City History Museum; Map p318; ☑0341-965 130; www.stadtgeschichtliches-museum-leipzig.de; Markt 1; adult/concession €6/4; ⊙10am-6pm Tue-Sun) Leipzig's beautiful Renaissance town hall is an atmospheric setting to recount the twists and turns of the city's history from its roots as a key medieval trading town to the present, including stops at the Battle of the Nations and the 1989 Peaceful Revolution. A nearby modern extension, the **Neubau** (Böttchergässchen 3; adult/concession €5/3.50; ⊙10am-6pm Tue-Sun), presents quality temporary exhibits, and is included on the combined ticket (adult/concession €10/8).

Bach-Museum Leipzig   MUSEUM
(Map p318; ☑0341-913 7202; www.bachmuseum leipzig.de; Thomaskirchhof 16; adult/concession/child under 16yr €8/6/free; ⊙10am-6pm Tue-Sun) This interactive museum does more than tell you about the life and accomplishments of Johann Sebastian Bach. Learn how to date a Bach manuscript, listen to baroque instruments or treat your ears to any composition he ever wrote. The 'treasure room' downstairs displays rare original manuscripts.

Thomaskirche   CHURCH
(Map p318; ☑0341-222 240; www.thomaskirche. org; Thomaskirchhof 18; tower €2; ⊙church 9am-6pm, tower 1pm, 2pm & 4.30pm Sat, 2pm & 3pm Sun Apr-Nov) Johann Sebastian Bach worked as a cantor in the Thomaskirche from 1723 until his death in 1750, and his remains lie buried beneath a bronze plate in front of the altar. The Thomanerchor (p324), once led by Bach, has been going strong since 1212

and now includes 100 boys aged eight to 18. The church tower can be climbed, though the real reason to come here is to absorb the great man's legacy, often played on the church's giant organ.

Völkerschlachtdenkmal
MONUMENT

(Monument to the Battle of the Nations; ☑0341-241 6870; www.stadtgeschichtliches-museum-leipzig. de; Strasse des 18 Oktober 100; adult/child €8/6; ⊙10am-6pm Apr-Oct, to 4pm Nov-Mar; ☐2 or 15 to Völkerschlachtdenkmal) Half a million soldiers fought – and one in five died – in the epic 1813 battle that led to the decisive victory of Prussian, Austrian and Russian forces over Napoléon's army. Built a century later near the killing fields, the Völkerschlachtdenkmal is a 91m colossus, towering sombrely like something straight out of Gotham City. Views from the top are monumental. If you need to bone up on your history, stop by the integrated Forum 1813 exhibit within the monument complex.

Galerie für Zeitgenössische Kunst
GALLERY

(Map p314; ☑0341-140 8126; www.gfzk-leipzig. de; Karl-Tauchnitz-Strasse 9-11; adult/concession per space €5/3, both spaces €8/4, Wed free; ⊙2-7pm Tue-Fri, noon-6pm Sat & Sun) Contemporary art in all media is the speciality of this gallery, presented in temporary exhibits in a minimalist container-like space and a late-19th-century villa.

Baumwollspinnerei
ARTS CENTRE

(Map p314; ☑0341-498 0222; www.spinnerei.de; Spinnerei Strasse 7; ⊙hours vary) FREE With about 100 resident artists, this sprawling industrial site, which grew around a 19th-century cotton mill, is a hub for contemporary art collectors, dealers and dedicated enthusiasts, although less so for average travellers. Yet, as a larger-than-life landmark in Plagwitz, it is worth snooping around – perhaps you'll find the next Botticelli in a scruffy workshop.

Augustusplatz
SQUARE

(Map p318) Massive Augustusplatz may look nondescript at best, and foreboding at worst, but it is actually flanked by some of Leipzig's most famous buildings, including the Gewandhaus (the city's main concert hall) and the opera house (p325). The 11-storey Kroch-Haus (Map p318; ☑0341-973 7015; www.gko. uni-leipzig.de/aegyptisches-museum; Augustusplatz; museum adult/concession €5/3; ⊙museum 1-5pm Thu & Fri, from 10am Sat & Sun), Leipzig's first high-

rise, is topped by a clock and two buff sentries. More eye-catching is the glass-fronted Paulinum (Map p318; Augustusplatz; ⊙11am-3pm Tue-Fri, Sunday Mass 10.30am-2.30pm), the university church and new campus building, constructed on the same spot as the medieval Paulinerkirche that was demolished in 1968 by GDR authorities.

Mendelssohn-Haus
MUSEUM

(Map p318; ☑0341-127 0294; www.mendelssohn-stiftung.de; Goldschmidtstrasse 12; adult/concession incl audioguide €8/6; ⊙10am-6pm) A key figure of the Romantic age, Felix Mendelssohn-Bartholdy was appointed music director of the Leipzig Gewandhausorchester in 1835 and held the position until shortly before his sudden death at age 38. Learn more in this intimate exhibit in the Biedermeier-furnished apartment where he lived with his family until his death in 1847. Concerts take place at 11am each Sunday.

☞ Tours

Leipzig Erleben
WALKING

(☑0341-710 4280; www.leipzig-erleben.com) Runs a 90-minute walking tour (per person €9) that covers the main sights in the centre with

---

SPOTLIGHT ON RICHARD WAGNER

Leipzig's musical legacy is partly hitched to the groundbreaking – and controversial – 19th-century composer Richard Wagner, who first saw the light of day on 22 May 1813 in a Leipzig townhouse on the street called the Brühl and later studied at the Alte Nikolaischule (Old St Nicholas School). It was in this city that he began his musical education and wrote his first compositions. Leipzig celebrated Wagner's bicentenary in 2013 with the opening of the Richard-Wagner-Museum (Map p318; www.kulturstiftung-leipzig.de/termine/wagner-ausstellung; Nikolaikirchhof 2; adult/student €3/1.50; ⊙noon-5pm Tue-Thu, Sat & Sun) in his old school on the Nikolaikirchhof. The interesting display focuses on Wagner's formative years in Leipzig from 1813 to 1834. An annual Richard Wagner Festival is held in late May each year, with public performances of his operas taking place in front of Oper Leipzig (p325).

SAXONY LEIPZIG

Central Leipzig

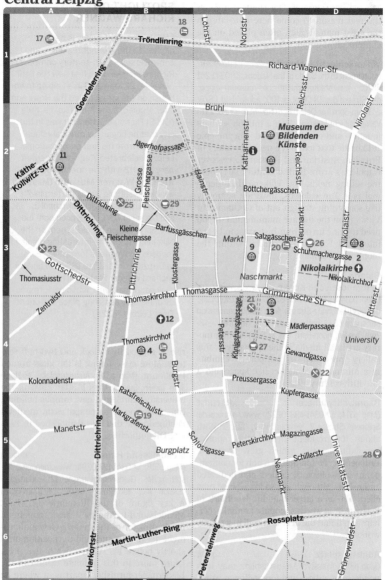

SAXONY LEIPZIG

narration in German and English. Tours depart from the tourist office (p325).

Trabi Erleben   DRIVING
(☏0341-1409 0922; www.trabi-stadtrundfahrt. de; per person €28-40) Explore Leipzig from behind the steering wheel or as a passenger in a GDR-built Trabi, on a 90-minute self-drive putt-putt with live commentary piped into your vehicle. Prior reservation is required; prices depend on the number of people.

Central Leipzig

✷ Festivals & Events

Leipziger Buchmesse LITERATURE
(www.leipziger-buchmesse.de; ⊘ Mar) One of the highlights of Leipzig's annual events calendar, held in late March. The second biggest literary festival in the country after Frankfurt.

Wave-Gotik-Treffen MUSIC
(www.wave-gotik-treffen.de; ⊘ May/Jun) On Whitsuntide, a black tide descends on Leipzig for the Wave-Gotik-Treffen, the world's largest goth festival, with a pagan village, a medieval market and lots of dark music. This is a fun time to visit the city, though you might feel a bit out of place without a black bridal veil.

Bachfest MUSIC
(Bach Festival; www.bach-leipzig.de) The 10-day Bach Festival takes place in late May or early June and attracts fans from around the world.

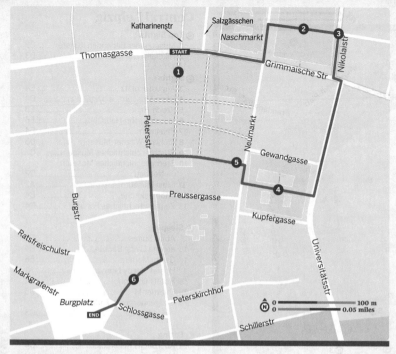

City Walk
Leipzig's Top Trading Palaces

START GRIMMAISCHE STRASSE
END BURGPLATZ
LENGTH 1KM; ONE HOUR

Leipzig's 500-year pedigree as a trading hub is splendidly reflected in its many historic arcades, courtyards and trade-fair palaces dotted around the city centre, each one flaunting its own character and design details. Trading arcades create an alternative street grid, an additional dimension in the city's layout that is not immediately apparent to outsiders.

The most famous arcade is the 1914 **①Mädlerpassage**, a lavish mix of neo-Renaissance and art nouveau and home to Auerbachs Keller, the restaurant featured in Goethe's *Faust*. Before setting off, fuel up with coffee and Leipziger Lerche, the city's signature dessert, at **Kümmel Apotheke** cafe (p323). On the way out, don't forget to touch the foot of the Faust statue near the Grimmaische Strasse exit for luck.

Make your way to Reichsstrasse and the gorgeously restored 1908 **②Speck's Hof**,

whose light-flooded atriums are decorated with murals, tiles and paintings by local artists. Exit onto Nikolaistrasse via the attached **③Hansa-Haus**, past a water-filled basin that's a copy of a 3500-year-old Ming Dynasty sound bowl. Wet your hands and run them over the two pommels to make the water fizz.

Follow Nikolaistrasse down to Universitätsstrasse and the 1893 **④Städtisches Kaufhaus**. It's on the site of Leipzig's first cloth exchange (Gewandhaus) and the original concert hall of the Gewandhaus Orchestra.

Exit onto Neumarkt and immediately enter the **⑤Messehofpassage**, which was the first post-WWII trade building to be completed in 1950. Remodelled a few years ago, the mushroom-shaped column near the Peterstrasse exit is the only vestige of the old arcade.

Turn left on Peterstrasse and head down to the **⑥Petersbogen**, an elegantly curving glass-covered arcade from 2001 that replaced the Juridicum Passage, which was destroyed in WWII. Before that, Leipzig's esteemed law school stood in this place for 500 years.

🛏 Sleeping

Hostel Blauer Stern
HOSTEL €

(Map p314; 📞0341-4927 6166; www.hostel blauerstern.de; Lindenauer Markt 20; dm/s/d €18/25/35; 📶) If you're interested in exploring Leipzig's alternative scene, this is a great option, in the western district of Plagwitz a young and arty slice of town. The thoughtfully decorated rooms all have an East German retro style, and big weekly discounts can make them a steal. Take tram 7 or 15 from Hauptbahnhof.

Hostel Sleepy Lion
HOSTEL €

(Map p318; 📞0341-993 9480; www.hostel-leipzig. de; Jacobstrasse 1; dm/d/apt from €14/46/62, linen €2.50, breakfast €4; @📶) This top-rated hostel gets our thumbs up with its clean and cheerfully painted en-suite rooms, supercentral location and clued-up staff. Every budget is catered for with dorms sleeping four to 10, as well as private rooms and spacious 4th-floor apartments with killer views. The kitchen is very basic, however, and not really suitable for self-caterers.

★ Meisterzimmer
BOUTIQUE HOTEL €€

(Map p314; 📞0341-3067 7099; www.meister zimmer.de; Spinnereistrasse 7; s/d from €80/90) Somewhere between a hotel and a designer Airbnb loft, this selection of minimalist but style-conscious rooms is inside a massive converted factory that houses half of Leipzig's creative industries. If you don't enjoy public areas in hotels, but love a light-bathed converted factory, this is the place for you. Booking ahead is essential. To get here, take the S-Bahn to Leipzig-Plagwitz.

Gwuni Mopera
B&B €€

(Map p318; 📞0341-6991 4463; Sternwartenstrasse 4; s/d from €65/70, breakfast €8; 📶) A tiny B&B hiding in the courtyard of a large Stalinesque edifice on Rossplatz, Gwuni Mopera is a subtly atmospheric option with creaky wooden floors, retro-styled furniture and art on the walls. Bathrooms are shared, but guests are too few to fight over them. The African-sounding name is in fact an acronym that includes four nearby landmarks.

Abito Suites
APARTMENT €€

(Map p318; 📞0341-985 2788; www.abito.de; Grimmaische Strasse 16; ste €140-170; 📶) This excellent option offers self-contained suites with some awesome views right in the heart of Leipzig. Spacious and modern luxury units feature Italian designer furniture, purple and gold accents and such lifestyle essentials as Illy espresso machines and a free minibar. There's no reception: check-in is via an automated system, so book ahead.

Quartier M
APARTMENT €€

(Map p318; 📞0341-2133 8800; www.apartment-leipzig.de; Markgrafenstrasse 10; apt €75-110; 🅿📶) The building oozes old-world flair but the roomy apartments with full kitchens are state-of-the-art and pack plenty of modern design cachet. Some units come with balcony or terrace. Rates drop significantly for stays over seven days and it's located above an organic supermarket.

arcona Living Bach14
HOTEL €€

(Map p318; 📞0341-496 140; http://bach14. arcona.de; Thomaskirchhof 13/14; d for 2 nights from €171; 📶) In this musically themed marvel, you'll sleep sweetly in sleek rooms decorated with sound-sculpture lamps, Bach manuscript wallpaper and colours ranging from subdued olive to perky raspberry. The quietest rooms are in the garden wing, while those in the historic front section have views of the famous Thomaskirche. The hotel has a two-night minimum stay policy.

Hotel Fürstenhof
HOTEL €€

(Map p318; 📞0341-1400; www.hotelfuerstenhof leipzig.com; Tröndlinring 8; d from €135; 🅰@📶🏊) The grande dame of the Leipzig hotel scene, with a 200-year-old pedigree, this understated place is the haunt of a low-key, old-money crowd. It has updated old-world flair, impeccable service, a gourmet restaurant and an oh-so-soothing grotto-style pool and spa – and it is just a short wander from most sights.

★ Steigenberger Grandhotel Handelshof
HOTEL €€€

(Map p318; 📞0341-350 5810; www.steigenberger. com; Salzgässchen 6; r from €182; 🅰@📶) Behind the imposing historic facade of a 1909 municipal trading hall, this exclusive boutique luxury joint outclasses most of Leipzig's hotels with its supercentral location, charmingly efficient team and modern rooms with crisp white-silver-purple colours, high ceilings and marble bathrooms. The stylish bi-level spa is the perfect bliss-out station.

🍴 Eating

★ Ouzeri Was Kost Das
GREEK €

(Map p314; 📞0341-8706 0377; www.facebook. com/OuzeriWasKostDas; Nonnenstrasse 5d; mezes

LEIPZIG MUSIC TRAIL

Bach, Mendelssohn-Bartholdy, Schumann, Wagner, Mahler and Grieg are among the many world-famous musicians who've left their mark on Leipzig, a legacy that to this day is upheld by the illustrious Gewandhausorchester (Gewandhaus Orchestra; p324) and the Thomanerchor (St Thomas Boys' Choir; p324). You can walk in the footsteps of these greats by following the 5km Leipziger Notenspur (Leipzig Music Trail) to the places where they lived and worked. At each of the 23 stops, there are information panels in English and German and phone numbers you can call to listen to music or additional commentary. There's also a 40km route designed to be followed by bike riders through further-flung areas of musical interest around Leipzig's suburbs. For details or to download a map, see http://notenspur-leipzig.de.

€2-8; ☺5.30-11pm) The subtly romantic canal-side setting succeeds in recreating the ambience of an island port taverna, but the concept is decidedly modern: a Greek version of a tapas bar, with the menu comprised entirely of small meze dishes that agree well with white wine or ouzo on a summer evening. Come with friends and share as many as you can.

Cafe Puschkin
CAFE €

(Map p314; ☑0341-392 0105; www.cafepuschkin. de; Karl-Liebknecht-Strasse 74; mains €5-12; ☺9am-2am) This charming old pub on the Südvorstadt neighbourhood's supercool Karli is a local institution. The selection of burgers, nachos and sausages won't blow you away, but it's good comfort food in a friendly and somewhat eccentric atmosphere. It's also a great breakfast spot following a night out here.

Kaiserbad
EUROPEAN €

(Map p314; ☑0341-3928 0894; www.kaiser bad-leipzig.de; Karl-Heine-Strasse 93; mains €8-15; ☺9am-2am; 🐾) A depot-sized dining hall next to the converted Westwerk powerplant, Kaiserbad is a result of the ongoing gentrification of the Plagwitz area, drawing more middle-aged and middle-class clientele than older local establishments. The menu is diverse and creative, leaning primarily

towards contemporary German and Italian cuisines. There are 19 kinds of beer on tap, including the surreal Cola-Weisen.

BiBaBo
GERMAN €

(Map p314; ☑0341-477 3350; http://bibabo.de; Engertstrasse 36; mains €7-14; ☺4-11pm) At the far end of Karli, this is an ultimate local, specialising in schnitzel and billiards. There are 14 kinds of schnitzel on the menu, from classic to mildly experimental, say with Roquefort cheese or spinach and gnocchi, to a completely outrageous pineapple curry option. Billiard tables are firmly occupied by locals, but there is darts for consolation.

Tobagi
KOREAN €

(Map p314; ☑0341-962 5836; Riemannstrasse 52; mains €8-11; ☺6-11pm) This unassuming Korean place just off the Karli is a lesson in not judging a book by its cover. Meet the eccentric and often cantankerous Korean owner before enjoying a superb meal of traditional dishes, including wonderful *bulgogi* (marinated grilled beef), rich *bibimbap* (rice mixed with egg, vegetables, chilli peppers, sliced meat and soybean paste) and an excellent spinach salad.

Die Versorger
CAFE €

(Map p314; www.die-versorger.com; Spinnerei strasse 7; mains €4-9; ☺8.30am-6pm Mon-Fri, 10am-7pm Sat) This charming garden cafe within Plagwitz's converted Baumwollspinnerei factory complex is also about the only place to have lunch nearby. Stop in for healthy daily specials and a variety of wraps, sandwiches, salads and soups.

Zest
VEGETARIAN €€

(Map p314; ☑0341-231 9126; www.zest-leipzig.de; Bornaische Strasse 54; mains €13-18; ☺5-11pm Mon, Wed & Thu, from 11am Fri-Sun; 🐾) You'd hardly expect to find such refined vegetarian fare in such unassuming and tiny premises, but here it is and its soy fillet brioche with yoghurt rice-flour muffin alone is worth heading to Connewitz for a lunch.

Pilot
INTERNATIONAL €€

(Map p318; ☑0341-9628 9550; www.enk-leipzig. de; Bosestrasse 1; mains €7.50-17; ☺9am-12.30am; 🐾) This retro-styled and quite charming establishment draws a bohemian crowd with its rustic menu, back-to-basic Saxon dishes and a splash of more contemporary specials and fresh salads. Its extensive drinks selection, including rich espresso from Trieste and a long tea list, is a further draw.

Telegraph CAFE €€

(Map p318; ☑0341-149 4990; www.cafe-telegraph. de; Dittrichring 18-20; mains €14-20; ☺8am-midnight; 🐾) Leipzig goes cosmopolitan at this elegantly high-ceilinged cafe with curved booths and wooden tables, a bilingual menu and a stack of international mags and dailies. It's a popular breakfast spot, available until a hangover-friendly 3pm. The menu is heavy on Austrian classics, and the omelette is simply fantastic.

Macis INTERNATIONAL €€

(Map p318; ☑0341-2228 7520; www.macis-leipzig. de; Markgrafenstrasse 10; mains lunch €15-22, dinner €22-29; ☺9am-2.30pm & 5.30-10.30pm Mon-Sat) 🥢 At this inspired port of call, affiliated with the adjacent baker and organic supermarket, only regionally sourced ingredients find their destiny in such internationally inspired dishes as lamb ragout, green haddock curry and black squid risotto.

★Stadtpfeiffer INTERNATIONAL €€€

(Map p318; ☑0341-217 8920; www.stadtpfeiffer. de; Augustusplatz 8; 4-/6-course menu €108/128; ☺6-11pm Tue-Sat) Petra and Deflef Schlegel give deceptively simple-sounding dishes the star treatment, and were deservedly the first in Leipzig to get the Michelin nod. Pairing punctilious artisanship with bottomless imagination, they create such exquisitely calibrated dishes as smoked Arctic char with foie gras or warm chocolate cake with lavender ice cream. It's a relaxed spot inside the Gewandhaus concert hall.

★Auerbachs Keller GERMAN €€€

(Map p318; ☑0341-216 100; www.auerbachs-keller-leipzig.de; Mädlerpassage, Grimmaische Strasse 2-4; mains Keller €16-28, Weinstuben €33-35; ☺Keller noon-11pm daily, Weinstuben 6-11pm Mon-Sat) Founded in 1525, Auerbachs Keller is one of Germany's best-known restaurants. It's cosy and touristy but the food's actually quite good and the setting memorable. There are two sections: the vaulted Grosser Keller for hearty Saxonian dishes and the four historic rooms of the Historische Weinstuben for upscale German fare. Reservations are highly advised.

In Goethe's *Faust,* Part I, Mephistopheles and Faust carouse here with students before riding off on a barrel. The scene is depicted on a carved tree trunk in what is now the Goethezimmer (Goethe Room), where the great writer allegedly came for 'inspiration'.

Max Enk GERMAN €€€

(Map p318; ☑0341-9999 7638; www.max-enk.de; Städtisches Kaufhaus, Neumarkt 9-19; mains €22-28, 5-course menu €69; ☺noon-midnight Mon-Sat, 11.30am-4pm Sun) People share laughs over hand-picked wines and plates of elegant comfort food kicked into high gear at this sleek outpost. The Wiener Schnitzel is excellent, the quality meats are grilled to perfection and the weekday multicourse lunches are a steal.

🍷 Drinking & Nightlife

There are several areas of Leipzig noted for their going-out options: in the city centre there's the boisterous Drallewatsch pub strip on narrow Barfussgässchen, as well as the more upmarket theatre district around Gottschedstrasse. The younger crowds tend to gravitate towards the Südvorstadt neighbourhood's long Karl-Liebknecht-Strasse (aka Südmeile) and Plagwitz's restaurant-and pub- packed Karl-Heine-Strasse.

★Distillery CLUB

(Map p314; ☑0341-3559 7400; www.distillery.de; Kurt-Eisner-Strasse 91; ☺11.30pm-late Fri & Sat; 🚊9 to Kurt-Eisner/A-Hoffmann-Strasse) One of eastern Germany's oldest techno clubs, Distillery has been going for over 20 years and remains among the best. With an unpretentious crowd, cool location, decent drinks prices and occasional star DJs (Ellen Allien, Carl Craig, Richie Hawtin), its popularity is easy to understand. As well as techno, there's house, drum'n'bass and hip-hop to be had here.

Kümmel Apotheke CAFE

(Map p318; ☑0341-960 8705; www.kuemmel -apotheke.de; Mädlerpassage, Grimmaische Strasse 2-4; ☺9.30am-10pm Mon-Thu, to 1am Fri & Sat, 10.30am-8pm Sun) Inside Mädlerpassage, this retro-styled cafe-cum-bar with red leather chairs and dark wood furniture is an inviting refuge from the commercial district's hustle and bustle. There are lots of coffee drinks on offer, many with alcohol. Try Leipziger Lerche, a famous local dessert.

Noch Besser Leben PUB

(Map p314; www.nochbesserleben.com; Merseburger Strasse 25; ☺4.30pm-late) Despite the address, the entrance this locally beloved bar can be found on Plagwitz's main drag, Karl-Heine-Strasse, and is a great, if smoky, spot to join a cool local crowd drinking an impressive selection of beer. It has a communal, friendly atmosphere, for which only the German word *gemütlich* (approximately translated as cosy) will do.

Beyerhaus
PUB

(Map p314; Ernst-Schneller-Strasse 6; ⊙7pm-2am) Just off the Karli, this large but extremely cosy pub is popular with a studenty, alternative crowd, who come here to drink beer under the two enormous glass chandeliers and enjoy the odd live musical performance. Friendly fun.

Cafe Waldi
BAR

(Map p314; ☑0341-462 5667; www.cafewaldi.de; Peterssteinweg 10; ⊙11.30am-late Mon-Fri, from 9am Sat & Sun; ☎) Despite its great-grandma's-living-room look – complete with big sofas, cuckoo clocks and mounted antlers – Waldi is an up-to-the-minute hang-out, where you can eat breakfast until 4pm, fuel up on coffee and a light meal, or nurse cocktails and pints until the wee hours. On weekends, DJs rock the upstairs area with house, indie and hip-hop.

Moritzbastei
BAR

(Map p318; ☑0341-702 590; www.moritzbastei.de; Universitätsstrasse 9; ⊙10am-late Mon-Fri, from noon Sat; ☎) This legendary (sub)cultural centre in a warren of cellars of the old city fortifications keeps an all-ages crowd happy with parties (almost nightly), concerts, art and readings. It harbours stylish cocktail and wine bars as well as a daytime cafe (dishes €3.50 to €6) that serves delicious coffee, along with healthy and wallet-friendly fare. There's a summer terrace, too.

Zum Arabischen Coffe Baum
CAFE

(Map p318; ☑0341-961 0060; www.coffe-baum.de; Kleine Fleischergasse 4; ⊙11am-midnight) One of Europe's oldest coffeehouses, this cosy multifloor warren has been going since 1720. It's an atmospheric, if rather touristy, spot to try the famous local treat called Leipziger Lerche (lark) – a marzipan-filled shortcrust pastry. Other mouth-watering cakes, light meals (mains €8 to €18) and alcohol are also available. The small, free 'museum' has over 500 coffee-related objects.

 LEIPZIG CARD

Use a Leipzig Card (1/3 days €11.90/23.50) for free or discounted admission to attractions, plus free travel on public transport. It's available from the tourist office and most hotels.

Flowerpower
PUB

(Map p314; ☑0341-961 3441; www.flower-power.de; Riemannstrasse 42; ⊙8pm-8am; ☎) It's party time any time at this dark, long-running psychedelic flashback to the '60s (cool pinball machines). Admission is always free and the music tends to be older than the international and up-for-it crowd. If you've run out of party options on a Tuesday morning, this is the destination for you.

Conne Island
CLUB

(www.conne-island.de; Koburger Strasse 3; ⊙4-10pm Mon-Sat, to 8pm Sun; ⊞9 to Koburger Brücke) Run by a collective, this cult location has defined Leipzig nightlife for ages with concerts and club nights that feed the gamut of musical appetites – punk to indie, techno to hip-hop. It's in the punkish-anarchist enclave of Connewitz.

Café Riquet
CAFE

(Map p318; ☑0341-961 0000; www.riquethaus.de; Schuhmachergässchen 1; ⊙9am-7pm) Two bronze elephants guard the entrance to this Viennese-style coffeehouse in a superb art nouveau building topped by an Asian-style turret. Good for a stylish coffee-and-cake break.

naTo
PUB

(Map p314; ☑0341-391 5539; www.nato-leipzig.de; Karl-Liebknecht-Strasse 46; ⊙7-11pm) The mother of Leipzig's alternative-music pub-clubs, with jazz, experimental and indie sounds alongside films and theatre. Great outdoor seating in summer.

Entertainment

Gewandhausorchester
CLASSICAL MUSIC

(Map p318; ☑0341-127 0280; www.gewandhausorchester.de; Augustusplatz 8) Led by Latvian conductor Andris Nelsons, the Gewandhaus is one of Europe's finest and oldest civic orchestras. With a history harkening back to 1743, it became an orchestra of European renown a century later under music director Felix Mendelssohn-Bartholdy.

Thomanerchor
CLASSICAL MUSIC

(Map p318; ☑0341-984 4211; www.thomaskirche.org; Thomaskirchhof 18; tickets €2) Leipzig's famous boys' choir performs Bach motets and cantatas at 6pm on Friday and 3pm on Saturday at the Thomaskirche (p316), and sings during Sunday services at 9.30am. Special concerts take place throughout the year. Performances are usually filled to capacity, so try to be there when doors open, 45 minutes before concerts begin.

Oper Leipzig
OPERA

(Map p318; ☎0341-126 1261; www.oper-leipzig.de; Augustusplatz 12) Leipzig's *Opernhaus* (opera house) has a 300-year-old pedigree, though the building only went up in the 1950s. The program is an eclectic mix of classics and contemporary works; the Gewandhausorchester provides the music.

ⓘ Information

The main post office is in the Hauptbahnhof.

Tourist Office (Map p318; ☎0341-710 4260; www.leipzig.travel; Katharinenstrasse 8; ⊗10am-6pm Mon-Fri, to 4pm Sat, to 3pm Sun) For room referral, ticket sales, maps and general information. Also sells the Leipzig Card.

ⓘ Getting There & Away

AIR

Leipzig-Halle Airport (☎0341-2240; www.leipzig-halle-airport.de) is about 21km west of Leipzig. It has domestic and international flights connecting it with many German cities as well as London and Istanbul.

CAR & MOTORCYCLE

Leipzig lies just south of the A14 Halle-Dresden autobahn and 15km east of the A9, which links Berlin to Nuremberg. All major international car hire agencies can be found at the airport, as well as several more at the Hauptbahnhof.

TRAIN

Deutsche Bahn has frequent services to Frankfurt (€88, 3¾ hours), Dresden (€26.50, 1¼ hours) and Berlin (€49, 1¼ hours). Tickets can be purchased for considerably less by booking online several days in advance.

ⓘ Getting Around

CAR & MOTORCYCLE

Leipzig's centre is a so-called *Umweltzone* (environmental zone), meaning you need to obtain an *Umweltplakette* (emissions sticker) if you brought your own car from abroad. Check www.umwelt-plakette.de for details.

PUBLIC TRANSPORT

Buses and trams are run by **LVB** (☎0341-194 49; www.lvb.de), which operates an **information kiosk** (Willy-Brandt-Platz; ⊗8am-8pm Mon-Fri, to 4pm Sat) outside the Hauptbahnhof. The central tram station is here as well. There's a second **LVB information kiosk** (Markgrafenstrasse 2; ⊗8am-8pm Mon-Sat). Single tickets cost €1.90 for up to four stops and €2.60 for longer trips; day passes are €7.40. The S-Bahn is run by Deutsche Bahn, but the ticketing system is integrated, so LVB tickets are valid on S-Bahn services within Leipzig.

TAXI

Taxis are expensive here. The minimum charge is €3.50, and each kilometre €2.50.

Chemnitz

☎0371 / POP 246,000

Like most of eastern Germany's cities, Chemnitz had to reinvent itself post-Wende, and has done so with some measure of success. Known from 1953 to 1990 as Karl-Marx-Stadt, the GDR gave it a Stalinist makeover, and smokestack industries once earned it the nickname of 'Saxon Manchester'. Such scars don't heal easily but Chemnitz has done a remarkable job, at least in its revitalised city centre that is now a pedestrianised glass-and-steel shopping and entertainment district.It doesn't draw many travellers, but some excellent museums and a friendly and progressive feel might tempt some to stop by.

⊙ Sights

Chemnitz's compact and largely pedestrianised centre is a pleasing mix of historic and modern, centred on the Markt. The dominant building is the stately 15th-century Altes Rathaus (Old Town Hall), whose distinctive tower sports an ornate Renaissance portal and a carillon with cute little figures re-enacting town history at 11am, 4pm and 7pm. The old town hall segues into the Neues Rathaus (New Town Hall, 1911), its imposing size best appreciated from Neumarkt, which is also flanked by the Galerie Roter Turm. This modern shopping mall with a pleasing terracotta facade was designed by architectural top dog Hans Kollhoff. The equally esteemed Helmut Jahn dreamed up the adjacent glass-and-steel Galeria Kaufhof department store.

★SMAC
MUSEUM

(Staatliches Museum für Archäologie Chemnitz; ☎0371-911 9990; www.smac.sachsen.de; Stefan-Heym-Platz 1; adult/concession €7/4; ⊗10am-6pm Mon-Wed & Fri-Sun, to 8pm Thu) Occupying a converted department store, this state-of-the-art museum is a brave attempt to celebrate all those crocks, bones and pieces of primitive jewellery found in the archaeology sections of history museums, which many visitors tend to overlook as they rush to admire treasures from later epochs. Here, the multimedia exhibition is organised as a journey through every cultural layer left by human civilisation, with each seemingly

CHEMNITZ'S SCHLOSSTEICH

About 1.3km north of Chemnitz's centre is the Schlossteich, an idyllic park-ringed pond with a music pavilion for summer concerts. As well as being a lovely place for a wander, there are two other standout attractions here. To get here, take Bus 76 from the city centre and get off at Schlossberg.

Schlosskirche (☎0371-369 550; http://schloss.kirche-chemnitz.info; Schlossplatz 7; ☺2.30-5.30pm Sat & Sun) This 12th-century Benedictine monastery has been recast into a weighty Gothic hall church and houses Hans Witten's intriguing sculpture *Christ at the Column* (1515).

Schlossbergmuseum (☎0371-488 4501; www.schlossbergmuseum.de; Schlossberg 12; adult/concession €6/4; ☺11am-6pm Tue-Sun) This late-Gothic monastery houses the city history museum, whose vaulted interior is a rich backdrop for Saxon 15th- and 16th-century sculpture.

unprepossessing object allowed to tell its fascinating story.

★ **Museum Gunzenhauser**　　　GALLERY
(☎0371-488 7024; www.kunstsammlungen-chemnitz.de; Stollberger Strasse 2; adult/concession €7/4.50; ☺11am-6pm Tue-Sun) A former 1930 bank building, built in austere New Objectivity style, is now a gallery of 20th-century art, most famous for its expressionist works by such key artists as Max Beckmann, Ernst Ludwig Kirchner and local boy Karl Schmidt-Rottluff. Pride of place, though, goes to a career-spanning collection of works by Otto Dix on the 3rd floor. It's a superb collection and shouldn't be missed by modern art lovers.

DAStietz　　　MUSEUM
(☎0371-488 4397; www.dastietz.de; Moritzstrasse 20) Beautifully renovated, this former 1913 department store now houses the city library as well as the **Neue Sächsische Galerie** (☎0371-367 6680; www.neue-saechsische-galerie.de; adult/child €4/free; ☺11am-5pm Thu-Mon, to 7pm Tue), which presents contemporary Saxon art, and the **Museum für Naturkunde** (Natural History Museum; ☎0371-488 4551;

www.naturkunde-chemnitz.de; adult/concession €4/2.50; ☺10am-5pm Mon, Tue, Thu & Fri, to 6pm Sat & Sun), whose most interesting exhibit, the Versteinerter Wald (petrified forest), can be admired for free in the atrium; some of the stony trunks are 290 million years old.

Henry Van de Velde Museum　　　MUSEUM
(☎0371-488 4424; www.kunstsammlungen-chemnitz.de; Parkstrasse 58; adult/child €3/free; ☺10am-6pm Wed & Fri-Sun) Around 2.5km south of the centre, this small but choice museum occupies the 1903 Villa Esche, which was Belgian artist Van de Velde's first commission in Germany. The dining room and music salon have been restored as period rooms, while upstairs you'll find a small collection of crafts and furniture. Take tram 4 to Haydnstrasse.

Kunstsammlungen Chemnitz　　　MUSEUM
(Chemnitz Art Museum; ☎0371-488 4424; www.kunstsammlungen-chemnitz.de; Theaterplatz 1; adult/concession €7/5; ☺11am-6pm Tue-Sun) Flanking Chemnitz' most beautiful square, the historic Theaterplatz, this lovely art museum stages large-scale temporary exhibits, sometimes drawn from its own collection of paintings, sculpture, graphics, textiles and crafts. Special strengths include Romantic painters (Caspar David Friedrich, Ludwig Richter) and sculptures by Degas, Rodin and Baselitz.

Karl Marx Monument　　　MONUMENT
(cnr Strasse der Nationen & Brückenstrasse) Things have rather turned against the founder of Communism since this 7m-high bronze head (one that catches the German philosopher on a very bad hair day) was erected in 1971. Behind Marx there's a huge frieze exhorting 'Workers of the world, unite!' in several languages. Attempts to remove the monument after the end of Communism were resisted by locals, however, and Marx's head remains a symbol of the city.

🛏 Sleeping

Biendo Hotel　　　HOTEL €
(☎0371-433 1920; www.biendo-hotel.de; Strasse der Nationen 12; s/d from €54/60; P 🛜) On the 5th and 6th floor of a GDR-era office building, this fantastic place is affordable for most visitors. Centrally located Biendo pitches itself somewhere between business and boutique hotel, with small but good-value rooms that enjoy contemporary furnishings and sweeping city views. The breakfast (€8), served in the light-bathed breakfast room, is worth it.

DJH Hostel
HOSTEL €

(☑ 0371-2780 9897; www.chemnitz-city.jugendher berge.de; Getreidemarkt 6; dm incl breakfast under/over 27yr €24/28; ⊘ reception 8-11am & 4-10pm; P @) If you like your hostels with a dash of quirk and history, this industrial-flavoured contender in a former converting station in the town centre should fit the bill. En-suite dorms sleep three to eight.

Hotel an der Oper
HOTEL €€

(☑ 0371-6810; www.hoteloper-chemnitz.de; Strasse der Nationen 56; s/d from €59/90; P ✳ ☎) With front-row views of the historic opera house, this renovated hotel spells comfort in soothing, good-sized rooms furnished in vanilla and chocolate hues. The chic cocktail bar has an impressive whisky selection, while the Scala restaurant has top-notch food and sumptuous views onto Theaterplatz.

✗ Eating

Cafe Michaelis
INTERNATIONAL €€

(☑ 0371-2733 7985; www.michaelis-chemnitz.de; Am Düsseldorfer Platz 11; mains €11-22; ⊘ 9am-10pm Mon-Thu, to 11pm Fri & Sat, 10am-9pm Sun) A century-old Chemnitz coffeehouse tradition, Cafe Michaelis remains famous for its mind-boggling selection of truly mouthwatering cakes. If you don't have a sweet tooth, opt for a crisp salad, homemade pasta or meaty main from the extensive menu. It offers a big terrace in summer.

Kellerhaus
GERMAN €€

(☑ 0371-335 1677; www.kellerhaus-chemnitz.de; Schlossberg 2; mains €10-20; ⊘ 11am-10pm) For a first-rate culinary journey at moderate prices, it's well worth heading out of the town centre to this half-timbered charmer at the foot of the historic Schlossberg quarter. Sit in the cosy cellar, the low-ceilinged main dining room or on the terrace.

Ratskeller
GERMAN €€

(☑ 0371-694 9875; www.ratskeller-chemnitz.de; Markt 1; mains €15-28; ⊘ 11am-midnight) The rustic, olde-worlde setting amid gorgeously painted vaulted ceilings just couldn't get any more charming, and this vast subterranean hall serves up decent German fare until late by local standards. In summer you can also eat outside on the Markt.

ⓘ Information

There are several banks with ATMs around the Markt.

Main Post Office (Strasse der Nationen 2-4; ⊘ 9am-7pm Mon-Fri, to 2pm Sat)
Tourist Office (☑ 0371-690 680; www.chemnitz-tourismus.de; Markt 1; ⊘ 9am-7pm Mon-Fri, 9am-4pm Sat, 11am-1pm Sun)

ⓘ Getting There & Around

CAR & MOTORCYCLE
The east–west A4 skirts Chemnitz, while the A72 heading south to the A9 (eg for Munich) originates nearby.

PUBLIC TRANSPORT
All trams and buses pass through the city-centre Zentralhaltestelle (central stop). Single tickets are €2.20, and a day pass is €4.40.

TRAIN
Chemnitz is linked by direct train to Dresden (€16, one hour) via Freiberg (€5, 30 minutes). There are also trains to Leipzig (€16, one hour) and Zwickau (€6.20, 30 minutes).

Freiberg

☑ 03731 / POP 42,000

Home to ancient silver mines and the world's oldest mining university, Freiberg boasts a pretty historical core complete with a castle, which houses a dazzling collection of gems and minerals from around the world. Other attractions include a visitable ore mine and a famous church organ – a magnet for music lovers from across Germany. With its own beer brand – Freiberger – and a fun-loving student population serviced by a couple of quality pubs, Freiberg definitely merits an overnight stay, although it can be easily done on a day trip out of Dresden or Chemnitz.

◉ Sights

★ Terra Mineralia
MUSEUM

(☑ 03731-394 654; www.terra-mineralia.de; Schlossplatz 4; adult/student €10/5, incl Krügerhaus €14/7; ⊘ 10am-5pm Mon-Fri, to 6pm Sat & Sun) Occupying a greater part of the 16th-century Freundenstein castle, this astounding collection of minerals makes human-made art seem insignificant compared to the genius of nature. The experience is akin to snorkelling over coral reefs – as you descend from the 5th floor, the dramatically dim-lit halls fill with thousands of colours radiating from dazzling gems. Each hall represents a continent where exhibits come

(Continued on page 330)

SAXONY FREIBERG

1

3

WESTEND61/GETTY IMAGES ©

VLADIMIR WRANGEL/SHUTTERSTOCK ©

1. Saxon Switzerland (p309)
Dramatic pinnacles of sandstone make for a climber's dream destination.

2. Leipzig (p313)
One of Europe's oldest civic orchestras, Gewandhausorchester (p324), makes its home in illustrious surrounds at the Oper Leipzig (p325).

3. Bautzen (p336)
Riders in the traditional Easter procession celebrated by Germany's Sorbian ethnic minority group.

(Continued from page 327)

from, with a separate section dedicated to meteorites.

The exhibition is a tribute to mineralogy enthusiast and heiress to the Wella cosmetics empire, Erika Pohl-Ströher, who donated her collection to Freiberg Bergakademie in 2004. An annexe to the museum, the adjacent Krügerhaus, contains a collection of minerals found in Germany. Audioguides are available for the main exhibition (€3) and Krügerhaus (€2).

Dom St Marien
CATHEDRAL

(✆03731-300 340; www.freiberger-dom.de; Untermarkt 1; adult/concession €4/3; ⊙10am-5pm Mon-Sat, from 11.30am Sun) Packed with touchingly naive wooden and stone sculpture, Freiberg's outstanding Lutheran cathedral contains the first large organ built by the famous master, Gottfried Silbermann, in 1714. Apart from the celebrated instrument, which is still in active use, highlights include the stone-carved Tulip pulpit (1505) and wooden figures of smart and foolish virgins adorning central columns (1505–20). Equally striking is the 15th-century pietà, a wooden sculpture of the Virgin Mary holding the body of Jesus taken from the cross.

Silberbergwerk Freiberg
MINE

(Reiche Zeche; ✆03731-394 571; www.silberbergwerk-freiberg.de; Fuchsmühlenweg 9; educational tour adult/concession €13/6, mining tour €18/10; ⊙9am-5pm Wed-Fri; ▣Linie D) People have been digging into the ore-rich rocks near Freiberg for 800 years. The result is a network of mines, one of which – Reiche Zeche – can be visited on a tour. Both tours on offer, the easier educational tour and the more physically challenging mining tour, take you into a 150m-deep black void and along unlit drives straight out of a suspense movie. The mining tour involves a steep climb up a claustrophobically narrow near-vertical slope.

Linie D buses depart for Silberbergwerk Freiberg (€2.20, half-hourly) from Freiberg Busbahnhof (near the train station).

✯ Festivals & Events

Bergstadtfest
PARADE

(www.bergstadtfest.de; ⊙last week of Jun) Drawing tens of thousands, Freiberg city festival involves an elaborate miners' parade, unrestrained beer consumption and lots of other street fun.

Mettensnicht
PARADE

(www.freiberg-service.de; ⊙Dec) Members of Freiberg's mining guild parade in traditional garb and take part in a special church service on the second Saturday of Advent.

🛏 Sleeping & Eating

Hotel ab Obermarkt
HOTEL €€

(✆03731-263 70; www.hotel-am-obermarkt.de; Waisenhausstrasse 2; s/d incl breakfast from €60/90; 🕿) Clearly not a purpose-built hotel, this 15th-century building off the main square used to house an orphanage, a wartime ration-card dispensary and a Soviet prison. In its current incarnation (since 1992), it features bland but perfectly passable rooms and a very friendly reception. The buffet breakfast is equally commendable.

Cafe Hartmann
CAFE €

(✆03731-228 07; www.cafe-hartmann.de; Petersstrasse 1a; mains €6-10; ⊙9am-6pm Mon-Fri, 9am-5pm Sat, 1pm-5pm Sun) An elegant old-school establishment just off the main square, this is the place to stop for a coffee or a light lunch and try Freiberg's signature desserts: Bauerhase pastry and Freiberger Eierschecke cheesecake.

Stadtwirtschaft
CZECH €€

(✆03731-419 113; www.stadtwirtschaft.de; Burgstrasse 18; mains €12-16; ⊙11am-midnight) Literally Bohemian (that is, related to the neighbouring part of Czechia), this easy-going place celebrates all things Czech - from *knedlki* dumplings and duck with sauerkraut to the Socialist-era Czech cartoon characters adorning the bar and dozens of beers fresh from the best *pivovars* (breweries) across the border.

❶ Getting There & Away

CAR & MOTORCYCLE

Freiberg lies on the 173 road between Dresden and Chemnitz, 52km from the former and 36km from the latter.

TRAIN

Trains for Dresden (€9.70, 30 to 45 minutes) and Chemnitz (€5, 30 minutes) depart from Freiberg (Sachs) Bahnhof every 30 minutes.

❶ Getting Around

Freiberg old town is 1km from the train station and best reached on foot. Linie D buses depart for Silberbergwerk Freiberg (€2.20, half-hourly) from the Busbahnhof (near the train station).

EASTERN SAXONY

The southeast corner of Germany, Eastern Saxony is a land of bucolic meadows and gentle hills that transform into low-lying mountains on the Czech border. Influenced by Slavic nations in the east and south, this is also the homeland of Germany's own Slavic minority, the Sorbs. Their cultural capital is Bautzen, home to the Sorbian museum and the venue of an annual Easter equestrian parade organised by the Sorbian community.

In the far east, divided between Germany and Poland, the magnificent town of Görlitz is a delight for architecture buffs. It's also just a great place to unwind for a few days, visiting museums and venturing further along the Polish border to the gardens of Bad Muskau, a masterpiece of landscape design. It's worth visiting the tiny town of Herrnhut, too, for its impressive collection of artefacts from all around the world amassed by Christian missionaries.

🛏 Sleeping

Görlitz is the best base for exploring the far east of Saxony, but much of the area can be easily covered out of Dresden, especially if you travel by car. There is enough accommodation to suit any budget in the main towns and plenty of country hotels scattered around the region.

❶ Getting There & Away

The main regional train line and the A5 autobahn run through Bautzen and Görlitz, with smaller roads branching off towards off-the-beaten-track attractions in the north and south.

Görlitz

📞 03581 / POP 56,000

Görlitz, Germany's easternmost city, is a dreamy coalescence of fabulous architecture, idyllic cobbled streets and an intriguing history. Having miraculously escaped destruction during WWII, Görlitz has over 4000 heritage buildings and is a veritable encyclopedia of European architectural styles, from the Renaissance to the 19th century.

The town was split between Germany and Poland in 1945, when the Allies drew a new border along the Neisse River. Görlitz' former eastern flank is now the Polish town of Zgorzelec, easily reached via a footbridge across the river (indeed, it's hard to tell you've even left Germany). The authorities on both sides tout Görlitz and Zgorzelec as a single tourist destination, with all the major sights located on the German side, while Poland lures visitors with cheaper food and accommodation options.

◉ Sights

Görlitz' sights cluster in the Altstadt, reached from the train station via Berliner Strasse or Jakobstrasse. It is organised around several squares, most notably the large Obermarkt and the smaller, cuter Untermarkt. From the latter, Neissstrasse leads down to the river and the footbridge to Zgorzelec.

◉ Obermarkt & Southern Altstadt

Art Nouveau Department Store   ARCHITECTURE

(www.kaufhaus-goerlitz.eu; Marienplatz; ☉2-6pm Thu, hours vary on public holidays) **FREE** Famously featuring in Wes Anderson's film *The Grand Budapest Hotel*, this architectural stunner is centred on a galleried atrium accented with wooden balustrades, floating staircases and palatial chandeliers, and lidded by an ornately patterned glass ceiling. Yet it stays empty, with long-overdue renovation repeatedly postponed due to regulatory issues. Until this begins in earnest, the building is open for visitors every Thursday and during public holidays.

Dreifaltigkeitskirche   CHURCH

(Klosterplatz 21; audioguide €2; ☉10am-6pm Mon-Sat, 11am-6pm Sun Apr-Oct, to 4pm Nov-Mar) Dominating the Obermarkt, this 15th-century former Franciscan monastery church is packed with medieval masterpieces, most notably the baroque high altar and the late Gothic 'Golden Mary' altar.

Reichenbacher Turm   VIEWPOINT

(www.museum-goerlitz.de; Platz des 17 Juni; adult/concession €3/2; ☉10am-5pm Tue-Thu, to 6pm Fri-Sun May-Oct) Climb the 165 steps to the top of this fortification tower that was inhabited by a sentry until 1904. En route, exhibits on the purpose of such sentries (eg keeping an eye out for fire or advancing marauders) provide a modest excuse to catch your breath.

◉ Untermarkt & Eastern Altstadt

Barockhaus   MUSEUM

(📞 03581-671 355; www.museum-goerlitz.de; Neissstrasse 30; adult/concession €5/3.50; ☉10am-5pm

Tue-Thu, to 6pm Fri-Sun) This museum will fascinate anyone with a taste for the odd with its curiously broad exhibits. Wealthy merchant Johann Christian Ameiss translated his wealth into this magnificent baroque residence that later became the seat of a prestigious scientific society. On the 1st floor, family rooms with period furnishings lead to cabinets brimming with baroque porcelain, art, glass, silver and other precious objects. Exhibits on the upper floor highlight society members' diverse research interests – including physics, archaeology and music.

Rathaus

HISTORIC BUILDING

Görlitz' town hall takes up the entire western side of the Untermarkt, but the oldest and most noteworthy section is the tower building with the curving Renaissance staircase fronted by a sculpture of the goddess Justitia. Take a moment to observe the lower of the two tower clocks and you'll notice that the helmeted soldier in the middle briefly drops his chin every minute.

Schlesisches Museum zu Görlitz

MUSEUM

(☑ 03581-879 10; www.schlesisches-museum. de; Brüderstrasse 8; adult/concession incl audio guide €6/4; ☉ 10am-5pm Tue-Sun) The splendid Schönhof, a 1526 Renaissance residence, forms the atmospheric backdrop to this comprehensive exhibit on the culture and history of Silesia, a region that's often found itself in the cross-hairs of political power players and repeatedly changed borders and identity over the past 1000 years. Fine art, fabulous glass and ceramics and objects from daily life complement the historical displays spread over 17 themed rooms in the historic main building and modern annexe.

Signage is only in German and Polish, meaning that the free audioguide is useful.

Peterskirche

CHURCH

(☑ 03581-428 7000; An der Peterskirche; ☉ 10am-6pm Mon-Sat, 11.45am-6pm Sun) Crowning Görlitz' skyline, this Gothic church is especially famous for its Sonnenorgel (Sun Organ), fashioned by Silesian-Italian Eugenio Casparini in 1703. It boasts 88 registers and 6095 pipes and derives its name from the 17 circular sun-shields integrated into the organ case.

🛏 Sleeping

★ Pension Miejski

PENSION €

(☑ in Poland 888 579 253; www.pensjonat-miejski.pl; Nowomiejjska 1, Zgorzelec; s/d/tr/apt

€33/38/48/55; P 🛜) Cross the footbridge onto the Polish side of the Neisse River, turn right and wander up the hill and you'll find this superb value-for-money option. There are eight impeccably maintained and spacious rooms done up in warm colours. Fast wi-fi, coffee and parking are all free, though book ahead for the last of these as there are limited spaces.

Pension Goldene Feder

PENSION €

(☑ 03581-684 3861; www.pension-goerlitz.de; Handwerk 12; d €60-70; P 🛜) A winner for fans of retro touches such as writing paper, quill and ink in your room, the 'Golden Feather' harmoniously mixes modern and vintage furnishings with art created by friends of the owner couple. Breakfast includes fruit and eggs from the family farm.

DJH Hostel

HOSTEL €

(☑ 03581-649 0700; www.goerlitz-city.jugendher berge.de; Peterstrasse 15; dm incl breakfast under/ over 27yr €26/30; ☉ check-in 4-9pm Apr-Sep, 5-8pm Oct-Mar; @ 🛜) This vast and modern hostel behind a historic facade is squarely aimed at groups. While it does boast an excellent Altstadt location, plenty of public and outdoor space and shiny en-suite rooms sleeping two to six, it feels a bit impersonal and charmless.

★ Hotel Börse

HOTEL €€

(☑ 03581-764 20; www.boerse-goerlitz.de; Unter-markt 16; s/d from €79/115; P @ 🛜) Four-poster beds, sparkling glass chandeliers, marble bathrooms, patterned parquet floors and elegant antiques are the hallmarks of this stylish hotel in an 18th-century Palais. With its absolutely perfect location, old-world atmosphere and surprisingly affordable rates, this is our best bet for a comfortable and memorable stay in Görlitz.

Rooms in the affiliated Gästehaus am Flüsterbogen (s/d €60/85) sport a similarly subtle romantic style but are a tad bigger. For a more contemporary feel, book into the nearby Herberge zum 6 Gebot (s/d €65/85), which translates as 'Inn of the 6th Commandment' (that would be the one about adultery). As a sweet touch of irony, rooms are named for such famous philanderers as Henry VIII and Casanova. Check-in and breakfast are all at the Hotel Börse.

Romantik Hotel Tuchmacher

HOTEL €€

(☑ 03581-473 10; www.tuchmacher.de; Peter-strasse 8; s/d/ste €102/132/188; P 🛜) In the most coveted rooms at this posh Renaissance charmer near the Peterskirche, you'll be sleeping beneath richly painted baroque ceilings, but others are just as nice with warm hues and classical furnishings. Roast in the hot tub or sauna before toasting the day over a sophisticated meal in the on-site restaurant.

✖ Eating

★ **Miódmaliny** EASTERN EUROPEAN €
(☑ in Poland 0756-418 090; http://miodmaliny.
pl; Daszyńskiego 17, Zgorzelec; mains €6-15;
⊙ 11.30am-11pm) A short walk to the Polish side of town and you can gorge on culinary delights with a big discount. Furnished as grandma's parlour, this cosy cafe is strong on Central European classics, with a local touch. Try Polish duck with apples or beef roulette, both served with Silesian dumplings, and don't bypass *nalewki* – delightful fruity liqueurs.

Senfladen SAXON €
(☑ 03581-764 909; www.senfladen-goerlitz.de; Brüderstrasse 5; snacks €2.50; ⊙ 10am-6pm) There is often a queue outside this little sausage joint coupled with a shop selling famous (and famously spicy) local mustard that comes in dozens of varieties. Apart from three types of wurst, they serve traditional *bullettes* (meatballs) and *fleischkäse* (meat loafs) – all lavishly seasoned with mustard of your choosing.

Vino e Cultura ITALIAN €€
(☑ 03581-879 6850; www.vinoecultura.de; Untermarkt 2; mains €16-21; ⊙ 3-11pm Tue-Fri, from noon Sat & Sun) The vaulted space right on the historic Untermarkt has been lavishly converted and is Görlitz's prime foodie destination. The menu, courtesy of the clearly ambitious French chef, is adventurous (try monkfish with paprika chutney or duck breast with caramelised apricots), the staff are charming and the entire place is a great leap forward for the local eating scene.

Filetto ITALIAN €€
(☑ 03581-421 131; www.filetto-goerlitz.de; Peterstrasse 1; mains €8-20; ⊙ 5pm-midnight Mon-Fri, noon-3pm & 5pm-midnight Sat, noon-3pm & 5-10pm Sun; ☎) This warm and friendly place in the heart of the old town has an Italian-leaning menu that is focused heavily on steaks and a simple list of French wines. It's cosy and oozes history (the building dates from 1530 and was once the town apothecary); it's a good idea to reserve a table in the evenings.

DON'T MISS

GÖRLITZ'S HOLY REPLICA

The **Heiliges Grab** (☑ 03581-315 864; www.heiligesgrab-goerlitz.de; Heilig-Grab-Strasse 79; €2; ⊙ 10am-6pm Mon-Sat, 11am-6pm Sun Apr-Sep, to 4pm Nov-Feb, to 5pm Mar & Oct) is a close replica of the Holy Sepulchre in Jerusalem as it looked in the Middle Ages during the time of the Crusades. Among the Crusaders was local boy Georg Emmerich, who made the trip primarily in atonement for knocking up the neighbour's daughter. Absolved from his sins, he returned, became the town mayor and, in 1480, instigated the construction of the Heiliges Grab.

It is part of a larger ensemble that also includes a double chapel and a salvation house, and marks the final stop in the Via Dolorosa (Stations of the Cross) pilgrimage path, which starts at the west portal of the Peterskirche and runs via Nikolaistrasse, Bogstrasse and Steinweg.

St Jonathan FUSION €€
(☑ 03581-421 082; Peterstrasse 16; mains €8-23; ⊙ 6-11pm Mon, noon-3pm & 6-11pm Tue-Sun) In a gorgeously attired dining space and atmospheric historic setting, St Jonathan offers delicious pasta, huge steaks and traditional regional dishes at linen-bedecked tables beneath a painted vaulted ceiling. For a romantic and unusual experience, book the table for two inside the fireplace.

Restaurant Lucie Schulte INTERNATIONAL €€
(☑ 03581-410 260; Untermarkt 22; mains €16-32; ⊙ noon-3pm & 6-11pm) In the romantic courtyard of the Flüsterbogen building, you'll find this upmarket place that is popular with locals and visitors alike. Despite the formal setting, there's room for some creativity: unusual flavour pairings and an impressive international wine list set the menu apart from many others in town.

❶ Information

Banks with ATMs are scattered throughout Görlitz, but are especially numerous around Postplatz.

Görlitz Tourist Office (☑ 03581-475 70; www.
visit-goerlitz.com; Obermarkt 32; ⊙ 9am-6pm Mon-Fri, to 5pm Sat, to 4pm Sun May-Oct, 9.30am-6pm Mon-Fri, to 2.30pm Sat & Sun

Nov-Apr) The main tourist office offers lots of information and has English-speaking staff.

I-Vent Private Tourist Office (☑ 03581-421 362; www.goerlitz-tourismus.de; Obermarkt 33; ☉ 9am-6pm Mon-Fri, 9.30am-5pm Sat, 9.30am-3pm Sun Apr-Oct, 9am-6pm Mon-Fri, 9.30am-3pm Sat Nov-Mar) A privately run office representing both Görlitz and Zgorzelec.

ℹ Getting There & Away

CAR & MOTORCYCLE

Görlitz is about 110km east of Dresden, just off the A4 autobahn; take exit 94 and follow the B6 to the B99 into town.

TRAIN

Trains run regularly between Görlitz and Dresden (€24, one to 1½ hours) via Bautzen (€8.80, 30 minutes). For Berlin (from €44, 2½ hours), change in Cottbus. Trains also run to Zittau (€7.60, 35 minutes). The train station is south of the old town; take Berliner Strasse to get there.

Zittau

☑ 03583 / POP 28,900

In the far southeast corner of Saxony, cradled by Poland and the Czech Republic, Zittau makes for an easy daytrip from Dresden or Görlitz. Its largely baroque Altstadt came through WWII mostly intact, though Cold War–era neglect is still evident in some places. The town is a major stop for religious pilgrims thanks to two precious late-medieval Lenten veils, which are ul-

trarare and stunning pieces of artistry. By contrast, the newest attraction is the bright and whimsical Pop Art Quarter, one of the largest of its kind in Germany.

South of Zittau, the Zittauer Gebirge is the smallest low-mountain range in Europe. With its idyllic gorges, thick forests and whimsical rock formations, it's great for hiking and clearing your head. You can drive or take the bus, but getting there is much more fun aboard the narrow-gauge Zittauer Schmalspurbahn, which has been steaming through the trees since 1890.

◉ Sights

Sights cluster around the Markt, which is about 1km south of the Hauptbahnhof via Bahnhofstrasse and Bautzener Strasse. With its baroque fountain, stately townhouses and imposing Italian palazzo-style Rathaus (town hall) by Prussian master builder Karl Friedrich Schinkel, it exudes a touch of lighthearted Mediterranean flair.

Pop-Art-Viertel   AREA
(Pop Art Quarter; www.mandauerglanz.de; btwn Grüne Strasse & Rosenstrasse) This once-drab cluster of GDR-era buildings has been transformed into a colourful and fanciful living theatre dreamed up by Berlin artist Sergej Alexander Dott. Highlights include giant sheep clambering around bright orange facades, and centaurs and angels standing guard over a pedestrianised walkway spanned by a massive double helix.

WORTH A TRIP

BAD MUSKAU

Squeezed against the border with Poland, sleepy Bad Muskau is a tiny spa-village with one big attraction. Unesco-listed **Muskauer Park** (☑ 035771-631 00; www.muskauer-park. de; Neues Schloss; park free, exhibit adult/concession €9/4.50, tower €4/2; ☉ exhibit 10am-6pm Apr-Oct) is the verdant masterpiece of 19th-century celebrity landscape gardener Prince Hermann von Pückler. 'Prince Pickle', as the English dubbed him, toiled on the park for nearly 30 years but never completed his 'painting with plants', because debt forced him to sell the estate in 1844. He nevertheless set the bar high for landscapers to follow, even compiling a meticulous instruction manual on landscaping techniques.

At a whopping 560 hectares, the folly-peppered park is too large to be fully explored on foot. Bike hire (€5 per day) is available at the well-signposted Schlossvorwerk, a leafy courtyard where you'll also find a cafe, gift shops and luggage lockers.

Bad Muskau is about 55km north of Görlitz. Coming by public transport, take an Ostdeutsche Eisenbahn train to Weisswasser (€7.80, 50 minutes), then change to bus 250 to Kirchplatz (€3, 20 minutes). Muskauer Park entrance is a short signposted walk away. Alternatively, it's possible on certain days from April to October to take a picturesque steam train ride from Weisswasser (€6.50 return) on the Waldeisenbahn Muskau (www. waldeisenbahn.de).

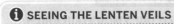

Museum Kirche zum Heiligen Kreuz
MUSEUM

(📋 03583-500 8920; www.zittauer-fastentuech er.de; Frauenstrasse 23; adult/concession €5/3; ⊘10am-5pm Apr-Oct, closed Mon Nov-Mar) This former church holds Zittau's most famous attraction, the 1472 Grosses Zittauer Fastentuch (Large Zittau Lenten Veil). The house-sized painted linen cloth shows a complete illustrated Bible in 90-odd scenes – Genesis to the Last Judgment. Its original purpose was to conceal the altar from the congregation during Lent. Ask for the accompanying voice-over to be played in English.

Also note the morbidly charming tombstones in the church cemetery.

Kulturhistorisches Museum Franziskanerkloster
MUSEUM

(📋 03583-554 790; www.zittauer-fastentuech er.de; Klosterstrasse 3; adult/concession €5/3; ⊘10am-5pm Apr-Oct, closed Mon Nov-Mar) The star exhibit at this museum is the 1573 Kleines Zittauer Fastentuch (Small Zittau Lenten Veil), which depicts the crucifixion scene framed by 40 symbols of the Passion of Christ, and is one of only seven such veils that have survived. The rest of the museum chronicles regional history.

Salzhaus
HISTORIC BUILDING

(www.salzhaus-zittau.de; Neustadt; ⊘8am-6.30pm) Overlooking fountain-studded Neustadt square, the weighty Salzhaus was originally a 16th-century salt storage house and now brims with market stalls, shops, restaurants and the public library.

Johanniskirche
CHURCH

(📋 03583-510 933; http://johannis-kirche-zittau. de; Johannisplatz 1; tower adult/concession €2/1; ⊘noon-6pm Mon-Fri, 10am-4pm Sat & Sun Apr-Oct, 10am-4pm Nov-Mar) Zittau's grand Church of St John has medieval roots, but the current version was designed by celebrated Prussian architect Karl Friedrich Schinkel, who added the wooden coffered ceiling, the neo-Gothic north tower and the baptismal font. It was consecrated in 1837. The south tower can be climbed for sweeping views of the mountains.

🍽 Sleeping & Eating

The tourist office should be able to help with accommodation in town and in Zittauer Gebirge.

ℹ SEEING THE LENTEN VEILS

Combination tickets to see both the large and small Lenten veils are €8 per adult (€5 concession). Tickets include English-language audio guides.

Hotel Dreiländereck
HOTEL €€

(📋 03583-5550; www.hotel-dle.de; Bautzener Strasse 9; s/d €73/95; 🅿 🛜) This one-time brewery on Zittau's pedestrianised commercial strip is a solid pick, with an old-school style – even if the green and gold colour schemes aren't to everyone's taste. The contemporary brasserie (mains €9 to €18) has vaulted ceilings and a large terrace.

★ Dornspachhaus
GERMAN €€

(📋 03583-795 883; www.dornspachhaus.de; Bautzner Strasse 2; mains €7-18; ⊘11.30am-2pm & 5.30-9.30pm) Zittau's oldest eatery dates from 1533 and oozes history, but it's not just a tourist piece – it serves delicious regional cuisine and has a lovely courtyard. A speciality is the Bohemian goulash, a creamy blend of slivered pork, pickles and mushrooms served in a bowl of bread, while during asparagus season you're spoiled for choice.

Seeger Schänke
GERMAN €€

(📋 03583-510 980; www.seeger-schaenke.de; Innere Weberstrasse 38; mains €10-14; ⊘11am-2pm & 6-10pm Mon-Fri, 6-10pm Sat & Sun) 'Seeger' is local dialect for 'clock', which explains the abundance of timepieces decorating this rustic pub that's often so crowded in the evenings that you have to wait for a table. There's a pleasant courtyard out the back, which is a great place for lunch in the sunshine during the summer months.

ℹ Information

Tourist Office (📋 03583-752 200; www.zittau. eu; Markt 1; ⊘9am-6pm Mon-Fri, 9am-1pm Sat, 10am-noon Sun May-Oct, closed Sun Nov-Apr) You'll find the tourist office inside the Rathaus.

ℹ Getting There & Away

CAR & MOTORCYCLE
Zittau is 36km south of Görlitz via the B99, and 48km southeast of Bautzen via the B96.

TRAIN
ODEG trains run to Görlitz (€7.60, 35 minutes), while Deutsche Bahn operates direct services to Dresden (€23.90, 1½ hours).

ZITTAU'S MOUNTAIN RAILWAY

The narrow-gauge **Zittauer Schmalspurbahn** (⏴03583-540 540; www.soeg-zittau.de; return trip €15), which has been steaming through the trees since 1890, departs year-round from a tiny timber station in front of Zittau train station and heads up to the sleepy resort villages of Oybin and Jonsdorf.

The historic locomotives split at Bertsdorf. The largest and nicest town is Oybin, which wraps around a beehive-shaped hill topped by a romantically ruined castle and monastery. Trains also stop at the Teufelsmühle (Devil's Mill), built for silver miners in the 17th century, from where a trail leads up to the Töpfer, a photogenic 582m-high mountain whose evocative sandstone formations have been nicknamed 'tortoise' or 'breeding hen'.

Bautzen

⏴ 03591 / POP 40,800

Rising high above the Spree River, with no fewer than 17 towers and much of the town fortification still ringing the Altstadt, Bautzen's skyline is a sight to behold. While its old town is now surrounded by a fairly unremarkable modern city, Bautzen is known across Germany for three things: its famous mustard, its two infamous prisons and its Slavic-speaking Sorbs, a protected (and endangered) ethnic minority group within Germany. Budyšin, as the Sorb language calls Bautzen, is home to several Sorb cultural institutions, and public signage is bilingual, though you'll be lucky to hear the language spoken.

◉ Sights

Gedenkstätte Bautzen   MEMORIAL

(⏴03591-404 74; www.gedenkstaette-bautzen.de; Weigangstrasse 8a; ⏰10am-4pm Mon-Thu, to 8pm Fri, to 6pm Sat & Sun) FREE Left exactly as it was in the late 1980s, the Bautzen II prison is now the Gedenkstätte Bautzen, dedicated to the victims of political oppression. You can see prisoner transport vans, recreated prison cells from the facility's various phases, the isolation wing and historical background exhibits.

Built in 1906 (alongside Bautzen I, which is still in use), Bautzen II became a notorious Stasi prison in the 1950s, controlled by the GDR Ministry of State Security. From 1956 to 1989, more than 2700 regime critics, would-be escapees and those who aided them, purported spies for the West and other political prisoners were incarcerated here.

Sorbisches Museum   MUSEUM

(⏴03591-270 8700; www.sorbisches-museum.de; Ortenburg 3-5; adult/concession €5/2.50; ⏰10am-6pm Tue-Sun) The Sorb national museum has collections and displays on every aspect of the history and culture of this ethnic minority. The exhibit kicks off with a general overview before documenting aspects of everyday life, such as customs and festivities, religion, architecture, music and dress. Upstairs, the focus is on Sorb language and literature, as well as on the emancipation movement of the 18th and 19th centuries. Unfortunately, there is no English labelling in the permanent exhibitions.

✯✯ Festivals & Events

Sorbian Easter   RELIGIOUS

(www.ostern-bautzen.de) On Easter Day, Sorbian men put on tall hats and frock coats, mount their richly decorated horses and ride through Bautzen and the surrounding villages, singing religious hymns. A major procession originates in Bautzen, meeting another one in the village of Radibor in the afternoon. Download a brochure from the website for exact schedules.

For several weeks prior to Easter, locals and tourists gather for the much-celebrated Sorbian Easter market, held in Postplatz in Bautzen during weekends, to shop for colourful Easter eggs.

✗ Eating

Bautzner Senfstube   GERMAN €€

(⏴03591-598 015; www.senf-stube.de; Schlossstrasse 3; mains €11-17; ⏰11am-10pm) Mustard bread, mustard salad dressing, mustard goulash, vanilla-mustard sauce, mustard potato mash – this restaurant is king when it comes to creative culinary uses of Bautzen's famous mustard. No worries if you're not a fan – there's a separate mustard-free menu as well.

Wjelbik   GERMAN €€

(⏴03591-420 60; www.wjelbik.de; Kornstrasse 7; mains €12-16; ⏰11am-3pm & 5.30-11pm Tue-Sat,

11am-3pm Sun) At this traditional restaurant, you'll be greeted Sorbian style, that is with a little bread and salt and a hearty *Witajće k nam!* (Welcome!). Enjoy the most Sorbian of dishes, 'Sorbian Wedding' (braised beef with horseradish sauce), in the dining room that manages modern and traditional in one go.

❶ Getting There & Away

CAR & MOTORCYCLE

The A4 linking Dresden with Görlitz runs just north of Bautzen.

TRAIN

Regional trains serve Bautzen from Görlitz (€8.20, 30 minutes) and Dresden (€14.30, one hour).

Herrnhut

📱 35873 / POP 3500

Surrounded by bucolic meadows, but visually an unremarkable little town, Herrnhut is an unlikely capital of the Moravian Brethren religious network, which has been engaged in missionary activity on all inhabited continents for almost three centuries. The group emerged as a union of fugitive Hussites, religious dissidents from Bohemia in modern Czechia, led by an enlightened German noble with a strong penchant for travel. Today it lures visitors with a remarkable collection of artefacts amassed by the Herrnhutter missionaries in places such as Australia and Greenland, and a factory celebrated as the birthplace of the Christmas stars that now decorate pretty much every German home in wintertime.

◉ Sights

★ Völkerkundemuseum   MUSEUM

(📱 351-4914 2000; http://voelkerkunde-herrnhut.skd.museum; Goethestrasse 1; adult/concession €3/2; ◷ 9am-5pm Tue-Sun) Even before they started travelling the world, the Herrnhutters were so obsessed with exotic lands they purchased items brought from Australia by Captain Cook's expedition. That collection was greatly expanded by curious missionaries, who brought back ritual objects from Tanzania, Buddhist *tangkas* from Kalmykia in Russia, walrus-bone toys from Greenland and much more. All of these are on display in the town's compact but rich ethnographic museum.

Heimatmuseum   MUSEUM

(📱 35873-307 33; www.herrnhut.de; Comeniusstrasse 6; ◷ 9am-5pm Tue-Fri, 10am-noon & 1-5pm Sat & Sun) If you want to learn more about the Moravian Brethren and its illustrious founder, Count Nicolaus Zinzendorf, head to Herrnhut's local history museum, which comes with a charming little garden. Sadly, signs are in German.

🛏 Sleeping & Eating

Few people stay overnight in Herrnhut, but there are a couple of hotels and guesthouses, some run by Moravian Brethren. Ask at museums.

Nostalgia Privatim   CAFE €

(📱 35873-360 970; www.nostalgia-privatim.com; Löbauer Strasse 55; mains €4.50-6.50; ◷ 7am-6pm Mon-Sat, 2-5pm Sun) Coming as a surprise here in Herrnhut, this cool Brooklyn-esque cafe inside the converted railway station building serves filling breakfasts and inexpensive midday meals. There's also ice cream, cakes and fresh bread baked on the premises.

🛍 Shopping

Hernhutter Sterne
Manufaktur   GIFTS & SOUVENIRS

(📱 35873-3640; www.herrnhuter-sterne.de; Oderwitzer Strasse 8; ◷ 9am-6pm Mon-Fri, 10am-5pm Sat) Now displayed at every other German home over Christmas, the Hernhutter stars – a Christian version of Chinese lanterns – were first produced in the 1850s by children at boarding schools, who regarded them as a symbol of homecoming. You can buy a star for yourself (€15 to €45) in this glassy edifice, where the heir of the original factory is based.

There is a free exhibition on the premises and a show workshop, where you are invited to look over the shoulder of workers producing stars and try your hand at making one.

❶ Getting There & Away

Herrnhut is located on the partly reconstructed 178 road that branches off the A4 towards Liberec in Czechia. Local bus 27 connects Herrnhut with Zittau Bahnhof (30 minutes, hourly).

SAXONY HERRNHUT

Munich

🎵 089 / POP 1.46 MILLION

Best Places to Eat

➡ Weinhaus Neuner (p369)

➡ Königsquelle (p367)

➡ Tantris (p371)

➡ Prinz Myshkin (p367)

➡ Esszimmer (p371)

Best Places to Stay

➡ Bayerischer Hof (p361)

➡ Flushing Meadows (p360)

➡ Hotel Laimer Hof (p363)

➡ Hotel Mandarin Oriental Munich (p361)

➡ Louis Hotel (p361)

Why Go?

The natural habitat of well-heeled power dressers and Lederhosen-clad thigh-slappers, Mediterranean-style street cafes and Mitteleuropa beer halls, highbrow art and high-tech industry, Germany's unofficial southern capital is a flourishing success story that revels in its own contradictions. If you're looking for Alpine clichés, they're all here, but the Bavarian metropolis has many an unexpected card down its Dirndl.

But whatever else this city is, it's popular. Statistics show Munich is enticing more visitors than ever, especially in summer and during Oktoberfest, when the entire planet seems to arrive to toast the town.

Munich's walkable centre retains a small-town air but holds some world-class sights, especially art galleries and museums. Throw in royal Bavarian heritage, an entire suburb of Olympic legacy and a kitbag of dark tourism, and it's clear why southern Germany's metropolis is such a favourite among those who seek out the past but like to hit the town once they're done.

When to Go

Shoulder seasons (April–June and September–October) are best, avoiding the heat of summer and the bitter winter temperatures. However, avoid late September and early October unless visiting Oktoberfest.

The Christmas market season is a good time to come, as is festival season over the summer.

History

It was Benedictine monks, drawn by fertile farmland and the closeness to Catholic Italy, who settled in what is now Munich. The city derives its name from the medieval Munichen (monks). In 1158 the Imperial Diet in Augsburg sanctioned the rule of Heinrich der Löwe, and Munich the city was born.

In 1240 the city passed to the House of Wittelsbach, which would govern Munich (and Bavaria) until the 20th century. Munich prospered as a salt-trading centre but was hit hard by plague in 1349. The epidemic subsided only after 150 years, whereupon the relieved Schäffler (coopers) initiated a ritualistic dance to remind burghers of their good fortune. The Schäfflertanz is performed every seven years but is re-enacted daily by the little figures on the city's Glockenspiel (carillon) on Marienplatz.

By the 19th century an explosion of monument building gave Munich its spectacular architecture and wide Italianate avenues. Things got out of hand after King Ludwig II ascended the throne in 1864, as spending for his grandiose projects (such as Schloss Neuschwanstein) bankrupted the royal house and threatened the government's coffers. Ironically, today they are the biggest money-spinners of Bavaria's tourism industry.

Munich has seen many turbulent times, but none like the first half of the 20th century. WWI practically starved the city to death, while the Nazis first rose to prominence here and WWII nearly wiped Munich off the map. The 1972 Olympic Games began as a celebration of a new democratic Germany but ended in tragedy when 17 people were killed in a terrorist hostage-taking incident. In 2006 the city won a brighter place in sporting history when it hosted the opening game of the FIFA World Cup.

Today Munich's claim to being the 'secret capital' of Germany is well founded. The city is recognised for its high living standards – with more millionaires per capita than any other German city except Hamburg – and for a cultural scene that rivals that of larger more important European capitals. Looking towards its 900th birthday, this great metropolis is striding affluently forward in the 21st century.

⊙ Sights

Munich's major sights cluster around the Altstadt, with the main museum district just north of the Residenz. However, it will take another day or two to explore bohemian Schwabing, the sprawling Englischer Garten, and trendy Haidhausen to the east. Northwest of the Altstadt you'll find cosmopolitan Neuhausen, the Olympiapark, and another of Munich's royal highlights – Schloss Nymphenburg.

⊙ Altstadt & Residenz

★ **Residenzmuseum**   MUSEUM
(Map p344; ☑ 089-290 671; www.residenz-muenchen. de; Residenzstrasse 1; adult/concession/under 18yr €7/6/free; ⊙ 9am-6pm Apr–mid-Oct, 10am-5pm mid-Oct–Mar, last entry 1hr before closing; Ⓤ Odeonsplatz) Home to Bavaria's Wittelsbach rulers from 1508 until WWI, the Residenz is Munich's number-one attraction. The amazing treasures, as well as all the trappings of the Wittelbachs' lifestyle over the centuries, are on display at the Residenzmuseum, which takes up around half of the palace. Allow at least two hours to see everything at a gallop.

Tours are in the company of a rather long-winded audioguide (free), and gone are the days when the building was divided into morning and afternoon sections, all of which means a lot of ground to cover in one go. It's worth fast-forwarding a bit to where the prescribed route splits into short and long tours, taking the long route for the most spectacular interiors. Approximately 90 rooms are open to the public at any one time, but as renovation work is ongoing, closures are inevitable, and you may not see all the highlights.

When wandering the Residenz, don't forget that only 50 sq metres of the building's roof remained intact at the end of WWII. Most of what you see today is a Wittelsbach postwar reconstruction.

The tours start at the Grottenhof (Grotto Court), home of the wonderful Perseusbrunnen (Perseus Fountain), with its namesake holding the dripping head of Medusa. Next door is the famous Antiquarium, a barrel-vaulted hall smothered in frescoes and built to house the Wittelsbachs' enormous antique collection. It's widely regarded as the finest Renaissance interior north of the Alps.

Further along the tour route, the neo-Byzantine Hofkirche was built for Ludwig I in 1826. After WWII only the red-brick walls were left; it reopened as an atmospheric concert venue in 2003.

Upstairs are the Kurfürstenzimmer (Electors Rooms), with some stunning Italian portraits and a passage lined with two dozen views of Italy, painted by local romantic artist Carl Rottmann. Also up here are François Cuvilliés' Reiche Zimmer (Rich Rooms), a

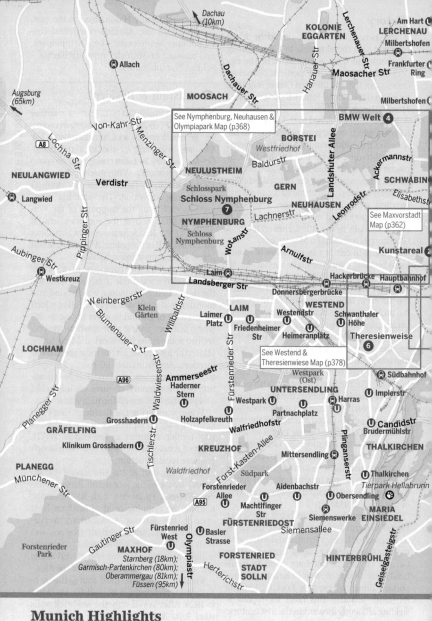

Munich Highlights

❶ Hofbräuhaus (p372) Raising a 1L stein at the mothership of authentic beer halls.

❷ Kunstareal (p354) Hitting up the south's leading art museums in one compact area.

❸ Residenzmuseum (p339) Revelling in the pomp and splendour of this top museum.

❹ BMW Welt (p354) Getting under the high-octane hood of BMW's latest models.

❺ Englischer Garten (p347) Watching daredevil surfers

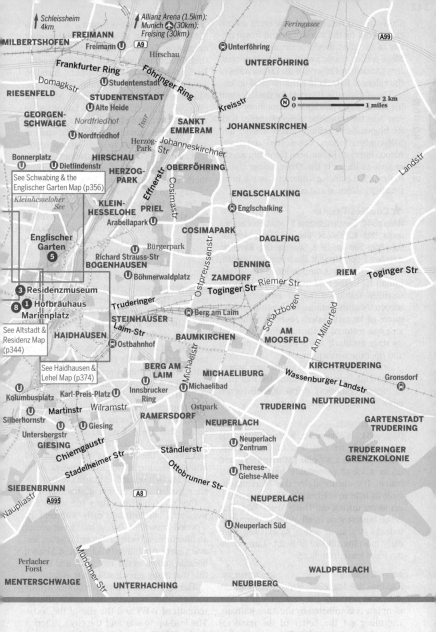

Schleissheim
4km

Allianz Arena (1.5km);
Munich (30km);
Freising (30km)

MILBERTSHOFEN

FREIMANN
Freimann Ⓤ A9

Hirschau

Ⓤ Unterföhring

UNTERFÖHRING

A99

Feringasee

Frankfurter Ring

Föhringer Ring

Domagkstr

Ⓤ Studentenstadt

Kreisstr

RIESENFELD

STUDENTENSTADT

Ⓤ Alte Heide

Nordfriedhof

**GEORGEN-
SCHWAIGE**

Isar

**SANKT
EMMERAM**

JOHANNESKIRCHEN

 ̂N 0   2 km
    0   1 miles

Ⓤ Nordfriedhof

Herzog-
Park

Johanneskirchner

Herzog-
Str

Bonnerplatz
Ⓤ

Ⓤ Dietlindenstr

HIRSCHAU

Landstr

See Schwabing & the
Englischer Garten Map (p356)

Kleinhesseloher
See

**HERZOG-
PARK**

Effnerstr

OBERFÖHRING

Cosimastr

**KLEIN-
HESSELOHE**

PRIEL

ENGLSCHALKING

Ⓤ Englschalking

**Englischer
Garten**
⑤

Arabellapark Ⓤ

Cosimastr

COSIMAPARK

DAGLFING

Ⓤ Bürgerpark

Richard Strauss-Str Ⓤ

BOGENHAUSEN

Ⓤ Böhmerwaldplatz

Ostpreussenstr

DENNING

ZAMDORF

RIEM

Toginger Str

③ **Residenzmuseum**

Toginger Str

Riemer Str

⑧① **Hofbräuhaus**
Marienplatz

Truderinger

STEINHAUSER

Schatzbogen

**AM
MOOSFELD**

Am Mitterfeld

KIRCHTRUDERING

Ⓤ Berg am Laim

See Altstadt &
Residenz Map
(p344)

Laim-Str

HAIDHAUSEN

Ⓤ Ostbahnhof

BAUMKIRCHEN

Michaelstr

Wassenburger Landstr

Gronsdorf

See Haidhausen &
Lehel Map (p374)

**BERG AM
LAIM**

MICHAELIBURG

Ⓤ Michaelibad

NEUTRUDERING

Ⓤ
Kolumbusplatz

Karl-Preis-Platz Ⓤ

Ⓤ Innsbrucker
Ring

Wilramstr

Ostpark

TRUDERING

**GARTENSTADT
TRUDERING**

Silberhornstr Ⓤ

Martinstr

RAMERSDORF

NEUPERLACH

Untersbergstr Ⓤ

Ⓤ Giesing

GIESING

Chiemgaustr

Ständlerstr

 ̈Ⓤ Neuperlach
Zentrum

**TRUDERINGER
GRENZKOLONIE**

Stadelheimer Str

Ottobrunner Str

Ⓤ Therese-
Giehse-Allee

NEUPERLACH

SIEBENBRUNN

Naupliastr

A995

A8

Ⓤ Neuperlach Süd

Perlacher
Forst

Münchner Str

WALDPERLACH

MENTERSCHWAIGE

UNTERHACHING

NEUBIBERG

---

negotiate an urban wave on
the artificial stream.

⑥ **Oktoberfest** (p360)
Raising several steins to a truly
Munich experience.

⑦ **Schloss Nymphenburg**
(p355) Revelling in the utter
grandeur of this commanding
palace.

⑧ **Marienplatz** (p342)
Taking in the heart and soul of
the Altstadt, the city's busiest
spot.

six-room extravaganza of exuberant rococo carried out by the top stucco and fresco artists of the day; they're a definite highlight. More rococo magic awaits in the *Ahnengallery* (Ancestors Gallery), with 121 portraits of the rulers of Bavaria in chronological order.

The *Hofkapelle*, reserved for the ruler and his family, fades quickly in the memory when you see the exquisite *Reichekapelle*, with its blue-and-gilt ceiling, inlaid marble and 16th-century organ. Considered the finest rococo interiors in southern Germany, another spot to linger is the *Steinzimmer* (Stone Rooms), the emperor's quarters, awash in intricately patterned and coloured marble.

★ **Cuvilliés-Theater**   THEATRE

(Map p344; Residenzstrasse 1; adult/concession/under 18yr €3.50/2.50/free; ⊙2-6pm Mon-Sat, 9am-6pm Sun Apr-Jul & Sep–mid-Oct, 9am-6pm daily Aug, 2-5pm Mon-Sat, 10am-5pm Sun Nov-Mar; 🚇Nationaltheater) Commissioned by Maximilian III in the mid-18th century, François Cuvilliés fashioned one of Europe's finest rococo theatres. Famous for hosting the premiere of Mozart's opera *Idomeneo*, the theatre was restored in the mid-noughties, and its stage regularly hosts high-brow musical and operatic performances.

Access is limited to the auditorium, where you can take a seat and admire the four tiers of loggias (galleries), dripping with rococo embellishment, at your leisure.

★ **Marienplatz**   SQUARE

(Map p344; ⑤ Marienplatz, Ⓤ Marienplatz) The epicentral heart and soul of the Altstadt, Marienplatz is a popular gathering spot and packs a lot of personality into a compact frame. It's anchored by the Mariensäule, built in 1638 to celebrate victory over Swedish forces during the Thirty Years' War. This is the busiest spot in all Munich, throngs of tourists swarming across its expanse from early morning till late at night. Many walking tours leave from here.

Altes Rathaus   HISTORIC BUILDING

(Old Town Hall; Map p344; Marienplatz; ⑤ Marienplatz, Ⓤ Marienplatz) The eastern side of Marienplatz is dominated by the Altes Rathaus. Lightning got the better of the medieval original in 1460 and WWII bombs levelled its successor, so what you see is really the third incarnation of the building designed by Jörg von Halspach of Frauenkirche fame. On 9 November 1938 Joseph Goebbels gave a hate-filled speech here that launched the nationwide *Kristallnacht* pogroms.

★ **Münchner Stadtmuseum**   MUSEUM

(City Museum; Map p344; www.muenchner-stadt museum.de; St-Jakobs-Platz 1; adult/concession/child €7/3.50/free, audioguide free; ⊙10am-6pm Tue-Sun; ⑤ Marienplatz, Ⓤ Marienplatz) Installed for the city's 850th birthday (2008), the Münchner Stadtmuseum's Typisch München (Typically Munich) exhibition – taking up the whole of a rambling building – tells Munich's story in an imaginative, uncluttered and engaging way. Exhibits in each section represent something quintessential about the city; a booklet/audioguide relates the tale behind them, thus condensing a long and tangled history into easily digestible themes.

Set out in chronological order, the exhibition kicks off with the monks who founded the city and ends with the postwar-boom decades. The first of five sections, Old Munich, contains a scale model of the city in the late 16th century (one of five commissioned by Duke Albrecht V; the Bayerisches Nationalmuseum (p349) displays the others), but the highlight here is the *The Morris Dancers*, a series of statuettes gyrating like 15th-century ravers. It's one of the most valuable works owned by the city.

Next comes New Munich, which charts the Bavarian capital's 18th- and 19th-century transformation into a prestigious royal capital and the making of the modern city. The *Canaletto View* gives an idea in oil paint of how Munich looked in the mid-18th century, before the Wittelsbachs (the German noble family that ruled Bavaria) launched their makeover. The section also takes a fascinating look at the origins of Oktoberfest and Munich's cuisine, as well as the phenomenon of the 'Munich Beauty' – Munich's womenfolk are regarded as Germany's most attractive.

City of Munich examines the weird and wonderful late 19th and early 20th century, a period known for *Jugendstil* (art nouveau) architecture and design, Richard Wagner, and avant-garde rumblings in Schwabing. Munich became known as the 'city of art and beer', a title that many agree it still holds today.

The fourth hall, Revue, becomes a little obscure, but basically deals with the aftermath of WWI and the rise of the Nazis. The lead-up to war and the city's suffering during WWII occupy the Feuchtwangersaal, where a photo of a very determined Chamberlain stands next to the other signatories to the 1938 Munich Agreement, which created parts of Czechoslovakia to Nazi Germany. This is followed by a couple of fascinating rooms that paint a portrait of the modern city, including nostalgic TV footage from the last 40 years.

Though the Typical Munich exhibition touches on the period, the rise of the Nazis has been rightly left as a powerful separate exhibition called Nationalsozialismus in München. This occupies an eerily windowless annexe.

★ Asamkirche
CHURCH

(Map p344; Sendlinger Strasse 32; ⊙9am-6pm; ⊠Sendlinger Tor, Ⓤ Sendlinger Tor) Though pocket sized, the late-baroque Asamkirche, built in 1746, is as rich and epic as a giant's treasure chest. Its creators, the brothers Cosmas Damian Asam and Egid Quirin Asam, dug deep into their considerable talent box to swathe every inch of wall space with gilt garlands and docile cherubs, false marble and oversized barley-twist columns.

The crowning glory is the ceiling fresco illustrating the life of St John Nepomuk, to whom the church is dedicated (lie down on your back in a pew to fully appreciate the complicated perspective). The brothers lived next door and this was originally their private chapel; the main altar could be seen through a window from their home.

Frauenkirche
CHURCH

(Church of Our Lady; Map p344; www.muenchner-dom.de; Frauenplatz 1; ⊙7.30am-8.30pm; Ⓢ Marienplatz) The landmark Frauenkirche, built between 1468 and 1488, is Munich's spiritual heart and the Mt Everest among its churches. No other building in the central city may stand taller than its onion-domed twin towers, which reach a skyscraping 99m. The south tower can be climbed, but has been under urgent renovation for several years.

The church sustained severe bomb damage in WWII; its reconstruction is a soaring passage of light but otherwise fairly spartan. Of note are the epic cenotaph (empty tomb) of Ludwig the Bavarian, just past the entrance, and the bronze plaques of Pope Benedict XVI and his predecessor John Paul II affixed to nearby pillars.

Heiliggeistkirche
CHURCH

(Church of the Holy Spirit; Map p344; Tal 77; ⊙7am-6pm; Ⓢ Marienplatz, Ⓤ Marienplatz) Gothic at its core, this baroque church on the edge of the Viktualienmarkt has fantastic ceiling frescoes created by the Asam brothers in 1720, depicting the foundation of a hospice that once stood next door. The hospice was demolished to make way for the new Viktualienmarkt.

Michaelskirche
CHURCH

(Church of St Michael; Map p344; www.st-michael-muenchen.de; Kaufingerstrasse 52; crypt €2; ⊙crypt 9.30am-4.30pm Mon-Fri, to 2.30pm Sat & Sun; ⊠Karlsplatz, Ⓢ Karlsplatz, Ⓤ Karlsplatz) It stands quiet and dignified amid the retail frenzy out on Kaufingerstrasse, but to fans of Ludwig II, the Michaelskirche is the ultimate place of pilgrimage. Its dank crypt is the final resting place of the Mad King, whose humble tomb is usually drowned in flowers.

Completed in 1597, St Michael's was the largest Renaissance church north of the Alps when it was built. It boasts an impressive unsupported barrel-vaulted ceiling, and the massive bronze statue between the two entrances shows the archangel finishing off a dragon-like creature, a classic Counter Reformation–era symbol of Catholicism triumphing over Protestantism. The building has been fully renovated and has never looked more impressive.

Viktualienmarkt
MARKET

(Map p344; ⊙Mon-Fri & morning Sat; Ⓤ Marienplatz, Ⓢ Marienplatz) Fresh fruit and vegetables, piles of artisan cheeses, tubs of exotic olives, hams and jams, chanterelles and truffles – Viktualienmarkt is a feast of flavours and one of central Europe's finest gourmet markets.

The market moved here in 1807 when it outgrew the Marienplatz, and many of the stalls have been run by generations of the same family. Put together a picnic and head for the market's very own beer garden for an alfresco lunch with a brew and to watch the traders in action.

St Peterskirche
CHURCH

(Church of St Peter; Map p344; Rindermarkt 1; church free, tower adult/child €3/2; ⊙tower 9am-6pm Mon-Fri, from 10am Sat & Sun; Ⓤ Marienplatz, Ⓢ Marienplatz) Some 306 steps divide you from the best view of central Munich from the 92m tower of St Peterskirche, central Munich's oldest church (1150). Inside awaits a virtual textbook of art through the centuries. Worth a closer peek are the Gothic St-Martin-Altar, the baroque ceiling fresco by Johann Baptist Zimmermann and rococo sculptures by Ignaz Günther.

Jüdisches Museum
MUSEUM

(Jewish Museum; Map p344; www.juedisches-museum-muenchen.de; St-Jakobs-Platz 16; adult/child €6/3; ⊙10am-6pm Tue-Sun; ⊠Sendlinger Tor, Ⓤ Sendlinger Tor) Coming to terms with its Nazi past has not historically been a priority

Altstadt & Residenz

0 | 200 m
0 | 0.1 miles

MAXVORSTADT

Alter Botanischer Garten

Palace of Justice

Hauptbahnhof (100m)

Streets & places

Königinstr
Von-der-Tann-Str
Franz-Josef-Str-Ring
Karl-Scharnagl-Ring
Thomas-Wimmer-Ring
Herzog-Rudolf-Str
Sigmundstr
Seitzstr
Galeriestr
Hofgarten
Hofgartenstr
Ludwigstr
Jägerstr
Oskar-von-Miller-Ring
Brienner Str
Odeonsplatz
Salvatorstr
Kardinal-Faulhaber-Str
Prannerstr
Promenadeplatz
Maffeistr
Theatinerstr
Residenzstr
Max-Joseph-Platz
Marstallplatz
Maximilianstr
Falckenbergstr
Stollbergstr
Hildegardstr
Neuturmstr
Herrnstr
Hochbrückenstr
Am Kosttor
Am Platzl
Pfisterstr
Alter Hof
Hofgraben
Altenhofstr
Burgstr
Münzstr
Braunaustr
Sparkassenstr
Ledererstr
Maderbraustr
Petersplatz
Marienplatz
Rosenstr
Sporerstr
Schäfflerstr
Filserbräugasse
Frauenplatz
Löwengrube
Augustinerstr
Kaufingerstr
Mazarstr
Ettstr
Maxburgstr
Pacellistr
Lenbachplatz
Sonnenstr
Max-Joseph-Str
Brienner Str
Ottostr
Maximiliansplatz
Barer Str
Karlstr
Sophienstr
Arcisstr
Elisenstr
Karlsplatz
Neuhauser Str
Eisenmannstr
Herzogspitalstr
Altheimer Eck
Hotterstr
Damenstiftstr
Adolf-Kolping-Str
Zweigstr
Schützenstr
Sonnenstr

Markers

2, 3, 5, 6, 8, 9, 10, 12, 14, 15, 16, 17, 19, 21, 22, 23, 24, 30, 35, 38, 39, 42, 44, 49, 50, 55, 58, 63, 67, 69, 70, 75, 76, 78, 79, 80, 82, 83, 87, 88, 89, 90

Cuvilliés-Theater

Residenzmuseum

Castles & Museums Infopoint

Landschaftsstr

Tourist Office – Marienplatz

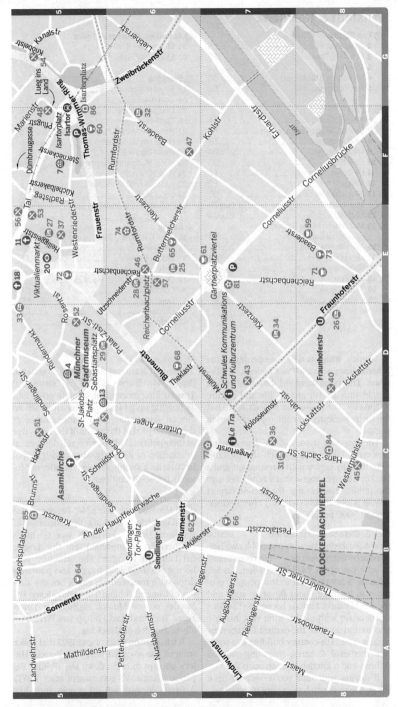

Altstadt & Residenz

in Munich, which is why the opening of the Jewish Museum in 2007 was hailed as a milestone. The permanent exhibition offers an insight into Jewish history, life and culture in the city. The Holocaust is dealt with, but the focus is clearly on contemporary Jewish culture.

The museum is part of the Jewish complex on St-Jakobs-Platz, which also includes a community centre with a restaurant and a bunker-like synagogue that's rarely open to the public. Munich has the second-largest Jewish population in Germany after Berlin's: around 9000 people.

Bier & Oktoberfestmuseum MUSEUM

(Beer & Oktoberfest Museum; Map p344; www.bier-und-oktoberfestmuseum.de; Sterneckerstrasse 2; adult/concession €4/2.50; ⊙1-6pm Tue-Sat; ⓈIsartor, ⓈIsartor) Head to this popular museum to learn all about Bavarian suds and the world's most famous booze-up. The four floors heave with old brewing vats, historic photos and some of the earliest Oktoberfest regalia. The 14th-century building has some fine medieval features, including painted ceilings and a kitchen with an open fire.

If during your tour you've worked up a thirst, the museum has its very own pub.

Monument to the Victims of National Socialism MONUMENT

(Map p344; Brienner Strasse; ⓊOdeonsplatz) This striking monument is made up of four Ts holding up a block-like cage in which an eternal flame gutters in remembrance of those who died at the hands of the Nazis due to their political beliefs, race, religion, sexual orientation or disability. Moved to this spot in 2014, it's a sternly simple reminder of Munich's not-so-distant past.

Feldherrnhalle HISTORIC BUILDING

(Field Marshalls Hall; Map p344; Residenzstrasse 1; ⓊOdeonsplatz) Corking up Odeonsplatz' southern side is Friedrich von Gärnter's Feldherrnhalle, modelled on the Loggia dei Lanzi in Florence. The structure pays homage to the Bavarian army and positively drips with testosterone; check out the statues of General Johann Tilly, who kicked the Swedes out of Munich during the Thirty Years' War; and Karl Philipp von Wrede, an ally turned foe of Napoléon.

It was here on 9 November 1923 that police stopped the so-called Beer Hall Putsch, Hitler's attempt to bring down the Weimar Republic (Germany's government after WWI). A fierce skirmish left 20 people, including

16 Nazis, dead. A plaque in the pavement of the square's eastern side commemorates the police officers who perished in the incident.

Hitler was subsequently tried and sentenced to five years in jail, but he ended up serving a mere nine months in Landsberg am Lech prison, where he penned his hate-filled manifesto, *Mein Kampf*.

Theatinerkirche　　　　　　　　CHURCH
(Map p344; Theatinerstrasse 22; ☺7am-9pm; Ⓢ Odeonsplatz) FREE The mustard-yellow Theatinerkirche, built to commemorate the 1662 birth of Prince Max Emanuel, is the work of Swiss architect Enrico Zuccalli. Also known as St Kajetan's, it's a voluptuous design with massive twin towers flanking a giant cupola. Inside, an ornate dome lords it over the Fürstengruft (royal crypt), the final destination of several Wittelsbach rulers, including King Maximilian II (1811–64).

❂ Schwabing & the Englischer Garten

★ **Englischer Garten**　　　　　　PARK
(English Garden; Map p356; Ⓤ Universität) The sprawling English Garden is among Europe's biggest city parks – it even rivals London's Hyde Park and New York's Central Park for size – and is a popular playground for locals and visitors alike. Stretching north from Prinzregentenstrasse for about 5km, it was commissioned by Elector Karl Theodor in 1789 and designed by Benjamin Thompson, an American-born scientist working as an adviser to the Bavarian government.

Paths meander around in dark stands of mature oak and maple before emerging into sunlit meadows of lush grass. Locals are mindful of the park's popularity and cyclists, walkers and joggers coexist amicably. Street musicians dodge balls kicked by children and students sprawl on the grass to chat about missed lectures.

Sooner or later you'll find your way to the Kleinhesseloher See, a lovely lake at the centre of the park. Work up a sweat while taking a spin around the lake's three little islands, then quaff a well-earned foamy one at the Seehaus beer garden (p375).

Several historic follies lend the park a playful charm. The wholly unexpected Chinesischer Turm (p375), now at the heart of Munich's oldest beer garden, was built in the 18th century during a pan-European craze

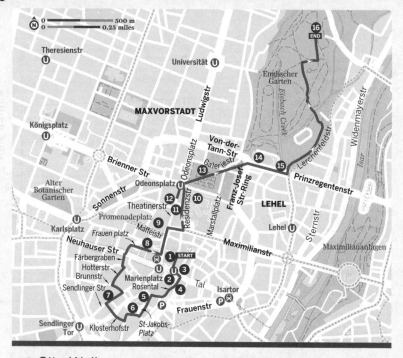

🏃 City Walk
Historic Centre & the Englischer Garten

START MARIENPLATZ
FINISH ENGLISCHER GARTEN
LENGTH 6KM, TWO HOURS

Kick off at central Marienplatz where the glockenspiel chimes from the ❶ **Neues Rathaus**, the impressive Gothic town hall. The steeple of the ❷ **St Peterskirche** (p343) affords great views of the old town, including the ❸ **Altes Rathaus** (p342). Turn left as you leave St Peters and walk down Petersplatz to the ❹ **Viktualienmarkt** (p343). Then head south to Sebastiansplatz and the ❺ **Münchner Stadtmuseum** (p342). The big cube opposite on St-Jakobs-Platz is Munich's synagogue, flanked by the ❻ **Jüdisches Museum** (p343).

From here follow Unterer Anger, turn right on Klosterhofstrasse, which continues as Schmidstrasse and reaches Sendlinger Strasse. Turn right for a peek inside the ❼ **Asamkirche** (p343). Backtrack a few steps on Sendlinger Strasse, turn left on Hackenstrasse, right on Hotterstrasse, past the tiny Hundskugel, the city's oldest restaurant, left on Altheimer Eck and right on Färbergraben. This takes you to Kaufinger Strasse, the Altstadt's shopping strip. Continue on Augustinerstrasse to the twin-onion-domed ❽ **Frauenkirche** (p343) with great views from the top. Lanes behind the church lead to Weinstrasse; turn left and continue on Theatinerstrasse, taking a break at the ❾ **Fünf Höfe** shopping arcade. Backtrack a few steps on Theatinerstrasse, then turn left on tiny Perusastrasse, which brings you to the ❿ **Residenz** (p339).

Continue north on Residenzstrasse to reach Odeonsplatz, dominated by the ⓫ **Feldherrnhalle** (p346), a shrine to war heroes. The mustard-yellow ⓬ **Theatinerkirche** (p347) contains the Wittelsbachs' crypt. Cross the ⓭ **Hofgarten** and take the underpass, then turn right on Prinzregentenstrasse and proceed past the ⓮ **Haus der Kunst** (p349). Just beyond, don't miss the ⓯ **surfers** (p347) riding the artificial wave on the Eisbach creek. Across the creek, turn left into the Englischer Garten and the multitiered ⓰ **Chinesischer Turm** (p375) for a well-deserved beer.

for all things oriental. Further south, at the top of a gentle hill, stands the heavily photographed Monopteros (1838), a small Greek temple whose ledges are often knee-to-knee with dangling legs belonging to people admiring the view of the Munich skyline.

Another hint of Asia awaits further south at the Japanisches Teehaus, built for the 1972 Olympics next to an idyllic duck pond. The best time to come is for an authentic tea ceremony celebrated by a Japanese tea master, though it's only open two days a month.

★ Bayerisches Nationalmuseum   MUSEUM
(Map p356; www.bayerisches-nationalmuseum.de; Prinzregentenstrasse 3; adult/concession/child €7/6/free, Sun €1; ⊙10am-5pm Tue, Wed & Fri-Sun, to 8pm Thu; ☐Nationalmuseum/Haus Der Kunst, ☐Nationalmuseum/Haus Der Kunst) Picture the classic 19th-century museum, a palatial neoclassical edifice overflowing with exotic treasure and thought-provoking works of art, a repository for a nation's history, a grand purpose-built display case for royal trinkets, church baubles and state-owned rarities – this is the Bavarian National Museum, a good old-fashioned institution for no-nonsense museum lovers. As the collection fills 40 rooms over three floors, there's a lot to get through here, so be prepared for at least two hours' legwork.

Most visitors start on the 1st floor, where hall after hall is packed with baroque, mannerist and Renaissance sculpture, ecclesiastical treasures (check out all those wobbly Gothic 'S' figures), Renaissance clothing and one-off pieces such as the 1000-year-old St Kunigunde's chest fashioned in mammoth ivory and gold. Climb to the 2nd floor to move up in history to the rococo, *Jugendstil* and modern periods, represented by priceless collections of Nymphenburg and Meissen porcelain, Tiffany glass, Augsburg silver and precious items used by the Bavarian royal family. Also up here is a huge circular model of Munich in the first half of the 19th century, shortly after it was transformed into a capital fit for a kingdom.

It's easy to miss, but the building's basement also holds an evocatively displayed collection of Krippen (nativity scenes), some with a Cecil B DeMille–style cast of thousands. Retold in paper, wood and resin, there are Christmas-story scenes here from Bohemia, Moravia and Tyrol, but the biggest contingent hails from Naples. Also here is the excellent museum shop.

DenkStätte Weisse Rose   MEMORIAL
(Map p356; www.weisse-rose-stiftung.de; Geschwister-Scholl-Platz 1; ⊙10am-5pm Mon-Fri, 11am-4.30pm Sat; ⓊUniversität) FREE This memorial exhibit to the Weisse Rose (White Rose; a nonviolent resistance group led by Munich University students Hans and Sophie Scholl to oppose the Nazis) is within the Ludwig-Maximilians-Universität. It's a moving story, and one of Munich's most heroic, told in photographs and exhibits from the period.

Haus der Kunst   MUSEUM
(House of Art; Map p356; www.hausderkunst.de; Prinzregentenstrasse 1; adult/concession €12/5; ⊙10am-8pm Fri-Wed, to 10pm Thu; ☐National museum/Haus Der Kunst, ☐Nationalmuseum/Haus Der Kunst) This austere fascist-era edifice was built in 1937 to showcase Nazi art, but now the Haus der Kunst presents works by exactly the artists whom the Nazis rejected and deemed degenerate. Temporary shows focus on contemporary art and design.

Ludwig-Maximilians-Universität   UNIVERSITY
(LMU; Map p356; www.uni-muenchen.de; Geschwister-Scholl-Platz 1; ⑤Universität) The oldest university in Bavaria Ludwig-Maximilians-Universität started out as a political football for its rulers. Founded in Ingolstadt in 1472, it moved to Landshut in 1800 before being lassoed to Munich in 1826 by newly crowned King Ludwig I. It has produced more than a dozen Nobel Prize winners, including Wilhelm Röntgen in 1901 (Physics) and Theodor Hänsch in 2005 (Physics).

The main building, by Friedrich von Gärtner of course, has cathedral-like dimensions and is accented with sculpture and other artworks. A flight of stairs leads to a light court with a memorial to *Die Weisse Rose*, the Nazi resistance group founded by Hans and Sophie Scholl. To get the full story, visit the small DenkStätte in the vaulted space behind.

Ludwigskirche   CHURCH
(Church of St Ludwig; Map p356; Ludwigstrasse 20; ⊙8am-8pm; ⑤Universität) The sombre twin-towered Ludwigskirche, built by Friedrich von Gärtner between 1829 and 1844, is a highly decorative, almost Byzantine, affair with one major showpiece: the *Last Judgment* fresco by the Nazarene painter Peter Cornelius in the choir. It's one of the largest in the world and an immodest – and thoroughly unsuccessful – attempt to outdo Michelangelo's version.

MAXIMILIANSTRASSE

It's pricey and pretentious, but no trip to Munich would be complete without a wander along Maximilianstrasse, one of the city's swishest boulevards. Starting at Max-Joseph-Platz, it's a 1km-long ribbon of style where well-heeled shoppers browse for Breguet and Prada and bored bodyguards loiter by Bentleys and Rolls Royces. It's also a haunt for Munich's many beggars. Several of the city's finest theatrical venues, including the Nationaltheater, the Kammerspiele and the GOP Varieté Theater, are also here.

Built between 1852 and 1875, Maximilianstrasse was essentially an ego trip for King Max II. He harnessed the skills of architect Friedrich von Bürklein to create a unique stylistic hotchpotch ranging from Bavarian rustic to Italian Renaissance and English Gothic. It even became known as the Maximilianic Style. That's the king gazing down upon his boulevard from his perch at the centre of the strip. Clinging to the base are four rather stern-looking children holding the coats of arms of Bavaria, Franconia, Swabia and the Palatinate.

☉ Maxvorstadt

★ **Alte Pinakothek**　　　MUSEUM
(Map p362; ☑ 089-238 0516; www.pinakothek.
de; Barer Strasse 27; adult/concession/child €7/5/
free, Sun €1, audioguide €4.50; ☉ 10am-8pm Tue, to
6pm Wed-Sun; ▣ Pinakotheken, ▣ Pinakotheken)
Munich's main repository of Old European
Masters is crammed with all the major players who decorated canvases between the 14th
and 18th centuries. This neoclassical temple
was masterminded by Leo von Klenze and is a
delicacy even if you can't tell your Rembrandt
from your Rubens. The collection is world
famous for its exceptional quality and depth,
especially when it comes to German masters.

The oldest works are altar paintings,
among which the standouts are Michael
Pacher's *Four Church Fathers* and Lucas
Cranach the Elder's *Crucifixion* (1503), an
emotional rendition of the suffering Jesus.

A key room is the Dürersaal upstairs.
Here hangs Albrecht Dürer's famous Christ-
like *Self-Portrait* (1500), showing the gaze of
an artist brimming with self-confidence. His
final major work, *The Four Apostles,* depicts
John, Peter, Paul and Mark as rather humble
men, in keeping with post-Reformation ideas. Compare this to Matthias Grünewald's
Sts Erasmus and Maurice, which shows the
saints dressed in rich robes like kings.

For a secular theme, inspect Albrecht Alt-
dorfer's *Battle of Alexander the Great* (1529),
which captures in great detail a 6th-century
war pitting Greeks against Persians.

There's a choice bunch of works by Dutch
masters, including an altarpiece by Rogi-
er van der Weyden called *The Adoration
of the Magi,* plus *The Seven Joys of Mary*
by Hans Memling, *Danae* by Jan Gossaert
and *The Land of Cockayne* by Pieter Brue-

gel the Elder. At 6m in height, Rubens' epic
Last Judgment is so big that Klenze custom-
designed the hall for it. A memorable portrait
is *Hélène Fourment* (1631), a youthful beauty
who was the ageing Rubens' second wife.

The Italians are represented by Botticelli, Rafael, Titian and many others, while
the French collection includes paintings
by Nicolas Poussin, Claude Lorrain and
François Boucher. Among the Spaniards are
such heavy hitters as Murillo and Velázquez,
and Greece's El Greco also features.

★ **Pinakothek der Moderne**　　MUSEUM
(Map p362; ☑ 089-2380 5360; www.pinakothek.
de; Barer Strasse 40; adult/child €10/free, Sun
€1; ☉ 10am-6pm Tue, Wed & Fri-Sun, to 8pm Thu;
▣ Pinakotheken, ▣ Pinakotheken)　Germany's
largest modern-art museum unites four significant collections under a single roof: 20th-
century art, applied design from the 19th
century to today, a graphics collection and an
architecture museum. It's housed in a spectacular building by Stephan Braunfels, whose
four-storey interior centres on a vast eye-like
dome through which soft natural light filters
throughout the blanched-white galleries.

The State Gallery of Modern Art has some
exemplary modern classics by Picasso, Klee,
Dalí and Kandinsky and many lesser-known
works that will be new to most visitors.
More recent big shots include Georg Baselitz, Andy Warhol, Cy Twombly, Dan Flavin
and the late enfant terrible Joseph Beuys.

In a world obsessed by retro style, the New
Collection is the busiest section of the museum. Housed in the basement, it focuses on
applied design from the industrial revolution
via art nouveau and Bauhaus to today. VW
Beetles, Eames chairs and early Apple Macs
stand alongside more obscure interwar items
that wouldn't be out of place in a Kraftwerk

video. There are lots of 1960s furniture, the latest spool tape recorders and an exhibition of the weirdest jewellery you'll ever see.

The State Graphics Collection has 400,000 pieces of art on paper, including drawings, prints and engravings by such artists as Leonardo da Vinci and Paul Cézanne. Because of the light-sensitive nature of these works, only a tiny fraction of the collection is shown at any given time.

Finally, there's the Architecture Museum, with entire studios of drawings, blueprints, photographs and models by such top practitioners as baroque architect Balthasar Neumann, Bauhaus maven Le Corbusier and 1920s expressionist Erich Mendelsohn.

★ **Museum Brandhorst** GALLERY
(Map p362; www.museum-brandhorst.de; Theresienstrasse 35a; adult/concession/child €7/5/free, Sun €1; ⊙10am-6pm Tue, Wed & Fri-Sun, to 8pm Thu; ⊠ Maxvorstadt/Sammlung Brandhorst, ⊠ Pinakotheken) A big, bold and aptly abstract building, clad entirely in vividly multihued ceramic tubes, the Brandhorst jostled its way into the Munich Kunstareal in a punk blaze of colour mid-2009. Its walls, its floor and occasionally its ceiling provide space for some of the most challenging art in the city, among it some instantly recognisable 20th-century images by Andy Warhol, whose work dominates the collection.

Pop Art's 1960s poster boy pops up throughout the gallery and even has an entire room dedicated to pieces such as his punkish *Self-Portrait* (1986), *Marilyn* (1962) and *Triple Elvis* (1963).

The other prevailing artist at the Brandhorst is the lesser-known Cy Twombly. His arrestingly spectacular splash-and-dribble canvases are an acquired taste, but this is the place to acquire it if ever there was one.

Elsewhere Dan Flavin floodlights various corners with his eye-watering light installations and other big names such as Mario Merz, Alex Katz and Sigmar Polke also make an appearance. Damien Hirst gets a look-in here and there.

Neue Pinakothek MUSEUM
(Map p362; ☎089-2380 5195; www.pinakothek.de; Barer Strasse 29; adult/child €7/free, Sun €1; ⊙10am-6pm Thu-Mon, to 8pm Wed; ⊠ Pinakotheken, ⊠ Pinakotheken) The Neue Pinakothek harbours a well-respected collection of 19th- and early-20th-century paintings and sculpture, from rococo to *Jugendstil* (art nouveau). All the world-famous household names get wall space here, including crowd-pleasing French

impressionists such as Monet, Cézanne and Degas as well as Van Gogh, whose boldly pigmented *Sunflowers* (1888) radiates cheer.

Perhaps the most memorable canvases, though, are by Romantic painter Caspar David Friedrich, who specialised in emotionally charged, brooding landscapes. There are also works by Gauguin, including *Breton Peasant Women* (1894), and Manet, including *Breakfast in the Studio* (1869). Turner gets a look-in with his dramatically sublime *Ostende* (1844).

Local painters represented in the exhibition include Carl Spitzweg and Wilhelm von Kobell of the Dachau School and Munich society painters such as Wilhelm von Kaulbach, Franz Lenbach and Karl von Piloty. Another focus is work by the Deutschrömer (German Romans), a group of neoclassicists centred on Johann Koch, who stuck mainly to Italian landscapes.

★ **Königsplatz** SQUARE
(Map p362; ⊠ Königsplatz, Ⓤ Königsplatz) Nothing less than the Acropolis in Athens provided the inspiration for Leo von Klenze's imposing Königsplatz, commissioned by Ludwig I and anchored by a Doric-columned Propyläen gateway and two temple-like museums. The Nazis added a few buildings of their own and used the square for their mass parades. Only the foundations of these structures remain at the eastern end of the square, rendered unrecognisable by foliage. Peaceful and green today, the square comes alive in summer during concerts and open-air cinema.

NS Dokuzentrum ARCHIVES
(National Socialism Documentation Centre; Map p362; ☎089-2336 7000; www.ns-dokuzentrum-muenchen.de; Max-Mannheimer-Platz 1; adult/concession €5/2.50; ⊙10am-7pm Tue-Sun; ⊠100, Königsplatz, Ⓤ Königsplatz) The mission of the NS Dokuzentrum, located right at the heart of what was once Nazi central in Munich, is to educate locals and visitors alike about the Nazi period and Munich's role in it. The excellent exhibition looks to find the answers to questions such as how did Hitler come to power, what led to the war, and why did democracy fail. Period documents, artefacts, films and multimedia stations help visitors form their own opinions on these questions.

Antikensammlungen MUSEUM
(Map p362; www.antike-am-koenigsplatz.mwn.de; Königsplatz 1; adult/child €6/free, Sun €1; ⊙10am-5pm Tue & Thu-Sun, to 8pm Wed; ⊠ Königsplatz, Ⓤ Königsplatz) This old-school museum is an

(Continued on page 354)

NIKADA/GETTY IMAGES ©

1. Oktoberfest (p360)
Munich's legendary beer festival is the largest in the world.

2. Marienplatz (p342)
The heart and soul of the Altstadt is the city's busiest spot.

3. BMW Welt (p354)
This showroom acts as a shop window for BMW's latest models

and a showcase for the company as a whole.

4. Hofbräuhaus (p372)
Beer guzzlers at Hofbräuhaus buy their *Mass* (1L tankard or stein of beer) with prepaid tokens, just like during Oktoberfest.

G.EVGENIJ/SHUTTERSTOCK ©

ROSS HELEN/SHUTTERSTOCK ©

3

DOMAGOJ KOVACIC/SHUTTERSTOCK ©

MUNICH'S KUNSTAREAL

The **Kunstareal** (Map p362; www.kunst areal.de; 🚇 Pinakotheken, 🚇 Pinakothek-en) is the compact Maxvorstadt area, roughly defined by Türkenstrasse, Schellingstrasse, Luisenstrasse and Karlstrasse, which is packed with southern Germany's finest art museums. These include the Alte Pinakothek (p350), the Museum Brandhorst (p351), the Neue Pinakothek (p351) and the Pinakothek der Moderne (p350).

(Continued from page 351)

engaging showcase of exquisite Greek, Roman and Etruscan antiquities. The collection of Greek vases, each artistically decorated with gods and heroes, wars and weddings, is particularly outstanding. Other galleries present gold and silver jewellery and ornaments, figurines made from terracotta and more precious bronze, and superfragile glass drinking vessels. Tickets for the museum are also valid for the Glyptothek.

Glyptothek   MUSEUM
(Map p362; www.antike-am-koenigsplatz.mwn.de; Königsplatz 3; adult/child €6/free, Sun €1; ⊙ 10am-5pm Fri-Sun, Tue & Wed, to 8pm Thu; 🚇 Königsplatz, Ⓤ Königsplatz) If you're a fan of classical art or simply enjoy the sight of naked guys without noses (or other pertinent body parts), make a beeline for the Glyptothek. One of Munich's oldest museums, it's a feast of art and sculpture from ancient Greece and Rome amassed by Ludwig I between 1806 and 1830, and it opens a surprisingly naughty window onto the ancient world. Tickets for the museum are also valid for the Antikensammlungen.

Lenbachhaus   MUSEUM
(Municipal Gallery; Map p362; 🕿 089-2333 2000; www.lenbachhaus.de; Luisenstrasse 33; adult/child incl audioguide €10/5; ⊙ 10am-8pm Tue, to 6pm Wed-Sun; 🚇 Königsplatz, Ⓤ Königsplatz) With its fabulous wing added by noted architect Norman Foster, this glorious gallery is the go-to place to admire the vibrant canvases of Kandinsky, Franz Marc, Paul Klee and other members of ground-breaking modernist group Der Blaue Reiter (The Blue Rider), founded in Munich in 1911.

Contemporary art is another focal point. An eye-catcher is a glass-and-steel sculpture by Olafur Eliasson in the soaring atrium. Many other big names are also represented, including Gerhard Richter, Sigmar Polke, Anselm Kiefer, Andy Warhol, Dan Flavin, Richard Serra and Jenny Holzer.

Tickets are also valid for special exhibits at the nearby Kunstbau, a 120m-long tunnel above the Königsplatz U-Bahn station.

Alter Botanischer Garten   PARK
(Map p362; Sophienstrasse 7; ⊙ 24hr; Ⓢ Karlsplatz, 🚇 Karlsplatz, Ⓤ Karlsplatz) The Old Botanical Garden is a pleasant place to soothe your soles and souls after an Altstadt shopping spree or to see out a long wait for a train away from the Hauptbahnhof. Created under King Maximilian in 1814, most of the tender specimens were moved in the early 20th century to the New Botanical Garden behind Schloss Nymphenburg, leaving this island of city-centre greenery.

The Neptunbrunnen (Neptune Fountain), on the south side, dates from the Nazi period when the garden was turned into a public park. The neoclassical entrance gate is called the Kleine Propyläen and is a leftover from the original gardens. The Old Botanical Gardens are also home to one of Munich's lower-profile beer gardens, Park-Cafe (p373).

⊙ Nymphenburg, Neuhausen & Olympiapark

★ **BMW Welt**   NOTABLE BUILDING
(BMW World; Map p368; 🕿 089-125 016 001; www.bmw-welt.de; Am Olympiapark 1; tours adult/child €7/5; ⊙ 7.30am-midnight Mon-Sat, from 9am Sun; Ⓤ Olympiazentrum) **FREE** Next to the Olympia park, the glass-and-steel, double-cone tornado spiralling down from a dark cloud the size of an aircraft carrier holds BMW Welt, truly a petrolhead's dream. Apart from its role as a prestigious car pick-up centre, this king of showrooms acts as a shop window for BMW's latest models and a show space for the company as a whole.

Straddle a powerful motorbike, marvel at technology-packed saloons and estates (no tyre kicking, please), browse the 'lifestyle' shop or take the 80-minute guided tour. On the Junior Campus, kids learn about mobility, fancy themselves car engineers and even get to design their own vehicle in workshops. Hang around long enough and you're sure to see motorbike stunts on the staircases and other petroleum-fuelled antics.

★ **Olympiapark**   SPORTSGROUND
(Olympic Park; Map p368; www.olympiapark.de; stadium tour adult/concession €8/6; ⊙ stadium

tours 11am, 1pm & 4pm Apr-Oct; Ⓤ Olympiazentrum) The area to the north of the city where soldiers once paraded and the world's first Zeppelin landed in 1909 found a new role in the 1960s as the Olympiapark. Built for the 1972 Olympic Summer Games, it has quite a small-scale feel, and some may be amazed that the games could once have been held at such a petite venue.

The complex draws people year-round with concerts, festivals and sporting events, and its swimming hall and ice-skating rink are open to the public. A good first stop is the Info-Pavilion, which has information, maps, tour tickets and a model of the complex. You can also rent a self-guided audio tour.

Olympiapark has two famous eye-catchers: the 290m **Olympiaturm** (Olympic Tower; adult/child €7/5; ☺9am-midnight) and the warped **Olympiastadion** (Olympic Stadium; ☺9am-8pm mid-May–mid-Sep, shorter hr rest of yr). Germans have a soft spot for the latter because it was on this hallowed turf in 1974 that the national soccer team – led by 'the Kaiser', Franz Beckenbauer – won the FIFA World Cup.

When the sky is clear, you'll quite literally have Munich at your feet against the breathtaking backdrop of the Alps from the top of the Olympiaturm.

★ **Schloss Nymphenburg**   PALACE
(Map p368; www.schloss-nymphenburg.de; castle adult/child €6/free, all sites €11.50/free; ☺9am-6pm Apr–mid-Oct, 10am-4pm mid-Oct–Mar; 🚋Schloss Nymphenburg) This commanding palace and its lavish gardens sprawl around 5km northwest of the Altstadt. Begun in 1664 as a villa for Electress Adelaide of Savoy, the stately pile was extended over the next century to create the royal family's summer residence. Franz Duke of Bavaria, head of the once royal Wittelsbach family, still occupies an apartment here.

The main palace building consists of a large villa and two wings of creaking parquet floors and sumptuous period rooms. Right at the beginning of the self-guided tour comes the high point of the entire Schloss, the Schönheitengalerie, housed in the former apartments of Queen Caroline. Some 38 portraits of attractive females chosen by an admiring King Ludwig I peer prettily from the walls. The most famous image is of Helene Sedlmayr, the daughter of a shoemaker, wearing a lavish frock the king gave her for the sitting. You'll also find Ludwig's beautiful, but notorious, lover Lola Montez, as well as 19th-century gossip-column celebrity Lady Jane Ellenborough and English beauty Lady Jane Erskine.

Further along the tour route comes the Queen's Bedroom, which still contains the sleigh bed on which Ludwig II was born, and the King's Chamber, resplendent with three-dimensional ceiling frescoes.

Also in the main building is the **Marstallmuseum** (adult/child €4.50/free), displaying royal coaches and riding gear. This includes Ludwig II's fairy tale–like rococo sleigh, ingeniously fitted with oil lamps for his crazed nocturnal outings. Upstairs is the world's largest collection of porcelain made by the famous Nymphenburger Manufaktur. Also known as the Sammlung Bäuml, it presents the entire product palette from the company's founding in 1747 until 1930.

The sprawling **palace grounds** (combined ticket for all 4 park buildings adult/child €4.50/3.50) behind Schloss Nymphenburg is a favourite spot with Münchners and visitors for strolling, jogging or whiling away a lazy afternoon. It's laid out in grand English style and accented with water features, including a large lake, a cascade and a canal, which is popular for feeding swans and for ice skating and ice curling when it freezes over in winter.

The park's chief folly, the Amalienburg, is a small hunting lodge dripping with crystal and gilt decoration; don't miss the amazing Spiegelsaal (hall of mirrors). The two-storey Pagodenburg was built in the early 18th century as a Chinese tea house and is swathed in ceramic tiles depicting landscapes, figures and floral ornamentation. The Badenburg is a sauna and bathing house that still has its original heating system. Finally, the Magdalenenklause was built as a mock hermitage in faux-ruined style.

BMW Museum   MUSEUM
(Map p368; www.bmw-welt.de; Am Olympiapark 2; adult/child €10/7; ☺10am-6pm Tue-Sun; Ⓤ Olympiazentrum) This silver, bowl-shaped museum comprises seven themed 'houses' that examine the development of BMW's product line and include sections on motorcycles and motor racing. Even if you can't tell a head gasket from a crankshaft, the interior design – with its curvy retro feel, futuristic bridges, squares and huge backlit wall screens – is reason enough to visit.

The museum is linked to two more architecturally stunning buildings: the BMW headquarters (closed to the public) and the BMW Welt showroom.

Schwabing & the Englischer Garten

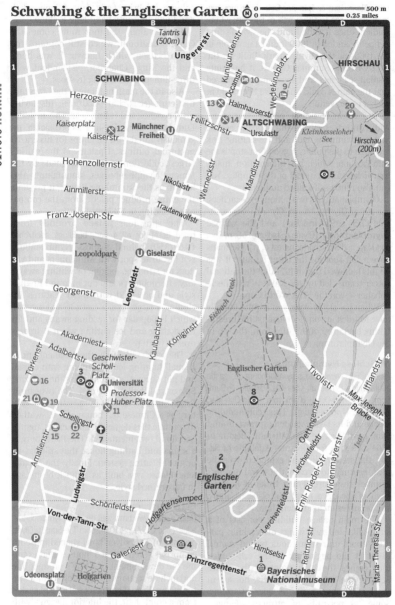

Tantris (500m)

Ungererstr

SCHWABING

HIRSCHAU

Herzogstr

Kunigundenstr

Wedekindplatz

10

9

20

Occamstr

Kaiserplatz

13

Haimhauserstr

Münchner Freiheit

12

Kaiserstr

14

ALTSCHWABING

Feilitzschstr

Ursulastr

Kleinhesseloher See

Hirschau (200m)

Hohenzollernstr

Mandlstr

5

Ainmillerstr

Nikolaistr

Werneckstr

Franz-Joseph-Str

Trautenwolfstr

Leopoldpark

Giselastr

Leopoldstr

Georgenstr

Eisbach Creek

Königinstr

Akademiestr

Kaulbachstr

17

Türkenstr

Adalbertstr

16

Geschwister-Scholl-Platz

Englischer Garten

3

Tivolistr

6

Universität

8

Ifflandstr

21

19

Professor-Huber-Platz

Max-Joseph-Brücke

Schellingstr

11

Oettingenstr

Isar

15

22

7

Amalienstr

Lerchenfeldstr

2

Ludwigstr

Englischer Garten

Lerchenfeldstr

Emil-Riedel-Str

Widenmayerstr

Maria-Theresia-Str

Schönfeldstr

Hofgartensemped

Von-der-Tann-Str

P

18

4

Himbselstr

Reitmorstr

Galeriestr

Prinzregentenstr

1

Odeonsplatz

Hofgarten

Bayerisches Nationalmuseum

Museum Mensch und Natur MUSEUM
(Museum of Humankind & Nature; Map p368; www.mmn-muenchen.de; Schloss Nymphenburg; adult/child €3.50/2.50; ⊙9am-5pm Tue, Wed & Fri, to 8pm Thu, 10am-6pm Sat & Sun; ⊡Schloss Nymphenburg) Kids will have plenty of ooh and aah moments in the Museum of Humankind & Nature, in the Schloss Nymphenburg north wing. Anything but old school, it puts a premium on interactive displays, models, audiovisual presentations and attractive animal dioramas. It's all in German, but few

Schwabing & the Englischer Garten

language skills are needed to appreciate the visuals.

◉ Haidhausen & Lehel

★ **Deutsches Museum** MUSEUM

(Map p374; ☎ 089-217 9333; www.deutsches-museum.de; Museumsinsel 1; adult/child €12/4; ◎ 9am-5pm; ⓪ Deutsches Museum) If you're one of those people for whom science is an unfathomable turn-off, a visit to the Deutsches Museum might just show you that physics and engineering are more fun than you thought. Spending a few hours in this temple to technology is an eye-opening journey of discovery, and the exhibitions and demonstrations will certainly be a hit with young, sponge-like minds.

There are tonnes of interactive displays (including glass-blowing and paper making), live demonstrations and experiments, model coal and salt mines, and engaging sections on cave paintings, geodesy, microelectronics and astronomy. In fact, it can be pretty overwhelming after a while, so it's best to prioritise what you want to see.

The place to entertain children aged three to eight is the fabulous Kinderreich, where 1000 activities await, from a kid-sized mouse wheel to interactive water fun. Get the littlies to climb all over a fire engine, build things with giant Lego, construct a waterway with canals and locks, or bang on a drum all day in a – thankfully – soundproof instrument room. Note that Kinderreich closes at 4.30pm.

Museum Fünf Kontinente MUSEUM

(State Museum of Ethnology; Map p374; www.museum-fuenf-kontinente.de; Maximilianstrasse 42; adult/child €5/free, Sun €1; ◎ 9.30am-5.30pm Tue-Sun; ⓪ Maxmonument) A bonanza of art and objects from Africa, India, the Americas, the Middle East and Polynesia, the State Museum of Ethnology has one of the most prestigious and complete ethnological collections anywhere. Sculpture from West and Central Africa is particularly impressive, as are Peruvian ceramics, Indian jewellery, mummy parts, and artefacts from the days of Captain Cook.

Museum Villa Stuck MUSEUM

(Map p374; ☎ 089-455 5510; www.villastuck.de; Prinzregentenstrasse 60; adult/concession €9/4.50; ◎ 11am-6pm Tue-Sun; ⓪ Friedensengel/Villa Stuck) Around the turn of the 20th century, Franz von Stuck was a leading light on Munich's art scene, and his residence is one of the finest *Jugendstil* homes you're ever likely to see. Stuck came up with the intricate design, which forges tapestries, patterned floors, coffered ceilings and other elements into a harmonious work of art. Today his glorious pad is open as a museum with changing exhibitions.

Sammlung Schack MUSEUM

(Map p374; www.sammlung-schack.de; Prinzregentenstrasse 9; adult/concession €4/3; ◎ 10am-6pm Wed-Sun; ⓪ Reitmorstrasse/Sammlung Schack) Count Adolf Friedrich von Schack (1815–94) was a great fan of 19th-century Romantic painters such as Böcklin, Feuerbach and von Schwind. His collection is housed in the former Prussian embassy, now the Schack-Galerie. A tour of the intimate space is like an escape into the idealised fantasy worlds created by these artists.

THE WHITE ROSE

Open resistance to the Nazis was rare during the Third Reich; after 1933, intimidation and the instant 'justice' of the Gestapo and SS served as powerful disincentives. One of the few groups to rebel was the ill-fated Weisse Rose (White Rose), led by Munich University student siblings Hans and Sophie Scholl.

The nonviolent White Rose began operating in 1942, its members stealing out at night to smear 'Freedom!' and 'Down with Hitler!' on the city's walls. Soon they were printing anti-Nazi leaflets on the mass extermination of the Jews and other Nazi atrocities. One read: 'We shall not be silent – we are your guilty conscience. The White Rose will not leave you in peace'.

In February 1943, Hans and Sophie were caught distributing leaflets at the university. Together with their best friend, Christoph Probst, the Scholls were arrested and charged with treason. After a summary trial, all three were found guilty and beheaded the same afternoon. Their extraordinary courage inspired the award-winning film *Sophie Scholl – Die Letzten Tage* (Sophie Scholl – The Final Days; 2005).

A memorial exhibit to the White Rose, DenkStätte (p349), is within Ludwig-Maximilian-Universität.

⊙ Westend & Theresienwiese

Deutsches Museum – Verkehrszentrum   MUSEUM
(Transport Museum; Map p378; www.deutsches-museum.de/verkehrszentrum; Am Bavariapark 5; adult/child €7/3; ⊙9am-5pm; Ⓤ Theresienwiese) An ode to the Bavarian obsession with getting around, the Transport Museum explores the ingenious ways humans have devised to transport things and each other. From the earliest automobiles to famous race cars and high-speed ICE trains, the collection is a virtual trip through transport history.

The exhibit is spread over three historic trade-fair halls near Theresienwiese, each with its own theme – Public Transportation, Travel, and Mobility & Technology. It's a fun place even if you can't tell a piston from a carburettor. Classic cars abound, vintage bikes fill an entire wall and there's even an old petrol station.

Theresienwiese   PARK
(Map p378; Ⓤ Theresienwiese) The huge Theresienwiese (Theresa Meadow), better known as Wies'n, southwest of the Altstadt, is the site of the Oktoberfest. At the western end of the 'meadow' is the Ruhmeshalle (Hall of Fame) FREE guarding solemn statues of Bavarian leaders, as well as the Bavariastatue (Statue of Bavaria; adult/child €3.50/2.50; ⊙9am-6pm Apr-mid-Oct, to 8pm during Oktoberfest), an 18m-high Amazon in the Statue of Liberty tradition, oak wreath in her hand and lion at her feet.

This iron lady has a cunning design that makes her seem solid, but actually you can climb via the knee joint up to the head for a great view of the Oktoberfest. At other times, views are not particularly inspiring.

🏃 Activities

Boating

A lovely spot to take your sweetheart for a spin is on the Kleinhesseloher See (p347) in the Englischer Garten. Rowing or pedal boats cost around €8 per half-hour for up to four people. Boats may also be hired at the Olympiapark (p354).

Cycling

Munich is an excellent place for cycling, particularly along the Isar River. Some 1200km of cycle paths within the city limits make it one of Europe's friendliest places for two-wheelers.

Skating

Iceskaters can glide alongside future medallists in the **Olympia-Eissportzentrum** (Map p368; ☑089-30670; www.olympiapark.de; Spiridon-Louis-Ring 21; adult/child per session €4.50/3; ⊙check website for times), hit the frozen canals in Nymphenburg (free) or twirl around at the **Münchner Eiszauber** (Map p344; www.muenchnereiszauber.de; adult €5-8.50, child €3.50-6; ⊙late Nov-late Jan; ⒢ Karlsplatz, Ⓢ Karlsplatz, Ⓤ Karlsplatz) ice rink on Karlsplatz.

Swimming

Bathing in the Isar River isn't advisable, due to strong and unpredictable currents (especially in the Englischer Garten), though many locals do. Better to head out of town to one of the many nearby swimming lakes, including the popular Feringasee (by car, take the S8 to Unterföhring, then follow signs), where the party never stops on hot summer days; the pretty Feldmochinger See (⑤ Feldmoching), which is framed by gentle mounds and has a special area for wheelchair-bound bathers (by car, take the S1 to Feldmoching); and the Unterföhringer See (Poschinger Weihen), which has warm water and is easily reached by bicycle via the Isarradweg cycele path or via the S8 to Unterföhring.

The best public-swimming-pool options, both indoors, are the **Olympia Schwimmhalle** (Map p368; www.swm.de; Coubertinplatz 1; 3hr pass adult/child €4.80/3.80; ⊗10am-7pm Mon, to 10pm Tue-Sun; ⑤ Olympiazentrum), where Mark Spitz famously won seven gold medals in 1972, and the spectacular **Müller'sches Volksbad** (Map p374; www.swm.de; Rosenheimer Strasse 1; adult/child €4.50/3.40; ⊗7.30am-11pm; 🚊 Am Gasteig), where you can swim in art nouveau splendour.

👉 Tours

For a budget tour of Munich's high-brow collections, hop aboard **bus 100 Museenlinie** (Map p378; www.mvv-muenchen.de), which runs from the Hauptbahnhof to the Ostbahnhof (east station) via 21 of the city's museums and galleries, including all the big hitters. As this is an ordinary bus route, the tour costs no more than a public-transport ticket.

★ Radius Tours & Bike Rental   TOURS
(Map p378; ☑089-543 487 7740; www.radius tours.com; Arnulfstrasse 3, Hauptbahnhof; ⊗8.30am-8pm; 🚊 Hauptbahnhof, Ⓤ Hauptbahnhof, ⑤ Hauptbahnhof) Entertaining and informative English-language tours include the two-hour Discover Munich walk (€15), the fascinating 2½-hour Third Reich tour (€17.50), and the three-hour Bavarian Beer tour (€36). The company also runs popular excursions to Neuschwanstein, Salzburg and Dachau and has hundreds of bikes for hire (€14.50 per day).

★ Walk on the Roof   WALKING
(Map p368; adult/concessions €43/33; ⊗2.30pm Apr-Oct) Can't make it to the Alps for a high-altitude clamber? No matter. Just head to the Olympic Stadium for a walk on the roof. Yup, the roof; that famously contorted steel and Plexiglas confection is ready for its close-up. Just like in the mountains, you'll be roped and hooked up to a steel cable as you clamber around under the eagle-eyed super-

vision of an experienced guide showering you with fascinating details about the stadium's architecture and construction.

SightRunning Munich   RUNNING
(☑0151-6136 5099; www.muenchen-sightrunning. de; Edelweissstrasse 6; 1hr tours €25-50) Hit the ground running with this novel way of seeing the sights in the company of an experienced guide-runner. There are running tours of Nymphenburg, the English Garden, Olympiapark and the Isar, or you can have one tailor made. All you need is a pair of trainers and the ability to run for an hour – so it's not for everyone.

Street Art Tour   CULTURAL
(☑089-4613 9401; www.streetarttour.org) Operated by an agency called Positive Propaganda, these fascinating street-art tours will show you a completely different side to Munich.

Mike's Bike Tours   CYCLING
(Map p344; ☑089-2554 3987; www.mikesbike tours.com; Bräuhausstrasse 10; classic tour €29; ⑤ Marienplatz, Ⓤ Marienplatz) This outfit runs various guided bike tours of the city as well as a couple of other themed excursions. The classic tour is around four hours long; the deluxe tour goes for five hours.

Munich Walk Tours   WALKING
(Map p362; ☑089-2423 1767; www.munich walktours.de; tours from €14; 🚊 Hauptbahnhof, ⑤ Hauptbahnhof, Ⓤ Hauptbahnhof) In addition to running an almost identical roster to Munich's other tour companies and acting as an agent for them (see website for times and prices), this place also runs cycling tours of the English Garden.

Vespa Munich   TOURS
(Map p368; ☑0151-517 251 69; www.vespa munich.com; Dom-Pedro-Strasse 26; full-day tour €59; ⊗office 10am-2pm daily, pick-ups 9am-6pm; 🚊 Leonrodplatz) Book in advance, pick up your vespa and spend the day bombing around Munich guided by the GPS unit provided. It's the latest fun way to see the city, but good luck on those freeways!

Grayline Hop-On-Hop-Off Tours   BUS
(Map p378; www.grayline.com/munich; adult/child from €20/11; ⊗hourly; Ⓤ Hauptbahnhof, ⑤ Hauptbahnhof) This well-known tour-bus company offers a choice of three tours, from one-hour highlights to the 2½-hour grand tour, as well as excursions to Ludwig II's castles, the Romantic Road, Dachau, Berchtesgaden, Zugspitze and Salzburg. All tours can be booked

MUNICH TOURS

online, and the buses are new. The main departure point is outside the Karstadt department store opposite the Hauptbahnhof.

✨ Festivals & Events

⭐ Starkbierzeit
BEER

(☺ Feb-Apr) Salvator, Optimator, Unimator, Maximator and Triumphator are not the names of gladiators but potent *Doppelbock* brews de-kegged only between Shrovetide and Easter. Many Bavarian breweries take part.

Frühlingsfest
BEER

(www.fruehlingsfest-muenchen.de; ☺ late Apr-early May) This mini-Oktoberfest kicks off the outdoor-festival season with two weeks of beer tents and attractions at the Theresienwiese.

⭐ Tollwood Festival
CULTURAL

(www.tollwood.de; ☺ late Jun-late Jul) Major world-culture festival with concerts, theatre, circus, readings and other fun events at the Olympiapark.

Filmfest München
FILM

(www.filmfest-muenchen.de; ☺ late Jun) This festival presents intriguing and often high-calibre fare by newbies and masters from around the world. Held at the Gasteig and cinemas around the city centre.

Opernfestspiele
MUSIC

(Opera Festival; www.muenchner-opern-festspiele. de; ☺ Jul) The Bavarian State Opera brings in top-notch talent from around the world for this month-long festival, which takes place at numerous venues around the city

Christopher Street Day
LGBT

(www.csd-munich.de; ☺ mid-Jul) Gay festival and parade culminating in a big street party on Marienplatz. Usually held on the second weekend in July.

Tanzwerkstatt Europa
PERFORMING ARTS

(www.jointadventures.net; ☺ mid-Aug) Performances and workshops for modern dance, drama and readings held over 10 days

Hans Sachs Strassenfest
LGBT

(www.hans-sachs-strassenfest.de; ☺ mid-Aug) This street party is held along Hans-Sachs-Strasse in the Glockenbachviertel.

⭐ Oktoberfest
BEER

(www.oktoberfest.de; ☺ mid-Sep-early Oct) Legendary beer-swilling party. Held on the Theresienwiese.

Munich Marathon
SPORTS

(www.generalimuenchenmarathon.de; ☺ mid-Oct) More than 10,000 runners from around the world take to the streets, finishing after just over 42km at the Olympiastadion.

⭐ Christkindlmarkt
CHRISTMAS MARKET

(www.christkindlmarkt.de; ☺ late Nov-Christmas Eve) Traditional Christmas market on Marienplatz, one of Germany's best.

🛏 Sleeping

Munich has the full range of accommodation options you would expect from a major city in Western Europe. Luxury hotels dot the centre, midrange places gather near the Hauptbahnhof. Room rates tend to be higher than in the rest of Bavaria, and they skyrocket during the Oktoberfest. However, midrange accommodation is cheaper here than in other major European cities.

🛏 Altstadt & Residenz

⭐ Flushing Meadows
DESIGN HOTEL €€

(Map p344; ☎ 089-5527 9170; www.flushing meadowshotel.com; Fraunhoferstrasse 32; studios around €150; P ❋ 🛜; Ⓢ Fraunhoferstrasse) Urban explorers keen on up-to-the-minute design cherish this new contender on the top two floors of a former postal office in the hip Glockenbachviertel. Each of the 11 concrete-ceilinged lofts reflects the vision of a locally known personality, while three of the five penthouse studios have a private terrace. Breakfast costs €10.50.

The panorama bar has quickly become the darling of the local in-crowd.

H'Otello B'01 München
BOUTIQUE HOTEL €€

(Map p344; ☎ 089-4583 1200; www.hotello.de; Baaderstrasse 1; s/d from €90/110; ❀ 🛜; Ⓑ Isartor, Ⓢ Isartor) Though now not as excitingly different as it once was, Munich's first boutique hotel is all about understated retro design and amiable service. Rooms won't fit a tonne of luggage but are nicely dressed in creamy hues, tactile fabrics and subtle lighting. Guests rave about the breakfast: a smorgasbord of fresh fruit, deli salads, smoked salmon and organic cheeses.

Hotel am Markt
HOTEL €€

(Map p344; ☎ 089-225 014; www.hotel-am-markt. eu; Heiliggeiststrasse 6; s/d from €90/122; 🛜; Ⓢ Marienplatz, Ⓤ Marienplatz) As supercentral as you could wish, this slender, medieval-style hotel occupies a gabled and turreted building overlooking the Viktualienmarkt.

Bedrooms are midrange business standard, some with cheap flatpack, others with vaguely antique-style furniture and wood-panelling. Bathrooms have been spruced up recently, and standards are generally good. There's a restaurant on-site.

Pension Gärtnerplatz
GUESTHOUSE €€

(Map p344; ☑089-202 5170; www.pensiongaertnerplatz.de; Klenzestrasse 45; s/d €86/142; ☎; Ⓤ Fraunhoferstrasse) Flee the urban hullabaloo to an Alpine fantasy land with alluring rooms boasting carved wood, painted bedsteads, woollen rugs and crisp, quality bedding. In one room a portrait of Ludwig II watches you as you slumber; breakfasts are organic.

Hotel am Viktualienmarkt
HOTEL €€

(Map p344; ☑089-231 1090; www.hotel-am-viktualienmarkt.de; Utzschneiderstrasse 14; s/d from €59/139; ☎; Ⓢ Marienplatz, Ⓤ Marienplatz) Elke and her daughter Stephanie run this good-value property with panache and a sunny attitude. The best of the 26 up-to-date rooms have wooden floors and framed poster art. All this, plus the city-centre location, makes it a superb deal.

★ Bayerischer Hof
HOTEL €€€

(Map p344; ☑089-212 00; www.bayerischerhof.de; Promenadeplatz 2-6; r €250-450; ☀☎☒; Ⓣ Theatinerstrasse) Around since 1841, this is one of the grande dames of the Munich hotel world. Rooms come in a number of styles, from busy Laura Ashley to minimalist cosmopolitan. The supercentral location and pool come in addition to impeccably regimented staff. Marble, antiques and oil paintings abound, and you can dine till you burst at any of the five fabulous restaurants.

★ Louis Hotel
HOTEL €€€

(Map p344; ☑089-411 9080; www.louis-hotel.com; Viktualienmarkt 6/Rindermarkt 2; r €179-320; ☎; Ⓢ Marienplatz) An air of relaxed sophistication pervades the scene-savvy Louis, where 72 good-sized rooms are furnished in nut and oak, natural stone and elegant tiles. Rooms come equipped with the latest technology. All have small balconies facing either the courtyard or the Viktualienmarkt. Views are also terrific from the rooftop bar and restaurant.

Breakfast costs a yodelling €28.50 extra, more than a room near the Hauptbahnhof.

Cortiina
HOTEL €€€

(Map p344; ☑089-242 2490; www.cortiina.com; Ledererstrasse 8; s/d from €199/231; Ⓟ☀☒; Ⓤ Marienplatz, Ⓢ Marienplatz) Tiptoeing between hip and haute, this hotel scores best with trendy, design-minded travellers. The street-level lounge usually buzzes with cocktail-swigging professional types, but all traces of hustle evaporate the moment you step into your minimalist, feng shui–inspired room.

★ Hotel Mandarin Oriental Munich
HOTEL €€€

(Map p344; ☑089-290 980; www.mandarinoriental.com; Neuturmstrasse 1; d from €650; Ⓟ☀@☎☒; Ⓢ Marienplatz, Ⓤ Marienplatz) These magnificent neo-Renaissance digs lure the world's glamorous, rich, powerful and famous with opulently understated rooms and top-notch service. Paul McCartney, Bill Clinton and Prince Charles have crumpled the sheets here. Service is polite almost to a fault.

Deutsche Eiche
HOTEL €€€

(Map p344; ☑089-231 1660; www.deutsche-eiche.com; Reichenbachstrasse 13; s/d from €79/169; ☎; Ⓡ Reichenbachplatz) The rainbow flag flutters brightly alongside the usual national pennants outside this traditionally gay outpost that invites style junkies of all sexual orientations to enjoy the slick rooms and first-class restaurant. There's a well-known sauna on the premises.

Hotel Blauer Bock
HOTEL €€€

(Map p344; ☑089-231 780; www.hotelblauerbock.de; Sebastiansplatz 9; s/d from €89/153; ☎; Ⓢ Marienplatz, Ⓤ Marienplatz) A pretzel's throw from the Viktualienmarkt, this simple hotel has cunningly slipped through the net of Altstadt gentrification to become one of the city centre's best deals, though prices have risen in recent years. It has a superb restaurant on the premises and parking in nearby garages.

Hotel Olympic
HOTEL €€€

(Map p344; ☑089-231 890; www.hotel-olympic.de; Hans-Sachs-Strasse 4; s €95-180, d €160-250; Ⓟ@☎; Ⓤ Müllerstrasse) If you're looking for a well-run place that's also small, friendly and peaceful with understated style, then this guesthouse-type hotel in a funky location might be for you. Rooms double up as mini art galleries and staff couldn't be more accommodating. Parking costs €15 a night.

🛏 Haidhausen & Lehel

Hotel Splendid-Dollmann
HOTEL €€

(Map p374; ☑089-238 080; www.hotel-splendid-dollmann.de; Thierschstrasse 49; s/d from

Maxvorstadt

€100/120; 🛜; 🚇 Lehel, Ⓤ Lehel) This small but posh Hotel Splendid-Dollmann delivers old-world charm and is sure to delight the romantically inclined. The mood is set at check-in where fresh orchids, classical music and friendly staff welcome you. Retire to antique-furnished rooms, the idyllic terraced garden or the regally furnished lounge. Rooms in front must deal with tram noise.

Hotel am Nockherberg HOTEL €€

(☎089-623 0010; www.nockherberg.de; Nockherstrasse 38a; s/d from €74/109; 🅿🛜; Ⓢ Kolumbusplatz) Located south of the Isar, this charming base puts you close to the Deutsches Museum, the bar- and restaurant-filled Gärtnerplatzviertel and the Gasteig Cultural Centre. The decor of the 48 rooms and suites is pleasingly modern in a generic kind of way, and all major modcons are accounted for. Booking directly with the hotel guarantees the best rates.

★ Hotel Ritzi HOTEL €€€

(Map p374; ☎089-414 240 890; www.hotel-ritzi.de; Maria-Theresia-Strasse 2a; s/d from €100/159; 🛜; 🚇 Maxmilianeum) At this charming art hotel next to a little park, creaky wooden stairs (no lift) lead to 25 rooms that transport you to the Caribbean, Africa, Morocco and other exotic lands. But it's the *Jugendstil* features of the building that really impress, as does the much-praised restaurant downstairs, with its Sunday brunch and well-chosen wine list.

Hotel Opéra HOTEL €€€

(Map p374; ☎089-210 4940; www.hotel-opera. de; St-Anna-Strasse 10; r €105-350; 🅿🛜; 🚇 Maxmonument, Ⓤ Lehel) Like the gates to heaven, a white double door opens at the touch of a tiny brass button at the Hotel Opéra. Beyond awaits a smart, petite cocoon of quiet sophistication with peaches-and-cream marble floors, a chandelier scavenged from the Vatican and uniquely decorated rooms. Parking is €20 extra.

Maxvorstadt

🛏 Maxvorstadt

Hotel Marienbad   HOTEL €€
(Map p362; ☎089-595 585; www.hotelmarien
bad.de; Barer Strasse 11; s €55-155, d €120-160;
Ⓟ 🛜; Ⓢ Ottostrasse) Back in the 19th century,
Wagner, Puccini and Rilke shacked up at the
Marienbad, which once ranked among Munich's finest hotels. The place is still friendly and well maintained, and the 30 rooms
flaunt an endearing jumble of styles, from
playful art nouveau to floral country Bavarian to campy 1960s utilitarian. Amenities are
of more recent vintage.

🛏 Nymphenburg, Neuhausen & Olympiapark

★ Hotel Laimer Hof   HOTEL €€
(Map p368; ☎089-178 0380; www.laimerhof.de;
Laimer Strasse 40; s/d from €65/85; Ⓟ 🛜; Ⓢ Ro-
manplatz) A mere a five-minute aristocratic
amble from Schloss Nymphenburg, this commendably tranquil refuge is run by a friendly team who take time to get to know their
guests. No two of the 23 rooms are alike, but
all boast antique touches, oriental carpets
and golden beds. Free bike rental, and coffee
and tea in the lobby. Breakfast costs €12.

🛏 Schwabing & the Englischer Garten

★ La Maison   DESIGN HOTEL €€
(Map p356; ☎089-3303 5550; www.hotel-la-mai
son.com; Occamstrasse 24; r from €109; Ⓟ ✳ 🛜;
Ⓤ Münchner Freiheit) Situated in the cool area
of Schwabing, this discerningly retro hotel
comes immaculately presented in shades of
imperial purple and ubercool grey. Rooms
at this sassy number wow with heated oak
floors, jet-black washbasins and starkly contrasting design throughout – though the operators can't resist putting a pack of gummy
bears on the expertly ruffed pillows! Cool
bar on ground level.

Gästehaus Englischer Garten   GUESTHOUSE €€
(Map p356; ☎089-383 9410; www.hoteleng
lischergarten.de; Liebergesellstrasse 8; s/d/apt
from €81/95/108; Ⓟ 🛜; Ⓤ Münchner Freiheit)
Cosily inserted into a 200-year-old ivy-clad
mill, this small guesthouse on the edge of
the Englischer Garten offers a Bavarian
version of the British B&B experience. Not
all rooms are en suite, and those with their
own facilities are considerably more expensive. The breakfast is a wallet-clouting
€10.50 extra.

🛏 Westend & Theresienwiese

★ Hotel Cocoon   DESIGN HOTEL €
(Map p378; ☎089-5999 3907; www.hotel-cocoon.
de; Lindwurmstrasse 35; s/d from €57/65; ⊝ 🛜;
Ⓢ Sendlinger Tor, Ⓤ Sendlinger Tor) Fans of retro design will strike gold in this central
lifestyle hotel. Things kick off in reception,
with its faux-'70s veneer and dangling '60s
ball chairs, and continue in the rooms. All
are identical, decorated in retro oranges and
greens and fully technologically equipped.

The glass showers stand in the sleeping area, with only a kitschy Alpine-meadow scene veiling life's vitals.

Wombats City Hostel Munich HOSTEL €

(Map p378; ☑089-5998 9180; www.wombats -hostels.com; Senefelderstrasse 1; dm/d from €25/95; P@🛜; 🚇Hauptbahnhof, Ⓤ Hauptbahnhof) Munich's top hostel is a professionally run affair with a whopping 300 dorm beds plus private rooms. Dorms are painted in cheerful pastels and outfitted with wooden floors, en-suite facilities, sturdy lockers and comfy pine bunks, all in a central location near the train station.

Pension Westfalia B&B €

(Map p378; ☑089-530 377; www.pension-west falia.de; Mozartstrasse 23; s/d from €45/60; 🛜; Ⓤ Goetheplatz) Only a stumble away from the Oktoberfest meadow, this stately four-storey house conceals a cosy, family-run guesthouse that makes a serene base for sightseeing (outside the beer fest). Rooms are reached by lift; the cheaper ones have corridor facilities.

Hotelissimo Haberstock HOTEL €€

(Map p378; ☑089-557 855; www.hotelissimo.com; Schillerstrasse 4; s/d from €74/104; 🛜; 🚇Hauptbahnhof, ⓈHauptbahnhof, ⓊHauptbahnhof) The cheery decor at this value-for-money pick reflects the vision of the owners, a husband-and-wife team with a feel for colour, fabrics and design. Easy-on-the-eye gold, brown and cream tones dominate the good-sized rooms on the lower floors, while upper rooms radiate a bolder, Mediterranean palette.

Hotel Mariandl HOTEL €€

(Map p378; ☑089-552 9100; www.mariandl. com; Goethestrasse 51; s €69-98, d €88-175; 🛜; 🚇Sendlinger Tor, ⓊSendlinger Tor) If you like your history laced with quirkiness, you'll simply be delighted with this rambling neo-Gothic mansion. It's an utterly charming place where rooms convincingly capture the *Jugendstil* period with hand-selected antiques and ornamented ceilings. Breakfast is served until 4pm in the Vienna-style downstairs cafe, which also hosts frequent live jazz or classical-music nights.

Demas City Hotel HOTEL €€

(Map p378; ☑089-693 3990; www.demas-city. de; Landwehrstrasse 19; s/d from €102/122; 🛜; 🚇Karlsplatz, ⓈKarlsplatz, ⓊKarlsplatz) The 44 rooms at this quiet sleeper near the Hauptbahnhof are done out in trendy greys and blacks, accentuated by flashes of bold colour.

Bathrooms are a snug fit and the location is uninspiring, but it's a decent, if vibe-less, place for centrally based snoozing, breakfasting and web-surfing.

Hotel Müller HOTEL €€

(Map p378; ☑089-232 3860; Fliegenstrasse 4; s/d from €79/109; 🛜; ⓈSendlinger Tor) This friendly hotel has big, bright, business-standard rooms and a good price-to-quality ratio, with five-star breakfasts and polite staff. Despite the city-centre location, the side-street position is pretty quiet.

Hotel Eder HOTEL €€

(Map p378; ☑089-554 660; www.hotel-eder. de; Zweigstrasse 8; s €55-180, d €65-230; P🛜; 🚇Hauptbahnhof, ⓈHauptbahnhof, ⓊHauptbahnhof) A slice of small-town Bavaria teleported to the slightly seedy area south of the Hauptbahnhof, this rustic oasis has its chequered curtains, carved-wood chairs and Sisi/Ludwig II portraits firmly in place for those who didn't come all this way for the cocktails. The unevenly sized rooms are slightly vanilla, but given the pricing, this is a good deal.

Alpen Hotel HOTEL €€

(Map p378; ☑089-559 330; www.alpenhotel-muenchen.de; Adolf-Kolping-Strasse 14; s/d from €119/139; 🛜; ⓈHauptbahnhof, 🚇Hauptbahnhof, 🚇Hauptbahnhof) Don't be fooled by the slightly gloomy corridors here – rooms are of a very high business standard, parading big bathrooms and every amenity you could need. The downstairs restaurant is a lively spot.

Hotel Uhland HOTEL €€

(Map p378; ☑089-543 350; www.hotel-uhland. de; Uhlandstrasse 1; s/d incl breakfast from €99/129; P🛜; ⓊTheresienwiese) Crisp, professionally run operation with well-maintained business-standard rooms, big breakfasts and attentive staff. Little touches such as musical instruments and real art on the walls mean bedrooms are far from bland. Parking is €5, but spaces are limited.

Meininger's HOSTEL, HOTEL €€

(Map p378; ☑089-5499 8023; www.meininger-hostels.de; Landsbergerstrasse 20; dm/s/d without breakfast from €30/75/95; 🛜; 🚇Holzapfelstrasse) About 800m west of the Hauptbahnhof, this energetic hostel-hotel has basic, clean, bright rooms with big dorms divided into two for a bit of privacy. Room rates vary depending on the date, events taking place in Munich, and occupancy. Breakfast is an extra €6.90; bike hire costs from €8 per day.

MUNICH FOR CHILDREN

(Tiny) hands down, Munich is a great city for children, with plenty of activities to please tots with even the shortest attention span. There are plenty of parks for romping around, swimming pools and lakes for cooling off, and family-friendly beer gardens with children's playgrounds for making new friends.

Deutsches Museum

Many of the city's museums have special kid-oriented programs, but the highly interactive Kinderreich at the Deutsches Museum (p357) specifically lures the single-digit set.

Tierpark Hellabrunn

Petting baby goats, feeding pelicans, watching falcons and hawks perform or even riding a camel should make for some unforgettable memories at the city zoo (Hellabrunn Zoo; ☑089-625 080; www.tierpark-hellabrunn.de; Tierparkstrasse 30; adult/child €15/6; ☉9am-6pm Apr-Sep, to 5pm Oct-Mar; ☒52 from Marienplatz, ☒Tiroler Platz, Ⓤ Thalkirchen).

SeaLife München

For a fishy immersion, head to this attraction (Map p368; www.visitsealife.com; Willi-Daume-Platz 1; adult/child gate prices €17.95/14.50; ☉10am-5pm Mon-Fri, to 6pm Sat & Sun; Ⓢ Olympiazentrum) in the Olympiapark.

Paläontologisches Museum

Dino fans will gravitate here (Palaeontological Museum; Map p362; www.palmuc.de; Richard-Wagner-Strasse 10; ☉8am-4pm Mon-Thu, to 2pm Fri; ☒Königsplatz, Ⓤ Königsplatz) FREE.

Museum Mensch und Natur

Budding scientists will find plenty to marvel at in this museum (p356) within the Schloss Nymphenburg.

Spielzeugmuseum

The Spielzeugmuseum (Toy Museum; Map p344; www.toymuseum.de; Marienplatz 15; adult/child €4/1; ☉10am-5.30pm; Ⓢ Marienplatz, Ⓤ Marienplatz) is of the look-but-don't-touch variety, but kids might get a kick out of seeing what toys grandma used to pester her parents for.

Münchner Marionettentheater

The adorable singing and dancing marionettes performing here (p379) have enthralled generations of wee ones.

Münchner Theater für Kinder

This theatre (p379) offers budding thespians a chance to enjoy fairy tales and children's classics in the style of *Pinocchio* and German children's classic *Max & Moritz*.

Hotel Königshof   HOTEL €€€
(Map p378; ☑089-551 360; www.koenigshof-hotel.de; Karlsplatz 25; d from €250; ❋☎; ☒Karlsplatz, Ⓢ Karlsplatz, Ⓤ Karlsplatz) Over-the-top luxury and obsessive attention to detail make the 'King's Court' a real treat if you like that sort of thing. Rooms range from better-than-average business standard to sumptuous belle époque–style quarters. A Michelin-starred restaurant and a stylish bar are on the premises, and some of the rooms have views of busy Karlsplatz (Stachus), giving the place a heart-of-the-action feel.

Anna Hotel   DESIGN HOTEL €€€
(Map p378; ☑089-599 940; www.geisel-privat hotels.de; Schützenstrasse 1; r from €165; ❋☎; ☒Karlsplatz, Ⓤ Karlsplatz, Ⓢ Karlsplatz) Urban

sophisticates love this well-positioned designer den, where you can retire to rooms dressed in sensuous furniture and regal colours, or tempered by teak, marble and mosaics and offering a more minimalist feel. The swanky restaurant-bar is a hive of dining activity.

Schiller 5   HOTEL €€€
(Map p378; ☑089-515 040; www.schiller5.com; Schillerstrasse 5; s/d from €119/163; ℗❋☎; Ⓢ Hauptbahnhof, ☒Hauptbahnhof, ☒Hauptbahnhof) Not only are the pads at this semiapartment hotel smartly trimmed, you also get a lot for your euro here in the shape of a well-equipped kitchenette, sound system, coffee machine and extra large bed in every room. Some guests complain of street noise, so try to bag a room away from the hustle below.

Sofitel Munich Bayerpost HOTEL €€€
(Map p378; ☑089-599 480; www.sofitel-munich.com; Bayerstrasse 12; r from €240; P☕❄@☎; ⓢHauptbahnhof, ⓡHauptbahnhof) The restored Renaissance facade of a former post office hides this high-concept jewel, which wraps all that's great about Munich – history, innovation, elegance, the art of living – into one neat and appealing package. Be sure to make time for the luxurious spa, where the grotto-like pool juts into the atrium lobby lidded by a tinted glass roof.

✖ Eating

Munich has southern Germany's most exciting restaurant scene. The best dishes make use of fresh regional, seasonal and organic ingredients. The Bavarian capital is also the best place between Vienna and Paris for internationally flavoured dining, especially for Italian, Afghan, Vietnamese and Turkish food, and even vegetarians can look forward to something other than noodles and salads.

✖ Altstadt & Residenz

Bratwurstherzl FRANCONIAN €
(Map p344; Dreifaltigkeitsplatz 1; mains €7-12; ⊙10am-11pm Mon-Sat; ⓢMarienplatz, ⓤMarienplatz) Cosy panelling and an ancient vaulted brick ceiling set the tone of this Old Munich tavern with a Franconian focus. Homemade organic sausages are grilled to perfection on an open beechwood fire and served on heart-shaped pewter plates. They're best enjoyed with a beer from the Hacker-Pschorr brewery.

Götterspeise CAFE €
(Map p344; Jahnstrasse 30; snacks from €3.50; ⊙8am-7pm Mon-Fri, to 6pm Sat; ⓡMüllerstrasse) The name of this cafe translates as 'food of the gods' and the food in question is that most addictive of treats, chocolate. Here it comes in many forms, both liquid and solid, but there are also teas, coffees and cakes and little outside perches for when the sun shines.

Küche am Tor GERMAN, ITALIAN €
(Map p344; Lueg Ins Land 1; mains around €9.50; ⊙noon-5pm Mon-Fri; ☑; ⓡIsartor, ⓢIsartor) No-nonsense, blink-and-you'd-miss-it lunch stop for local office workers. The comfortingly short menu contains mostly German fare, but also includes Mediterranean touches such as pesto, tuna and *salsiccia* (Italian sausage). Mostly a tourist-free zone.

Wiener Cafe CAFE €
(Map p344; cnr Reichenbachstrasse & Rumfordstrasse; snacks €2-5; ⊙8.30am-6pm Mon-Fri, 8am-5pm Sat; ⓡReichenbachplatz) The only cool thing about this delightfully old-fashioned coffeehouse, which serves cakes, snacks and drinks, is the marble tabletops.

Cordo Bar TAPAS €
(Map p344; www.cordo-bar.de; Ickstattstrasse 1a; tapas €2.90-10, mains €4.50-15; ⊙4pm-1am Mon-Thu, to 2am Fri & Sat, to midnight Sun; ☎; ⓤFraunhoferstrasse) Choose between the raw-wood streetside seats or the darkwood-and-tiles interior at this atmospheric tapas bar. The small plates ooze with Iberian imagination and can be paired with any of 13 cocktails for a refined night out.

Schmalznudel CAFE €
(Cafe Frischhut; Map p344; Prälat-Zistl-Strasse 8; pastries €2.10; ⊙8am-6pm Mon-Sat; ⓢMarienplatz, ⓤMarienplatz) This incredibly popular institution serves just four traditional pastries, one of which, the *Schmalznudel* (an oily type of doughnut), gives the place its local nickname. All baked goodies you munch here are crisp and fragrant, as they're always fresh off the hotplate. They're best eaten with a steaming pot of coffee on a winter's day.

★Weisses Brauhaus BAVARIAN €€
(Map p344; ☑089-290 1380; www.weisses-brauhaus.de; Tal 7; mains €7-20; ⊙8am-12.30am; ⓢMarienplatz, ⓤMarienplatz) One of Munich's classic beer halls, this place is charged in the evenings with red-faced, ale-infused hilarity, with Alpine whoops accompanying the rabble-rousing oompah band. The *Weisswurst* (veal sausage) here sets the standard; sluice down a pair with the unsurpassed Schneider *Weissbier,* but only before noon. Understandably very popular and reservations are recommended after 7pm.

★Fraunhofer BAVARIAN €€
(Map p344; ☑089-266 460; www.fraunhofertheater.de; Fraunhoferstrasse 9; mains €5-20; ⊙4.30pm-1am; ☑; ⓡMüllerstrasse) With its screechy parquet floors, stuccoed ceilings, wood panelling and virtually no trace that the last century even happened, this wonderfully characterful inn is perfect for exploring the region with a fork. The menu is a seasonally adapted checklist of southern German favourites but also features at least a dozen vegetarian dishes and the odd exotic ingredient. Cash only.

The tiny theatre at the back stages great shows and was among the venues that pioneered a modern style of *Volksmusik* (folk music) back in the '70s and '80s.

★ Prinz Myshkin
VEGETARIAN €€

(Map p344; ☑ 089-265 596; www.prinzmyshkin.com; Hackenstrasse 2; mains €9-20; ⊙ 11am-12.30am; ☑; ⑤ Marienplatz, Ⓤ Marienplatz) This place is proof, if any were needed, that the vegetarian experience has well and truly left the sandals, beards and lentils era. Ensconced in a former brewery, Munich's premier meat-free dining spot occupies a gleamingly whitewashed, vaulted space where health-conscious eaters come to savour imaginative dishes such as curry-orange-carrot soup, unexpectedly good curries and 'wellness desserts'.

Königsquelle
EUROPEAN €€

(Map p344; ☑ 089-220 071; www.koenigsquelle. com; Baaderplatz 2; mains €10-27; ⊙ 5pm-1am Sun-Fri, from 7pm Sat; ⓠ Isartor, ⓠ Isartor, ⑤ Isartor) This wood-panelled Munich institution is well loved for its attentive service, expertly prepared food and dark, well-stocked hardwood bar containing what must be the Bavarian capital's best selection of malt whiskies, stacked high behind the bar. The only-just decipherable handwritten menu hovers somewhere mid-Alps, with anything from schnitzel to linguine and goat's cheese to cannelloni to choose from.

Cafe Luitpold
CAFE €€

(Map p344; www.cafe-luitpold.de; Briennerstrasse 11; mains €10-19; ⊙ 8am-7pm Mon, to 11pm Tue-Sat, 9am-7pm Sun; 🖀; Ⓤ Odeonsplatz) A cluster of pillarbox-red streetside tables and chairs announces you've arrived at this stylish but not ubercool retreat. It offers a choice of three spaces: a lively bar, a less boisterous columned cafe and a cool palm-leaved atrium. Good for a daytime coffee-and-cake halt or a full evening blowout with all the trimmings.

Les Deux Brasserie
INTERNATIONAL €€

(Map p344; ☑ 089-710 407 373; www.les deux-muc.de; Maffaistrasse 3a; mains €7-17; ⊙ noon-10pm; ⑤ Marienplatz) Below the eponymous fine-dining restaurant, Les Deux's ground-floor brasserie is perfect for taking a tasty break without breaking the budget. Choose from such classics as miniburgers, club sandwich or Icelandic cod and chips, or go for one of the more elaborate weekly specials. If the weather permits, tables spill into the courtyard.

Tegernseer Tal
BAVARIAN €€

(Map p344; ☑ 089-222 626; www.tegernseer-tal8. com; Tal 8; mains €10-20; ⊙ 9.30am-1am Sun-Wed,

to 3am Thu-Sat; 🖀; ⑤ Marienplatz, Ⓤ Marienplatz) A blond-wood interior illuminated by a huge skylight makes this a bright alternative to Munich's dark-panelled taverns. And with Alpine Tegernseer beer on tap and an imaginative menu of regional food, this is generally a lighter, calmer more refined beer-hall experience with a less raucous ambience.

Bamyan
AFGHANI €€

(Map p344; www.bamyan.de; Hans-Sachs-Strasse 3; mains €9.50-20; ⊙ 5pm-1am Sun-Fri, from 11.30am Sat; ⓠ Müllerstrasse) The terms 'happy hour', 'cocktail' and 'chilled vibe' don't normally go together with the word 'Afghan', but that's exactly the combination you get at this exotic hang-out, named after the Buddha statues infamously destroyed by the Taliban in 2001. The gastro-award-winning Central Asian soups, kebabs, rice and lamb dishes, and big salads are eaten at handmade tables inlaid with ornate metalwork.

OskarMaria
INTERNATIONAL €€

(Map p344; www.oskarmaria.com; Salvatorplatz 1; mains €9-23; ⊙ 10am-midnight Mon-Sat, to 7pm Sun; ☑; Ⓤ Odeonsplatz) The bookish cafe at the Literaturhaus cultural centre is a commendably stylish spot, with high ceilings, rows of small central European cafe tables and sprightly waiters. The more highbrow atmosphere will be appreciated by those who prefer their eateries (virtually) tourist free, and the menu features international staples plus several Bavarian favourites.

Fedora
ITALIAN €€

(Map p344; www.fedorabar.de; Ledererstrasse 3; mains around €10, pizzas €10-15; ⊙ 11.30am-11pm Mon-Thu, to midnight Fri & Sat, 5-10pm Sun; 🖀; ⑤ Marienplatz, Ⓤ Marienplatz) Occupying the vaulted spaces of the 13th-century Zerwirkgewölbe, this Italian job named after the famous hat does a decent pizza and has an open kitchen where you can watch cooks load it up. Tables bearing chequered tablecloths spread out from a big bar, and there's plenty of sunny street-side seating.

Vegelangelo
VEGETARIAN €€

(Map p344; ☑ 089-2880 6836; www.vegelangelo.de; Thomas-Wimmer-Ring 16; mains €13-19, set menu €22-34; ⊙ noon-2pm Tue-Thu, 6pm-late Mon-Sat; ☑; ⓠ Isartor, ⑤ Isartor) Reservations are compulsory at this petite vegie spot, where Indian odds and ends, a piano and a small Victorian fireplace distract little from the superb meat-free cooking, all of which can be converted to suit vegans. There's a set-menu-only policy Friday

Nymphenburg, Neuhausen & Olympiapark

MUNICH

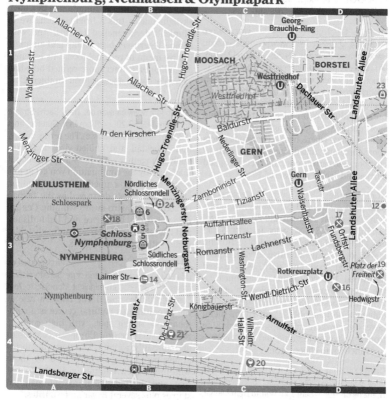

Nymphenburg, Neuhausen & Olympiapark

Alois Dallmayr
FOOD HALL €€

(Map p344; ☑ 089-213 50; www.dallmayr.de; Dienerstrasse 14; ⊙ 9.30am-7pm Mon-Sat; ⑤ Marienplatz, Ⓤ Marienplatz) A pricey gourmet delicatessen right in the thick of the Altstadt action, Alois Dallmayr is best known for its coffee but has so much more, including cheeses, ham, truffles, wine, caviar and exotic foods from every corner of the globe.

Einstein
JEWISH €€

(Map p344; ☑ 089-202 400 332; www.einstein -restaurant.de; St-Jakobs-Platz 18; mains €19-20; ⊙ noon-3pm & 6pm-midnight Sat-Thu, 12.30-3pm Fri; 🛜; Ⓡ Marienplatz, Ⓤ Marienplatz) Reflected in the plate-glass windows of the Jewish Museum, this is the only kosher eatery in the city centre. The ID-and-bag-search entry process is worth it for the restaurant's uncluttered lines, smartly laid tables, soothing ambience and menu of well-crafted Jewish dishes. Reservations online only.

Conviva im Blauen Haus
INTERNATIONAL €€

(Map p344; www.conviva-muenchen.de; Hildegardstrasse 1; 3-course lunch €8-10, dinner mains €10-22; ⊙ 11am-1am Mon-Sat, from 5pm Sun; ☑; Ⓡ Kammerspiele) The industrially exposed interior and barely dressed tables mean nothing distracts from the great food at this theatre restaurant. The daily-changing menus make the most of local seasonal ingredients and are reassuringly short. The lunch menu is a steal.

★ Weinhaus Neuner
BAVARIAN €€€

(Map p344; ☑ 089-260 3954; www.weinhaus- neuner.de; Herzogspitalstrasse 8; mains €20-25; ⊙ noon-midnight; ⑤ Karlsplatz, Ⓤ Karlsplatz) This Munich institution has been serving Bavarian-Austrian classics and a long wine list for well over 100 years. Take a break from the hop-infused frenzy and pork knuckle to enjoy schnitzel and *Tafelspitz* (boiled veal or beef), helped along with a Franconian Riesling or a Wachau Grüner Veltiner amid the understated surroundings. Reservations advised.

Galleria
ITALIAN €€€

(Map p344; ☑ 089-297 995; www.ristorante- galleria.de; Sparkassenstrasse 11; mains €17.50- 30; ⊙ noon-2.30pm & 6-11pm; ⑤ Marienplatz, Ⓤ Marienplatz) Munich has a multitude of Italian eateries, but Galleria is a cut above the rest. The compact interior hits you first, a multihued, eclectic mix of contemporary art and tightly packed tables. The menu throws up a few surprises – some dishes contain very un-Italian ingredients, such as

and Saturday. No prams allowed and no tap water served, but it does accept Bitcoin.

Kochspielhaus
INTERNATIONAL €€

(Map p344; ☑ 089-5480 2738; www.kochspiel haus.de; Rumfordstrasse 5; breakfast €7.50-16, mains €8.50-17; ⊙ 7am-6pm Sun-Tue, to 10pm Wed- Sat; ⑤ Fraunhoferstrasse) Attached to a gourmet bakery called Backspielhaus, this modern country-style lair accented with massive candles packages only superfresh, top-quality ingredients into clever pasta, meat and fish dishes. Also a great spot for breakfast.

Deutsche Eiche
INTERNATIONAL €€

(Map p344; ☑ 089-231 1660; www.deutsche -eiche.com; Reichenbachstrasse 13; mains €9-17; ⊙ 7am-1am; Ⓡ Reichenbachplatz) A Munich institution and gay central, this was once filmmaker Rainer Werner Fassbinder's favourite hang-out. It's still a popular spot and packs in a mixed crowd for its schnitzels, salads and prompt service.

curry and coconut. Reservations are pretty much essential in the evening.

🍴 Haidhausen & Lehel

Wirtshaus in der Au
BAVARIAN €€

(Map p374; ☑089-448 1400; www.wirtshaus inderau.de; Lilienstrasse 51; mains €10-22; ⊙5pm-midnight Mon-Fri, from 10am Sat & Sun; 🚇Deutsches Museum) This Bavarian tavern's simple slogan is 'Beer and dumplings since 1901', and it's this time-honoured staple – dumplings – that's the speciality here (the tavern even runs a dumpling-making course in English). Once a brewery, the space-rich dining area has chunky tiled floors, a lofty ceiling and a crackling fireplace in winter. When spring springs, the beer garden fills.

Sir Tobi
BAVARIAN €€

(Map p374; ☑089-3249 4825; www.sirtobi -muenchen.de; Sternstrasse 16; mains €9-20; ⊙11.30am-3pm Mon-Fri, 5.30pm-midnight Thu-Sat; 🗣; 🚇Lehel) This Bavarian bistro serves delicious, slow-food versions of southern German and Austrian dishes in an environment of crisp white tablecloths and fresh flowers. The service here is particularly good.

Fischhäusl
SEAFOOD €€

(Map p374; Wiener Platz; mains €7-15; ⊙9.30am-6pm Tue-Fri, 9am-2.30pm Sat; 🚇Wiener Platz) Part of the food market on Wiener Platz, this kiosk with a few seats is one of the best spots in Munich to lunch on fish, which is prepared simply on a grill and served with salad, potatoes and white wine.

Dreigroschenkeller
BAVARIAN €€

(Map p374; Lilienstrasse 2; mains €10-20; ⊙5pm-1am Sun-Thu, to 3am Fri & Sat; 🚇Deutsches Museum) A quirky, labyrinthine brick-cellar pub with rooms – based upon Bertolt Brecht's *Die Dreigroschenoper* (The Threepenny Opera) – ranging from a prison cell to a red satiny salon. There are several types of beer to choose from and an extensive menu of hearty Bavarian favourites.

🍴 Maxvorstadt

Il Mulino
ITALIAN €€

(Map p362; www.ristorante-ilmulino.de; Görresstrasse 1; mains €6-20; ⊙11.30am-midnight; Ⓢ Josephsplatz) This much-loved neighbourhood classic has been feeding Italophiles and immigrants from the beautiful country for over three decades. All the expected pastas and pizzas are present and correct, though the daily specials will likely tickle

the palate of more curious eaters. Somewhat surprisingly 'The Mill' was declared Bavarian restaurant of the year in 2017.

🍴 Nymphenburg, Neuhausen & Olympiapark

Ruffini
CAFE €

(Map p368; www.ruffini.de; Orffstrasse 22; meals €7-10; ⊙10am-midnight Tue-Sun; 🗣; 🚇Neuhausen) Well worth the effort of delving deep into Neuhausen to find it, this cafe is a fun place to be no matter where the hands of the clock are. On sunny days the self-service rooftop terrace gets busy with locals – few tourists make it out here. Regular music events, from rock to classical.

Eiscafé Sarcletti
GELATO €

(Map p368; www.sarcletti.de; Nymphenburger Strasse 155; ⊙9am-11.30pm May-Aug, shorter hours Sep-Apr; Ⓤ Rotkreuzplatz) Ice-cream addicts have been getting their gelato fix at this Munich institution since 1879. Choose from more than 50 mouth-watering flavours, from not-so-plain vanilla to buttermilk and mango.

Zauberberg
INTERNATIONAL €€

(Map p368; Hedwigstrasse 14; 3-course dinner menu around €45; ⊙6.30pm-1am Tue-Sat; 🚇Albrechtstrasse) Far off the tourist track, this 40-seat locals' favourite will put your tummy into a state of contentment with its elegant, well-composed international creations. Single plates are available, but in order to truly sample the chef's talents, you should order a multicourse menu.

Chopan
AFGHANI €€

(Map p368; ☑089-1895 6459; www.chopan.de; Elvirastrasse 18a; mains €8-20; ⊙6pm-midnight; Ⓤ Maillingerstrasse) Munich has a huge Afghan community, whose most respected eatery is this much-lauded restaurant done out in the style of a Central Asian caravanserai, with rich fabrics, multihued glass lanterns and geometric patterns. In this culinary Aladdin's cave, you'll discover an exotic menu of lamb, lentils, rice, spinach and flatbread in various combinations. No alcohol.

Schlosscafé im Palmenhaus
CAFE €€

(Map p368; ☑089-175 309; www.palmenhaus.de; Schloss Nymphenburg 43; mains €10-17; ⊙11am-6pm Tue-Fri, from 10am Sat & Sun; 🚇Schloss Nymphenburg) The glass-fronted 1820 palm house where Ludwig II used to keep his exotic house plants warm in winter is now a high-ceilinged and pleasantly scented cafe serving soups, salads, sandwiches and other light meals. It's just behind Schloss Nymphenburg.

★ **Esszimmer** MEDITERRANEAN €€€
(Map p368; ☑ 089-358 991 814; www.bmw-welt.com; BMW Welt, Am Olympiapark 1; 4/5 courses €130/145; ⊙ from 7pm Tue-Sat; ※ ♠; Ⓤ Olympiazentrum) It took Bobby Bräuer, head chef at the gourmet restaurant at BMW World, just two years to gain his first Michelin star. Munich's top dining spot is the place to sample high-octane French and Mediterranean morsels, carnivore and wholly vegetarian, served in a trendily dark and veneered dining room above the i8s and 7 Series. Life in the gastronomic fast lane.

✖ Schwabing & the Englischer Garten

Cafe an der Uni CAFE €
(Map p356; Ludwigstrasse 24; mains around €9; ⊙ 8am-1am Mon-Fri, from 9am Sat & Sun; ♠ ☑; Ⓢ Universität) Anytime is a good time to be at charismatic CADU. Enjoy breakfast (served until a hangover-friendly 10pm!), a cuppa Java or a Helles in the lovely garden hidden by a wall from busy Ludwigstrasse.

★ **Cochinchina** ASIAN €€
(Map p356; ☑ 089-3898 9577; www.cochinchina.de; Kaiserstrasse 28; mains around €20; ⊙ 11.30am-2.30pm & 6pm-midnight; ♠; Ⓤ Münchner Freiheit) Bearing an old name for southern Vietnam, this cosmopolitan Asian fusion restaurant is Munich's top place for Vietnamese and Chinese concoctions. The food is consumed in a dark, dramatically exotic space devoted to the firefly and splashed with colour in the shape of Chinese vases and lamps. The traditional *pho* soup is southern Germany's best.

Potting Shed BURGERS €€
(Map p356; www.thepottingshed.de; Occamstrasse 11; mains €5-18; ⊙ from 6pm Tue-Sat; Ⓤ Münchner Freiheit) This relaxed hang-out serves tapas, gourmet burgers and cocktails to an easygoing evening crowd. The burger menu whisks you round the globe, but it's the 'Potting Shed Special', involving an organic beef burger flambéed in whisky, that catches the eye on the simple but well-concocted menu.

Ruff's Burger & BBQ BURGERS €€
(Map p356; Occamstrasse 4; burgers €5.50-16, other mains €9-19; ⊙ 11.30am-11pm Mon-Wed, to midnight Thu-Sat, to 10pm Sun; ♠; Ⓤ Münchner Freiheit) Munich's obsession with putting a bit of fried meat between two buns is celebrated

at this Schwabing joint, where the burgers are 100% Bavarian beef – except, of course, for the token veggie version. Erdinger and Tegernseer beer and mostly outdoor seating.

★ **Tantris** INTERNATIONAL €€€
(☑ 089-361 9590; www.tantris.de; Johann-Fichte-Strasse 7; menu from €100; ⊙ noon-3pm & 6.30pm-1am Tue-Sat Oct-Dec, closed Tue Jan-Sep; ♠; Ⓤ Dietlindenstrasse) Tantris means 'the search for perfection' and here, at one of Germany's most famous restaurants, it's not far off it. The interior design is full-bodied '70s – all postbox reds, truffle blacks and illuminated yellows. The food is sublime and the service is sometimes as unobtrusive as it is efficient. The wine cellar is probably Germany's best. Reservations essential.

✖ Westend & Theresienwiese

★ **Marais** CAFE €
(Map p378; www.cafe-marais.de; Parkstrasse 2; dishes €5-13; ⊙ 8am-8pm Tue-Sat, 10am-6pm Sun; ☑; ⬛ Holzapfelstrasse) Is it a junk shop, a cafe or a sewing shop? Well, Westend's oddest coffeehouse is in fact all three, and everything you see in this converted haberdashery – the knick-knacks, the cakes and the antique chair you're sitting on – is for sale.

Bodhi VEGAN €€
(Map p378; ☑ 089-4114 2458; www.bodhivegan.de; Ligsalzstrasse 23; mains €9.50-17; ⊙ 5pm-midnight; ☑; Ⓤ Schwanthalerhöhe) This vegan restaurant has an uncluttered, wood-rich interior where health-conscious diners feast on meat-and-dairy-free pastas, burgers, salads, soya steaks and tofu-based dishes. Whether those same wellness fanatics swill it all down with the large selection of cocktails and whisky is something you'll have to see for yourself.

La Vecchia Masseria ITALIAN €€
(Map p378; Mathildenstrasse 3; mains €10-20, pizzas €7.50-12; ⊙ 11.30am-11.30pm; ⬛ Sendlinger Tor, Ⓢ Sendlinger Tor) In an area traditionally settled by Italians, this is one of Munich's longest-established Italian *osterie*. Choose between the small beer garden out front or the earthy, rurally themed dining room with its chunky wood tables, antique tin buckets, baskets and clothing irons, all conjuring up the ambience of an Apennines farmhouse. All pizzas are €5.99 on Sundays.

Dinner Hopping MULTICUISINE €€€
(Map p378; www.dinnerhopping.de; Arnulfstrasse 1, departure & arrival point next to the Hauptbahnhof;

dinner experience from €129; ⊙6.30-10.15pm; 🚇Hauptbahnhof, Ⓤ Hauptbahnhof, Ⓢ Hauptbahnhof) Be driven around Munich in an old yellow US schoolbus as you enjoy either an Italian, American or Bavarian three-course dinner accompanied by a live act. It may sound gimmicky, but the food gets rave reviews.

🍺 Drinking & Nightlife

Munich is truly a great place for boozers. Raucous beer halls, snazzy hotel lounges, chestnut-canopied beer gardens, DJ bars, designer cocktail temples – the variety is huge. And no matter where you are, you won't be far from an enticing cafe to get a caffeine-infused pick-me-up. Munich has some of Europe's best nightclubs with exciting venues for almost every musical taste.

🍺 Altstadt & Residenz

★Hofbräuhaus   BEER HALL
(Map p344; 📞089-2901 36100; www.hofbraeuhaus.de; Am Platzl 9; ⊙9am-midnight; 🚇Kammerspiele, Ⓢ Marienplatz, Ⓤ Marienplatz) Even if you don't like beer, every visitor to Munich should make a pilgrimage to the mothership of all beer halls, if only once. Within this major tourist attraction, you'll discover a range of spaces in which to do your *Mass* lifting: the horse chestnut–shaded garden, the main hall next to the oompah band, tables opposite the industrial-scale kitchen and quieter corners.

One unusual feature is that you can buy your beer with prepaid beer tokens, just like during Oktoberfest. There's an interesting gift shop on the premises, and the Hofbräuhaus prides itself on being open every day of the year, even Christmas day.

★Pacha   CLUB
(Map p344; www.pacha-muenchen.de; Maximiliansplatz 5; ⊙7pm-6am Thu, 11pm-6am Fri & Sat; 🚇Lenbachplatz) One of a gaggle of clubs at Maximiliansplatz 5, this nightspot with its cherry logo is one of Munich's hottest nights out, with the DJs spinning their stuff till well after sunrise.

★Schumann's Bar   BAR
(Map p344; 📞089-229 060; www.schumanns.de; Odeonsplatz 6-7; ⊙8am-3am Mon-Fri, 6pm-3am Sat & Sun; Ⓢ Odeonsplatz) Urbane and sophisticated, Schumann's shakes up Munich's nightlife with libational flights of fancy in an impressive range of concoctions. It's also good for weekday breakfasts. Cash only.

Augustiner-Grossgaststätte   BEER HALL
(Map p344; 📞089-2318 3257; www.augustiner-restaurant.com; Neuhauser Strasse 27; ⊙9am-11.30pm) This sprawling place has a less raucous atmosphere and superior food to the usual offerings. Altogether it's a much more authentic example of an old-style Munich beer hall, but with the added highlight of a tranquil arcaded beer garden out back.

★MilchundBar   CLUB
(Map p344; www.milchundbar.de; Sonnenstrasse 27; ⊙10pm-7am Mon-Thu, 11pm-9am Fri & Sat; 🚇Sendlinger Tor, Ⓤ Sendlinger Tor) One of the hottest addresses in the city centre for those who like to spend the hours between supper and breakfast boogieing to an eclectic mix of nostalgia hits during the week and top DJs at the weekends.

Viktualienmarkt   BEER GARDEN
(Map p344; Viktualienmarkt 6; ⊙9am-10pm; Ⓤ Marienplatz, Ⓢ Marienplatz) After a day of sightseeing or stocking up on tasty nibbles at the Viktualienmarkt (p343), find a table at this chestnut-shaded beer garden surrounded by stalls, a Munich institution since 1807. All of Munich's breweries take turns serving here, so you never know what's on tap.

Rote Sonne   CLUB
(Map p344; www.rote-sonne.com; Maximiliansplatz 5; ⊙from 11pm Thu-Sun; 🚇Lenbachplatz) Named for a 1969 Munich cult movie starring it-girl Uschi Obermaier, the Red Sun is a fiery nirvana for fans of electronic sounds. A global roster of DJs keeps the dance floor packed and sweaty until the sun rises.

Braunauer Hof   BEER HALL
(Map p344; www.wirtshaus-im-braunauer-hof.de; Frauenstrasse 42; ⊙10am-midnight Mon-Sat, to 10pm Sun; 🚇Isartor, Ⓢ Isartor) Near the Isartor, drinkers can choose between the traditional Bavarian interior or the beer garden out the back, which enjoys a surprisingly tranquil setting despite its city-centre location. Most come for the Paulaner beer in the evening, but the €8.50 lunch menu is commendable value for money.

Trachtenvogl   CAFE
(Map p344; www.trachtenvogl.de; Reichenbachstrasse 47; ⊙9am-10pm; 📶; 🚇Fraunhoferstrasse) At night you'll have to shoehorn your way into this buzzy lair favoured by a chatty, boozy crowd of scenesters, artists and students. Daytimes are mellower – all the better to sample its seasonal menu and check out

the incongruous collection of knick-knacks left over from the days when this was a traditional garment shop.

Baader Café
CAFE

(Map p344; www.baadercafe.de; Baaderstrasse 47; ⊙9.30am-1am Sun-Thu, to 2am Fri & Sat; 🐾; ᄆFraunhoferstrasse) Around since the mid-'80s, this literary think-and-drink place lures all sorts, from short-skirts to tweed jackets, who linger over daytime coffees and nighttime cocktails. It's normally packed, even on winter Wednesday mornings, and is popular among Brits who come for the authentic English breakfast.

Cafe Pini
CAFE

(Map p344; www.cafepini.de; Klenzestrasse 45; ⊙8am-11pm Mon-Fri, from 9am Sat, 9am-7pm Sun; ᄆFraunhoferstrasse) *Bibite, panini, giornali* (drinks, sandwiches, newspapers) is the holy trinity served up at this Italian cafe, which takes you back to the days of the *Wirtschaftswunder* when Italian *gastarbeiter* (foreign workers) flooded into Munich to rebuild the city after WWII. Take a break, pull up a vintage seat and enjoy the area's most authentic Italian coffee.

Niederlassung
BAR

(Map p344; ☑089-3260 0307; www.niederlassung.org; Buttermelcherstrasse 6; ⊙7pm-1am Tue-Thu, to 3am Fri & Sat, to midnight Sun; ⑤Fraunhoferstrasse, ᄆIsartor) From Adler Dry to Zephyr, this gin joint stocks an impressive 80 varieties of juniper juice in an unpretentious setting filled with books and sofas and humming with indie sounds. There's even a selection of different tonic waters to choose from. Happy hour from 7pm to 9pm and after midnight.

Zephyr Bar
COCKTAIL BAR

(Map p344; www.zephyr-bar.de; Baaderstrasse 68; ⊙8pm-1am Sun-Thu, to 3am Fri & Sat; ⑤Fraunhoferstrasse) At one of Munich's best bars, Alex Schmaltz whips up courageous potions with unusual ingredients such as homemade cucumber-dill juice, sesame oil or banana-parsley puree. Cocktail alchemy at its finest, and a top gin selection to boot.

Del Fiore
CAFE

(Map p344; www.delfiore.de; Gärtnerplatz 1; ⊙10am-midnight; 🐾; ᄆReichenbachplatz) Come to this buzzing Italian coffeehouse, the only one with outdoor seating on the Gärtnerplatz, where there's standing room only from the first rays of late winter to the

last of autumn. Great people-watching possibilities all day long.

🍺 Haidhausen & Lehel

Biergarten Muffatwerk
BEER GARDEN

(Map p374; www.muffatwerk.de; Zellstrasse 4; ⊙from noon mid-Mar–mid-Oct; ᄆAm Gasteig) Think of this one as a progressive beer garden with reggae instead of oompah, civilised imbibing instead of brainless guzzling, organic meats, fish and vegetables on the grill, and the option of chilling in lounge chairs. Opening hours are open-ended, meaning some very late finishes.

Hofbräukeller
BEER HALL

(Map p374; ☑089-459 9250; www.hofbraeukeller.de; Wiener Platz; ⊙10am-midnight; ᄆWiener Platz) One of the original beer halls, this wood-panelled, staunchly traditional tavern serves nine different types of the finest Hofbräu, including two alcohol-free versions and always a seasonal brew. Out back is what was, many claim, Munich's first beer garden.

🍺 Maxvorstadt

★Alter Simpl
PUB

(Map p362; ☑089-272 3083; www.altersimpl.com; Türkenstrasse 57; ⊙11am-3am Mon-Fri, to 4am Sat & Sun; ᄆSchellingstrasse) Thomas Mann and Hermann Hesse used to knock 'em back at this well-scuffed and wood-panelled thirst parlour. A bookish ambience still pervades, making this an apt spot at which to curl up with a weighty tome over a few Irish ales. The curious name is an abbreviation of the satirical magazine *Simplicissimus*.

Augustiner Keller
BEER GARDEN

(Map p362; www.augustinerkeller.de; Arnulfstrasse 52; ⊙10am-1am Apr-Oct; 🖰; ᄆHopfenstrasse) Every year this leafy 5000-seat beer garden, about 500m west of the Hauptbahnhof, buzzes with fairy-lit thirst-quenching activity from the first sign that spring may have *gesprungen*. The ancient chestnuts are thick enough to seek refuge under when it rains, or else lug your mug to the actual beer cellar. Small playground.

Park-Cafe
BEER GARDEN

(Map p362; www.parkcafe089.de; Sophienstrasse 7; ⊙11am-11pm; ᄆLenbachplatz) A hidden gem, this typical Munich beer garden in the Alter Botanischer Garten serves Hofbräu suds and lots of filling food.

Haidhausen & Lehel

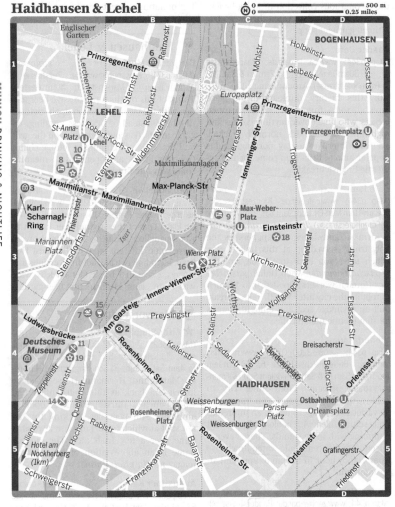

Eat the Rich BAR

(Map p362; www.eattherich.de; Hessstrasse 90; ⏰7pm-1am Thu, to 4am Fri & Sat; Ⓤ Theresienstrasse) Strong cocktails served in half-litre glasses quickly loosen inhibitions at this sizzling nightspot, a great place to crash when the party's winding down everywhere else. Food is served till 3am on weekends.

🍺 Nymphenburg, Neuhausen & Olympiapark

Hirschgarten BEER GARDEN

(Map p368; www.hirschgarten.de; Hirschgarten 1; ⏰11.30am-1am; 🚋Kriemhildenstrasse, Ⓢ Laim)

The Everest of Munich beer gardens can seat up to 8000 Augustiner lovers, making it Bavaria's biggest – an accolade indeed. It's in a lovely spot in a former royal hunting preserve and rubs up against a deer enclosure and a carousel. Steer here after visiting Schloss Nymphenburg – it's only a short walk south of the palace.

Backstage CLUB

(Map p368; www.backstage.eu; Reitknechtstrasse 6; Ⓢ Hirschgarten) Refreshingly nonmainstream, this groovetastic club has a chilled night beer garden and a shape-shifting line-up of punk, nu metal, hip-hop, dance hall

Haidhausen & Lehel

and other alternative sounds, both canned and live.

🍺 Schwabing & the Englischer Garten

⭐ **Chinesischer Turm**　　　BEER GARDEN

(Map p356; ☎089-383 8730; www.chinaturm.de; Englischer Garten 3; ⏰10am-11pm late Apr-Oct; 🚌Chinesischer Turm, 🚋Tivolistrasse) This one's hard to ignore because of its English Garden location and pedigree as Munich's oldest beer garden (open since 1791). Camera-toting tourists and laid-back locals, picnicking families and businesspeople sneaking a sly brew clomp around the wooden pagoda, showered by the strained sounds of possibly the world's drunkest oompah band.

P1　　　CLUB

(Map p356; www.p1-club.de; Prinzregentenstrasse 1; ⏰11pm-4am Tue-Sat; 🚌Nationalmuseum/Haus der Kunst) If you make it past the notorious face control at Munich's premier late spot, you'll encounter a crowd of Bundesliga reserve players, Q-list celebs and quite a few Russian speakers too busy seeing and being seen to actually have a good time. But it's all part of the fun, and the decor and summer terrace have their appeal.

Hirschau　　　BEER GARDEN

(www.hirschau-muenchen.de; Gysslingstrasse 15; ⏰noon-11pm Mon-Fri, from 11am Sat & Sun; Ⓤ Dietlindenstrasse) This mammoth beer garden in the northern half of the English Garden can seat 1700 quaffers and hosts live music almost every day in the summer months. When the picnic is over, dispatch the kids to the large playground while you indulge in some tankard caressing.

Cafe Zeitgeist　　　CAFE

(Map p356; Türkenstrasse 74; ⏰9am-1am Sun-Thu, to 3am Fri & Sat; 🚌Schellingstrasse) Go with the zeitgeist and take a pew at this perfect spot where you can enjoy a hearty breakfast or pore over coffee and cake as you watch, from a shady courtyard, the steady flow of students and hipsters wandering along Türkenstrasse.

Seehaus　　　BEER GARDEN

(Map p356; Kleinhesselohe 3; ⏰10am-1am; Ⓢ Münchner Freiheit) On the shores of the English Garden's Kleinhesseloher See, Seehaus has a family-friendly beer garden with an attached restaurant that can be described as almost-upmarket.

Black Bean　　　CAFE

(Map p356; Amalienstrasse 44; ⏰7am-7pm Mon-Fri, from 8am Sat & Sun; 🛜; Ⓤ Universität) If you thought the only decent brew Bavarians could mash was beer, train your Arabica radar to this regional retort to Starbucks. The organic coffee gets tops marks, as do the muffins.

Schall & Rauch　　　BAR

(Map p356; Schellingstrasse 22; ⏰10am-1am Sun-Thu, to 3am Fri & Sat; 🛜; Ⓤ Universität) The few battered cafe chairs and vintage barstools get bagged quickly at this small, friendly, open-fronted bar, meaning drinkers often spill out onto Schellingstrasse even during the day. With a long menu of drinks and an easygoing feel, this is a relaxing place for lunch or a last weekend drink at 2am.

OUT & ABOUT IN MUNICH

Homosexuality is legal in Bavaria, but the scene, even in Munich, is tiny compared to, say, Berlin or Cologne. Homosexuality is widely accepted, and gays will experience no hostility in the capital. There are websites aplenty, but most are in German only. Try www. gay-web.de or, for women, www.lesarion.de. The **Schwules Kommunikations und Kulturzentrum** (Map p344; ☑ 089-856 346 400; www.subonline.org; Müllerstrasse 14; ☺ 7-11pm Sun-Thu, to midnight Fri, 8pm-1am Sat; ⓓ Müllerstrasse) in the city centre is a gay information agency. Lesbians can also turn to **Le Tra** (Map p344; ☑ 089-725 4272; www.letra.de; Angertorstrasse 3; ☺ 2.30-5pm Mon & Wed; ⓓ Müllerstrasse).

The main street parties of the year are Christopher Street Day (p360), held on Marienplatz on the second weekend in July, and the Hans Sachs Strassenfest (p360), held in mid-August along Hans-Sachs-Strasse in the Glockenbachviertel.

Bars & Clubs

Ochsengarten (Map p344; www.ochsengarten.de; Müllerstrasse 47; ☺ 8pm-3am Sun-Thu, 8pm-late Fri & Sat; ⓓ Müllerstrasse) The first bar to open in the Bavarian capital where you have to be clad in leather, rubber, lycra, neopren or other kinky attire to get in. Gay men only.

Edelheiss (Map p344; www.edelheiss.de; Pestalozzistrasse 6; ☺ 3pm-1am Mon-Thu, to 3am Fri & Sat; ⓓ Sendlinger Tor, Ⓤ Sendlinger Tor) A laid-back cafe by day, Edelheiss has vibrant gay party nights, especially at weekends.

Prosecco (Map p344; www.prosecco-munich.de; Theklastrasse 1; ☺ from 10pm; ⓓ Müllerstrasse) Fun venue for dancing, cruising and drinking that attracts a mixed bunch of party people with quirky decor and a cheesy mix of music (mostly '80s and charts).

NY Club (Map p362; www.nyclub.de; Elisenstrasse 3; ☺ 11pm-7am Thu-Sat; ⓓ Hauptbahnhof, Ⓤ Hauptbahnhof, Ⓢ Hauptbahnhof) After a move to near the Old Botanical Gardens, it's again 'Raining Men' at Munich's hottest gay dance temple, where you can party away with Ibiza-style abandon on the cool, main floor.

🍺 Westend & Theresienwiese

★ **Augustiner Bräustuben**　　BEER HALL
(Map p378; ☑ 089-507 047; www.braeustuben. de; Landsberger Strasse 19; ☺ 10am-midnight; ⓓ Holzapfelstrasse) Depending on the wind direction, the bitter-sweet aroma of hops envelops you as you approach this traditional beer hall inside the Augustiner brewery. The Bavarian fare is superb, especially the *Schweinshaxe* (pork knuckle). Due to the location, the atmosphere in the evenings is slightly more authentic than that of its city-centre cousins, with fewer tourists at the long tables.

★ **Harry Klein**　　CLUB
(Map p378; ☑ 089-4028 7400; www.harryklein club.de; Sonnenstrasse 8; ☺ from 11pm; ⓓ Karlsplatz, Ⓢ Karlsplatz, Ⓤ Karlsplatz) Follow the gold-lined passageway off Sonnenstrasse to what some regard as one of the best *Elektro-clubs* in the world. Nights here are an amazing alchemy of electro sound and visuals, with live video art projected onto the walls Kraftwerk-style and blending to awe-inspiring effect with the music.

Strom Club　　CLUB
(Map p378; www.strom-muc.de; Lindwurmstrasse 88; ☺ from 8pm, see website for dates; Ⓤ Poccistrasse) Indie rock, postpunk, and underground are the speciality of this industrial club near the Theresienwiese. Live bands, both local and international, and DJs keep the crowd jumping till the early hours.

☆ Entertainment

As you might expect from a major metropolis, Munich's entertainment scene is lively and multifaceted, though not particularly edgy. You can hobnob with high society at the opera or the chic P1 disco, hang with the kids at an indie club, catch a flick alfresco or watch one of Germany's best soccer teams.

Tickets to cultural and sporting events are available at venue box offices and official ticket outlets, such as Zentraler Kartenvorverkauf (p378). Outlets are also good for online bookings, as is München Ticket (p378), which shares premises with the tourist office.

Cinemas

For show information check any of the listings publications. Movies presented in their original language are denoted in listings by the acronym OF *(Originalfassung)* or OV *(Originalversion);* those with German subtitles are marked OmU *(Original mit Untertiteln).*

Museum-Lichtspiele   CINEMA
(Map p374; ☑ 089-482 403; www.museum-licht-spiele.de; Lilienstrasse 2; ⓖ Deutsches Museum) Cult cinema with wacky interior and screenings of the *Rocky Horror Picture Show* (11.10pm Friday and Saturday nights). Shows English-language movies.

Cinema   CINEMA
(Map p362; ☑ 089-555 255; www.cinema-muenchen.de; Nymphenburger Strasse 31; Ⓤ Stiglmaierplatz) Cult cinema with all films in English.

Classical & Opera

Bayerische Staatsoper   OPERA
(Bavarian State Opera; Map p344; ☑ 089-2185 1025; www.staatsoper.de; Max-Joseph-Platz 2; ⓖ Nationaltheater) One of the world's best opera companies, the Bavarian State Opera performs to sell-out crowds at the Nationaltheater (Map p344) in the Residenz and puts the emphasis on Mozart, Strauss and Wagner. In summer it hosts the prestigious Opernfestspiele (p360). The opera's house band is the Bayerisches Staatsorchester, in business since 1523 and thus Munich's oldest orchestra.

Münchner Philharmoniker   CLASSICAL MUSIC
(Map p374; ☑ 089-480 985 500; www.mphil.de; Rosenheimer Strasse 5; ⓖ mid-Sep–Jun; ⓖ Am Gasteig) Munich's premier orchestra regularly performs at the Gasteig Cultural Centre (Map p374; ☑ tickets 089-548 181 81; www.gasteig.de). Book tickets early, as performances usually sell out.

BR-Symphonieorchester   CLASSICAL MUSIC
(☑ 089-590 001; www.br-so.com) Charismatic Lithuanian maestro Mariss Jansons has rejuvenated this orchestra's playlist and often performs with its choir at such venues as the Gasteig and the Prinzregententheater (Map p374; ☑ 089-218 502; www.theaterakademie.de; Prinzregentenplatz 12; Ⓢ Prinzregentenplatz).

Staatstheater am
Gärtnerplatz   PERFORMING ARTS
(Map p344; ☑ 089-2185 1960; www.gaertner platztheater.de; Gärtnerplatz 3; ⓖ Reichenbachplatz) Spruced up to southern German standards for its 150th birthday in November 2015, this grand theatre specialises in light opera, musicals and dance.

Jazz

Jazzclub Unterfahrt
im Einstein   LIVE MUSIC
(Map p374; ☑ 089-448 2794; www.unterfahrt.de; Einsteinstrasse 42; ⓖ from 9pm; Ⓤ Max-Weber-Platz) Join a diverse crowd at this long-established, intimate club for a mixed bag of acts ranging from old bebop to edgy experimental. The Sunday open-jam session is legendary.

Jazzbar Vogler   JAZZ
(Map p344; www.jazzbar-vogler.com; Rumfordstrasse 17; €2-6; ⓖ 7pm-midnight Mon-Thu, to 1am Fri & Sat; ⓖ Reichenbachplatz) This intimate watering hole brings some of Munich's baddest cats to the stage. You never know who'll show up for Monday's jam session, and Tuesday to Thursday are live piano nights, but the main acts take to the stage on Friday and Saturday. Cash only.

Café am Beethovenplatz   JAZZ
(Map p378; ☑ 089-552 9100; Goethestrasse 51; ⓖ 9am-1am; Ⓢ Sendlinger Tor) Downstairs at the Hotel Mariandl (p364), this is Munich's oldest music cafe. It has an eclectic menu of sounds ranging from bossa nova to piano to Italian *canzoni* (songs). Reservations advised.

Theatre

Bayerisches Staatsschauspiel   THEATRE
(☑ 089-2185 1940; www.residenztheater.de) This leading ensemble has gone alternative in recent years, staging Shakespeare, Schiller and other tried-and-true playwrights in 21st-century garb and the like. Performances are in the Residenztheater (Map p344; Max-Joseph-Platz 2; ⓖ Nationaltheater), the Theater im Marstall (Map p344; Marstallplatz 4; ⓖ Kammerspiele) and the Cuvilliés-Theater (p342).

Münchner Kammerspiele   THEATRE
(Map p344; ☑ 089-2339 6600; www.muenchner -kammerspiele.de; Maximilianstrasse 26; ⓖ Kammerspiele) A venerable theatre with an edgy bent, the Kammerspiele delivers provocative interpretations of the classics as well as works by contemporary playwrights. Performances are in a beautifully refurbished art nouveau theatre at Maximilianstrasse 26 and in the Neues Haus (Map p344; Falckenbergstrasse 1; ⓖ Kammerspiele), a 21st-century glass cube nearby.

Deutsches Theater   THEATRE
(Map p378; ☑ 089-5523 4444; www.deutsches-theater.de; Schwanthalerstrasse 13; Ⓤ Hauptbahnhof, Ⓢ Hauptbahnhof) On wide and bustling Schwanthalerstrasse, Munich's

Westend & Theresienwiese

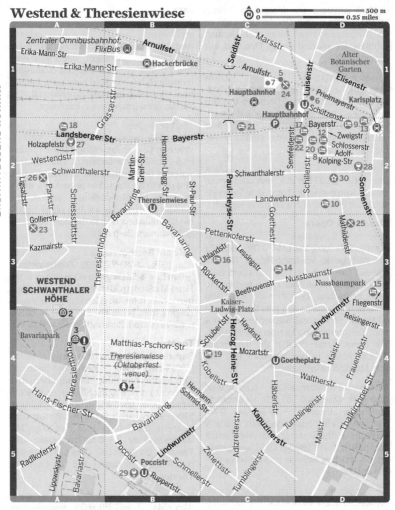

answer to London's West End hosts touring road shows such as *Dirty Dancing*, *The Gruffalo* and *Mamma Mia*.

GOP Varieté Theater THEATRE
(Map p374; ☎089-210 288 444; www.variete.de; Maximilianstrasse 47; Ⓜ Maxmonument) Hosts a real jumble of acts and shows, from magicians to light comedies to musicals.

Zentraler Kartenvorverkauf – Marienplatz BOOKING SERVICE
(Map p344; ☎089-5450 6060; www.zkv-muenchen.de; Marienplatz; ⊗9am-8pm Mon-Sat; Ⓤ Marienplatz) One of the best places to buy tickets to cultural and sporting events. Located in the entrance to the U·STYLE Galeria Kaufhof clothes shop in Marienplatz U-Bahn station.

München Ticket BOOKING SERVICE
(Map p344; ☎089-5481 8181; www.muenchen ticket.de; Marienplatz; ⊗10am-8pm Mon-Sat; Ⓤ Marienplatz, Ⓢ Marienplatz) Tickets for cultural and sporting events in Munich are available from this office within the Neues Rathaus. Enter from Dienerstrasse.

Westend & Theresienwiese

MUNICH SHOPPING

Puppet & Children's Theatre

Münchner Theater für Kinder THEATRE
(Map p362; ☑089-594 545; www.mtfk.de; Dachauer Strasse 46; ⊘3pm daily, 10am Sat, Sun & school holidays; ⓖStiglmaierplatz) At the Münchner Theater für Kinder budding thespians can enjoy fairy tales and children's classics à la *Max & Moritz* and *Pinocchio*.

Münchner Marionettentheater PUPPET THEATRE
(Map p344; ☑089-265 712; www.muema-theater.de; Blumenstrasse 32; ⊘3pm Mon, Wed & Fri, 8pm Sat; ⓖMüllerstrasse) The adorable singing and dancing marionettes performing at the Münchner Marionettentheater have enthralled generations of wee ones.

Spectator Sports

★ FC Bayern München FOOTBALL
(☑089-6993 1333; www.fcbayern.de; Allianz Arena, Werner-Heisenberg-Allee 25, Fröttmaning; ⓤFröttmaning) Germany's most successful team both domestically and on a European level plays home games at the impressive Allianz Arena, built for the 2006 World Cup. Tickets can be ordered online.

EHC München ICE HOCKEY
(Map p368; www.ehc-muenchen.de; Olympia Eishalle, Olympiapark; ⓤOlympiazentrum) It's not one of Germany's premier ice-hockey outfits, but EHC München's games at the Olympic ice rink are exciting spectacles nonetheless;

the team features several Canadian and American players.

🔒 Shopping

Munich is a fun and sophisticated place to shop that goes far beyond chains and department stores. If that's what you want, head to Neuhauser Strasse and Kaufingerstrasse. Southeast of there, Sendlinger Strasse has smaller and somewhat more individual stores. The Glockenbachviertel and Schwabing have many intriguing stores specialising in vintage clothing, books and antiques.

★ Globetrotter SPORTS & OUTDOORS
(Map p344; www.globetrotter.de; Isartorplatz 8-10; ⊘10am-8pm Mon-Sat; ⓤIsartor, ⓢIsartor) Munich's premier outdoors and travel stockist is worth a browse even if you've never pulled on a pair of hiking boots. The basement boasts a lake for testing out kayaks and there's a travel agent and even a branch of the Alpenverein, as well as every travel and outdoor accessory you could ever possibly need. Stocks the best range of maps and guides in the city.

★ Munich Readery BOOKS
(Map p362; www.readery.de; Augustenstrasse 104; ⊘11am-8pm Mon-Fri, 10am-6pm Sat; ⓤTheresienstrasse) With Germany's biggest collection of secondhand English-language titles, the Readery is the place to go in Bavaria for holiday reading matter. In fact we think this may be the only such secondhand bookshop

between Paris and Prague. The shop holds events such as author readings, and there's a monthly book club. See the website for details.

Pick & Weight
CLOTHING

(Map p356; Schellingstrasse 24; ⊙noon-8pm Mon-Sat; Ⓤ Universität) Part of a small national chain, Pick & Weight sells top-notch vintage clothing for between €25 and €95 per kilo. The men's and women's attire, plus accessories, are of the highest quality, and the shop is crammed with exquisite yesteryear pieces.

★ Holareidulijö
CLOTHING

(Map p362; www.holareidulijoe.com; Schellingstrasse 81; ⊙noon-6.30pm Tue-Fri, 10am-1pm Sat May-Sep, 2-6pm Thu & Fri, 11am-1pm Sat Oct-Apr; ⓢ Schellingstrasse) This rare secondhand traditional-clothing store (the name is a phonetic yodel) is worth a look even if you don't intend buying. Apparently, wearing hand-me-down Lederhosen greatly reduces the risk of chafing.

Loden-Frey
CLOTHING

(Map p344; ☏089-210 390; www.lodenfrey.com; Maffeistrasse 5-7; ⊙10am-8pm Mon-Sat; ⓢ Theatinerstrasse) The famous cloth producer stocks a wide range of Bavarian wear and other top-end clothes. The Lederhosen and Dirndl outfits are a cut above the discount night-out versions and prices are accordingly high.

Porzellan Manufaktur Nymphenburg
CERAMICS

(Map p368; ☏089-1791 970; www.nymphenburg.com; Nördliches Schlossrondell 8; ⊙10am-5pm Mon-Fri; ⓢ Schloss Nymphenburg) Traditional and contemporary porcelain masterpieces by the royal manufacturer. Prices are high.

Manufactum
HOMEWARES

(Map p344; www.manufactum.de; Dienerstrasse 12; ⊙9.30am-7pm Mon-Sat; ⓢ Marienplatz, Ⓡ Marienplatz) Anyone with an admiration for top-quality design from Germany and further afield should make a beeline for this store. Last-a-lifetime household items compete for shelf space with retro toys, Bauhaus lamps and times-gone-by stationery. The stock changes according to the season.

Words' Worth Books
BOOKS

(Map p356; www.wordsworth.de; Schellingstrasse 3; ⊙9am-8pm Mon-Fri, 10am-4pm Sat; ⓢ Schellingstrasse) You will find tonnes of English-language books, from secondhand novels to the latest bestsellers, at this excellent and long-established bookstore.

7 Himmel
CLOTHING

(Map p344; www.siebterhimmel.com; Hans-Sachs-Strasse 17; ⊙11am-7pm Mon-Fri, 10am-6pm Sat; ⓢ Müllerstrasse) Couture cool-hunters will be in seventh heaven (a translation of the boutique's name) when browsing the assortment of fashions and accessories by indie labels sold at surprisingly reasonable prices.

Schuster
SPORTS & OUTDOORS

(Map p344; Rosenstrasse 1-5; ⊙10am-8pm Mon-Sat; ⓢ Marienplatz, Ⓤ Marienplatz) Get tooled up for the Alps at this sports megastore boasting seven shiny floors of equipment, including cycling, skiing, travel and camping paraphernalia.

Bottles & Glashaus
GLASS

(Map p344; www.bottles.de; Josephspitalstrasse 1; ⊙10am-7pm Mon-Fri, to 6pm Sat; ⓢ Sendlinger Tor, Ⓤ Sendlinger Tor) If it's made of glass, this wonderfully stocked backstreet shop sells it, from jam jars to wine glasses, marbles to vases, paperweights to Venetian-style beads.

Flohmarkt im Olympiapark
MARKET

(Map p368; Olympiapark; ⊙7am-4pm Fri & Sat; ⓢ Olympiapark West) Large flea market held outside the Olympiastadion.

Stachus Passagen
MALL

(Map p344; www.stachus-passagen.de; Karlsplatz/Stachus; ⊙9.30am-8pm Mon-Sat; ⓢ Karlsplatz, ⓢ Karlsplatz, Ⓤ Karlsplatz) Europe's biggest underground shopping mall, with 36 escalators and 250,000 shoppers a day wandering its 58 mainstream shops.

❶ Information

DANGERS & ANNOYANCES

During Oktoberfest crime and staggering drunks are major problems, especially around the Hauptbahnhof. It's no joke: drunks in a crowd trying to make their way home can get violent, and there are around 100 cases of assault every year. Leave early or stay cautious – if not sober – yourself.

Strong and unpredictable currents make cooling off in the Eisbach creek in the Englischer Garten more dangerous than it looks. Exercise extreme caution; there have been deaths.

Fast-moving bikes in central Munich are a menace. Make sure you don't wander onto bike lanes, especially when waiting to cross the road and when alighting from buses and trams.

EMERGENCY

Ambulance	☏192 22
Fire	☏112
Police	☏110

INTERNET ACCESS

As across the rest of Europe, internet cafes are generally a thing of the past. Wi-fi is widespread and often free. Most public libraries offer internet access to nonresidents. Check www.muenchner-stadtbibliothek.de (in German) for details.

MEDICAL SERVICES

The US and UK consulates can provide lists of English-speaking doctors.

Ärztlicher Hausbesuchdienst (☑089-555 566; www.ahd-hausbesuch.de; ⏲24hr) Doctor for home and hotel visits.

Bereitschaftsdienst der Münchner Ärzte (☑116 117; ⏲24hr) Evening and weekend nonemergency medical services with English-speaking doctors.

Emergency dentist (☑089-3000 5515; ⏲24hr)

Emergency pharmacy (www.apotheken.de) Online referrals to the nearest open pharmacy. Most pharmacies have employees who speak passable English, but there are several designated international pharmacies with staff fluent in English, including **Internationale Ludwigs-Apotheke** (☑089-550 5070; www.ludwigsapo.de; Neuhauser Strasse 11; ⏲9am-8pm Mon-Sat; Ⓤ Marienplatz).

Schwabing Hospital (☑089-30 680; Kölner Platz 1; Ⓤ Scheidplatz) Accident and Emergency department.

MONEY

ATMs abound in the city centre, though not all take every type of card. All major credit cards are widely accepted.

Reisebank (Bahnhofplatz 2; ⏲7am-10pm; ⒮Hauptbahnhof, Ⓤ Hauptbahnhof, ⒮Hauptbahnhof) Best place to change and withdraw money at the Hauptbahnhof.

POST

Post office (Map p344; Alter Hof 6-7; ⏲9am-6.30pm Mon-Fri, 9.30am-12.30pm Sat; Ⓤ Marienplatz, ⒮Marienplatz) For additional branches, search www.deutschepost.de.

TOURIST INFORMATION

There are branches of the tourist office at the **Hauptbahnhof** (Map p378; ☑089-21 800; www.muenchen.de; Bahnhofplatz 2; ⏲9am-8pm Mon-Sat, 10am-6pm Sun; ⒮Hauptbahnhof, Ⓤ Hauptbahnhof, ⒮Hauptbahnhof) and on the **Marienplatz** (Map p344; ☑089-2339 6500; www.muenchen.de; Marienplatz 2; ⏲9am-7pm Mon-Fri, to 4pm Sat, 10am-2pm Sun; Ⓤ Marienplatz, ⒮Marienplatz).

Castles & Museums Infopoint (Map p344; ☑089-2101 4050; www.infopoint-museen-bayern.de; Alter Hof 1; ⏲10am-6pm Mon-Sat; Ⓤ Marienplatz, ⒮Marienplatz) Central information point for museums and palaces throughout Bavaria.

ⓘ MUNICH CITY TOUR CARD

The **Munich City Tour Card** (www.citytourcard-muenchen.com; 1/3 days €12.90/24.90) includes all public transport in the *Innenraum* (Munich city – zones 1 to 4, marked white on transport maps) and discounts of between 10% and 50% for over 80 attractions, tours, eateries and theatres. These include the Residenz, the BMW Museum and the Bier & Oktoberfestmuseum. It's available at some hotels, tourist offices, Munich public transport authority (MVV) offices and U-Bahn, S-Bahn and DB vending machines.

ⓘ Getting There & Away

AIR

Munich Airport (MUC; ☑089-975 00; www.munich-airport.de), aka Flughafen Franz-Josef Strauss, is second in importance only to Frankfurt for international and domestic connections. The main carrier is Lufthansa, but over 80 other companies operate from the airport's two runways, from major carriers such as British Airways and Emirates to minor operations such as Luxair and Air Malta.

Only one major airline from the UK doesn't use Munich's main airport – Ryanair flies into Memmingen's **Allgäu Airport** (FMM; ☑08331-984 2000; www.allgaeu-airport.de; Am Flughafen 35, Memmingen), 125km to the west.

BUS

The **Zentraler Omnibusbahnhof** (Central Bus Station, ZOB; Map p378; www.muenchen-zob.de; Arnulfstrasse 21; ⒮Hackerbrücke) next to the Hackerbrücke S-Bahn station handles the vast majority of international and domestic coach services. There's a Eurolines/Touring office, a supermarket and various eateries on the 1st floor; buses depart from ground level.

The main operator out of the ZOB is now low-cost coach company **Flixbus** (Map p378; ☑030 300 137 300; www.flixbus.com; Zentraler Omnibusbahnhof, Arnulfstrasse 21), which links Munich to destinations across Germany and beyond.

A special Deutsche Bahn express coach leaves for Prague (€70, 4¾ hours, three daily) from the ZOB.

TRAIN

Train connections from Munich to destinations in Bavaria are excellent and there are also numerous services to more distant cities within Germany and around Europe. All services leave from the **Hauptbahnhof** (Central Station).

Staffed by native English speakers, **Euraide** (www.euraide.de; Desk 1, Reisezentrum,

Hauptbahnhof; ⊙10am-7pm Mon-Fri Mar-Apr & Aug-Dec, 9.30am-8pm May-Jul; 🚇 Hauptbahnhof, Ⓤ Hauptbahnhof, Ⓢ Hauptbahnhof) is a friendly agency based at the Hauptbahnhof that sells all DB (Deutsche Bahn) products, makes reservations and creates personalised rail tours of Germany and beyond.

Connections from Munich:

Augsburg €14.60 to €20, 30 to 50 minutes, thrice hourly

Baden-Baden €80, four hours, hourly (change in Mannheim)

Berlin €150, 5¼ hours, hourly

Cologne €147, 4½ hours, hourly

Frankfurt €105, 3¼ hours, hourly

Freiburg €100, 4½ hours, hourly (change in Mannheim or Karlsruhe)

Nuremberg €40-€60, one hour, twice hourly

Regensberg €29.70, 1½ hours, hourly

Vienna €99, four hours, every two hours

Würzburg €74, two hours, twice hourly

Zürich €84, 4¾ hours, thrice daily

❶ Getting Around

Central Munich is compact enough to explore on foot. The outlying suburbs are easily reachable by public transport, which is extensive and efficient.

TO/FROM THE AIRPORT

Munich Airport Linked by S-Bahn (S1 and S8) to the Hauptbahnhof. The trip costs €10.80, takes about 40 minutes and runs every 20 minutes almost 24 hours a day. The Lufthansa Airport Bus shuttles at 20-minute intervals between the airport and Arnulfstrasse, next to the Hauptbahnhof, between 5.15am and 7.55pm. The trip takes about 45 minutes and costs €10.50 (return €17). A taxi from Munich Airport to the Altstadt costs €50 to €70.

Allgäu Airport The Allgäu Airport Express also leaves from Arnulfstrasse at the Hauptbahnhof, making the trip up to seven times a day. The journey takes one hour 40 minutes and the fare is €13 (return €19.50).

CAR & MOTORCYCLE

Driving in central Munich can be a nightmare; many streets are one-way or pedestrian only, ticket enforcement is Orwellian and parking is a nightmare. Car parks (indicated on the tourist-office map) charge about €1.70 to €2.20 per hour.

PUBLIC TRANSPORT

Munich's efficient public-transport system is composed of buses, trams, the U-Bahn and the S-Bahn. It's operated by MVV (www.mvv-muenchen.de), which maintains offices in the U-Bahn stations at Marienplatz, the Hauptbahnhof, Sendlinger Tor, the Ostbahnhof and Poccistrasse. Staff hand out free network maps and timetables, sell tickets and answer questions.

Automated trip planning in English is best done online. The U-Bahn and S-Bahn run almost 24 hours a day, with perhaps a short gap between 2am and 4am. Night buses and trams operate in the city centre.

Tickets & Fares

The city-of-Munich region is divided into four zones, with most places of visitor interest (except Dachau and the airport) conveniently clustering within the white *Innenraum* (inner zone).

Single tickets cost €2.70. Children aged between six and 14 pay a flat €1.40 regardless of the length of the trip. Day passes are €6.70 for individuals and €12.80 for up to five people travelling together; a weekly pass called an IsarCard costs €15.40. Bikes cost €3 to take aboard and may only be taken on *U-Bahn* and S-Bahn trains, but not during the 6am to 9am and 4pm to 6pm rush hours.

Bus drivers sell single tickets and day passes, but tickets for the U-Bahn and S-Bahn and other passes must be purchased from vending machines at stations or MVV offices. Tram tickets are available from vending machines on board. Most tickets must be stamped (validated) at station platform entrances and on board buses and trams before use. The fine for getting caught without a valid ticket is €40.

TAXI

Taxis cost €3.70 at flag fall plus €1.90 per kilometre and are not much more convenient than public transport. Luggage is sometimes charged at €1.50 per piece. Ring a taxi on 216 10 or 194 10. Taxi ranks are indicated on the city's tourist map.

AROUND MUNICH

Dachau

📋 08131 / POP 46,900

Officially called **KZ-Gedenkstätte Dachau** (Dachau Concentration Camp Memorial Site; 📋 08131-669 970; www.kz-gedenkstaette-dachau.de; Peter-Roth-Strasse 2a, Dachau; ⊙9am-5pm) **FREE**, this was the Nazis' first concentration camp, built by Heinrich Himmler in March 1933 to house political prisoners. All in all, it 'processed' more than 200,000 inmates, killing at least 43,000, and is now a haunting memorial. Expect to spend two to three hours here to fully absorb the exhibits. Note that children aged under 12 may find the experience too disturbing.

The place to start is the **visitors centre**, which houses a bookshop, a cafe and a tour-booking desk where you can pick up an audioguide (€4). It's on your left as you enter the main gate. Two-and-a-half-hour tours (€3.50) also run from here at 11am and

1pm (extra tours run at 12.15pm on Sunday between July and September).

You pass into the compound itself through the Jourhaus, originally the only entrance. Set in wrought iron, the infamous, chilling slogan 'Arbeit Macht Frei' (Work Sets You Free) hits you at the gate.

The museum is at the southern end of the camp. Here, a 22-minute English-language documentary runs at 10am, 11.30am, 12.30pm, 2pm and 3pm and uses mostly postliberation footage to outline what took place here. Either side of the small cinema extends an exhibition relating the camp's harrowing story, from a relatively orderly prison for religious inmates, leftists and criminals to an overcrowded concentration camp racked by typhus, and its eventual liberation by the US Army in April 1945.

Disturbing displays include photographs of the camp, its officers and prisoners (all male until 1944), and of horrifying 'scientific experiments' carried out by Nazi doctors. Other exhibits include a whipping block, a chart showing the system of prisoner categories (Jews, homosexuals, Jehovah's Witnesses, Poles, Roma and other 'asocial' people) and documents on the persecution of 'degenerate' authors banned by the party. There's also a lot of information on the rise of the Nazis and other concentration camps around Europe, a scale model of the camp at its greatest extent and numerous uniforms and everyday objects belonging to inmates and guards.

Outside, in the former roll-call square, is the International Memorial (1968), inscribed in English, French, Yiddish, German and Russian, which reads 'Never Again'. Behind the exhibit building, the bunker was the notorious camp prison where inmates were tortured. Executions took place in the prison yard.

Inmates were housed in large barracks, now demolished, which used to line the main road north of the roll-call square. In the camp's northwestern corner is the crematorium and gas chamber, disguised as a shower room but never used. Several religious shrines, including a timber Russian Orthodox church, stand nearby.

ⓘ Getting There & Away

Dachau is about 16km northwest of central Munich. The S2 makes the trip from Munich Hauptbahnhof to the station in Dachau in 22 minutes. You'll need a two-zone ticket (€5.80) or four strips of a *Streifenkarte* (multiple-journey ticket). Here change to bus 726 alighting at the KZ-Gedenkstätte stop (with almost everyone else).

Schleissheim

📞 089 / POP 11,600

When you've exhausted all possibilities in central Munich, the northern suburb of Schleissheim is well worth the short S-Bahn trip for its three elegant palaces and a high-flying aviation museum, a great way to entertain the kids on a rainy afternoon.

◉ Sights

★ **Neues Schloss Schleissheim** PALACE
(New Palace; www.schloesser-schleissheim.de; Max-Emanuel-Platz 1; adult/concession €4.50/3.50, all 3 palaces €8/6; ⊙9am-6pm Tues-Sun Apr-Sep, 10am-4pm Oct-Mar; 🚇Mittenheimer Strasse) The crown jewel of Schleissheim's palatial trio is the Neues Schloss Schleissheim. This pompous pile was dreamed up by Prince-Elector Max Emanuel in 1701 in anticipation of his promotion to emperor. It never came. Instead he was forced into exile for over a decade and didn't get back to building until 1715. Cash-flow problems required the scaling back of the original plans, but given the palace's huge dimensions and opulent interior, it's hard to imagine where exactly the cuts fell.

Some of the finest artists of the baroque era were called in to create such eye-pleasing sights as the ceremonial staircase, the Victory Hall and the Grand Gallery. There are outstanding pieces of period furniture, including the elector's four-poster bed, intricately inlaid tables, and a particularly impressive ceiling fresco by Cosmas Damian Asam.

The palace is home to the Staatsgalerie (State Gallery), a selection of European baroque art drawn from the Bavarian State Collection, including works by such masters as Peter Paul Rubens, Anthony van Dyck and Carlo Saraceni. The most impressive room here is the Grand Galerie.

Schloss Lustheim PALACE
(www.schloesser-schleissheim.de; adult/concession €3.50/2.50, all 3 palaces €8/6; ⊙9am-6pm Tues-Sun Apr-Sep, 10am-4pm Oct-Mar; 🚇Mittenheimer Strasse) While construction of Prince-Elector Max Emanuel's Neues Schloss Schleissheim was going on, the elector and his retinue resided in the fanciful hunting palace of Schloss Lustheim, on a little island in the eastern Schlosspark. It now provides an elegant setting for porcelain masterpieces from Meissen belonging to the Bayerisches Nationalmuseum.

MUNICH SCHLEISSHEIM

Altes Schloss Schleissheim PALACE
(www.schloesser-schleissheim.de; Maximilian-
shof 1; adult/concession €3/2, all 3 palaces €8/6;
⊙9am-6pm Tues-Sun Apr-Sep, 10am-4pm Oct-
Mar; ⊡ Mittenheimer Strasse) The Altes Schloss
Schleissheim is a mere shadow of its Renaissance self, having been altered and refashioned in the intervening centuries. It
houses paintings and sculpture depicting
religious culture and festivals all over the
world, including an impressive collection of
more than 100 nativity scenes.

Flugwerft Schleissheim MUSEUM
(www.deutsches-museum.de/flugwerft; Ferdinand-
Schulz-Allee; adult/child €7/3; ⊙9am-5pm; ⊡ Mit-
tenheimerstrasse) The Flugwerft Schleissheim,
the aviation branch of the Deutsches Museum, makes for a nice change of pace and
aesthetics from Schleissheim's regal palaces. Spirits will soar at the sight of the lethal
Soviet MiG-21 fighter jet, the Vietnam-era
F-4E Phantom and a replica of Otto Lilien-
thal's 1894 glider, with a revolutionary wing
shaped like Batman's cape. Kids can climb
into an original cockpit, land a plane and
even get their pilot's licence.

ℹ Getting There & Away

To get to Schleissheim, take the S1 (direction
Freising) to Oberschleissheim (€5.80), then
walk along Mittenheimer Strasse for about 15
minutes towards the palaces. On weekdays only,
bus 292 goes to the Mittenheimer Strasse stop.

By car, take Leopoldstrasse north until it becomes Ingolstädter Strasse. Then take the A99
to the Neuherberg exit, at the southern end of
the airstrip.

Starnberger Fünf-Seen-Land

Once a royal retreat and still a popular place
of residence for the rich and famous, the
Fünf-Seen-Land (Five Lakes District) is set
in a glacial plain and makes a fast and easy
escape from the urban bustle of Munich. Organised tourism in these parts is very much
a seasonal affair, but any time is good for
hiking and cycling.

Starnberg is the biggest and most famous
body of water here. The other lakes – Ammersee, Pilsensee, Wörthsee and Wesslinger
See – are smaller and offer more secluded
charm. Swimming, boating and windsurfing are popular activities on all lakes, and
the area is also riddled with a whopping

493km of bike paths and 185km of hiking
trails.

◉ Sights & Activities

★**Kloster Andechs** MONASTERY
(⌨08152-3760; www.andechs.de; Bergstrasse
2, Andechs; ⊙8am-6pm Mon-Fri, 9am-6pm Sat,
9.45am-6pm Sun) FREE Founded in the 10th
century, the gorgeous hilltop monastery of
Andechs has long been a place of pilgrimage, though today more visitors come to
slurp the Benedictines' fabled ales.

Marienmunster ABBEY
(⌨08807-948 940; Klosterhof 10a, Diessen) FREE
A real gem in the baroque architectural style,
Diessen's Marienmunster was built between
1732 and 1739 by the famous architect of the
period, Johann Michael Fischer. The highlights are the stucco and fresco decoration
as well as altarpieces by Tiepolo and Straub.

Buchheim Museum MUSEUM
(www.buchheimmuseum.de; Am Hirschgarten 1,
Bernried; adult/concession €8.50/4; ⊙10am-6pm
Tue-Sun Apr-Oct, to 5pm Nov-Mar) Art fans should
make a special trip to this museum on the
western shore of Starnberger See, espcially if
they have an interest in expressionism. The
Buchheim collection features expressionist
paintings as well as folk items. The building
is set in parkland on the water's edge.

Bike It CYCLING
(⌨08151-746 430; www.bikeit.de; Bahnhofstrasse
1, Starnberg) This all-things-bike company
runs guided bike tours from around €25.

ℹ Information

Starnberger Fünf-Seen-Land Tourist Office
(⌨08151-906 00; www.sta5.de; Hauptstrasse
1, Starnberg; ⊙8am-6pm Mon-Fri, 9am-1pm
Sat May-Oct, 9.30am-5pm Mon-Fri Nov-Apr)
Tourist office covering the entire lakes region.

Tourist Office – Herrsching (⌨08151-
906 040; www.sta5.de; Bahnhofsplatz 3,
Herrsching; ⊙9am-1pm & 2-6pm Mon-Fri, 9am-
1pm Sat May-Sep, 10am-1pm Mon-Fri Oct-Apr)
Tourist office for the Ammersee area.

ℹ Getting There & Away

Starnberg is a half-hour ride on the S6 train from
Munich Hauptbahnhof (€5.80).

From Easter to mid-October **Bayerische-
Seen-Schifffahrt** (⌨08151-8061; www.seen-
schifffahrt.de) runs boat services from Starnberg
to other lakeside towns as well as offering longer
cruises. Boats dock behind the S-Bahn station in
Starnberg.

Bavaria

POP 12.4 MILLION

Best Places to Eat

➡ Bürgerspital Weinstube (p411)

➡ Gaststätte St Bartholomä (p406)

➡ Albrecht Dürer Stube (p434)

➡ Perlacht Acht (p422)

➡ Mittermeier (p415)

Best Places to Stay

➡ Bayerischer Hof (p457)

➡ Hotel Schloss Ort (p462)

➡ Elements Hotel (p453)

➡ Dinkelsbühler Kunst-Stuben (p417)

➡ Schlosshotel Harburg (p420)

Why Go?

From the cloud-shredding Alps to the fertile Danube plain, the Free State of Bavaria is a place that keeps its clichéd promises. Story-book castles bequeathed by an oddball king poke through dark forest, cowbells tinkle in flower-filled meadows, the thwack of palm on Lederhosen accompanies the clump of frothy stein on timber bench, and medieval walled towns go about their time-warped business.

But diverse Bavaria offers much more than the chocolate-box idyll. Learn about Bavaria's state-of-the-art motor industry in Ingolstadt, discover its Nazi past in Nuremberg and Berchtesgaden, sip world-class wines in Würzburg, get on the Wagner trail in Bayreuth or seek out countless kiddy attractions across the state. Destinations are often described as possessing 'something for everyone', but in Bavaria's case this is no exaggeration.

And, whatever you do in Germany's southeast, every occasion is infused with that untranslatable feel-good air of *Gemütlichkeit* (cosiness) that makes exploring the region such an easygoing experience.

When to Go

A winter journey along an off-season, tourist-free Romantic Road really sees the snow-bound route live up to its name. Come the spring, tuck into some seasonal fare as Bavaria goes crazy for asparagus during *Spargelzeit* (from late March). The summer months are all about the beer garden, and this is obviously the best time to savour the region's unsurpassed brews in the balmy, fairy-lit air. Autumn is the time to experience the dreamy haze of the Bavarian Forest and the bustle of Bavaria's cities, revived after the summer's time out.

Bavaria Highlights

1 **Schloss Neuschwanstein**
(p388) Indulging your romantic fantasies at this fairy-tale castle.

2 **Zugspitze**
(p394) Rack-and-pinioning your way to the top of Germany's highest peak.

3 **Berchtesgaden**
(p404) Perching at the Eagle's Nest to enjoy show-stopping Alpine vistas.

4 **Bavarian Forest**
(p464) Striking a trail through the tranquil wilds of this national park.

5 **Dinkelsbühl**
(p416) Going full circle around the town walls of this quaint town.

6 **Königssee**
(p404) Messing around on the waters of this achingly picturesque lake.

7 **Nuremberg**
(p425) Revisiting Bavaria's Nazi past.

8 Savouring a cold one in some of the hundreds of superb **beer gardens, breweries and brewpubs** across the region.

History

For centuries Bavaria was ruled as a duchy in the Holy Roman Empire, a patchwork of nations that extended from Italy to the North Sea. In the early 19th century, a conquering Napoleon annexed Bavaria, elevated it to the rank of kingdom and doubled its size. The fledgling nation became the object of power struggles between Prussia and Austria and, in 1871, was brought into the German Reich by Bismarck.

Bavaria was the only German state that refused to ratify the Basic Law (Germany's near constitution) following WWII. Instead, Bavaria's leaders opted to return to its prewar status as a 'free state', and drafted their own constitution. Almost ever since, the *Land* (state) has been ruled by the Christlich-Soziale Union (CSU), the arch-conservative party that is peculiar to Bavaria. Its dominance of the politics of a single *Land* is unique in postwar Germany, having ruled for all but five of the last 50 years without the need to form a coalition with anyone else. Its sister party, the CDU, operates in the rest of the country by mutual agreement.

❶ Getting There & Around

Munich is Bavaria's main transport hub, second only to Frankfurt in flight and rail connections. Rail is the best way to reach Munich from other parts of Germany, and the best means of getting from the Bavarian capital to other parts of Bavaria. Air links within Bavaria are much less extensive.

Without your own set of wheels in Eastern Bavaria and the Alps, you'll have to rely on bus services, which peter out in the evenings and at weekends. Trips along the Romantic Road can be done by tour bus, although again a car is a better idea. Several long-distance cycling routes cross Bavaria and the region's cities are some of the most cycle friendly in the world, so getting around on two wheels could not be easier.

BAVARIAN ALPS

Stretching west from Germany's remote southeastern corner to the Allgäu region near Lake Constance, the Bavarian Alps (Bayerische Alpen) form a stunningly beautiful natural divide along the Austrian border. Ranges further south may be higher, but these mountains shoot up from the foothills so abruptly that the impact is all the more dramatic.

The region is pocked with quaint frescoed villages, spas and health retreats, and possibilities for skiing, snowboarding, hiking, canoeing and paragliding – much of it year-round. The ski season lasts from about late December until April, while summer activities stretch from late May to November.

One of the largest resorts in the area is Garmisch-Partenkirchen, one of urban Bavaria's favourite getaways. Berchtesgaden, Füssen and Oberstdorf are also good bases.

❶ Getting Around

There are few direct train routes between main centres, meaning buses are the most efficient method of public transport in the Alpine area. If you're driving, sometimes a short cut via Austria works out to be quicker (such as between Garmisch-Partenkirchen and Füssen or Oberstdorf).

Füssen

📞 08362 / POP 15,400

Nestled at the foot of the Alps, tourist-busy Füssen is the southern climax of the Romantic Road, with the nearby castles of Neuschwanstein and Hohenschwangau the highlight of many a southern Germany trip. But having 'done' the country's most popular tourist route and seen Ludwig II's fantasy palaces, there are several other reasons to linger longer in the area. The town of Füssen is worth half a day's exploration and, from here, you can easily escape from the crowds into a landscape of gentle hiking trails and Alpine vistas.

◉ Sights

★ **Schloss Neuschwanstein** CASTLE
(📞 tickets 08362-930 830; www.neuschwanstein. de; Neuschwansteinstrasse 20; adult/child €13/ free, incl Hohenschwangau €25/free; ⏰ 9am-6pm Apr–mid-Oct, 10am-4pm mid-Oct–Mar) Appearing through the mountaintops like a mirage, Schloss Neuschwanstein was the model for Disney's *Sleeping Beauty* castle. King Ludwig II planned this fairy-tale pile himself, with the help of a stage designer rather than an architect. He envisioned it as a giant stage on which to recreate the world of Germanic mythology, inspired by the operatic works of his friend Richard Wagner. The most impressive room is the Sängersaal (Minstrels' Hall), whose frescos depict scenes from the opera *Tannhäuser*.

Built as a romantic medieval castle, work started in 1869 and, like so many of Ludwig's grand schemes, was never finished. For all the coffer-depleting sums spent on it, the king spent just over 170 days in residence.

Completed sections include Ludwig's Tristan and Isolde–themed bedroom, dominated by a huge Gothic-style bed crowned with intricately carved cathedral-like spires; a gaudy artificial grotto (another allusion to Tannhäuser); and the Byzantine-style Thronsaal (Throne Room) with an incredible mosaic floor containing over two million stones. The painting opposite the (throneless) throne platform depicts another castle dreamed up by Ludwig that was never built (he planned many more). Almost every window provides tour-halting views across the plain below.

The tour ends with a 20-minute film on the castle and its creator, and there's a reasonably priced cafe and the inevitable gift shops.

For the postcard view of Neuschwanstein and the plains beyond, walk 10 minutes up to Marienbrücke (Mary's Bridge), which spans the spectacular Pöllat Gorge over a waterfall just above the castle. It's said Ludwig enjoyed coming up here after dark to watch the candlelight radiating from the Sängersaal.

★ **Schloss Hohenschwangau** CASTLE
(☑08362-930 830; www.hohenschwangau.de; Alpseestrasse 30; adult/child €13/free, incl Neuschwanstein €25/free; ⊗8am-5pm Apr–mid-Oct, 9am-3pm mid-Oct–Mar) King Ludwig II grew up at the sun-yellow Schloss Hohenschwangau and later enjoyed summers here until his death in 1886. His father, Maximilian II, built this palace in a neo-Gothic style atop 12th-century ruins left by Schwangau knights. Far less showy than Neuschwanstein, Hohenschwangau has a distinctly lived-in feel where every piece of furniture is a used original. After his father died, Ludwig's main alteration was having stars, illuminated with hidden oil lamps, painted on the ceiling of his bedroom.

It was at Hohenschwangau where Ludwig first met Richard Wagner. The Hohenstaufensaal features a square piano where the hard-up composer would entertain Ludwig with excerpts from his latest creation. Some rooms have frescos from German mythology, including the story of the Swan Knight, *Lohengrin*. The swan theme runs throughout.

Hohes Schloss CASTLE, GALLERY
(Magnusplatz 10; adult/child €6/free; ⊗galleries 11am-5pm Tue-Sun Apr-Oct, 1-4pm Fri-Sun Nov-Mar) The Hohes Schloss, a late-Gothic confection and one-time retreat of the bishops of Augsburg, towers over Füssen's compact historical centre. The north wing of the palace contains the Staatsgalerie (State Gallery), with regional paintings and sculpture from the 15th and 16th centuries. The Städtische

Gemäldegalerie (City Paintings Gallery) below is a showcase of 19th-century artists.

Tegelbergbahn CABLE CAR
(www.tegelbergbahn.de; one-way/return €13.30/20.60; ⊗9am-5pm) For fabulous views of the Alps and the Forggensee, take this cable car to the top of the Tegelberg (1730m), a prime launching point for hang-gliders and parasailers. From here it's a wonderful hike down to the castles (two to three hours; follow the signs to Königsschlösser). To get to the valley station, take RVO bus 73 or 78 (www.rvo-bus.de) from Füssen Bahnhof.

Museum Füssen MUSEUM
(Lechhalde 3; adult/child €6/free; ⊗11am-5pm Tue-Sun Apr-Oct, 1-4pm Fri-Sun Nov-Mar) Below the Hohes Schloss, and integrated into the former Abbey of St Mang, this museum highlights Füssen's heyday as a 16th-century violin-making centre. You can also view the abbey's festive baroque rooms, Romanesque cloister and the St Anna Kapelle (AD 830) with its famous 'Dance of Death' paintings.

🛏 Sleeping

Old Kings Hostel HOSTEL €
(☑08362-883 4090; www.oldkingshostel.com; Franziskanergasse 2; dm €22, d from €44; ☎) This great design hostel tucked away in the mesh of lanes in the old town has two dorms and three doubles, all with a different quirky, but

---

CASTLE TICKETS & TOURS

Schloss Neuschwanstein and Schloss Hohenschwangau can only be visited on guided tours (in German or English), which last about 35 minutes each (Hohenschwangau is first). Strictly timed tickets are available from the Ticket Centre (☑08362-930 830; www.hohenschwangau.de; Alpseestrasse 12; ⊗7.30am-5pm Apr–mid-Oct, 8.30am-3pm mid-Oct–Mar) at the foot of the castles. In summer, come as early as 8am to ensure you get in that day.

Enough time is left between tours for the steep 30- to 40-minute walk between the castles. Alternatively, you can take a horse-drawn carriage, which is only marginally quicker.

Tickets for the Museum of the Bavarian Kings (p390) can be bought at the Ticket Centre and at the museum itself.

All Munich's tour companies run day excursions out to the castles.

DON'T MISS

MUSEUM DER BAYERISCHEN KÖNIGE

Palace-fatigued visitors often head straight for the bus stop, coach park or nearest beer after a tour of the castles, most overlooking this worthwhile **museum** (Museum of the Bavarian Kings; www.museumderbayerischenkoenige.de; Alpseestrasse 27; adult/child €11/free; ⊙9am-5pm), installed in a former lakeside hotel 400m from the castle ticket office (heading towards Alpsee lake). The architecturally stunning museum is packed with historical background on Bavaria's former first family and well worth the extra legwork.

The big-window views across the stunningly beautiful lake (a great picnic spot) to the Alps are almost as stunning as the Wittelsbach bling on show, including Ludwig II's famous blue-and-gold robe.

not overplayed, theme. Kitchen, continental breakfast, laundry service and local beer are all available and the whole place is kept very neat and tidy.

Bavaria City Hostel   HOSTEL €

(☑08362-926 6980; www.hostelfuessen.com; Reichenstrasse 15; dm/d from €18/44; ☜) The BCH is a colourful, well-run place created out of a part of the Zum Goldenen Posthorn Hotel. Dorms hold four to six people, and while bright, the themes will be a touch 'in-your-face' for some. The nine-bed dorm has a smooth, Japanese-Oriental thing going on, while the Mountain Lodge is an Alpine dream. Staff can help with most things such as tours and tickets.

★Hotel Sonne   DESIGN HOTEL €€

(☑08362-9080; www.hotel-fuessen.de; Prinzregentenplatz 1; s/d from €90/110; ℙ☜) Although traditional looking from outside, this Altstadt favourite offers an unexpected design-hotel experience within. Themed rooms feature everything from swooping bed canopies to big-print wallpaper, huge pieces of wall art to sumptuous fabrics. The public spaces are littered with pieces of art, period costumes and design features – the overall effect is impressive and slightly unusual for this part of Germany.

Altstadthotel Zum Hechten   HOTEL €€

(☑08362-916 00; www.hotel-hechten.com; Ritterstrasse 6; s €60-85, d €95-120; ℙ☜) This is one of Füssen's oldest hotels and one of its friendliest. Public areas are traditional in style, while the bedrooms are bright and modern with beautifully patterned parquet floors, large beds and sunny colours. The small but classy spa is great for relaxing after a day on the trail.

Fantasia   DESIGN HOTEL €€

(☑08362-9080; www.hotel-fantasia.de; Ottostrasse 1; s €40-80, d €50-100; ☜) This late-19th-century former holiday home for nuns and monks has been converted into a quirky design hotel. The lounge is straight out of a design magazine; the rooms are slightly less wild, but still boast huge ceiling prints of Schloss Neuschwanstein and idiosyncratic furniture. There's a pleasant garden in which to unwind after a hard day's castle hopping.

Steakhaus   GUESTHOUSE €€

(☑08362-509 883; www.steakhouse-fuessen.de; Tiroler Strasse 31; s/d €30/85; ℙ☜) These budget rooms above a restaurant a 10-minute walk south of Füssen town centre, towards the border with Austria, will win no prizes for decor or character, but the location at the Lechfall gorge, with uncluttered views of the Alps, River Lech and surrounding forests, can be pure magic.

✖ Eating

Vinzenzmurr   BAVARIAN €

(Reichenstrasse 35; all dishes under €6; ⊙8am-6pm Mon-Fri, 7.30am-1pm Sat) Füssen branch of the Munich butcher and self-service canteen offering no-nonsense portions of *Leberkäse* (meatloaf) in a bun, goulash soup, *Saures Lüngerl* (goat or beef lung with dumplings), bratwurst and schnitzel as well as something for those crazy vegetarians. No coffee or desserts.

Restaurant Ritterstub'n   GERMAN €€

(☑08362-7759; www.restaurant-ritterstuben.de; Ritterstrasse 4; mains €10-18.50; ⊙11.30am-10pm Tue-Sun) This convivial pit stop has value-priced salads, snacks, lunch specials, fish, schnitzel and gluten-free dishes, and even a cute kids' menu. The medieval knight theme can be a bit grating but does little to distract from the filling food when you arrive hungry from the peaks.

Beim Olivenbauer AUSTRIAN, ITALIAN €€
(☑ 08362-6250; www.beim-olivenbauer.de; Ottostrasse 7; mains €8-19; ⊙ 11.30am-11.30pm) The Tyrol meets the Allgäu at this fun eatery, its interior a jumble of Doric columns, mismatched tables and chairs, multihued paint and assorted rural knick-knackery. Treat yourself to a wheel of pizza and a glass of Austrian wine, or go local with a plate of *Maultaschen* (pork and spinach ravioli) and a mug of local beer.

Zum Franziskaner BAVARIAN €€
(Kemptener Strasse 1; mains €6.50-18; ⊙ 11.30am-10pm) This popular restaurant specialises in *Schweinshaxe* (pork knuckle) and schnitzel, prepared in more varieties than you can imagine. There's some choice for non-carnivores such as *Käsespätzle* (rolled cheese noodles) and salads. When the sun shines the outdoor seating shares the pavement with the 'foot-washing' statue.

Zum Hechten BAVARIAN €€
(Ritterstrasse 6; mains €8-19; ⊙ 10am-10pm) Füssen's best hotel restaurant has six different spaces to enjoy and keeps things regional with a menu of Allgäu staples like schnitzel and noodles, Bavarian pork-themed favourites, and local specialities such as venison goulash from the Ammertal.

❶ Information

Tourist Office (☑ 08362-938 50; www. fuessen.de; Kaiser-Maximilian-Platz; ⊙ 9am-5pm Mon-Fri, 9.30am-3.30pm Sat) Very professionally run operation where staff field questions about the castles with a smile. Can also help find rooms.

BAVARIA FÜSSEN

LUDWIG II, FAIRY-TALE KING

Every year on 13 June, a stirring ceremony takes place in Berg, on the eastern shore of Lake Starnberg. A small boat quietly glides towards a cross just offshore and a plain wreath is fastened to its front. The sound of a single trumpet cuts the silence as the boat returns from this solemn ritual in honour of the most beloved king ever to rule Bavaria: Ludwig II.

The cross approximately marks the spot where Ludwig died under mysterious circumstances in 1886. His early death capped the life of a man at odds with the harsh realities of a modern world no longer in need of a romantic and idealistic monarch.

Prinz Otto Ludwig Friedrich Wilhelm was a sensitive soul, fascinated by romantic epics, architecture and music, but his parents, Maximilian II and Marie, took little interest in his musings and he suffered a lonely and joyless childhood. In 1864, at 18 years old, the prince became king. He was briefly engaged to the sister of Elisabeth (Sisi), the Austrian empress, but, as a rule, he preferred the company of men. He also worshipped composer Richard Wagner, whose Bayreuth opera house was built with Ludwig's funds.

Ludwig was an enthusiastic leader initially, but Bavaria's days as a sovereign state were numbered, and he became a puppet king after the creation of the German Reich in 1871 (which had its advantages, as Bismarck gave Ludwig a hefty allowance). Ludwig withdrew completely to drink, draw up castle plans and view concerts and operas in private. His obsession with French culture and the Sun King, Louis XIV, inspired the fantastical palaces of Neuschwanstein (p388), Linderhof (p393) and Herrenchiemsee (p402) – lavish projects that spelt his undoing.

Contrary to popular belief, it was only Ludwig's purse – and not the state treasury – that was being bankrupted. However, by 1886 his evergrowing mountain of debt and erratic behaviour had put him at odds with his cabinet. The king, it seemed, needed to be 'managed'.

In January 1886, several ministers and relatives arranged a hasty psychiatric test that diagnosed Ludwig as mentally unfit to rule (this was made easier by the fact that his brother had been declared insane years earlier). That June, he was removed to Schloss Berg on Lake Starnberg. A few days later the dejected bachelor and his doctor took a Sunday evening lakeside walk and were found several hours later, drowned in just a few feet of water.

No one knows with certainty what happened that night. There was no eyewitness nor any proper criminal investigation. The circumstantial evidence was conflicting and incomplete. Reports and documents were tampered with, destroyed or lost. Conspiracy theories abound. That summer the authorities opened Neuschwanstein to the public to help pay off Ludwig's huge debts. King Ludwig II was dead, but the myth, and a tourist industry, had been born.

❶ Getting There & Away

BUS

The **Deutsche Touring** (www.touring.de, www.romantic-road.com) **Romantic Road Coach** (p407) leaves from outside Füssen train station (stop 3) at 8am. It arrives in Füssen at 8.30pm.

TRAIN

If you want to do the castles in a single day from Munich, you'll need to start very early. The first train leaves Munich at 4.48am (€28.40, change in Kaufbeuren), reaching Füssen at 6.49am. Otherwise, direct trains leave Munich once every two hours throughout the day.

❶ Getting Around

BUS

RVO buses 78 and 73 (www.rvo-bus.de) serve the castles from Füssen Bahnhof (€4.40 return, eight minutes, at least hourly). Buy tickets from the driver.

Oberammergau

📞 08822 / POP 5400

Quietly quaint Oberammergau occupies a wide valley surrounded by the dark forests and snow-dusted peaks of the Ammergauer Alps. The centre is packed with traditional painted houses, woodcarving shops and awestruck tourists who come here to learn about the town's world-famous Passion Play. It's also a great budget base for hikes and cross-country skiing trips into easily accessible Alpine backcountry.

⊙ Sights

Passionstheater   THEATRE
(📞 08822-941 36; www.passionstheater.de; Othmar-Weis-Strasse 1; tour adult/child €6/2, combined tour & Oberammergau Museum entry €8/3; ⊙ 10am-5pm Tue-Sun) The Passionstheater, where the Passion Play is performed, can be visited as part of a guided tour. The tour provides ample background on the play's history and also lets you peek at the costumes and

sets. Ask the tourist office about music, plays and opera performances that take place here over the summer.

Oberammergau Museum   MUSEUM
(📞 08822-941 36; www.oberammergaumuseum.de; Dorfstrasse 8; adult/child €3.50/1.50, combined museum entry & Passiontheater tour adult/concession €6/5; ⊙ 10am-5pm Tue-Sun Apr-Oct) This is one of the best places to view exquisite examples of Oberammergau's famously intricate woodcarving art. The village has a long tradition of craftspeople producing anything from an entire nativity scene in a single walnut shell to a life-size Virgin Mary. If you get the urge to take some home, plenty of specialist shops around town sell pricey pieces.

Pilatushaus   NOTABLE BUILDING
(📞 08822-949 511; Ludwig-Thoma-Strasse 10; ⊙ 1-6pm Tue-Sun mid-May–mid-Oct) **FREE** Aside from the Passion Play, Oberammergau's other claim to fame is its Lüftmalerei, the eye-popping house facades painted in an illusionist style. The pick of the crop is the amazing Pilatushaus, whose painted columns snap into 3D as you approach. It contains a gallery of glass traditional painting on the 1st floor and several workshops where you can watch demonstrations of local crafts.

🎎 Festivals & Events

★ **Passion Play**   THEATRE
(www.passionplay-oberammergau.com) A blend of opera, ritual and Hollywood epic, the Passion Play has been performed every year ending in a zero (plus some extra years for a variety of reasons) since the late 17th century as a collective thank you from the villagers for being spared the plague.

Half the village takes part, sewing amazing costumes and growing hair and beards for their roles (no wigs or false hair allowed). The next performances will take place between May and October 2020, but tours of

---

WORTH A TRIP

KLOSTER ETTAL

Ettal would be just another bend in the road were it not for this famous **monastery** (www.kloster-ettal.de; Kaiser-Ludwig-Platz 1, Ettal; ⊙ 8.30am-noon & 1.15-5.45pm Mon-Sat, 9-10.45am & 2.30-5.30pm Sun). The highlight here is the sugary rococo basilica housing the monks' prized possession, a marble Madonna brought from Rome by Ludwig der Bayer in 1330. However, some might argue that the real high point is sampling the monastically distilled Ettaler Klosterlikör, an equally sugary herbal digestif.

Ettal is 5km south of Oberammergau, an easy hike along the Ammer River. Otherwise take bus 9606 from Garmisch-Partenkirchen or Oberammergau.

SCHLOSS LINDERHOF

A pocket-sized trove of weird treasures, Schloss Linderhof (www.schlosslinderhof.de; adult/child €8.50/free; ⊙9am-6pm Apr–mid-Oct, 10am-4.30pm mid-Oct–Mar) was Ludwig II's smallest but most sumptuous palace, and the only one he lived to see fully completed. Finished in 1878, the palace hugs a steep hillside in a fantasy landscape of French gardens, fountains and follies. The reclusive king used the palace as a retreat and hardly ever received visitors here. Linderhof was inspired by Versailles and dedicated to Louis XIV, the French 'Sun King'.

Linderhof's myth-laden, jewel-encrusted rooms are a monument to the king's excesses that so unsettled the governors in Munich. The private bedroom is the largest, heavily ornamented and anchored by an enormous 108-candle crystal chandelier weighing 500kg. An artificial waterfall, built to cool the room in summer, cascades just outside the window. The dining room reflects the king's fetish for privacy and inventions. The king ate from a mechanised dining board, whimsically labelled 'Table, Lay Yourself', that sank through the floor so that his servants could replenish it without being seen.

Created by the famous court gardener Carl von Effner, the gardens and outbuildings, open April to October, are as fascinating as the castle itself. The highlight is the oriental-style Moorish Kiosk, where Ludwig, dressed in oriental garb, would preside over nightly entertainment from a peacock throne. Underwater light dances on the stalactites at the Venus Grotto, an artificial cave inspired by a stage set for Wagner's *Tannhäuser*. Now sadly empty, Ludwig's fantastic conch-shaped boat is moored by the shore.

Linderhof is about 13km west of Oberammergau and 26km northwest of Garmisch-Partenkirchen. Bus 9622 travels to Linderhof from Oberammergau nine times a day. If coming from Garmisch-Partenkirchen change in Ettal or Oberammergau. The last service from Linderhof is just before 6pm but, if you miss it, the 13km vista-rich hike back to Oberammergau is an easygoing amble along the valley floor through shady woodland.

the Passionstheater enable you to take a peek at the costumes and sets any time.

The theatre doesn't lie dormant in the decade between Passion Plays – ask the tourist office about music, plays and opera performances that take place here over the summer.

Sleeping & Eating

Gästehaus Richter
B&B €

(☎08822-935 765; www.gaestehaus-richter.de; Welfengasse 2; s €36-42, d €70-85; ☞) The best deal in Oberammergau, this family-run guesthouse offers well-maintained rooms with some traditional Alpine elements, guest kitchen and a hearty breakfast.

DJH Hostel
HOSTEL €

(☎08822-4114; www.oberammergau.jugendherberge.de; Malensteinweg 10; dm from €23) This oddly wood-clad hostel provides immaculate en suite rooms, a guest kitchen and a filling Alpine breakfast.

Hotel Turmwirt
HOTEL €€

(☎08822-926 00; www.turmwirt.de; Ettalerstrasse 2; s/d from €90/115; ☞) This well-maintained hotel next to the church has pristine business-standard rooms, some with Alpine views from the balconies and bits of woodcarving art and traditional Alpine furniture throughout.

Mundart
BAVARIAN €€

(☎08822-949 7565; www.restaurant-mundart.de; Bahnhofstrasse 12; mains €13-21; ⊙5-11pm Wed-Fri, from 11am Sat & Sun; ☞) Mouth-wateringly light, 21st-century versions of Bavarian classics await at this trendy, baby-blue and grey themed restaurant near the train station. The menu is reassuringly brief, prices reasonable and the service the best in the village. Always a choice of dishes for noncarnivores.

❶ Information

Tourist Office (☎08822-922 740; www.ammergauer-alpen.de; Eugen-Papst-Strasse 9a; ⊙9am-6pm Mon-Fri, to 1pm Sat & Sun, closed Sat & Sun Nov-Mar)

❶ Getting There & Away

Hourly trains connect Munich with Oberammergau (change at Murnau; €22, 1¾ hours). Hourly RVO bus 9606 goes direct to Garmisch-Partenkirchen via Ettal; change at Echelsbacher Brücke for Füssen.

Garmisch-Partenkirchen

☎08821 / POP 27,150

The double-barrelled resort of Garmisch-Partenkirchen is blessed with a fabled setting just a snowball's throw from the Alps and is a top hang-out for outdoorsy types, skiing fans and day-trippers from Munich. To say you 'wintered in Garmisch' still has an aristocratic ring, and the area offers some of the best skiing in the land, including runs on Germany's highest peak, the Zugspitze (2962m).

The towns of Garmisch and Partenkirchen were merged for the 1936 Winter Olympics and, to this day, host international skiing events. Each retains its own distinct character: Garmisch has a more 21st-century feel, while Partenkirchen has retained its old-world Alpine village vibe.

⊙ Sights

★ Zugspitze
MOUNTAIN

(Map p395; www.zugspitze.de; return adult/child €56/32; ⊙ train 8.15am-2.15pm) On good days, views from Germany's rooftop extend into four countries. The round trip starts in Garmisch aboard a cogwheel train (Zahnradbahn) that chugs along the mountain base to the Eibsee, an idyllic forest lake. From here, the Eibsee-Seilbahn, a supersteep cable car, swings to the top at 2962m. When you're done admiring the views, the Gletscherbahn cable car takes you to the Zugspitze glacier at 2600m, from where the cogwheel train heads back to Garmisch.

Partnachklamm
CANYON

(Map p395; www.partnachklamm.eu; adult/child €5/2; ⊙ 8am-6pm May & Oct, 6am-10pm Jun-Sep, 9am-6pm Nov-Apr) A top attraction around Garmisch is this narrow and dramatically beautiful 700m-long gorge with walls rising up to 80m. The trail hewn into the rock is especially spectacular in winter when you can walk beneath curtains of icicles and frozen waterfalls.

Jagdschloss Schachen
CASTLE

(Map p395; ☑ 08822-920 30; adult/child €4.50/free; ⊙ tours 11am, 1pm, 2pm & 3pm Jun-Sep) A popular hiking route is to King Ludwig II's hunting lodge, Jagdschloss Schachen, which can be reached via the Partnachklamm in about a four-hour hike (10km). A plain wooden hut from the outside, the interior is surprisingly magnificent; the Moorish Room is something straight out of *Arabian Nights*.

Kirchdorf Wamberg
VILLAGE

(Map p395; Wamberg) For an easy hike accompanied by achingly quaint, chocolate-box views head to Germany's highest Kirchdorf (basically a hamlet with a church where services are held). You can walk from near the hospital (around 45 minutes) or take the Eckbauerbahn lift then walk along the path heading northeast through some exquisite Alpine scenery. The views from the village are worth the effort.

🏃 Activities

★ Zugspitzbahn
RAIL

(Map p396; www.zugspitze.de; return adult/concession €56/32) You can climb Germany's highest mountain on foot...or you can take the train! Trains leave from a special station next to G-P's main train terminus. The first train in the morning departs at 8.15am, the last service from the top at 4.30pm with hourly trains in between.

Deutscher Alpenverein
HIKING

(Map p396; ☑ 08821-2701; www.alpenverein-gapa.de; Carl-Reiser-Strasse 2; ⊙ 4-6pm Tue, 10am-noon Wed & Fri, 4-7pm Thu) The German Alpine Club offers guided hikes and courses and its website is a mine of detailed, expertly updated local information, albeit in German only.

Bergsteigerschule Zugspitze
HIKING

(Map p395; ☑ 08821-589 99; www.bergsteiger-schule-zugspitze.de; Am Kreuzeckbahnhof 12a; ⊙ 8am-noon & 1-5pm Mon-Fri) A mountaineering school offering guided hikes and courses. Located at the lower station of the Alpspitzbahn, southwest of the town.

Skischule
SKIING

(Map p396; ☑ 08821-4931; www.skischule-gap.de; Am Hausberg 8) Offers a high standard of skiing courses as well as equipment hire.

Alpensport Total
SKIING

(Map p396; ☑ 08821-1425; www.alpensporttotal.de; Marienplatz 18; ⊙ 8am-6pm) Winter ski school and hire centre that organises other outdoor activities in the warmer months.

🛏 Sleeping

DJH Hostel
HOSTEL €

(Map p395; ☑ 08821-967 050; www.garmisch.jugendherberge.de; Jochstrasse 10; dm from €26; P @ 🛜) The standards at this smart, immaculately maintained hostel are as good as at some chain hotels. Rooms have Ikea-style furnishings and fruity colour schemes, and there are indoor and outdoor climbing walls if the Alps are not enough. Located 4.5km north of the town.

Transfers from the train station cost a whopping €65 so either walk or catch bus 3 or 4 from outside the train station to Burgrain.

Around Garmisch-Partenkirchen

Around Garmisch-Partenkirchen

★ **Reindl's Partenkirchner Hof**   HOTEL €€
(Map p396; ☎08821-943 870; www.reindls.de;
Bahnhofstrasse 15; s/d €100/150; P 🛜) Reindl's
may not look worthy of its five stars from
street level, but this elegant, tri-winged luxury hotel is stacked with perks, a wine bar
and a top-notch gourmet restaurant. Renovated to perfection on a rolling basis, the
rooms are studies in folk-themed elegance
and some enjoy gobsmacking Alpine views
to get you in the mood.

Gasthof zum Rassen   HOTEL €€
(Map p395; ☎08821-2089; www.gasthof-rassen.
de; Ludwigstrasse 45; s/d from €70/90; P 🛜)
This beautifully frescoed 14th-century
building is home to a great option in this
price bracket, where the simply furnished,
contemporary rooms contrast with the traditionally frilly styling of the communal
areas. The cavernous event hall, which was
formerly a brewery, houses Bavaria's oldest
folk theatre.

Garmisch-Partenkirchen

Garmisch-Partenkirchen

Hotel Garmischer Hof   HOTEL €€
(Map p396; ☎ 08821-9110; www.garmischer-hof.de; Chamonixstrasse 10; s €75-85, d €85-200; 🅿🛜♨) Owned by the Seiwald family since 1928, many a climber, skier and Alpine adventurer has creased the sheets at this welcoming inn. Rooms are elegant and cosy with some traditional Alpine touches, the buffet breakfast is served in the vaulted cafe-restaurant, and there's a spa and sauna providing après-ski relief.

Hostel 2962   HOSTEL €€
(Map p396; ☎ 08821-909 2674; www.hostel 2962-garmisch.com; Partnachauenstrasse 3; dm/d from €25/70; 🛜) Touted as a hostel, the somewhat vibe-less 2962 is essentially a typical Garmisch hotel with seven dorms, but a good choice nonetheless. If you can get into one of the four- or five-bed rooms, it's the cheapest sleep in town. Breakfast is an extra €6 if you stay in a dorm.

🍴 Eating

⭐ **Gasthof Fraundorfer**   BAVARIAN €€
(Map p395; ☎ 08821-9270; www.gasthof-fraun dorfer.de; Ludwigstrasse 24; mains €5-23; ⊗7am-midnight Thu-Mon, from 5pm Wed) If you've travelled to the Alps to experience yodelling, knee slapping and beetroot-faced locals squeezed into Lederhosen, you just arrived at the right address. Steins of frothing ale fuel the increasingly raucous atmosphere as the evening progresses and monster portions of plattered pig meat push belt buckles to the limit. Decor ranges from baroque cherubs to hunting trophies and the 'Sports Corner'. Unmissable.

Zum Wildschütz   BAVARIAN €€
(Map p396; Bankgasse 9; mains €9-20; ⊗11.30am-11pm) The best place in town for fresh venison, rabbit, wild boar and other seasonal game dishes, this place is, not surprisingly, popular with hunters. The Tyrolean and south Bavarian takes on schnitzel aren't bad either. If you prefer your victuals critter free, look elsewhere.

Zirbel   PUB FOOD €€
(Map p396; www.zirbel-stube.de; Promenadestrasse 2; mains €8-20; ⊗5pm-1am) A bit away from the tourist promenade and guarded by a grumpy-looking woodcarved bear, this locally popular, low-beamed and rustically themed pub serves noodle dishes, salads and schnitzel, all helped down with Hofbräu beer. Sadly, it's only open in the evenings.

Bräustüberl
GERMAN €€

(Map p396; ☑ 08821-2312; www.braeustueberl
-garmisch.de; Fürstenstrasse 23; mains €6-19; ⊙ from
5pm Mon-Fri, from 10am Sat & Sun) This quintessentially Bavarian tavern dating from 1663
is the place to cosy up with some local nosh,
served by Dirndl-trussed waitresses, while the
enormous enamel coal-burning stove revives
snow-chilled extremities. Live music and theatre take place in the upstairs hall.

Hofbräustüberl
BAVARIAN, CROATIAN €€

(Map p396; Chamonixstrasse 2; mains €11-20;
⊙11.30am-3pm & 5-11pm; ☎) Balkan spice
meets with German heartiness at this Ba-
varian-Yugoslav restaurant right in the thick
of things. Despite the seemingly *echt-Bayern*
(authentic Bavarian) name, the long menu is
a mixed bag of Alps and Adriatic, the interi-
or understated and quite formal, the service
top notch. The wines from the former Yugoslavia are a rare treat.

❶ Information

Mountain Rescue (☑ 08821-3611, 112; www.
bergwacht-bayern.de; Auenstrasse 7) Mountain
rescue station.

Post Office (Map p396; Bahnhofstrasse 30;
⊙8am-6pm Mon-Fri, to 1pm Sat)

Tourist Office (Map p396; ☑ 08821-180 700;
www.gapa.de; Richard-Strauss-Platz 2; ⊙9am-
5pm Mon-Fri, to 3pm Sat) Friendly staff hand
out maps, brochures and advice.

❶ Getting There & Around

Garmisch-Partenkirchen has hourly connections
from Munich (€22, one hour 20 minutes); special
packages, available from Munich Hauptbahnhof,
combine the return trip with a Zugspitze day ski
pass (around €60).

RVO bus 9606 (www.rvo-bus.de) leaves from
the **bus station** (Map p396; Bahnhofstrasse)
at 9.40am, reaching the Füssen castles at Neuschwanstein and Hohenschwangau two hours
later. On the way back take the 4.18pm bus 9651
and change onto the 9606 at Echelsbacher
Brücke. The same connection runs at 5.18pm for
those who want more time. The 9606 also runs
hourly to Oberammergau (40 minutes).

For bike hire, try **Bikecenter** (Map p396;
☑ 08821-549 46; www.bikeverleih.de; Ludwigstrasse 90; ⊙9am-6.30pm Mon-Fri, to 6pm Sat).

Mittenwald

☑ 08823 / POP 7400

Nestled in a cul-de-sac under snowcapped
peaks, sleepily alluring Mittenwald, 20km
southeast of Garmisch-Partenkirchen, is the
most natural spot imaginable for a resort.

Known far and wide for its master violin
makers, the citizens of this drowsy village
seem almost bemused by its popularity. The
air is ridiculously clean, and on the main
street the loudest noise is a babbling brook.

◉ Sights & Activities

Geigenbaumuseum
MUSEUM

(www.geigenbaumuseum-mittenwald.de; Ballen-
hausgasse 3; adult/child €5.50/2; ⊙10am-5pm
Tue-Sun Feb–mid-Mar & mid-May–mid-Oct, shorter
hours rest of year) Matthias Klotz (1653–1743)
is the man credited with turning Mittenwald
into an internationally renowned centre of
violin making. Learn more about him, the
craft and the instrument itself in the engagingly organised Geigenbaumuseum. There's
still a violin-making school in town today
and the film showing the many steps required in fashioning the instrument is truly
fascinating. The museum is also the venue
for occasional concerts.

Erste Skischule Mittenwald
SKIING

(☑ 08823-3582; www.skischule-mittenwald.de;
Bahnhofsplatz 14; ⊙8am-6pm) Equipment hire
and ski/snowboard instruction.

🛏 Sleeping & Eating

Hotel-Gasthof Alpenrose
HOTEL €€

(☑ 08823-927 00; www.alpenrose-mittenwald.de;
Obermarkt 1; s €34-63, d €80-105; ☎) A purely
Alpine affair, the friendly Hotel-Gasthof Alpenrose has cosy, old-style rooms, a folksy
restaurant and live Bavarian music almost
nightly. Staff can arrange horse-riding trips
for all ages.

Gaststätte Römerschanz
BAVARIAN €€

(Innsbrucker Strasse 30; mains €7-17; ⊙10am-
midnight Wed-Mon; ☎) A short walk from the
Obermarkt, the much-lauded Gaststätte
Römerschanz has a cosy, seasonally decorated interior and Mittenwald's tastiest food
served gourmet-style on odd-shaped plates.

🍷 Drinking

Postkeller
PUB

(www.brauereigaststaette-postkeller.de; Innsbrucker Strasse 13; ⊙10am-late Fri-Tue, from 5pm Thu)
This modern pub belongs to Mittenwald's
very own brewery, and is hence the best
place to try the local lager. It claims to be
Germany's highest altitude brewery.

❶ Information

Tourist Office (☑ 08823-339 81; www.mitten
wald.de; Dammkarstrasse 3; ⊙8.30am-6pm

Mon-Fri, 9am-noon Sat, 10am-noon Sun mid-May–mid-Oct, shorter hours rest of the year) The professional team here keeps a well-maintained website and can help out with just about anything in the Mittenwald area.

ⓘ Getting There & Away

Mittenwald is served by trains from Garmisch-Partenkirchen (€4.90, 20 minutes, hourly), Munich (€22, 1¾ hours, hourly) and Innsbruck (€11.10, one hour, every two hours), across the border in Austria. Otherwise RVO bus 9608 connects Mittenwald with Garmisch-Partenkirchen (30 minutes) several times a day.

Oberstdorf

☐ 08322 / POP 9700

Spectacularly situated in the western Alps, the Allgäu region feels a long, long way from the rest of Bavaria, both in its cuisine (more *Spätzle* than dumplings) and the dialect, which is closer to the Swabian of Baden-Württemberg. The Allgäu's chief draw is the car-free resort of Oberstdorf, a major skiing centre that's just a short hop from Austria.

🏃 Activities

Oberstdorf is almost ringed by towering peaks and offers some top-draw hiking. In-the-know skiers value the resort for its friendliness, lower prices and less-crowded pistes. The village is surrounded by 70km of well-maintained cross-country trails and three ski fields: the Nebelhorn, Fellhorn/Kanzelwand and Söllereck. For ski hire and tuition, try **Alpin Skischule** (☐ 08322-952 90; www.alpinskischule.de; Bahnhofplatz 1a; ⊙8.30am-6pm) opposite the train station or **Erste Skischule Oberstdorf** (☐ 08322-3110; www.skischule-oberstdorf.de; Freiherr-von-Brutscher-Strasse 4).

Eissportzentrum Oberstdorf   ICE SKATING
(☐ 08322-700 5003; www.eissportzentrum-oberstdorf.de; Rossbichlstrasse 2-6) The Eissportzentrum Oberstdorf, behind the Nebelhorn cable-car station, is the biggest ice-skating complex in Germany, with three separate rinks. Check the website for public skating session times.

🛏 Sleeping

Oberstdorf is chock-full of private guesthouses, but owners are usually reluctant to rent rooms for just a single night, even in the quieter shoulder seasons.

Oberstdorf Hostel   HOSTEL €
(☐ 08322-987 8400; www.oberstdorf-hostel.de; Mühlbachstrasse 12; dm/s/d from €20/20/65; P🖤) This very family-friendly hostel in the village of Tiefenbach is around 10 minutes by car from Oberstdorf train station. Rooms with up to six beds are spotless, there's a playground for the kiddies and lots of activities going on. Prices include breakfast and there's a very good-value family package that includes dinner, too.

DJH Hostel   HOSTEL €
(☐ 08322-987 50; www.oberstdorf.jugendherberge. de; Kornau 8; dm €24; 🖤) A relaxed, 200-bed chalet-hostel with commanding views of the Allgäu Alps. Take bus 1 from the bus station in front of the Hauptbahnhof to the Reute stop; it's in the suburb of Kornau, near the Söllereck chairlift.

Haus Edelweiss   APARTMENT €€
(☐ 08322-959 60; www.edelweiss.de; Freibergstrasse 7; apt €50-145; P⊜🖤) As crisp and sparkling as freshly fallen alpine snow, this recently completed apartment hotel just a couple of blocks from the tourist office has 19 pristine, self-contained flats with fully equipped kitchens, ideal for stays of three nights or more. Generally the longer you tarry, the fewer euros per night you spend.

Weinklause   GUESTHOUSE €€
(☐ 08322-969 30; www.weinklause.de; Prinzenstrasse 10; s/d from €75/100; P🖤) Willing to take one-nighting hikers at the drop of a felt hat, this superb lodge offers all shapes and sizes of room and apartment, some with kitchenettes, others with jaw-dropping, spectacular alpine views. A generous breakfast is served in the restaurant, which comes to life most nights with local live music.

🍴 Eating & Drinking

Restaurant-Cafe Allgäu   BAVARIAN €€
(☐ 08322-809 657; www.restaurant-cafe-allgäu.de; Pfarrstrasse 10; mains €12-20; ⊙11.30am-10pm Wed-Sun; 🖤) For the best local Allgäu dishes, head to this long-established, knick-knack-filled restaurant where the pork knuckle, schnitzel, *Kartoffelrösti* (potato fritter) and of course signature *Käsespätzle* all come in Alpine portions. There are plenty of vegetarian dishes and superb local beer on tap.

★Oberstdorfer Dampfbierbrauerei   BREWERY
(www.dampfbierbrauerei.de; Bahnhofplatz 8; ⊙11am-1am Wed-Sun) Knock back a few

'steamy ales' at Germany's southernmost brewery, right next to the train station. The brewery runs free tours in German at 11am every Wednesday.

ℹ Information

Tourist Office (☎ 08322-7000; www.oberst dorf.de; Prinzregenten-Platz 1; ☺9am-5pm Mon-Fri, 9.30am-noon Sat) The tourist office and its **branch office** (☎ 08322-7000; Bahn-hofplatz; ☺10am-5pm) at the train station runs a room-finding service.

ℹ Getting There & Away

There are direct Alex trains from Munich (€22.70, 2½ hours, every two hours), otherwise change in Buchloe or Kempten. The train station is a short walk north of the town centre on Bahnhofstrasse.

Bad Tölz

☎ 08041 / POP 18,500

Situated some 40km south of central Munich, Bad Tölz is a pretty spa town straddling the Isar River. The town's gentle inclines provide a delightful spot for its attractive, frescoed houses and the quaint shops of the old town. At weekends city folk flock here to wander the streets and for hiking trips along the river. Bad Tölz is also the gateway to the Tölzer Land region and its emerald-green lakes, the Walchensee and the Kochelsee.

◉ Sights & Activities

Cobblestoned and car-free, Marktstrasse is flanked by statuesque townhouses with ornate overhanging eaves that look twice as high on the sloping street.

Kalvarienberg　　　　　LANDMARK
(Cavalry Church; Kalvarienberg) Above the town, on Kalvarienberg, looms Bad Tölz' landmark, the twin-towered Kalvarienbergkirche. This enormous baroque structure stands side by side with the petite Leonhardikapelle (Leonhardi Chapel; 1718), the destination of the town's well-known Leonhardifahrt (Leonardi pilgrimage).

Stadtmuseum　　　　　MUSEUM
(☎ 8041-504 688; Marktstrasse 48; adult/child €2/1.50; ☺10am-5pm Tue-Sun) The Stadtmuseum covers all aspects of local culture and history, with a fine collection of painted armoires (the so-called Tölzer Kasten), a 2m-tall, single-stringed *Nonnengeige* (marine trumpet), examples of traditional glass painting and a cart used in the Leonhardifahrt.

Blomberg　　　　　HIKING
Southwest of Bad Tölz, the Blomberg (1248m) is a family-friendly mountain that has easy hiking and a fun Alpine slide in summer and a natural toboggan track in winter. Unless you're walking, getting up the hill involves, weather permitting, a chairlift ride aboard the **Blombergbahn** (www.blombergbahn.de; top station adult/child return €11/5; ☺9am-5pm).

Over 1km long, the fibreglass Alpine toboggan track snakes down the mountain from the middle station. You zip down at up to 50km/h through the 17 hairpin bends on little wheeled bobsleds with a joystick to control braking. A long-sleeved shirt and jeans are recommended to provide a little protection. To reach Blomberg, take RVO bus 9612 from the train station to the Blombergbahn stop.

✷ Festivals & Events

Leonhardifahrt　　　　　CULTURAL
(www.toelzer-leonhardifahrt.bayern; ☺6 Nov) Every year on 6 November, residents pay homage to the patron saint of horses, Leonhard. The famous Leonhardifahrt is a pilgrimage up to the Leonhardi chapel on Kalvarienberg, where townsfolk dress up in traditional costume and ride dozens of garlanded horse carts to the strains of brass bands.

🛏 Sleeping & Eating

Posthotel Kolberbräu　　　　HOTEL €€
(☎ 08041-768 80; www.kolberbraeu.de; Marktstrasse 29; s/d from €50/90; ☼) Posthotel Kolberbräu is a very well-appointed, 30-room inn set amid the bustle of the main street, with hefty timber furniture, a classic Bavarian restaurant and a tradition going back four centuries.

Gasthof Zantl　　　　　BAVARIAN €€
(www.gasthof-zantl.de; Salzstrasse 31; mains €8-18; ☺5pm-late Fri-Mon, plus 11am-2.30pm Sat & Sun) One of Bad Tölz' oldest buildings, this convivial tavern has a predictably pork-heavy menu, with ingredients sourced from local villages as much as possible. There's a sunny beer garden out front.

ℹ Information

Tourist Office (☎ 08041-793 5156; www.bad-toelz.de; Marktstrasse 48; ☺10am-5pm Tue-Sun)

ℹ Getting There & Away

The private **Bayerische Oberlandbahn** (BOB; ☎ 08024-997 171; www.meridian-bob-brb. de) runs trains between Bad Tölz and Munich

(Continued on page 402)

BAVARIA BAD TÖLZ

Romantic Residences

© BAYERISCHE SCHLOSSERVERWALTUNG WWW.SCHLOESSER.BAYERN.DE / TAKASHI IMAGES/SHUTTERSTOCK ©

Think Southern Germany and the Alps, think story-book castles and noble palaces, hilltop ruins and Renaissance splendour – few places on earth boast such a treasure trove of medieval and aristocratic architecture and visiting these stately piles is a key part of any visit to the region.

Schloss Neuschwanstein

One of the world's most romantic castles (p388), King Ludwig II's 19th-century folly inspired Walt Disney's citadel as well as millions of tourists to visit this corner of the Alps. All turrets and pointed towers rising dreamily from the alpine forests, if Bavaria has a single unmissable sight, this is it.

1. Würzburg Residenz (p407), Würzburg **2.** Schloss Linderhof (p393), Oberammergau **3.** Kaiserburg (p425), Nuremberg

Würzburg Residenz

Würzburg's Unesco-listed palace (p407) is one of the country's most exquisite chunks of aristocratic baroque, built by a stellar name of the period, Balthasar Neumann. The highlight of the huge building is without doubt the Grand Staircase whose ceiling boasts the world's largest fresco.

Schloss Linderhof

Another of Ludwig II's wistful follies, this lavish though compact palace (p393) was the only one of his creations he saw finished. The remote location in the foothills of the Alps only heightens the effect of the eye-pleasing symmetry of the outside and the quirkiness of the interior.

Kaiserburg

One of Bavaria's most historically significant fortresses, Nuremberg's Kaiserburg (p425) lords it over the old town of the state's second city. A tour takes you back to medieval times when Nuremberg was one of the key cities in the Holy Roman Empire, the castle was used as a safe box for the empire's trinkets.

(Continued from page 399)

Hauptbahnhof (€13.90, 50 minutes, at least hourly). Alternatively, take the S2 from central Munich to Holzkirchen, then change to the BOB. In Holzkirchen make sure you board the Bad Tölz–bound portion of the train.

Chiemsee

✓ 08051

The Chiemsee is Bavaria's biggest lake (if you don't count Bodensee which is only partially in the state) and its natural beauty and water sports make the area popular with de-stressing city dwellers – many affluent Munich residents own weekend retreats by its shimmering waters. However, the vast majority of foreign visitors arrive at the shores of the Bavarian Sea – as Chiemsee is often called – in search of King Ludwig II's Schloss Herrenchiemsee.

The towns of Prien am Chiemsee and, about 5km south, Bernau am Chiemsee (both on the Munich–Salzburg rail line) are good bases for exploring the lake. Of the two towns, Prien is by far the larger and livelier.

◉ Sights

★ **Schloss Herrenchiemsee** CASTLE
(✓ 08051-688 70; www.herren-chiemsee.de; adult/child €11/free; ⊘ tours 9am-6pm Apr-Oct, 9.40am-4.15pm Nov-Mar) An island just 1.5km across the Chiemsee from Prien, Herreninsel is home to Ludwig II's Versailles-inspired castle. Begun in 1878, it was never intended as a residence, but as a homage to absolutist monarchy, as epitomised by Ludwig's hero, Louis XIV. Ludwig spent only 10 days here and even then was rarely seen, preferring to read at night and sleep all day. The palace is typical of Ludwig's creations, its design the product of his romantic obsessions and unfettered imagination.

Ludwig splurged more money on this palace than on Neuschwanstein and Linderhof combined, but when cash ran out in 1885, one year before his death, 50 rooms remained unfinished. Those that were completed outdo each other in opulence. The vast Gesandtentreppe (Ambassador Staircase), a double staircase leading to a frescoed gallery and topped by a glass roof, is the first visual knock-out on the guided tour, but that fades in comparison to the stunning Grosse Spiegelgalerie (Great Hall of Mirrors). This tunnel of light runs the length of the garden (98m, or 10m longer than that in Versailles). It sports 52 candelabra and 33 great glass chandeliers with 7000 candles,

which took 70 servants half an hour to light. In late July it becomes a wonderful venue for classical concerts.

The Paradeschlafzimmer (State Bedroom) features a canopied bed perching altar-like on a pedestal behind a golden balustrade. This was the heart of the palace, where morning and evening audiences were held. But it's the king's bedroom, the Kleines Blaues Schlafzimmer (Little Blue Bedroom), that really takes the cake. The decoration is sickly sweet, encrusted with gilded stucco and wildly extravagant carvings. The room is bathed in a soft blue light emanating from a glass globe at the foot of the bed. It supposedly took 18 months for a technician to perfect the lamp to the king's satisfaction.

Admission to the palace also entitles you to a spin around the König-Ludwig II-Museum, where you can see the king's christening and coronation robes, more blueprints of megalomaniac buildings and his death mask.

To reach the palace, take the hourly or half-hourly ferry from Prien-Stock or from Bernau-Felden. From the boat landing on Herreninsel, it's about a 20-minute walk through pretty gardens to the palace. Palace tours (in German or English) last 30 minutes.

Fraueninsel ISLAND
A third of this tiny island is occupied by **Frauenwörth Abbey** (www.frauenwoerth.de; Fraueninsel; admission free, tours €4) **FREE**, founded in the late 8th century, making it one of the oldest abbeys in Bavaria. The 10th-century church, whose free-standing campanile sports a distinctive onion-dome top (11th century), is worth a visit. Opposite the church is the AD 860 Carolingian **Torhalle** (admission €2; ⊘ 10am-6pm May-Oct). It houses medieval objets d'art, sculpture and changing exhibitions of regional paintings from the 18th to the 20th centuries.

🏃 Activities

The swimming beaches at Chieming and Gstadt (both free) are the easiest to reach, on the lake's eastern and northern shores respectively. A variety of boats are available for hire at many beaches. In Prien, **Bootsverleih Stöffl** (✓ 08051-2000; www.stoeffl.de; Seestrasse 120, Prien; ⊘ Easter-Oct) is possibly the best company to approach.

Prienavera SWIMMING
(✓ 08051-609 570; www.prienavera.de; Seestrasse 120, Prien; 4hr pass adult/child €12/7, day pass

€14/8; ⊘10am-10pm Mon-Fri, 9am-10pm Sat & Sun) The futuristic-looking glass roof by the harbour in Prien-Stock shelters Prienavera, a popular pool complex with a wellness area, water slides and a restaurant.

🛏 Sleeping

Panorama Camping Harras   CAMPGROUND €
(☑08051-904 613; www.camping-harras.de; Harrasser Strasse 135; per person/tent/car from €9.40/5.80/3.40) This camping ground is scenically located on a peninsula 3km south of Prien with its own private beach. There is water-sports equipment for hire and the restaurant-beer garden has a delightful lakeside terrace.

Hotel Bonnschlössl   HOTEL €€
(☑08051-961 400; www.bonnschloessl.de; Ferdinand-Bonn-Strasse 2, Bernau; s €50-75, d €85-180; ℗🐕) Built in 1477, this pocket-size 21-room palace hotel with faux turrets once belonged to the Bavarian royal court. Rooms are stylish, if slightly overfurnished, and there's a wonderful terrace with a rambling garden. There's a small spa area, a library and a lobby bar, but no restaurant.

Luitpold am See   HOTEL €€
(☑08051-609 100; www.luitpold-am-see.de; Seestrasse 101, Prien; s €60-80, d €115-155; 🐕) Right on the lake shore in Prien, the 54 rooms at this excellent hotel offer a good price to standard ratio, with their pristine bathrooms, wood-rich furnishings and pretty views. There's an on-site restaurant and *Konditorei* (cafe-bakery) and reception can help out with travel arrangements, tours and the like.

🍴 Eating

Alter Wirt   BAVARIAN €€
(www.alter-wirt-bernau.de; Kirchplatz 9, Bernau; mains €10-19; ⊘8am-11pm Tue-Sun) This massive half-timbered inn with seven centuries of history, situated on Bernau's main street, plates up south German meat slabs and international standards to a mix of locals and tourists. For dessert why not try *Heisse Liebe* ('Hot Love') – vanilla and chocolate ice cream with hot raspberry sauce and cream.

Westernacher am See   BAVARIAN €€
(☑08051-4722; www.westernacher-chiemsee.de; Seestrasse 115, Prien; mains €5.50-18.50; ⊘8am-11pm) This busy lakeside dining haven has multiple personalities, with a cosy restaurant, cocktail bar, cafe, beer garden and glassed-in winter terrace. The long menu is an eclectic affair combining pizzas, Bavarian favourites, Italian pasta, Thai curries and Chiemsee fish dishes.

Sallers Badehaus   BAVARIAN €€
(☑08051-966 3450; www.sallers-badehaus.de; Rathausstrasse 11; mains €8-20; ⊘11am-11pm Mon-Fri, from 9am Sat & Sun; 🐕) Near the Chiemsee Tourist Office and the lake shore, this fancy restaurant, contemporary beer hall and garden has quirky decor and gourmet-style fare priced for all wallet capacities.

ℹ Information

Bernau Tourist Office (☑08051-986 80; www.bernau-am-chiemsee.de; Aschauer Strasse 10, Bernau; ⊘9am-6pm Mon-Fri, 9am-noon Sat, slightly shorter hours mid-Sep–mid-Jul)

Chiemsee Tourist Office (☑08051-965 550; www.chiemsee-alpenland.de; Felden 10; ⊘10am-12.30pm & 1.30-6.30pm Mon-Fri) On the southern lake shore, near the Bernau-Felden autobahn exit.

Prien Tourist Office (☑08051-690 50; www.tourismus.prien.de; Alte Rathausstrasse 11, Prien; ⊘8.30am-6pm Mon-Fri, to 4pm Sat, closed Sat Oct-Apr)

ℹ Getting There & Away

If you're day tripping to Herrenchiemsee, conveniently interconnecting transport is available. To explore more, you'll need a set of wheels.

Meridian trains run from Munich to Prien (€20.50, 55 minutes, hourly) and Bernau (€21.50, one hour, hourly). Hourly RVO bus 9505 connects the two lake towns.

ℹ Getting Around

Local buses run from Prien Bahnhof to the harbour in Stock. You can also take the historic **Chiemseebahn** (www.chiemsee-schifffahrt.de; return €4), one of the world's oldest narrow-gauge steam trains (1887).

Chiemsee-Schifffahrt (☑08051-6090; www.chiemsee-schifffahrt.de; Seestrasse 108) operates half-hourly to hourly ferries from Prien with stops at Herreninsel, Fraueninsel, Seebruck and Chieming on a schedule that changes seasonally. You can circumnavigate the entire lake and make all these stops (getting off and catching the next ferry that comes your way) for €13. Children aged six to 15 get a 50% discount.

Chiemgau Biking (☑08051-961 4973; www.chiemgau-biking.de; Chiemseestrasse 84, Bernau; per day from €9; ⊘8.30am-6pm Mon-Fri, 9am-1pm Sat) and **Bike Rental Fritz Müller** (☑08051-961 4948; www.fahrradverleih-chiemsee.de; Felden 12, Bernau; per day from €9), both in Bernau, hire out bikes and run bike tours of the lake area.

Berchtesgaden

☑ 08652 / POP 7800

Plunging deep into Austria and framed by six high-rise mountain ranges, the Berchtesgadener Land is a drop-dead-gorgeous corner of Bavaria steeped in myths and legends. Local lore has it that angels given the task of distributing the earth's wonders were startled by God's order to get a shift on and dropped them all here by accident. These most definitely included the Watzmann (2713m), Germany's second-highest mountain, and the pristine Königssee, perhaps Germany's most photogenic body of water.

Much of the area is protected by law within the Berchtesgaden National Park, which was declared a biosphere reserve by Unesco in 1990. The village of Berchtesgaden is the obvious base for hiking circuits into the park.

Away from the trails, the area has a more sinister aspect – the mountaintop Eagle's Nest was a lodge built for Hitler and is now a major dark-tourism destination while the Dokumentation Obersalzberg chronicles the region's Nazi past.

◉ Sights

★ **Eagle's Nest** HISTORIC SITE
(Kehlsteinhaus; ☑ 08652-29 69; www.kehlstein haus.de; Obersalzberg; tour €30.50; ⊙ buses 8.30am-4.50pm mid-May–Oct) Located at 1834m above sea level, the Eagle's Nest was built as a mountaintop retreat for Hitler, and gifted to him on his 50th birthday. It took around 3000 workers a mere two years to carve the precipitous 6km-long mountain road, cut a 124m-long tunnel and a brass-panelled lift through the rock, and build the lodge itself (now a restaurant). It can only be reached by special shuttle bus from the Kehlsteinhaus bus station.

On clear days, views from the top are breathtaking. If you're not driving, bus 838 makes the trip to the shuttle bus stop from the Berchtesgaden Hauptbahnhof every half-hour.

At the mountain station, you'll be asked to book a spot on a return bus. Allow at least two hours to get through lines, explore the lodge and the mountaintop, and perhaps have a bite to eat. Tours including the bus and guide can be booked online in advance.

★ **Königssee** LAKE
(Schönau am Königsee) Gliding serenely across the wonderfully picturesque, emerald-green Königssee makes for some unforgettable memories and photo opportunities. Cradled by steep mountain walls some 5km south of Berchtesgaden, the Königssee is Germany's highest lake (603m), with drinkably pure waters shimmering into fjordlike depths. Bus 841/843 makes the trip out here from the Berchtesgaden train station roughly every hour.

Escape the hubbub of the bustling lakeside tourist village of Schönau by taking an electric boat tour (p406) to St Bartholomä, a quaint onion-domed chapel on the western shore. At some point, the boat will stop while the captain plays a horn towards the Echo Wall – the sound will bounce seven times. From St Bartholomä, an easy trail leads to the wondrous Eiskapelle (ice chapel) in about one hour.

You can also skip the crowds by meandering along the lake shore. It's a nice and easy 3.5km return walk to the secluded Malerwinkel (Painter's Corner), a lookout famed for its picturesque vantage point.

★ **Dokumentation Obersalzberg** MUSEUM
(☑ 08652-947 960; www.obersalzberg.de; Salzbergstrasse 41, Obersalzberg; adult/child €3/free, audioguide €2; ⊙ 9am-5pm daily Apr-Oct, 10am-3pm Tue-Sun Nov-Mar, last entry 1hr before closing) In 1933 the tranquil Alpine settlement of Obersalzberg (3km from Berchtesgaden) in essence became the second seat of Nazi power after Berlin, a dark period that's given the full historical treatment at this superb exhibition. Various rooms document the forced takeover of the area, the construction of the compound and the daily life of the Nazi elite. All facets of Nazi terror are dealt with, including Hitler's near-mythical appeal, his racial politics, the resistance movement, foreign policy and the death camps.

Berchtesgaden National Park NATIONAL PARK
(www.nationalpark-berchtesgaden.de) Forty years old in 2018, the wilds of this 210-sq-km park still offer some of the best hiking in Germany. A good introduction is a 2km trail up from St Bartholomä beside the Königssee to the notorious Watzmann-Ostwand, where scores of mountaineers have met their deaths. Another popular hike goes from the southern end of the Königssee to the Obersee.

For details of routes visit the **national park office** (Haus der Berge; ☑ 08652-979 0600; www.haus-der-berge.bayern.de; Hanielstrasse 7; exhibition €4; ⊙ 9am-5pm), or buy a copy of the Berchtesgadener Land (sheet 794) map in

HITLER'S MOUNTAIN RETREAT

Of all the German towns tainted by the Third Reich, Berchtesgaden has a burden heavier than most. Hitler fell in love with nearby Obersalzberg in the 1920s and bought a small country home, later enlarged into the imposing Berghof.

After seizing power in 1933, Hitler established a part-time headquarters here and brought much of the party brass with him. They bought, or often confiscated, large tracts of land and tore down farmhouses to erect a 7ft-high barbed-wire fence. Obersalzberg was sealed off as the fortified southern headquarters of the NSDAP (National Socialist German Workers' Party). In 1938, British prime minister Neville Chamberlain visited for negotiations (later continued in Munich), which led to the infamous promise of 'peace in our time' at the expense of Czechoslovakia's Sudetenland.

Little is left of Hitler's Alpine fortress today. In the final days of WWII, the Royal Air Force levelled much of Obersalzberg, though the Eagle's Nest, Hitler's mountaintop eyrie, was left strangely unscathed. The historical twist and turns are dissected at the impressive Dokumentation Obersalzberg.

the Kompass series, available across Germany or online.

Salzbergwerk
HISTORIC SITE

(www.salzzeitreise.de; Bergwerkstrasse 83; adult/child €17/9.50; ⊙9am-5pm Apr-Oct, 11am-3pm Nov-Mar) Once a major producer of 'white gold', Berchtesgaden has thrown open its salt mines for fun-filled 1½-hour tours. Kids especially love donning miners' garb and whooshing down a wooden slide into the depths of the mine. Down below, highlights include mysteriously glowing salt grottoes and crossing a 100m-long subterranean salt lake on a wooden raft. Take hourly bus 840 from Berchtesgaden train station.

🏃 Activities

Jenner-Königssee Area
SKIING

(www.jennerbahn.de; daily pass €33) The Jenner-Königssee area at Königssee is the biggest and most varied of five local ski fields. For equipment hire and courses, try Skischule Treff-Aktiv (☑08652-66710; www.skischule-treffaktiv.de; Jennerbahnstrasse 16).

Watzmann Therme
SPA

(☑08652-946 40; www.watzmann-therme.de; Bergwerkstrasse 54; 2hr/4hr/day €11.70/15.40/17.70; ⊙10am-10pm) The Watzman Therme is Berchtesgaden's thermal wellness complex, with several indoor and outdoor pools and various hydrotherapeutic treatment stations, a sauna and inspiring Alpine views.

☞ Tours

Eagle's Nest Tours
TOURS

(☑08652-649 71; www.eagles-nest-tours.com; Königsseer Strasse 2; €55; ⊙1.15pm mid-May–Oct) This highly reputable outfit offers a fascinat-

ing overview of Berchtesgaden's Nazi legacy. Guest are taken not only to the Eagle's Nest but around the Obersalzberg area and into the underground bunker system. The four-hour English-language tour departs from the tourist office, across the roundabout opposite the train station. Booking ahead is advisable in July and August.

🛏 Sleeping

DJH Hostel
HOSTEL €

(☑08652-943 70; www.berchtesgaden.jugendherberge.de; Struberberg 6; dm from €23; 🛜) This 265-bed hostel is situated in the suburb of Strub, and has great views of Mt Watzmann. It's a 25-minute walk from the Hauptbahnhof or a short hop on bus 839.

KS Hostel Berchtesgaden
HOSTEL €

(☑08652-979 8420; www.hostel-berchtesgaden.de; Bahnhofplatz 4; dm from €23; Ⓟ🛜) This basic hostel above a Burger King is actually attached to the railway station, making it good for arrival and departure as well as for accessing buses to the sights. Rooms are spartan but there's cycle storage, free parking and common rooms on all floors.

★Hotel Reikartz
Vier Jahreszeiten
HOTEL €€

(☑08652-9520; www.hotel-vierjahreszeiten-berchtesgaden.de; Maximilianstrasse 20; r from €70; ⊙reception 7am-11pm; Ⓟ🛜🞉) For a taste of Berchtesgaden's storied past, stay at this traditional lodge where Bavarian royalty once crumpled the sheets. Rooms are very well kept and the south-facing (more-expensive) quarters offer dramatic views of the peaks. After a day's sightseeing, dinner in the hunting lodge–style Hubertusstuben restaurant is a real treat.

Hotel Edelweiss HOTEL **€€**
(☑ 08652-979 90; www.edelweiss-berchtesgaden.
com; Maximilianstrasse 2; d incl breakfast €110-
200; 🖥 🛜 🌊) In the heart of town, the Edelweiss is a sleek affair. The style could be
described as modern Bavarian, meaning
a combination of traditional woodsy flair
and factors such as a luxe spa, a rooftop terrace restaurant-bar with widescreen Alpine
views and an outdoor infinity pool. Rooms
are XL-sized and most have a balcony.

Hotel Bavaria HOTEL **€€**
(☑ 08652-966 10; www.hotelbavaria.net;
Sunklergässchen 11; s/d from €50/110; 🅿) Belonging to the same family for well over a
century, this professionally run hotel offers
a romantic vision of Alpine life with rooms
bedecked in frilly curtains, canopied beds,
heart-shaped mirrors and knotty wood galore. Five of the pricier rooms have private
whirlpools. Breakfast is a gourmet affair,
with sparkling wine and both hot and cold
delectables.

Hotel Krone HOTEL **€€**
(☑ 08652-946 00; www.hotel-krone-berchtes
gaden.de; Am Rad 5; s €45-55, d €80-120; @ 🛜 🌊)
Within ambling-distance of Berchtesgaden
centre, this family-run gem provides almost
unrivalled views of the valley and the Alps
beyond. The timber-rich cabin-style rooms
are generously cut affairs, with carved ceilings, niches and bedsteads all in aromatic
pine. Take breakfast on the suntrap terrace
for a memorable start, and end the day with
a sauna or Roman steam bath.

🍴 Eating

⭐ **Gaststätte St Bartholomä** BAVARIAN **€€**
(☑ 08652-964 937; www.bartholomae-wirt.de; St
Bartholomä; mains €10-20; ⊙ open according to
the boat tour timetable) Perched on the shore
of the Königssee, and accessible by boat
tour (☑ 08652-963 60; www.seenschifffahrt.de;
Schönau; return boat €15; ⊙ boats 8am-5.15pm
mid-Jun–mid-Sep, shorter hours rest of the year),
this is a tourist haunt that actually serves
delicious food made with ingredients picked,
plucked and hunted from the surrounding
forests and the lake. Savour generous platters of venison in mushroom sauce with
dumplings and red sauerkraut in the large
beer garden or indoors.

⭐ **Bräustübl** BAVARIAN **€€**
(☑ 08652-976 724; www.braeustueberl-bercht
esgaden.de; Bräuhausstrasse 13; mains €7-17;

⊙ 10am-midnight) Past the vaulted entrance
painted in Bavaria's white and blue diamonds this lively but cosy beer hall–beer
garden is run by the local brewery. Expect
a carnivorous feast with favourites such as
pork roast and the house speciality: breaded calf's head (tastes better than it sounds).
On Friday and Saturday, an oompah band
launches into knee-slapping action.

Le Ciel INTERNATIONAL **€€€**
(☑ 08652-975 50; www.restaurant-leciel.de; Hinter-
eck 1; mains €30-40; ⊙ 6.30-10.30pm Wed-Sat; 🛜)
Don't let the Hotel InterConti location turn
you off: Le Ciel really is as heavenly as its
French name suggests and it has the Michelin star to prove it. Testers were especially
impressed by Ulrich Heimann's knack for
spinning regional ingredients into inspired
gourmet compositions. Service is smooth
and the circular dining room is magical.

ℹ️ Information

Post Office (Franziskanerplatz 2; ⊙ 9am-noon
& 2-5pm Mon-Fri, 9am-noon Sat)

Tourist Office (☑ 08652-896 70; www.bercht
esgaden.com; Königsseer Strasse 2; ⊙ 8.30am-
6pm Mon-Fri, 9am-5pm Sat, shorter hours mid-
Oct–Mar) Near the train station, this helpful
office has information on the entire region.

ℹ️ Getting There & Around

Berchtesgaden is south of the Munich–Salzburg
A8 autobahn. Travelling from Munich by train involves a change from Meridian to BLB (Berchtesgadener Land Bahn) trains at Freilassing (€36.40,
2½ hours, at least hourly connections). The best
option between Berchtesgaden and Salzburg is
RVO bus 840 (45 minutes), which leaves from the
train station in both towns roughly hourly.

The train station in Berchtesgaden is around 15
minutes' walk from the village centre. The Eagle's
Nest, Königssee and Dokumentation Obersalzberg all require trips by bus if you don't have your
own transport. Seeing all the sights in a day without your own transport is virtually impossible.

THE ROMANTIC ROAD

From the vineyards of Würzburg to the foot
of the Alps, the almost 400km-long Romantic
Road (Romantische Strasse) draws two million visitors every year, making it by far the
most popular of Germany's holiday routes.
This well-trodden trail cuts through a cultural and historical cross-section of southern
Germany as it traverses Franconia and clips
Baden-Württemberg in the north before
plunging into Bavaria proper to end at Lud-

wig II's crazy castles. Expect lots of Japanese signs and menus, tourist coaches and kitsch galore, but also a fair wedge of *Gemütlichkeit* and geniune hospitality from those who earn their living on this most romantic of routes.

ⓘ Getting There & Away

Though Frankfurt is the most popular gateway for the Romantic Road, Munich is a good choice as well, especially if you decide to take the bus.

With its gentle gradients between towns, the Romantic Road is ideal for the holidaying cyclist. Bikes can be hired at many train stations; tourist offices keep lists of bicycle-friendly hotels that permit storage, or check out Bett und Bike (www.bettundbike.de) predeparture.

Direct trains run from Munich to Füssen every two hours, more often if you change in Buchloe. Rothenburg is linked by train to Würzburg, Munich, Augsburg and Nuremberg, with at least one change needed in Steinach to reach any destination.

ⓘ Getting Around

It is possible to do this route using train connections and local buses, but the going is complicated, tedious and slow on weekdays, virtually impossible at weekends. The ideal way to travel is by car, though many foreign travellers prefer to take Deutsche Touring's **Romantic Road Coach** (www.romanticroadcoach.de), which can get incredibly crowded in summer. From April to October the special coach runs daily in each direction between Frankfurt and Füssen (for Neuschwanstein); the entire journey takes around 12 hours. There's no charge for breaking the journey and continuing the next day.

Tickets are available for short segments of the trip, and reservations are only necessary during peak-season weekends. Reservations can be made through travel agents, **Deutsche Touring** (www.touring.de, www.romantic-road.com) and Deutsche Bahn's Reisezentrum offices in the train stations. If you stayed on the coach all the way from Frankfurt to Füssen (a pointless exercise), the total fare would be €158. The average fare from one stop to the next is around €5.

Coaches can accommodate bicycles but you must give three working days' notice. Students, children, pensioners and rail-pass holders qualify for discounts of between 10% and 50%.

For detailed schedules and prices, see www. romanticroadcoach.de.

Würzburg

🗗 0931 / POP 126,000

Straddling the Main River, scenic Würzburg is renowned for its art, architecture and delicate wines. The definite highlight is the Residenz, one of Germany's finest baroque buildings, though there's plenty more to see besides. A large student population guarantees a lively scene, and plenty of hip nightlife pulsates through its cobbled streets. The city is also the northern terminus of the Romantic Road, Germany's most popular tourist route.

History

Würzburg was a Franconian duchy when, in 686, three Irish missionaries tried to persuade Duke Gosbert to convert to Christianity, and ditch his wife. Gosbert was mulling it over when his wife had the three bumped off. When the murders were discovered decades later, the martyrs became saints and Würzburg was made a pilgrimage city, and, in 742, a bishopric.

For centuries the resident prince-bishops wielded enormous power and wealth, and the city grew in opulence under their rule. Their crowning glory is the Residenz, one of the finest baroque structures in Germany and a Unesco World Heritage Site.

In WWII 90% of the city centre was flattened. Authorities originally planned to leave the ruins as a reminder of the horrors of war, but a valiant rebuilding project saw the city restored almost to its pre-war glory.

⊙ Sights

★**Würzburg Residenz** PALACE
(www.residenz-wuerzburg.de; Balthasar-Neumann-Promenade; adult/child €7.50/free; ⊙ 9am-6pm Apr-Oct, 10am-4.30pm Nov-Mar, 45min English tours 11am & 3pm, plus 1.30pm & 4.30pm Apr-Oct) The vast Unesco-listed Residenz, built by 18th-century architect Balthasar Neumann as the home of the local prince-bishops, is one of Germany's most important and beautiful baroque palaces. Top billing goes to the brilliant zigzagging *Treppenhaus* (Staircase) lidded by what still is the world's largest fresco, a masterpiece by Giovanni Battista Tiepolo depicting allegories of the four then-known continents (Europe, Africa, America and Asia).

The structure was commissioned in 1720 by prince-bishop Johann Philipp Franz von Schönborn, who was unhappy with his old-fashioned digs up in Marienberg Fortress, and took almost 60 years to complete. Today the 360 rooms are home to government institutions, university faculties and a museum, but the grandest 40 have been restored for visitors to admire.

Besides the Grand Staircase, you can feast your eyes on the ice-white stucco-adorned

Würzburg

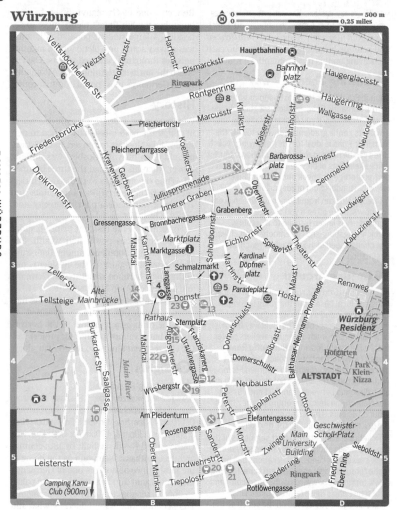

Weisser Saal (White Hall) before entering the *Kaisersaal* (Imperial Hall), canopied by yet another impressive Tiepolo fresco. Other stunners include the gilded stucco *Spiegelkabinett* (Mirror Hall), covered with a unique mirror-like glass painted with figural, floral and animal motifs (accessible by tour only).

In the residence's south wing, the *Hofkirche* (Court Church) is another Neumann and Tiepolo co-production. Its marble columns, gold leaf and profusion of angels match the Residenz in both splendour and proportions.

Entered via frilly wrought-iron gates, the *Hofgarten* (Court Garden; open until dusk, free) is a smooth blend of French- and English-style landscaping teeming with whimsical sculptures of children, mostly by court sculptor Peter Wagner. Concerts, festivals and special events take place here during the warmer months.

The complex also houses collections of antiques, paintings and drawings in the Martin-von-Wagner Museum (no relation to Peter) and, handily, a winery in the atmospheric cellar, the Staatlicher Hofkeller Würzburg, that is open for tours with tasting.

Würzburg

Festung Marienberg FORTRESS
(tour adult/child €3.50/free; ⊗ tours 11am, 2pm, 3pm & 4pm Tue-Sun, plus 10am & 1pm Sat & Sun mid-Mar–Oct, 11am, 2pm & 3pm Sat & Sun Nov–mid-Mar) Enjoy panoramic city and vineyard views from this hulking fortress whose construction was initiated around 1200 by the local prince-bishops who governed here until 1719. Dramatically illuminated at night, the structure was only penetrated once, by Swedish troops during the Thirty Years' War, in 1631. Inside, the Fürstenbaumuseum (closed November to mid-March) sheds light on its former residents' opulent lifestyle, while the Mainfränkisches Museum presents city history and works by local late-Gothic master carver Tilman Riemenschneider and other famous artists.

Neumünster CHURCH
(www.neumuenster-wuerzburg.de; Schönbornstrasse; ⊗ 6am-6.30pm Mon-Sat, from 8am Sun) In the Altstadt, this satisfyingly symmetrical church stands on the site where three ill-fated Irish missionaries who tried to convert Duke Gosbert to Christianity in 686 met their maker. Romanesque at its core, it was given a thorough baroque restyle by the Zimmermann brothers and is typical of their work. The interior has busts of the three martyrs (Kilian, Colonan and Totnan) on the high altar and the tomb of St Kilian lurks in the well-lit crypt.

Dom St Kilian CHURCH
(www.dom-wuerzburg.de; Domstrasse 40; ⊗ 8am-7pm Mon-Sat, to 8pm Sun) FREE This highly unusual cathedral has a Romanesque core that has been altered many times over the centuries. The elaborate stucco work of the chancel contrasts starkly with the bare whitewash of the austere Romanesque nave that is capped with a ceiling that wouldn't look out of place in a 1960s bus station. The whole mishmash creates quite an impression and is possibly Germany's oddest cathedral interior. The Schönbornkapelle by Balthasar Neumann returns a little baroque order to things.

Museum im Kulturspeicher MUSEUM
(✆ 0931-322 250; www.kulturspeicher.de; Veitshöchheimer Strasse 5; adult/child €3.50/2; ⊗ 1-6pm Tue, 11am-6pm Wed & Fri-Sun, 11am-7pm Thu) In a born-again historic granary right on the Main River, you'll find this absorbing art museum with choice artworks from the 19th to the 21st centuries. The emphasis is on German impressionism, neorealism and contemporary art, but the building also houses the post-1945 constructivist works of the Peter C Ruppert collection, a challenging assembly of computer art, sculpture, paintings and photographs.

Grafeneckart MEMORIAL
(Domstrasse) FREE Adjoining the Rathaus, the 1659-built Grafeneckart houses a scale model of the WWII bombing. It starkly depicts the extent of the damage to the city following the night of 16 March 1945, when 1000 tons of explosives were dropped on the city and 5000 citizens lost their lives in just 20 minutes. Viewing it and reading the potted history of events before you climb up to the fortress overlooking the city gives you an appreciation of Würzburg's astonishing recovery.

Museum am Dom MUSEUM
(www.museum-am-dom.de; Kiliansplatz; adult/child €4/free; ⊗ 10am-5pm Tue-Sun) Housed in a beautiful building by the cathedral, this worthwhile

museum displays collections of modern art on Christian themes. Works of international renown by Joseph Beuys, Otto Dix and Käthe Kollwitz are on show, as well as masterpieces of the Romantic, Gothic and baroque periods.

Röntgen Gedächtnisstätte   MUSEUM
(www.wilhelmconradroentgen.de; Röntgenring 8; ⊙ 8am-7pm Mon-Fri, to 5pm Sat) FREE Wilhelm Conrad Röntgen discovered X-rays in 1895 and was the winner of the very first Nobel Prize in 1901. His preserved laboratory forms the heart of this small exhibition that is complemented by a film on Röntgen's life and work in English.

🎊 Festivals & Events

Mozart Fest   MUSIC
(☑ 0931-372 336; www.mozartfest-wuerzburg.de; ⊙ mid-May–late Jun) Germany's oldest Mozart festival takes place at the Residenz, the Kiliansdom, the Mainfranken Theater and several other venues including some of the city's wine taverns.

Africa Festival   CULTURAL
(☑ 0931-150 60; www.africafestival.org; ⊙ early Jun) Held on the meadows northwest of the river at Mainwiesen, this is Germany's best festival of Afro music with acts from almost 60 countries across Africa and the Caribbean taking part.

Hoffest am Stein   WINE
(www.hoffest-am-stein.de; ⊙ Jul) Popular wine and music festival held in the first half of July at the Weingut am Stein.

Stramu   MUSIC
(www.stramu-wuerzburg.de; ⊙ Sep) This street music festival claims to be Europe's largest stage-free music event attracting over 400 acts from all over the world.

🛌 Sleeping

Babelfish   HOSTEL €
(☑ 0931-304 0430; www.babelfish-hostel.de; Haugerring 2; dm €25, s/d €65/80; ⊙ reception 8am-midnight; 🛜) With a name inspired by a creature in Douglas Adams' *The Hitchhiker's Guide to the Galaxy*, this uncluttered and spotlessly clean hostel has 74 beds spread over two floors and a sunny rooftop terrace. The communal areas are an inviting place to down a few beers in the evening and there's a well-equipped kitchen. Breakfast costs €5.90.

DJH Hostel   HOSTEL €
(☑ 0931-467 7860; www.wuerzburg.jugendher berge.de; Fred-Joseph-Platz 2; dm from €25) At the foot of the fortress, this well-equipped, wheelchair-friendly hostel has room for over 230 snoozers in three- to eight-bed dorms.

Camping Kanu Club   CAMPGROUND €
(☑ 0931-725 36; www.kc-wuerzburg.de; Mergentheimer Strasse 13b; per person/tent €4/3) Around 2km to the south of Würzburg, this is the closest camping ground to the town centre. Take tram 3 or 5 to the Judenbühlweg stop, which is on its doorstep.

Hotel Zum Winzermännle   HOTEL €€
(☑ 0931-541 56; www.winzermaennle.de; Domstrasse 32; s €60-80, d €90-110; P 🛜) This family-run converted winery is a feel-good retreat in the city's pedestrianised heart. Rooms are well furnished, if a little on the old-fashioned side; some among those facing the quiet courtyard have balconies. Communal areas are bright and often seasonally decorated. Breakfast costs €7.

Hotel Poppular   HOTEL €€
(☑ 0931-322 770; www.hotelpoppular.de; Textorstrasse 17; r €70-100; P 🛜) Relatively basic, city-centre hotel above a wine restaurant where rooms have a vague Scandinavian feel about them and are immaculately kept. All in all an excellent deal for the location within suitcase-dragging distance of the Hauptbahnhof and often massively discounted on popular booking websites. For walkers-in reception closes at 10pm.

Hotel Rebstock   HOTEL €€€
(☑ 0931-309 30; www.rebstock.com; Neubausstrasse 7; s/d from €115/250; ❄ 🛜) Würzburg's top digs, in a squarely renovated rococo townhouse, has 70 unique, stylishly finished rooms with the gamut of amenities, impeccable service and an Altstadt location. A pillow selection and supercomfy 'gel' beds should ease you into slumberland, perhaps after a fine meal in the dramatic bistro or the slick Michelin-star Kuno 1408 restaurant.

🍴 Eating

For a town of its size, Würzburg has an enticing selection of wine taverns, beer gardens, cafes and restaurants, with plenty of student hang-outs among them.

Juliusspital Bäckerei   BAKERY €
(Juliuspromenade 19; snacks €2-5; ⊙ 5am-6pm Mon-Sat, 8am-5pm Sun) Würzburg has tens of cafe-bakeries, but this high-ceilinged, colourful affair within the Juliusspital is great for very early starters whose trains leave

before hotel breakfast is laid out. Seasonally decorated, it's warm and welcoming, though sells the same range of baked goods and sandwiches as every other place.

Uni-Café
CAFE €

(Neubaustrasse 2; snacks €4-8; ☺8am-1am Mon-Sat, from 9am Sun; 🐦) Hugely popular contemporary cafe on two levels, with a student-priced, daily-changing menu of burgers, baguettes and salads plus a buzzy bar and much full-mouthed and animated waffling.

Capri & Blaue Grotto
ITALIAN €

(Elefantengasse 1; pizzas €7.50-9.50, other mains €4.50-13; ☺11.30am-2pm & 5-11pm Tue-Fri, evenings only Sat & Sun) This outpost of the *bel paese* has been plating up pronto pasta and pizza since 1952 – it was in fact Germany's first ever pizzeria.

★ Bürgerspital Weinstube
FRANCONIAN €€

(✑0931-352 880; www.buergerspital-weinstuben. de; Theaterstrasse 19; mains €7-25; ☺10am-midnight) If you are going to eat out just once in Würzburg, the aromatic and cosy nooks of this labyrinthine medieval place probably provide the top local experience. Choose from a broad selection of Franconian wines (some of Germany's best) and wonderful regional dishes and snacks, including *Mostsuppe* (a tasty wine soup). Buy local whites in the adjoining wine shop.

Juliusspital
FRANCONIAN €€

(www.weinstuben-juliusspital.de; Juliuspromenade 19; mains €8-30; ☺11am-midnight) This attractive *Weinstube* (traditional wine tavern) features fabulous (if pricey) Franconian fish and even better wines. Ambient lighting, scurrying waiters and walls occupied by oil paintings make this the place to head to for a special do.

Backöfele
FRANCONIAN €€

(✑0931-590 59; www.backoefele.de; Ursulinergasse 2; mains €7-23; ☺noon-midnight Mon-Thu, to 1am Fri & Sat, to 11pm Sun) This old-timey warren has been serving hearty Franconian food for decades. Find a table in the cobbled courtyard or one of four historic rooms, each candlelit and uniquely furnished with local flair. Featuring schnitzel, snails, bratwurst in wine, wine soup with cinnamon croutons, venison, boar and other local favourites, the menu makes for mouth-watering reading. Bookings recommended.

Alte Mainmühle
FRANCONIAN €€

(✑0931-167 77; www.alte-mainmuehle.de; Mainkai 1; mains €11-23; ☺10am-midnight; 🐦) Accessed

straight from the old bridge, people cram into this old mill to savour modern twists on Franconian classics (including popular river fish). In summer the double terrace beckons – the upper one delivers pretty views of the bridge and Marienberg Fortress; in winter retreat to the snug timber dining room. Year-round guests spill out onto the bridge itself, Aperol spritz in hand.

🍷 Drinking & Entertainment

Wine is the tipple of choice in Würzburg, much of it made with grapes from the surrounding hills. Juliusspital and Bürgerspital Weinstube are the best places to sample the local minerally whites. Meanwhile Sandstrasse is the place to head for a weekend night out for its gathering of studenty venues, live music, bars and kebab shops.

Sternbäck
PUB

(www.facebook.com/sternbaeck; Sterngasse 2; ☺9am-1am) This atmospheric, low-lit pub serves Distelhäuser beer and dishes up bratwurst and *Flammkuchen* (Alsatian pizza) under a modern fresco of fat-faced drinkers. It's an intimate and convivial place to enjoy a beer when you've had your fill of Würzburg's monastery-like wine taverns.

Kult
BAR

(Landwehrstrasse 10; ☺6pm-1am Mon, from 10am Tue-Sun) Enjoy a tailor-made breakfast, munch a cheap lunch or party into the wee hours at Würzburg's coolest cafe. The unpretentious interior, with its salvaged tables and old beige benches, hosts regular fancy-dress parties, table-football tournaments and other offbeat events. DJs take over at weekends.

MUCK
BAR

(www.cafe-muck.de; Sanderstrasse 29; ☺9am-1am) This very popular and long-established student cafe serves a hangover-busting breakfast and morphs into something of an informal party after nightfall.

Odeon Lounge
CLUB

(www.odeon-lounge.de; Augustinerstrasse 18; ☺from 11pm Wed, Fri & Sat) Mainstream club in a former cinema at the heart of the Augustinerstrasse student nightlife district. Expect '90s parties, local DJs, R'n'B nights and a 'midlife' night you may, er, want to avoid.

Standard
LIVE MUSIC

(www.standard-wuerzburg.com; Oberthürstrasse 11a; ☺11.30am-1am Mon-Wed, to 3am Thu-Sat, 3pm-1am Sun) Soulful jazz spins beneath a corrugated-iron ceiling and stainless-steel fans, while bands and DJs play a couple of times a week in a second downstairs bar.

ℹ️ Information

Post Office (Paradeplatz 4; ⊙8.30am-6pm Mon-Fri, 9am-noon Sat)

Tourist Office (📞0931-372 398; www.wuerz burg.de; Marktplatz 9; ⊙10am-6pm Mon-Fri, to 2pm Sun May-Oct, closed Sun & slightly shorter hours Nov-Apr) Within the attractive Falkenhaus this efficient office can help you with room reservations and tour booking.

ℹ️ Getting There & Away

BUS

The Romantic Road Coach (p407) stops at the **main bus station** (Bahnhofplatz) next to the Hauptbahnhof, and at Residenzplatz. Budget coach company Flixbus (www.flixbus.de) links Würzburg with destinations across Germany and beyond including Nuremberg and Munich.

TRAIN

Train connections from **Würzburg train station** (Bahnhofplatz) include Bamberg (€22, one hour, twice hourly), Frankfurt (€20 to €36, one hour, hourly), Munich (€74, two hours, twice hourly) and Nuremberg (€20, one hour, twice hourly). For Rothenburg ob der Tauber (€15.70, one hour, hourly), change in Steinach.

Rothenburg ob der Tauber

📞09861 / POP 11,100

A true medieval gem, Rothenburg ob der Tauber (meaning 'above the Tauber River') is a top tourist stop along the Romantic Road. With its web of cobbled lanes, higgledy-piggledy houses and towered walls, the town is the archetypal fairy-tale Germany. Urban conservation orders here are the strictest in Germany – and at times it feels like a medieval theme park – but all's forgiven in the evenings, when the lamplight casts its spell long after the last tour buses have left.

◉ Sights

Mittelalterliches Kriminalmuseum   MUSEUM
(Medieval Crime & Punishment Museum; www.kriminalmuseum.eu; Burggasse 3; adult/concession €7/4; ⊙10am-6pm Apr-Oct, 1-4pm Nov-Mar) The star attractions at this gruesomely fascinating museum are medieval implements of torture and punishment. Exhibits include chastity belts, masks of disgrace for gossips, a cage for cheating bakers, a neck brace for quarrelsome women and a beer-barrel pen for drunks. You can even snap a selfie in the

stocks. The museum has 50,000 exhibits making it the biggest of its kind in Europe.

Jakobskirche   CHURCH
(Church of St Jacob; Klingengasse 1; adult/child €2.50/1.50; ⊙9am-5pm Apr-Oct, shorter hours Nov-Mar) One of the few places of worship in Bavaria to charge admission, Rothenburg's Lutheran parish church was begun in the 14th century and finished in the 15th. The building sports some wonderfully aged stained-glass windows but the top attraction is Tilman Riemenschneider's Heilig Blut Altar (Altar of the Holy Blood). The gilded cross above the main scene depicting the Last Supper incorporates Rothenburg's most treasured reliquary – a rock crystal capsule said to contain three drops of Christ's blood.

Deutsches Weihnachtsmuseum   MUSEUM
(Christmas Museum; 📞09861-409 365; www.weihnachtsmuseum.de; Herrngasse 1; adult/child/family €4/2.50/7; ⊙10am-5pm Easter-Christmas, shorter hours Jan-Easter) If you're glad Christmas comes but once every 365 days, then stay well clear of the Käthe Wohlfahrt Weihnachtsdorf (p416), a Yuletide superstore that also houses this Christmas Museum. This repository of all things 'Ho! Ho! Ho!' traces the development of various Christmas customs and decorations, and includes a display of 150 Santa figures, plus lots of retro baubles and tinsel .

Stadtmauer   HISTORIC SITE
(Town Wall) With time and fresh legs, a 2.5km circular walk around the unbroken ring of town walls gives a sense of the importance medieval people placed on defending their settlements. A great lookout point is the eastern tower, the **Röderturm** (Rödergasse; adult/child €2/1; ⊙9am-5pm Mar-Oct & Dec), but for the most impressive views head to the western side of town, where a sweeping view of the Tauber Valley includes the Doppelbrücke, a double-decker bridge.

Reichsstadtmuseum   MUSEUM
(www.reichsstadtmuseum.rothenburg.de; Klosterhof 5; adult/child €6/5; ⊙9.30am-5.30pm Apr-Oct, 1-4pm Nov-Mar) Highlights of the Reichsstadtmuseum, housed in a former Dominican convent, include the Rothenburger Passion (1494), a cycle of 12 panels by Martinus Schwarz, and the oldest convent kitchen in Germany, as well as weapons and armour. Outside the main entrance (on your right as you're facing the museum), you'll see a spinning barrel, where the nuns distributed

Rothenburg ob der Tauber

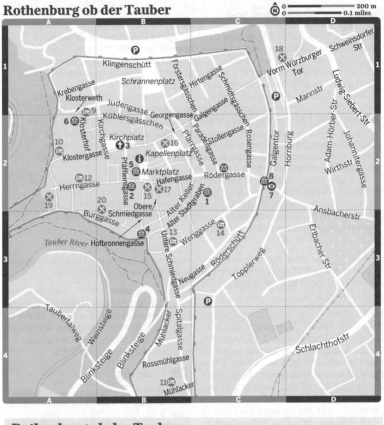

Rothenburg ob der Tauber

bread to the poor – and where women would leave babies they couldn't afford to keep.

Alt-Rothenburger Handwerkerhaus HISTORIC BUILDING
(www.alt-rothenburger-handwerkerhaus.de; Alter Stadtgraben 26; adult/child €3/1.50; ⊙11am-5pm Mon-Fri, from 10am Sat & Sun Easter-Oct, 2-4pm daily Dec) Hidden down a little alley is the Alt-Rothenburger Handwerkerhaus, where numerous artisans – including coopers, weavers, cobblers and potters – have their workshops today, and mostly have had for

BOTTOMS UP FOR FREEDOM

In 1631 the Thirty Years' War – pitching Catholics against Protestants – reached the gates of Rothenburg ob der Tauber. Catholic General Tilly and 60,000 of his troops besieged the Protestant market town and demanded its surrender. The town resisted but couldn't stave off the onslaught of marauding soldiers, and the mayor and other town dignitaries were captured and sentenced to death.

And that's about where the story ends and the legend begins. As the tale goes, Rothenburg's town council tried to sate Tilly's bloodthirstiness by presenting him with a 3L pitcher of wine. Tilly, after taking a sip or two, presented the councillors with an unusual challenge, saying, 'If one of you has the courage to step forward and down this mug of wine in one gulp, then I shall spare the town and the lives of the councilmen!' Mayor Georg Nusch accepted – and succeeded! And that's why you can still wander though Rothenburg's wonderful medieval lanes today.

It's pretty much accepted that Tilly was really placated with hard cash. Nevertheless, local poet Adam Hörber couldn't resist turning the tale of the Meistertrunk (champion drinker) into a play, which, since 1881, has been performed every Whitsuntide (Pentecost), the seventh Sunday after Easter. It's also re-enacted several times daily by the clock figures on the tourist office building.

the house's more than 700-year existence. It's half museum, half active workplace and you can easily spend an hour or so watching the artisans at work.

Rathausturm   HISTORIC BUILDING
(Town Hall Tower; Marktplatz; adult/child €2/0.50; ☺9.30am-12.30pm & 1-5pm Apr-Oct, 10.30am-2pm & 2.30-6pm Sun-Thu, to 7pm Fri & Sat Dec, noon-3pm Sat & Sun Jan-Mar & Nov) The Rathaus on Marktplatz was begun in Gothic style in the 14th century and was completed during the Renaissance. Climb the 220 steps of the medieval town hall to the viewing platform of the Rathausturm to be rewarded with widescreen views of the Tauber.

⚜ Festivals & Events

Historisches Festspiel 'Der Meistertrunk'   THEATRE
(www.meistertrunk.de; ☺late May) Takes place on Whitsuntide, with parades, dances and a medieval market. The highlight is the re-enactment of the mythical *Meistertrunk* story. The *Meistertrunk* play itself is performed three more times: once during the Reichsstadt-Festtage (early September), when the city's history is re-enacted in the streets, and twice during the Rothenburger Herbst, an autumn celebration (October).

Historischer Schäfertanz   DANCE
(Historical Shepherds' Dance; www.schaefertanz rothenburg.de; Marktplatz; ☺Apr-Oct) Involving colourfully dressed couples, this less-than-spectacular traditional dance

event takes places on Marktplatz several times between April and October.

Christmas Market   CHRISTMAS MARKET
(www.rothenburg.de; ☺Advent) The Rothenburger Reiterlesmarkt as it's officially known is the town's Christmas market, one of the most romantic in Germany. It's set out around the central Marktplatz during Advent.

🛏 Sleeping

Hotel Raidel   HOTEL €
(☎09861-3115; www.gaestehaus-raidel.de; Wenggasse 3; s/d €45/70; ☏) With 500-year-old exposed beams studded with wooden nails, antiques throughout and a welcoming owner, as well as musical instruments for the guests to play, this is the place to check in if you're craving some genuine romance on the Romantic Road.

DJH Hostel   HOSTEL €
(☎09861-941 60; www.rothenburg.jugend herberge.de; Mühlacker 1; dm from €23; ☏) Rothenburg's youth hostel occupies two enormous old buildings in the south of town. It's agreeably renovated and extremely well equipped, but you can sometimes hear the screams of noisy school groups from outside.

Kreuzerhof Hotel Garni   GUESTHOUSE €€
(☎09861-3424; www.kreuzerhof-rothenburg.de; Millergasse 2-6; s €55-65, d €75-110; ☏) Away from the tourist swarms, this quiet family-run B&B has charming, randomly furnished rooms with antique touches in a medieval townhouse and annexe. There's free tea and

coffee and the generous breakfast is really an energy-boosting set-up for the day.

Altfränkische Weinstube
HOTEL €€

(☑ 09861-6404; www.altfraenkische.de; Klosterhof 7; d €80-130; ☏) This very distinctive, 650-year-old inn has eight wonderfully romantic, realistically priced rural-style rooms with exposed half-timber, bath-tubs and most with four-poster or canopied beds. From 6pm onwards, the tavern serves up sound regional fare with a dollop of medieval cheer.

★ Hotel Herrnschlösschen
HOTEL €€€

(☑ 09861-873 890; www.hotel-rothenburg.de; Herrngasse 20; r from €225; ☏) Occupying a 900-year-old mansion, this top-class hotel is a blend of ancient and new, with Gothic arches leaping over faux-retro furniture and ageing oak preventing ceilings from crashing down onto chic 21st-century beds. The hotel's restaurant has established itself as one of the town's most innovative dining spots and there's an exquisite baroque garden out back for a spot of R&R.

★ Burg-Hotel
HOTEL €€€

(☑ 09861-948 90; www.burghotel.eu; Klostergasse 1-3; s €100-135, d €125-195; P ✴ ☏) Each of the 17 elegantly furnished guest rooms at this boutique hotel built into the town walls has its own private sitting area. The lower floors shelter a decadent spa with tanning beds, saunas and rainforest showers, and a cellar with a Steinway piano; while phenomenal valley views unfurl from the breakfast room and stone terrace.

The owners also run the hotel across the road where there are 14 more modern rooms and a restaurant. There is parking (€10 per day) and bikes for rent (€7.50 per day).

✖ Eating

Gasthof Goldener Greifen
FRANCONIAN €€

(☑ 09861-2281; www.gasthof-greifen-rothenburg. de; Obere Schmiedgasse 5; mains €8-17; ☉ 11.30am-10pm; ☏) Erstwhile home of Heinrich Toppler, one of Rothenburg's most famous medieval mayors (the dining room was his office), the 700-year-old Golden Griffin is the locals' choice in the touristy centre. A hearty menu of Franconian favourites is served in an austere semimedieval setting and out back in the sunny and secluded garden. There's also a long kids' menu, a rarity in Bavaria.

Weinstube zum Pulverer
FRANCONIAN €€

(☑ 09861-976 182; Herrngasse 31; mains €8-15; ☉ 5pm-late Wed-Fri, from noon Sat & Sun) The ornately carved timber chairs in this ancient wood-panelled wine bar (allegedly Rothenburg's oldest) are works of art. The simple but filling dishes, like soup in a bowl made of bread, gourmet sandwiches and cakes, are equally artistic. There's also a piano for postprandial self-expression.

Zur Höll
FRANCONIAN €€

(☑ 09861-4229; www.hoell.rothenburg.de; Burggasse 8; mains €7-20; ☉ 5-11pm Mon-Sat) This medieval wine tavern is in the town's oldest original building, with sections dating back to AD 900. The menu of regional specialities is limited but refined, though it's the superb selection of Franconian wines that people really come for.

Gasthof Butz
GERMAN €€

(☑ 09861-2201; Kapellenplatz 4; mains €7-16; ☉ 11.30am-2pm & 6-9pm Fri-Wed; ☏) For a quick, no-nonsense goulash, schnitzel or roast pork, lug your weary legs to this locally adored, family-run inn in a former brewery. In summer two flowery beer gardens beckon. It also rents a dozen simply furnished rooms.

★ Mittermeier
BAVARIAN, INTERNATIONAL €€€

(☑ 09861-945 430; www.villamittermeier.de; Vorm Würzburger Tor 7; mains €10-30; ☉ 6-10.30pm Tue-Sat; P ☏) Supporter of the slow food movement and a regular in the Michelin Guide, this hotel restaurant pairs punctilious artisanship with top-notch ingredients, sourced regionally whenever possible. There are five different dining areas including a black-and-white tiled 'temple', an alfresco terrace and a barrel-shaped wine cellar. The wine list is one of the best in Franconia. Book ahead.

🛍 Shopping

Käthe Wohlfahrt Weihnachtsdorf
CHRISTMAS DECORATIONS

(www.wohlfahrt.com; Herrngasse 1; ☉ 10am-5pm Mon-Sat) With its mind-boggling assortment of Yuletide decorations and ornaments, this huge shop lets you celebrate Christmas every day. Many of the items are handcrafted with

---

SNOWBALLS

Rothenburg's most obvious speciality is Schneeballen, ribbons of dough loosely shaped into balls, deep-fried then coated in icing sugar, chocolate and other dentist's foes. Some 27 different types are produced at Diller's Schneeballen (Hofbronnengasse 16; ☉ 10am-6pm). A more limited range is available all over town.

amazing skill and imagination; prices are correspondingly high. This is the original shop of a chain that has spread across Rothenburg and all of Germany.

ℹ Information

Post Office (Rödergasse 11; ⏰9am-1pm Mon-Fri, to noon Sat, plus 2-5.30pm Mon, Tue, Thu & Fri)

Tourist Office (☑ 09861-404 800; www.tourismus.rothenburg.de; Marktplatz 2; ⏰9am-6pm Mon-Fri, 10am-5pm Sat & Sun May-Oct, 9am-5pm Mon-Fri, 10am-1pm Sat Nov-Apr) Helpful office offering free internet access.

ℹ Getting There & Away

BUS

The Romantic Road Coach (p407) stops in the main bus park at the Hauptbahnhof and on the more central Schrannenplatz.

TRAIN

You can go anywhere by train from Rothenburg, as long as it's Steinach. Change there for services to Würzburg (€15.70, one hour and 10 minutes). Travel to and from Munich (from €29, three to four hours) can involve up to three different trains, making a day trip from the capital unfeasible.

ℹ Getting Around

The city has five car parks right outside the walls. The town centre is essentially closed to nonresident vehicles, though hotel guests are exempt.

Dinkelsbühl

☑ 09851 / POP 11,600

Some 40km south of Rothenburg, immaculately preserved Dinkelsbühl proudly traces its roots to a royal residence founded by Carolingian kings in the 8th century. Saved from destruction in the Thirty Years' War and ignored by WWII bombers, this is arguably the Romantic Road's quaintest and most authentically medieval halt. For a good overall impression of the town, walk along the fortified walls with their 18 towers and four gates.

◉ Sights

Haus der Geschichte   MUSEUM
(House of History; www.hausdergeschichte-dinkelsbuehl.de; Altrathausplatz 14; adult/child €4/2; ⏰9am-6pm Mon-Fri, 10am-5pm Sat & Sun May-Oct, 10am-5pm Nov-Apr) Dinkelsbühl's history comes under the microscope at the Haus der Geschichte, which occupies the 14th-century former town hall. Highlights include an interesting section on the Thirty Years' War and a

gallery with paintings depicting Dinkelsbühl at the turn of the century. Audioguides are included in the ticket price.

Münster St Georg   CHURCH
(www.st-georg-dinkelsbuehl.de; Marktplatz 1; ⏰9am-7pm) Standing sentry over the heart of Dinkelsbühl is one of southern Germany's greatest late-Gothic hall churches. Rather austere from the outside, the interior stuns with an incredible fan-vaulted ceiling. A curiosity is the Pretzl Window donated by the bakers' guild; it's located in the upper section of the last window in the right aisle.

Museum of the 3rd Dimension   MUSEUM
(☑ 09851-6336; www.3d-museum.de; Nördlinger Tor; adult/child €10/6; ⏰11am-5pm daily May-Jun & Sep-Oct, Sat & Sun Nov-Mar, 10am-6pm daily Jul-Aug) Located just outside the easternmost town gate, this is an engaging place to entertain young minds, bored with the Romantic Road's twee medieval pageant. Inside there are three floors of holographic images, stereoscopes and attention-grabbing 3D imagery. The slightly inflated admission includes a pair of red-green-tinted specs.

✹ Festivals & Events

Kinderzeche   CULTURAL
(www.kinderzeche.de; ⏰mid-Jul) In the third week of July, the 10-day Kinderzeche celebrates how, during the Thirty Years' War, the town's children persuaded the invading Swedish troops to spare Dinkelsbühl from a ransacking. The festivities include a pageant, re-enactments in the festival hall, lots of music and other merriment.

🛏 Sleeping

Campingpark 'Romantische Strasse'   CAMPGROUND €
(☑ 09851-7817; www.campingplatz-dinkelsbuehl.de; Kobeltsmühle 6; per tent/person €9.30/4.40) This camping ground is set on the shores of a swimmable lake 1.5km northeast of the Wörnitz Tor.

DJH Hostel   HOSTEL €
(☑ 09851-555 6417; www.dinkelsbuehl.jugendherberge.de; Koppengasse 10; dm from €26; 🛜) Dinkelsbühl's renovated 25-room hostel in the western part of the Altstadt occupies a beautiful 15th-century half-timbered granary.

★ Dinkelsbühler Kunst-Stuben   GUESTHOUSE €€
(☑ 09851-6750; www.kunst-stuben.de; Segringer Strasse 52; s €65, d €80-90, ste €100; 🅿@🛜)

Personal attention and charm by the bucketload make this guesthouse, situated near the westernmost gate (Segringer Tor), one of the best on the entire Romantic Road. Furniture (including the four-posters) is all handmade by Voglauer, the cosy library is perfect for curling up in with a good book, and the suite is a matchless deal for travelling families. The artist owner will show his Asia travel films if enough guests are interested.

Deutsches Haus HOTEL **€€**
(☑ 09851-6058; www.deutsches-haus.net; Weinmarkt 3; r from €105; ☜) Concealed behind the town's most ornate and out-of-kilter facade, the 19 elegant rooms at this central inn opposite the Münster St Georg flaunt antique touches and big 21st-century bathrooms. Downstairs Dinkelbühl's hautiest restaurant serves game and fish prepared according to age-old recipes.

Gasthof Goldenes Lamm HOTEL **€€**
(☑ 09851-2267; www.goldenes.de; Lange Gasse 26-28; s €55-70, d €80-105; P ☜) Operated by the same family for four generations, this stress-free, bike-friendly oasis has pleasant rooms at the top of a creaky staircase, plus a rooftop garden deck with plump sofas. The attached wood-panelled restaurant plates up Franconian-Swabian specialities, including a vegetarian selection.

✖ Eating

Haus Appelberg FRANCONIAN, INTERNATIONAL **€€**
(☑ 09851-582 838; www.haus-appelberg.de; Nördlinger Strasse 40; dishes €6-12; ☉ 6pm-midnight Mon-Sat; ☜) At this 40-cover wine restaurant owners double up as cooks to keep tables supplied with traditional dishes such as local fish, Franconian sausages and *Maultaschen* (pork and spinach ravioli). On warm days swap the rustic interior for the secluded terrace, a fine spot for some evening idling over a Franconian white.

The eight rooms upstairs are of a very high standard with antique touches.

Weib's Brauhaus PUB FOOD **€€**
(www.weibsbrauhaus.de; Untere Schmiedgasse 13; mains €5.90-18.50; ☉ 11am-1am Thu-Mon, 6pm-1am Wed; ☝) A female brewer presides over the copper vats at this half-timbered pub-restaurant, which has a good-time vibe thanks to its friendly crowd of regulars. Many dishes are made with the house brew, including the popular *Weib's Töpfle* ('woman's pot') – pork in beer sauce with croquettes.

ⓘ Information

Tourist Office (☑ 09851-902 440; www.tourismus-dinkelsbuehl.de; Altrathausplatz 14; ☉ 9am-6pm Mon-Fri, 10am-5pm Sat & Sun May-Oct, 10am-5pm Nov-Apr) Located in the Haus der Geschichte. Lots of brochures available for download from the website.

ⓘ Getting There & Away

Despite a railway line cutting through the town, Dinkelsbühl is not served by passenger trains. Regional bus 501 to Nördlingen (50 minutes, eight daily) stops at the ZOB Schwedenwiese bus station. Reaching Rothenburg is a real test of patience without your own car. Change from bus 805 to a train in Ansbach, then change trains in Steinach. The Europabus stops right in the Altstadt at Schweinemarkt.

Nördlingen

☑ 09081 / POP 20,000

Delightfully medieval, Nördlingen receives slightly fewer tourists than its better-known neighbours and manages to retain an air of authenticity, which is a relief after some of the Romantic Road's kitschy extremes. The town lies within the Ries Basin, a massive impact crater gouged out by a meteorite more than 15 million years ago. The crater – some 25km in diameter – is one of the best preserved on earth, and has been declared a special 'geopark'. Nördlingen's 14th-century walls, all original, mimic the crater's rim and are almost perfectly circular.

Incidentally, if you've seen the 1970s film *Willy Wonka and the Chocolate Factory*, you've already looked down upon Nördlingen from a glass elevator.

ⓞ Sights

You can circumnavigate the entire town in around an hour on top of the walls. Access points are near the old gates into the old town.

St Georgskirche CHURCH
(www.kirchengemeinde-noerdlingen.de; Marktplatz; tower adult/child €3.50/2.50; ☉ 9am-5pm Easter-Oct, 10.30am-12.30pm Tue-Sat, 9.30am-12.30pm Sun rest of the year, tower at least 10am-4pm daily) Dominating the heart of town, the immense late-Gothic St Georgskirche got its baroque mantle in the 18th century and seems to have been under restoration ever since. To truly appreciate Nördlingen's circular shape and the dished-out crater in which it lies, scramble up the 350 steps of the church's 90m-tall Daniel Tower, by far the town's tallest structure.

Bayerisches Eisenbahnmuseum
MUSEUM

(www.bayerisches-eisenbahnmuseum.de; Am Hohen Weg 6a; adult/child €6/3; ◉noon-4pm Tue-Sat, 10am-5pm Sun May-Sep, noon-4pm Sat, 10am-5pm Sun Oct-Mar) Half museum, half junkyard retirement home/graveyard for locos that have long puffed their last, this trainspotter's paradise occupies a disused engine depot across the tracks from the train station (no access from the platforms). The museum runs steam and old diesel trains up to Dinkelsbühl, Feuchtwangen and Gunzenhausen several times a year; see the website for details.

Rieskrater Museum
MUSEUM

(www.rieskrater-museum.de; Eugene-Shoemaker-Platz 1; adult/child €4.50/2.50, ticket also valid for Stadtmuseum; ◉10am-4.30pm Tue-Sun, closed noon-1.30pm Nov-Mar) Situated in an ancient barn, this unique museum explores the formation of meteorite craters and the consequences of such violent collisions with Earth. Rocks, including a genuine moon rock (on permanent loan from NASA), fossils and other geological displays shed light on the mystery of meteors.

Stadtmuseum
MUSEUM

(Vordere Gerbergasse 1; adult/child €4.50/2.50, ticket also valid for Rieskrater Museum; ◉1.30-4.30pm Tue-Sun Apr-early Nov) Nördlingen's worthwhile municipal museum covers an ambitious sweep of human existence on the planet, from the early Stone Age to 20th-century art, via the 1634 Battle of Nördlingen during the Thirty Years' War, Roman endeavours in the area and the town's once-bustling mercantile life.

Stadtmauermuseum
MUSEUM

(An der Löpsinger Mauer 3, Löpsinger Torturm; adult/child €2/1.40; ◉10am-4.30pm Tue-Sun Apr-Oct) Head up the spiral staircase of the Löpsinger Torturm for an engaging exhibition on the history of the town's defences, an apt place to kick off a circuit of the walls.

⭐ Festivals & Events

Nördlinger Pfingstmesse
FAIR

(Kaiserwiese; ◉Jun) The largest annual celebration is the 10-day Nördlinger Pfingstmesse (or often just Nördlinger Messe) that starts two weekends after Whitsuntide (Pentecost). It takes place at the Kaiserwiese to the north of the town and involves 200 stalls and countless fairground attractions.

🛏 Sleeping

Kaiserhof Hotel Sonne
HOTEL €€

(☑09081-5067; www.kaiserhof-hotel-sonne.de; Marktplatz 3; s €55-75, d €80-120; [P][🅰]) Right on the main square, Nördlingen's most famous digs once hosted crowned heads and their entourages, but they have quietly gone to seed in the past two decades. However, rooms are still packed with character, mixing 20th-century comforts with traditional charm, and the atmospheric regional restaurant downstairs is definitely worth a shot.

Art Hotel Ana Flair
DESIGN HOTEL €€

(☑09081-290 030; www.ana-hotels.com; Bürgermeister-Reiger-Strasse 14; s/d from €65/85; [🅰]) One of the few hotels outside the historical walls, the crisply contemporary Ana Flair, right opposite the train station, is the latest addition to the town's hotel scene. The 39 rooms blend retro-styling with 21st-century layouts and materials, the communal areas throw a little bit of Swabian tradition into the mix and there's a reasonably priced restaurant for lazy evenings.

Breakfast is normally included making this a pretty good deal all round.

Jugend & Familengästehaus
GUESTHOUSE €€

(JUFA; ☑09081-290 8390; www.jufa.eu; Bleichgraben 3a; s/d from €55/75; [P][@][🅰]) Located just outside the town walls, this shiny, 186-bed hotel-hostel-guesthouse is spacious and clean-cut. There are two- to six-bed rooms, ideal for couples or families, and facilities include bicycle hire and a cafe. Unless you are travelling with an entire handball team in tow, staff are not permitted to sell beds in dorms to individual travellers, no matter how hard you plead.

🍴 Eating

La Fontana
ITALIAN €

(Bei den Kornschrannen 2; mains €7-10.50; ◉11am-11pm Tue-Sun; [🅰]) Nördlingen's most popular restaurant is this large Italian pizza-pasta place occupying one end of the terracotta Kornschrannen building as well as tumbling tables out onto Schrannenstrasse. The menu is long, the service swift and when the sun is shining there's no lovelier spot to fill the hole.

Cafe-buch.de
CAFE €

(Weinmarkt 4; snacks from €2; ◉10am-6pm Mon, Tue & Thu-Sat, from 11am Sun, from noon Wed) That winning combination of coffee, cakes and secondhand books makes this cafe a pleasing midstroll halt for literary types and a nice break from the medieval onslaught for everyone else.

Café Radlos CAFE €€
(www.cafe-radlos.de; Löpsinger Strasse 8; mains €5.50-16; ⊙11.30am-2pm & 5pm-1am Wed-Mon; 🖝🍴) More than just a place to tuck into tasty pizzas and pastas, this convivially random cafe, Nördlingen's coolest haunt, parades cherry-red walls that showcase local art and photography exhibits. Kids have their own toy-filled corner, while you relax with board games, soak up the sunshine in the beer garden or surf the web.

ⓘ Information

Geopark Ries Information Centre (www.geopark-ries.de; Eugene-Shoemaker-Platz; ⊙10am-4.30pm Tue-Sun) Has a free exhibition on the Ries crater.

Tourist Office (📞04081-841 16; www.noerdlingen.de; Marktplatz 2; ⊙9am-6pm Mon-Thu, to 4.30pm Fri, 10am-2pm Sat Easter-Oct, plus 10am-2pm Sun Jul & Aug, closed Sat & Sun rest of year) Staff sell the Nördlinger TouristCard (€12.50) that saves you around €8 if you visit everything in town.

ⓘ Getting There & Away

The Europabus stops at Schäfflesmarkt not far from the St Georgskirche. Bus 501 runs to Dinkelsbühl from the new bus station (50 minutes, seven daily).

Train journeys to and from Munich (€30, two hours) and Augsburg (€16, 1¼ hours) require a change in Donauwörth.

Donauwörth

📞0906 / POP 19,750
Sitting pretty at the confluence of the Danube and Wörnitz rivers, Donauwörth rose from its humble beginnings as a 5th-century fishing village to its zenith as a Free Imperial City in 1301. Three medieval gates and five town wall towers still guard it today, and faithful rebuilding – after WWII had destroyed 75% of the medieval old town – means steep-roofed houses in a rainbow of colours still line its main street, Reichstrasse.

Reichstrasse is around 10 minutes' walk north of the train station. Turn right onto Bahnhofstrasse and cross the bridge onto Ried Island.

⊙ Sights

Liebfraukirche CHURCH
(Reichstrasse) At the western end of Reichstrasse rises this 15th-century Gothic church

with original frescos and a curiously sloping floor that drops 120cm. Swabia's largest church bell (6550kg) swings in the belfry.

Käthe-Kruse-Puppenmuseum MUSEUM
(www.kaethe-kruse.de; Pflegstrasse 21a; adult/child €2.50/1.50; ⊙11am-6pm Tue-Sun May-Sep, 2-5pm Thu-Sun Oct-Apr) This nostalgia-inducing museum fills a former monastery with old dolls and dollhouses by world-renowned designer Käthe Kruse (1883–1968). Donauwörth is home to the Käthe Kruse doll factory, so many of the 150 exhibits you see here were made locally.

Rathaus HISTORIC BUILDING
(Rathausgasse) Work on Donauwörth's landmark town hall began in 1236, but it has seen many alterations and additions over the centuries. At 11am and 4pm daily, the carillon on the ornamented step gable plays a composition by local legend Werner Egk (1901–83) from his opera *Die Zaubergeige* (The Magic Violin). The building also houses the tourist office.

Heilig-Kreuz-Kirche CHURCH
(Heilig-Kreuz-Strasse) Overlooking the grassy banks of the shallow River Wörnitz, this soaring baroque confection has for centuries lured the faithful to pray before a chip of wood, said to come from the Holy Cross, installed in the ornate-ceilinged Gnadenkappelle (Grace Chapel).

🛏 Sleeping & Eating

Drei Kronen HOTEL €€
(📞09851-706 170; www.hotel3kronen.com; Bahnhofstrasse 25; s/d €85/120, apt per person €90; 🅿🖝) Situated opposite the train station a little way along Bahnhofstrasse, the 'Three Crowns' has the town's most comfortable, if slightly cramped, rooms and a lamplit restaurant. There's also an apartment with kitchen.

Posthotel Traube BAVARIAN €€
(Kapellstrasse 14-16; mains €5-17; ⊙11am-2pm & 5-10pm Mon-Fri & Sun, closed Sat) Choose from a cafe, coffeehouse, restaurant or beer garden at this friendly, multitasking hotel where Mozart stayed as a boy in 1777. The schnitzel, cordon bleu and local carp in beer sauce are where your finger should land on the menu.

Cafe Rafaello ITALIAN €€
(www.raffaello-donauwoerth.de; Fischerplatz 1; mains €7-25; ⊙10am-midnight) On Ried Island, this Italian job specialising in seafood uses Apennines kitsch to recreate *la dolce vita* to

HARBURG

Looming over the Wörnitz River, the medieval covered parapets, towers, turrets, keep and red-tiled roofs of the 12th-century **Schloss Harburg** (www.burg-harburg.de; Burgstrasse 1; courtyard admission €3, tour €4; ⊙10am-5pm mid-Mar–Oct) are so perfectly preserved they almost seem like a film set. Tours tell the building's long tale and evoke the ghosts that are said to use the castle as a hang-out.

The walk to Harburg's cute, half-timbered Altstadt from the castle takes around 10 minutes, slightly more the other way as you're heading uphill. A fabulous panorama of the village and castle can be admired from the 1702 Stone Bridge spanning the Wörnitz.

One of the most truly romantic places to stay on the RR, part of Harburg Castle has been transformed into a very comfortable **hotel** (☑09080-968 60; www.burg-harburg.de; Burgstrasse 1; d from €85; 🅿🛜) that combines the ancient architecture of this millennium-old burg with antique furniture and 21st-century plumbing. All of the rooms are different and some have idyllic views of the castle courtyard and the surrounding hills.

The Europabus stops in the village (outside the Gasthof Grüner Baum) but not at the castle. Hourly trains run to Nördlingen (€4.90, 15 minutes) and Donauwörth (€4, 12 minutes). The train station is about a 30-minute walk from the castle.

southern German tastes. The endless menu has something for everyone.

ℹ Information

Tourist Office (☑09851-789 151; www.donauwoerth.de; Rathausgasse 1; ⊙9am-noon & 1-6pm Mon-Fri, 3-5pm Sat & Sun May-Sep, shorter hours Mon-Fri, closed Sat & Sun Oct-Apr)

ℹ Getting There & Away

The Romantic Road Coach (p407) stops by the Liebfraukirche.

Train connections from Donauwörth include Augsburg (€7, 30 minutes, twice hourly), Harburg (€4, 11 minutes, twice hourly), Ingolstadt (€12.90, 45 minutes, hourly) and Nördlingen (€7.20, 30 minutes, hourly).

Augsburg

☑0821 / POP 289,600

The largest city on the Romantic Road (and Bavaria's third largest), Augsburg is also one of Germany's oldest, founded by the step-children of Roman emperor Augustus over 2000 years ago. As an independent city state from the 13th century, it was also one of its wealthiest, free to raise its own taxes, with public coffers bulging on the proceeds of the textile trade. Banking families such as the Fuggers and the Welsers even bankrolled entire countries and helped out the odd skint monarch. However, from the 16th century, religious strife and economic decline plagued the city. Augsburg finally joined the Kingdom of Bavaria in 1806.

Shaped by Romans, medieval artisans, bankers, traders and, more recently, industry and technology, this attractive city of spires and cobbles is an easy day trip from Munich or an engaging stop on the Romantic Road, though one with a grittier, less quaint atmosphere than others along the route.

◉ Sights

Fuggerei   HISTORIC SITE
(www.fugger.de; Jakober Strasse; adult/concession €4/3; ⊙8am-8pm Apr-Sep, 9am-6pm Oct-Mar) The legacy of Jakob Fugger 'The Rich' lives on at Augsburg's Catholic welfare settlement, the Fuggerei, which is the oldest of its kind in existence. Around 200 people live here today and their rent remains frozen at 1 Rhenish guilder (now €0.88) per year, plus utilities and three daily prayers. Residents wave to you as you wander through the car-free lanes of this gated community flanked by its 52 pin-neat houses (containing 140 apartments) and little gardens.

To see how residents lived before running water and central heating, one of the apartments now houses the **Fuggereimuseum** (Mittlere Gasse 14; admission incl with entry to the Fuggerei; ⊙9am-8pm Mar-Oct, to 6pm Nov-Apr), while there's a modern apartment open for public viewing at Ochsengasse 51. Interpretive panels are in German but you can ask for an information leaflet in English or download it from the website before you arrive.

St Anna Kirche   CHURCH
(Im Annahof 2, off Annastrasse; ⊙noon-6pm Mon, 10am-12.30pm & 3-6pm Tue-Sat, 10am-12.30pm & 3-5pm Sun May-Oct, slightly shorter hours Nov-Apr) **FREE** Often regarded as the first Renaissance

church in Germany, the rather plain-looking (and well-hidden) St Anna Kirche is accessed via a set of cloisters lined with tombstones. The church contains a bevy of treasures, as well as the sumptuous Fuggerkapelle, where Jacob Fugger and some of his relatives lie buried, and the lavishly frescoed Goldschmiedekapelle (Goldsmiths' Chapel; 1420).

The church played an important role during the Reformation. In 1518 Martin Luther, in town to defend his beliefs before the papal legate, stayed at what was then a Carmelite monastery. His rooms have been turned into the Lutherstiege, a very informative exhibition about the Reformation and Luther's life.

Brechthaus   MUSEUM
(☑ 0821-324 2779; Auf dem Rain 7; adult/concession €3.50/2.50; ☺ 10am-5pm Tue-Sun) Opened in 1998 to celebrate local boy Bertolt Brecht's 100th birthday, this house museum is the birthplace of the famous playwright and poet, where he lived for the first two years of his life (from 1898 to 1900) before moving across town. Among the displays are old theatre posters and a great series of life-size chronological photos, as well as his mother's bedroom.

Maximilianmuseum   MUSEUM
(☑ 0821-324 4102; www.kunstsammlungen-museen. augsburg.de; Philippine-Welser-Strasse 24; adult/child €7/free; ☺ 10am-5pm Tue-Sun) The Maximilianmuseum occupies two patrician townhouses joined by a statue-studded courtyard covered by a glass-and-steel roof. Highlights include a fabulous collection of Elias Holl's original wooden models for his architectural creations, and a collection of gold and silver coins. However, the real highlights here are the expertly curated temporary exhibitions on a variety of Bavarian themes.

Dom Mariä Heimsuchung   CHURCH
(Hoher Weg; ☺ 7am-6pm) Augsburg's cathedral has its origins in the 10th century but was Gothicised and enlarged in the 14th and 15th centuries. The star treasures here are the so-called 'Prophets' Windows'. Depicting David, Daniel, Jonah, Hosea and Moses, they are among the oldest figurative stained-glass windows in Germany, dating from the 12th century. Look out for four paintings by Hans Holbein the Elder, including one of Jesus' circumcision.

Rathausplatz   SQUARE
The heart of Augsburg's Altstadt, this large, pedestrianised square is anchored by the Augustusbrunnen, a fountain honouring the Roman emperor; its four figures represent the Lech River and the Wertach, Singold and Brunnenbach brooks.

Rising above the square are the twin onion-domed spires of the Renaissance Rathaus (Rathausplatz), built by Elias Holl from 1615 to 1620 and crowned by a 4m-tall pine cone, the city's emblem (also an ancient fertility symbol). Upstairs is the Goldener Saal (Golden Hall; adult/child €2.50/1.50; ☺ 10am-6pm), a huge banquet hall with an amazing gilded and frescoed coffered ceiling.

For panoramic views over Rathausplatz and the city, climb to the top of the Perlachturm (adult/child €2/1; ☺ 10am-6pm Apr-Nov), a former guard tower, and also an Elias Holl creation.

Jüdisches Kulturmuseum   MUSEUM
(☑ 0821-513 658; www.jkmas.de; Halderstrasse 6-8; adult/child €4/2; ☺ 9am-6pm Tue-Thu, to 4pm Fri, 10am-5pm Sun) About 300m east of the main train station, as you head towards the Altstadt, you'll come to the Synagoge Augsburg, an art nouveau temple built between 1914 and 1917 and housing a worthwhile Jewish museum. Exhibitions here focus on Jewish life in the region, presenting religious artefacts collected from defunct synagogues across Swabia.

🛏 Sleeping

As you might expect for a city of Augsburg's size, you can find every type of accommodation here, even a large hostel. The city could be used as an alternative base for Oktoberfest, though hotel owners pump up their prices just as much as their Munich counterparts do.

Übernacht   HOSTEL €
(☑ 0821-4554 2828; www.uebernacht-hostel.de; Karlstrasse 4; dm/d from €19/50; 🖥) Professionally run, 21st-century operation spread over three floors of a former office block with a wide selection of bright dorms, doubles and apartments, some en suite, some with shared facilities. Amenities are hotel standard and there's a superb kitchen for guest use. Book ahead in summer and during Oktoberfest.

Gästehaus SLEPS   GUESTHOUSE €
(☑ 0821-780 8890; www.sleps.de; Unterer Graben 6; s/d from €42/65; 🖥) The SLEPS is simply the singles and doubles at Augsburg's youth hostel (*Jugendherberge*), rebranded as a guesthouse. Rooms still have that whiff of institutional occupation about them but are

bright, clean and quiet. For these prices the decent buffet breakfast is a real bonus these days.

★ Dom Hotel   HOTEL €€

(☏ 0821-343 930; www.domhotel-augsburg.de; Frauentorstrasse 8; s €80-150, d €100-180; P ⊖ 🛜 🏊) Augsburg's top choice packs a 500-year-old former bishop's guesthouse (Martin Luther and Kaiser Maxmilian I stayed here) with 57 rooms, all different but sharing a stylishly understated air and pristine upkeep; some have cathedral views. The big pluses here, however, are the large swimming pool and fitness centre. Parking is an extra €6.

Hotel am Rathaus   HOTEL €€

(☏ 0821-346 490; www.hotel-am-rathaus-augsburg.de; Am Hinteren Perlachberg 1; s €70-105 d €105-145; 🛜) With a central location just steps from Rathausplatz and Maximilianstrasse, this boutique hotel has 31 rooms with freshly neutral decor and a sunny little breakfast room. Attracts a business-oriented clientele, so watch out for special weekend deals (almost a third off normal rates).

Steigenberger Drei Mohren Hotel   HOTEL €€€

(☏ 0821-503 60; www.augsburg.steigenberger.de; Maximilianstrasse 40; r from €150; P ⊖ ❄ @ 🛜) Proud dad Leopold Mozart stayed here with his prodigious offspring in 1766 and it remains by far Augsburg's oldest and grandest hotel. The punctiliously maintained rooms are the last word in soothing design and come with marble bathrooms and original art. Dine in-house at the gastronomic extravaganza that is Maximilians, a great place to swing by for Sunday brunch.

Eating

In the evening, Maximilianstrasse is the place to tarry, with cafes tumbling out onto the pavements and Augsburg's young and beautiful watching the world go by. Fastfood joints gather around the Königsplatz and along Frauenstrasse.

Anno 1578   CAFE €

(Fuggerplatz 9; mains €5-11; ⊗ 9am-7pm Mon-Sat; 🛜) Munch on blockbuster breakfasts, lunchtime burgers and sandwiches, or just pop by for a cappuccino or ice cream at this trendy cafe under ancient neon-uplit vaulting. The central table, a huge chunk of timber, is a great place to meet locals and other travellers.

★ Perlacht Acht   MEDITERRANEAN €€

(☏ 0821-2480 5265; www.perlachacht.de; Am Perlachberg 8; mains €10-17; ⊗ noon-11pm Mon-Fri, 9.30am-11pm Sat & Sun; 🛜) Run by a young local couple, this superb restaurant has its focus firmly on light, flavoursome dishes with a sunny Mediterranean bent. Take a seat at one of the hefty olive-wood tables to enjoy handmade pastas, tomato risotto with smoked mozarella and crispy pork belly with orange, fennel and gnocchi.

Antico Duomo   ITALIAN €€

(www.antico-duomo.de; Frauentorstrasse 2; mains €7-26; ⊗ 11am-11pm; 🛜) This Italian job opposite the cathedral has a pink Vespa scooter in the window, attractively laid tables and leathery chairs, seated on which you can enjoy something tasty from the *bel paese*. The menu runs the full gamut of Italian cuisine and there's plenty of prosecco and Valpolicella to wash it all down.

Bauerntanz   GERMAN €€

(Bauerntanzgässchen 1; mains €8-20; ⊗ 11am-11.30pm) Belly-satisfying helpings of creative Swabian and Bavarian food – *Spätzle* (local pasta) and more *Spätzle* – are plated up by friendly staff at this prim Alpine tavern with lace curtains, hefty timber interior and chequered fabrics. When the sun makes an appearance, everyone bails for the outdoor seating.

★ August   INTERNATIONAL €€€

(☏ 0821-352 79; Johannes-Haag-Strasse 14; dinner €169; ⊗ from 7pm Wed-Sat) Most Augsburgers have little inkling their city possesses two Michelin stars, both of which belong to chef Christian Grünwald. Treat yourself to tasty smears and blobs that make up some of Bavaria's most innovative cooking, served in the beautifully renovated dining room of a small mansion east of the city centre. Reserve well ahead.

🍷 Drinking & Nightlife

City Club   CAFE

(www.cityclub.name; Konrad-Adenauer-Allee 9; ⊗ from 2pm Tue-Sun) For some grungy student drinking action, head to this cafe near the tram interchange with its mismatched furniture, vegie pizzas and almost nightly DJs.

Thing   BEER GARDEN

(www.mein-thing.de; Vorderer Lech 45; ⊗ 6pm-1am Mon-Thu, to 2am Fri & Sat, 5pm-midnight Sun) Augsburg's coolest beer garden sports totem poles and often gets crowded in the evenings. Serves great burgers and beer.

WIESKIRCHE

Located in the village of Wies, just off the B17 between Füssen and Schongau, the Wieskirche ([☎] 08862-932 930; www.wieskirche.de; ⊙ 8am-8pm Apr-Oct, to 5pm Nov-Mar) is one of Bavaria's best-known baroque churches and a Unesco World Heritage Site. About a million visitors a year flock to see its pride and joy, the monumental work of the legendary artist-brothers Dominikus and Johann Baptist Zimmermann.

In 1730, a farmer in Steingaden, about 30km northeast of Füssen, witnessed the miracle of his Christ statue shedding tears. Pilgrims poured into the town in such numbers over the next decade that the local abbot commissioned a new church to house the weepy work. Inside the almost circular structure, eight snow-white pillars are topped by gold capital stones and swirling decorations. The unsupported dome must have seemed like God's work in the mid-17th century, its surface adorned with a pastel ceiling fresco celebrating Christ's resurrection.

From Füssen, regional RVO bus 73 (www.rvo-bus.de) makes the journey six times daily. The Romantic Road Coach (p407) also stops here long enough in both directions to have a brief look round then get back on. By car, take the B17 northeast and turn right (east) at Steingaden.

⭐ Entertainment

Augsburger Puppenkiste   THEATRE
([☎] 0821-450 3450; www.augsburger-puppenkiste. de; Spitalgasse 15; tickets from €9.50) The celebrated puppet theatre holds performances of modern and classic fairy tales that even non–German speakers will enjoy. Advance bookings essential.

ℹ Information

Post Office (Halderstrasse 29; ⊙ 8am-6.30pm Mon-Fri, 9am-1pm Sat) At the Hauptbahnhof.

Tourist Office ([☎] 0821-502 0723; www. augsburg-tourismus.de; Rathausplatz; ⊙ 8.30am-5.30pm Mon-Fri, 10am-5pm Sat, 10am-3pm Sun Apr-Oct, slightly shorter hours Mon-Fri Nov-Mar) This office multitasks as a citizen's advice point so staff can be slightly distracted.

ℹ Getting There & Away

The Romantic Road Coach (p407) stops at both the Hauptbahnhof and the Rathaus.

Augsburg has rail connections with Donauwörth (€13, 20 to 40 minutes, three hourly), Munich (€14.60 to €20, 30 to 50 minutes, three hourly), Nuremberg (€19 to €62, one to two hours, hourly) and Ulm (€20 to €25.50, 45 minutes to one hour, three hourly). Direct services go to Füssen (€22, two hours, every two hours), otherwise change in Buchloe.

ℹ Getting Around

From the train station take tram 3, 4 or 6 (€1.80) to the central interchange at Königsplatz where all Augsburg's tram routes converge. Trams 1 and 2 run from there to Ratshausplatz.

Landsberg am Lech

[☎] 08191 / POP 28,800

Lovely Landsberg am Lech is often overlooked by Romantic Road trippers on their town-hopping way between Füssen to the south and Augsburg to the north. But it's for this very absence of tourists and a less commercial ambience that this walled town, prettily set on the River Lech, is worth a halt, if only a brief one.

Landsberg can claim to be the town where one of the German language's best-selling books was written. Was it a work by Goethe, Remarque, Brecht? No, unfortunately, it was Hitler. It was during his 264 days of incarceration in a Landsberg jail, following the 1923 beer-hall putsch, that Adolf penned his hate-filled *Mein Kampf,* a book that sold an estimated seven million copies when published. The jail later held Nazi war criminals and is still in use.

⊙ Sights

Landsberg's hefty medieval defensive walls are punctuated by some beefy gates, the most impressive of which are the 1425 Bayertor to the east and the Renaissance-styled Sandauer Tor to the north. The tall Schmalztor was left centrally stranded when the fortifications were moved further out and still overlooks the main square and the 500 listed buildings within the town walls.

Johanniskirche   CHURCH
(Vorderer Anger 215) If you've already seen the Wieskirche to the south, you will instantly

recognise this small baroque church as a creation by the same architect, Dominikus Zimmermann, who lived in Landsberg and even served as its mayor.

Stadtpfarrkirche Mariä Himmelfahrt
CHURCH

(Georg-Hellmair-Platz) This huge 15th-century church with its slender bell tower was built by Matthäus von Ensingen, architect of Bern Cathedral. The barrel nave is stuccoed to baroque perfection, while a cast of saints populates columns and alcoves above the pews. Gothic-era stained glass casts rainbow hues on the church's most valuable work of art, the 15th-century *Madonna with Child* by local sculptor Lorenz Luidl.

Heilig-Kreuz-Kirche
CHURCH

(Von-Helfenstein-Gasse) Head uphill from the Schmalztor to view this beautiful baroque Jesuit church, the interior of which is a hallucination in broodily dark gilding and glorious ceiling decoration.

Neues Stadtmuseum
MUSEUM

(www.museum-landsberg.de; Von-Helfenstein-Gasse 426; adult/child €3/1.50; ☺2-5pm Tue-Fri, from 11am Sat & Sun May-Jan, closed Feb-Apr) Housed in a former Jesuit school, Landsberg's municipal museum chronicles the area's past from prehistory to the 20th century, and displays numerous works of local art, both religious and secular in nature.

🛏 Sleeping & Eating

Stadthotel Augsburger Hof
HOTEL €€

(☑08191-969 596; www.stadthotel-landsberg.de; Schlossergasse 378; s €45-70, d €90; ☐🗐) The 15 en suite rooms at this highly recommended traditional inn are a superb deal, and have chunky pine beds and well-maintained bathrooms throughout. The owners and staff are a friendly bunch, and the breakfast is a filling set-up for the day. Cycle hire and cycle-friendly.

Weidekind
INTERNATIONAL €€

(☑08191-979 7083; www.weidekind-landsberg.de; Bahnhofsplatz 1; mains €7-15; ☺7am-6pm Mon, to 10pm Tue-Thu, to 11.30pm Fri, 5.30-11.30pm Sat, 10am-6pm Sun; 🗐) Arguably Landsberg's best eatery is in the *Bürgerbahnhof,* the publicly owned train station. Savour imaginative dishes, stylishly served in the 21st-century interior, all bare lamp bulbs and exposed brick walls, as you watch people buy their tickets for the next train. The building has a great vibe (Deutsche Bahn would have replaced it with a ticket machine) and it's well worth stopping by.

Lechgarten
BAVARIAN €€

(www.lechgarten.de; Hubert-von-Herkomer-Strasse 73; mains €5-11; ☺3-11pm Mon-Fri, noon-11pm Sat & Sun Apr-Oct) Lansberg's top beer garden on the tree-shaded banks of the River Lech has 250 seats, beer from Andechs Monastery and hearty beer-garden fare. Live music summer weekends, pretty river views any time.

❶ Information

Tourist Office (☑08191-128 246; www.landsberg.de; Hauptplatz 152; ☺9am-12.30pm & 1.30-6pm Mon-Fri, 11.30am-5pm Sat & Sun May-Oct, shorter hours Nov-Apr) Within the wonderfully stucco'ed Rathaus.

❶ Getting There & Away

The Romantic Road Coach (p407) stops on the Hauptplatz.

The **train station** (Bahnhofsplatz) is just across the Lech from the historical centre. Landsberg has connections to Augsburg (€9.70, 50 minutes, hourly), Füssen (€17.80, 1½ hours, every two hours), with a change at Kaufering, and Munich (€14.60, 55 minutes, twice hourly), with a change at Kaufering.

NUREMBERG & FRANCONIA

Somewhere between Ingolstadt and Nuremberg, Bavaria's accent mellows, the oompah bands play that little bit quieter and wine competes with beer as the local tipple. This is Franconia (Franken) and, as every local will tell you, Franconians, who inhabit the wooded hills and the banks of the Main River in Bavaria's northern reaches, are a breed apart from their brash and extroverted cousins to the south.

In the northwest, the region's winegrowers produce some exceptional whites, sold in a distinctive teardrop-shaped bottle called the *Bocksbeutel.* For outdoor enthusiasts, the Altmühltal Nature Park offers wonderful hiking, biking and canoeing. But it is Franconia's old royalty and incredible cities – Nuremberg, Bamberg and Coburg – that draw the biggest crowds.

❶ Getting There & Away

The region has excellent rail links with the rest of Bavaria and neighbouring *Länder.* Nuremberg Airport (p436) handles flights from tens of destinations around Europe.

Nuremberg

📞 0911 / POP 511,600

Nuremberg (Nürnberg), Bavaria's second-largest city and the unofficial capital of Franconia, is an energetic place where the nightlife is intense and the beer is as dark as coffee. As one of Bavaria's biggest draws it is alive with visitors year-round, but especially during the spectacular Christmas market.

For centuries, Nuremberg was the undeclared capital of the Holy Roman Empire and the preferred residence of most German kings, who kept their crown jewels here. Rich and stuffed with architectural wonders, it was also a magnet for famous artists, though the most famous of all, Albrecht Dürer, was actually born here. 'Nuremberg shines throughout Germany like a sun among the moon and stars,' gushed Martin Luther. By the 19th century, the city had become a powerhouse in Germany's industrial revolution.

The Nazis saw a perfect stage for their activities in working class Nuremberg. It was here that the fanatical party rallies were held, the boycott of Jewish businesses began and the infamous Nuremberg Laws outlawing German citizenship for Jewish people were enacted. On 2 January 1945, Allied bombers reduced the city to landfill, killing 6000 people in the process.

After WWII the city was chosen as the site of the war crimes tribunal, now known as the Nuremberg Trials. Later, the painstaking reconstruction – using the original stone – of almost all the city's main buildings, including the castle and old churches in the Altstadt, returned the city to some of its former grandeur.

⊙ Sights

Most major sights are within the Altstadt and can be covered on foot. Only a few, such as the Reichsparteigelände and the Memorium Nuremberg Trials exhibition, require a trip by public transport.

★**Kaiserburg**   CASTLE
(Imperial Castle; 📞 0911-244 6590; www.kaiser burg-nuernberg.de; Auf der Burg; adult/child incl Sinwell Tower €7/free; Palas & Museum €5.50/free; ⊙ 9am-6pm Apr-Sep, 10am-4pm Oct-Mar) This enormous castle complex above the Altstadt poignantly reflects Nuremberg's medieval might. The main attraction is a tour of the renovated residential wing (Palas) to see the lavish Knights' and Imperial Hall, a Romanesque double chapel and an exhibit on the inner workings of the Holy Roman Empire. This segues to the Kaiserburg Museum, which focuses on the castle's military and building history. Elsewhere, enjoy panoramic views from the Sinwell Tower or peer 48m down into the Deep Well.

For centuries the castle, which has origins in the 12th century, also sheltered the crown jewels (crown, sceptre, orb etc) of the Holy Roman Empire, which are now kept at Hofburg palace in Vienna. It also played a key role in the drawing up of Emperor Charles IV's Golden Bull, a document that changed the way Holy Roman Emperors were elected. The exhibition contains an original statue taken from Prague's Charles Bridge of Charles IV who spent a lot of time in both Bohemia and Franconia during his reign.

★**Deutsche Bahn Museum**   MUSEUM
(📞 0800-3268 7386; www.dbmuseum.de; Lessingstrasse 6; adult/child €6/3; ⊙ 9am-5pm Tue-Fri, 10am-6pm Sat & Sun) Forget Dürer and wartime rallies, Nuremberg is a railway town at heart. Germany's first passenger trains ran between here and Fürth, a fact reflected in the unmissable German Railways Museum. which explores the history of Germany's legendary rail system. The huge exhibition that continues across the road is one of Nuremberg's top sights, especially if you have a soft spot for things that run on rails.

If you have tots aboard, head straight for KIBALA (Kinder-Bahnland, Children's Railway World), a section of the museum where lots of hands-on, interactive choo-choo-themed attractions await. There's also a huge model railway, one of Germany's largest, set in motion every hour by a uniformed controller.

The main exhibition charting almost two centuries of rail history starts on the ground floor and continues with more recent exhibits on the first. Passing quickly through the historically inaccurate beginning (as every rail buff knows, the world's first railway was the Stockton–Darlington, not the Liverpool–Manchester), highlights include Germany's oldest railway carriage dating from 1835 and lots of interesting Deutsche Reichsbahn paraphernalia from the former East Germany.

However, the real meat of the show is the two halls of locos and rolling stock. The first hall contains Ludwig II's incredible rococo rail carriage, dubbed the 'Versailles of the rails', as well as Bismarck's considerably less ostentatious means of transport. There's also Germany's most famous steam loco,

Nuremberg

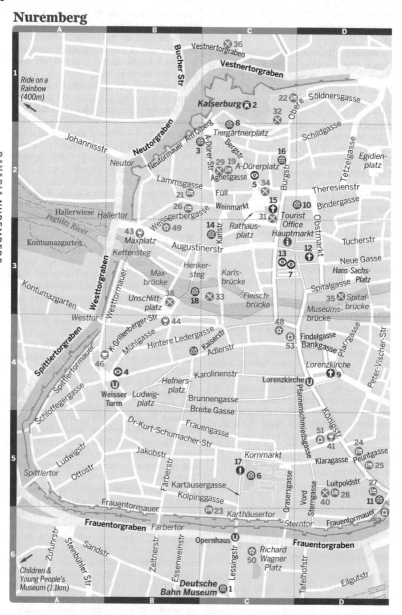

the Adler, built by the Stephensons in New-castle-upon-Tyne for the Nuremberg–Fürth line. The second hall across the road from the main building houses some mammoth engines, some with their Nazi or Deutsche Reichsbahn insignia still in place.

Germanisches
Nationalmuseum   MUSEUM

(German National Museum; ☏ 0911-133 10; www. gnm.de; Kartäusergasse 1; adult/child €8/5; ☉ 10am-6pm Tue & Thu-Sun, to 9pm Wed) Spanning prehistory to the early 20th century,

Highlights of the eclectic collection include Dürer's anatomically detailed *Hercules Slaying the Stymphalian Birds* and the world's oldest terrestrial globe and pocket watch as well as 20th-century design classics and baroque dollhouses.

Reichsparteitagsgelände HISTORIC SITE

(Luitpoldhain; ☑ 0911-231 7538; www.museen.nuern berg.de/dokuzentrum; Bayernstrasse 110; grounds free, Documentation Centre adult/child incl audioguide €6/1.50; ⊙ grounds 24hr, Documentation Centre 9am-6pm Mon-Fri, 10am-6pm Sat & Sun) If you've ever wondered where the infamous B&W images of ecstatic Nazi supporters hailing their Führer were taken, it was here in Nuremberg. Much of the grounds were destroyed during Allied bombing raids, but enough remain to get a sense of the megalomania behind it, especially after visiting the excellent Dokumentationszentrum (Documentation Centre). It's served by tram 8 from the Hauptbahnhof.

In the north wing of the partly finished Kongresshalle (Congress Hall), the Documentation Centre examines various historical aspects, including the rise of the NSDAP, the Hitler cult, the party rallies and the Nuremberg Trials.

East of here is the Zeppelinfeld, where most of the big Nazi parades, rallies and events took place. It is fronted by a 350m-long grandstand, the Zeppelintribüne, where you can still stand on the very balcony from where Hitler incited the masses. It now hosts sporting events and rock concerts, though this rehabilitation has caused controversy.

The grounds are bisected by the 2km-long and 40m-wide Grosse Strasse (Great Road), which was planned as a military parade road. Zeppelinfeld, Kongresshalle and Grosse Strasse are all protected landmarks for being significant examples of Nazi architecture.

The Reichsparteitagsgelände is about 4km southeast of the city centre.

Memorium Nuremberg Trials MEMORIAL

(☑ 0911-3217 9372; www.memorium-nuremberg. de; Bärenschanzstrasse 72; adult/child incl audio guide €6/1.50; ⊙ 9am-6pm Mon & Wed-Fri, 10am-6pm Sat & Sun Apr-Oct, slightly shorter hours Nov-Mar) Göring, Hess, Speer and 21 other Nazi leaders were tried for crimes against peace and humanity by the Allies in Schwurgerichtssaal 600 (Court Room 600) of this still-working courthouse. Today the room forms part of an engaging exhibit detailing the background, progression and impact of the trials using film, photographs, audiotape

this museum is the German-speaking world's biggest and most important museum of Teutonic culture. It features works by German painters and sculptors, an archaeological collection, arms and armour, musical and scientific instruments, and toys.

Nuremberg

and even the original defendants' dock. To get here, take the U1 towards Bärenschanze and get off at Sielstrasse.

The initial and most famous trial, held from 20 November 1945 until 1 October 1946, resulted in three acquittals, 12 sentences to death by hanging, three life sentences and four long prison sentences. Hermann Göring, the Reich's field marshall, famously cheated the hangman by taking a cyanide capsule in his cell hours before his scheduled execution.

Although it's easy to assume that Nuremberg was chosen as a trial venue because of its sinister key role during the Nazi years, it was actually picked for practical reasons since the largely intact Palace of Justice was able to accommodate lawyers and staff from all four Allied nations.

Note that Court Room 600 is still used for trials and may be closed to visitors.

Spielzeugmuseum   MUSEUM
(Toy Museum; Karlstrasse 13-15; adult/child €6/1.50; ⊙10am-5pm Tue-Fri, to 6pm Sat & Sun) Nuremberg has long been a centre of toy manufacturing, and the large Spielzeugmuseum presents toys in their infinite variety – from innocent hoops to blood-and-guts computer games, historical wooden and tin toys to Barbie et al. Kids and kids at heart will delight in the imaginatively designed play area.

Way of Human Rights   MONUMENT
(Kartäusergasse) Next to the Germanisches Nationalmuseum, 30 austere, 8m-tall concrete columns, each bearing one article of the Universal Declaration of Human Rights in a different language (plus German), run the entire length of Kartäusergasse. This spectacle is the work of Israeli artist Dani Karavan and is even more relevant in today's central Europe than it was when he won the competition to design the look of the street in the early 1990s.

Albrecht-Dürer-Haus   MUSEUM
(☎0911-231 2568; Albrecht-Dürer-Strasse 39; adult/child €6/1.50; ⊙10am-5pm Tue, Wed & Fri, to 8pm Thu, to 6pm Sat & Sun, to 5pm Mon Jul-Sep)

Dürer, Germany's most famous Renaissance draughtsperson, lived and worked at this site from 1509 until his death in 1528. Enjoy the slightly OTT multimedia show before embarking on an audioguide tour of the four-storey house narrated by 'Agnes', Dürer's wife. Highlights are the hands-on demonstrations in the recreated studio and print shop on the 3rd floor and, in the attic, a gallery featuring copies and originals of Dürer's work. The museum gift shop across the street is a source of original, highbrow souvenirs.

Ehekarussell Brunnen   FOUNTAIN
(Am Weissen Turm) At the foot of the fortified Weisser Turm (White Tower; now the gateway to the U-Bahn station of the same name) stands this large and startlingly grotesque sculptural work depicting six interpretations of marriage (from first love to quarrel to death-do-us-part), all based on a verse by Hans Sachs, the medieval cobbler-poet. You soon realise why the artist faced a blizzard of criticism when the fountain was unveiled in 1984; it really is enough to put anyone off tying the knot.

Sachs' poem can be found chiselled into a large pink marble heart on the tower side of the fountain.

St Sebalduskirche   CHURCH
(www.sebalduskirche.de; Winklerstrasse 26; ⊙9.30am-4pm Jan-Mar, to 6pm Apr-Dec) Nuremberg's oldest church was hoisted skywards in rusty pink-veined sandstone in the 13th century. Its exterior is replete with religious sculptures and symbols; check out the ornate carvings over the Bridal Doorway to the north, showing the Wise and Foolish Virgins. Inside, the bronze shrine of St Sebald (Nuremberg's own saint) is a Gothic and Renaissance masterpiece that took its maker, Peter Vischer the Elder, and his two sons more than 11 years to complete (Vischer is in it, too, sporting a skullcap).

Lorenzkirche   CHURCH
(Lorenzplatz; ⊙9am-5pm Mon-Sat, 1-4pm Sun, guided tours in German 11am & 2pm Mon-Sat, 2pm Sun) FREE Dark and atmospheric, the Lorenzkirche has dramatically downlit pillars, taupe stone columns, sooty ceilings and many artistic highlights. Check out the 15th-century tabernacle in the left aisle – the delicate carved strands wind up to the vaulted ceiling. Remarkable also are the stained glass (including a rose window 9m in diameter) and Veit Stoss' *Engelsgruss* (Annunciation), a wooden carving with life-size figures

suspended above the high altar. Some of the free German-language tours climb the tower, normally out of bounds to visitors.

Stadtmuseum Fembohaus   MUSEUM
(☎0911-231 2595; Burgstrasse 15; adult/child €6/1.50; ⊙10am-5pm Tue-Fri, to 6pm Sat & Sun) Offering an entertaining overview of the city's history, highlights of the Stadtmuseum Fembohaus include the restored historic rooms of this 16th-century merchant's house. Other sections look at aspects of Nuremberg's past and the 'A Crown – Power – History' exhibition gives you a potted history of the city in 30 minutes in the company of a special audioguide, an excellent and commendably digestable idea.

Neues Museum   MUSEUM
(☎0911-240 269; www.nmn.de; Luitpoldstrasse 5; adult/child €6/5; ⊙10am-6pm Fri-Wed, to 8pm Thu, closed Mon) The aptly named New Museum showcases contemporary art and design from the 1950s onwards, with resident collections of paintings, sculpture, photography and video art complemented by world-class travelling shows. Equally stunning is the award-winning building itself, with a dramatic 100m curved glass facade that, literally and figuratively, reflects the stone town wall opposite.

Jüdisches Museum Franken   JEWISH, MUSEUM
(☎0911-977 4853; www.juedisches-museum.org; Königstrasse 89; adult/child €3/free; ⊙Tue-Sun 10am-5pm) A quick U-Bahn ride away in the adjoining town of Fürth is the Jüdisches Museum Franken. Fürth once had the largest Jewish congregation of any city in southern Germany, and this museum chronicles the history of Jewish life in the region from the Middle Ages to today. To reach the museum, take the U1 to the Rathaus stop in Fürth.

Felsengänge   HISTORIC SITE
(Underground Cellars; www.historische-felsengaenge. de; Bergstrasse 19; tours adult/concession/child under 7 €7/6/free; ⊙tours hourly 11am-5pm Mon-Fri, 10am-5pm Sat & Sun) Deep beneath the Albrecht Dürer Monument on Albrecht-Dürer-Platz lurks the chilly Felsengänge. Departing from the brewery shop at Bergstrasse 19, tours descend to this four-storey subterranean warren, which dates from the 14th century and once housed a brewery and a beer cellar. During WWII, it served as an air-raid shelter. Tours take a minimum of three people and last 60 to 70 minutes. Take a jacket against the damp chill.

BAVARIA NUREMBERG

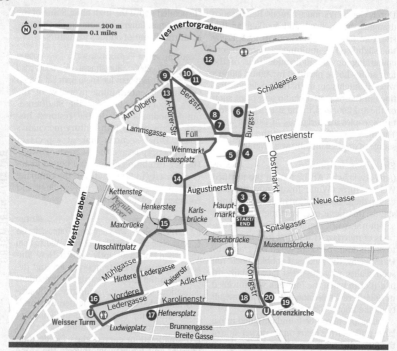

🚶 Walking Tour
Nuremberg Altstadt

START HAUPTMARKT
END HAUPTMARKT
LENGTH 2.5KM, TWO HOURS

This leisurely circuit covers the historic centre's key sights, taking as long as you like.

Start at the **①** **Hauptmarkt** (p431), the main square. At the eastern end is the ornate Gothic **②** **Pfarrkirche Unsere Liebe Frau** (p431), also called the Frauenkirche. Nearby the **③** **Schöner Brunnen** (p431) fountain rises from the cobblestones. Walk north to the **④** **Altes Rathaus**, the old town hall, with its Lochgefängnisse (medieval dungeons). Opposite is the 13th-century **⑤** **St Sebalduskirche** (p429), with the bronze shrine of St Sebald inside. Just up Burgstrasse, the **⑥** **Stadtmuseum Fembohaus** (p429) covers the highs and lows of Nuremberg's past. Backtrack south and turn right into Albrecht-Dürer-Platz, with the **⑦** **Albrecht Dürer Monument**. Directly beneath are the **⑧** **Felsengänge** (p431), tunnels once used as beer cellars and an air-raid shelter.

Moving up Bergstrasse, you'll reach the massive **⑨** **Tiergärtnertor**, a 16th-century tower. Nearby is the half-timbered **⑩** **Pilatushaus**. A few steps east is the **⑪** **Historischer Kunstbunker** (p431) where precious art was stored in WWII. Looming over the whole scene is the **⑫** **Kaiserburg** (p425). Go south to the **⑬** **Albrecht-Dürer-Haus** (p429), where the Renaissance genius lived and worked. Continue south along Albrecht-Dürer-Strasse, turn left around behind Sebalduskirche to Karlsstrasse, to reach the **⑭** **Spielzeugmuseum**, with generations of nostalgia-inducing playthings.

Cross the Karlsbrücke to enjoy a view of the **⑮** **Weinstadl** (p431). Continue across the Henkersteg and south to Vordere Ledergasse, leading to the amazing **⑯** **Ehekarussell Brunnen** (p429). Head east on Ludwigplatz past the **⑰** **Peter-Henlein-Brunnen**, with a statue of the first watchmaker, and along Karolinenstrasse to the city's oldest house, **⑱** **Nassauer Haus**, at No 2, and the massive **⑲** **Lorenzkirche** (p429), with a 15th-century tabernacle with a suspended carving of the Annunciation. The **⑳** **Tugendbrunnen** (Fountain of the Seven Virtues) is on the northern side of the church.

Historischer Kunstbunker HISTORIC BUILDING

(Historical Art Shelter; ✏911-2360 2731; www.
felsengaenge-nuernberg.de; Obere Schmiedgasse 52; adult/concession/child under 7 €7/6/
free; ⏱tours 2.30pm daily, plus 5.30pm Fri & Sat,
11.30am Sun) The Historischer Kunstbunker
is a climate-controlled bomb shelter deep
under the Burgberg that was used to protect art treasures during WWII. Priceless
masterpieces by Albrecht Dürer, sculptor
Veit Stoss and Martin Behaim, the maker
of a bafflingly accurate 15th-century globe,
were kept safe here from the Allied bombs
raining down on the city. The 75-minute
tour tells the story of how the bunker was
created from old beer cellars long before the
war began and which treasures were kept
safe down there.

Schöner Brunnen FOUNTAIN

(Beautiful Fountain; Hauptmarkt) Standing like
a space probe on the northwestern corner
of the square is the 19m (62ft) Schöner
Brunnen. A replica of the late 14th-century
original, it is a stunning golden vision of 40
electors, religious heroes and other allegorical figures. The original, made of badly erod-
ed sandstone, stands in the Germanisches
Nationalmuseum.

Pfarrkirche Unsere Liebe Frau CHURCH

(Frauenkirche; Hauptmarkt) At the eastern end
if the Hauptmarkt stands this ornate Gothic
church, also called the Frauenkirche. Its clock's
figures also spring into action every day at noon.

Weinstadl & Henkersteg HISTORIC BUILDING

On the northern side of the Pegnitz, near
the Karlsbrücke, is the impressive half-
timbered Weinstadl, an old wine depot with
two half-timbered storeys jutting out over
the river. It's had a storied life, ranging from
lepers' refuge to student dorm. Crossing
the river is the covered timber Henkersteg
(Hangman's Bridge), built to keep the hangman's exposure to disease to a minimum.

Mittelalterliche
Lochgefängnisse HISTORIC BUILDING

(Medieval Dungeons; ✏0911-2312690; https://mus
euun.nuernberg.de/lochgefaengnisse; adult/child
€3.50/1.50; ⏱tours 10am-4.30pm Tue-Sun) Beneath the Altes Rathaus (1616–22), a hulk of
a building with lovely Renaissance-style interiors, you'll find the macabre Mittelalter-
liche Lochgefängnisse. This 12-cell death
row and torture chamber must be seen on
a guided tour (held every half-hour) and
might easily put you off lunch.

Hauptmarkt SQUARE

(Hauptmarkt) This bustling square in the heart
of the Altstadt is the site of daily markets
as well as the famous *Christkindlsmarkte*
(Christmas markets). At the eastern end is
the ornate Gothic Frauenkirche (church).
Daily at noon crowds crane their necks to
witness the clock's figures enact a spectacle
called the Männleinlaufen (Little Men Dancing). Rising from the square like a Gothic
spire is the sculpture-festooned Schöner
Brunnen (Beautiful Fountain). Touch the
golden ring in the ornate wrought-iron gate
for good luck.

☞ Tours

Geschichte für Alle CULTURAL

(✏0911-307 360; www.geschichte-fuer-alle.de;
adult/concession €8/7) An intriguing range of
themed English-language tours by a nonprofit association. The 'Albrecht Dürer' and
'Life in Medieval Nuremberg' tours come
highly recommended.

Old Town Walking Tours WALKING

(✏0170-141 1223; www.nuernberg-tours.de; tour
€10; ⏱1pm May-Oct) English-language Old
Town walking tours are run by the tourist
office – tours leave from the Hauptmarkt
branch and take two hours.

Nuremberg Tours WALKING

(www.nurembergtours.com; adult/concession
€22/19; ⏱11.15am Mon, Wed & Sat Apr-Oct)
Four-hour walking and public transport
tours taking in the city centre and the Reichsparteitagsgelände (p427). Groups meet
at the entrance to the Hauptbahnhof.

🎊 Festivals & Events

Christkindlesmarkt CHRISTMAS MARKET

(www.christkindlesmarkt.de) From late November to Christmas Eve, the Hauptmarkt is tak-
en over by what most regards as Germany's
top Christmas market. Yuletide shoppers descend on the 'Christmas City' from all over
Europe to seek out unique gifts at the scores
of colourful timber trinket stalls that fill the
square.

🛏 Sleeping

Five Reasons HOSTEL €

(✏0911-9928 6625; www.five-reasons.de; Frauen-
tormauer 42; dm/d from €18/50; @ 🛜) This crisp,
21st-century 90-bed hotel-hostel boasts spotless dorms, the trendiest hostel bathrooms
you are ever likely to encounter, premade
beds, card keys, fully equipped kitchen, a

BAVARIA NUREMBERG

small bar and very nice staff. Breakfast is around €5 extra depending on what option you choose. Overall a great place to lay your head in a very central location.

Probst-Garni Hotel PENSION €
(☎0911-203 433; www.hotel-garni-probst.de; Luitpoldstrasse 9; s/d €55/70; 📶) A creaky lift from street level takes you up to this realistically priced, centrally located guesthouse, run for over 70 years by three generations of Probsts. The 33 gracefully old-fashioned rooms are multihued and high-ceilinged but some are more renovated than others. Breakfast is an extra €6.50.

Knaus-Campingpark CAMPGROUND €
(☎0911-981 2717; www.knauscamp.de; Hans-Kalb-Strasse 56; per tent/person €7/8.70; 📶) A camping ground near the lakes not far from the Dokumentationszentrum Reichsparteitagsgelände, southeast of the city centre. Take the S-Bahn to Nürnberg Frankenstadion.

DJH Hostel HOSTEL €
(☎0911-230 9360; www.nuernberg.jugendherberge.de; Burg 2; dm from €35) Open year-round, this impressive youth hostel is one of Germany's best and a real trip-stopper with a standard of facilities many four-star hotels would envy. Fully revamped a decade ago, the ancient Kornhaus is a dramatic building itself, but now flaunts crisply designed corridors, well-maintained dorms with super-modern bathrooms, a canteen, bar and very helpful staff.

★ **Hotel Deutscher Kaiser** HOTEL €€
(☎0911-242 660; www.deutscher-kaiser-hotel.de; Königstrasse 55; s/d from €90/110; 📶) Aristocratic in its design and service, this centrally located treat of a historic hotel has been in the same family since the turn of the 20th century. Climb the castle-like granite stairs to find rooms of understated simplicity, flaunting oversize beds, Italian porcelain, silk lampshades and real period furniture (*Biedermeier* and *Jugendstil*).

Agneshof HOTEL €€
(☎0911-214 440; www.agneshof-nuernberg.de; Agnesgasse 10; s/d from €85/105; P 📶) Tranquilly located in the antiques quarter near the St Sebalduskirche, the Agneshof's public areas have a sophisticated, artsy touch. The 74 box-ticking rooms have whitewashed walls and standard hotel furniture; some at the top have views of the Kaiserburg. There's a state-of-the-art wellness centre, and a pretty summer courtyard garden strewn with deck-chairs.

Hotel Victoria HOTEL €€
(☎0911-240 50; www.hotelvictoria.de; Königstrasse 80; s/d from €80/100; P 📶) A hotel since 1896, the Victoria is a solid option in a central location. With its early-21st-century bathrooms and now ever so slightly dated decor, the price is about right. Popular with business travellers. Parking costs €14.

Hotel Elch HOTEL €€
(☎0911-249 2980; www.hotel-elch.com; Irrer strasse 9; s/d from €55/70; 📶) Occupying a 14th-century, half-timbered house near the Kaiserburg, the Elch has a boutique wing and a 21st-century reception and restaurant giving you the choice between fairy-tale 'historic' and slick 'boutique', the latter of which costs a bit more.

Burghotel HOTEL €€
(☎0911-238 890; www.burghotel-nuernberg.de; Lammsgasse 3; s/d from €65/85; @ 📶 🏊) The mock-Gothic reception area and lantern-lit corridors (watch your head) indicate you're in for a slightly different hotel experience here. The small singles and doubles have strange '50s-style built-in timber furniture reminiscent of yesteryear train carriages, old-fashioned bedhead radios and chunky TVs, while some much larger 'comfort' rooms under the eaves have spacious sitting areas and more up-to-date amenities.

Art & Business Hotel HOTEL €€
(☎0911-232 10; www.art-business-hotel.com; Gleissbühlstrasse 15; s/d from €60/90; 📶) No need to be an artist or a businessperson to sleep at this up-to-the-minute place, a short amble from the Hauptbahnhof. From the trendy bar to the latest in slate bathroom styling, design here is bold, but not overpoweringly so. From reception follow the cool carpeting to your room, a well-maintained haven unaffected by traffic noise despite the city-centre frenzy outside.

Hotel Drei Raben BOUTIQUE HOTEL €€€
(☎0911-274 380; www.hoteldreiraben.de; Königstrasse 63; s/d from €100/160; P ❄ 📶) The design of this classy charmer builds upon the legend of the three ravens perched on the building's chimney stack, who tell stories from Nuremberg lore. Art and decor in the 'mythical theme' rooms reflect a particular tale, from the life of Albrecht Dürer to the first railway.

NUREMBERG FOR KIDS

No city in Bavaria has more for kids to see and do than Nuremberg. Every two months the region even produces a thick 'what's on' magazine called Frankenkids (www.frankenkids.de) focusing specifically on things to do with children. Keeping the little ones entertained in these parts really is child's play.

Museums

Children & Young People's Museum (☎ 0911-600 040; www.kindermuseum-nuernberg.de; Michael-Ende-Strasse 17; adult/family €7.50/19.50; ⏲ 2-5.30pm Sat, 10am-5.30pm Sun Sep-Jun) Educational exhibitions and lots of hands-on fun – just a pity it's not open more often.

School Museum (☎ 0911-530 2574; Äussere Sulzbacher Strasse 62; adult/child €6/1.50; ⏲ 9am-5pm Tue-Fri, 10am-6pm Sat & Sun) Recreated classroom plus school-related exhibits from the 17th century to the Third Reich.

Deutsche Bahn Museum (p425) Feeds the kids' obsession for choo-choos.

Play

Playground of the Senses (www.erfahrungsfeld.nuernberg.de; Wöhrder Wiese; adult/child €8.50/7; ⏲ 9am-6pm Mon-Fri, 1-6pm Sat, 10am-6pm Sun May–mid-Sep) Some 80 hands-on 'stations' designed to educate children in the laws of nature, physics and the human body. Take the U2 or U3 to Wöhrder Wiese.

Toys

Playmobil (☎ 0911-9666 1700; www.playmobil-funpark.de; Brandstätterstrasse 2-10; admission €11.90; ⏲ 10am-6pm mid-Feb–Mar, 9am-6pm Apr, 9am-7pm May–mid-Sep) This theme park has life-size versions of the popular toys. It's located 9km west of the city centre in Zirndorf; take the S4 to Anwanden, then change to bus 151. Free admission if it's your birthday. Special 'Kleine Dürer' (Little Dürer; €2.99) figures are on sale here and at the tourist office.

Käthe Wohlfahrt Christmas shop (p436) The Nuremberg branch of this year-round Christmas shop.

Spielzeugmuseum (p429) Some 1400 sq metres of Matchbox, Barbie, Playmobil and Lego, plus a great play area.

Germanisches Nationalmuseum (p427) Has a toy section and holds ocassional tours for children.

✕ Eating

Café am Trödelmarkt CAFE €
(Trödelmarkt 42; dishes €4-10; ⏲ 9am-6pm Mon-Sat, 10am-6pm Sun) A gorgeous place on a sunny day, this multilevel waterfront cafe overlooks the covered Henkersteg bridge. It's especially popular for its continental breakfasts, and has fantastic cakes, as well as good blackboard lunchtime specials between 11am and 2pm.

Naturkostladen Lotos ORGANIC, BUFFET €
(www.naturkostladen-lotos.de; Am Unschlittplatz 1; dishes €4-9; ⏲ 9am-6.30pm Mon-Fri, to 5pm Sat; ⏲) Unclog arteries and blast free radicals with a blitz of grain burgers, spinach soup or vegan pizza at this strictly bio health-food shop. The fresh bread and cheese counter is a treasure chest of nutritious picnic supplies.

Suppdiwupp CAFETERIA €
(Lorenzer Strasse 27; soups & mains €4-7; ⏲ 11am-6pm Mon-Thu, to 4pm Fri, noon-5pm Sat) This fragrantly spicy lunch stop has outdoor seating, a weekly changing menu and a choice of nonliquid mains (sandwiches, salads) if you don't fancy one of the 16 types of broth. Very popular early afternoon so get there early.

Wurst Durst GERMAN €
(Luitpoldstrasse 13; dishes €3.50-6; ⏲ 11am-6pm Tue-Thu, to 5am Fri & Sat) Wedged in between the facades of Luitpoldstrasse, this tiny snack bar offers some munchies relief in the form of Belgian fries, sausages and trays of *Currywurst*.

American Diner AMERICAN €
(Gewerbemuseumsplatz 3; burgers €6-11; ⊗ 11.30am-11.30pm Sun-Thu, to 12.30am Fri & Sat) This retro diner is one of several eateries within the Cinecitta Cinema complex, Germany's biggest multiplex. It serves filling prefilm burgers.

★**Albrecht Dürer Stube** FRANCONIAN €€
(☑ 0911-227 209; www.albrecht-duerer-stube.de; cnr Albrecht-Dürer-Strasse & Agnesgasse; mains €6-15.50; ⊗ 6pm-midnight Mon-Sat plus 11.30am-2.30pm Fri & Sun) This unpretentious and intimate restaurant has a Dürer-inspired dining room, prettily laid tables, a ceramic stove keeping things toasty and a menu of Nuremberg sausages, steaks, sea fish, seasonal specials, Franconian wine and *Landbier* (regional beer). Booking ahead at weekends is highly recommended, as there aren't many tables.

Goldenes Posthorn FRANCONIAN €€
(☑ 0911-225 153; Glöckleinsgasse 2, cnr Sebalder Platz; mains €6-14; ⊗ 11.30am-11.30pm) Push open the heavy copper door to find a real culinary treat that has hosted royals, artists and professors (including Albrecht Dürer) since 1498. You can't go wrong sticking with the miniature local sausages, but the pork shoulder and also the house speciality – vinegar-marinated ox cheeks – are all good value for money.

Heilig-Geist-Spital BAVARIAN €€
(☑ 0911-221 761; www.heilig-geist-spital.de; Spitalgasse 16; mains €7-18; ⊗ 11.30am-11pm) Lots of dark carved wood, a herd of hunting trophies and a romantic candlelit half-light make this former hospital, suspended over the Pegnitz, one of the most atmospheric dining rooms in town. Sample the delicious, seasonally changing menu inside or out in the pretty courtyard, a real treat if you are looking for somewhere traditional to dine.

Bratwursthäusle FRANCONIAN €€
(http://die-nuernberger-bratwurst.de; Rathausplatz 1; meals €7.50-11.50; ⊗ 11am-10pm) Seared over a flaming beech-wood grill, the little links sold at this rustic inn next to the Sebalduskirche arguably set the standard across the land. You can dine in the timbered restaurant or on the terrace with views of the Hauptmarkt. Service can be flustered at busy times and it's cash only when the bill comes.

Hexenhäusle GERMAN €€
(☑ 0911-4902 9095; www.hexenhaeusle-nuernberg. com; Vestnertorgraben 4; mains €7-12; ⊗ 5-11pm

Tue-Thu, 11am-11pm Fri & Sat, 11am-9pm Sun) The half-timbered 'Witches Hut' ranks among Nuremberg's most enchanting inns and beer gardens. Tucked next to a sturdy town gate at the foot of the castle, it serves the gamut of grilled fare, dumplings and other Franconian rib-stickers with big mugs of local Zirndorfer and Tucher beer. Also has a small beer garden.

Marientorzwinger GERMAN €€
(www.wirtshaus-marientorzwinger.de; Lorenzer Strasse 33; mains €7-17; ⊗ 11.30am-1am) The last remaining *Zwinger* eatery (a tavern built in a *Zwinger*, a narrow space between two defensive walls) in Nuremberg is an atmospheric place to chomp on a mixed bag of sturdy regional specials in the simple wood-panelled dining room or the leafy beer garden. Fürth-brewed Tucher is the ale of choice here.

Burgwächter FRANCONIAN, INTERNATIONAL €€
(☑ 0911-2348 9844; www.burgwaechter-nuernberg.de; Am Ölberg 10; mains €9-20; ⊗ 11am-10pm; ☑) Refuel after a tour of the Kaiserburg with prime steaks, bratwurst with potato salad, and vegetarian-friendly Swabian filled pastas and salads, as you feast your eyes on the best terrace views from any Nuremberg eatery or drinking spot. With kiddies in tow, ask for *Kloss* (a simple dumpling with sauce for €3.90).

🍷 Drinking & Nightlife

Cafe Katz BAR
(Hans-Sachs-Platz 8; ⊗ 11am-1am Sun-Thu, to 2am Fri & Sat) From the outside this place looks like a secondhand furniture shop, the vitrines packed with 1970s coffee tables, old school desks and 1980s high-back chairs. But the La Marzocco espresso machine gives the game away as this is one of Nuremberg's coolest cafes, an on-trend spot to see, be seen and enjoy a drink and/or a vegie or vegan meal amid retro furnishings.

Kloster PUB
(Obere Wörthstrasse 19; ⊗ 5pm-1am) One of Nuremberg's best drinking dens is all dressed up as a monastery replete with ecclesiastic knick-knacks including coffins emerging from the walls. The monks here pray to the god of *Landbier* (regional beer) and won't be up at 5am for matins, that's for sure.

Kettensteg BEER GARDEN
(Maxplatz 35; ⊗ 11am-11pm) At the end of the chain bridge and in the shadow of the Hal-

letor you'll find this classic Bavarian beer garden complete with its gravel floor, folding slatted chairs, fairy lights, tree shade and river views. Zirndorfer, Lederer and Tucher beers are on tap and some of the food comes on heart-shaped plates.

Treibhaus   CAFE
(Karl-Grillenberger-Strasse 28; light meals €6-10; ⊙9am to last customer; ⊛) Off the path of most visitors, this bustling cafe is a Nuremberg institution and one of the most happening places in town. Set yourself down in the sun on a yellow director's chair out front or warm yourself with something strong around the huge zinc bar inside. Visitors heap praise on the big breakfasts served here.

Meisengeige   BAR
(Am Laufer Schlagturm 3; ⊙3.30pm-midnight Mon-Wed, to 1am Thu, to 2am Fri & Sat, 1.30pm-midnight Sun) The pub attached to a small foreign- and art-film cinema of the same name is a characterful old place (bentwood chairs, potted plants and big mirrors) for an evening beer, even if you aren't going to see a film. Located right by the Laufer Schlagturm, one of the medieval gates into the city.

Barfüsser Brauhaus   BEER HALL
(Königstrasse 60; ⊙11am-1am Mon-Fri, to 2am Sat) This cellar beer hall deep below street level is a popular spot to hug a mug of site-brewed ale, bubbling frothily in the copper kettles that occupy the cavernous vaulted interior. The traditional trappings of the huge quaffing space clash oddly with the polo shirts of the swift-footed waiting staff, but that's our only criticism.

☆ Entertainment

Mata Hari Bar   LIVE MUSIC
(www.mataharibar.de; Weissgerbergasse 31; ⊙from 8pm Wed-Sun) This bar with live music and DJ nights is a Nuremberg institution. After 9pm it's usually standing room only and the party goes on well into the early hours.

Staatstheater   THEATRE
(☑0911-231 3808; www.staatstheater-nuernberg.de; Richard-Wagner-Platz 2) Nuremberg's magnificent state theatre serves up an impressive mix of dramatic arts. The renovated art nouveau opera house presents opera and ballet, while the Kammerspiele offers a varied program of classical and contemporary plays. The Nürnberger Philharmoniker also performs here.

Filmhaus   CINEMA
(www.kunstkulturquartier.de; Königstrasse 93) This small indie picture house, part of the large Cultural Quarter complex, shows foreign-language movies, plus reruns of cult German flicks and films for kids.

Hirsch   LIVE MUSIC
(☑0911-429 414; www.der-hirsch.de; Vogelweiherstrasse 66) This converted factory, 2.5km south of the Hauptbahnhof, hosts live alternative music almost daily, both big-name acts and local names. Take the U1 or U2 to Plärrer, then change to tram 4, alighting at Dianaplatz.

Mach1   CLUB
(☑0911-246 602; www.macheins.club; Kaiserstrasse 1-9; ⊙from 10pm Fri & Sat) This centrally located temple to dance has been around for decades, but is still one of the most popular venues at weekends. Mostly mainstream music and a young crowd.

🛍 Shopping

Käthe Wohlfahrt
Christmas Shop   CHRISTMAS DECORATIONS
(www.wohlfahrt.com; Königstrasse 8; ⊙10am-6pm Mon-Sat) The Nuremberg branch of Germany's chain of Christmas shops selling pricey Yuletide decorations 365 days a year.

Bier Kontor   ALCOHOL
(An der Mauthalle 2; ⊙11am-2pm & 2.30-7pm Mon-Sat) This small shop just off the tourist drag stocks a whopping 350 types of beer, from local Franconian suds to Hawaiian ales, fruity Belgian concoctions to British porters. And staff really know their stuff when it comes to the amber nectar.

Handwerkerhof   MARKET
(www.handwerkerhof.de; Am Königstor; ⊙9am-6.30pm Mon-Fri, 10am-4pm Sat Apr-Dec, shorter hours Jan-Mar) A recreation of an old-world Nuremberg crafts quarter, the Handwerkerhof is a walled tourist market by the Königstor. If you're in the market for souvenirs you may find some decent merchandise here such as gingerbread wooden toys and traditional ceramics, and there is plenty of bratwurst to go round, too.

ℹ Information

Post Office (Josephsplatz 3; ⊙9am-6.30pm Mon-Fri, to 2pm Sat)

ReiseBank (Hauptbahnhof; ⊙8am-9pm Mon-Fri, 8am-12.30pm & 1.15-4pm Sat & Sun)

> ### ❶ NÜRNBERG + FÜRTH CARD
>
> Available to those staying overnight in either city, the Nürnberg + Fürth Card (€28) is good for two days of public transport and admission to all museums and attractions. It can only be purchased from tourist offices or online from Nuremberg's official tourism website.

Convenient place to change money at the Hauptbahnhof.

Tourist Office Hauptmarkt (📞 0911-233 60; www.tourismus.nuernberg.de; Hauptmarkt 18; ⊙ 9am-6pm Mon-Sat, 10am-4pm Sun) Hauptmarkt branch of the tourist office. Has extended hours during Christkindlesmarkt that takes place on its doorstep.

Tourist Office Künstlerhaus (📞 0911-233 60; www.tourismus.nuernberg.de; Königstrasse 93; ⊙ 9am-7pm Mon-Sat, 10am-4pm Sun) Publishes the excellent *See & Enjoy* booklet, a comprehensive guide to the city.

❶ Getting There & Away

AIR

Nuremberg's **Albrecht Dürer Airport** (NUE; 📞 0911-937 00; www.airport-nuernberg.de; Flughafenstrasse), 5km north of the centre, is served by regional and international carriers, including Ryanair, Lufthansa, Air Berlin and Air France.

BUS

Buses to destinations across Europe leave from the **main bus station** (ZOB) near the Hauptbahnhof. There's a Touring/Eurolines office nearby. Flixbus (www.flixbus.com) links Nuremberg with countless destinations in Germany and beyond. Special Deutsche Bahn express coaches to Prague (from €10, 3½ hours, seven daily) leave from the ZOB.

TRAIN

Nuremberg is connected by train to Berlin (from €80, three to 3½ hours, hourly), Frankfurt (€30 to €60, 2¼ hours, at least hourly), Hamburg (from €80, 4½ hours, hourly) and Munich (€40 and €60, one hour, twice hourly). Services also go to Cheb (€34, 1¾ hours, every two hours), for connections to Prague, and Vienna (from €90, four to 5½ hours, every two hours).

❶ Getting Around

TO/FROM THE AIRPORT

U-Bahn 2 runs every few minutes from the Hauptbahnhof to the airport (€2.75, 13 minutes). A taxi to the airport will cost about €20.

BICYCLE

Nuremberg has ample bike lanes along busy roads and the Altstadt is pretty bike friendly. For bike hire, try the excellent **Ride on a Rainbow** (📞 0911-397 337; www.ride-on-a-rainbow.de; Adam-Kraft-Strasse 55; per day from €9).

PUBLIC TRANSPORT

The best transport around the Altstadt is at the end of your legs. Timed tickets on the VGN bus, tram and U-Bahn/S-Bahn networks cost from €1.30. A day pass costs €8.10. Passes bought on Saturday are valid all weekend.

Bamberg

📞 0951 / POP 75,800

A disarmingly beautiful architectural masterpiece with an almost complete absence of modern eyesores, Bamberg's entire Altstadt is a Unesco World Heritage Site and one of Bavaria's unmissables. Generally regarded as one of Germany's most attractive settlements, the town is bisected by rivers and canals and was built by archbishops on seven hills, earning it the inevitable sobriquet of 'Franconian Rome'. Students inject some liveliness into its streets, pavement cafes, pubs and no fewer than 10 breweries cooking up Bamberg's famous smoked beer, but it's usually wide-eyed tourists who can be seen filing through its narrow medieval streets. The town can be tackled as a day trip from Nuremberg, but, to really do it justice and to experience the romantically lit streets once most visitors have left, consider an overnight stay.

◉ Sights

★**Bamberger Dom**   CATHEDRAL
(www.erzbistum-bamberg.de; Domplatz; ⊙ 9.30am-6pm Apr-Oct, to 5pm Nov-Mar) Beneath the quartet of spires, Bamberg's cathedral is packed with artistic treasures, most famously the slender equestrian statue of the Bamberger Reiter (Bamberg Horseman), whose true identity remains a mystery. It overlooks the tomb of cathedral founders, Emperor Heinrich II and his wife Kunigunde, splendidly carved by Tilmann Riemenschneider. The marble tomb of Clemens II in the west choir is the only papal burial site north of the Alps. Nearby, the Virgin Mary altar by Veit Stoss also warrants closer inspection.

Founded by Heinrich II in 1004, the cathedral's current appearance dates to the early 13th century and is the outcome of a Romanesque-Gothic duel between church architects after the original and its immediate successor

Bamberg

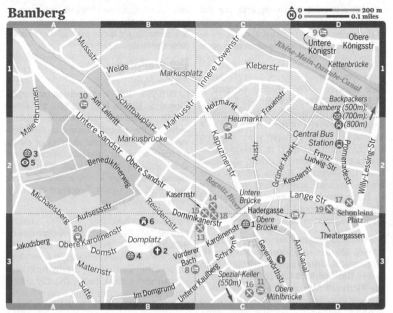

⊙ 0   200 m
0   0.1 miles

Bamberg

⊙ Sights
1 Altes Rathaus	C3
2 Bamberger Dom	B3
3 Fränkisches Brauereimuseum	A2
4 Historisches Museum	B3
5 Kloster St Michael	A2
6 Neue Residenz	B3

🛏 Sleeping
7 Alt Bamberg	D3
8 Barockhotel am Dom	B3
9 Hotel Europa	D1
10 Hotel Residenzschloss	A1
11 Hotel Sankt Nepomuk	C3
12 Hotel Wohnbar	C2

🍴 Eating
13 Alt Ringlein	C3
14 Ambräusianum	C2
15 Bäckerei Seel	C2
16 Klosterbräu	C3
17 Messerschmidt	D2
18 Schlenkerla	C3
19 Zum Sternla	D2

🍷 Drinking & Nightlife
20 Torschuster	A3

burnt down in the 12th century. The pillars have the original light hues of Franconian sandstone thanks to Ludwig I, who eradicated all postmedieval decoration in the early 19th century.

Altes Rathaus   HISTORIC BUILDING
(Old Town Hall; Obere Brücke; adult/child €6/5; ⊙10am-4.30pm Tue-Sun) Like a ship in dry dock, Bamberg's 1462 Old Town Hall was built on an artifical island in the Regnitz River, allegedly because the local bishop had refused to give the town's citizens any land for its construction. Inside you'll find the Sammlung Ludwig, a collection of precious

porcelain, but even more enchanting are the richly detailed frescos adorning its facades – note the cherub's leg cheekily protruding from the eastern facade.

Historisches Museum   MUSEUM
(☎0951-519 0746; www.museum.bamberg.de; Domplatz 7; adult/child €7/1; ⊙10am-5pm Tue-Sun May-Oct) Bamberg's main museum fills the Alte Hofhaltung (old court hall), a former prince-bishops' palace near the cathedral, with a mixed bag of exhibits. These include a model of the pilgrimage church Vierzehnheiligen and the Bamberger Götzen, ancient stone sculptures found in the region. Often

of greater interest are the expertly curated special exhibitions, which examine aspects of the region's past in more detail.

In winter the museum is often only open for special exhibitions.

Neue Residenz
PALACE

(New Residence; ☑ 0951-519 390; Domplatz 8; adult/child €4.50/free; ⊙ 9am-6pm Apr-Sep, 10am-4pm Oct-Mar) This splendid episcopal palace gives you an eyeful of the lavish lifestyle of Bamberg's prince-bishops who, between 1703 and 1802, occupied its 40-odd rooms that can only be seen on guided 45-minute tours (in German). Tickets are also good for the Bavarian State Gallery, with works by Lucas Cranach the Elder and other Old Masters. The baroque Rose Garden delivers fabulous views over the town.

Fränkisches Brauereimuseum
MUSEUM

(☑ 0951-530 16; www.brauereimuseum.de; Michaelsberg 10f; adult/concession €4/3.50; ⊙ 1-5pm Wed-Fri, 11am-5pm Sat & Sun Apr-Oct) Located in the Kloster St Michael, this comprehensive brewery museum exhibits over 1000 period mashing, boiling and bottling implements, as well as everything to do with local suds, such as beer mats, tankards, enamel beer signs and lots of photos and documentation. If the displays have left you dry mouthed, quench your thirst in the small pub.

Kloster St Michael
MONASTERY

(Franziskanergasse 2; ⊙ 9am-6pm Apr-Oct) Above Domplatz, at the top of Michaelsberg, is the Benedictine Kloster St Michael, a former monastery and now an aged people's home. The monastery church is essential Bamberg viewing, both for its baroque art and the meticulous depictions of nearly 600 medicinal plants and flowers on the vaulted ceiling. The manicured garden terraces behind the church – former monastical vineyards – provide splendid city panoramas.

The entire complex was completely under wraps at the time of research as it underwent thorough renovation work that may take a number of years.

☞ Tours

BierSchmecker Tour
WALKING

(www.bier.bamberg.info; adult €22.50) Possibly the most tempting tour of the amazingly varied offerings at the tourist office is the self-guided BierSchmecker Tour. The price includes entry to the Fränkisches Brauereimuseum (depending on the route taken), plus five beer vouchers valid in five pubs and breweries, an English information booklet, a route map and a souvenir stein. Not surprisingly, it can take all day to complete the route.

🛏 Sleeping

Alt Bamberg
HOTEL €

(☑ 0951-986 150; www.hotel-alt-bamberg.de; Habergasse 11; s/d from €45/65; �🖥) Often heavily discounted on popular booking websites, the no-frills rooms at this well-located, old-school hotel are digs of choice for euro-watching nomads. Some rooms share showers, the breakfast is an ample spread and there's a well-respected Greek restaurant downstairs. Reception closes between 11am and 3pm.

Backpackers Bamberg
HOSTEL €

(☑ 0951-222 1718; www.backpackersbamberg.de; Heiliggrabstrasse 4; dm €17-20, s/d €30/45; 🖥) Bamberg's backpacker hostel is a well-kept affair, with clean dorms, a fully functional kitchen and a quiet, family-friendly atmosphere (staff stress this is not a party hostel). Make sure you let the hostel know when you're arriving, as it's left unstaffed for most of the day. It's located 400m north along Luitpoldstrasse from the Luitpoldbrücke.

Campingplatz Insel
CAMPGROUND €

(☑ 0951-563 20; www.campinginsel.de; Am Campingplatz 1; tents €4-8, adult/car €7/4; 🖥) If rustling nylon is your abode of choice, this well-equipped site, in a tranquil spot right on the river, is the sole camping option. Take bus 918 to Campingplatz.

★ Hotel Sankt Nepomuk
HOTEL €€

(☑ 0951-984 20; www.hotel-nepomuk.de; Obere Mühlbrücke 9; s/d from €90/130; 🅿🖥) Aptly named after the patron saint of bridges, this is a classy establishment in a half-timbered former mill right on the Regnitz. It has a superb restaurant (mains €15 to €30) with a terrace and 24 new-fangled rooms of recent vintage. Breakfast is an extra €5.

Hotel Residenzschloss
HOTEL €€

(☑ 0951-609 10; www.residenzschloss.com; Untere Sandstrasse 32; r from €100; 🅿🖥) Bamberg's grandest digs occupy a palatial building formerly used as a hospital. But have no fear, as the swanky furnishings – from the Roman-style steam bath to the flashy piano bar – have little in common with institutional care. High-ceilinged rooms are business standard though display little historical charm. Take bus 916 from the ZOB.

Hotel Wohnbar   BOUTIQUE HOTEL €€
(📞0951-5099 8844; www.wohnbar-bamberg.de; Stangsstrasse 3; s/d from €60/80; 🅿🛜) 'Carpe Noctem' (Seize the Night) is the motto of this charming 10-room retreat with boldly coloured, contemporary rooms near the university quarter. Those in the 'economy' category are a very tight squeeze. Parking costs €10 per day, breakfast €8.50.

Barockhotel am Dom   HOTEL €€
(📞0951-540 31; www.barockhotel.de; Vorderer Bach 4; s/tw from €85/100; 🅿🛜) The sugary facade, a sceptre's swipe from the Dom, gives a hint of the baroque heritage and original details within. The 19 rooms have sweeping views of the Dom or the roofs of the Altstadt, and breakfast is served in a 14th-century vault.

Hotel Europa   HOTEL €€
(📞0951-309 3020; www.hotel-europa-bamberg. de; Untere Königstrasse 6-8; d from €105; 🛜) This spick-and-span but unfussy affair just outside the Altstadt gets kudos for its friendliness, comfy beds and opulent breakfast, served in the winter garden or sunny courtyard. Rooms at the front are noisier but may overlook the cathedral and the red-tiled roofs of the Altstadt. Some are a bit small.

✖ Eating

★**Schlenkerla**   GERMAN €
(📞0951-560 60; www.schlenkerla.de; Dominikanerstrasse 6; mains €7-13; ⊙9.30am-11.30pm) Beneath wooden beams as dark as the superb *Rauchbier* poured straight from oak barrels, locals and visitors gather around a large ceramic stove to dig into scrumptious Franconian fare at this legendary flower-festooned tavern. Staff will pass beers through a tiny window in the entrance for those who just want to taste a beer but not sit.

★**Klosterbräu**   PUB FOOD €
(Obere Mühlbrücke 1-3; mains €7-13; ⊙11.30am-10pm Mon-Sat, to 2pm Sun) This beautiful half-timbered brewery is Bamberg's oldest. It draws *Stammgäste* (regulars) and tourists alike who wash down filling slabs of meat and dumplings with its excellent range of ales in the unpretentious dining room.

Zum Sternla   FRANCONIAN €
(📞0951-287 50; www.sternla.de; Lange Strasse 46; mains €5-12; ⊙4-11pm Tue, 11am-11pm Wed-Sun) Bamberg's oldest *Wirtshaus* (inn; established 1380) bangs out bargain-priced staples including pork dishes, steaks, dumplings and

DON'T MISS

KLEIN VENEDIG

A row of diminutive, half-timbered cottages once inhabited by fisherfolk (hence the street's name meaning 'fishery') comprises Bamberg's Klein Venedig (Little Venice), which hems the Regnitz's east bank between Markusbrücke and Untere Brücke. The little homes balance on poles set right into the water and are fronted by tiny gardens and terraces (wholly unlike Venice, but who cares), the river flowing sluggishly past just centimetres below ground level.

Klein Venedig is well worth a stroll but looks at least as pretty from a distance, especially in summer when red geraniums spill from flower boxes. Good vantage points include the Untere Brücke near the Altes Rathaus, and Am Leinritt on the opposite bank.

sauerkraut, as well as specials, but it's a great, nontouristy place for a traditional *Brotzeit* (snack), or just a pretzel and a beer. The menu is helpfully translated from Franconian into German.

Spezial-Keller   GERMAN €
(📞0951-548 87; www.spezial-keller.de; Sternwartstrasse 8; dishes €6-14; ⊙3pm-late Tue-Fri, from noon Sat, from 10.30am Sun) The walk into the hills past the cathedral to this delightful beer garden is well worth it, both for the malty *Rauchbier* and the sweeping views of the Altstadt. In winter the action moves into the cosy, wood-panelled tavern warmed by a traditional wood-burning tiled stove.

Bäckerei Seel   BAKERY €
(Dominikanerstrasse 8; snacks from €1.50; ⊙6am-6pm Mon-Fri, 7am-4pm Sat) This old town bakery is the place to go for early starters who need breakfast at 6am. It stocks a delicious range of pastries and sandwiches, but if you want to eat on the premises it's standing only.

Alt Ringlein   FRANCONIAN €€
(www.altringlein.com; Dominikanerstrasse 9; mains €7-20; ⊙11am-11pm; 🛜) Serving gourmet-ish takes on the most traditional of Franconian fare, this bastion of beer, meat and *Kloss* (Franconian dumplings) has one of the most impressive dining rooms in town, all chunky

carved wood chairs and dark-wood panelling. Service is swift and polite and there's a beer garden out back for summertime sipping.

Messerschmidt   FRANCONIAN €€
(☑ 0951-297 800; Lange Strasse 41; mains €12-25; ☺ 11am-10pm; ☞) This stylish gourmet eatery may be ensconced in the house where aviation engineer Willy Messerschmidt was born, but there's nothing 'plane' about dining here. The place oozes old-world charm, with dark woods, white linens and traditionally formal service. Sharpen your molars on platters of roast duck and red cabbage out on the alfresco terrace overlooking a pretty park, or in the attached wine tavern.

Ambräusianum   PUB FOOD €€
(☑ 0951-509 0262; Dominikanerstrasse 10; mains €9-14; ☺ 11am-11pm Tue-Sat, to 9pm Sun) Bamberg's only brewpub is, as you might expect, a traditional affair and does a killer schnitzel plus pork knuckle and *Flammkuchen* (Alsatian pizza) that'll have you waddling out the door. Many just come for the home-brewed beer, but if you're not into downing tankards you can just have a taster rack for €3.

🍷 Drinking & Nightlife

Torschuster   BAR
(Obere Karolinenstrasse 10; ☺ 7.30-1pm) Amid the palaces and ecclesiastic institutions of the Domberg stands this small pub serving beers from all of Bamberg's breweries and a good selection of whisky. Old enamel advertising signs decorate the walls but the main attraction here is the friendly owner Thomas' eclectic vinyl collection that doesn't go much past the mid-80s. All in all an after-dark antidote to medieval tavern life. Take bus 910 to Torschuster.

ℹ️ Information

Post Office (Ludwigstrasse 25; ☺ 9am-6pm Mon-Fri, to 12.30pm Sat)

Tourist Office (☑ 0951-297 6200; www.bamberg.info; Geyerswörthstrasse 5; ☺ 9.30am-6pm Mon-Fri, to 4pm Sat, to 2.30pm Sun) Large professional office with parking, toilets and a children's playground all nearby. Staff sell the Bambergcard (€14.90), valid for three days of free bus rides and free museum entry.

ℹ️ Getting There & Around

Bamberg has rail connections to Berlin (from €60, 2¾ hours, hourly), Munich (€25, two hours, every two hours or change in Nuremberg),

Nuremberg (€20, 40 minutes, up to four hourly) and Würzburg (€22, one hour, twice hourly).

Several buses, including 901, 902 and 931, connect the train station with the **central bus station** (ZOB; Promenadestrasse), which has a handy 12-hour left-luggage facility. Bus 910 goes from the ZOB to Domplatz.

Bayreuth
☑ 0921 / POP 73,000

Even without its Wagner connections, Bayreuth would still be an interesting detour from Nuremberg or Bamberg for its streets of sandstone baroque architecture and impressive palaces. But it's for the annual Wagner Festival that 60,000 opera devotees make a pilgrimage to this neck of the *Wald*.

Bayreuth's glory days began in 1735 when Wilhelmine, sister of King Frederick the Great of Prussia, was forced to marry stuffy Margrave Friedrich. Bored with the local scene, the cultured Anglo-oriented Wilhelmine invited the finest artists, poets, composers and architects in Europe to court. The period bequeathed some eye-catching buildings, still on display for all to see.

⊙ Sights

★**Markgräfliches Opernhaus**   THEATRE
(Opernstrasse 14; adult/child €8/free; ☺ 9am-6pm Apr-Sep, 10am-4pm Oct-Mar) Designed by Giuseppe Galli Bibiena, a famous 18th-century architect from Bologna, Bayreuth's opera house is one of Europe's most stunningly ornate baroque theatres. Germany's largest opera house until 1871, it has a lavish interior smothered in carved, gilded and marbled wood. However, Richard Wagner considered it too modest for his serious work and conducted here just once.

This grand old dame spent most of the past decade under wraps, receiving a multimillion euro facelift but reopened its door in early 2018. It was declared a Unesco World Cultural Heritage Site in 2012.

Richard Wagner Museum   MUSEUM
(Haus Wahnfried; ☑ 0921-757 2816; www.wagnermuseum.de; Richard-Wagner-Strasse 48; adult/child €8/free; ☺ 10am-6pm Jul & Aug, to 5pm Tue-Sun Sep-Jun) In the early 1870s King Ludwig II, Wagner's most devoted fan, gave the composer the cash to build Haus Wahnfried, a pleasingly symmetrical minimansion on the northern edge of the Hofgarten. The building now houses the Richard Wagner Museum, Ludwig's bronze bust stand-

BAVARIA BAYREUTH

BAYREUTH'S FAMOUS WAGNER FESTIVAL

The Wagner Festival (www.bayreuther-festspiele.de; ☉late Jul & Aug) has been a summer fixture in Bayreuth for over 140 years and is generally regarded as the top Wagner event anywhere in the world. The festival lasts for 30 days, with each performance attended by an audience of just over 1900. Demand is insane, with an estimated 500,000 fans vying for less than 60,000 tickets.

The vast majority of tickets go onto the open market in an online free-for-all. Every ticket is snapped up in seconds, a fact that has angered many a Wagner society, which used to get preferential treatment. Alternatively, it is still possible to lay siege to the box office 2½ hours before performances begin in the hope of snapping up cheap returned tickets, but there's no guarantee you'll get in.

ing prominently outside. Crisply renovated in the early part of the decade, the bulk of the exhibition looks at Wagner's life and work. Another section in the new building examines the history of the Bayreuth Wagner Festival.

Behind the house, hidden behind a ring of rhododendron bushes, lies the completely unmarked, ivy-covered tomb containing Wagner and his wife Cosima. The sandstone grave of his loving canine companion Russ stands nearby.

Festspielhaus
THEATRE
(☎0921-787 80; www.bayreuth.de; Festspielhügel 1-2; adult/concession €7/5; ☉tours 2pm Nov-Apr, 10am & 2pm Sep & Oct, no tours May-Aug) North of the Hauptbahnhof, the main venue for Bayreuth's annual Wagner Festival is the Festspielhaus, constructed in 1872 with King Ludwig II's backing. The structure was specially designed to accommodate Wagner's massive theatrical sets, with three storeys of mechanical works hidden below stage. It's still one of the largest opera venues in the world. To see inside you must join the daily tour. Take bus 305 to Am Festspielhaus.

Neues Schloss
PALACE
(☎0921-759 690; Ludwigstrasse 21; adult/child €5.50/free; ☉9am-6pm Apr-Sep, 10am-4pm Oct-Mar) Opening into the vast Hofgarten, the Neues Schloss lies a short distance south of the main shopping street, Maximilianstrasse. A riot of rococo style, the margrave's residence after 1753 features a vast collection of 18th-century Bayreuth porcelain. The annual VIP opening of the Wagner Festival is held in the Cedar Room. Also worth a look is the Spiegelscherbenkabinett (Broken Mirror Cabinet), which is lined with irregular shards of broken mirror – supposedly Margravine Wilhelmine's response to the vanity of her era.

Eremitage
PARK
(Eremitagestrasse) Around 6km east of the centre lies the Eremitage, a lush park girding the Altes Schloss (adult/child €4.50/free; ☉9am-6pm Apr-Sep), the summer residence that belonged to 18th-century margrave Friedrich and his wife Wilhelmine. Visits to the palace are by guided tour only and take in the Chinese Mirror room where Countess Wilhelmine penned her memoirs. Also in the park is horseshoe-shaped Neues Schloss (not to be confused with the one in town), which centres on the amazing mosaic Sun Temple with gilded Apollo sculpture. Take bus 302 from the Hauptbahnhof.

Maisel's Bier-Erlebnis-Welt
BREWERY, MUSEUM
(☎0921-401 234; www.maisel.com/museum; Kulmbacher Strasse 40; tours adult/concession €8/5; ☉tours 2pm & 6pm) For a fascinating look at the brewing process, head to this enormous museum next door to the brewery of one of Germany's top wheat-beer producers – Maisel. The one-hour guided tour takes you into the bowels of the 19th-century plant, with atmospheric rooms filled with 4500 beer mugs and amusing artefacts. Visits conclude with a glass of sweet-cloudy Weissbier (wheat beer).

🛏 Sleeping

DJH Hostel
HOSTEL €
(☎0921-764 380; www.bayreuth.jugendherberge. de; Universitätsstrasse 28; dm from €23; 🗝) This excellent 140-bed hostel near the university has comfortable, fresh rooms, a relaxed atmosphere and heaps of guest facilities such as a multipurpose sports ground and beach volleyball court.

Goldener Löwe
HOTEL €€
(☎0921-746 060; www.goldener-loewe.de; Kulmbacher Strasse 30; s €40-105, d €75-140; 🅿😊🗝) Outside the summer months (rates increase

(Continued on page 444)

OLIVER FOERSTNER/SHUTTERSTOCK ©

1. Celle (p706) 2. Beilstein (p611)
3. Quedlinburg (p268) 4. Wismar (p207)

LCRMS/SHUTTERSTOCK ©

Small-Town Charmers

Tourist-trail faves like Heidelberg, Rothenburg ob der Tauber and Oberammergau exude charm and quaintness from every crooked lane, cobbled stone or medieval facade. Alas, all too often they also drown in the sheer volume of visitors. If you crave beauty along with (relative) serenity, consider folding one of these much-lesser-known but no less lovely towns into your itinerary.

Quedlinburg

On the edge of the Harz Mountains, Quedlinburg (p268) is a symphony in half-timber whose original medieval layout is graced by over 1300 listed buildings. The first German king, Henry I, was buried in the hilltop Romanesque Stiftskirche St Servatius in 936.

Wismar

This Baltic seaside town (p207) was a Hanseatic League hot shot, and its historic wealth is still reflected in its distinctive silhouette, characterised by elaborately decorated red-brick Gothic town houses and churches. It's a delightful, lively place that's best enjoyed by kicking back over a beer by the harbour or in a cool cafe.

Celle

Compact Celle's old town (p706) teems with timber-framed houses boasting ornate, painted gables and is punctuated by a palace that blends Renaissance and baroque elements. In a lovely setting on the southern fringes of the Lüneburg Heath, Celle is a mere 40km northeast of Hanover.

Beilstein

Scoring high on the 'romance meter', pint-sized Beilstein (p611) on the Mosel is perfect for putting on the brakes during a busy itinerary. Take to the high ground on a vineyard trek to the requisite ruined hilltop castle, then soak up the fairy-tale flair along with a glass of wine in the cluster of higgledy-piggledy medieval houses.

(Continued from page 441)

considerably mid-July to end of August) this is a great little deal within easy walking distance of the sights. Rooms are tiny but impeccably kept, the Michelin-reviewed restaurant downstairs is tempting and there's free parking. The owners seem to have a bit of a jam fetish, every guest receiving a free jar.

Hotel Goldener Hirsch
HOTEL €€

(☑0921-1504 4000; www.bayreuth-goldener-hirsch.de; Bahnhofstrasse 13; s €65-85, d €85-110; P ❀ 🕿) Just across from the train station, the 'Golden Reindeer' looks a bit stuffy from the outside, but once indoors you'll discover crisp, well-maintained rooms with contemporary furniture and unscuffed, whitewashed walls. Some of the 40 rooms have baths. Parking is free and the price includes breakfast.

Hotel Goldener Anker
HOTEL €€€

(☑0921-787 7740; www.anker-bayreuth.de; Opernstrasse 6; s €100-140, d €170-235; P ❀ 🕿) Bayreuth's top address since 1753 stands just a few metres from the opera house and oozes refined elegance, with many of the rooms decorated in traditional style with heavy curtains, dark woods and antique touches. There's a swanky restaurant at ground level, the service is impeccable and there is fresh fruit waiting for you on arrival.

✗ Eating

Kraftraum
CAFE €

(Sophienstrasse 16; mains €5.50-11; ⊗8am-1am Mon-Fri, from 9am Sat & Sun; ☑) This vegetarian eatery has plenty to tempt even the most committed meat eaters, including pastas, jacket potatoes, soups and huge salads. The retro-ish, shabby-chic interior empties on sunny days when everyone plumps for the alfresco seating out on the cobbles. Tempting weekend brunches (€15.50) always attract a large crowd.

Hansl's Wood Oven Pizzeria
PIZZA €

(www.hansls-holzofenpizzeria.de; Friedrichstrasse 15; pizzas €5.20-11; ⊗10am-10.30pm) The best pizza in town is found at this tiny place tucked away in a corner of the square near the Stadthalle. There's next to no chance of a seat at mealtimes, so grab a takeaway.

Torten Schmiede
CAFE €

(Ludwigstrasse 10; ⊗12.30-6pm Tue-Fri & Sun, 10am-6pm Sat) Bayreuth has lots of cafes, but with its car-boot sale of retro furniture,

homemade cakes and 'street art' on the walls, this tiny cafe is something that's a bit different. Enjoy your shot of caffeine and cake on a 1960s living room chair, or trendily streetside on a cushioned pallet.

Rosa Rosa
BISTRO €

(Von-Römer-Strasse 2; mains €4-11; ⊗5pm-1am; ☑) Join Bayreuth's chilled crowd at this alternatively minded bistro-cum-pub for belly-filling portions of salad, pasta and vegie fare, as well as seasonal dishes from the big specials board, or just a Frankenwälder beer in the evening. The poster-lined walls keep you up to date on the latest acts to hit town.

Oskar
FRANCONIAN, BAVARIAN €€

(Maximilianstrasse 33; mains €6-15; ⊗8am-1am Mon-Sat, from 9am Sun; 🕿) At the heart of the pedestrianised shopping boulevard, this multitasking, open-all-hours bar-cafe-restaurant is Bayreuth's busiest eatery. It's good for a busting Bavarian breakfast, a light lunch in the covered garden cafe, a full-on dinner feast in the dark-wood restaurant, or a *Landbier* (regional beer) and a couple of tasty Bayreuth bratwursts anytime you feel.

🍺 Drinking & Nightlife

Brauhaus Schinner
PUB

(www.buergerbraeu-schinner.de; Richard-Wagner-Strasse 38; ⊗5pm-midnight Tue-Sat, 10.30am-2pm Wed-Sat) The pub belonging to Bayreuth's Schinner brewery is a reassuringly old-fashioned affair with great, fresh-tasting beer but slightly pricey food. The speciality here is Braunbier, a dark bitter brew specific to Bayreuth.

ℹ Information

The **Bayreuth Card** (72hr €12.90) is good for unlimited trips on city buses, entry to eight museums and a two-hour guided city walk (in German). The card covers one adult and up to two children under 15.

Post Office (Hauptbahnhof, Bürgerreutherstrasse 1; ⊗8am-6.30pm Mon-Fri, 8.30am-1pm Sat)

Tourist Office (☑0921-885 88; www.bayreuth-tourismus.de; Opernstrasse 22; ⊗9am-7pm Mon-Fri, to 4pm Sat, plus 10am-2pm Sun May-Oct) Has a train ticket booking desk and a worthwhile gift shop. Also sells the Bayreuth Card (72 hours €12.90) that is good for unlimited trips on city buses and entry to eight museums.

ℹ Getting There & Away

Most rail journeys between Bayreuth and other towns in Bavaria require a change in Nuremberg

(€12, one hour, twice hourly), including Munich (€30 to €71, two hours, twice hourly). There are direct services to Bamberg (€22, 1½ hours, twice hourly) or change in Lichtenfels

Coburg

📞 09561 / POP 41,000

If marriage is diplomacy by another means, Coburg's rulers were masters of the art. Over four centuries, the princes and princesses of Saxe-Coburg wed themselves into the dynasties of several European states, most prominently, Great Britain. In 1857, Albert of Saxe-Coburg-Gotha took his vows with first cousin Queen Victoria, founding the present British royal family. The British royals quietly adopted the less-German name of Windsor during WWI.

With its Victoria connections and cosy, small-town atmosphere, Coburg makes for an enjoyable escape from Nuremberg and other big cities. Also, if you've developed a taste for Franconian sausages, Coburg has one of the best.

◉ Sights

★ **Veste Coburg**   FORTRESS
(www.kunstsammlungen-coburg.de;   adult/concession €8/6; ⊙ 9.30am-5pm daily Apr-Oct, 1-4pm Tue-Sun Nov-Mar) Towering above Coburg's centre is a story-book medieval fortress, the Veste Coburg. With its triple ring of fortified walls, it's one of the most impressive fortresses in Germany, though it attracts few foreign visitors. It houses the vast collection of the Kunstsammlungen, with works by star painters such as Rembrandt, Dürer and Cranach the Elder. The elaborate Jagdintarsien-Zimmer (Hunting Marquetry Room) is a superlative example of carved woodwork.

Protestant reformer Martin Luther, hoping to escape an imperial ban, sought refuge at the fortress in 1530. His former quarters have a writing desk and, in keeping with the Reformation, a rather plain bed.

★ **Schloss Ehrenburg**   CASTLE
(www.schloesser-coburg.de; Schlossplatz; adult/child €4.50/free; ⊙ tours at least hourly 9am-6pm Tue-Sun Apr-Sep, 10am-4pm Tue-Sun Oct-Mar) The erstwhile residence of the Coburg dukes, Ehrenburg is a must for fans of the British monarchy – it was here that Prince Albert spent his childhood and Queen Victoria made several long visits. She stayed in a room with Germany's first flushing toilet

(1860, suitably illuminated) and the bed she slept in is still present. Another highlight is the splendid Riesensaal (Hall of Giants), which has a baroque ceiling supported by 28 statues of Atlas.

It was in the Riesensaal that Queen Vic met up with Emperor Franz Joseph. Depictions of Britain's most famous monarch, who once declared that Coburg would have been her natural choice of home had she not become queen, can be found throughout the lavish building. Tours take 45 minutes and are in German only but info sheets are provided in other languages.

Marktplatz   SQUARE
Coburg's epicentre is the magnificent Markt, a beautifully renovated square radiating a colourful, aristocratic charm. The fabulous Renaissance facades and ornate oriels of the Stadthaus (townhouse) and the Rathaus vie for attention, while a greening bronze of Prince Albert, looking rather more flamboyant and Teutonically medieval than the Brits are used to seeing Queen Victoria's husband, calmly surveys the scene.

Coburger Puppenmuseum   MUSEUM
(www.coburger-puppenmuseum.de; Rückerstrasse 2-3; adult/child €4/2; ⊙ 11am-4pm Apr-Oct, closed Mon Nov-Mar) Filling a huge townhouse, this delightfully old-fashioned museum boasts a huge nostalgia-inducing collection. The downstairs section is like a museum of German childhood with lots of different toys from the late 19th and early 20th centuries. Upstairs you'll find the collection of dolls, dollhouses, miniature kitchens and chinaware, some from as far away as Japan. Aptly named 'Hallo Dolly', the stylish cafe next door is ideally situated for restoring calm after all those eerie glass eyes.

🎊 Festivals & Events

Samba Festival   DANCE
(www.samba-festival.de; ⊙ mid-Jul) Believe it or not, Coburg hosts Europe's largest Samba Festival every year, an incongruous venue if ever there was one. This orgy of song and dance attracts almost 100 bands and up to 200,000 scantily clad, bum-wiggling visitors, many from the Portuguese-speaking world.

🛏 Sleeping & Eating

Hotelpension Bärenturm   GUESTHOUSE €€
(📞 09561-318 401; www.baerenturm-hotelpension. de; Untere Anlage 2; s/d from €75/90; 🅿 🛜) For those who prefer their complimentary

pillow pack of gummy bears served with a touch of history, Coburg's most characterful digs started life as a defensive tower that was expanded in the early 19th century to house Prince Albert's private tutor. Each of the 15 rooms is a gem boasting squeaky parquet floors, antique-style furniture and regally high ceilings.

The Square
HOTEL €€

(☑ 09561-705 8520; www.hotelthesquare.com; Ketschengasse 1; s/d from €75/85; P ☎) What The Square lacks in character it more than makes up for in space and facilities. Each room has a kitchen, or corridor access to one, some have baths and the three large apartments cost the same as a double. You can also choose your view – the Prince Albert bronze out front on the Marktplatz or the pretty Stadtkirche out back.

Café Prinz Albert
CAFE €

(Ketschengasse 27; snacks & cakes €2-5; ⊙7.30am-6pm Mon-Fri, from 8am Sat) This long-established cafe on Albertsplatz is a good snack stop mid-sightseeing. The breakfast menu has a historical theme – the 'Martin Luther' (€3.20) is a sober, modest affair compared to the more lavish 'Prinz Albert' (€8.90).

Tie
VEGETARIAN €€

(Leopoldstrasse 14; mains €10-20; ⊙from 5pm Tue-Sun; ☑) A five-minute walk east of the Marktplatz, this vegetarian restaurant plates up imaginative food crafted from fresh organic ingredients. Dishes range from vegetarian classics to Asian inspirations, with the odd fish or meat dish for the unconverted. Seasonally set tables and temporary art exhibitions on the walls add colour to the simple decor.

❶ Information

Tourist Office (☑ 09561-898 000; www.coburg-tourist.de; Herrngasse 4; ⊙9am-5pm Mon-Fri, 10am-2pm Sat & Sun) Helpful office where staff sell the CObook (€14.90), a five-day ticket good for 13 sights in Coburg and around as well as local public transport. English audioguides (€3.50) to the city are also available here.

❶ Getting There & Around

Coburg has rail connections to Bamberg (€12.90, one hour, hourly), Bayreuth (€20.10, 1½ hours, hourly) and Nuremberg (€22, 1¾ hours, hourly).

The **Veste-Express** (www.geckobahn.de; one-way/return €3.50/5; ⊙10am-5pm Apr-Oct) tourist train leaves the tourist office every 30 minutes for the Veste Coburg. Otherwise it's a steep, 3km climb.

Altmühltal Nature Park

The Altmühltal Nature Park is one of Germany's largest nature parks and covers some of Bavaria's most eye-pleasing terrain. The Altmühl River gently meanders through a region of little valleys and hills before joining the Rhine-Main Canal and eventually emptying into the Danube. Outdoor fun on well-marked hiking and biking trails is the main reason to head here, but the river is also ideal for canoeing. There's basic camping in designated spots along the river, and plenty of accommodation in the local area.

The park takes in 2900 sq km of land southwest of Regensburg, south of Nuremberg, east of Treuchtlingen and north of Eichstätt. The eastern boundaries of the park include the town of Kelheim.

North of the river, activities focus around the towns of Kipfenberg, Beilngries and Riedenburg.

🏃 Activities

Canoeing & Kayaking

The most beautiful section of the river is from Treuchtlingen or Pappenheim to Eichstätt or Kipfenberg, about a 60km stretch that you can do lazily in a kayak or canoe in two to three days. There are lots of little dams along the way, as well as some small rapids about 10km northwest of Dollnstein, so make sure you are up for little bits of portaging. Signs warn of impending doom, but locals say that, if you heed the warning to keep to the right, you'll be safe.

You can rent canoes and kayaks in just about every town along the river. Expect to pay about €15/25 per day for a one-/two-person boat, more for bigger ones. Staff will sometimes haul you and the boats to or from your embarkation point for a small fee.

You can get a full list of boat-hire outlets from the Informationszentrum Naturpark Altmühltal.

San-Aktiv Tours
CANOEING

(☑ 09831-4936; www.san-aktiv-tours.com; half-/full-day tour €22/28) San-Aktiv Tours is the largest and best-organised of the canoe-hire companies in the park, with a network of vehicles to shuttle canoes, bicycles and people around the area. Trips through the park run from April to October, and you can canoe alone or join a group. Packages generally include the canoe, swim vests, maps, instructions and transfer back to the embarkation point.

Cycling & Hiking

With around 3000km of hiking trails and 800km of cycle trails criss-crossing the landscape, foot and pedal are the best ways to strike out into the park. Cycling trails are clearly labelled and have long rectangular brown signs bearing a bike symbol. Hiking-trail markers are yellow. The most popular cycling route is the Altmühltal Radweg, which runs parallel to the river for 166km. The Altmühltal-Panoramaweg, stretching 200km between Gunzenhausen and Kelheim, is a picturesque hiking route, which crosses the entire park from west to east.

You can rent bikes in almost every town within the park, and prices are more or less uniform. Most bike-hire agencies will also store bicycles. Ask for a list of bike-hire outlets at the Informationszentrum Naturpark Altmühltal.

Located in Eichstätt, Kanuuh (☑08421-2110; www.kanuuh.de; Am Graben 22) will bring the bikes to you, or take you and the bikes to anywhere in Altmühltal Nature Park for an extra fee.

Rock Climbing

The worn cliffs along the Altmühl River offer some appealing terrain for climbers of all skill levels. The medium-grade 45m-high rock face of Burgsteinfelsen, located between the towns of Dollnstein and Breitenfurt, has routes from the fourth to eighth climbing levels, with stunning views of the valley. The Dohlenfelsen face near the town of Wellheim has a simpler expanse that's more suitable for children. The Informationszentrum Naturpark Altmühltal can provide more details on the region's climbing options.

ℹ Information

The park's main information centre is in Eichstätt, a charmingly historic town at the southern end of the park that makes an excellent base for exploring.

Informationszentrum Naturpark Altmühltal
(☑08421-987 60; www.naturpark-altmuehltal. de; Notre Dame 1, Eichstätt; ◷9am-5pm Mon-Sat, 10am-5pm Sun Apr-Oct, 8am-noon & 2-4pm Mon-Thu, 8am-noon Fri Nov-Mar) Has information on Altmühltal Nature Park and can help with planning an itinerary. The website has

tons of information on every aspect of the park, including activities and accommodation.

ℹ Getting There & Away

There are bus and train connections between Eichstätt and all the major milestones along the river including, from west to east, Gunzenhausen, Treuchtlingen and Pappenheim.

BUS

From mid-April to October the FreizeitBus Altmühltal-Donautal takes passengers and their bikes around the park. Buses normally run three times a day from mid-April to early October. Route 1 runs from Regensburg and Kelheim to Riedenburg on weekends and holidays only. Route 2 travels between Eichstätt, Beilngries, Dietfurt and Riedenburg, with all-day service on weekends and holidays and restricted service on weekdays. All-day tickets, which cost €11 for passengers with bicycles and €8 for those without (or €25/18 per family with/without bicycles) are bought from the driver.

TRAIN

Hourly trains run between Eichstätt Bahnhof and Treuchtlingen (€7.10, 25 minutes), and between Treuchtlingen and Gunzenhausen (€4.50, 15 minutes). RE trains from Munich that run through Eichstätt Bahnhof also stop in Dollnstein, Solnhofen and Pappenheim.

Eichstätt

☑08421 / POP 13,500

Hugging a tight bend in the Altmühl River, Eichstätt radiates a tranquil Mediterranean-style flair with cobbled streets meandering past elegantly Italianate buildings and leafy piazzas. Italian architects, notably Gabriel de Gabrieli and Maurizio Pedetti, rebuilt the town after Swedes razed the place during the Thirty Years' War (1618–48) and it came through WWII virtually without a graze. Since 1980 many of its baroque facades have played host to faculties belonging to Germany's sole Catholic university.

Eichstätt is pretty enough, but is really just a jumping off and stocking up point for flits into the wilds of Altmühltal Nature Park. You'll be chomping at the bit, eager to hit a trail or grab a paddle, if you stay more than a day.

◉ Sights

Dom   CHURCH
(www.bistum-eichstaett.de/dom; Domplatz; ◷7.15am-7.30pm) Eichstätt's centre is dominated by the richly adorned Dom. Standout features include an enormous 16th-century stained-glass window by Hans Holbein the

Elder, and the carved sandstone Pappenheimer Altar (1489–97), depicting a pilgrimage from Pappenheim to Jerusalem. The seated statue is of St Willibald, the town's first bishop. The adjoining Domschatzmuseum includes the robes of 8th-century English-born bishop St Willibald and baroque Gobelin tapestries.

Willibaldsburg
CASTLE

(☑ 08421-4730; Burgstrasse 19; adult/child €4.50/free; ⊘ 9am-6pm Tue-Sun Apr-Oct, 10am-4pm Tue-Sun Nov-Mar) The walk or drive up to the hilltop castle of Willibaldsburg (1355) is worth it for the views across the valley from the formally laid-out Bastiongarten; many locals also head up here on sunny days for the nearby beer garden. The castle itself houses two museums, the most interesting of which is the Jura-Museum, specialising in fossils and containing a locally found archaeopteryx (the oldest-known fossil bird), as well as aquariums with living specimens of the fossilised animals.

Domschatzmuseum
MUSEUM

(Cathedral Treasury Museum; ☑ 08421-507 42; www.dioezesanmuseum-eichstaett.de; Residenzplatz 7; adult/concession €3/1.50, Sun €1; ⊘ 10.30am-5pm Wed-Fri, 10am-5pm Sat & Sun Apr-Nov) The worthwhile Domschatzmuseum includes the robes of 8th-century English-born bishop St Willibald and baroque Gobelin tapestries illustrating scenes from the life of St Walburga. There's lots of church silver and gold to admire and religious paintings galore.

Fürstbischöfliche Residenz
PALACE

(Residenzplatz 1; admission €1; ⊘ 7.30am-noon Mon-Fri, 2-4pm Mon-Wed, 2-5.30pm Thu) The prince-bishops lived it up at the baroque Residenz, built between 1725 and 1736 by Gabriel de Gabrieli. Inside, the stunning main staircase and a hall of mirrors stick in the mind. In the square outside rises a late 18th-century golden statue of the Madonna atop a 19m-high column.

Kloster St Walburga
CONVENT

(www.abtei-st-walburg.de; Westenstrasse) The final resting place of St Willibald's sister, the Kloster St Walburga is a popular local pilgrimage destination. Every year between mid-October and late February, water oozes from Walburga's relics in the underground chapel and drips down into a catchment. The nuns bottle diluted versions of the so-called *Walburgaöl* (Walburga oil) and give it away to the faithful.

A staircase from the lower chapel leads to an off-limits upper chapel where you can catch a glimpse through the grill of beautiful ex-voto tablets and other trinkets left as a thank you to the saint. The main St Walburga Church above has a glorious rococo interior.

🛏 Sleeping & Eating

DJH Hostel
HOSTEL €

(☑ 08421-980 410; www.eichstaett.jugendherberge.de; Reichenaustrasse 15; dm from €21; 🛜) This comfy 122-bed youth hostel provides pretty views of the Altstadt, and is peddle- and paddle-friendly.

Municipal Camping Ground
CAMPGROUND €

(☑ 08421-908 147; www.eichstaett.de; Pirkheimerstrasse; per campsite €10; ⊘ Apr-Oct) This basic camping ground is on the northern bank of the Altmühl River, 1km southeast of the town centre.

★ Hotel Adler
HOTEL €€

(☑ 08421-6767; www.adler-eichstaett.de; Marktplatz 22; s €60-65, d €85-110; 🅿 🛜) A superb ambience reigns in this ornate 300-year-old building, Eichstätt's top digs. Sleeping quarters are bright and breezy, and the generous breakfast buffet is a proper set up for a day on the trail or river. Despite the posh feel, this hotel welcomes hiker and bikers.

Fuchs
HOTEL €€

(☑ 08421-6789; www.hotel-fuchs.de; Ostenstrasse 8; s €45-70, d €75-85; 🅿 🛜) This central, family-run hotel, with underfloor heating in the bathrooms, adjoins a cake shop with a sunny dining area. It's convenient to a launch ramp on the river where you can put in, and you can lock your canoe or kayak in the garage.

★ Gasthof Krone
BAVARIAN €€

(www.krone-eichstaett.de; Domplatz 3; mains €6.50-18.50; ⊘ 10am-midnight) The top place to source real local sustenance is this large, multilevel dining hall serving the best local food such as house sausages, river trout and seasonal salads. The local Hofmühl beer goes down a treat after a day on the water.

Trompete
BAVARIAN, ITALIAN €€

(☑ 08421-981 70; www.braugasthof-trompete.de; Ostenstrasse 3; mains €5-16.50; ⊘ 7am-1am Mon-Fri, from 7.30am Sat & Sun) From breakfast to your last cocktail of the day, this friendly inn, just a short walk to the southeast of the centre, is a sure-fire option at any time of day. The menu features some *echt*-Bavarian dishes such as Altmühltal trout and *Ochsenbraten* (roast beef) as well as a long list of pizzas and pastas.

❶ Information

Post Office (Domplatz 7; ⊙ 9am-12.30pm & 1.30-5pm Mon-Fri, 9am-noon Sat)

Tourist Office (☑ 08421-600 1400; www.eichstaett.de; Domplatz 8; ⊙ 10am-5pm Mon-Fri, to 4pm Sat, to 1pm Sun May-Sep, shorter hours & closed Sun rest of the year) Professionally run office with cycle hire and walking tours.

❶ Getting There & Away

Eichstätt has two train stations. Main-line trains stop at the Bahnhof, 5km from the centre, from where coinciding diesel services shuttle to the Stadtbahnhof (town station). Trains run to Ingolstadt (€7, 25 minutes, hourly) and Nuremberg (€21.30, 1½ hours, every two hours).

REGENSBURG & THE DANUBE

The sparsely populated eastern reaches of Bavaria may live in the shadow of Bavaria's big-hitting attractions, but they hold many historical treasures to rival their neighbours. Top billing goes to Regensburg, a former capital, and one of Germany's prettiest and liveliest cities. From here the Danube gently winds its way to the Italianate city of Passau. Landshut was once the hereditary seat of the Wittelsbach family, and the region has also given the world a pope – Benedict XVI – who was born in Marktl am Inn. Away from the towns, the Bavarian Forest broods in semiundiscovered remoteness.

Regensburg

☑ 0941 / POP 148,600

The capital of the Oberpfalz region of Bavaria, Regensburg dates back to Roman times and was the first capital of Bavaria. Two thousand years of history bequeathed the city some of the region's finest architectural heritage, a fact recognised by Unesco in 2006. Though big on the historical wow factor, today's Regensburg is a laid-back, studenty and unpretentious sort of place and its tangle of old streets is a joy to wander.

◉ Sights

★ **Schloss Thurn und Taxis** CASTLE
(www.thurnundtaxis.de; Emmeramsplatz 5; tours adult/child €13.50/11; ⊙ tours hourly 10.30am-

MUSEUM OF BAVARIAN HISTORY

Regensburg is set to acquire a major new attraction in mid-2019 – the Museum of Bavarian History. The architecturally striking building (other, less favourable, descriptions have been used) has been bolted together around 250m east of the Steinerne Brücke, altering the historical appearance of the riverfront. As well as the supercontemporary look of the structure, the wisdom of placing a major attraction in such a flood-prone location has also been questioned.

4.30pm late Mar-early Nov, to 3.30pm Sat & Sun Nov-Mar) In the 15th century, Franz von Taxis (1459–1517) assured his place in history by setting up the first European postal system, which remained a monopoly until the 19th century. In recognition of his services, the family was given the former Benedictine monastery St Emmeram, henceforth known as Schloss Thurn und Taxis. It was soon one of the most modern palaces in Europe and featured such luxuries as flushing toilets. Today it is the world's largest inhabited building.

The palace complex also contains the Schatzkammer (Treasury). The jewellery, porcelain and precious furnishings on display belonged, for many years, to the wealthiest dynasty in Germany. The fortune, administered by Prince Albert II, is still estimated at well over €1 billion.

★ **Dom St Peter** CHURCH
(www.bistum-regensburg.de; Domplatz; ⊙ 6.30am-7pm Jun-Sep, to 6pm Apr, May & Oct, to 5pm Nov-Mar) It takes a few seconds for your eyes to adjust to the interior of Regensburg's soaring landmark, the Dom St Peter, one of Bavaria's grandest Gothic cathedrals with stunning kaleidoscopic stained-glass windows and an opulent, silver-sheathed main altar. The cathedral is home of the Domspatzen, a 1000-year-old boys' choir that accompanies the 10am Sunday service (only during the school year). The Domschatzmuseum (Cathedral Treasury) brims with monstrances, tapestries and other church treasures.

★ **Golf Museum** MUSEUM
(☑ 0941-510 74; www.golf-museum.com; Tändlergasse 3; adult/child €7.50/5; ⊙ 10am-6pm Mon-Sat) Claiming to be Europe's best golf museum

Regensburg

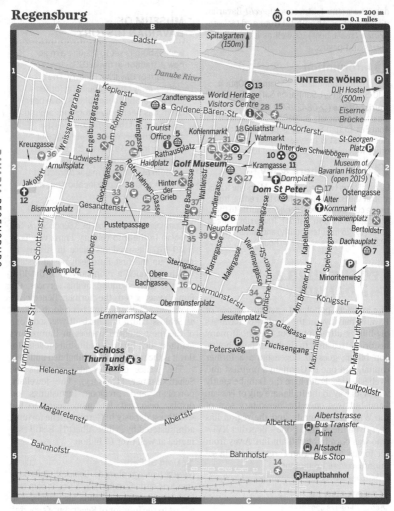

(not counting Scotland, home to the British Golf Museum), this fine repository of wooden clubs, ivory tees and yellowing score cards (including one belonging to King George V of England) backswings its way through golf's illustrious past – interesting, even if you think a green fee is something to do with municipal recycling. The entrance is in an antiques shop.

Altes Rathaus HISTORIC BUILDING
(Old Town Hall; Rathausplatz; adult/child €7.50/4; ☉ tours in English 3pm Easter-Oct, 2pm Nov & Dec, in German every 30min) From 1663 to 1806,

the Reichstag (imperial assembly) held its gatherings at Regensburg's old town, an important role commemorated by an exhibit in today's Reichstagsmuseum. Tours take in the lavish assembly hall and the original torture chambers in the cellar. Buy tickets at the tourist office in the same building. Note that access is by tour only. Audioguides are available for English speakers in January and February.

Steinerne Brücke BRIDGE
(Stone Bridge) An incredible feat of engineering for its day, Regensburg's 900-year-

Regensburg

BAVARIA REGENSBURG

old Stone Bridge was at one time the only fortified crossing of the Danube. Damaged and neglected for centuries (especially by the buses that once used it) the entire expanse has undergone renovation in recent years.

Schottenkirche St Jakob CHURCH
(Jakobstrasse 3) The sooty 12th-century main portal of the Schottenkirche St Jakob is considered one of the supreme examples of Romanesque architecture in Germany. Its reliefs and sculptures form an iconography that continues to baffle the experts. Sadly it's protected from further pollution by an ageing glass structure that makes the whole thing an eyesore. However, this is more than made up for inside, where pure, tourist-free Romanesque austerity prevails.

Alte Kapelle CHURCH
(Alter Kornmarkt 8) South of the Dom, the humble exterior of the graceful Alte Kapelle belies the stunning interior with its rich rococo decorations. The core of the church, however, is about 1000 years old, although the vaulted ceilings were added in the Gothic period. The church is open only during services but you can always peek through the wrought-iron grill.

Porta Praetoria RUINS
(Unter den Schwibbögen) Just north of the Dom, the arched gate called Porta Praetoria is the most impressive reminder of Regensburg's Roman heritage. It was built in AD 179 by Emperor Marcus Aurelius as part of the Castra Regina. To see more remains of the Roman wall, stroll along Unter den Schwibbögen.

Document Neupfarrplatz HISTORIC SITE
(☑ 0941-507 3417; Neupfarrplatz) Excavations in the mid-1990s revealed remains of Regensburg's once-thriving 16th-century Jewish quarter, along with Roman buildings, gold coins and a Nazi bunker. The subterranean Document Neupfarrplatz only provides access to a small portion of the excavated area, but tours feature a worthwhile multimedia presentation (in German) about the square's history. Back up above, on the square itself, a work by renowned Israeli artist Dani Karavan graces the site of the former synagogue. Contact the tourist office for tickets and tour details.

Historisches Museum MUSEUM
(Dachauplatz 2-4; adult/child €5/2.50; ⊙10am-4pm Tue-Sun) A medieval monastery provides a suitably atmospheric backdrop for the city's history museum. The collections plot

the region's story from cave dweller to Roman, and medieval trader to 19th-century burgher.

Oskar Schindler Plaque
MEMORIAL

(Am Watmarkt 5) Oskar Schindler lived in Regensburg for years, and today one of his houses bears a plaque to his achievements, as commemorated in Steven Spielberg's epic dramatisation *Schindler's List*.

Roman Wall
HISTORIC SITE

The most tangible reminder of the ancient rectangular Castra Regina (Regen Fortress), where the name 'Regensburg' comes from, is the remaining Roman wall, which follows Unter den Schwibbögen and veers south onto Dr-Martin-Luther-Strasse. Dating from AD 179 the rough-hewn Porta Praetoria arch is the tallest Roman structure in Bavaria and formed part of the city's defences for centuries.

Kepler-Gedächtnishaus
MUSEUM

(Kepler Memorial House; Keplerstrasse 5; adult/child €2.20/1.10; ☺10.30am-4pm Sat & Sun) Disciples of astronomer and mathematician Johannes Kepler should visit the house he lived in while resident in Regensburg.

🏃 Activities

Schifffahrt Klinger
BOATING

(☎0941-521 04; www.schifffahrtklinger.de; cruises adult/child from €9/5.50; ☺Apr-late Oct) The name of the company's 50-minute Strudelfahrt river tour of the city may invoke a few giggles but is an enjoyable experience, as is the cruise to Walhalla.

Bikehaus
BICYCLE RENTAL

(☎0941-599 8194; www.fahrradverleih-regensburg.de; Bahnhofstrasse 18; bikes per day €15; ☺10am-7pm Mon-Sat) At Bikehaus you can rent anything from kiddies bikes to fully saddled tourers and tandems for a novel city tour. You'll need a €100 deposit which is returned when you give the bike back.

🎉 Festivals & Events

Dult
BEER

(www.r-dult.de; ☺May & Aug/Sep) Major Oktoberfest-style beer party with brewery tents, carousel rides, entertainment, sausages and vendors on the Dultplatz.

Weihnachtsmarkt
CHRISTMAS MARKET

(www.regensburg.de; ☺Dec) The Christmas market has stalls selling roasted almonds, gingerbread and traditional wooden toys.

Held at Neupfarrplatz and Schloss Thurn und Taxis during Advent.

🛏️ Sleeping

Brook Lane Hostel
HOSTEL €

(☎0941-696 5521; www.hostel-regensburg.de; Obere Bachgasse 21; dm/s/d from €16/40/50, apt per person €55; 🐾) Regensburg's only backpacker hostel has its very own convenience store, which doubles up as reception, but it isn't open 24 hours, so late landers should let staff know in advance. Dorms do the minimum required, but the apartments and doubles are applaudable deals, especially if you're travelling in a two- or more-some. Access to kitchens and washing machines throughout.

DJH Hostel
HOSTEL €

(☎0941-466 2830; www.regensburg.jugendherberge.de; Wöhrdstrasse 60; dm from €22; 🐾) Regensburg's 190-bed DJH hostel occupies a beautiful old building on a large island about a 10-minute walk north of the Altstadt.

Hotel am Peterstor
HOTEL €

(☎0941-545 45; www.hotel-am-peterstor.de; Fröhliche-Türken-Strasse 12; s/d from €40/50; 🐾) The pale-grey decor might be grim but the location is great, the price is right and staff go out of their way to assist. Make sure you get a nonsmoking room, as some still have a pong of secondhand smoke. Breakfast is an optional €5 extra, parking €8. Payment on arrival.

★ Elements Hotel
HOTEL €€

(☎941-2007 2275; www.hotel-elements.de; Alter Kornmarkt 3; d from €105; 🐾) Four elements, four rooms, and what rooms they are! 'Fire' blazes in plush crimson; while 'Water' is a wellness suite with a jacuzzi; 'Air' is playful and light and natural wood; and stone and leather reign in colonial-inspired 'Earth'. Breakfast in bed costs an extra €10.

★ Hotel Orphée
HOTEL €€

(☎0941-596 020; www.hotel-orphee.de; Untere Bachgasse 8; s €40-120, d €80-155; 🐾) Behind a humble door lies a world of genuine charm, unexpected extras and ample attention to detail. The striped floors, wrought-iron beds, original sinks and common rooms with soft cushions and well-read books give the feel of a lovingly attended home. Check-in and breakfast is nearby in the Cafe Orphée at Untere Bachgasse 8. Additional rooms are available above the cafe.

Hotel Goldenes Kreuz
HOTEL €€

(☑ 0941-558 12; www.hotel-goldeneskreuz.com; Haidplatz 7; s €90-135, d €110-160; ☎) Surely the best deal in town, the nine fairy-tale rooms each bear the name of a crowned head and are fit for a kaiser. Huge mirrors, dark antique and Bauhaus furnishings, four-poster beds, chubby exposed beams and parquet flooring produce a stylishly aristocratic opus in leather, wood, crystal and fabric. Breakfast is in the house chapel.

Zum Fröhlichen Türken
HOTEL €€

(☑ 0941-536 51; www.hotel-zum-froehlichen-tuerk en.de; Fröhlichen-Türken-Strasse 11; s/d €60/90; ☎) With its comfortable, clean quarters, unstinting breakfast and mild-mannered staff, the 'Jolly Turk' will bring a smile to any price-conscious traveller's face. The pricier rooms have private bathrooms.

Goliath Hotel
HOTEL €€

(☑ 0941-200 0900; www.hotel-goliath.de; Goliathstrasse 10; d from €135; P ❄ ☎) Bang in the heart of Regensburg's historical core, the 41 rooms at the Goliath are all differently conceived and pristinely serviced. Some have little extras such as bathroom–bedroom windows and big baths. It's a cool pad, but doesn't go the whole boutique hog and staff are surprisingly old school.

Hotel Roter Hahn
HOTEL €€€

(☑ 0941-595 090; www.roter-hahn.com; Rote-Hahnen-Gasse 10; s/d from €110/140; P ☎) A bulky beamed ceiling and a glassed-in Roman stone well (staff appear to be oblivious of its provenance) greet you in the lobby of the 'Red Rooster', contrasting with streamlined rooms offering freshly maintained amenities. The downside here is the extras – parking costs a hefty €20 a night, as does breakfast.

✖ Eating

★ Historische Wurstkuchl
GERMAN €

(☑ 0941-466 210; www.wurstkuchl.de; Thundorfer-strasse 3; 6 sausages €9.60; ☉ 9am-7pm) Completely submerged several times by the Danube's fickle floods, this titchy eatery has been serving the city's traditional finger-size sausages, grilled over beech wood and dished up with its own sauerkraut and sweet grainy mustard, since 1135 and lays claim to being the world's oldest sausage kitchen.

Spaghetteria Aquino
ITALIAN €

(www.spaghetteria-regensburg.de; Am Römling 12; dishes €6.50-11.50; ☉ 5.30pm-midnight Mon-Fri, 11.30am-midnight Sat, 11.30am-3pm & 5.30pm-midnight Sun; ☎ ☑) Get carbed up at this former 17th-century chapel, where you can splatter six types of pasta with 24 types of sauce, and get out the door for the cost of a cocktail in Munich. The all-you-can-eat buffets (€7) are a cheap way to fill up at lunchtime. There are 14 different pizzas to choose from as well as vegan spaghetti dishes.

Dampfnudel Uli
CAFE €

(Watmarkt 4; dishes €5-8; ☉ 10.01am-5.01pm Wed-Fri, to 3.01pm Sat) This quirkily old-fashioned little noshery serves a mean Dampfnudel (steamed doughnut) with custard in a Gothic chamber lined with photos of beer steins (tankards) at the base of the Baumburger Tower.

★ Dicker Mann
BAVARIAN €€

(☑ 0941-573 70; www.dicker-mann.de; Krebsgasse 6; mains €9-21; ☉ 9am-1am; ☎) The 'Chubby Chappy', a stylish, tranquil and very traditional inn, is one of the oldest restaurants in town, allegedly dating back to the 14th century. All the staples of Bavarian sustenance are plated up plus a few other dishes for good measure. On a balmy eve, be sure to bag a table in the lovely beer garden out back.

★ Café Orphée
FRENCH €€

(Untere Bachgasse 8; mains €10-26; ☉ 8am-1am) Claiming to be the Frenchiest bistro east of the Rhine – it really is like being teleported to 1920s Paris – this visually pleasing, always bustling eatery is bedecked in faded red velvet, dark wood and art nouveau posters. Light-lunch fare populates a handwritten menu of appetising Gallic favourites with slight Bavarian touches for sturdiness. Best breakfast menu in Bavaria.

Leerer Beutel
EUROPEAN €€

(☑ 0941-589 97; www.leerer-beutel.de; Bertold-strasse 9; mains €12-28; ☉ 6pm-1am Mon, 11am-1am Tue-Sat, 11am-3pm Sun) Subscriber to the slow food ethos, the cavernous restaurant at the eponymous cultural centre offers an imaginatively mixed menu of Bavarian, Tyrolean and Italian dishes, served indoors or out on the car-free cobbles. From Tuesday to Friday, clued-in locals invade for the two-course lunches for €7.20.

Haus Heuport
INTERNATIONAL €€

(www.heuport.de; Domplatz 7; mains €11.50-22; ☉ 10am-midnight Mon-Fri, from 9am Sat & Sun; ☑) Enter an internal courtyard (flanked

WORTH A TRIP

WALHALLA

Modelled on the Parthenon in Athens, the Walhalla (www.walhalla-regensburg.de; Walhalla strasse 48, Donaustauf; adult/child €4/free; ⊙9am-6pm Apr-Oct, 10am-noon & 1-4pm Nov-Mar) is a breathtaking Ludwig I monument dedicated to the giants of Germanic thought and deed. Marble steps seem to lead up forever from the banks of the Danube to this dazzling marble hall, with a gallery of 127 heroes in marble.

The collection includes a few dubious cases, such as astronomer Copernicus, born in a territory belonging to present-day Poland. The most recent addition (2009) was romantic poet Heinrich Heine, whose works were set to music by Strauss, Wagner and Brahms.

To get here take the Danube Valley country road (unnumbered) 10km east from Regensburg to the village of Donaustauf, then follow the signs. Alternatively, you can take a two-hour boat cruise with Schifffahrt Klinger (p452), which includes a one-hour stop at Walhalla, or take bus 5 from Regensburg Hauptbahnhof.

by stone blocks where medieval torches were once extinguished) and climb up the grand old wooden staircase to this space-rich Gothic dining hall for eye-to-eye views of the Dom St Peter and an internationally flavoured culinary celebration. The Sunday breakfast buffet runs to a hangover-busting 2pm. Always busy.

Weltenburger am Dom   BAVARIAN €€

(☎0941-586 1460; www.weltenburger-am-dom. de; Domplatz 3; dishes €7-20; ⊙11am-11pm; 🖎) Tightly packed gastropub with a mouth-watering menu of huge gourmet burgers, sausage dishes, beer hall and garden favourites such as *Obazda* (cream cheese on pretzels) and *Sauerbraten* (marinated roast meat), dark beer goulash and a few token desserts. Make sure you're hungry before you come as portions are huge.

★Storstad   INTERNATIONAL €€€

(☎0941-5999 3000; www.storstad.de; Watmarkt 5; 3 courses from €40; ⊙noon-2pm, plus 6.30-9.30pm Tue-Thu, from 6pm Fri & Sat; 🖎) If you are looking for something a bit more creative on your plate than hunks of pork and dumplings, book a table at this 21st-century gourmet restaurant. The menus feature rare ingredients for Bavaria such as lamb, cod and mackerel, enjoyed paired with German and other European wine in the ultramodern, if rather overlit, dining room.

🍷 Drinking & Nightlife

★Cafebar   BAR

(www.cafebar-regensburg.de; Gesandtenstrasse 14; ⊙8am-midnight Mon-Wed, to 1am Thu & Fri, 9am-1am Sat, 1pm-midnight Sun) This time-warped, tightly squeezed blast from the past in

Jugendstil tile, cast iron and stained glass has been filling with newspaper-reading caffeine fans at first rays and ethanol fans after sundown for over three decades.

Kneitinger   PUB

(www.kneitinger.de; Arnulfsplatz 3; ⊙9am-midnight) Kneitinger is Regensburg's local beer and there's no better place to head in the city for some hearty home cooking, delicious house suds and outrageous oompah frolics than the brewery's own tavern. It's been in business since 1530.

Wirtshaus im Alten Augustiner Kloster   BEER GARDEN

(www.hacker-pschorr-regensburg.de; Neupfarrplatz 15; ⊙10am-11.30pm) This popular fairy-lit beer garden and restaurant is ideally located in the heart of the city. Order a Munich-brewed Hacker-Pschorr lager and pack it away with some traditional south German fare in the sprawling garden or cavernous interior.

Félix   CAFE

(www.cafefelix.de; Fröhliche-Türken-Strasse 6; ⊙9am-2am Sun-Thu, 10am-3am Fri & Sat) Early-bird's breakfast and after-dark trendoids leaf through the lengthy drinks menu behind the curvaceous neo-baroque frontage of this open-all-hours cafe with a welcoming air. You'd be lucky to get a seat here at lunchtime so arrive early.

Spitalgarten   BEER GARDEN

(☎0941-847 74; www.spitalgarten.de; St Katharinenplatz 1; ⊙10am-11pm) A veritable thicket of folding chairs and slatted tables by the Danube, this is one of the best places in town for some alfresco quaffing. It claims to have brewed beer (today's Spital) here since 1350, so it probably knows what it's doing by now.

Paletti BAR
(Gesandtenstrasse 6, Pustetpassage; ⊘8am-2am; ☎) Tucked into a covered passageway off Gesandtenstrasse, this buzzy Italian cafe-bar that has not changed since the 1960s teleports you back to the postwar years when many Italian immigrants made Bavaria their home.

Hemingway's BAR
(www.hemingways.de; Obere Bachgasse 5; ⊘9am-1am Sun-Thu, to 2am Fri & Sat) Black wood, big mirrors and lots of photos of Papa himself add to the cool atmosphere of this swish, art-deco-style cafe-bar.

Moritz BAR
(www.cafemoritz.com; Untere Bachgasse 15; ⊘7.30am-1am Mon-Sat, from 9am Sun) Take some Gothic cross vaulting, paint it high-visability tunnel orange, throw in some killer cocktails and invite a millennial crowd – and you've got Moritz!

❶ Information

Use the **Regensburg Card** (24/48hr €9/17) for free public transport and discounts at local attractions and businesses. Available at the tourist office.

Post Office (Domplatz; ⊘9.30am-noon & 2-6pm Mon-Fri, to noon Sat)

Tourist Office (☑0941-507 4410; https://tourismus.regensburg.de; Rathausplatz 4; ⊘9am-6pm Mon-Fri, to 4pm Sat, 9.30am-4pm Sun Apr-Oct, to 2.30pm Sun Nov-Mar; ☎) In the historic Altes Rathaus. Sells tickets, tours, rooms and an audioguide for self-guided tours.

World Heritage Visitors Centre (☑0941-507 4410; www.regensburg-welterbe.de; Weisse-Lamm-Gasse 1; ⊘10am-7pm) Visitors centre by the Steinerne Brücke, focusing on the city's Unesco World Heritage Sites. Interesting interactive multimedia exhibits.

❶ Getting There & Away

TRAIN
Train connections from Regensburg:

Frankfurt am Main €70, three hours, every two hours

Landshut €14.50, 40 minutes, at least hourly

Munich €29.70, 1½ hours, hourly

Nuremberg €23.20, one to two hours, two hourly

Passau €26.40 to €31, one hour, every two hours or change in Plattling

❶ Getting Around

BICYCLE
Bikehaus (p452) rents anything from kiddies bikes to fully saddled tourers and tandems for a novel city tour. You'll need a €100 deposit that is returned when you give the bike back.

BUS
On weekdays the Altstadtbus (€1.10) somehow manages to squeeze its way through the narrow streets between the Hauptbahnhof and the **Altstadt** every 10 minutes between 9am and 7pm. The **bus transfer point** (Albertstrasse) is one block north of the Hauptbahnhof. Tickets for all city buses (except the Altstadtbus) cost €2.40 for journeys in the centre; an all-day ticket costs €5 at ticket machines.

Ingolstadt

☑0841 / POP 133,600

Even by Bavaria's high standards, Danube-straddling Ingolstadt is astonishingly affluent. Auto manufacturer Audi has its headquarters here, flanked by a clutch of oil refineries on the outskirts, but industry has left few marks on the medieval centre, with its cobblestone streets and historic, if slightly overrenovated, buildings. Ingolstadt's museum-church has the largest flat fresco ever made, and few people may know that its old medical school figured in the literary birth of Frankenstein, the monster by which all others are judged.

⊙ Sights

Asamkirche Maria de Victoria CHURCH
(☑0841-305 1830; Neubaustrasse 11; adult/child €3/2; ⊘9am-noon & 12.30-5pm Tue-Sun Mar-Oct, plus Mon May-Sep, 1-4pm Tue-Sun Nov-Feb) The Altstadt's crown jewel is the Asamkirche Maria de Victoria, a baroque masterpiece designed by brothers Cosmas Damian and Egid Quirin Asam between 1732 and 1736. The church's mesmerising trompe l'oeil ceiling, painted in just six weeks in 1735, is the world's largest fresco on a flat surface.

Audi Factory FACTORY
(☑0800-283 4444; www.audi.com; Ettinger Strasse; adult/child €7/3.50; ⊘10.30am, 12.30pm & 2.30pm Mon-Fri in German, 11.30am Mon-Fri in English) Ingolstadt is home to the famous Audi factory that sprawls to the north of the city centre. The two-hour 'Production in a Nutshell' tours of the plant take you through

the entire Audi production process, from the metal press to the testing station.

Audi Forum – Museum Mobile MUSEUM
(☑0800-283 4444; www.audi.de/foren; Ettinger Strasse 40; adult/child €4/free; ☺9am-6pm Mon-Fri, 10am-4pm Sat & Sun) The excellent Audi Forum exhibits on three floors chart Audi's humble beginnings in 1899 to its latest dream machines such as the R8. Some 50 cars and 20 motorbikes are on display, including prototypes that glide past visitors on an open lift. Take half-hourly bus 11 to the terminus from the Hauptbahnhof or Paradeplatz.

Liebfrauenmünster CHURCH
(Kreuzstrasse; ☺8am-6pm) Ingolstadt's biggest church was established by Duke Ludwig the Bearded in 1425 and enlarged over the next century. This classic Gothic hall church has a pair of strangely oblique square towers that flank the main entrance. Inside, subtle colours and a nave flooded with light intensify the magnificence of the high-lofted vaulting and the blossoming stonework of several side chapels.

Museum für Konkrete Kunst MUSEUM
(Museum of Concrete Art; ☑0841-305 1875; www.mkk-ingolstadt.de; Tränktorstrasse 6-8; adult/concession €5/3; ☺10am-5pm Tue-Sun) This unique art museum showcases works and installations from the Concrete Movement, all of a bafflingly abstract nature and certainly an acquired taste. The movement was defined and dominated by interwar artists Max Bill and Theo van Doesburg whose works make up a large share of the collections.

Lechner Museum MUSEUM
(☑0841-305 2250; www.lechner-museum.de; Esplanade 9; adult/concession €5/3; ☺11am-5pm Thu-Sun) This unusual art museum highlights works cast in steel, a medium that's more expressive than you might think. Exhibits are displayed in a striking glass-covered factory hall dating from 1953.

Deutsches Medizinhistorisches Museum MUSEUM
(German Museum of Medical History; ☑0841-305 2860; www.dmm-ingolstadt.de; Anatomiestrasse 18-20; adult/concession €3/2; ☺10am-5pm Tue-Sun) Located in the stately Alte Anatomie (Old Anatomy) at the university, this sometimes rather gory museum chronicles the evolution of medical science as well as the many (scary) instruments and techniques used. Unless you are, or have been, a medical student, pack a strong stomach for the visit.

Closed for renovations until 2020.

Neues Schloss PALACE
(New Palace) The ostentatious Neues Schloss was built for Duke Ludwig the Bearded in 1418. Fresh from a trip to wealth-laden France, Ludwig borrowed heavily from Gallic design and created a residence with 3m-thick walls, Gothic net vaulting and individually carved doorways. One guest who probably didn't appreciate its architectural merits was future French president Charles de Gaulle, held as a prisoner of war here during WWI.

Today the building houses the **Bayerisches Armeemuseum** (Bavarian Military Museum; ☑0841-937 70; www.armeemuseum.de; Paradeplatz 4; adult/concession €3.50/3, Sun €1; ☺9am-5.30pm Tue-Fri, 10am-5.30pm Sat & Sun) with exhibits on long-forgotten battles, armaments dating back to the 14th century and legions of tin soldiers filling the rooms.

The second part of the museum is in the **Reduit Tilly** across the river. This 19th-century fortress has an undeniable aesthetic, having been designed by Ludwig I's chief architect. It was named after Johann Tilly – a field marshal of the Thirty Years' War, who was known as the 'butcher of Magdeburg' –

THE BIRTH OF FRANKENSTEIN

Mary Shelley's *Frankenstein*, published in 1818, set a creepy precedent in the world of monster fantasies. The story is well known: young scientist Viktor Frankenstein travels to Ingolstadt to study medicine. He becomes obsessed with the idea of creating a human being and goes shopping for parts at the local cemetery. Unfortunately, his creature is a problem child and sets out to destroy its maker.

Shelley picked Ingolstadt because it was home to a prominent university and medical faculty. In the 19th century, a laboratory for scientists and medical doctors was housed in the Alte Anatomie (now the Deutsches Medizinhistorisches Museum). In the operating theatre, professors and their students carried out experiments on corpses and dead tissue, though perhaps one may have been inspired to work on something a bit scarier...

and features exhibits covering the history of WWI and post-WWI Germany.

The museum complex also houses the **Bayerisches Polizeimuseum** (Donaulände 1; adult/concession €3.50/3, Sun €1; ⊙9am-5.30pm Tue-Fri, 10am-5.30pm Sat & Sun), which lives in the Turm Triva, built at the same time as the Reduit Tilly. Exhibitions trace the story of Bavarian police and their role in various episodes of history such as the Third Reich and the Cold War.

A combined ticket is available at each museum that covers entry to all three museums (adult/concession €7/5).

Kreuztor
HISTORIC BUILDING

(Kreuzstrasse) The Gothic Kreuztor (1385) was one of the four main gates into the city until the 19th century and its redbrick fairytale outline is now the emblem of Ingolstadt. This and the main gate within the Neues Schloss are all that remain of the erstwhile entrances into the medieval city, but the former fortifications, now flats, still encircle the centre.

🛏 Sleeping

Ingolstadt has lots of hotels aimed at business travellers, which can be an advantage at weekends when rates tumble.

DJH hostel
HOSTEL €

(☑0841-305 1280; www.ingolstadt.jugendherberge.de; Friedhofstrasse 4; dm from €20) This beautiful, cheap, well-equipped and wheelchair-friendly hostel crams 84 beds into a renovated redbrick fortress (1828), about 150m west of the Kreuztor.

★Kult Hotel
DESIGN HOTEL €€

(☑0841-95100; www.kult-hotel.de; Theodor-Heuss-Strasse 25; d from €130; P🖥) The most eye-catching feature of rooms at this exciting design hotel, 2km northeast of the city centre, is the painted ceilings, each one a slightly saucy work of art. Otherwise fittings and furniture come sleek, room gadgets are the latest toys, and the restaurant constitutes a study in cool elegance.

Bayerischer Hof
HOTEL €€

(☑0841-934 060; www.bayerischer-hof-ingolstadt. de; Münzbergstrasse 12; s €70-85, d €85-100; 🖥) Located around a Bavarian eatery, the 34 rooms here are filled with hardwood furniture, TVs and modern bathrooms. Rates come down at weekends making it a good deal for lone travellers as almost half the rooms are business-traveller-oriented singles.

Hotel Anker
HOTEL €€

(☑0841-300 50; www.hotel-restaurant-anker. de; Tränktorstrasse 1; s/tw €70/90; 🖥) Bright rooms, a touch of surrealist art and a commendably central location make this family-run hotel a good choice. When checking in, try to avoid arriving at meal times, when staff are busy serving in the traditional restaurant downstairs.

Enso Hotel
HOTEL €€€

(☑0841-885 590; www.enso-hotel.de; Bei der Arena 1; s/d from €100/130; P🖥) Located just across the Danube from the city centre, the 176 business-standard rooms here come in bold dashes of lip-smacking red and soot black, with acres of retro faux veneer. Traffic noise is barely audible despite the location at a busy intersection. Amenities include a commendable Italian restaurant-bar and a fitness room.

🍴 Eating & Drinking

Local drinkers are proud that Germany's Beer Purity Law of 1516 was issued in Ingolstadt, the 500th anniversary of which the city celebrated in 2016. Herrnbräu, Nordbräu or Ingobräu are the excellent local brews.

Weissbräuhaus
PUB FOOD €€

(☑0841-328 90; Dollstrasse 3; mains €7-19; ⊙11am-midnight) This beer hall with a modern feel plates up standard Bavarian fare as well as the delicious signature *Weissbräupfändl* (pork fillet with homemade noodles). The beer garden with a charming fountain out back is a pleasant place to while away a balmy evening.

Zum Daniel
BAVARIAN €€

(☑0841-352 72; Roseneckstrasse 1; mains €8-17; ⊙9am-midnight Tue-Sun) In a wonderfully Bavarian step-gabled townhouse, Ingolstadt's oldest inn is a lovingly run, Michelin-reviewed local institution serving what many claim to be the town's best pork roast and seasonal specials.

Stella D'Oro
ITALIAN €€€

(☑0841-794 3737; www.stelladoro.de; Griesbadgasse 2; mains €15-30; ⊙11.30am-2.30pm & 5.30-11pm Mon-Sat) Ingolstadt has more Italian eateries than some Italian towns, so if you're going for *la dolce vita,* you might as well go for the best. The brief menu at this smart Italian job features a well-curated selection of meat, fish and pasta, though a starter here costs the same as a main elsewhere.

Kuchlbauer PUB

(☑0841-335 512; www.zum-kuchlbauer-ingolstadt. de; Schäffbräustrasse 11a; ⊙11.30am-11pm Sun-Fri, to 1am Sat) This unmissable brewpub is half museum, half tavern with oodles of brewing knick-knacks lining the walls. The house beer comes in wheat, dark and Helles varieties.

Neue Galerie Das MO BAR

(☑0841-339 60; www.dasmo.de; Bergbräustrasse 7; ⊙10.30am-midnight Sun-Wed, to 2am Thu-Sat; ☏) This trendy haunt puts on occasional art exhibitions, but it's the walled beer garden in the shade of mature chestnut trees that punters really come for. The international menu offers everything from grilled meats to schnitzel and *Obazda*. Vegetarians are well catered for.

❶ Information

Post Office (Am Stein 8; ⊙8.30am-6pm Mon-Fri, 9am-1pm Sat)

Tourist Office Hauptbahnhof (☑0841-305 3005; www.ingolstadt-tourismus.de; Elisabeth-strasse 3; ⊙8.30am-6.30pm Mon-Fri, 9.30am-1pm Sat) Branch of the tourist office at the main train station.

Tourist Office Rathausplatz (☑0841-305 3030; www.ingolstadt-tourismus.de; Moritzstrasse 19; ⊙9am-6pm Mon-Fri, 10am-2pm Sat & Sun, shorter hours & closed Sun Nov-Mar) Centrally located visitors centre next to the Rathaus.

❶ Getting There & Around

When arriving by train from the north (from Eichstätt and Nuremberg), **Ingolstadt Nord station** (Am Nordbahnhof) is nearer to the historical centre than the Hauptbahnhof. Trains from the south arrive at the **Hauptbahnhof** (Elisabethstrasse). Ingolstadt has connections to Munich (€20, 40 minutes to one hour, twice hourly), Nuremberg (€20 to €33, 30 to 45 minutes, half-hourly) and Regensburg (€16.60, one hour, hourly).

Buses 10, 11 and 18 run every few minutes between the city centre and the Hauptbahnhof, 2.5km to the southeast.

Freising

☑08161 / POP 47,900

For 1000 years Freising was the spiritual and cultural epicentre of southern Bavaria. Now the nearest town to the airport, it's become something of a bedroom community for Munich but retains the feel of a traditional market town. In 1821 the bishop bowed to the inevitable and moved his seat to Munich. Freising sank in the ecclesiastical ranking but hung onto its religious gems, the main reasons to visit today. The town was a major way station in the life of Pope Benedict, who studied and taught at the university, was ordained here as a priest and later became archbishop here.

◉ Sights

Dom St Maria und St Korbinian CATHEDRAL

(www.freisinger-dom.de; Domberg; ⊙8am-6pm Fri-Wed, from 2pm Thu) Looming over the old town is the Domberg, a hub of religious power with the twin-towered Dom St Maria und St Korbinian as its focal point. The restored church interior in whitewash, ochre and delicate rose is a head-turning stucco masterpiece by the Asam brother megastars, whose baroque frescos grace the most pious ceilings of Bavaria. Remnants from the Gothic era include the choir stalls and a *Lamentation of Christ* painting in the left aisle.

The altar painting by Rubens is a copy of the original in the Alte Pinakothek museum in Munich.

Don't miss the crypt, not so much to view Korbinian's mortal remains as to admire the forest of pillars, no two of which are carved alike. The Bestiensäule (Beast Pillar) features an epic allegory of Christianity fighting the crocodile-like monsters of evil.

East of the Dom are the cloisters, where the halls drip with fancy stucco and 1000 years' homage in marble plaques to the bishops of Freising. The baroque hall of the cathedral library was designed by none other than François Cuvilliés, of Cuvilliés-Theatre fame.

Diözesan Museum MUSEUM

(www.dimu-freising.de; Domberg 21; adult/conces-sion €6/4; ⊙10am-5pm Tue-Sun May-Oct) At the western end of the Domberg you'll find Germany's largest ecclesiastical museum. The building contains a Fort Knox–worthy collection of bejewelled gold vessels, reliquaries and ceremonial regalia, as well as some exquisite nativity scenes. Pride of place goes to the *Lukasbild,* a 12th-century Byzantine icon set in its own diminutive silver altar. Rubens and other masters await upstairs.

⌖ Tours

Staatsbrauerei Weihenstephan BREWERY

(www.weihenstephaner.de; Alte Akademie 2; tours with/without beer tasting €11/8; ⊙10am Mon-Wed & 1.30pm Tue) Southwest of the Domberg, a former Benedictine monastery hosts, among other university faculties, a respected college of beer brewing. Also here is the Staatsbrauerei Weihenstephan, a brewery founded in 1040, making it the world's oldest still in operation. Guided tours trace a millenium of brewery history in the museum, which is followed by a behind-the-scenes spin around the hallowed halls and concluded with a beer tasting (if you've paid extra). Tours must be booked ahead online.

❶ Information

Tourist Office (☏ 08161-544 4111; www.freising.de; Rindermarkt 20; ☺9am-6pm Mon-Fri, to 1pm Sat) For information, visit the tourist office, from which staff run a range of guided tours in English, including airport tours for kids, beer tours, and a tour that follows in the steps of Pope Benedict.

❶ Getting There & Away

Freising is about 35km northeast of Munich at the northern terminus of the S1 (€8.70, 40 minutes) and is also frequently served by faster regional trains (€8.70, 25 minutes). The Domberg and Altstadt are a 10-minute walk from the train station.

Landshut

☏ 0871 / POP 62,000

A worthwhile halfway halt between Munich and Regensburg, or a place to kill half a day before a flight from nearby Munich Airport, Landshut (pronounced 'Lants-hoot') was the hereditary seat of the Wittelsbach family in the early 13th century, and capital of the Dukedom of Bavaria-Landshut for over a century. Apart from a brief episode as custodian of the Bavarian University two centuries ago, Landshuters have since been busy retreating into provincial obscurity, but the town's blue-blooded past is still echoed in its grand buildings, a historical pageant with a cast of thousands and one seriously tall church.

◎ Sights

Burg Trausnitz CASTLE
(☏ 0871-924 110; www.burg-trausnitz.de; adult/child €5.50/free; ☺tours 9am-6pm Apr-Sep, 10am-4pm Oct-Mar) Roosting high above the Altstadt is Burg Trausnitz, Landshut's star attraction. The 50-minute guided tour (in German with English text) takes you through the Gothic and Renaissance halls and chambers, ending at an alfresco party terrace with bird's-eye views of the town below. The tour

includes the Kunst- und Wunderkammer (Room of Art and Curiosities), a typical Renaissance-era display of exotic curios assembled by the local dukes.

St Martin Church CHURCH
(www.st.martin-landshut.de; Altstadt; ☺7.30am-6pm Apr-Sep, to 5pm Oct-Mar) Rising in Gothic splendour at the southern end of the Altstadt is Landshut's record-breaking St Martin Church: its spire is the tallest brick structure in the world at 130.6m and took 55 years to build. It's by far Bavaria's tallest church with Regensburg's Dom a full 25m shorter.

Stadtresidenz PALACE
(Altstadt 79; adult/child €3.50/free; ☺tours in German hourly 9am-6pm Apr-Sep, 10am-4pm Oct-Mar, closed Mon) Gracing the Altstadt is the Stadtresidenz, a Renaissance palace built by Ludwig X that hosts temporary exhibitions on historical themes. Admission is by guided tour only.

✦ Festivals & Events

Landshuter Hochzeit FESTIVAL
(www.landshuter-hochzeit.de; ☺Jul) Every four years, the town hosts the Landshuter Hochzeit (next held in 2021 and 2025), one of Europe's biggest medieval bashes. It commemorates the marriage of Duke Georg der Reiche of Bavaria-Landshut to Princess Jadwiga of Poland in 1475.

⬛ Sleeping

DJH Hostel HOSTEL €
(☏ 0871-234 49; www.landshut.jugendherberge.de; Richard-Schirrmann-Weg 6; dm from €22; ☏) This clean, well-run 100-bed hostel occupies an attractive old villa up by the castle, with views across town.

Goldene Sonne HOTEL €€
(☏ 0871-925 30; www.goldenesonne.de; Neustadt 520; s/d from €70/90; ❖☏) True to its name, the 'Golden Sun' fills a magnificently gabled, six-storey townhouse with light. Rooms sport stylishly lofty ceilings, ornate mirrors and renovated bathrooms. There's a fancy Bavarian restaurant on-site.

Zur Insel HOTEL €€
(☏ 0871-923 160; www.insel-landshut.de; Badstrasse 16; s/d from €70/85; ☏) Housed in a former mill on a large island in the Isar, this is a good-value place to kip with 15 simple folksy rooms and a wood-panelled restaurant.

Eating

Tigerlilly Supperclub
ITALIAN €€

(www.tigerlilly-supperclub.com; Altstadt 362; mains €7-18; ⊙10am-midnight Mon, Wed & Thu, to 2am Fri & Sat, 11am-10pm Sun; 🕿) With its retro-styling, long communal benches and happy staff, Tigerlilly is a breath of trendy air in conservative Landshut. The menu has a definite Italian leaning with well-executed pizzas, salads and pastas galore.

Augustiner an der St Martins Kirche
BAVARIAN €€

(www.landshut-augustiner.de; Kirchgasse 251; mains €5-17; ⊙10am-midnight) This dark-wood tavern at the foot of the St Martin's spire is the best place in town to down a meat-dumpling combo, washed along with a frothy Munich wet one. It also does a mean Nuremberg Bratwurst.

Alt Landshut
BAVARIAN €€

(Isarpromenade 3; mains €6-15; ⊙11am-11pm) Sunny days see locals linger over an Augustiner and some neighbourhood nosh outside by the Isar. In winter you can retreat to the simple whitewashed dining room.

Information

Tourist Office (☑0871-922 050; www.land shut.de; Altstadt 315; ⊙9am-6pm Mon-Fri, 10am-4pm Sat Apr-Oct, 9am-5pm Mon-Fri, 10am-2pm Sat Nov-Feb)

Getting There & Away

TO/FROM THE AIRPORT
The airport bus (€13, 45 minutes) leaves hourly from near the tourist office and the train station between 3am and 10pm.

TRAIN
Landshut is a fairly major stop on the Munich–Regensburg main-line. Services include Munich (€17.30, one hour, twice hourly), Passau (€22, 1½ hours, hourly) and Regensburg (€14.50, 40 minutes, at least hourly).

Passau

☑0851 / POP 51,100

The power of flowing water has quite literally shaped the picturesque town of Passau on the border with Austria. Its Altstadt is stacked atop a narrow peninsula that jabs its sharp end into the confluence of three rivers: the Danube, the Inn and the Ilz. The rivers brought wealth to Passau, which for centuries was an important trading centre, especially for Bohemian salt, central Europe's

'white gold'. Christianity, meanwhile, generated prestige as Passau evolved into the largest bishopric in the Holy Roman Empire. The Altstadt remains pretty much as it was when the powerful prince-bishops built its tight lanes, tunnels and archways with an Italianate flourish, but the western end (around Nibelungenplatz) has received a modern makeover with shopping malls centred on the hang-glider-shaped central bus station (ZOB).

Passau is a Danube river-cruise halt and is often bursting with day visitors. It's also the convergence point of several long-distance cycling routes.

Sights

Dom St Stephan
CHURCH

(www.bistum-passau.de; Domplatz; ⊙6.30am-7pm) There's been a church on this spot since the late 5th century, but what you see today is much younger thanks to the fire of 1662, which ravaged much of the medieval town, including the cathedral. The rebuilding contract went to a team of Italians, notably the architect Carlo Lurago and the stucco master Giovanni Battista Carlone. The result is a top-heavy baroque interior with a posse of saints and cherubs gazing down at the congregation from countless cornices and capitals.

The building's acoustics are perfect for its main attraction, the world's largest organ, which perches above the main entrance. This monster of a wind instrument contains an astonishing 17,974 pipes and it's an amazing acoustic experience to hear it in full puff. Half-hour organ recitals take place at noon daily Monday to Saturday (adult/child €5/2) and at 7.30pm on Thursday (adult/child €10/5) from May to October and for a week around Christmas. Show up at least 30 minutes early to ensure you bag a seat.

Dreiflusseck
LANDMARK

(Three River Corner) The very nib of the Altstadt peninsula, the point where the rivers merge, is known as the Dreiflusseck. From the north the little Ilz sluices brackish water down from the peat-rich Bavarian Forest, meeting the cloudy brown of the Danube as it flows from the west and the pale snow-melt jade of the Inn from the south to create a murky tricolour. The effect is best observed from the ramparts of the Veste Oberhaus.

Veste Oberhaus
FORTRESS

(☑0851-396 800; www.oberhausmuseum.de; adult/child €5/4; ⊙9am-5pm Mon-Fri, 10am-6pm

Sat & Sun mid-Mar–mid-Nov) A 13th-century defensive fortress, built by the prince-bishops, Veste Oberhaus towers over Passau with patriarchal pomp. Not surprisingly, views of the city and into Austria are superb from up here. Inside the bastion is the Ober-hausmuseum, a regional history museum where you can uncover the mysteries of medieval cathedral building, learn what it took to become a knight and explore Passau's period as a centre of the salt trade. Displays are labelled in English.

Passauer Glasmuseum _MUSEUM_
(☑0851-350 71; www.glasmuseum.de; Schrottgasse 2, Hotel Wilder Mann; adult/child €7/5; ☉9am-5pm) Opened by Neil Armstrong, of all people, Passau's warren-like glass museum is filled with some 30,000 priceless pieces of glass and crystal from the baroque, classical, art nouveau and art deco periods. Much of what you see hails from the illustrious glassworks of Bohemia, but there are also works by Tiffany and famous Viennese producers. Be sure to pick up a floor plan as it's easy to get lost.

Altes Rathaus _NOTABLE BUILDING_
(Old Town Hall; Rathausplatz 2) An entrance in the side of the Altes Rathaus flanking Schrottgasse takes you to the **Grosser Rathaussaal** (Great Assembly Room; adult/child €2/1.50; ☉8am-noon Mon-Fri, plus 1-4pm Mon & Tue, 1-5pm Thu), where large-scale paintings by 19th-century local artist Ferdinand Wagner show scenes from Passau's history with melodramatic flourish. You can also sneak into the adjacent Small Assembly Room for a peek at the ceiling fresco, which features allegories of the three rivers.

The rest of the Rathaus is a grand Gothic affair topped by a 19th-century painted tower. A carillon chimes several times daily (hours are listed on the wall, alongside historical flood-level markers).

Museum Moderner Kunst _MUSEUM_
(☑0851-383 8790; www.mmk-passau.de; Bräugasse 17; adult/child €6/4; ☉10am-6pm Tue-Sun, to 4pm Mon Jun-Sep) Gothic architecture contrasts with 20th- and 21st-century artworks at Passau's Modern Art Museum. The rump of the permanent exhibition is made up of cubist and expressionist works by Georg Philipp Wörlen, who died in Passau in 1954 and whose architect son, Hanns Egon Wörlen, set up the museum in the 1980s. Temporary exhibitions normally showcase big-hitting German artists and native styles and personalities from the world of architecture.

Römermuseum _MUSEUM_
(☑0851-347 69; www.stadtarchaeologie.de; Lederergasse 43; adult/child €4/2; ☉10am-4pm Tue-Sun Mar–mid-Nov) Roman Passau can be viewed from the ground up at this Roman fort museum. Civilian and military artefacts unearthed here and elsewhere in Eastern Bavaria are on show and the ruins of Kastell Boiotro, which stood here from AD 250 to 400, are still in situ; some of the towers are still inhabited. There's a castle-themed kids' playground nearby.

Tours

Wurm + Köck _BOATING_
(☑0851-929 292; www.donauschiffahrt.de; Höllgasse 26; city tour €8.90) From March to early November, Wurm + Köck operates cruises to the Dreiflusseck from the docks near Rathausplatz, as well as a whole host of other sailings to places along the Danube. The most spectacular vessel in the fleet is the sparkling _Kristallschiff_ (Crystal Ship), decorated ostentatiously inside and out with Swarovski crystals.

🛏 Sleeping

Pension Rössner _GUESTHOUSE €_
(☑0851-931 350; www.pension-roessner.de; Bräugasse 19; s/d €35/60; P 🖥) This immaculate place, in a restored mansion near the tip of the peninsula, offers great value for money and a friendly, cosy ambience. Each of the 16 rooms is uniquely decorated and many overlook the fortress. There's bike hire (€10 per day) and parking (€5 per day). Breakfast can be taken on the terrace overlooking the Danube for €7 extra. Booking recommended.

DJH Hostel _HOSTEL €_
(☑0851-493 780; www.passau.jugendherberge.de; Oberhaus 125; dm from €23; 🖥) Beautifully renovated 129-bed hostel and one of Bavaria's best DJHs, right in the fortress.

HendlHouseHotel _HOTEL €_
(☑0851-330 69; www.hendlhouse.com; Grosse Klingergasse 17; s/d €50/70; 🖥) With their light, unfussy decor and well-tended bathrooms, the 15 pristine rooms at this Altstadt hotel offer a high quality-to-price ratio. Buffet breakfast is served in the downstairs restaurant.

Camping Passau _CAMPGROUND €_
(☑0851-414 57; www.camping-passau.de; Halser Strasse 34; per person €9.50; ☉May-Sep) Tent-only camping ground idyllically set on

WORTH A TRIP

MARKTL AM INN

On a gentle bend in the Inn River, some 60km southwest of Passau, sits the drowsy settlement of Marktl am Inn. Few outside Germany (or indeed Bavaria) had heard of it before 19 April 2005, the day when its favourite son, Cardinal Joseph Ratzinger, was elected Pope Benedict XVI. Literally overnight the community was inundated with reporters, devotees and the plain curious, all seeking clues about the pontiff's life and times. It's for these papal associations that people still flock to Marktl, though not in the numbers they once did.

Geburtshaus (✆ 08678-747 680; www.papsthaus.eu; Marktplatz 11; adult/child €3.50/free; ☉ 10am-noon & 2-6pm Tue-Fri, 10am-6pm Sat & Sun Easter-Oct), the simple but pretty Bavarian home where Cardinal Joseph Ratzinger (Pope Benedict XVI) was born in 1927 and lived for the first two years of his life before his family moved to Tittmoning, now houses an exhibition dedicated to the ex-pope. Things kick off with a film (in English) tracing the pontiff's early life, career and the symbols he selected for his papacy. You then head into the house proper, where exhibits expand on these themes. The modest room where Ratzinger came into the world is on the upper floor.

The **Heimatmuseum** (✆ 08678-8104; Marktplatz 2; adult/child €2/1.50) is in possession of a golden chalice and a skullcap that was used by Pope Benedict XVI in his private chapel in Rome. It is only open to groups of five or more by prior arrangement; visitors should call the **tourist office** (✆ 08678-748 820; www.marktl.de; Marktplatz 1; ☉ 10am-noon & 1-3pm) at least a day ahead to arrange entry. His baptismal font can be viewed at the **Pfarrkirche St Oswald** (Marktplatz 6), which is open for viewing except during church services.

Marktl is a very brief stop on an Inn-hugging branch line of the train service between Simbach and the junction at Mühldorf (€6.90, 20 minutes), from where there are regular direct connections to Munich, Passau and Landshut.

the Ilz River, 15 minutes' walk from the Altstadt. Catch bus 1 or 2 to Ilzbrücke.

Pension Vicus
GUESTHOUSE €

(✆ 0851-931 050; www.pension-vicus.de; Johann-Bergler-Strasse 2; s €45-50, d €65-80; P ☎) A bright, colour-splashed, family-run pension on the southern side of the Inn. Rooms have small kitchenettes and there's a supermarket next door. Breakfast is an extra €7. Take frequent bus 3 or 4 from the ZOB to the Johann-Bergler-Strasse stop.

★ Hotel Schloss Ort
BOUTIQUE HOTEL €€

(✆ 0851-340 72; www.hotel-schloss-ort.de; Im Ort 11; s/d from €70/90; P ☎) The most characterful place to sleep in Passau, this 800-year-old medieval palace by the Inn River conceals a tranquil boutique hotel, stylishly done with polished timber floors, crisp white cotton sheets and wrought-iron bedsteads. Many of the 18 rooms enjoy river views and breakfast is served in the vaulted restaurant.

Hotel König
HOTEL €€

(✆ 0851-3850; www.hotel-koenig.de; Untere Donaulände 1; s €70-95, d €90-140; P ☎) This riverside property puts you smack in the heart of the Altstadt and near all the sights. The

41 timber-rich rooms – many of them enormous – spread out over two buildings and most come with views of the Danube and fortress. Parking is €10 a night.

Hotel Wilder Mann
HOTEL €€

(✆ 0851-350 71; www.wilder-mann.com; Höllgasse 1; s €60-150, d €95-220; P ☎) Sharing space with the Glasmuseum (p461), this historic hotel boasts former guests ranging from Empress Elisabeth (Sisi) of Austria to Yoko Ono. In the rooms, folksy painted furniture sits incongrously with 20th-century telephones and 21st-century TVs. The building is a warren of staircases, passageways and linking doors, so make sure you remember where your room is.

Guests receive a miserly discount to the museum but breakfast is normally included.

Eating

Cafe Greindl
CAFE €

(www.greindl-passau.de; Wittgasse 8; light meals €6-10; ☉ 7am-6pm Mon-Sat, from 11am Sun) The affluent *Kaffee-und-Torte* society meet daily at this bright, flowery cafe that oozes Bavarian *Gemütlichkeit*. The staff pride themselves on their seasonal decor and the service is excellent. The early opening makes this a sure-fire breakfast option.

Café Kowalski
CAFE €

(☑0851-2487; www.cafe-kowalski.de; Oberer Sand 1; mains €8-18; ☺9.15am-1am Mon-Sat, 10am-midnight Sun; ☎) Chat flows as freely as the wine and beer at this cool, retro-furnished cafe, a kicker of a nightspot. The giant burgers, schnitzels and big breakfasts are best consumed on the terrace overlooking the Ilz River.

★ Culinarium Passau
MEDITERRANEAN €€

(☑0851-9890 8270; www.culinarium-passau.de; Lederergasse 16; mains €14-24, 3-/4-course menu €37/46; ☺5-11pm Tue-Sat) Choose between seasonal and Mediterranean menus with paired wine and a regularly changing à la carte menu at this gourmet, evening-only restaurant with leaping brick vaulting on the southern side of the Inn. Diners rave about the service and laud praise on the standard of the dishes.

★ Heilig-Geist-Stifts-Schenke
BAVARIAN €€

(☑0851-2607; www.stiftskeller-passau.de; Heilig-Geist-Gasse 4; mains €10-20; ☺11am-midnight, closed Wed; ☎) Not only does this historical inn have a succession of walnut-panelled ceramic-stove-heated rooms, a candlelit cellar (from 6pm) and a vine-draped garden, but the food is equally inspired. Amid the river fish, steaks and seasonal dishes there are quite gourmet affairs such as beef fillet in flambéed cognac sauce. Help it all along with one of the many Austrian and German wines in stock.

Diwan
CAFE €€

(☑0851-490 3280; Niebelungenplatz 1, 9th fl, Stadtturm; mains €6-14; ☺9am-7pm Mon-Sat, 1-6pm Sun) It's all aboard the high-speed lift from street level to this trendy, high-perched cafe-lounge at the top of the Stadtturm, with by far the best views in town. From the tangled rattan and plush cappuccino-culture sofas you can see it all – the Dom St Stephan, the rivers, the Veste Oberhaus – while you tuck into the offerings of the changing seasonal menu.

Drinking & Nightlife

Andorfer Weissbräu
BEER GARDEN

(☑0851-754 444; Rennweg 2; ☺9.30am-midnight Tue-Sun) High on a hill 1.5km north of the Altstadt, this rural beer garden attached to the Andorfer brewery serves filling Bavarian favourites, but the star of the show is the outstanding *Weizen* (wheat beer) and *Weizenbock* (strong wheat beer) brewed

metres away. Take bus 7 from the ZOB to Ries-Rennweg.

Caffè Bar Centrale
CAFE

(Rindermarkt 7; ☺8am-10pm) Venetian bar that has to spill out onto the cobbles of the Rindermarkt as it's so tiny inside. It may be small, but there's a huge drinks menu and it's a fine place to head for a first or last drink. The Italian soundtrack fits nicely with the Italianate surroundings.

ℹ Information

Post Office (Bahnhofstrasse 1; ☺9.30am-8pm Mon-Sat)

Tourist Office (☑0851-955 980; www.tourism. passau.de; Rathausplatz 3; ☺8.30am-6pm Mon-Fri, 9am-4pm Sat & Sun Easter–mid-Oct, shorter hours mid-Oct–Easter) Passau's main tourist office is located in the Altstadt. There's another smaller office opposite the **Hauptbahnhof** (Bahnhofstrasse 28; ☺9am-5pm Mon-Thu, to 4pm Fri, 10.30am-3.30pm Sat & Sun Easter-Sep, shorter hours Oct-Easter). Both branches sell the PassauCard.

ℹ Getting There & Away

BUS

A lonely bus leaves at 3.45am for the Czech border village of Železná Ruda (2¾ hours), though it arrives too late for connections to Prague. However, you can reach Pilsen.

TRAIN

Rail connections from Passau include Munich (€38.70, 2¼ hours, hourly), Nuremberg (€50, two hours, every two hours), Regensburg (€26.40 to €31, one hour, every two hours), or change in Plattling, and Vienna (€58, 2¾ hours, every two hours).

ℹ Getting Around

Central Passau is sufficiently compact to explore on foot. The CityBus links the Bahnhof with the Altstadt (€1) up to four times an hour. Longer trips within Passau cost €2; a day pass costs €4.50.

The walk up the hill to the Veste Oberhaus or the DJH Hostel, via Luitpoldbrücke and Ludwigsteig path, takes about 30 minutes. From April to October, a shuttle bus operates every 30 minutes from Rathausplatz (€2).

There are several public car parks near the train station, but only one in the Altstadt at Römerplatz.

Bavarian Forest

Together with the Bohemian Forest on the Czech side of the border, the Bavarian Forest (Bayerischer Wald) forms the largest continuous woodland area in Europe. This inspiring landscape of peaceful rolling hills and rounded tree-covered peaks is interspersed with seldom-disturbed valleys and stretches of virgin woodland, providing a habitat for many species long since vanished from the rest of Central Europe. A large area is protected as the surprisingly wild and remote Bavarian Forest National Park (Nationalpark Bayerischer Wald).

Although incredibly good value, the region sees few international tourists and remains quite traditional. A centuries-old glass-blowing industry is still active in many of the towns along the Glasstrasse (Glass Road), a 250km holiday route connecting Waldsassen with Passau. You can visit the studios, workshops, museums and shops, and stock up on traditional and contemporary designs.

The centrally located town of Zwiesel is a natural base, but other settlements along the Waldbahn such as Frauenau and Grafenau are also worth considering if relying on public transport.

○ Sights

Bavarian Forest National Park   NATIONAL PARK
(Nationalpark Bayerischer Wald; www.nationalpark-bayerischer-wald.de) A thickly wooded paradise for lovers of fresh air, the Bavarian Forest National Park extends for around 24,250 hectares along the Czech border, from Bayerisch Eisenstein in the north to Finsterau in the south. Its thick forest, most of it mountain spruce, is criss-crossed by hundreds of kilometres of marked hiking, cycling and cross-country skiing trails, some of which now link up with a similar network across the border. The region is home to deer, wild boar, fox, otter and countless bird species.

Around 1km northeast of the village of Neuschönau stands the **Hans-Eisenmann-Haus** (☑08558-961 50; www.nationalpark-bayerischer-wald.de; Böhmstrasse 35; ☺9am-6pm May-Nov, to 5pm Dec-Apr), the national park's main visitors centre. The free exhibition has displays designed to shed light on topics such as pollution and tree growth. There's also a children's discovery room, shop and library.

Museumsdorf Bayerischer Wald   MUSEUM
(☑08504-8482; www.museumsdorf.com; Am Dreiburgensee, Tittling; adult/child €7/5; ☺10am-6pm Apr-Oct) On the southern edge of the Bavarian Forest is Tittling, home to this 20-hectare open-air museum displaying 150 typical Bavarian Forest timber cottages and farmsteads from the 17th to the 19th centuries. Exhibitions inside the various buildings range from clothing and furniture to pottery and farming implements. Take frequent RBO bus 6124 to Tittling from Passau Hauptbahnhof.

Glasmuseum   MUSEUM
(☑09926-941 020; www.glasmuseum-frauenau.de; Am Museumspark 1, Frauenau; adult/child €5/free; ☺9am-5pm Tue-Sun) Frauenau's dazzlingly modern Glasmuseum covers four millennia of glass-making history, starting with the ancient Egyptians and ending with modern glass art from around the world. Demonstrations and workshops for kids are regular.

Gläserne Wald   PUBLIC ART
(Glass Forest; www.glaeserner-wald.de; Weissenstein, Regen) One of the more unusual sights along the Glass Route is the Gläserne Wald near the small town of Regen. Here glass artist Rudolf Schmid has created a forest of glass trees, some up to 8m tall. The trees, in a number of transparent shades, are set in a flowery meadow next to Weissenstein Castle and are an intriguing sight.

JOSKA Bodenmais   CULTURAL CENTRE
(☑09924-7790; www.joska.com; Am Moosbach 1, Bodenmais; ☺9.30am-6pm Mon-Fri, to 5pm Sat year-round, 10am-5pm Sun May-Oct) FREE The glass highlight of the small town of Bodenmais is JOSKA Bodenmais, a crystal theme park complete with crystal shops, public artworks, beer garden, year-round Christmas market, crystal gallery and a workshop where visitors can try their hand at glass-blowing.

Waldmuseum   MUSEUM
(☑09922-503 706; www.waldmuseum.zwiesel.de; Kirchplatz 3, Zwiesel; adult/child €6/1; ☺10am-4pm Thu-Mon) Housed in a former brewery, Zwiesel's 'Forest Museum' has exhibitions on local customs, flora and fauna, glass-making and life in the forest.

⚡ Activities

Two long-distance hiking routes cut through the Bavarian Forest: the European Distance Trails E6 (Baltic Sea to the Adriatic Sea) and E8 (North Sea to the Carpathian Mountains). There are mountain huts all along the way. Another popular hiking trail is the Gläserne Steig (Glass Trail) from Lam to Grafenau.

WEIDEN

A worthwhile trip from Regensburg and one of the largest towns in the Oberpfalz region in northeast Bavaria, sleepy Weiden sees few visitors save for the odd Czech coming over the border to shop. The pleasantly historical town centre is an easygoing stroll but the star attraction is the **International Ceramics Museum** (www.dnstdm.de; Luitpoldstrasse 25; adult/child €4/3; ⊙10am-1.30pm & 2-4.30pm), housed in a spare baroque monastery building right in the town centre. The permanent exhibition covers eight millennia of pottery, porcelain and faience including ancient Chinese and Egyptian artefacts. The temporary exhibitions here are selected from only top-notch travelling shows from around the world.

The **train station** (Bahnhofstrasse) is 800m southwest of the centre. Weiden has connections to Nuremberg (€22.60, 70 minutes, hourly), Regensburg (€20.50, 70 minutes, at least hourly) and Munich (€43.30, 2¾ hours, every 2 hours or change in Regensburg).

BAVARIA BAVARIAN FOREST

Whatever route you're planning, maps produced by Kompass – sheets 185, 195 and 197 – are invaluable companions. They are available from tourist offices, some bookshops and the park visitors centre.

The Bavarian Forest has seven ski areas, but downhill skiing is low-key, even though the area's highest mountain, the Grosser Arber (1456m), occasionally hosts European and World Cup ski races. The major draw here is cross-country skiing, with over 2000km of prepared routes through the ranges.

🛏 Sleeping

DJH Hostel   HOSTEL €
(☎08553-6000; www.waldhaeuser.jugendherberge.de; Herbergsweg 2, Neuschönau; dm from €23; 🛜) The Bavarian Forest National Park's sole hostel is an ideal base for hikers, bikers and cross-country skiers.

★ Das Reiners   HOTEL €€
(☎08552-964 90; www.dasreiners.de; Grüb 20, Grafenau; r from €105; P🛜☒) This elegant hotel in Grafenau is good value for the weary traveller. The stylish rooms are spacious and most have balconies. Guests are treated to a pool and sauna, and scrumptious buffet meals. Half-board and other deals are available.

Hotel Zur Waldbahn   HOTEL €€
(☎09922-8570; www.zurwaldbahn.de; Bahnhofplatz 2, Zwiesel; s €65-70, d €90-110; P🛜) Many of the rooms at this characteristic inn, opposite Zwiesel train station, run by three generations of the same family, open to balconies with views over the town. The breakfast buffet is an especially generous spread and even includes homemade jams. The restaurant

serves traditional local fare and is probably the best in town.

Ferienpark Arber   HOLIDAY PARK €€
(☎09922-802 595; www.ferienpark-arber.de; Waldesruhweg 34, Zwiesel; cabin from €100) This convenient and well-equipped camping ground around 500m north of Zwiesel train station has cabins for rent. The tariff includes service charges and a hefty €39 cleaning fee so it's best for those looking to stay at least a week, making this their base.

🍴 Eating & Drinking

Dampfbräu   BAVARIAN €€
(☎09922-4737; Stadtplatz 6, Zwiesel; mains €6-15; ⊙11.30am-11.30pm; 🛜) The best place for some substantial East Bavarian fare and excellent 'steam' beer is this brewpub right in the centre of Zwiesel near the bridge. The traditional woodclad interior, dumpling-and-meat-heavy menu and pleasant countryside service make this a superb place to end a day in the Bavarian Forest.

Gasthaus Mühlhiasl   BAVARIAN €€
(Museumsdorf Bayerischer Wald, Am Dreiburgensee, Tittling; mains €7-19; ⊙10am-6pm Apr-Oct) The rustic restaurant at the Museumsdorf Bayerischer Wald in Tittling sports traditionally laid tables under some of the chunkiest beams you'll ever see. The menu is east Bavarian to the core with lots of forest inhabitants, mushrooms and dumplings to choose from.

❶ Information

Tourist Office Grafenau (☎08552-962 343; www.grafenau.de; Rathausgasse 1, Grafenau; ⊙8am-5pm Mon-Thu, to 1pm Fri, 10-11.30am & 3-5pm Sat, 9.30-11.30am Sun)

Tourist Office Zwiesel (☑ 09922-500 1692; www.zwiesel.de; Stadtplatz 27, Zwiesel; ⊗ 8.30-11.30am & 1.30-4pm Mon-Thu, 8.30am-noon Fri)

❶ Getting There & Around

From Munich, Regensburg or Passau, Zwiesel is reached by rail via Plattling (55 minutes, hourly); most trains continue to Bayerisch Eisenstein on the Czech border, with connections to Prague. The scenic Waldbahn shuttles directly between Zwiesel and Bodenmais, and Zwiesel and Grafenau.

There's also a tight network of regional buses, though service can be infrequent. The Igel-Bus, operated by Ostbayernbus (www.ostbayernbus. de), navigates around the national park on three routes. A useful one is the Lusen-Bus (€5/12.50 per one/three days), which leaves from Grafenau Hauptbahnhof and travels to the Hans-Eisenmann-Haus, the DJH Hostel and the Lusen hiking area.

The best value is usually the Bayerwald-Ticket (€9), a day pass good for unlimited travel on bus and train across the forest area. It's available from the park visitors centre, stations and tourist offices throughout the area.

Straubing

☑ 09421 / POP 47,100

Some 30km southeast of Regensburg, Danube-straddling Straubing enjoyed a brief heyday as part of a wonky alliance that formed the short-lived Duchy of Straubing-Holland. As a result, the centre is chock-a-block with historical buildings that opened new horizons in a small town. In August, the demand for folding benches soars during the Gäubodenfest.

◉ Sights

Ursulinenkirche   CHURCH
(www.kloster.ursulinen-straubing.de; Burggasse 40) The interior of the Ursulinenkirche was designed by the Asam brothers in their final collaboration. Its ceiling fresco depicts the martyrdom of St Ursula surrounded by allegorical representations of the four continents known at the time.

Gäubodenmuseum   MUSEUM
(☑ 09421-9446 3222; www.gaeubodenmuseum.de; Frauenhoferstrasse 23; adult/child €4/1; ⊗ 10am-

4pm Tue-Sun) This intimate museum is one of Germany's most important repositories of Roman treasure. Displays include imposing armour and masks for both soldiers and horses, probably plundered from a Roman store.

St Jakobskirche   CHURCH
(www.st-jakob-straubing.de; Pfarrplatz) St Jakobskirche is a late-Gothic hall church with original stained-glass windows, but also a recipient of a baroque makeover, courtesy of the frantically productive Asam brothers.

✪ Festivals & Events

Gäubodenfest   FESTIVAL
(www.gaeubodenvolksfest-straubing.de; ⊗ mid-Aug) The Gäubodenfest is a 10-day blow-out that once brought together grain farmers in 1812, but today draws over 20,000 drinkers.

🛏 Sleeping & Eating

Asam Hotel   HISTORIC HOTEL €€
(☑ 09421-788 680; www.hotelasam.de; Wittelsbacherhöhe 1; s/d from €90/115; ▣ 🛜) This four-star treat a few streets south of the train station is Straubing's top address with sleek, 21st century rooms and a fine-dining restaurant.

Weissbierhaus   BAVARIAN €
(Theresienplatz 32; mains €6-15; ⊗ 9am-11pm) Simple, cosy and friendly, this authentic little place on the main square, with views from the outdoor seating of Straubing's grand architecture, is the place to enjoy a meat and dumpling combination and a local beer.

❶ Information

Tourist Office (☑ 09421-9446 0199; www. straubing.de; Fraunhoferstrasse 27; ⊗ 9am-5pm Mon-Wed & Fri, to 6pm Thu, 10am-2pm Sat)

❶ Getting There & Away

Surprisingly, Straubing has no direct train connections to Regensburg. First take the train to Radldorf then change to connecting bus (€10.50, 45 minutes, hourly). For Passau (€17.50, one hour, hourly) and Munich (€29, two hours, hourly) change at Plattling or Neufahrn.

Stuttgart & the Black Forest

POP 12.6 MILLION

Best Places to Eat

➡ Restaurant Bareiss (p500)

➡ Schwarzwaldstube (p500)

➡ Rebers Pflug (p484)

➡ Olivo (p475)

➡ Café Schäfer (p517)

Best Places to Stay

➡ Hotel Belle Epoque (p494)

➡ Glückseligkeit Herberge (p524)

➡ Hotel Oberkirch (p509)

➡ Brickstone Hostel (p487)

➡ Hotel Scholl (p483)

Why Go?

If one word could sum up Germany's southwesternmost region, it would be 'inventive'. Baden-Württemberg gave the world relativity (Einstein), DNA (Miescher) and the astronomical telescope (Kepler). It was here that Bosch invented the spark plug; Gottlieb Daimler the gas engine; and Count Ferdinand the zeppelin. And where would we be without Black Forest gateau, cuckoo clocks and the ultimate beer food, the pretzel?

Beyond the high-tech urban pleasures of 21st-century Stuttgart lies a region still ripe for discovery. On the city fringes, country lanes roll into vineyards and lordly baroque palaces, spa towns and castles steeped in medieval myth. Swinging south, the Black Forest (*Schwarzwald* in German) looks every inch the Grimms' fairy-tale blueprint. Wooded hills rise sharply above church steeples, looming over half-timbered villages and a crochet of tightly woven valleys. It is a perfectly etched picture of sylvan beauty, a landscape refreshingly oblivious to time and trends.

When to Go

Snow dusts the heights from January to late February, attracting downhill and cross-country skiers to the higher peaks in the Black Forest. In late February, around Shrove Tuesday, pre-Lenten *Fasnacht* parades bring carnival shenanigans and elaborate costumed characters to the region's towns and villages.

Enjoy cool forest hikes, riverside bike rides, splashy fun on lakes Constance and Titisee, lazy afternoons in beer gardens and open-air festivals galore during summer.

From late September to October the golden autumn days can be spent rambling in woods, mushrooming and snuggling up in Black Forest farmhouses.

Stuttgart & the Black Forest Highlights

1 Stuttgart (p468)
Tuning into modern-day Germany in this city of high culture, fast cars and beer festivals.

2 Baden-Baden (p490)
Wallowing in thermal waters and art nouveau grandeur in the belle of the Black Forest.

3 Lake Constance (p520)
Kayaking, hiking or cycling

between Swiss, German and Austrian borders.

4 Ulm (p484) Being wowed by the world's tallest cathedral steeple in Einstein's home town.

5 Triberg (p516)
Going cuckoo for clocks, Black Forest gateau and Germany's highest waterfall.

6 Black Forest (p490)
Striding into thickly wooded

hills and valleys on mile after glorious mile of walking trails.

7 Tübingen (p480)
Rowing your boat merrily along the Neckar River and living it up, Goethe-style, in this student town.

8 Schauinsland Peak (p512) Hitching a ride above the treetops to this peak for rousing views over the forest to the not-so-distant Alps.

STUTTGART

♫ 0711 / POP 628,032

Ask many Germans their opinion of Stuttgarters and they'll have plenty of things to say: they are road hogs, speeding along the autobahn; they are sharp-dressed executives

with a Swabian drawl; they are tight-fisted homebodies who slave away to *schaffe, schaffe, Häusle baue* (work, work, build a house).

So much for the stereotypes: the real Stuttgart is less superficial than legend would have it. True, some good-living locals like their cars fast and their restaurants fancy, but most are just as happy getting their boots dirty in the surrounding vine-clad hills and hanging out with friends in the rustic confines of a *Weinstube* (wine tavern) or a tree-shaded *Biergarten*. In the capital of Baden-Württemberg, city slickers and country kids walk hand in hand, with no need to compromise.

History

Whether with trusty steeds or turbocharged engines, Stuttgart was born to ride – it was founded as the stud farm Stuotgarten around AD 950. Progress was swift: by the 12th century Stuttgart was a trade centre, by the 13th century a blossoming city and by the early 14th century the seat of the Württemberg royal family. Count Eberhard im Bart added sheen to Swabian suburbia by introducing the *Kehrwoche* in 1492, the communal cleaning rota still revered today.

The early 16th century brought hardship, peasant wars, plague and Austrian rulers (1520–34). A century later, the Thirty Years' War devastated Stuttgart and killed half its population.

In 1818, King Wilhelm I launched the first Cannstatter Volksfest to celebrate the end of a dreadful famine. An age of industrialisation dawned in the late 19th and early 20th centuries, with Bosch inventing the spark plug and Daimler pioneering the gas engine. Heavily bombed in WWII, Stuttgart was painstakingly reconstructed and became the capital of the new state of Baden-Württemberg in 1953. Today it is one of Germany's greenest and most affluent cities.

◉ Sights

Stuttgart's main artery is the shopping boulevard Königstrasse, running south from the Hauptbahnhof (p478). Steep grades are common on Stuttgart's hillsides: more than 500 city streets end in *Stäffele* (staircases).

★**Staatsgalerie Stuttgart**   GALLERY
(☑0711-470 400; www.staatsgalerie.de; Konrad-Adenauer-Strasse 30-32; adult/concession €7/5; ☺10am-6pm Tue, Wed & Fri-Sun, to 8pm Thu; Ⓤ Staatsgalerie) Neoclassical meets contemporary at the Staatsgalerie, which bears British architect James Stirling's curvy, colourful imprint. Alongside big-name exhibitions, the gallery harbours a stellar collection of European art from the 14th to the 21st centuries, and American post-WWII avant-gardists. Highlights include works by Miró, Picasso,

Matisse, Kandinsky and Klee. Special billing goes to masterpieces such as Dalí's *The Sublime Moment* (1938), Rembrandt's pensive, chiaroscuro *Saint Paul in Prison* (1627), Max Beckmann's utterly compelling, large-scale *Resurrection* (1916) and Monet's diffuse *Fields in the Spring* (1887).

Schlossplatz   SQUARE
(Ⓤ Schlossplatz) Stuttgart's pride and joy is this central square, dominated by the exuberant three-winged Neues Schloss, an impressive, Versailles-inspired baroque palace that houses government ministries. In summer, the square plays host to open-air concerts and festivals, such as the Sommerfest (www.stuttgarter-sommerfest.de; ☺early Aug); in winter it twinkles with its Christmas market (p473).

Schloss Solitude   PALACE
(☑0714-118 6400; www.schloss-solitude.de; Solitude 1; adult/concession €4/2; ☺10am-5pm Tue-Sun Apr-Oct, 1.30-4pm Tue-Sat & 10am-4pm Sun Nov-Mar; Ⓢ Feuersee) Domed Schloss Solitude, perched above Stuttgart, was built in 1763 for Duke Karl Eugen of Württemberg as a hunting pleasure and summer residence. Blending rococo and neoclassical styles, it's a lavish confection, with an opulently frescoed, chandelier-lit, gilded interior: top billing goes to the pearly white, stucco-encrusted Weisse Saal (White Hall).

Kunstmuseum Stuttgart   GALLERY
(☑0711-2161 9600; www.kunstmuseum-stuttgart.de; Kleiner Schlossplatz 1; adult/concession €6/4; ☺10am-6pm Tue-Thu, Sat & Sun, to 9pm Fri; Ⓤ Schlossplatz) Occupying a shimmering glass cube, this gallery presents high-calibre special exhibits alongside a permanent gallery filled with a prized collection of works by Otto Dix, Willi Baumeister and Stuttgart-born abstract artist Alfred Hölzel. For far-reaching views over the city, head up to the Cube (p476) cafe and restaurant.

Schlossgarten   GARDENS
(Ⓤ Neckartor) A terrific park for a wander right in the heart of the city, Stuttgart's sprawling Schlossgarten threads together the Mittlerer Schlossgarten (Middle Palace Garden), with its fine beer garden for summer imbibing, the sculpture-dotted Unterer Schlossgarten (Lower Palace Garden; Ⓤ Stöckach), and the Oberer Schlossgarten (Upper Palace Garden; Ⓤ Charlottenplatz), home to stately landmarks such as the Staatstheater (p477) and the glass-fronted Landtag (State Parliament; Ⓤ Charlottenplatz).

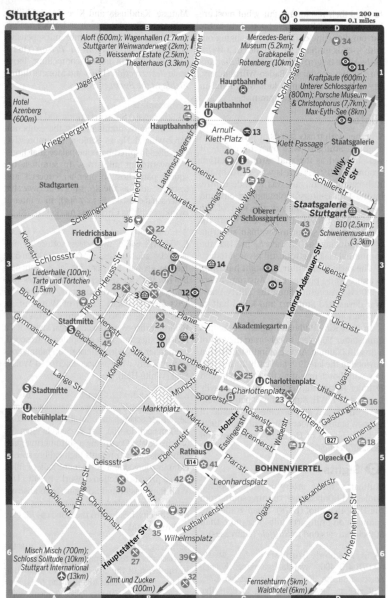

Aloft (600m); Wagenhallen (1.7km);
Stuttgarter Weinwanderweg (2km);
Weissenhof Estate (2.5km);
Theaterhaus (3.3km)

Mercedes-Benz
Museum (5.2km);
Grabkapelle
Rotenberg (10km)

Kraftpaule (600m);
Unterer Schlossgarten
(800m); Porsche Museum
& Christophorus (7.7km);
Max-Eyth-See (8km)

Hotel
Azenberg
(600m)

Liederhalle (100m);
Tarte und Törtchen
(1.5km)

B10 (2.5km);
Schweinemuseum
(3.3km)

Misch Misch (700m);
Schloss Solitude (10km);
Stuttgart International
(13km)

Fernsehturm (5km);
Waldhotel (6km)

Zimt und Zucker
(100m)

Weissenhof Estate MUSEUM

(📞0711-257 9187; www.weissenhofmuseum.de; Rathenaustrasse 1-3; adult/concession €5/2, guided tours €5/4; ⏰11am-6pm Tue-Fri, 10am-6pm Sat & Sun, guided tours 3pm Tue-Sat, 11am & 3pm Sun; Ⓤ Killesberg) Architecture enthusiasts are thrilled by the recent opening of the Weissenhof Estate, following many years of restoration. Built in 1927 for the Deutscher Werkbund exhibition, the estate showcases the pioneering modern architecture of the age, bearing the clean aesthetic imprint of 17 prominent architects, among them Ludwig Mies van der Rohe, Le Corbusier and Walter

Stuttgart

Gropius. Two of Le Corbusier's residential units have received Unesco World Heritage status. Guided tours are in German only.

Fernsehturm   TOWER
(☏0711-9291 4743; www.fernsehturm-stuttgart. de; Jahnstrasse 120, Stuttgart-Degerloch; adult/ concession €7/4; ☺10am-11pm Mon-Thu, 9am-11pm Fri & Sat; ⓤ Ruhbank (Fernsehturm)) Whether you think it a marvel or a monstrosity, the 217m-high Fernsehturm is one of Stuttgart's most visible landmarks, with its needle-thin concrete spire poking up above the city. Built in 1956, it was the world's first TV tower and the prototype for all to come. It goes without saying that the 360° views from the lookout platform and panoramic cafe are a knock-out, reaching over the city (particularly impressive when illuminated) to the Swabian Alps beyond.

Mercedes-Benz Museum   MUSEUM
(☏0711-173 0000; www.mercedes-benz.com; Mercedesstrasse 100; adult/concession €10/5; ☺9am-6pm Tue-Sun, last admission 5pm; ⓢ Neckarpark) A futuristic swirl on the cityscape, the

Mercedes-Benz Museum takes a chronological spin through the Mercedes empire. Look out for legends such as the 1885 Daimler Riding Car (the world's first gasoline-powered vehicle) and the record-breaking Lightning Benz that hit 228km/h at Daytona Beach in 1909.

Porsche Museum   MUSEUM
(☏0711-9112 0911; www.porsche.com/museum; Porscheplatz 1; adult/concession €8/4; ☺9am-6pm Tue-Sun; ⓢ Neuwirtshaus) Looking like a pearly white spaceship preparing for lift-off, the barrier-free Porsche Museum is a car-lover's dream. Audioguides race you through the history of Porsche from its 1948 beginnings. Stop to glimpse the 911 GT1 that won Le Mans in 1998. Call ahead for details of the factory tours that can be combined with a museum visit.

Turmforum   VIEWPOINT
(www.s21erleben.de; Im Hauptbahnhof; ☺9am-7pm Mon-Wed & Fri, 10am-9pm Thu, 10am-6pm Sat & Sun; ⓤ Hauptbahnhof) FREE Some of the best views of Stuttgart are from the the top of the tower jutting out from the main train station. A free lift (elevator) deposits you right

DON'T MISS

STUTTGARTER WEINWANDERWEG

To taste the region's fruity Trollingers and citrusy Rieslings, factor in a stroll through the vineyards surrounding Stuttgart. The Stuttgarter Weinwanderweg (www.stuttgarter -weinwanderweg.de; U Maybachstrasse) comprises several walking trails that thread through winegrowing villages. One begins at Pragsattel station (on the U5 or U6 line) and meanders northeast to Max-Eyth-See, affording fine views from Burgholzhofturm. Visit the website for alternative routes, maps and distances.

From October to March, look out for a broom above the door of Besenwirtschaften (Besa for short). Run by winegrowers, these rustic boltholes are atmospheric places to chat with locals while sampling the latest vintage and Swabian home cooking. Some operate every year but most don't. Check the Besen Kalender website (www.besenkalender. de) during vintage season.

below the revolving Mercedes star. You also get a bird's-eye view of 'Stuttgart 21', a huge – and controversial – revamp of the main train station. Exhibits on floors 3, 5 and 7a explain the details.

Landesmuseum Württemberg MUSEUM

(☑ 0711-8953 5111; www.landesmuseum-stuttgart. de; Schillerplatz 6, Altes Schloss; ⊙ 10am-5pm Tue-Sun; U Charlottenplatz) **FREE** An archway leads to the turreted 10th-century Altes Schloss, where this museum features regional archaeology and architecture. The historic booty includes Celtic jewellery, neolithic pottery, diamond-encrusted crown jewels and rare artefacts. Time your visit to see, from the arcaded courtyard, the rams above the clock tower lock horns on the hour. Entry to the permanent collection is free.

Wilhelma Zoologisch-Botanischer Garten ZOO

(www.wilhelma.de; Rosensteinpark; adult/ concession €16/8, after 4pm & Nov-Feb €11/5.50; ⊙ 8.15am-6pm, to 4pm in winter; U Wilhelma) Wilhelma Zoologisch-Botanischer Garten is a quirky mix of zoo and botanical gardens. Kid magnets include semistriped okapis, elephants, penguins and a petting farm. Greenhouses sheltering tree ferns, camellias and Amazonian species are among the botanical highlights. Sniff out the gigantic bloom of the malodorous titan arum in the Moorish Villa.

Württembergischer Kunstverein GALLERY

(☑ 0711-223 370; www.wkv-stuttgart.de; Schlossplatz 2; adult/concession €5/3; ⊙ 11am-6pm Tue & Thu-Sun, to 8pm Wed; U Schlossplatz) Identified by its copper cupola, this gallery stages thought-provoking contemporary art exhibitions. There are free guided tours (in German) at 3pm on Sundays.

Planetarium Stuttgart PLANETARIUM

(☑ 0711-216 890; www.planetarium-stuttgart.de; Willy-Brandt-Strasse 25; adult/concession €8/5; ⊙ Tue-Sun; U Staatsgalerie) This pyramid-shaped planetarium uses up-to-the-minute technology to virtually propel you into outer space, with highly realistic projections of constellations and planets, plus plenty of background on astronomy. There are a number of different shows, many with fancy laser and music displays. Show times vary; check the website for latest listings. English audioguides are available.

Grabkapelle Rotenberg CHAPEL

(www.grabkapelle-rotenberg.de; Württembergstrasse 340; adult/child €4/2; ⊙ 10am-5pm Tue-Sat, to 6pm Sun Apr-Nov; 🚍 61) When King Wilhelm I of Württemberg's beloved wife Katharina Pavlovna, daughter of a Russian tsar, died at the age of 30 in 1819, the king tore down the family castle and built this burial chapel. The king was also interred in the neoclassical Russian Orthodox chapel decades later. Modelled on the Pantheon, no less, and built from local sandstone, its pure-white interior is striking, with pillars and statues of the four evangelists lifting visitors' gaze to the dome.

Schweinemuseum MUSEUM

(☑ 0711-6641 9600; www.schweinemuseum.de; Schlachthofstrasse 2a; adult/concession €5.90/5; ⊙ 11am-7.30pm; U Schlachthof) Billing itself as the world's biggest pig museum, the Schweinemuseum is one heck of a pigsty: 50,000 paintings, lucky trinkets, antiques, cartoons, piggy banks and a veritable mountain of cuddly toys cover the entire porcine spectrum. Since opening in the city's century-old former slaughterhouse, the kitsch-cool museum has drawn crowds to its exhibits spotlighting everything from pig worship to wild-boar hunting rituals.

👉 Tours

CityTour Stuttgart
BUS

(adult/concession €15/12; ⊘ blue tour 10am-4pm year-round, green tour 11am-4.40pm Apr-Oct; Ⓤ Hauptbahnhof) Departing roughly hourly from the tourist office (p478), the blue tour trundles through the city centre past icons such as Schlossplatz (p469) and the Mercedes-Benz Museum (p471). The new green tour takes in lesser-known corners in the south and west of Stuttgart.

Neckar-Käpt'n
BOATING

(www.neckar-kaeptn.de; Wilhelma; Ⓤ Wilhelma) From early May to late October, Neckar-Käpt'n runs cruises on the Neckar River, departing from its dock at Wilhelma in Bad Cannstatt on the U14.

✨ Festivals & Events

Christopher Street Day
LGBT

(www.csd-stuttgart.de; ⊘ mid-Jul) Held over the course of two weeks, Christopher Street Day is southern Germany's biggest gay and lesbian festival, with concerts, gala dinners, club nights, events and a huge (and hugely flamboyant) parade. The parade begins on Erwin-Schoettle-Platz and makes its way through the centre.

Weindorf
WINE

(www.stuttgarter-weindorf.de; ⊘ late Aug–early Sep) A 12-day event where winemakers sell the year's vintages from hundreds of booths, accompanied by Swabian grub, cultural events, live music and kids' activities. Some 500 wines hailing from the vines in Baden-Württemberg are there for the sniffing, swirling and tasting. Begins on the last weekend in August; held in Schillerplatz, Kirchstrasse and Marktplatz.

Cannstatter Volksfest
BEER

(www.cannstatter-volksfest.de; Cannstatter Wasen; ⊘ late Sep–mid-Oct; Ⓤ Cannstatter Wasen) Stuttgart's answer to Oktoberfest, Cannstatter Volksfest is a beer-guzzling bash held over three consecutive weekends from late September to mid-October. It lifts spirits with oompah music, fairground rides and fireworks. In 2018, the festival pulled out the stops for its 200th anniversary.

Weihnachtsmarkt
CHRISTMAS MARKET

(www.stuttgarter-weihnachtsmarkt.de; ⊘ late Nov-late Dec) One of Germany's biggest Christmas markets brings festive twinkle to Marktplatz, Schillerplatz (Ⓤ Schlossplatz) and Schlossplatz (p469).

🛏 Sleeping

Hostel Alex 30
HOSTEL €

(☏ 0711-838 8950; www.alex30-hostel.de; Alexanderstrasse 30; dm €25-29, s/d €43/64; Ⓟ 🛜; Ⓤ Olgaeck) Fun-seekers on a budget should thrive at this popular hostel within walking distance of the city centre. Rooms are kept spic and span, and the bar, sun deck and communal kitchen are ideal for swapping stories with fellow travellers. Light sleepers might want to pack earplugs for thin walls and street noise. Breakfast costs €8.

Aloft
DESIGN HOTEL €€

(☏ 0711-8787 5000; www.aloftstuttgarthotel.com; Milaneo Shopping Mall, Heilbronner Strasse 70; d €95-293; 🛜; Ⓤ Stadtbibliothek) It looks pretty nondescript from outside but don't be fooled – this newcomer to Stuttgart's hotel scene is a slick, open-plan design number, with lots of retro-cool touches, pops of colour and terrific views. Rooms ramp up the modern-living factor with creature comforts from Bliss Spa toiletries to coffee-making facilities.

Hotel Azenberg
HOTEL €€

(☏ 0711-225 5040; www.hotelazenberg.de; Seestrasse 114-116; s €85-135, d €100-160; Ⓟ 🛜 🏊; 🚌 43) This family-run choice has individually designed quarters with themes swinging from English country manor to Picasso. There's a pool, tree-shaded garden and little spa for relaxing moments. Breakfast will set you back an extra €11.50. Take bus 43 from Stadtmitte to Hölderlinstrasse.

City Hotel
HOTEL €€

(☏ 0711-210 810; www.cityhotel-stuttgart.de; Uhlandstrasse 18; s €87-109, d €101-139; Ⓟ 🛜; Ⓤ Olgaeck) Eschew the anonymity of Stuttgart's cookie-cutter chains for this intimate hotel just off Charlottenplatz. Rooms are light, clean and modern, if slightly lacklustre. Breakfast on the terrace in summer is a bonus.

Steigenberger Graf Zeppelin
HOTEL €€€

(☏ 0711-204 80; www.stuttgart.steigenberger.de; Arnulf-Klett-Platz 7; d €180-282, ste €260-4000; Ⓟ ✳ 🛜 🏊; Ⓤ Hauptbahnhof) While its concrete facade won't bowl you over, inside is a different story. This five-star pad facing the Hauptbahnhof (p478) is luxury all the way with stylish rooms, Zen-style spa and the Michelin-starred restaurant, Olivo (p475).

Waldhotel
HOTEL €€€

(☏ 0711-185 720; www.waldhotel-stuttgart.de; Guts-Muths-Weg 18; s €126-185, d €145-300, ste €260-362; Ⓟ 🛜; Ⓤ Waldau) A serene hideaway just a short U-Bahn hop from the centre, the Waldhotel snuggles up to the forest on the fringes of Stuttgart. Many of the bright, contemporary, parquet-floored rooms open onto balconies or terraces, and there's a spa for postsightseeing chilling. It's a five-minute stroll to the iconic Fernsehturm (p471).

Kronenhotel
HOTEL €€€

(☑0711-225 10; www.kronenhotel-stuttgart.de; Kronenstrasse 48; s €115-125, d €160-190; P ✳ @ 🛜; U Hauptbahnhof) A 1km walk north of central Königstrasse, this hotel outclasses most in the city with its terrific location, good-natured staff, well-appointed rooms and sauna. Breakfast is above par, with fresh fruit, eggs and bacon, smoked fish and pastries.

Der Zauberlehrling
BOUTIQUE HOTEL €€€

(☑0711-237 7770; www.zauberlehrling.de; Rosenstrasse 38; s €160-250, d €180-420; P 🛜; U Olgaeck) The dreamily styled rooms at the 'Sorcerer's Apprentice' offer soothing quarters after a day on the road. Each one interprets a different theme (Mediterranean siesta, sunrise, *1001 Nights*), through colour, furniture and features such as canopy beds, clawfoot tubs, tatami mats or fireplaces. Breakfast costs €19.

Ochsen Hotel
HISTORIC HOTEL €€€

(☑0711-407 0500; www.ochsen-online.de; Ulmer Strasse 323; s €92-143, d €124-175; P 🛜; U Inselstrasse) It's worth going the extra mile to this charismatic 18th-century hotel. At the pricier end of the spectrum, the spacious, warm-hued rooms have whirlpool tubs for a postsightseeing bubble. The wood-panelled restaurant dishes up appetising Swabian grub (mains €10 to €18) from *Maultaschen* (pork and spinach ravioli) to pork with *Spätzle* (egg noodles).

Hotel am Schlossgarten
HOTEL €€€

(☑0711-202 60; www.hotelschlossgarten.com; Schillerstrasse 23; d €160-250, ste €240-620; P ✳ 🛜; U Hauptbahnhof) Sidling up to the Schloss, this Hotel am Schlossgarten has handsome, park-facing rooms flaunting the luxuries that justify the price tag. Book a table at Michelin-starred Zirbelstube (tasting menus €109 to €139) for classy French dining in subtly lit, pine-panelled surrounds.

✖ Eating

Stuttgart has raised the bar in the kitchen, with chefs putting an imaginative spin on local, seasonal ingredients. The city boasts a half-dozen Michelin-starred restaurants.

Zimt und Zucker
CAFE €

(www.zimtundzucker-stuttgart.de; Weissenburgstrasse 2c; cake & light meals €3.50-12; ⊙10am-5.30pm Tue-Sun; U Österreichischer Platz) Cheerily decorated with cartoon murals and candy-bright colours that make it look like a kid has been let loose on the interior design, this laid-back cafe is filled with sugar, spice and all things nice. It serves speciality teas, delectable cakes and tortes, as well as great breakfasts (pancakes, muesli, fruit bowls) and daily lunch specials (Tuesday to Friday).

Super Jami
VEGAN €

(☑0711-3209 9749; www.super-jami.de; Bopserstrasse 10; snacks & light mains €5-10.50; ⊙11.30am-4pm Mon-Wed, 11.30am-4pm & 5.30-9.30pm Thu & Fri; U Österreichischer Platz) Comic-strip murals bring a splash of colour to this cool, laid-back vegan deli. Great-value day specials such as Sri Lankan hoppers filled with *thel dala* (spicy devilled potatoes) go for €9.70 a pop, but there's more besides – superfood salads, wraps, chilli sin carne, Belgian waffles and the like.

Platzhirsch
INTERNATIONAL €

(☑0711-76162508;www.facebook.com/Platzhirsch. Stuttgart; Geissstrasse 12; mains €6.20-11.80; ⊙11am-2am Mon-Thu, 11am-3am Fri & Sat, 2pm-1am Sun; U Rathaus) Combining a breath of country air with a pinch of urban cool, wood-panelled Platzhirsch always has a good buzz and, in summer, a packed terrace. Dig into mains such as parmesan *Knödel* (dumplings) in thyme-honey sauce, and saffron risotto with prawns. Lunch specials go for a wallet-friendly €6.90 to €7.80.

Tarte und Törtchen
DESSERTS €

(www.tarteundtoertchen.de; Gutbrodstrasse 1; sweets & breakfast €2.50-13.50; ⊙7am-6pm Tue-Fri, 9am-5pm Sat, 10am-5pm Sun; U Schwab-/Bebelstrasse) For desserts that are edible works of art, it's worth the short U-Bahn ride out of town to this rather fabulous patisserie. The cakes and pastries are decadent indeed: from fruit tarts to zingy citrus mousses and mille-feuilles. And it's a petite, elegant space for a leisurely breakfast, with its white walls, chandeliers and mishmash of vintage furniture.

Stuttgarter Markthalle
MARKET €

(Market Hall; www.markthalle-stuttgart.de; Dorotheenstrasse 4; ⊙7am-6.30pm Mon-Fri, 7am-5pm Sat; U Charlottenplatz) Olives, cheeses, spices, patisserie, fruit and veg, wine and tapas – it's all under one roof at this large art nouveau market hall, which also has snack stands.

Reiskorn

INTERNATIONAL €€

(☏0711-664 7633; www.das-reiskorn.de; Tor-strasse 27; mains €11-15.50; ☺5-10pm Tue-Sat; ☑; Ⓤ Rathaus) With a bamboo-green retro interior and an easygoing vibe, this imaginative culinary globetrotter serves everything from celery schnitzel with mango-gorgonzola cream to meltingly tender beef braised in chocolate-clove sauce, and banana and yam curry. There are plenty of vegetarian and vegan choices. It's always busy.

Academie der Schönsten Künste

INTERNATIONAL €€

(☏0711-242 436; www.academie-der-schoensten-kuenste.de; Charlottenstrasse 5; mains €11-24; ☺8am-midnight Mon-Sat, to 8pm Sun; Ⓤ Charlottenplatz) A breakfast institution since the 1970s, the Academy has evolved into a darling French-style bistro where dishes revolve around market-fresh fare but also include such tried-and-true classics as schnitzel with pan-fried potatoes and *Flammekuchen* (Alsatian pizza). Sit inside among bright canvases or in the charismatic courtyard.

Ochs'n'Willi

GERMAN €€

(☏0711-226 5191; www.ochsn-willi.de; Kleiner Schlossplatz 4; mains €12-30; ☺11am-11.30pm; Ⓤ Börsenplatz) A warm, woody hunter's cottage restaurant just this side of twee, Ochs'n'Willi delivers gutsy portions of Swabian and Bavarian fare. Dig into pork knuckles with lashings of dumplings and kraut, spot-on *Maultaschen* (pasta pockets) or rich, brothy *Gaisburger Marsch* (beef stew). There's a terrace for warm-weather dining.

Amadeus

INTERNATIONAL €€

(☏0711-292 678; http://amadeus-stuttgart.de; Charlottenplatz 17; mains €12-30; ☺11.30am-11pm Mon-Fri, 9am-11pm Sat, 10am-10pm Sun; Ⓤ Charlottenplatz) Once an 18th-century orphanage dishing up gruel, this chic, bustling, bistro-style restaurant now serves glorious Swabian food such as *Maultaschen* (pork and spinach ravioli) and Riesling-laced *Kutteln* (tripe), as well as salads and international dishes from wok noodles to burritos. The terrace is a big draw in summer. Lunch specials go for between €8 and €11.

Alte Kanzlei

GERMAN €€

(☏0711-294 457; www.alte-kanzlei-stuttgart.de; Schillerplatz 5a; mains €12-25; ☺9.30am-11.30pm Mon-Fri, 9am-11.30pm Sat & Sun; Ⓤ Schlossplatz) Empty tables are rare as gold dust at this convivial, high-ceilinged restaurant, with a terrace spilling out onto Schillerplatz (p473).

DON'T MISS

BEAN DISTRICT

To really slip under Stuttgart's skin, mosey through one of the city's lesser-known neighbourhoods. Walk south to Hans-im-Glück Platz, centred on a fountain depicting the caged Grimms' fairy-tale character Lucky Hans, and you'll soon reach the boho-flavoured **Bohnenviertel** (Bean District; www.bohnenviertel.net; Ⓤ Rathaus). A facelift has restored the neighbourhood's cobbled lanes and gabled houses, which harbour idiosyncratic galleries, workshops, bookshops, wine taverns and cafes.

Feast on Swabian favourites such as *Spanferkel* (roast suckling pig) and *Flädlesuppe* (pancake soup), washed down with regional tipples.

Weinhaus Stetter

GERMAN €€

(☏0711-240 163; www.weinhaus-stetter.de; Rosen-strasse 32; mains €10-17; ☺3-11pm Mon-Fri, noon-3pm & 5.30-11pm Sat; Ⓤ Charlottenplatz) This traditional wine tavern in the Bohnenviertel quarter serves up no-nonsense Swabian cooking, including flavoursome *Linsen und Saiten* (lentils with sausage), beef roast with onion and *Kässpätzle* (eggy pasta topped with onions and cheese) in a convivial atmosphere. The attached shop sells around 500 different wines.

★ Weinstube am Stadtgraben

GERMAN €€€

(☏0711-567 006; www.weinstube-stadtgraben.de; Am Stadtgraben 6, Stuttgart-Bad Cannstatt; 4-course menu €45; ☺6-10pm; Ⓤ Daimlerplatz) The Swabian food served at this warm, rustic, wood-beamed wine tavern in Bad Cannstatt is the real deal, albeit with a refined touch. Expect dishes that go with the seasons – be it spot-on suckling pig in dark beer sauce, fresh fish with pumpkin purée or duck breast with red cabbage and spinach dumplings. The wines hail from local vines.

★ Olivo

MODERN EUROPEAN €€€

(☏0711-204 8277; www.olivo-restaurant.de; Arnulf-Klett-Platz 7; mains around €40, 4-course lunch/dinner €98/132; ☺noon-1.30pm & 6.30-9.30pm Wed-Fri, 6.30-9.30pm Tue & Sat; Ⓤ Hauptbahnhof) Young, sparky chef Nico Burkhardt works his stuff at Steigenberger's minimalist-chic, Michelin-starred restaurant. Olivo is lauded for its exquisitely presented, French-inspired specialities such as Périgord goose liver with sheep's milk yoghurt, brioche crumble and woodruff, or beautifully cooked Breton turbot with ricotta and wild garlic.

5 GASTRONOMY €€€

(☑0711-6555 7011; www.5.fo; Bolzstrasse 8; 3- to 8-course menus €84-176; ⊗restaurant 6.30-9.30pm Mon-Sat, lounge bar 9am-11pm Mon-Thu, to 1am Fri & Sat, to 10pm Sun; Ⓤ Börsenplatz) This glossy, nouveau-chic restaurant and lounge walks the culinary high wire with a Michelin star and chef Claudio Urru presiding over the stove. Food is masterful, clever and presented in the newfangled, ingredient-listed style: dandelion with radish, wasabi and sesame; textures of *skrei* (Arctic cod) with shallots and spiced nuts; or figs with sorrel, acacia honey, bergamot and cacao.

Christophorus GASTRONOMY €€€

(☑0711-9112 1911; www.porsche.com/museum; Porscheplatz 5, Porsche Museum; mains €35-65, 4-/5-course menu €82/105; ⊗11.30am-3pm & 5.30pm-midnight Tue-Sat; Ⓢ Neuwirtshaus) Not only the cars at the Porsche Museum have va-va-voom. Christophorus is a sophisticated, grown-up affair, with red leather banquettes and linen-draped tables. Prime cuts of US beef grilled to perfection and more refined Med-style dishes, such as pickled char with asparagus panna cotta, and lamb with olive polenta, are paired with top-notch wines, served with finesse.

Cube INTERNATIONAL €€€

(☑0711-280 4441; www.cube-restaurant.de; Kleiner Schlossplatz 1; mains €19-30; ⊗noon-5pm & 6pm-midnight; Ⓤ Schlossplatz) The food is stellar but it actually plays second fiddle to the dazzling decor, refined ambience and stunning views at this glass-fronted cube atop the Kunstmuseum (p469). Lunches are perky, fresh and international, while dinners feature more Asian-inspired cuisine: red Thai curry, duck cooked two ways and yellowfin tuna with bean risotto. Lunch specials are a steal at €9.95.

Délice GASTRONOMY €€€

(☑0711-640 3222; www.restaurant-delice.de; Hauptstätter Strasse 61; 5-course tasting menu €109; ⊗7pm-midnight Mon-Fri; Ⓤ Österreichischer Platz) Natural, integral flavours sing in specialities such as red shrimp with tomato, wild herbs and sesame, and saddle of lamb with fennel, avocado and Roman-style dumplings at this incredibly intimate, barrel-vaulted Michelin-starred restaurant. It's the combined vision of chef Andreas Hettinger and passionate sommelier Evangelos Pattas, who will talk you through the award-winning Riesling selection.

🍸 **Drinking & Nightlife**

⭐ **Schwarz Weiss Bar** COCKTAIL BAR

(www.schwarz-weiss-bar.de; Wilhelmstrasse 8a; ⊗7pm-3am Sun-Thu, to 5am Fri & Sat; Ⓤ Österreichischer Platz) Jazz creates a mellow mood at this slinky little cocktail bar, with barrel-vaulted ceilings, stone walls and dim lighting. The mixologists seem to put a pinch of magic into the succinct, everchanging list of cocktails – from 'The Maker' (bourbon, elderberry, Madeira, ginger, bergamot and bitters) to 'Naschi-Äffle' (Monkey 47 gin with pear juice, lavender, honey and ginger).

⭐ **Kraftpaule** MICROBREWERY

(www.kraftpaule.de; Nikolausstrasse 2; ⊗4-10pm Tue-Fri, 11am-10pm Sat; Ⓤ Stöckach) Competition is stiff but for our money this might just be Stuttgart's coolest new-wave craft microbrewery and bar. The bartenders really know their stuff, the selection of beers – from IPAs to stouts, single hop brews and wheat beers – is *wunderbar,* and the vibe easygoing in the bare-wood-tabled and terracotta-tiled interior. Check the website for details on tastings.

Misch Misch COFFEE

(www.misch-misch.de; Tübinger Strasse 95; ⊗8am-6pm Mon-Thu, 8am-7pm Fri, 10am-7pm Sat; Ⓤ Marienplatz) If you're serious about your beans, this new retro-flavoured cafe just south of the centre is surely a little slice of heaven. As tiny and well loved as your own living room, here you can sip a mighty fine espresso, mocha or cold brew – and perhaps nibble on delicious carrot cake. If you like the house blend, you can buy the beans to take home.

Sky Beach BAR

(www.skybeach.de; Königstrasse 6, top fl Galeria Kaufhof; ⊗noon-12.30am Mon-Sat, 1-11.30pm Sun Apr-Sep; Ⓤ Hauptbahnhof) When the sun comes out, Stuttgarters live it up at this urban beach, complete with sand, cabana beds, DJs spinning mellow lounge beats and grandstand city views. It's on the top floor of the department store Galeria Kaufhof.

Wagenhallen CLUB

(www.wagenhallen.de; Innerer Nordbahnhof 1; Ⓤ Wagenhallen Nordbahnhof) Swim away from the mainstream at this postindustrial space 2km north of the centre, where club nights, gigs and workshops skip from Balkan-beat parties to poetry slams. There's a relaxed beer garden for summertime quaffing. Undergoing renovation at the time of writing, the Wagenhallen reopened in late 2018.

Biergarten im Schlossgarten BEER GARDEN
(www.biergarten-schlossgarten.de; Am Schlossgarten 18; ⊗ 10.30am-1am May-Oct; 🐾; Ⓤ Hauptbahnhof) Toast to summer with beer and pretzels at Stuttgart's best-loved, 2000-seat beer garden in the green heart of the Schlossgarten (p469). Regular live music on Sundays gets steins a-swinging.

Palast der Republik BEER GARDEN
(☑ 0711-226 4887; www.facebook.com/Palast Stuttgart; Friedrichstrasse 27; ⊗ 11am-2am Mon-Thu, 11am-3am Fri & Sat, 3pm-2am Sun; Ⓤ Börsenplatz) Once a public toilet, this not-so-very-palatial kiosk-bar now offers a very different kind of piss-up. Everyone from students to bankers has a soft spot for *the* local hot spot for chilling under the trees and meeting friends, cold beer in hand.

Ciba Mato LOUNGE
(Wilhelmsplatz 11; ⊗ 5pm-1am Sun-Thu, to 3am Fri & Sat; Ⓤ Österreichischer Platz) There's more than a hint of Buddha Bar about this scarlet-walled, Asia-infused space. It's a slinky spot to sip a gingertini or pisco punch, or to hang out Bedouin-style in the *shisha* tent and nibble on fusion food. The terrace deck is a summertime magnet.

Paul & George COCKTAIL BAR
(www.paulandgeorge.de; Weberstrasse 3; ⊗ 6pm-1.30am; Ⓤ Rathaus) Housed in a building dating to 1889 and exuding its very own brand of old-school glamour and boho flair, Paul & George is named after the architects of this one-time tavern on Weberstrasse. With Thonet-style Bentwood chairs, bare brick walls and bow-tied waiters, it's an intimate spot for a craft gin, beer or highball.

Ribingurūmu BAR
(Theodor-Heuss-Strasse 4; ⊗ 3pm-2am Mon-Thu, to 3am Fri & Sat, to midnight Sun; Ⓤ Börsenplatz) A chilled-out crowd hangs out over jam-jar cocktails in Ribingurūmu, which exudes an 'old-skool' vibe with its vintage furnishings.

☆ Entertainment

For the low-down on events, grab a copy of German-language monthly *Lift Stuttgart* (www.lift-online.de) from the tourist office (p478) or news kiosks, or listings magazine *Prinz* (www.prinz.de/stuttgart). Events tickets can be purchased at the tourist office.

Liederhalle CONCERT VENUE
(☑ 0711-202 7710; www.liederhalle-stuttgart.de; Berliner Platz 1; Ⓤ Berliner Platz) Jimi Hendrix and Sting are among the stars who have performed at this culture and congress centre. The 1950s venue stages big-name classical and pop concerts, cabaret and comedy.

Staatstheater PERFORMING ARTS
(☑ 0711-202 090; www.staatstheater-stuttgart.de; Oberer Schlossgarten 6; Ⓤ Schlossplatz) Stuttgart's grandest theatre presents a top-drawer program of ballet, opera, theatre and classical music.

Kiste JAZZ
(☑ 0711-1603 4970; www.kiste-stuttgart.de; Hauptstätter Strasse 35; ⊗ 6pm-2am Mon-Thu, 7pm-3am Fri & Sat; Ⓤ Rathaus) Jam-packed at weekends, this hole-in-the-wall bar is Stuttgart's leading jazz venue, with nightly concerts starting at 9pm or 10pm.

Bix Jazzclub LIVE MUSIC
(☑ 0711-2384 0997; www.bix-stuttgart.de; Leonhardsplatz 28; ⊗ 7pm-1am Tue-Thu, to 2am Fri & Sat; Ⓤ Rathaus) Suave chocolate-gold tones and soft lighting set the scene for first-rate jazz acts at Bix, swinging from big bands to soul and blues.

Theaterhaus THEATRE
(☑ 0711-402 0720; www.theaterhaus.com; Siemensstrasse 11; Ⓤ Maybachstrasse) This dynamic theatre stages live rock, jazz and other music genres, as well as theatre and comedy performances.

🔒 Shopping

Mooch around plane-tree-lined Königstrasse, Germany's longest shopping mile, or Königsbau Passagen on Schlossplatz (p469) and the Dorotheen Quartier for high-street brands, design and department stores. Calwer Strasse channels boutique shopping, Stiftstrasse designer labels. The casual Bohnenviertel (p475) is the go-to quarter for antiques, art galleries, vintage garb and Stuttgart-made crafts and jewellery.

Dorotheen Quartier MALL
(www.dorotheen-quartier.de; Holzstrasse; ⊗ 10am-8pm Mon-Fri, 9.30am-8pm Sat; Ⓤ Rathaus) A good one for rainy-day shopping, this architecturally striking new mall houses a host of design, high-street and fashion stores such as Diesel, American Vintage, Gant, MaxMara and BoConcept, as well as cafes, a bakery and a sushi bar and grill.

ℹ DISCOUNT CARD

Get a **StuttCard** (24/48/72 hours without VVS – public transport – ticket €15/20/25, with VVS ticket €25/35/45) for free entry to most museums, plus discounts on events, activities and guided tours. Sold at the tourist office and some hotels.

Feinkost Böhm   FOOD & DRINKS
(www.feinkost-boehm.de; Kronprinzstrasse 6; ⊙10am-8pm Mon-Thu, 9am-8pm Fri & Sat; Ⓤ Schlossplatz) Böhm is a foodie one-stop shop with regional wine, beer, chocolate and preserves, and an appetising deli.

Königsbau Passagen   SHOPPING CENTRE
(Königstrasse 26; ⊙10am-8pm Mon-Sat; Ⓤ Schlossplatz) Overlooking Schlossplatz (p469) is the classical, colonnaded Königsbau, reborn as an upmarket shopping mall, the Königsbau Passagen.

ℹ Information

Airport Tourist Office (🖉 0711-222 8100; Stuttgart Airport; ⊙8am-7pm Mon-Fri, 9am-1pm & 1.45-4.30pm Sat, 10am-1pm & 1.45-5.30pm Sun) The tourist office branch at Stuttgart Airport (p478) is situated in Terminal 3, Level 2 (Arrivals).

Post Office (Bolzstrasse 3; ⊙10am-8pm Mon-Fri, 9am-4pm Sat) Just northwest of the Schlossplatz.

Stuttgart Tourist Office (🖉 0711-222 80; www.stuttgart-tourist.de; Königstrasse 1a; ⊙9am-8pm Mon-Fri, to 6pm Sat, 10am-5pm Sun) The staff can help with room bookings (for a €3 fee) and public transport enquiries. Also has a list of vineyards open for tastings.

ℹ Getting There & Away

AIR
Stuttgart Airport (SGT; 🖉 0711-9480; www.stuttgart-airport.com), a major hub for Eurowings, is 13km south of the city. There are four terminals, all within easy walking distance of each other.

TRAIN
Long-distance IC and ICE destinations departing from **Stuttgart Hauptbahnhof** include Berlin (€130 to €154, 5½ hours), Frankfurt (€50 to €66, 1¼ hours) and Munich (€54, 2¼ hours). There are frequent regional services to Tübingen (€15.10, 43 minutes to one hour), Schwäbisch Hall (€16.60, 70 minutes) and Ulm (€21.90 to €27, one hour).

ℹ Getting Around

TO/FROM THE AIRPORT
Very frequent S2 and S3 trains take about 30 minutes from the airport to the **Hauptbahnhof** (€4.20).

PUBLIC TRANSPORT
From slowest to fastest, Stuttgart's VVS (www.vvs.de) public transport network consists of a Zahnradbahn (rack railway), buses, the Strassenbahn (tramway), Stadtbahn lines (light-rail lines beginning with U; underground in the city centre), S-Bahn lines (suburban rail lines S1 through to S6) and RegionalBahn lines (regional trains beginning with R). On Friday and Saturday there are night buses (beginning with N) with departures from Schlossplatz at 1.11am, 2.22am and 3.33am.

For travel within the city, single tickets are €2.50 and four-ride tickets (4er-Ticket) cost €9.70 for one zone. For short hops of three stops or less, a *Kurzstrecken* ticket (€1.40) suffices. A day pass, good for two zones (including, for instance, the Mercedes-Benz and Porsche Museums), is better value at €7 for one person and €12.30 for a group of between two and five.

LUDWIGSBURG

🖉 07141 / POP 92,973

This neat, cultured town was the childhood home of the dramatist Friedrich Schiller. Duke Eberhard Ludwig put it on the global map in the 18th century by erecting a chateau to out-pomp them all – the sublime, Versailles-inspired Residenzschloss. With its whimsical palaces and gardens, Ludwigsburg is baroque in overdrive and a flashback to when princes wore powdered wigs and lords went a-hunting.

◎ Sights & Activities

★ **Residenzschloss**   PALACE
(🖉 07141-186400; www.schloss-ludwigsburg.de; Schlossstrasse 30; tour adult/concession €7/3.50, museums incl audioguide €3.50/1.80; ⊙10am-5pm daily mid-Mar–mid-Nov, 10am-5pm Tue-Sun mid-Nov–mid-Mar) Nicknamed the 'Swabian Versailles', the Residenzschloss is an extravagant 452-room baroque, rococo and Empire affair. The 90-minute chateau tours (in German) leave every half-hour; there are English tours at 1.15pm and 3.15pm daily.

The 18th-century feast continues with a spin around the staggeringly ornate scarlet-and-gold Karl Eugen Apartment, and three museums showcasing everything from exquisite baroque paintings to fashion accessories and majolica.

The Residenzschloss, on Schlossstrasse (the B27), lies 400m northeast of the central Marktplatz.

Blühendes Barock
GARDENS

(www.blueba.de; Mömpelgardstrasse 28; adult/concession €9/4.50; ⊘7.30am-8.30pm, closed early Nov–mid-Mar) Appealing in summer is a fragrant stroll amid the herbs, rhododendrons and gushing fountains of the Blühendes Barock gardens. Admission includes entry to the Märchengarten.

Marktplatz
SQUARE

Dominated by a twin-spired, powderpuff-pink church and rimmed by arcaded houses, Ludwigsburg's striking market square was laid out in the 18th century in the baroque style by the Italian architect of the age, Donato Giuseppe Frisoni.

Schloss Favorite
PALACE

(www.schloss-favorite-ludwigsburg.de; Favoritepark 1) Sitting in parkland a five-minute walk north of the Residenzschloss is the petite baroque palace Schloss Favorite, built between 1717 and 1723 for Duke Eberhard Ludwig. It was mostly used as a hunting palace and summer residence. The interior of the palace is largely neoclassical in style and graced with Empire-style furniture.

The palace was undergoing extensive restoration at the time of writing and is set to reopen in mid 2019.

Märchengarten
AMUSEMENT PARK

(☑07414-910 2252; Mömpelgardstrasse 28; adult/concession €9/4.50; ⊘9am-6pm, closed early Nov–mid-Mar) Kids drag their parents to this fairy-tale theme park to visit the witch with a Swabian cackle at the gingerbread house and admire themselves in Snow White's magic mirror. Should you want Rapunzel to let down her hair, get practising: *Rapunzel, lass deinen Zopf herunter.* (The gold-tressed diva only understands well-pronounced German!). Admission includes entry to the Blühendes Barock.

✕ Eating & Drinking

Alte Sonne
ALSATIAN €€

(☑07141-643 6480; http://alte-sonne.de; Bei der Katholischen Kirche 3; mains €17-30; ⊘noon-2.30pm & 6-10.30pm Wed-Sun; ✐) The most refined address in Ludwigsburg is the Alte Sonne, where the menu plays up regional, seasonal ingredients in attractively presented dishes that are a nod to the chef's native Alsace, be it leek and Riesling soup, cod in a speck crust with orange, celery, walnuts and smoked trout ravioli, or blueberry sorbet laced with Alsatian Muscat wine.

Ludwigsburger Brauhaus
BEER GARDEN

(www.brauhaus-ludwigsburg.de; Bahnhofstrasse 17; ⊘11am-11pm) On Solitudeplatz, this brewpub serves home brews (by the glass, litre or metre) in cosy, wood-panelled surrounds in winter and in its popular beer garden in summer.

ℹ Information

Ludwigsburg Tourist Office (☑07141-910 2252; www.mik-ludwigsburg.de; Eberhardtstrasse 1; ⊘10am-6pm) Ludwigsburg's tourist office has excellent material in English on lodgings, festivals and events such as the baroque Christmas market.

ℹ Getting There & Around

S-Bahn trains (local trains operating within a city and its suburban area) from Stuttgart serve the Hauptbahnhof, 750m southwest of the centre.

Stuttgart's S4 and S5 S-Bahn lines go directly to Ludwigsburg's Hauptbahnhof (€3.97, 10 minutes), 750m southeast of the centre. There are frequent links to the Residenzschloss on buses 421, 425 and 427. On foot, the chateau is 1km from the train station.

SWABIAN ALPS REGION

Often eclipsed by the Black Forest to the west and the Bavarian Alps to the southeast, the Swabian Alps (*Schwäbische Alb* in German) are wholly deserving of more attention. Ulm, where the Danube swiftly flows, forms the boundary in the south, while the Neckar runs past half-timbered towns, limestone crags, beech woods, juniper-cloaked heaths, hilltop ducal castles and robber-knight ruins further north.

The region is a geologist's dream – 200 million years ago it had more volcanoes than almost anywhere else on earth; today it holds Unesco World Heritage Geopark status. The karst landscape is riddled with caves, where rare fossils and ice age art (including the 30,000-year-old *Löwenmensch* on display in Museum Ulm; p485) have been discovered.

In 2017, the Swabian Jura Caves and ice age art received Unesco World Heritage status for having some of the world's oldest figurative art, dating from 43,000 to 33,000 years ago.

Tübingen

📞 07071 / POP 87,464

Liberal students and deeply traditional *Burschenschaften* (fraternities) singing ditties for beloved Germania, ecowarriors, artists and punks – all have a soft spot for this bewitchingly pretty Swabian city, where cobbled lanes lined with half-timbered townhouses twist up to a turreted castle. It was here that Joseph Ratzinger, now Pope Benedict XVI, lectured on theology in the late 1960s; that Friedrich Hölderlin studied stanzas, Johannes Kepler planetary motions, and Goethe the bottom of a beer glass.

The finest days unfold slowly in Tübingen: lingering in Altstadt cafes, punting on the plane-tree-lined Neckar River and pretending, as the students so diligently do, to work your brain cells in a chestnut-shaded beer garden.

⊙ Sights & Activities

★ Schloss Hohentübingen
CASTLE

(📞 07071-297 7579; www.unimuseum.uni-tue bingen.de; Burgsteige 11; guided tour of wine cellar adult/concession €5/3; ⊙10am-6pm Wed-Sun May-Sep, to 5pm Oct-Apr) FREE On its perch above Tübingen, this turreted 16th-century castle has a terrace overlooking the Neckar River, the Altstadt's triangular rooftops and the vine-streaked hills beyond. An ornate Renaissance gate leads to the courtyard and the laboratory where Friedrich Miescher discovered DNA in 1869.

Besides a clutch of museums, the finest of which is the Museum Alte Kulturen (adult/concession €5/3; ⊙10am-5pm Wed, Fri-Sun, to 7pm Thu), the castle's highlights include the immense, 84,000-litre *Grosse Fass* wine vat – one of the world's oldest, dating to 1564 – which can only be visited on guided tours at 2pm, 3pm, 4pm and 5pm (book ahead online).

Am Markt
SQUARE

Half-timbered townhouses frame the Altstadt's main plaza Am Markt, a much-loved student hang-out. Rising above it is the 15th-century Rathaus (town hall), which is opposite the Neptunbrunnen. Keep an eye out for No 15, where a white window frame identifies a secret room where Jews hid in WWII.

Kloster Bebenhausen
MONASTERY

(www.kloster-bebenhausen.de; adult/concession €5/2.50, incl guided tour €7/3.50, audioguide €2; ⊙9am-6pm Apr-Oct, 10am-noon & 1-5pm Tue-Sun Nov-Mar, guided tours 2pm & 3pm Sat & Sun Apr-Oct) Founded in 1183 by Rudolph I, Count Palatine of Tübingen, Kloster Bebenhausen is one of southern Germany's finest medieval Cistercian monasteries. Beautifully situated on the wooded fringes of Naturpark Schönbuch, it became a royal hunting retreat post-Reformation. A visit takes in the intricately frescoed summer refectory, the Gothic abbey church and intricate star vaulting and half-timbered facades in the cloister. The monastery interior can only be visited by guided tour.

Bebenhausen is 7km north of Tübingen via the L1208. Buses run at least twice hourly (€2.30, 15 minutes).

Rathaus
LANDMARK

(Am Markt 1) Drawing the gaze high above Am Markt, Tübingen's 15th-century Rathaus sports a riotous, exuberantly frescoed baroque facade and an astronomical clock.

Stiftskirche St Georg
CHURCH

(Am Holzmarkt; ⊙9am-4pm) FREE The late-Gothic Stiftskirche shelters the tombs of the Württemberg dukes and some dazzling late-medieval stained-glass windows.

Cottahaus
LANDMARK

(Münzgasse 15) The Cottahaus is the one-time home of Johann Friedrich Cotta, who first published the works of Schiller and Goethe. A bit of a lad, Goethe conducted detailed research on Tübingen's pubs during his weeklong stay in 1797. The party-loving genius is commemorated by the plaque '*Hier wohnte Goethe*' (Goethe lived here). On the wall of the grungy student digs next door is perhaps the more insightful sign '*Hier kotzte Goethe*' (Goethe puked here).

Kunsthalle
GALLERY

(📞 07071-969 10; www.kunsthalle-tuebingen. de; Philosophenweg 76; adult/concession €7/5; ⊙11am-7pm Tue, to 6pm Wed-Sun) The streamlined Kunsthalle stages first-rate exhibitions of mostly contemporary art; in recent times, everything from Post-Minimalist art to hyper realistic sculpture has been thrown into the spotlight. Buses 5, 13 and 17 run from central Tübingen to the Kunsthalle stop.

Hölderlinturm
MUSEUM

(Bursagasse 6) You can see how the dreamy Neckar views from this silver-turreted tower fired the imagination of Romantic poet Friedrich Hölderlin, resident here from 1807 to 1843. It now contains a museum tracing his life and work. Due to extensive renovation work, the museum is closed until late 2019.

NATURPARK SCHÖNBUCH

For back-to-nature hiking and cycling, make for this 156-sq-km, lushly forested **nature reserve** (www.naturpark-schoenbuch.de; Kloster Bebenhausen; ☉information centre 9am-5pm Tue-Fri, 10am-5pm Sat & Sun). It's interwoven with 560km of marked trails. With a bit of luck and a pair of binoculars, you might catch a glimpse of black woodpeckers and yellow-bellied toads. The nature reserve's beech and oak woods fringe the village of Bebenhausen and its well-preserved Cistercian abbey (p480).

Bebenhausen, 7km north of Tübingen via the L1208, is the gateway to Naturpark Schönbuch. Buses run at least twice hourly (€2.30, 15 minutes).

Wurmlinger Kapelle   WALKING
(☉chapel 10am-4pm May-Oct) A great hike is the *Kreuzweg* (way of the cross) to the 17th-century Wurmlinger Kapelle, perched atop a 475m hill, about 6km southwest of Tübingen. A footpath loops up through well-tended vineyards to the whitewashed pilgrimage chapel, from where there are long views across the Ammer and Neckar valleys. The tourist office (p482) has leaflets (€1).

✭✭ Festivals & Events

Stocherkahnrennen   SPORTS
(http://stocherkahnrennen.germania-strassburg. de; ☉late May) Students in fancy dress do battle on the Neckar at May's hilarious Stocherkahnrennen punt race, where jostling, dunking and even snapping your rival's oar are permitted. The first team to reach the Neckarbrücke wins the race, the title and as much beer as they can sink. The losers have to down half a litre of cod liver oil. Arrive in good time to snag a prime spot on **Platanenallee**.

🛏 Sleeping

Hotel am Schloss   HISTORIC HOTEL €€
(☎07071-929 40; www.hotelamschloss.de; Burgsteige 18; s €99, d €128-148, tr/q €225/290; 🅿🛜) So close to the castle you can almost touch it, this flower-bedecked hotel has dapper rooms ensconced in a 16th-century building. The hotel's cosy Mauganeschtle restaurant excels in hearty Swabian grub.

Hotel Krone   HOTEL €€
(☎07071-133 10; www.krone-tuebingen.de; Uhlandstrasse 1; s €109, d €139-169, ste €189-239, f €204-229; 🛜) Occupying a late-9th-century house right in the heart of Tübingen, this four-star hotel has been given a contemporary facelift, but some original features remain, such as the stained-glass windows in the open fire-warmed lobby. Muted colours and clean lines define the spacious rooms, and

the plush top-floor spa has a sauna, infrared cabins and a roof terrace.

Hotel La Casa   HOTEL €€€
(☎07071-946 66; www.lacasa-tuebingen.de; Hechinger Strasse 59; s €186-205, d €215-289, ste €269-400; 🛜🛝) Tübingen's swishest hotel is a 15-minute stroll south of the Altstadt. Contemporary rooms designed with panache come with welcome tea, coffee and soft drinks. Breakfast is a smorgasbord of mostly organic goodies. The crowning glory is the top-floor spa with tremendous city views.

🍴 Eating

Kornblume   VEGETARIAN €
(☎07071-920 9317; Haaggasse 15; snacks & light meals €3-8; ☉8.30am-6pm Mon-Fri, to 3pm Sat; 🍴) Vegetarians and health-conscious locals squeeze into this hobbit-like cafe for wholesome soups, freshly squeezed juice, organic salads by the scoopful and day specials such as rye pancakes with vegetables, and sweet potato-chard curry.

Meze Akademie   MEZE €€
(☎07071-938 7746; http://mezeakademie.com; Hechinger Strasse 67; meze €7.50-18; ☉noon-2.30pm & 5.30-11pm Mon-Fri, noon-2.30pm & 3.30-11pm Sat) Creative riffs on Greek meze (small dishes to share) take centre stage at this slick restaurant, with an open-plan design and bistro-style seating at bare wood tables. The menu seesaws with the seasons, so expect anything from wild boar sausage with caramelised onion and poached egg to more classic *dolmadakia* (stuffed vine leaves) and baked feta with tomato marmalade.

Mauganeschtle   GERMAN €€
(☎07071-929 40; www.hotelamschloss.de; Burgsteige 18, Hotel am Schloss; mains €12-26.50; ☉noon-2.30pm & 6pm-midnight) It's a stiff climb up to this restaurant at Hotel am Schloss (p481), but worth every step. Suspended above the rooftops of Tübingen, the

> **DON'T MISS**
>
> ## MESSING ABOUT ON THE RIVER
>
> There's nothing like a languid paddle along the sun-dappled Neckar River in summer. Hire a row boat, canoe, pedalo or punt at **Bootsvermietung Märkle** (Eberhardsbrücke 1; ⊘ 11am-6pm Apr-early Oct, to 9pm Jul & Aug), or sign up at the tourist office (p482) for **punting** (adult/child €7/5; ⊘ 1pm daily, plus 5pm Sat May-Sep) around the Neckarinsel. The summer's most hilarious fest is the Stocherkahnrennen (p481) punt race, where students in fancy dress paddle hell for leather to be the first to the bridge.

terrace is a scenic spot for the house speciality, *Maultaschen* (pasta pockets), with fillings such as lamb, trout, porcini and veal.

Neckarmüller
PUB FOOD €€

(☏ 07071-278 48; www.neckarmueller.de; Gartenstrasse 4; mains €7.50-15; ⊘ 10am-1am Mon-Sat, to 11.45pm Sun) Overlooking the Neckar, this cavernous microbrewery is a summertime magnet for its chestnut-shaded beer garden. Come for home brews by the metre and beer-laced dishes from (tasty) Swabian roast to (interesting) tripe stew. Day specials go for €6.50.

 Drinking & Nightlife

Weinhaus Beck
BAR

(www.weinhaus-beck.de; Am Markt 1; ⊘ 8am-11pm) There's rarely an empty table at this wine shop and tavern beside the Rathaus (p480). It's a convivial place to enjoy regional and international wines (choose from 600 different varieties) or coffee and cake.

Kuckuck
BAR

(www.kuckuck-bar.de; Fichtenweg 5; ⊘ 8pm-2am Mon-Thu, to 5pm Fri & Sat, to 1am Sun) 'Cuckoo' is the name of this upbeat, student-driven bar and club, with plenty of good vibes and a young, fun crowd. The drinks are insanely cheap – €1.50 for a beer and €3 for a cocktail. It's a 3km trek north of town so hop in a taxi if you don't fancy the walk.

Bartista
COCKTAIL BAR

(www.bartista.de; Kirchgasse 19; ⊘ 6pm-1am Mon-Thu, to 3am Fri & Sat, 8pm-1am Sun) A pinch of 1920s flair goes a long way at this stylish little bar with red walls, candelabra and cosy

armchairs for conversing. Cocktails are what it's all about here, such as the house special Tübingen Gardens – a zesty blend of lemon juice, elderflower syrup, lavender-infused gin and soda.

Schwärzlocher Hof
BEER GARDEN

(www.hofgut-schwaerzloch.de;Schwärzloch1; ⊘ 11am-10pm Wed-Sun) Scenically perched above the Ammer Valley, a 2km trudge west of town, this farmhouse is famous for its beer garden and home-pressed *Most* (cider).

Storchen
CAFE

(Ammergasse 3; ⊘ 3pm-1am Mon-Thu & Sun, to 2am Fri, 11am-2am Sat) Mind your head climbing the stairs to this easygoing student hangout, serving enormous mugs of milky coffee and cheap local brews under wooden beams.

 Information

Post Office (Beim Nonnenhaus 14; ⊘ 9am-7pm Mon-Fri, to 6pm Sat) In the Altstadt.
Tübingen Tourist Office (☏ 07071-913 60; www.tuebingen-info.de; An der Neckarbrücke 1; ⊘ 9am-7pm Mon-Fri, 10am-4pm Sat, plus 11am-4pm Sun May-Sep)

 Getting There & Away

Tübingen is an easy train ride from Stuttgart (€15.10, one hour, at least two per hour) and Ulm (€26.50 to €37, two hours, roughly twice hourly). Trains depart from the **Hauptbahnhof**, 500m south of the Altstadt on the opposite side of the Neckar River.

Burg Hohenzollern

Rising dramatically from an exposed crag, with its medieval battlements and riot of towers and silver turrets often veiled in mist, **Burg Hohenzollern** (www.burg-hohenzollern.com; tour adult/concession €12/8, grounds admission without tour adult/concession €7/5; ⊘ tours 10am-5.30pm mid-Mar–Oct, to 4.30pm Nov–mid-Mar) is darned impressive from a distance, but up close it looks more contrived. Dating to 1867, this neo-Gothic castle is the ancestral seat of the Hohenzollern family, the first and last monarchical rulers of the short-lived second German Empire (1871–1918).

History buffs should take a 35-minute German-language tour, which takes in towers, overblown salons replete with stained glass and frescos, and the dazzling *Schatzkammer* (treasury). The grounds command tremendous views over the Swabian Alps.

Frequent trains link Tübingen, 28km distant, with Hechingen, about 4km northwest of the castle.

Schwäbisch Hall

📞 0791 / POP 38,827

Out on its rural lonesome near the Bavarian border, Schwäbisch Hall is an unsung gem. This medieval time capsule of higgledy-piggledy lanes, soaring half-timbered houses built high on the riches of salt, and covered bridges that criss-cross the Kocher River is story-book stuff.

Buzzy cafes and first-rate museums add to the appeal of this town, known for its rare black-spotted pigs and the jangling piggy banks of its nationwide building society.

◉ Sights

★ Kunsthalle Würth   GALLERY
(www.kunst.wuerth.com; Lange Strasse 35; ☉10am-6pm daily, guided tours 11.30am & 2pm Sun) FREE The brainchild of industrialist Reinhold Würth, this contemporary gallery is housed in a striking limestone building that preserves part of a century-old brewery. Stellar temporary exhibitions have recently spotlighted hidden treasures from the Academy of Fine Arts in Vienna including masterpieces by Dürer, Botticelli, Rembrandt, Rubens, Klimt and Hundertwasser. Guided tours (in German) and audioguides cost €6.

Am Markt   SQUARE
On Am Markt square, your gaze is drawn to the ornate Rathaus (Town Hall) and to the terracotta-hued Widmanhaus at No 4, a remnant of a 13th-century Franciscan monastery. It's also presided over by the late-Gothic Kirche St Michael (☉noon-5pm Mon, 10am-5pm Tue-Sat, 11.30am-5pm Sun) FREE and Gotischer Fischbrunnen.

Neubau   LANDMARK
Towering above Pfarrgasse is the steep-roofed, 16th-century Neubau, built as an arsenal and granary and now used as a theatre. Ascend the stone staircase for dreamy views over red-roofed houses to the former city fortifications, the covered Roter Steg bridge and the Henkerbrücke (Hangman's Bridge).

Hohenloher Freilandmuseum   MUSEUM
(📞0791-971 010; www.wackershofen.de; Wackershofen; adult/concession €8/6; ☉9am-6pm May-Sep, 10am-5pm Tue-Sun rest of year) One

place you can be guaranteed of seeing a black-spotted pig is this open-air farming museum, a sure-fire hit with the kids with its traditional farmhouses, orchards and animals. It's 6km northwest of Schwäbisch Hall and served by bus 7.

Hällisch-Fränkisches Museum   MUSEUM
(📞0791-751 360; Keckenhof 6; ☉10am-5pm Tue-Sun) FREE This well-curated museum traces Schwäbisch Hall's history with a collection of shooting targets, Roman figurines and rarities including an exquisite hand-painted wooden synagogue interior from 1738 and a 19th-century mouse guillotine.

🛏 Sleeping & Eating

★ Hotel Scholl   HOTEL €€
(📞0791-975 50; www.hotel-scholl.de; Klosterstrasse 2-4; d €89-149; 🖥) A charming pick behind Am Markt, this family-run hotel has rustic-chic rooms with parquet floors and granite or marble bathrooms. Most striking of all is the attic penthouse with its beams, free-standing shower and far-reaching views over town. Breakfast is a fine spread of cold cuts, fruit and cereals.

Der Adelshof   HISTORIC HOTEL €€
(📞0791-758 90; www.hotel-adelshof.de; Am Markt 12; s €95-100, d €125-225; P🖥) This centuries-old pad is as posh as it gets in Schwäbisch Hall, with a wellness area and plush quarters, from the red-walled romance of the Chambre Rouge to the four-poster Turmzimmer. Its beamed Ratskeller restaurant (mains €18 to €27) knocks up spot-on local specialities such as saddle of veal with mushrooms, and pork tenderloin with lentils and Spätzle (egg noodles).

Entenbäck   BISTRO €€
(📞0791-9782 9182; Steinerner Steg 1; mains €12-32; ☉5-11pm Tue, 11am-2.30pm & 5-11pm Wed-Sat; 🖥) This inviting bistro receives high praise for its Swabian-meets-Mediterranean menu, from cream of Riesling soup to duck-filled Maultaschen (pasta pockets) and roast beef with onions and Spätzle. There's also a succinct vegetarian menu.

Schwein & Weinbar   GERMAN €€
(📞0791-931 230; www.rebers-pflug.de; Weckriedener Strasse 2; €9.50-24.50; ☉6.30-9pm Mon & Tue, noon-2pm & 6-9pm Wed-Sat) A relaxed and more reasonably priced alternative to the Michelin-starred finery of Rebers Pflug, this chic wine-bar/bistro under the same roof has a highly decent selection of light

meals – all expertly prepared – from dry-aged beef burgers to *Gaisburger Marsch* (Swabian beef stew). There are some excellent regional wines represented.

Brauerei-Ausschank
Zum Löwen   PUB FOOD €€
(⧉0791-204 1622; Mauerstrasse 17; mains €10-17; ⊙11.30am-2pm & 5.30-11pm Fri-Tue) Down by the river, this brewpub attracts a jovial bunch of locals who come for freshly tapped Haller Löwenbrauerei brews and hearty nosh such as Swabian *Maultaschen* (pasta pockets) topped with a fried egg, and pork cooked in beer-cumin sauce.

★ Rebers Pflug   INTERNATIONAL €€€
(⧉0791-931 230; www.rebers-pflug.de; Weckriedener Strasse 2; mains €18.50-42, 3- to 7-course menu €65-115; ⊙6.30-9pm Mon & Tue, noon-2pm & 6-9pm Wed-Sat; ⧉) Hans-Harald Reber presides over the stove at this 19th-century country house, one of Schwäbisch Hall's Michelin-starred haunts. He puts an imaginative spin on seasonal, regional numbers such as local venison with chanterelles and parsley root *Spätzle* (egg noodles), and suckling pig cooked two ways with plum jus and sweet-potato cream. Vegetarians are also well catered for.

ⓘ Information

Schwäbisch Hall Tourist Office (⧉0791-751 246; www.schwaebischhall.de; Am Markt 9; ⊙9am-6pm Mon-Fri, 10am-3pm Sat & Sun May-Sep, 9am-5pm Mon-Fri Oct-Apr) On the Altstadt's main square.

ⓘ Getting There & Away

There are two train stations here. Trains from Stuttgart (€16.60, one hour, hourly) arrive at **Hessental**, on the right bank about 7km south of the centre and linked to the Altstadt by bus 1. Trains from Heilbronn go to the left-bank **Bahnhof Schwäbisch Hall**, a short walk along Bahnhofstrasse from the centre.

Ulm
⧉0731 / POP 122,636

Starting with the statistics: Ulm has the crookedest house (as listed in *Guinness World Records*) and one of the narrowest (4.5m wide), the world's oldest zoomorphic sculpture (aged 30,000 years), tallest cathedral steeple (161.5m high), and is the birthplace of the physicist, Albert Einstein.

This idiosyncratic city will win your affection with everyday encounters, particularly in summer as you pedal along the Danube and the Fischerviertel's beer gardens hum with animated chatter. One *Helles* (pale lager) too many and you may decide to impress the locals by attempting the tongue twister: 'In Ulm, um Ulm, und um Ulm herum' ('In Ulm, around Ulm and all around Ulm').

⊙ Sights

★ Ulmer Münster   CATHEDRAL
(www.ulmer-muenster.de; Münsterplatz; organ concerts adult/concession €8/4, tower adult/concession €5/3.50; ⊙9am-7pm Apr-Sep, 10am-5pm Oct-Mar) **FREE** 'Ooh, it's so big'... First-time visitors gush as they strain their neck muscles gazing

---

SWABIAN MENU DECODER

As the Swabian saying goes: *Was der Bauer net kennt, frisst er net* (What the farmer doesn't know, he doesn't eat) – so find out before you dig in:

Bubespitzle Officially called *Schupfnudeln*, these short, thick potato noodles – vaguely reminiscent of gnocchi – are browned in butter and tossed with sauerkraut. Sounds appetising until you discover that *Bubespitzle* means 'little boys' penises'.

Gaisburger Marsch A strong beef stew served with potatoes and *Spätzle*.

Maultaschen Giant ravioli pockets, stuffed with leftover ground pork, spinach, onions and bread mush. The dish is nicknamed *Herrgottsbeschieserle* (God trickster) because it was a sly way to eat meat during Lent.

Saure Kuddle So who is for sour tripe? If you don't have the stomach, try the potato-based, meat-free *saure Rädle* (sour wheels) instead.

Spätzle Stubby egg-based noodles. These are fried with onions and topped with cheese in the calorific treat *Käsespätzle*.

Zwiebelkuche Autumnal onion tart with bacon, cream and caraway seeds, which pairs nicely with *neuer Süsser* (new wine) or *Moschd* (cider).

up to the Münster. It is. And rather beautiful. Celebrated for its 161.5m-high steeple, this Goliath of cathedrals, the world's tallest, took 500 years to build from the first stone laid in 1377. Note the hallmarks on each stone, inscribed by cutters who were paid by the block. Those intent on cramming the Münster into one photo, filigree spire and all, should lie on the cobbles.

Only by puffing up 768 spiral steps to the tower's 143m-high viewing platform can you appreciate the Münster's dizzying height. There are terrific views of the Black Forest and, on cloud-free days, the Alps.

The Israelfenster, a stained-glass window above the west door, commemorates Jews killed during the Holocaust. The Gothic-style wooden pulpit canopy eliminates echoes during sermons. Biblical figures and historical characters such as Pythagoras embellish the 15th-century oak choir stalls. The Münster's regular organ concerts are a musical treat.

Museum Ulm   MUSEUM
(☑0731-161 4330; www.museumulm.de; Marktplatz 9; adult/concession €8/6; ☉11am-5pm Tues, Wed, Fri-Sun, to 8pm Thu) This museum is a fascinating romp through ancient and modern art, history and archaeology. Standouts include the 20th-century Kurt Fried Collection, starring Klee, Picasso and Lichtenstein works shown in rotating exhibitions. Archaeological highlights are tiny Upper Palaeolithic figurines unearthed in caves in the Swabian Alps, including the 30,000-year-old ivory Löwenmensch (lion man), the world's oldest zoomorphic sculpture. There's free entry on the first Friday of the month.

Marktplatz   SQUARE
Lording it over the square, the 14th-century **Rathaus** (Town Hall; 7am-6pm Mon-Thu, to 2pm Fri) FREE sports a step-gabled, lavishly frescoed Renaissance facade. Out front is the **Fischkastenbrunnen**, where fishmongers once dumped their catch to be sold at market. The Rathaus' architectural antithesis is the cutting-edge glass pyramid of the **Stadtbibliothek**, the city's main library.

Fischerviertel   AREA
The charming Fischerviertel, Ulm's old fishers' and tanners' quarter, is slightly southwest of the centre. Beautifully restored half-timbered houses huddle along the two channels of the Blau River. Harbouring art galleries, rustic restaurants, courtyards and the crookedest house in the world – as well

as one of the narrowest – the cobbled lanes are ideal for a leisurely saunter.

Stadtmauer   AREA
South of the Fischerviertel, along the Danube's north bank, runs the red-brick Stadtmauer (city wall), the height of which was reduced in the 19th century after Napoleon decided that a heavily fortified Ulm was against his best interests. Walk it for fine views over the river, the Altstadt and the slightly off-centre **Metzgerturm** (Butcher's Tower; Unter der Metzig).

Einstein Fountain & Monument   FOUNTAIN
(Zeughausgasse 15) A nod to Ulm's most famous son, this fiendishly funny bronze fountain by Jürgen Goertz shows a wild-haired, tongue-poking-out Albert Einstein, who was born in Ulm but left when he was one year old. Standing in front of the 16th-century **Zeughaus** (Arsenal; Am Zeughaus), the rocket-snail creation is a satirical play on humanity's attempts to manipulate evolution for its own self-interest. Nearby, at Zeughaus 14, is a single stone bearing the inscription *Ein Stein* (One Stone).

Synagogue   SYNAGOGUE
(Weinhof 2) Fitting neatly into Ulm's ensemble of eye-catching contemporary architecture, this free-standing synagogue was built for the Jewish community and completed in 2012. The architecturally striking edifice sits on the Weinhof, close to the former synagogue that was destroyed during Kristallnacht in 1938. At night its main window shimmers with the Star of David pattern.

Kunsthalle Weishaupt   GALLERY
(www.kunsthalle-weishaupt.de; Hans-und-Sophie-Scholl-Platz 1; adult/concession €6/4; ☉11am-5pm Tues, Wed, Fri-Sun, to 8pm Thu) The glass-fronted Kunsthalle Weishaupt contains the private collection of Siegfried Weishaupt, which is presented in rotating exhibitions. The accent is on modern and pop art, with bold paintings by Klein, Warhol and Haring.

Stadthaus   LANDMARK
(www.stadthaus.ulm.de; Münsterplatz 50) Designed by Richard Meier, the contemporary aesthetic of the concrete-and-glass Stadthaus is a dramatic contrast to the Münster. The American architect caused uproar by erecting the postmodern building alongside the city's Gothic giant but the result is striking. The Stadthaus stages exhibitions and events, houses the tourist office (p489) and a **cafe** (www.cafe-restaurant-stadthaus.de;

Ulm

Ulm

⊙8am-midnight Mon-Thu, 8am-1am Fri & Sat, 9am-midnight Sun).

Museum der Brotkultur
MUSEUM

(www.museum-brotkultur.de; Salzstadelgasse 10; adult/concession €4/3; ⊙10am-5pm) How grain grows, what makes a good dough and other bread-related mysteries are unravelled at the Museum of Bread Culture. The collection celebrates bread as the staff of life over millennia and across cultures, displaying curios from mills to Egyptian corn mummies.

🏃 Activities

Ulm Stories
AMUSEMENT PARK

(www.ulmstories.de; Kramgasse 3; flight €5; ⊙10am-6pm Tue-Sat) Ever dreamt of flying? Then you're going to love Ulm Stories, a new full-body flight simulator where you can get a virtual sparrow's-eye view of the cityscape as it would have looked in 1890, darting precariously close to the Münster's (p484) spires and the rooftops of the Altstadt.

Legoland
AMUSEMENT PARK

(www.legoland.de; Legoland-Allee 1, Günzburg; adult/concession €45.50/40.50; ⊙10am-6pm late Mar-early Nov) A sure-fire kid-pleaser, this pricey Lego-themed amusement park has shows, splashy rides and a miniature world built from 25 million Lego bricks. Note that it's around 20% cheaper to purchase tickets online in advance. Legoland is in Günzburg, 37km east of Ulm, just off the A8.

🛏 Sleeping

Brickstone Hostel
HOSTEL €

(☎0731-708 2559; www.brickstone-hostel.de; Schützenstrasse 42, Neu-Ulm; dm €19-21, s/d €32/46; 🐾) We love the homely vibe at this beautifully restored art nouveau house in Neu-Ulm. The high-ceilinged rooms are kept spotless and backpacker perks include a self-catering kitchen with free coffee and tea, plus an honesty bar, bike rental and a cosy lounge with book exchange. Bed linen costs an extra €3. Take bus 7 to Schützenstrasse from the Hauptbahnhof (p490).

★Hotel Schiefes Haus
B&B €€

(☎0731-967 930; www.hotelschiefeshausulm.de; Schwörhausgasse 6; s €125, d €148-160; 🐾) There was a crooked man and he walked a crooked mile...presumably to the world's most crooked hotel. Fear not – this early 16th-century, half-timbered rarity is not about to topple into the Blau. Up those creaking wooden stairs, in your snug, beamed room, you won't have to buckle yourself to the bed thanks to spirit levels and specially made height adjusters.

Hotel Restaurant Löwen
HOTEL €€

(☎0731-388 5880; www.hotel-loewen-ulm.de; Klosterhof 41; s €91, d €126-136, ste €138; P🐾) It's amazing what you can do with a former monastery and an eye for design. Exposed beams and stone add an historical edge to streamlined rooms with parquet floors. Breakfast is a hearty spread of homemade jam, eggs, freshly baked bread and cold cuts. Take tram 1 from central Ulm to Söflingen.

Hotel Schmales Haus
B&B €€

(☎0731-6027 2595; www.hotelschmaleshaus. de; Fischergasse 27; s/d €119/149, ste €183-229; P) Measuring a mere 4.5m across, this half-timbered 'narrow house' is a one-off. The affable Heides have transformed the slender 16th-century pad into a gorgeous

SPOT THE SPARROW

You can't move for *Spatzen* (sparrows) in the German language. You can eat like one (*essen wie ein Spatz*) and swear like one (*schimpfen wie ein Rohrspatz*); there are *Spatzenschleuder* (catapults), *Spätzles* (little darlings) and *Spatzenhirne* (bird brains). Nicknamed *Spatzen*, Ulm residents are, according to legend, indebted to the titchy bird for the construction of their fabulous Münster (p484).

The story goes that the half-baked builders tried in vain to shove the wooden beams for the minster sideways through the city gate. They struggled, until a sparrow fluttered past with straw for its nest. Enlightened, the builders carried the beams lengthways, completed the job and placed a bronze statue of a sparrow at the top to honour the bird.

Today there are sparrows everywhere in Ulm: on postcards, in patisseries, at football matches (team SSV Ulm are dubbed 'die Spatzen') and, above all, in the colourful sculptures dotting the Altstadt.

B&B, with exposed beams, downy bedding and wood floors in the three rooms.

Hotel am Rathaus & Hotel Reblaus
HOTEL €€

(☑ 0731-968 490; www.rathausulm.de; Kronengasse 10; s €78-125, d €98-140, q €149-175, s/d without bathroom €66/76; ☏) Just paces from the Rathaus (p485), these family-run twins ooze individual charm in rooms with flourishes including stucco and Biedermeier furnishings. Light sleepers take note: the walls are thin and the street can be noisy.

Becker's Boutique Hotel
BOUTIQUE HOTEL €€€

(☑ 0731-3885 0250; www.beckershotel.de; Münsterplatz 24; d €149-179; ☏) The Münster (p484) bells are your wake-up call at this supercentral new boutique hotel. There are just seven rooms, tastefully done out in crisp whites, blues and greens, with luxurious fabrics, parquet floors and walk-in rain showers. Lots of thought has gone into little details, including express app check-ins, generous made-to-order breakfasts, and toiletries hailing from a local soap factory.

✕ Eating

Fräulein Lecker
GERMAN €

(☑ 0731-3996 6494; https://fraeuleinlecker.de; Sterngasse 14; tasting plates €6-10, sushi set €7.90; ☺ 4-11pm Mon-Thu, to midnight Fri & Sat) Almost Scandi in style with its clean-lined simplicity, this wine-store-bar-bistro lit by funky bottle lights is a great place to try (and buy) local wines with region-driven snacks – from tasting platters of cheeses and hams to *Dinnete* (a Swabian take on tarte flambée) and German sushi (substituting pearl barley for rice). As the name suggests, it's all *lecker* (yum).

Dean & David
DELI €

(☑ 0731-1439 3174; https://deananddavid.de; Hafengasse 3; snacks & light meals €5-13; ☺ 9.30am-9pm Mon-Sat; ✎) This is a great find for vegetarians, vegans and frankly anyone looking for a healthy bite while exploring central Ulm. The slickly modern deli-cafe rustles up interesting salads (from mango prawn to vegan superfood and grilled veggie), sandwiches, curries, soups, freshly squeezed juices and green smoothies at wallet-friendly prices. Allergies are catered for.

Animo
CAFE €

(☑ 0731-964 2937; www.cafe-animo.de; Syrlinstrasse 17; day specials around €7; ☺ 7.30am-6pm Tue-Fri, 9am-6pm Sat & Sun; ✎) Snuggled away in a *Topferei* (potter's workshop), Animo is a relaxed cafe, with homemade cakes and vegetarian specials (creative salads, pasta, risotto and the like) – all served in beautifully detailed porcelain. Also hosts regular cultural events.

★ Zur Forelle
GERMAN €€

(☑ 0731-639 24; www.ulmer-forelle.de; Fischergasse 25; mains €17.50-27.50; ☺ 11.30am-2.30pm & 5pm-midnight Mon-Fri, 11am-midnight Sat, 11am-10pm Sun) Since 1626, this low-ceilinged tavern has been convincing wayfarers (Einstein included) of the joys of seasonal Swabian cuisine. Ablaze with flowers in summer, this wood-panelled haunt by the Blau prides itself on its namesake *Forelle* (trout), kept fresh under the bridge and served in a number of different guises alongside menu staples such as schnitzel and beef roulade.

Gerberhaus
MEDITERRANEAN €€

(☑ 0731-175 5771; www.gerber-haus.de; Weinhofberg 9; mains €10-29; ☺ 11.30am-2.30pm & 5.30-10pm) This warm, inviting woodcutter's cottage hits the mark with its delicious mix of Swabian and Italian-inspired dishes. Plump for a river-facing table and sample clean, bright flavours such as home-smoked salmon carpaccio, or Swabian old favourites including *Kässpätzle* and *Maultaschen* (regional take on ravioli). Day specials cost as little as €7.

Zunfthaus der Schiffleute
GERMAN €€

(☑0731-644 11; www.zunfthaus-ulm.de; Fischergasse 31; mains €10-28.50; ☺11.30am-midnight; ☻) Looking proudly back on a 600-year tradition, this timber-framed restaurant sits by the river. The menu speaks of a chef who loves the region, with Swabian favourites such as *Katzagschroi* (beef, onions, egg and fried potatoes) and meaty one-pot *Schwäbisches Hochzeitssüppchen*.

Zur Lochmühle
GERMAN €€

(☑0731-673 05; www.lochmuehle.com; Gerbergasse 6; mains €12.50-24; ☺11am-midnight) The watermill has been churning the Blau since 1356 at this rustic half-timbered pile. Plant yourself in the riverside beer garden for Swabian classics such as crispy roast pork, *Schupfnudeln* (potato noodles) and brook trout with lashings of potato salad.

Barfüsser
PUB FOOD €€

(☑0731-602 1110; Neue Strasse 87-89; mains €8-23; ☺9am-1am Sun-Thu, to 2am Fri & Sat) Hearty fare such as *Käsespätzle* (cheese noodles) and pork roast soak up the prize-winning beer, microbrewed in Neu-Ulm, at this brewpub. There are also some excellent craft beers to sample. The lunch special goes for €6.90.

Da Franco
ITALIAN €€€

(☑0731-305 85; www.da-franco.de; Neuer Graben 23; mains €23-29; ☺10.30am-midnight Tue-Sun) If you fancy a break from the norm, give this little Italian place a whirl. There is a seasonal touch to authentic dishes such as swordfish with clams, and veal escalope with asparagus, all cooked and presented with style.

🍷 Drinking & Entertainment

Rosebottel
BAR

(www.rosebottel.de; Zeitblomstrasse 21; ☺8pm-1am Mon-Sat) Ranked in the *Mixology Bar Guide* as one of Germany's best bars, Rosebottel time-warps you back to a more decadent age with its dark wood panelling, antique furniture and cosy, candlelit nooks. Come for the creative cocktails and impressive array of gins mixed with Rosebottel's own small-batch lemonades infused with ginger, fruits and botanicals.

Naschkatze
CAFE

(http://cafenaschkatze.de; Marienstrasse 6, Neu-Ulm; ☺8am-7pm Mon-Fri, 9am-6pm Sat, 10am-6pm Sun) Naschkatze, or 'sweet-toothed', is a fitting name for this vintage-cool cafe, where Ulmers come to lap up the retro vibe, coffee and homemade cakes.

Cabaret Eden
CLUB

(http://cabareteden.de; Karlstrasse 71; ☺7pm-1am Thu, 11pm-5am Fri & Sat) Once a striptease bar, Cabaret Eden has reinvented itself as an alternative club, with everything from DJs spinning hip-hop and drum 'n' bass to yoga nights where asanas (postures) are practised to electronica beats. It's close to Ulm Ost station.

Café im Kornhauskeller
CAFE

(Hafengasse 19; ☺8am-midnight Mon-Sat, 9am-10pm Sun) Arty cafe with an inner courtyard for coffee, breakfast, light bites or ice cream. It's also a chilled spot for a beer or glass of wine in the evening.

Roxy
CONCERT VENUE

(☑0731-968 620; www.roxy.ulm.de; Schillerstrasse 1) This huge cultural venue, housed in a former industrial plant 1km south of the Hauptbahnhof (p490), has a concert hall, cinema, disco, bar and special-event forum. Take tramline 1 to Ehinger Tor.

❶ Information

Post Office (Bahnhofplatz 2; ☺8.30am-6.30pm Mon-Fri, 9am-1pm Sat) To the left as you exit the **Hauptbahnhof** (p490).

Ulm Tourist Office (☑0731-161 2830; www.tourismus.ulm.de; Münsterplatz 50, Stadthaus; ☺9am-6pm Mon-Sat, 11am-3pm Sun Apr-Dec, 9.30am-6pm Mon-Fri, to 4pm Sat Jan-Mar) Ulm's main tourist office has plenty of info on the city and its surrounds. It can help book rooms and arrange guided tours.

❶ CITY SAVER

If you're planning on ticking off most of Ulm's major sights, consider investing in a good-value **UlmCard** (1/2 days €12/18), available at the tourist office, which covers public transport in Ulm and Neu-Ulm, a free city tour or rental of the itour audioguide, entry to all museums, plus numerous other discounts on tours, attractions and restaurants.

❶ Getting There & Away

Ulm is about 90km southeast of Stuttgart and 150km west of Munich, near the intersection of the north–south A7 and the east–west A8.

Ulm is well-served by ICE and EC trains; major destinations include Stuttgart (€21.90 to €27, one hour, several hourly) and Munich (€34 to €40, 1¼ hours, several hourly).

Ulm's **bus station** (Friedrich-Ebert-Strasse) is near the **Hauptbahnhof** (Bahnhofplatz).

❶ Getting Around

Ulm's ecofriendly trams run on renewable energy. There's a **local transport information counter** (www.swu-verkehr.de; Neue Strasse 79; ⊙9am-6pm Mon-Fri, to 2pm Sat) in the centre of town. A single/day ticket for the bus and tram network in Ulm and Neu-Ulm costs €2.20/4.40.

Should you wish to zip around on two wheels, you can hire sturdy city bikes from the tourist office (p489) for €12 per day.

THE BLACK FOREST

As deep, dark and delicious as its famous cherry gateau, the Black Forest gets its name from its canopy of evergreens. With deeply carved valleys, thick woodlands, luscious meadows, stout timber farmhouses and wispy waterfalls, it looks freshly minted for a kids' bedtime story. Wandering on its many miles of forest trails, you half expect to bump into a wicked witch or huntsman, and might kick yourself for not bringing those breadcrumbs to retrace your tracks...

Measuring 160km from top to bottom, the Black Forest is a ludicrously lovely expanse of hills, lakes and forest, topping out at 1493m Feldberg. It reaches from the spa town of Baden-Baden to the Swiss border, and from the Rhine almost to Lake Constance. This corner of the country is made for slow touring: on foot, by bicycle or behind the wheel of a car on one of many twisty roads with sensational views.

Baden-Baden

📋 07221 / POP 54,160

Baden-Baden's curative waters and air of old-world luxury have attracted royals, the rich and celebrities over the years – Barack Obama and Bismarck, Queen Victoria and Victoria Beckham included. This Black Forest town boasts grand colonnaded buildings and whimsically turreted art nouveau villas

spread across the hillsides and framed by forested mountains.

The bon vivant spirit of France, just across the border, is tangible in the town's open-air cafes, chic boutiques and pristine gardens fringing the Oos River. And with its temple-like thermal baths – which put the *Baden* (bathe) in Baden – and palatial casino, the allure of this grand dame of German spa towns is as timeless as it is enduring.

◉ Sights

★ **Museum Frieder Burda**　　GALLERY
(📋 07221-398 980; www.museum-frieder-burda.de; Lichtentaler Allee 8b; adult/concession €13/11; ⊙10am-6pm Tue-Sun) A Joan Miró sculpture guards the front of this architecturally innovative gallery, designed by Richard Meier. The star-studded collection of modern and contemporary art features Picasso, Gerhard Richter and Jackson Pollock originals; these are complemented by temporary exhibitions. There are free short guided tours at noon, 2pm and 4pm on Saturdays.

Casino　　HISTORIC BUILDING, CASINO
(📋 07221-302 40; www.casino-baden-baden.de; Kaiserallee 1; admission €5, guided tour €7; ⊙2pm-2am Sun-Thu, to 3.30am Fri & Sat, guided tours 9.30-11.45am Apr-Oct, 10am-11.30am Nov-Mar) The sublime casino seeks to emulate – indeed, outdo – the gilded, chandelier-lit splendour of Versailles. Marlene Dietrich called it 'the most beautiful casino in the world'. Gents must wear a jacket and tie. If you're not much of a gambler and want to simply marvel at the opulence, hook onto a 40-minute guided tour.

Lichtentaler Allee　　GARDENS
This 2.3km ribbon of greenery, threading from Goetheplatz to Kloster Lichtenthal, is quite a picture: studded with fountains and sculptures and carpeted with flowers (crocuses and daffodils in spring, magnolias, roses and azaleas in summer). Shadowing the sprightly Oosbach River, its promenade and bridges are made for aimless ambling. The avenue concludes at the Kloster Lichtenthal.

Trinkhalle　　LANDMARK
(Pump Room; Kaiserallee 3; ⊙10am-5pm Mon-Sat, 2-5pm Sun) Standing proud above a manicured park, this neoclassical pump room was built in 1839 as an attractive addition to the Kurhaus (p493). The 90m-long portico is embellished with 19th-century frescos of local legends. Baden-Baden's elixir of youth, some say, is the free curative mineral water

The Black Forest

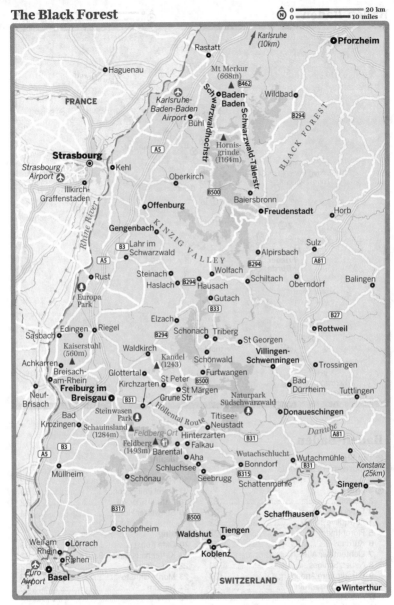

that gushes from a faucet linked to the Friedrichsbad spring.

Staatliche Kunsthalle
GALLERY

(☎07221-3007 6400; www.kunsthalle-baden-baden. de; Lichtentaler Allee 8a; adult/concession €7/5, Fri free; ☺10am-6pm Tue-Sun) Sidling up to the Museum Frieder Burda is this gallery, which showcases rotating exhibitions of contemporary art in neoclassical surrounds. Previous exhibitions include the works of Nigerian artist Emeka Ogboh and the experimental creations of Chinese artist Liang Shuo.

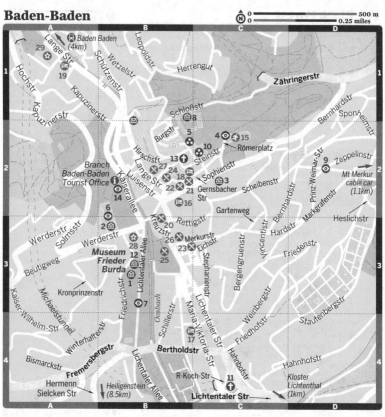

Baden-Baden

Baden-Baden

Fabergé Museum MUSEUM
(☑07221-970 890; www.faberge-museum.de;
Sophienstrasse 30; adult/concession €18/12;
⊙10am-6pm) Admittedly it's not everyone's
cup of tea, but if you happen to find Fabergé
fascinating, you're going to love this museum devoted to its impossibly ornate imperial Easter eggs, jewellery and gem-encrusted
animals made for Russian tsars in the late
19th and early 20th centuries.

Florentinerberg RUINS
(Höllengasse) The Romans used to cool off at
this hill; check out the ruins of the original
baths at its foot. Nowadays, on the same site,
the serene botanical gardens nurture wisteria, cypress trees, orange and lemon groves.

Paradies am Annaberg GARDENS
(Das Paradies) These Italianate gardens are
the perfect spot to unwind, with their soothing fountains and waterfalls. There are fine
views of the Altstadt and wooded hills from
these heights. Bus 205 to Friedrichshöhe
runs nearby.

Mt Merkur VIEWPOINT
(funicular one-way/return €2/4; ⊙10am-10pm)
Though modest in height, the 668m Mt
Merkur commands widescreen views of
Baden-Baden and the Murg Valley. It's a
popular spot for paragliding, gentle hiking
and family picnics. Buses 204 and 205 stop
near the funicular, which has been trundling
to the top since 1913.

Kurhaus LANDMARK
(www.kurhaus-baden-baden.de; Kaiserallee 1) Corinthian columns and a frieze of mythical
griffins grace the belle époque facade of the
Kurhaus, which towers above well-groomed
gardens. An alley of chestnut trees, flanked
by two rows of boutiques, links the Kurhaus
with Kaiserallee.

Stiftskirche CHURCH
(Marktplatz; ⊙8am-6pm) **FREE** The centrepiece of cobbled Marktplatz is this pink
church, a hotchpotch of Romanesque, late
Gothic and, to a lesser extent, baroque
styles. Its foundations incorporate some ruins of the former Roman baths. Come in the
early afternoon to see its stained-glass windows cast rainbow patterns across the nave.

Römische Badruinen RUINS
(Römerplatz; adult/child €2.50/1; ⊙11am-noon &
3-4pm mid-Mar–mid-Nov) The beauty-conscious
Romans were the first to discover the healing
properties of Baden-Baden's springs in the city

they called Aquae Aureliae. Slip back 2000
years at one of the oldest and best-preserved
Roman bathing complexes in the country.
Multilingual audioguides are available.

Russische Kirche CHURCH
(Russian Church; Lichtentaler Strasse 76; admission
€1; ⊙10am-6pm) Beautiful, if a little incongruous, Baden-Baden's Byzantine-style 1882
Russian church is lavishly adorned with
frescos and topped with a brilliantly golden
onion dome.

Neues Schloss HISTORIC BUILDING
(Schlossstrasse) Vine-swathed steps lead
from Marktplatz to the 15th-century Neues
Schloss, the former residence of the Baden-
Baden margraves, which is set to reopen at
some point in the distant future. The lookout
is still accessible, and affords far-reaching
views over Baden-Baden's rooftops and spires
to the Black Forest beyond.

🏃 Activities

⭐**Friedrichsbad** SPA
(☑07221-275 920; www.carasana.de; Römerplatz
1; 3hr ticket €25, incl soap-&-brush massage €37;
⊙9am-10pm, last admission 7pm) If it's the body
of Venus and the complexion of Cleopatra
you desire, abandon modesty to wallow in
thermal waters at this palatial 19th-century
marble-and-mosaic-festooned spa. As Mark
Twain said, 'after 10 minutes you forget time;
after 20 minutes, the world', as you slip into
the regime of steaming, scrubbing, hot-cold
bathing and dunking in the Roman-Irish
bath.

Panoramaweg HIKING
If you want to appreciate Baden-Baden and
the northern Black Forest from its most photogenic angles, walk all or part of the 40km
Panoramaweg, a high-level ridge trail weaving through orchards and woodlands past
waterfalls and viewpoints. The five-stage
hike begins at the Bernharduskirche, close
to the centre of town. For details and maps,
visit the tourist office's (p495) website.

Caracalla Spa SPA
(☑07221-275 940; www.carasana.de; Römerplatz
11; 2/3hr €16/19, day ticket €23; ⊙8am-10pm, last
admission 8pm) This modern, glass-fronted spa
has a cluster of indoor and outdoor pools,
grottoes and surge channels, making the
most of the mineral-rich spring water. For
those who dare to bare, saunas range from
the rustic 'forest' to the roasting 95°C 'fire'
variety.

🛏 Sleeping

Hotel am Sophienpark HISTORIC HOTEL €€
(📞 07221-3560; www.hotel-am-sophienpark.de; Sophienstrasse 14; s €99-140, d €150-160, ste €300, f €150-199; P 🛜) Overlooking attractively tended gardens right in the heart of Baden-Baden, this hotel has retained all the grace and character of the belle époque, with Juliet balconies and a mansard roof. The interior brims with period features, such as the impressive wrought-iron staircase, which sweeps up to generously sized rooms that swing from contemporary to romantic and chandelier-lit in style.

Hotel am Markt HISTORIC HOTEL €€
(📞 07221-270 40; www.hotel-am-markt-baden.de; Marktplatz 18; s €65-88, d €105-128, apt €110-138; P 🛜) Sitting pretty in front of the Stiftskirche (p493), this hotel, which is almost three centuries old, has 23 homely, well-kept rooms. It's quiet up here apart from your wake-up call of church bells, but then you wouldn't want to miss out on the great breakfast.

Rathausglöckel HOTEL €€
(📞 07221-906 10; www.rathausgloeckel.de; Steinstrasse 7; s €80-100, d €115-139, ste €135-300; P 🛜) Right in the thick of things, this friendly family-run hotel occupies a 16th-century townhouse. The attractively renovated rooms (some with rooftop views) are dressed in muted tones with pine furniture – those on the 3rd floor command the best views over Baden-Baden's rooftops. Breakfast is a generous spread of fresh bread, fruit and pastries, homemade jam and bacon and eggs.

Heiligenstein HOTEL €€
(📞 07221-961 40; www.hotel-heiligenstein.de; Heiligensteinstrasse 19a; s €90-95, d €122-145; P) It's worth going the extra mile (or seven) to this sweet hotel overlooking vineyards. Pared-back, earthy-hued rooms come with balconies, and guests can put their feet up in the spa and gardens. The highly regarded restaurant (mains €16 to €27) serves local, seasonally inspired fare, from freshly caught trout to venison with blackcurrant sauce and asparagus.

Schweizer Hof HOTEL €€
(📞 07221-304 60; www.schweizerhof.de; Lange Strasse 73; s €69-89, d €99-145, ste €135-185; P 🛜) Sitting on one of Baden-Baden's smartest streets, this above-par hotel is a real find, with 40 dapper, recently updated rooms, chandelier-lit spaces, and a garden with sun lounges for chilling. The buffet breakfast is a rich affair.

Hotel Belle Epoque LUXURY HOTEL €€€
(📞 07221-300 660; www.hotel-belle-epoque.de; Maria-Viktoria-Strasse 2c; s €170-185, d €240-305, ste €389-685; 🛜) Nestling in manicured parkland, this neo-Renaissance villa is one of Baden-Baden's most characterful five-star pads. Antiques lend a dash of old-world opulence to the individually designed rooms. Rates include afternoon tea, with scones, cakes and fine brews served on the terrace or by the fireplace.

🍴 Eating

Café König CAFE €
(Lichtentaler Strasse 12; cake €3.50-5, lunch specials €11-19; ⏰ 8.30am-6.30pm) Liszt and Tolstoy once sipped coffee at this venerable cafe, which has been doing a brisk trade in Baden-Baden's finest cakes, tortes, pralines and truffles for over 250 years. Black Forest gateau topped with clouds of cream; fresh berry tarts; or moist nut cakes – oh, decisions!

Kaffeehaus Baden-Baden CAFE €
(Gernsbacher Strasse 24; snacks €3-6; ⏰ 9.30am-6pm Mon-Fri, 10.30am-6pm Sat, 1-6pm Sun) The aroma of freshly roasted coffee fills this artsy cafe, a laid-back spot for an espresso or chai latte and a slice of freshly baked cake. Its shop sells speciality teas, coffees, chocolate, organic preserves and handmade ceramics.

Weinstube im Baldreit GERMAN €€
(📞 07221-231 36; Küferstrasse 3; mains €12.50-19; ⏰ 5-10pm Tue-Sat) Well hidden down cobbled lanes, this wine-cellar restaurant is tricky to find, but worth looking for. Baden-Alsatian fare such as *Flammkuchen* (Alsatian pizza) topped with Black Forest ham, Roquefort and pears is expertly matched with local wines. Eat in the ivy-swathed courtyard in summer, and the vaulted interior in winter.

Monte Christo TAPAS €€
(📞 07221-393 434; http://monte-christo-baden-baden.de; Eichstrasse 5; tapas €6-17, mixed tapas plate €20; ⏰ 6pm-1am Tue-Sat) Bare wood tables, soft lighting and decorative tiles create a cosy feel at this tapas bar, where punchy Spanish flavours – from baked sheep's cheese with olives, garlic and rosemary to sweet-potato chips with fig aioli – are served with generosity, panache and fine Riojas. There's always a buzz – even after most restaurants in town have closed – and for good reason.

La Casserole
FRENCH €€

(☑07221-222 21; Gernsbacher Strasse 18; mains €16-21; ☺11.30am-3pm & 5-10pm Thu-Sat, 5-10pm Mon-Wed) Lace curtains, cheek-by-jowl tables and flickering candles create the classic bistro tableau at intimate La Casserole. Go for satisfying Alsatian specialities such as beef cheeks braised in Pinot Noir until tender, served with *Spätzle* (thick egg-based noodles).

★ Nigrum
GASTRONOMY €€€

(☑07221-397 9008; www.restaurant-nigrum. de; Baldreitstrasse 1; 3-/5-/8-course menu €65/85/115; ☺6pm-midnight Tue-Sat) This dark, seductive, gold-kissed glamour puss of a restaurant has insiders whispering Michelin star. Profound, season-driven flavours here are presented in the new-fangled way according to primary ingredients. The tasting menus don't disappoint – be it braised, meltingly soft Iberian pork cheek or salmon confit with octopus. It's all beautifully cooked and served with flair.

Schneider's Weinstube & Vinothek
GERMAN €€€

(☑07221-976 6929; www.schneiders-weinstube. de; Merkurstrasse 3; mains €20-29; ☺5-11pm Mon-Sat) A charmingly old-school choice, Schneider's brings you the best of Badisch food and Pinot wines to the table. You'll receive a heartfelt welcome in the warmly lit space, where the menu swings with the seasons – from pike-perch with potato salad to braised wild boar with cranberry sauce. Check out the day specials on the blackboard.

Rizzi
INTERNATIONAL €€€

(☑07221-258 38; www.rizzi-baden-baden.de; Augustaplatz 1; mains €16-38; ☺noon-1am) Book well ahead to snag a table at this insanely popular restaurant, housed in a pastel-pink villa overlooking the Lichtentaler Allee (p490). In summer, the tree-shaded patio is the place to sip excellent wines while tucking into choice steaks. Other menu favourites include organic schnitzels, pepped-up pastas and homemade burgers. Lunch specials go for between €8 to €14.

☆ Entertainment

Festspielhaus
CONCERT VENUE

(☑07221-301 3101; www.festspielhaus.de; Beim Alten Bahnhof 2, Robert-Schuman-Platz) Ensconced in an historical train station and fabled for its acoustics, the Festspielhaus is Europe's second-biggest concert hall, seating 2500 theatregoers, and a lavish tribute to

DON'T MISS

TEN YEARS YOUNGER

Rheumatism, arthritis, respiratory complaints, skin problems – all this and a host of other ailments can, apparently, be cured by Baden-Baden's mineral-rich spring water. If you'd rather drink the stuff than bathe in it, head to the **Fettquelle** (Römerplatz; ☺24hr) fountain at the base of a flight of steps near Römerplatz, where you can fill your bottle for free. It might taste like lukewarm bathwater but if it makes you feel 10 years younger, who cares?

Baden-Baden's musical heritage. Under the direction of Andreas Mölich-Zebhauser, the grand venue hosts a world-class program of concerts, opera and ballet.

Baden-Badener Philharmonie
CLASSICAL MUSIC

(☑07221-932 791; www.philharmonie.baden-baden.de; Solmsstrasse 1) The revered Philharmonie Baden-Baden frequently performs in the Kurhaus (p493).

Baden-Baden Theater
THEATRE

(☑07221-932 700; www.theater.baden-baden.de; Goetheplatz) The Baden-Baden Theater is a neo-baroque confection of white-and-red sandstone with a frilly interior that looks like a miniature version of the Opéra-Garnier in Paris. It forms the gateway to Lichtentaler Allee (p490) and stages an eclectic line-up of German-language productions.

❶ Information

Branch Baden-Baden Tourist Office (Kaiserallee 3; ☺10am-5pm Mon-Sat, 2-5pm Sun; ☎) In the Trinkhalle (p490). Sells events tickets. Free wi-fi.

Main Baden-Baden Tourist Office (☑07221-275 200; www.baden-baden.com; Schwarzwaldstrasse 52, B500; ☺9am-6pm Mon-Sat, to 1pm Sun) Situated 2km northwest of the centre. If you're driving from the northwest (from the A5) this place is on the way into town. Sells events tickets.

Post Office (Lange Strasse 44; ☺9am-7pm Mon-Fri, to 2pm Sat) Located inside Kaufhaus Wagener.

❶ Getting There & Around

Karlsruhe-Baden-Baden Airport (Baden Airpark; ☑07229-662 000; www.badenairpark.de), 15km west of Baden-Baden, serves destinations

DON'T MISS

SILENT HEIGHTS

Escape the crowds and enjoy the view at these Baden-Baden lookouts and trails.

Neues Schloss (p493) A stately 15th-century residence with views over the rooftops of Baden-Baden to the dark woods of the Black Forest.

Mt Merkur (p493) Hiking and picnicking high above Baden-Baden at this lookout, reached by funicular.

Florentinerberg (p493) Uplifting views over city and forest-draped hill from these former Roman baths and botanical gardens.

Paradies am Annaberg (p493) Landscaped gardens in the Italian style, with falls and far-reaching forest views.

Panoramaweg (p493) A 40km hike starting in Baden-Baden, which dips into the most scenic bits of the northern Black Forest.

including London Stansted, Edinburgh, Rome and Malaga by Ryanair.

Buses to Black Forest destinations depart from the bus station, next to the **Hauptbahnhof** (Ooser Bahnhofstrasse).

Baden-Baden is on a major north–south rail corridor. Twice-hourly destinations include Freiburg (€23.70 to €40, 45 to 90 minutes) and Karlsruhe (€11 to €16, 15 to 30 minutes).

Local buses run by **Stadtwerke Baden-Baden** (www.stadtwerke-baden-baden.de; Waldseestrasse 24) cost €2/6.40 for a single/24-hour ticket. A day pass for up to five people is €10.60. Bus 201 (every 10 minutes) and other lines link the Bahnhof with Leopoldsplatz. Bus 205 runs roughly hourly between the Bahnhof and the airport (p495) from Monday to Friday, less frequently at weekends.

Karlsruhe

☑ 0721 / POP 307,755

When planning this radial city in 1715, the margraves of Baden placed a mighty baroque palace smack in the middle – an urban layout so impressive it became the blueprint for Washington, DC.

Laid-back and cultured, Karlsruhe grows on you the longer you linger, with its rambling parks and museums crammed with futuristic gizmos and French Impressionist paintings. The suburbs dotted with art nouveau town-

houses are a reminder that France is just 15km away. Some 43,000 students keep the beer cheap and the vibe upbeat in the pubs, and the wheels of innovation in culture and technology turning.

◉ Sights

★**Schloss**   PALACE

(Schlossbezirk 10) From the baroque-meets-neoclassical Schloss, Karlsruhe's 32 streets radiate like the spokes of a wheel. Karl Wilhelm, margrave of Baden-Durlach, named his epicentral palace Karlsruhe (Karl's retreat) when founding the city in 1715. Destroyed during WWII, the grand palace was sensitively rebuilt. In warm weather, locals play *pétanque* on the fountain-strewn Schlossplatz parterre. The palace harbours the Badisches Landesmuseum.

Edging north, the Schlossgarten is a relaxed spot for walks and picnics.

Badisches Landesmuseum   MUSEUM

(☑0721-926 6514; www.landesmuseum.de; Schlossbezirk 10; adult/concession €4/3, after 2pm Fri free; ⊙10am-5pm Tue-Thu, to 6pm Fri-Sun) The treasure-trove Badisches Landesmuseum, inside the Schloss, shelters the jewel-encrusted crown of Baden's grand-ducal ruling family, and spoils of war from victorious battles against the Turks in the 17th century. Scale the tower for a better look at Karlsruhe's circular layout and for views stretching to the Black Forest.

Kunsthalle Karlsruhe   GALLERY

(☑0721-926 3359; www.kunsthalle-karlsruhe.de; Hans-Thoma-Strasse 2-6; adult/concession €12/9; ⊙10am-6pm Tue & Wed & Fri-Sun, to 9pm Thu) The outstanding State Art Gallery presents a world-class collection, from the canvases of late-Gothic German masters such as Matthias Grünewald and Lucas Cranach the Elder to Impressionist paintings by Degas, Monet and Renoir. Step across to the Orangerie to view works by German artists including Georg Baselitz and Gerhard Richter.

Kloster Maulbronn   MONASTERY

(Maulbronn Monastery; www.kloster-maulbronn.de; Maulbronn; adult/concession/family €7.50/3.80/18.80; ⊙9am-5.30pm Mar-Oct, 9.30am-5pm Tue-Sun Nov-Feb) Billed as the best-preserved medieval monastery north of the Alps, this one-time Cistercian monastery was founded by Alsatian monks in 1147. It was born again as a Protestant school in 1556 and designated a Unesco World Heritage Site in

1993. Its famous graduates include the astronomer Johannes Kepler. Aside from the Romanesque-Gothic portico in the monastery church and the weblike vaulting of the cloister, it's the insights into monastic life that make this place so culturally stimulating.

Maulbronn is 37km east of Karlsruhe, near the Pforzheim Ost exit on the A8. From Karlsruhe, take the S4 to Bretten Bahnhof and from there bus 700.

Zentrum für Kunst und Medientechnologie
MUSEUM

(ZKM; ☑ 0721-810 00; www.zkm.de; Lorenzstrasse 19; adult/concession €6/4; ⊙ 10am-6pm Wed-Fri, 2-6pm Sat, 11am-6pm Sun) Set in a historical munitions factory, the ZKM is a mammoth exhibition and research complex fusing art and emerging electronic media technologies. The interactive Medienmuseum has media art displays, including a computer-generated 'legible city' and real-time bubble simulations. The Museum für Neue Kunst hosts first-rate temporary exhibitions of post-1960 art. Served by tram 2, the ZKM is 2km southwest of the Schloss and a similar distance northwest of the Bahnhof (p498).

Marktplatz
SQUARE

The grand neoclassical Marktplatz is dominated by the Ionic portico of the 19th-century **Evangelische Stadtkirche** and the dusky-pink **Rathaus**. The iconic red-stone **pyramid** is an incongruous tribute to Karl Wilhelm, margrave of Baden-Durlach, and marks his tomb.

Museum beim Markt
MUSEUM

(☑ 0721-926 6578; Karl-Friedrich-Strasse 6; adult/concession €4/3; ⊙ 11am-5pm Tue-Thu, 10am-6pm Fri-Sun) At the northern tip of Marktplatz, Museum beim Markt presents an intriguing stash of post-1900 applied arts, from art nouveau to Bauhaus.

🛏 Sleeping

bbKarlsruhe Hostel
HOSTEL €

(☑ 015 785 073 050; www.bbkarlsruhe.de; Karlstrasse 132a; dm/s/d €30/50/64) Artsy, individually decorated rooms with a retro feel and paintings on the walls make this one of Karlsruhe's most enticing budget picks. Bathrooms are shared, as is the kitchen. It's a 10-minute walk northwest of the Bahnhof (p498). The nearest tram stop is Kolpingplatz.

Hotel Rio
HOTEL €€

(☑ 0721-840 80; www.hotel-rio.de; Hans-Sachs-Strasse 2; s €78-119, d €86-132; 🅿🖥) Service can be

brusque but this is still one of your best bets for spotless, contemporary quarters in Karlsruhe. Breakfast is worth the extra €6 – eggs, salmon, the works. Take the tram to Mühlburger Tor.

Acora Hotel
HOTEL €€

(☑ 0721-850 90; www.acora.de; Sophienstrasse 69-71; s €80-121, d €100-152; 🅿🖥) Chirpy staff make you feel at home at this apartment-hotel, featuring bright, modern rooms equipped with kitchenettes.

🍴 Eating & Drinking

Vogelbräu
PUB FOOD €

(☑ 0721-377 571; www.vogelbraeu.de/karlsruhe/lokal.html; Kapellenstrasse 50; mains €7-10; ⊙ 10am-midnight) Quaff a cold one with regulars by the copper vats or in the leafy beer garden of this microbrewery. The unfiltered house pils washes down hale and hearty food such as goulash, dumplings and bratwurst with beer sauce. The tram to Durlacher Tor stops close by.

DeliBurgers
BURGERS €

(☑ 0721-6699 1055; www.deliburgers.de; Akademiestrasse 39; burgers €7-10; ⊙ 11.30am-9.30pm) DeliBurgers does what it says on the tin: top-quality beef burgers, grilled to your taste, with gourmet toppings and organic buns. Everything is made right here – from the sauces to the fluffy hand-cut fries. It's near the Europaplatz tram stop.

Casa do José
PORTUGUESE €€

(☑ 0721-9143 8018; www.casadojose.de; Kriegsstrasse 92; mains €14-24.50; ⊙ 5-11pm Tue-Fri, 11.30am-11pm Sat & Sun) A slice of Portugal in the heart of Karlsruhe, Casa do José extends a heartfelt *bemvindo* (welcome). The look is modern-rustic, with beams suspended above bistro tables in a light interior. *Petiscos* (Portuguese tapas) such as salt-cod fritters and fried garlic sausage are an appetising prelude to dishes such as *cataplana de peixe e marisco* (paprika-spiked fish and shellfish stew).

Kommödchen
INTERNATIONAL €€€

(☑ 0721-350 5884; www.kommoedchen-ka.de; Marienstrasse 1; mains €20-30; ⊙ 6pm-midnight Tue-Sun) A drop of good old-fashioned sophistication in Karlsruhe's southern Südstadt neighbourhood, Kommödchen keeps things cosy with soft lamplight, bistro seating, portraits festooning the walls and warm service. Matched with great wines, the menu has Mediterranean and Asian overtones in dishes such as red tuna carpaccio with lemon-herb dressing, and grilled tiger prawns with mango-coconut sauce.

Oberländer Weinstuben
GERMAN €€€

(✆0721-250 66; www.oberlaender-weinstube.de; Akademiestrasse 7; 3-course lunch/dinner €30/51, mains €19-26; ⊙noon-3pm & 6pm-midnight Tue-Sat) This highly atmospheric pick brings together an elegant wood-panelled tavern and a flowery courtyard. Fine wines marry perfectly with seasonal winners such as slow-cooked ox cheeks, goose ravioli with salsify and nut-butter foam, and rack of venison with pumpkin – all cooked with flair and served with finesse.

Phono
CRAFT BEER

(http://phono.bar; Karl-Wilhelm-Strasse 6; ⊙6pm-11.45pm Mon, to 1am Tue-Wed, to 2am Thu-Fri, 8pm-2am Sat) This vintage-cool craft beer bar in Karlsruhe's Oststadt hums with folk thirsty for unusual brews – and here there are 70 to try from all over the world. Phono also hosts events from tastings to DJ sets. Take the tram to Durlacher Tor. From here it's a 300m walk northeast.

ℹ Information

Karlsruhe Tourist Office (✆0721-3720 5383; www.karlsruhe-tourismus.de; Bahnhofplatz 6; ⊙8.30am-6pm Mon-Fri, 9am-1pm Sat) Across the street from the **Bahnhof**. Sells the Karlsruhe Card (24/48/72hr card €18.50/22.50/26.50) offering free or discounted entry to museums and other attractions as well as unlimited use of public transport. A cheaper version of the card (24/48/72hr card €12.50/16.50/20.50) excludes public transport.

Post Office (Poststrasse 3; ⊙9am-6.30pm Mon-Fri, 9.30am-1pm Sat) East of the **Bahnhof**.

ℹ Getting There & Around

Destinations well-served by train from the **Bahnhof** include Baden-Baden (€11.50 to €16.50, 15 minutes) and Freiburg (€29 to €37, one hour).

The **Bahnhof** is linked to the **Marktplatz** (p497), 2km north, by tram and light-rail lines 2, 3, S1, S11, S4 and S41. Single tickets cost €2.50; a 24-Stunden-Karte (24-hour unlimited travel card) costs €6.40 (€10.60 for up to five people).

Freudenstadt

✆07441 / POP 22,579

Duke Friedrich I of Württemberg built a new capital here in 1599, which was bombed to bits in WWII. The upshot is that Freuden-stadt's centre is underwhelming, though its magnificent setting in the Black Forest is anything but.

Freudenstadt marks the southern end of the Schwarzwaldhochstrasse (Black Forest Highway) and is a terminus for the gorgeous Schwarzwald-Tälerstrasse (Black Forest Valley Road), which runs from Rastatt via Alpirsbach.

◉ Sights

Stadtkirche
CHURCH

(Marktplatz; ⊙10am-5pm) **FREE** In the south-west corner of Marktplatz looms the 17th-century red-sandstone Stadtkirche, with an ornate 12th-century Cluniac-style baptismal font, Gothic windows, Renaissance portals and baroque towers. The two naves are at right angles to each other, an unusual design by the geometrically minded Duke Friedrich I.

Marktplatz
SQUARE

Lovers of statistics will delight in ticking off Germany's biggest square (216m by 219m, for the record), dislocated by a T-junction of heavily trafficked roads. At the heart of Freudenstadt, it harbours rows of shops, cafes with alfresco seating and a playground.

🏃 Activities

While you won't linger for Freudenstadt's sights, the deep forested valleys on its fringes are worth exploring. Scenic hiking trails include a 12km uphill walk to Kniebis (www.kniebis.de) on the Schwarzwaldhoch-strasse, where there are superb Kinzig Valley views. Ask the tourist office (p500) for details.

Jump on a mountain bike to tackle routes such as the 85km Kinzigtal-Radweg, taking in dreamy landscapes and half-timbered villages, or the 60km Murgtal-Radweg over hill and dale to Rastatt. Both valleys have bike trails and it's possible to return to Freudenstadt by train.

Pfau Schinken
FOOD

(✆07445-6482; www.pfau-schinken.de; Alte Post-strasse 17, Herzogsweiler; ⊙7.30am-12.30pm & 2-6pm Mon-Fri, 7.30am-12.30pm Sat, guided tours 2.30pm & 4.30pm Tue, 11.30am Sat) When you smell the tantalising aroma of *Schwar-zwälder Schinken* (Black Forest ham), you know you've arrived at Pfau, which lends insight into the curing and smoking process on its guided tours. It's a 10-minute drive north of Freudenstadt on the B28.

Panorama-Bad   SWIMMING
(www.panorama-bad.de; Ludwig-Jahn-Strasse 60;
adult/concession 3hr pass €7.30/6.20; ⊙9am-
10pm Mon-Sat, to 8pm Sun) The glass-fronted
Panorama-Bad is a relaxation magnet with
pools, steam baths and saunas.

🛏 Sleeping

Camping Langenwald   CAMPGROUND €
(⏹07441-2862;   www.camping-langenwald.de;
Strasburger Strasse 167; per person/tent €8.60/10;
⊙Easter-Oct; 🗷) This leafy site has a so-
lar-heated pool and a nature trail. There's
plenty to keep the kids amused, including a
playground, table football and volleyball. It's
served by bus 12 to Kniebis.

Warteck   HOTEL €€
(⏹07441-919 20; www.warteck-freudenstadt.
de; Stuttgarter Strasse 14; s €70-82, d €81-114,
tr €146-178; P🛜) In the capable hands of
the Glässel family since 1894, this hotel
sports modern, gleamingly clean rooms.
The real draw here, however, is the elegant
wood-panelled restaurant (mains €14.50 to
€39), which serves market-fresh fare such
as beetroot tortellini and rack of venison
with wild mushrooms.

Hotel Adler   HOTEL €€
(⏹07441-915 252; www.adler-fds.de; Forststrasse
15-17; s €70-105, d €100-130, ste €150; P🛜) This
family-run hotel near the Marktplatz has
well-kept, recently renovated rooms with
parquet floors, transparent bathroom par-
titions and pops of lime green. The restaurant (mains €12 to €17) dishes up appetising

regional grub such as *Zwiebelrostbraten*
(roast beef with onions).

Hotel Grüner Wald   SPA HOTEL €€€
(⏹07441-860 540; www.gruener-wald.de; Kinzig-
talstrasse 23, Lauterbad; s €92-102, d €174-210, ste
€220-304; P🛜🗷) Nuzzling between forest
and meadows, this eco-conscious spa hotel
in Lauterbad, 2km south of Freudenstadt,
is a terrific pick for a relaxing break, with
warm-toned, country-style rooms done
out in wood and natural fabrics, affording
knock-out views from their balconies. The
spa has an indoor pool, relaxation area with
waterbeds, saunas and steam room. There's
a pretty garden with hammocks.

🍴 Eating

Speckwirt   GERMAN €
(⏹07441-919 5680; www.speckwirt-fds.de; Marktplatz 45; mains €7.50-13.50, lunch special €7.90;
⊙9am-10pm; 🛜🍴) Speckwirt has winged
Black Forest tradition into the 21st century with its new-wave-rustic decor of basket
lights, forest murals on the wall and chunky
pine trappings. Come for good old-fashioned
grub along the lines of *Maultasche* (Swabian-
style ravioli) in speck sauce to a *Vesperbrett*
(sharing platter) of Black Forest ham and sausage. Children's menus (€4.50 to €6.50) are
available.

Turmbräu   GERMAN €€
(www.turmbraeu.de; Marktplatz 64; mains €8-28;
⊙11am-midnight Sun-Thu, to 3am Fri & Sat) For a
lively night out in Freudenstadt, this is your
place, with a microbrewery that doubles as a

HIKING THE BLACK FOREST

As locals will tell you, you need to hit the trails to really see the Black Forest. From gentle
half-day strolls to multiday treks, we've cherry-picked the region for a few of our favourites. Local tourist offices can help out with more info and maps, or check out the free
tour planner at www.wanderservice-schwarzwald.de.

It's also worth checking out the Schwarzwaldverein (www.schwarzwaldverein.de),
where well-marked paths criss-cross the darkest depths of the Black Forest.

The ultimate long-distance trail is the 280km **Westweg**, marked with a red diamond,
stretching from Pforzheim in the northern Black Forest to Basel in Switzerland. Highlights feature the steep Murg Valley, Titisee and 1493m Feldberg. But if you have less
time (and energy), these shorter hikes are terrific alternatives:

Panoramaweg (p493)

Gütenbach-Simonswäldertal (p517)

Wutachschlucht (p515)

Feldberg–Steig (p513)

Martinskapelle (p518)

beer garden. Pull up a chair in ye-olde barn to munch hearty grub such as goulash, stubby pork knuckles with sauerkraut, and *Bierkrustenbraten* (pork roast with beer sauce) while guzzling Turmbräu brews – a 5L barrel costs €39.

★ **Schwarzwaldstube** MODERN EUROPEAN €€€ (☎ 07442-4920; www.traube-tonbach.de; Tonbachstrasse 237, Baiersbronn-Tonbach; tasting menus €180-225, cookery courses around €200; ⏲ 7pm-midnight Wed, noon-2pm & 7-9pm Thu-Sun) Schwarzwaldstube commands big forest views from its rustically elegant dining room. Head chef Torsten Michel performs culinary magic, carefully sourcing ingredients and presenting with an artist's flair. The tasting menu goes with the seasons, but might begin with a palate-awakening confit of Arctic cod with red-bell pepper ginger crust, followed by suckling veal with smoked bone marrow and Périgord truffle.

If you fancy getting behind the stove, sign up for one of the cookery classes, which revolve around a theme or techniques including pasta-making and preparing pâtés. The website has details and dates.

Schwarzwaldstube has three Michelin stars. It's located in the village of Tonbach, 11km north of Freudenstadt.

★ **Restaurant Bareiss** MODERN EUROPEAN €€€ (☎ 07442-470; www.bareiss.com; Hermine-Bareiss-Weg 1, Baiersbronn-Mitteltal; lunch menu €105, dinner menus €185-225; ⏲ noon-2pm & 7-9.30pm Wed-Sun) Claus-Peter Lumpp has consistently won plaudits for his brilliantly composed, French-inflected menus at Restaurant Bareiss. On paper, dishes such as sautéed langoustine with almond cream, and fried fillet of suckling calf and sweetbreads with chanterelles seem deceptively simple; on the plate they become things of beauty, rich in textures and aromas and presented with an artist's eye for detail.

Restaurant Bareiss has three Michelin stars. It's situated 11km north of Freudenstadt.

❶ Information

Freudenstadt Tourist Office (☎ 07441-864 730; www.freudenstadt.de; Marktplatz 64; ⏲ 9am-6pm Mon-Fri, 10am-3pm Sat, 10am-1pm Sun; ☎) Hotel reservations are free.

❶ Getting There & Away

Freudenstadt's focal point is the Marktplatz (p498) on the B28. The town has two train stations: the *Stadtbahnhof*, five minutes' walk north of Marktplatz, and the Hauptbahnhof, 2km southeast of Marktplatz at the end of Bahnhofstrasse.

Trains on the Ortenau line, serving Offenburg and Strasbourg, depart hourly from the Hauptbahnhof and are covered by the 24-hour Europass. The pass represents excellent value at €11.90 for individuals and €19 for families. Trains go roughly hourly to Karlsruhe (€19.60, 1½ to two hours) from the *Stadtbahnhof* and Hauptbahnhof.

Kinzigtal

Shaped like a horseshoe, the Kinzigtal (Kinzig Valley) begins south of Freudenstadt and shadows the babbling Kinzig River south to Schiltach, west to Haslach and north to Offenburg. Near Strasbourg, 95km downriver, the Kinzig is swallowed up by the mighty Rhine. The valley's inhabitants survived for centuries on mining and shipping goods by raft.

This Black Forest valley is astonishingly pretty, with hills brushed with thick larch and spruce forest or ribboned with vines; its half-timbered villages look every inch the Grimms' fairy tale. For seasonal colour, come in autumn (for foliage) or spring (for fruit blossom).

❶ Getting There & Away

The B294 follows the Kinzig from Freudenstadt to Haslach, from where the B33 leads north to Offenburg. If you're going south, pick up the B33 to Triberg and beyond in Hausach.

An hourly train line links Freudenstadt with Offenburg (€16.20, 1¼ hours), stopping in Alpirsbach (€3.95, 16 minutes), Schiltach (€6.80, 26 minutes), Hausach (€9.60, 42 minutes), Haslach (€11.30, 50 minutes) and Gengenbach (€14.80, one hour). From Hausach, trains run roughly hourly southeast to Triberg (€6.70, 21 minutes), Villingen (€12.90, 44 minutes) and Konstanz (€31.60, two hours). For Konstanz, it's cheaper to buy the Baden-Württemberg Ticket (€24).

Alpirsbach

☎ 07444 / POP 6337

Nudging the wooded hills of the Upper Kinzigtal, Alpirsbach is presided over by a splendid Benedictine monastery. Lore has it that the town itself is named after a quaffing cleric who, when a glass of beer slipped clumsily from his hand and rolled into the river, exclaimed: *All Bier ist in den Bach!* (All the beer is in the stream!). A prophecy, it seems, as today Alpirsbacher Klosterbräu is brewed from pure spring water.

⊙ Sights

★ Monkey 47   DISTILLERY

(☑ 07455-946 870; www.monkey47.com; Äusserer Vogelsberg 7, Lossburg) FREE Embracing the global craft gin craze, Monkey 47 has scooped awards for its batch-distilled, handcrafted dry gin, with piney, peppery notes. Distillery tours are free, but the early monkey gets the banana – it's by appointment only. See the website for details. The distillery is 11km north of Alpirsbach on the L408.

Kloster Alpirsbach   MONASTERY

(www.kloster-alpirsbach.de; Klosterplatz 1; adult/concession €6/3; ⊙10am-5.30pm Mon-Sat, 11am-5.30pm Sun) All the more evocative for its lack of adornment, this 11th-century former Benedictine monastery effectively conveys the simple, spiritual life in its Romanesque three-nave church, spartan cells and Gothic cloister, which hosts candlelit concerts from June to August. It's amazing what you can find under the floorboards, as the museum reveals with its stash of 16th-century clothing, caricatures (of artistic scholars) and lines (of misbehaving ones).

Alpirsbacher Klosterbräu   BREWERY

(☑ 07444-670; www.alpirsbacher.com; Marktplatz 1; tours €7-12.20; ⊙tours 2.30pm) Alpirsbacher Klosterbräu is brewed from pure spring water. Brewery tours at 2.30pm, taking a behind-the-scenes peek at the brewing process, are in German, though guides may speak English. Two beers are thrown in for the price of a €7 ticket, while more expensive €12.20 tickets include bratwurst and a glass of beer schnapps.

⊨ Sleeping & Eating

Hotel Rössle   HISTORIC HOTEL €€

(☑ 07444-956 040; www.roessle-alpirsbach.de; Aischbachstrasse 5; s €58, d €88-98, tr €120, f €170; P🐾) This welcoming family-run number lodges in a half-timbered house a couple of minutes' stroll from the monastery. Light, spacious rooms are done out in modern Black Forest style, with pale wood, forest-green tones and stag-embossed cushions. Connecting rooms are available for families. There's a highly regarded, region-focused restaurant (mains €19 to €26) and a lounge warmed by an open fire.

Muggelcaf   CAFE €

(☑ 07444-956 5970; http://muggelcaf.com; Marktstrasse 10; light bites €6.50-13; ⊙11am-10pm Sun-Thu, to 1am Fri & Sat) *Harry Potter* fans might

like the name of this cheery, central cafe-bar, housed in a half-timbered building. Come for light meals including salads, burgers and tarte flambée, and Alpirsbacher Klosterbräu brews.

ⓘ Information

Alpirsbach Tourist Office (☑ 07444-951 6281; www.stadt-alpirsbach.de; Krähenbadstrasse 2; ⊙9-11.30am Mon, Wed & Fri, 2-5.30pm Tue & Thu) The tourist office can supply hiking maps and, for cyclists, information on the 85km Kinzigtalradweg from Offenburg to Lossburg.

Schiltach

☑ 07836 / POP 3803

Sitting snugly at the foot of wooded hills and on the banks of the Kinzig and Schiltach rivers, medieval Schiltach looks too ludicrously pretty to be true. The meticulously restored half-timbered houses, which once belonged to tanners, merchants and raft builders, are a riot of crimson geraniums in summer.

Being at the confluence of the two rivers, logging was big business here until the 19th century and huge rafts were built to ship timber as far as the Netherlands. The willow-fringed banks now attract grey herons and kids who come to splash in the shallow waters when the sun's out.

⊙ Sights

Marktplatz   SQUARE

Centred on a trickling fountain, the sloping, triangular Marktplatz is Schiltach at its picture-book best. The frescoes of its step-gabled 16th-century Rathaus depict scenes from local history.

Schlossbergstrasse   STREET

Clamber south up Schlossbergstrasse, pausing to notice the plaques that denote the trades of one-time residents, such as the *Strumpfstricker* (stocking weaver) at No 6, and the sloping roofs where tanners once dried their skins. Up top there are views over Schiltach's red rooftops.

Museum am Markt   MUSEUM

(Marktplatz 13; ⊙11am-5pm Apr-Oct, Sat & Sun only Nov-Mar) FREE Museum am Markt is crammed with everything from antique spinning wheels to Biedermeier costumes. Highlights include the cobbler's workshop and an interactive display recounting the tale of the devilish Teufel von Schiltach, who, as local lore has it, was responsible for the raging fire that reduced the town to ashes in the 16th century.

(Continued on page 504)

MATT MUNRO/LONELY PLANET ©

MEINZAHN/GETTY IMAGES ©

1. Schwarzwälder Freilichtmuseum Vogtsbauernhof (Black Forest Open Air Museum; p504)

Farmhouses have been painstakingly reconstructed in this self-contained early-17th-century farmstead to create an authentic farming hamlet, complete with reenactors in traditional costumes.

2. Trinkhalle (p490)

Baden Baden's neoclassical pump room features a 90m-long portico embellished with 19th-century frescos.

3. Triberger Wasserfälle (p516)

Germany's highest waterfalls drop a total of 163m over seven tiers.

4. Weltgrösste Kuckucksuhr (p517)

It took clockmaker Joseph Dold three years to build the so-called 'world's oldest-largest cuckoo clock' in Schonach, just outside Triberg.

ANDREY_POPOV/SHUTTERSTOCK ©

(Continued from page 501)

Schüttesäge Museum
MUSEUM

(Hauptstrasse 1; ⊘ 11am-5pm daily Apr-Oct) FREE The riverfront Schüttesäge Museum focuses on Schiltach's rafting tradition with reconstructed workshops, a watermill generating hydroelectric power for many homes in the area and touchy-feely exhibits for kids, from different kinds of bark to forest animals.

🛏 Sleeping & Eating

Adler 1604
BOUTIQUE HOTEL €€

(☑ 07836-957 5800; http://adler1604.com; Hauptstrasse 20; s €90, d €120-130; P 🄿 🛜) Occupying a lovingly converted half-timbered house, dating to (you guessed it!) 1604, this Schiltach newcomer has hit the ground running. In the capable hands of the Meiers, the boutique hotel keeps things intimate with eight newly renovated rooms, featuring perks including Nespresso makers, fresh fruit and honesty bars. Top billing goes to the romantic *Erker* (bay window) rooms.

Zur Alten Brücke
GUESTHOUSE €€

(☑ 07836-2036; www.altebruecke.de; Schramberger Strasse 13; s/d/apt €60/90/110; P 🛜) You'll receive a warm welcome at this riverside guesthouse. The pick of the bright, cheery rooms overlook the Schiltach. Michael cooks up seasonal, regional fare in the kitchen and there's a terrace for summer imbibing.

Weyssses Rössle
GUESTHOUSE €€

(☑ 07836-387; www.weysses-roessle.de; Schenkenzeller Strasse 42; s €62, d €86-98; P 🛜) Rosemarie and Ulrich continue the tradition of 19 generations in this 16th-century inn. Countrified rooms decorated with rosewood and floral fabrics also feature stylish bathrooms and wi-fi. Its restaurant (menus €25 to €42) serves locally sourced, organic fare.

ⓘ Information

Schiltach Tourist Office (☑ 07836-5850; www.schiltach.de; Marktplatz 6; ⊘ 9am-noon & 2-4pm Mon-Thu, 9am-noon Fri) The tourist office in the Rathaus can provide info and free internet access. Local hiking options are marked on an enamel sign just opposite.

Gutach

☑ 07831 / POP 2267

Slumbering at the foot of thickly wooded hills and identified by its rambling hip-roofed, shingle-clad farmhouses ablaze with geraniums in summer, little Gutach is a fine rural escape for hiking, cycling and family

holidays. It's in a side valley that forks south of the Kinzigtal.

One of the village's main claims to fame is that it's the original home of the Bollenhut bonnet.

◉ Sights

★ Vogtsbauernhof
MUSEUM

(Black Forest Open-Air Museum; ☑ 07831-935 60; www.vogtsbauernhof.org; Wählerbrücke 1, Gutach; adult/concession/child/family €10/9/5.50/28; ⊘ 9am-6pm late Mar-early Nov, to 7pm Aug, last entry 1hr before closing) The Schwarzwälder Freilichtmuseum spirals around the Vogtsbauernhof, a self-contained early-17th-century farmstead. Farmhouses shifted from their original locations have been painstakingly reconstructed here, using techniques such as thatching and panelling, to create this authentic farming hamlet and preserve age-old Black Forest traditions. There are free guided tours at 2.30pm daily in German, and at 1pm daily in July and August in English.

Duravit Design Centre
MUSEUM

(www.duravit.de; Werderstrasse 36, Hornberg; ⊘ 8am-6pm Mon-Fri, noon-4pm Sat) FREE If giant cuckoo clocks and Black Forest gateau no longer thrill, how about a trip to the world's largest loo? Drive on the B33 to Hornberg and there, in all its lavatorial glory, stands the titanic toilet dreamed up by designer Philippe Starck. Even if you have no interest in designer urinals or home jacuzzis, the centre's worth visiting for the tremendous view across the Black Forest from the 12m-high ceramic loo. The design centre is 3.5km south of Gutach.

🛏 Sleeping

Zur Mühle
CAMPGROUND €

(☑ 07834-775; www.camping-kirnbach.de; Talstrasse 79, Wolfach/Kirnbach; camping per adult/child/tent €4.90/3.50/7) A chilled spot to pitch a tent, with lovely views over wooded hills, this campground has plenty of shade, a stream where kids can paddle and walking trails heading off into the forest. It's 5.5km east of the Vogtsbauernhof.

Gasthaus zum Hirsch
GUESTHOUSE €

(☑ 07831-228; www.hirsch-gutach.de; Hirschgasse 2; s/d/f €47/69/95) This stout half-timbered house shelters simple pine-clad quarters, which are a little dated but perfectly comfortable. Spacious family rooms are available. The restaurant (mains €15 to €21) plays up Black Forest and Badisch flavours in dishes such as venison goulash with *Spätzle* (egg pasta) and whole-baked trout with almond butter. There's an appealing terrace in summer.

ℹ️ Getting There & Away

Gutach is in the side valley that runs south of the Kinzigtal. The B33 runs through it, linking it to Triberg, 13.5km south.

From nearby Hausach there are regular trains to towns such as Gengenbach (€4.30, 18 minutes) and Triberg (€6.70, 21 minutes).

Haslach

📞 07832 / POP 6934

An enticingly mellow little town with lanes stacked with medieval timber-framed houses, Haslach makes a laid-back base for dipping into the Kinzigtal on foot or by bike. Haslach's 17th-century former Capuchin monastery houses its pride and joy, the **Schwarzwälder Trachtenmuseum** (Black Forest Costume Museum; Klosterstrasse 1; adult/concession €3/2.50; ⊙10am-12.30pm & 1.30-5pm Tue-Sun Apr-Oct, 10am-12.30pm & 1.30-5pm Tue-Fri Nov-Mar), showcasing flamboyant costumes and outrageous hats, the must-have accessories for the well-dressed Fräulein of the 1850s. Look out for the Black Forest Bollenhut, a straw bonnet topped with pom poms (red for unmarried women, black for married) and the Schäppel, a fragile-looking crown made from hundreds of beads and weighing up to 5kg.

Haslach is 18km south of Gengenbach via the B33 or by train (€4.30, 13 minutes). The centrally located Bahnhof is just on the northern edge of the Altstadt.

Gengenbach

📞 07803 / POP 10,941

If ever a Black Forest town could be described as chocolate-box, it would surely be Gengenbach, with its scrumptious Altstadt of half-timbered townhouses framed by vineyards and orchards. It's fitting, then, that director Tim Burton made this the home of gluttonous Augustus Gloop in the 2005 blockbuster *Charlie and the Chocolate Factory* (though less so that he called it Düsseldorf).

👁️ Sights & Activities

Marktplatz SQUARE

Between the town's two tower-topped gates sits the triangular Marktplatz, dominated by the Rathaus, an 18th-century pink-and-cream confection. The fountain bears a statue of a knight, a symbol of Gengenbach's medieval status as a Free Imperial City.

Engelgasse STREET

The best way to discover Gengenbach's historical centre is with a serendipitous mooch through its narrow backstreets, such as the gently curving Engelgasse, off Hauptstrasse, lined with listed half-timbered, shuttered houses draped in vines and bedecked with scarlet geraniums in summer.

Kloster Gengenbach MONASTERY

(Klosterstrasse 4; ⊙dawn to dusk) FREE Amble along Klosterstrasse to check out the former Benedictine monastery. A calm *Kräutergarten* (herb garden), stippled with fragrant and medicinal herbs, can be visited behind its walls.

Weinpfad WALKING

Stop by the tourist office (p506) for info on the hour-long Weinpfad, a wine trail beginning in the Altstadt that threads through terraced vineyards to the Jakobskapelle, a 13th-century hilltop chapel commanding views as far as Strasbourg on clear days.

🎇 Festivals & Events

⭐ **Gengenbach**
Advent Calendar CHRISTMAS

(Rathaus, Marktplatz; ⊙Dec) Every December, Gengenbach rekindles childhood memories of opening tiny windows when the Rathaus morphs into the world's biggest Advent calendar. At 6pm daily, one of 24 windows is opened to reveal a festive scene. Previously, the tableaux have been painted by well-known artists and children's-book illustrators including Marc Chagall, Andy Warhol and Tomi Ungerer.

🛏️ Sleeping & Eating

DJH Hostel HOSTEL €

(📞0781-317 49; www.jugendherberge-schloss-ortenberg.de; Burgweg 21, Ortenberg; dm €22.50-29.50; 🅿🛜) The Hogwarts gang would feel at home in the 12th-century Schloss Ortenberg, rebuilt in whimsical neo-Gothic style complete with lookout tower and wood-panelled dining hall. A staircase sweeps up to dorms with Kinzig Valley views. From Gengenbach station, take bus 7134 or 7160 to Ortenberg, and get off at the 'Schloss/Freudental' stop.

Weinhotel Pfeffer und Salz HOTEL €€

(📞07803-934 80; www.pfefferundsalz-gengenbach.de; Mattenhofweg 3; s/d/tr €60/90/122; 🅿🛜) On a vineyard spreading just north of Gengenbach, Pfeffer und Salz is an appealingly converted Black Forest farmhouse with pretty gardens, views and a playground. The rooms are light, contemporary and decorated in warm colours – and above all supremely peaceful. Wine tastings can be arranged. Half board costs an extra €21.

Stadthotel Pfeffermühle
HOTEL €€

(📞 07803-933 50; www.stadthotel-gengenbach.de; Oberdorfstrasse 24; s/d €60/90; 🅿 🛜) In a snug half-timbered house dating to 1476, close to one of the Altstadt gate towers, this neat-and-tidy hotel is a bargain. Decorated with antique knick-knacks, the wood-panelled restaurant (mains €14 to €22) serves up regional favourites such as Black Forest trout and *Sauerbraten* (pot roast).

★ Die Reichsstadt
BOUTIQUE HOTEL €€€

(📞 07803-966 30; www.die-reichsstadt.de; Engelgasse 33; d €160-194, ste €214-244; 🅿 🛜) This boutique stunner on Engelgasse wings you to story-book heaven. Its 16th-century exterior conceals a pure, contemporary aesthetic, where clean lines, natural materials and subtle cream-caramel shades are enlivened with eye-catching details. A spa, sparkling wine on arrival, free fruit in your room and one of the top restaurants in town complete this pretty picture.

Gasthof Hirsch
GERMAN €€

(📞 07803-3387; www.hirschgengenbach.de; Grabenstrasse 34; mains €18-23.50; ⊙ 8am-2pm & 5-11pm Thu-Mon) This is a warm, woody tavern in the old-school mould, with black-and-white photos on the walls, soft lamplight and cheek-by-jowl tables. The kitchen reels out Badisch and Swabian soul food, from spinach *Knödel* (dumplings) to venison goulash with *Spätzle* (eggy pasta), matched with Pinot and Riesling wines from the region.

Zum Turm
GERMAN €€

(📞 07803-1496; www.zum-turm.de; Hauptstrasse 39; mains €9-15; ⊙ 5pm-midnight Tue-Fri, 11am-1pm Sat, 11am-10pm Sun) Behind a pretty half-timbered facade, Zum Turm attracts a faithful crowd for the great beer on tap and by the bottle (including local Alpirsbacher brews), the warm, woody atmosphere and the menu of straightforward grub – *Flammkuchen* in many guises, steaks, salads and Badisch specialities such as crispy pork knuckles.

ℹ Information

Gengenbach Tourist Office (📞 07803-930 143; www.gengenbach.info; Im Winzerhof; ⊙ 9am-12.30pm & 1.30-5pm Mon-Fri year-round, plus 10am-noon Sat May-Oct & Dec)

The tourist office is in a courtyard just off Hauptstrasse.

ℹ Getting There & Away

Regular trains run from Gengenbach to Kinzigtal towns including Schiltach (€9.50, 35 minutes) as well as other destinations including Offenburg (€2.50, nine minutes), Freiburg (€16.20, one hour) and Villingen-Schwenningen (€17.30, one hour). The Bahnhof is a two-minute walk west of the Altstadt.

Freiburg

✓ 0761 / POP 226,393

Sitting plump at the foot of the Black Forest's wooded slopes and vineyards, Freiburg is a sunny, cheerful university town, its medieval Altstadt a story-book tableau of gabled townhouses, cobblestone lanes and cafe-rimmed plazas. Party-loving students spice up the local nightlife.

Blessed with 2000 hours of annual sunshine, this is Germany's warmest city. Indeed, while neighbouring hilltop villages are still shovelling snow, the trees in Freiburg are clouds of white blossom, and locals are already imbibing in canal-side beer gardens. This eco-trailblazer has shrewdly tapped into that natural energy to generate nearly as much solar power as the whole of Britain, making it one of the country's greenest cities.

◉ Sights

★ Freiburger Münster
CATHEDRAL

(Freiburg Minster; www.freiburgermuenster.info; Münsterplatz; tower adult/concession €2/1.50; ⊙ 10am-5pm Mon-Sat, 1-7pm Sun, tower 9.30am-5pm Mon-Sat, 1-5pm Sun) With its lacy spires, cheeky gargoyles and intricate entrance portal, Freiburg's 11th-century minster cuts an impressive figure above the market square. It has dazzling kaleidoscopic stained-glass windows that were mostly financed by medieval guilds and a high altar with a masterful triptych by Dürer protégé Hans Baldung Grien. Square at the base, the tower becomes an octagon higher up and is crowned by a filigreed 116m-high spire. On clear days you can spy the Vosges Mountains in France.

Closer to the ground, near the main portal in fact, note the medieval wall measurements used to ensure that merchandise (eg loaves of bread) were the requisite size.

Note that the cathedral is closed for visits during services (exact times are available at the info desk inside).

Augustinermuseum
MUSEUM

(☑ 0761-201 2501; www.freiburg.de; Augustinerplatz 1; adult/concession/child €7/5/free; ⊙ 10am-5pm Tue-Thu, Sat & Sun, to 7pm Fri) Dip into the past as represented by artists working from the Middle Ages to the 19th century at this superb museum in a sensitively modernised monastery. The Sculpture Hall on the ground floor is especially impressive for its fine medieval sculptures and masterpieces by Renaissance artists Hans Baldung Grien and Lucas Cranach the Elder. Head upstairs for eye-level views of mounted gargoyles.

Schlossberg
VIEWPOINT

(Schlossbergring; cable car one-way/return €3.30/5.50; ⊙ 9am-10pm daily Mar-Oct, closed Tue Nov-Feb) The forested Schlossberg dominates Freiburg. Take the footpath opposite the Schwabentor, leading up through sun-dappled woods, or hitch a ride on the recently restored *Schlossbergbahn* cable car. For serious hikers, several trails begin here including those to St Peter (17km) and Kandel (25km).

Rathausplatz
SQUARE

(Town Hall Square) Join locals relaxing in a cafe by the fountain in chestnut-shaded Rathausplatz, Freiburg's prettiest square. Pull out your camera to snap pictures of the square's ox-blood-red 16th-century Altes Rathaus (Old Town Hall) that houses the tourist office (p511); the step-gabled 19th-century Neues Rathaus (New Town Hall); and the medieval Martinskirche church with its modern interior.

Schwabentor
GATE

(Schwabenring) The 13th-century Schwabentor, on the Schwabenring, is a massive city gate with a mural of St George slaying the dragon, and tram tracks running under its arches. It's one of two intact medieval gates in Freiburg.

Museum für Stadtgeschichte
MUSEUM

(☑ 0761-201 2515; Münsterplatz 30; adult/concession €3/2; ⊙ 10am-5pm Tue-Sun) The sculptor Christian Wentzinger's baroque townhouse, east of the Historisches Kaufhaus, now shelters this museum, spelling out in artefacts Freiburg's eventful past. Inside, a wrought-iron staircase guides the eye to an elaborate ceiling fresco.

Archäologisches Museum
MUSEUM

(☑ 0761-201 2574; www.freiburg.de; Rotteckring 5; adult/concession €4/3; ⊙ 10am-5pm Tue-Sun) This archaeology-focused museum is inside the neo-Gothic Colombischlössle. From the skylit marble entrance, a cast-iron staircase ascends to a stash of finds from Celtic grave offerings to Roman artefacts and Stone Age statuettes.

Museum für Neue Kunst
GALLERY

(☑ 0761-201 2583; Marienstrasse 10; adult/concession €3/2; ⊙ 10am-5pm Tue-Sun) Across the Gewerbekanal from the Altstadt, this gallery highlights 20th-century Expressionist and abstract art, including emotive works by Oskar Kokoschka and Otto Dix.

Historisches Kaufhaus
HISTORIC BUILDING

(Münsterplatz) Facing the Münster's south side and embellished with polychrome tiled turrets is the arcaded brick-red Historisches Kaufhaus, an early 16th-century merchants' hall. The coats of arms on the oriels and the four figures above the balcony symbolise Freiburg's allegiance to the House of Habsburg.

☞ Tours

Freiburg Kultour
TOURS

(☑ 017 661 266 675; www.freiburg-kultour.com; adult/concession €10/8; ⊙ 2.30-4pm Fri, 10.30am-noon Sat, 11.30am-1pm Sun) Kultour offers 1½-to two-hour walking tours of the Altstadt and the Münster in German and English. Book online or call ahead. The meeting point is on Rathausplatz. A number of self-guided tours are available to download on its website.

🛏 Sleeping

Black Forest Hostel
HOSTEL €

(☑ 0761-881 7870; www.blackforest-hostel.de; Kartäuserstrasse 33; dm €18-28, s/d €44/64, linen €4; ⊙ reception 7am-1am; @) Boho budget digs with chilled common areas, a shared kitchen, bike rental, musical instruments and a ping-pong table. There's no wi-fi but you can check email using the internet terminals. It's a five-minute walk from the town centre.

COLD FEET OR WEDDED BLISS?

As you wander the Altstadt, watch out for the gurgling *Bächle,* streamlets once used to water livestock and extinguish fires. Today they provide welcome relief for hot feet on sweltering summer days. Just be aware that you could get more than you bargained for: legend has it that if you accidentally step into the *Bächle,* you'll marry a Freiburger or a Freiburgerin.

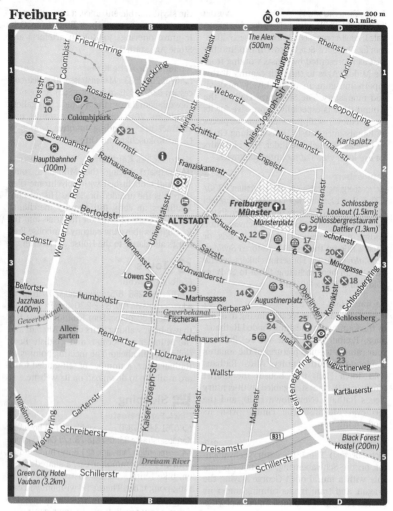

The Alex　　　　　　　　　　BOUTIQUE HOTEL €€
(☏ 0761-296 970; www.the-alex-hotel.de; Rhein-strasse 29; d €94-148; 🅿 ✳ 🕾) The Alex stands head and shoulders above most hotels in town. Its clean, contemporary aesthetic includes lots of plate glass, blonde wood, natural materials and a muted palette of colours. Besides modern rooms with rain showers, there's a bar, Winery29, where you can try locally produced wines.

Green City Hotel Vauban　　　　HOTEL €€
(☏ 0761-888 5740; http://hotel-vauban.de; Paula-Modersohn-Platz 5; d €96-116, apt €150; 🕾) 🍃 This ecofriendly hotel fits in neatly to Freiburg's Vauban neighbourhood, a shining model of sustainability with its PlusEnergy housing and car-free streets. The light, bright rooms are furnished with local woods and plump white bedding. The pick of the doubles have balconies. To reach it, take tram 3 from Freiburg Hauptbahnhof to Freiburg Paula-Modersohn-Platz.

Hotel Barbara　　　　　　　HISTORIC HOTEL €€
(☏ 0761-296 250; www.hotel-barbara.de; Poststrasse 4; s €80-98, d €114-156, apt €139-212; 🕾) A grandfather clock, curvy staircases and high ceilings give this art nouveau townhouse a nostalgic feel. It's a homely, family-run place with

Freiburg

old-fashioned, pastel-hued rooms, homemade jams and eggs to order at breakfast. There's no lift so be prepared to lug your bags.

Hotel Schwarzwälder Hof
HOTEL €€

(☑0761-380 30; www.schwarzwaelder-hof.com; Herrenstrasse 43; s €70-85, d €99-120, f €150-180; 🛜) This bijou hotel has an unrivalled style-for-euro ratio. A wrought-iron staircase sweeps up to stylish rooms furnished in classic, modern or traditional style. Some have postcard views of the Altstadt; others are suitable for families (cots are also available on request). There's also an on-site restaurant.

Hotel am Rathaus
HOTEL €€

(☑0761-296160; www.am-rathaus.de; Rathausgasse 4-8; s €85-105, d €110-173; 🅿🛜) Right in the thick of things on Rathausplatz (p507), this neat hotel has spacious, neutral-toned rooms with homely touches like books and free tea and coffee in the lounge; ask for a rear-facing room if you're a light sleeper.

Hotel Minerva
HOTEL €€

(☑0761-386 490; www.minerva-freiburg.de; Poststrasse 8; s €65-99, d €133-155, tr €180; 🛜) All curvaceous windows and polished wood, this art nouveau charmer is five minutes' trudge from the Altstadt. The sleek, contemporary rooms feature free wi-fi. Breakfast is a generous spread of fresh fruit, cold cuts, pastries, cereals and eggs.

★ Hotel Oberkirch
HISTORIC HOTEL €€€

(☑0761-202 6868; www.hotel-oberkirch.de; Münsterplatz 22; s €119-139, d €159-199; 🅿) Wake up to views of the Münster (p506) at this green-shuttered hotel. The country-style rooms feature floral wallpaper, though some have recently been revamped. The dark-wood downstairs tavern (mains €17 to €25) does a roaring trade in hearty Badisch fare such as venison ragout with *Knödel* (dumplings).

🍴 Eating

Edo's Hummus Küche
VEGETARIAN €

(http://edoshummus.com; Atrium Augustinerplatz; light meals €2.50-8.50; ⊙11.30am-9pm Mon-Sat; 🖉) Edo's pulls in the midday crowds with superb homemade hummus served with warm pitta, as well as lentils, fava bean salad and falafel. The basic hummus plate for €4.90 is a meal in itself.

Vegetage
VEGETARIAN €

(Rathausgasse 4, Bursengalerie; buffet €2.20 per 100g; ⊙11.30am-3pm Mon-Sat; 🖉) For a quick, wholesome vegetarian lunch this buffet takes some beating. The freshly squeezed juices pack a vitamin punch. It's on the 1st floor of a little covered arcade just off central Rathausplatz (p507).

Markthalle
MARKET €

(www.markthalle-freiburg.de; Martinsgasse 235; light meals €4-8; ⊙8am-8pm Mon-Thu, to midnight Fri & Sat) Eat your way around the world – from curry to sushi, oysters to antipasti – at the food counters in this historical market hall, nicknamed 'Fressgässle'.

Gasthaus zum Kranz
GERMAN €€

(☑0761-217 1967; www.gasthauszumkranz.de; Herrenstrasse 40; mains €15-26; ⊙11.30am-3pm Mon,

DON'T MISS

EUROPE IN MINIATURE

Germany's largest theme park, **Europa-Park** (www.europapark.de; Europa-Park-Strasse 2, Rust; adult/concession €49.50/42.50; ⊙ 9am-6pm Apr-early Nov, to 8pm Aug–mid-Sep, 11am-7pm late Nov-early Jan), located 35km north of Freiburg near Rust, is Europe in miniature. Get soaked fjord-rafting in Scandinavia before nipping across to England to race at Silverstone, or Greece to ride the water roller coaster Poseidon. Aside from white-knuckle thrills, the park's Children's World amuses tots with labyrinths and Viking ships.

When Mickey waltzed off to Paris, Europa-Park even got its own mousy mascot, Euromaus.

Shuttle buses (hourly in the morning) link Ringsheim train station, on the Freiburg–Offenburg line, with the park. By car, take the A5 exit to Rust (57b).

11.30am-3pm & 5.30pm-midnight Tue-Sat, noon-3pm & 5.30pm-midnight Sun) There's always a good buzz at this rustic, quintessentially Badisch tavern. Pull up a hefty chair at one of the even heftier timber tables for well-prepared regional favourites such as roast suckling pig, *Maultaschen* (pork and spinach ravioli) and *Sauerbraten* (beef pot roast with vinegar, onions and peppercorns). Service can be hit-and-miss.

Englers Weinkrügle   GERMAN €€
(✆ 0761-383 115; Konviktstrasse 12; mains €9-19; ⊙ 11.30am-2pm & 5.30pm-midnight Tue-Sun) A warm, woody Baden-style *Weinstube* (wine tavern) with wisteria growing out front and regional flavours on the menu. The trout in various guises (for instance, with Riesling or almond butter sauce) is delicious.

Martin's Bräu   PUB FOOD €€
(✆ 0761-387 000; www.martinsbräu-freiburg.de; Martinsgässle; mains €9-18; ⊙ 11am-midnight Sun-Thu, to 1am Fri & Sat) Home-brewed pilsners and craft beers wash down meaty snacks from ox-tongue salad to suckling pig and enormous bratwursts. Copper vats gleam in the wood-panelled interior. You'll find it off Kaiser-Joseph-Strasse.

Enoteca Trattoria   ITALIAN €€
(✆ 0761-389 9130; www.enoteca-freiburg.de; Schwabentorplatz 6; mains €16-30; ⊙ 6pm-midnight Mon-Sat) This is the trattoria of the two Enoteca twins (the more formal restaurant is at Gerberau 21). The chef here always hits the mark with authentic Italian dishes such as *taleggio* ravioli with Frascati sauce and glazed pear.

★**Kreuzblume**   INTERNATIONAL €€€
(✆ 0761-311 94; www.hotel-kreuzblume.de; Konviktstrasse 31; mains €18-32, 3-course menu €42.50; ⊙ 6-11pm Wed-Sun; ✐) Situated on a flower-festooned lane, Kreuzblume is a pocket-sized restaurant with clever backlighting, slick monochrome decor and a menu fizzing with bright, sunny flavours. It attracts a rather food-literate clientele. Each dish combines just a few hand-picked ingredients in bold and tasty ways: apple, celery and chestnut soup, say, or roast duck breast with wild herb salad. Service is top notch.

★**Wolfshöhle**   MEDITERRANEAN €€€
(✆ 0761-303 03; www.wolfshoehle-freiburg.de; Konviktstrasse 8; mains €23-49, 3-course lunch/dinner €35/63; ⊙ noon-2pm & 6-9.30pm Tue-Sat) With tables set up on a pretty square, Wolfshöhle is a summer-evening magnet. The menu whisks you off on a gastronomical tour of the Mediterranean, with well-executed, beautifully presented dishes listed in the modern, ingredient-driven way: Jerusalem artichoke with black truffle and hazelnut, for instance, or sea bass with saffron and clams. The €35, three-course lunch offers a good introduction.

Zirbelstube   GASTRONOMY €€€
(✆ 0761-210 60; www.colombi.de; Rotteckring 16; mains €34-48; ⊙ noon-2pm & 7pm-midnight Tue-Sat) Freiburg's bastion of fine dining is this Michelin-starred restaurant, decorated in warm Swiss pine. Chefs of exacting standards allow each ingredient to shine in specialities such as glazed rack of venison with caramelised pineapple, and cod confit with cauliflower cooked three ways – all perfectly matched with quality wines.

Schlossbergrestaurant Dattler   GERMAN €€€
(✆ 0761-137 1700; http://dattler.de; Am Schlossberg 1; mains €20-34; ⊙ 9.15am-11pm Wed-Sun; ✐) For special occasions, this refined restaurant atop the Schlossberg (p507) has panoramic windows affording compelling surround views of Freiburg's spire-studded cityscape. The food is pretty impressive, with the chef keeping things regional in dishes

such as *Badisches Rahmtöpfle* (pork medallions with mushrooms and homemade *Spätzle*). There's plenty to appeal to vegetarians and vegans.

Drinking & Entertainment

Schlappen
PUB

(www.schlappen.com; Löwenstrasse 2; ☺11am-1am Mon-Wed, to 2am Thu, to 3am Fri & Sat, 3pm-1am Sun) In historical digs and crammed with antiques and vintage theatre posters, this rocking, friendly boozer has made the magic happen for generations of students. The drinks – a good array of beers, gins, absinthes and whiskies – are affordable and the terrace heaves in summer.

Alte Wache
WINE BAR

(www.alte-wache.com; Münsterplatz 38; ☺10am-7pm Mon-Fri, to 4pm Sat) Right on the square, this 18th-century guardhouse serves local Müller-Thurgau and Pinot Noir wines at the tasting tables. See the website for details of the regular food and wine events.

Hausbrauerei Feierling
MICROBREWERY

(www.feierling.de; Gerberau 46; ☺11am-midnight Sun-Thu, 11am-1am Fri & Sat) This stream-side microbrewery and beer garden is a relaxed spot to quaff a cold one under the chestnut trees in summer or next to the copper vats in winter. Snacks including pretzels and sausages (snacks €3 to €9.50) soak up the malty, organic brews.

Greiffenegg-Schlössle
BEER GARDEN

(Schlossbergring 3; ☺11am-midnight Mar-Oct) All of Freiburg is at your feet from this chestnut-shaded beer garden atop Schlossberg (p507). Perfect sunset spot.

Juri's
COCKTAIL BAR

(www.juris-bar.de; Schwabentorplatz 7; ☺6pm-2am Wed-Sat & Mon) What a find this mulberry-hued wine and cocktail bar is, with its cushion-strewn nooks and candlelit tables. It does a head-spinning range of wines and cocktails from gin basil smashes (gin, basil, sugar and lemon) to Sloppy Joe mojitos made with mint rum.

Jazzhaus
LIVE MUSIC

(☎0761-349 73; www.jazzhaus.de; Schnewlinstrasse 1) Under the brick arches of a wine cellar, this venue hosts first-rate jazz, rock and world music concerts at least a couple of nights a week (see the website for details). It morphs into a club from 11pm to 3am on Friday and Saturday nights.

ℹ Information

Available at the tourist office, the three-day **WelcomeKarte**, covering all public transport and the **Schauinslandbahn** (www.schauinslandbahn.de; Schauinslandstrasse, Oberried; return adult/child €12.50/8, one-way €9/6; ☺9am-5pm Oct-Jun, to 6pm Jul-Sep) cable car, costs €26/16 per adult/child.

Freiburg Tourist Office (☎0761-388 1880; www.visit.freiburg.de; Rathausplatz 2-4; ☺8am-8pm Mon-Fri, 9.30am-5pm Sat, 10.30am-3.30pm Sun Jun-Sep, 8am-6pm Mon-Fri, 9.30am-2.30pm Sat, 10am-noon Sun Oct-May) Pick up the three-day WelcomeKarte (€26).

Post Office (Eisenbahnstrasse 58-62; ☺8.30am-6.30pm Mon-Fri, 9am-2pm Sat)

ℹ Getting There & Around

AIR

Freiburg shares **EuroAirport** (BSL; ☎France +33 3 89 90 31 11; www.euroairport.com) with Basel (Switzerland) and Mulhouse (France); get there on the airport bus. The airport is 71km south of Freiburg via the A5 motorway. Low-cost airline easyJet and Ryanair fly from here.

BICYCLE

Bike paths run along the Dreisam River, leading westward to Breisach and then into France. **Freiburg Bikes** (☎0761-202 3426; www.freiburgbikes.de; Wentzingerstrasse 15; city bike 4hr/day €10/15, mountain/e-bike per day €22/30; ☺9.30am-1pm & 2-7pm Mon-Sat, 10am-1pm & 2-6pm Sun Jun-Sep, reduced hours rest of year), across the bridge from the Hauptbahnhof, rents bikes and sells cycling maps.

BUS

The **airport bus** (☎0761-500 500; www.freiburger-reisedienst.de; one-way/return €19.90/39) goes hourly from Freiburg's bus station to **EuroAirport**. The journey takes roughly an hour.

Südbaden Bus (www.suedbadenbus.de) and RVF (www.rvf.de) operate bus and train links to towns and villages throughout the southern Black Forest. Single tickets for one/two/three zones cost €2.30/4/5.70; a 24-hour Regio24 ticket costs €5.80 for one person and €8.20 for two to five people. Buses depart from the Hauptbahnhof.

TRAIN

Freiburg is on a major north–south rail corridor, with frequent departures from the **Hauptbahnhof** for destinations such as Basel (€19.10 to €26.60, 45 minutes) and Baden-Baden (€23.70 to €40, 45 minutes to 1½ hours). There's a local connection to Breisach (€5.70, 26 minutes, at least hourly).

STUTTGART & THE BLACK FOREST FREIBURG

Schauinsland

One of the best vantage points in the Black Forest, with soul-stirring views reaching over forest, valley and to the Alps beyond on cloud-free days, the 1284m **peak** (www.bergwelt-schauinsland.de) of Schauinsland is an easy day trip from Freiburg, a mere cable car (p511) ride away. Up top, walking trails are plentiful and morph into cross-country ski tracks in winter. The peak is topped by a lookout tower commanding fabulous views to the Rhine Valley and Alps, plus walking, cross-country and cycling trails that allow you to capture the scenery from many angles. You can bounce downhill from Schauinsland on the 8km off-road **scooter track** (www.rollerstrecke.de; Schauinsland Peak; €25; ⊙ 2pm & 5pm Sun May-Jun, Sat & Sun Jul, Sep & Oct, Wed-Sun Aug), one of Europe's longest; it takes around an hour from top to bottom station.

On a quiet perch above the rippling hills of the Black Forest, **Die Halde** (☑ 07602-944 70; www.halde.com; Oberried-Hofsgrund; d incl full board €280-304; P @ 🖼) is a rustic-chic retreat, with an open fire crackling in the bar, calm rooms dressed in local wood and a glass-walled spa overlooking the valley. Martin Hegar cooks market-fresh dishes from trout to wild boar with panache in the wood-panelled restaurant (mains €24-35).

St Peter

☑ 07660 / POP 2583

As if cupped in celestial hands, the twin-spired baroque abbey church of St Peter thrusts up above meadows and hills plaited with dark-green spruce forest and interwoven with hiking trails.

In this serene, back-to-nature village on the southern slopes of Mt Kandel (1243m), folk are deeply committed to time-honoured traditions. On religious holidays, villagers from toddlers to pensioners still proudly don colourful, handmade *Trachten* (folkloric costumes).

The town's most outstanding landmark is this former **Benedictine abbey** (Klosterhof 11; guided tours adult/concession €6/2; ⊙ tours 11.30am Sun, 11am Tue, 2.30pm Thu), a rococo jewel designed by Peter Thumb of Vorarlberg. Many of the period's top artists collaborated on the sumptuous interior of the twin-towered red-sandstone church, including Joseph Anton Feuchtmayer, who

carved the gilded Zähringer duke statues affixed to pillars. Guided tours (in German) to the monastery complex include the rococo library.

The **tourist office** (☑ 07652-120 60; www.hochschwarzwald.de; Klosterhof 11; ⊙ 9am-noon & 3-5pm Mon-Fri; 🕿) is under the archway leading to the Klosterhof (the abbey courtyard). A nearby information panel shows room availability.

St Peter is on the Schwarzwald Panoramastrasse, a 70km-long route from Waldkirch (17km northeast of Freiburg) to Feldberg with giddy mountain views.

By public transport, the best way to get from Freiburg to St Peter is to take the train to Kirchzarten (13 minutes, twice hourly) and then bus 7216 (23 minutes, twice hourly). Local public transport is free with the KONUS guest card.

Breisach

☑ 07667 / POP 15,500

Rising above vineyards and the Rhine, Breisach is where the Black Forest spills into Alsace. Given its geographical and cultural proximity to France, it's little surprise that the locals share their neighbours' passion for a good bottle of plonk.

From the cobbled streets lined with pastel-painted houses you'd never guess that 85% of the town was flattened in WWII, so successful has been the reconstruction.

◉ Sights & Activities

St Stephansmünster   CHURCH
(Münsterplatz; ⊙ 9am-5pm Mon-Sat) **FREE**
Plonked on a hill above the centre for all to behold in wonder, the Romanesque and Gothic St Stephansmünster shelters a faded fresco cycle, Martin Schongauer's *The Last Judgment* (1491), and a magnificent altar triptych (1526) carved from linden wood. From the tree-shaded square outside, the Schänzletreppe steps lead down to the Gutgesellentor, the gate where Pope John XXIII was scandalously caught fleeing the Council of Constance in 1415.

Neuf-Brisach   FORTRESS
Vauban's French fortified town of Neuf-Brisach (New Breisach), a Unesco World Heritage Site, sits 4km west of Breisach. Shaped like an eight-pointed star, the town was commissioned by Louis XIV in 1697 to strengthen French defences and prevent

the area from falling to the Habsburgs. It was conceived by Sébastien Le Prestre de Vauban (1633–1707). Take bus 1076 from Breisach station to get here.

BFS BOATING
(www.bfs-info.de; Rheinuferstrasse; ☉Apr-Sep) Boat excursions along the Rhine are run by BFS. A one-hour harbour tour costs €12.

🛏 Sleeping

DJH Hostel HOSTEL €
(☑07667-7665; www.jugendherberge-breisach. de; Rheinuferstrasse 12; dm €23.90-30.40; P🖥) On the banks of the Rhine, this hostel has first-rate facilities, including a barbecue hut, volleyball court and access to the swimming pool next door.

ℹ Information

Breisach Tourist Office (☑07667-940 155; http://tourismus.breisach.de; Marktplatz 16; ☉9am-12.30pm & 1.30-6pm Mon-Fri, 10am-3pm Sat) The tourist office can advise on wine tasting and private rooms in the area.

ℹ Getting There & Around

Breisach's train station, 500m southeast of Marktplatz, serves Freiburg (€5.70, 26 minutes, at least hourly) and towns in the Kaiserstuhl. Buses go to Colmar, 22km west.

Breisach is a terrific base for free-wheeling over borders. Great rides include crossing the Rhine to the delightful French town of Colmar, or pedalling through terraced vineyards to Freiburg. Hire an e-bike from the centrally located **Fahrradverleih Breisach** (☑07667-287 1183; http://fahrrad verleih-breisach.de; Fischerhalde 5a; per half-/full day €25/30; ☉10am-2pm & 5-7pm Mon-Sat).

Feldberg

☑07655, 07676, 07652 / POP 1880
At 1493m, Feldberg is the Black Forest's highest mountain, and one of the few places here with downhill skiing. The actual mountaintop is treeless and not particularly attractive but on clear days the view southward towards the Alps is mesmerising.

Feldberg is also the name given to a cluster of five villages, of which Altglashütten is the hub.

Feldberg-Ort is around 9km west of Altglashütten, right in the heart of the 42-sq-km nature reserve that covers much of the mountain. Most of the ski lifts are here, including the scenic *Feldbergbahn* chairlift to the Bismarckdenkmal (Bismarck monument).

◉ Sights & Activities

Todtnauer Wasserfall WATERFALL
(Todtnau; adult/concession €2/1; ☉daylight hours) Head south on the Freiburg–Feldberg road and you'll glimpse the roaring Todtnauer Wasserfall. While the 97m falls are not as high as those in Triberg (p516), they're every bit as spectacular, tumbling down sheer rock faces and illuminating the velvety hills with their brilliance. Hike the zigzagging 9km trail to Aftersteg for views over the cataract. Take care on paths in winter when the falls often freeze solid. The waterfall's car park is on the L126.

Feldbergbahn CABLE CAR
(www.feldbergbahn.de; Dr-Pilet-Spur 17; adult/concession return €9.50/6.60; ☉9am-5pm Jul-Sep, to 4.30pm May, Jun & Oct) A cable car whisks you to the 1493m summit of Feldberg in minutes. The panorama unfolding at the top reaches across the patchwork meadows and woods of the Black Forest all the way to the Vosges and Swiss and French Alps on clear days.

Feldberg–Steig HIKING
Orbiting the Black Forest's highest peak, the 1493m Feldberg, this 12km walk traverses a nature reserve that's home to chamois and wildflowers. On clear days, the views of the Alps are glorious. It's possible to snowshoe part of this route in winter.

Haus der Natur HIKING
(☑07676-933 630; www.naturpark-suedschwarz wald.de; Dr-Pilet-Spur 4; ☉10am-5pm) The eco-conscious Haus der Natur can advise on the area's great hiking opportunities, including the rewarding 12km Feldberg–Steig to the Feldberg summit. In winter, Feldberg's snowy heights are ideal for a stomp through twinkling woods. Strap on snowshoes for the 3km Seebuck-Trail or more challenging 9km Gipfel-Trail. The Haus der Natur rents snowshoes for €10/5 per day for adults/children.

🛏 Sleeping & Eating

Naturfreundehaus HOSTEL €
(☑07676-336; www.naturfreundehaus-feldberg. de; Am Baldenweger Buck; dm €15.50) 🌿 In a Black Forest farmhouse a 30-minute walk from Feldberg's summit, this back-to-nature hostel uses renewable energy and serves fair-trade and organic produce at breakfast (€6). Surrounding views of wooded hills and comfy, pine-clad dorms make this a great spot for hiking in summer, and skiing and snowshoeing in winter.

KAISERSTUHL

Squeezed between the Black Forest and the French Vosges, the low-lying volcanic hills of the Kaiserstuhl in the Upper Rhine Valley yield highly quaffable wines, including fruity *Spätburgunder* (Pinot Noir) and *Grauburgunder* (Pinot gris) varieties.

The grapes owe their quality to a unique microclimate, hailed as Germany's sunniest, and fertile loess (clay and silt) soil that retains heat during the night. Nature enthusiasts should look out for rarities including sand lizards, praying mantis and European bee-eaters.

The Breisach tourist office (p513) can advise on cellar tours, wine tastings, bike paths such as the 55km Kaiserstuhl-Tour circuit, and trails such as the Winzerweg (Wine Growers' Trail), an intoxicating 15km hike from Achkarren to Riegel.

The *Kaiserstuhlbahn* does a loop around the Kaiserstuhl. Stops (where you may have to change trains) include Sasbach, Endingen, Riegel and Gottenheim. The area is 15km northeast of Breisach.

Landhotel Bierhäusle   GUESTHOUSE €€

(07655-306; www.bierhaeusle-feldberg.de; Ortsstrasse 22, Feldberg-Falkau; d €99-120, tr €118-138; P🐾📶👶) A winner for families, this enticing chalet-style guesthouse has dreamy views over forested hills, and immaculate country-style rooms done out in florals and pine. The best open onto balconies. For kids, there are games, a playground, trampoline and animals (goats, rabbits and guinea pigs) to pet. Breakfast is a good spread of bread, cold cuts, homemade jam, eggs and fruit.

Schwarzwaldhaus   GERMAN €€

(07655-933 833; www.das-schwarzwaldhaus.com; Falkauer Strasse 3, Feldberg-Altglashütten; mains €11-21, 2-course lunch €10.90; ⊙11am-3pm & 6-10pm Fri-Tue, 6-10pm Thu; 🐾👶) With dark wood panelling, low beams, banquette seating and a *Kachelofen* (ceramic tiled oven), the Schwarzwaldhaus is a rustic tavern in the traditional Black Forest mould. Mains swing from perfectly crisp schnitzel to venison goulash with bread dumplings, with half portions and specials for kids and vegetarians available.

ℹ Information

Feldberg Tourist Office (07652-120 60; Kirchgasse 1, Altglashütten; ⊙9am-noon & 1-5pm Mon-Fri; 📶) Altglashütten's Rathaus harbours the tourist office, with stacks of info on activities, plus rucksacks, pushchairs and GPS devices for hire from €2 to €5 per day.

ℹ Getting There & Away

Bärental and Altglashütten are stops on the *Dreiseenbahn*, linking Titisee with Seebrugg (Schluchsee). From the train station in Bärental, bus 7300 makes trips at least hourly to Feldberg-Ort (€2.25, 21 minutes).

From late December until the end of the season, shuttle buses run by Feldberg SBG link Feldberg and Titisee with the ski lifts (free with a lift ticket or Gästekarte).

Titisee-Neustadt

07651 / POP 12,083

Titisee is a cheerful summertime playground with a name that makes English-speaking travellers giggle. The iridescent blue-green glacial lake, rimmed by forest, has everyone diving for their cameras or into the ice-cool water. Though a tad on the touristy side in the peak months, a quick stroll along these shores brings you to quiet bays and woodland trails that are blissfully crowd-free.

🏃 Activities

Seepromenade   WALKING, WATER SPORTS

Wander along the flowery Seestrasse promenade and you'll soon leave the crowds and made-in-China cuckoo clocks behind to find secluded bays ideal for swimming and picnicking. A lap of the lake is 7km. Hire a rowing boat or pedalo at one of the set-ups along the lake front; expect to pay around €12 per hour.

Strandbad Titisee   SWIMMING

(Strandbadstrasse 1; ⊙9am-7pm Jun-Sep) FREE This lake-front lido has a pool and children's pool, a slide, floating raft and a volleyball area, as well as lawns for sunbathing. Action Forest rents kayaks and stand-up paddle boards here for €10/18 per half/full hour.

Badeparadies   SPA

(www.badeparadies-schwarzwald.de; Am Badeparadies 1; 3hr €20, incl sauna complex €24; ⊙10am-10pm Mon-Thu, to 11pm Fri, 9am-10pm Sat & Sun) This huge, glass-canopied leisure and wellness centre is a year-round draw. You can lounge, cocktail in hand, by palm-fringed lagoons in Palmenoase, race down white-knuckle slides with gaggles of overexcited kids in Galaxy, or strip off in themed saunas with waterfalls and Black Forest views in the adults-only Wellnessoase.

Bootsvermietung Titisee
BOATING

(www.boote-titisee.de; Seestrasse 37; €26/49 per half-hour/hour) For a novel way to paddle across the lake, rent one of the so-called 'donuts', giant rings with space for the whole family. It also rents out electric boats.

Sleeping & Eating

Neubierhäusle
PENSION €€

(☑ 07651-8230; www.neubierhaeusle.de; Neustädter Strasse 79; d €85-95, apt €148-178; P ❂) Big forest views, piny air and pastures on the doorstep – this farmhouse is the perfect country retreat. Dressed in local wood, the light-filled rooms are supremely comfy, while apartments have space for families. Your hosts lay on a hearty breakfast (included in the room rate), and you can help yourself to free tea and fruit throughout the day.

Action Forest Active Hotel
GUESTHOUSE €€

(☑ 07651-825 60; www.action-forest-hotel.de; Neustädter Strasse 41; s €55-60, d €100-110, tr €120-140, q €140-170; P ❂) You can't miss this green-fronted guesthouse, snuggled up against the forest. It's run by a friendly family and contains spacious, light-filled rooms (including generously sized triples and quads for families), fitted out with country-style pine furnishings.

Bergseeblick
PENSION €€

(☑ 07675-929 4440; https://bergseeblick.com; Erlenweg 3; s €40, d €75-95, tr €95, f €125; P ❂) But a two-minute stroll from the shores of Titisee, this family-friendly guesthouse has recently modernised rooms – some big enough for families – done out in neutral colours and chunky pine furnishings. The lounge with complimentary drinks and snacks is a nice touch, and the generous breakfast includes fresh rolls, pastries, fruit, cold cuts and cooked options.

Hotel Bären
HOTEL €€€

(☑ 07651-8060; www.baeren-titisee.de; Neustädter Strasse 35; d €182-252; P ❂ ☲) Run by the welcoming Sauter family, this streamlined hotel fuses contemporary living with traditional local materials (note the wood shingling on the facade). The bright, spacious rooms have warm tones and ultramodern bathrooms, and open onto balconies with fine Black Forest views. There's an impressive spa area with an indoor pool, sauna and steam room and barefoot path.

Villinger Feinkost
DELI €

(☑ 07651-1401; www.feinkost-villinger.de; Hauptstrasse 6, Neustadt; lunch €9.50-14; ⊙ 7.30am-9pm Mon-Wed, to 10.30pm Thu-Sat) Market-fresh food prepared in creative ways, local sourcing and a nicely chilled setting make this upbeat bistro and deli one of the best picks in town. Lunch specials swing from brook trout with polenta to *Käsespätzle* (cheese-topped noodles) and beef bourguignon – all tasty and cracking value.

ℹ Information

Titisee-Neustadt Tourist Office (☑ 07652-120 60; www.hochschwarzwald.de; Strandbadstrasse 4; ⊙ 9am-5pm Mon-Fri; ❂) The tourist office stocks walking and cycling maps, and has pushchairs and backpacks available to hire (€3 to €5). Free wi-fi.

ℹ Getting There & Around

While the *Höllentalbahn* undergoes extensive restoration work in 2018, there is a restricted train service. From Titisee train station, there are frequent services on bus 7257 to Schluchsee (40 minutes) and bus 7300 to Feldberg–Bärental (13 minutes). The train station in Titisee is just 200m north of the lake.

Local public transport is free with the KONUS guest card.

Ski-Hirt (☑ 07651-922 80; Titiseestrasse 28, Neustadt; ⊙ 9am-6.30pm Mon-Fri, to 4pm Sat) rents reliable bikes and ski equipment, and can supply details on local cycling options.

Schluchsee

☑ 07656 / POP 2440

Photogenically poised above its namesake lake – the Black Forest's largest – and rimmed by forest, Schluchsee tempts you outdoors with pursuits such as swimming, windsurfing, hiking, cycling and, ahem, skinny-dipping from the secluded bays on the western shore. The otherwise sleepy resort jolts to life with sunseekers in summer and cross-country skiers in winter.

🏃 Activities & Tours

Wutachschlucht
HIKING

(www.wutachschlucht.de) This wild gorge, carved out by a fast-flowing river and flanked by near-vertical rock faces, lies near Bonndorf, close to the Swiss border and 20km east of Schluchsee. The best way to experience its unique microclimate, where you might spot orchids, ferns, rare butterflies and lizards, is on this 13km trail leading from Schattenmühle to Wutachmühle.

Aqua Fun Strandbad SWIMMING
(Freiburger Strasse 16; adult/concession €4/2.70; ⊙9am-7pm May-Sep) Popular with families, this lake-front lido has a heated pool, water slide and rapid river, a sandy beach and a volleyball court.

MS Schluchsee BOATING
(www.seerundfahrten.de; Freiburger Strasse; ⊙10.30am-4.45pm late Apr-Oct) Boat tours around Schluchsee make stops in Aha, Seebrugg and the Strandbad. A 75-minute round trip costs €10/5 for adults/children. You can hire rowing boats and pedalos for €6/10 per half/full hour.

🛏 Sleeping & Eating

Gasthof Hirschen GUESTHOUSE €€
(☑07656-989 40; www.hirschen-fischbach.de; Schluchseestrasse 9, Fischbach; s €65-70, d €136; 🅿🛈) It's worth going the extra mile to this farmhouse, prettily perched on a hillside in Fischbach, 4km north of Schluchsee. The simple, quiet rooms are a good-value base for summer hiking and modest winter skiing. There's also a sauna, playground and a restaurant (mains €13 to €21) dishing up regional fare.

Heger's Parkhotel Flora SPA HOTEL €€€
(☑07656-974 20; www.parkhotel-flora.de; Sonnhalde 22; s €160 d €240-256, ste €266-342; 🅿🛈🏊) This luxe spa hotel has beautiful views of the wooded hills from its gardens and outdoor pool, a lounge warmed by an open fire and modern, generously sized rooms. After a day's hiking in the hills, the spa area, with its salt inhalation room and anti-ageing vinotherapy treatments is just the ticket. There's also a refined restaurant.

Parkhotel Flora EUROPEAN €€
(☑07656-974 20; www.parkhotel-flora.de; mains €18.50-32.50; ⊙6-9.30pm Mon-Fri, noon-1.30pm & 6-9.30pm Sat & Sun; 🍴) At the hotel of the same name, this elegant restaurant majors in well-executed regional and international dishes, from Black Forest trout in almond butter to rabbit ragout with Pinot blanc. These are married with Kaiserstuhl wines from the family vineyard. In summer, try to wangle a table

on the garden terrace. The menu caters for allergies and vegetarians.

Seehof INTERNATIONAL €€
(☑07656-988 9965; http://seehof-schluchsee.de; Kirchsteige 4; mains €14.50-27; ⊙11.30am-10.30pm) Seehof is an inviting spot for a bite to eat, with a terrace overlooking the lake. Its menu is packed with local fish and meat mains, salads, pizzas and ice cream.

🛈 Information

Schluchsee Tourist Office (☑07652-120 60; www.schluchsee.de; Fischbacher Strasse 7, Haus des Gastes; ⊙9am-4pm Mon-Fri) Schluchsee's tourist office hands out maps and has info on activities and accommodation.

🛈 Getting There & Around

Bus 913 runs regularly to Feldberg–Altglashütten (10 minutes) and Titisee (29 minutes). Bus 7257 links Schluchsee three or four times daily with the Neustadt and Titisee train stations (40 minutes). Local public transport is free with the KONUS guest card.

City, mountain and e-bikes can be rented for €13/14/25 per day at **Müllers** (www.staumauer-schluchsee.de; An der Staumauer 1; ⊙10am-6pm Apr-Oct). An hour's pedalo/rowing boat/motor boat hire costs €8/8/17.

Triberg

☑07722 / POP 4787

Home to Germany's highest waterfall, heir to the original 1915 Black Forest gateau recipe, and nesting ground of the world's biggest cuckoos, Triberg leaves visitors reeling with superlatives. It was here that in bleak winters past folk huddled in snowbound farmhouses to carve the clocks that would drive the world cuckoo, and here that in a flash of brilliance the waterfall was harnessed to power the country's first electric street lamps in 1884.

◎ Sights & Activities

★ **Triberger Wasserfälle** WATERFALL
(adult/concession €5/4.50) Niagara they ain't but Germany's highest waterfalls do exude their own wild romanticism. The Gutach River feeds the seven-tiered falls, which drop a total of 163m and are illuminated until 10pm. A paved trail accesses the cascades. Pick up a bag of peanuts at the ticket counter to feed the tribes of inquisitive red squirrels. Entry is cheaper in winter. The falls are located in central Triberg.

Stöcklewaldturm TOWER
(www.stoecklewaldturm.de; admission €0.50; ⊙10am-8pm Wed-Sun May-Sep, 11am-7pm Wed-Sun Oct-Apr) A steady and attractive 6.5km walk through spruce forest and pastures from Triberg's waterfall brings you to this 1070m-high 19th-century lookout tower, where the 360° views stretch from the Swabian Alps to the snowcapped Alps. The car park on the L175 is a 10-minute stroll from the tower. Footpaths head off in all directions from the summit, one of which leads to a woodsy cafe (snacks €2.50-7).

Eble Uhren–Park LANDMARK
(www.uhren-park.de; Schonachbach 27; adult/child €2/free; ⊙9am-6pm Mon-Sat, 10am-6pm Sun) The *Guinness World Records*–listed world's largest cuckoo clock occupies an entire house, but is mostly a gimmick to lure shoppers inside a large clock shop. It's still interesting to get a glimpse of its supersized mechanism and hear the call of the whopping 4.5m cuckoo.

Haus der 1000 Uhren MUSEUM
(House of 1000 Clocks; ☑07722-963 00; www.hausder1000uhren.de; Hauptstrasse 79; ⊙9.30am-6pm May-Sep, 10am-5pm Oct-Apr) A glockenspiel bashes out melodies and a cuckoo greets his fans with a hopelessly croaky squawk on the hour at the kitschy House of 1000 Clocks, a wonderland of clocks from traditional to trendy. The latest quartz models feature a sensor that sends the cuckoo to sleep after dark!

Weltgrösste Kuckucksuhr LANDMARK
(First World's Largest Cuckoo Clock; www.dold-urlaub.de; Untertalstrasse 28, Schonach; adult/child €2/1; ⊙10am-noon & 1-5pm Tue-Sun) A rival to the hotly contested giant-cuckoo-clock crown, the so-called 'world's oldest-largest cuckoo clock' kicked into gear in 1980 and took local clockmaker Joseph Dold three years to build by hand. A Dold family member is usually around to explain the mechanism.

Gütenbach-Simonswäldertal HIKING
Gütenbach, 22km south of Triberg, is the trailhead for one of the Black Forest's most beautiful half-day hikes. It leads to Simonswäldertal, 13km distant. A forest trail threads to Balzer Herrgott, where a tree has grown into a sandstone figure of Christ. Walking downhill from here to Simonswälder Valley, fir-draped hills rise like a curtain before you.

Sanitas Spa SPA
(☑07722-860 20; www.sanitas-spa.de; Gartenstrasse 24; 2hr pass €15, half day €26-30, full day €45-50; ⊙10am-10pm) Fronted by wraparound windows overlooking Triberg's forested hills, Parkhotel Wehrle's day spa is gorgeous. This is a serene spot to wind down in, with its spacily lit kidney-shaped pool, exquisitely tiled hammams, steam rooms, whirlpool and waterbed meditation room. Treatments vary from *rhassoul* clay wraps to reiki. Admission is cheaper on weekdays. Towel and robe hire is available for €8.

🍴 Sleeping & Eating

Gasthaus Staude GUESTHOUSE €€
(☑07722-4802; http://gasthaus-staude.com; Obertal 20, Triberg-Gremmelsbach; s €55, d €86-104; ⓟ🛜) A beautiful example of a 17th-century Black Forest farmhouse, with its hip roof, snug timber-clad interior and wonderfully rural setting in the forest, Gasthaus Staude is worth going the extra mile for. The rooms are silent and countrified, with chunky wood furnishings – the most romantic one has a four-poster bed. It's a 15-minute drive east of town on the B500.

Parkhotel Wehrle HISTORIC HOTEL €€€
(☑07722-860 20; www.parkhotel-wehrle.de; Gartenstrasse 24; s €95-115, d €159-265; ⓟ🛜🏊) Standing proud on Triberg's main drag for the past 400 years, this historical hotel has quarters with a baroque or Biedermeier touch, some beautifully furnished with antiques and the best with Duravit whirlpool tubs. The hotel's restaurant is highly regarded. Guests have entry to the fabulous Sanitas Spa.

★Café Schäfer CAFE €
(☑07722-4465; www.cafe-schaefer-triberg.de; Hauptstrasse 33; cakes €3-4; ⊙9am-6pm Mon, Tue, Thu & Fri, 8am-6pm Sat, 11am-6pm Sun) Confectioner Claus Schäfer uses the original 1915 recipe for Black Forest gateau to prepare this sinful treat that layers chocolate cake perfumed with cherry brandy, whipped cream and sour cherries and wraps it all in more cream and shaved chocolate. Trust us, it's worth the calories.

Parkhotel Wehrle Restaurant GERMAN €€€
(www.parkhotel-wehrle.de; Gartenstrasse 24; mains €15-24; ⊙6-9pm daily, noon-2pm Sun) Hemingway once waxed lyrical about the trout he ordered at this venerable restaurant.

ℹ️ Information

Triberg's main drag is the B500, which runs more or less parallel to the Gutach River. The town's focal point is the Marktplatz, a steep 1.2km uphill walk from the Bahnhof.

Triberg Tourist Office (☑ 07722-866 490; www.triberg.de; Wallfahrtstrasse 4; ⊙ 9am-5pm Mon-Fri, 10am-5pm Sat & Sun) Inside the Schwarzwald-Museum. Stocks walking (€3), cross-country ski trail (€2) and mountain bike (€6.90) maps.

❶ Getting There & Away

From the Bahnhof, 1.5km north of the centre, the *Schwarzwaldbahn* train line loops southeast to Konstanz (€27.50, 1½ hours, hourly), and northwest to Offenburg (€13.50, 46 minutes, hourly).

Bus 7150 travels north through the Gutach and Kinzig valleys to Offenburg; bus 7265 heads south to Villingen via St Georgen. Buses also depart from the Bahnhof.

Martinskapelle

A road twists scenically up a remote valley to Martinskapelle at 1085m, so named because of the little whitewashed chapel that has stood here in some shape or form since around AD 800. A beautiful swath of forest, interwoven with marked walking trails in summer and cross-country ski tracks in winter, unfolds at the top. It's a serene place for slipping away from the crowds.

A scenic and easygoing 10km loop walk begins at the Martinskapelle. The well-marked path wriggles through forest to tower-topped Brendturm (1149m), which affords views from Feldberg to the Vosges and the Alps on cloud-free days. Continue via Brendhäusle and Rosseck for a stunning vista of overlapping mountains and forest.

It's worth spending the night up here at the Kolmenhof (☑ 07723-931 00; www.kolmen hof.de; An der Donauquelle; s/d €55/115; 🅿 🛜 🐕) to appreciate the total sense of calm, early morning forest walks and views. The closest town of real note is Triberg, where there are more accommodation choices.

Bus 7270 runs roughly hourly from the Marktplatz in Triberg to Escheck (€2.30, 20 minutes); from here it's a 4.5km walk to Martinskapelle.

Villingen-Schwenningen

☑ 07721 / POP 84,674

Villingen and Schwenningen trip simultaneously off the tongue, yet each town has its own flavour and history. Villingen once belonged to the Grand Duchy of Baden and Schwenningen to the duchy of Württemberg, conflicting allegiances that apparently can't be reconciled. Villingen, it must be said, is the more attractive of the twin towns.

Encircled by impenetrable walls that look as though they were built by the mythical local giant, Romäus, Villingen's Altstadt is a late-medieval time capsule, with cobbled streets and handsome patrician houses. Though locals nickname it the *Städtle* (little town), the name seems inappropriate during February's mammoth week-long *Fasnacht* (carnival) celebrations.

◎ Sights & Activities

Upper Danube Valley Nature Reserve NATURE RESERVE (Naturpark Obere Donau; www.naturpark-obere-donau.de) Theatrically set against cave-riddled limestone cliffs, dappled with pine and beech woods that are burnished gold in autumn, and hugging the Danube's banks, this reserve bombards you with rugged splendour. Stick to the autobahn, however, and you'll be none the wiser. To fully explore the nature reserve, slip into a bicycle saddle or walking boots, and hit the trail.

One of the finest stretches is between Fridingen and Beuron, a 12.5km ridge-top walk of three to four hours. The signposted, easy-to-navigate trail runs above ragged cliffs, affording eagle's-eye views of the meandering Danube, which has almost 2850km to go before emptying into the Black Sea. The vertigo-inducing outcrop of Laibfelsen is a great picnic spot. From here, the path dips in and out of woodlands and meadows flecked with purple thistles. In Beuron the big draw is the working Benedictine abbey, one of Germany's oldest, dating to 1077. The lavish stuccoed-and-frescoed church is open to visitors: see www.beuron.de for details.

Fridingen and Beuron lie on the L277, 45km east of Villingen.

Franziskaner Museum MUSEUM (www.franziskanermuseum.de; Rietgasse 2; adult/concession €5/3; ⊙ 1-5pm Tue-Sat, 11am-5pm Sun) Next to the 13th-century Riettor gate tower and occupying a former Franciscan monastery, the Franziskaner Museum skips merrily through Villingen's history and heritage. Standouts include Celtic artefacts unearthed at Magdalenenberg, 30 minutes' walk south of Villingen's centre.

Münsterplatz
SQUARE

The Münsterplatz is presided over by the step-gabled Altes Rathaus (Old Town Hall) and Klaus Ringwald's Münsterbrunnen, a bronze fountain and a tongue-in-cheek portrayal of characters that have shaped Villingen's history. The square throngs with activity on Wednesday and Saturday mornings when market stalls are piled high with local bread, meat, cheese, fruit and flowers.

Münster
CATHEDRAL

(Münsterplatz; ☉9am-6pm) **FREE** The main crowd-puller in Villingen's Altstadt is the red-sandstone, 12th-century Münster with its disparate spires: one overlaid with coloured tiles, the other spiky and festooned with gargoyles. The Romanesque portals with haut-relief doors depict dramatic biblical scenes.

Kneippbad
SWIMMING

(Am Kneippbad 1; adult/concession €4.50/3; ☉6.30am-8pm Mon-Fri, 8am-8pm Sat & Sun mid-May–early Sep) If the sun's out, take a 3km walk northwest of the Altstadt to this forest lido, a family magnet with its outdoor pools, slides and volleyball courts.

🍽 Sleeping & Eating

Rindenmühle
HOTEL €€€

(☎07721-886 80; www.rindenmuehle.de; Am Kneippbad 9; s €94-120, d €160-185; P🐾) This converted watermill houses one of Villingen's smartest hotels, with forest walks right on its doorstep and a recently added spa and fitness area. Rooms are slick and decorated in muted hues. In the restaurant (mains €19 to €32), Martin Weisser creates award-winning flavours using home-grown organic produce, including chickens, geese and herbs from his garden.

OM
VEGETARIAN €

(☎07721-204 3690; www.om-cafe.de; Obere Strasse 12; lunch special €6.90; ☉noon-2.30pm Mon, noon-8pm Tue-Sat; 🥗) Doubling up as a yoga studio and boutique, this cafe brings the warm colours and boho flavour of India to central Villingen. On the lunch menu are healthy, vegetarian dishes from curries and stir-fries to soups, salads and spicy lentil dishes.

Gasthaus Löwen
ITALIAN €€

(☎07721-404 1926; www.loewenvillingen.de; Obere Strasse 10; mains €14-24; ☉10.30am-2.30pm & 6-10.30pm Tue-Sat; 🥗) This German-Italian bistro creates a modern mood with its brick floor, bare wood tables, globe lights and moulded chairs. Hailing originally from Venice, the friendly owners are firm believers in slow food and organic ingredients, so expect such season-driven taste sensations as home-made gnocchi with artichokes, and tuna sashimi with beetroot sorbet. Day specials are chalked up on a blackboard.

ℹ Information

Villingen Tourist Office (☎07721-822 340; www.wt-vs.de; Rietgasse 2; ☉10am-5pm Mon-Sat, 11am-5pm Sun) In the Franziskaner Museum. E-bikes are available for rent for €10/20 per half/full day.

ℹ Getting There & Around

Villingen's Bahnhof, situated on the eastern edge of the Altstadt, is on the scenic train line from Konstanz (€22.20, 70 minutes) to Triberg (€6.50, 23 minutes) and Offenburg (€20.30, 70 minutes). Trains to Stuttgart (€29.90 to €31.50, two hours) involve a change in Rottweil, and to Freiburg (€21.30 to €31.60, two hours) a change in Donaueschingen.

From Villingen Bahnhof, buses 7265 and 7270 make regular trips north to Triberg. Frequent buses (eg line 1) link Villingen with Schwenningen.

Rottweil
☎0741 / POP 24,915

Baden-Württemberg's oldest town is the Roman-rooted Rottweil, founded in AD 73. But a torrent of bad press about the woofer with a nasty nip means that most folk readily associate the town with the Rottweiler, which was indeed bred here as a hardy butchers' dog until recently. Fear not, the Rottweiler locals are much tamer. And the town is something of an unsung beauty, with its medieval Altstadt buttressed by towers and lined with gabled houses.

◉ Sights

★ Testturm
TOWER

(Berner Feld 60; adult/concession €9/5; ☉10am-6pm Fri & Sun, to 8pm Sat) Sticking out like a sore thumb, the futuristic, environmentally progressive Testturm is the brainchild of steel-engineering giant Thyssenkrupp, who aims to speed up skyscraper construction. At a whopping 246m high, it's the tallest elevator test tower in the world. At the time of research, it was open to the public, with Germany's highest visitor platform (232m) commanding staggering 360° views of the Black Forest, Swabian Alps and – on clear days – the Swiss Alps .

Schwarzes Tor GATE

(Schwarzer Graben) The sturdy 13th-century Schwarzes Tor is the gateway to Hauptstrasse and the well-preserved Altstadt, a cluster of red-roofed, pastel-painted houses. The town gate is the starting point for the pre-Lenten *Fasnacht* celebrations.

Sidling up to it, the curvaceous Hübschen Winkel townhouse will make you look twice with its 45° kink.

Münster Heilig-Kreuz CATHEDRAL

(Münsterplatz; ⊙9am-7pm) FREE Standing proud on Münsterplatz, the late-Romanesque, three-aisled Münster-Heiliges-Kreuz features some striking Gothic stonework and cross-ribbed vaulting. The cathedral reopened in late 2017 following extensive renovation work.

🛏 Sleeping & Eating

Hotel Bären HOTEL €€

(☑0741-174 600; Hochmaurenstrasse 1; s €83-108, d €120-135; 🅿🤖) Standing head and shoulders above most hotels in town, the Bären extends a *herzlich Willkommen* (warm welcome). Its spacious contemporary rooms, most recently revamped, are done out in blonde wood, clean lines and pops of colour. Breakfast is a highly decent spread of fresh breads and fruits, cold cuts and cereals.

Wandelbar CAFE €

(☑0741-3488 6724; www.wandel-bar.com; Neckartal 67; light bites €6-10; ⊙11.30am-7pm Tue & Wed, 11.30am-1am Thu & Fri, 2pm-1am Sat, 2-7pm Sun) Wandelbar is one of Rottweil's coolest haunts, with a high-ceilinged, stone-walled, gallery-style interior, retro furniture and bold art on the walls. It takes you through from morning espresso to afternoon *Kaffee und Kuchen* (with delicious homemade cakes) and evening cocktails. Or go for snacks such as tapas, paninis and tarte flambée.

🛈 Information

Rottweil Tourist Office (☑0741-494 280; www.rottweil.de; Hauptstrasse 21; ⊙9.30am-5.30pm Mon-Fri, to 12.30pm Sat) Can advise on accommodation, tours and biking the Neckartal-Radweg.

🛈 Getting There & Away

Rottweil is just off the A81 Stuttgart–Singen motorway. Trains run at least hourly to Stuttgart (€25.50, 1½ hours) and Villingen (€3.80, 30 minutes) from the Bahnhof, 1.2km southeast of the Altstadt.

Unterkirnach

☑07721 / POP 2534

Nuzzling among velvety green hills, low-key Unterkirnach is a winner with families and anyone into their outdoor sports. In summer, the village is a terrific starting point for forest hikes, with 130km of marked walking trails, while in winter there are 50km of *Loipen* (cross-country ski tracks) and some terrific slopes to sledge.

Kids can slide and climb to their heart's content at the all-weather Spielscheune (www.spielscheune-unterkirnach.de; Schlossbergweg 4; admission €4.50; ⊙2-6pm Mon & Wed-Fri, 11am-6pm Sat & Sun; 🚻), or toddle uphill to the farm to meet inquisitive goats and Highland cattle (feeding time is 3pm).

When you stay overnight, you'll automatically receive the KONUS guest card, which means the indoor pool, Spielscheune, play barn, guided walks (ask the tourist office (☑07721-800 837; www.unterkirnach.de; Villinger Strasse 5; ⊙9am-12.30pm & 2-5pm Mon-Fri) for details), ski lifts (in winter) and local transport are free.

Unterkirnach is on a minor road that runs just south and parallel of the B33 between Triberg and Villingen.

Bus 61 runs roughly one an hour between Unterkirnach and Villingen (€3.50, 16 minutes).

LAKE CONSTANCE

Nicknamed the *schwäbische Meer* (Swabian Sea), Lake Constance – Central Europe's third-largest lake – straddles three countries: Germany, Austria and Switzerland. Formed by the Rhine Glacier during the last ice age and fed and drained by that same sprightly river today, this whopper of a lake measures 63km long by 14km wide and up to 250m deep. There is a certain novelty in the fact that this is the only place in the world where you can wake up in Germany, cycle across to Switzerland for lunch and make it to Austria in time for afternoon tea, strudel and snapshots of the Alps.

Taking in meadows and vineyards, orchards and wetlands, beaches and Alpine foothills, the lake's landscapes are like a 'greatest hits' of European scenery. Culture? It's all here, from baroque churches to Benedictine abbeys, Stone Age dwellings to Roman forts, and medieval castles to zeppelins.

Lake Constance

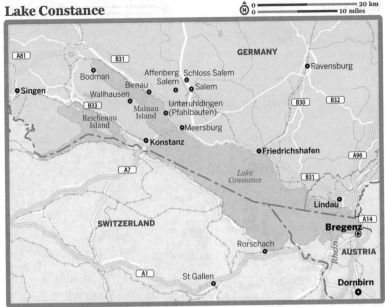

ℹ Getting There & Around

The most enjoyable way to cross the lake is by ferry. **Konstanz** is the main hub but Meersburg and Friedrichshafen also have ferry options.

Although most towns have a train station (Meersburg is an exception), in some cases buses provide the only land connections. **Bodensee Ticket** (www.bodensee-ticket.com), which groups all Lake Constance-area public transport, publishes a free *Fahrplan* (timetable) with schedules for all train, bus and ferry services. A day pass (€18.50/26 for one/all zones) gets you access to land transport around Lake Constance, including areas in Austria and Switzerland. It's sold at train stations and ferry docks. Children pay half price.

CAR FERRY

The roll-on roll-off **Konstanz–Meersburg car ferry** (www.sw.konstanz.de; car up to 4m incl driver/bicycle/pedestrian €9.40/5.30/3) runs 24 hours a day, except when high water levels prevent it from docking. The ferry runs every 15 minutes from 5.35am to 8.50pm, every 30 minutes from 8.50pm to midnight and every hour from midnight to 5.35am. The crossing, affording superb views from the top deck, takes 15 minutes.

The car ferry dock in Konstanz, served by local bus 1, is 4km northeast of the centre along Mainaustrasse. In Meersburg, car ferries leave from a dock 400m northwest of the old town.

PASSENGER FERRY

The most useful lines are run by German **BSB** (☑ 07531-364 00; www.bsb-online.com; Hafenstrasse 6, Konstanz) and Austrian **Vorarlberg Lines** (www.vorarlberg-lines.at; Seestrasse 4, Bregenz). BSB ferries link Konstanz with ports such as Meersburg (€6.10, 30 minutes), Friedrichshafen (€13.30, 1¾ hours), Lindau (€17.30, three hours) and Bregenz (€18.60, 3½ hours); children aged six to 15 years pay half price. The website lists timetables in full.

Der Katamaran (☑ 07531-363 9320; www.der-katamaran.de; Passenger Ferry Dock, Konstanz; adult/6-14yr €10.50/5.70) is a sleek passenger service that takes 50 minutes to make the Konstanz–Friedrichshafen crossing. It runs hourly from 6am to 7pm, plus hourly from 8pm to midnight on Fridays and Saturdays from mid-May to early October.

Konstanz

☑ 07531 / POP 82,859

Sidling up to the Swiss border, bisected by the Rhine and outlined by the Alps, Konstanz sits prettily on the northwestern shore of Lake Constance. Roman emperors, medieval traders and the bishops of the 15th-century Council of Constance have all left their mark on this alley-woven town, mercifully spared from the WWII

Konstanz

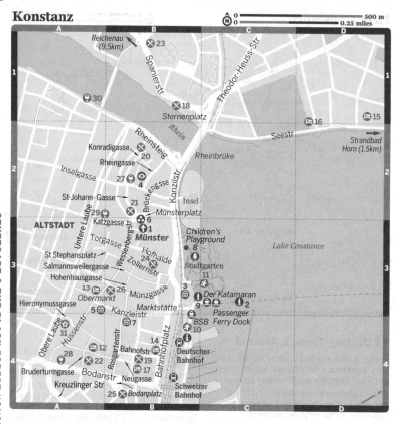

Konstanz

◎ Top Sights

◎ Sights

◑ Activities, Courses & Tours

◲ Sleeping

⊗ Eating

◒ Drinking & Nightlife

✦ Entertainment

bombings that obliterated other German cities.

◉ Sights

★ Münster
CATHEDRAL

(Münsterplatz 1; tower adult/child €2/1; ⊙10am-6pm, tower 10am-5pm Mon-Sat, 12.30-5.30pm Sun) Crowned by a filigreed spire and looking proudly back on 1000 years of history, the sandstone Münster was the church of the Diocese of Konstanz until 1821. Its interior is an architectural potpourri of Romanesque, Gothic, Renaissance and baroque styles. Standouts include the 15th-century Schnegg, an ornate spiral staircase in the northern transept, to the left of which a door leads to the 1000-year-old crypt. From the crypt's polychrome chapel, you enter the sublime Gothic cloister.

Mainau
GARDENS

(www.mainau.de; adult/concession €21/12 summer, €10/6 winter; ⊙10am-7pm late Mar-late Oct, to 5pm rest of year) Jutting out over the lake and bursting with flowers, the lusciously green islet of Mainau is a 45-hectare Mediterranean garden dreamed up by the Bernadotte family, relatives of the royal house of Sweden.

Around two million visitors flock here every year to admire sparkly lake and mountain views from the baroque castle, and wander sequoia-shaded avenues and hothouses bristling with palms and orchids.

Römersiedlung
RUINS

(Münsterplatz; tour €1; ⊙tours 6pm Sun) The glass pyramid in front of the Münster shelters the Römersiedlung, the 3rd-century-AD remains of the Roman fort Constantia that gave the city its name. You'll only get a sneak peek from above, so join one of the guided tours that begin at the tourist office (p526) for a touch of magic as a staircase opens from the cobbles and leads down to the ruins.

Rathaus
HISTORIC BUILDING

(City Hall; Kanzleistrasse) Slightly south of the Münster, the flamboyantly frescoed Renaissance Rathaus occupies the former linen weavers' guildhall. Behind it you'll find a peaceful arcaded courtyard.

Niederburg
AREA

Best explored on foot, Konstanz' cobbled heart Niederburg stretches north from the Münster to the Rhine. The twisting lanes lined with half-timbered townhouses are the place to snoop around galleries and antique shops.

Imperia
STATUE

At the end of the pier, giving ferry passengers a come-hither look from her rotating pedestal, stands *Imperia*. Peter Lenk's 9m-high sculpture of a buxom prostitute, said to have plied her trade in the days of the Council of Constance, was inspired by a short story by Honoré de Balzac, *La Belle Impéria*. In her clutches are hilarious sculptures of a naked (and sagging) Pope Martin V and Holy Roman Emperor Sigismund, symbolising religious and imperial power.

Rosgartenmuseum
MUSEUM

(www.rosgartenmuseum-konstanz.de; Rosgartenstrasse 3-5; adult/concession €3/1.50, 1st Sun of the month & after 2pm Wed free; ⊙10am-6pm Tue-Fri, to 5pm Sat & Sun) The one-time butchers' guildhall now harbours the Rosgartenmuseum, spotlighting regional art and history, with an emphasis on medieval panel painting and sculpture. Most of the information is given in German only.

Konzilgebäude
HISTORIC BUILDING

(Council Building; Konzilstrasse) Look out for the white, dormered Konzilgebäude, built in 1388, which served as a granary and warehouse before Pope Martin V was elected here in 1417. Today it's a conference and concert hall.

Stadtgarten
PARK

With its landscaped flower beds, plane trees and children's playground, the Stadtgarten is a fine place to kick back and enjoy dreamy views out over Lake Constance.

Zeppelin Monument
MONUMENT

(Stadtgarten) The Zeppelin Monument shows airship inventor Count Ferdinand von Zeppelin in an Icarus-like pose. He was born in 1838 on the Insel islet.

Reichenau
ISLAND

(www.reichenau-tourismus.de) In AD 724 a missionary named Pirmin founded a Benedictine monastery on Reichenau, a 4.5km-by-1.5km island (Lake Constance's largest) about 11km west of Konstanz. During its heyday, from 820 to 1050, the so-called Reichenauer School produced stunning illuminated manuscripts and vivid frescos. Today, three surviving churches provide silent testimony to Reichenau's Golden Age. Thanks to them, this fertile islet of orchards and wineries was declared a Unesco World Heritage Site in 2000.

Strandbad Horn
BEACH

(Eichhornstrasse 100; ⊗ mid-May–Sep; 🚌) **FREE**
This lake-front beach, 4km northeast of the centre, has sunbathing lawns, a kiddie pool, playground, volleyball courts and a naturist area.

🏃 Activities

La Canoa
CANOEING

(www.lacanoa.com; Robert-Bosch-Strasse 4; canoe/kayak/SUP 3hr €15/20/30, per day €25/30/45; ⊗10am-12.30pm & 2-6pm Tue-Fri, 10am-4pm Sat) La Canoa has canoe, kayak and SUP rental points in all major towns on the lake; see the website for details.

Bootsvermietung Konstanz
BOATING

(Stadtgarten; per hour €12-32; ⊗11am-7pm Easter–mid-Oct) This boat rental in the Stadtgarten (p523) has pedalos for trundling across the lake.

🛏 Sleeping

Glückseeligkeit Herberge
GUESTHOUSE €

(☑07531-902 2075; www.herberge-konstanz.de; Neugasse 20; s €40-60, d €60-80; 🛜) What a sweet deal this little guesthouse is. Housed in a period building in the Altstadt, it shelters petite but attractively decorated rooms. The attic room has direct access to the roof terrace, which peers over a jumble of rooftops to the cathedral spire. There's also a shared lounge, kitchen and patio. E-bikes are available for rental.

Hotel Halm
HOTEL €€

(☑07531-1210; www.hotel-halm-konstanz.de; Bahnhofplatz 6; s €70-120, d €90-140; 🛜) A joyous hop and skip from the lake and Altstadt, this late-19th-century pile has warm, elegantly furnished rooms with marble bathrooms; upgrade if you want a balcony with a lake view. Its pride and joy is its lavish Moorish Hall, serving Middle Eastern cuisine. There's also a small sauna for a postsightseeing steam.

Hotel Barbarossa
HISTORIC HOTEL €€

(☑07531-128 990; www.hotelbarbarossa.de; Obermarkt 8-12; s €70-90, d €115-170, f €180-200; 🛜) This 600-year-old patrician house features parquet-floored, individually decorated rooms, which are bright and appealing if a tad on the small side. The terrace has views over Konstanz' rooftops and spires. The first-floor Weinstube restaurant (mains €20 to €24) serves food with a Mediterranean slant in a historic, wood-panelled parlour.

Villa Barleben
HISTORIC HOTEL €€€

(☑07531-942 330; www.hotel-barleben.de; Seestrasse 15; s €76.50-165, d €100-325; 🅿🛜) Gregariously elegant, this 19th-century villa's sunny rooms and corridors are sprinkled with antiques and ethnic art. The rambling lakefront gardens are ideal for dozing in a *Strandkorb* (wicker beach lounger), G&T in hand, or enjoying lunch on the terrace.

Viva Sky
HOTEL €€€

(☑07531-692 3620; www.hotel-viva-sky.de; Sigismundstrasse 19; s €90-150, d €129-179, apt €149-169, f €179-199, ste €179-219; 🅿🛜) An arresting panorama of Konstanz' Altstadt spreads out before you from the top floor of this stylish newcomer. It might look nondescript from outside, but inside, rooms are very comfortable, with parquet floors and themed touches. The pick of them have balconies with fine views, while the top suite ups the romance with a whirlpool bath and four-poster bed.

Riva
BOUTIQUE HOTEL €€€

(☑07531-363 090; www.hotel-riva.de; Seestrasse 25; s €110-230, d €200-320, ste €320-660; 🅿🛜🏊) This ultrachic contender has crisp white spaces, glass walls and a snail-like stairwell. Zen-like rooms with hardwood floors feature perks such as free minibars. A rooftop pool, spa area and gym, and a gourmet restaurant and terrace overlooking the lake, seal the deal.

🍴 Eating

★ Voglhaus
CAFE €

(☑07531-918 9520; www.das-voglhaus.de; Wessenbergstrasse 8; light meals €5-9.50; ⊗9am-6.30pm Mon-Sat, 11am-6pm Sun; 🍴) Locals flock to the 'bird house' for its chilled vibe and contemporary wood-and-stone interior, warmed by an open fire in winter. Wood-oven bread with spreads, wholegrain bagels, wraps and cupcakes pair nicely with smoothies and speciality coffees such as the Hansel and Gretel (with gingerbread syrup). Day specials swing from yellow curry to pasta bowls.

Ess Bar
INTERNATIONAL €

(☑07531-804 3475; www.essbar-konstanz.de; Bahnhofstrasse 15; light meals €10-12; ⊗noon-1am Tue-Thu, to 2am Fri & Sat) The packed tables speak volumes at this minimalist-chic, monochrome-toned bistro, with banquette seating and a pavement terrace for summer-day dining. The menu packs flavour punches in tapas-style dishes including Asian-style oysters with chilli, lime and ginger; spinach risotto with parmesan; and pulled pork with miso aioli – all bang on the money. Order a few – sharing is the way to go.

Sol
VEGETARIAN €

(✏️ 07531-936 4990; www.sol-konstanz.de; Ebertplatz 4; snacks & mains €4-10; ⏰ 10am-10pm; 🚶) Over the Rhine just north of the Altstadt, this cool and wholesome cafe has a chilled vibe, with exposed stone walls and an open deli kitchen. The menu plays up regional and organic ingredients in bites including quinoa burgers, falafel, homemade cake, vegan ice cream and smoothies. Go easy on the spicy sauce, though – it's seriously hot stuff.

Tamara's Weinstube
GERMAN €

(✏️ 07531-284 318; http://tamaras-weinstube.de; Zollernstrasse 6-8; light bites & meals €5-13.50; ⏰ 4pm-midnight Mon-Sat) With stone walls, low wood beams, soft lighting and a traditional *Kachelofen* (tiled oven), this wine bar is as cosy as they come. It's a terrific spot for an evening of Badisch wines and regional grub such as ox salad with onions and gherkins, homemade potato salad, pork knuckles and farm-fresh bratwurst.

Constanzer Wirtshaus
GERMAN €€

(✏️ 07531-363 0130; www.constanzer-wirtshaus. de; Spanierstrasse 3; mains €10-19; ⏰ 11am-midnight; 🚶) On the banks of the Rhine where it flows into Lake Constance, this delightfully old-school tavern has bags of character, with its vaulted interior and waterfront terrace. Classic German food such as veal goulash, *Schweinebraten* (regional pork roast with bread dumplings) and *Kässpätzle* (noodles topped with cheese and fried onions) marry well with the house brews and Lake Constance wines.

Münsterhof
GERMAN €€

(✏️ 07531-363 8427; Münsterplatz 3; mains €11-20; ⏰ 11.30am-1am Sun-Fri, to 3am Sat; 🚶) Tables set up in front of the Münster (p523), a slick bistro interior and a lunchtime buzz have earned Münsterhof a loyal local following. Dishes from cordon bleu with pan-fried potatoes to asparagus-filled *Maultaschen* (pasta pockets) in creamy chive sauce are substantial and satisfying. The €8.40 lunch special is great value.

Tolle Knolle
INTERNATIONAL €€

(✏️ 07531-175 75; Bodanplatz 9; mains €11.50-19; ⏰ 11am-midnight) On a fountain-dotted square with alfresco seating, this art-slung restaurant lives up to its 'great potato' moniker. Potatoes come in various guises: with *Wiener Schnitzel*, beer-battered fish and on the signature pizza.

La Bodega
TAPAS €€

(✏️ 07531-277 88; Schreibergasse 40; tapas €5-10.50; ⏰ 5pm-1am Tue-Sat) Squirrelled away in Niederburg, this candy-bright bodega with a pocket-sized terrace whips up tapas from *papas canarias* (Canarian potatoes) to stuffed calamari.

San Martino Gourmet
GASTRONOMY €€€

(✏️ 07531-284 5678; www.san-martino.net; Bruderturmgasse 3; mains €42-56, 5-course menu €160; ⏰ 6-10pm Tue-Sat) A class act with space for just 16 lucky diners, this Michelin-starred restaurant rests against the old city walls. Jochen Fecht's season-inspired food allows each ingredient to shine in dishes such as wood sorrel with Monkey 47 gin and bergamot, and nose-to-tail veal with soubise and Shimeji mushrooms.

🍸 Drinking & Entertainment

Klimperkasten
BAR

(Bodanstrasse 40; ⏰ 6pm-1am Mon-Thu, to 3am Fri & Sat) Indie kids, garage and old-school fans all hail this retro cafe, which gets clubbier after dark when DJs work the decks. Occasionally hosts gigs.

Schwarze Katz
BAR

(Katzgasse 8; ⏰ 6pm-1am Tue-Thu & Sun, to 2am Fri & Sat) Found the Black Cat? You're in luck. A relaxed mood, friendly crowd and reasonably priced drinks (including Black Forest Alpirsbacher beer) make this a Konstanz favourite.

Strandbar Konstanz
BAR

(http://strandbar-konstanz.de; Webersteig 12; ⏰ noon-11pm Apr & May, noon-midnight Jun-Aug, 2-10pm Sep) Konstanz gets its summer groove on down at this beach bar, with sand, deckchairs, DJ beats, long drinks and good vibes on the banks of the Rhine.

Brauhaus Johann Albrecht
PUB

(http://konstanz.brauhaus-joh-albrecht.de; Konradigasse 2; ⏰ 11.30am-midnight) This stepgabled microbrewery is a relaxed haunt for quaffing craft beers. There's a terrace for summer imbibing.

K9
CULTURAL CENTRE

(www.k9-kulturzentrum.de; Hieronymusgasse 3) Once a medieval church, this is now Konstanz' most happening cultural venue, with a line-up skipping from salsa nights and film screenings to gigs, club nights and jive nights. See the website for schedules.

ℹ️ Information

Konstanz Tourist Office (☑ 07531-133 030; www.konstanz-tourismus.de; Bahnhofplatz 43, Hauptbahnhof; ☺ 9am-6.30pm Mon-Fri, 9am-4pm Sat, 10am-1pm Sun Apr-Oct, 9.30am-6pm Mon-Fri Nov-Mar) Located at the Hauptbahnhof. Inside you can pick up a walking-tour brochure (€1) and city map (€0.50); outside there's a hotel reservation board and free hotel telephone.

ℹ️ Getting There & Away

Konstanz is the main ferry hub – for passengers and for cars (p521) – for Lake Constance.

Konstanz' **Hauptbahnhof** (Bahnhofplatz) is the southern terminus of the scenic *Schwarzwaldbahn*, which trundles hourly through the Black Forest, linking Offenburg with towns such as Triberg and Villingen. To reach Lake Constance's northern shore, you usually have to change in Radolfzell. The Schweizer Bahnhof has connections to destinations throughout Switzerland.

ℹ️ Getting Around

The city centre is a traffic headache, especially on weekends. Your best bet is the free Park & Ride lot 3km northwest of the Altstadt, near the airfield on Byk-Gulden-Strasse, where your only outlay will be for a bus ticket.

Local buses cost €2.35 for a single ticket, and day passes are €4.60/7.90 for an individual/family; see www.sw.konstanz.de for timetables. Bus 1 links the Meersburg car-ferry dock with the Altstadt. If you stay in Konstanz for at least two nights, your hotelier will give you a Gästekarte entitling you to free local bus travel.

Bikes can be hired from **Kultur-Rädle** (☑ 07531-273 10; Bahnhofplatz 29; per day/week €13/70; ☺ 9am-12.30pm & 2.30-6pm Mon-Fri, 10am-4pm Sat year-round, plus 10am-12.30pm Sun Easter-Sep), close to the tourist office.

Meersburg

☑ 07532 / POP 5776

Tumbling down vine-streaked slopes to Lake Constance and crowned by a perkily turreted medieval castle, Meersburg lives up to all those clichéd knights-in-armour, damsel-in-distress fantasies. And if its tangle of cobbled lanes and half-timbered houses filled with jovial banter doesn't sweep you off your feet, the local Pinot Noir served in its cosy *Weinstuben* (wine taverns) will.

👁️ Sights & Activities

Burg Meersburg   CASTLE
(Schlossplatz 10; adult/concession €12.80/10; ☺ 9am-6.30pm Mar-Oct, 10am-6pm Nov-Feb) Looking across Lake Constance from its lofty perch, Burg Meersburg is an archetypal medieval stronghold, complete with keep, drawbridge, knights' hall and dungeons. Founded by Merovingian king Dagobert I in the 7th century, the fortress is among Germany's oldest, no mean feat in a country with a *lot* of old castles. The bishops of Konstanz used it as a summer residence between 1268 and 1803.

Meersburg Therme   SPA
(☑ 07532-440 2850; www.meersburg-therme.de; Uferpromenade 12; thermal baths 2hr adult/concession €9/8.50, incl sauna 3hr €18/17.50; ☺ 10am-10pm Mon-Thu, to 11pm Fri & Sat, 9am-10pm Sun) It's a five-minute walk east along the Uferpromenade to this lake-front spa, where the 34°C thermal waters, water jets and Swiss Alp views are soothing. Those who dare to bare all can skinny-dip in the lake and steam in saunas that are replicas of Unteruhldingen's Stone Age dwellings (p531).

Neues Schloss   CASTLE
(www.neues-schloss-meersburg.de; Schlossplatz 13; adult/concession €5/2.50; ☺ 9.30am-6pm Apr-Oct, noon-5pm Sat & Sun Nov-Mar) In 1710 Prince-Bishop Johann Franz Schenk von Stauffenberg, perhaps tired of the dinginess and rising damp, swapped the Altes Schloss for the dusky-pink, lavishly baroque Neues Schloss. A visit to the now state-owned palace takes in the extravagant bishops' apartments replete with stucco work and frescos, Bathasar Neumann's elegant staircase, and gardens with inspirational lake views.

Lakefront   HARBOUR
(Seepromenade) Stroll the harbour for classic snaps of Lake Constance or to hire a pedalo. On the jetty, you can't miss – though the pious might prefer to – Peter Lenk's satirical *Magische Säule* (Magic Column). The sculpture is a hilarious satirical depiction of characters who have shaped Meersburg's history, including buxom wine-wench Wendelgart and poet Annette von Droste-Hülshoff.

Vineum   MUSEUM
(www.vineum-bodensee.de; Vorburggasse 13; adult/concession €5.50/3; ☺ 11am-6pm Tue-Sun Apr-Oct,

11am-6pm Sat & Sun Nov-Mar) Housed in the 400-year-old Heilig-Geist-Spital (Hospice of the Holy Spirit), this new museum presents an intriguing interactive romp through the history of winemaking in and around Meersburg – from sniffing the different aromas to tasting 16 locally produced wines in the Vinemathek.

Sleeping & Eating

Meersburg goes with the seasons, with most places closing from November to Easter.

Landhaus Ödenstein   GUESTHOUSE €€
(☎07532-6142; www.oedenstein.de; Droste-Hülshoff-Weg 25; s €67-99, d €99-155; P🇸) Spectacularly plonked on a hill above vine-cloaked slopes, this family-run guesthouse has knock-out views of Lake Constance and spotless, light-filled rooms with pine furnishings – the pick of which have balconies. A pretty garden, warm welcome and generous breakfasts sweeten the deal.

Gasthof zum Bären   GUESTHOUSE €€
(☎07532-432 20; www.baeren-meersburg.de; Marktplatz 11; s €52, d €96-118; P🇸) Straddling three 13th- to 17th-century buildings, this guesthouse receives glowing reviews for its classic rooms, spruced up with stucco work, ornate wardrobes and lustrous wood; corner rooms No 13 and 23 are the most romantic. The rustic tavern (mains €9 to €18) serves Lake Constance fare such as *Felchen* (whitefish).

Romantik
Residenz am See   BOUTIQUE HOTEL €€€
(☎07532-800 40; www.hotel-residenz-meersburg.com; Uferpromenade 11; s €129-141, d €234-294, apt €344-384; P🇸) Sitting with aplomb on the promenade, this romantic hotel is a class act. The higher you go, the better the view from the warm-hued rooms facing the vineyards or lake. All room rates include breakfast, minibar and a four-course dinner in Residenz restaurant. The hotel also houses the Michelin-starred Casala, offering sophisticated Mediterranean cuisine. Bikes/e-bikes can be rented for €12/25 per day.

Badische Weinstube   GERMAN €€
(☎07532-496 42; www.badische-weinstube.com; Unterstadtstrasse 17; mains €14-28; ⊙5-11pm Wed-Sun) Close to the lake front, this wine tavern combines a mock-rustic interior with a pavement terrace. Try the homemade fish soup flavoured with saffron and garlic, followed by Lake Constance *Felchen* (white fish) in

❶ BODENSEE ERLEBNISKARTE

The three-day **Bodensee Erlebniskarte** (adult/child €74/37, not including ferries €41/21), available at area tourist and ferry offices from late March to mid-October, allows free travel on almost all boats and mountain cableways on and around Lake Constance (including its Austrian and Swiss shores). It also includes free entry to more than 160 tourist attractions and museums. There are also seven-day (adult/child €99/49) and 14-day (adult/child €144/72) versions.

almond butter or *Zwiebelrostbraten* (onion roast) with *Spätzle* (egg noodles).

Winzerstube zum Becher   GERMAN €€
(☎07532-9009; www.winzerstube-zum-becher.de; Höllgasse 4; mains €10.50-26; ⊙noon-2pm & 6-10pm Tue-Sun) Vines drape the facade of this wood-panelled bolthole, run by the same family since 1884. Home-grown Pinot Noirs accompany Lake Constance classics such as whitefish in almond-butter sauce. The terrace affords Altes Schloss views.

Casala   MEDITERRANEAN €€€
(☎07532-800 40; www.hotel-residenz-meersburg.com; Uferpromenade 11; tasting menus €90-135; ⊙6.30-9pm Thu-Sun; 🌱) At the Romantik Residenz am See hotel's Michelin-starred restaurant, chef Markus Philippi brings sophisticated Mediterranean cuisine to the table. One of the menus is vegetarian.

❶ Information

Meersburg Tourist Office (☎07532-440 400; www.meersburg.de; Kirchstrasse 4; ⊙9am-noon & 2-4.30pm Mon-Fri) Housed in a one-time Dominican monastery.

❶ Getting There & Away

Meersburg, which lacks a train station, is 18km west of Friedrichshafen.

From Monday to Friday, eight times a day, express bus 7394 makes the trip to Konstanz (€4, 40 minutes) and Friedrichshafen (€4.55, 30 minutes). Bus 7373 connects Meersburg with Ravensburg (€6, 40 minutes, four daily Monday to Friday, two Saturday). Meersburg's main bus stop is next to the Mariä-Heimsuchung church on Stettener Strasse (on the northern edge of the Altstadt).

OFF THE BEATEN TRACK

ONE LAKE, TWO WHEELS, THREE COUNTRIES

When the weather warms, there's no better way to explore Bodensee (Lake Constance) than with your bum in a saddle. The well-marked **Bodensee Radweg** (Bodensee Cycle Path; www. bodensee-radweg.com) is a 273km loop of Lake Constance, taking in vineyards, meadows, orchards, wetlands and historic towns. There are plenty of small beaches where you can stop for a refreshing dip in the lake. See the website for itineraries and maps.

Bike hire is available in most towns for between €10 and €20 per day. While the entire route takes roughly a week, ferries and trains also make it possible to cover shorter chunks, such as Friedrichshafen–Konstanz–Meersburg, in a weekend.

The 24-hour **Konstanz–Meersburg Car Ferry** (p521) leaves from a dock 400m northwest of the old town

Friedrichshafen

📞 07541 / POP 59,108

Zeppelins, the cigar-shaped airships that first took flight in 1900 under the stewardship of high-flying Count Ferdinand von Zeppelin, will forever be associated with Friedrichshafen. An amble along the flowery lake-front promenade and a visit to the museum that celebrates the behemoth of the skies are the biggest draws of this industrial town, which was heavily bombed in WWII and rebuilt in the 1950s.

⊙ Sights & Activities

★ **Zeppelin Museum** MUSEUM
(www.zeppelin-museum.de; Seestrasse 22; adult/concession €9/5; ⊙9am-5pm daily May-Oct, 10am-5pm Tue-Sun Nov-Apr) Near the eastern end of Friedrichshafen's lake-front promenade is the Zeppelin Museum, housed in the Bauhaus-style former *Hafenbahnhof* (harbour station), built in 1932. The centrepiece is a full-scale mock-up of a 33m section of the *Hindenburg* (LZ 129), the largest airship ever built, measuring an incredible 245m long and outfitted as luxuriously as an ocean liner. The hydrogen-filled craft tragically burst into flames, killing 36, while landing in New Jersey in 1937.

Schlosskirche CHURCH
(www.schlosskirche-fn.de; Schlossstrasse 2; ⊙9am-6pm Easter-late Oct) **FREE** The western end of Friedrichshafen's promenade is anchored by the twin-onion-towered baroque Schlosskirche. It's the only accessible part of the Schloss and is still inhabited by the ducal family of Württemberg.

Zeppelin NT SCENIC FLIGHTS
(📞07541-590 00; www.zeppelinflug.de; Messestrasse 132; 30/45/60/90/120-min flight €245/380/455/640/825) Real airship fans will justify the splurge on a trip in a high-tech, 12-passenger Zeppelin NT. Shorter trips cover lake destinations such as **Schloss Salem** (www.salem.de; Schlossbezirk 1; adult/concession €9/4.50; ⊙9.30am-6pm Mon-Sat, 10.30am-6pm Sun Apr-Oct) and Lindau, while longer ones drift across to Austria or Switzerland. Take-off and landing are in Friedrichshafen.

🛏 Sleeping & Eating

Gasthof Rebstock GUESTHOUSE €€
(📞07541-950 1640; www.gasthof-rebstock-fn. de; Werastrasse 35; s/d/tr/q €65/80/95/110; 🛜) Geared up for cyclists and offering bike rental (€8 per day), this family-run hotel has a beer garden and humble but tidy rooms with pine furnishings. It's 750m northwest of the *Stadtbahnhof*.

Aika Seaside Living BOUTIQUE HOTEL €€€
(📞07541-378 357; www.aika-cafe.de; Karlstrasse 38; d €139-219, ste €260-350; 🛜) Well, it might not be the 'seaside' exactly, but Aika comes up trumps with its large, spacious, wood-floored rooms and slick, contemporary neutral-palette suites, which come with fabulous views of the lake. The cafe downstairs has one of the best terraces in town.

Aika CAFE €
(www.aika-cafe.de; Karlstrasse 38; snacks €3-8; ⊙8.30am-8pm Mon-Fri, 9am-8pm Sat, 9.30am-8pm Sun) Slick and monochrome, this deli-cafe has a lakeside terrace for lingering over a speciality coffee, breakfast, homemade ice cream, cake or sourdough sandwich.

Beach Club CAFE €
(www.beachclub-fn.de; Uferstrasse 1; snacks €6-10; ⊙9am-midnight Apr-Oct) This lake-front shack is the place to unwind on the deck, cocktail in hand, and admire the *Klangschiff* ('sound

ship') sculpture and the not-so-distant Alps. Revive over salads, sandwiches, tarte flambée, tapas and ice cream.

s'Wirtshaus am See   GERMAN €€
(☑ 07541-388   5989;   www.swirtshaus.de; Seestrasse 18; mains €13-26; ☺ 9am-11pm; 🖥️🚗) Right on the lake front, this restaurant goes in for the new-wave rustic look, with a sleek blonde-wood interior, contemporary fireplace and funky stag antler lights. The Swabian menu includes dishes such as *Allgäuer Käsesuppe* (cheese soup), bratwurst in dark beer sauce, and roast chicken with lashings of potato salad. Try to snag a table on the terrace in summer.

❶ Information

Friedrichshafen Tourist Office (☑ 07541-2035 5444; www.friedrichshafen.info; Bahnhofplatz 2; ☺ 9am-1pm & 2-6pm Mon-Fri, 9am-1pm Sat) On the square outside the *Stadtbahnhof*. Staff can book zeppelin flights.

❶ Getting There & Around

Friedrichshafen's **airport** (☑ 07541-2840; www.bodensee-airport.eu; Am Flugplatz 64) is served by airlines including easyJet, British Airways and Lufthansa.

There are ferry options, including a catamaran to Konstanz. Sailing times are posted on the waterfront just outside the Zeppelin Museum.

From Monday to Friday, seven times a day, express bus 7394 makes the trip to Konstanz (1¼ hours) via Meersburg (30 minutes). Birnau and Meersburg are also served almost hourly by bus 7395.

Friedrichshafen is on the Bodensee (Lake Constance)–Gürtelbahn train line, which runs along the lake's northern shore from Radolfzell to Lindau. There are also regular services on the Bodensee-Oberschwaben-Bahn to Ravensburg (€6, 14 to 20 minutes).

Trains and buses depart from the Bahnhof, which is 500m west of the Altstadt.

Ravensburg

☑ 0751 / POP 49,830

Ravensburg has puzzled the world for the past 125 years with its jigsaws and board games. The medieval Altstadt has toy-town appeal, studded with turrets, robber-knight towers and gabled patrician houses. For centuries, dukes and wealthy merchants polished the cobbles of this Free Imperial City – now it's your turn.

◉ Sights & Activities

Museum Humpis-Quartier   MUSEUM
(www.museum-humpis-quartier.de; Marktstrasse 45; adult/concession €5/3; ☺ 11am-6pm Tue, Wed & Fri-Sun, to 8pm Thu) Seven exceptional late-medieval houses set around a glass-covered courtyard shelter a permanent collection focusing on Ravensburg's past as a trade centre, based on the lives of four historic characters. Free audioguides provide some background.

Marienplatz   SQUARE
The heart of the Altstadt is the elongated, pedestrianised Marienplatz, framed by sturdy towers such as the round Grüner Turm, with its lustrous tiled roof, and frescoed patrician houses, such as the late-Gothic, step-gabled Waaghaus. The 15th-century Lederhaus, with its elaborate Renaissance facade, was once the domain of tanners and shoemakers.

Liebfrauenkirche   CHURCH
(Church of Our Lady; Kirchstrasse 18; ☺ 9am-6pm) **FREE** Rising high above Marienplatz, the weighty, late-Gothic Liebfrauenkirche conceals some fine examples of 15th-century stained glass and a gilt altar.

Mehlsack   TOWER
(Mehlsackweg; ☺ 11am-4pm Sat & Sun Aug-Sep) **FREE** The all-white Mehlsack (flour sack) is a tower marking the Altstadt's southern edge. A steep staircase leads up to the Veitsburg, a quaint baroque castle that now harbours a restaurant of the same name, with outlooks over Ravensburg's mosaic of red-tiled roofs.

Ravensburger Spieleland   AMUSEMENT PARK
(www.spieleland.de; Mecklenbeuren; adult/concession €34.50/32.50; ☺ 10am-6pm Apr-Oct) Kids in tow? Take them to this board-game-inspired theme park, with attractions including giant rubber-duck racing, cow milking against the clock, rodeos and Alpine rafting. By car it's 10 minutes south of Ravensburg on the B467.

🛏️ Sleeping & Eating

Hotel zum Engel   B&B €€
(☑ 0751-363 6130; www.engel-ravensburg.de; Marienplatz 71; s €90-107, d €120-156; 🖥️) Following a recent makeover, the Engel (angel) is flying once again. The location on Marienplatz square is unbeatable, the welcome friendly and the rooms tastefully decorated, with wood floors, soft pastel hues and original features including exposed wood beams and vintage furnishings.

Gasthof Obertor
GUESTHOUSE €€

(☑0751-366 70; www.hotelobertor.de; Markt-strasse 67; s €78-98, d €126-136, f €196; P 🛜) The affable Rimpps take pride in their lem-on-fronted patrician house. Obertor stands head and shoulders above most Altstadt guesthouses, with spotless rooms, a sauna area and generous breakfasts.

Waldhorn
HISTORIC HOTEL €€€

(☑0751-361 20; http://waldhorn.de; Marienplatz 15; s €119-129, d €159-199; 🛜) The Waldhorn creaks with history and its light, appealingly restored rooms make a great base for exploring the Altstadt. Breakfast is served in the wood-beamed restaurant, lodged in the 15th-century vintners' guildhall.

Cafe Glücklich
CAFE €

(http://cafeglueecklich.com; Grüner-Turm-Strasse 25; light meals €6-12; ⊙9am-6pm Mon-Sat; ☑) *Glücklich* means 'happy' and most customers are that indeed at this sweet, easygoing cafe, decked out with floral wallpaper and mismatched vintage furniture. Nab a table for homemade treats prepared with regional ingredients – from breakfast burgers to green smoothies, vegan waffles, tortes, tarts and chai. The staff can advise on allergy-free options.

Mohren
INTERNATIONAL €

(☑0751-1805 4310; www.mohren-ravensburg.de; Marktstrasse 61; mains €9-22.50; ⊙10.30am-midnight Mon-Fri, 9.30am-midnight Sat) 'Contemporary rustic' best sums up Mohren, with its bright feel, exposed red brick and log piles. The menu wings you from antipasti to steaks, Swabian classics and Thai curries, all playfully presented and revealing the chef's pride in careful sourcing.

Gleis 9
INTERNATIONAL €€

(☑0751-3594 3720; http://gleis9-rv.de; Escher-Wyss-Strasse 9; mains €13-17; ⊙5pm-midnight Tue-Thu & Sun, to 3am Fri & Sat) In a warehouse right behind Ravensburg's main train station, on what was once platform 9, this industrial-cool pick has a cool backlit, red-brick, lounge-style interior. The menu stays on track with street food: goat's cheese with pesto, chicken gyros, pulled pork with slaw, sweet potato fries – you name it. DJ beats pick up as the night wears on.

❶ Information

Ravensburg Tourist Office (☑0751-828 00; www.ravensburg.de; Lederhaus, Marienplatz 35; ⊙9am-5.30pm Mon-Fri, 9.30am-2pm Sat)

The office is located right in the heart of town on Marienplatz.

❶ Getting There & Away

The train station is six blocks west of the tourist office along Eisenbahnstrasse. Ravensburg is on the train line linking Friedrichshafen (€6, 15 minutes, at least twice hourly) with Ulm (€20.10, 1¼ hours, at least hourly) and Stuttgart (€36.50, two hours, at least hourly).

Lindau

☑08382 / POP 25,249

Brochures rhapsodise about Lindau being Germany's 'Garden of Eden' and the 'Bavarian Riviera'. Paradise and southern France it ain't, but it is pretty special. Cradled in the southern crook of Lake Constance and almost dipping its toes into Austria, this is a good-looking, outgoing little town, with a candy-coloured postcard of an Altstadt, clear-day Alpine views and lake-front cafes that use every sunray to the max.

⊙ Sights

Seepromenade
AREA

In summer the harbourside promenade has a happy-go-lucky air, with its palms, bobbing boats and folk sunning themselves in pavement cafes.

Out at the harbour gates, looking across to the Alps, is Lindau's signature 36m-high Neuer Leuchtturm and, just in case you forget which state you're in, a statue of the Bavarian lion. The square, tile-roofed 13th-century **Mangturm** (Old Lighthouse) guards the northern edge of the sheltered port.

Stadtmuseum
MUSEUM

(www.kultur-lindau.de; Marktplatz 6; adult/concession €8/3.50; ⊙10am-6pm) Lions and voluptuous dames dance across the trompe l'oeil facade of the flamboyantly baroque Haus zum Cavazzen, which contains this museum, showcasing a fine collection of furniture, weapons and paintings. The museum also hosts stellar temporary exhibitions; previous shows have included works by Picasso, Chagall, Matisse, Emil Nolde, Klee and August Macke.

Neuer Leuchtturm
VIEWPOINT

(New Lighthouse; Hafenplatz; adult/concession €1.80/0.70; ⊙10am-7.30pm) Climb 139 steps to the top of this 36m-high lighthouse for cracking views out over Lindau and Lake

Constance, especially on clear days when the Alps are visible on the horizon. The lighthouse shines at night.

Peterskirche
CHURCH

(Oberer Schrannenplatz; ⊘variable) **FREE** Looking back on a 1000-year history, this enigmatic church is now a war memorial, hiding exquisite time-faded frescoes of the Passion of Christ by Hans Holbein the Elder. The cool, dimly lit interior is a quiet spot for contemplation. Next door is the turreted 14th-century Diebsturm, once a tiny jail.

Altes Rathaus
LANDMARK

(Old Town Hall; Bismarckplatz 4) Lindau's biggest architectural stunner is the step-gabled Altes Rathaus, built in 1422 in flamboyant Gothic style. Decorated many centuries later in 1930, its facade is a frescoed frenzy of cherubs, merry minstrels, galleons, fishermen, farmers and sea monsters.

🛏 Sleeping

Hotel Anker
GUESTHOUSE €€

(☏08382-260 9844; www.anker-lindau.com; Bindergasse 15; s €59-69, d €85-169; 🕸) Shiny parquet floors, citrus colours and artwork have spruced up the charming and peaceful rooms at this central guesthouse, tucked down a cobbled lane. Rates include a hearty breakfast. There is no lift.

Hotel Garni-Brugger
HISTORIC HOTEL €€

(☏08382-934 10; www.hotel-garni-brugger.de; Bei der Heidenmauer 11; s €60-88, d €94-135, tr €118-148, q €128-165; 🕸) This 18th-century hotel has bright rooms done up in floral fabrics and pine, which are comfortable enough if nothing flash. The family go out of their way to please. Guests can unwind in the little spa with steam room and sauna (€10) in the cooler months.

Helvetia
BOUTIQUE HOTEL €€€

(☏08382-9130; www.hotel-helvetia.com; Seepromenade; r €220-380; 🕸🏊) With an unbeatable location right on the lake front with a stellar view of the lighthouse, Helvetia is a superchic boutique number, with a mix of highly stylish rooms with themes swinging from the Swiss Alps to Oriental Spa (with own sauna). Or you can notch up the fancy factor by staying the night in a private yacht in the harbour.

Hotel Alte Schule
HOTEL €€€

(☏08382-911 4444; www.hotelalteschule-lindau.de; Alter Schulplatz 2; s €75-95, d €120-220, ste €180-

WORTH A TRIP

PFAHLBAUTEN

Awarded Unesco World Heritage status in 2011, the **Pfahlbauten** (Pile Dwellings; www.pfahlbauten.de; Strandpromenade 6, Unteruhldingen; adult/concession €10/8; ⊘9am-6.30pm Apr-Sep, to 5pm Oct, 9am-5pm Sat & Sun Nov) represent one of 11 prehistoric pile dwellings around the Alps. Based on the findings of local excavations, the carefully reconstructed dwellings catapult you back to the Stone and Bronze Ages, from 4000 to 850 BC. A spin of the lakefront complex takes in stilt dwellings that give an insight into the lives of farmers, fishers and craftspeople. Kids love the hands-on activities from axe-making to fire-starting using flints.

250; P🕸) A recent makeover has brought this hotel bang up to date. Housed in a listed 15th-century building, the themed rooms zoom in on different places around Lake Constance, from the flowery exuberance of Insel Mainau to the rustic-cool, mountain-themed Pfänder. Regional and organic produce incuding pastries, eggs to order and fresh orange juice, appear at breakfast.

Alte Post
HOTEL €€€

(☏08382-934 60; www.alte-post-lindau.de; Fischergasse 3; s €75-95, d €140-190, f €180-210; 🕸) This 300-year-old coaching inn was once a stop on the Frankfurt–Milan mail run. Well-kept, light and spacious, the newly revamped rooms (including those suitable for families) have solid oak floors and furnishings. Downstairs is a beer garden and a highly regarded restaurant (mains €10 to €22).

🍴 Eating & Drinking

Engelstube
GERMAN €€

(☏08382-5240; www.engel-lindau.de; Schafgasse 4; mains €14-21; ⊘11am-3pm & 5-11pm) Dark wood panelling and plenty of rustic touches keep the vibe cosy at this smart wine tavern, which looks proudly back on more than 600 years of history. Regional dishes such as Lake Constance fish with herbs, and roast Bavarian ox are cooked to a T. Try to snag a spot on the pavement terrace in summer.

Weinstube Frey
GERMAN €€

(☏08382-947 9676; Maximilianstrasse 15; mains €16-22; ⊘11.30am-10pm) This 500-year-old

WORTH A TRIP

AFFENBERG SALEM

No zoo-like cages, no circus antics, just happy Barbary macaques free to roam in a near-natural habitat: that's the concept behind conservation-oriented **Affenberg Salem** (www.affenberg-salem.de; Mendlishauser Hof, Salem; adult/concession €9/6; ⊙9am-6pm mid-Mar-Oct). Trails interweave the 20-hectare woodlands, where you can feed tailless monkeys one piece of special popcorn at a time, observe their behaviour (you scratch my back, I'll scratch yours...) and get primate close-ups at hourly feedings. The park is also home to storks; listen for bill clattering and look out for their nests near the entrance.

wood-panelled wine tavern oozes Bavarian charm with its cosy nooks. Dirndl-clad waitresses serve up regional wines and fare such as Lake Constance whitefish with market veg, and *Zwiebelrostbraten* (onion beef roast). Sit out on the terrace when the sun's out.

Grosstadt CAFE €€
(☑08382-504 2998; www.grossstadt-lindau.de; In der Grub 27; light meals €6-16; ⊙9am-1am; ☺☒)
There's always a good buzz at this retro-flavoured cafe, full of intimate nooks and crannies and with a terrace spilling out onto the cobbles. The menu is a winning mix of speciality coffees, wraps, soups, creative salads, bagels and deli-style dishes such as marinated feta with rocket, with vegan and gluten-free options. It morphs into a chilled bar by night.

Valentin MEDITERRANEAN €€€
(☑08382-504 3740; https://valentin-lindau.de; In der Grub 28; mains €20-31, day specials €11.50-13.50; ⊙6-11pm; ☒) With a deft hand, the chef sources local, seasonal, largely organic ingredients to go into his Med-style dishes at this chic vaulted restaurant. Dishes such as ayurvedic spinach soup, octopus with chorizo, cabbage and sweet potato, and chocolate molten cake with pumpkin ice cream are beautifully prepared and presented. Vegetarians and vegans are well catered for.

37° CAFE
(Bahnhofplatz 1; ⊙10am-8pm Tue-Sun) Part boutique, part boho-chic cafe, 37° combines a high-ceilinged interior with a cracking lake-facing pavement terrace. Pull up a candy-coloured chair for cold drinks and light bites such as tapas, quiche and soups.

Kunst Café CAFE
(http://kunst-cafe.info; Maximilianstrasse 48; ⊙10am-6pm Mon-Sat, noon-6pm Sun) Eat and drink among art and antiques at this rather elegant cafe, where oil paintings festoon walls and chandeliers hang from stuccoed

ceilings. It's a nicely chilled choice for a beer, coffee and a slice of homemade cake or snacks such as tarte flambée.

ⓘ Information

Post Office (Zeppelinstrasse 6, REWE Markt; ⊙7am-8pm Mon-Sat) Post office in REWE supermarket.
Lindau Tourist Office (☑08382-260 030; www.lindau.de; Alfred-Nobel-Platz 1; ⊙10am-noon & 2-5pm Mon-Fri, 10am-4pm Sat & Sun) Lindau's tourist office is handily situated near the main train station.

ⓘ Getting There & Away

Lindau is on the B31 and connects to Munich by the A96. The precipitous Deutsche Alpenstrasse (German Alpine Rd), which winds giddily eastward to Berchtesgaden, begins here.

Lindau is at the eastern terminus of the Bodensee–Gürtelbahn train line, which goes along the lake's north shore via Friedrichshafen (€8, 18 to 35 minutes) westward to Radolfzell, and the southern terminus of the Südbahn to Ulm (€27.90, 1½ to two hours) via Ravensburg (€12.50, one hour).

The lake front **Hauptbahnhof** (Am Bahnhof 1) is right in the heart of the Altstadt.

ⓘ Getting Around

The compact, walkable *Insel* (island), home to the town centre and harbour, is connected to the mainland by the Seebrücke, a road bridge at its northeastern tip, and by the Eisenbahndamm, a rail bridge open to cyclists and pedestrians. The **Hauptbahnhof** lies to the east of the island, a block south of the pedestrianised, shop-lined Maximilianstrasse.

Buses 1 and 2 link the Hauptbahnhof to the main bus hub, known as ZUP. A single ticket costs €2.20; a day pass is €4.40.

Bikes and tandems can be rented at **Unger's Fahrradverleih** (☑08382-943 688; www.fahr rad-unger.de; Inselgraben 14; per day bikes €6-12, tandems €18, electro-bikes €20; ⊙9am-1pm & 3-6pm Mon-Fri, 9am-1pm Sat & Sun Mar-Oct).

Frankfurt & Southern Rhineland

Best Places to Eat

➜ Gollner's (p562)

➜ Kalinski (p626)

➜ Urgestein (p590)

➜ Zur Herrenmühle Heidelberg (p577)

➜ Restaurant Burg Landshut (p615)

Best Places to Stay

➜ Hotel Jagdschloss Kranichstein (p569)

➜ Deidesheimer Hof (p591)

➜ Hotel Villa Marstall (p576)

➜ Hotel Villa Hügel (p621)

➜ Jakobsberg (p603)

Why Go?

In this enchanting corner of Germany, the finer things in life take pride of place: good food, great wine, glorious walking and cycling, and exceptional art everywhere, from magnificent museums to quirky street sculptures.

Vineyards ribbon the steep-sided Romantic Rhine and Moselle valleys, as well as the wisteria-draped German Wine Route, the country's warmest region. All three areas are strewn with hilltop castles, dark forests and scores of snug wineries for sampling exquisite crisp whites.

History abounds here, from the preserved Roman amphitheatre and thermae in Germany's oldest city, Trier; to crooked half-timbered medieval villages; spectacular palaces; centres of learning like the ancient university city of Heidelberg, Goethe's birthplace – the finance and trade-fair hub of Frankfurt; and momentous industrial and engineering legacies – including the invention of the printing press in Mainz, and the bicycle and automobile in Mannheim: that continue to influence the world today.

When to Go

Frankfurt's attractions can be enjoyed at any time of the year, but you'll pay a fortune for accommodation if your visit coincides with a big trade fair. Nearby towns can provide a cheaper base, but you should still book *well* ahead.

The Moselle and Rhine valleys teem with visitors from May to August but are very quiet from November to March, when many establishments close, although towns with Christmas markets are lively in December.

Along the German Wine Route, village wine festivals are held on weekends from March to mid-November; the grape harvest in September and October is especially atmospheric.

Frankfurt & Southern Rhineland Highlights

1 River cruise
(p545) Floating past Frankfurt's medieval church spires and glittering skyscrapers aboard a river cruise.

2 Hiking in Rüdesheim (p599) Catching a cable car uphill to head out on a hike through vineyards along the castle-studded Romantic Rhine.

3 Schloss Heidelberg (p573) Wandering the ruins and gardens of Heidelberg's romantic red-sandstone castle.

4 Mainzer Dom (p563) Marvelling at the towering Romanesque cathedral in Mainz.

5 Kaiser-Friedrich-Therme (p560) Soaking in the steaming spring-fed pools of Wiesbaden's *Jugendstil* (art nouveau) thermal baths.

6 Roman sites (p616) Travelling back to the time of the gladiators at the remarkable Roman ruins in Germany's oldest city, Trier.

7 Cycling in the Moselle Valley (p607) Pedalling along the banks of the gently winding, wine-tavern-lined Moselle.

8 HockenheimRing (p585) Zooming around Germany's famed Formula One Grand Prix race track.

❶ Getting There & Away

Frankfurt is the region's main gateway. Frankfurt Airport (p557) is a major hub, with flights to destinations across the globe. The smaller Frankfurt-Hahn Airport (p558), served by low-cost carriers, is inconvenient for Frankfurt itself but is handy for the Moselle Valley.

Frankfurt's Hauptbahnhof has train services throughout Germany and to European destinations. Direct services include Amsterdam (the Netherlands); Basel, Zürich, Bern and Interlaken (Switzerland); Milan (Italy); Vienna, Salzburg, Innsbruck and Graz (Austria).

❶ Getting Around

Your own wheels (two or four) are ideal for exploring this region.

Boats travel along the Rhine and Moselle rivers.

Trains are the most efficient form of public transport between major destinations; in smaller places, local buses fill the gaps.

BICYCLE

The region is a cycling paradise. Delightful long-distance bike trails (www.radwanderland.de and www.radroutenplaner.hessen.de) run along the Rhine, the Moselle and the German Wine Route, and in Saarland. Many follow decommissioned rail lines, with gentle gradients. Almost all cities and towns have bike rental options.

Tourist offices can supply cycling maps that include elevation charts, and outline your public transport options (so, for example, you can catch a ride up the hill and cycle back down).

Bicycles can be taken aboard all regional trains for no charge except between 6am and 9am from Monday to Friday, when you need a special ticket (from €1.80). You can also take bikes aboard ferries for a small charge (€1 to €2.50).

TRAIN

Day passes often work out to be significantly cheaper than standard one-way fares, especially for groups. Buy them from train stations' ticket counters or ticket machines.

Hessenticket (One day €35) Allows a group of up to five people travelling together to take regional trains (those designated RB, RE and IRE, ie any trains except D, IC, EC or ICE) anywhere within the German federal state of Hesse, plus Mainz and Worms, any time after 9am (all day on Saturday, Sunday and public holidays) – an incredible deal.

Rheinland-Pfalz-Ticket (One day for one person €24, additional person €6) Valid from 9am to 3am the next morning (all day on weekends and holidays) for up to five people travelling together in both Rhineland-Palatinate and Saarland, plus adjacent parts of Hesse (including Wiesbaden) and Baden-Württemberg (including Mannheim). Parents and grandparents can bring along their children or grandchildren under the age of 14 for free.

Baden-Württemberg-Ticket (One day for one person €24, additional person €6) For travel in the Heidelberg area. Same conditions as the Rheinland-Pfalz-Ticket.

For route maps and bookings, visit www.bahn.de.

FRANKFURT REGION

This densely populated region takes in the cities of Frankfurt am Main, Darmstadt, Mainz and Wiesbaden.

Frankfurt am Main

📱 069 / POP 732,688

Glinting with glass, steel and concrete skyscrapers, Frankfurt-on-the-Main (pronounced 'mine') is unlike any other German city. The focal point of a conurbation of 5.5 million inhabitants, 'Mainhattan' is a high-powered finance and business hub, home to one of the world's largest stock exchanges and the gleaming headquarters of the European Central Bank, and famously hosts some of the world's most important trade fairs, attracting thousands of business travellers.

Yet at its heart, Frankfurt is an unexpectedly traditional and charming city, with half-timbered buildings huddled in its quaint medieval Altstadt (old town), cosy apple-wine taverns serving hearty regional food, village-like neighbourhoods filled with outdoor cafes, boutiques and street art, and beautiful parks, gardens and riverside paths. The city's cache of museums is second in Germany only to Berlin's, and its nightlife and entertainment scenes are bolstered by a spirited student population.

History

Around two millennia ago Frankfurt was a site of Celtic and Germanic settlement, and later – in the area known today as the Römerberg – a Roman garrison town.

Mentioned in historical documents as far back as AD 794, Frankfurt was an important centre of power in the Holy Roman Empire. With the election of Frederick I (Barbarossa) in 1152, the city became the customary site of the selection of German kings. International trade fairs – attracting business from

FRANKFURT IN...

One Day

Begin in Frankfurt's historic heart at the **Kaiserdom**, visiting its **museum** and, if you're feeling active, climbing its tower. See more of medieval Frankfurt at the **Römerberg** (p538). Head west for lunch with river views at glass-framed restaurant **Main Nizza** (p550). Then delve deeper into the city's rich past at the **Historisches Museum Frankfurt** (p538).

Cross the river to Alt-Sachsenhausen for Frankfurt specialities and a glass of traditional *Apfelwein* (apple wine) at **Dauth-Schneider** (p551). Hop between the bars and clubs lining cobbled Klappergasse, or catch a jazz or blues concert at **Summa Summarum** (p555).

Two Days

Start your second day along the riverside Museumsufer (Museum Bank), whose row of museums cover everything from **fine arts** (p542) to **film** (p543). Set amid parkland, the **Maincafé** (p554) makes a peaceful stop for lunch.

In the afternoon, take a scenic **river cruise** (p545), then browse the aromatic food stalls at the **Kleinmarkthall** (p549). Catch an early dinner in the candlelit cellar of **Zu den 12 Aposteln** (p550) and be sure to try its home-brewed beers. Then zip up the lift inside the soaring **Main Tower** (p539) to its observation deck for sweeping views of the city skyline after dark. Stay for **cocktails** (p539), or pre-book to take in a performance at the **Städtische Bühnen** (p555) cultural complex.

---

the Mediterranean to the Baltic – were held here from the 12th century.

In 1372 Frankfurt became a 'free imperial city', a status it enjoyed almost uninterrupted until the Prussian takeover of 1866. A stock exchange began operating in Frankfurt in 1585, and it was here that the Rothschild banking family began its ascent in the 1760s.

Frankfurt has a strong Jewish history – in 1933, its Jewish community, with 30,000 members, was Germany's second largest. Around town, you may see brass squares the size of a cobblestone embedded in the pavement. These *Stolpersteine* ('stumbling blocks') serve as memorials to Jews deported by the Nazis by marking their last place of residence.

About 80% of Frankfurt's medieval city centre was destroyed – and over 1000 people were killed – by Allied bombing raids in March 1944. The area around the Römerberg has since been reconstructed.

Today, Frankfurt is a thriving, contemporary city still focused on trade fairs and finance.

◉ Sights

Note that most of Frankfurt's museums are closed on Mondays; exceptions include the Goethe-Haus (p539) and Senckenberg Museum (p544).

◉ Altstadt

The city's historic core centres on the Dom and the lively, tourist-mobbed Römerberg, a medieval public square ringed by reconstructed half-timbered buildings.

★ Kaiserdom CATHEDRAL
(Imperial Frankfurt Cathedral; www.dom-frankfurt.de; Domplatz 1; tower adult/child €3/1.50; ⊙ church 9am-8pm Sun-Thu, from 1pm Fri, tower 9am-6pm Apr-Oct, 10am-5pm Nov-Apr; Ⓤ Dom|Römer) Frankfurt's red-sandstone cathedral is dominated by a 95m-high Gothic tower, which can be climbed via 328 steps. Construction began in the 13th century; from 1356 to 1792, the Holy Roman Emperors were elected (and, after 1562, consecrated and crowned) in the *Wahlkapelle* at the end of the right aisle (look for the 'skull' altar). The cathedral was rebuilt both after an 1867 fire and after the bombings of 1944, which left it a burntout shell.

It's dedicated to the apostle St Bartholomew, hence its official name, Kaiserdom St Bartholomäus.

The on-site **Dommuseum** (Cathedral Museum; ☑ 069-1337 6186; www.dommuseum-frankfurt.de; museum adult/child €4/2, cathedral tours €4/2; ⊙10am-5pm Tue-Fri, from 11am Sat & Sun, cathedral tours 3pm Tue-Sun) has a small collection of precious liturgical objects.

Frequent concerts, including organ recitals take place here; schedules are listed on the Dom's website.

★ Römerberg
SQUARE

(Ⓤ Dom|Römer) The Römerberg is Frankfurt's old central square. Ornately gabled half-timbered buildings, reconstructed after WWII, give an idea of how beautiful the city's medieval core once was. In the square's centre is the Gerechtigkeitsbrunnen (Fountain of Justice). The Römerberg is especially lovely as a backdrop for the Christmas market (p546) in December.

Römer
HISTORIC BUILDING

(Römerberg; Ⓤ Dom|Römer) The photogenic Römer (old town hall) consists of three step-gabled 15th-century houses. In the time of the Holy Roman Empire, it was the site of celebrations during the election and coronation of emperors. Today it houses the office of Frankfurt's mayor and serves as the registry office. The barrel-vaulted Kaisersaal (Emperor's Hall; ☑ 069-2123 4814; adult/child €2/0.50; ☺10am-1pm & 2-5pm, closed during events) is accessed from Limpurgergasse via a courtyard and carved red-sandstone spiral staircase.

Museum für Moderne Kunst
MUSEUM

(MMK; Museum of Modern Art; ☑ 069-2123 0447; www.mmk-frankfurt.de; Domstrasse 10; adult/child €12/6, all three sites €16/8; ☺10am-6pm Tue & Thu-Sun, to 8pm Wed; Ⓤ Dom|Römer) The outstanding Museum of Modern Art focuses on European and American art from the 1960s to the present, with frequent temporary exhibits. The permanent collection (not always on display) includes works by Roy Lichtenstein, Claes Oldenburg and Joseph Beuys. Free English-language tours on varying topics take place at 4pm every Saturday. The main premises are referred to as MMK1; there are another two exhibition spaces, MMK2 (in the TaunusTurm at Taunustor 1) and MMK3 (opposite MMK 1 at Domstrasse 3).

The distinctive MMK1 building is dubbed the 'slice of cake' because of its triangular footprint.

Schirn Kunsthalle
MUSEUM

(www.schirn.de; Römerberg; ☺10am-7pm Tue & Fri-Sun, to 10pm Wed & Thu; Ⓤ Dom|Römer) Some of Germany's most topical and talked-about art exhibitions take place at this modern and contemporary art museum, such as retrospectives of artists like Kandinsky, Chagall, Kahlo, Giacometti and Klein, as well as digital art, and themes such as 'artists and prophets'. The building's interlocking structures include a domed rotunda main entrance hall and a 140m-long central exhibition building designed to resemble the Uffizi building in Florence. Admission prices depend on the exhibition; pre-purchase tickets to avoid queueing.

Alte Nikolaikirche
CHURCH

(www.alte-nikolaikirche.de; Römerberg; ☺10am-8pm Apr-Sep, to 6pm Oct-Mar; Ⓤ Dom|Römer) Topped by a single spire, this red-sandstone Protestant church – begun in the 13th century – is situated on the south side of Römerberg and was one of the few Altstadt structures to survive WWII almost intact. In the tranquil interior, under late-Gothic vaulting, are stone carvings and 14th- and 15th-century gravestones.

Historisches Museum Frankfurt
MUSEUM

(Historical Museum; www.historisches-museum. frankfurt.de; Saalhof 1; adult/child €8/free; ☺10am-6pm Tue & Thu, to 9pm Wed, 11am-7pm Sat & Sun; Ⓤ Dom|Römer) Showcasing Frankfurt's long and fascinating history, the city's revamped Historical Museum occupies a five-building complex completed in 2017. Its main permanent collection, *Frankfurt Then?*, spans daily life, finance, trade, military, science, children's toys, photography, paintings, graphic prints, ceramics, sculptures, media, fashion, textiles, furniture, musical instruments and technology, arranged thematically rather than chronologically. *Frankfurt Now!* features a scale model of the city based on contemporary residents' impressions by artist Herman Helle.

Junges Museum Frankfurt
MUSEUM

(Young Museum Frankfurt; ☑ 069-2123 5154; www. kindermuseum.frankfurt.de; Historisches Museum Frankfurt, Saalhof 1; adult/child €4/2; ☺10am-6pm Tue, Thu & Fri, to 9pm Wed, 11am-7pm Sat & Sun; ☒; Ⓤ Römer) Formerly Frankfurt's Children's Museum, this museum dedicated to kids and families became the Junges Museum Frankfurt (Young Museum) in 2018 when it reopened at its original premises at the Historisches Museum Frankfurt. Exhibitions change regularly; it also runs various arts, crafts and other hands-on workshops.

◉ Innenstadt

The Innenstadt (inner city), Frankfurt's financial, business and commercial heart, is bounded by the park-lined Main River to the south and elsewhere by a narrow, semi circular band of parks. They follow the route of the city's medieval walls, torn down between 1806 and 1812.

Museum Judengasse
MUSEUM

(www.museumjudengasse.de; Battonnstrasse 47; adult/child €6/free, multimedia guide €2; ⊙10am-8pm Tue, to 6pm Wed-Sun; ⓤKonstablerwache) Most of Frankfurt's medieval Jewish ghetto – Europe's first, dating from 1460 – on narrow Judengasse (Jews' Street) was destroyed by a French bombardment in 1796, but you can get a sense of local Jewish life during the 15th to 18th centuries from the excavated remains of houses and ritual baths. Laws confining Frankfurt's Jews to the ghetto were repealed in 1811. Renovated in 2016, the museum here spotlights the former residents' interactions with Frankfurt's Christian residents, the city council and the emperor.

Also here is the Old Jewish Cemetery; about a third of the cemetery's original tombstones, dating from the 13th century to 1828, survived Nazi depredations; many still lean at crazy angles. The exterior of the cemetery's western wall is known as the Wand der Namen (Wall of Names) because it is studded with row upon row of metal cubes bearing the names of 11,000 Frankfurt Jews who died in the Holocaust. Visitors often place pebbles atop the cubes to indicate, in accordance with Jewish tradition, that the deceased are still remembered.

Alte Oper
ARCHITECTURE

(Old Opera House; www.alteoper.de; Opernplatz 1; ⓤAlte Oper) Inaugurated in 1880, the Italian Renaissance-style Alte Oper anchors the western end of the Zeil-Fressgass pedestrian zone. Burnt out in 1944, it narrowly avoided being razed and replaced with 1960s cubes. It was finally reconstructed between 1976 and 1981 to resemble the original, with statues of Goethe and Mozart gracing its ornate facade. Other than the mosaics in the lobby, the interior – closed except during concerts (p555) – is modern.

Main Tower
VIEWPOINT

(☎069-3650 4878; www.maintower.de; Neue Mainzer Strasse 52-58; adult/child €7.50/5; ⊙10am-9pm Sun-Thu, to 11pm Fri & Sat Apr-Oct, 10am-7pm Sun-Thu, to 9pm Fri & Sat Nov-Mar, cocktail lounge 9pm-midnight Tue-Thu, to 1am Fri & Sat; ⓤAlte Oper) Frankfurt's skyline wouldn't be the same without the Main Tower, one of the tallest and most distinctive high-rises in town. A great place to get a feel for 'Mainhattan' is 200m above street level, on the tower's observation platform, reached by lift in a mere 45 seconds. Pre-booking tickets online saves time queuing, but be prepared for airport-type security. It closes during adverse weather.

You can also take in the cityscape from the 53rd-floor restaurant (☎069-3650 4777; www.maintower-restaurant.de; 2-/3-course lunch menus €31/39, 3-/4-/5-course dinner menus €79/92/105, with paired wines €109/130/152; ⊙noon-3pm & 6pm-midnight Tue-Thu, to 1am Fri, 6pm-1am Sat) or the adjacent cocktail lounge.

Goethe-Haus
HISTORIC BUILDING

(www.goethehaus-frankfurt.de; Grosser Hirschgraben 23-25; adult/child €7/3, audioguide €3; ⊙10am-6pm Mon-Sat, to 5.30pm Sun; ⓤWilly-Brandt-Platz) Completely rebuilt after WWII (only the cellar survived Allied bombing), the birthplace of Johann Wolfgang von Goethe (1749–1832) is furnished in the haute-bourgeois style of Goethe's time, based on an inventory taken when Goethe's family sold the property. One of the few pieces that actually belonged to the great writer, philosopher and statesman is a puppet theatre given to him at age four. The Goethe-Museum (included in admission) displays seminal paintings from Goethe's era.

Jüdisches Museum
MUSEUM

(Jewish Museum; www.juedischesmuseum.de; Untermainkai 14-15; ⓤWilly-Brandt-Platz) Frankfurt's Jüdisches Museum is set in the one-time residence of the Rothschild family, the Rothschildpalais. It's closed for renovations until 2019. When it reopens, it will pick up from the Museum Judengasse, which covers Jewish history until 1800, with displays on the period from 1800 to the present day.

Frankfurt Stock Exchange
NOTABLE BUILDING

(Börse; ☎069-2111 1515; www.deutsche-boerse.com; Börsenplatz 4; ⓤHauptwache) The famous old Börse, built in 1843, is an impressively colonnaded neoclassical structure. The porch is decorated with allegorical statues of the five continents. A new visitor centre is expected to open in 2019, and will offer guided tours.

In the square out front, a sculpture entitled Bulle und Bär depicts a showdown between a bull and a bear.

FRANKFURT & SOUTHERN RHINELAND FRANKFURT AM MAIN

Central Frankfurt

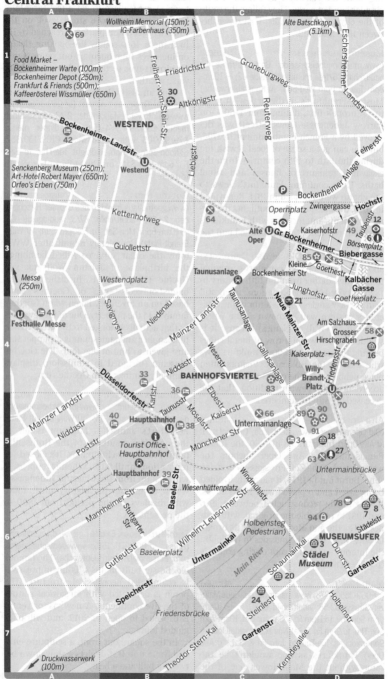

Wollheim Memorial (150m);
IG-Farbenhaus (350m);

Alte Batschkapp
(5.1km)

Food Market –
Bockenheimer Warte (100m);
Bockenheimer Depot (250m);
Frankfurt & Friends (500m);
Kaffeerösterei Wissmüller (650m)

WESTEND

Bockenheimer Landstr

Senckenberg Museum (250m);
Art-Hotel Robert Mayer (650m);
Orfeo's Erben (750m)

Westend

Kettenhofweg

Guiollettstr

Messe
(250m)

Westendplatz

Festhalle/Messe

Savignystr

Niedenau

Düsseldorferstr

Karlstr

Mainzer Landstr

Niddastr

Poststr

Mannheimer Str

Gutleutstr

Stuttgarter Str

Speicherstr

Friedensbrücke

Druckwasserwerk
(100m)

Freiherr-vom-Stein-Str

Friedrichstr

Altkönigstr

Liebigstr

Mainzer Landstr

Weserstr

Niddastr

Taunusstr

Moselstr

Elbestr

Hauptbahnhof

Tourist Office -
Hauptbahnhof

Hauptbahnhof

Baseler Str

Wiesenhüttenplatz

Wilhelm-Leuschner-Str

Untermainkai

Baselerplatz

Theodor-Stern-Kai

Grüneburgweg

Reuterweg

Bockenheimer Anlage

Opernplatz

Alte Oper

Gr Bockenheimer Str

Kaiserhofstr

Kleine Bockenheimer Str

Kleine Goethestr

Taunusanlage

Taunusanlage

Neue Mainzer Str

Junghofstr

Kaiserstr

Münchener Str

Untermainanlage

Windmühlstr

Holbeinsteg
(Pedestrian)

Main River

Schaumainkai

Steinlestr

Gartenstr

Eschersheimer Landstr

Fellnerstr

Hochstr

Zwingergasse

Börsenplatz

Biebergasse

Goethestr

Kalbächer Gasse

Goetheplatz

Am Salzhaus

Grosser Hirschgraben

Kaiserplatz

Willy-Brandt-Platz

Friedensstr

Untermainbrücke

MUSEUMSUFER

Städel Museum

Städelstr

Durerstr

Gartenstr

Holbeinstr

Kennedyallee

FRANKFURT & SOUTHERN RHINELAND FRANKFURT FRANKFURT AM MAIN

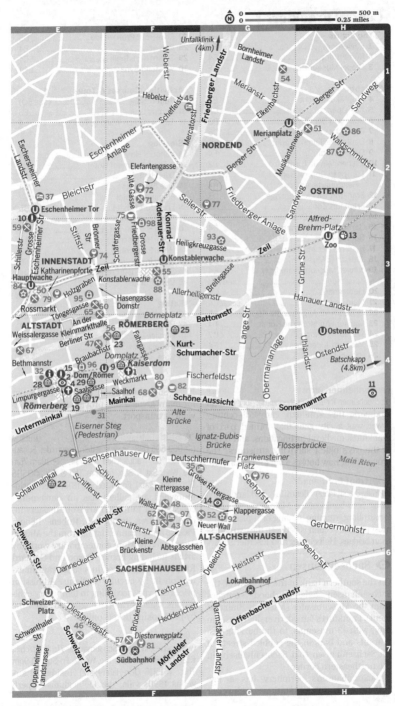

Central Frankfurt

Eschenheimer Turm
TOWER

(Eschenheimer Tor 1; U Eschenheimer Tor) A local landmark, this 47m-high, early-15th-century tower was a city gate that formed part of Frankfurt's medieval fortifications, and is one of the city's oldest surviving structures. The ground floor now houses a bar and restaurant.

Riverfront Promenade
PARK

(U Willy-Brandt-Platz) Beautiful parkland runs along both banks of the Main River – perfect for strolling, running, cycling or a picnic. The most popular section is between the two pedestrian bridges, Holbeinsteg and Eiserner Steg.

◉ Sachsenhausen

On the southern bank of the Main River, the Sachsenhausen neighbourhood stretches from the Museumsufer (Museum Embankment), Frankfurt's famed, riverside 'museum row', with 13 museums, to the buzzing restaurants and bars in the cobbled streets of Alt-Sachsenhausen (old Sachsenhausen) in the northeastern corner.

Sachsenhausen's periphery has a few U-Bahn and S-Bahn stations (Schweizer Platz, Südbahnhof and Lokalbahnhof) but for many areas trams provide the most convenient transport.

★ Städel Museum
MUSEUM

(☎069-605 098; www.staedelmuseum.de; Schaumainkai 63; adult/child €16/14; ☺10am-7pm Tue, Wed, Sat & Sun, to 9pm Thu & Fri; ☐15|16 Otto-Hahn-Platz) Founded in 1815, this world-renowned art gallery has an outstanding collection of European art from masters including Dürer, Rembrandt, Rubens, Renoir, Picasso and Cézanne, dating from the Middle Ages to today. More contemporary works by artists including Francis Bacon and Gerhard Richter are showcased in a subterranean extension lit by circular skylights. Admission prices can vary according to temporary exhibitions. Queues can be lengthy, so save time by pre-booking tickets online.

Liebieghaus
MUSEUM

(www.liebieghaus.de; Schaumainkai 71; adult/child €12/10; ☺10am-6pm Tue, Wed & Fri-Sun, to 9pm Thu; ☐15|16 Otto-Hahn-Platz) Inside a gorgeous 1890s villa, the Liebieghaus' superb

FRANKFURT & SOUTHERN RHINELAND FRANKFURT AM MAIN

sculpture collection encompasses Greek, Roman, Egyptian, medieval, Renaissance and baroque works, plus some items from East Asia. Special exhibitions (extra charges may apply) sometimes displace parts of the permanent collection. There's a beautiful cross-vaulted cafe on site.

Museum für Angewandte Kunst MUSEUM
(Museum of Applied Arts; ☑069-2123 1286; www.museumangewandtekunst.de; Schaumainkai 17; adult/child €12/6; ☺10am-6pm Tue & Thu-Sun, to 8pm Wed; 🚊15|16 Schweizerstrasse-Gartenstrasse) Contemporary trends in design and fashion are featured alongside displays of beautiful furniture, textiles, metalwork, glass and ceramics from Europe (including *Jugendstil*) and Asia at Frankfurt's Museum of Applied Arts. It's set amid lush gardens in the 1804-built Villa Metzler; there's a swish on-site bistro with outdoor seating.

Deutsches Filmmuseum MUSEUM
(www.deutsches-filminstitut.de; Schaumainkai 41; adult/child €7/5; ☺10am-6pm Tue & Thu-Sun, to 8pm Wed; 🚊15|16|19 Schweizerstrasse-Gartenstrasse) Permanent and changing exhibitions chart the history of cinema, film-making, and specific genres and artists at this dynamic museum. Signs are in English and German; there's also an art-house cinema (☑069-961 220 220; ☺Tue-Sun).

Frau Rauscher Brunnen FOUNTAIN
(Klappergasse; 🚊14|18 Frankensteiner Platz) Inspired by a local song about apple wine, the Frau Rauscher Brunnen – a statue of a fierce-looking, apple-wine-jug-wielding woman – periodically sprays a stream of water onto the footpath during the warmer months; when the street's busy, you'll often see pedestrians get drenched.

Museum Giersch MUSEUM
(☑069-1382 1010; www.museum-giersch.de; Schaumainkai 83; adult/child €6/4; ☺noon-7pm Tue-Thu, 10am-6pm Fri-Sun; 🚊15|16 Otto-Hahn-Platz) Lesser-known Frankfurt-area artists from the 19th and early 20th centuries are the focus of the special exhibitions at this neoclassical riverside villa, with displays spanning painting, photography, sculpture and graphic art, along with architecture and applied art.

Deutsches Architekturmuseum MUSEUM
(DAM; www.dam-online.de; Schaumainkai 43; adult/child €9/4.50; ⊙ 11am-6pm Tue & Thu-Sun, to 8pm Wed; 🚇 16 Schweizerstrasse-Gartenstrasse) Germany's architecture museum mounts three temporary exhibitions at a time, which often focus on a particular architect or firm. Not much relates to Frankfurt, though. Signs are in English and German.

⊙ Messe, Westend & Bockenheim

Heading northwest from the Innenstadt along Bockenheimer Landstrasse brings you to the leafy Westend neighbourhood's parks and stately residential streets lined with grand 19th-century apartments and mansions.

At the area's southwestern edge is the trade fair ground known as the **Messe** (www.messefrankfurt.com; Ludwig-Erhard-Anlage 1; **S** Messe), which is frenetic during events and desolate outside them. To the north lies the monumental IG-Farbenhaus, which anchors the Westend campus of Goethe Universität (Frankfurt University).

Bockenheimer Landstrasse leads to Bockenheim, centred on the lively main shopping street, Leipziger Strasse.

★ **Senckenberg Museum** MUSEUM
(☑ 069-754 20; www.senckenberg.de; Senckenberganlage 25; adult/child €10/5, audioguide €3; ⊙ 9am-5pm Mon, Tue, Thu & Fri, to 8pm Wed, to 6pm Sat & Sun; **U** Bockenheimer Warte) Life-size dinosaur mock-ups guard the front of Frankfurt's natural history museum. Inside the early 1900s neo-baroque building, exhibits cover palaeontology (including fossils from the Grube Messel site; p572), biology and geology. Most have English signs.

PalmenGarten PARK
(www.palmengarten.de; Siesmayerstrasse 63; adult/child €7/3; ⊙ 9am-6pm Feb-Oct, to 4pm Nov-Jan; **U** Palmengartenstrasse) Established in 1871, Frankfurt's botanical PalmenGarten (palm garden) is filled with tropical hothouses, rose gardens, a bamboo grove and rock garden. There are playgrounds for kids, a pond with row boats (May to September) and a mini-gauge train. Open-air concerts take place here in summer. A second entrance is located on Palmengartenstrasse.

IG-Farbenhaus HISTORIC BUILDING
(☑ 069-7982 2472; www.uni-frankfurt.de; Grüneburgplatz 1; ⊙ 7am-10pm Mon-Sat; **U** Holzhausenstrasse) The monumental seven-storey IG-Farbenhaus was erected in 1931 as the headquarters of IG-Farben (pronounced 'ee geh far-behn'), the mammoth German chemicals conglomerate whose constituent companies included Agfa, BASF, Bayer and Hoechst. After Hitler took power, Jewish scientists and executives were fired, and the company's products soon became central to the Nazi war effort.

Inside, on the 1st to 5th floors at cross wing Q4, you can check out an informative historical exhibit (in English and German) with photographs and illustrations.

From 1941 to 1944, staff based in this building kept the Final Solution running smoothly by carrying out the work of co-ordinating the production of the company's most notorious product, Zyklon-B, the cyanide-based killing agent used in the gas chambers of Auschwitz.

After the war, IG-Farbenhaus served briefly as the headquarters of General Dwight D Eisenhower, Supreme Commander of Allied Forces in Europe, and later as the headquarters of US occupation forces ('the Pentagon in Europe') and as a CIA bureau.

In 1995, with the Cold War over, US forces handed the building back to Germany's federal government. After refurbishment, it became the focal point of the new Westend campus of Johann-Wolfgang-Goethe-Universität – and a bastion of the spirit of free inquiry and humanism that Nazism tried to extinguish.

Seven of its nine floors are served by two paternoster lifts, whose open cabins keep cycling around like rosary beads. Signs warn that these historic elevators are not safe for children, pets and people wearing back-packs or skates.

About 50m from the southwest corner of the building (to the left as you approach the main entrance) stands the **Wollheim Memorial** (www.wollheim-memorial.de; Norbert-Wollheim-Platz; ⊙ 8am-6pm; **U** Holzhausenstrasse).

Under the trees in front of IG-Farbenhaus, panels show photographs of German Jews, later sent to Buna/Monowitz, enjoying life in the years before the Holocaust, unaware of what was to come.

Westend Synagogue SYNAGOGUE
(Westend Shtibel, Beit HaMidrash; ☑ 069-768 036 100; www.jg.ffm.de; Freiherr-vom-Stein-Strasse 30; ⊙ by appointment; **U** Westend) Frankfurt's largest synagogue was built between 1908 and 1910 by Lichtenstein-born architect Franz

Roeckle (1879–1953), who trained in Stuttgart before settling in Frankfurt. Damaged in the 1938 pogroms and WWII bombing raids, its interior was restored between 1948 and 1950, but restoration of its exterior wasn't completed until 1994. On its gable, a medallion features a heraldic lion holding a shield bearing the Star of David in its paw.

◉ Ostend

The neighbourhoods east of the Innenstadt and the Nordend are known as the Ostend. Hanauer Landstrasse runs through the Osthafen ('eastern harbour') area.

Frankfurt Zoo   ZOO
(Zoologischer Garten; ☑069-2123 3735; www. zoo-frankfurt.de; Bernhard-Grzimek-Allee 1; adult/ child €10/5; ⊙9am-7pm Apr-Oct, to 5pm Nov-Mar; 🚸; Ⓤ Zoo) Dating from 1874, Frankfurt's 11-hectare zoo is home to some 4500 animals, with houses for primates, nocturnal creatures, birds and amphibians. There's a petting zoo for kids, along with playgrounds, a picnic area, and a handful of family-friendly dining options.

European Central Bank
Headquarters   NOTABLE BUILDING
(www.ecb.europa.eu; Sonnemannstrasse 20; Ⓤ Ostbahnhof) The European Central Bank (ECB) relocated in 2014 from Frankfurt's Eurotower into these striking 180m-high headquarters on the site of the city's former wholesale market. Free 90-minute guided visits are possible; you need to reserve at least four weeks in advance by emailing visitor. centre@ecb.europa.eu, and bring a passport or national ID card.

☞ Tours

★Primus Linie   BOATING
(www.primus-linie.de; Mainkai; adult/child one-way €9.80/5.50, full circuit €12.80/5.50; ⊙11am-5pm Mar–mid-Nov, 11am-4pm Sat & Sun mid-Nov–Feb; Ⓤ Dom|Römer) Gliding past Frankfurt's landmarks aboard a boat is one of the most peaceful ways to see the city. Primus Linie runs 50-minute sightseeing cruises from the Mainkai boat docks both upstream and down; for the best skyline views, take the full 100-minute circuit. It also hosts various dinner cruises and party cruises – schedules are posted online.

Ebbelwei-Express   TOURS
(Apple Wine Express; www.ebbelwei-express.com; adult/child €8/3.50; ⊙1.30-6.45pm Sat & Sun)

This loveable vintage tram's one-hour circuit takes in both banks of the Main between the zoo and the Messe. You can jump on at any of its 23 stops (a map is posted on its website) but you can't break your journey. Tickets include *Ebbelwei* (apple wine in Frankfurt dialect) or juice, and pretzels.

Kulturothek   WALKING
(☑069-281 010; www.kulturothek-frankfurt.de; An der Kleinmarkthalle 7-9; tours €8-25; ⊙office 10am-6pm Mon-Fri, 11am-4pm Sat; Ⓤ Hauptwache) Engaging tours (some in English) take in the city and its institutions, such as the European Central Bank and the IG-Farbenhaus, as well as the food-filled Kleinmarkthalle. Departure points for individual tours vary. Book ahead.

Tourist Office Walking Tours   WALKING
(www.frankfurt-tourismus.de; Römerberg 27; 1hr city tour €10.90, with Main Tower entry €16.90, 1½hr old town tour €12.90; ⊙Mar-Dec; Ⓤ Dom|Römer) Various walking tours of Frankfurt depart from the Römer tourist office (p557), providing historical context for this hyper-modern city. Annual schedules are posted on the tourist office website, which also sells tickets.

✯ Festivals & Events

Christopher Street Day   LGBT
(Pride; www.csd-frankfurt.de; ⊙mid-Jul; Ⓤ Konstablerwache) The Christopher Street Day incorporates a colourful Pride parade, as well as a *Strassenfest* (street festival) at Konstablerwache.

Museumsuferfest   CULTURAL
(Museum Embankment Festival; www.museums uferfest.de; ⊙Aug) Held on both banks of the Main, this huge three-day cultural festival held over the last weekend in August draws some 2.5 million people for discounted museum entry, tours, workshops, music and dance performances, stalls selling handicrafts, jewellery and clothing, and open-air art exhibitions. Each year has a different theme, such as 'Modern Art' or 'Children'.

Apfelweinfestival   WINE
(www.frankfurt-tourismus.de; Rossmarkt; ⊙Aug; Ⓤ Hauptwache) Frankfurt celebrates its famous *Apfelwein* (apple wine) with a 10-day festival on the Rossmarkt with live music, local-dialect poetry and storytelling. Stalls provide tastings and sell bottles, along with apple wine accoutrements such as a traditional ribbed glass or *Bembel* (blue-painted grey jug).

ℹ TRADE FAIRS

Frankfurt is famous around the world for its *Messen* (trade fairs), held at the southern edge of the Westend district on the ground of the Messe (p544).

If you're in Frankfurt during one of the really big trade fairs, you'll experience a city transformed. Accommodation prices skyrocket, getting a table at many restaurants, even casual establishments, requires advance booking, and you'll overhear conversations – in strange jargon, sprinkled with obscure acronyms – about parts of the global economy that usually fly under the radar.

Check www.frankfurt-tourismus.de for a list of upcoming trade fairs.

Rheingauer Weinmarkt   WINE

(Rhine District Wine Festival; www.frankfurt-tourismus.de; ☺Aug-Sep; ⓤAlter Oper) More than 600 wines from the Rheingau wine-growing region are available to taste and buy from 30 stalls at this 10-day festival. It sets up around Grosse Bockenheimer Strasse in the pedestrianised Fressgass area.

Frankfurt Book Fair   FAIR

(Frankfurter Buchmesse; www.buchmesse.de; Messe; ☺mid-Oct; ⓢMesse) The world's largest book fair takes place over five days in mid-October. Two days are open to the general public, featuring author readings, poetry slams and more; tickets are sold on the website.

Christmas Market   CHRISTMAS MARKET

(Weihnachtsmarkt; Römerberg; ☺10am-9pm Mon-Sat, from 11am Sun late Nov-22 Dec; ⓤDom|Römer) Atmospherically set in the Altstadt, Frankfurt's Christmas market has choirs, ornament stalls, traditional foods and steaming mugs of *Glühwein*.

🛏 Sleeping

Supply and demand reign supreme in Frankfurt's accommodation pricing. The city's hotels cater mainly to business travellers and so tend to drop rates on weekends (Friday, Saturday and Sunday nights), on public holidays and in July and August – but they soar during trade fairs.

The tourist office has a free hotel booking service. You can find furnished rooms and apartments through a *Mitwohnzentrale* (accommodation finding service), such as www.city-residence.de.

During major trade fairs, prices can triple or even quadruple. To keep costs down during fairs, many travellers stay outside the city and commute using Frankfurt's fast, easy public transport system. In neighbouring cities such as Darmstadt, Wiesbaden and Mainz, which are an hour or less by S-Bahn from the trade fair grounds, prices rise less dramatically than in Frankfurt itself. You'll still need to book well ahead.

During trade fairs, Frankfurt's tourist office can arrange private rooms (single/double €60/85, with private bathroom €65/90).

🛏 Train Station Area

The Bahnhofsviertel (the area around the main train station, the Hauptbahnhof) has lots of moderately priced places to stay, few of them noteworthy but all of them just a short walk from most of the city's major sights. The Hauptbahnhof is a major S-Bahn (commuter rail), U-Bahn (metro/subway) and Strassenbahn (tram) hub, making it easy to reach both the airport and the Messe.

Be aware, however, that Frankfurt's extremely sleazy red-light area, where drug users congregate, is just east of the station, on and around Elbestrasse and Taunusstrasse.

Five Elements   HOSTEL €

(☎069-2400 5885; www.5elementshostel.de; Moselstrasse 40; dm/s/d/apt from €22.50/34.50/82.90/134.50; 🖥; ⓡHauptbahnhof) The location mightn't be Frankfurt's most salubrious, but once you're inside the turn-of-the-20th-century gabled building it's a sanctuary of parquet floors, boldly coloured walls and designer furniture. Facilities include a laundry and 24-hour bar with a billiard table; breakfast costs €6.50. The private apartment, sleeping up to four people, has a private bathroom and kitchen.

Frankfurt Hostel   HOSTEL €

(☎069-247 5130; www.frankfurt-hostel.com; Kaiserstrasse 74, 3rd fl; dm/s/d from €21/49/59; @🖥; ⓡHauptbahnhof) Reached via a pre-war marble-and-tile lobby and a mirrored lift, this lively, 200-bed hostel has a chill-out area for socialising, a small shared kitchen, squeaky wooden floors, free lockers and a free breakfast buffet. Dorm rooms, two of which are female-only, have three to 10 metal bunks.

Hotel Excelsior   HOTEL €

(☎069-256 080; www.hotelexcelsior-frankfurt.de; Mannheimer Strasse 7-9; s/d from €68/82;

P @ 🛜; 🚉 Hauptbahnhof) While the decor won't make you swoon, the excellent value just might, especially the freebies: minibar, breakfast, phone calls within Germany, and coffee, tea, fruit and cakes in the lobby. The lift is slow, but handy if you're hauling luggage.

25hours Hotel by Levi's
DESIGN HOTEL €€

(☑ 069-256 6770; www.25hours-hotels.com; Niddastrasse 58; d from €112; P 🏱 🛜; 🚉 Hauptbahnhof) Inspired by Levi's (yes, the jeans brand), this hip hotel has a rooftop terrace, free bike hire, and a Gibson Music Room for jamming on drums and guitars. Its 76 rooms are themed by decade, from the 1930s (calm colours) to the 1980s (tiger-print walls, optical-illusion carpets). Be aware that its denim-blue bathrooms have no doors. Breakfast costs €18.

Hotel Hamburger Hof
HOTEL €€

(☑ 069-2713 9690; www.hamburgerhof.com; Poststrasse 10-12; d/ste from €131/167; 🏱 @ 🛜; 🚉 Hauptbahnhof) Directly across the road from the train station to the north (away from the grittiest part of the neighbourhood), this stylish three-star hotel has a burgundy-accented lobby and 62 comfortable rooms with contemporary furnishings and sparkling bathrooms.

🛏 Altstadt

The centre of the centre offers easy access to the Dom, the parks along the river and the Innenstadt, but properties here are limited and come at a premium.

Steigenberger Frankfurter Hof
HISTORIC HOTEL €€€

(☑ 069-215 02; www.steigenberger.com; Am Kaiserplatz; d/ste from €235/359; 🏱 @ 🛜; Ⓤ Willy-Brandt-Platz) Dating from 1876, this palatial hotel is a truly monumental place to rest your head. In addition to its 261 luxurious rooms and 42 even more luxurious suites, there are four gourmet restaurants, one of which has a Michelin star, a cigar lounge where 48 different kinds of rum are served fireside, a gym, a sun terrace and Frankfurt's largest spa.

🛏 Innenstadt

Staying in the inner city puts you close to the historic sites of the Altstadt, Frankfurt's tallest buildings, fine shopping and plenty of cultural venues, restaurants and nightlife, but it doesn't come cheap.

Adina Apartment Hotel
HOTEL €€

(☑ 069-247 4740; www.adinahotels.com; Wilhelm-Leuschner-Strasse 6; studio/1-bed/2-bed apt from €147/228/282; 🏱 🏱 🛜 🔁; 🚊 11|12 Weser-strasse|Münchener Strasse) Handy for self-caterers and families, the spacious one- and two-bedroom apartments in this high-rise overlooking the Main River come with full kitchens (grocery delivery can be arranged) and small balconies or roof terraces. Guests have free use of the indoor pool.

Fleming's Hotel
HISTORIC HOTEL €€€

(☑ 069-427 2320; www.flemings-hotels.com; Eschenheimer Tor 2; d/ste from €156/248; 🏱 🏱 @ 🛜; Ⓤ Eschenheimer Tor) Classic 1950s elegance stretches from the stainless steel, neon and black-and-white marble of the lobby all the way up to the panoramic 7th-floor restaurant (p551), linked by a rare, hop-on-hop-off paternoster lift/elevator. The 200 rooms are quietly luxurious, and some are huge. Amenities include a fitness room, sauna and steam bath, as well as limited parking (reserve spaces ahead).

🛏 Sachsenhausen

A short stroll across the bridge from the city centre, the southern side of the river is brilliantly positioned for art along the Museumsufer (Museum Embankment) and bars and taverns in Alt-Sachsenhausen.

Hotel Royal
HOTEL €

(☑ 069-460 920 600; www.hotel-royal-frankfurt.net; Wallstrasse 17; s/d/tr from €65/75/90; 🏱 🛜; 🚊 14|18 Frankensteiner Platz) Locations don't come better than the Royal's, a stone's throw from the bars of Alt-Sachsenhausen (weekends can be noisy – ask for a rear-facing room). It's an easy walk to the Museumsufer, riverfront promenade and city centre. The rooms' decor is dated but they're comfortable and spotlessly clean, and service goes above and beyond. Reserve its limited parking ahead.

DJH Hostel
HOSTEL €

(☑ 069-610 0150; www.jugendherberge.de; Deutschherrnufer 12; dm €19.50-33, s/d/f from €38.50/54/67.50; @ 🛜; 🚊 14|18 Frankensteiner Platz) Advance bookings are advisable for Frankfurt's bustling, 433-bed *Jugendherberge* (youth hostel), situated within easy walking distance of the city centre and Alt-Sachsenhausen's nightspots. Dorm rooms are single-sex; family rooms have three or four beds. There are washing machines, but no cooking facilities.

🛏 Messe, Westend |& Bockenheim

The area immediately surrounding the Messe is home to surprisingly few hotels, so even trade fair-goers who can afford Frankfurt's sky-high 'Messe rates' usually stay elsewhere in the centre, nearer to restaurants and other amenities.

★Hotel Hessischer Hof   LUXURY HOTEL €€€

(☑069-754 00; www.grandhotel-hessischerhof.com; Friedrich-Ebert-Anlage 40; d/ste from €255/385; P✳@🛜; ⓊFesthalle|Messe) Owned by descendants of the landgraves, electors and grand dukes of the House of Hessen, and opened in 1952, this 121-room hotel is filled with over 1500 antiques from the family collections. It's renowned for its old-world luxury and superb service. There's a gym, roof terrace and late-night Jimmy's Bar (p554). Breakfast costs €34.

Hotel Palmenhof   HOTEL €€€

(☑069-753 0060; www.palmenhof.com; Bockenheimer Landstrasse 89-91; s/d/ste from €140/190/220; P🛜; ⓊWestend) In the heart of the leafy Westend, this *Jugendstil* red-sandstone establishment, constructed in 1890, offers 45 understated rooms with a mix of modern and classical furnishings; those at the rear have balconies. Breakfast costs €16.

🛏 Nordend & Bornheim

Northeast of the Innenstadt, this villagey part of town is ideal for enjoying a traditional Frankfurt-style meal, a mug of beer or a glass of apple wine.

★Villa Orange   BOUTIQUE HOTEL €€

(☑069-405 840; www.villa-orange.de; Hebelstrasse 1; s/d from €140/170; P✳🛜; 🚉12|18 Friedberger Platz) 🌿 Offering a winning combination of tranquillity, modern German design and small-hotel comforts (such as a quiet corner library), this century-old, tangerine-coloured villa has 38 spacious rooms, some with free-standing baths and four-poster beds. Everything is organic – the sheets, the soap and the bountiful buffet breakfast (included in the rate) – with bikes also available to hire.

Art-Hotel Robert Mayer   DESIGN HOTEL €€

(☑069-9709 1010; www.de.arthotel-frankfurt.de; Robert-Mayer-Strasse 44; s/d from €86/97; P🛜; 🚉3|4 Nauheimer Strasse) Each of the 12 rooms at this 1905-built art nouveau hotel was designed by a different Frankfurt artist, with a mix of classical and contemporary styles. The age of the building means there's no lift, but limited underground parking is available (book ahead).

🛏 Ostend

25hours Goldman   BOUTIQUE HOTEL €€

(☑069-4058 6890; www.25hours-hotels.com; Hanauer Landstrasse 127; d from €149; @🛜; 🚉11 Osthafenplatz) The 49 original 22-sq-metre rooms at this hypercreative place were each designed by a local personality, while the 48 most recent rooms are inspired by New York's United Nations HQ. Amenities include free coffee, a top-notch Mediterranean restaurant and free bikes. Beehives on the roof produce house-brand honey.

🍴 Eating

During trade fairs, getting a restaurant table generally requires making reservations a day or more ahead.

While you're in town, be sure to try Frankfurt's distinctive local specialities including *Handkäse mit Musik* ('hand-cheese with music') and *Frankfurter Grüne Sosse* (Frankfurt green sauce).

🍴 Train Station Area

Pizzeria Montana   PIZZA €

(☑069-2648 6714; www.montana-pizzeria.de; Weserstrasse 14; pizzas €7-11; ⓗ11.30am-10pm Mon-Wed, to 11pm Thu & Fri, noon-11pm Sat, noon-10pm Sun; 🛜🖉; 🚉11|12 Weser|Münchener Strasse) Colourful Pizzeria Montana has vivid blue walls framing a communal table down one side and stool seating along the other, with a bright yellow wood-fired pizza oven painted like a Pac-Man. Cooked for just 60 seconds in a 450-degree Celsius oven, crispy thin-crust pizzas topped with premium ingredients include plenty of vegetarian options.

★Druckwasserwerk   GERMAN €€€

(☑069-2562 8770; www.restaurant-druckwasserwerk.de; Rotfeder-Ring 16; mains €19-41; ⓗ11.30am-3pm & 3.30pm-midnight Mon-Fri, 6pm-midnight Sat, 10am-11pm Sun; 🛜; ⓊHauptbahnhof) Dating from 1899, this neo-Romanesque pump house in the rapidly rejuvenating industrial area of Westhafen, on the Main 1.2km southwest of the Hauptbahnhof, is now a spectacular restaurant serving superior German cuisine. The soaring interior

DON'T MISS

FRANKFURT MARKETS

Aromatic stalls inside the bustling traditional **Kleinmarkthalle** (www.kleinmarkthalle. de; Hasengasse 5-7; ☺8am-6pm Mon-Fri, to 4pm Sat; Ⓤ Dom|Römer) sell artisan smoked sausages, cheeses, roasted nuts, breads, pretzels, loose-leaf teas, pastries, cakes and chocolates, along with fruit, vegetables, spices, fresh pasta, olives, meat, poultry and, downstairs, fish. It's unmissable for picnickers or self-caterers, or anyone wanting to experience Frankfurt life. The upper-level wine bar opens to a terrace.

Other food markets:

Erzeugermarkt Konstablerwache (Konstablerwache Farmers Market; www.erzeugermarkt-konstablerwache.de; Konstablerwache; ☺10am-8pm Thu, 8am-5pm Sat; Ⓤ Konstablerwache) 🥬

Food Market – Bockenheimer Warte (Bockenheimer Warte; ☺8am-6pm Thu; Ⓤ Bockenheimer Warte)

Food Market – Südbahnhof (Diesterwegplatz; ☺8am-6pm Tue & Fri; Ⓤ Südbahnhof)

Flohmärkte (www.hfm-frankfurt.de; ☺9am-2pm Sat) Hundreds of tables and pavement-spread blankets are piled high with second-hand goods at this flea market; come early for finds. It takes place on alternate weeks in Sachsenhausen, along the Schaumainkai riverfront between the Eiserner Steg and Hobeinsteg pedestrian bridges; and at the Osthafen, along Lindleystrasse, 1.3km east of U-Bahn Ostbahnhof.

has exposed-brick walls, metal girders, crank shafts and pulleys, a monumental chandelier and mezzanine seating. Outside there's an ephemeral umbrella-shaded terrace and beach with Tahiti-imported sand.

✖ Altstadt

Restaurants and cafes immediately surrounding the Römerberg cater mainly to tourists, but nearby you'll find some very local – and atmospheric – dining options.

Bitter & Zart CAFE €
(☏069-9494 2846; www.bitterundzart.de; Braubachstrasse 14; dishes €4-8.80; ☺10am-7pm Mon-Sat, 11am-6pm Sun; Ⓤ Dom|Römer) Walk past the shelves piled high with chocolate pralines to order espresso brewed from Frankfurt-roasted beans, hot chocolate and luscious cakes such as lemon, carrot or *Frankfurt Kränzen* (butter-cream), with gluten-free options available.

Karin CAFE €
(☏069-295 217; www.cafekarin.de; Grosser Hirschgraben 28; dishes €3.50-9.60; ☺9am-9pm Mon-Fri, to 7pm Sat, 10am-6pm Sun; Ⓤ Hauptwache) Across from the Goethe-Haus, Karin serves German and international dishes and nine different breakfasts named for different Frankfurt neighbourhoods, from 'City' (croissant and marmalade) to 'Bornheim' (bread roll, salami, eggs and cheese). Changing exhibits by local artists grace the walls. Cash only.

Fisch Franke SEAFOOD €€
(☏069-296 261; www.fischfranke.de; Domstrasse 9; mains €14-26, sandwiches €4-5.50; ☺9am-9pm Mon-Fri, to 5pm Sat; Ⓤ Dom|Römer) In a large, light-filled space, 1920-established Fisch Franke serves standout fish dishes: ocean perch with new potatoes and green sauce, pollock with spinach and cheese sauce, langoustines with lemon butter, and its signature seafood chowder. Self-caterers should stop by the attached fishmonger and deli, which does fantastic takeaway sandwiches (eg pickled herring or prawn with tangy Marie Rose sauce).

Salzkammer AUSTRIAN €€
(☏069-1539 3000; www.salzkammerffm.de; Weissadlergasse 15; mains €13-27; ☺11am-11pm Mon-Sat; Ⓤ Hauptwache) Warm timbers give this restaurant a cosy atmosphere, and it has a beautiful umbrella-shaded terrace. But it's the traditional Austrian food that leaves a lasting impression, from Styrian fried chicken to three different sizes of schnitzel with cranberry sauce and fried potatoes, beef broth with liver dumplings, and *Kaiserschmarrn* – caramelised, shredded pancakes with *Zwetschgenröster* (plum compote).

Mozart Café CAFE €€
(www.cafemozart-frankfurt.de; Töngesgasse 23-25; cakes €3-5.50, mains €8.50-18.50; ☺8am-9pm Mon-Sat, from 9am Sun; Ⓤ Hauptwache) Take a seat on a red leather wing chair inside or at

the Paris-cafe-style pavement tables to enjoy coffee and cake or something more substantial, such as grilled perch, steaks, stews and meal-sized salads – the menu changes depending on what's fresh at the markets.

✕ Innenstadt

The Innenstadt has some of Frankfurt's best dining options. The pedestrianised avenue linking the Alte Oper and the western end of the Zeil – officially called Kalbächer Gasse and Grosse Bockenheimer Strasse – is dubbed 'Fressgass' ('eat street') because of its gourmet shops and restaurants. Seating spills outside in warm weather.

Käsestube Gutes aus Milch   CHEESE €

(☑ 069-2691 6814; www.gutesausmilch.com; Schillerstrasse 30; cheese tastings per piece €2.50-5.50; ⊙ 11am-3.15pm & 4-7pm Tue & Wed, to 8pm Thu, 11am-8pm Fri, 11am-6pm Sat; Ⓤ Eschenheimer Tor) Over 150 cheeses from the surrounding Hesse state (and another 50 from further afield) are sold at this fabulous cheese specialist, alongside regional wines. You can taste both, either at the communal timber table inside the airy, exposed-brick shop, or at tables on the pavement, with a range of platters and wine-pairing options available.

Vevay   VEGETARIAN €

(www.vevay.net; Neue Mainzerstrasse 20; dishes €5.50-15; ⊙ 10am-11pm Mon-Sat; ☑; Ⓤ Willy-Brandt-Platz) 🖋 Even diehard carnivores might be converted after tucking into this stylish cafe's creative vegetarian and vegan dishes: tempeh with three-bean and coconut salad with mango and avocado salsa; oat and chickpea burger with quinoa and cucumber salad; rice noodle salad with tofu, snow peas and asparagus; and raw poppyseed chocolate cake. Bio-organic ingredients are primarily sourced from local farms.

You can also pick up dishes to take away in bio-degradable packaging.

Ebert's Suppenstube   CAFE €

(www.erbert-feinkost.de; Grosse Bockenheimer Strasse 31; dishes €2.50-6.50; ⊙ 11am-7pm Mon-Fri, to 6pm Sat; Ⓤ Alte Oper) Soups made on the premises are the speciality of this terrific city-centre spot, with varieties like liver dumpling, lentil and local sausage, beef and ravioli, and vegetable. Other dishes include meatloaf, and pork loin served in a bread roll. There are tables indoors and out – and almost constant queues. Its butcher and deli are directly opposite.

★ Zu den 12 Aposteln   GERMAN €€

(☑ 069-288 668; www.12aposteln-frankfurt.de; Rosenbergerstrasse 1; mains €9-24; ⊙ 11.30am-1am; Ⓤ Konstablerwache) Glowing with sepia-toned lamplight, the 12 Apostles has ground-floor and cellar dining rooms serving traditional German dishes: *Matjes* (herring) with sour cream, apple and fried onion; roast pork knuckle with pickled cabbage; Frankfurter schnitzel with *Grüne Sosse* (green sauce); and *Käsespätzle* (handmade cheese noodles with onions). It brews its own light and dark beers on the premises.

Main Nizza   EUROPEAN €€

(☑ 069-2695 2922; www.mainnizza.de; Untermainkai 17; mains €15.50-24; ⊙ 11.30am-2.30pm & 6-10pm Mon-Fri, 11.30am-10pm Sat & Sun; 🐾✎🚼; Ⓤ Willy-Brandt-Platz) A striking glass-box design gives this restaurant uninterrupted views over the Main from inside (even interior-facing tables have mirrors to draw in the river and parkland) as well as from its two outdoor terraces. Upmarket European dishes might include sea bass with roast cauliflower and Riesling sauce or honey-marinated duck breast with artichoke gnocchi; good kids' and vegetarian menus are available.

Café Hauptwache   GERMAN €€

(☑ 069-2199 8627; http://web.cafe-hauptwache. de; An der Hauptwache 15; mains €12-36; ⊙ 10am-11pm Mon-Sat, noon-10pm Sun; Ⓤ Hauptwache) One of Frankfurt's most beautiful buildings to have escaped WWII's destruction is this 1730-built baroque city guardhouse. A restaurant since 1904, it's enveloped by summer terraces and dwarfed by surrounding skyscrapers. Classical German fare includes grilled pork ribs with sauerkraut and mash, and potato soup with Frankfurt sausage.

Seven Swans   VEGETARIAN €€€

(☑ 069-2199 6226; www.sevenswans.de; Mainkai 4; 5-/6-course menu €79/89; ⊙ 7-11pm Tue-Sat May-Aug, from 6.30pm Sep-Apr, bar to 1am; ✎; 🚋 11|12 Börneplatz|Stolzestrasse) 🖋 One of Frankfurt's narrowest buildings, at 3.8m wide, houses this inconspicuous restaurant (look for the teensy silver plaque on the facade). Produce from its own permaculture garden stars on gourmet vegetarian and vegan set menus (no à la carte) featuring dishes such as roast fennel with black cabbage and smoked sunflower seeds, and sweet carrot with lavender goat's milk custard.

On the ground floor, its 16-seat bar, the Tiny Cup, mixes monthly changing craft cocktails.

Fleming's Club
INTERNATIONAL €€€

(☑069-427 2320; www.flemings-hotels.com; Eschenheimer Tor 2; mains €16-38; ⊙4-11pm Mon-Sat, from noon Sun, bar to 1am; ✿☎; ⓊEschenheimer Tor) Stunning city views and equally stunning food await at this 7th-floor restaurant and bar, reached from the lobby of Fleming's Hotel (p547) via a paternoster lift that will make you feel like you're in a 1930s movie. Start with dishes like lobster soup with pastis foam, followed by mains such as rib-eye steak with Béarnaise sauce and potato gratin.

Save room for desserts like *Bienenstich* (a buttercream-filled yeast cake topped with roasted almonds) accompanied by spiced figs and mandarin sorbet.

Buffalo
STEAK €€€

(☑069-285 796; www.buffalo-steakhaus.de; Kaiserhofstrasse 18-20; mains €10.50-51; ⊙11.30am-11pm Mon-Sat; ⓊAlte Oper) Founded in 1973, this renowned steakhouse serves some of Frankfurt's most succulent sirloin, tenderloin and rib-eye steaks, ranging from 180g to 450g, all shipped fresh from Argentina. There's an impressive international wine list. Unless you'll be dining from 3pm to 6pm, reservations are a must. It's hidden down the stairs leading to tiny Zwingerstrasse.

✖ Sachsenhausen

Frankfurt's densest concentration of places to drink and eat is in Alt-Sachsenhausen. Head to bar- and restaurant-packed streets such as Grosse Rittergasse, Kleine Rittergasse, Klappergasse and Wallstrasse. Seven blocks southwest, the southern end of shop-lined Schweizer Strasse also has a string of restaurants.

L'Atelier des Tartes
CAFE €

(Kleine Brückenstrasse 3; dishes €3.30-9.50; ⊙11am-7pm Tue-Sat; ☎☑; 🚇14|18 Frankensteiner Platz) Heavenly aromas fill this chic polished-concrete cafe. French owner Aurélie bakes tarts both savoury (potato and brie, mushroom and asparagus, and pear, Roquefort and walnut) and sweet (apple with cinnamon and vanilla, strawberry, rhubarb and cranberry) and serves soups and creative salads (such as quinoa, butternut squash and charred orange). You can browse French design magazines while you dine.

Bizziice
ICE CREAM €

(www.bizzi-ice.com; Wallstrasse 26; ice cream per scoop €1.60; ⊙11am-10pm May-Sep, to 7pm Oct-Apr; ☎; 🚇14|18 Frankensteiner Platz) 🌿 Organic milk, fruit, veggies and nuts are used to make the ice creams served at this tile-floored space. Original flavour combinations include carrot and agave, mango and chilli, rhubarb and quark, and cinnamon- and nutmeg-spiced chocolate. The coffee is excellent too.

★ Dauth-Schneider
GERMAN €€

(☑069-613 533; www.dauth-schneider.de; Neuer Wall 5; mains €8-13.50; ⊙11.30am-midnight; 🚊Lokalbahnhof) With a history stretching back to 1849 (the basement housed an apple winery), this convivial tavern is a wonderful place to sample both the local drop and classic regional specialities such as *Sulz Fleisch* (cold meat and jelly terrine), *Gekochte Haspel* (pickled pork knuckle) with sauerkraut, and various tasting platters. Tables fill the tree-shaded terrace in summer.

Lobster
BISTRO €€

(☑069-612 920; www.lobster-weinbistrot.de; Wallstrasse 21; mains €17-35; ⊙6-10.30pm Mon-Sat, bar to 1am; 🚇14|18 Frankensteiner Platz) In a one-time grocery and milk shop from the 1950s, this cosy 'wine bistro' chalks its daily French-influenced meat, fish and shellfish specials (including its namesake lobster) on the blackboard. Three dozen wines are available by the glass. There are just seven tables, so reservations are a must.

Adolf Wagner
GERMAN €€

(☑069-612 565; www.apfelwein-wagner.com; Schweizer Strasse 71; mains €10-19.50; ⊙11am-midnight; ⓊSchweizer Platz) Hang your coat on a hook along the wood-panelled wall of this apple wine tavern, take a seat at a long table and order something local from the menu – *Handkäse mit Musik* or schnitzel with *Frankfurter Grüne Sosse* along with a jug of *Apfelwein*. It's been run by the same family since 1931.

✖ Messe, Westend & Bockenheim

Few places to eat are located right around the Messe, given this part of the city fluctuates wildly between throngs during fairs and scarcely a soul the rest of the time.

Near the Westend campus of Goethe Universität, you will find restaurants along

FRANKFURT SPECIALITIES

Frankfurt's local delicacies are best experienced in the cosy surrounds of the city's traditional apple wine taverns.

➡ *Ebbelwei* (or *Ebbelwoi;* Frankfurt dialect for *Apfelwein*)

Many Frankfurters derive great pleasure from savouring a glass of tangy, slightly carbonated apple wine with the alcohol content of a strong beer. Visitors, though, may find that the tart golden liquid, served straight up or *gespritzt* (with sparkling water), is something of an acquired taste (that doesn't resemble apples at all). It's traditionally served in a *Bembel,* a grey earthenware jug painted with cobalt-blue detailing.

➡ *Handkäse mit Musik* ('hand-cheese with music')

This opaque cheese, marinated in oil and vinegar with chopped raw onions and cumin seeds, is served with dark bread and butter. As you might imagine, this potent mixture tends to give one a healthy dose of wind – the release of which is the 'music'.

➡ *Frankfurter Grüne Sosse* (Frankfurt green sauce)

Made from parsley, sorrel, dill, burnet, borage, chervil and chives mixed with boiled, sieved eggs and sour cream or yoghurt, this delicious green sauce is usually slathered on eggs, boiled potatoes or schnitzel.

Feldbergstrasse, which is lined with impressive Wilhelmian-era buildings.

In Bockenheim, inexpensive eateries and ethnic takeaways line Leipziger Strasse. The streets southwest of Bockenheimer Warte have reasonably priced restaurants and bars.

Frankfurt & Friends   CAFE €€

(www.frankfurtandfriends.de; Jordanstrasse 1; mains €10.50-24, sandwiches €8-12.50; ⊙noon-11pm Mon-Fri, from 11am Sat & Sun; 🖉; Ⓤ Bockenheimer Warte) Nine different burgers – including a veggie burger, Frankfurt & Friends burger with bacon and cheese, and Tex-Mex burger with guacamole and jalapeño peppers – are among the choices at this minimalist cafe, along with gourmet sandwiches, omelettes and gluten-free pastas. In the evening you can cook your own steak on sizzling 'hot rock' lava-stone slabs.

There's an outside patio with warm, woolly blankets in winter.

Siesmayer   CAFE €€

(🖉069-9002 9200; www.palmengarten-gastronomie.de; Siesmayerstrasse 59; pastries €4-7.50, dishes €11-23; ⊙8am-7pm; Ⓤ Palmengartenstrasse) Experience highly civilised Westend life at this elegant cafe, whose lovely patio is surrounded by the greenery of the PalmenGarten (p544). A glass case displays French-style pastries; there are also soups, schnitzels and gourmet sandwiches (such as pastrami, pickles and sauerkraut or shredded roast pork with caramelised sweet po-

tato and apple sauce). It's located on a street lined with 19th-century mansions.

Mon Amie Maxi   FRENCH €€€

(🖉069-7140 2121; www.mook-group.de/monamie maxi; Bockenheimer Landstrasse 31; mains €17-34; ⊙noon-3pm & 6-10.30pm Sun-Fri, 6.30-10.30pm Sat; Ⓤ Alte Oper) In a gorgeous belle époque space with bare boards, butter-coloured walls and an elevated front terrace, this grande dame specialises in seafood, including oysters (per half-dozen from €20) and sumptuous platters: Les Misérables (€35); Le Royal with a half-lobster (€90), and Le Maxi with a whole lobster (€150); and the monumental Le Mook with Alaskan king crab (€300).

French classics include escargot, foie gras, sole meunière, bouillabaisse and steak tartare.

🍴 Nordend & Bornheim

Offering a slice of everyday Frankfurt life, Berger Strasse is home to authentic and atmospheric bars and restaurants, especially around Merianplatz. The stretch of Berger Strasse just north of Rendeler Strasse is known as Alt-Bornheim (old Bornheim).

Sandweg, which runs parallel to Berger Strasse, also has inexpensive restaurants.

Café Kante   CAFE €

(www.cafe-kante.de; Kantstrasse 13; dishes €3.50-7.50; ⊙7am-8pm Mon-Fri, to 7pm Sat, 8.30am-7pm Sun; Ⓤ Merianplatz) The tantalising aromas of baking breads, cakes and croissants engulf you as you enter this tiny space filled with vintage bric-a-brac. Fantastic coffee too.

Eckhaus
GERMAN €€

(☑069-491 197; www.eckhaus-frankfurt.de; Bornheimer Landstrasse 45; mains €10.90-19.90; ◉5.30-10.30pm Mon-Sat, 5-10pm Sun; Ⓤ Merianplatz) With smoke-stained walls and ancient floorboards, this cornerstone of the neighbourhood is as old-school as they come. Don't miss its hallmark *Kartoffelrösti* (shredded potato pancake).

Drinking & Nightlife

Frankfurt's lively drinking and nightlife scenes span snug traditional apple wine taverns, many of which are also great places to eat, to chic cocktail bars, raucous pubs and pumping clubs.

Dozens of bars spill onto the cobbled streets of Alt-Sachsenhausen, particularly around Kleine Rittergasse.

In summer, open-topped boat bars line up along the Main River's banks.

Altstadt

Naïv
BAR

(www.naiv-frankfurt.de; Fahrgasse 4; ◉bar 5pm-1am Mon-Fri, from 10am Sat & Sun, shop 3-7pm Wed-Fri, from 1.30pm Sat; ▣11|12 Börneplatz|Stolzestrasse) At any one time this contemporary bar (and attached shop) has between 90 to 120 craft beers from around the world – everywhere from Hawaii to Norway – in addition to three house beers (bio, cellar, and honey lager) and sophisticated street-food-inspired fare. Even the slightest ray of sunshine sees the sprawling front terrace packed with locals.

Six-hour brewing courses (per person €99) in English and German include 2L to take with you, as well as tastings and lunch.

Sugar Mama
CAFE

(Kurt-Schumacher-Strasse 2; ◉11am-10pm Mon-Thu, to 11pm Fri, 10am-11pm Sat, to 10pm Sun; ▣11|12 Börneplatz|Stolzestrasse) Mismatched vintage furniture – '70s couches, rocking chairs, timber packing crates and cushioned cane armchairs – creates an outdoor lounge room on the pavement terrace fronting this hippie-chic cafe. Herbal teas range from lemon and ginger to lavender, rooibos, mint and peach; it also serves soy lattes, iced cappuccinos, and snacks such as quiches, cakes, brownies and cookies. Cash only.

Mantis
BAR

(www.mantis-roofgarden.de; Katharinenpforte 6; ◉10am-1am Mon-Thu, to 2am Fri & Sat, noon-11pm Sun; Ⓤ Hauptwache) Mantis' ground floor houses a buzzing, curvilinear glass-fronted bar and grill, while the 1st-floor lounge bar opens to a garden with a retractable roof. There's a huge range of wines, champagnes and cocktails such as the house speciality, Mantis Mai Tai, made with 23-year-old Guatemala Zacapa rum and apricot brandy.

Innenstadt

Apfelwein Klaus
PUB

(www.apfelweinklaus.de; Kaiserhofstrasse 18; ◉11.30am-2.30pm & 5pm-midnight Mon-Fri, 5pm-midnight Sat; Ⓤ Alte Oper) Over a century old, this charming little stone vaulted cellar has communal benches where you can strike up a conversation with locals over a jug of apple wine and inexpensive home-cooked Frankfurt specialities. Enter via Zwingergasse.

Espresso Bar
COFFEE

(www.theespressobar.de; Schäfergasse 42; ◉8.30am-7pm Mon-Fri, from 9.30am Sat; Ⓤ Konstablerwache) Vintage fittings including copper lights and baristas in long white laboratory coats make this hole-in-the-wall an atmospheric stop for an expertly brewed espresso. Inside it's standing room only but there are a couple of tables on the pavement.

Cave
CLUB

(www.the-cave.rocks; Brönnerstrasse 11; ◉10pm-4am Sun & Thu, to 6am Fri & Sat; Ⓤ Eschenheimer Tor) At Frankfurt's number-one rock club, DJs (who take requests) play alternative rock as well as punk and metal in two barrel-vaulted cellars. Things really get going around midnight. No dress code.

Sachsenhausen

Bootshaus Dreyer
BAR

(www.bootshaus-dreyer.de; Schaumainkai 7; ◉11am-midnight Apr-Oct; ▣16 Schweizerstrasse-Gartenstrasse) Festooned with geranium-filled flower boxes, the top deck of this summertime boat bar is a sensational spot for an apple wine or beer on a balmy evening while watching the sun set over the dramatic skyline and the city lights reflecting on the river. Cash only.

Südbahnhof
CLUB

(www.suedbahnhof.de; Südbahnhof; Ⓤ Südbahnhof) This *Musik-Lokal*, inside the Südbahnhof

S-Bahn station, is known for its '30-Plus' parties (9pm to 3am Saturday), open to anyone who's been around for at least three decades. It also often hosts dances for seniors (4pm to 8pm Monday) and live music on Sunday afternoons.

Maincafé CAFE
(www.maincafe.net; Schaumainkai 50; ☉10am-2am Mar-late Oct; ⊡16 Otto-Hahn-Platz) Hidden away between the embankment and the water's edge, this cafe set in a grassy riverfront park with dazzling views of the city-centre skyline is an idyllic spot for a coffee, beer or glass of apple wine.

Fichtekränzi PUB
(www.fichtekraenzi.de; Wallstrasse 5; ☉5pm-1am Mon-Sat, from 4pm Sun; ⊡14|18 Frankensteiner Platz) Founded in 1849, Fichtekränzi is an authentic apple wine tavern with wood-panelled walls, smoke-stained murals, long tables, long benches, a beer garden and a high-spirited atmosphere. Classic dishes include *Handkäse mit Musik*, schnitzel and apple strudel. Cash only.

ⓔ Messe, Westend & Bockenheim

Jimmy's Bar BAR
(www.grandhotel-hessischerhof.com; Friedrich-Ebert-Anlage 40; ☉8pm-4am, closed Sun & Mon

---

LGBT FRANKFURT

The beating heart of gay and lesbian Frankfurt is north of the Zeil around Schäfergasse and, a block further north, Alte Gasse, with a bevy of clubs and cafes. For the low-down on the scene, check out www.inqueery.de or www.travelgayeurope.com/frankfurt.

Gay pride peaks during mid-July's Christopher Street Day (p545).

Bar Central (Elefantengasse 11-13; ☉8pm-2am Sun-Thu, to 3am Fri & Sat; ⓤKonstablerwache) Frankfurt's most popular gay bar, stylish Bar Central has regular themed nights including jazz on Sundays. Cash only.

La Gata (www.club-la-gata.de; Seehofstrasse 3; ☉8pm-1am Mon, Wed & Thu, 9pm-3am Fri & Sat; ⊡14|18 Frankensteiner Platz) Opened in 1971, this intimate spot is Frankfurt's sole women-only lesbian bar.

Aug; ⓤFesthalle|Messe) Wood panelling, leather armchairs, a live pianist from 10pm to 3am, and expertly mixed cocktails make this cigar bar in the basement of the Hotel Hessischer Hof (p548) a classy spot for night owls. Food is served until 3am.

Kaffeerösterei Wissmüller CAFE
(www.kaffeeroesterei-wissmueller.de; Leipziger Strasse 39; ☉8am-5pm Mon-Wed & Fri, to 6.30pm Thu, 9am-4pm Sat; ⓤLeipziger Strasse) The aroma of freshly roasted coffee lures you through a covered alley and cobbled courtyard to this hidden spot. Kaffeerösterei Wissmüller has been roasting *Stern* ('star') coffee on the site since 1948, with beans sourced from 17 different countries including Brazil, Colombia, Kenya and Guatemala. Savour a cup at upturned barrels covered with hessian coffee sacks.

ⓔ Nordend & Bornheim

★Le Panther CLUB
(www.lepanther.club; Seilerstrasse 34; ☉5pm-2am Mon-Thu, to 4am Fri-Sun May-Sep, 10pm-2am Thu, 6pm-4am Fri & Sat Nov-Apr; ⓤKonstablerwache) Noise levels aren't a problem at this spectacular club, which occupies an 1808 villa surrounded by manicured gardens with fountains, ponds and lounges. The ground-floor dance floor is overlooked by a wraparound upper-level balcony and candle-lit lounge. The cocktails feature fresh herbs from its vertical garden, and organic juices and mixers. Check the website for parties and events.

☆ Entertainment

Frankfurt is a magnet for the entire Rhine-Main region, with a diverse range of cultural events. Thursday is a big night out for workers who commute to Frankfurt for the week and go 'home' on Friday.

Websites with nightlife events and cultural listings include the following:

➡ Journal Frankfurt (www.journal-frankfurt.de)

➡ Prinz Frankfurt (www.prinz.de/frankfurt)

➡ Frizz (www.frizz-frankfurt.de)

➡ Strandgut (www.strandgut.de)

Nachtleben LIVE MUSIC
(☏069-206 50; https://batschkapp.tickets.de; Kurt-Schumacher Strasse 45; ☉10.30am-2am Mon-Wed, to 4am Thu-Sat, 7pm-2am Sun;

Ⓤ Konstablerwache) Tucked away in the south-eastern corner of Konstablerwache, Nachtleben has a cafe with a terrace on the ground floor and hosts concerts that showcase alternative and indie bands, as well as parties ranging from Britpop to techno, and indietronic to hip-hop, depending on the night.

Städtische Bühnen
PERFORMING ARTS

(☑069-2124 9494; www.buehnen-frankfurt.de; Untermainanlage 11; Ⓤ Willy-Brandt-Platz) The city's huge cultural complex includes Oper Frankfurt (www.oper-frankfurt.de), Frankfurt's main opera company, and Schauspiel Frankfurt (www.schauspielfrankfurt.de; Neue Mainzer Strasse 17), its largest theatre company. Tickets can be booked by phone or online.

Bockenheimer Depot
DANCE

(☑069-2124 9494; www.buehnen-frankfurt.de; Carlo-Schmid-Platz 1; Ⓤ Bockenheimer Warte) This century-old former tram depot hosts innovative dance performances as well as Städtische Bühnen theatre and opera productions.

Batschkapp
LIVE MUSIC

(☑069-9521 8410; https://batschkapp.tickets.de; Gwinnerstrasse 5; Ⓤ Gwinnerstrasse) Since 1976, when it began staging live bands (rock, soul, et al), the legendary 'Batsch' has seen 'em come and go. Its main premises are in the Frankfurter Kulturzentrum, 8km northeast of the Hauptbahnhof; other concert venues include the Alte Batschkapp ('old Batschkapp') premises at Maybachstrasse 24, 8km north of the Hauptbahnhof (S-Bahn Eschersheim), and Nachtleben.

Jazzkeller
JAZZ

(☑069-288 537; www.jazzkeller.com; Kleine Bockenheimer Strasse 18a; DJs & jam nights €5, concerts from €15; ◷9pm-1am Tue-Thu, to 3am Fri & Sat, 8pm-1am Sun; Ⓤ Alte Oper) Check out the walls for photos of jazz greats who've played at this venue since it opened in 1952. In addition to concerts, there are jam sessions on Wednesdays, and DJs on Fridays, with dancing to Latin, funk and soul. It's hidden away in a cellar across from Goethestrasse 27.

Mouson
PERFORMING ARTS

(Künstlerhaus Mousonturm; ☑069-405 8950; www.mousonturm.de; Waldschmidtstrasse 4; Ⓤ Merianplatz) This rambling former soap factory serves as a forum for younger artists, and hosts contemporary dance, theatre (sometimes in English) and cabaret, as well as concerts by up-and-coming bands. Schedules are posted online.

ℹ️ TICKETS FOR CULTURAL EVENTS

Last-minute tickets can generally be purchased an hour or so before performance time at each venue's *Abendkasse* (evening ticket window).

Tickets for rock, pop and classical concerts, operas, musicals, plays and sports events (except football/soccer) are available from Frankfurt Ticket (☑069-134 0400; www.frankfurtticket.de; An der Hauptwache; ◷10am-7pm Mon-Fri, to 4pm Sat; Ⓤ Hauptwache). Tickets ordered through its website can be printed out; you can also collect tickets at venues' box offices.

Alte Oper
CLASSICAL MUSIC

(Old Opera House; www.alteoper.de; Opernplatz 1; ◷Sep-Jun; Ⓤ Alte Oper) The Alte Oper hosts frequent concerts of symphonic and chamber music in its two halls, which seat 2450 and 720 respectively. Pop, jazz, singer-songwriter and world music acts also play here.

Tigerpalast
CABARET

(☑069-920 0220; www.tigerpalast.de; Heiligkreuzgasse 16-20; ◷7pm & 10pm Tue-Thu, 7.30pm & 10.30pm Fri & Sat, 4.30pm & 8pm Sun mid-Aug–mid-Jun; Ⓤ Konstablerwache) Hugely enjoyable even if you don't speak German, Tigerpalast is a top venue for cabaret and *Varieté* theatre, with programs that often include acrobats, circus and magic performances.

English Theatre
THEATRE

(☑069-2423 1620; www.english-theatre.de; Gallusanlage 7; tickets €27-50; ◷box office 10am-6pm Mon-Sat, 3-5pm Sun; Ⓤ Willy-Brandt-Platz) Continental Europe's largest English-language theatre company stages first-rate plays and musicals, with top actors hired after casting calls in London and New York.

Mampf
JAZZ

(☑069-448 674; www.mampf-jazz.de; Sandweg 64; ◷6pm-1am Sun-Thu, to 2am Fri & Sat; Ⓤ Merianplatz) Cool jazz permeates this tiny, 1972-opened jazz-club/pub. Live concerts take place most nights – check the calendar for details.

Summa Summarum
LIVE MUSIC

(www.facebook.com/Summa.Summarum.Musikkeller; Klappergasse 3; ◷9pm-1am Tue, Fri & Sat; 🚊14|18 Lokalbahnhof) This *Musikkeller* (music cellar), an intimate basement venue with vaulted stone ceilings and just half a dozen tables, features a wide-ranging program of jazz, singer-songwriters (blues, rock etc) and more. The music lasts from about 9pm to midnight.

Orfeo's Erben
CINEMA

(☏ 069-7076 9100; www.orfeos.de; Hamburger Allee 45; adult/child €10/7; 🚌 17 Nauheimer Strasse) Orfeo's Erben screens non-dubbed art-house films (celluloid and digital).

🛍 Shopping

The pedestrianised Zeil is the main shopping precinct, with high-street chains and malls. For the city's most chic fashion and jewellery boutiques, head to nearby Goethestrasse and its surrounding streets. Fressgass, the pedestrian zone between Opernplatz and Börsenstrasse, is filled with tantalising gourmet shops.

Young clothing designers have shops in Sachsenhausen around the intersection of Brückenstrasse and Wallstrasse.

★ Handwerkskunst am Römer
GIFTS & SOUVENIRS

(www.handwerkskunst-frankfurt.com; Braubachstrasse 39; ⊙10am-8pm Mon-Sat, from 11am Sun; Ⓤ Dom|Römer) Exquisite handcrafted souvenirs at this long-established shop include traditional toy-soldier nutcrackers, adorable 'smokers' (incense burners) depicting peddlers, miners, organ-grinders and so on, cuckoo clocks, music boxes, tiny wooden figurines and Christmas decorations.

There's a second shop at Hasengasse 9.

Töpferei Maurer
CERAMICS

(www.keramik-maurer.de; Wallstrasse 5; ⊙9am-6pm Mon-Fri, to 1pm Sat; 🚌 Lokalbahnhof) At this traditional Sachsenhausen ceramics manufacturer, you can buy an authentic *Bembel* made either here on the premises or at Töpferei Maurer's larger factory nearby. The iconic blue-painted, grey-coloured jugs range from thimble-sized to barrel-like (mounted on cast-iron stands to facilitate pouring the apple wine).

Frankfurter Fass
FOOD & DRINKS

(www.frankfurter-fass.de; Töngesgasse 38; ⊙10am-6.30pm Mon-Fri, to 4pm Sat; Ⓤ Hauptwache) Pick up *Apfelwein*, as well as apple brandy, regional wines, vinegars, oils, spirits, salts, mustard and other local delicacies like Frankfurt bonbons filled with cider liqueur, at this emporium.

Kleidoskop
FASHION & ACCESSORIES

(www.kleidoskop.de; Töngesgasse 38; ⊙11am-7pm Mon-Fri, to 6pm Sat; Ⓤ Hauptwache) Women's clothes, shoes, handbags and belts by Frankfurt's young, up-and-coming designers are stocked at this stark, stylish boutique, along with a handful of high-end European labels.

Wohnen und Spielen
TOYS

(www.wohnenundspielen.de; Grosse Friedberger Strasse 32; ⊙10am-7pm Mon-Fri, to 5pm Sat; Ⓤ Konstablerwache) A Frankfurt institution, this toy shop has been delighting kids for decades with handcrafted dolls, pull-along wooden toys, teddy bears and jigsaws as well as musical instruments.

ℹ Information

ACCESSIBLE TRAVEL

For details on access to sights, activities, the Messe and public transport, visit www.frankfurt-tourismus.de/en/Frankfurt-for/Travellers-with-handicaps. The same site has information and links for information on using the public transport system. While buses have ramps, not all U-Bahn and S-Bahn stations have lifts/elevators yet.

The website www.frankfurt-inklusiv.de also has useful information in English.

DANGERS & ANNOYANCES

In general, Frankfurt is a safe city, but there are some places where you should exercise extra caution.

➡ The area east of the Hauptbahnhof is a base for Frankfurt's trade in sex and illegal drugs, and has *Druckräume* (safe injecting rooms) for drug-users.

➡ Elbestrasse and Taunusstrasse have the city's largest concentration of sex shows, go-go bars, short-time hotels, sleazy casinos and shifty characters.

➡ Police and private security guards frequently patrol the train station and the surrounding streets, but keep your wits about you, and stay alert for pickpockets and petty thieves.

DISCOUNT CARDS

Benefits of the **Frankfurt Card** (one/two days for one person €10.50/15.50, for up to five people €22/32) include free public transport (including to/from the airport), up to 50% discount at museums and the PalmenGarten, and discounts at the zoo and on opera and theatre tickets.

You can order the card online and print it out. It's also available at the airport's **Hotels & Tours** (www.frankfurt-airport.com; terminal 1, arrival hall B, Frankfurt Airport; ⊙6am-10pm; 🚌 Flughafen Regionalbahnhof) desk (so you can use it for the train ride into the city), the **tourist office**, the **Verkehrsinsel** (☑ 069-2424 8024; www.rmv.de; Zeil 129; ⊗ 9am-8pm Mon-Fri, 9.30am-6pm Sat; Ⓤ Hauptwache) and some hotels.

Many museums are free on the last Saturday of the month ('SaTOURday'), when there are also special events and exhibitions for children (except in August and December). Information is online at www.kultur-frankfurt.de.

A great option for museum buffs, the **Museumsufer Ticket** (adult/child/family €18/10/28) gets you into 34 museums over two consecutive days. Pick it up from participating museums or from the tourist office.

MEDICAL SERVICES

To find a *Notdienstapotheke* (emergency service pharmacy) open after-hours, check the window of any pharmacy or visit www.aponet.de. Pharmacies at the Hauptbahnhof and the airport are open until late at night.

Unfallklinik (Centre for Trauma Surgery; ☑ 069-475 2033; www.bgu-frankfurt.de; Friedberger Landstrasse 430; ⊗ 24hr; ☒ 30 Unfallklinik) Accident and emergency treatment, 5km northeast of the centre.

Vertragsärztlicher Bereitschaftsdienst (VBF; ☑ 116 117; www.bereitschaftsdienst-hessen.de; ⊗ 24hr) Doctors make house (or hotel) calls.

TOURIST INFORMATION

Frankfurt's tourist office has two city branches:

Tourist Office – Hauptbahnhof (☑ 069-2123 8800; www.frankfurt-tourismus.de; Main Hall, Hauptbahnhof; ⊗ 8am-9pm Mon-Fri, 9am-6pm Sat & Sun; ☒ Hauptbahnhof) At the main train station.

Tourist Office – Römer (☑ 069-2123 8800; www.frankfurt-tourismus.de; Römerberg 27; ⊗ 9.30am-5.30pm Mon-Fri, to 4pm Sat & Sun; Ⓤ Dom|Römer) Smallish office in the central square.

ⓘ Getting There & Away

AIR

Located 12km southwest of the centre, **Frankfurt Airport** (FRA; www.frankfurt-airport.com; Hugo-Eckener-Ring; 🕾; ☒ Flughafen Regionalbahnhof) is Germany's busiest, with the highest cargo turnover and the third-highest passenger numbers in Europe (after London's Heathrow and Paris' Charles de Gaulle). Its two terminals are linked by the free SkyLine elevated railway (every two to three minutes), and free buses (every 10 minutes). Left-luggage lockers are available (per two/24 hours €4.50/7).

Frankfurt-Hahn Airport (HHN; www.hahn-airport.de; Lautzenhausen) is 124km west of Frankfurt. Low-cost carriers have flights to/from European destinations including Dublin and London-Stansted, as well as Morocco.

BUS

Eurolines (www.eurolines.de) and Flixbus (www.flixbus.com) can take you inexpensively to cities across Germany and throughout Europe. Both companies use Frankfurt Airport and the main **bus station** (Mannheimer Strasse 15; ☒ Hauptbahnhof) at the Hauptbahnhof; Flixbus also uses the Südbahnhof in Sachsenhausen for some services.

CAR & MOTORCYCLE

Major car rental companies have desks at both Frankfurt Airport and Frankfurt-Hahn Airport.

At the Hauptbahnhof, Avis, Europcar, Hertz and Sixt have offices next to the tourist office.

TRAIN

Hauptbahnhof The main train station, about 1km west of the Altstadt and 1km southeast of the Messe, is Germany's most frequented, with convenient trains to pretty much everywhere. Left luggage lockers are available (per 72 hours small/large €3/5).

Major services include:

Berlin (€90, four hours, two per hour)

Cologne (€39, 1¼ hours, up to four per hour Monday to Saturday, up to three per hour Sunday)

Heidelberg €19.90 to €29.90, one hour to 1½ hours, hourly)

Mainz (€8.50, 40 minutes, frequent)

Munich (€60, 3¼ hours, hourly)

Nuremberg (€36, 2¼ hours, up to two per hour)

Stuttgart (€34, 1½ hours, up to two per hour)

Frankfurt Airport Fernbahnhof From Frankfurt Airport's long-distance train station (Terminal 1), you can travel directly to destinations across Germany, often by fast IC and ICE trains.

Direct services include:

Cologne (€40, one hour, up to four per hour Monday to Saturday, up to three per hour Sunday)

Munich (€60, 3½ hours, up to two per hour)

Nuremberg (€36, 2¼ hours, up to two per hour)

Stuttgart (€34, 1¼ hours, up to two per hour Monday to Saturday, hourly Sunday)

ⓘ Getting Around

TO/FROM THE AIRPORT
Frankfurt Airport

Train The Flughafen Regionalbahnhof (airport regional train station; Terminal 1) handles regional train and S-Bahn connections; services begin at about 4.30am and end at 1.30am.

S-Bahn commuter rail lines S8 and S9 shuttle between the airport and city centre (one-way €4.90, 11 minutes, every 15 minutes), stopping at Hauptbahnhof, Hauptwache and Konstablerwache, as well as (in the other direction) Wiesbaden and Mainz. To get to Darmstadt, change to the S3.

Intercity trains use the airport's modern, glass-roofed Fernbahnhof (long-distance train station).

Bus Bus 61 links the Südbahnhof in Sachsenhausen with Terminals 1 and 2 every 15 minutes (€4.90, 15 minutes, every 15 minutes Monday to Friday, every 30 minutes on Saturday and Sunday).

Taxi A taxi from the airport to the city centre costs between €25 to €35.

Frankfurt-Hahn Airport

Frankfurt-Hahn Airport (p557) is linked to Frankfurt, Heidelberg and the Moselle Valley by **bus** (www.bohr.de; ticket €19, luggage €8).

BICYCLE

Cycling is a great way to get around Frankfurt, which is crisscrossed with designated bike lanes.

Call-a-Bike (☑ 069-4272 7722; www.callbike-interaktiv.de; annual subscription €3, bike hire per 30min/24hr/72hr €1/15/40) To use Deutsche Bahn's share bicycle scheme, register online or by phone with your credit card number, then go to one of Frankfurt's city-wide Call-a-Bike Stations and use the app or make a phone call to get the lock code to pick up a bicycle.

Next Bike (☑ 030-6920 5046; www.nextbike.de; per 30min €1) After registering with a credit card, go to one of Frankfurt's dozens of pick-up points throughout the city and use the app to get the lock code.

CAR & MOTORCYCLE

Traffic flows smoothly in central Frankfurt. Signs indicate the way to the nearest *Parkhaus* (parking garage) and the number of spaces left. City-centre street parking is generally limited to one hour.

In many areas, parking on one side of the street is reserved for *Bewohner* (local residents) whose cars have a special sticker. Signs list the hours during which restrictions apply.

PUBLIC TRANSPORT

Frankfurt's excellent transport system, part of the RMV (Rhein-Main-Verkehrsverbund; www.rmv.de) network, integrates all bus, *Strassenbahn* (tram), S-Bahn (commuter rail) and U-Bahn (metro/subway) lines.

➡ Tickets can be purchased at transit stops from *Fahrkartenautomaten* (ticket machines). Zone 50 encompasses most of Frankfurt, ex-

cluding the airport. Machines accept euro coins and notes (up to €10 or €20) and chip-and-pin credit cards, which excludes many US-issued cards (and even some international chip-and-pin cards).

➡ An *Einzelfahrt* (single-ride) ticket costs adult/child €2.75/1.55; it's time-stamped when you buy it and so is valid only for travel you begin immediately. For trips of less than 2km, buy a *Kurzstrecke* (short-distance journey) ticket (adult/child €2.05/1.25).

➡ A *Tageskarte* (all-day ticket), valid from the start of service until 5am the next day, costs €5.35 (€9.55 including the airport); a *Gruppentageskarte* (all-day group ticket), for up to five people is just €11.30 (€16.60 including the airport) – a superb deal.

➡ A *Wochenkarte* (weekly pass, valid for any seven consecutive days), sold at the airport's DB ticket office and available from some ticket machines, costs €25.70 (including the airport) and is also great value.

➡ Nachtbus (www.nachtbus-frankfurt.de) lines have numbers beginning with 'n' and leave from Konstablerwache half-hourly (hourly for some suburban destinations) from 12.50am to 4am daily. Tickets cost the same as for daytime transport, or you can use an all-day ticket or weekly pass.

➡ Inspectors frequently check to make sure passengers have valid tickets. The fine for travelling *schwarz* ('black', ie without a ticket) is €40.

TAXI

Taxis have a €3.50 flagfall; trips costs €2 per kilometre for the first 15km, and €1.75 for every subsequent kilometre, with a waiting charge of €33 per hour. A fifth passenger costs €7 extra.

There are taxi ranks throughout the city. Firms include **Taxi Frankfurt** (☑ 069-230 001; www.taxi-frankfurt.de) and **Time Car** (☑ 069-203 04; www.timecar.de).

Wiesbaden

☑ 0611 / POP 289,544

Lined with magnificent neoclassical buildings that were rebuilt after WWII, Wiesbaden, the state capital of Hesse, is one of Europe's oldest spa towns, with hot springs still flowing today. It's 40km west of Frankfurt, across the Rhine from Mainz.

Wiesbaden's name translates as 'meadow baths', reflecting both its thermal baths and beautiful expanses of parkland. The city lies at the eastern edge of the Rheingau wine-growing region, which stretches along the Rhine's right (northern) bank west to the Rüdesheim area of the Romantic Rhine.

Renowned Russian novelist Fyodor Dostoevsky (1821–81) amassed huge debts at the city's gambling tables in the 1860s, which inspired his masterpiece, *The Gambler*.

Home to the European headquarters of the US Army, Wiesbaden has a strong US military presence, with around 19,000 US citizens based here.

◎ Sights

Wiesbaden's walkable city centre is 1km north (along Bahnhofstrasse) from the Hauptbahnhof.

A good place to start exploring Wiesbaden is the Schlossplatz, home to several monuments and landmarks including the neoclassical Stadtschloss (1840), built for Duke Wilhelm von Nassau and now home of the Hessischer Landtag (Hessian state parliament).

Schloss Freudenberg   MUSEUM
(www.schlossfreudenberg.de; Freudenbergstrasse 220-226, Dotzheim; adult/child €14/7; ⊘9am-5pm Mon-Fri, 11am-6pm Sat & Sun Mar-Oct, 10am-5pm Mon-Fri, 11am-6pm Sat & Sun Nov-Feb) Challenge all your senses at Schloss Freudenberg, a century-old mansion 3.5km southwest of Wiesbaden's centre that's been turned into a hands-on, experiential *Erhfahrungsfeld* (Experience Field). Inspired by the ideas of Rudolf Steiner, exhibits change regularly, and may include an ice chamber, where you can experience a winter storm at -22°C, or a barefoot path. All are family-friendly. At the *Dunkelbar* (dark bar) you can order a drink in total darkness.

Marktkirche   CHURCH
(www.marktkirche-wiesbaden.de; Schlossplatz 4; ⊘2-6pm Tue, Thu & Fri, 10-11.30am & 2-6pm Wed, 10-11am & noon-2pm Sat, 2-5pm Sun Mar-Dec, shorter hours Jan & Feb) The Protestant neo-Gothic Marktkirche, built of bright red bricks between 1853 and 1862, was the first all-brick building to be built in the region. Its glockenspiel (carillon) has 49 bronze bells weighing between 13kg and 2200kg; it rings at 9am, noon, 3pm and 5pm daily. Schedules for regular organ concerts are posted on the website.

Kochbrunnen   SPRING
(Kranzplatz) If you're game to taste-test the hot spa waters for which the city is known (and named), which are said to have wonderful pharmacological powers, head to the Kochbrunnen. Inside the stone pavilion are four free-flowing spouts. A sign recommends drinking no more than 1L a day, though if you can down more than a mouthful you deserve a beer.

There's another hot springs tap at the Bäckerbrunnen (Grabenstrasse 28), a little brick building a block south of Goldgasse.

Museum Wiesbaden   MUSEUM
(⊘0611-335 2250; www.museum-wiesbaden.de; Friedrich-Ebert-Allee 2; adult/child €6/free, incl temporary exhibitions €10/free; ⊘10am-5pm Wed & Fri-Sun, to 8pm Tue & Thu) Paintings from the 12th to 19th centuries and some 100 works by the Russian expressionist Alexej von Jawlensky (1864–1941), who lived in Wiesbaden for the last 20 years of his life, are highlights of Wiesbaden's art museum. They sit alongside late-20th-century installations, objects, sculptures and paintings, and a natural sciences section featuring geological, mineral and botanical exhibits. The dazzling gilded hall mosaic dates from just before WWI.

Kurhaus Wiesbaden   HISTORIC BUILDING
(www.wiesbaden.de; Kurhausplatz 1; ⊘24hr, closed during events) Built in 1907, the neoclassical Kurhaus is now the city's convention centre. Ornate interior spaces include the **main hall**, with its marble floor, granite columns, Greco-Roman statuary and sparkling dome mosaics, and the casino (p562).

Altes Rathaus   HISTORIC BUILDING
(Old Town Hall; Marktstrasse 16) Overlooking the Schlossplatz, the Altes Rathaus (1610) is Wiesbaden's oldest building. It houses the representative rooms of the Hessischer Landtag (Hessian state parliament) and is closed to the public, other than the vaulted wine bar in the cellar.

Neues Rathaus   NOTABLE BUILDING
(New Town Hall; Schlossplatz 6) Across the Schlossplatz from the Altes Rathaus is the Neues Rathaus (1887). Its interior is closed to the public.

Marktbrunnen   FOUNTAIN
(Löwenbrunnen, Market Fountain; Schlossplatz) On the Schlossplatz, the Marktbrunnen dates from 1753 and was restored in 2016.

Michelsberg Synagogue Memorial   MEMORIAL
(www.am-spiegelgasse.de; Michelsberg 24) The site of Wiesbaden's largest pre-war synagogue, built in 1869 and destroyed in 1938, is marked by a memorial that includes an outline of the structure (in dark paving

Wiesbaden

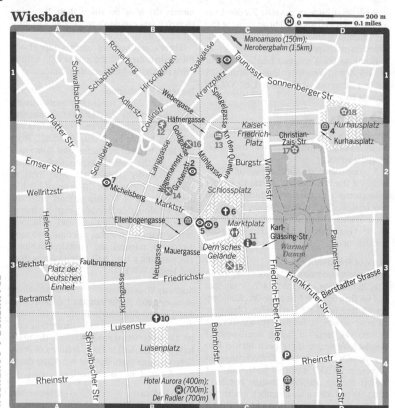

stones on the footpaths and street) and historic photos and biographical information on 1507 Wiesbaden Jews who perished in the Holocaust.

St-Bonifatius-Kirche CHURCH
(www.bonifatius-wiesbaden.de; Luisenstrasse 27; ⊙8am-7pm) The soaring steeples of this Gothic Revival church, reaching 68m high, make it a local landmark. Construction started in 1844 and it was consecrated in 1849, but its facade wasn't completed until 1856 and its steeples in 1866.

Russische Orthodoxe Kirche CHURCH
(Russian Orthodox Church; www.roc-wiesbaden. de; Christian-Spielmann-Weg 1; entry by donation; ⊙10am-6pm Mon-Fri, to 4.45pm Sat, 12.30-6pm Sun May-Oct, 10am-5pm Apr, to 4pm Nov-Mar) The five glinting gold onion domes of this Russian Orthodox Church, constructed between 1847 and 1855, rise above a canopy of trees 600m southeast of the Neroberg hill.

The church was built by Duke Adolph von Nassau to house the funerary monument of his wife, Elisabeth Michailowna, and their daughter, who died during childbirth.

🏃 Activities

⭐ **Kaiser-Friedrich-Therme** THERMAL BATHS
(☑0611-318 078; www.wiesbaden.de; Langgasse 38-40; per hour adult/child May-Aug €5/3, Sep-Apr €6.50/4.50; ⊙10am-10pm, to midnight Fri & Sat Sep-Apr, women only Tue) Built in 1913 as a municipal bathhouse on the site of a Roman steam bath, these gorgeous baths, still run by the city, let you experience 'Irish-Roman' spa culture with saunas and pools fed by water naturally heated to 66.4°C. Bathrobes and towels can be rented; swimsuits are banned in the sauna (you can wear a towel) and optional elsewhere.

Shower before entering the pools. The minimum age for the sauna is 16, but kids can access the bathing area.

Wiesbaden

City Walking Tour WALKING
(www.wiesbaden.de; Marktplatz 1; adult/child €6.50/4.80; ⊙10.30am & 2.30pm Sat May-Oct, 10.30am Sat Feb-Apr & Nov) Wiesbaden's tourist office (p562) runs 90-minute walking tours of the city in English and German; it also has an English-only tour at 2pm Saturday from June to September.

🛏 Sleeping

Genteel Wiesbaden has some appealing family-run and boutique options.

Hotel Aurora HOTEL €
(☑0611-373 728; www.aurora-wiesbaden.de; Untere Albrechtstrasse 9; s/d/studio from €67/77/120; P🛜) This gem, in a late 19th-century building with high ceilings (but no lift), is just 500m north along Bahnhofstrasse from the Hauptbahnhof, but peaceful and quiet. Its 31 rooms are individually decorated. The pretty courtyard garden has umbrella-shaded tables, where breakfast (€12) is served in fine weather. Baby cots are available; kids under six stay free.

DJH Hostel HOSTEL €
(☑0611-486 57; www.wiesbaden.jugendherberge. de; Blücherstrasse 66; dm/s/d/q €29/33.50/74/142; 🛜) Behind its functional exterior, this modernised 236-bed hostel 1.2km west of the city centre has squeaky-clean rooms and helpful staff. Amenities include table football, billiards, air hockey and a barbecue area. Wi-fi is in public areas only. From the Hauptbahnhof or the city centre, take bus 14 to Gneisenaustrasse.

Citta Trüffel Hotel BOUTIQUE HOTEL €€
(☑0611-990 5510; www.citta-hotel.de; Webergasse 6-8; s/d from €110/140; ❄🛜) Just 300m north of Marktplatz on the edge of the Altstadt, this ultra-stylish business hotel's 30 sleek, spacious rooms have natural materials, cool neutral colour schemes, designer lighting and parquet floors, as well as huge, state-of-the-art bathrooms. Some rooms open onto balconies.

🍴 Eating

Restaurant-lined Goldgasse, a block north of the Stadtschloss, is the heart of Wiesbaden's dining district.

Trüffel Feinkost DELI €
(www.trueffel.net; Webergasse 6-8; dishes €6.80-11.80; ⊙9am-7pm Mon-Fri, 8am-4pm Sat) Gourmet goods at this tantalising deli range from 150 cheeses, 150 cured meats, antipasti and artisan breads to ready-to-eat dishes like bratwurst and potato salad, and schnitzel with rosemary potatoes. It also stocks cakes, pastries, chocolates, wines and liqueurs.

Food Market MARKET €
(Dern'sches Gelände; ⊙7am-2pm Wed & Sat) Food stalls set up twice weekly next to the tourist office on the Schlossplatz.

das!Burger BURGERS €€
(☑0611-5808 9030; www.das-burger.com; Grabenstrasse 16; burgers €9-13; ⊙11am-10pm Tue-Sat, from noon Sun) 🌿 Towering burgers made with locally sourced produce include the Alamo (cheddar, beef, onion rings, pickles and BBQ sauce), Farmhouse (bacon, beef, tomato, fried egg and goats cheese), and the brilliantly named Lousy Hunter (seared halloumi cheese, pickled red onions, grilled peppers and courgette, and olive and mushroom tapenade, cooked on its own grill). There's a fantastic range of craft beers.

WORTH A TRIP

NEROBERG

About 2km northwest of the centre, the Neroberg is a 245m-high hill, accessible by the **Nerobergbahn** (www.eswe-verkehr.de; Wilhelminenstrasse 51; one-way/return adult €4/5, child €2.50/3; ⏲ 9am-8pm May-Aug, 10am-7pm Apr, Sep & Oct) funicular (linked to the Hauptbahnhof by bus 1). Neroberg is home to one of the oldest vineyards in the area and an outdoor swimming complex, **Opelbad** (☑ 0611-318 079; www.wiesbaden.de; Neroberg 2; adult/child €8.20/3; ⏲ 7am-8pm May-Sep).

Ristorante Comeback   ITALIAN €€

(☑ 0611-373 802; www.ristorante-comeback.de; Goldgasse 13; mains €11.50-25.50; ⏲ 11.30am-11pm Sun-Thu, to midnight Fri & Sat; ✔) Classical Italian *secondi* (mains) at this elegant restaurant include rabbit braised in Mirto (myrtle liqueur) and red wine, sage-pesto-stuffed chicken breast, and calamari, tomato, black olive and caper stew. White-clothed tables fill the candle-lit stone interior and the terrace of the pedestrianised street. If you can't decide between the handmade pastas, you can order two half-portions.

★ Gollner's   GERMAN €€€

(☑ 0611-541 409; www.gollners.de; Am Schlossberg 20, Sonnenberg; mains €21-38; ⏲ noon-2.30pm & 6-10.30pm Wed-Sun) Above the pretty village of Sonnenberg, 4km northeast of Wiesbaden, this sublime fine-dining restaurant occupies a 1201-built hilltop castle, Burg Sonnenberg. Umbrella-shaded tables cover the panoramic terrace, with valley views to Wiesbaden. Artistically presented steaks, schnitzels and fish dishes are matched with impeccably chosen wines from around the world. From central Wiesbaden, take bus 18; a taxi costs around €13.

Drinking & Entertainment

Manoamano   COCKTAIL BAR

(www.manoamano-bar.de; Taunusstrasse 31; ⏲ 7pm-2am Mon-Sat) Wiesbaden's coolest cocktail bar has a 9m-long LED light wall, custom-made luminescent panels on its walls and ceiling, and amazing cocktails: elderflower Collins made with Wiesbaden-distilled Amato gin, chocolate martinis and raspberry mojitos, as well as seasonal specials and infused vodkas.

Hessisches Staatstheater   PERFORMING ARTS

(☑ 0611-132 325; www.staatstheater-wiesbaden.de; Christian Zais Strasse 3) The Hessian State Theatre puts on operas, operettas, ballet, classical music, musicals, plays and events for children.

Kulturzentrum Schlachthof   LIVE MUSIC

(☑ 0611-974 450; www.schlachthof-wiesbaden.de; Murnaustrasse 1) Live music and top-name DJs make this venue a huge draw for music lovers, with events most nights.

Murnau Filmtheater   CINEMA

(www.murnau-stiftung.de; Murnaustrasse 6; tickets adult/child €7/6) Arthouse films screen in their original languages at this cinema 500m south of the Hauptbahnhof.

Spielbank Wiesbaden   CASINO

(Wiesbaden Casino; ☑ 0611-536 100; www.spielbank-wiesbaden.de; Kurhausplatz 1; table room €2.50, slot rooms free; ⏲ table room 2.45pm-3am Sun-Thu, to 4am Fri & Sat, slot rooms noon-4am) Dostoevsky gambled at this historic casino. To do the same (or have a drink at its bars), men will need a jacket, a button-down shirt and non-sports shoes; ties are not required (jackets can be rented from the cloak room). Table games include French and American roulette, poker and blackjack. You must be over 18 and have ID.

❶ Information

DISCOUNT CARDS

The two-day **Wiesbaden Card** (per one/five people €9/17) includes free public transport in both Wiesbaden and Mainz, and discounts on city tours, museums, and pool and spa entry. Buy it at the tourist office.

TOURIST INFORMATION

Tourist Office (☑ 061-172 9930; www.wiesbaden.de; Marktplatz 1; ⏲ 10am-6pm Mon-Sat, 11am-3pm Sun Apr-Sep, Mon-Sat Oct-Mar) Main office. If you're travelling with kids, pick up a *Leisure Guide for Families*. There's a second **information point** (☑ 0611-4502 2408; Bahnhofsplatz; ⏲ 6am-8pm Mon-Fri, 10am-5.30pm Sat) at the Hauptbahnhof.

❶ Getting There & Away

Frequent S-Bahn trains link Wiesbaden with Frankfurt's Hauptbahnhof (€8.50). S1 (42 minutes) goes direct; S8 and S9 serve Frankfurt Airport (€4.90, 30 minutes) before continuing to the Hauptbahnhof. S8 also serves Mainz (€2.80, 13 minutes), a major rail hub.

DB trains also serve Frankfurt (€8.50, 40 minutes). An all-day ticket for travel between Wiesbaden and Frankfurt, including the use of local trams and buses, costs €16.55.

❶ Getting Around

BICYCLE

Der Radler (☑ 0611-9881 9555; www.der-radler-wiesbaden.de; Hauptbahnhof; per hr/day €4/10, electric bikes €5/20, helmets €3, child seats €3; ☺ 8am-6pm Mon-Fri, 9am-1pm Sat May-Sep, 8am-6pm Mon-Fri Oct-Apr) Hires bicycles. From the train station, take the exit next to Track 11 and turn left. Ask staff about city and regional bicycle tours in summer.

BUS

Buses linking the Hauptbahnhof with the city centre include 1, 4, 8, 14, 27 and 47. A single ticket costs €2.80; a short-trip ticket (maximum three stops) costs €1.75. A day pass for one/up to five people costs €5.35/10.30. The **Eswe Verkehr bus information office** (☑ 0611-4502 2450; www.eswe-verkehr.de; platforms A & B, Hauptbahnhof; ☺ 6am-7pm Mon-Fri, 10am-5pm Sat) has transport maps.

TAXI

Taxi Wiesbaden (☑ 0611-999 99; www.taxi-wiesbaden.de)

Mainz

☑ 06131 / POP 209,779

Strategically situated at the confluence of the Rhine and Main Rivers, Mainz has been the capital of the German federal state of Rhineland-Palatinate since 1946. This lively city has a sizeable university, pretty pedestrian precincts and a *savoir vivre* dating from Napoleon's occupation (1797–1814). Strolling along the Rhine and sampling local wines in a half-timbered Altstadt tavern are as much a part of any Mainz visit as viewing the fabulous Dom, Chagall's ethereal windows in St-Stephan-Kirche (p565), or the first printed Bible in the bibliophile paradise of the Gutenberg Museum.

◉ Sights

The broad Marktplatz, Mainz' central market square, and the adjacent Liebfrauenplatz are together the focal point of the Altstadt. South of the squares, pedestrian-only Augustinerstrasse is lined with handsome five-storey houses (some half-timbered) and shops.

★ **Heiligtum der Isis und Mater Magna** ARCHAEOLOGICAL SITE
(☑ 06131-600 7493; www.roemisches-mainz.de; Römerpassage 1; ☺ 10am-6pm Mon-Sat) FREE
In a darkened, dungeon-like space, a glass walkway leads you around this extraordinary Roman archaeological site, which was discovered in 1999 during the construction of the Römerpassage shopping mall. Brilliantly illuminated artefacts discovered during excavations include ceremonial bowls, Roman tablets, statues, coins and dried fruits like figs from other climates. Signs are in German but an English brochure is available. The easy-to-miss, office-like entrance is on the mall's ground floor, just inside the western entrance.

★ **Mainzer Dom** CHURCH
(☑ 06131-253 412; www.mainzerdom.bistummainz.de; Markt 10; ☺ 9am-6.30pm Mon-Fri, to 4pm Sat, 12.45-6.30pm Sun Mar-Oct, 9am-5pm Mon-Fri, to 3pm Sat, 12.45-3pm & 4-5pm Sun Nov-Feb) Topped by an octagonal tower, Mainz' immense cathedral, built from deep red sandstone in the 12th century, is quintessentially Romanesque. Its predecessor went through a literal baptism by fire when it burned down in 1009 on the day of its consecration. Over the centuries seven coronations were held here. Sunday hours can vary.

Check its online schedule for classical concerts (adult seated/standing €10/5, child free).

★ **Gutenberg-Museum Mainz** MUSEUM
(☑ 06131-122 503; www.gutenberg-museum.de; Liebfrauenplatz 5; adult/child €5/2, audioguide €3.50; ☺ 9am-5pm Tue-Sat, from 11am Sun) A heady experience for book lovers, the Gutenberg Museum commemorates native son Johannes Gutenberg, who in the 15th century ushered in the information age here by perfecting moveable type. Highlights include very early printed masterpieces – kept in a walk-in vault – such as three extremely rare (and valuable) examples of Gutenberg's original 42-line Bible. Many of the signs are in English, as is a 15-minute film.

Try out Gutenberg's technology yourself at the museum's **Druckladen** (Print Shop; ☺ 9am-5pm Mon-Fri, 10am-3pm Sat) across tiny Liebfrauenstrasse.

★ **Landesmuseum Mainz** MUSEUM
(☑ 06131-285 70; www.landesmuseum-mainz.de; Grosse Bleiche 49-51; adult/child €6/3, audio/multimedia guide €1/2; ☺ 10am-5pm Wed-Sun, to 8pm Tue) Highlights of this well laid-out state

FRANKFURT & SOUTHERN RHINELAND MAINZ

Mainz

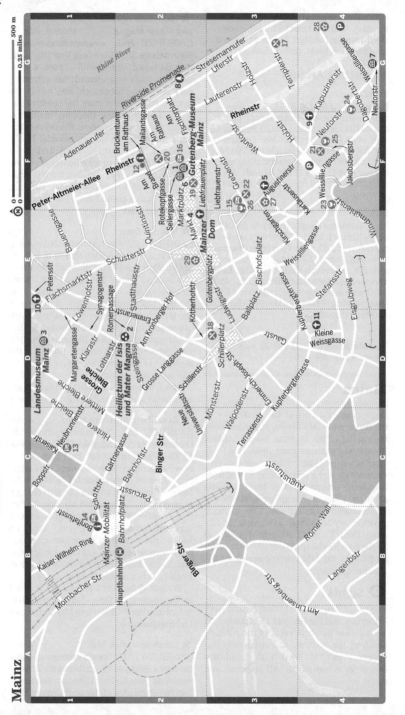

500 m
0.25 miles

Rhine River

Riverside Promenade

Stresemannufer

Uferstr

Rheinstr

Gutenberg-Museum Mainz

Mainzer Dom

Landesmuseum Mainz

Heiligtum der Isis und Mater Magna

Binger Str

Mainz

museum include an ensemble of exquisite *Jugendstil* pieces, outstanding collections of Renaissance and 20th-century German paintings, and baroque porcelain and furniture. Rare artefacts from the Merovingian and Carolingian periods include 4th- to 7th-century tombstones in Latin. Mainz' illustrious medieval Jewish community is represented by gravestones from the 11th to 13th centuries.

St-Ignazkirche CHURCH
(www.bistummainz.de; Kapuzinerstrasse 36; ⊙9am-6pm Apr-Oct, to 5pm Nov-Mar) Dating from 1773, this church marks the transition from rococo to neoclassicism – the baroque baldachin (over the altar) and organ sit in a space defined by Corinthian columns and a neoclassical dome.

St-Stephan-Kirche CHURCH
(www.st-stephan-mainz.bistummainz.de; Kleine Weissgasse 12; ⊙10am-5pm Mon-Sat, from noon Sun Mar-Oct, 10am-4.30pm Mon-Sat, from noon Sun Nov-Feb) This would be just another Gothic church rebuilt after WWII were it not for the nine brilliant-blue, stained-glass windows created by the Russian-Jewish artist Marc Chagall (1887–1985) in the final years of his life, which serve as a symbol of Jewish–Christian reconciliation.

Museum für Antike Schiffahrt MUSEUM
(Museum of Ancient Seafaring; ☎06131-286 6316; http://web.rgzm.de; Neutorstrasse 2b; ⊙10am-

6pm Tue-Sun) FREE The extraordinary remains of five wooden ships of the Romans' Rhine flotilla, used around AD 300 to thwart the Germanic tribes then threatening Roman settlements, are the centrepiece of this museum. Also on display are two full-size replicas of Roman ships and a collection of scale-model ships kids will love. Signs are in English.

Augustinerkirche CHURCH
(www.priesterseminar-mainz.de; Augustinerstrasse 34; ⊙9am-5pm Mon-Fri, 8am-2pm Sat) Part of the local Catholic seminary, the classically baroque Augustinerkirche, built from 1768 to 1772, was unscathed by WWII so all its rich decor is original, including its elaborate organ loft and a delicate ceiling fresco by Johann Baptist Enderle.

St-Peterskirche CHURCH
(www.bistummainz.de; Petersstrasse 3; ⊙9am-6pm Apr-Oct, to 5pm Nov-Mar) Completed in 1762, the Church of St Peter is a worthy showcase for the exuberant glory of the rococo style, with a richly adorned and gilded pulpit and altars, putti-decorated columns and a white-and-pink colour scheme.

Riverfront Promenade PARK
(Adenauer-Ufer, Stresemann-Ufer & Templerstrasse) A parade of barges along the Rhine pass by Mainz' riverfront promenade. This is one of the city's great spots for cycling, strolling or picnicking.

☞ Tours

Tourist Office Walking Tours WALKING
(tours €10; ⊙ English tour 2pm Sat Nov-Apr) Informative guides take you on two-hour walking tours of the city departing from the tourist office (p568).

🛏 Sleeping

Hostel accommodation, apartments and hotels can fill quickly. The tourist office (p568) has an accommodation service; bookings can be made in person, by phone or online.

DJH Hostel HOSTEL €
(☑ 06131-853 32; www.jugendherberge.de; Otto-Brunfels-Schneise 4; dm/s/d from €23.50/29/58; P 🖥) On the grounds of the leafy urban oasis Mainzer Volkspark, footsteps from the riverfront, this modernised 173-bed hostel has one-, two- and four-bed rooms, all with private bathrooms. Great amenities include a barbecue area, kids' playground, and a bar, bistro and cafe. It's 3.3km southeast of the Hauptbahnhof; take bus 62 or 63 to the Am Viktorstift stop.

Guesthouse Mainz APARTMENT €€
(☑ 06131-270 270; www.guesthouse-mz.de; Kaiserstrasse 20; s/d/tr studios from €99/119/139; ⊙ reception 7am-8pm Mon-Fri, to 11pm Sat & Sun; 🖥) Contemporary, light-filled studio apartments come with well-equipped kitchenettes with hotplates, fridges, microwaves and coffeemakers, making them a perfect base for exploring the city and region. Call ahead if you'll be arriving outside reception hours.

Hotel Hof Ehrenfels HOTEL €€
(☑ 06131-971 2340; www.hof-ehrenfels.de; Grebenstrasse 5-7; s/d/apt from €82/102/182; 🖥) Housed in a 15th-century Carmelite convent, this hotel has spectacular views of the Dom (though its bells can be loud). Its 22 rooms are spacious and modern; there's also a three-person apartment with a kitchenette. Unwind in the walled courtyard garden with umbrella-shaded tables. Its *Weinhaus* has a lengthy local wine list.

Hotel Schwan HOTEL €€
(☑ 06131-144 920; www.mainz-hotel-schwan.de; Liebfrauenplatz 7; s/d €87/114; 🖥) You can't get more central than the historic Hotel Schwan. The same family has had a property here since 1463; the current building dates from 1628, and Kaiser Joseph II stayed here in 1777. Its 22 well-lit rooms have baroque-style furnishings. Vegetarian, vegan and gluten-free breakfast options are available with advance notice.

Hotel Hammer HOTEL €€
(☑ 06131-965 280; www.hotel-hammer.com; Bahnhofplatz 6; s/d from €102/112; ✳ @ 🖥) Handy for the train station, the 37-room, business-oriented Hammer has 37 soundproof rooms with plum-toned fabrics, natural timbers and bright bathrooms. The free sauna is a welcome bonus. Bike storage is available.

🍴 Eating

Restaurants are scattered throughout the historic centre and on Templerstrasse along the waterfront. Inexpensive cafes and snack bars can be found near the Hauptbahnhof (eg along Bahnhofstrasse) and, south of the Dom, along Augustinerstrasse.

Food Market MARKET €
(Marktplatz & Liebfrauenplatz; ⊙ 7am-2pm Tue, Fri & Sat) Along the north and east sides of the Dom, this big, open-air market's colourful stalls spill over with fruit, vegetables, cheeses, sausages, breads and ready-to-eat dishes.

★ Zur Kanzel EUROPEAN €€
(☑ 06131-237 137; www.zurkanzel.de; Grebenstrasse 4; mains €8-23.50; ⊙ 5-11pm Mon-Fri, noon-4pm & 6-11pm Sat) Germany meets France in seasonally changing dishes like grilled tuna with Riesling and sage sauce, garlic-crusted rack of lamb with wilted spinach, schnitzel with Frankfurt-style *Grüne Sosse,* and rump steak with herb butter, as well as garlic snails. There's a lovely summer courtyard. Cash only.

Weinstube Lösch GERMAN €€
(☑ 06131-220 383; www.weinstube-loesch.de; Jakobsbergstrasse 9; mains €8.80-26.80; ⊙ 3pm-midnight Tue-Fri, from 2pm Sat, 2-11pm Sun) Traditional, timber-lined Lösch is a wonderful spot for local specialities, such as *Kartoffeleintopf mit Speck und Fleischwurst* (sausage casserole with bacon and cabbage) and *Kartoffelklösse Gefüllt Wahlweise mit Leberwurst* (medallions of pork with liver-stuffed potato dumplings). It serves its own wines from its Bingen estate, alongside other local vintages. Tables set up on the cobblestones in summer.

Heiliggeist BISTRO €€
(☑ 06131-225 757; www.heiliggeist-mainz.de; Mailandsgasse 11; mains €14-33; ⊙ 6-11pm Mon-Fri,

from 9am Sat & Sun) Soaring Gothic vaults make this 15th-century former hospital a fabulously atmospheric spot to try inventive twists on German cuisine: wild garlic and Riesling soup, pork tenderloin with herb *Spätzle* (hand-rolled noodles), rib-eye with forest mushrooms, and apple strudel with spicy *Killepitsch* (herb and berry liqueur) ice cream. Weekend breakfast is served until 4pm.

Bellpepper
EUROPEAN €€€

(☑ 06131-731 1537; www.bellpepper.de; Templerstrasse 6; mains €16-34; ⊘12.30-2.30pm & 6.30-10pm Mon-Thu, to 10.30pm Fri & Sat, to 9.30pm Sun; ☎ ⚥) Sunlight streams in through the glass walls and ceiling of this upmarket restaurant overlooking the Rhine. Watch the chefs in the open kitchen prepare showstoppers such as pike-perch fillet with roasted blood sausage and sauerkraut, and hazelnut crème brûlée with champagne nougat dust. Vegetarian and vegan menus are available.

El Chico
STEAK €€€

(☑ 06131-238 440; Kötherhofstrasse 1; mains €15.50-28.50; ⊘6-11pm; ☎) Widely considered to serve Mainz' finest steaks (from Argentina) and lamb chops (from New Zealand), as well as desserts like flaky apple strudel, El Chico has the ambience of an intimate bistro, with fresh flowers and candles on the tables. Its popularity means reservations are essential all week, year round.

🍷 Drinking & Nightlife

There are some atmospheric wine bars in the old town, along with pubs and bars. For more extensive nightlife options, head to Frankfurt.

Spiritus
COCKTAIL BAR

(Neutorstrasse 5; ⊘8pm-1am Sun-Thu, to 3am Fri & Sat) Hefty ceiling beams and a bar made from recycled timbers blend the old and new at this hip little drinking den. Over 300 infused spirits are used in its daily changing cocktail menu, including blackberry-infused whisky, white chocolate-infused rum and stinging nettle-infused gin.

Weingut Michel
WINE BAR

(www.michel-wein.de; Jakobsbergstrasse 8; ⊘4pm-midnight) Mainz' only *Weingut* (winery) to exclusively serve its own wines occupies a vine-draped stone building that's housed a wine bar since 1756. Along with superb whites including Riesling and blanc

de noir, there are feisty reds (dornfelder, merlot) and sparkling wines.

Eisgrub-Bräu
MICROBREWERY

(www.eisgrub.de; Weisslilliengasse 1a; ⊘11.30am-midnight Sun-Thu, to 1am Fri & Sat) Take a seat in this down-to-earth microbrewery's warren of vaulted chambers or on the heated pavement terrace and order a mug of *Dunkel* (dark) or *Hell* (light) – or, if you're planning to settle in for a while – a 3L or 5L *Bierturm* (beer tower).

Weinstube Hottum
WINE BAR

(Grebenstrasse 3; ⊘4pm-midnight) Behind a plain, olive-green-painted facade is one of the Altstadt's cosiest wine taverns. Dating from 1791, it serves wines purely from the Rheingau and Rheinhessen regions.

☆ Entertainment

Mainz is large and lively enough to have a diverse range of cultural offerings. The tourist office has event guides and sells tickets. Gigs are listed online at Der Mainzer (www.dermainzer.net).

KuZ
LIVE MUSIC

(KulturZentrum; ☑ 06131-635 6463; www.kuz.de; Dagobertstrasse 20b) Concerts by German and international bands, dance parties, theatre for kids... the happening KulturZentrum (cultural centre) has it and more. It's housed in a red-brick building that began life in the 19th century as a military laundry.

Frankfurter Hof
LIVE MUSIC

(☑ 06131-242 914; www.frankfurter-hof-mainz.de; Augustinerstrasse 55) See performances by up-and-coming artists and big-name international acts at this cultural venue. Some events take place at other venues around the city, such as open-air summer concerts.

Staatstheater
PERFORMING ARTS

(☑ 06131-285 1222; www.staatstheater-mainz.com; Gutenbergplatz 7) The state theatre stages plays, opera and ballet. Students get significant discounts.

ℹ️ Information

DISCOUNT CARDS

Valid for two days, the **Mainz Cardplus** (per one/five people €11.95/25) gets you admission to museums (some are free anyway), a walking tour, unlimited public transport in both Mainz and Wiesbaden, plus various discounts. Buy it from the tourist offices in Mainz (p568) or Wiesbaden (p562).

TOURIST INFORMATION

Tourist Office (☑ 06131-242 888; www.mainz-tourismus.com; Rheinstrasse 55; ⊙ 9am-5pm Mon-Fri, 10am-4pm Sat)

❶ Getting There & Away

Train From the Hauptbahnhof, S-Bahn line S8 goes frequently via Frankfurt airport (€4.90, 20 minutes) to Frankfurt's Hauptbahnhof (€8.50, 40 minutes). A day ticket that takes in both Mainz and Frankfurt, including S-Bahn commuter trains, local trams and buses, costs €16.55.

A major rail hub, Mainz's Hauptbahnhof has at least hourly regional services to Bingen (€11, 30 minutes) and other Romantic Rhine towns, as well as to Koblenz (€22, one hour, every 30 minutes), Saarbrücken (€34.80, 2¼ hours, up to three per hour) and Worms (€14.10, 25 to 40 minutes, up to three per hour).

Bus Buses to Hahn Airport (www.bohr.de; one-way €16, 70 minutes, up to 19 per day) depart from in front of the Hauptbahnhof.

❶ Getting Around

Bicycle Zweirad Boxx (☑ 06131-901 7757; www.zweiradboxx.de; Nackstrasse 14; per day bicycles €8-15, tandem or electric bikes €25; ⊙ 10am-6pm Mon, Wed & Fri, 2-7pm Tue & Thu, 10am-2pm Sat Mar-Oct, 10am-6pm Mon, Wed & Fri, 10am-2pm Sat Nov-Jan) rents bikes.

Bus & Tram Mainz operates its bus and tram system jointly with Wiesbaden. Single tickets cost €2.80; short tickets (maximum three stops) cost €1.75. Day passes for individuals/groups of up to five are €5.35/10.30. Buy tickets on board or from ticket machines. Details on public transport in the region are available at **Mainzer Mobilität** (☑ 06131-127 777; www.mainzer-mobilitat.de; Bahnhofplatz 6a; ⊙ 7am-7pm Mon-Fri, 9am-2pm Sat).

Darmstadt

☑ 06151 / POP 157,437

Beautiful *Jugendstil* (art nouveau) architecture and excellent museums are the biggest draws of this strollable city 35km south of Frankfurt.

Famed for its technical university, Darmstadt is a designated *Wissenschaftsstadt* (City of Science). The super-heavy element Darmstadtium was first created at Darmstadt's GSI Helmholtzzentrum für Schwerionenforschung (GSI Helmholtz Centre for Heavy Ion Research) in 1994. The city's glass-and-stone conference centre is also called the Darmstadtium.

In 2017, Darmstadt won Germany's first ever Digital City award for its investment in a sustainable digital future; already, the power supply for the entire tram network has been converted to 100% green electricity.

The surrounding area has some fascinating sights, including the Unesco-listed archaeological site Grube Messel (p572), and fabled castle Burg Frankenstein (p572).

◉ Sights

Mathildenhöhe   ARTS CENTRE

(☑ 06151-132 778; www.mathildenhoehe.eu; Olbrichweg 13; museum adult/child €5/3; ⊙ 11am-6pm Tue-Sun Apr-Sep, to 5pm Oct-Mar) Established in 1899 at the behest of Grand Duke Ernst Ludwig, the former *Künstlerkolonie* (artists' colony) at Mathildenhöhe is famous for its Darmstädter *Jugendstil* architecture. Its on-site museum displays supremely elegant *Jugendstil* furniture, tableware, textiles, ceramics and jewellery.

Prices for temporary exhibitions vary. The area is surrounded by a lovely hilltop park with fountains; on the western slope is a Russian Orthodox chapel. From the centre, take bus F.

Free one-hour tours in English take place at 4pm on the first Thursday of each month.

Schlossmuseum   MUSEUM

(☑ 06151-240 35; www.schlossmuseum-darmstadt.de; Marktplatz 15; adult/child €4/2.50; ⊙ 10am-5pm Fri-Sun, tours every 90min) Ornate furnishings, carriages and paintings pack the Schlossmuseum, one block east of Luisenplatz. It occupies the southeast corner of the Schloss complex, one-time residence of the landgraves and grand dukes of Hessen-Darmstadt. Rebuilt after WWII damage, it is now part of Darmstadt's university, the Technische Universität Darmstadt. The only way to visit is on one-hour tours (in German; some guides speak English).

Hessisches Landesmuseum   MUSEUM

(☑ 06151-165 7000; www.hlmd.de; Friedensplatz 1; adult/child €6/free; ⊙ 10am-6pm Tue, Thu & Fri, to 8pm Wed, 11am-5pm Sat & Sun) An exceptional selection of works by pop artist Joseph Beuys is the highlight of the wide-ranging art collection at the Hesse State Museum. Other displays include art nouveau pieces from around the world, along with artworks spanning the prehistoric, early history and medieval eras. There's an extensive zoological section and fossils from the nearby Grube Messel (p572) pit. The museum is two blocks northeast of Luisenplatz.

Kirche Hl Maria Magdalena   CHURCH
(Russian Orthodox Church; ☎ 06151-424 235; www.darmstadt-church.de; Nikolaiweg 18; ⏲ 10am-1pm & 2-4pm Tue-Sat, 2-4pm Sun) Mathildenhöhe's western slope is graced by the three golden onion domes of this mosaic-adorned Russian Orthodox church. It was built from 1897 to 1899 for the last Russian Tsar, Nicholas II, who married Darmstdt-born Princess Alix von Hessen (Grand Duke Ernst Ludwig's younger sister) in 1894.

Luisenplatz   SQUARE
Darmstadt's focal point is the 18th-century Luisenplatz, a veritable hive of activity thanks to the adjacent shopping precinct, which stretches south from the Luisencenter shopping mall.

In the centre of Luisenplatz, a 39m-high column, erected in 1844, holds aloft a statue of Grand Duke Ludwig I of Hesse and the Rhine (1753–1830). The square itself is named after his wife, Grand Duchesse Louise (1761–1829).

Luisenplatz is 1.5km east of the Hauptbahnhof, linked by trams 2, 3 and 5.

🏃 Activities

Jugendstilbad   SWIMMING
(www.jugendstilbad.de; Mercksplatz 1; pools 2hr/4hr/all day €7.30/9.60/11.90, incl spa €10.80/13.60/16, incl spa & saunas €16.80/19.60/23.30; ⏲ 10am-10pm) This historic swimming and spa complex looks as gorgeous as it did when it opened in 1909. It has a year-round outdoor pool, superb *Jugendstil* indoor pool, children's pools and 10 dry and wet saunas. Some areas are *textilfrei* (clothing-free). You can rent a towel (€5) and bathrobe (€5).

Naturfreibad Grosser Woog   SWIMMING
(Landgraf-Georg-Strasse 121, Woogsviertel; adult/child €3.50/1.70; ⏲ 8am-10pm Jun-Sep, to 8pm Apr, May & Oct) For open-air swimming in warm weather, head to this natural lake 1.4km east of the city centre.

Tourist Office Tours   TOURS
(☎ 06151-134 513; www.darmstadt-tourismus.de; tours from €5) The tourist office (p572) runs tours (some in English) of the city, Matildenhöhe and Burg Frankenstein, as well as various factory tours and excursions to places otherwise off-limits to the public such as the German meteorological service, EUMETSAT. Departure points vary; schedules are posted online.

🛏 Sleeping

DJH Hostel   HOSTEL €
(☎ 06151-452 93; www.darmstadt.jugendherberge.de; Landgraf-Georg-Strasse 119; dm €27-31.50; 🛜) This basic, 128-bed hostel has a superb setting on the shores of the Grosser Woog lake, 1km east of the city centre (there's no direct public transport). On site are two lock-up bike sheds and a drying room. Wi-fi is in public areas only.

★ Hotel Jagdschloss Kranichstein   HISTORIC HOTEL €€
(☎ 06151-130 670; www.hotel-jagdschloss-kranichstein.de; Kranichstein Strasse 261; s/d/ste from €89/109/179; 🅿 @ 🛜) Set on 4.2 hectares of forest and parkland 5km northeast of Darmstadt, this 1580-built hunting lodge is now a magnificent hotel, with contemporary countrified rooms throughout the estate's buildings. Breakfast costs €18; epicurean options include a game-specialist restaurant, bar/bistro, and *Bierstube* (tavern) in the armoury, opening to a beer garden, plus gourmet hampers for summer picnicking in the grounds.

Hotel Darmstadt   HOTEL €€
(☎ 06151-281 00; www.bestwestern.de; Grafenstrasse 31; s/d from €119/139; 🅿 ❄ @ 🛜) The entrance, through a parking garage, is unpromising, but inside, this Best Western's lobby is pristine and its 77 quiet, neutral-toned rooms are spacious, modern and comfortable. Kids under 12 stay free in their parents' room. Best of all is the central location, just two blocks southwest of Luisenplatz.

Hotel Prinz Heinrich   HOTEL €€
(☎ 06151-813 70; www.hotel-prinz-heinrich.de; Bleichstrasse 48; s/d €70/85; 🛜) A traditional atmosphere, friendly service, modern bathrooms, comfy beds and outsized photos on the walls make this 60-room hotel a great-value choice. Singles are small but serviceable. Breakfast costs €9. It's midway between the Hauptbahnhof and Luisenplatz.

🍴 Eating

In the warm season you'll find outdoor cafes two blocks southeast of Luisenplatz on the Marktplatz.

★ Elisabeth   CAFE €
(☎ 06151-278 7858; www.suppkult.de; Schulstrasse 14; dishes €4.50-6.80; ⏲ 11am-4pm Mon-Sat; 🍴) Hidden down a passageway in a

(Continued on page 572)

GUENTER ALBERS/SHUTTERSTOCK ©

1. Kölner Dom (p629) 2. Allianz Arena, home of FC Bayern München (p379) 3. Schloss Neuschwanstein (p388) 4. Jüdisches Museum (p85)

YURI TURKOV/SHUTTERSTOCK ©

Architectural Icons

From Roman amphitheatres to glass-and-steel skyscrapers, Germany abounds with fine architecture representing a rainbow of styles and reflecting the era and culture in which it was built. Marvel at architects' vision, builders' ingenuity, changes in taste and innovations in materials and technology as you discover Instagram-worthy landmarks wherever you go.

Schloss Neuschwanstein

Bavarian King Ludwig II was not quite of this world and neither is his most sugary palace (p388), a turreted mirage rising from the thickly forested Alpine foothills. Germany's most photographed castle reflects the king's obsession with Teutonic mythology and medieval grandeur, inspired by the operas of Richard Wagner.

Kölner Dom

The blueprint for the mighty Cologne cathedral (p629) was drafted in the 13th century, but it took more than 600 years to complete this spirit-lifting masterpiece with its filigree twin towers, luminous stained-glass windows and priceless artwork.

Jüdisches Museum, Berlin

Berlin's Jewish Museum (p85) by Daniel Libeskind is essentially a 3D metaphor for the tortured history of the Jewish people. Its zigzag outline symbolises a broken Star of David, while on the inside three intersecting walkways – called axes – represent the fates of Jews during the Nazi years.

Allianz Arena, Munich

Germany's winningest football (soccer) team, the FC Bayern München, plays home games in this breathtaking stadium (p379) designed by the Swiss firm of Herzog & de Meuron (2006). Its most striking feature is the facade, which consists of 2784 shimmering white, diamond-shaped pillows that can be illuminated in different colours.

(Continued from page 569)

picnic-table-filled courtyard, this wonderful spot specialises in homemade soups like pork meatballs and split green peas, curried apple and potato, lentil, carrot and leek, and roast tomato with sheep's cheese, all served with home-baked sourdough or rye bread. Soups change daily. It's also possible to order salads as meals. Finish off with fabulous cakes.

City Braustüb'l GERMAN €€
(📞 06151-255 11; www.city-braustuebl.de; Wilhelminenstrasse 31; mains lunch €6.25-7.25, dinner €8.50-18.50; ⏰ 11am-midnight; 🐾) At this classic brewery-affiliated restaurant – with wood-plank floors, hops hanging from the rafters and a beer garden out back – you can wash down hearty German dishes with a Darmstädter beer brewed over near the Hauptbahnhof.

☆ Entertainment

Centralstation LIVE MUSIC
(📞 06151-780 6999; www.centralstation-darmstadt.de; Im Carree; ⏰ 11am-2am Mon-Thu, to 4am Fri & Sat) The city's first electric power plant, built in 1888, is now a multipurpose cultural centre hosting concerts (especially jazz but also pop and classical), along with comedy, puppetry shows and DJs. There's an upstairs cocktail lounge.

Goldene Krone LIVE MUSIC
(📞 06151-213 52; www.goldene-krone.de; Schustergasse 18; ⏰ 7pm-3am Mon-Wed, to 5am Thu-Sat, to 2am Sun) An long-time student favourite, this sociable bar is known for its nightly concerts as well as dance parties, many held on Friday and Saturday nights starting at 9pm. Enter via Holzstrasse. Cash only.

❶ Information

DISCOUNT CARDS
The **Darmstadt Card** (one/two days €6/9) buys you unlimited use of public transport and reduced-price entry to museums. It's sold at the tourist office.

TOURIST INFORMATION
Tourist Office (📞 06151-134 513; www.darmstadt-tourismus.de; Luisenplatz 5; ⏰ 10am-6pm Mon-Fri, to 4pm Sat, plus to 2pm Sun Apr-Sep) Darmstadt's tourist office is in the northeastern corner of the Luisencenter shopping mall. It sells cultural events tickets. An excellent free app, which can be downloaded from the website, has a map with walking tours, an audio tram tour, an events calendar and more.

❶ Getting There & Around

Frequent S-Bahn (S3) trains link Darmstadt with Frankfurt's Hauptbahnhof (€8.50, 35 minutes), but it's faster to take one of DB's RB, IC or ICE trains (€9.50, 16 minutes).

A day ticket that takes in both cities, including local trams and buses, costs €16.55.

Trams 2, 3 and 5 link the Hauptbahnhof with Luisenplatz. A single ticket costs €2.15. Tickets are sold on board and at ticket machines.

Around Darmstadt

★ Grube Messel ARCHAEOLOGICAL SITE
(Messel Pit; 📞 0615-971 7590; www.grube-messel.de; Rossdörfer Strasse 108, Messel; visitor centre adult/child €10/8, 1/2hr tour €9/7; ⏰ 10am-5pm, tours by reservation) A Unesco World Heritage Site, this one-time coal and oil shale quarry 10km northeast of Darmstadt is renowned for its superbly preserved animal and plant remains from the Eocene era (some 47 million years ago). Early horses found here illustrate the evolutionary path towards the modern beast. A picturesque half-timbered house 3km south of the visitor centre houses a fossil-filled **museum** (📞 0615-951 19; www.messelmuseum.de; Langgasse 2, Messel; ⏰ 11am-5pm daily Apr-Oct, Sat & Sun Nov-Mar) FREE. You can visit the pit with a German-speaking guide or pre-arrange an English-speaking tour (extra €20 per group).

Some 40,000 fossils have been unearthed to date. Other interesting finds from the site are showcased at the Hessisches Landesmuseum (p568) in Darmstadt and the Senckenberg Museum (p544) in Frankfurt.

Burg Frankenstein CASTLE
(📞 06151-501501; www.frankenstein-restaurant.de; Ralphweg, Mühltal; entry by donation; ⏰ 9am-sunset except during events) Built by Lord Konrad II Reiz von Breuberg around 1250, this hulking, partly ruined hilltop castle was visited by Mary Shelley on her German travels in 1814, inspiring the title of her famous novel and its protagonist. Tours are in German but you're free to walk around the castle and grounds. It's home to a panoramic restaurant and hosts events, including one of Europe's largest Halloween parties. From Darmstadt, it's 13km south, high up in the forest, via the B426.

Other events here include medieval banquets, costumed adventure castle days, live music including jazz, magic shows, and theatre nights for adults and children – schedules are posted online.

HEIDELBERG REGION

The ancient university city of Heidelberg is the most high-profile city in this region, but Speyer, Worms and Mannheim also harbour plenty of architectural and cultural treasures.

Heidelberg is the region's main gateway. Mannheim, Speyer and Worms are also well served by trains.

Heidelberg

📞 06221 / POP 159,914

Surrounded by forest, Germany's oldest and most famous university town is renowned for its baroque Altstadt, beautiful riverside setting and evocative half-ruined hilltop castle, which draw 11.9 million visitors a year. They follow in the footsteps of the late 18th- and early-19th-century romantics, most notably the poet Goethe and Britain's William Turner, who was inspired by Heidelberg to paint some of his greatest landscapes.

In 1878, Mark Twain began his European travels with a three-month stay in Heidelberg, recounting his observations in *A Tramp Abroad* (1880). Heidelberg's rich literary history, along with its thriving contemporary scene, saw it named a Unesco City of Literature in 2014.

Heidelberg's Altstadt has a red-roofed townscape of remarkable architectural unity. After having been all but destroyed by French troops under Louis XIV (1690s), it was rebuilt during the 18th century. Unlike many German cities, it emerged from WWII almost unscathed.

⦿ Sights

Heidelberg's Altstadt runs along the left (south) bank of the Neckar River from Bismarckplatz east to the hillside Schloss. One of Europe's longest pedestrian zones, the 1600m-long Hauptstrasse, runs east–west through the Altstadt, about 200m south of the Neckar, passing a series of picturesque public squares, many with historic or modern fountains. Superb views of the town extend from the north (right) bank of the Neckar in Neuenheim.

★ **Schloss Heidelberg**   CASTLE
(📞06221-658 880; www.schloss-heidelberg.de; Schlosshof 1; adult/child incl Bergbahn €7/4, tours €5/2.50, audioguide €5; ⦿grounds 24hr, castle 8am-6pm, English tours hourly 11.15am-4.15pm Mon-Fri, from 10.15am Sat & Sun Apr-Oct, fewer tours Nov-Mar) Towering over the Altstadt, Heidelberg's ruined Renaissance castle cuts a romantic figure, especially across the Neckar River when illuminated at night. Along with fabulous views, attractions include the Deutsches Apotheken-Museum. The castle is reached either via a steep, cobbled trail in about 10 minutes or by taking the **Bergbahn** (cogwheel train) from Kornmarkt station. The only way to see the less-than-scintillating interior is by tour. After 6pm you can stroll the grounds for free.

Once you arrive up top, you'll be struck by the far-reaching views over the Neckar River and the Altstadt rooftops. Show your ticket to enter the Schlosshof, the castle's central courtyard, which is framed by reconstructed Gothic and Renaissance buildings with elaborate facades. The most eye-catching belongs to the Friedrichsbau, which is festooned with life-size sculptures of kings and emperors.

You can't miss the enormous wine cask, the Grosses Fass, with a capacity of 221,726L.

Deutsches Apotheken-Museum   MUSEUM
(German Pharmacy Museum; www.schloss-heidelberg.de; Schlosshof, Schloss Heidelberg; incl in Schloss Heidelberg ticket; ⦿10am-6pm Apr-Oct, to 5.30pm Nov-Mar) The German Pharmacy Museum, off the Schlosshof at Schloss Heidelberg, illustrates the history of Western pharmacology, in which Germany played a central role. Exhibits include pharmacies from the early 1700s and the Napoleonic era. Children can use a mortar and a pestle to blend their own herbal tea. Most signs are in English.

Heiliggeistkirche   CHURCH
(📞06221-980 30; www.ekihd.de; Marktplatz; tower adult/child €2/1; ⦿church 11am-5pm Mon-Sat, from 12.30pm Sun, tower 11am-5pm Mon-Sat, from 12.30pm Sun Apr-Oct, 11am-3pm Fri & Sat, from 12.30pm Sun Nov-Mar) For bird's-eye views, climb the 208 stairs to the top of the tower of Heidelberg's famous church, constructed between 1398 and 1441. It was shared by Catholics and Protestants from 1706 until 1936 (it's now Protestant). Designed in 1984 by Johannes Schreiter, its predominantly red stained-glass window features the equation $E = mc^2$ followed by the date 06/08/1945 (the bombing of Hiroshima). The church hosts regular concerts (adult/child from €10/6) and half-hour organ recitals (€4/2); check the website for schedules.

Marktplatz   SQUARE
The Marktplatz is the focal point of Altstadt street life.

Hercules Fountain FOUNTAIN
(Marktplatz) In the middle of the Marktplatz is the Hercules fountain; in medieval times petty criminals were chained to it and left to face the populace.

Kurpfälzisches Museum MUSEUM
(www.museum-heidelberg.de; Hauptstrasse 97; adult/child Tue-Sat €3/1.80, Sun €1.80/1.20; ☉10am-6pm Tue-Sun) The city-run Palatinate Museum chronicles Heidelberg's eventful past, particularly the Roman period – exhibits include original wood beams from a 3rd-century bridge. To learn about really ancient history, check out the replica of the 600,000-year-old jawbone of *Homo heidelbergensis* (Heidelberg Man), unearthed some 18km southeast in 1907 (the original is stored at the university's palaeontology institute). Most of the museum's late 15th- to 20th-century paintings and sculptures are by artists from or associated with the region.

Ruprecht-Karls-Universität UNIVERSITY
(Heidelberg University; www.uni-heidelberg.de; Grabengasse) Established in 1386 by Count Palatine Ruprecht I, Germany's oldest and most prestigious university comprises 12 faculties with 30,000 German and international students, and has an esteemed alumni that includes a roll-call of Nobel Laureates. The most historic facilities are around Universitätsplatz, dominated by the Alte Universität (1712–28; on the south side) and the Neue Universität (1931; on the north side), the 'old' and 'new' university buildings respectively. Nearby stands the Löwenbrunnen (Lions Fountain).

Universitätsmuseum MUSEUM
(www.uni-heidelberg.de; Grabengasse 1; adult/child incl Studentenkarzer €3/2.50; ☉10am-6pm Tue-Sun Apr-Sep, to 4pm Tue-Sat Oct-Mar) The three-room University Museum, inside the Alte Universität building of Ruprecht-Karls-Universität, has paintings, portraits, documents and photos from the university's mostly illustrious history. Only the signs on the Third Reich period are in English, but the ticket price includes an English audioguide. Tickets also include admission to the adjacent Alte Aula, a neo-Renaissance hall whose rich decoration dates from 1886, and the Studentenkarzer.

Studentenkarzer HISTORIC SITE
(Student Jail; ☑ 06221-541 2813; www.uni-heidelberg.de; Auginergasse 2; adult/child incl Universitätsmuseum €3/2.50; ☉10am-6pm Tue-Sun Apr-Oct, to 4pm Mon-Sat Nov-Mar) From 1823 to 1914, students convicted of misdeeds such as public inebriation, loud nocturnal singing, freeing the local pigs or duelling were sent to this student jail for at least 24 hours. Judging by the inventive wall graffiti, some found their stay highly amusing. Delinquents were let out to attend lectures or take exams. In certain circles, a stint in the Karzer was considered a rite of passage.

Universitätsbibliothek MUSEUM
(www.uni-heidelberg.de; Plöck 107-109; ☉10am-6pm) FREE The University Library was built in massive Wilhelmian style from 1901 to 1905. Upstairs you can see rare books and prints from its superb collections in the corner Ausstellungsraum (exhibition room).

Jesuitenkirche CHURCH
(www.heidelberg-neckartal.de; Schulgasse 4; church free, Schatzkammer adult/child €3/2.50; ☉church 9.30am-6pm May-Sep, to 5pm Oct-Apr, Schatzkammer 10am-5pm Tue-Sat, from 1pm Sun Jun-Oct, Sat & Sun Nov-May) Rising above an attractive square just east of Universitätsplatz, the red-sandstone Jesuits' church, with an all-white interior, is a fine example of 18th-century baroque. The *Schatzkammer* (treasury) displays precious religious artefacts. Look out for regular concerts.

Alte Brücke BRIDGE
(Karl-Theodor-Brücke) Heidelberg's 200m-long 'old bridge', built in 1786, connects the Altstadt with the river's right bank and the Schlangenweg (Snake Path), whose switchbacks lead to the Philosophenweg.

Next to the tower gate on the Altstadt side of the bridge, look for the brass sculpture of a monkey holding a mirror. It's the 1979 replacement of the original 17th-century sculpture.

Philosophenweg TRAIL
(Philosophers' Walk; Neckar River north bank) Winding past monuments, towers, ruins, a beer garden, and an enormous *Thingstätte* (amphitheatre) built by the Nazis in 1935, the 2.5km-long Philosophers' Walk has captivating views of Heidelberg's Schloss, especially at sunset when the city is bathed in a reddish glow. Access is easiest via the steep Schlangenweg from Alte Brücke. Don't attempt to drive up as the road is narrow and there's nowhere to turn around at the top.

Botanischer Garten der Universität   PARK
(University Botanical Garden; ☑06221-545 783; http://botgart.hip.uni-heidelberg.de; Im Neuenheimer Feld 340; ⊙gardens dawn-dusk, hothouses 9am-4pm Mon-Thu, to 2.30pm Fri, 10am-5pm Sun) **FREE** Established in 1593 as a medicinal garden, the University Botanical Garden – part of the university's right-bank Neuenheimer Feld campus, 2.5km northwest of Bismarckplatz – now has over 14,000 plant species. Orchids, bromeliads, ferns and Madagascan succulents thrive in the hothouses; alpine, bog and heath are among the outdoor environments, along with a vineyard.

Neuenheim River Bank   PARK
(Uferstrasse) The Neckar's grassy northern bank between Theodor-Heuss-Brücke and Ernst-Walz-Brücke is a favourite student hang-out when the weather is warm.

🏃 Activities

Bootsverleih Simon   BOATING
(☑06221-411 925; Uferstrasse 3; per hour 3-/4-person pedalo €15/18; ⊙2pm-dusk Mon-Fri, from 1pm Sat & Sun Apr-early Oct) To take to the river under your own steam, hire a pedalo on the north shore of the Neckar, just east of Theodor-Heuss-Brücke.

👉 Tours

Tourist Office Walking Tours   WALKING
(www.heidelberg-marketing.de; adult/child €9/7; ⊙English tours 10.30am Thu-Sat Apr-Oct) English-language tours (1½ hours) taking in the Altstadt's highlights depart from the Marktplatz tourist office (p579).

Solarschiff   CRUISE
(www.hdsolarschiff.com; Alte Brücke; adult/child €9/3.50; ⊙10am-6pm Tue-Sun Mar-Oct) 🌿 One of the most peaceful ways to appreciate Heidelberg's charms is to get out on the river. Solarschiff's solar-panelled boat engine is silent – all you hear during a 50-minute cruise, apart from onboard commentary in English and German, is the water and the distant sounds of the city.

Rhein-Neckar Fahrgastschifffahrt   CRUISE
(Weisse Flotte; ☑06221-201 81; www.weisse-flotte-heidelberg.de; to Neckarsteinach return adult/child €17/8; ⊙10am-6pm Easter-Oct) Daytrips run up and down the Neckar to Neckarsteinach (1½ hours).

The company also runs a six-stop ferry along the Neckar, from the Ernst-Walz-Brücke to the Alte Brücke (adult/child per stop €2/0.50, entire length €4/2, hop-on hop-off €10/5), and a cruise to Mannheim and Worms (adult/child €21/9.50, three hours).

⭐ Festivals & Events

Heidelberger Schlossbeleuchtung   FIREWORKS
(Castle Illumination; ⊙10.15pm on 1st Sat Jun, 2nd Sat Jul & 1st Sat Sep) The Schloss, the Alte Brücke and the Altstadt are lit up by fantastic fireworks that commemorate the French assault on the Schloss in 1693. The best views are from both banks of the Neckar, west of the Alte Brücke.

Heidelberger Herbst   STREET CARNIVAL
(⊙10am-11pm last Sat in Sep) Heidelberg's huge street party has music, arts and crafts, buskers, food and general merrymaking throughout the Altstadt on the last Saturday of September, with events also taking place the following day.

Weihnachtsmarkt   CHRISTMAS MARKET
(⊙11am-10pm late Nov-22 Dec) Around 140 stalls take over the Altstadt's public squares, including the Marktplatz, Universitätsplatz and the Kornmarkt, during Heidelberg's magical Christmas market.

🛏 Sleeping

Heidelberg's popularity means finding a bed can be tricky, so booking ahead is advisable any time of year, but particularly in summer and during the Christmas season.

Lotte   HOSTEL €
(☑06221-735 0725; www.lotte-heidelberg.de; Burgweg 3; dm/d/tr from €23/64/81; 🖥) Directly opposite the Kornmarkt station of the Bergbahn up to the castle, with plenty of pubs, bars and restaurants nearby, this cosy independent hostel has five dorms (four mixed, one female-only), two doubles and a triple. All are en suite. There's a self-catering kitchen, laundry, bike storage and board games (but no TV); rates include a basic breakfast.

Steffis Hostel   HOSTEL €
(☑06221-778 2772; www.hostelheidelberg.de; Alte Eppelheimer Strasse 50; dm/d/tr from €22/50/64; ⊙reception 8am-10pm; @🖥) In a 19th-century tobacco factory a block north of the Hauptbahnhof, accessed via an industrial-size lift, Steffis offers bright, well-lit dorms and rooms, a sociable lounge, a spacious kitchen and an old-school hostel vibe. Breakfast costs €3. Perks include tea, coffee and free

bike rental. From May to September there's a two-night minimum stay at weekends.

★ **Hotel Villa Marstall** HISTORIC HOTEL **€€**
(☑ 06221-655 570; www.villamarstall.de; Lauerstrasse 1; s/d/ste from €115/135/165; ⊘ reception 7am-10pm Mon-Sat, 8am-6pm Sun; ❋ ⚛) A 19th-century neoclassical mansion directly overlooking the Neckar River, Villa Marstall is a jewel with cherrywood floors, solid-timber furniture and amenities including a lift. Its 18 exquisite rooms are decorated in whites, creams and bronzes, and come with in-room fridges (perfect for chilling a bottle of regional wine). A sumptuous breakfast buffet (€12) is served in the red-sandstone vaulted cellar.

★ **Arthotel Heidelberg** BOUTIQUE HOTEL **€€**
(☑ 06221-650 060; www.arthotel.de; Grabengasse 7; s €109-172, d €125-198; **P** ❋ ⚛) This charmer is a winning blend of historic setting and sleek contemporary design. Equipped with huge bathrooms (tubs!), the 24 rooms are spacious and purist – except for three that sport painted ceilings from 1790. There's a courtyard as well as a roof garden (but avoid rooms below it in summer, when you can hear people walking above). Breakfast costs €13.50.

Hotel Goldene Rose HOTEL **€€**
(☑ 06221-905 490; www.hotel-goldene-rose.de; St-Anna-Gasse 7; s/d from €100/115; ⚛) At the western end of the Hauptstrasse, this rose-toned, gold-trimmed hotel has 37 surprisingly modern rooms that are compact but quiet, comfortable and well kept.

Hotel Goldener Hecht HOTEL **€€**
(☑ 06221-536 80; www.hotel-goldener-hecht.de; Steingasse 2; s/d from €69/85; ⚛) Right by the Alte Brücke, this atmospheric hotel has just 13 rooms, six with bridge views; the three corner rooms are bright and gorgeous. One drawback to being so central: it can be noisy at night, especially on summer weekends. Goethe was once turned away for lack of space, so book ahead. Breakfast costs €12.

Denner Hotel HOTEL **€€**
(☑ 06221-604 510; www.denner-hotel.de; Bergheimer Strasse 8; s/d from €91/119; ⚛) Just 100m east of the Hauptstrasse, Denner has 18 uniquely decorated rooms, with details such as designer furniture, hardwood floors and stencilled walls; some have four-poster beds. Rooms 14 and 26 have neoclassical balconies overlooking Bismarckplatz. No breakfast is available but there are cafes nearby.

Kulturbrauerei Hotel HOTEL **€€**
(☑ 06221-502 980; www.heidelberger-kulturbrauerei.de; Leyergasse 6; s/d/ste from €100/120/150; ⚛) This stylish Altstadt hotel above the eponymous microbrewery (p579) has 43 romantic cream-coloured rooms with polished parquet floors, classical furniture and large windows. Breakfast is €12 for hotel guests (€15 for non-guests).

Hotel Regina HOTEL **€€**
(☑ 06221-536 40; www.hotel-regina.de; Luisenstrasse 6; s €75-105, d €89-145; ⚛) Central but quiet, just west of the Altstadt and 200m west of Bismarckplatz, the welcoming Regina occupies a brick-and-stone building built a century ago that opens to a small, greenery-filled courtyard. The 15 rooms have bright, all-tile bathrooms and blackout curtains.

Hotel zum Ritter St Georg HISTORIC HOTEL **€€**
(☑ 06221-705 050; www.hotel-ritter-heidelberg.com; Hauptstrasse 178; s/d from €79/109; ⚛) Set in an ornate, late-Renaissance mansion built by a Huguenot cloth merchant in 1592, Hotel zum Ritter St Georg's cheaper rooms are an anticlimax after the opulent facade, but the spacious superior (23 to 28 sq metres) and deluxe (28 to 35 sq metres) rooms, some with church views, are bright and really lovely. Breakfast costs €15.

Hotel am Kornmarkt HOTEL **€€**
(☑ 06221-905 830; www.hotelamkornmarkt.de; Kornmarkt 7; s/d/tr/q €78/90/130/140, without bathroom s/d €68/75; ⚛) In a fantastic location just a block from the Marktplatz, this hotel is low on frills but great value. Behind its baroque facade, the 20 rooms are comfortable and spotless; some have Kornmarkt views. Breakfast costs €10.

★ **Hip Hotel** BOUTIQUE HOTEL **€€€**
(☑ 06221-208 79; www.hip-hotel.de; Hauptstrasse 115; d/tr/ste from €140/200/230; @ ⚛) Snooze in a Fijian beach shack complete with sandy bay, a woodsy Canadian hunter's cottage, or a topsy-turvy Down Under room where everything (paintings, doors, bed) is upside down. In an age in which cities are awash in 'theme hotels', this 27-room place is both genuinely creative and heaps of fun. The Amsterdam room is wheelchair-accessible. Breakfast costs €12.

✖ Eating

The Altstadt, especially around Steingasse and Untere Strasse, is chock-full of restaurants, cafes, pubs and beer gardens. Cosy restaurants frequented by locals are tucked away on the side streets south of the Hauptstrasse and west of the Kornmarkt.

Many of Heidelberg's traditional pubs are also atmospheric places to dine on hearty German cuisine.

Gundel   BAKERY €
(www.gundel-heidelberg.de; Hauptstrasse 212; dishes €2-8; ⊙ cafe 8.30am-6.30pm Tue-Fri, 8am-6pm Sat & Sun, bakery 6am-7pm Tue-Fri, 7am-6pm Sat & Sun) Gundel's bakery section has 30 kinds of bread and rolls, as well as delectable pastries. It's a great stop to stock up for a river or forest picnic; alternatively you can dine in at the wicker-chair-filled cafe, which serves light bites like salads, soups, quiches, sausages, pickled herring fillets and jacket potatoes.

Joe Molese   DINER €
(www.joemolese.com; Steingasse 16a; dishes €5-12; ⊙noon-11pm) Sandwiches – like pastrami, tomato and honey-mustard vinaigrette; brie, arugula and truffle oil; or wild smoked salmon with lemon juice and olive oil – are the standout at Joe's, but it also has fantastic salads, chicken drumsticks, burgers and buffalo wings. Black-and-white chequerboard tiling and fire-engine-red walls give it a souped-up New York deli vibe. Cash only.

Smoothies range from strawberry-and-basil to pineapple-and-lime, or you can order beer, wine and cocktails.

Unter Freunden   PIZZA €
(Märzgasse 2; pizza per slice €1.20-3.40; ⊙10am-8pm Mon & Wed-Sat; 🕏🍴) Pizza *al taglio* (by the slice) is the speciality of this hip whitewashed space. Toppings include pear and gorgonzola, mortadella (Italian sausage) with artichoke and buffalo mozzarella, and hummus with figs, aubergine and pecorino, plus at least one vegan option per day. Pair it with smoothies like Bloody Hell (beetroot, lemon juice, orange and flax seed).

There are tables inside and out on the pavement, or pick up a slice to take away.

Gelato Go   GELATO €
(www.gelatogo.de; Hauptstrasse 100; gelato from €1.30; ⊙10am-midnight) The Hauptstrasse is sprinkled with ice cream shops but Gelato Go trumps them all (hence the constant queue out the door, even in winter). In addition to the classics, flavours span sea salt caramel, crème brûlée, lemon vodka, chest-

nut and watermelon. Most of the flavours are organic and several are gluten-free.

Die Kuh Die Lacht   BURGERS €
(www.diekuhdielacht.com; Hauptstrasse 133; burgers €7-10; ⊙11.30am-10pm Mon-Thu, to 11pm Fri & Sat, noon-9pm Sun; 🍴) This sleek burger joint's 19 different, all-natural burgers are handmade on the premises. Choices include chicken caesar, barbecued beef, a Mexican burger with beans and corn, as well as veggie options such as a tofu burger and a falafel burger.

Schnitzelbank   GERMAN €€
(☑06221-211 89; www.schnitzelbank-heidelberg. de; Bauamtsgasse 7; mains €15-22; ⊙5pm-11.30pm Mon-Fri, from 11.30am Sat & Sun, bar to 1am) Small and often jam-packed, this cosy wine tavern has you sampling the local tipples (all wines are regional) and cuisine while crouched on wooden workbenches from the time when this was still a cooperage. It's these benches that give the place its name, incidentally, not the veal and pork schnitzel on the menu.

Café Weinstube Burkardt   CAFE €€
(☑06221-166 620; www.facebook.com/cafeburkardt; Untere Strasse 27; mains €12-23.50; ⊙kitchen 11.30am-2pm & 6-10pm, cafe 9am-11pm) Charming Burkardt's has a superb selection of wines from the Heidelberg region available by the glass, and first-rate food, such as risotto with asparagus and mushrooms or apricot and lamb ragout. The courtyard abuts the house where Friedrich Ebert, German President during the Weimar Republic, was born.

★'S' Kastanie   EUROPEAN €€€
(☑06221-728 0343; www.restaurant-s-kastanie. de; Elisabethenweg 1; 2-course lunch menu €10, 3-/4-/5-course dinner menus €43/46.50/58, mains €17-29.50; ⊙11.30am-2.30pm & 6-10pm Wed-Fri, 5-10pm Sat, 11.30am-8pm Sun; 🍴) A panoramic terrace provides sweeping views of the river at this gorgeous 1904-built former hunting lodge with stained glass and timber panelling, set in the forest near the castle. Chef Sven Schönig's stunning creations include octopus carpaccio with grilled watermelon and cauliflower mousse or feather-light goat's cheese soufflé with wild garlic sauce. Vegetarian and vegan choices are available.

★Zur Herrenmühle
Heidelberg   GERMAN €€€
(☑06221-602 909; www.herrenmuehle.net; Hauptstrasse 239; mains €28.50-36, 3-/4-course

WORTH A TRIP

SCHLOSS SCHWETZINGEN

The enchanting gardens of **Schloss Schwetzingen** (Schwetzingen Palace; ✆ 06221-658 880; www.schloss-schwetzingen.de; Schlossstrasse, Schwetzingen; adult/child gardens €6/3, incl Schloss tour €11/5.50; ◷ gardens 9am-8pm Apr-Oct, to 5pm Nov-Mar, English palace tours 2pm Mon-Fri, noon, 2pm & 4pm Sat & Sun Apr-Oct), the grand baroque-style summer residence of Prince-Elector Carl Theodor (1724–1799), are wonderful for a stroll, especially on a sunny day. The only way to see the furnished Schloss interior is on a 90-minute guided tour. Download the free brochure *Schwetzingen Castle Garden* or buy it at the ticket desk (€1.50). Schloss Schwetzingen is 10km west of Heidelberg and 8km south of Mannheim (served by buses), just east of the A6.

Of Versailles-like proportions and inspiration, the palace gardens blend French formality and meandering, English-style landscaping. Scattered around the gardens are burbling fountains and 'follies', architectural flights of fancy. Among them is an ersatz *Moschee* (mosque), an extraordinary pink complex decorated with Turkish crescents, that mixes 18th-century German baroque with 'exotic' styling inspired by Constantinople. As you wander, keep an eye out for strutting peacocks.

There are cafes on site.

menus €62/68; ◷ 6-9.30pm Mon-Sat, noon-4pm & 6-9.30pm Sun) A flour mill from 1690 has been turned into an elegant and highly cultured place to enjoy refined 'country-style' cuisine, such as saffron-crusted dorade royale with baby spinach and creamed potato, beneath weighty, 300-year-old wooden beams with candles flickering on the tables. Book ahead.

Weisser Bock   FUSION €€€

(✆ 06221-900 00; www.weisserbock.de; Grosse Mantelgasse 24; mains €21.50-36; ◷ 5-10pm Mon-Thu, from 11.30am Fri & Sat) Dark-wood panelling, linen-bedecked tables and low lighting make an elegant backdrop for newly interpreted classical dishes. Each is prepared with fresh ingredients that play off each other: scallop tartare with wasabi or wild garlic and chilli prawns for starters, followed by pancetta-wrapped monkfish with saffron foam, and dark chocolate cake with elderflower sorbet.

🍷 Drinking & Nightlife

Heidelberg's student population fuels the party, especially at the weekend. On the Neuenheim river bank, a favourite student hang-out in warm weather, cafes sell snacks and drinks including beer. For a pub crawl, you can't beat pedestrianised Untere Strasse, which student revellers keep lively until very late on weekends.

Zum Roten Ochsen   PUB

(Red Ox Inn; www.roterochsen.de; Hauptstrasse 217; ◷ 5pm-midnight Mon-Wed, from 11.30am Thu-Sat) Fronted by a red-painted, blue-grey-shuttered facade, Heidelberg's most historic student pub has black-and-white frat photos on the dark wooden walls and names carved into the tables. Along with German luminaries, visitors who've raised a glass here include Mark Twain, John Wayne and Marilyn Monroe. Live piano plays from 7.30pm, with plenty of patrons singing along.

Traditional dishes focus on regional fare, such as deer ragout with cranberries, croquettes and red cabbage.

Vetter's Alt Heidelberger Brauhaus   BREWERY

(www.brauhaus-vetter.de; Steingasse 9; ◷ 11.30am-midnight Sun-Thu, to 2am Fri & Sat; 🛜) The gleaming copper kettles at this dark-wood pub contain house beers including *Helles* (blond), *Dunkles Hefeweizen* (dark wheat beer), *Doppel Bock* (double bock) and seasonal brews like Oktoberfest's amber *Märzen*. Soak them up with heaping portions of hearty traditional German dishes.

Frollein Bent   BAR

(www.bentbar.de; Neckarmünzgasse 1; ◷ 2pm-midnight Tue-Sun Apr-Sep, from 5pm Fri-Sun Oct-Mar) With just 13 seats, the interior of this retro-style bar can be cramped, but its big draw is its sun-drenched terrace on a riverfront square – a fabulously scenic spot to enjoy an Italian Sequella coffee, a Brazilian-invented, German-adopted caipirinha, or other cocktails like mojitos and G&Ts. There are more seats around the corner at its second location at Leyergasse 2.

Chocolaterie Yilliy
CAFE

(www.chocolaterie-heidelberg.de; Haspelgasse 7; ⊙10am-8pm) Especially when the weather is on the chilly side, this is a wonderful spot to warm up with a wickedly thick house-speciality hot chocolate in flavours such as hazelnut, Cointreau, chilli or praline. The airy space has a laid-back lounge-room vibe, with a book swap, piano, regular acoustic gigs and rotating exhibitions by local artists.

KulturBrauerei
MICROBREWERY

(www.heidelberger-kulturbrauerei.de; Leyergasse 6; ⊙7am-11pm) With its wood-plank floor, chairs from a Spanish monastery, black iron chandeliers and an enchanting beer garden, this brewpub is an atmospheric spot to taste the house brews, including many seasonal specialities, and local dishes such as home-made sausages with cream cheese, radish and dark bread.

Destille
PUB

(www.destilleonline.de; Untere Strasse 16; ⊙noon-2am Sun-Thu, to 3am Fri & Sat) An enormous tree frames the bar of this mellow pub, which is famed for its *Warmer Erpel* ('warm duck'; spicy schnapps). It also serves various other schnapps, such as green melon, as well as *Apfelwein* (apple wine).

☆ Entertainment

The city's effervescent cultural scene includes concerts, films, and dance and theatre performances. Venues sell tickets online, or buy them from **Zigaretten Grimm** (☑06221-209 09; www.duerninger.de; Sophienstrasse 11; ⊙9am-7pm Mon-Fri, 10am-5pm Sat).

Karlstorbahnhof
ARTS CENTRE

(☑06221-978 911; www.karlstorbahnhof.de; Am Karlstor 1; ⊙Sep-Jul) Within an old train station, beloved cultural centre Karlstorbahnhof has an art-house cinema screening original-language films; theatre, cabaret and comedy performances (some in English); a nightclub hosting DJs and parties; and a diverse range of concerts. It's 100m east of the Karlstor, the towering stone gate at the eastern end of the Altstadt.

Gloria und Gloriette
CINEMA

(☑06221-253 19; www.gloria-kamera-kinos.de; Hauptstrasse 146; tickets €6.50-8) Right on the Hauptstrasse, this cute little cinema with just 131 seats shows art-house films, some in English.

Deutsch-Amerikanisches Institut
ARTS CENTRE

(German-American Institute; ☑06221-607 30; www.dai-heidelberg.de; Sofienstrasse 12; ⊙ticket office 1-6pm Mon-Fri) The German-American Institute hosts concerts, lectures and films several times a week; many events are in English.

🛍 Shopping

Stroll along traffic-free Hauptstrasse for souvenirs, brand-name shops and fine window displays, or delve into the backstreets to find one-off galleries and speciality shops.

L'Épicerie
FOOD & DRINKS

(www.lepicerie.de; Hauptstrasse 35; ⊙1-7pm Mon, from 11am Tue-Fri, 10am-6pm Sat) In a courtyard off Hauptstrasse, L'Épicerie is filled with luscious pralines, spices, oils and preserves, and accoutrements such as pepper mills, mortars and pestles.

Heidelberger Zuckerladen
FOOD

(www.zuckerladen.de; Plöck 52; ⊙noon-7pm Tue-Fri, 11am-5pm Sat) This old-time sweet shop is filled with bonbons, liquorice laces and fizzy sherbet.

Bären Treff
FOOD

(www.baeren-treff.de; Hauptstrasse 144; ⊙10am-6pm Mon-Sat) This entire shop is dedicated to chewy gummi bear sweets (with free samples). A poster on the wall shows how they're made.

ℹ Information

DISCOUNT CARDS

The **Heidelberg Card** (one/two/four days €15/17/19) entitles you to unlimited public transport use, free admission to the Schloss (including the Bergbahn cogwheel railway) and discounts for museums, tours and more. A two-day family card for up to two adults and three children costs €36. Pick it up from the tourist office or some hotels.

TOURIST INFORMATION

Tourist Office – Hauptbahnhof (☑06221-5844 444; www.heidelberg-marketing.de; Willy-Brandt-Platz 1; ⊙9am-7pm Mon-Sat, 10am-6pm Sun Apr-Oct, 9am-6pm Mon-Sat Nov-Mar) Right outside the main train station.

Tourist Office – Marktplatz (www.heidelberg-marketing.de; Marktplatz 10; ⊙8am-5pm Mon-Fri) At the Rathaus (Town Hall) in the old town.

Tourist Office – Neckarmünzplatz (☑06221-5840 244; www.heidelberg-marketing.de; Obere Neckarstrasse 31; ⊙9am-6pm Mon-Sat,

10am-5pm Sun Apr-Oct, 10am-5pm Mon-Sat Nov-Mar) By the river on Neckarmünzplatz.

ⓘ Getting There & Away

Heidelberg is 93km south of Frankfurt.

TRAIN

From the **Hauptbahnhof** (Willy-Brandt-Platz), 3km west of the Schloss, there are up to three services per hour to/from Frankfurt (€19.90 to €29.90, one to 1½ hours) and Stuttgart (€23.90 to €39.90, 40 minutes to one hour), as well as S-Bahn services to Mannheim (€5.80, 30 minutes, two per hour) and Speyer (€10.90, 50 minutes, every 30 minutes). From Mannheim you can connect to German Wine Route towns.

BUS

The fastest way to reach Frankfurt airport (p557) is the **Lufthansa Airport Shuttle** (☑ 06152-976 9099; www.frankfurt-air-port-shuttles.de; Crowne Plaza Hotel, Kurfürsten-Anlage 1-3; one-way €24; ⊙ 5am-6.30pm). It runs every 90 minutes; journey time is one hour.

To get to Frankfurt-Hahn airport (p557), you can take the **Hahn Express** (☑ 06204-608 2400; www.holger-tours.de; one-way €22; 2¼ hours, five daily), which stops at the Hauptbahnhof.

ⓘ Getting Around

Heidelberg's network of trams and buses is operated by VRN (www.vrn.de).

Tram 5 and buses 10, 33, 34, 41 and 42 link the Hauptbahnhof with Bismarckplatz – Heidelberg's main public transport hub – and parts of the Altstadt. The quickest way from the Hauptbahnhof to the eastern part of the Altstadt is to take an S-Bahn train one stop to the Altstadt station.

Speyer

☑ 06232 / POP 50,284

Scarcely damaged during WWII, the handsome town of Speyer is crowned by a magnificent Romanesque cathedral. Its centre is home to some outstanding museums and the remains of a medieval synagogue, and is easily explored on foot.

History

First a Celtic settlement, then a Roman market town, Speyer gained prominence in the Middle Ages under the Salian emperors, hosting 50 imperial parliament sessions (1294–1570).

In 1076, the king and later Holy Roman Emperor Heinrich IV, having been excommunicated by Pope Gregory VII, launched his penitence walk to Canossa in Italy from Speyer. He crossed the Alps in the middle of winter, an action that warmed the heart of the pope, who revoked his excommunication. He lies buried in the Kaiserdom.

In 1529, pro-Luther princes 'protested' a harsh anti-Luther edict issued by the Diet of Speyer, thereby starting the use of the term 'Protestant'.

⊙ Sights

Roman troops and medieval emperors once paraded down 'Via Triumphalis'. Now known as Maximilianstrasse, Speyer's pedestrian-only shopping strip is 800m long, linking the Kaiserdom with the Altpörtel. Striking baroque buildings along Maximilianstrasse include the Rathaus (at No 13), with its red-orange facade and lavish rococo 1st floor (open for concerts and events), and the Alte Münze (Old Mint; at No 90).

★ Altpörtel   GATE

(Maximilianstrasse 55; adult/child €3/2; ⊙ 10am-noon & 2-4pm Mon-Fri, 10am-5pm Sat & Sun Apr-Oct) The 55m-high, 13th-century Altpörtel, the city's western gate, is the only remaining part of the town wall. Its clock dates from 1761. Climbing 154 steps to the top of the Altpörtel rewards you with breathtaking views on a clear day. On the second floor, a permanent exhibition covers the history of Speyer.

★ Kaiserdom   CATHEDRAL

(www.dom-zu-speyer.de; Domplatz; crypt adult/child €3.50/1, tower €6/3; ⊙ cathedral & crypt 9am-7pm Mon-Sat, 11.30am-5.30pm Sun Apr-Oct, 9am-5pm Mon-Sat, 11.30am-5.30pm Sun Nov-Mar, tower 10am-5pm Mon-Sat, noon-5pm Sun Apr-Oct) Begun in 1030 by Emperor Konrad II of the Salian dynasty, this extraordinary Romanesque cathedral has been a Unesco World Heritage Site since 1981. Its square red towers and green copper dome float majestically above Speyer's rooftops; you can climb the 304 steps of the southwest tower to reach the 60m-high viewing platform for a spectacular panorama. Other highlights include the fascinating crypt and 19th-century paintings in the Kaisersaal.

Atmospheric organ concerts (adult/child €10/5) often take place here.

The cathedral's interior is startling for its awesome dimensions (it's an astonishing 134m long); walk up the side aisles to the elevated altar area to get a true sense of its vastness.

To the right of the altar, steps lead down to the crypt, whose candy-striped Romanesque arches – like those on the west front – recall Moorish architecture (ask for an English-language brochure). Stuffed into a side room, up some stairs, are the sandstone sarcophagi of eight emperors and kings, along with some of their queens. Tours (adult/child including crypt entry €7.50/4) of the cathedral and crypt take place in English by online reservation from April to October.

Behind the Dom, the large Domgarten (cathedral park) stretches towards the Rhine.

★ Judenhof   RUINS
(Jews' Courtyard; www.verkehrsverein-speyer.de; Kleine Pfaffengasse 21; ruins adult/child €3/free, museum €3/1; ⏰10am-5pm Apr-Oct, 10am-4pm Tue-Sun Nov-Mar) A block south of the Rathaus, the 'Jews' Courtyard' is one of the most important medieval Jewish sites in Germany: the remains of a Romanesque-style synagogue that was consecrated in 1104 and used until 1450. Highlights include the 13th-century women's section, a *Mikwe* (ritual bath) from the early 1100s – the oldest, largest and best preserved north of the Alps – and a small museum covering the city's medieval Jewish community. Signs are in English and German.

Technik Museum   MUSEUM
(⏰06232-670 80; www.technik-museum.de; Am Technik Museum 1; adult/child museum €16/13, IMAX €12/8, both €21/17; ⏰9am-6pm Mon-Fri, to 7pm Sat & Sun) At this technology extravaganza, 1km south of the Kaiserdom, you can climb aboard a Lufthansa Boeing 747-230 mounted 20m off the ground (and walk out on its wing), a 1960s U-boat that's claustrophobic even on dry land, and a mammoth Antonov An-22 cargo plane with an all-analogue cockpit and a nose cone you can peer out of. Other highlights include the Soviet space shuttle *Buran*. Its IMAX cinema with a domed screen shows science-related films.

There are also military jets and helicopters from both sides of the former Iron Curtain, and a superb collection of vintage automobiles and fire engines.

The Wilhelmsbau showcases some extraordinary automated musical instruments – all in working order – including a Hupfeld Phonoliszt-Violina, a piano that also bows and fingers two violins, and a Roland orchestrion (1928), which simulates the sound of a soprano accompanying an orchestra.

Dreifaltigkeitskirche   CHURCH
(Trinity Church; www.dreifaltigkeit-speyer.de; Grosse Himmelsgasse 3a) Consecrated in 1717, 200 years to the day after Luther posted his 95 Theses, this harmonious church half a block north of Maximilianstrasse is a superb example of Protestant baroque. Almost all the rich interior decor is original. The double-sided front pews, installed in 1890, allow worshippers to face the altar and then shift sides to see the pulpit during the sermon. Look out for organ recitals.

Historisches Museum der Pfalz   MUSEUM
(Historical Museum of the Palatinate; ⏰06232-620 000; www.museum.speyer.de; Domplatz 4; adult/child incl audioguide €7/3; ⏰10am-6pm Tue-Sun) Exhibits at this treasure-packed museum across from the Kaiserdom include the Goldener Zeremonialhut von Schifferstadt, an ornate gilded hat shaped like a giant thimble, which dates from the Bronze Age (c 1300 BC), and Celtic artefacts such as two bronze wheels (c 800 BC). In the Wine Museum, an amphora from about AD 325 contains what may be the world's oldest wine. Emperor Konrad II's surprisingly simple 11th-century bronze crown is the prized exhibit of the Domschatz (cathedral treasury).

🏃 Activities

Several excellent cycling paths fan out around Speyer. The Kaiser-Konrad-Radweg links Speyer's Kaiserdom with Bad Dürkheim's Rathaus (32.5km each way), on the German Wine Route; the 120km Salier-Radweg circuit also takes in Worms. Starting from Basel in Switzerland, the 420km-long Veloroute Rhein follows the Rhine north to Worms.

The tourist office has cycling information; alternatively, visit Outdoor Active (www.outdooractive.com) for downloadable links, maps and more.

Radsport Stiller   CYCLING
(⏰06232-759 66; www.stiller-radsport.de; Gilgenstrasse 24; standard/electric bike hire per day €15/25; ⏰9.30am-12.30pm & 2-6.30pm Mon-Fri, 9am-3pm Sat, 1-5pm Sun) This first-rate bike shop hires bikes and can provide maps and touring advice.

🛏 Sleeping

There are good midrange hotels in the Altstadt and around the Technik Museum.

DJH Hostel
HOSTEL €

(☑ 06232-615 97; www.jugendherberge.de; Geibstrasse 5; dm/d €30/73; ☞) On the banks of the Rhine next to the Bademaxx swimming complex, Speyer's DJH has 176 beds spread across 51 rooms, all with private bathrooms, and wi-fi in public areas. It's linked to the Hauptbahnhof and city centre by buses 564 and 565; get off at the Bademaxx stop.

★ Hotel Domhof
HOTEL €€

(☑ 06232-132 90; www.hoteldomhof.de; Bauhof 3; s/d from €92/130; P ✳ @ ☞) A hotel has stood on this spot next to the Kaiserdom since the Middle Ages, hosting emperors, kings and councillors over the centuries. The current incarnation opened in 1990 – Speyer's 2000th anniversary. Wrapped around an ivy-covered, cobbled courtyard, its 49 autumnal-hued rooms have parquet floors, bright bathrooms and leafy views. There's an excellent brewery restaurant on site. Breakfast costs €12.50.

Families will appreciate the playground, cots on request, and free stays for kids under seven.

Maximilian
APARTMENT €€

(☑ 06232-100 2516; www.maximilian.bar; Korngasse 15; s/d/apt from €66.50/75/110; ☞) Bang in the centre of town by the Altpörtel, cafe/bistro Maximilian (which doubles as reception) has three attractive guest rooms in the same building, two of which have balconies. Wi-fi can be somewhat patchy. Around the corner, on Karmeliterstrasse, it also rents out two contemporary duplex apartments with well-equipped kitchens, sleeping two adults.

Hotel Speyer
HOTEL €€

(☑ 06232-671 00; www.hotel-speyer.de; Am Technik Museum 1; caravan site €25, s/d €70/80; P ☞) Part of the Technik Museum (p581) complex, this motel-like establishment has 108 practical rooms (some of which face the museum's Boeing 747) as well as a 90-space caravan park (no tents). Guests at both the hotel and the caravan park get discounted Technik Museum entry.

Hotel Zum Augarten
HOTEL €€

(☑ 06232-754 58; www.augarten.de; Rheinhäuser Strasse 52; s/d from €85/105; P ☞) In a suburban setting 1.7km south of the town centre, this tangerine-coloured, family-run hotel offers a warm welcome. Its 16 rooms are modern and some have soothing plum-toned colour schemes.

✗ Eating & Drinking

When the weather's warm, outdoor cafe terraces set up along Maximilianstrasse and nearby streets such as Kleine Pfaffengasse.

Maximilianstrasse and its surrounds have plenty of cafes and bars.

★ Rabennest
GERMAN €€

(☑ 06232-623 857; www.weinstube-rabennest.de; Korngasse 5; mains €8-19; ☉ 11am-11pm Mon-Sat, to 9pm Sun) A half-timbered, green-shuttered building houses this timber-panelled winery, which serves Palatinate vintages and specialities such as *Leberknödel* (liver meatballs in beef broth) and *Pfälzer Bauernsteak* (pork steak with mushrooms, onions and bacon). In summer tables set up on the cobblestones out front. Reservations are recommended.

Domhof-Hausbrauerei
GERMAN €€

(☑ 06232-674 40; www.domhof.de; Grosse Himmelsgasse 6; mains €12-24.50; ☉ 11.30am-10pm Mon-Fri, from 11am Sat & Sun; ☞ ♦) Just beside the Kaiserdom, this historic brewery has a courtyard beer garden shaded by chestnut trees. Regional specialities, some prepared using the three beers brewed on the premises (light, dark and wheat), include fried local sausages with sauerkraut cooked in light beer, and liver dumplings in dark-beer-and-beef broth. Small portions of adult dishes are available for kids.

Maximilian
CAFE €€

(www.maximilian.bar; Korngasse 15; mains €10.50-22; ☉ 8am-11pm Mon-Fri, from 9am Sat & Sun, bar to midnight Sun-Wed, to 1am Thu-Sat) Always buzzing, this local favourite by the Altpörtel serves 12 different breakfasts, from traditional German spreads to eggs Benedict and French toast, various lunch specials, and an à la carte menu spanning sausage platters, steaks, burgers and pastas.

Alter Hammer
WINE BAR

(www.alter-hammer.de; Leinpfad 1c; ☉ 11.30am-9.30pm; ☞) On the grassy banks of the Rhine, this half-timbered manor house has a sprawling, 360-seat summer beer garden canopied by linden trees. Its lengthy local wine list includes house-made *Glühwein* in winter. Traditional German fare, vegetarian options and a kids' menu make it a perfect place to while away a few hours. Cash only.

ℹ Information

Tourist Office (☑ 06232-142 392; www.speyer.de; Maximilianstrasse 13; ☉ 9am-5pm Mon-Fri, 10am-3pm Sat, 10am-2pm Sun Apr-Oct,

9am-5pm Mon-Fri, 10am-noon Sat Nov-Mar)
Situated 200m west of the Kaiserdom, next to
the historic Rathaus.

ⓘ Getting There & Around

S-Bahn (S3 and S4) trains link the Hauptbahnhof
with Mannheim (€5.80, 25 minutes, every 30
minutes) and Heidelberg (€10.90, 50 minutes,
every 30 minutes). Change at Mannheim to
reach the German Wine Route towns.

Buses 564 and 565, run by VRN (www.vrn.de),
link the Hauptbahnhof, Maximilianstrasse, the
Dom, Festplatz, the Technik Museum and the
DJH youth hostel at 10- to 15-minute intervals
from 6am (9am on Sunday) to 8pm. A single
ticket costs €1.20.

The bike-share scheme **VRNnextbike** (www.
vrnnextbike.de; per 30 min €1; ⊘24hr) has
bikes at docking stations around town. Sign up
via the app or at a station using your credit card.

Radsport Stiller (p581) hires bikes and can
provide maps and touring advice.

Mannheim

☑ 0621 / POP 305,780

Situated between the Rhine and Neckar
Rivers, near their confluence, Mannheim
has an energetic cultural scene and decent shopping in its busy city centre, along
with a landmark palace, the Barockschloss
Mannheim.

The city's surrounding factories and
heavy industry plants (automotive, chemicals, pharmaceuticals, engineering, agricultural and construction machinery) mean
this isn't Germany at its prettiest, but they
are a reminder of the drivers of the German
economy.

Two important transportation firsts took
place in Mannheim: Karl Drais created the
world's first bicycle in 1817, and Karl Benz
built the world's first automobile to combine
an internal combustion engine and integrated chassis in 1885; the three-wheeled vehicle
was patented in 1886.

⊙ Sights

★ **Barockschloss Mannheim** PALACE
(☑ 06221-658 880; www.schloss-mannheim.de;
cnr Bismarckstrasse & Breite Strasse; adult/child
incl audioguide €7/3.50, incl guided tour €9/4.50;
⊘10am-5pm Tue-Sun) Mannheim's most famous sight is the yellow and red sandstone
Schloss, Germany's largest baroque palace.
Now occupied by the University of Mannheim, the 450m-long structure was built
over the course of 40 years in the mid-1700s

but was almost completely destroyed during
WWII.

Off the main courtyard are the Schloss
Museum (included in your ticket) and the
baroque **Schlosskirche** (www.alt-katholisch.
de; Bismarckstrasse 14; ⊘10am-5pm).

In the Schloss Museum, you can see the
impressively rococo Kabinettsbibliothek,
saved from wartime destruction thanks
to having been stored off-site, and several
pseudo-baroque halls – each a feast of stucco, marble, porcelain and chandeliers – rebuilt after the war.

Kunsthalle Museum MUSEUM
(www.kuma.art; Friedrichsplatz 4) Mannheim's
premier gallery is a vast repository of modern and contemporary art by masters such
as Cézanne, Degas, Manet, Kandinsky and
Rodin. The permanent collection has often
been stored away to make space for blockbuster exhibitions, but that changed with
the opening of a new €70 million metal-
encased, glass-roofed, 16,000-sq-metre exhibition space.

Jesuitenkirche CHURCH
(Jesuit Church; www.jesuitenkirche.de; A4, 2;
⊘9am-7pm) A sumptuously ornate baroque
vision, glowing with gold leaf, the Jesuitenkirche was built between 1733 and 1760.
When Mozart spent time in Mannheim in
the late 1700s, he praised its acoustics and
atmosphere. Like the rest of the city, the
church suffered damage during WWII, but
it has since been fully restored.

Friedrichsplatz PARK
Five blocks northeast of the Hauptbahnhof,
Friedrichsplatz is an oasis of manicured
lawns, lovely flower beds and art-nouveau
fountains. Its centrepiece is the 60m-high
Wasserturm (Water Tower), a bit of
19th-century civil architecture that has become one of the city's symbols. An elegant
ensemble of red sandstone edifices, many
with arcades, lines the perimeter.

ⓘ Orientation

Mannheim is famous for its quirky – indeed,
unique – chessboard street layout. The city centre, which measures 1.5km by 1.5km, is divided
into four quadrants by two perpendicular, largely
pedestrianised shopping streets, the north–
south Breite Strasse and the east–west Planken.
At their intersection is the grassy Paradeplatz,
with a fountain in the middle.

The streets don't have names. Instead, each
rectilinear city block has an alphanumeric

designation. Starting at the Schloss, as you move north the letters go from A up to K for blocks west of Breite Strasse and from L to U for blocks east of it. The numbers rise from 1 to 7 as you move away – either east or west – from Breite Strasse. The result is addresses such as 'Q3, 16' or 'L14, 5' (the latter numeral specifies the building) that sound a bit like galactic sectors.

🛏 Sleeping

Accommodation is limited; Heidelberg, 23km southeast, has more atmospheric options.

Arabella Pension
PENSION €

(☑ 0621-230 50; www.pension-arabella-mannheim.de; M2, 12; s/d/tr with shared bathroom from €28/46/63; 🖭) Centrally situated just two blocks north of the Schloss, the Arabella has 18 bright, spacious, ultra-budget rooms with shared bathrooms (and no breakfast). Reception is closed Sunday afternoon – call ahead if you'll be arriving then.

Maritim Hotel
LUXURY HOTEL €€

(☑ 0621-158 80; www.maritim.de; Friedrichsplatz 2; d/ste from €136/228; 🅿❄@🖭🛋) Built in 1901 in the sumptuous style of the Renaissance, this grand hotel overlooks Friedrichsplatz. Its 173 rooms are more austere than the exterior would suggest, but they're spacious, and many have balconies or terraces. Amenities include a swimming pool, sauna and steam bath, two upmarket restaurants and a piano bar with music most nights. Breakfast costs €21.

Central Hotel
HOTEL €€

(☑ 0621-123 00; www.centralhotelmannheim.de; Kaiserring 26-28; s €68-145, d €78-165; 🅿🖭) The aptly named Central Hotel, just two blocks north of the Hauptbahnhof, offers snazzy design at reasonable prices. Its 34 rooms are bright and modern, though singles can be small. For a cityscape panorama, ask for one of the three corner rooms. Breakfast costs €10.

🍴 Eating

Mannheim's Marktplatz is flanked by cafes with al fresco seating in summer.

Südlandhaus
DELI €

(☑ 0621-243 02; www.suedlandhaus.de; P3, 8-9; ⊙9.30am-7pm Mon-Fri, to 5.30pm Sat) Filled with German and international wines, cheeses, breads, sausages, hams, olives, liqueurs and chocolates, this aromatic food emporium is an ideal place to pick up picnic fare.

Café Prag
CAFE €

(E4, 17; dishes €1.60-7.90; ⊙10am-6pm Mon-Sat) A former tailor's shop and cigar store, built in 1902, is now an arty cafe with *Jugendstil* woodwork, cranberry-red walls and a pre-war Central European feel. Smooth jazz on the stereo makes a perfect backdrop for enjoying an espresso with a croissant or rhubarb cake, or focaccia with toppings like pastrami and horseradish or avocado and alfalfa. Cash only.

Wochenmarkt
MARKET €

(www.wochenmarkt-mannheim.de; Marktplatz; ⊙8am-2pm Tue & Thu, to 3pm Sat) Lively farmers markets set up on the Marktplatz three times weekly, selling fresh fruit, vegetables, fish, spices, wine, flowers and snacks to eat on the go as you browse the stalls.

Café Journal
CAFE €€

(☑ 0621-271 02; www.cafejournal-mannheim.de; H1, 15; mains €6.80-17.80; ⊙8.30am-11.30pm Mon-Sat, from 9.30am Sun) In a prime people-watching location on Mannheim's Marktplatz, French-styled Café Journal serves dishes ranging from asparagus-stuffed pancakes and schnitzel to grilled fish and burgers. Breakfast (scrambled eggs, pastries, muesli and cheese and meat platters) is available until 3pm. Live jazz plays every Wednesday evening and Sunday afternoon.

Gasthaus Zentrale
GERMAN €€

(☑ 0621-202 43; N4, 15; mains €7-14.50; ⊙9.30am-midnight, bar to 1am) Dark and rustic, and opening to a terrace in warm weather, this welcoming place rustles up salads, steaks, schnitzel and other pub favourites. Great-value daily specials (not available Sunday) cost €6 to €10.

ℹ Information

Tourist Office (☑ 0621-293 8700; www.visit-mannheim.de; Willy-Brandt-Platz 5; audioguide 3 hrs/1 day €7.50/10; ⊙9am-7pm Mon-Fri, 10am-1pm Sat) Just across the square from the Hauptbahnhof. An audioguide tour of the city is available.

ℹ Getting There & Away

Mannheim is a major rail hub on the Hamburg–Basel line serving Frankfurt (€20.70, 50 minutes, up to four per hour). S-Bahn trains link the Hauptbahnhof with Heidelberg (€5.80, 30 minutes, two per hour).

The bike-share scheme **VRNnextbike** (www.vrnnextbike.de; per 30 min €1; ⊙24hr) has bikes at docking stations around Mannheim.

HOCKENHEIMRING

The hallowed **HockenheimRing** (☑ 06205-950 222; www.hockenheimring.de; Am Motodrom, Hockenheim; Insider Tour adult/child €12/6.50; ☺ Insider Tour 11am except race days) , 22km southwest of Heidelberg just east of the A6, has three circuits and stands accommodating up to 120,000 fans. It hosts some of Germany's most famous car races, including the Formula One German Grand Prix (in even-numbered years).

Motorsports fans can get a look behind the scenes on a 90-minute Insider Tour (in German; English audioguide €2). Tickets are sold at the **Motor Sport Museum** (☑ 06205-950 222; www.hockenheimring.de; Am Motodrom, Hockenheim; adult/child €6/3; ☺ 10am-5pm Apr-Oct, 10am-5pm Sun Nov-Mar, longer hours on race days) – reservations are required between December and March.

If roaring along on a speed-limitless Autobahn doesn't get the adrenaline pumping any more, you can take to the Hockenheim track when it isn't being used for a race. Action Track Days (per person from €249) see you do three laps on the Grand Prix course with a professional driver in a superfast racing car, eg a Porsche GT3, a Mercedes AMG GTS or a Ferrari 458. Race'n'roll (€429) lets you drive a superfast race car yourself (with a professional instructor as your passenger).

Sign up via the app or at a station using your credit card.

Worms

☑ 06241 / POP 82,102

On the Rhine's western bank, the port town of Worms (pronounced 'vorms', rhyming with 'forms') has played a key role at pivotal moments in European history. In AD 413 it became capital of the short-lived Burgundian kingdom whose rise and fall was chronicled in the epic 12th-century poem *Nibelungenlied*.

After the Burgundians, virtually every other tribe in the area had a go at ruling Worms, including the Huns, the Alemans and the Franks. The city flourished in the 9th century under the Frankish leader Charlemagne. The most impressive reminder of the city's medieval heyday is its majestic, late-Romanesque Dom. In 1521, it was in Worms that Martin Luther refused to recant his teachings, paving the way for Protestantism.

A Jewish community, renowned for the erudition of its rabbis, thrived here from the 10th century until the 1930s, earning Worms the moniker 'Little Jerusalem'.

◉ Sights

Kaiserdom CHURCH
(Dom St Peter und St Paul; www.wormser-dom.de; Domplatz; ☺ 9am-5.45pm Apr-Oct, 10am-4.45pm Nov-Mar) Worms' skyline is dominated by the four towers and two domes of the magnificent Kaiserdom, built in the 11th and 12th

centuries in the late-Romanesque style, and consecrated in 1018. Inside, the lofty dimensions impress as much as the lavish, canopied high altar (1742) in the east choir, designed by the baroque master Balthasar Neumann. Details of concerts are listed on the website. It's closed to tourists during Sunday morning mass.

In the cathedral's south transept, a scale model shows the enormity of the original complex. Nearby stairs lead down to the stuffy crypt, which holds the stone sarcophagi of several members of the Salian dynasty of Holy Roman emperors.

Museum der Stadt Worms MUSEUM
(City Museum; ☑ 06241-853 4105; www.worms.de; Weckerlingplatz 7; adult/child €3/1.50, temporary exhibition prices vary; ☺ 10am-5pm Tue-Sun) Exhibits at Worms' city museum bring its fascinating history to life. Highlights include Bronze Age women's jewellery, a superb collection of delicate Roman glass excavated from local graves, and a section on the Middle Ages.

Luther Memorial MEMORIAL
(Lutherplatz) On Lutherplatz, on the northwest edge of the half-oval-shaped Altstadt, the Luther Memorial honours the Protestant reformer, who refused to recant his beliefs here in Worms in 1521. Cast in bronze, the monument depicts Luther standing on a central stone pillar, surrounded by scholars, lords and personifications of key Reformation cities. Designed by Dresden artist Ernst Rietschel, it was completed by his students in 1868 following the artist's death in 1861.

JEWISH HISTORY IN WORMS

Starting in the 900s, Jewish life in Worms – known as Varmaiza in medieval Jewish texts – was centred on the Judengasse, in the northeast corner of the Altstadt. Today, it's where you'll find a medieval synagogue, a 12th-century ritual bath and Worms' Jewish museum.

Before 1933, 1100 Jews lived in the city. A Jewish community was re-established in the late 1990s.

For more information, visit www.worms.de, which has a dedicated Jewish Worms section in English.

Nibelungen Museum   MUSEUM

(☑06241-853 4120; www.nibelungenmuseum.de; Fischerpförtchen 10; adult/child incl audio guide €5.50/3.50; ⊙10am-5pm Tue-Fri, to 6pm Sat & Sun) The *Nibelungenlied* is the ultimate tale of love and hate, treasure and treachery, revenge and death, with a cast including dwarves, dragons and bloodthirsty *Überfrauen* (superwomen). Richard Wagner set the poem to music, Fritz Lang turned it into a silent movie in 1924 and the Nazis abused its mythology, seeing in dragon-slayer Siegfried the quintessential German hero. The Nibelungen Museum's multimedia exhibit seeks to rescue the epic from the Nazi manipulations.

Alter Jüdenfriedhof   CEMETERY

(Willy-Brandt-Ring 21; ⊙8am-8pm Sun-Fri Jun-Sep, to 4pm Oct-May, closed Jewish holidays) Inaugurated in 1076, the Old Jewish Cemetery, also known as the Heiliger Sand ('holy sand'), is one of the oldest Jewish burial grounds in Europe. The most revered gravestone is that of Talmudic commentator Rabbi Meir of Rothenburg (1215–93).

Alte Synagoge   SYNAGOGUE

(Rashi Shul; ☑06241-853 4707; Synagogenplatz, Judengasse; ⊙10am-12.30pm & 1.30-5pm Apr-Oct, 10am-noon & 2-4pm Nov-Mar, closed to visitors Sat morning) Worms' famous Old Synagogue, founded in 1034, was destroyed in the 1938 pogroms, but in 1961 it was reconstructed primarily using stones from the original. Men are asked to cover their heads inside.

In the garden, stone steps lead down to an extraordinary, Romanesque-style *Mikwe* (ritual bath) built in the 1100s; it's closed for renovations until 2019.

Jüdisches Museum   MUSEUM

(Raschi-Haus; ☑06241-853 4701; Hintere Judengasse 6; adult/child €1.50/0.80; ⊙10am-12.30pm & 1.30-5pm Tue-Sun Apr-Oct, to 4.30pm Nov-Mar) Behind Worms' Alte Synagoge, the Jewish Museum introduces the city's storied Jewish community through exhibits such as parchment manuscripts, documents and plans, and a *menorah* (seven-armed candlestick), as well as a model of the synagogue depicting its location around the year 1600. The museum also sells several informative English booklets on Jewish Worms.

🏃 Activities

Radhaus-Mihm   CYCLING

(☑06241-242 08; www.radhaus-worms.de; Von Steuben-Strasse 8; bike hire per day €5; ⊙9.30am-12.30pm & 1.30-6pm Mon-Fri, 10am-1pm Sat Feb-Oct, to 5pm Mon-Fri, 10am-1pm Sat Nov-Jan) Accessed via a tunnel under the tracks from the Hauptbahnhof, Radhaus-Mihm hires bikes and provides advice on cycling routes.

🎊 Festivals & Events

Nibelungen-Festspiele   CULTURAL

(www.nibelungenfestspiele.de; ⊙late Jul–mid-Aug) The saga of the Burgundian kingdom is celebrated at this two-week festival, featuring theatre productions on an open-air stage in front of Worms' Cathedral.

🛏 Sleeping

Accommodation in Worms is limited; Mainz and Heidelberg have more options.

DJH Hostel   HOSTEL €

(☑06241-257 80; www.jugendherberge.de; Dechaneigasse 1; dm/s/d €22.50/28/56; 🅿🛜) In a superb location facing the south side of the Dom, this 126-bed hostel has spick-and-span rooms with private bathrooms. There are four lounge areas, a beer garden and a bistro, as well as free parking out the front. Wi-fi is in public areas only.

Parkhotel Prinz Carl   HOTEL €€

(☑06241-3080; www.parkhotel-prinzcarl.de; Prinz-Carl-Anlage 10-14; s/d/ste from €90/133/153; 🅿🛜) Housed in two barracks built during the reign of the last Kaiser, the Prinz Carl has 90 spacious, comfortable rooms including ones especially designed for business travellers, with good-sized desks. There's a classy restaurant and bar inside the former American military church. It's peacefully situated on the northern edge of town near a chestnut-shaded park.

Kriemhilde
HOTEL €€

(☑ 06241-911 50; www.hotelkriemhilde.de; Hofgasse 2-4; s/d/q from €45/80/105; 🛜) Wake up to the peal of the Dom bells at this family-run inn. It faces the north side of the mighty cathedral, which can be glimpsed from some of the 17 streamlined, sparingly furnished rooms and from the terrace. There's a wine cellar and restaurant serving hearty German cuisine.

✖ Eating

Restaurants cluster around Domplatz and Marktplatz.

Café TE
INTERNATIONAL €

(☑ 06241-304 4852; Bahnhofstrasse 5; mains €5-17.50; ⊙ 4-9pm Mon-Sat, to 8pm Sun, bar to 1am Sun-Thu, to 2am Fri & Sat; 🛜) Just south of the Hauptbahnhof, sociable TE ('Trans Europa') has communal tables within a huge building. It's a student favourite for its different special each night (Monday is burger night, Tuesday is steak night and so on). This restaurant is cash only.

Schnitzelhütt
GERMAN €€

(☑ 06241-594 343; www.schnitzelhuett.de; Rathenaustrasse 31; mains €7-23; ⊙ 11.30am-10pm Mon-Sat, to 9pm Sun; 🛜👶) No fewer than 27 varieties of pork or chicken schnitzel are served at this exposed brick-and-timber city-centre restaurant with barrel tables: Gorgonzola-topped, Dijon mustard-doused, slathered in sherry-cream sauce, Swiss-style with cheese and ham, Hawaiian-style with pineapple, plus a fiery *Teufelsschnitzel* ('devil schnitzel') with corn, kidney beans, pepperoni, olives and fresh chilli. Other dishes include rump steaks, burgers and meal-sized salads.

Mini kids' meals are available.

Trattoria-Pizzeria Pepe e Sale
ITALIAN €€

(☑ 06241-258 36; www.pepe-e-sale.de; Wollstrasse 12; pizzas & pasta €6.50-11, mains €10-22; ⊙ 11am-11.30pm; 🐾) This long-established Italian-run trattoria/pizzeria serves dozens of varieties of pizzas and pastas along with Italian mains such as veal in Marsala or Sambuca-cream sauce. Chunky wooden tables and open wine racks fill the dining room, which opens to a summer pavement terrace.

🍺 Drinking & Nightlife

You'll find cafes and bars around the Hauptbahnhof, Domplatz and Marktplatz.

★ Hagenbräu
MICROBREWERY

(www.hagenbraeu.de; Am Rhein 3; ⊙ 10am-11pm Mon-Fri, from 9am Sat & Sun Mar-Oct, 11.30am-11pm Tue-Sat, 10am-9pm Sun Nov-Feb) Producing four varieties of beer each month (light, dark, wheat beer and a seasonal brew such as potato beer), this half-timbered microbrewery is one of several hugely popular beer gardens along the Rhine, just north of the bridges, with plane-tree-shaded tables stretching down to the water's edge. Filling Rheinhessisch-style fare is served until an hour before closure.

Nearby is a **statue of Hagen** tossing the Nibelung treasure into the Rhine.

Strand Bar 443
BEER GARDEN

(www.strandbar443-worms.de; Am Rhein 9; ⊙ 2-10pm Mon-Fri, from 1pm Sat & Sun Apr-Sep) Tiki huts and sandy beaches lined with sun lounges are the last thing you'd expect to find along the Rhine, but this beach bar sees this stretch of riverbank transformed into a tropical paradise come summer. There's a big barbecue area, DJs most nights and great cocktails (plus soft drinks for the kids). Hours can vary depending on the weather.

ⓘ Information

Tourist Office (☑ 06241-853 7306; www.worms.de; Neumarkt 14; ⊙ 9am-6pm Mon-Fri, 10am-2pm Sat & Sun Apr-Oct, 9am-5pm Mon-Fri Nov-Mar) Can arrange guided city tours and book accommodation; also sells local event tickets.

ⓘ Getting There & Away

Frequent trains serve Worms. Destinations include:

Darmstadt (€17.80, 1½ hours, half-hourly)
Deidesheim (€9.20, one hour, half-hourly)
Frankfurt (€14.60, 1¼ hours, half-hourly)
Mainz (€12.50, 26 minutes, half-hourly)
Mannheim (€5.80, 25 minutes, half-hourly)
Speyer (€10.90, 45 minutes, half-hourly)

ⓘ Getting Around

The bike-share scheme **VRNnextbike** (www.vrnnextbike.de; per 30 min €1; ⊙ 24hr) has bikes at docking stations around Worms. Sign up via the app or at a station using your credit card.

Accessed via a tunnel under the tracks from the Hauptbahnhof, Radhaus-Mihm hires bikes and provides advice on cycling routes.

The tourist office sells cycling maps.

FRANKFURT & SOUTHERN RHINELAND WORMS

WORTH A TRIP

LORSCH ABBEY

Founded around AD 760, **Lorsch Abbey** (Kloster Lorsch; ☎ 06251-514 40; www.kloster-lorsch.de; Nibelungenstrasse 35, Lorsch; adult/child €6/4; ◉ 10am-5pm Tue-Sun, English tours hourly 11am-4pm Tue-Sun Mar-Oct, Sat & Sun Nov-Feb), in the charming village of Lorsch, was an important religious site in its Carolingian heyday (8th to 10th centuries). Preserved medieval buildings include the rare, Carolingian-era Königshalle and the Altenmünster. Museum exhibits cover the history of the abbey, life in Hesse, and tobacco, which was cultivated in Lorsch in the late 17th century.

Lorsch is 30km south of Darmstadt via the A5 or picturesque Bergstrasse (B3); light rail links it with Worms (€4.10, 25 minutes, hourly). The station is 1km north of the abbey.

GERMAN WINE ROUTE

One of Germany's oldest touring routes, the Deutsche Weinstrasse was inaugurated in 1935. It traverses the heart of the Palatinate (Pfalz) – a region of vine-covered hillsides, rambling forests, ruined castles, picturesque hamlets and, of course, exceptional wine estates. It's blessed with a moderate climate that allows almonds, figs, kiwi fruit and even lemons to thrive.

Starting in Schweigen-Rechtenbach, on the French border, the route winds north – through Germany's largest contiguous wine-growing area – for 85km to Bockenheim an der Weinstrasse (not to be confused with the Frankfurt district of Bockenheim), 15km west of Worms. The Pfälzerwald, the hilly forest that runs along the route's western edge, was declared a Unesco Biosphere Reserve in 1993 (along with France's adjacent Vosges du Nord area). Hiking and cycling trails abound.

The Palatinate is a renowned culinary destination, with a strong French influence, thanks to its proximity to France.

🏃 Activities

Tourist offices can supply lists of visitable wineries, or check www.deutsche-weinstrasse.de. For hiking in the Pfälzerwald, visit www.pfaelzerwald.de.

🎊 Festivals & Events

The German Wine Route is especially pretty during the spring bloom (March to mid-May). *Weinfeste* (wine festivals) run from March to mid-November (especially on weekends); check with tourist offices for dates. The grape harvest (September and October) is also a lively time to visit.

ⓘ Getting There & Away

The **Rhein-Haardtbahn** (www.vrn.de) light rail line links Bad Dürkheim with Mannheim (€5.80, 50 minutes, at least hourly). Change at Mannheim for Frankfurt (€21 to €24, 1¾ hours, frequent).

The RNV-Express goes to Heidelberg's Hauptbahnhof and Bismarckplatz (€10.90, 1¼ hours, every 30 minutes). The trip from Speyer requires a change at Schifferstadt (€9.20, one hour, every 30 minutes).

ⓘ Getting Around

The German Wine Route is most easily explored by car. Cycling here is also a pleasure, thanks to a multitude of *Radwanderwege* (bike paths and cycle-friendly back roads; see www.radwanderland.de) such as the Radweg Deutsche Weinstrasse. Tourist offices sell various excellent cycling maps and have details on bike rentals.

Germany's superb transport network also means it's possible to get almost everywhere – including to trail heads – by public transport. Local trains that take bicycles link Deidesheim and Bad Dürkheim (€2.60, six minutes, every 30 minutes) and head south to Neustadt an der Weinstrasse (€4.10, 18 minutes) and beyond. Bikes travel free after 9am.

Neustadt an der Weinstrasse

☎ 06321 / POP 52,999

Vineyards fan out around Neustadt, a busy wine-producing town at the heart of the German Wine Route. A half-timbered Altstadt and historic hilltop castle make it an unmissable stop.

◉ Sights & Activities

Neustadt's largely pedestrianised Altstadt teems with half-timbered houses, especially along Mittelgasse, Hintergasse, Metzgergasse and Kunigundenstrasse. It's anchored by the Marktplatz, a cobbled square flanked by the baroque Rathaus and the Gothic Stiftskirche.

★ **Hambacher Schloss**   CASTLE
(Hambacher Castle; ☎ 06321-926 290; www.hambacher-schloss.de; Schlossstrasse, Wolfsburg;

adult/child €5.50/2.50, incl tour €9/6, audioguide €3; ⊙ castle 10am-6pm Apr-Oct, 11am-5pm Nov-Mar, tours hourly 11am-4pm Apr-Oct, 11am, noon & 2pm Sat & Sun Nov-Mar) Atop a forested Pfälzerwald hill 6km southwest of the centre, this 'cradle of German democracy' is where idealistic locals, Polish refugees and French citizens held massive protests for a free, democratic, united Germany on 27 May 1832, hoisting the black, red and gold German flag for the first time. An exhibition commemorates the event, known as the Hambacher Fest. Audioguides and 45-minute guided tours are available in English. Bus 502 (17 minutes, hourly) runs from the Hauptbahnhof.

Other tours include architecture, children's tours, and tours for the visually impaired. There's a restaurant (p590) at the castle.

Stiftskirche
CHURCH

(📞 06321-841 79; www.evpfalz.de; Marktplatz 2; church tours adult/child €3/1, tower tours €3/1; ⊙ 11am-3pm Mon-Sat, from noon Sun, church tour 4pm Fri, tower tour noon Sat) Built from red sandstone, the 14th- and 15th-century Gothic Stiftskirche has been shared by Protestant and Catholic congregations since 1708. Renovations in 2005 revealed frescos from 1410 that offer a snapshot of life at the time, with bakers, craftspeople and market traders. Guided tours take you into the 51m-high tower, reached by 184 steps. Many tours are in English – phone ahead to confirm your spot.

Weingut Kriegshaeuser
WINE

(📞 06321-836 09; www.kriegshaeuser-wein.de; Kreuzstrasse 4, Diedesfeld; ⊙ 10am-6pm Mon-Fri, to 5pm Sat, to noon Sun Apr-Oct, shorter hours Nov-Mar) A beautiful half-timbered building houses this *Weingut*, which offers tastings of its Riesling, pinot blanc, spät, cabernet dorsa and sparkling wines from its vineyards dating from 1594. It's just off the Weinstrasse (L512) 5km south of the centre.

🛌 Sleeping

Places to sleep are limited in Neustadt itself, but there are appealing options in the surrounding countryside.

Gästehaus-Weingut Helbighof
GUESTHOUSE €€

(📞 06321-327 81; www.helbighof.de; Andergasse 40; d from €85; 🅿 🛜) Beneath the Hambacher Schloss amid sprawling vineyards, this charming family-run win ery has just five

WORTH A TRIP

BURG TRIFELS

Thought to be of Celtic origins, this enormous red-sandstone **hilltop castle** (📞 06346-8470; www.burgen-rlp. de; K2, Annweiler am Trifels; adult/child €3/2; ⊙ 10am-6pm mid-Mar–Oct, to 5pm Sat & Sun Feb–mid-Mar & Nov) was first documented in 1081. Between 1125 and 1298 it was the repository of imperial treasures including, allegedly, a nail from Jesus' cross and a tooth from John the Baptist. Richard the Lionheart (Richard I of England) was imprisoned here from 1193 to 1194 for insulting Leopold V, Duke of Austria. Today, the castle's displays include a replica of the imperial crown jewels.

Recent excavations have uncovered the remains of a wooden castle believed to date from Saxon times. One-hour guided tours (adult/child €10/7) in English take place at 3pm on Saturdays from May to October.

guest rooms, so book well ahead. The pick is room 3, with balconies on two sides. Its superb wines are sold at an honour bar; a sun terrace overlooks the vines. Turn right after Andergasse 36, then immediately left to reach the driveway. Cash only.

🍴 Eating

Look for restaurants around Marktplatz, and along Hauptstrasse and Hintergasse.

Bruno's
BURGERS €

(📞 06321-355 4426; www.brunos-lieblings-gerichte.de; Zwerchgasse 17; burgers €7-12.50; ⊙ noon-3pm Tue, noon-3pm & 5.30-9pm Wed-Fri, 2-9pm Sat; 🛜) Picnic tables made from reclaimed timbers cover the pavement outside this photogenic half-timbered building. In the muralled interior, Bruno's sizzles up inventive burgers such as Red Hot Chilli Pepper, with bacon and fiery jalapeño peppers, and veggie favourite Three Cheese High, with halloumi, goats cheese and cheddar smothered in mango and lemongrass chutney.

Herve's Crêperie
CRÊPES €

(📞 06321-398 651; www.hervescreperie.de; Hauptstrasse 121; savoury galettes €4.50-6.80, sweet crêpes €2.70-7; ⊙ 11.30am-9pm Wed-Fri, to 4pm Sat) In a contemporary, airy space in the town centre, this authentic Breton-run crêperie serves savoury buckwheat-flour galettes like *forestière* (with mushrooms and cream sauce) and *tricolore* (rustique, St-Agur blue and raclette cheese with cranberry jam), and sweet crêpes such as caramelised apples with calvados and salted caramel, accompanied by bowls of traditional cider.

Restaurant 1832   GERMAN **€€**
(☑ 06321-959 7880; www.hambacherschloss.de; Hambacher Schloss, Schlossstrasse, Wolfsburg; mains €16-23; ◷ 10am-6pm Apr-Oct, from 11am Nov-Mar) Inside the Hambacher Schloss, opening to a courtyard, Restaurant 1832 serves dishes such as *Saumagen* (stuffed pig's stomach) with Riesling bread, roasted duck breast with glazed chestnuts, and goat's cheese gratin with lavender honey. Its trio of ice creams – dark chocolate, banana and raspberry – reflect the black, yellow and red German flag first raised at the castle in 1832.

★ **Urgestein**   GERMAN **€€€**
(☑ 06321-489 060; www.restaurant-urgestein.de; Rathausstrasse 6; 5-/6-course menus €100/120, with paired wines €140/160; ◷ 6-10pm Tue-Sat) For a gastronomic extravaganza, book a table at Benjamin Peifer's Michelin-starred, vaulted brick cellar restaurant within a half-timbered house in the town centre. Over 300 wines complement exquisite

dishes like pickled trout with sauerkraut and horseradish, followed by steamed liver dumplings with Riesling foam, hay-roasted pigeon with foie gras mousse, and nougat ganache with hazelnut yoghurt.

Live jazz plays in the summer courtyard. Upstairs, are six spacious guest rooms (doubles from €100).

❶ Information

Tourist Office (☑ 06321-926 892; www.neustadt.eu; Hetzelplatz 1; ◷ 9.30am-6pm Mon & Wed-Fri, to 2pm Tue & Sat Apr-Oct, 9.30am-5pm Mon & Wed-Fri, to 2pm Tue Nov-Mar) Diagonally across Bahnhofplatz from the Hauptbahnhof, with information on local sights, hiking, cycling and wine festivals.

❶ Getting There & Away

Light rail links Neustadt an der Weinstrasse with Deidesheim (€2.50, 10 minutes, every 30 minutes) and Bad Dürkheim (€4.10, 20 minutes, every 30 minutes).

Deidesheim

☑ 06326 / POP 3779
Draped with pale purple-flowering wisteria in the springtime, diminutive Deidesheim is one of the German Wine Route's most picturesque – and upmarket – villages. Perfect for a romantic getaway, it offers plenty of opportunities for wine tasting, relaxed strolling and sublime dining.

GERMAN WINE ROUTE GATES

Deutsches Weintor (German Wine Gate; Weinstrasse, Schweigen-Rechtenbach) There's no missing the start of the German Wine Route, which is marked by this towering stone gate, the 1936-built Deutsches Weintor. Inside is one of Germany's largest wine cooperatives. The adjacent **Vinothek** (☑ 06342-224; www.weintor.de; Weinstrasse 4, Schweigen-Rechtenbach; wine tasting per glass €2-5; ◷ 10am-6pm Mar-Dec, from 1pm Mon-Thu, from 10am Fri Jan & Feb) doubles as a tourist information office.

Haus der Deutschen Weinstrasse (House of the German Wine Route; www.haus-der-deutschen-weinstrasse.net; Weinstrasse 91b, Bockenheim an der Weinstrasse) Spanning the road at the northern edge of the village of Bockenheim an der Weinstrasse, in Roman *castrum* style, is the modern, brick-and-tile Haus der Deutschen Weinstrasse, built in 1995 as a counterpart to the Deutsches Weintor at the route's starting point. There's a restaurant inside, but you'll find better dining options elsewhere.

Bockenheimer Weinstube (☑ 06359-409 0050; www.bockenheimerweinstube.de; Weinstrasse 91, Bockenheim an der Weinstrasse; mains €8.50-23; ◷ 5-10pm Wed-Sat, from 11.30am Sun Apr-Oct, shorter hours Nov-Mar) You can just drop by to try local wines by the glass, but top-notch local specialities at this rustic *Weinstube* include *Saumagen* (pig's stomach) stuffed with whole chestnuts, *Bratwurst* with sauerkraut, and *Flammkuchen* (regional pizza). When the sun is shining, the sweetest seats are in the vine-draped, flower-filled summer courtyard.

Deidesheim is a 'Cittaslow' town, an extension of the Slow Food movement that aims to rebalance modern life's hectic pace not only through 'ecogastronomy' but also local arts, crafts, nature, cultural traditions and heritage.

◉ Sights

Museum für Weinkultur   MUSEUM
(Museum of Wine Culture; 📞 06326-981 561; www.weinkultur-deidesheim.de; Marktplatz 9; ⏰ 3-6pm Wed-Fri, 2-5pm Sat Apr-Dec) FREE A Marktplatz landmark with a canopied outdoor staircase, the Altes Rathaus (old town hall) dates from the 16th century. Inside is the three-storey Museum of Wine Culture, featuring displays on winemakers' traditional lifestyle and naive-art portrayals of the German Wine Route. An English brochure is available. Look out for wine tastings.

Deutsches Film-und
Fototechnik Museum   MUSEUM
(German Film & Photography Museum; 📞 06326-6568; www.dftm.de; Weinstrasse 33; adult/child €4/2.50; ⏰ 10am-4pm Thu, 2-6pm Fri & Sat, 11am-6pm Sun) Down an alleyway across from the Rathaus, this museum has an impressive collection of historic photographic and movie-making equipment, with over 5000 exhibits in all. Check out the vintage film-dispensing vending machine by the entrance. Film screenings (in German) occasionally take place here; the schedule is posted on the website.

Geissbockbrunnen   FOUNTAIN
(Goat Fountain; Bahnhofstrasse) Near the tourist office, this whimsical fountain celebrates a quirky local tradition. For seven centuries, the nearby town of Lambrecht has had to pay an annual tribute of one goat for using pastureland belonging to Deidesheim. The presentation of this goat, which is auctioned off to raise funds for local cultural activities, culminates in the Geissbockversteigerug.

Pfarrkirche St Ulrich   CHURCH
(www.pfarrei-deidesheim.de; Marktplatz; ⏰ 8am-5pm) Right on the Marktplatz, this late Gothic, three-nave columned church with beautiful stained-glass windows was built between 1440 to 1480, and is the only remaining large mid-15th-century church in the Palatinate.

🏃 Activities

Deidesheim is home to over a dozen winemakers (some closed Sunday) that welcome visitors – look for signs reading *Weingut* (winery), *Verkauf* (sale) and *Weinprobe* (wine tasting) and ring the bell. Many are located along the small streets west of Pfarrkirche St Ulrich.

The tourist office has maps for several signposted walking routes and cycling routes through vineyards and the Pfälzerwald.

🎉 Festivals & Events

Weihnachtsmarkt   CHRISTMAS MARKET
(Bahnhofstrasse; ⏰ 5-9pm Fri, from 2pm Sat, from 11am Sun late Nov-late Dec) Deidesheim is famed for its picturesque Christmas market, the region's largest, with over 100 stalls selling quality decorations, toys and gifts, along with sweets, ready-to-eat dishes and warming mugs of mulled wine. It's held on the four weekends before Christmas.

Geissbockversteigerug   CULTURAL
(Goat Festival; ⏰ Tue after Pentecost) In medieval times, the nearby village of Lambrecht paid Deidesheim one goat as rent for pasture rights in Deidesheim's forest, a tradition that has evolved into this lively 'goat festival'. Each year, a goat is paraded around town before being auctioned; there are also wine tastings and special menus at restaurants.

🍽️ Sleeping & Eating

Some of the loveliest accommodation along the German Wine Route is located in Deidesheim, with prices to match; Bad Dürkheim, 6.5km to the north, has cheaper options.

Deidesheim is a culinary hotspot, with a couple of Michelin-starred restaurants. The town's speciality, *Saumagen* (stuffed pig's stomach), appears on menus everywhere.

Hotel Ritter von Böhl   HOTEL €€
(📞 06326-972 201; www.ritter-von-boehl.de; Weinstrasse 35-39; s/d/ste from €60/98/112; ⏰ reception 8am-6pm; P 🛜) Set around a wisteria-wrapped courtyard, this hotel occupies a former charity hospital founded in 1494. It has 44 rose, pale yellow and white-toned rooms and a bright breakfast atrium where you can start the day with pastries and breads from the on-site bakery.

★ Deidesheimer Hof   BOUTIQUE HOTEL €€€
(📞 06326-968 70; www.deidesheimerhof.de; Am Marktplatz; s/d/ste from €127/167/257; P ❄ 🛜) In a story-book gabled building dating from the 16th century, the renowned Deidesheimer

Hof hotel has 28 individually decorated, ultra-spacious rooms (the smallest are 25 sq metres), and two fine restaurants: regional specialist St Urban (mains €17.50-31.50; ⊙noon-2pm & 6-9pm), and, in the vaulted basement, the Michelin-starred Schwarzer Hahn (mains €33-59, 4-/5-/6-/7-course menus €118/125/145/159, with paired wines €165/185/210/229; ⊙6-10pm Tue-Sat). Breakfast costs €21.

Ketschauer Hof BOUTIQUE HOTEL €€€
(☑06326-700 00; www.ketschauer-hof.com; Ketschauerhofstrasse 1; s/d/ste from €195/230/350; ❋🛜) Start your stay with a glass of Riesling at this one-time winemaker's mansion, which has been turned into a romantic 17-room hotel that blends traditional luxury with contemporary styling. Also here are two gourmet restaurants, the Michelin-starred LA Jordan (4-/5-/7-course menus €85/125/155; ⊙6.30-9.30pm Tue-Sat) and French Bistro 1718 (mains €14.50-28; ⊙noon-2.30pm & 6-10pm Tue-Sun), along with an in-house spa and sauna. Reserve well ahead for weekend stays.

Turmstüb'l GERMAN €€
(☑06326-981 081; www.turmstuebel.de; Turmstrasse 3; mains €10-17; ⊙6pm-midnight Tue-Sat, noon-11pm Sun) Tucked down an alley opposite the church, this artsy wine bar serves seasonal dishes like white asparagus with poached eggs and parsley, and regional specialities such as *Zwiebelkuchen* (bacon and onion cake) as well as over a dozen wines by the glass.

Drinking & Nightlife

Weincafe Kostbar COFFEE
(www.weincafe-kostbar.de; Weinstrasse 58; ⊙9.30am-6pm Mon, Tue & Fri-Sun, to 2pm Wed; 🛜) Run by Deidesheim local Markus Badura, whose intricate coffee etchings have seen him crowned the German latte art champion, this laid-back cafe has artworks created with coffee on the walls (all for sale), and cushions covered in hessian coffee sacks. Ten preparation methods are available; you can also book three-hour latte art courses (from €99) in English or German.

Shopping

Wine shopping aside, galleries and artisans' studios (such as jewellery makers and potters) can be visited along the Kunst und Kultur (Art and Culture) Circuit; look for dark-blue-on-yellow 'K' signs.

Weingut Geheimer Rat Dr von Bassermann-Jordan WINE
(☑06325-6006; www.bassermann-jordan.de; Kirchgasse 10; ⊙8am-6pm Mon-Fri, 10am-3pm Sat & Sun) One of Deidesheim's oldest and most prestigious wineries, dating back nearly three centuries, produces exceptional Riesling and sauvignon blanc in particular, and organises guided vineyard walks, vaulted cellar tours and culinary events – check the website for schedules.

Gold Schmiede Krack JEWELLERY
(www.krackschmuck.de; Marktplatz 6; ⊙10am-12.30pm & 3-7pm Tue-Fri, 10am-5pm Sat) This goldsmith has been family-run for five generations. It handcrafts beautiful rings, earrings, bracelets, brooches, necklaces and cufflinks on site.

❶ Information

Tourist Office (☑06326-967 70; www.deidesheim.de; Bahnhofstrasse 5; ⊙9am-12.30pm & 1.30-5pm Mon-Thu, to 6pm Fri, 9am-12.30pm Sat Apr-Oct, 9am-noon & 2-5pm Mon-Fri Nov-Mar) Situated 150m across the car park from the Bahnhof.

❶ Getting There & Away

Light rail connects Deidesheim with Bad Dürkheim (€2.60, 10 minutes, every 30 minutes) and Neustadt an der Weinstrasse (€2.60, 10 minutes, every 30 minutes).

Bad Dürkheim

☑06322 / POP 18,499

Adorned with splashy fountains, the attractive spa town of Bad Dürkheim is famous for its salty thermal springs and lovely parks. It hosts what's claimed to be the world's largest wine festival, and is also home to the world's largest wine barrel, the Dürkheimer Fass – with a diameter of 13.5m and volume of 1,700,000L – which contains a restaurant.

◎ Sights & Activities

Glorious walking options include Weinwanderwege (vineyard trails) from St Michaels kapelle, a chapel atop a little vine-clad hill northeast of the tourist office, to Honigsäckel and the Hochmess vineyards (a 6km circuit), and forest trails to two historic ruins, Limburg and Hardenburg (4km west of town). The tourist office has maps.

The 130km-long Kaiser-Konrad-Radweg bike path to Speyer starts here.

Kurpark PARK

(Mannheimer Strasse) Between the Hauptbahnhof and the tourist office lies the grassy Kurpark, an azalea- and wisteria-filled public garden where you'll find the tiny Isenach River, with landscaped banks and a children's playground.

Salinarium SWIMMING

(06322-935 865; www.salinarium.de; Kurbrunnenstrasse 28; per day pools adult/child €6.80/3.90, saunas €14.40/11; pools 9am-5.45pm Mon, to 10pm Tue-Thu, to 11pm Fri, to 9pm Sat & Sun, saunas noon-10pm Mon, 10am-10pm Tue-Thu, to 11pm Fri, to 9pm Sat & Sun) Water babies of all ages will love the city-run Salinarium, a complex of outdoor (April to September) and indoor swimming pools. There's a 100m-long spiral water slide, whirlpools, a children's pool and seven saunas. Lockers require a €1 deposit.

From 2018 to 2020, the complex is undergoing an expansion but will remain open throughout.

Festivals & Events

Dürkheimer Wurstmarkt WINE

(www.duerkheimer-wurstmarkt.de; Sep) The Dürkheimer Wurstmarkt ('sausage market', named for the area where it's held, which once hosted the town's eponymous Wurst market) bills itself as the world's largest wine festival, with amusement rides, food tents, live music and fireworks. Much of the action takes place around the enormous Dürkheimer Riesenfass wine barrel. It's held on the second and third weekends in September.

Sleeping

Bad Dürkheim makes an ideal overnight stop, with a good selection of reasonably priced hotels.

Landhaus Fluch HOTEL €€

(06322-2488; www.landhaus-fluch.de; Seebacher Strasse 95; s/d from €80/89;) In the leafy neighbourhood of Seebach, 1.3km southwest of the centre, this welcoming family-run hotel has forest trails leading into the Pfälzerwald on its doorstep. Its 25 comfortable rooms open to balconies or ground-floor terraces. Fuel up for a hike at breakfast with a buffet-style spread of local cheeses, meats and more.

Kurparkhotel CASINO HOTEL €€

(06322-7970; www.kurpark-hotel.de; Schlossplatz 1-4; s/d from €122/162;) Occupying a yellow, neoclassical building on the edge of the Kurpark, this landmark hotel has 113 unexpectedly contemporary, spacious rooms, all with minibars and most with balconies overlooking the Kurpark's manicured gardens. Rates include spa use and casino entry, and drop for stays of longer than one night.

Hotel Weingarten PENSION €€

(06322-940 10; www.hotelweingarten.de; Triftweg 11a-13; s/d from €86/122; reception 3-6pm;) Next door to a winery owned by the same family, the aptly named 'wine garden' has 18 lovingly cared-for rooms, some with balconies, and two saunas. Breakfast includes homemade jam and local produce. Call ahead if you'll be arriving outside reception hours. On weekends there's a minimum two-night stay. It's 1km northeast of the train station along Manheimer Strasse.

Marktschänke HOTEL €€

(06322-952 60; www.marktschaenke-bad duerkheim.de; Marktgasse 1; s/d/studio from €70/98/130;) Centrally situated some 250m southwest of the train station off the Obermarkt, this cosy spot has seven streamlined rooms (six doubles, plus a studio suite with two balconies). Its restaurant serves Palatinate-meets-Mediterranean cuisine and has a local following.

Eating & Drinking

Restaurants with warm-season terraces can be found on Römerplatz and along nearby Kurgartenstrasse. Many of the surrounding hiking trails lead to small restaurants hidden in the forest; details of openings and maps are available from the tourist office.

Weinrefugium GERMAN €€

(06322-921 20; https://restaurant-weinrefugium.jimdosite.com; Schlachthausstrasse 1a; mains €15.70-25, 3-/4-course menu €37/42, with paired wines €52/62; 6-10pm Mon-Sat) Situated inside a charming mustard-coloured, charcoal-trimmed building, Weinrefugium serves exquisitely presented dishes incorporating locally grown flowers, herbs and vegetables. Smoked catfish with dill and Riesling sauce and *Blutwurst Saumagen* (pig's stomach stuffed with blood sausage) are highlights; set menus with matching local wines are fantastic value. Its summer courtyard is draped with grape vines and ivy.

Restaurant Dürkheimer Fass   GERMAN €€
(✍ 06322-2143; www.duerkheimer-fass.de; St Michaels-Allee 1; mains €14.50-26; ⊙11am-11pm Thu-Tue Apr-Oct, shorter hours Nov-Mar; 🚗) This convivial spot occupies the landmark Dürkheimer Riesenfass, the world's largest wine barrel, which has had a restaurant inside since a master cooper built it out of 200 pine trees in 1934. Dishes range from *Leberk Nödel* (liver dumplings) to *Jäger-schnitzel* (schnitzel with forest mushroom sauce) and *Zander* (perch fillet) with *Grüne Sosse* (green sauce). There's a summer beer garden.

Petersilie Bier & Weinstube   WINE BAR
(✍ 06322-4394; www.weinstube-petersilie.de; Römerplatz 12; ⊙11.30am-10pm) On the town's liveliest square, Petersilie is a great spot to try local wines (including organic wines) by the glass, or to knock back a frothy beer. Umbrella-shaded tables spill onto the square in warm weather. Bar snacks include gold-medal-winning *Pfälzer Saumagen* (chestnut-stuffed pig's stomach pâté), *Flammkuchen* (regional-style pizza) and potato soup.

ℹ Information

Tourist Office (✍ 06322-935 140; www.bad-duerkheim.com; Kurbrunnenstrasse 14; ⊙9am-6pm Mon-Fri, 9.30am-3pm Sat & Sun Feb-Dec, 9am-6pm Mon-Fri Jan) Has a useful walking-tour map in English.

ℹ Getting There & Away

Bad Dürkheim is linked by light rail to Deidesheim (€2.60, 10 minutes, every 30 minutes), Mannheim (€5.80, 50 minutes, at least hourly) and Neustadt an der Weinstrasse (€4.10, 18 minutes, every 30 minutes).

ROMANTIC RHINE VALLEY

Between Rüdesheim and Koblenz, the Rhine cuts deeply through the Rhenish slate mountains, meandering between hillside castles and steep fields of wine-producing grapes. This is Germany's landscape at its most dramatic – forested hillsides alternate with craggy cliffs and near-vertical terraced vineyards. Idyllic villages appear around each bend, their half-timbered houses and Gothic church steeples seemingly plucked from the world of fairy tales.

Medieval castles perch high above the river. Most were built by a mafia of local robber barons – knights, princes and even bishops – who extorted tolls from merchant ships by blocking their passage with iron chains. Time and French troops under Louis XIV laid waste to many of the castles, but several were restored in the 19th century, when Prussian kings, German poets and British painters discovered the area's beauty. In 2002, Unesco designated these 65 km of riverscape, known as the Oberes Mittelrheintal, as a World Heritage Site.

🏃 Activities

Cycling

The **Rhein-Radweg** (www.rheinradweg.eu) stretches for 1233km from Andermatt in Switzerland to the Hoek van Holland, near Rotterdam. Between Bingen and Koblenz it runs along both banks. It links up with two other long-distance bike paths: the 127km-long **Nahe-Hunsrück-Mosel-Radweg** (www.naheradweg.de), which follows the Nahe River from Bingen southwest to Selbach, and the 311km-long **Mosel-Radweg** (www.maare-moselradweg.de), which runs along the banks of the Moselle River from Koblenz to Traben-Trarbach, Bernkastel-Kues and Trier, and on to Metz in France.

Bicycles can be taken on regional trains, car ferries and river ferries, making it possible to ride one way (such as down the valley) and take public transport the other.

Hiking

The Rhine Valley is superb territory for hikers. Almost every village has hiking options – tourist offices can supply suggestions and maps. A one-way hike can be turned into a circuit by combining walking with ferries, trains and buses.

There are two challenging but beautiful long-distance hiking trails that run along the Romantic Rhine, with variants continuing downriver to Bonn and upriver to Mainz and beyond, including the 199km **RheinBurgenWeg** (www.rheinburgenweg.com), linking Rolandseck, near Bonn, with Bingen, passing some 40 castles; and the 320km **Rheinsteig** (www.rheinsteig.de), linking Wiesbaden with Bonn – the prettiest section of this tough, hilly trail is between Rüdesheim and Loreley.

🛏 Sleeping & Eating

A popular summer and early autumn tourist destination, the area all but shuts down in winter. Hotel prices are highest on weekends from May to mid-October.

Booking ahead is a good idea during the busy summer months. In winter, many places reduce their hours or close altogether.

🔾 Getting There & Away

Mainz and Koblenz are the main access points; both are served by frequent train services to Frankfurt and other major German cities.

🔾 Getting Around

BOAT

River travel is a relaxing and very romantic way to see the castles, vineyards and villages of the Romantic Rhine.

From about Easter to October (winter services are very limited), passenger ships run by **Köln-Düsseldorfer** (KD; ☑ 0221-208 8318; www.k-d.com) link Rhine villages on a set timetable.

You can travel to the next village or all the way from Rüdesheim to Koblenz (one-way/return €42.30/49.20, downstream 5½ hours, upstream eight hours)

Within the segment you've paid for (for example, Boppard–Rüdesheim), you can get on and off as many times as you like, but make sure to ask for a free stopover ticket each time you disembark.

Return tickets usually cost only slightly more than one-way. Children under four travel for free; children under 13 pay a flat €6 regardless of distance. To bring along a bicycle, there's a supplement of €2.80.

Many rail passes (such as Eurail) get you a free ride or discount on normal KD services, although you still need to register at the ticket counter.

Several smaller companies also send passenger boats up and down the river:

Bingen-Rüdesheimer (www.bingen-ruedesheimer.de)

Hebel Linie (www.hebel-linie.de)

Loreley Linie (www.loreley-linie.com)

Rössler Linie (http://roesslerlinie.de)

Ferry Crossings

No bridges span the Rhine between Koblenz and Mainz; the only way for drivers to cross the river along this stretch is by *Autofähre* (car ferry).

Services generally operate every 15 or 20 minutes during the day and every 30 minutes early in the morning and late at night.

Car ferry crossings:

Bingen–Rüdesheim (www.bingen-ruedesheim.de; car & driver €4.50, passenger €1.30, bicycle & rider €2.50, pedestrian €2; ⊙5.30am-9.50pm Sun-Thu, to 12.50am Fri & Sat May-Oct, 5.30am-9.50pm Nov-Apr)

Boppard–Filsen (www.faehre-boppard.de; car & driver €4.50, passenger €1.30, bicycle & rider €2.50, pedestrian €2; ⊙6.30am-10pm Jun-Aug, to 9pm Apr, May & Sep, to 8pm Oct-Mar)

Niederheimbach–Lorch (www.mittelrhein-faehre.de; car & driver €4.50, passenger €1.30, bicycle & rider €2.50, pedestrian €2; ⊙6am-10.50pm Apr-Oct, to 6.50pm Nov-Mar)

Oberwesel–Kaub (www.faehre-kaub.de; car & driver €4.50, passenger €1.30, bicycle & rider €2.50, pedestrian €2; ⊙6am-8pm Mon-Sat, 8am-8pm Sun Apr-Sep, 6am-7pm Mon-Sat, 8am-7pm Sun Oct-Mar)

St Goar–St Goarshausen (www.faehre-loreley.de; car & driver €4.50, passenger €1.30, bicycle & rider €2.50, pedestrian €2; ⊙5.30am-10.30pm Mon-Fri, from 6.20am Sat, from 7.20am Sun May-Sep, shorter hours Oct-Apr)

Passenger-only ferry crossings:

Bingen-Rüdesheim Passenger Ferry (www.bingen-ruedesheimer.de; adult/child €2.50/1.25, bicycle €1.20; ⊙10am-5.30pm Mon-Fri, 8.45am-6.55pm Sat & Sun late Mar-early Nov)

Fährboot (www.faehre-kaub.de; Kaub; adult/child €3/1.50; ⊙10am-6pm Tue-Sun Apr-Oct, to 5pm Mar, to 5pm Sat & Sun Nov, Jan & Feb) Serves **Pfalzgrafstein** (p600)

BUS & TRAIN

Bus and train travel is a convenient way to village-hop, get to a trail head, or return to your lodgings at the end of a hike or bike ride.

Villages on the Rhine's left bank (eg Bingen, Bacharach, Oberwesel and Boppard) are served regularly by local trains on the Koblenz–Mainz service.

Right-bank villages such as Rüdesheim, Assmannshausen, Kaub, St Goarshausen and Braubach are linked hourly to Koblenz' Hauptbahnhof and Wiesbaden by the RheingauLinie.

It takes about 1½ hours to travel by train from Koblenz, along either riverbank, to Mainz or Wiesbaden.

Rüdesheim Region

☑ 06722 / POP 9892

Some three million day-tripping coach tourists descend on Rüdesheim each year. The town centre – and especially its most famous feature, a medieval alley known as Drosselgasse – is kitschy and colourful, but there's also wonderful walking in the greater area, which is part of the Rheingau wine region, famed for its superior Rieslings.

◉ Sights

Kloster Eberbach　　　　　　　MONASTERY
(☑ 06723-917 8150; www.kloster-eberbach.de; Eltville; monastery adult/child incl audioguide €9/5, guided tour & Vinothek wine tastings €29.50-46.50;

FRANKFURT & SOUTHERN RHINELAND RÜDESHEIM REGION

Romantic Rhine Valley

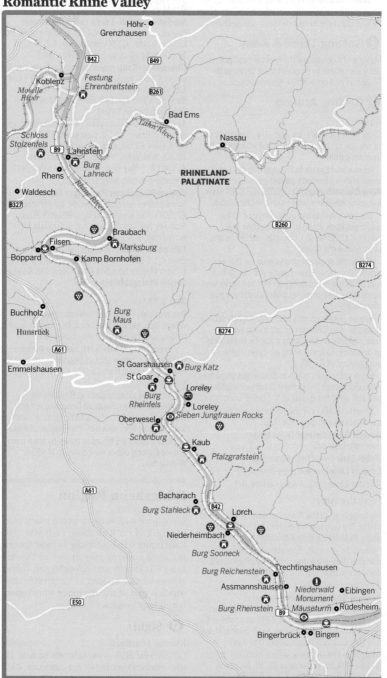

Höhr-Grenzhausen

B42

B49

Koblenz

B261

Festung Ehrenbreitstein

Moselle River

Bad Ems

Lahn River

Nassau

Schloss Stolzenfels

B9 Lahnstein

RHINELAND-PALATINATE

Rhens

Burg Lahneck

Rhine River

Waldesch

B327

B260

B274

Braubach

Marksburg

Filsen

Boppard

Kamp Bornhofen

Buchholz

Hunsrück

Burg Maus

B274

A61

Emmelshausen

St Goarshausen *Burg Katz*

St Goar

Loreley

Burg Rheinfels

Loreley

Oberwesel

Sieben Jungfrauen Rocks

Schönburg

Kaub

Pfalzgrafstein

A61

Bacharach

B42 Lorch

Burg Stahleck

Niederheimbach

Burg Sooneck

Trechtingshausen

Burg Reichenstein

Assmannshausen

Niederwald Monument

Eibingen

E50

Mäuseturm

Rüdesheim

Burg Rheinstein

B9

Bingerbrück

Bingen

⊙ monastery 10am-7pm Mon-Fri, from 9am Sat & Sun Apr-Oct, 11am-6pm Nov-Mar, Vinothek 10am-7pm Apr-Oct, to 6pm Nov-Mar) Dating from the 12th century, this one-time Cistercian monastery, in an idyllic little valley 15km northeast of Rüdesheim, went through periods as a hospital, jail, sheep pen and accommodation for WWII refugees. Today you can explore the 13th- and 14th-century **Kreuzgang** (cloister), the monks' baroque **refectory** and their vaulted Gothic **Mönchsdormitorium** (dormitory), as well as the austere Romanesque **Klosterkirche** (basilica).

At the **Vinothek** you can taste and buy the superb wines produced by the government-owned Hessische Staatsweingüter (Hessian State Winery).

Guided English-language tours of the monastery including tastings at the Vinothek last 1½ to two hours; higher-priced tours include a classical music performance.

Weinmuseum MUSEUM
(Wine Museum; ☑ 06722-2348; www.rheingauer-weinmuseum.de; Rheinstrasse 2; adult/child incl audioguide €5/3; ⊙ 10am-6pm Mar-Oct) The 1000-year-old Brömserburg castle near the Bingen car-ferry dock now houses this museum, filled with winemaking and wine-drinking paraphernalia from Roman times onwards. A six-glass tasting flight costs €14. Great river views extend from the tower.

Siegfried's Mechanisches Musikkabinett MUSEUM
(☑ 06722-492 17; www.smmk.de; Oberstrasse 29; tour adult/child €7.50/4; ⊙ 10am-4pm Mar-Dec) Situated 50m to the left from the top of Drosselgasse, this fun museum has a collection of 350 18th- and 19th-century mechanical musical instruments that play themselves as you're shown around on the compulsory 45-minute tour.

✿ Festivals & Events

Weihnachtsmarkt CHRISTMAS MARKET
(⊙ 23 Nov-23 Dec) Rüdesheim is famous for its *Weihnachtsmarkt* (Christmas market), with 120 stalls crowding Drosselgasse and Oberstrasse.

🛏 Sleeping

★ **Rüdesheimer Schloss** BOUTIQUE HOTEL €€
(☑ 06722-905 00; www.ruedesheimer-schloss.com; Steingasse 10; s/d/ste from €99/139/169; 🅿 🛜) Truly good places to sleep and eat are thin on the ground in central Rüdesheim,

but this 18th-century building has 26 stunning contemporary rooms designed by local and regional artists. Its restaurant is excellent, serving dishes like cheese and Riesling soup, veal liver with truffled mash, and roast duck stuffed with dates and figs, with a live pianist and after-dinner dancing.

Hotel Jagdschloss
Niederwald HISTORIC HOTEL **€€**
(☑ 06722-710 60; www.niederwald.de; Jagdschloss Niederwald 1; s/d/ste from €86/126/193; P 🛜 ☲) Up in the hills amid sprawling forest 4.7km west of Rüdesheim, this former hunting lodge dates from 1764, though its 52 understated rooms and suites have modern decor. Amenities include an indoor swimming pool and a sauna, and a restaurant serving dishes such as wild boar stew with forest mushrooms.

✖ Eating & Drinking

Restaurants line Drosselgasse and Oberstrasse.

Weingut Georg Breuer WINERY
(☑ 06722-472 25; www.georg-breuer.com; Grabenstrasse 8; ⊙ 10am-6pm) All-organic wines produced by this 1880-established winery are mostly Rieslings but there are also some pinot noir, pinot gris, orléans and heunisch varieties, with labels created by local artists. Tastings (three glasses for €9.50) take place in the vaulted cellar; pre-book for one-hour vineyard hikes (€15).

ℹ Information

Tourist Office (☑ 06722-906 150; www.ruedesheim.de; Rheinstrasse 29a; ⊙ 9am-6pm Mon-Fri, 10am-4pm Sat & Sun Apr-Sep, shorter hours Oct-Mar) At the eastern edge of the town centre.

ℹ Getting There & Away

Rüdesheim is connected to Bingen by passenger (p595) and car (p595) ferries.

Trains travel to Wiesbaden (€6.30, 45 minutes, hourly) and Koblenz (€15.10, 80 minutes, hourly).

Bingen

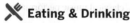 06721 / POP 24,987

Thanks to its strategic location at the confluence of the Nahe and Rhine Rivers, Bingen has been coveted by warriors and merchants since its founding by the Romans in 11 BC. These days it's a busy working town that's less touristy – and less cute – than its smaller neighbours.

⊙ Sights

Museum am Strom MUSEUM
(www.bingen.de; Museumsstrasse 3; adult/child €3/2; ⊙ 10am-5pm Tue-Sun) On Bingen's riverside promenade, this one-time power station now displays exhibits on Rhine romanticism, both engraved and painted. Other highlights include a set of surgical instruments – from scalpels and cupping glasses to saws – left behind by a Roman doctor in the 2nd century AD.

Mäuseturm CASTLE
(⊙ closed to the public) The Mouse Tower, on an island near the confluence of the Nahe and Rhine, is where – according to legend – Hatto II, the 10th-century archbishop of Mainz, was devoured alive by mice as punishment for his oppressive rule. In fact, the name is probably a mutation of *Mautturm* (toll tower), which reflects the building's medieval function.

ℹ Information

Tourist Office (☑ 06721-184 205; www.bingen.de; Rheinkai 21; ⊙ 9am-6pm Mon-Fri, to 5pm Sat, 10am-1pm Sun May-Oct, shorter hours Nov-Apr) Can advise on river cruises and vineyards in the area.

ℹ Getting There & Away

Bingen has two train stations: the Hauptbahnhof, just west of the Nahe in Bingerbrück; and the more central Bahnhof Bingen Stadt, just east of the town centre. Trains from both stations serve Mainz (€10.50, 25 minutes, up to four per hour) and Koblenz (€14.60, 50 minutes, two per hour). Change in Mainz for Wiesbaden.

Passenger ferries (p595) to Rüdesheim leave from the town centre's riverfront promenade; car ferries (p595) dock 1km upriver (east) from the centre.

Burg Rheinstein

In the 1820s, privately owned Rheinstein, 6km downriver from Bingen, became the first **Rhine castle** (☑ 06721-6348; www.burg-rheinstein.de; B9, Trechingshausen; adult/child €5.50/3.50; ⊙ 10am-5.30pm Mon, 9.30am-6pm Tue-Sun mid-Mar–Oct, noon-4pm Sat & Sun Nov) to be converted – by Prussian royalty (a branch of the Hohenzollerns) – into a romantic summer residence complete with turrets and battlements. Today, the neo-Gothic interior is furnished more or less as it was over a century ago. Highlights include a tiny chapel, the Rittersaal (Knights' hall), and 14th- to

VINEYARD WALKS

For a stunning Rhine panorama, head up the wine slopes west of Rüdesheim to the **Niederwald Monument**. Erected between 1877 and 1883, this bombastic monument celebrates the Prussian victory in the Franco-Prussian War and the creation of the German Reich, both in 1871. You can walk up via the Rüdesheimer Berg vineyards – signposted trails include one that begins at the P2 car park (one block above Oberstrasse) – but to save climbing 203 vertical metres, it's faster to glide above the vineyards aboard the 1400m-long **Seilbahn** (Kabinenbahn; www.seilbahn-ruedesheim.de; Oberstrasse 37; adult/child one-way €5.50/3, return €8/4, with Sesselbahn €9/4.50; ☺ 9.30am-7pm Jul & Aug, to 6pm Mon-Fri, to 7pm Sat & Sun Jun & Sep, shorter hours mid-Mar–May & Oct-Dec) cable car.

From the monument, a network of trails leads to destinations such as the **Jagdschloss** (2km), a one-time hunting lodge that's now a **hotel** and restaurant; and, down the hill, the romantic ruin of **Burg Ehrenfels** (Ruine Ehrenfels).

North of the Jagdschloss, you can follow part of the Rheinsteig long-distance path down to **Assmannshausen**, a village 7km downriver from Rüdesheim that's known for its *Spätburgunder* (pinot noir). Or you can head down to Assmannshausen on the **Sesselbahn** (Sessellift; www.seilbahn-assmannshausen.de; Niederwaldstrasse 34; adult/child one-way €5/2.50, return €7/3.50, with Seilbahn €8/4; ☺ 10am-5.30pm Mon-Fri, to 6pm Sat & Sun May-Sep, 10am-5pm Mon-Fri, to 5.30pm Sat & Sun Mar, Apr & Oct) and return to Rüdesheim on foot (via hillside vineyards and Burg Ehrenfels), by train or by passenger ferry (p595).

A round-trip **Ring-Ticket** (adult/child €18/9) includes the Seilbahn, the Sesselbahn and the ferry.

19th-century stained-glass windows brought from churches in Cologne and Düsseldorf.

A path leads from parking places along the B9. Also here are two apartments for rent (per night from €65; minimum stay two nights), and a tavern.

Burg Reichenstein

Looming above the village of Trechtingshausen, 8km downriver from Bingen, mighty **Burg Reichenstein** (☑06721-6117; www.burg-reichenstein.com; Burgweg 24, Trechtingshausen; adult/child €5.50/3.50; ☺10am-6pm Tue-Sun) harbours a lavish collection of furnishings, armour, hunting trophies (including one of Germany's largest collection of antlers) and cast-iron oven slabs. To get a taster of what living here would be like, book into one of its 21 individually designed rooms (single/double/suite from €99/119/159). Its fine-dining restaurant has seasonal regional menus and monumental views.

Bacharach

☑06743 / POP 1880

One of the prettiest of the Rhine villages, tiny Bacharach – 24km downriver from Bingen – conceals its considerable charms be-

hind a 14th-century wall. From the B9, pass through one of the thick arched gateways under the train tracks to reach its medieval old town filled with half-timbered buildings.

◉ Sights

The best way to get a sense of the village and its hillside surrounds is to take a stroll on top of the walls – it's possible to walk almost all the way around the centre.

Wernerkapelle　　　　　　　　RUINS
(www.bacharach.de) Built from red sandstone between 1289 and 1430 in the shape of a clover leaf, the Gothic Wernerkapelle was partially destroyed in 1689 during the Palatine War of Succession. By 1787, the chapel's roof, vaults and cellar walls had been removed, but it underwent several partial restorations between 1847 and 1996. Still roofless, the ruins are especially photogenic when illuminated at night. Take the pathway from the south side of Peterskirche.

Postenturm　　　　　　　　　　TOWER
(www.bacharach.de; Blücherstrasse; ☺24hr)
FREE Once part of the city's 14th-century fortifications and now surrounded by vineyards, this tower on the upper section of the wall affords panoramic views from the top, reached by scaling 58 steps.

Peterskirche　　　　　　　　　CHURCH
(Blücherstrasse 1; ☺10am-6pm Mar-Sep, to 4pm Nov-Feb) This late-Romanesque-style Protestant church, completed in 1269, has some columns with vivid capitals – look for the naked woman with snakes sucking her breasts (a warning about the consequences of adultery), at the altar end of the left aisle.

🛏 Sleeping

★ DJH Burg Stahleck　　　　　HOSTEL €
(☑06743-1266; www.jugendherberge.de; Burg Stahleck, Stahleckstrasse; dm/s/d from €22.50/34.50/69; Ⓟ@) In a dream setting inside a hillside 12th-century medieval castle, Burg Stahleck, this hostel has 170 beds in rooms for one to four people, almost all with private bathrooms. There's pinball and ping-pong but – due to the thick castle walls – patchy wi-fi. To get here, walk along the town walls or drive up Blücherstrasse for 1km.

Rhein Hotel　　　　　　　　HOTEL €€
(☑06743-1243; www.rhein-hotel-bacharach.de; Langstrasse 50; s/d/ste from €90/110/160; Ⓟ❄🛜) Right on the town's medieval ramparts in a half-timbered building, this family-run hotel has 14 well-lit rooms with original artworks that are named for the vineyards they overlook. Rooms facing the river, and therefore the train tracks, have double-glazing. Guests can borrow bikes for free. Its Stübers Restaurant is top-notch.

🍴 Eating & Drinking

Restaurants concentrate along Oberstrasse. Oberstrasse and Blücherstrasse have wine taverns.

Stübers Restaurant　　　　　GERMAN €€
(☑06743-1243; www.rhein-hotel-bacharach.de; Langstrasse 50; mains €14-24; ☺5.30-9pm Mon-Sat, noon-2pm & 5.30-9pm Sun early Mar-early Dec; 🖐) At the Rhein Hotel, slow food-focused Stübers specialises in regional dishes such as *Rieslingbraten* (Riesling-marinated braised beef) and *Steeger Hinkelsdreck* (chicken-liver pâté with red wine, toasted almonds and grape jelly), with small versions of German favourites for kids. Although the terrace overlooks the Rhine, it's metres from the railway line, so dining inside is a more peaceful experience.

★ Zum Grünen Baum　　　　　WINE BAR
(www.weingut-bastian-bacharach.de; Oberstrasse 63; ☺noon-10pm Apr-Oct, shorter hours Nov-Mar) Dating from 1421, this olde-worlde tavern serves some of Bacharach's best whites; the

Weinkarussel (€22.50) lets you sample 15 of them. Its nearby Weingut, by contrast, is state of the art. Owner Friedrich Bastian is a renowned opera singer, so music (and culinary) events take place year-round, including on Bastian's private river island with its own vineyard.

🛍 Shopping

Weingut Fritz Bastian　　　　　WINE
(☑06743-937 8530; www.weingut-bastian-bacharach.de; Koblenzer Strasse 1; ☺11am-6pm Fri-Sun Apr-Oct, shorter hours Nov-Mar) On the corner of Rosenstrasse in the town centre, the stark icy-white walls, exposed slate and wooden beams at Friedrich Bastian's Weingut provide a stunning backdrop for his wines (tastings available), and a contemporary counterpoint for his cosy nearby tavern, Zum Grünen Baum.

ℹ Information

Tourist Office (☑06743-919 303; www.rhein-nahe-touristik.de; Oberstrasse 10; ☺9am-5pm Mon-Fri, 10am-3pm Sat & Sun Apr-Oct, 9am-1pm Mon-Fri Nov-Mar) Has information about the area, including details of day hikes through the vineyards.

ℹ Getting There & Away

Trains link Bacharach with Koblenz (€11.60, 35 minutes, up to two per hour) and Mainz (€13.70, 40 minutes, up to two per hour).

Pfalzgrafstein

Across the river from the village of Kaub, the boat-shaped toll castle **Pfalzgrafstein** (☑06774-745; www.burg-pfalzgrafenstein.de; adult/child €4/2.50, audioguide €1; ☺10am-6pm Tue-Sun mid-Mar–Oct, to 5pm Feb–mid-Mar & Nov), built in 1326, perches on an island in the middle of the Rhine. A once-dangerous rapid here (since modified) forced boats to use the right-hand side of the river, where a chain forced ships to stop and pay a toll. Pick up an audioguide to learn more about its lengthy history. It's reached by the Fährboot (p595) passenger ferry, next to Kaub's car ferry dock.

Oberwesel

☑06744 / POP 2834
Oberwesel is known for its 3km-long medieval town wall, sporting the remains of 16 guard towers, that wraps around much of the picturesque Altstadt; a path lets you walk along the top of most of it. The old

town is separated from the river by the rail line, laid in 1857.

◉ Sights

St-Martins-Kirche
CHURCH

(www.pfarreiengemeinschaft-oberwesel.de; Martinsberg; ⊙10am-6pm) Easily spotted on a hillside at the northern end of town is the enormous early 14th-century St-Martins-Kirche, popularly known as the 'white church'. It has painted ceilings, a richly sculpted main altar and a tower that once formed part of the town's defences.

Liebfrauenkirche
CHURCH

(www.pfarreiengemeinschaft-oberwesel.de; Kirchstrasse; ⊙10am-noon & 2-5pm Apr-Oct, 2-4pm Nov-Mar) In the southern Altstadt, the High Gothic Liebfrauenkirche, known as the 'red church' for the colour of its facade, dates from the early 14th century and has an impressive gilded altar.

Oberwesel Kulturhaus
MUSEUM

(☑06744-714 726; www.kulturhaus-oberwesel.de; Rathausstrasse 23; adult/child €3/1; ⊙10am-5pm Tue-Fri, from 2pm Sat & Sun Apr-Oct, 10am-2pm Tue-Fri Nov-Mar) Every April, Oberwesel crowns not a *Weinkönigin* (wine queen), as in most Rhine towns, but a *Weinhexe* (wine witch) – a good witch who is said to protect the vineyards. Photos of all the *Weinhexen* crowned since 1946 are on display in the cellar of Oberwesel's Kulturhaus, whose local history exhibits feature ice age skeletons of mammoths, aurochs (extinct wild cattle) and prehistoric horses found in the area, along with 19th-century engravings of the Romantic Rhine and models of Rhine riverboats.

⊨ Sleeping

DJH Hostel
HOSTEL €

(☑06744-933 30; www.jugendherberge.de; Am dem Schönburg; dm/s/d from €23.50/35.50/58; [P][⊛][⊚]) Commanding views stretch from the terrace and some of the rooms of this modern, 269-bed hostel perched near the Schönburg, a steep 800m walk south from the town centre. Amenities include an indoor swimming pool, panoramic terrace, barbecue, campfire area, table tennis, billiards and pinball.

Hotel Römerkrug
HOTEL €€

(☑06744-949 0772; www.roemerkrug-oberwesel.de; Marktplatz 1; d from €72; [⊚]) Facing the Rathaus in the prettiest part of town, the half-timbered Römerkrug is run by three generations of a friendly local family. Its five

individually decorated rooms have antique furnishings; some have features such as chandeliers and ancient roof beams. Lock-up bike storage is available. French/German cuisine is served at its on-site restaurant.

Schönburg
CASTLE €€€

(☑06744-939 30; www.hotel-schoenburg.com; Auf Schönburg; s/d/ste from €140/250/350; [P][⊚]) Sumptuous Schönburg's 25 palatial rooms are richly furnished with antiques and chandeliers; some have four-poster beds and open fireplaces. Parking is 250m below the castle, but you and your luggage can travel to the property by electric cart. The gastronomic restaurant is also open to non-guests by reservation.

✗ Eating & Drinking

Restaurants surround the Rathaus. You'll find wine taverns and bars around the Rathaus and tucked up in the hillsides.

★ Günderode Haus
GERMAN €

(☑06744-714 011; www.guenderodefilmhaus.de; Siebenjungfrauenblick; dishes €4-11; ⊙11am-7pm Tue-Sat, 10am-6pm Sun Apr-Oct, shorter hours Nov-Mar) Hidden sky-high up a steep vineyard-striped hillside, Günderode Haus' flagstone terrace with sweeping views over the Rhine is an incredible spot for traditional dishes like wild boar sausages with rosemary potatoes, or a glass of wine or beer. From Oberwesel, take the K93 east for 600m, turn right (north) onto the K95; after 1km, the car park is on your right.

Historische Weinwirtschaft
WINE BAR

(www.ci-it.de/weinwirtschaft; Liebfrauenstrasse 17; ⊙4-10pm Mon & Thu-Sat, from noon Sun) A half-timbered, slate-walled house with exposed timber ceiling beams and creaky timber floors is a fantastically atmospheric setting for sampling local wines. In summer, picnic tables shaded by magnolias fill the ivy-clad courtyard.

❶ Information

Tourist Office (☑06744-710 624; www.oberwesel.de; Rathausstrasse 3; ⊙9am-1pm & 2-5pm Mon-Thu, to 6pm Fri, to 1pm Sat Jun-Oct, Mon-Fri Apr & May, shorter hours Nov-Mar)

❶ Getting There & Away

Trains run to/from Koblenz (€14.80, 30 minutes, two per hour) and Mainz (€12.50, 55 minutes, two per hour).

Loreley & St Goar Region

📞 06771 / POP 4457

The most fabled spot along the Romantic Rhine, Loreley is an enormous, almost vertical slab of slate that owes its fame to a mythical maiden whose siren songs are said to have lured sailors to their death in the river's treacherous currents. Heinrich Heine told the tale in his 1824 poem *Die Lorelei*.

The nearby village of St Goarshausen, 2.5km north, is lorded over by the sprawling ruins of Burg Rheinfels, once the mightiest fortress on the Rhine. It's linked by car ferry with its twin across the river, St Goar.

◎ Sights

Loreley Besucherzentrum　　　　MUSEUM
(📞 06771-599 093; www.loreley-besucherzentrum. de; Loreleyring 7; adult/child €2.50/1.50; ☺ 10am-5pm Mar-Oct) On the edge of the plateau above the Loreley outcrop, 4km southeast of St Goarshausen, this visitors centre covers the Loreley myth and local flora, fauna, shipping and winemaking traditions through an English-signed multimedia exhibit and German-language 3D film. Major works underway here include new walking trails, an improved viewing platform 190m above the river and a hotel; all are due for completion by late 2019.

From April to October, bus 535 runs from St Goarshausen's Marktplatz. Alternatively, the 400-step Treppenweg begins at the base of the breakwater.

Burg Rheinfels　　　　　　　　FORTRESS
(📞 06741-7753; www.st-goar.de; Schlossberg 47; adult/child €5/2.50, guided mine tour €7/free; ☺ 9am-6pm Apr-Oct, to 5pm Mar & Nov, guided mine tours by reservation) Once the mightiest fortress on the Rhine, Burg Rheinfels was built in 1245 by Count Dieter V of Katzenelnbogen as a base for his toll-collecting operations. Its size and labyrinthine layout are astonishing. Kids (and adults) will love exploring the subterranean tunnels and galleries, accessed by lantern-lit guided English-language tunnel tours; check the website for schedules. Entry fees are cash only. To reach the sprawling ruins, it's a 550m uphill walk; allow 20 minutes. The complex also incorporates a hotel.

Lorelei Sculpture　　　　　　SCULPTURE
At the tip of a narrow breakwater jutting into the Rhine, a bronze sculpture of Loreley's famous maiden perches lasciviously atop a rocky platform. Access to the breakwater car park is 2.5km south of St Goarshausen. From the car park, you can walk the 600m out to the sculpture, from where there are fantastic views of both riverbanks, but be aware that the rough path is made from jagged slate, and the gentler sandy lower path is often underwater.

Burg Maus　　　　　　　　　CASTLE
(Burg Peterseck; ☺ closed to the public) Two rival castles stand either side of the village of St Goarshausen. Burg Peterseck was built by the archbishop of Trier to counter the toll practices of the powerful Katzenelnbogen family. The latter responded by building a much bigger castle high on the other side of town, Burg Neukatzenelnbogen (dubbed Burg Katz, meaning 'Cat Castle'). Highlighting the obvious imbalance of power between the Katzenelnbogens and the archbishop, Burg Peterseck was soon nicknamed Burg Maus ('Mouse Castle').

🛌 Sleeping & Eating

Romantik Hotel Schloss Rheinfels　　HISTORIC HOTEL €€
(📞 06741-8020; www.schloss-rheinfels.de; Schlossberg 47; s/d/ste from €110/140/270; 🅿 🛜 🏊) Part of the Burg Rheinfels (p602) castle complex is occupied by a romantic hotel with 64 rooms and suites that range in size from tiny to palatial. All have antique-style furnishings; pricier rooms come with a river view. The hotel has three restaurants: one rustic, one semi-formal and one gourmet. Cots and babysitting services can be arranged. Breakfast costs €18.

Weinhotel Landsknecht　　　　GERMAN €€
(📞 06741-2011; www.hotel-landsknecht.de; Aussiedlung Landsknecht 4; mains €15.50-29.50, 4-course dinner menu €44; ☺ noon-2.30pm & 6-9pm Mar–mid-Dec; 🛜) The dining room and terrace at this wonderful spot 1.5km north of St Goar feel like being aboard a cruise boat, with close-up, uninterrupted river views. Delicious home cooking spans pickled salmon with quince mousse, to schnitzel with mushroom and Riesling sauce, and red-wine-marinated plums with rosemary and vanilla ice cream. Many of its rooms (single/double/family from €70/90/140) also have Rhine views.

❶ Getting There & Around

Koblenz is linked by train with St Goar (€8.30, 25 minutes, hourly) and St Goarshausen (€8.10,

30 minutes hourly). Wiesbaden has trains to/from St Goarshausen (€14.40, one hour, hourly). Mainz has trains to/from St Goar (€14.60, one hour, hourly).

The top of the Loreley outcrop can be reached in the following ways:

Car It's a 4km uphill drive from St Goarshausen.

Shuttle bus One-way from St Goarshausen's Marktplatz costs €2.65; there are up to two buses per hour from 10am to 7pm March to October.

Walk The Treppenweg, a strenuous, 400-step stairway, begins 2.5km upriver from St Goarshausen at the base of the breakwater.

Boppard

06742 / POP 15,404

Scenically located on a horseshoe bend in the river, Boppard (pronounced bo-*part*) is one of the Romantic Rhine's prettiest towns, not least because its riverfront and historic centre aren't split by the rail line but are both on the same side of the tracks. Many of its charming half-timbered buildings house snug wine taverns serving Riesling from grapes grown nearby, in some of the Rhine's steepest vineyards.

⊙ Sights

Severuskirche   CHURCH
(Kronengasse; ⊗ 8am-6pm Apr-Oct, to 5pm Nov-Mar) The impressive late Romanesque 13th-century Severuskirche is built on the site of Roman military baths. Inside are polychrome wall paintings, a hanging cross from 1225 in the choir, and spiderweb-like vaulted ceilings.

Marktplatz   SQUARE
Just off Boppard's main commercial street, the pedestrianised, east–west oriented Oberstrasse, is the ancient Marktplatz, today a favourite local hang-out.

Rheinallee   WATERFRONT
Lined with boat docks, hotels, cafes, restaurants and wine taverns, Boppard's beautiful pedestrian promenade runs along the riverfront. There are grassy areas for picnicking and a children's playground upriver from the car-ferry dock.

Römer-Kastell   ARCHAEOLOGICAL SITE
(Roman Fort, Römerpark; cnr Angertstrasse & Kirchgasse; ⊗ 24hr) FREE A block south of the Marktplatz, the Roman Fort has 55m of original 4th-century Roman wall, and graves from the Frankish era (7th century). A wall panel shows what the Roman town of Bodobrica looked like 1700 years ago.

🛏 Sleeping

Hotels line the Rheinallee, Boppard's riverfront promenade.

★ **Jakobsberg**   RESORT €€
(🖉 06742-8080; www.jakobsberg.de; Im Tal der Loreley; s/d/ste from €101/121/199; 🅿 🛜 🌊) Stupendous views extend over the Rhine from this resort 13km north of Boppard via the small town of Spay. Its 101 rooms, spanning 20 sq metres to a whopping 65 sq metres, have stylish light-wood furnishings; some open to balconies or terraces. There's an 18-hole golf course, spa, beer garden, two restaurants and wines from its own vineyards.

Hotel Bellevue   HOTEL €€
(🖉 06742-1020; www.bellevue-boppard.de; Rheinallee 41; s/d/tr/ste from €85/115/130/187; 🅿 🛜 🌊) Built in 1910, this beautiful *Jugendstil* hotel has a charming original lift with a bench seat and 93 rooms, many with balconies overlooking the Rhine. The relaxing indoor swimming pool, along with a steam bath, sauna and gym, are all free for guests. Its gourmet restaurant, Le Chopin, serves elevated German cuisine. Breakfast will cost you €22.

Hotel Günther   HOTEL €€
(🖉 06742-890 90; www.hotelguenther.de; Rheinallee 40; s/d incl breakfast from €65/80; ⊗ Jan-Nov; @ 🛜) Watch boats and barges glide along the mighty Rhine from this bright, welcoming waterfront hotel: of its 19 plain but perfectly comfortable rooms, 15 have river-facing balconies. It hires bikes to guests and has lock-up storage if you're bringing your own wheels.

🍴 Eating & Drinking

Chocobar   CAFE €
(Kronengasse 20; dishes €4-11.50; ⊗ 10am-6pm Apr-Oct, shorter hours Nov-Mar) Facing the Marktplatz, with a large outdoor terrace spilling onto the square, this is a terrific bet for breakfast, including a 'chocolate breakfast' of a croissant, chocolate spread, three chocolate truffles, and hot chocolate (traditional, orange, chilli or caramel). It also serves panini, *Flammkuchen* (Alsatian pizza) and cakes, and sells handmade imported chocolates.

DON'T MISS

HILLSIDE HIKES

Outdoor enthusiasts can tackle some superb hillside hiking trails that fan out from Boppard; the tourist office has maps.

Vierseenblick & Gedeonseck The peculiar geography of the Four-Lakes-View panoramic outlook creates the illusion that you're looking at four separate lakes, rather than a single river. The nearby Gedeonseck affords views of the Rhine's hairpin curve. To get up here you can either hike for 1.4km or – to save 240 vertical metres – take the 20-minute Sesselbahn (Chairlift; ☑ 06742-2510; http://sesselbahn-boppard.de; Mühltal 12; adult/child one-way €5.50/3, return €8.50/4.50; ☺ 10am-6pm mid-Apr–Sep, shorter hours Oct & Nov) chairlift over the vines from the upriver edge of town.

Klettersteig This 2½- to three-hour cliffside adventure hike (a 6.2km round-trip) begins at the upriver edge of town right next to the Sesselbahn. Decent walking or climbing shoes are a must; optional climbing equipment can be rented at the Aral petrol station (☑ 06742-2447; Koblenzer Strasse 237; climbing equipment hire per day €5, plus €20 deposit; ☺ 6am-9pm Mon-Fri, 8am-9pm Sat & Sun). Some vertical sections involve ladders; less vertiginous alternatives are available – except at the Kletterwand, a hairy section with steel stakes underfoot. It's possible to walk back to town via the Vierseenblick.

Hunsrück Trails Germany's steepest scheduled railway route, the Hunsrückbahn (www.hunsrueckbahn.de; Hauptbahnhof; adult/child one-way €2.90/1.75, bicycle free; ☺ hourly 10am-6pm Apr-Oct, to 4pm Nov-Mar), travels through five rail tunnels and across two viaducts on its 8km journey from Boppard's Bahnhof to Buchholz (a section continues for 7km from Buchholz to Emmelshausen, though there's little to see here). From Buchholz, many people hike back via the Mörderbachtal to Boppard, but Buchholz is also the starting point for an excellent 17km hike via the romantic Ehrbachklamm (Ehrbach gorge) to Brodenbach (on the Moselle), from where you can take a bus to Koblenz, with connections to Boppard.

Severus Stube GERMAN €€
(☑ 06742-3218; www.facebook.com/Severusstube; Untere Marktstrasse 7; mains €10.50-21.50; ☺ 5.30-10.30pm Mon, Tue & Thu, to 11pm Fri, 11.30am-2.30pm & 5.30-11pm Sat & Sun Apr-Oct, shorter hours Nov-Mar) Smoked trout roasted in herb butter, pheasant with roast potatoes and bacon, braised beef in horseradish sauce, and warm apple strudel with vanilla custard are among the dishes served at high-backed wooden booths in Severus Stube's cosy, timber-panelled dining room, and on the cobbled laneway in summer. Reservations are recommended.

Weinhaus Heilig Grab WINE BAR
(www.heiliggrab.de; Zelkesgasse 12; ☺ 3pm-midnight Wed-Mon) Across the street from the Hauptbahnhof, Boppard's oldest wine tavern, dating back over 200 years, offers a cosy setting for sipping 'Holy Sepulchre' Rieslings. In summer you can sit outside under the chestnut trees, where live music plays on weekends. It also has five guest rooms (doubles €73 to €89).

Weingut Felsenkeller WINE BAR
(www.felsenkeller-boppard.de; Mühltal 21; ☺ 3-11pm Mon, Wed, Thu & Sun, to midnight Fri & Sat Apr-Oct, shorter hours Nov-Mar) Across the street from the Sesselbahn (p604) station, next to a little stream, this homey place serves its own and other local growers' wines along with hearty German fare like schnitzels.

ⓘ Information

Tourist Office (☑ 06742-3888; www.boppard-tourismus.de; Marktplatz; ☺ 9am-6.30pm Mon-Fri, 10am-2pm Sat May-Sep, 9am-5pm Mon-Fri Oct-Apr)

ⓘ Getting There & Away

Trains link Boppard with Koblenz (€13.60, 15 minutes, two per hour) and Mainz (€16.40, 1¼ hours, two per hour).

Braubach

High above Braubach are the dramatic towers, turrets and crenellations of the 700-year-old Marksburg (☑ 02627-206; www.marksburg.

de; Braubach; adult/child €7/5; ⊙10am-5pm mid-Mar–Oct, 11am-4pm Nov–mid-Mar), which is unique among the Rhine fortresses as it was never destroyed. The compulsory tour takes in the citadel, the Gothic hall and the large kitchen, plus a grisly torture chamber, with its hair-raising assortment of pain-inflicting nasties. English tours take place at 3pm and 4pm from mid-March to October.

Koblenz

☑ 0261 / POP 112,586

At the confluence of the Rhine and Moselle Rivers and the convergence of three low mountain ranges – the Hunsrück, the Eifel and the Westerwald – the Romans founded a military stronghold they named Confluentes for the site's supreme strategic value. Modern-day Koblenz is a park- and flower-filled city that serves as both the northern gateway to the Romantic Rhine Valley and the northeastern gateway to the Moselle Valley, making it an ideal starting point for exploring the region.

◉ Sights

Koblenz' Altstadt, most of it rebuilt after WWII, surrounds the northern end of Löhrstrasse, the city's main pedestrian-only shopping street. Its intersection with Altengraben is known as Vier Türme (Four Towers) because each of the 17th-century corner buildings sports an ornately carved and painted oriel.

★ Festung Ehrenbreitstein   FORTRESS

(☑0261-6675 4000; www.tor-zum-welterbe.de; adult/child €7/3.50, incl cable car €13.80/6.20, audioguide €2; ⊙10am-6pm Apr-Oct, to 5pm Nov-Mar) On the right bank of the Rhine, 118m above the river, this fortress proved indestructible to all but Napoleonic troops, who levelled it in 1801. To prove a point, the Prussians rebuilt it as one of Europe's mightiest fortifications. There are fabulous views from its ramparts and viewing platform. Inside are several museums, including an excellent regional museum, photography museum and archaeological museum, as well as restaurants, bars and cafes. It's accessible by car, on foot or by cable car (☑0261-2016 5850; www.seilbahn-koblenz.de; Rheinstrasse 6; adult/child return €9.90/4.40, incl Festung Ehrenbreitstein €13.80/6.20; ⊙9.30am-7pm Jul-Sep, to 6pm Easter-Jun & Oct, 10am-5pm Nov-Easter).

Mittelrhein-Museum   MUSEUM

(www.mittelrhein-museum.de; Zentralplatz 1; adult/child €12/free; ⊙10am-6pm Tue-Sun) Spread over 1700 sq metres of the striking glass Forum Confluentes building, Koblenz' Mittelrhein-Museum's displays span 2000 years of the region's history, including artworks, coins, ceramics, porcelain, furniture, miniature art, textiles, militaria and more. Don't miss the collection of 19th-century landscape paintings of the Romantic Rhine by German and British artists.

Deutsches Eck   SQUARE

At the point of confluence of the Moselle and the Rhine, the 'German Corner' is dominated by a soaring statue of Kaiser Wilhelm I on horseback, in the bombastic style of the late 19th century. After the original was destroyed in WWII, the stone pedestal remained empty – as a testament to lost German unity – until, post-reunification, a copy was re-erected in 1993. Flowery parks stretch southwest, linking up with a grassy riverfront promenade running southward along the Rhine.

Basilika St Kastor   BASILICA

(www.sankt-kastor-koblenz.de; Kastorhof 4; ⊙9am-6pm) Adjoining a lovely formal garden is Koblenz' oldest church, Basilika St Kastor. Established in the 9th century, it was rebuilt in the 12th century. In 1991, Pope John Paul II raised its status to a minor basilica. The entrance is on the west side.

Liebfrauenkirche   CHURCH

(www.liebfrauen-koblenz.de; An der Liebfrauenkirche 16; ⊙8am-6pm Mon-Sat, from 8.30am Sun) In the Altstadt, the arched walkway at Am Plan square's northeastern corner leads to the Catholic Liebfrauenkirche, built in a harmonious hotchpotch of styles. Of Romanesque origin, it has a Gothic choir (check out the stained glass), painted vaulting above the central nave, and baroque onion-domed turrets. It was destroyed in 1944 and rebuilt in 1955.

Ludwig Museum   MUSEUM

(www.ludwigmuseum.org; Danziger Freiheit 1; adult/child €6/free; ⊙10.30am-5pm Tue-Sat, 11am-6pm Sun) Once the property of the Order of the Teutonic Knights, the Deutschherrenhaus is now home to the Ludwig Museum, which showcases post-1945 and contemporary art, including works by Picasso, Frank Stella, Jasper Johns, Grimanesa Amorós, Jean Dubuffet and Christian Boltanski.

Schloss Stolzenfels   CASTLE
(www.schloss-stolzenfels.de; Schlossweg; adult/
child €5/3; ⊘ 10am-6pm mid-Mar–Oct, to 5pm
Feb–mid-Mar & Nov) A vision of crenellated
towers, ornate gables and medieval-style
fortifications, Schloss Stolzenfels rises above
the Rhine's left bank 5km south of the city
centre. In 1823, the future Prussian king
Friedrich Wilhelm IV had the castle – ruined by the French – rebuilt as his summer
residence; guests included Queen Victoria.
Today, the rooms remain largely as the king
left them, with paintings, weapons, armour
and furnishings from the mid-19th century.
Take bus 650 from the Hauptbahnhof.

Historiensäule   SCULPTURE
(History Column; Josef-Görres-Platz) The Historiensäule portrays 2000 years of Koblenz
history in 10 scenes perched one atop the
other – the WWII period, for instance, is
represented by a flaming ruin. There's an
English-language panel to provide context.

☞ Tours

Romantic Old Town Walking Tour   WALKING
(☑ 0261-194 33; www.koblenz-touristik.de; adult/
child €7/3.50; ⊘ English tours 3pm Sat Apr-Oct)
Departing from the tourist office, this two-
hour tour takes you through the Altstadt,
stopping at sights such as the Basilika St
Kastor and Liebfrauenkirche, as well as
Deutsches Eck. Tours in German run more
frequently.

KD Cruises   BOATING
(☑ 0261-310 30; www.k-d.com; Konrad-Adenauer-
Ufer; ⊘ Easter-Oct) KD operates popular
cruises from Koblenz along the Rhine to
Rüdesheim (one-way/return €42.20/49.20).
It also runs trips southwest along the Moselle
to Cochem (one-way/return €38.20/44.20).

🛏 Sleeping

DJH Hostel   HOSTEL
(☑ 0261-972 870; www.jugendherberge.de; Festung
Ehrenbreitstein; dm/s/d from €23.50/35.50/62;
@ 🕏) Within the thick walls of the immense
Festung Ehrenbreitstein (p605) fortress,
Koblenz' DJH hostel has 157 beds in one-,
two- and four-bed en-suite rooms. Wi-fi is
available in public areas. Guests ride the cable car (p605) to reach it for free.

Hotel Stein   BOUTIQUE HOTEL €€
(☑ 0261-963 530; www.hotel-stein.de; Mayener
Strasse 126; s/d from €85/110; 🅿 🕏) Decorated
in zesty colours such as tangerine contrasted

with dark timbers, Stein's 30 contemporary
rooms are all soundproofed for a peaceful
night's sleep. The hotel is situated across
the Moselle River 2km north of Koblenz' city
centre. Michelin-starred restaurant Schiller's is on the ground floor.

Hotel Morjan   HOTEL €€
(☑ 0261-304 290; www.hotel-morjan.de; Konrad
Adenauer Ufer; s/d/tr/f from €75/95/135/150;
🅿 @ 🕏) In an unbeatable location facing the
Rhine about 300m south of the Deutsches
Eck, this late-20th-century hotel has 42
bright minibar-equipped rooms, half with
river views and some with balconies. Parking is (very) limited but free.

Hotel Jan van Werth   HOTEL €€
(☑ 0261-365 00; www.hoteljanvanwerth.de; Von-
Werth-Strasse 9; s/d from €56/92, without bathroom
from €47/69; 🕏) This long-time budget favourite, with a lobby that feels like someone's
living room, offers exceptional value. No surprise, then, that its 17 cute, colourful rooms
are often booked out; definitely reserve
ahead. It's 600m north of the Hauptbahnhof.

🍴 Eating

Koblenz has some excellent places to dine,
including Michelin-starred establishments.
Restaurants congregate in the Altstadt, especially along the streets south of Florinsmarkt, and by the Rhine.

Winninger Weinstube   GERMAN €
(☑ 0261-387 07; www.winninger-weinstube.de;
Rheinzollstrasse 2; mains €7-14.50; ⊘ 4pm-midnight
Tue-Thu, from noon Fri-Sun May-Sep, 4-11pm Tue-
Sun Oct-Apr; 🕏) A cavernous stone building
that once housed a museum is now a restaurant and wine bar serving local specialities such as *Koblenzer Saumagen* (stuffed
pig's stomach), Riesling-marinated pork
knuckle, liver and potato dumplings and
Flammkuchen with both sweet and savoury
topping options. Wines come from its own
vineyard in Winningen just upstream along
the Moselle.

Look out for its Eiswein ('ice wine'), made
from grapes harvested after the first frost.

Einstein   CAFE €€
(☑ 0261-914 4999; www.einstein-koblenz.de; Fir-
mungstrasse 30; mains €9.50-24, Sun brunch
€21.90; ⊘ 9am-10pm Mon-Sat, from 10am Sun,
bar to midnight Sun-Thu, to 2am Fri & Sat) Grilled
calf's liver with masala jus; gilthead, tiger
prawn and lime risotto; ribbon noodles with
feta, spinach and tomatoes; and chocolate

cannelloni with almond mascarpone and orange sorbet are among the choices at this elegant crimson-toned cafe/bar. It also has lighter bites like soups and salads. Book ahead for Sunday's brunch buffet. Live music often plays on weekends.

Schiller's EUROPEAN €€€
(☑ 0261-963 530; www.hotel-stein.de; Hotel Stein, Mayener Strasse 126; 4-/5-/6-course menus €79/98/119, with paired wines €107/133/161, 5-course veg menu €89, with paired wines €124; ☺6-10pm Tue-Sat) At the Hotel Stein, 2km north of the city centre across the Moselle, Michelin-starred Schiller's utilises premium ingredients like white asparagus, scampi, foie gras, truffles and smoked sea urchin roe in its artistically presented menus (vegetarian menus are available). Wines are sourced exclusively from the Moselle and Rhine valleys.

It also runs four-hour cooking courses in English and German (€149) creating a four-course menu that you and a companion can enjoy afterwards, even if they're not cooking themselves.

Da Vinci INTERNATIONAL €€€
(☑ 0261-921 5444; www.davinci-koblenz.de; Deinhardplatz 3; 4-/5-/7-/9-course menus €85/99/125/155, with paired wines €111/131/169/205; ☺5.30-11pm Wed-Sat, noon-2.30pm & 5.30-11pm Sun) At this refined Michelin-starred restaurant, inspired multi-course menus served at white-clothed tables might include Riesling-cured salmon with trout roe and pickled asparagus, or lamb with sweet potato doughnuts and caramelised shallots. The mostly local wine list is extensive; bookings are recommended. Tables cover the terrace in summer.

🍷 Drinking & Nightlife

Münzplatz has a large concentration of bars. There are also numerous places for a coffee or beer along the Rhine riverfront. The city is lively after dark; cocktail bars and nightclubs are scattered throughout the Altstadt.

Alte Weinstube Zum Hubertus WINE BAR
(www.weinhaus-hubertus.de; Florinsmarkt 6; ☺3.30-11pm Mon, Wed & Thu, noon-midnight Fri-Sun) Specialising in Rhine and Moselle wines by the glass and/or bottle, rustic Alte Weinstube Zum Hubertus occupies a half-timbered house dating from 1689, with an open fireplace, antique furniture and dark-wood panelling. In summer, seating

spills onto the square. Classic German dishes include braised pork.

ℹ️ Information

Tourist Office (☑ 0261-194 33; www.koblenz-touristik.de; Zentralplatz 1; ☺10am-6pm) In the Forum Confluentes.

ℹ️ Getting There & Away

TRAIN

Koblenz has two train stations, the main **Hauptbahnhof** on the Rhine's left bank about 1km south of the city centre, and **Koblenz-Ehrenbreitstein** on the right bank (right below Festung Ehrenbreitstein).

Regional trains serve villages on both banks of the Romantic Rhine, including Bingen (€14.60, 50 minutes, two per hour).

Direct Hauptbahnhof services include:
➡ Bonn (€17, 40 minutes, up to four per hour)
➡ Cologne (€20, 50 minutes, up to three per hour)
➡ Frankfurt (€31, 1½ hours, up to four per hour)
➡ Mainz (€22, one hour, every 30 minutes)
➡ Trier (€24, 1½ to two hours, two per hour)

BUS

Some Romantic Rhine villages are also served by buses (www.rmv-bus.de) that stop outside the Hauptbahnhof. Bus 650 goes to Boppard via Schloss Stolzenfels (€7.10, 40 minutes, two per hour), while bus 570 goes to Braubach/Marksburg (€8.20, 35 minutes, two per hour).

The Fahrplan Rhein-Mosel-Bus services link Koblenz with Frankfurt-Hahn Airport (€11.50, 1¼ hours, six per day).

BOAT

Several boat companies have docks on Konrad-Adenauer-Ufer, which runs along the Rhine south of the Deutsches Eck.

ℹ️ Getting Around

Bus 1 (€1.90, 13 minutes, two per hour, hourly after 8pm) links the Hauptbahnhof with the Deutsches Eck.

MOSELLE VALLEY

Wending between vertiginous vine-covered slopes, the Moselle (Mosel in German) is narrower than its neighbour, the Rhine, and has a more intimate charm. The German section of the river, which rises in France then traverses Luxembourg, flows for 195km from Trier to Koblenz on a slow, winding course, with entrancing scenery around

Moselle Valley

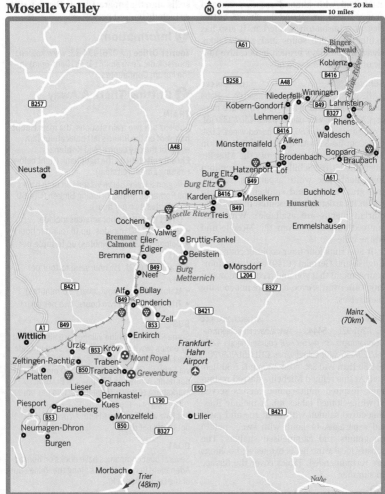

every hairpin bend: vine-ribboned hillsides, colourful half-timbered medieval villages, crumbling hilltop castles, elegant *Jugendstil* (art nouveau) villas, and ancient wine warehouses.

In spring pale-purple wisteria flowers, trailing from stone houses, anticipate the bunches of grapes that will ripen in autumn. Wonderful walking trails allow you to explore the Moselle's precipitous banks, where you'll find Europe's (and reputedly the world's) steepest vineyard, the Bremmer Calmont just north of Bremm, with a 65-degree gradient.

Activities

To sample the Moselle's exceptional wines, look for signs reading *Weingut, Weinprobe, Wein Probieren, Weinverkauf* and *Wein zu Verkaufen*.

Cycling

Superb cycling paths (www.mosel-radweg-etappen.com) traverse the countryside along and near the Moselle, including the 311km-long **Mosel-Radweg**, which runs from Bussan in France, skirting the Luxembourg border, to Koblenz. Tourist offices have maps.

Hiking

The Moselle Valley is especially scenic walking country. Variants of the **Mosel Erlebnis Route** follow the entire Moselle Valley along both banks of the river.

Expect some steep climbs if you venture away from the river, such as on the 185km-long **Moselhöhenweg**, which sticks to high ground, but offers spectacular vistas.

The website www.mosellandtouristik.de has comprehensive information; bookshops and tourist offices carry brochures and maps.

✨ Festivals & Events

From around April to mid-November, numerous wine festivals take place in the towns and villages; for a complete list visit www.mosel-weinfeste.de.

🍴 Sleeping & Eating

Summer (July to August) and autumn (September to October) are peak season in the Moselle. Almost all towns in the valley have a summertime camping ground, most right on the breeze-cooled riverbanks; book ahead. Christmas aside, from November to around Easter the majority of towns are very quiet, and some hotels close. You can book accommodation at www.mosellandtouristik.de.

Sublime Moselle wines are used extensively in dishes throughout the valley. Trier and Cochem have the widest variety of dining options. In smaller villages, many places reduce their hours or close altogether outside peak season.

ℹ Getting There & Away

Frankfurt-Hahn Airport (p557) is just 21km east of Traben-Trarbach. A shuttle bus (Rhein-Mosel-Bus; www.hahn-airport.de) links the airport with the railhead of Bullay (€8.20, 45 minutes, up to 11 daily); two shuttle-bus services continue on to Cochem (€9.90, 1¼ hours).

The **Hochmoselbrücke** (High Moselle Bridge), linking Ürzig and Zeltingen-Rachtig, with a 158m-high carriageway stretching above the river, is part of a new highway connection, the 'Hochmoselübergang' (B50), providing a fast link to the Frankfurt area and beyond. Environmental concerns saw it beset by delays, but it was completed in late 2018. Learn more at www.hochmoseluebergang.rlp.de.

ℹ Getting Around

Driving is the easiest way to see the Moselle, which, unlike the Romantic Rhine, is spanned by plenty of bridges.

The valley is also well served by public transport.

TRAIN

The rail line linking Koblenz with Trier (€25.20, 1½ to two hours, at least hourly) follows the Moselle (and stops at its villages) only as far upriver as Bullay before veering inland (Koblenz–Bullay €11.80, 45 minutes, hourly; Trier–Bullay €12.10, 45 minutes, two per hour).

From Bullay, small shuttle trains run along a spur line that terminates in Traben-Trarbach (€3, 20 minutes, hourly).

BUS

The villages between Traben-Trarbach and Trier, including Bernkastel-Kues, are served year-round by bus 333 (www.moselbahn.de, day ticket €6, six daily Monday to Friday, three daily Saturday and Sunday).

From April to October the popular RegioRadler bus service has bicycle trailers (bicycle per trip €2.80; online reservations recommended).

BOAT

Kolb (www.moselrundfahrten.de) is the Moselle's main boat operator, offering sightseeing cruises as well as one-way transport. Most services run from April to October.

Alken

☑ 02605 / POP 651

Dominated by a majestic castle, Alken is one of the Moselle's oldest villages, tracing its roots to Celtic and Roman times. It's also one of the valley's prettiest, with geranium-filled window boxes emblazoning half-timbered houses, and vestiges of medieval walls. Its twin town, Kattenes, is across the river.

◉ Sights

Burg Thurant   CASTLE
(☑02605-2004; www.thurant.de; adult/child €4/2.50; ☺10am-6pm May-Sep, to 5pm Mar, Apr & Sep–mid-Nov) Built on Roman foundations from 1197, this mighty castle on the hilltop above Alken has an intriguing history. From 1246 to 1248 it was fought over by the archbishops of Cologne and Trier, and divided in two parts (separated by a wall). The peace agreement dated 17 September 1248 is one of the oldest surviving documents in the German language. Fascinating displays include medieval torture devices; the watchtower is accessible by ladder. Leaflets are available in English.

If you want to stay, there's a kitchen-equipped apartment (from €170) sleeping six people in a half-timbered wing, with a terrace overlooking the Moselle.

HATZENPORT

Occupying a 1547 half-timbered building in the little village of Hatzenport, wonderfully local **Weinhaus Ibald** (☑02605-2043; www.weinhaus-ibald.de; Moselstrasse 34, Hatzenport; ⊙noon-10pm daily Easter-Oct, to 8pm Fri-Sun Nov-Mar; 🛜) specialises in Rieslings, sparkling Spätlese, dornfelder reds and *Fruchsaft* (fruit wine); the ultimate spot for a glass is on the vine-shaded terrace.

Food ranges from homemade onion soup to sausage platters and gorgeous cakes including rhubarb topped with meringue. You can also stay in simple but comfortable rooms (doubles from €70).

🛏 Sleeping & Eating

There are a handful of inns in Alken and across the river in Kattenes, and an apartment in the castle itself. Nearby options include Cochem, 27km southwest, and Koblenz, 23km northeast.

Hotel-Gasthaus Burg Thurant　　HOTEL€
(☑02605-849 8580; www.turmgasthaus.de; Moselstrasse 15; s/d €55/78) Next to the old bell tower (once part of the medieval walls), this charmer has stylish rooms with iron beds, pewter and sky-blue fabrics, and bright, white modern bathrooms. Two of its four rooms overlook the river; the other two have castle views. Its restaurant, with a fireplace and exposed stone walls, serves excellent local food and wine.

Winzerstube Brachtendorf　　GERMAN€
(☑02605-2805; www.winzerhofbrachtendorf.de; Moselstrasse 13; mains €6-11.50; ⊙4pm-midnight Mon & Wed-Fri, from 2pm Sat & Sun; 🛜) The river-facing summer terrace at Winzerstube Brachtendorf makes an ideal spot to sample the Brachtendorf family's wines, peach liqueur and apple-and-pear brandy. Dishes baked in a stone oven include *Griebenschmalz* (lard spread, served in a clay pot with bread), *Tresterfleisch* (wine-marinated pork) and *Winzersülze* (pork jelly, accompanied by warm potato salad). Double rooms start from €75.

❶ Getting There & Away

The train station is in Kattenes. There are hourly services to Cochem (€7.10, 25 minutes) and Koblenz (€4.90, 25 minutes).

Burg Eltz

At the head of the beautiful Moselle side-valley the Eltz, Burg Eltz (☑02672-950 500; www.burg-eltz.de; Burg-Eltz-Strasse 1, Wierschem; tour adult/child €9/6.50; ⊙9.30am-5.30pm Apr-Oct) is one of Germany's most romantic medieval castles. Never destroyed, this fairy-tale vision of turrets, towers, oriels, gables and half-timber has jutted forth from a rock framed by thick forest for nearly 900 years and is still owned by the original family. The decorations, furnishings, tapestries, fireplaces, paintings and armour you see during the 40-minute tour (English brochures provided; English-language tours by appointment) are also centuries old.

From the Eltz car park it's a shuttle bus ride (€2; four daily May to October, four on Saturday and Sunday only in April) or 1.3km walk to the castle. From Koblenz, boats and trains also go to Moselkern village, from where it's a lovely 5km walk to the castle.

Cochem

☑02671 / POP 5332
Cochem, with its bank of pastel-coloured, terrace-fronted restaurants lining the waterfront, tangle of narrow alleyways and dramatic castle precipitously perched on a rock, is one of the Moselle's most visited towns.

◉ Sights

Bundesbank Bunker　　HISTORIC SITE
(☑02671-915 3540; www.bundesbank-bunker.de; Am Wald 35; adult/child €10/5, shuttle bus one-way/return €2.50/4; ⊙tours hourly 11am-3pm May-Oct, every two hours 11am-4pm Nov-Apr) Camouflaged as residential buildings and built to survive a nuclear war, this extraordinary Cold War secret bunker owned by the German Federal Bank was stocked with 15 billion Deutsche Marks to roll out in the event of war. One-hour guided tours descend 100 steps into the bunker, where the year-round temperature is 12 degrees Celsius (bring a jacket). From May to October, shuttle buses run from the tourist office; otherwise it's a steep 1km walk or drive from the centre.

Reichsburg　　CASTLE
(☑02671-255;www.reichsburg-cochem.de;Schlossstrasse 36; tours adult/child €6/3; ⊙tours 9am-5pm mid-Mar–Oct, shorter hours Nov–mid-Mar) Like many others in the area, Cochem's original 11th-century castle fell victim to French

troops in 1689, then stood ruined for centuries until wealthy Berliner Louis Ravene snapped it up for a pittance in 1868 and had it restored to its current – if not always architecturally faithful – glory. The 40-minute tours (some in English; leaflet/audioguide otherwise available) take in the decorative rooms that reflect 1000 years' worth of tastes and styles.

In summer, various themed tours, such as musical or ghost tours, are available; check the website for details. Its restaurant hosts four-hour banquets (including castle tour adult/child €49/24.50) on Friday and Saturday evenings, attended by costumed staff, with wine served in a clay tumbler that you get to keep, culminating in a knighting ceremony.

🛏 Sleeping

Hotel Traumblick HOTEL €€
(📞 02671-603 7888; www.hotel-traumblick.de; Bergstrasse 6; d from €90; 🅿 🛜) The pick of the airy, light-toned rooms at this stylishly renovated, family-run hotel have balconies with stunning views of Cochem's castle and the river below; others face the mountain behind. There's a lift in the building and bike storage on site.

🍴 Eating

The waterfront Moselpromenade and, one street back, cobbled Bernstrasse, on the western side of the river, have the densest concentration of restaurants.

Alt Thorschenke GERMAN €€
(📞 02671-7059; www.thorschenke.de; Brückenstrasse 3; mains €10.50-19; ⊙ 11am-9pm; 🛜) Wedged into the old medieval walls, away from the busy riverfront restaurants, this is a diamond find for regional specialities, such as herring with apple and onions, pork neck with mustard-cream sauce, and several different types of schnitzel – accompanied by wines from local producers. Upstairs are 27 small but charming rooms (doubles from €99), some with four-poster beds.

🛍 Shopping

★ VinoForum WINE
(📞 02671-917 1777; www.vinoforum-ernst.de; Moselstrasse 12-13, Ernst; ⊙ 10am-6pm Apr-Oct, 1-5pm Nov-Mar) Barrels are suspended from the ceiling at this ultra-contemporary *Vinothek*. Taste and buy exceptional wines made from grapes grown on the hillside behind

and in the surrounding area, and look out for events, such as brunches, dinners and jazz concerts on the elevated terrace overlooking the Moselle. It's in the hamlet of Ernst, 4km east of Cochem.

Vinothek Walter J Oster WINE
(📞 02671-605 710; www.weingutoster.de; Herrenstrasse 5; ⊙ 10am-6pm) Winemakers for 15 generations, the Oster family has vineyards located in the Moselle's prized Bremmer Calmont, Neefer Frauenberg and Ediger Elzhofberg areas. Along with wines, the family also produces liqueurs, brandies, gins, vinegars and oils (tastings available).

Ask about tours of its factory, 20km upstream at St Aldegund, or its vineyards.

ℹ Information

Tourist Office (📞 02671-600 40; www.ferienland-cochem.de; Endertplatz 1; ⊙ 9am-5pm Mon-Sat, 10am-3pm Sun mid-Jun–Sep, shorter hours Oct–mid-Jun) Can suggest local wineries and hikes, and provide transport advice.

ℹ Getting There & Away

Cochem is a key Moselle Valley transport hub and has excellent connections.

Shuttle buses (€9.90, 1¼ hours, two daily) link Cochem with Frankfurt-Hahn Airport (p558).

By train, destinations include Koblenz (€11.80, 40 minutes, two per hour), Trier (€14.90, 55 minutes, two per hour) and Bullay (€3.80, 10 minutes, two per hour), from where buses serve villages further upstream.

Kolb (www.moselrundfahrten.de) runs boats along the river from April to October.

Beilstein
📞 02673 / POP 140

On the right bank of the Moselle about 50km upriver from Koblenz, Beilstein is a pint-sized village straight out of a storybook. Centred on the Marktplatz, dating from 1322, its cluster of half-timbered houses are surrounded by steep vineyards.

⊙ Sights

Karmeliterkirche St Josef CHURCH
(www.st-josef-beilstein.de; Klostertreppe; ⊙ 8am-6pm) Up a steep set of stairs from Fürst-Metternich Strasse, this baroque 17th-century Carmelite monastery church has a spectacular interior with a vaulted ceiling supported by soaring apricot-coloured columns. The Kloster restaurant/cafe has a sheltered inner courtyard as well as a panoramic terrace.

GERMANY'S LARGEST SUSPENSION BRIDGE

Stretching 360m at a height of 100m above ground, Germany's largest suspension bridge, **Hängeseilbrücke Geierlay** (www.geierlay.de; Geierlay Kastellauner Strasse, Mörsdorf; ⊘24hr), isn't for the faint-hearted but the valley views are spectacular. Walking trails criss-cross the area. From the car park at Mörsdorf, a 1.2km path leads to the bridge.

Burg Metternich RUINS
(📞02673-936 39; www.burg-metternich.de; adult/child €2.50/1; ⊘9am-6pm Apr-Nov) Above Beilstein looms Burg Metternich, a ruined hilltop castle reached via a footpath off Im Mühlental (at the top of cobbled Bachstrasse). Built in 1129, it was destroyed by French troops during the Nine Years' War (1688–97). Today you can visit the ruins and have a glass of local wine at the courtyard cafe.

🛏 Sleeping

Hotel Altes Zollhaus HOTEL €€
(📞02673-1850; www.hotel-lipmann.de; Moselstrasse 26; d from €85; ⊘Apr-Oct; 🅿🛜) Right by the river, this historic half-timbered former toll house contains snug rooms with floral fabrics, a beautiful slate bar, a vine-draped river-view terrace, and a restaurant serving hearty German and international fare. The Lipmann family, whose record of hosting visitors in Beilstein stretches back to 1795, runs another flowery hotel on the hillside, Hotel Am Klosterberg.

🍴 Eating & Drinking

Charming wine taverns and traditional restaurants are a hallmark of Beilstein.

Zehnthauskeller WINE BAR
(📞02673-900 907; www.zehnthauskeller.de; Marktplatz 1; ⊘11am-10pm Tue-Sat, from noon Sun; 🛜) Starting in 1574, the Zehnthauskeller was used to store wine delivered as a tithe; it now houses a romantically dark, vaulted wine cellar where you can try a variety of wines and traditional German dishes served by Dirndl-wearing staff. Live music plays on summer evenings.

ℹ Information

Tourist information is available on the village website www.beilstein-mosel.de. Note that Beilstein has no ATMs.

ℹ Getting There & Away

Buses link Beilstein with Cochem (€3.80, 20 minutes, every two hours).

From April to October, ferries run by Kolb (www.moselrundfahrten.de) stop here.

Traben-Trarbach

📋 06541 / POP 5768

Elegant Traben-Trarbach makes an excellent base for exploring the valley by bike or car. A major centre of the wine trade a century ago, the town's winemakers still welcome visitors for tastings and sales.

Traben, on the Moselle's left bank, is the commercial hub. It lost its medieval appearance to three major fires but was well compensated with beautiful *Jugendstil* villas, many of them designed by Berlin architect Bruno Möhring, whose works also include the ornate 1898 bridge gate, Brückentor, across the river in Trarbach. The two towns united in 1904.

Both banks of the Moselle have grassy riverfront promenades that are perfect for strolling.

◉ Sights

Grevenburg RUINS
(Trarbach) The Grevenburg castle, built in the mid-1300s, sits high in the craggy hills above Trarbach, with incredible valley views. Because of its strategic importance, it changed hands 13 times, was besieged six times, and destroyed seven times – no wonder that two walls are all that remain. It's reached via a steep 500m-long footpath, the **Sponheimer Weg**, that begins a block north of the bridge (there's no access by car). Its cafe serves wine, beer and *Flammkuchen* (Alsatian pizza).

Buddha Museum MUSEUM
(www.buddha-museum.de; Bruno-Möhring-Platz 1, Trarbach; adult/child €15/7.50; ⊘10am-6pm Tue-Sun) A magnificent 1906 *Jugendstil* former winery, designed by Bruno Möhring, is the unlikely home of the Buddha Museum, which has a beautifully presented collection of over 2000 wood, bronze and paper statues of the Buddha from all over Asia. Upstairs the peaceful rooftop garden has Moselle views.

Tickets are valid all day.

Mont Royal RUINS
(Traben) Above Traben are the remains of the vast Mont Royal fortress, constructed

between 1687 and 1698 and designed by Vauban for Louis XIV as a base from which to project French power. Ruinously expensive, it was dismantled before completion by the French themselves under the Treaty of Ryswick. The 1.5km-long footpath up to the ruins begins at the upper end of Römerstrasse.

Mittelmosel-Museum MUSEUM
(☎06541-9480; Casinostrasse 2, Trarbach; adult/child €2.50/1; ⏱10am-5pm Tue-Sun Easter-Oct) A 1755 baroque villa proud of having hosted Johann Wolfgang von Goethe for a few hours in 1792 is now home to Traben-Trarbach's local history museum. Displays include furniture, 18th- and 19th-century period costumes, works of art and archaeological finds unearthed in the area.

Activities

From Traben-Trarbach, Bernkastel-Kues is 24km upriver by car but, because of the Moselle's hairpin curve, just 6.5km over the hill on foot. The walk up through the forest from Traben-Trarbach and down through the vineyards to Bernkastel-Kues is wonderfully scenic. Pick up a map from the tourist office.

Contact the tourist office for details of wine tastings and cellar tours.

Weingut Louis Klein WINE
(☎06541-6246; www.klein-wein.de; Enkircher Strasse 20, Trarbach; 90-min cellar tour incl tastings €8; ⏱10am-6pm Mon-Sat, to noon Sun, tours by reservation) Along with whites like Riesling, rivaner and pinot blanc, Louis Klein is one of the few Moselle wine producers to specialise in reds, including pinot meunier, pinot noir, cabernet dorio, cabernet sauvignon, merlot and dornfelder. It occupies a monumental stone warehouse on the river; you can also arrange tastings in the vineyard among the vines.

Tours

Underground Traben-Trarbach WINE
(☎06541-839 80; www.traben-trarbach.de; tour €8; ⏱by appointment Fri, Sat & Mon Aug-Oct, Mon & Fri Apr-Jul, every 2nd Fri Nov-Mar) In the early 1900s, Traben-Trarbach was Europe's second-largest wine-trading centre (after Bordeaux) and consequently expanded its storage with cellars – some up to 100m long and several storeys deep – below the towns' streets. Fascinating 90-minute English- and German-language guided tours departing from the tourist office (p614) take you beneath the *Jugendstil* buildings into the cellar network, emerging in hidden gardens and vineyards.

Sleeping

Central Hotel HOTEL €
(☎06541-6238; www.centralhotel-traben.de; Bahnstrasse 43, Traben; s/d/tr from €45/78/96, apt per week from €360; P 📶) In the same family for three generations, this welcoming hotel 50m east of the tourist office, bang in the centre of Traben, has a handy lift and 33 modest but spotless rooms, as well as three apartments sleeping up to five for weekly rental.

DJH Hostel HOSTEL €
(☎06541-9278; www.jugendherberge.de; Hirtenpfad 6, Traben; dm/d €22.50/56; P @ 📶) All rooms at this modern, 172-bed hostel have private bathrooms. Wi-fi is in common areas only. It's a 1.2km walk up the hillside from the train station, past the fire station.

Hotel Bellevue HISTORIC HOTEL €€
(☎06541-7030; www.bellevue-hotel.de; An der Mosel 11, Traben; s/d/ste from €95/140/175; 📶 🏊) Topped by a Champagne-bottle-shaped slate turret, this river-facing *Jugendstil* hotel was built in 1903 by Bruno Möhring, with an oak staircase in the lobby and beautiful stained-glass windows in its gourmet restaurant, Belle Epoque. Individually designed rooms are overwhelmingly romantic. There's a minimum two-night stay on weekends year-round and minimum three-night stay at any time July to October and December.

Amenities include bike and canoe hire, a pool and a sauna.

BOAT & BIKE COMBO

From April to October, boats run by Kolb (www.moselrundfahrten.de) link Bernkastel with Traben-Trarbach (one-way/return €16/22, two hours, up to two daily). You can take along a bicycle for €2, making it easy to sail one way and ride the 24km back.

In Traben-Trarbach, **Zweirad Wagner** (☎06541-1649; www.zweirad-wagner.de; Brückenstrasse 42, Trarbach; standard/electric bike per day €10/25; ⏱8am-12.30pm & 2-6pm Mon-Fri, 9am-1pm Sat Apr-Oct, shorter hours Nov-May) rents bikes; in Bernkastel-Kues try Fun Bike Team (p616).

✗ Eating & Drinking

Charming wine taverns are located on both sides of the river. A local (non-alcoholic) speciality is the local bottled spring water, Trabacher.

★ Alte Zunftscheune   GERMAN €€

(☎06541-9737; www.zunftscheune.de; Neue Rathausstrasse 15, Traben; mains €9-23; ⊙5-11pm Tue-Sat, 11.30am-3pm & 5-11pm Sun Easter-Oct, 6-11pm Fri, 5-11pm Sat & Sun Nov-Easter; ☑) Dine on delicious Moselle-style dishes such as homemade black pudding and liver sausage, pork medallions with Riesling cream sauce, or grilled rump steak with asparagus and fried potatoes in a series of wonderfully atmospheric rooms chock-full of rustic bric-a-brac, with beautiful timber staircases. Its cellar still has its original 1890s lighting. Reservations are recommended. This restaurant is cash only.

Die Graifen   MEDITERRANEAN €€€

(☎06541-811 075; www.graifen.de; Wolfer Weg 11, Trabach; mains €18-32; ⊙5-10pm Wed-Fri, 12.30-2.30pm & 5-10pm Sat, 12.30-2.30pm & 5-9pm Sun) In a prime riverside setting, Die Graifen has a shaded summer garden and glass-roofed, gas-heated winter garden. The menu is inspired: wild boar mousse with beetroot carpaccio, braised veal with truffled potato cakes, homemade avocado and spinach tortellini with buffalo mozzarella and tomato foam, and dark praline ice cream with hazelnut and nougat brûlée.

ⓘ Information

Tourist Office (☎06541-839 80; www.traben-trarbach.de; Am Bahnhof 5, Traben; ⊙10am-5pm Mon-Fri, 11am-3pm Sat May-Aug, 10am-6pm Mon-Fri, 11am-3pm Sep & Oct, 10am-4pm Mon-Fri Nov-Apr; ☎) Adjacent to the train station.

ⓘ Getting There & Away

Traben is home to the end-of-the-line train station, which is linked by small shuttle trains to the railhead of Bullay (€3, 20 minutes, hourly), from where there are connections to Koblenz and Trier.

Bernkastel-Kues

☑ 06531 / POP 6987

These charming twin towns are the hub of the *Mittelmosel* (Middle Moselle) region. Bernkastel, on the right (eastern) bank, is a symphony in half-timber, stone and slate,

and teems with wine taverns. Kues, the birthplace of theologian Nicolaus Cusanus (1401–64), is less quaint but is home to some key historical sights and has a lovely riverfront promenade.

⊙ Sights

★ Kloster Machern   BREWERY

(☎06532-95150; www.brauhaus-kloster-machern.de; An der Zeltinger Brücke, Zeltingen-Rachtig; museum adult/child €3/1.50; ⊙museum 10am-6pm, bar 11am-1am, shop noon-5pm Easter-Oct, shorter hours Nov-Easter) The Moselle might be better known for its wine, but a former Cistercian monastery, founded in the 13th century, now houses this extraordinary brewery, with a bar made from a copper vat and strung with dry hops, a wicker-chair-filled terrace, and excellent local cuisine. Brews, including a *Dunkel* (dark), *Hell* (light) and *Hefe-Weizen* (wheat beer), are also sold at its shop. Also here is a museum exhibiting religious iconography, plus puppets, toys and model railways. It's 7km northwest of Bernkastel-Kues.

Marktplatz   SQUARE

(Bernkastel) Bernkastel's pretty Marktplatz, a block inland from the bridge, is enclosed by a romantic ensemble of half-timbered houses with beautifully decorated gables. Look for the iron handcuffs, to which criminals were attached, on the facade of the 1608-built Rathaus.

Burg Landshut   RUINS

(☎06531-972 770; www.burglandshut.de; Bernkastel; ⊙noon-9pm Thu-Tue) A rewarding way to get your heart pumping is to head from Marktplatz up to this ruined 13th-century castle, framed by vineyards and forests on a bluff above Bernkastel. It's a very steep 750m from town; allow 30 minutes. You'll be rewarded with glorious valley views. The spectacularly renovated restaurant was unveiled in 2018; during restoration, a 4th-century Roman tower's foundations were also discovered. An hourly shuttle bus from the riverfront costs €5 uphill, €3.50 downhill, or €7 return.

Pfarrkirche St Michael   CHURCH

(www.pfarrei.de; Mandatstrasse 8, Bernkastel; ⊙9am-6pm Apr-Oct, shorter hours Nov-May) Facing the bridge, this partly 14th-century-Gothic church has an ornate interior and some colourful stained glass. The tower was originally part of the town's fortifications.

St-Nikolaus-Hospital HISTORIC BUILDING
(www.cusanus.de; Cusanusstrasse 2, Kues; guided
tour €7; ☺9am-6pm Sun-Fri, to 3pm Sat, guided
tour 10.30am Tue & 3pm Fri Apr-Oct) FREE Most
of Kues' sights, including the Mosel Vinothek
and Mosel-Weinmuseum, are conveniently
grouped near the bridge in the late-Gothic
St-Nikolaus-Hospital, an old-age home founded by Cusanus in 1458 for 33 men (one for
every year of Jesus' life). You're free to explore
the cloister and Gothic *Kapelle* (chapel) at leisure, but the treasure-filled library can only be
seen on a guided tour.

Mosel-Weinmuseum MUSEUM
(Moselle Wine Museum; ☑06531-4141; www.mosel
weinmuseum.de; Cusanusstrasse 2, Kues; adult/
child €5/2.50; ☺10am-6pm mid-Apr–Oct, 2-5pm
Nov–mid-Apr) Part of the St-Nikolaus-Hospital
complex, this small museum has interactive
screens (best appreciated by German speakers) and features such as an Aromabar (you
have to guess what you're smelling). The
main event, though, is the adjacent Vinothek.

🏃 Activities

For a gentle bike ride, the Mosel-
Maare-Radweg (www.maare-moselradweg.
de), linking Bernkastel-Kues with Daun (in
the Eifel Mountains), follows an old train
line, so the gradients are reasonable. From
April to October, you can take the Regio-
Radler bus (adult/bicycle €12.60/3, 1½
hours, every two hours) to the top and ride
the 58km back down to Bernkastel-Kues.

Weingut Dr Pauly-Bergweiler WINE
(☑06531-3002; www.pauly-bergweiler.com; Gestade 15; wine tastings €11.50; ☺wine tastings by
reservation 1-6pm Mon-Fri, from 2pm Sat) Tastings
of renowned wines produced by Dr Pauly-Bergweiler can take place in an atmospheric vaulted cellar, chapel and baroque
hall. It's popular with groups, so book ahead.

Mosel Vinothek WINE
(☑06531-4141; www.moselvinothek.de; Cusanusstrasse 2; wine tasting per person summer/winter
€18/12; ☺10am-6pm Apr-Oct, 11am-5pm Feb, Mar,
Nov & Dec) In the cellar of the Vinothek within the St-Nikolaus-Hospital complex, you
can sample from a list of over 160 vintages.
In winter the selection is more limited but
cheaper.

MTB Trailscout CYCLING
(☑017 620 730 681; www.mtbtour-mosel.de; tours
from €25; ☺Easter-Oct) Guided mountain-bike
tours offer a local perspective of the valley

(English tours are possible by arrangement).
Two- to three-hour beginner tours cover
25km; experienced (and fit!) mountain bikers can take a challenging six-hour, 50km
tour. Departure points vary. Rates don't
include bikes or compulsory helmets; rent
both from Fun Bike Team (p616), or Fahrräder Wildmann (p616).

🛏 Sleeping

**★ Christiana's Wein
& Art Hotel** BOUTIQUE HOTEL €€
(☑06531-6627; www.wein-arthotel.de; Lindenweg
18, Kues; s/d/ste from €69/89/111; ꟼ❉৪) Each
of the 17 rooms at this sleek hotel is named
after a Moselle vineyard (with correspond-
ing wines in each minibar), and features
dramatic outsized photos of wine glasses
or barrels. Bathrooms are state of the art;
higher-priced rooms have spas and/or balconies. Its steakhouse restaurant overlooks
the vines. Lock-up bike storage is available.

Doctor Weinstube HISTORIC HOTEL €€
(☑06531-96650; www.doctor-weinstube-bernkas
tel.de; Hebegasse 5, Bernkastel; s/d from
€76/129; ৪) Spacious rooms in this partly
half-timbered building in the heart of the
Altstadt have light-toned fabrics and contemporary bathrooms; some have exposed
wooden beams. Post-cycling, unwind in its
two saunas. Local sausages, Hunsrück deer
and other specialities are served at the hotel's restaurant; the vaulted cellar contains
a bar hosting live music on summer weekends (thick stone walls provide effective
soundproofing).

🍴 Eating

Bernkastel has restaurants along the waterfront and in the Altstadt's squares and narrow, pedestrian-only streets. In Kues there
are several restaurants near the bridge.

★ Restaurant Burg Landshut GERMAN €€
(☑06531-972 770; www.burglandshut.de; Burg
Landshut, Bernkastel; mains €14-25; ☺noon-
2pm & 6-9pm Thu-Tue Easter-Nov) Opened in
2018 in the ruined castle Burg Landshut,
this state-of-the-art restaurant is worth the
steep climb (or shuttle-bus ride) for modern German cuisine such as sauerkraut and
blood-sausage soup, and pike-perch with
bacon and cabbage mash, topped off by
desserts like Black Forest mousse with berry coulis and Riesling sorbet with poached
local peaches. Panoramic views unfold over
town.

Rotisserie Royale   EUROPEAN €€

(☑06531-6572; www.rotisserie-royale.de; Burgstrasse 19, Bernkastel; mains €14.50-24.50, 5-course dinner menu €46.50; ☺noon-2pm & 5-9pm Thu-Tue) Seriously good cooking inside this half-timbered house spans starters like pan-fried foie gras on a potato-and-apple rösti or sautéed calf's liver with black truffle foam, followed by mains such as catfish-stuffed cabbage with white asparagus mousse, and desserts like chocolate ganache on eggnog foam with walnut sorbet to finish.

🍷 Drinking & Nightlife

★**Weinstube Spitzhäuschen**   WINE BAR

(☑06531-7476; www.spitzhaeuschen.de; Karlstrasse 13, Bernkastel; ☺4-10pm Mon-Fri, from 3pm Sat & Sun Easter-Oct, 3-10pm Sat Nov-Dec, other times by appointment) Wine bars don't come any cuter than this crooked half-timbered building (the Moselle's oldest, dating from 1416), which resembles a giant bird house: its narrow base is topped by a much larger, precariously leaning upper floor which allowed carriages to pass through the narrow alley to the marketplace. Taste over 50 of the Schmitz family's local wines; small snacks are available.

🛍 Shopping

Bonbon Willi   FOOD

(www.bonbon-willi.de; Burgstrasse 8, Bernkastel; ☺11am-5.30pm Mon-Sat) Watch sweets being boiled and crafted using century-old techniques and tools at this traditional shop. Some of the more unusual flavours include Riesling and *Federweiser* (red wine); it also makes liquorice, marzipan and chocolates.

ℹ Information

Tourist Office (☑06531-500 190; www.bernkastel.de; Gestade 6, Bernkastel; audioguides 3 hrs/1 day €6/8; ☺9am-5pm Mon-Fri, from 10am Sat, to 1pm Sun May-Oct, 9.30am-4pm Mon-Fri Nov-Apr) Reserves hotel rooms, sells hiking and cycling maps, and has an ATM. It also rents out audioguides to explore the two towns.

ℹ Getting There & Away

Buses run to Bullay (€12.60, 1¼ hours, three daily) and Trier (€11.55, 2¼ hours, three daily).

Boats operated by **Kolb** (☑06531-4719; www.moselrundfahrten.de; ☺Apr-Oct) link Bernkastel with Traben-Trarbach (one-way/return €16/22, two hours, up to two daily). One-way bicycle transport costs €2.

ℹ Getting Around

In Bernkastel, **Fun Bike Team** (☑06531-940 24; www.funbiketeam.de; Schanzstrasse 22, Bernkastel; standard/electric bike per day €12/25; ☺9am-1pm & 2-6.30pm Mon-Fri, 9am-2pm Sat Apr-Oct, shorter hours Nov-Mar) rents bicycles.

Zeltingen-Rachtig–based **Fahrräder Wildmann** (☑06532-954 367; www.fahrraederwildmann.de; Uferallee 55, Zeltingen-Rachtig; standard/electric bike hire per day €10/22, bike transport from €80; ☺9am-noon & 4-6pm Wed-Mon Apr-Oct, shorter hours Nov-Mar), 5km northwest of Bernkastel-Kues, hires bikes, and has pick-up, drop-off and luggage-transport services.

Trier

☑0651 / POP 114, 914

With an astounding nine Unesco World Heritage sites, Germany's oldest city shelters the country's finest ensemble of Roman monuments, among them a mighty gate, amphitheatre, elaborate thermal baths, imperial throne room, and the country's oldest bishop's church, which retains Roman sections. Architectural treasures from later ages include Germany's oldest Gothic church, and Karl Marx' baroque birthplace.

Trier's proximity to both Luxembourg and France is apparent in its cuisine and the local esprit, enlivened by some 15,000 students from its renowned university. The mostly pedestrianised city centre is filled with cafes and restaurants, many inside gorgeous Gothic or baroque buildings, while wineries are scattered throughout the surrounding vineyards.

👁 Sights

★**Porta Nigra**   ROMAN SITE

(adult/child €4/2.50; ☺9am-6pm Apr-Sep, to 5pm Mar & Oct, to 4pm Nov-Feb) Trier's most famous landmark, this brooding 2nd-century Roman city gate – blackened by time, hence the name, Latin for 'black gate' – is a marvel of engineering, since it's held together by nothing but gravity and iron clamps. In the 11th century, the structure was turned into a church to honour Simeon, a Greek hermit who spent six years walled up in its east tower. After his death in 1134, he was buried inside the gate and later became a saint.

★**Konstantin Basilika**   ROMAN SITE

(Constantine's Throne Room; ☑0651-9949 1200; www.konstantin-basilika.de; Konstantinplatz 10;

FRANKFURT & SOUTHERN RHINELAND TRIER

☺10am-6pm Mon-Sat, 1-6pm Sun Apr-Oct, 10am-noon & 2-4pm Tue-Sat, 1-3pm Sun Nov-Mar) FREE Constructed around AD 310 as Constantine's throne room, the brick-built basilica is now an austere Protestant church. With built-to-impress dimensions (some 67m long, 27m wide and 33m high), it's the largest single-room Roman structure still in existence. Its organ, with 87 registers and 6500 pipes, generates a seven-fold echo.

★**Liebfrauenbasilika**   CHURCH
(Church of Our Lady; www.trierer-dom.de; Liebfrauenstrasse; ☺10am-6pm Mon-Fri, to 4.30pm Sat, 12.30-6pm Sun Apr-Oct, 11am-5pm Mon-Fri, to 4.30pm Sat, 12.30-5pm Sun Nov-Mar) Germany's oldest Gothic church was built in the 13th century. It has a cruciform structure supported by a dozen pillars symbolising the 12 Apostles (look for the black stone from where all 12 articles of the Apostle's Creed painted on the columns are visible) and some colourful post war stained glass.

★**Trierer Dom**   CATHEDRAL
(☑0651-979 0790; www.trierer-dom.de; Liebfrauenstrasse 12; ☺6.30am-6pm Apr-Oct, to 5.30pm Nov-Mar) Looming above the Roman palace of Helena (Emperor Constantine's mother), this cathedral is Germany's oldest bishop's church and still retains Roman sections. Today's edifice is a study in nearly 1700 years of church architecture with Romanesque, Gothic and baroque elements. Intriguingly, its floorplan is of a 12-petalled flower, symbolising the Virgin Mary.

To see some dazzling ecclesiastical equipment and peer into early Christian history, head upstairs to the **Domschatz** (Cathedral Treasury; ☑0651-710 5378; www.trierer-dom. de/bauwerk/domschatz; adult/child €1.50/0.50; ☺10am-6pm Mon-Sat, from 12.30pm Sun Apr-Oct & Dec, 11am-4pm Tue-Sat, from 12.30pm Sun Nov & Jan-Mar) or around the corner to the **Museum am Dom Trier** (☑0651-710 5255; www.bistum-trier.de/museum; Bischof-Stein-Platz 1; adult/child €3.50/2; ☺9am-5pm Tue-Sat, from 1pm Sun).

★**Rheinisches Landesmuseum**   MUSEUM
(Roman Archaeological Museum; www.landesmuseum-trier.de; Weimarer Allee 1; adult/child incl audioguide €8/4; ☺10am-5pm Tue-Sun) A scale model of 4th-century Trier and rooms filled with tombstones, mosaics, rare gold coins (including the 1993-discovered Trier Gold Hoard, the largest preserved Roman gold hoard in the world, with over 2600 gold coins) and some fantastic glass are highlights of this museum, which affords an extraordinary look at local Roman life.

★**Kaiserthermen**   ROMAN SITE
(Imperial Baths; Weberbachstrasse 41; adult/child €4/2.50; ☺9am-6pm Apr-Sep, to 5pm Mar & Oct, to 4pm Nov-Feb) Get a sense of the layout of this vast Roman thermal bathing complex with its striped brick-and-stone arches from the corner lookout tower, then descend into an underground labyrinth consisting of cavernous hot and cold water baths, boiler rooms and heating channels.

★**Amphitheatre**   ROMAN SITE
(Olewiger Strasse; adult/child €4/2.50; ☺9am-6pm Apr-Sep, to 5pm Mar & Oct, to 4pm Nov-Feb) Trier's mighty Roman amphitheatre could accommodate 20,000 spectators for gladiator tournaments and animal fights. Beneath the arena are dungeons where prisoners sentenced to death waited next to starving beasts for the final showdown.

Basilika St Matthias   ABBEY
(St Matthias Abbey; ☑0651-170 90; www.abteistmatthias.de; Matthiasstrasse 85; ☺8am-7pm) Magnificent St Matthias Abbey is thought to be Germany's oldest Christian church. Begun in 1127, when the relics of the Apostle Matthias (Judas' successor) were found here, it was added to over the ensuing centuries. Treasures include the Holy Cross Chapel's Staurotheke (1240), containing a piece of Christ's cross. Steps on either side of the Romanesque–Gothic interior lead to the crypt, home to the sarcophagi of the abbey's first two bishops, Eucharius and Valerius, and St Matthias' relics.

Barbarathermen   ROMAN SITE
(Barbara Baths; Südallee; ☺9am-6pm Apr-Sep, to 5pm Oct-Mar, to 4pm Nov-Feb) FREE Named for a former monastery on this site, these Roman baths were built in the 2nd century AD. Information panels line a walkway through the atmospheric ruins.

Palastgarten   PARK
Stretching south from Konstantinplatz, the lawns, daffodil beds, statues and fountains of the formal Palace Garden are perfect for a stroll, especially on warm summer days. The pink and gold rococo confection at the northern end is the **Kurfürstliches Palais** (Prince Electors' Palace; interior closed to the public).

Trier

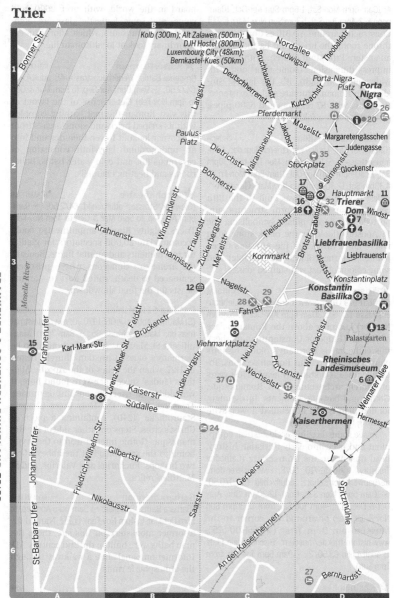

Kolb (300m); Alt Zalawen (500m);
DJH Hostel (800m);
Luxembourg City (48km);
Bernkastel-Kues (50km)

Nordallee

Bonner Str

Ludwigstr

Theobaldstr

Deutschherrenstr

Bruchhausenstr

Langstr

Pferdemarkt

Porta-Nigra-
Platz

**Porta
Nigra**
◉ 5   26

38
ⓘ● 20

Paulus-
Platz

Dietrichstr

Kutzbachstr

Moselstr

Jakobstr

Margaretengässchen

Judengasse

Böhmerstr

Walramsneustr

Stockplatz

35

Simeonstr

Glockenstr

9

17

Trierer
Dom

Hauptmarkt   11

Windstr

16
32
18

30
⊗ 7
4

Liebfrauenbasilika

Liebfrauenstr

Krahnenstr

Windmühlenstr

Frauenstr

Johannisstr

Zuckerbergstr

Metzelstr

Fleischstr

Kornmarkt

Brotstr

Grabenstr

Palaststr

Konstantinplatz

**Konstantin
Basilika** ◉ 3

10

Nagelstr

12

28
29

31

**Rheinisches
Landesmuseum**

6

Palastgarten

13

Krahnenufer

Karl-Marx-Str

Feldstr

Brückenstr

Hindenburgstr

Fahrstr

19

Viehmarktplatz

Neustr

Weberbachstr

Pützenstr

Wechselstr

37

36

Moselle River

Lorenz-Kellner-Str

Kaiserstr

Südallee

8

15

Kaiserthermen
2

Hermesstr

Weimarer Allee

Johanniterufer

Friedrich-Wilhelm-Str

Gilbertstr

24

Nikolausstr

Saarstr

Gerberstr

An den Kaiserthermen

Spitzmühle

St-Barbara-Ufer

27

Bernhardstr

Stadtmuseum
Simeonstift

MUSEUM

(📞651-718 1459; www.museum-trier.de; Simeon-
strasse 60; adult/child incl audioguide €5.50/4;
🕙10am-5pm Tue-Sun) Adjoining the Porta
Nigra, in the 11th-century priests' residence

Simeon's College (retaining an original
1060-laid oak beam floor in the double-
storey cloister), Trier's city museum brings
alive two millennia of local history through
paintings, sculptures, porcelain, textiles and
more. Highlights include the Trier Kino

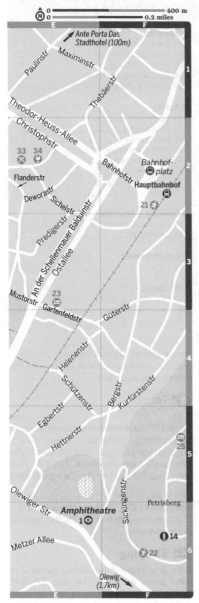

Hauptmarkt
SQUARE

Anchored by a 1595 fountain dedicated to St Peter and the Four Virtues, Trier's central market square is surrounded by medieval and Renaissance architectural treasures such as the Rotes Haus, and the Steipe, which now houses the Spielzeugmuseum, as well as the Gothic St-Gangolf-Kirche.

Small market stalls (flowers, sausages etc) set up most days, except Sunday.

Museum Karl-Marx-Haus
MUSEUM

(www.fes.de/museum-karl-marx-haus; Brückenstrasse 10; adult/child €5/3.50; ⊗9am-6pm Apr-Oct, 1-5pm Mon, 10am-5pm Tue-Sun Nov-Mar) Revamped in 2018 on the 200th anniversary of Marx' birth, the early-18th-century baroque town house in which the author of *The Communist Manifesto* and *Das Kapital* was born in 1818 now houses exhibits covering his life, work, allies and enemies, social democracy, his decades of exile in London, where he died in 1883, and his intellectual and political legacy.

Spielzeugmuseum
MUSEUM

(Toy Museum; ☑651-758 50; www.spielzeug museum-trier.de; Dietrichstrasse 50/51; adult/child €5/2.50; ⊗11am-5pm Tue-Sun; ⊕) Upstairs in the historic Steipe building on the Hauptmarkt, the Spielzeugmuseum is chock-full of miniature trains, dolls, wooden soldiers and other childhood delights. It's also accessible from Hauptmarkt 14; an entrance for visitors with limited mobility is located at Jakobstrasse 4-5.

Thermen am Viehmarkt
ROMAN SITE

(Forum Baths; Viehmarktplatz; adult/child €4/2.50; ⊗9am-5pm Tue-Sun) Found by accident in 1987 during the construction of a parking garage, and buried beneath WWII air-raid shelters, the remains of a 17th-century Capucinian monastery, one-time vineyards and cemeteries, these thermal baths are sheltered by a dramatic glass cube.

Römerbrücke
ROMAN SITE

(Roman Bridge; Karl Marx Strasse) Spanning the Moselle, Germany's oldest bridge uses 2nd-century stone pilings (AD 144–152), built from black basalt from the Eifel mountains, which have been holding it up since legionnaires crossed on chariots.

St-Gangolf-Kirche
CHURCH

(⊗7am-6pm) Topped by a 62m-high tower, the Gothic St-Gangolf-Kirche was built in the early 15th century on the site of a

(Trier Cinema), where you can see almost 80 short films of Trier, some made as far back as 1904. Admission includes an audioguide, with a special audioguide available for children.

Trier

14th-century tower. It's reached via a flowery portal on the Hauptmarkt.

Rotes Haus   HISTORIC BUILDING
(Red House; Dietrichstrasse 53; ⊘interior closed to the public) On the Hauptmarkt, the Rotes Haus was the house of the bakers' guild master and secretary of the cathedral chapter, Johann Wilhelm Polch.

🏃 Activities

Weinkulturpfad   HIKING
(Wine Culture Path) Panoramic views unfold from Petrisberg, the vine-covered hill just east of the Roman amphitheatre. Halfway up, the Weinkulturpfad leads through the grapes to Olewig (1.6km). Next to the Petrisberg/Aussicht stop for buses 4 and 85, a multilingual panel (Sickingenstrasse) traces local history from the first known human habitation (30,000 years ago) through the last ice age to the Romans.

Radstation   CYCLING
(Fahrradservicestation; ☑0651-148 856; www.bues-trier.de; Bahnhofsplatz; adult/child/electric bike per day from €12/6/30; ⊙9am-6pm May-Sep, 10am-6pm Mon-Fri, to 2pm Sat Oct-Apr) Bikes in tip-top condition can be rented at the Hauptbahnhof's Radstation, next to track 11. Staff are enthusiastic about cycling and can provide tips on routes.

☞ Tours

Kolb   CRUISE
(☑0651-26 666; www.moselrundfahrten.de; Georg-Schmitt-Platz 2; ⊙May-Oct) Choose from a range of river tours such as a 4¼-hour trip to Bernkastel (one-way/return €25/35). Trips leave from the boat docks (Zurlaubener Ufer).

City Walking Tour   WALKING
(adult/child €7.90/4.50; ⊙1pm May-Oct) Guided 75-minute walking tours in English begin at the tourist office.

🛏 Sleeping

Trier is a popular weekend getaway and hotel prices rise on Friday and Saturday. Options range from hostels and inexpensive family-run properties to some excellent city-centre independent and chain hotels and boutique gems in the vine-ribboned surrounds.

Evergreen Hostel   HOSTEL €
(☑1578 856 9594, 0651-6998 7026; www.evergreen-hostel.de; Gartenfeldstrasse 7; dm from €19,

s/d from €44/56, without bathroom from €40/50; ⊘reception 8-11am & 2-7pm May-Oct, 9-11am & 3-6pm Nov-Apr; @ 🕾) This laid-back indie hostel has a piano, well-equipped self-catering kitchen and attractive, spacious rooms, most with private bathrooms. Breakfast costs €8. Outside reception hours, call ahead to arrange your arrival.

★ **Hotel Villa Hügel** BOUTIQUE HOTEL €€
(🖉0651-937 100; www.hotel-villa-huegel.de; Bernhardstrasse 14; s/d from €118/163; P @ 🕾 ☒) You can begin the day with sparkling wine over breakfast at this chic 1914-built hillside villa, and end it luxuriating in the indoor or rooftop pools and Finnish sauna. The 45 rooms are decorated with honey-toned woods; higher-category 'relax' rooms have balconies. Panoramic views extend from its glass-walled gourmet restaurant and flower-filled summer terrace.

Becker's DESIGN HOTEL €€
(🖉0651-938 080; www.beckers-trier.de; Olewiger Strasse 206; hotel s €95-125, d €140-190, ste €210-240, Weinhaus s/d €85/110; P ✳ @ 🕾) In the peaceful wine district of Olewig, across the creek from the old monastery church, 3km southeast of the centre, classy Becker's pairs supremely tasteful rooms – ultramodern in its hotel, rustically traditional in its Weinhaus – with stellar dining (p623).

Hotel Petrisberg HOTEL €€
(🖉0651-4640; www.hotel-petrisberg.de; Sickingenstrasse 11; s €75, d €110, apt €195; P @ 🕾) Incredible views of the city and Roman Amphitheater extend from this traditional, hillside-perched hotel; try for a front room, which comes with a balcony that's idyllic for enjoying a glass of Moselle (the in-house honour bar has wine and beer). It's a great option for cyclists, with lock-up bike storage. A zigzag path leads down the hill into Trier.

Hotel Deutscher Hof HOTEL €€
(🖉0651-977 80; www.hotel-deutscher-hof.de; Südallee 25; s/d from €64/80; P @ 🕾) At the city centre's southern edge, this comfortable, value-priced pad has softly lit and warmly decorated rooms. In summer enjoy breakfast (€9) on the terrace; on colder days head to the sauna (per day €6.50).

Hotel Römischer Kaiser HOTEL €€
(🖉0651-977 0100; www.friedrich-hotels.de; Porta-Nigra-Platz 6; s/d/tr from €93/116/156; P 🕾) Convenient for the train station and the old city, this 1894-built hotel offers 43 bright,

comfortable rooms with solid wood furnishings, parquet floors and spacious bathrooms. Breakfast (€9.50) is a lavish spread; there's an excellent in-house restaurant.

Ante Porta Das Stadthotel HOTEL €€
(🖉0651-436 850; www.hotel-anteporta.de; Paulinstrasse 66; s/d/f from €59/69/100; P 🕾) Named for the landmark Porta Nigra, a 500m walk southwest, this sparkling-clean hotel has contemporary rooms and public areas accented in vibrant jade green. Breakfast costs €9. Gated on-site parking is available but limited so reserve ahead.

🍴 Eating

In the warmer months, cafes fill the Altstadt's public squares, including the Hauptmarkt and Kornmarkt. Summer dining is also popular along the river near the boat docks.

BurgerAMT BURGERS €
(🖉0651-99466341;www.facebook.com/Burgeramt Trier; Nagelstrasse 18; burgers €7-11; ⊘11.30am-9pm Sun-Thu, to 11pm Fri & Sat; 🕾 ♪) Huge burgers at this hip restaurant with a ceiling plastered in music and movie posters include vegetarian options with halloumi or vegetable patties, and a portobello mushroom vegan burger, cooked on a separate grill. Local specialities include a Luxemburger (beef, smoked-bacon marmalade, Limburger cheese and fennel). Sides span coleslaw to sweet potato fries; there are craft beers, milkshakes and Fritz-kola.

Zuppa SOUP €
(www.zuppa-trier.de; Sichelstrasse 18; soup €3-5.50; ⊘11am-7.30pm Mon-Fri, noon-4pm Sat; ♪) Five different soups served with sourdough bread are the mainstay of this bright little hole in the wall: two vegetarian, one vegan and two meat-based. Soups change daily but might include lentil and spinach, potato with pork sausage, curried pumpkin, and asparagus and cabbage. Finish off with semolina or almond cake.

Kartoffel Kiste GERMAN €
(www.kistetrier.de; Fahrstrasse 13-14; mains €7-17; ⊘11.30am-10pm; ♪ ♨) Fronted by a bronze fountain, local favourite Kartoffel Kiste specialises, as its name suggests, in baked, breaded, gratinéed, soupified and sauce-doused potatoes. If you're after something heartier (albeit pricier), it also does great schnitzel and steaks. There are 220 seats inside and, in warmer weather, another 120 on the terrace.

CYCLE TOURING: FIVE RIVERS IN FIVE DAYS

Trier makes an ideal base for day trips by bike, with five different riverside bike paths (www.radwanderland.de) to choose from. Trains and RegioRadler buses (www.mosel-bahn.de), which have bike trailers, make it possible to ride one way (ie downhill) and take public transport the other.

Esterbauer (www.esterbauer.com) publishes Bikeline cycling guides with maps.

Kylltal-Radweg From Losheimergraben on the Belgian border, this route parallels the Cologne-Trier railway line 121.4km southeast along the Kyll (pronounced *kool*) River. Take the train between Erdorf and Kyllburg (five to seven minutes) to avoid a killer hill.

Mosel-Radweg (www.radweg-reisen.com) Beginning in Metz in France, the 311km Mosel-Radweg passes through Trier before continuing downriver to Koblenz. Parts are served by bus.

Ruwer-Hochwald-Radweg (www.ruwer-hochwald-radweg.de) This 50km bike path runs along a one-time rail line from Hunsrück, following the Ruwer River (a tributary of the Moselle) through picturesque wine-growing country to Ruwer, 19km southeast of Trier. Some bus services are available.

Saar-Radweg Starting in Strasbourg in France, this route runs 210km along the mostly gorgeous, partly industrial Saar River via Saarbrücken to Konz, 9km southwest of Trier, where the Saar and Moselle rivers meet.

Sauertal-Radweg From Ettelbruck in Luxembourg, this 61.2km path follows a de-commissioned rail line north along the Sauer River to Wasserbillig, 13km west of Trier. Northern variants follow the Prüm and Nims Rivers. Buses serve some areas.

Children's dishes, such as Bob the Builder (small pork schnitzel) or Pippi Longstocking (sausages and fries) are €5.

Food Market
MARKET €

(Viehmarktplatz; ⊙7am-2pm Tue & Fri Apr-Sep, from 8am Oct-Mar) The city centre's largest outdoor market is a perfect place to pick up fresh local produce for a riverside picnic.

★ Weinwirtschaft Friedrich-Wilhelm
GERMAN €€

(☑0651-994 7480; www.weinwirtschaft-fw.de; Weberbach 75; mains €12.50-27.50; ⊙11.30am-2.30pm & 5.30-10pm Mon-Fri, 11.30am-10pm Sat & Sun) A historic former wine warehouse with exposed brick and joists now houses this superb restaurant. Creative dishes incorporate local wines, such as trout poached in sparkling white wine with mustard sauce and white asparagus, or local sausage with Riesling sauerkraut and fried potatoes. Vines trail over the trellis-covered garden; the attached wine shop is a great place to stock up.

Alt Zalawen
GERMAN €€

(☑0651-286 45; www.altzalawen.de; Zurlaubener Ufer 79; mains €6-18; ⊙kitchen 11am-10pm, closed Sun Nov-Mar; 🐾) The pick of the cluster of bar/restaurants right on the riverfront, with terraces extending to the path running along the grassy bank, timber-panelled Alt Zalawen is a picturesque spot for traditional German specialities (schnitzels, sausages, *Spätzle*) and local Trierer Viez cider.

Weinstube Kesselstatt
GERMAN €€

(☑0651-411 78; www.weinstube-kesselstatt.de; Liebfrauenstrasse 10; mains €8-20; ⊙kitchen 11.30am-2.30pm & 6-10pm Sun-Fri, 11.30am-10pm Sat, bar 10am-midnight) Dining on quality regional produce – and sampling the local whites – is a serious pleasure at this charming *Weinstube*, either in the barrel-filled, dark-timber interior housing a huge wooden wine press, or in the tree-shaded, flower-filled summer garden facing the cathedral. Seasonal specialities utilise ingredients like mushrooms, game or asparagus. Order at the bar.

Zum Domstein
INTERNATIONAL €€

(☑0651-744 90; www.domstein.de; Hauptmarkt 5; mains €9-18.50, Roman menu €17-31; ⊙11.30am-9.30pm, Roman menu from 5.30pm) Feast like a Roman on dishes based on the recipes of 1st-century local chef Marcus Gavius Apicius: mulled Moselle white wine followed by barley soup, pine-nut-stuffed sausage, artichokes with boiled eggs, ham with figs and almonds, and wine-sautéed pears with custard, honey and green peppercorns. During the day it serves more conventional German and international fare.

★ **Weinhaus Becker** INTERNATIONAL €€€
(📞 0651-938 080; www.beckers-trier.de; Olewiger Strasse 206; 1-/3-course lunch menu €18/28, 3-/4-course dinner menu €45/58, mains €21-34; ⏰ noon-2pm & 6-10pm Tue-Sun) Within the Becker's (p621) hotel complex, 3km southeast of the centre, this supremely elegant wine-house serves sublime internationally influenced dishes like cod with pumpkin, banana and macadamia nuts, or quail with parsnip foam and roasted mushrooms, accompanied by (very) local wines made from grapes grown on the hillside opposite. Also here is the ultragourmet, twin-Michelin-starred Becker's Restaurant (5-/8-course dinner menu €125/158; ⏰ 7-9pm Tue-Sat).

🍷 Drinking & Nightlife

Traditional *Weinstuben* (wine taverns) scatter throughout the Olewig district, 3km southeast of the centre.

Weingut Georg Fritz von Nell WINERY
(📞 0651-323 97; www.vonnell.de; Im Tiergarten 12; ⏰ cellar door tastings 5.15-6pm, wine bar 6pm-midnight Wed-Sat) To appreciate the Riesling, rivaner, Elbling and chardonnay at this rustic seven-generation *Weingut* without worrying about driving, its bus can pick you up from Trier's tourist office (per person including four tastings €10; reserve ahead). Otherwise make your own way 2.5km southeast of Trier's centre. Its walled courtyard is lovely on summer evenings.

Weinhaus Minarski WINE BAR
(📞 0651-998 0621; www.weinhaus-minarski.de; Kochstrasse 8; ⏰ 10am-noon & 3-8pm Tue & Wed, to midnight Thu & Fri, 10am-midnight Sat) Whites, reds, rosés and sparkling wines from local and regional vineyards are available by the glass or bottle at this stylish city-centre wine bar. Regular themed evenings might include 'scampi and riesling' or Spanish tapas.

Zebra Club CLUB
(www.trierwirdwild.de; Stockplatz 2a; ⏰ 11pm-6am Thu, 10pm-7am Fri, 11pm-7am Sat) Set over two storeys in a baroque stone building, Zebra is Trier's best club, with international DJs spinning hip-hop, dance, house and electronica.

☆ Entertainment

The tourist office has details on concerts and other cultural activities and sells tickets.

TuFa PERFORMING ARTS
(📞 0651-718 2410; www.tufa-trier.de; Wechselstrasse 4-6) Housed in a former *Tuchfabrik* (towel factory), this vibrant cultural events venue hosts cabaret, live music of all sorts, theatre and dance performances.

🛍 Shopping

Kleine Fluchten SPORTS & OUTDOORS
(www.kleinefluchtenoutdoor.de; Margaretengässchen 4; ⏰ 10am-7pm Mon-Fri, to 4pm Sat) Stock up on everything you need for a vineyard hike or other outdoor activities at this independent outdoors shop. Along with clothing and footwear, it has a great range of tents, sleeping bags, rucksacks, compasses, cooking equipment and more, mostly by German brands.

Hop Shop DRINKS
(Neustrasse 63; ⏰ noon-7pm Tue-Sat) Over 250 craft beers are stocked at this specialist boutique, most of them German, such as liquorice oatmeal stout from Pax Bräu, Sunday Pale Ale from And Union, Backbone Splitter IPA from Hanscraft & Co and Baltic ale from Insel Bräuerei. A small fridge has ready-to-drink cold brews.

ℹ Information

DISCOUNT CARDS

The **Antiquities Card** (including Rheinisches Landesmuseum and 2/4 Roman sites €12/18) is a great deal for Trier's most interesting antiquities. It's sold at the tourist office and each site.

Using the **TrierCard** (adult/family €9.90/21) for three consecutive days you get 10% to 25% off museum and monument admissions, unlimited use of public transport, and other discounts. Buy it at the tourist office.

TOURIST INFORMATION

Tourist Office (📞 0651-978 080; www.trier-info.de; An der Porta Nigra; ⏰ 9am-6pm Mon-Sat, 10am-5pm Sun Mar-Dec, 10am-5pm Mon-Sat Jan & Feb)

ℹ Getting There & Around

Trier has frequent train connections to Saarbrücken (€20.90, one to 1½ hours, two per hour) and Koblenz (€24, 1½ to two hours, two per hour).

There are also regular trains to Luxembourg City (€19.40, 50 minutes, at least hourly), with onward connections to Paris (€80, 3½ to 4½ hours, at least hourly).

The city centre is easily explored on foot. Buses (www.vrt-info.de) cost €2; a public transport day pass costs €5.90. The Olewig wine district is served by buses 6, 16 and 81. There are bus stops on Bahnhofsplatz.

Bikes in tip-top condition can be rented at the Hauptbahnhof's Radstation (p620), next to track 11, and from the tourist office, as well as many hotels.

SAARLAND

The French influence on this border region is readily apparent. While the tiny federal state of Saarland is now solidly within German boundaries, many locals are bilingual and the standard greeting is not 'hallo' but 'salü', from the French 'salut'. Their French heritage, although somewhat imposed, means Saarlanders have an appreciation of good cuisine, fine wine and a laid-back lifestyle – 'Saarvoir vivre', it's called.

Over the centuries, France and Germany have played ping pong with Saarland, coveting it for its valuable natural resources. In the 20th century, the region came under French control twice – after each of the world wars – but in both cases (in referendums held in 1935 and 1955) its people voted in favour of rejoining Germany.

Long a land of coal and heavy industry, Saarland has in recent decades cleaned up its air and streams and reoriented its economy towards technology and industrial heritage tourism.

Activities

Rolling hills and forest cover much of the Saarland countryside. Cycling paths include the 356km, circular Saarland-Radweg and the 110km Saar-Radweg (VeloRoute Saar-LorLux), along the (mostly) beautiful Saar River. Walking is also superb here.

ⓘ Getting There & Away

Saarbrücken is the main transport hub, with rail and bus connections to destinations in Germany, France and Luxembourg.

Saarbrücken

☏ 0681 / POP 179,709

Saarland's capital has considerable charm. Vestiges of its 18th-century heyday as a royal residence under Prince Wilhelm Heinrich (1718–68) survive in the baroque town houses and churches designed by his prolific court architect, Friedrich Joachim Stengel.

Saarbrücken is home to the main Universität des Saarlandes (Saarland University)

campus, whose 17,000-plus students add to the city's dynamic energy.

◉ Sights

From the Hauptbahnhof, at the northwestern end of the city centre, pedestrian-only Reichsstrasse and its continuation Bahnhofstrasse – the attractive main shopping street – lead 1km southeast to St Johanner Markt.

Moderne Galerie   MUSEUM
(☏ 0681-996 40; www.kulturbesitz.de; Bismarckstrasse 11-15; adult/child €7/free; ⊘ 10am-6pm Tue & Thu-Sun, to 10pm Wed) One of Saarland's cultural highlights, the Saarland Museum's Moderne Galerie covers European art from the late 1800s to the present, and is especially noteworthy for its works of German Impressionism (Slevogt, Corinth and Liebermann), French Impressionism (Monet, Sisley, Renoir and more) and expressionism (Kirchner, Marc and von Jawlensky). The Galerie der Gegenwart focuses on contemporary art.

Alte Sammlung   MUSEUM
(☏ 0681-954 050; www.kulturbesitz.de; Schlossplatz 16; adult/child €5/free, after 3pm Tue free; ⊘ 10am-6pm Tue & Thu-Sun, to 10pm Wed) The Saarland Museum's Alte Sammlung ('old collection') displays a millennium's worth of paintings, porcelain, tapestries and sculptures from southwest Germany and the Alsace and Lorraine regions of France.

Basilika St Johann   CHURCH
(www.pfarrei-st-johann.de; Gerberstrasse 31; ⊘ 9.30am-7.15pm Mon, Fri & Sat, from 8.30am Tue, Thu & Sun, 8.30am-5pm Wed) This dazzlingly baroque Catholic church, designed by Friedrich Joachim Stengel and completed in 1758, wows you with its gleaming gold altars, pulpit, organ case and overhead ray-burst design – and with its legions of ubercute putti. As you face the facade, the entrance is to the left around the side on Türkenstrasse.

Historisches Museum Saar   MUSEUM
(☏ 0681-506 4506; www.historisches-museum.org; Schlossplatz 15; adult/child €6/free; ⊘ 10am-6pm Tue & Thu-Sun, to 8pm Wed) The Saarbrücker Schloss' basement and a modern annex house the well-designed Museum of Regional History. The section covering Saarland from 1870 to the 1950s includes a 1904 film of Saarbrücken street life. From here you can descend to the castle's massive bastions and Kasematten (casemates; English brochure available). Other exhibits look at

Saarland under French rule (1920–35) and during the Nazi regime.

Museum für Vor- und Frühgeschichte
MUSEUM

(Museum of Early History & Prehistory; ☑0681-954 050; www.kulturbesitz.de; adult/child €5/free, after 3pm Tue free; ☉10am-6pm Tue & Thu-Sun, to 10pm Wed) The standout exhibit at this museum covering the Romans, the Celts and their predecessors is resplendent gold jewellery from around 400 BC, discovered in the tomb of a Celtic princess at Bliesbruck-Reinheim.

Museum in der Schlosskirche
MUSEUM

(☑0681-954 050; www.kulturbesitz.de; Am Schlossberg 6; ☉10am-6pm Tue & Thu-Sun, to 10pm Wed) **FREE** Inside a desanctified late-Gothic church, the Museum in der Schlosskirche features religious art from the 13th to 19th centuries. Highlights include the elaborate tombs of three 17th- and 18th-century princes.

Schlossplatz
SQUARE

Crossing the Saar River via the footbridge Alte Brücke takes you to the Stengel-designed baroque Schlossplatz, around which you'll find the city's ensemble of museums. The dominant building here is the **Saarbrücker Schloss**, which incorporates several architectural styles from Renaissance to baroque to neoclassical. The northern wing was once used by the Gestapo as offices and detention cells.

St Johanner Markt
SQUARE

The heart of Saarbrücken, historic St Johanner Markt is a long, narrow public square anchored by an ornate fountain designed by Friedrich Joachim Stengel and flanked by some of the town's oldest buildings.

Ludwigskirche
CHURCH

(www.ludwigskirche.de; Ludwigsplatz; ☉11am-5pm Tue-Sat, to 3pm Sun) The star at Friedrich Joachim Stengel's handsome Ludwigsplatz, flanked by stately baroque town houses, is his architectural masterpiece, Ludwigskirche. A Protestant church built in 1775 and rebuilt after its destruction in WWII, it sports a facade festooned with biblical figures and a brilliant white interior with stylish stucco decoration.

🏃 Activities

BBQ Donuts
BOATING

(☑0681-9331 7094; www.saarsspass.de; Schillerplatz; 2hr boat hire from €67.60; ☉Mar-Oct) A unique

---

WORTH A TRIP

SAARSCHLEIFE
....

The most scenic spot along the Saar River is the Saarschleife, 60km northwest of Saarbrücken, where the river makes a spectacular, almost unbelievable hairpin turn, flowing 10km to return to a point just 2km from where it started. In a large nature park 6km northwest of Mettlach, the 42m-high viewing platform **Baumwipfelpfad Saarschleife** (☑06865-186 4810; www.baumwipfelpfad-saarschleife.de; Cloef-Atrium, Meltlach-Orscholz; adult/child €10/8, guided tour €3; ☉9.30am-7pm May-Sep, to 6pm Apr & Oct, to 4pm Nov-Mar, guided tour by reservation) is reached by a 1.25km elevated walkway above the forest from the car park. Both the walkway and viewing platform are wheelchair accessible.

---

way to get out on the river is to hire a 'bbq donut' – a circular, umbrella-shaded boat powered by a 4hp engine (no boat licence necessary) with a charcoal barbecue grill at its centre and an inbuilt sound system. Boats accommodate up to 10 people. Buy barbecue packs (sausages, steaks, sauces) from its kiosk or bring your own. Plates, cutlery, tongs etc are provided.

🛏 Sleeping

Hotel Madeleine
HOTEL €

(☑0681-857 780; www.hotel-madeleine.de; Cecilienstrasse 5; s/d from €65/71; @🖢) 🖉 Impressively eco-conscious, this central, family-operated hotel has 31 bright rooms with bold wallpapering, fabrics and furniture like clear-plastic chairs that are comfortable if compact (doubles are 12 to 14 sq metres). Several rooms have church views. Breakfasts are mostly organic, with vegetarian and vegan options.

DJH Hostel
HOSTEL €

(☑0681-330 40; www.jugendherberge.de; Meerwiesertalweg 31; dm/d €24.50/60; 🅿🖢) Peacefully set back from the road 1.7km northeast of the city centre, this modern, 192-bed hostel has en suite rooms and dorms, a barbecue area and a lockable bike storage room. Wi-fi is in public areas only. It's served by buses 101 and 150 from the Rathaus and bus 124 from the Hauptbahnhof (Monday to Friday only).

VÖLKLINGER HÜTTE

The hulking former ironworks of Völklinger Hütte (☑06898-910 0100; www.voelklinger-huette.org; Rathausstrasse 75-79, Völklingen; adult/child €17/free, after 4pm Tue free; ☺10am-7pm Apr-Oct, to 6pm Nov-Mar), 14km northwest of Saarbrücken, are one of Europe's great heavy-industrial relics. Opened in 1873, 17,000 people worked here by 1965 – the height of Germany's post-WWII boom. The plant blasted its last pig iron in 1986 and was declared a Unesco World Heritage Site in 1994.

Trains link Saarbrücken with Völklingen station (10 minutes), from where it's a three-minute walk.

Both Dickensian and futuristic, dystopian and a symbol of renewal, the plant's massive scale dwarfs humans, who nevertheless managed to master the forces of fire, wind and earth in order to smelt iron, without which civilisation as it is today could not exist. Fine views of the whole rusty ensemble can be had from atop a 45m blast furnace (helmet provided). Parts of the vast complex are being reclaimed by trees, shrubs and mosses. Brochures and all signs are in German, English and French.

Colourful works of modern art make a particularly cheerful impression amid the ageing concrete and rusted pipes, beams, conveyors and car-sized ladles. Check out the website for details on exhibitions and events (like summertime jazz concerts). At night, the compound is luridly lit up like a vast science-fiction set.

★**Hotel am Triller** DESIGN HOTEL €€
(☑0681-580 000; www.hotel-am-triller-saarbruecken.de; Trillerweg 57; s/d/ste from €84/99/149; P@🐾🔉) Uphill from Schlossplatz, Triller has art-filled public areas and 110 creative rooms, some with themes such as Musée de Paris, the seductive, red-clad Moulin Rouge, Planet Ocean with porthole-shaped paintings of reefs and fish, and Saarlegenden, featuring Saarland legends in comic-book form above the bed. Its all-organic Mediterranean restaurant, Panorama, has 270-degree views over the city. Breakfast costs €14.50.

Hotel Stadt Hamburg HOTEL €€
(☑0681-379 9890; www.hotel-stadt-hamburg-saarbruecken.de; Bahnhofstrasse 71-73, 3rd fl; s/d from €70/90; P🔉) Artist-owned Hotel Stadt Hamburg has 24 rooms decorated with colourful original watercolours, oils and collages. It can be noisy at night due to the cafes downstairs but the trade-off is the central location and on-site parking (book ahead).

✗ Eating

Saarbrücken's restaurant and cafe scene centres on St Johanner Markt and nearby streets Saarstrasse, Am Stiefel and Kappenstrasse, with cheaper eats along Kaltenbachstrasse.

★**Kalinski** GERMAN €
(www.kalinskibrueder.de; Kaltenbachstrasse 4; dishes €2-8.50; ☺noon-11pm Mon-Thu, to 2am Fri & Sat, 1-10pm Sun) 🍴 Saarbrücken's hippest hang-out is this *Wurstwirtschaft*, which sizzles up street-food-style *Currywurst* (including a fabulous tofu and wheatgerm vegetarian sausage with spicy tomato sauce), pulled pork burgers, *Spätzle*, and meatballs, accompanied by potato or sweet-potato fries and craft beers. Everything, down to the condiments, is preservative-free and made daily on the premises from local produce. Seats spill onto the front pavement.

Brot und Seele BAKERY €
(Kaltenbachstrasse 6; breads & pastries €0.80-4.50, salads & sandwiches €4-10; ☺7.30am-10pm Mon-Fri, from 8am Sat, from 10am Sun) Breads including sourdoughs, soft pretzels and gluten-free loaves are baked continuously throughout the day at this contemporary bakery. Creative sandwiches (such as tofu, roast beetroot and corn; or chicken, Emmental and paprika mayo) and salads (eg roast beef, carrot, radish and walnuts) are made to order. There are three tables inside, with more on the pavement out front in summer.

Zum Stiefel GERMAN €€
(☑0681-936 450; www.der-stiefel.de; Am Stiefel 2; mains €11.50-24.50; ☺restaurant noon-2pm & 6-10pm Mon-Sat, brewery 11.45am-11pm Mon-Thu, to midnight Fri & Sat, 5.30-10pm Sun) One kitchen covers two dining options at this brewery and German restaurant. Zum Stiefel features good-value classic German and *saarländische* dishes, including *Gefüllde* (meat-filled potato dumplings). Next door (the entrance is around the corner), Stiefel-Bräu,

Saarbrücken's oldest microbrewery, also serves meals (from Monday to Saturday) and three beers brewed according to an old Broch family recipe.

🍷 Drinking & Entertainment

The city's lively student nightlife district concentrates around the intersection of Nauwieserstrasse and Cicilienstrasse.

★ Baker Street   BAR

(www.bakerstreetsb.de; Mainzer Strasse 8; ⊙6pm-midnight Mon-Thu, to 2am Fri, noon-2am Sat, 10am-midnight Sun) Named for Sherlock Holmes' fictional home, this is a fabulous Victorian-era-themed bar with crackling open fireplaces. It bills itself as a 'criminal tea room and pub'. Vintage furniture including studded leather couches and book-lined shelves fill Watson's Club; homemade scones with clotted cream are served in the Tea Room; and you can sip British ales like Newcastle Brown in the colonial-style Adventure Salon.

Events range from murder mystery nights to magic shows.

Jules Verne   BAR

(Mainzer Strasse 39; ⊙5pm-midnight Wed & Thu, 3pm-2am Fri, 10am-2am Sat, 10am-10pm Sun; 🛜) Filled with mismatched flea-market-sourced furniture, this free-wheeling bar has jazz and blues concerts, stand-up comedy nights and film screenings. Local craft beers, regional German wines and cocktails are complemented by a small menu of two or three daily dishes, such as schnitzel with red cabbage sauerkraut.

Garage   LIVE MUSIC

(www.garage-sb.de; Bleichstrasse 11-15; ⊙nightclub 11pm-5am Fri & Sat) Industrial 1920s brick surrounds provide great acoustics at this live music venue, where punk, alternative, metal and rock bands take to the stage. Concerts generally start around 7pm. On weekends it also hosts a small nightclub, Kleiner Klub (www.kleinerklub.de) with dance, techno and reggae nights.

Staatstheater   THEATRE

(☑0681-309 2486; www.theater-saarbruecken.de; Schillerplatz; ⊙box office 10am-6pm Mon-Fri, to 2pm Sat) The grandiose, golden-hued Staatstheater was built on Hitler's orders to thank the Saarlanders for their 1935 vote to rejoin Germany. It opened in 1938 with Richard Wagner's *The Flying Dutchman* and today presents opera, ballet, classical music concerts, drama and musicals.

ℹ Information

Tourist Office (☑0681-9590 9200; www.saarbruecken.de; Rathausplatz 1; ⊙9am-6pm Mon-Fri, 10am-4.30pm Sat) Inside the Rathaus St-Johann, a red-brick neo-Gothic structure built from 1897 to 1900, this helpful office has region-wide info and sells cycling guides and tickets for cultural events.

ℹ Getting There & Around

Saarbrücken's Hauptbahnhof has rail connections to Mainz (€24, 2¼ hours, at least hourly) and Trier (€20.90, 1¼ hours, two per hour), via Völklingen.

Trains run south to the lovely French city of Metz (€17.40, one hour, 10 daily) – ideal for a cross-border day-trip.

Saarbrücken has an integrated bus and rail network (www.saarbahn.de) that also includes one tram line, called S1. Tickets within the city cost €2.60 (€1.90 for up to five stops); a day pass for one/five people costs €5.80/11.60.

Cologne & Northern Rhineland

POP 17.9 MILLION (NORTH RHINE–WESTPHALIA)

Best Places to Eat

➡ Salon Schmitz (p640)

➡ Altes Gasthaus Leve (p685)

➡ Bei Oma Kleinmann (p640)

➡ Am Knipp (p659)

➡ Brauerei im Füchschen (p665)

➡ Münstermann Kontor (p666)

Best Places to Stay

➡ Hopper Hotel et cetera (p638)

➡ Qvest Hideaway (p639)

➡ Klever Tor (p669)

➡ Factory Hotel (p684)

➡ 25hours Hotel Das Tour (p665)

➡ Hotel Drei Könige (p658)

Why Go?

Cologne's iconic Dom has twin towers that might as well be exclamation marks after the word 'welcome'. Flowing behind the cathedral, the Rhine provides a vital link for some of the region's highlights – Düsseldorf, with its great nightlife, architecture and shopping; and Bonn, the former capital, which hums to Beethoven. Away from the river, Aachen still echoes to the beat of the Holy Roman Empire and Charlemagne.

Much of Germany's 20th-century economic might stemmed from the northern Rhineland industrial region known as the Ruhrgebiet. Now that the mines are closed and the steelworks are silent, cities such as Essen and Bochum are transforming them into progressive cultural playgrounds. Dortmund is literally scoring with its Bundesliga (Premier League) football team, the national soccer museum and beer making tradition. In the flat northern reaches, Xanten's archaeological excavations bring Roman history to life, while Münster is an endlessly interesting and vibrant student town.

When to Go

Although the region has plenty of beer gardens and restaurants that delight in warm weather, much of what's best happens indoors so you can visit any time.

Come in summer for outdoor explorations such as cycling along the Rhine, hiking the Red Wine Trail in the Ahr Valley, or rambling around the forests of the Eifel National Park or the Sauerland.

Summertime is also peak festival season, with plenty of music, fireworks, fun fairs and other shenanigans filling the calendar.

Sure it's cold in December but the Christmas markets will warm you up. Just a couple of months later, Cologne's Carnival is one of Europe's best, with Düsseldorf's not far behind.

COLOGNE

📞 0221 / POP 1,075 MILLION

Cologne (Köln) offers a mother lode of attractions, led by its famous cathedral whose filigree twin spires dominate the skyline. The city's museum landscape is especially strong when it comes to art but also has something in store for fans of chocolate, sports and even Roman history. Cologne's people are known for their liberalism and joie de vivre; it's easy to have a good time with them in the beer halls of the Altstadt or during Carnival.

Cologne is like a living textbook on history and architecture: drifting about town you'll stumble upon an ancient Roman wall, medieval churches galore, nondescript postwar buildings, avant-garde structures and a new postmodern quarter right on the Rhine.

Germany's fourth-largest city was founded by the Romans in 38 BC and given the lofty name Colonia Claudia Ara Aggripinensium. It grew into a major trading centre, a tradition solidified in the Middle Ages and upheld today.

◉ Sights

Plan on a couple of days to explore Cologne's wealth of sights. The city maintains an excellent website (www.museenkoeln.de) with info on most of Cologne's museums. The **MuseumsCard** (per person/family €18/30) is good for one-time admission to all municipal museums on two consecutive days.

◉ Altstadt

The Altstadt hugs the riverbank between two bridges, the Hohenzollernbrücke and Deutzer Brücke. You can easily spend a few hours just strolling and soaking it all in.

★**Kölner Dom**   CATHEDRAL
(Cologne Cathedral; 📞 0221-9258 4720; www. koelner-dom.de; Domkloster 4; tower adult/ concession €4/2; ⊙6am-9pm May-Oct, to 7.30pm Nov-Apr, tower 9am-6pm May-Sep, to 5pm Mar, Apr & Oct, to 4pm Nov-Feb; 🚊5, 16, 18 Dom/ Hauptbahnhof) Cologne's geographical and spiritual heart – and its single-biggest tourist draw – is the magnificent Kölner Dom. With its soaring twin spires, this is the Mt Everest of cathedrals, jam-packed with art and treasures. For an exercise fix, climb the 533 steps up the Dom's south tower to the base of the steeple that dwarfed all buildings in Europe until Gustave Eiffel built a certain tower in Paris. The Domforum

visitor centre is a good source of info and tickets.

The Dom is Germany's largest cathedral and must be circled from the outside to truly appreciate its dimensions. Note how its lacy spires and flying buttresses create a sensation of lightness and fragility despite its mass and height.

This feeling of airiness continues inside, where a phalanx of pillars and arches supports the lofty nave. Soft light filters through the medieval stained-glass windows, as well as a much-lauded recent window by contemporary artist Gerhard Richter in the right transept. A kaleidoscope of 11,500 squares in 72 colours, Richter's abstract design has been called a 'symphony of light'; in the afternoon especially, when the sun hits it just so, it's easy to understand why.

The pièce de résistance among the cathedral's bevy of treasures is the Shrine of the Three Kings behind the main altar, a richly bejewelled and gilded sarcophagus said to hold the remains of the kings who followed the star to the stable in Bethlehem where Jesus was born. The bones were spirited out of Milan in 1164 as spoils of war by Emperor Barbarossa's chancellor and instantly turned Cologne into a major pilgrimage site.

Other highlights include the Gero Crucifix (970), notable for its monumental size and an emotional intensity rarely achieved in those early medieval days; the choir stalls from 1310, richly carved from oak; and the altar painting (c 1450) by Cologne artist Stephan Lochner.

During your climb up to the 95m-high viewing platform on the south tower, take a breather and admire the 24-tonne Peter Bell (1923), the largest free-swinging working bell in the world.

To get more out of your visit, invest €1 in the information pamphlet or join a guided tour.

ⓘ DOM INDEPTH

Join a **guided tour** (📞0221-9258 4730; www.koelner-dom.de; Kardinal-Höffner-Platz; adult/concession €8/6; ⊙tours in English 10.30am & 2.30pm Mon-Sat, 2.30pm Sun Apr-Oct, less often rest of year; 🚊5, 16, 18 Dom/Hauptbahnhof) to get more out of your visit to Kölner Dom. Tours meet inside the main portal. No reservations are needed.

Cologne & Northern Rhineland Highlights

1 Kölner Dom
(p629) Feeling your spirits soar as you gaze up at the loftiness of Cologne's majestic cathedral.

2 Cologne's beer halls (p641) Losing count of the little glasses of *Kölsch* beer you've had in the city's atmospheric pubs.

3 Düsseldorf's art museums Drinking in European art before comparing the city's iconic *Altbier* brew to rival Cologne's *Kölsch.*

4 Zeche Zollverein (p671) Experiencing a 21st-century spin on the Industrial Age at this Unesco-honoured former coal mine in Essen.

5 Aachen (p655) Stepping back to the Middle Ages with memories of Charlemagne around every corner.

6 Münster (p680) Enjoying the city's vibrant life where great history combines with youthful pleasures.

7 Rotweinwanderweg (p653) Stumbling along this trail leading through the beautiful Ahr Valley linking villages and wineries.

8 Soest (p689) Basking in the ethereal green glow of the pristine medieval town's native limestone churches.

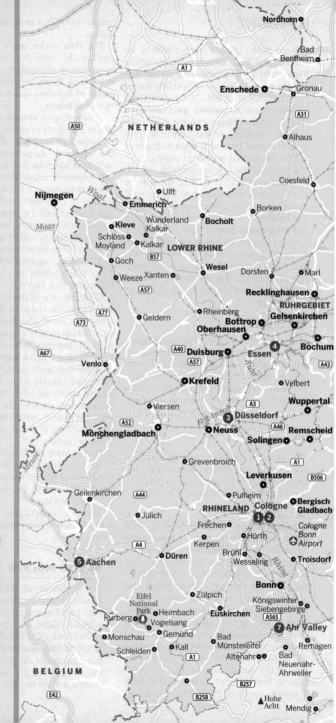

Domschatzkammer
MUSEUM

(Cathedral Treasury; ☑ 0221-1794 0530; www.dombau-koeln.de; Domkloster 4; adult/concession €6/3; ☺ 10am-6pm; ⛟ 5, 16, 18 Dom/Hauptbahnhof) Reliquaries, robes, sculptures and liturgical objects are handsomely presented in medieval vaulted rooms below the main floor of the Dom. Standouts include a Gothic bishop's staff from 1322 and a 15th-century sword.

The main entrance is on the north side of the cathedral, but there's also access from the left transept inside.

★ Wallraf-Richartz-Museum & Fondation Corboud
MUSEUM

(☑ 0221-2212 1119; www.wallraf.museum; Obenmarspforten; adult/concession €9/5.50; ☺ 10am-6pm Tue-Sun; ⛟ 1, 7, 9 Heumarkt, ⛟ 5 Rathaus) One of Germany's finest art museums, the Wallraf-Richartz presents a primo collection of European art from the 13th to the 19th centuries in a minimalist cube designed by the late OM Ungers. All the marquee names are here – Rubens and Rembrandt to Manet and Monet – along with a prized sampling of medieval art, most famously Stefan Lochner's *Madonna in Rose Bower*, nicknamed the 'Mona Lisa of Cologne'.

Museum Ludwig
MUSEUM

(☑ 0221-2212 6165; www.museum-ludwig.de; Heinrich-Böll-Platz; adult/concession €12/8, more during special exhibits; ☺ 10am-6pm Tue-Sun; ⛟ 5, 16, 18 Dom/Hauptbahnhof) A mecca of modern art, Museum Ludwig presents a tantalising mix of works from all major genres. Fans of German expressionism (Beckmann, Dix, Kirchner) will get their fill here as much as those with a penchant for Picasso, American pop art (Warhol, Lichtenstein) and Russian avant-garde painter Alexander Rodchenko. Rothko and Pollock are highlights of the abstract collection, while Gursky and Tillmanns are among the reasons the photography section is a must-stop.

A free audioguide may be downloaded from the website.

★ Römisch-Germanisches Museum
MUSEUM

(Roman Germanic Museum; ☑ 0221-2212 4438; www.roemisch-germanisches-museum.de; Roncalliplatz 4; adult/concession/under 18yr €6.50/3.50/free; ☺ 10am-5pm Tue-Sun; ⛟ 5, 16, 18 Dom/Hauptbahnhof) Sculptures and ruins displayed outside the entrance are merely the overture to a full symphony of Roman

artefacts found along the Rhine. Highlights include the giant Poblicius tomb (AD 30–40), the magnificent 3rd-century Dionysus mosaic, and astonishingly well-preserved glass items. Insight into daily Roman life is gained from toys, tweezers, lamps and jewellery, the designs of which have changed surprisingly little since Roman times.

Plenty of remnants of the Roman city survive around the museum, including a street leading to the harbour and two wells. Other vestiges from the ancient settlement include a Roman arch from the former town wall outside the Dom (p629) and the nearby **Römerturm** (Roman Tower; Burgmauer 5; ⛟ 5, 16, 18 Dom/Hauptbahnhof).

Kolumba
MUSEUM

(☑ 0221-933 1930; www.kolumba.de; Kolumbastrasse 4; adult/child €5/free; ☺ noon-5pm Wed-Mon; ⛟ 5 Rathaus) Art, history, architecture and spirituality form a harmonious tapestry in this spectacular collection of the Archdiocese of Cologne's religious treasures. Called Kolumba, the building encases the ruins of the late-Gothic church of St Kolumba, its layers of foundations going back to Roman times, and the Madonna in the Ruins chapel, built on the site in 1950. Exhibits span the arc of religious artistry from the early days of Christianity to the present. Don't miss the 12th-century carved ivory crucifix.

Other exhibits include Coptic textiles, Gothic reliquaries and medieval painting juxtaposed with works by Bauhaus legend Andor Weiniger in edgy room installations.

The museum is yet another magnificent design by Swiss architect Peter Zumthor, 2009 winner of the Pritzker Prize, the 'architectural Oscar'.

Museum für Angewandte Kunst
MUSEUM

(MAKK, Museum of Applied Arts; ☑ 0221-2212 6714; www.makk.de; An der Rechtschule; adult/concession €5/2.50; ☺ 11am-6pm Tue-Sun; ⛟ 5, 16, 18 Appellhofplatz, Dom/Hauptbahnhof) If Aalto, Eames and Olivetti are music to your ears, you should swing by the Museum of Applied Arts, which displays a prestigious and extensive collection of classic and innovative objects in its newly reopened Design section. The historical collection upstairs, meanwhile, will remain closed for restoration for the foreseeable future.

Historisches Rathaus
HISTORIC BUILDING

(Rathausplatz; ☺ 8am-4pm Mon, Wed & Thu, to 6pm Tue, to noon Fri; ⛟ 5 Rathaus) **FREE** Dating to the 15th century and much restored, the old city hall has fine bells that ring daily at noon and 5pm. The Gothic tower is festooned with statues of old city notables, and the plaza out front is popular with wedding parties. Note that the main entrance is closed until at least January 2019 because of construction work. Follow signs to the temporary entrance.

MiQua Archaeological Zone HISTORIC SITE
(http://miqua.lvr.de; Rathausplatz; 📍5 Rathaus) The square in front of Cologne's historical town hall has for years been ripped open as archaeologists unearthed fabulous finds from Roman times and the medieval Jewish quarter. The area is being developed to include a Jewish museum that will extend underground beneath the Rathausplatz. It will incorporate the Roman Praetorium and a Jewish *mikveh* (ritual bath). Completion may happen in 2021.

Praetorium & Roman Sewer HISTORIC SITE
(www.museenkoeln.de; Kleine Budengasse 2; adult/concession €3.50/3; ⊙10am-5pm Tue-Sun; 📍5 Rathaus) Remnants of the Praetorium (governor's palace), the political power nexus of Roman Cologne, have been discovered beneath the medieval town hall. In a well-done exhibit you can discover parts of the foundation along with an old sewer system and items spanning 2000 years unearthed during the excavations.

Church of Gross St Martin CHURCH
(An Gross-St-Martin 9; ⊙9.30am-7.30pm Tue-Sat, noon-7.15pm Sun; 📍5 Rathaus) FREE Winning top honours for Cologne's most handsome church exterior is Gross St Martin, with an ensemble of four slender turrets grouped around a central spire towering above Fischmarkt in the Altstadt.

Dating to the 12th century, it was built on the foundations of a Roman storage hall, which was then on an island in the Rhine.

Church of St Ursula CHURCH
(📞0221-788 0750; Ursulaplatz; treasury adult/concession €2/1; ⊙10am-noon & 3-5pm Mon-Sat, 3-4.30pm Sun; 📍Dom/Hauptbahnhof, Hansaring) If you look at Cologne's coat of arms, you'll see what looks like 11 apostrophes. In fact, the squiggles represent St Ursula and 11,000 virgins who were martyred in Cologne in the 4th century. Today's basilica stands atop the Roman graveyard where the virgins' remains were allegedly found during the building's construction. In the 17th century, the richly ornamented baroque Goldene

Kammer (Golden Chamber) was built to house their relics.

Roman Arch MONUMENT
(Kardinal-Höffner-Platz; 📍5, 16, 18 Dom/Hauptbahnhof) This arch outside the Dom (p629) is a rare vestige of Cologne's ancient Roman city wall and once formed the northern gateway into the colony.

Duftmuseum im Farina-Haus PERFUME
(📞0221-399 8994; www.farina-haus.de; Obenmarspforten 21; tour adult/child €5/free; ⊙10am-7pm Mon-Sat, to 4pm Sun; 🚇Heumarkt) Credit for inventing eau de cologne is usually given to Johann Maria Farina and dated to 1709. This private museum in the original factory building takes you on a 'scent'-sory journey through 300 years of perfume making. It can be visited on guided 45-minute tours (some in English) offered on the hour.

◉ South of the Altstadt

South of Deutzer Brücke await a couple of high-profile riverside museums.

Schokoladenmuseum MUSEUM
(Chocolate Museum; 📞0221-931 8880; www.schokoladenmuseum.de; Am Schokoladenmuseum 1a; adult/student/child €11.50/9/7.50; ⊙10am-6pm Tue-Fri, 11am-7pm Sat & Sun, last entry 1hr before closing; 📍133 Schokoladenmuseum) This boat-shaped, high-tech temple to the art of chocolate making has plenty of engaging exhibits on the 5000-year cultural history of the 'elixir of the gods' (as the Aztecs called it) as well as on the cocoa-growing process. The walk-through tropical forest is a highlight, although most visitors are more enthralled by the glass-walled miniature production facility and a sample at the chocolate fountain.

You can also learn about the mysteries of truffle making, find out how chocolate bunnies are born, have a bespoke chocolate bar created in the workshop and, of course, stop

---

DIGGING UP THE PAST

The area around Cologne's historical city hall (Altes Rathaus) has been a major construction site while a new U-Bahn line is being built. During this time, massive archaeological excavations have unearthed many new discoveries about Cologne's Roman and Jewish past.

Cologne

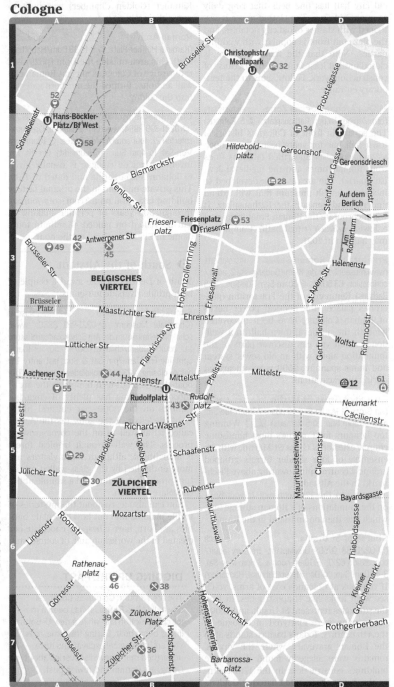

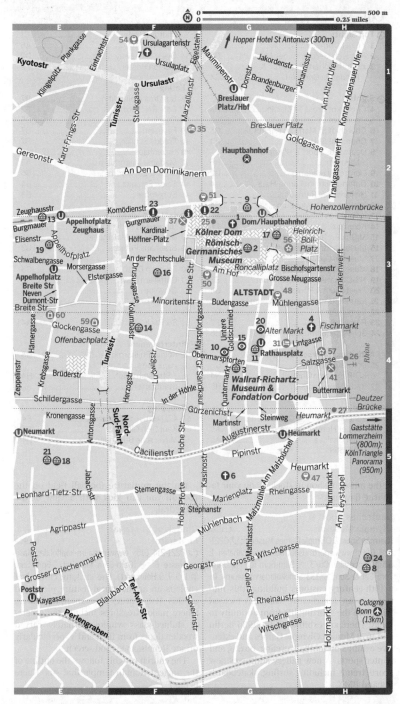

Cologne

in the museum shop to stock up on your favourite flavours.

Deutsches Sport & Olympia Museum
MUSEUM

(German Sport & Olympic Games Museum; ☑ 0221-336 090; www.sportmuseum.de; Im Zollhafen 1; adult/concession €6/3; ☺ 9am-6pm Tue-Fri, 11am-7pm Sat & Sun; ☐ 133 Schokoladenmuseum) In a 19th-century customs building, this museum is an imaginative Germany-focused tribute to the sporting life from antiquity to today. There are exhibits on the 1936 Berlin and 1972 Munich Olympic Games and extensive exhibits on football, cycling, boxing and winter sports. A new gallery addresses new sports trends including surfing, skateboarding and BMX.

On the miniature football field on the rooftop you can kick with a view of the cathedral.

Church of St Maria im Kapitol
CHURCH

(☑ 0221-214 615; www.maria-im-kapitol.de; Kasinostrasse 6; ☺ 10am-6pm Mon-Sat, 1-6pm Sun; ☐ 1, 5, 7, 9 Heumarkt) The striking clover-leaf choir is an architectural feature pioneered at this 11th-century Romanesque church, where major treasures include the ethereal stained-glass window, ornately carved wooden doors from 1065 and a spectacularly ornate Renaissance rood screen.

The church roughly follows the outline of the ancient Roman temple that stood here before.

West of the Altstadt

The area west of busy Tunisstrasse is dotted with several excellent museums, especially near Neumarkt.

Museum Schnütgen MUSEUM

(☑ 0221-2212 2310; www.museum-schnuetgen. de; Cäcilienstrasse 29; adult/concession €6/3.50; ◷ 10am-6pm Tue, Wed & Fri-Sun, to 8pm Thu; ℙ; Ⓤ Neumarkt) The Museum Schnütgen is an exquisite repository of medieval religious art and sculpture from the Rhineland region presented within the serene ambience of the Romanesque Cäcilienkirche, one of Cologne's oldest churches. Outstanding works include the Parler Bust, a crucifix from St George and the ivory Comb of St Heribert.

A combination ticket with the adjacent Rautenstrauch-Joest-Museum costs €10 (concession €7).

Rautenstrauch-Joest-Museum MUSEUM

(Cultures of the World Museum; ☑ 0221-2213 1356; www.museenkoeln.de/rautenstrauch-joest-museum; Cäcilienstrasse 29-33; adult/concession €7/4.50; ◷ 10am-6pm Tue, Wed & Fri-Sun, to 8pm Thu; ℙ; ⌂ 3, 4, 16, 18 Neumarkt) This ethno-museum makes a bold opening statement with a huge rice barn from Sulawesi filling its cavernous lobby. Beyond here are three floors of theme-based exhibits (art, living, death and the afterlife, religions etc) on the cultures of the world; fear not about getting your knuckles rapped – many are interactive and you're encouraged to touch.

Käthe Kollwitz Museum MUSEUM

(☑ 0221-227 2899; www.kollwitz.de; Neumarkt 18-24; adult/concession €5/2; ◷ 10am-6pm Tue-Fri, 11am-6pm Sat & Sun; ⌂ 1, 3, 4, 5, 7, 9 Neumarkt) Käthe Kollwitz (1867–1945) was a famous early 20th-century German artist whose social and political awareness lent a tortured power to her lithographs, graphics, woodcuts, sculptures and drawings. This museum presents an extensive overview of her work, including the famous cycle called *Ein Weberaufstand* (A Weavers' Revolt, 1897).

Enter through an arcade, then take the glass-walled lift to the 4th floor.

NS-Dokumentationszentrum MUSEUM

(NS-DOK; ☑ 0221-2212 6332; www.museenkoeln. de/ns-dokumentationszentrum; Appellhofplatz 23-25; adult/concession €4.50/2; ◷ 10am-6pm Tue-Fri, 11am-6pm Sat & Sun; ⌂ 3, 4, 5, 16, 18 Appellhofplatz) Cologne's Third Reich history is poignantly and exhaustively documented in the NS Documentation Centre housed in the very building that served as the headquarters of the local Gestapo (Nazi secret police). The basement prison, where scores of people were interrogated, tortured and killed, is now a memorial site.

Kölnisches Stadtmuseum MUSEUM

(Cologne City Museum; ☑ 0221-2212 2398; www. koelnisches-stadtmuseum.de; Zeughausstrasse 1-3; adult/concession €5/3; ◷ 10am-8pm Tue, to 5pm Wed-Sun; ⌂ 3, 4, 5, 16, 18 Appellhofplatz) The Kölnisches Stadtmuseum, in the former medieval armoury, explores all facets of Cologne's history. Although the permanent exhibit remains closed while undergoing rehabilitation following water damage suffered in 2017, the dedicated curators mount excellent themed temporary exhibits that shed light on the things that make Cologne unique.

Church of St Gereon CHURCH

(☑ 0221-474 5070; www.stgereon.de; Gereonshof 2; ◷ 10am-6pm Mon-Fri, to 5.30pm Sat, 1-6pm Sun; ⌂ 12, 15 Christophstrasse/Mediapark) The most eccentric looking of Cologne's many Romanesque churches, St Gereon grew from a late-Roman chapel into this massive complex lidded by a 10-sided dome decorated with delicate ribbed vaulting. This translates into a stunning architectural ensemble filled with treasures, beautiful stained-glass windows and red-and-gold dome ceiling.

👉 Tours

KD-Panoramafahrt BOATING

(☑ 0221-258 3011; www.k-d.com; Frankenwerft; adult/concession €10.40/6; ◷ 10.30am-6pm Apr-Oct; ⌂ 1, 5, 7, 9 Heumarkt, ⌂ 5 Rathaus) KD is one of several operators offering one-hour spins on the Rhine taking in the splendid

COLOGNE & NORTHERN RHINELAND COLOGNE

BIRDS-EYE VIEWS

The noise of the city fades to a quiet hum on the viewing platform located at a lofty 103m atop the **KölnTriangle office tower** (☑ 02234-992 1555; www. koelntrianglepanorama.de; Ottoplatz 1; adult/under 12 €3/free; ◷ 11am-11pm Mon-Fri, 10am-11pm Sat & Sun May-Sep, noon-8pm Mon-Fri, 10am-8pm Sat & Sun Oct-Apr; ℙ; Ⓤ Köln Messe/Deutz) on the right Rhine bank across from the Cologne Cathedral (p629). The building, with its shiny glass and aluminum facade, is an eye-catcher in its own right.

COLOGNE FOR CHILDREN

Cologne is an enjoyable place to visit if you're travelling with little ones. The city has plenty of parks and playgrounds, a zoo, beer gardens with play areas, museums with child-friendly exhibits, and restaurants that welcome tots with special menus.

➡ Satisfy everyone's sweet tooth at the Schokoladenmuseum (p633).

➡ The Kölner Dom (p629) is imposing at any age.

➡ Listen to the Glockenspiel at 4711 House of Fragrances (p643)

➡ Take a boat tour (p637) on the Rhine

➡ Ride the lift up the KölnTriangle (p637)

➡ Go underground at a Roman governor's palace (p633)

city panorama. Tours leave every 90 minutes from docks in the Altstadt. Buy tickets online or at the office at the docks.

Radstation Tours CYCLING
(☑0221-139 7190; www.radstationkoeln.de; Marksmannsgasse, Deutzer Brücke; tours incl bike rental €22.50; ⊙1.30pm Apr-Oct; ☐1, 5, 7, 9 Heumarkt) This bike rental (bikes from three hours/day €6/11; ⊙5.30am-10.30pm Mon-Fri, 6.30am-8pm Sat, 8am-8pm Sun; Ⓤ Köln Dom/Hbf) place also runs German/English three-hour bicycle tours that tick off Cologne's main sights on a 15km route.

★ Festivals & Events

Street Food Festival FOOD & DRINK
(www.street-food-festival.de; Heliosstrasse 35-37; €2; ⊙noon-10pm Sat, to 8pm Sun, 1st weekend of month Mar-Sep; ☐3, 4, 13 Venloer Strasse/Gürtel) Eat your way around the world from dozens of trucks and stalls at this food frenzy held monthly on the grounds of an old electric light factory (Heliosgelände) in the northwestern suburb of Ehrenfeld.

🛏 Sleeping

Cologne often hosts trade shows (especially in spring and autumn) when hotel rates can double or even triple. Otherwise, you'll find good-value options throughout the walkable central area. Note that a 5 per cent city tax is added to your hotel bill (business travellers are exempt).

Pension Otto PENSION €
(☑015 785 952 825; www.pensionotto.de; Richard-Wagner-Strasse 18; d €70-80; ➡☎; ☐ Moltkestrasse) This charmingly renovated 1st-floor pension in a 100-year-old apartment building in the trendy Belgisches Viertel is run with panache and personal dedication. The five rooms have contemporary flair, art-

sy touches and high ceilings. The owner is happy to point the compass to the coolest places in town. Breakfast is available (€3.50 to €8).

Station Hostel HOSTEL €
(☑0221-912 5301; www.hostel-cologne.de; Marzellenstrasse 44-56; dm €18-26, s/d from €35/52; @☎; ☐ Hauptbahnhof) Not for introverts, this is as classic a hostel as hostels should be: central, convivial and economical. A lounge gives way to clean, colourful rooms sleeping one to six people in single aluminium-frame beds with reading lamps. Check-in is next to the adjacent Station cafe-bar, which serves breakfast, snacks and cold beer. Some private rooms have their own bathrooms.

★ **25hours Hotel The Circle** HOTEL €€
(☑0221-162 530; www.25hours-hotels.com; Im Klapperhof 22-24; d €120-220; Ⓟ➡✳☎; Ⓤ Friesenplatz) The Cologne edition of this mod lifestyle hotel chain occupies a listed circular building (a former insurance company headquarters) and is bathed in a retro-futuristic design theme. Past the vast lobby with bike rental and DJ corner are good-sized rooms that bulge with quirk, character and zeitgeist-capturing amenities such as Bluetooth speakers.

Catch cathedral views from the 8th-floor restaurant-bar.

★ **Hopper Hotel et cetera** HOTEL €€
(☑0221-924 400; www.hopper.de; Brüsseler Strasse 26; d €90-95; Ⓟ➡@☎☎; ☐ Moltkestrasse) A waxen monk welcomes you to this former monastery that now sports 50 stylish, minimalist rooms with eucalyptus floors, cherry-wood furniture and marble baths along with fridges and iPod docking stations. The sauna in the vaulted cellar is great for reliving the day's exploits, as is the

restaurant in the former chapel with trompe l'oeil apse and garden. Breakfast €13.

Hopper Hotel St Antonius
HOTEL €€

(☎0221-166 00; www.hopper.de; Dagobertstrasse 32; d €95-100; P❄@🅟🛜🐾; Ⓤ Ebertplatz) History and high-tech mix nicely at this 54-room retreat in a historical journeyman's hostel with plenty of eye candy for the style-conscious. The romantic courtyard garden and small spa in the brick-vaulted cellar are great bliss-out spots, while the mounted photographs add artsy splashes.

Optional – and opulent – breakfast is €13 and served in the on-site L.Fritz restaurant, which is popular with locals.

Midtown Hotel
BOUTIQUE HOTEL €€

(☎0221-139 850; http://themidtownhotel.de; Kaiser-Wilhelm-Ring 48; d from €130; P🛜; 🚊 Christophstrasse/Mediapark) Once drab now fab, this hotel on the busy ring road flaunts a passion for contemporary style that is reflected in the owner-designed furniture, atmospheric colour concepts and houndstooth-patterned carpets. None of the 40 rooms, spread across seven floors, are alike, but all guests get to greet the day with the same breakfast bonanza.

Hotel Chelsea
HOTEL €€

(☎0221-207 150; www.hotel-chelsea.de; Jülicher Strasse 1; s/d from €65/80; P❄@🛜; 🚊136, 146 Roonstrasse, 🚊16, 18 Neumarkt) Those fancying an artsy vibe will be well sheltered in this self-titled 'hotel different'. Originals created by international artists in exchange for lodging grace the public areas and 39 rooms. Those on the eye-catching deconstructivist top floor come with air-con and a small terrace.

The cafe, which hosted wild art parties in the '80s and '90s, is excellent. New elevator.

Lint Hotel
HOTEL €€

(☎0221-920 550; www.lint-hotel.de; Lintgasse 7; d from €120; ⊙reception 7am-11pm Mon-Fri, to 6pm Sat & Sun; ❄🛜🐾; 🚊Rathaus) This cute, contemporary and intimate hotel in the heart of the Altstadt has 18 rooms with hardwood floors, warm colours and lots of wood. Outside of reception hours, keys are dispensed from a safety box. Breakfast is €10.

⭐ Qvest Hideaway
DESIGN HOTEL €€€

(☎0221-278 5780; www.qvest-hotel.com; Gereonskloster 12; d from €150; ❄🛜; 🚊Christophstrasse/Mediapark) This dazzling alchemy of historical setting and up-to-the-minute design touches is hidden within the neo-Gothic

ribbed vaults and stone pillars of the former city archives. The carefully chosen art, design classics, midcentury furniture and amenities are likely to inspire loads of decorating ideas (hint: there's a shop that sells some of the objects). Optional breakfast is €20.

🍴 Eating

Multicultural Cologne offers culinary journeys around the world. Make tasty discoveries in Belgisches Viertel and the streets in and around Zülpicher Platz and Ehrenstrasse. Sample traditional Rhenish dishes including *Himmel un Ääd* (mashed potato with blood sausage and apple) at atmospheric beer halls. For street food fans, there's the weekly Meet & Eat Markt and the monthly Street Food Festival.

Freddy Schilling
BURGERS €

(☎0221-1695 5515; www.freddyschilling.de; Kyffhäuserstrasse 34; burgers €7-10; ⊙11.30am-10pm Sun-Thu, to 11pm Fri & Sat; 🚊9 Dasselstrasse/Bf Süd) A wholewheat bun provides a solid framework for the moist patties made with beef from happy cows and drizzled with Freddy's homemade 'special' sauce. Pair it with a side of hand-cut fries or *Rosis* (butter-and-rosemary-tossed baby potatoes). The vegan burger is a toothsome meat-free alternative.

Madame Miammiam
BAKERY €

(☎0221-271 9242; www.madamemiammiam.de; Antwerpener Strasse 39; treats from €3; ⊙11am-2pm Tue-Thu, to 7pm Fri & Sat, 1-5pm Sun; 🚊3, 4, 5, 12, 15 Friesenplatz) This luscious bakery specialises in stunning wedding cakes but also has a mouth-watering range of cupcakes, petit fours, cookies and tarts on display in its little cake shop. Pick your fave, then find a spot on Brüsseler Platz to savour your little treat.

LOCAL KNOWLEDGE

THURSDAY FOOD FRENZY

A combination of farmers market and street-food fair, Meet & Eat (www.meet-and-eat.koeln; Rudolfplatz; ⊙4-9pm Thu; Ⓤ Rudolfplatz) draws locals of all ages to Rudolfplatz on Thursday evenings. Aside from fresh produce, you can pick up homemade pesto, chutney, organic cheeses and other artisanal products or sit down at a covered table for a vegan sausage or succulent burger.

Engelbät

EUROPEAN €

(☏ 0221-246 914; www.engelbaet.de; Engelbertstrasse 7; crêpes €5.50-9; ⊙ 11am-midnight Mon-Thu, to 1am Fri & Sat; ☑; ☐ 9, 12, 15 Zülpicher Platz) This cosy restaurant-pub is famous for its habit-forming crêpes, which come in 50 varieties – sweet or savoury, meat or vegetarian and vegan. Also popular for its breakfasts (served until 3pm) and salads with homemade dressing.

★ Salon Schmitz

EUROPEAN €€

(☏ 0221-139 5577; www.salonschmitz.com; Aachener Strasse 28-34; mains from €10; ⊙ 9am-1am Sun-Thu, open end Fri & Sat; ☐ 1, 7, 12, 15 Rudolfplatz) Spread over three historical row houses, the Schmitz empire is your one-stop shop for excellent food and drink. Greet the day with a lavish breakfast in the retro-hip 1950s and '60s setting of the Salon; order cake, quiche or a hot dish in the Metzgerei, a historical butcher's shop turned deli; or indulge in a fine brasserie-style dinner in the art-nouveau-styled Bar.

It's a perfect pit stop for relaxed chats over coffee, cocktails or creative meals. There are plenty of tables outside.

★ Bei Oma Kleinmann

GERMAN €€

(☏ 0221-232 346; www.beiomakleinmann.de; Zülpicher Strasse 9; mains €13-24; ⊙ 5pm-midnight Tue-Thu & Sun, to 1am Fri & Sat; ☐ 9, 12, 15 Zülpicher Platz) Named for its long-time owner, who was still cooking almost to her last day at age 95 in 2009, this perennially booked, graffiti-covered restaurant serves oodles of schnitzel, made either with pork or veal and paired with homemade sauces and sides. Pull up a seat at the small wooden tables for a classic Cologne night out.

Feynsinn

INTERNATIONAL €€

(☏ 0221-240 9210; www.cafe-feynsinn.de; Rathenauplatz 7; dinner mains €10-23; ⊙ 9am-1am Mon-Thu, to 2am Fri, 9.30am-2am Sat, 10am-1am Sun; ☐ 9, 12 15 Zülpicher Platz) This well-respected Zülpicher Viertel restaurant is an excellent pit stop at any time of the day. Come for extravagant breakfasts, light lunches and creative cakes or a dinner menu that weaves organic seasonal ingredients into sharp-flavoured dishes. Get a table overlooking the park for a meal or just a drink.

Gaststätte Lommerzheim

GERMAN €€

(☏ 0221-814 392; Siegesstrasse 18; mains €10-19; ⊙ 11am-2.30pm & 4.30pm-midnight Mon & Wed-Sat, 10.30am-2.30pm & 4.30pm-midnight Sun; ☐ 1, 7, 9 Deutzer Freiheit) The best reason to wander east across the Hohenzollernbrücke railway bridge over the Rhine is this delightfully old-school pub serving some of the finest pork chops around. Just tell the waiter what sides you want (fries, potato salad etc), then quaff some local beer while you wait for your thick juicy chop.

The pub was founded in 1959 by Hans Lommerzheim, who became a local cult figure. He died in 2004 but has been honoured with a memorial fountain in the beer gaden.

Haxenhaus

GERMAN €€

(☏ 0221-947 2400; www.haxenhaus.de; Frankenwerft 19; mains €12.50-22; ⊙ 11.30am-1am; ☐ 5 Rathaus, ☐ 1, 5, 7, 9 Heumarkt) While the Altstadt has no shortage of mediocre restaurants aimed at beer-swilling tourists, this old place stands out for its classic local and German fare, and is especially famous for its *Haxen* – roast pork knuckles. The menu features a mind-boggling 14 varieties (including a Chinese version) but we recommend sticking with the classic Limburger *Haxe*.

Patio tables have river views.

Café Reichard

CAFE €€

(☏ 0221-257 8542; www.cafe-reichard.de; Unter Fettenhennen 11; mains €6-15; ⊙ 8.30am-8pm; ☐ Dom/Hauptbahnhof) There are plenty of cafes around the Dom (p629), but this slightly hidden one is a true luxe gem with a pedigree going back to 1855. It's best for its luscious cakes but also serves a breakfast buffet, a salad buffet and a decent selection of cooked German dishes. Great people-watching from the terrace tables.

Sorgenfrei

EUROPEAN €€€

(☏ 0221-355 7327; www.sorgenfrei-koeln.com; Antwerpener Strasse 15; per course €16, 3-/4-course dinner €44/58; ⊙ 6pm-midnight Mon-Sat; ☐ 3, 4, 5, 12, 15 Friesenplatz) Dishes are prepared with the same attention to detail (yet lack of pretension) found throughout this casual fine-dining treasure. An excellent wine list, charming hosts and a feel-good ambience make Sorgenfrei a locally adored foodie destination.

Devotees swear by the *steak frites* starring Argentinian entrecôte and homemade fries.

Drinking & Nightlife

Cologne's huge array of thirst parlours range from grungy to grand. Centres of action include the Altstadt, student-flavoured Zülpicher Viertel, trendy Friesenplatz and Belgisches

KÖLSCH BEER & ICONIC BEER HALLS

Cologne has its own style of beer, *Kölsch,* which is light, hoppy, slightly sweet and served cool in *Stangen,* skinny, straight glasses that only hold 0.2L. In traditional Cologne beer halls and pubs you don't order beer so much as subscribe; the constantly prowling waiters will keep dropping off the little glasses of beer until you indicate you've had enough by placing a beer mat on top of your glass.

A ceaseless flow of *Stangen* filled with *Kölsch,* along with earthy humour and platters of meaty local foods, are the hallmarks of Cologne's iconic beer halls. Look for the days when each place serves glorious potato pancakes (*Rievkooche* or *Reibekuchen* in the local dialect).

Brauerei zur Malzmühle (☑0221-9216 0613; https://brauereizurmalzmuehle.de; Heumarkt 6; ⊘11.30am-midnight Mon-Thu, to 1.30am Fri, noon-1am Sat, 11am-11pm Sun; ☑1, 5, 7, 9 Heumarkt) Expect plenty of local colour at this convivial, family-run beer hall attached to a brewery in business since 1858. It serves the popular *Mühlen Kölsch* which has a robust, malty taste. If you prefer a less potent brew, try the *Koch'sches Malzbier* (malt beer, 2% alcohol). Good menu of traditional Cologne brewpub fare (mains €10 to €22.50).

Päffgen (☑0221-135 461; www.paeffgen-koelsch.de; Friesenstrasse 64-66; ⊘10am-midnight Sun-Thu, to 12.30am Fri & Sat; ☑5 Friesenplatz) Busy and boisterous, Päffgen has been pouring *Kölsch* since 1883 and hasn't lost step since. In summer you can enjoy the refreshing brew and local specialities (€4.30 to €15.50) beneath starry skies in the beer garden.

Biergarten Rathenauplatz (☑0221-801 7349; www.rathenauplatz.de/biergarten; Rathenauplatz 30; ⊘noon-11.30pm Apr-Sep; ☑9, 12, 15 Zülpicher Platz) A large, leafy park has one of Cologne's best places for a drink: a community-run beer garden. Tables sprawl under huge old trees, while simple snacks such as salads and very good *Frikadelle* (spiced hamburger) issue forth from a cute little hut.

Prices are cheap and proceeds help maintain the park. There's even a playground to keep the kiddies occupied.

Brauhaus Peters (☑0221-257 3950; www.peters-brauhaus.de; Mühlengasse 1; ⊘11am-12.30am; ☑5 Rathaus) This beautifully restored 19th-century pub draws a crowd knocking back their *Kölsch* in a web of highly individualistic nooks, including a little 'chapel' and a room lidded by a kaleidoscopic stained-glass ceiling. On Tuesdays after 5pm, insiders invade for the freshly made potato pancakes (*Rievkooche* in local dialect, €5.60 to €12.20).

The wood carving over the main entrance translates as: 'Hops and malt, God preserves'. Outside tables abound. Lunch mains are €9; dinner goes for €15 to €30.

Früh am Dom (☑0221-261 3215; www.frueh-am-dom.de; Am Hof 12-18; ⊘11am-midnight Mon-Fri, 9am-midnight Sat & Sun; ☑5, 16, 18 Dom/Hauptbahnhof) This warren of a beer hall near the Dom (p629) epitomises Cologne earthiness and is a great place to sample the typical *Kölsch* beer. Knock them back and tuck into hearty pub grub amid loads of knickknacks or out on the flower-filled terrace next to a fountain.

Snacks go for €4.50 to €7.30; mains are €9 to €22.50.

Schreckenskammer (☑0221-132 581; www.schreckenskammer.com; Ursulagartenstrasse 11; ⊘11am-1.45pm & 4.30-10.30pm Mon-Thu, to midnight Fri & Sat; ☑5, 16, 18 Dom/Hauptbahnhof, ☑12, 15 Hansaring) Empty chairs are a rare sight at this locals' favourite with a pedigree going back to 1442. There's a fine beer garden, excellent food (mains €9 to €20), and should you need divine inspiration for just one more glass, the Romanesque St Ursula (p633) is just across the square.

Gaffel am Dom (☑0221-913 9260; www.gaffelamdom.de; Bahnhofsvorplatz 1; ⊘11am-midnight Sun-Thu, to 2am Fri & Sat; ☑5, 16, 18 Dom/Hauptbahnhof) Right in the shadow of the Dom (p629), this rambling beer hall pours traditional *Kölsch* beer for up to 1200 thirsty guests. Hearty Rhenish dishes, including some of the city's best potato pancakes, provide sustenance (from €7.20).

Viertel, and multicultural Ehrenfeld. Next to Berlin, Cologne has one of the best club scenes for electronic music; the best venues are located outside the Ring.

★Odonien   CLUB
(☑0221-972 7009; www.odonien.de; Hornstrasse 85; ☺beer garden 5pm-late Thu-Sat May-Sep; ⑤Nippes) The brainchild of artist Odo Rumpf, this subculture playground is creative lab, beer garden, concert venue, club, art centre, alfresco cinema and urban garden all rolled into one. In summer, there are few more inspiring places to kick back with a cold *Kölsch* than amid Odo's bizarre metal sculptures. On weekends, techno and house electrify the three dance floors.

Bring the kids – there's a playground to keep them busy.

Gewölbe   CLUB
(www.facebook.com/Gewoelbeklub; Hans-Böckler-Platz 2; ☺11.30pm-6am Fri & Sat; ⓊHans-Böckler-Platz/Bf West) The name translates as Vault so it's quite apropos that you have to negotiate a maze of small rooms to arrive at the main floor at this underground club in Belgisches Viertel. Once there, join in as top DJs shower shiny happy people with house and techno streaming from an amazing sound system until the wee hours.

Bootshaus   CLUB
(www.bootshaus.tv; Auenweg 173; ☺11pm-6am Fri, 10pm-6am Sat; 📖150 Thermalbad) Bootshaus is the offshoot of Warehouse, one of Cologne's oldest techno clubs (1991) and regularly

hosts DJ royalty such as David Guetta, Ellen Allien and Jeff Mills alongside its 14 resident spinmeisters. Drift off into the night on three floors, including the BLCKBX with its starry LED sky, plus an outdoor chill zone with snack stand.

Voted 11th best club in the world's top 100 by the prestigious *DJ Mag* in 2018. Catch bus 150 at Deutz/Messeplatz.

Frieda Bar   BAR
(☑0221-8000 6186; www.frieda-bar.de; Antwerpener Strasse 53; ☺7pm-3am Mon-Thu, 8pm-5am Fri & Sat; ⓊFriesenplatz) Even if punk and stoner rock are not usually your thing, you'll get a warm and fuzzy feeling in this campy pub-style bar that pours *Kölsch* instead of Guinness for an unpretentious tattooed crowd. It's a welcome change from the electro beats dominating other Belgian Quarter watering holes.

Six Pack   BAR
(☑0221-254 587; Aachener Strasse 33; ☺8pm-3am or later; 📖1, 7 Moltkestrasse) An institution in the Belgisches Viertel, Six Pack is a worthy stop on any Cologne pub crawl. Pass through the battered door, belly up to the super-long bar and pick from several dozen varieties of beer, all served by the bottle from a giant fridge. It gets seriously jammed after midnight.

☆ Entertainment

With two major orchestras, an opera house and numerous theatres, Cologne has a terrific highbrow cultural scene, along with

---

CARNIVAL IN COLOGNE: FOOLS, FLOATS & REVELRY

Known as the 'fifth season', Karneval (Carnival; www.koelnerkarneval.de) in Cologne is one of the best parties in Europe and a thumb in the eye of the German work ethic. Every year at the onset of Lent (late February/early March), a year of painstaking preparation culminates in the 'three crazy days' – actually more like six.

It all starts with *Weiberfastnacht*, the Thursday before Ash Wednesday, when women rule the day (and do things such as chopping off the ties of their male colleagues/bosses). The party continues through the weekend, with more than 50 parades of ingenious floats and wildly dressed lunatics dancing in the streets. By the time it all comes to a head with the big parade on *Rosenmontag* (Rose Monday), the entire city has come unglued. Those still capable of swaying and singing will live it up one last time on Shrove Tuesday before the curtain comes down on Ash Wednesday.

'If you were at the parade and saw the parade, you weren't at the parade', say the people of Cologne in their inimitable way. Translated, this means that you should be far too busy singing, drinking and roaring the Carnival greeting '*Alaaf!*' to notice anything happening around you. Swaying and drinking while crammed like sardines in a pub, or following other costumed fools behind a huge bass drum leading to God-only-knows-where, you'll be swept up in one of the greatest parties known to the world.

concerts, musicals and literature and film festivals. For listings consult *Kölner Illustrierte* (mainstream, www.koelner.de) and *StadtRevue* (alternative, www.stadtrevue. de). Buy tickets at www.koelnticket.de.

Kölner Philharmonie
CLASSICAL MUSIC

(⏰ 0221-280 280; www.koelner-philharmonie.de; Bischofsgartenstrasse 1; concert tickets €14-48; ⓤ Köln Dom/Hbf) The Kölner Philharmonie is a grand modern concert hall that presents a wide range of aural treats, from classical to jazz and chansons. It's also the home base of two world-class classical orchestras, the Gürzenich Orchester and the WDR Sinfonieorchester.

Free 30-minute lunchtime concerts take place once or twice on weekdays. Check the website.

Club Bahnhof Ehrenfeld
LIVE MUSIC

(http://cbe-cologne.de; Bartholomäus-Schink-Strasse 65/67; ⓢ varies; ⌂ 3, 4 Venloer Strasse/Gürtel, ⓢ Venloer Strasse/Gürtel) An institution in Cologne's alternative scene, this club in the hip cross-cultural Ehrenfeld borough has programming as eclectic as the crowd. Depending on the day, dance parties, poetry slams, concerts or flea markets lure punters to three cavernous spaces below the train tracks. Nice beer garden to boot.

Stadtgarten
LIVE MUSIC

(⏰ 0221-952 9940; www.stadtgarten.de; Venloer Strasse 40; ⌂ 3, 4, 5, 12, 15 Friesenplatz, ⌂ 3, 4, 5 Hans-Böckler-Platz) For more than 30 years, this well-respected venue has treated music fans to up to 400 concerts a year – mostly jazz, but also folk, indie and pop – on three stages. It's attached to a pleasant cafe-restaurant with a beer garden that serves light meals and cold drinks all day long.

As of 2018, it receives sizeable government subsidies towards the goal of turning it into the European Centre for Jazz and Contemporary Music and to help position Cologne as a top destination for jazz.

Gebäude 9
LIVE MUSIC

(⏰ 0221-2801; www.gebaeude9.de; Deutz-Mülheimer Strasse 127-129; ⓤ KölnMesse) Although a bit dated and grungy, this ex-factory remains an essential concert venue in town with concerts covering the entire sound spectrum from indie rock to hip-hop. The calendar also includes the occasional party, play, film or festivals. It's in Deutz, on the right bank of the Rhine.

Papa Joe's Jazzlokal 'Em Streckstrump'
LIVE MUSIC

(⏰ 0221-257 7931; www.papajoes.de; Buttermarkt 37; ⓢ 8pm-3am; ⌂ 5 Rathaus) **FREE** Traditional jazz – Dixieland, New Orleans, Swing – riffs nightly in this museum-like place where the smoky brown walls are strewn with yesteryear's photographs. There really is a Joe and he is a true jazz lover. Try Streckes, the house brew.

There's a second, less intimate location, Papa Joe's Klimperkasten, on Alter Markt.

🔒 Shopping

Cologne is a popular shopping destination with a fun mix of eccentric boutiques, designer and vintage stores, plus the usual selection of chain and department stores. And of course there are classic outlets for its famous eau de cologne.

Kauf Dich Glücklich
FASHION & ACCESSORIES

(⏰ 0221-2774 8020; www.kaufdichgluecklich-shop. de; Neue Langgasse 2; ⓢ 10.30am-8pm Mon-Sat; ⓤ Appellhofplatz) With a branch in Berlin, this small indie boutique chain now supplies the same quality threads, accessories and jewellery to Cologne's fashion-forward men and women. Look for their own KDG label alongside brands from around Germany and Europe with particular emphasis on Scandinavia.

Mayersche Buchhandlung
BOOKS

(⏰ 0221-203 070; www.mayersche.de; Neumarkt 2; ⓢ 9.30am-8pm Mon-Sat; ♿; ⌂ 1, 3, 4, 5 7, 9 Neumarkt) Huge bookstore with a cafe, a good range of English-language books and an entire floor dedicated to children's books and toys, complete with carousel and pirate ship.

4711 House of Fragrances
PERFUME

(⏰ 0221-2709 9910; www.4711.com; Glockengasse 4; ⓢ 9.30am-6.30pm Mon-Fri, to 6pm Sat; ⓤ Appellhofplatz) A classic gift for Grandma is a bottle of eau de cologne, invented in, yes, Cologne in the late 18th century. The most famous is 4711, named after the address where it was first created. The building now houses a flagship store and a museum where you can marvel at a giant Gobelin tapestry and stop by the Fragrance Fountain.

Note the carillon outside with characters from Prussian lore parading hourly from 9am to 9pm.

COLOGNE & NORTHERN RHINELAND NOERTHEN RHINELAND

ⓘ FREE PUBLIC WI-FI

There is free public wi-fi in the area around the Dom (p629) and other city centre areas such as Neumarkt, Friesenplatz or Rudolfplatz. Look for the Hotspot.Koeln network and sign up.

If you're really into colognes, enquire about tours, creating your own scent at a seminar and indulging in a 'fragrance menu'.

ⓘ Information

The **KölnCard** (24 hours, €9) offers free public transport and discounted admission, tours, meals and entertainment. It's available at the **tourist office** (☑ 0221-346 430; www.cologne-tourism.com; Kardinal-Höffner-Platz 1; ⊙ 9am-8pm Mon-Sat, 10am-5pm Sun; Ⓤ Köln Dom/Hbf), in many hostels and hotels and at public transport ticket vending machines as well as online at www.cologne-tourism.com/book-buy/koelncard. If there's more than three of you, buy the group ticket for €19.

The **MuseumsCard** (per person/family €18/30) offers one-time admission to all municipal museums over two consecutive days.

ⓘ Getting There & Away

AIR

About 18km southeast of the city centre, **Köln Bonn Airport** (CGN; Cologne Bonn Airport; ☑ 02203-404 001; www.koeln-bonn-airport.de; Kennedystrasse; ⊞ Köln/Bonn Flughafen) has direct flights to 130 cities and is served by numerous airlines, with destinations across Europe.

BUS

Cologne's central bus station near the Hauptbahnhof has been closed to long-distance coaches such as those operated by Flixbus. The nearest stops are 'Köln Nord' in Leverkusen (S6 to/from Cologne's Hauptbahnhof), and 'Köln Süd' at Köln Bonn Airport (S13 to/from Hauptbahnhof).

TRAIN

Cologne's beautiful **Hauptbahnhof** (www.bahnhof.de/bahnhof-de/Köln_Hbf-1032796; Trankgasse 11; ⊞ 16, 18 Breslauer Platz/Hbf, ⊞ 5 Dom/Hbf) sits just a frankincense waft away from the landmark Dom (p629). Services are fast and frequent in all directions and include fast Thalys and ICE trains to Brussels (€59, two hours) where you can connect to the Eurostar for London) and Paris.

Flixtrain also operates a route all the way to Hamburg via Düsseldorf, the Ruhrgebiet and Münster.

ⓘ Getting Around

Walking and using public transport are the best ways of getting around Cologne.

TO/FROM THE AIRPORT

The S13, RE6 and RE8 trains connect the airport and the Hauptbahnhof every 20 minutes (€2.80, 15 minutes). Taxis charge about €35.

BICYCLE

Cologne's public transport network **KVB** (Kölner Verkehrsbetriebe; ☑ 01806-50 40 30; www.kvb.koeln) also maintains a bike-sharing system (KVB-Rad). You need to sign up (free), then pick up a bike by typing in the bike number or scanning the QR code and then opening the lock with the four-digit lock code sent via the app. Bikes may be left at any main street or street crossing within the city. For full details, see www.kvb-rad.de.

You can also rent bicycles for longer periods from Radstation (p638) on the edge of the Altstadt.

PUBLIC TRANSPORT

Cologne's mix of buses, trams (Stadtbahn), U-Bahn and S-Bahn trains is operated by **KVB** in cooperation with Bonn's system. Short trips (up to four stops) cost €1.90, longer ones €2.40. Day passes are €7.10 for one person and €10 for up to five people travelling together. Buy your tickets from the machines at stations and aboard trams; be sure to validate them. KVB's website has a journey planner.

TAXI

Flagfall is €3.50; the kilometre rate is €1.70 to €1.90. Taxis can be hailed in the street, ordered by phone (0221-2882 or 0221-194 10) or picked up at a taxi rank.

NORTHERN RHINELAND

North of Koblenz, the scenery bordering the Rhine is not quite as romantic as along the Middle Rhine further south. Instead the river takes on the mightiness of an urban stream as it courses through such cities as Bonn, Cologne and Düsseldorf. Many towns in the region started out as Roman settlements some 2000 years ago, and it was also the Romans who gave the Rhine its name (*rhenus* in Latin).

Cultural travellers will be richly rewarded with such sightseeing gems as the magnificent cathedrals in Cologne and Aachen and the richly endowed art museums in

Düsseldorf, Cologne and Bonn. Rhenish *joie de vivre* means that you'll never be far from a party, be it in a quaint beer hall or a hot-stepping nightclub.

❶ Getting There & Around

The Rhineland is criss-crossed by a spider web of autobahns and country roads. It's linked to other cities in Germany and beyond by train and bus. Between April and October, boats operated by **KD Deutsche Rheinschiffahrt** (🎫 0221-208 8318; www.k-d.com) travel between Cologne and Linz on a set timetable.

The region's cities and towns are connected by a comprehensive public transport network operated by the **Verkehrsverbund Rhein-Sieg** (VRS; 🎫 01806-50 40 30; www.vrsinfo.de).

Brühl

🎫 02232 / POP 44,300

Brühl wraps an astonishing number of riches into a pint-sized package. The town, halfway between Cologne and Bonn, languished in relative obscurity until the 18th century, when archbishop-elector Clemens August (term 1723–61) – a friend of Casanova and himself a lover of women, parties and palaces – made it his residence. His two made-to-impress rococo palaces, at opposite ends of the elegant Schlosspark, landed on Unesco's list of World Heritage Sites in 1984. Brühl's other big drawcard is Phantasialand, one of Europe's oldest theme parks.

◉ Sights & Activities

Brühl's two palaces are a wonderful stroll apart on a wide 2.5km promenade through the Schlosspark. Schloss Augustusburg is close to the train station and presents a dramatic vision as you arrive.

⭐ Schloss Augustusburg   PALACE
(Schloss Brühl; 🎫 02232-440 00; www.schloss bruehl.de; Max-Ernst-Allee; adult/concession incl tour €8.50/7, combined ticket with Jagdschloss Falkenlust €13/10; ⏰ 9am-noon & 1.30-4pm Tue-Fri, 10am-5pm Sat & Sun, closed Dec-Jan; 🅿; 🚍18 Brühl Mitte, 🚆Bahnhof Brühl) The favourite palace of archbishop and prince-elector Clemens August, Schloss Augustusburg is a precious rococo symphony designed by François Cuvilliés. It was further embellished by other big-name 18th-century architects including Balthasar Neumann, who dreamt up the ceremonial staircase – a dizzying symphony of stucco, sculpture and faux marble. On guided tours you'll learn

fascinating titbits about hygiene, dating and other aspects of daily life at court.

It is surrounded by a magnificent baroque garden as well as a lavish landscape garden created by Peter Joseph Lenné.

Jagdschloss Falkenlust   HISTORIC BUILDING
(🎫 02232-440 00; www.schlossbruehl.de; An Schloss Falkenlust; adult/concession incl audioguide €6.50/5, combined ticket with Schloss Augustusburg €13/10; ⏰ 9am-noon & 1.30-4pm Tue-Fri, 10am-5pm Sat & Sun, closed Dec-Jan; 🅿; 🚍18 Brühl Mitte) Part of Brühl's park-and-palace ensemble, Jagdschloss Falkenlust is a petite rococo jewel designed by François Cuvilliés as a hunting palace. This is where prince-bishop Clemens August liked to indulge his fancy for falconry, followed by lavish banquets in an opulently furnished setting, which has largely survived in original condition.

Also a gem is the adjacent chapel, which is awash with shells, minerals and crystals. Another building houses an exhibit on falconry and a re-created falconer's workshop.

Max Ernst Museum   MUSEUM
(🎫 02232-579 30; www.maxernstmuseum.com; Comesstrasse 42; adult/concession/under 18yr €7/4/free; ⏰ 11am-6pm Tue-Sun; 🅿; 🚍18 Brühl Mitte, 🚆 Bahnhof Brühl) A short stroll from the palaces is the Max Ernst Museum, where nine rooms trace all creative phases of the Brühl-born Dadaist and surrealist (1891–1976). Pride of place goes to the 36 'D-paintings' that Ernst created as an expression of love for his fourth wife Dorothea Tanning. Another highlight is the spooky collage novels, which are graphic works exploring the darkest crevices of the subconscious.

An audioguide may be rented for €2.

⭐ Phantasialand   AMUSEMENT PARK
(🎫 02232-366 00; www.phantasialand.de; Berggeiststrasse 31-41; day pass adult/child 4-11yr/under 4yr €47.50/37/free; ⏰ 9am-6pm Apr-Jun, Sep & Oct, to 8pm Jul-Aug, 11am-8pm late Nov-mid-Jan; 🚍18 Brühl Mitte, 🚆Brühl) Founded in 1967, Phantasialand is one of Europe's oldest, most popular and best Disneyland-style amusement parks. In six themed areas – Chinatown, Berlin, Mexico, Fantasy, Mystery and Deep in Africa – you can travel around (and out of) the world on roller coasters, 3D rides, simulators, water rides and other thrills; there are also song-and-dance shows.

There are plenty of lunch-losing rides along with tamer ones for kids and nervous

COLOGNE & NORTHERN RHINELAND BRÜHL

Nellies. Some rides have minimum height requirements.

Shuttle buses (return €3, 20 minutes) leave from Brühl's train station and the Brühl Mitte tram stop at least once hourly.

🍴 Eating

The town centre around Markt, a short walk west of Schloss Augustusburg (p645), has a bunch of restaurants and cafes.

Glaewe's Restaurant　INTERNATIONAL **€€€**
(☑ 02232-135 91; www.glaewesrestaurant.de; Balthasar-Neumann-Platz 28-30; mains €22; ⊙ 6-10pm daily, noon-3pm Sun) Some things never go out of style, including this local gastro-stalwart. Run by a charming couple for around 30 years, the cosy, elegant space serves updated German food with more than a hint of Mediterranean influences. Regulars sit at the bar. It's a bit hidden inside a small shopping centre.

ℹ Information

Brühl Tourist Office (☑ 02232-793 45; www. bruehl.de; Uhlstrasse 1; ⊙ 9am-7pm Mon-Fri year-round, 9am-1pm Sat Nov-Apr, 9am-4pm Sat & 1-5pm Sun May-Oct)

ℹ Getting There & Around

Brühl is regularly served by regional trains from Cologne (€3.90, 15 minutes) and Bonn (€5.10, 12 minutes). The Hauptbahnhof is opposite **Schloss Augustusburg** (p645), with the compact town centre west of (behind) the palace. Shuttle buses to **Phantasialand** (p645) leave from outside the train station, which also has a **bike rental outlet** (☑ 02232-950 761; Max-Ernst-Allee 2; bicycle per day from €8.50; ⊙ 6am-8pm Mon-Fri, 8am-8pm Sat, 8am-6pm Sun).

Bonn

☑ 0228 / POP 322,000

When this relaxed city on the Rhine became West Germany's 'temporary' capital in 1949 it surprised many, including its own residents. When in 1991 a reunited German government decided to move to Berlin, it shocked many, especially Bonn's own residents.

More than a generation later, Bonn is doing just fine, thank you. It has a healthy economy and lively urban vibe. For visitors, the birthplace of Ludwig van Beethoven has plenty of note, not least the great composer's birth house, a string of top-rated museums, a lovely riverside setting and the nostalgic feel of the old government quarter. Expect

a big line-up of special events in 2020 – Beethoven's 250th birthday.

⊙ Sights

Bonn can be seen on an easy day trip from Cologne or as a stop on the busy Rhine railway line. There is a concentration of sights in the Altstadt, while the big museums along Museumsmeile are just a quick tram ride away.

⊙ Altstadt

You can easily explore all of Bonn's old town on foot.

★ **Beethoven-Haus Bonn**　MUSEUM
(Beethoven House; ☑ 0228-981 7525; www.beethoven-haus-bonn.de; Bonngasse 20; adult/concession €6/4.50; ⊙ 10am-6pm Apr-Oct, 10am-5pm Mon-Sat, 11am-5pm Sun Nov-Mar) Star composer Ludwig van Beethoven was born in 1770 in this rather humble townhouse, where today original scores, letters, paintings and instruments, including his last grand piano, offer insight into his work, routines and feelings. Of special note are the huge ear trumpets he used to combat his growing deafness. Tickets are also good for the new media exhibit in the adjacent building, where you can experience the composer's genius during a spacey, interactive 3D multimedia tour.

Contemplate his life in a near-hidden garden out back, and stroke your inner Schroeder (of *Peanuts* fame) in the Beethoven-bust-filled gift shop.

Münster Basilica　CATHEDRAL
(☑ 0228-985 880; www.bonner-muenster.de; Münsterplatz; ⊙ closed for renovation) The landmark Münster Basilica was built on the graves of the two martyred Roman soldiers who later got promoted to be the city's patron saints. It got its Gothic look in the 13th century but the Romanesque origins survive beautifully in the cloister. Both church and cloister are closed for restoration until at least 2019.

Beethoven Monument　MONUMENT
(Münsterplatz) A buttercup-yellow baroque Palais (palace; now the post office) forms a photogenic backdrop for the Beethoven Monument, unveiled in 1845, 75 years after the composer's death.

Altes Rathaus　HISTORIC BUILDING
(Old Town Hall; Markt) Overlooking the triangular Markt square, the rococo Altes Rathaus absolutely glistens with silver and gold trim. Politicians from Charles de Gaulle to John F

Kennedy have waved to the crowds from its double-sided staircase.

Kurfürstliches Schloss HISTORIC BUILDING
(Electoral Palace; Regina-Pacis-Weg) The palatial 1705 Kurfürstliche Residenz was once the immodest home of the prince-electors of Cologne and has been part of Bonn's university since 1818. Its south side opens up to the expansive Hofgarten (Palace Garden), a popular gathering place for students.

Arithmeum MUSEUM
(☑0228-738 790; www.arithmeum.de; Lennéstrasse 2; adult/child €3/2; ☺11am-6pm Tue-Sun) If memories of math class give you nightmares, this museum may not be for you. If they don't, you may well find this expansive collection of mechanical calculating machines – from the abacus to early computers by Hollerith and Babbage – quite fascinating. The science aspect is complemented by changing art exhibits, usually with a geometric constructivist bent. Work your way down from the top floor of the large minimalist glass-and-steel cube.

LandesMuseum Bonn MUSEUM
(Rhineland Regional Museum; ☑0228-207 00; www.landesmuseum-bonn.lvr.de; Colmantstrasse 14; adult/concession/under 18yr €8/6/free; ☺11am-6pm Tue-Fri & Sun, from 1pm Sat) The LandesMuseum charts the cultural history of the region back to the days of the Neanderthals. Each of the seven themed galleries brims with fascinating treasures, including a 40,000-year-old Neanderthal skull, a rare blue Roman glass vessel from the 1st century AD and, in the new 'Celts in the Rhineland' exhibit, gold jewellery unearthed from the grave of a Celtic princess.

◉ Museumsmeile

★ Haus der Geschichte MUSEUM
(Museum of History; ☑0228-916 5400; www.hdg. de; Willy-Brandt-Allee 14; ☺9am-7pm Tue-Fri, 10am-6pm Sat & Sun; ℗; 🚋16, 63, 66 Heussallee/Museumsmeile) FREE The Haus der Geschichte der Bundesrepublik Deutschland presents a smart, fun romp through recent German history, starting from the end of WWII. Walk through the fuselage of a Berlin airlift *Rosinenbomber* plane, watch classic clips in a 1950s cinema, imagine free love in a VW microbus, examine Erich Honecker's arrest warrant, stand in front of a piece of the Berlin Wall or watch John F Kennedy's famous *'Ich bin ein Berliner'* speech.

Bundeskunsthalle ARTS CENTRE
(Kunst-und Ausstellungshalle der Bundesrepublik Deutschland; ☑0228-917 1200; www.bundeskunst halle.de; Friedrich-Ebert-Allee 4; varies, under 18yr free; ☺10am-9pm Tue & Wed, to 7pm Thu-Sun; 🚋16, 63, 66, 68 Heussallee/Museumsmeile) Adjoining the Kunstmuseum Bonn, the Bundeskunsthalle (Federal Art Hall) is another striking space that brings in blockbuster exhibits from around the world. Despite the name, the hall doesn't necessarily showcase serious art; it also has exhibits that delve into the realms of history, science, technology and the environment.

The building itself, by Viennese architect Gustav Peichl, is striking and easily recognised by the three sky-blue glass-tipped cones jutting from the rooftop garden. The 16 columns represent the 16 states of Germany.

Kunstmuseum Bonn MUSEUM
(Bonn Art Museum; ☑0228-776 260; www.kunst museum-bonn.de; Friedrich-Ebert-Allee 2; adult/ concession €7/3.50; ☺11am-6pm Tue & Thu-Sun, to 9pm Wed; ℗; 🚋16, 63, 66, 68 Heussallee/Museumsmeile) Beyond its dramatic foyer, the Kunstmuseum Bonn presents 20th-century works, especially by August Macke and other Rhenish expressionists, as well as such post-WWII avant-gardists as Beuys, Baselitz and Kiefer. It has a vigorous schedule of special exhibitions showcasing various facets of contemporary art.

Competing with the art is the stark beauty of the building itself. Blueprinted by Axel Schultes, a Berlin-based architect, it juxtaposes airiness with strict geometric structures that play with light and shadow. Note especially the dramatic main staircase, the shape of which resembles an hourglass.

Deutsches Museum Bonn MUSEUM
(☑0228-302 255; www.deutsches-museum-bonn. de; Ahrstrasse 45; adult/concession €9/5; ☺10am-5pm Tue-Fri & Sun, noon-5pm Sat; ℗; 🚋16, 63 Hochkreuz/Deutsches Museum Bonn) Did you know that the airbag and MP3 technology were invented in Germany? You will, after visiting the Deutsches Museum Bonn. This pint-size subsidiary of the blockbuster Munich mothership highlights German research and technology since WWII with plenty of buttons to push and knobs to pull.

The 100 or so exhibits highlight achievements in six scientific fields: physics, chemistry, biology, medical technology, ecology, and aviation and space travel. The museum is around 6km south of the city centre.

THE FORMER FEDERAL GOVERNMENT DISTRICT

From 1949 to 1999, the nerve centre of West German political power lay in Bonn's Bundesviertel, about 1.5km southeast of the Altstadt along Adenauerallee. These days the former government quarter has reinvented itself as the home of the United Nations and other international and federal institutions. The airy and modern Plenary Hall, where the Bundestag (German parliament) used to convene, now hosts international conferences. Nearby, the high-rise nicknamed Langer Eugen (Tall Eugen), where members of parliament kept their offices, is now a UN campus. Officially retaining their former purposes are the stately Villa Hammerschmidt, now the secondary official seat and residence of the German president, and the neoclassical Palais Schaumburg, which has the same function for the German chancellor. Explore the district on the Weg der Demokratie (Path of Democracy; www.wegderdemokratie.de) self-guided tour.

Museum Koenig   MUSEUM
(☑0228-912 20; www.zfmk.de; Adenauerallee 160; adult/concession €5/2.50; ☉10am-6pm Tue & Thu-Sun, to 9pm Wed, last entry 1hr before closing; ℗; ☐16, 63 Museum König) The Museum Koenig is a natural history museum but it's hardly your usual dead-animal zoo. The 'Savannah' exhibit re-creates an entire habitat with theatrical flourishes: elephants drinking at a watering hole, a jaguar holed up with its kill and vultures surveying the scene from above. In the 'Rainforest' diorama elephants come 'alive' through telescopes while a colossal sea elephant watches over the 'Arctic' exhibit, and a condor with a 3m wingspan surveys the 'World of Birds'.

☉ Nordstadt

Also referred to as Northern Altstadt, Nordstadt is a former working-class quarter where the web of narrow streets has grown pockets of hipness. Cafes, restaurants, boutiques and galleries have sprouted along Breite Strasse, Heerstrasse and the connecting side streets. The quarter is prettiest in spring when the cherry trees are in bloom.

August Macke-Haus   MUSEUM
(☑0228-655 531; www.august-macke-haus.de; Hochstadenring 36; adult/concession €9.50/6; ☉11am-5pm Tue, Wed & Fri-Sun, 1-8pm Thu; ☐602 Eifelstrasse/August Macke-Haus, ☐6, 18, 63 Bonn-West/August Macke-Haus) The expressionist painter August Macke (1887–1914) lived and worked in this house in the three years before his untimely death on the battlefields in WWI. Soak up the master's aura in his recreated studio and see some originals; the finest works, though, are not far away at the Kunstmuseum Bonn (p647).

☉ Poppelsdorf & Around

About 2km south of the Altstadt, elegant and leafy Poppelsdorf is anchored by Schloss Poppelsdorf, a palace now used by the university. Students and neighbourhood folk populate the bars and restaurants along Clemens-August-Strasse, which runs south of the palace towards the hillside Kreuzbergkirche.

Doppelkirche Schwarzrheindorf   CHURCH
(☑0228-461 609; Dixstrasse 41; ☉9am-11am Tue, Wed & Fri-Sun, 3.30-6.30pm Thu; ☐550, 640 Schwarzrheindorf-Kirche) The 12th-century Doppelkirche Schwarzrheindorf is a magnificent 'double church' where the nobility would sit on the upper level and peek down on the common parishioners through an octagonal opening in the floor. Considered one of the most beautiful Romanesque churches in Germany, its architecture is truly impressive, as is the restored Old Testament fresco cycle in the lower church.

The church is on the right bank of the Rhine in the suburb of Schwarzrheindorf, about 3km from the city centre.

Kreuzbergkirche   CHURCH
(Stationsweg 21; ☉9am-6pm Apr-Oct, to 5pm Nov-Mar; ℗; ☐602, 603 Kreuzberg) This rococo gem is lavishly decorated with gilded faux marble, frescoes and a Balthasar Neumann–designed version of the Holy Steps.

It's about a 1km walk from the bus stop.

☞ Tours

The tourist office (p650) runs a variety of guided themed bus and walking tours.

KD Deutsche Rheinschiffahrt   BOATING
(☑0228-632 134; www.k-d.com; Brassertufer) This boat company runs regular ferries up and down the Rhine. A popular day trip is the Siebengebirgs-Tour (€10.60, one hour),

which travels past beautiful scenery, vine-yards, castles and romantic wine villages. Boats leave from the Alter Zoll landing docks in the city centre.

Bonner Personen Schiffahrt   BOATING
(☑0228-636 363; www.bonnschiff.de; Brassertufer; ☺Apr-Oct) This local company runs boat trips on a fixed timetable upriver as far as St Goarshausen several times daily. From Bonn, a popular day trip destination is the 45-minute trip to Königswinter (one way €9.50, return €12).

Bonn Walking Tour   WALKING
(☑0228-775 000; Windeckstrasse 1; adult/concession €9/5; ☺11.30am Sat May-Oct, 4pm Fri Jul-Sep) Walk in the footsteps of Romans, Beethoven and the prince-bishops on this 90-minute English-language ramble through the Altstadt. Tours leave from the tourist office (p650).

Big City Tour   TOURS
(Windeckstrasse 1; adult/concession €16/8; ☺2pm daily Apr-Oct, Sat Nov-Mar) On weekends, the tourist office (p650) runs a variety of guided city tours, including the popular Big City Tour which covers all major sights by bus and on foot in the course of 2½ hours. Tours leave from the tourist office. In season, it's best to book ahead.

🛏 Sleeping

Bonn accommodation is like the city – spread out. There are some decent places in the Altstadt and a few atmospheric hotels along the Rhine. For assistance, contact the tourist office (p650) or check out www.bonnhotels.de where bookings include a free local transport ticket during your stay. Note that a 5% city tax is added to your hotel bill unless you're travelling on business.

Max Hostel   HOSTEL €
(☑0228-8234 5780; http://max-hostel.de; Maxstrasse 7; dm €20-24, s/d €39/50; ☺check-in 4-8pm; P🐶; 🚋62, 62 Stadthaus) Choose from brightly decorated rooms with one to eight quality beds with reading lamps at this modern, welcoming 48-bed hostel. It's in a quiet location just north of the old centre, yet close to bars and restaurants. Bathrooms are shared. The breakfast buffet is €6.80, bed linen is €2.50 and wi-fi costs €3 per 24 hours.

The hostel is about 500m from the nearest tram stop.

Villa Esplanade   HOTEL €€
(☑0228-983 800; www.hotel-villa-esplanade. de; Colmantstrasse 47; d incl breakfast €107-164; P😊🐶) Inside a stately late-19th-century building, this charming hotel close to the train station has 17 bright rooms with lofty ceilings, wooden floors and fridges. Get ready for a day on the tourist track with a breakfast buffet served in a lovely room with ornate stucco ceilings.

Hotel Löhndorf   HOTEL €€
(☑0228-634 726; www.hotel-loehndorf-bonn. de; Stockenstrasse 6; d incl breakfast €110-160; P😊@🐶) This 13-room property is wonderfully quiet and within strolling distance of the Hofgarten and the Rhine. There's a cheery breakfast room and a bamboo-lined patio. Bonus: a handy honour bar in the lounge and free access to the next-door gym and sauna. Wallet watchers should ask about the economy singles with shared bathrooms.

Ameron Hotel Königshof   HOTEL €€€
(☑0228-260 10; www.hotel-koenigshof-bonn.de; Adenauerallee 9; r €93-242; P😊❋🐶) Sit back on the leafy terrace and enjoy sweeping views of the Rhine from this luxurious yet understated hotel. Rooms in five sizes have inviting beds and a homey elegance. There are good walks along the river and strolls in the neighbouring Stadtgarten. Rates include access to a Technogym fitness room and the sauna.

The stylish restaurant, Oliveto, is known for its Med-influenced fare.

🍴 Eating

The largely pedestrianised Altstadt brims with options. For offbeat choices head to Heerstrasse and Wolfsstrasse just northwest of the Altstadt.

Cafe Blüte   CAFE
(☑0228-9629 9944; www.cafeblüte.de; Heerstrasse 61; ☺noon-7pm Tue-Sun; 🐶) Walls lined with the colourful containers of the owner's favorite teas overlook mismatched but comfy chairs and tables at this neighbourhood favourite. The spread of delicious home-made cakes changes daily. If you're in the mood for savoury stuff, order a crisp *Flammkuchen* (Alsatian pizza). All furniture and decorations are also for sale.

Bottler Cafe & Brasserie   BRASSERIE €€
(☑0228-9090 2999; Vivatsgasse 8; mains €8-20; ☺9am-8pm Mon-Sat, 10am-6pm Sun) Right

across from Bonn's landmark Sterntor, the old city gate, is this good all-arounder. Whether it's a quick breakfast, coffee and a cake (great pastries!) or a more elaborate seafood or pasta meal, Bottler is a dependable pit stop.

Brauhaus Bönnsch
GERMAN €€

(☑ 0228-650 610; www.boennsch.de; Sterntorbrücke 4; mains €10-22; ⊙ 11am-1am Mon-Thu, to 3am Fri & Sat;) The unfiltered ale is a must at this congenial brewpub adorned with photographs of famous politicians great and failed, from Willy Brandt to, yes, Arnold Schwarzenegger. Schnitzel, Rhenish specialities and and fry-ups dominate the menu, but the *Flammkuchen* (tarte flambée) is always a crowd-pleaser.

There's a small children's menu with a complimentary scoop of vanilla ice cream.

Cafe Spitz
CAFE €€

(☑ 0228-974 30; www.spitz-bonn.de; Sterntorbrücke 10; mains €12-21; ⊙ 9am-1am Mon-Thu, to 2am Fri & Sat, to midnight Sun) This spare and stylish place is often mobbed, especially during the after-work cocktail happy hour. The menu revolves around salad, pizza and pasta supplemented by changing blackboard specials. The corner location affords great people-watching from the outdoor tables.

🍷 Drinking & Nightlife

As befits a former capital, Bonn has a nicely cosmopolitan bar scene. Aside from traditional brewpubs you'll find lots of wine bars, craft beer bars and cocktail bars for elevated imbibing. The Altstadt has lots of promising locations. The local blog www.welovepubs.de (in German) is a good source.

Biergarten Alter Zoll
BEER GARDEN

(☑ 0228-241 243; http://alterzoll.de; Brassertufer 1, Stadtgarten; ⊙ 11am-midnight Apr-Oct) Here's a Bonn drinking game: every time a barge passes below this beer garden with gorgeous views of the Rhine, have a drink. You won't

last an hour. It's in Bonn's Stadtgarten, a little leafy gem next to the Altstadt with an old bastion overlooking the river. The beer and sausages here are standard but the surroundings are anything but. Snacks from €3.20

Limes
PUB

(☑ 0228-555 2768; www.limes-musikcafe-bonn.de; Theaterstrasse 2; ⊙ 7pm-1am or later Mon-Sat; 🚌 61, 65 Wilhelmsplatz) This cult pub north of the Altstadt has a bewildering menu of 50 beers plus discounted daily specials along with foosball and occasional live music.

Pawlow
BAR

(☑ 0228-653 603; Heerstrasse 64; ⊙ 11am-1am Sun-Thu, to late Fri & Sat) Generations of bon vivants have followed the Pavlovian bell to this northern Altstadt institution. A cafe in the daytime with a fine terrace (good breakfast!), it morphs into a bar at night when electro, punk and '60s sounds heating up a chatty, boozy crowd.

☆ Entertainment

Kammermusiksaal
CLASSICAL MUSIC

(☑ 0228-981 7515; www.beethoven.de; Bonngasse 24-26; tickets €26-45) This chamber music hall is part of the Beethoven House (p646) complex. Buy tickets online at www.bonnticket.de.

Beethovenhalle
CONCERT VENUE

(☑ 0228-22 20; www.beethovenhalle.de; Wachsbleiche 17) Bonn's premier concert hall is closed for renovation until 2020.

ℹ Information

Bonn Tourist Office (☑ 0228-775 000; www.bonn-region.de; Windeckstrasse 1; ⊙ 10am-6pm Mon-Fri, to 4pm Sat, to 2pm Sun) Lots of free information and combined bus-and-walking tours in English (adult/concession €16/8).

ℹ Getting There & Away

AIR

Köln Bonn Airport (p644) is 20km north of central Bonn and has direct flights to 130 cities across Europe. Express bus SB60 shuttles between here and Bonn's Hauptbahnhof every 20 minutes (€7.90, 30 minutes). A taxi ride costs about €55.

BOAT

You can travel the Rhine by boat, to/from Cologne and south to/from Koblenz and beyond. KD Deutsche Rheinschiffahrt (p648) and Bonner Personen Schiffahrt (p649) are the main operators.

ℹ TICKET TO SAVINGS

The Bonn Regio WelcomeCard (24hr per person/family €10/19) offers better value than most schemes. Besides unlimited public transport, it includes free (rather than reduced) admission to over 20 museums, plus discounts on tours, thermal baths and more. It's sold at the tourist office and at some hotels.

BUS

Flixbus (🚌 16, 18, 63, 66, 68 Heussallee/Museumsmeile) stops on Joseph-Beuys-Allee near the museums, about 2km south of the city centre.

TRAIN

Bonn is linked to Cologne many times hourly by U-Bahn lines U16 and U18 (€7.90, 54 minutes) as well as by regional trains (26 minutes) and long-distance IC and ICE trains.

❶ Getting Around

Buses, trams and the U-Bahn make up the public transport system, which is operated by the VRS (p645). It is linked to the Cologne network and is divided into zones. All you need to travel within Bonn is a City Ticket (€2.90 per trip or €8.60 for a 24-hour pass). All tickets must be validated upon boarding.

Radstation (📞 0228-981 4636; www.radstationbonn.de; Quantiusstrasse; per day from €10, e-bikes €25; ⏱ 6am-10pm Mon-Fri, from 7am Sat, from 8am Sun Mar-Oct, shorter hours Nov-Feb) at the train station rents bicycles.

For a taxi, call 📞 0228-555 555.

South of Bonn

Siebengebirge

Steeped in legend, the densely forested hills of the Siebengebirge (Seven Mountains) rise above the right bank of the Rhine, just a few kilometres south of Bonn. Closer inspection actually reveals about 40 peaks, but only the seven most prominent give the region its name.

At 461m, the Ölberg may be the highest, but the 321m Drachenfels is the most heavily visited of these 'mountains'. From the main town of Königswinter, a nostalgic cogwheel **train** (📞 02223-920 90; www.drachenfelsbahn-koenigswinter.de; Drachenfelsstrasse 53, one way/return adult €8/10, child €5/5.50; ⏱ 9am-7pm May-Sep, 10am-6pm Mar & Oct, 9am-6pm Apr, shorter hours Nov-Feb) chugs uphill to the Drachenfels plateau with stops at the **Nibelungenhalle** (📞 02223-241 50; www.nibelungenhalle.de; Drachenfelsstrasse 107, adult/concession/child €5/4/3; ⏱ 10am-6pm mid-Mar–Oct, 11am-4pm Sat & Sun Nov–mid-Mar; 🅿; 🚌 66 Königswinter Fähre/Sea Life Aquarium), which celebrates the composer Richard Wagner, and the fairy-tale **Schloss Drachenburg** (📞 02223-901 970; www.schloss-drachenburg.de; Drachenfelsstrasse 118; adult/concession €7/5; ⏱ 11am-6pm Mar-Jun & Oct, to 7pm Jul-Sep, noon-

5pm Nov, noon-9pm Sat & noon-8pm Sun Dec). At the top you can enjoy views, restaurants and Burg Drachenfels, a ruined medieval castle. If you want to get your heart pumping, you can also hike up along a paved path.

Königswinter is served by tram 66 from Bonn Hauptbahnhof. A more atmospheric approach is by one of the ferry boats (p649) that depart from Bonn's Brassertufer between April and October.

Remagen

At the end of WWII, as the Allies raced across France and Belgium to rid Germany of Nazism, the Wehrmacht tried frantically to stave off defeat by destroying all bridges across the Rhine. The bridge at Remagen, however, lasted long enough for Allied troops to cross the river, contributing significantly to the collapse of Hitler's western front. One of the bridge's surviving basalt towers now houses the **Friedensmuseum** (Peace Museum Bridge; 📞 02642-218 63; www.bruecke-remagen.de; An der Alten Rheinbrücke 11; adult/child €3.50/1; ⏱ 10am-5pm Mar, Apr & mid-Nov, to 6pm May-Oct; 🅿), with a well-presented exhibit on Remagen's pivotal role in WWII.

The Friedensmuseum is a 15-minute walk along the Rhine promenade south from the Remagen train station, which has frequent services from Bonn (23 minutes, €3.90).

The Ahr Valley & the Eifel

The Eifel, a rural area of gentle hills, tranquil villages and volcanic lakes, makes for a lovely respite from the mass tourism of the Moselle and Rhine Valleys. Its subtle charms are best sampled on a bike ride or a hike, though it also has a few headline attractions, including a national park (p654) with a Nazi-era castle-turned-peace-institution (p654), a world-class car racing track (p653), a serene wine region, the Ahr Valley and a dazzling Romanesque abbey (p652).

The Ahr River has carved a scenic 90km valley stretching from Blankenheim, in the High Eifel, to its confluence with the Rhine near Remagen. This is Germany's most famous red-wine region – growing *Spätburgunder* (Pinot Noir) in particular – with vineyards clinging to steeply terraced slopes along both banks. The quality is high but the yield small, so very few wine labels ever

MARIA LAACH ABBEY CHURCH

Serenely tucked within beautiful Eifel countryside, **Abteikirche Maria Laach** (Maria Laach Abbey Church; ☎ 02652-590; www.maria-laach.de; Maria Laach; ⊙ visitor centre 10am-12.30pm & 1-5pm Mon-Sat, 10am-5pm Sun Mar-Oct, reduced hours Nov & Dec, closed Jan & Feb; **P**) **FREE** is one of the finest examples of a Romanesque church in Germany. Part of a 900-year-old Benedictine abbey, it is next to a volcanic lake, the Laacher See, surrounded by a 21-sq-km nature reserve. Attending prayer services is worthwhile if only to listen to the monks' ethereal chanting in Latin and German. Before entering the compound, drop by the visitors centre for information on the abbey and the lake area.

You enter the church via a large *Vorhalle* (portico; restored in 2009), a feature not usually found north of the Alps. Note the quirky carvings on and above the capitals and the Löwenbrunnen (Lion Fountain), reminiscent of Moorish architecture. The interior is surprisingly modest, in part because the original furnishings were lost during the 1800s. In the west apse lies the late-13th-century, recumbent, statue-adorned tomb of abbey founder Heinrich II of Palatine. The east apse shelters the high altar with its wooden canopy; overhead is an early-20th-century Byzantine-style mosaic of Christ donated by Kaiser Wilhelm II. The entrance to the 11th-century crypt is to the left of the choir.

Across the path from the Klostergaststätte restaurant, a 20-minute film looks at the life of the resident 46 monks, who take the motto *Ora et labora* (pray and work) very seriously indeed. They pray five times a day and earn a living from economic activities such as growing organic apples and raising house plants, available for purchase in the Klostergärtnerei nursery.

Various trails take walkers up the forested hill behind the abbey; options for circumambulating the Laacher See include the lakefront Ufer-Rundweg (8km) and the more strenuous Höhenrundweg (15km).

Next to the car park, a small shop sells fruits and vegetables grown by the monks, as well as other organic edibles.

Maria Laach is about 30km northwest of Koblenz and 22km southeast of Bad Neuenahr and Ahrweiler. The nearest train station is in Andernach from where bus 310 travels to the abbey in 25 minutes. Parking is €2.

make it beyond the area – all the more reason to visit and sample them for yourself.

ℹ Getting There & Away

The fire-engine-red Vareo trains (www.vareo.de) operate several lines in the Ahr Valley and the Eifel, including the Ahrtalbahn from Bonn to Ahrbrück and the Eifelstrecke between Cologne and Trier via Kall.

Bad Neuenahr and Ahrweiler

☎ 02641 / POP 27,500

The hub of the Ahr Valley, Bad Neuenahr and Ahrweiler are a bit of an odd couple: two small towns joined together by government edict. The spouse listed second, **Ahrweiler**, should come first in terms of appeal. It's an attractive medieval town encircled by a wall and criss-crossed by pedestrianised lanes lined with half-timbered houses.

Bad Neuenahr, by contrast, is a spa town. Although its healing waters have been sought out by the moneyed and the famous (including Karl Marx and Johannes Brahms) for a century and a half, it's rather on the bland side.

◉ Sights & Activities

Dokumentationsstätte Regierungsbunker   HISTORIC SITE
(Government Bunker Documentation Site; ☎ 02641-911 7053; www.regbu.de; Am Silberberg 0; adult/student/child €9/6/free; ⊙ 10am-6pm Wed, Sat, Sun & holidays early Mar–mid-Nov, last entry 4.30pm; **P**) During the Cold War, there was no vast top-secret bunker complex bored into the Ahr Valley hillside – at least not officially. Now, however, you can see the truth at the museum set up along a 200m section of the nuclear-proof former 'Emergency Seat of the Constitutional Organs of the Federal Republic of Germany'. Tours last 90 minutes; bring a jacket – it's chilly inside.

There's a real *Dr Strangelove* quality to what comforts the bureaucrats thought would be good to have at hand as the world ended.

Museum Roemervilla MUSEUM
(☑ 02641-5311; www.museum-roemervilla.de; Am Silberberg 1; adult/concession €6/3; ⊙ 10am-5pm Tue-Sun Apr–mid-Nov, closed mid-Nov–Mar) Ahrweiler's Roman roots spring to life at the Museum Roemervilla on the northwest edge of town. Protected by a lofty glass and wood structure are the surprisingly extensive 2nd- to 3rd-century ruins – a veritable Rhenish mini-Pompeii – which reveal the posh standard of living enjoyed by wealthy Romans.

St Laurentiuskirche CHURCH
(☑ 02641-347 37; http://laurentius-aw.de; Marktplatz) Laurentiuskirche goes back to the 13th century, making it one of the oldest hall churches in the Rhineland. It's beautifully decorated with floral frescoes from the 14th century, old wood carvings and luminous stained-glass windows, some of which show farmers working their vineyards.

Rotweinwanderweg WALKING
(Red Wine Hiking Trail; www.ahr-rotweinwanderweg. de) Well-signed paths abound throughout the Ahr Valley's vineyards. Wander amid the grapes and soak up the hillside views from Bad Bodendorf in the east to Altenahr in the west. The full length is almost 36km; it's broken up by wine tasting rooms and cute villages with train stops. The 6.7km Bad Neuenahr–Ahrweiler segment loops up beautifully into the hills.

For the route, check the website or pick up a brochure at the tourist offices.

Ahr Thermen SPA
(☑ 02641-911 760; www.ahr-thermen.de; Felix-Rütten-Strasse 3; day pass €17; ⊙ 9am-10pm Sun-Thu, to 11pm Fri & Sat) Neuenahr owes its status as a spa centre to the mineral water that bubbles up from the earth's volcanic belly and feeds the pools at this popular spa with 31°C water. Besides the pools, you can test the waters in a surge channel and whirlpools or pick up some steam in the sauna (bathing suits not allowed).

Towels and bathrobes may be rented for a small fee.

🍴 Sleeping & Eating

Kleine Herberge GUESTHOUSE €
(☑ 02641-378 1024; www.kleineherberge.de; Adenbachhutstrasse 8, Ahrweiler; d incl breakfast €58-69; ⊛) Just inside the Adenbachtor, the gate closest to the train stop, this 1898 house has been turned into a stylish two-room guesthouse. There's a garden out the back where you can chill out after hillside wanderings.

★ **Prümer Gang** BOUTIQUE HOTEL €€
(☑ 02641-4757; www.pruemergang.de; Niederhutstrasse 58, Ahrweiler; d incl breakfast €131-143; P⊛🐾) After a day of rambling and wine drinking, this charismatic boutique hotel will feel like a warm, welcome refuge.

WORTH A TRIP

NÜRBURGRING: A RACING LEGEND

The Nürburgring historic race-car track (☑ tollfree 0800 20 83 200; www.nuerburgring.de; Nürburgring Blvd 1, Nürburg; Green Hell tourist rides €25 Mon-Thu, €30 Sat & Sun; ⊙ info centre 9am-6pm) has hosted many spectacular races with legendary drivers since its completion in 1927. The 20.8km, 73-curve Nordschleife (North Loop) dates back to the 1920s and was one of the most difficult ever built, earning the respectful moniker 'Green Hell' from racing legend Jackie Stewart. With your own car or motorcycle, you can channel your inner Lewis Hamilton on the track nearly every day. See www.greenhell driving.nuerburgring.de for details.

After Niki Lauda's near-fatal crash in 1976, the German Grand Prix moved to the Hockenheimring near Mannheim, but in 1995 Formula One returned (in odd-numbered years) to the 5148m Grand-Prix-Strecke (South Loop), built in 1984. The complex hosts dozens of races a year. On select dates, it's also possible to do a tourist drive on the Grand Prix track. Another option is to join a pro driver in a high-performance machine such as a BMW M5 for a 'co-pilot ride' starting at €295; non-race periods only.

The Info°Center (☑ 0800 20 83 200; www.nuerburgring.de; ring°boulevard; ⊙ 9am-6pm) is the hub for all things Nürburgring: learn about the circuit, find out all the ways you can go fast, pick up pre-booked tickets and more.

The Nürburgring is off the B258, reached via the B257 from Altenahr. It is 60km west of Koblenz via the A61 and B412.

There are a dozen airy rooms with comfy mattresses and crisp sheets. Before retiring, unwind with free mineral water and tea in the sauna or steam room or treat yourself to creative, seasonal fare in the elegant yet relaxed restaurant.

Hotel & Restaurant Hohenzollern
HOTEL €€

(☑02641-9730; www.hotelhohenzollern.com; Am Silberberg 50, Ahrweiler; d incl breakfast €125-155; P⊝☎) At this elegant hillside hotel, right on the Rotweinwanderweg (p653; Red Wine Hiking Trail), the nicest rooms have a balcony with unbeatable valley views; you can save a bunch by booking one that opens out over the vineyards. The formal top-end restaurant serves market-fresh regional fare and is popular among locals for special occasions. Free sauna.

Das Kleine Caféhaus
CAFE €

(☑02641-5061; www.daskleinecafehaus.de; Niederhutstrasse 65, Ahrweiler; snacks €2.50-9; ⊝8.30am-6pm) Before your wine adventure begins – or when you need a break – fortify yourself at this top-class cafe with big breakfast spreads, homemade cakes, toothsome soups, fresh salads and light bistro classics. Nice people-watching from the sidewalk tables.

❶ Information

Ahrweiler Tourist Office (☑02641-917 10; www.ahrtal.de; Blankartshof 1; ⊝9am-12.30pm & 1.30-5pm Mon-Fri, 10am-3pm Sat & Sun)

Bad Neuenahr Tourist Office (☑02641-917 10; www.ahrtal.de; Hauptstrasse 80; ⊝9am-5pm Mon-Fri, 10am-3pm Sat & Sun)

❶ Getting There & Away

Hourly RB30 trains serve the towns from Bonn (€5.10, 36 minutes) via Remagen.

Altenahr
☑02643 / POP 1850

Surrounded on all sides by craggy peaks, steep vineyards and rolling hills, Altenahr may just be the most romantic spot in the Ahr Valley. The landscape is best appreciated by taking a 20-minute uphill walk from the Bahnhof to the 11th-century Burgruine Are, a ruined hilltop castle with a weather-beaten stone tower standing guard over the valley.

Altenahr is the western terminus of the Rotweinwanderweg (p653). A dozen more trails, including the 5km Geologischer Wanderweg, can be picked up in the village centre, where the main sight is the Romanesque Pfarrkirche Maria Verkündigung (Church of the Annunciation), which partly dates back to the late 1100s.

⬚ Sleeping & Eating

Hotel Zum Schwarzen Kreuz
HOTEL €

(☑02643-1534; www.zumschwarzenkreuz.de; Brückenstrasse 5-7; d incl breakfast €78; P⊝☎⊛) In the heart of town, this half-timbered old-school hotel offers a retro feel, a quiet library with overstuffed chairs and 30 rooms (some

---

OFF THE BEATEN TRACK

NAZI CASTLE TURNED PEACE CENTRE

In the middle of the serene Eifel National Park (Nationalpark Eifel; ☑02444-915 740; www.nationalpark-eifel.de; P) looms a hulking modern castle with a dark history. Ordensburg Vogelsang (☑02444-915 790; www.vogelsang-ip.de; Vogelsang 70, Schleiden; exhibits adult/concession €8/6 each, combination ticket €12/6, tours adult/concession €8/6; ⊝visitor centre 10am-5pm, tours 2pm daily, 11am Sat & Sun; P; ⬚SB82, SB63 Vogelsang IP Forum)was built by the Nazis as a party elite leadership training college and is one of the largest remaining Third Reich buildings. In 2006 it was developed into an international centre of tolerance and peace. The spanking new visitors centre (⊝10am-5pm) has two excellent exhibits on the compound's Nazi-era period and on the natural history of the Eifel National Park.

After WWII Vogelsang was used as a military training site by the Belgian army. You're free to explore the grounds on your own or to join a guided tour (in German). Don't miss climbing up the tower to take in the immense size of the complex and how it fits into the idyllic surrounds.

To get there by public transport, take a train to Kall or Simmerath, which will be met by the Eifel National Park shuttle SB62 or SB63, respectively. Both go straight to Vogelsang. See www.vrsinfo.de for timings.

with balconies), as well as a restaurant serving specialities from the Eifel region (mains €9 to €20) and *Flammkuchen* (Alsatian pizza). Free wi-fi in public areas only.

Ruland GERMAN €€
(☑02643-8318; www.hotel-ruland.de; Brückenstrasse 6; mains €10-24; ⊗noon-2.30pm & 5-9.30pm Mon-Fri, noon-9.30pm Sat & Sun) Elegant without being stuffy, this restaurant in the eponymous hotel cooks up German food with a seasonal, contemporary kick. The menu changes often but may include roast corn-fed chicken with ginger and lemongrass, or fried pike-perch with onion-Riesling marinade. Excellent local wines, naturally.

❶ Information

Altenahr Tourist Office (☑02643-8448; www.altenahr-ahr.de; Altenburger Strasse 1a; ⊗10am-3pm Mon-Fri) Limited hours and info.

❶ Getting There & Away

From Bonn, regional train line RB30 runs hourly through the Ahr Valley via Remagen (€7.90, one hour).

Aachen

☑0241 / POP 254,000

Aachen has been around for millennia. The Romans nursed their war wounds and stiff joints in the steaming waters of its mineral springs, but it was Charlemagne who put the city firmly on the European map. The emperor, too, enjoyed a dip now and then, but it was more for strategic reasons that he made Aachen the geographical and political capital of his vast Frankish Empire in 974 – arguably the first empire with European dimensions.

Today, Aachen is still a quintessentially international city that has a unique appeal because of its location in the border triangle with the Netherlands and Belgium. Charlemagne's legacy lives on in the stunning Dom, which in 1978 became Germany's first Unesco World Heritage Site, as well as in the new Centre Charlemagne and the Route Charlemagne (p658) walking trail.

Aachen has a lively vibe that's further enhanced by a large student population.

⊙ Sights

Appreciating the Dom and wandering Aachen's medieval streets can easily fill a day. Everything is reachable on foot.

REDECORATING THE DOM

Like the stereotypical suburban housewives who never know when to leave well enough alone, the caretakers of the Dom have been on a centuries-long remodelling binge. The result is that very little of what you see dates from Charlemagne's time. For instance, the interior of the main part of the church was redone for the umpteenth time in the 19th century, when vast amounts of Byzantine gilt and stained glass were introduced. At that time, churches across Europe thought to be as old as the Dom were scoured for design ideas, which explains why you can see echoes of Istanbul's Hagia Sophia in the Aachen Dom.

The inside of the dome overhead dates from the 17th century – and on it goes. Other than possibly the hidden relics and Charlemagne's bones, the oldest authenticated item in the Dom is the 12th-century chandelier, which was a gift from Emperor Friedrich Barbarossa.

★**Aachener Dom** CATHEDRAL
(☑0241-4770 9110; www.aachendom.de; Münsterplatz; tours adult/concession €4/3; ⊗7am-7pm Apr-Dec, to 6pm Jan-Mar) It's impossible to overestimate the significance of Aachen's magnificent cathedral. The burial place of Charlemagne, it's where more than 30 German kings were crowned and where pilgrims have flocked since the 12th century. Before entering the church, stop by Dom Information (☑0241-4770 9145; Johannes-Paul-II-Strasse 1; ⊗10am-5pm Jan-Mar, to 6pm Apr-Dec) for info and tickets for tours and the cathedral treasury (p657). English tours run daily at 2pm.

The oldest and most impressive section is Charlemagne's palace chapel, the Pfalzkapelle, an outstanding example of Carolingian architecture. Completed in 800, the year of the emperor's coronation, it's an octagonal dome encircled by a 16-sided ambulatory supported by antique Italian pillars. The colossal brass chandelier was a gift from Emperor Friedrich Barbarossa, during whose reign Charlemagne was canonised in 1165.

Pilgrims have poured into town ever since that time, drawn as much by the cult surrounding Charlemagne as by its prized relics: Christ's loincloth from when he was

Aachen

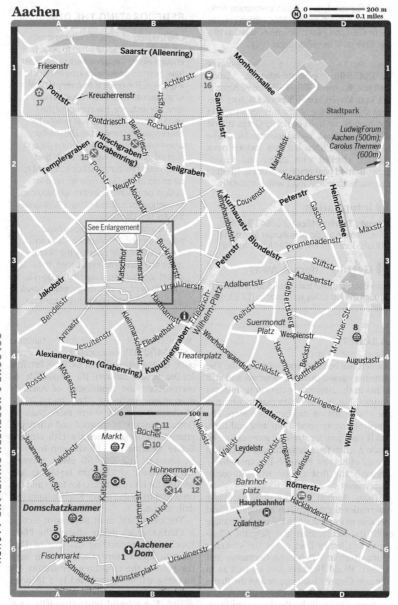

COLOGNE & NORTHERN RHINELAND AACHEN

crucified, Mary's cloak, the cloth that John the Baptist's decapitated head was wrapped in, and swaddling clothes from when Jesus was an infant. These are displayed once every seven years (next in 2021) and draw 100,000 or more of the faithful.

To accommodate these regular floods of visitors, a Gothic choir was docked to the chapel in 1414 and filled with such treasures as the Pala d'oro – a gold-plated altar-front depicting Christ's Passion – and the jewel-encrusted gilded copper pulpit, both fash-

Aachen

ioned in the 11th century. At the far end is the gilded shrine of Charlemagne that has held the emperor's remains since 1215. In front, the equally fanciful shrine of St Mary shelters the four relics.

Unless you join a guided tour, you'll barely get a glimpse of the white marble of Charlemagne's imperial throne in the upstairs gallery. Reached via six steps – just like King Solomon's throne – it served as the coronation throne of 30 German kings between 936 and 1531.

★ **Domschatzkammer**   MUSEUM
(Cathedral Treasury; ☎0241-4770 9127; www.aachener-domschatz.de; Johannes-Paul-II-Strasse 2; adult/concession €5/4; ☺10am-2pm Mon, to 5pm Tue-Sun Jan-Mar, 10am-2pm Mon, to 6pm Tue-Sun Apr-Dec) Aachen's cathedral treasury is a veritable mother lode of gold, silver and jewels. Of particular importance are the silver-and-gold bust of Charlemagne and a 10th-century bejewelled processional cross known as the Lotharkreuz; both featured in the coronation ceremonies held at the cathedral between 936 and 1531. Other highlights include a 1000-year-old relief-decorated ivory situla (a pail for holy water) and the marble sarcophagus that held Charlemagne's

bones until his canonisation; the relief shows the rape of Persephone.

Get tickets at Dom Information.

Centre Charlemagne   MUSEUM
(☎0241-432 4956; www.centre-charlemagne.eu; Katschhof 1; adult/concession €6/3; ☺10am-5pm Tue-Sun) A modern triangular building in the midst of where the great man walked, this museum looks at not only the life and times of Charlemagne but also Aachen's dramatic history. Multimedia exhibits bring key periods to life, from the Roman era onward. Begin your Route Charlemagne walk here; there is a huge amount of info in English.

Rathaus   HISTORIC BUILDING
(Town Hall; ☎0241-432 7310; http://rathaus-aachen.de; Markt; adult/concession/under 22 incl audioguide €6/3/free; ☺10am-6pm) Fifty life-sized statues of German rulers, including 30 kings crowned in Aachen between 936 and 1531 AD, adorn the facade of Aachen's splendid Gothic town hall. Inside, the undisputed highlight is the vaulted coronation hall where the post-ceremony banquets were held. Note the epic 19th-century frescoes and replicas of the imperial insignia: a crown, orb and sword (the originals are in Vienna).

The Rathaus was built in the 14th century atop the foundations of Charlemagne's palace, of which the eastern tower, the Granusturm, is the oldest part to survive.

Suermondt Ludwig Museum   MUSEUM
(☎0241-479 8040; www.suermondt-ludwig-museum.de; Wilhelmstrasse 18; adult/concession/under 22yr €8/4/free; ☺10am-5pm Tue-Sun) The Suermondt Ludwig Museum is especially proud of its medieval sculpture but also has fine works by Cranach, Dürer, Macke, Dix and other masters. An oddly fascinating highlight is the room of curiosities with such items as a stuffed shark and a falcon mummy on display.

It's all beautifully presented in a 19th-century town mansion.

Ludwig Forum Aachen   MUSEUM
(☎0241-180 7104; www.ludwigforum.de; Jülicher Strasse 97-109; adult/concession/under 22 €5/3/free; ☺10am-5pm Tue, Wed, Fri-Sun, to 8pm Thu; ▣1, 11, 16, 21, 36, 52 Ludwig Forum, Blücherplatz) In a former umbrella factory, the well-respected Ludwig Forum trains the spotlight on American and European contemporary art (Warhol, Richter, Holzer, Penck, Haring) and also stages progressive changing exhibits. Among the most eye-catching works is

ROUTE CHARLEMAGNE

The Route Charlemagne (www.route-charlemagne.eu) is a self-guided walk designed to showcase Aachen's 1200-year tradition as a European city of culture and science. It links key sites around town, including the cathedral, the Rathaus, the Grashaus (the former town hall) and the Elisenbrunnen hot springs. Each stop has exhibits on a particular theme (such as history, power, religion) to show the connection between Charlemagne's times and today.

Pick up a map (€1, or download for free) at the logical starting place for the tour, the Centre Charlemagne, or at the tourist office .

the sculpture *Supermarket Lady* (1971) by Duane Hanson, a poignant critique of mass consumption.

Katschhof SQUARE

(Katschhof) It's worth finding a comfy spot in which to sit and contemplate this deeply historic square. At the north end is the backside of the Rathaus; across from it is the Dom and its complex of buildings. To the west is a mishmash of old buildings that have parts dating back to when this was part of Charlemagne's palace.

Activities & Tours

In fine weather, get off the asphalt and onto the trails of the densely forested spa garden north of the Altstadt. A brisk 20-minute walk takes you up the 264m-high **Lousberg** hill, where the entire city panorama unfolds before you. Get there by cutting north on Kupferstrasse from Ludwigsallee, then left on Belvedereallee.

Carolus Thermen SPA

(☑0241-182 740; www.carolus-thermen.de; Stadtgarten/Passstrasse 79; 4½hr/all day without sauna €18/36 Mon-Fri, €19/38 Sat & Sun, with sauna €33/36 Mon-Fri, €35/38 Sat & Sun; ☺9am-11pm, last entry 9.30pm; ☐34, 51 Carolus Thermen/Ungarnplatz) Oriental pools, honey rubs, deep-tissue massages and soothing saunas are among the relaxation options at the Carolus Thermen, a snazzy bathing complex on the edge of the Stadtpark (city park) fed by Aachen's mineral springs. Bathing suits are a no-no inside the saunas.

Tickets for shorter sessions (from 2.5 hours) are also available.

★ Aachener Dom Guided Tour TOURS

(adult/concession €4/3; ☺tours 11am-5.30pm Mon-Fri, 1-5pm Sat & Sun, 2pm tour in English daily) The only way to see Charlemagne's throne and learn about the cathedral's complicated past is on one of these excellent tours, which take you into parts of the incense-scented interior you can't otherwise visit. Book at Dom Information (p655).

🛏 Sleeping

There are good overnight choices around the Dom and the historical quarters. Chain hotels dot the ring roads.

A&O Aachen HOSTEL, HOTEL €

(☑0241-4630 73300; www.aohostels.com; Hackländerstrasse 5; dm/s/d from €22/60/65; ℗🐾) It's vast and utilitarian, and you can't beat this flashpacker haven's location next to the train station and close to the centre. All rooms have private bathrooms and there is a lift, a bar and a pool table. Families can check into large rooms with a double and a bunk bed and there's a communal kiddie play corner as well.

At busy times rates can soar past those of plusher digs in town.

Hotel Drei Könige HOTEL €€

(☑0241-483 93; www.h3k-aachen.de; Büchel 5; d €129-169; 🐾🐾🐾) The sunny Mediterranean design and quirky touches are an instant mood-lifter at this family-run favourite with its super-central location. Some of the 10 rooms are a tad wee. Breakfast, on the 4th floor, comes with dreamy views over the rooftops and the cathedral (p655).

Aquis Grana City Hotel HOTEL €€

(☑0241-4430; www.hotel-aquis-grana.de; Büchel 32; d incl breakfast €100-165; ℗🐾🐾🐾) The best quarters at this gracious hotel have terrace and balcony views of the cathedral or town hall. But even in the most modest of the 98 rooms, you couldn't be any closer to the heart of town. The hotel offers a full range of services, including a bar and a restaurant.

🍴 Eating

Aachen is the birthplace of the famous (and tasty) *Printen,* crunchy spiced cookies (a bit like gingerbread) spiked with herbs or nuts and drenched in chocolate or icing. You'll find them sold in bakeries and supermarkets across town.

★ Café zum Mohren
CAFE €

(☑0241-352 00; www.cafezummohren.de; Hof 4; mains €4.50-10; ⊙10am-7pm) This darling cafe just off the tourist trail is famous for its cakes, especially a wicked chocolate one called *Krippekratz* (local slang for 'devil') and sumptuous ice-cream cakes. Also a good spot for breakfast or light meals. Outside tables overlook a courtyard flanked by Roman columns.

Alt-Aachener Café-Stuben
CAFE €

(Cafe Van den Daele; ☑0241-357 24; www.van-den-daele.de; Büchel 18; treats from €3; ⊙9am-6pm Mon-Sat, 10am-6pm Sun) Leather-covered walls, tiled stoves and antiques forge the yesteryear feel of this rambling cafe established in 1890 (the building goes back to 1655). It's famous for its house-made *Printen,* which come in a dozen varieties, but also wows eyes and belly with its tantalising array of cakes and a Belgian speciality called *Reisfladen* (pie filled with rice pudding).

★ Am Knipp
GERMAN €€

(☑0241-331 68; www.amknipp.de; Bergdriesch 3; mains €9-24; ⊙5-10.30pm Mon & Wed-Fri, 6-10.30pm Sat & Sun; ☎) Hungry grazers have stopped by this traditional inn since 1698, and you too will have a fine time enjoying hearty German cuisine served amid a flea market's worth of knick-knacks or, if weather permits, in the big beer garden.

Magellan
MEDITERRANEAN €€

(☑0241-401 6440; https://magellan-aachen.de; Pontstrasse 78; mains €7.50-22; ⊙10am-1am Sun-Thu, to 2am Fri & Sat) This restaurant-bar comes with a lovely hidden garden right near the centre of town. There's even a little stream running past garden tables where you can enjoy refreshments and food with Mediterranean flair, including a number of delicious Turkish dishes.

Locals turn out in droves for the weekend brunch buffets (Saturday/Sunday €9.90/13.90).

🍷 Drinking & Entertainment

The main bar-hopping drag is student-flavoured Pontstrasse (locals say 'Ponte').

For listings, pick up the free magazine *Klenkes* (www.klenkes.de) in cafes and the tourist office.

Cafe & Bar Zuhause
BAR

(☑0241-9278 9974; www.zuhause-aachen.de; Sandkaulstrasse 109/11; ⊙6pm-midnight Mon-Fri, 2pm-midnight Sat & Sun) This living-room-style cafe brims with books and leafy plants. It's an inviting refuge for winding down on vintage sofas or for meeting locals over a cold beer and a soccer match on the big screen.

Apollo Kino & Bar
BAR, CLUB

(☑0241-900 8484; www.apollo-aachen.de; Pontstrasse 141-149; movie tickets €6-7.50; ⊙movies daily, party Tue-Sat) This cavernous basement joint does double duty as an art-house cinema and a sweaty dance club that draws mainly from Aachen's huge student population. DJs play a potpourri of sounds that varies by night – salsa to '80s, funk to house. Drink specials fuel the vibe.

ℹ Information

Aachen Tourist Office (☑0241-180 2950; www.aachen-tourist.de; Friedrich-Wilhelm-Platz; ⊙10am-6pm Mon-Fri, to 2pm Sat & Sun Apr-Dec, shorter hours Jan-Mar)

There's free wi-fi ('Aachen WiFi') in the centre around the Dom (p655); no password needed.

ℹ Getting There & Away

Regional trains to Cologne (€17.50, one hour) run twice hourly from the **Hauptbahnhof** (www.bahnhof.de/bahnhof-de/Aachen_Hbf-1027760; Bahnhofsplatz), with some proceeding beyond. Aachen is a stop for high-speed trains to/from Brussels (€40, 1¼ hours) and Paris.

Flixbus has two stops: **Aachen West** (Kühlwetterstrasse 18; ▣ Aachen Westbahnhof), about 1.5km north of the cathedral, and **Aachen Hüls**

> ### ℹ CULTURE DEALS
>
> Museum hounds can save a bundle by picking up the Six for Six museum pass, which is good for one-time admission to the Centre Charlemagne, the Ludwig Forum, the Suermondt Ludwig Museum, the Couven Museum (☑0241-432 4421; www.couven-museum. de; Hühnermarkt 17; adult/concession/under 22yr €6/3/free; ⊙10am-5pm Tue-Sun) and the Internationales Zeitungsmuseum as well as the Rathaus. Available at any of these sites, it costs €14 (concession €10) and is good for six months.
>
> Consider yourself double-lucky if you're 21 or under: in that case, admission is completely free.

(Wilmersdorfer Strasse; 🚌 23, 47 Wilmersdorfer Strasse), about 4.5km east of the city centre.

ℹ Getting Around

From the Hauptbahnhof (p659) it's a 10- to 15-minute signed walk to the tourist office (p659) and the Altstadt.

Bus tickets for travel within central Aachen cost €1.70; drivers sell tickets. For timetable information, check www.aseag.de.

Radstation (📞 0241-9903 3216; Bahnhofstrasse 22; bikes per day from €5, e-bikes €10; 🕐 5.30am-10.30pm Mon-Fri, 10am-6.30pm Sat & Sun) by the train station rents bikes.

Düsseldorf

📞 0211 / POP 628,000

Düsseldorf impresses with boundary-pushing architecture, zinging nightlife and an art scene to rival many higher-profile cities. It's a posh and modern city that seems all buttoned-up business at first glance: banking, advertising, fashion and telecommunications are among the fields that have made North Rhine–Westphalia's capital one of Germany's wealthiest cities. Yet all it takes is a few hours of bar-hopping around the Altstadt (the historical quarter along the Rhine) to realise that locals have no problem letting their hair down once they shed those Armani jackets.

The Altstadt claims fame as the 'longest bar in the world' but some focus has moved to Medienhafen (p664), a redeveloped harbour area home to international avant-garde architecture. Older neighbourhoods are also evolving, including the now-hip Flingern and the vibrantly creative Unterbilk, especially along Lorettostrasse. And the new underground Wehrhahn line's six stations are an eye-catching blend of architecture, design and art.

⊙ Sights

⊙ Altstadt

Düsseldorf's Altstadt, a mostly pedestrianised web of lanes cuddling up to the Rhine, is rightly (in)famous for its lively nightlife but also has lots of sights, from a grand baroque church to museums on art, film and ceramics, and a lively river promenade.

★ **K20 Grabbeplatz**　　　　　　MUSEUM
(📞 0211-838 1204; www.kunstsammlung.de; Grabbeplatz 5; adult/concession/child €12/10/2.50;

🕐 10am-6pm Tue-Fri, 11am-6pm Sat & Sun; Ⓤ Schadowstrasse) A collection that spans the arc of 20th-century artistic vision gives the K20 an enviable edge in the art world. It encompasses major works by Picasso, Matisse and Mondrian and more than 100 paintings and drawings by Paul Klee. Americans represented include Jackson Pollock, Andy Warhol and Jasper Johns. Düsseldorf's own Joseph Beuys has a major presence as well.

A combination ticket with sister museum K21 Ständehaus costs €18 (concession/child €14/4). The two museums make up the **Kunstsammlung Nordrhein-Westfalen**.

★ **K21 Ständehaus**　　　　　　MUSEUM
(📞 0211-838 1204; www.kunstsammlung.de; Ständehausstrasse 1; adult/concession/child €12/10/2.50; 🕐 10am-6pm Tue-Fri, 11am-6pm Sat & Sun; Ⓤ Graf-Adolf-Platz) A stately 19th-century parliament building forms a fabulously dichotomous setting for the cutting-edge art of the K21 – a collection only showcasing works created after the 1980s. Large-scale film and video installations and groups of works share space with site-specific rooms by an international cast of artists including Andreas Gursky, Candida Höfer, Bill Viola and Nam June Paik.

Kunsthalle Düsseldorf　　　　GALLERY
(Art Hall; 📞 0211-899 6240; www.kunsthalle-duesseldorf.de; Grabbeplatz 4; adult/concession/under 18yr €6/3/free; 🕐 11am-6pm Tue-Sun; Ⓤ Heinrich-Heine-Allee) A Brutalist '60s cube built from prefabricated blocks of concrete houses the Kunsthalle, which hosts bleeding-edge contemporary art shows. The bookstore is superb.

Andreaskirche　　　　　　　　CHURCH
(📞 0211-136 340; www.dominikaner-duesseldorf.de; Andreasstrasse 27; 🕐 7.30am-6.30pm Mon-Sat, 8.30am-7pm Sun; Ⓤ Heinrich-Heine-Allee) This early baroque church, built from 1622 to 1629, is drenched in fanciful white stucco. Six baroque saint sculptures from the original altar are integrated into the sanctuary. More religious art awaits in the treasury in the upstairs gallery. A great time to visit is for the free organ concert at 4.30pm on Sundays.

Mahn- und Gedenkstätte Düsseldorf　　MEMORIAL
(Memorial Düsseldorf; 📞 0211-899 6205; www.gedenk-dus.de; Mühlenstrasse 6; 🕐 11am-5pm Sun-Fri, 1-5pm Sat; Ⓤ Heinrich-Heine-Allee) FREE Just west of the central Marktplatz, this memorial

trains the spotlight on local persecution and resistance during the Third Reich. It reopened in 2015 after a complete reconstruction and expansion. The permanent exhibit addresses the topic of Düsseldorf's children and youth in the Third Reich.

Marktplatz SQUARE

(U Heinrich-Heine-Allee) The historical Marktplatz is framed by the Renaissance Rathaus (1573) and accented by a bronze equestrian statue of Jan Wellem. The art-loving 17th-century ruler lies buried nearby in the Andreaskirche.

⊙ Along the Rhine

Rheinuferpromenade WATERFRONT

(Rhine River Walk; 🚌 726 Alter Hafen, Mannesmannufer, U Benrather Strasse) Burgplatz marks the northern end of the Rheinuferpromenade, where cafes and benches fill with people in fine weather, creating an almost Mediterranean feel.

Museum Kunstpalast MUSEUM

(🖉 0211-5664 2100; www.smkp.de; Ehrenhof 5; adult/child €5/4, special exhibits vary; ⊙ 11am-6pm Tue, Wed, Fri-Sun, to 9pm Thu; U Tonhalle/Ehrenhof) The Kunstpalast stages changing exhibitions drawn from its well-respected art collection and often presented in paradigm-shifting ways. As such, old masters may find themselves juxtaposed with modern iconoclasts and non-Western works to reveal unexpected connections between the ages and artistic trends.

Concerts are held in the grand Robert Schumann Saal music hall.

NRW-Forum Düsseldorf GALLERY

(🖉 0211-892 6690; www.nrw-forum.de; Ehrenhof 2; adult/concession/under 17 €6/4/1 Tue-Thu, €8/5/1 Fri-Sun; ⊙ 11am-8pm Tue-Thu, to 9pm Fri, 10am-9pm Sat, 10am-6pm Sun; U Tonhalle/Ehrenhof) For innovative artistic expression, head to the NRW-Forum Düsseldorf; it primarily deals in cutting-edge media, including digital art, and mounts zeitgeist-capturing exhibits that blur the boundaries between genres.

St Lambertuskirche CHURCH

(Church of St Lambert; 🖉 0211-300 4990; www.lambertuspfarre.de; Stiftsplatz; ⊙ 8am-5pm; U Tonhalle/Ehrenhof) The twisted tower of the 14th-century St Lambertuskirche shadows treasures that span several centuries. Look for the Gothic tabernacle, the Renaissance

LOCAL KNOWLEDGE

HAVE A FLING WITH FLINGERN

Once all working-class, Flingern, east of the Hauptbahnhof (p668), is now the centre of all things stylish and cool in Düsseldorf. Its core drag, Ackerstrasse, is alive with harbingers of hipsterism; owner-run indie boutiques, homey cafes and minimalist-chic restaurant bars. Famous local band Kraftwerk's old Kling-Klang-Studio is also here, rebooted as an edgy sound lab.

Getting here is easy: from the Hauptbahnhof it's either a 15-minute walk via Worringer Strasse or a short ride on tram 709 or 719 to Wetterstrasse (head north for a couple of minutes to get to Ackerstrasse).

marble tombs, baroque altars and modern windows.

Schlossturm & SchifffahrtMuseum HISTORIC BUILDING

(Palace Tower & Navigation Museum; 🖉 0211-899 4195; http://freunde-schifffahrtmuseum.de; Burgplatz 30; adult/concession €3/1.50; ⊙ 11am-6pm Tue-Sun; U Heinrich-Heine-Allee, Tonhalle/Ehrenhof) Looking a bit forlorn by the river, the Schlossturm is all that's left of the electors' palace, which burned down in 1872. Recently restored, it houses a multimedia exhibit about shipping and trading on the Rhine and a cafe in the top of the tower.

Hetjens Museum MUSEUM

(German Ceramics Museum; 🖉 0211-899 4210; www.duesseldorf.de/hetjens; Schulstrasse 4; adult/concession/under 18yr €4/2/free; ⊙ 11am-5pm Tue & Thu-Sun, to 9pm Wed; U Benrather Strasse) A short detour off the Rheinuferpromenade takes you to the Hetjens Museum, famous for its comprehensive survey of 8000 years of ceramic art from around the world. A German or English audioguide is available for €2.

Filmmuseum MUSEUM

(🖉 0211-899 2232; www.duesseldorf.de/film museum; Schulstrasse 4; adult/concession/under 18yr €5/2.50/free, free for all during last 30min; ⊙ 11am-6pm Tue-Sun; U Heinrich-Heine-Allee, Benrather Strasse) This small musuem trains the spotlight on the technology, history and mystery of movie-making. Its Black Box art-house cinema presents retrospectives, rare flicks and silent movies with live organ accompaniment.

Düsseldorf

COLOGNE & NORTHERN RHINELAND DÜSSELDORF

Düsseldorf
International
(8km)

Joseph-Beuys-Ufer

Fischerstr

Nordstr

Duisburger Str

Rochusstr

11

Scheibenstr

Inselstr

Arnoldstr

Feldstr

Sternstr

Rosenstr

Mozartstr

12 Ehrenhof

Oederallee

Kaiserstr

Taubenstr

19

Oberkasseler
Brücke

Tonhalle

36

Hofgartenrampe

Fritz-Roeber-Str

Jägerhofstr

Gartenstr

Hofgarten

Maxim-Weyhe-Allee

Reiterkaserne

Altestadt

Ritterstr

32 24

Ratinger Str

Liefergasse

Stiftsplatz

6

Jan-
Wellem-Platz

Gustaf-
Gründgens-
Platz

Schossstr

Rheinuferpromenade

16

Grabbeplatz

Mühlenstr

1 K20
Grabbeplatz

Rhine

15 Burgplatz

Kurze Str

Marktplatz

Mertensgasse

9 Andreasstr

31

8

3

34

Heinrich-
Heine-
Allee

Schadow-
platz

Schadowstr

14

Zollstr

10

Marktstr

Hunsrückenstr

Cornelius
platz

Tourist Office – Altstadt

Rheinartstr

ALTSTADT

33

Berger Str

Wallstr

Grabenstr

Königsallee

Heinrich-Heine-Allee

Blumenstr

Marienstr

4

Schulstr

5

Bäckerstr

23

Berger Allee

Bäckergasse

Bilker Str

25 Carlsplatz

Benratherstr

CARLSTADT

Steinstrasse/Königsallee

Steinstr

Kreuzstr

Rheinkniebrücke

35

26

Mediciplatz

Bastionstr

Königsallee

Grünstr

Berliner Allee

Stresemannstr

22

Kasernenstr

Breite Str

7

Thomasstr

Horion-
platz

Bahnstr

Alexanderstr

29

13

Apolloplatz

Mannesmannufer Rathausufer

Südstr

Hohe Str

Graf-
Adolf-
Platz

Graf-Adolf-Str

Adersstr

Ernst-
Reuter-
Platz

Adersstr

21

Neusserstr

Kavalleriestr

Poststr

Haroldstr

Luisenstr

Luisenstr

Hüttenstr

Pionierstr

Reichsstr

Ständehausstr

2 K21
Ständehaus

Elisabethstr

Friedrichstr

Talstr

Herzogstr

Jahnstr

Medienhafen
(1.5km)

Fürstenwall

Fürstenwall

18

KIT
GALLERY

(Kunst im Tunnel; ☎0211-892 0769; www.kunst-im-tunnel.de; Mannesmannufer 1b; adult/concession €4/3; ⊙11am-6pm Tue-Sun; 🚊706, 708, 709 Landtag/Kniebrücke) Young artists – many from the local art academy – get the nod in this underground exhibition space housed in a spectacularly adapted tunnel below the Rheinuferpromenade (p661). The entrance is via a glass pavilion.

Rheinturm   TOWER
(Rhine Tower; ☑ 0211-863 2000; Stromstrasse 20; adult/concession €9/7, half-price with minimum spend; ⊙ 10am-midnight Sun-Thu, to 1am Fri & Sat; ⬜ 726, 732 Stadttor, ⬜ 706, 709 Stadttor) Spearing the sky at the southern end of the Rheinuferpromenade (p661), the Rheinturm, which is brilliantly lit at night, and has an observation deck at the 164m level of its overall height of 240m. There are various cafes and bars, and a revolving restaurant. Intriguingly, the circular portholes along the tower's shaft form a decimal clock.

⊙ Königsallee & Hofgarten

Nowhere does Düsseldorf's reputation as a fashion capital find better expression than on its chic Königsallee. Along with Rodeo Drive and Fifth Avenue, the Kö, as it is fondly called, has long been one of the world's most illustrious shopping avenues. Those who worship at the altar of ritzy brand names will be in heaven on this tree-lined catwalk of couture whose northern end spills into Daniel Libeskind's striking Kö-Bogen, a sinuously geometric shopping mall completed in 2013. It flanks the Hofgarten (Ⓤ Schadowstrasse), which provides a breezy respite from urbanity.

⊙ Medienhafen

This once-dead old harbour area has been reborn as the Medienhafen (Am Handelshafen; ⬜ 726,732 Erftstrasse/Grand Bateau), a hip quarter filled with architecture, restaurants, bars, hotels and clubs. Once-crumbling warehouses have been turned into high-tech office buildings and now rub shoulders with bold new structures designed by celebrated international architects, including Frank Gehry.

⊙ Schloss Benrath

Schloss Benrath   MUSEUM
(☑ 0211-892 1903; www.schloss-benrath.de; Benrather Schlossallee 100-106; day pass adult/concession/child €14/10/4; ⊙ museums 11am-5pm Mon-Fri, to 6pm Sat Apr-Oct, 11am-5pm Tue-Sun Nov-Mar; Ⓟ; Ⓤ Urdenbacher Allee) About 10km south of the city centre, Schloss Benrath is a park-and-palace ensemble where elector Carl Theodor, a man of deep pockets and

good taste, came to relax and frolic in the late 18th century. Designed by Frenchman Nicolas de Pigage, the three-winged palace centres on the residential tract (Corps de Logis), where tours offer a glimpse of the elector's lifestyle. Tours in English run at 3pm Tuesday to Sunday; tours in German are more frequent.

The other wings contain an old-school natural history museum and a museum of European garden history that may well grow on you. The day pass includes the Corps de Logis as well as access to the park and the two museums. If you don't want to see everything, separate tickets are available as well.

⚲ Tours

Hop On Hop Off City Tour   BUS
(☑ 0211-1720 2854; www.duesseldorf-tourismus. de/city-tours; Tourist Office, Immermannstrasse 65; 1-/2-day pass adult & 2 children €15/21; ⊙ 10.30am-4.30pm) This bus tour of the city, operated by the tourist office (p668), is a good way to get a handle on the sprawl of Düsseldorf in 90 minutes. There are a few caveats: the 'Hop On Hop Off' aspect is slightly dubious as you can wait a long time between buses, and the roof may stay closed even on nice days.

⌸ Sleeping

Düsseldorf's hotels cater primarily to business travellers, which explains why prices can triple during big trade shows held not only here but as far away as Cologne and Essen. Fortunately, bargains abound on weekends and in summer.

Backpackers Düsseldorf   HOSTEL €
(☑ 0211-302 0848; www.backpackers-duesseldorf. de; Fürstenwall 180; dm €18.50-25, s/d €32/50; ⊙ reception 8am-10pm; Ⓟ @ 🛜; Ⓤ Kirchplatz) Düsseldorf's adorable indie hostel sleeps 60 in clean four- to 10-bed dorms outfitted with individual backpack-sized lockers. Bathrooms are shared. It's a low-key place with a kitchen and a relaxed lounge where cultural and language barriers melt quickly. The vending machine is filled with beer. Rates include a small breakfast; linen costs €3.

Boutique Hotel Berial   BOUTIQUE HOTEL €
(☑ 0211-490 0490; www.boutique-hotel-duesseldorf.de; Gartenstrasse 30; s/d incl breakfast from €55/70; @ 🛜; ⬜ 707 Schloss Jägerhof) This well-kept property is run with a personal touch and puts you minutes from the Hof-

garten – perfect for jogging off your jet lag. The 40 rooms sport stylish designer furniture, an easy-on-the-eyes colour scheme and extra-comfy box spring beds. Breakfast is a sumptuous spread. Superb value for money.

Hotels Sir & Lady Astor
BOUTIQUE HOTEL €€

(☑ 0211-173 370, 0211-936 090; www.sir-astor.de; Kurfürstenstrasse 18 & 23; d €81-96; ⊜ ✳ @ ⓢ; Ⓤ Hauptbahnhof) Never mind the ho-hum setting on a residential street near the Hauptbahnhof (p668): this charismatic twin boutique hotel brims with class and charm. Check-in is at Sir Astor, furnished in 'Scotland-meets-Provence' style with plaid carpets in public areas and rooms where the bedside wall is covered with swirling floral wallpaper. The decor's similar in the Lady Astor guesthouse across the street

Breakfast is an extra €9.

Hotel Windsor
HOTEL €€

(☑ 0211-914 680; www.windsorhotel.de; Grafenberger Allee 36; d from €81; Ⓟ ✳ ⓢ; Ⓤ Wehrhahn, Uhlandstrasse) The Windsor's design commits itself to the British country tradition. Behind the sandstone facade of this 100-year-old mansion await 18 rooms where you can unwind surrounded by antiques, fleur-de-lis carpets and sedate prints. Some rooms have air-con; those facing the garden are quietest.

Optional breakfast is €9 and served in a sunny room with a coffered ceiling and plaid wallpaper.

Max Hotel Garni
PENSION €€

(☑ 0211-386 800; www.max-hotelgarni.de; Adersstrasse 65; s/d €75/90; ⊜ @ ⓢ ✳; ⓡ 708, 709 Stresemannplatz) Upbeat, contemporary and run with personal flair, this charmer is a favourite Düsseldorf bargain. The 11 good-sized rooms are brightened by playful green colour accents. Rates include coffee, tea, soft drinks and a local public transport pass; breakfast costs €7.50. The reception isn't always staffed, so call ahead to arrange an arrival time.

25hours Hotel Das Tour
HOTEL €€€

(☑ 0211-900 9100; www.25hours-hotels.com; Louis-Pasteur-Platz 1; r €130-210; Ⓟ ✳ ⓢ; Ⓤ Wehrhahn) Part of new Le Quartier Central, a reurbanised freight yard about 2km north of the Hauptbahnhof (p668), this hip new contender is an ironic marriage of French *savoir vivre* and German engineering. While 'German' rooms have a cutting-edge cool design, the 'French' ones brim with

playful, ironic touches. A highlight is the Paris Club bi-level restaurant-bar on the upper floors.

Optional breakfast is €21.

Eating

Düsseldorf has a rich international and contemporary dining scene, including some of the most authentic Japanese food outside of Tokyo. Travelers with a hankering for rib-sticking Rhenish cuisine will be in heaven in traditional Altstadt brewpubs.

Sulis Cafe
CAFE €

(☑ 0211-5985 1470; www.suliscafe.de; Tussmannstrasse 5; dishes €4-13; ⊙ 10am-6pm Tue-Fri, from 9am Sat & Sun; ⓢ ✎; ⓡ 704 Tussmannstrasse) This locally adored cafe is especially lovely in summer when half the 'hood comes out to sip java and eat yummy cheesecake or carrot cake (both homemade of course) on the sunny terrace. Otherwise, the wooden tables and high ceiling provide a relaxed backdrop for breakfast, build-your-own salads and soups. Service is charming and swift.

Bäckerei Hinkel
BAKERY €

(☑ 0211-8620 3413; www.baeckerei-hinkel.de; Hohe Strasse 31; snacks from €2; ⊙ 6am-6.30pm Mon-Fri, to 4pm Sat; ⓡ 703, 706 Benrather Strasse) This traditional bakery is an institution that has people queuing patiently for its excellent breads and cakes. Buy the fixings for a perfect picnic – it blows away anything you've had from a train station chain bakery.

Bistro Zicke
INTERNATIONAL €

(☑ 0211-324 056; www.bistro-zicke.de; Bäckerstrasse 5a; dishes €6-12; ⊙ 9am-1am; ✎; Ⓤ Benrather Strasse, bus 726 Alter Hafen) Arty types jam this staple in a quiet corner tucked away from the Altstadt bustle. Linger over breakfast (served until 3pm, on weekends till 4pm) or come for fresh and tasty soups, salads and various hot plates that change daily. Marble tables add class.

★ Brauerei im Füchschen
GERMAN €€

(☑ 0211-137 4716; www.fuechschen.de; Ratinger Strasse 28; mains €9-17; ⊙ 9am-1am Mon-Thu, to 2am Fri & Sat, to midnight Sun; Ⓤ Tonhalle/Ehrenhof) Boisterous, packed and drenched with local colour – the 'Little Fox' in the Altstadt is all you expect a Rhenish beer hall to be. The kitchen is especially famous for its mean *Schweinshaxe* (roast pork leg) served in a high-ceilinged interior that echoes with the mirthful roar of people enjoying their meals.

This is one of the best *Altbier* breweries in town, in business since 1848.

Cafe Beethoven
CAFE €€

(☎ 0211-679 0973; http://beethoven-flingern.de; Ackerstrasse 106; ⊙ 10am-midnight Mon-Sat, to 11pm Sun; 🖪; Ⓤ Uhlandstrasse) This Flingern classic caters to an easy-going local crowd who whoop it up on the terrace when the weather plays along. It's a great spot for breakfast, a crispy lunch salad, homemade cakes or a plate of linguini (mains €9 to €19). Or come just for coffee or a cocktail. Huge weekend breakfast buffet and kids' menu.

Restaurant Takumi
JAPANESE €€

(☎ 0211-179 933; www.facebook.com/Takumi Dusseldorf; Immermannstrasse 28; ramen €10-16; ⊙ 11.30am-10.30pm Mon-Fri, to 10pm Sat & Sun; Ⓤ Oststrasse) All you need to know about this hole-in-the-wall is that it's always packed elbow-to-elbow with Düsseldorf's expat Japanese community salivating over an authentic taste of home: slurp-worthy noodle soups. The Sapporo ramen imported from Japan swim in a hearty and complex broth made from pig bones and vegetables along with various other ingredients.

Pepella
GEORGIAN €€

(☎ 0211-445 208; http://pepella-duesseldorf.de; Augustastrasse 30; mains €8.50-14.50; ⊙ 5-10pm Tue-Sat, noon-10pm Sun; ⑤ Düsseldorf Zoo) Georgia (the country, not the US state) is a cultural and geographical bridge between east and west, which is also reflected in its cuisine. It's meat-centric fare that gets pizzazz from fragrant spices and herbs. If you've never had Georgian food, Pepella is a good place to lose your virginity, so to speak. Also try the Georgian wines.

Markt am Carlsplatz
MARKET €€

(www.carlsplatz-markt.de; Carlsplatz; mains €5-20; ⊙ 8am-6pm Mon-Fri, to 4pm Sat; ⍟; Ⓤ Benrather Strasse) A former fruit and vegetable market has been transformed into a foodies' playground. Scores of cafes, artisanal food vendors, stand-up takeaways and others dish up a huge range of food that's always fresh, regional and seasonal. Look forward to some happy grazing: a wurst here, a glass of wine there, fresh berries over there...

★ Münstermann Kontor
EUROPEAN €€€

(☎ 0211-130 0416; www.muenstermann-kontor. de; Hohe Strasse 11; mains €16-32; ⊙ 11am-10pm Tue-Fri, to 6pm Sat; Ⓤ Benrather Strasse) This legendary delicatessen has spawned a buzzy bistro serving some of Düsseldorf's best seasonal and locally sourced fare. Day after day the place hums with loyalists hungry for seasonally rotating dishes that manage to be both creative and down to earth. The vibe is noisy and energetic; try for a sidewalk table to enjoy the Hohe Strasse scene.

Sila Thai
THAI €€€

(☎ 0211-860 4427; www.sila-thai.com; Bahnstrasse 76; mains €16-25; ⊙ noon-3pm & 6pm-1am; 🚌 708, 709 Stresemannplatz) Even simple curries become culinary poetry at this Thai gourmet temple with its fairy-tale setting of carved wood, rich fabrics and imported sculpture. Like a trip to Thailand without the long flight. Book ahead and try the crispy duck with sweet basil and Penang shrimp.

🍷 Drinking & Nightlife

The Altstadt is nicknamed the 'world's longest bar' for a reason but other fun drinking grounds include the Medienhafen (p664) and Ackerstrasse in Flingern. Düsseldorf's beverage of choice is a smooth, copper-hued ale called *Altbier* served in small 0.25L glasses. Some locals chase it with a shot of Killepitsch, a potent blood-red schnapps blend of some 90 fruits, herbs and spices.

★ Salon des Amateurs
CLUB

(☎ 0211-171 2830; www.salondesamateurs.de; Grabbeplatz 4; ⊙ from 9pm Fri & Sat; Ⓤ Heinrich-Heine-Allee) At one of the country's most progressive dance clubs, the music skews heavily towards non-mainstream electronic and improvisational acts, which makes for a nice contrast to the '60s vintage look. The glass-fronted club with its wooden floor and leather sofas was founded by three Düsseldorf Academy artists and draws a crowd that's as eclectic as the music.

It's tucked below the Kunsthalle (p660).

★ Zum Uerige
BEER HALL

(☎ 0211-866 990; www.uerige.de; Berger Strasse 1; ⊙ 10am-midnight; Ⓤ Heinrich-Heine-Allee) Local colour by the bucketful (despite the high tourist contingent) is what awaits at this cavernous *Altbier* brewpub. The suds flow so quickly from giant copper vats that the waiters – called *Köbes* – simply carry huge trays of brew and plonk down a glass whenever they spy an empty. Even on a cold day, the outside tables are alive with merriment.

Brauerei Kürzer
BEER HALL

(☎ 0211-322 696; www.brauerei-kuerzer.de; Kurze Strasse 18-20; ⊙ 3pm-1am Mon-Thu, to 3am Fri,

LOCAL KNOWLEDGE

WHERE TO DRINK IN THE ALTSTADT

With its 'world's longest bar' hype, the Altstadt may seem like one big festive drunk, but there are distinct personalities to various streets. Here's a guide as you go on the prowl.

Andreasstrasse A good place to find a classy cafe or restaurant with a free table outside.

Berger Strasse Excellent casual restaurants and what seems like a hectare of outdoor tables.

Bolker Strasse A nightmare of fake ethnic restaurants geared towards the undiscerning; bad bars and a mural of a man pooping.

Hunsrückenstrasse Fake Irish bars – need we say more?

Rheinartstrasse The merry crowds spilling out of Zum Uerige set the tone.

Kurze Strasse Slightly mellow; restaurants with tables outside, not a mob scene.

Mertensgasse Quieter than others, few outside tables, several late-night clubs.

2pm-3am Sat, 2pm-midnight Sun; ⓤ Heinrich-Heine-Allee) In 2010 Düsseldorf's established breweries got competition from this new kid on the block. No-fuss Brauhaus Kürzer captures the design zeitgeist with exposed brick walls and look-at-me glass barrels. The *Altbier* is delish, as is the mix of classic and modern pub grub, from roast pork knuckle to vegan burgers. This place is proof that even tradition can move with the times.

Stone im Ratinger Hof CLUB
(☏ 0211-210 7828; www.stone-club.de; Ratinger Strasse 10; cover varies; ◷10pm-5am Fri & Sat; ⓤ Tonhalle/Ehrenhof) In the 1980s, Ratinger Hof was the hub of Düsseldorf's underground scene and a birthplace of German punk. A techno temple in the '90s, it's again the place for indie and alt rock. Depending on the night, tousled boho types, emos in skinny jeans and sneaker-wearing students thrash it out to everything from noise pop to indietronic to punk'n'roll.

Melody Bar COCKTAIL BAR
(☏ 0211-329 057; Kurze Strasse 12; ◷9pm-3am Wed-Sat; ⓤ Heinrich-Heine-Allee) After 10pm you may have to shoehorn your way into this jewel of a cocktail bar that's a tiny island of sophistication amid the boisterous Altstadt thirst parlours. The drinks are excellent, and there's a respectable whisky selection, charming owners and a mixed and convivial crowd.

☆ Entertainment

Check listings site Coolibri (www.coolibri.de) for current goings-on in 'D-Town'.

Tonhalle CLASSICAL MUSIC
(☏ 0211-899 6123; www.tonhalle.de; Am Ehrenhof 1; ⓤ Tonhalle/Ehrenhof) As a former planetarium the Tonhalle has always trained the spotlight on the stars. Today it's the Düsseldorf Symphony Orchestra and the heavyweights of jazz, soul and chanson that shine beneath its ribbed metal-blue dome .

ZAKK LIVE MUSIC
(☏ 0211-973 0010; www.zakk.de; Fichtenstrasse 40; tram 706 Fichtenstrasse, ⓤ Kettwiger Strasse) This action-oriented non-profit cultural centre in an old factory has been around since 1977 and is still the go-to place for non-mainstream indie and alternative artists and progressive and eclectic programming.

AK 47 LIVE MUSIC
(☏ 016 0379 2815; www.ak47-dusseldorf.com; Kiefernstrasse 23; ⓤ Kettwiger Strasse) Like punk rock? Go here. Enough said.

Düsseldorfer Marionetten-Theater PUPPET THEATRE
(☏ 0211-328 432; www.marionettentheater-duesseldorf.de; Bilker Strasse 7; tickets €14-24; ⓤ Benrather Strasse) Generations of kids and adults have been enthralled by the adorable marionettes that sing, dance and act their way through beautifully orchestrated operas and fairy tales at this venerable venue. Pure magic.

Deutsche Oper am Rhein OPERA
(☏ 0211-892 5211; http://operamrhein.de; Heinrich-Heine-Allee 16a; tickets €19-90; ⓤ Heinrich-Heine-Allee) Düsseldorf has an opera tradition going back to 1875. Its ensemble presents both opera and ballet here and in the sister venue in nearby Duisburg.

ℹ Information

The **DüsseldorfCard** (24/48/72 hours €9/14/19) offers free public transport and free or discounted admission rates on museums, tours, food and events. It's available online at www.duesseldorf-tourismus.de and at the tourist offices.

Düsseldorf Tourist Office – Hauptbahnhof (☑ 0211-1720 2844; www.duesseldorf-touris mus.de; Immermannstrasse 65b; ⏰ 9.30am-7pm Mon-Fri, to 5pm Sat; Ⓤ Hauptbahnhof)

Tourist Office – Altstadt (☑ 0211-1720 2840; www.duesseldorf-tourismus.de; cnr Marktstrasse & Rheinstrasse; ⏰ 10am-6pm; Ⓤ Heinrich-Heine-Allee)

ℹ Getting There & Away

AIR

Düsseldorf International Airport (DUS; ☑ 0211-4210; www.dus.com; Ⓡ Düsseldorf Flughafen) has three terminals and is served by a wide range of airlines.

BUS

Düsseldorf's **central bus station** (Worringer Strasse 140; Ⓤ Hauptbahnhof), about 250m north of the Hauptbahnhof main exit, is served by Flixbus, Eurolines and other intercity coach companies.

TRAIN

Düsseldorf is part of a dense S-Bahn and regional train network in the Rhine–Ruhr region. ICE/IC trains departing from its **Hauptbahnhof** (www.bahnhof.de/bahnhof-de/Düsseldorf_Hbf-1021118; Konrad-Adenauer-Platz 14; Ⓤ Hauptbahnhof) head to Berlin (€116, 4¼ hours), Hamburg (€86, 3½ hours), Frankfurt (€86, 1¾ hours) and many other destinations.

The green Flixtrain stops in Düsseldorf between Cologne and Hamburg.

ℹ Getting Around

The Hauptbahnhof is on the southeastern edge of the city centre. From here it's about a 20-minute walk along Bismarckstrasse and Blumenstrasse to the Königsallee, with the Altstadt just beyond. Alternatively, any U-Bahn from the Hauptbahnhof to Heinrich-Heine-Allee will put you right in the thick of things.

TO/FROM THE AIRPORT

Düsseldorf International Airport is about 10km north of the Hauptbahnhof. S-Bahn, regional RE and long-distance trains connect the airport with Düsseldorf's Hauptbahnhof and cities beyond every few minutes.

The SkyTrain links the airport terminals with the Flughafen station. A Kurzstrecke ticket (€1.60) must be bought before boarding.

A taxi into town costs about €30; phone ☑ 0211-212 121.

BICYCLE

In the southeast corner of the train station, **Radstation** (☑ 0211-514 4711; www.rad station-duesseldorf.de; Willi-Becker-Allee 8a, Hauptbahnhof; rental per day from €13; ⏰ 7am-8pm Mon-Fri, from 10am Sat & Sun; Ⓤ Hauptbahnhof) rents a range of bikes.

A natural first place to ride is the Rheinuferpromenade (p661).

PUBLIC TRANSPORT

Rheinbahn (www.rheinbahn.de) operates an extensive network of U-Bahn trains, trams and buses throughout Düsseldorf. Tickets (single ride/day pass €2.70/7) are available from bus drivers and orange vending machines at U-Bahn and tram stops, and must be validated upon boarding.

TAXI

Flagfall is €4.50 with each kilometre charged at €2.20; phone ☑ 0211-212 121.

Niederrhein (Lower Rhine)

North of Düsseldorf, the Rhine widens and embarks on its final headlong rush towards the North Sea, traversing the sparsely populated Lower Rhine (Niederrhein). It's a flat, windswept plain that feels like Holland without the windmills and yields a few offbeat surprises. The main town is Xanten, famous for its Roman ruins and medieval Altstadt (old town).

ℹ Getting There & Around

The region's tiny **Weeze Airport** (☑ 02837-666 111; www.airport-weeze.de; Flughafen-Ring 1, Weeze), a hub for Ryanair, is about 30km southwest of Xanten.

Regional RB31 trains shuttle between Duisburg as far as Xanten, but from here on all other destinations are served by buses that operate on a limited schedule. Go to www.vrr.de for a journey planner.

Having a car is helpful for getting around this region. Being flat, it's also conducive to bicycling.

Xanten

☑ 02801 / POP 21,500

Xanten, the main town in the Lower Rhine, has a pedigree going all the way back to its founding as a Roman military camp in 12 BC. Within a century it grew into a respectable town called Colonia Ulpia Traiana. At its peak, some 15,000 people milled about town, enjoying a surprisingly high standard of living.

Xanten's medieval heyday is best symbolised by the majestic Dom that dominates the tangled old centre with its stately gates, cheerful mills and historical fountains. The town is also the mythological birthplace of Siegfried, the dragon-slaying hero of the 12th-century Nibelungen epic, which became the subject of Richard Wagner's *The Ring of the Nibelung* opera cycle 700 years later.

◉ Sights

Xanten's medieval core is small enough to explore on foot. The archaeological park is about 1km northwest of the town centre.

★Archäologischer Park   MUSEUM
(Archaeological Park; ☑ 02801-988 9213; www.apx. lvr.de; Am Rheintor; adult/concession/under 18yr incl RömerMuseum €9/6/free; ☺9am-6pm Mar-Oct, to 5pm Nov, 10am-4pm Dec-Feb; ℗; ☒SL42 Am Rheintor) The Roman Colonia Ulpia Traiana has been reborn as an archaeological park, an open-air museum that features faithfully reconstructed buildings to help visitors visualise what the Roman town looked like. The self-guided tour takes you past such sites as the Amphitheatre, which seats 12,000 people during Xanten's summer music festival; the Spielehaus, where you can play early versions of backgammon and Nine Men's Morris; a Roman hostel complete with hot baths and a restaurant; and the majestic Hafentempel (Harbour Temple).

Also scattered around the grounds are pavilions that zero in on such themes as the life of gladiators, Roman building techniques and the power structure between emperors, citizens and slaves. Kids will enjoy the two imaginative playgrounds, one a Roman fort, the other water-themed (bring a towel).

To make better sense of the park, it's well worth taking a spin around the adjoining RömerMuseum before your visit.

★RömerMuseum   MUSEUM
(☑02801-988 9213; www.apx.lvr.de; Siegfriedstrasse; adult/concession/under 18yr incl Archäologischer Park €9/6/free; ☺9am-6pm Mar-Oct, to 5pm Nov, 10am-4pm Dec-Feb; ℗; ☒SL42 Am Rheintor) For a deeper understanding of the Roman presence in the region and the ruins in the adjacent Archaeological Park, the

engaging RömerMuseum is a must. In a striking building, the often hands-on exhibit covers a 400-year period, kicking off with the arrival of the Roman legions and ending with the colony's 4th-century demise at the hands of marauding Germanic tribes.

Make your way along the floating ramps to learn how the Roman folk earned their money, worshipped, educated their kids, played and buried their dead. A highlight among the locally excavated treasures is the Roman ship.

The museum, which is located about 1.3km northwest of Xanten's train station and town centre, was built on the foundations of the Roman town baths, which have been partly excavated and can be admired in an adjacent hall.

Dom St Viktor   CHURCH
(☑02801-713 10; www.sankt-viktor-xanten.de; Kapitel 8; ☺10am-6pm Mon-Sat, 12.30-6pm Sun Mar-Oct, noon-5pm Mon-Fri, 10am-5pm Sat, 12.30-6pm Sun Nov-Feb) The crown jewel of Xanten's Altstadt is the Dom St Viktor, which has Romanesque roots but is now largely Gothic. It is framed by a walled close, called an 'Immunity', which can only be entered from the Markt. The soaring five-nave interior brims with treasures, reflecting the wealth Xanten enjoyed in the Middle Ages. Foremost is the Marienaltar, halfway down the right aisle, with a base featuring an intricately carved version of the *Tree of Jesse* by Heinrich Douvermann (1535).

Siegfriedmuseum Xanten   MUSEUM
(☑02801-772 200; www.siegfriedmuseum-xanten. de; Kurfürstenstrasse 9; adult/concession/under 18yr €4/3/free; ☺10am-5pm) The *Nibelungenlied* (Song of the Nibelungs) is an epic medieval poem about love, jealousy, murder and revenge that shot to international stardom in the 19th century when the composer Richard Wagner turned it into the equally epic four-part opera *Der Ring des Nibelungen*. The hero of the convoluted plot is Siegfried the dragon slayer who, so goes the myth, was born in Xanten. This modern museum near the Dom lays out the poem's characters, stories and myths in engaging fashion.

⌸ Sleeping

★Klever Tor   APARTMENT €
(☑02801-772 200; www.xanten.de; Klever Strasse 39; apt €65-95; ℗☺☂) A romantic place to spend the night is the striking Klever Tor, a

SPOTLIGHT ON JOSEPH BEUYS

With its Rapunzel towers and Romeo-and-Juliet balcony, neo-Gothic **Schloss Moyland** (☎02824-951 060; www.moyland.de; Am Schloss 4, Bedburg-Hau; adult/concession €7/3; ⊙11am-6pm Tue-Fri, 10am-6pm Sat & Sun Apr-Sep, 11am-5pm Tue-Sun Oct-Mar, garden open daily; 🅿; 🚌44 Schloss Moyland) is an unexpected sight amid the dull expanses of the Lower Rhine flatlands. Although its history begins in the 14th century, the 'medieval' fairy-tale looks are actually a 19th-century creation. Today, the castle houses a private modern-art collection with a focus on works by Joseph Beuys. The labyrinthine interior is smothered in drawings, paintings and etchings.

For a breather, take a spin around the lovely park with its old trees, hortensias and wacky sculptures.

Schloss Moyland is about 20km northwest of Xanten. Take bus 44 from the train station (€5.90, 28 minutes). The Schloss is then a 10-minute walk from the bus stop.

14th-century town gate that's been converted into modern holiday flats with kitchens. Book through the tourist office, which also has other such gems on offer. One-night stays incur a €20 surcharge.

Hotel van Bebber
HOTEL €€

(☎02801-6623; www.hotelvanbebber.de; Klever Strasse 12; d €109-129; 🅿🌐🐕) Notables including Queen Victoria and Churchill have slept in this old-school 35-room hotel. Rooms pair historical open beams and antiques with a nice range of mod-cons. Those in the deluxe category have views of the Dom, plus four-poster beds and big tubs. A generous (but optional) breakfast is €12 per person.

🍴 Eating

From simple bistros to a Michelin-starred restaurant, Xanten has a surprisingly diverse cuisine scene that belies its size. In sunny weather, you can picnic among the Roman ruins in the Archaeological Park.

Petersilchen
VEGETARIAN €€

(☎02801-1484; www.petersilchen-xanten.de; Klever Strasse 23-25; mains €12-16; ⊙5.30-10pm Wed & Thu, noon-10pm Fri-Sun May-Oct, to 9pm Nov-Apr; 🍃) Stepping inside the 'little parsley' (as the name translates) is like getting a hug from an old friend. An old piano and fresh flowers set the tone for the plant-based menu that travels around the world. Dig into lasagne with lentil bolognese, couscous with falafel or wok-tossed vegetables with ginger and seitan.

Zur Börse
GERMAN €€

(☎02801-1441; http://zurboersexanten.de; Markt 12; mains €7-19; ⊙11am-10pm, closed Tue Oct-Mar) Waiters bustle between tables inside and out

at this smart restaurant in the very heart of town. Although the interior is modern, the menu is thick with classic dishes, including regional faves such as lima bean and bacon stew, braised kale and marinated pot roast.

ℹ️ Information

Xanten Tourist Office (☎02801-772 200; www.xanten.de; Kurfürstenstrasse 9; ⊙10am-6pm Mon-Fri Apr-Oct, to 5pm Nov-Mar, 10am-5pm Sat & Sun year-round) Right in the Altstadt.

ℹ️ Getting There & Around

Xanten is served by hourly RB31 trains on a spur line from Duisburg (€12.50, 45 minutes). Bus 44 runs from Xanten to Kalkar (€5.90, 20 minutes).

Xanten's compact Altstadt is about 500m northeast of the train station via Hagenbuschstrasse or Bahnhofstrasse. The Archäologischer Park (p669) is a further 1km northwest of the old town and served by bus. To explore the surrounds, renting a bicycle is ideal. **Fahrrad am Niederrhein** (☎02801-984 9642; http://fahr radamniederrhein.de; Bahnhofstrasse 47; rental per day bike/e-bike from €9/23.50; ⊙12.30-8pm Mon, Wed & Thu, to 9.30pm Fri-Sun) in the train station rents bikes.

THE RUHRGEBIET

Once known for its belching steelworks and filthy coal mines, the Ruhrgebiet – a sprawling post-industrial region of 53 cities and 5.1 million people – has worked hard in recent decades to reboot for a high-tech future.

Rather than eschew their lowbrow heritage, the people of the Ruhrgebiet have embraced it by recasting dormant furnaces, steelworks, coking plants and other vestiges of the Industrial Age in creative ways. For travellers, the Ruhrgebiet delivers a trainload of surprises and unique sights, locations and experiences. You can see cutting-edge art in a huge converted gas tank, free-climb around a blast furnace or hear classical music in a gas power station. You can also feast your eyes on old masters, majestic churches and great architecture ranging from Gothic to Bauhaus to postmodern.

ℹ Information

The Ruhr.TopCard (adult/child €54/35, www.ruhrtopcard.de) gives free public transport, free admission to 96 attractions and 50% discount on a further 53 attractions (including theme parks, museums and tours) during the course of a calendar year. It's available from local tourist offices.

The region's tourist authority, Ruhr Tourismus (www.ruhr-tourismus.de) has an excellent website although, alas, it's only in German (for now).

ℹ Getting Around

The Ruhrgebiet's comprehensive public transport web consists of the U-Bahn, buses and trams; its cities are linked by frequent S-Bahn and regional trains. Transport authority VRR (www.vrr.de) has a handy journey planner.

Essen

☏ 0201 / POP 589,700

It's taken a few decades, but Germany's seventh-largest city has mastered the transition from coal and steel powerhouse – spearheaded by the Krupp empire – to post-industrial city of commerce and culture. Visitors will be richly rewarded on their stopover. A visit with Van Gogh? Go to the Museum Folkwang (p674). Emperor Otto III's gem-studded childhood crown? Head for the cathedral (p674) treasury. A Unesco-listed Bauhaus-style former coal mine with a fabulous museum? Look no further than Zeche Zollverein. Add to that a verdant green belt and half-timbered medieval quarters and you may find it hard to believe you're in the Ruhrgebiet.

◉ Sights

Essen's sights are scattered about. If you only have time for one, make it Zeche Zollverein with its myriad attractions. With more time, have a wander around the city centre. The Hauptbahnhof's Nord (north) exit drops you

right onto the main drag, the pedestrianised Kettwiger Strasse.

◉ Zollverein

★ Zeche Zollverein HISTORIC BUILDING

(Zollverein Coal Mine; ☏ 0201-830 3636; www.zollverein.de; Gelsenkirchener Strasse 181; ⊗ grounds 6am-midnight, visitors centre 10am-6pm; ☐ 107 Essen Zollverein) **FREE** A key site along the Ruhr area's Industrial Heritage Trail (www.route-industriekultur.de), the former Zollverein coal mine was a marvel of efficiency while in operation from 1932 until 1986. In 2001, Unesco declared the Bauhaus-style complex a World Heritage Site. Since closing, the sprawling site has since been rebooted as a cultural centre with museums, performance spaces, artists' studios, cafes and some unusual playgrounds. A major focus is the excellent Ruhr Museum in the old coal-wash plant.

Be sure to explore the rambling grounds, which encompass dozens of industrial buildings spread out over a wooded expanse with some park-like areas. Attractions include sculptures and installations, workshops and galleries, a seasonal swimming pool and ice-skating rink (€7), and a solar-powered Ferris wheel. Cafes and restaurants are scattered about. If you don't want to walk, rent a bicycle near the visitors centre (p676).

★ Ruhr Museum MUSEUM

(☏ 0201-2468 1444; www.ruhrmuseum.de; Fritz-Schupp-Allee 15; adult/concession €8/5, audioguide €3; ⊗ 10am-6pm; ☐ 107 Essen Zollverein) The former coal-wash plant at the Unesco-listed Zeche Zollverein provides a suitably atmospheric setting for accessible and engaging exhibits on the history, nature and culture of the Ruhr Region. Just as the coal was transported on conveyor belts, a long escalator whisks you up to the foyer from where you descend into the dark bowels of the building.

The exhibition spreads across three floors and starts in the present to provide a window into modern daily life in the Ruhr area. The next floor jumps back in time to look at the region's pre-industrial roots before examining, in often fascinating detail, how the once-agricultural region morphed into the largest coal and steel production area in Europe. With its raw stone walls, steep steel stairs, shiny aluminium ducts and industrial machinery, the space itself has all the drama and mystique of a movie set (*Blade Runner* comes to mind).

(Continued on page 674)

COLOGNE & NORTHERN RHINELAND ESSEN

Historic Marvels

Germany's history has been shaped by many players. Hear the whispers of the past as you nose around medieval castles, crane your neck to take in lofty cathedrals and explore the cobbled tangle of towns founded centuries before Columbus set sail. If only stones could talk...

Beauteous Bamberg

Germany teems with towns drenched in history, but Bamberg (p436) is a particularly delightful web of medieval lanes, with a lordly cathedral, well-kept historic buildings and some of Germany's best beer. The Altes Rathaus is a shutterbug favourite.

Europe's Roots

Few people have shaped Europe as much as Charlemagne. And few German cathedrals have as illustrious a history as Aachen's (p655), where the Frankish king-turned-emperor is buried and which witnessed the coronations of over 30 kings between AD 936 and 1531.

Joyful Sanctuaries

Lift your spirits at the heavenly rococo Wieskirche pilgrimage church (p423), rising like a vision from an emerald Bavarian meadow. With angels flitting across frescoed ceilings and an altar that is a symphony of colour, its beauty will resonate even with nonbelievers.

Fairy-tale Fantasy

Before touring Schloss Neuschwanstein in Füssen, glimpse an insight into 'Mad' King Ludwig II's mind on a spin around his childhood home, Schloss Hohenschwangau (p389). A romantic neo-gothic extravaganza, it is festooned with mythological murals and still furnished in the original 19th-century style.

1 Altes Rathaus (p438), Bamberg 2 Aachener Dom (p655) 3 Wieskirche (p423), Bavaria 4 Schloss Hohenschwangau (p389), Füssen

(Continued from page 671)

Tickets also include access to the Panorama Roof, which lets you appreciate the vastness of the colliery grounds.

Red Dot Design Museum   MUSEUM

(☑0201-301 0460; www.red-dot.org; Gelsenkirchener Strasse 181; adult/concession/under 12yr €6/4/free; ☑11am-6pm Tue-Sun, last entry 5pm; P; ☑107 Essen Zollverein) Part of the Zeche Zollverein (p671) colliery-turned-cultural centre, this museum showcases the best in contemporary design in the former stoker's hall, creatively adapted by British architect Norman Foster. In a perfect marriage of space and function, this four-storey maze incorporates many of the original fixtures: bathtubs balance on grated walkways, bike helmets dangle from snake-like heating ducts, and beds perch atop a large oven. All objects are winners of the Red Dot award, the Oscar of the design world.

◉ City Centre & Around

★Museum Folkwang   MUSEUM

(☑0201-884 5444; www.museum-folkwang.de; Museumsplatz 1; ☑10am-6pm Tue, Wed, Sat & Sun, to 8pm Thu & Fri; ☑Philharmonie) FREE A grand dame among Germany's art repositories, the Museum Folkwang has sparkling digs designed by top British architect David Chipperfield. Galleries radiate out from inner courtyards and gardens of the glass-fronted building, providing a progressive setting for the works of 19th-century German and French masters. You'll find barely a big name missing from the permanent collection, which has artwork from brooding landscapes by German Romantics such as Caspar David Friedrich to boldly hued impressionist works by Monet and Van Gogh.

Dom Essen   CATHEDRAL

(☑0201-220 4206; www.domschatz-essen.de; Burgplatz 2; treasury adult/concession €4/3; ☑church 6.30am-6.30pm Mon-Fri, 9am-7.30pm Sat & Sun, treasury 11am-5pm Tue-Sun) Essen's medieval Dom is an island of quiet engulfed by the commercialism of pedestrianised Kettwiger Strasse, the main shopping strip. It has a priceless collection of Ottonian works, all about 1000 years old. Not to be missed is a hauntingly beautiful Golden Madonna, set in her own midnight-blue chapel, which matches the colour of her eyes. The treasury presents more fancy baubles, including a crown worn by Holy Roman Emperor Otto III, in a contemporary, intimate fashion.

Alte Synagoge   CULTURAL CENTRE

(☑0201-884 5218; www.alte-synagoge.essen.de; Steeler Strasse 29; ☑10am-6pm Tue-Sun) FREE The grand Alte Synagoge served as the hub of Essen's Jewish community between 1913 and 1938 and miraculously survived WWII largely intact. A memorial site since 1980, it now harbours the House of Jewish Culture with exhibits, concerts and discussions. A free audioguide (also in English) provides useful background information.

◉ Werden

Lining a pastoral stretch of the Ruhr, the half-timbered houses and cobbled lanes of the suburb of Werden offer insight into what a pre-industrial Ruhrgebiet must have looked like. The village today mixes low-key modernity with a sprinkling of medieval structures, most notably Basilika St Ludgerus. Take a breather in the lovely park on an island in the river.

The S6 follows a leafy route to Werden from the Hauptbahnhof.

Basilika St Ludgerus   CHURCH

(☑0201-491 801; www.schatzkammer-werden.de; Brückstrasse 54; treasury adult/concession €3/2; ☑treasury 10am-noon & 3-5pm Tue-Sun; P; ☑S6 Werden) Werden's main sight is the solid stone St Ludgerus (1175), a beautiful late-Romanesque church named for the Frisian missionary buried here. It has an impressive exterior as well as a commendable treasury housed in the old abbey. Standouts include the bronze crucifix forged locally around AD 1060.

🛏 Sleeping

Essen is a trade-fair city and hotel prices spike accordingly. Good deals can often be had on weekends. The more charming places are in the suburbs.

★Mintrops Stadt Hotel Margarethenhöhe   HOTEL €€

(☑0201-438 60; www.mintrops-stadthotel.de; Steile Strasse 46; r €70-150; P ☕ ☎; ☑17 Laubenweg) A former Krupp guesthouse has been reborn as a cheerful 30-room hotel where no two rooms are alike but all are filled with light, art and designer touches. We especially like the four 'Ruhrkultur' rooms where the design evokes people and aspects of local culture in a stylish way.

The gourmet restaurant grows much of its own ingredients. The hotel is about 5km

THE KRUPP DYNASTY: MEN OF STEEL

Steel and Krupp are virtual synonyms. So are Krupp and Essen. For it's this bustling Ruhrgebiet city that is the ancestral seat of the Krupp family and the headquarters of one of the most powerful corporations in Europe.

It all began rather modestly in 1811 when Friedrich Krupp and two partners founded a company to process 'English cast steel' but, despite minor successes, he left a company mired in debt upon his death in 1826. Enter his son Alfred, then a tender age of 14, who would go on to become one of the seminal figures of the Industrial Age.

It was through the production of the world's finest steel that the 'Cannon King' galvanised a company that – by 1887 – employed more than 20,000 workers. In an unbroken pattern of dazzling innovation, coupled with ruthless business practices, Krupp produced steel and machinery that was essential to the world economy.

But Krupp also provided womb-to-tomb benefits to its workers at a time when the term 'social welfare' had not yet entered the world's vocabulary.

Krupp will forever be associated, however, with the Third Reich. Not only did the corporation supply the hardware for the German war machine, it also provided much of the financial backing that Hitler needed to build up his political power base. Krupp plants were prime targets for Allied bombers. After the war, the firm slowly lost its way and in 1999 merged with former arch-rival Thyssen.

An excellent source for an understanding of what the Krupp family has meant to Germany is William Manchester's brilliant chronicle *The Arms of Krupp* (1964).

south of the centre in the Margarethen-höhe, a garden-like art nouveau workers' colony.

Georges Boutique Hotel & Boardinghouse BOUTIQUE HOTEL **€€**
(☑ 0201-7473 7219; www.georges-essen.de; Florastrasse 15b; d incl breakfast €99; ⊜ 🛜; Ⓤ Messe Ost/Gruga-Halle) This chic hotel puts you within stumbling distance of the bars and restaurants on Rüttenscheider Strasse. Each room is slightly different but all pack nice design touches and such mod-cons as iPod docking stations, rainforest showers and tea and coffee-making tools. Street-facing rooms can be noisy and the self-check-in makes for a lonely arrival.

✖ Eating

The city centre is devoid of interesting restaurants and is also dead after dark. Instead, point your compass south to the Rüttenscheider Strasse ('Rü'), where you can pick from dozens of eateries and bars.

Take the U11 or tram 107 to Martinstrasse or Rüttenscheider Stern.

Orkide Döner TURKISH **€**
(☑ 0201-797 408; Klarastrasse 1; dishes €3.50-11; ⊘ 11.30am-10pm Mon-Sat; Ⓤ Rüttenscheider Stern) People come from all over, passing a lot of other doner kebab places on the way, to enjoy Orkide's piquant goodness. Germany's favourite fast food is given great treatment in an appropriately casual setting. The sauces and fillings are just that much better than the rest.

Miamamia CAFE **€€**
(☑ 0201-874 2562; www.miamamia.de; Rüttenscheider Strasse 183; mains €6-16; ⊘ 9am-10pm; Ⓤ Rüttenscheider Stern) This feel-good cafe is beautifully situated in an old house and quite possibly serves the best coffee in town. Join the locals as they indulge in deep conversation over breakfast, drop by for a salad or light lunch or get tempted by the gorgeous homemade cakes. Retreat to tables in the garden or soak up the Rü scene out front.

☆ Entertainment

Zeche Carl LIVE PERFORMANCE
(☑ tickets 0201-834 4410; www.zechecarl.de; Wilhelm-Nieswandt-Allee 100; ⊘ cafe & beer garden 5-11pm Tue-Sat, 11am-11pm Sun; Ⓤ Karlsplatz) The machine hall and washrooms of a former coal mine have been restyled as an alternative cultural centre with live concerts, parties, cabaret, theatre and art exhibits. The cafe has a beer garden plus a wide range of small and large plates.

ℹ Information

Essen Tourist Office (☑ 0201-887 2333, 0201-194 33; www.essen.de; Am Hauptbahnhof 2; ⊘ 9am-5pm Mon-Fri, 10am-1pm Sat)

❶ CULTURAL TRAM

Essen's major sights are spread out, but all are easily accessible by U-Bahn, S-Bahn or trams. The handiest line is tram 107 (www.kulturlinie107.de), which links Zollverein (p671), the city centre, Museum Folkwang (p674) and the Rüttenscheider Strasse dining and nightlife district.

Ruhr.VisitorCenter Essen (☑ 0201-246 810; www.zollverein.de; Fritz-Schupp-Allee 14, Zeche Zollverein; ⊙10am-6pm; 🚊107 Essen Zollverein)

❶ Getting There & Away

There are frequent cross-country ICE and IC trains in all directions as well as RE and S-Bahn trains departing every few minutes to other cities in the region such as Düsseldorf. The Flixtrain also stops in Essen on its route from Cologne to Hamburg.

Flixbus and other coach companies stop outside the south exit of the Hauptbahnhof.

Dortmund

☑ 0231 / POP 586,000

Football (soccer) is a major Dortmund passion. Borussia Dortmund, the city's Bundesliga (premier league) team, has won the national championships an impressive eight times. So it's actually quite appropriate that Dortmund was chosen as the site of the German Football Museum, which opened in 2015. Other attractions include several treasure-filled churches and high-calibre art museums.

As the largest city in the Ruhrgebiet, Dortmund once built its prosperity on coal, steel and beer. These days, the mines are closed and the steel mills quiet, with more zeitgeist-compatible high-tech industries having taken their place. Only the breweries are going as strong as ever, churning out oceans of beer and ale, much of it for export.

⊙ Sights

★ **Deutsches Fussball Museum** MUSEUM
(German Football Museum; ☑ 0231-476 4660; www.fussballmuseum.de; Platz der Deutschen Einheit 1; adult/concession €17/14; ⊙10am-6pm Tue-Sun) This vast shrine to the nation's passion and obsession is a place of pilgrimage not only for German football fans. Inside a

futuristic building next to the Hauptbahnhof (p678) is an emotional multimedia and sometimes interactive tribute to the game and Germany's role in shaping its history. Learn about stars such as Franz Beckenbauer, relive historic matches or fancy yourself a commentator.

The treasure chamber holds replicas of the four World Cups and three European trophies won by the Mannschaft (Germany's national team). Online tickets are a couple of euro cheaper.

Dortmunder U CULTURAL CENTRE
(☑ 0231-502 4723; www.dortmunder-u.de; Leonie-Reygers-Terrasse; ⊙ Tue, Wed, Sat & Sun 11am-6pm, to 8pm Thu & Fri) **FREE** You can see it from afar – the golden 'U' atop the tower once used for beer storage by the now defunct Union Brauerei. Once one of Dortmund's largest and most famous breweries, the protected landmark has been reborn as a progressive centre for art and creativity in the digital age. Tenants include the prestigious art museum Museum am Ostwall and the Hartware Medienkunstverein (adult/concession €5/2.50), an organisation dedicated to promoting an appreciation for Brutalist architecture.

Cineasts are drawn to the art-house cinema on the ground floor.

★ **Museum am Ostwall** MUSEUM
(☑ 0231-502 4723; www.museumamostwall. dortmund.de; Dortmunder U, Leonie-Reygers-Terrasse 2; adult/concession/under 18yr €5/2.50/ free; ⊙ Tue, Wed, Sat & Sun 11am-6pm, to 8pm Thu & Fri) The 4th and 5th floors of the Dortmunder U creative complex are home to the Museum am Ostwall, an art-world star thanks to its far-reaching collection of all major 20th- and 21st-century genres, from expressionism to art informel, fluxus to op art and concrete art. This translates into works by Macke, Nolde, Beuys and Paik as well as such living artists as Jochen Gerz, and Anna and Bernhard Blume.

Reinoldikirche CHURCH
(☑ 0231-882 3013; www.sanktreinoldi.de; Ostenhellweg 2; tower €1.50; ⊙10am-6pm Mon-Sat, 1-6pm Sun, tower noon-3pm Sat) Dating from 1280, the Reinoldi church is named after the city's patron saint. As the story goes, after Reinold was martyred in Cologne, the carriage containing his coffin rolled all the way to Dortmund, stopping on the site of the church. There's a statue of him, opposite Charlemagne, at the entrance to the choir.

Marienkirche CHURCH

(☑ 0231-526 548; www.st-marien-dortmund.de; Ostenhellweg; ⊘10am-noon & 2-4pm Tue, Wed & Fri, to 6pm Sat, to 1pm Sat) Marienkirche is the oldest of Dortmund's churches, and its Romanesque origins are still visible in the round-arched nave. The star exhibit here is the Marienaltar (1420), with a delicate triptych by local son Conrad von Soest. In the northern nave is the equally impressive Berswordt Altar (1385). Both were saved from wartime destruction; the churches all needed massive reconstruction.

Petrikirche CHURCH

(☑ 0231-721 4173; www.stpetrido.de; Westenhellweg; ⊘11am-5pm Tue-Fri, 10am-4pm Sat) The 14th-century Petrikirche's showstopper is the massive Antwerp altar (1520), featuring 633 individually carved and gilded figurines in scenes depicting the Easter story. Note that the altar is closed in summer, exposing only the panels' painted outer side.

Brauerei-Museum Dortmund MUSEUM

(Brewery Museum; ☑ 0231-840 0200; www.braue reierlebnis-dortmund.de; Steigerstrasse 16; adult/concession €5/2.50; ⊘10am-5pm Tue, Wed, Fri & Sun, to 8pm Thu, noon-5pm Sat; P) Dortmund is not only famous for its football team but also has a long tradition of beer-making. This museum is in the machine and production halls of the former Hansa Brewery pay tribute to this legacy and trace the history of commercial brewing. A 1920s bar, a beer truck from 1922 and bottling machines from the 1950s are among the original historical items on display.

Mahn- und Gedenkstätte Steinwache MEMORIAL

(☑ 0231-502 5002; www.ns-gedenkstaetten.de; Steinstrasse 50; ⊘10am-5pm Tue-Sun) FREE This municipal memorial uses the original rooms and cells of a Nazi prison as a backdrop for a grim exhibit about Dortmund during the Third Reich. Over 66,000 people were imprisoned here, many tortured and killed. It's north of the Hauptbahnhof (p678), just beyond the multiplex cinema.

🍴 Sleeping & Eating

With about 7000 hotel rooms, Dortmund has plenty of places to hang your hat. Rates spike during trade shows, big football matches and special events. Unless you're traveling on business, a city tax of 7.5% is added to your hotel bill.

Coffee Fellows Hotel Dortmund HOTEL €€

(☑ 0231-5450 9870; www.coffee-fellows-hotel.com; Schwarze-Brüder-Strasse 1; d €90-120; ⊖🐾🛜🛇) If the idea of smelling the coffee when you wake up appeals to you, check into the first hotel created by the German Coffee Fellow cafe chain. Rooms sport cosy, contemporary looks with their charcoal and white hues, patterned carpet and little desk. Don't skip the wonderful breakfast in the coffee shop downstairs (€7.90).

Cityhotel Dortmund HOTEL €€

(☑ 0231-477 9660; www.cityhoteldortmund.de; Grafenhof 6; s/d incl breakfast from €75/90; P⊖@🛜🛇) Behind an inconspicuous facade hides this jewel close to shopping and sights. Bold patterns and cheerful Mediterranean colours create welcoming flair in the public areas and although none of the 50 rooms will hold a ton of luggage, beds are comfy and there's a kettle to make coffee or tea with.

Wenkers am Markt GERMAN €€

(☑ 0231-527 548; www.wenkers.de; Betenstrasse 1; mains €13-30; ⊘11am-midnight Sun-Thu, to 1am Fri & Sat) A legendary place for quaffing before and after football matches, Wenkers has a sea of tables outside on a central square and serves German classics in gut-busting portions. It's one of the oldest breweries in Westphalia and has been in the business since 1430.

Zum Alten Markt GERMAN €€

(☑ 0231-572 217; www.altermarkt-dortmund.de; Markt 3; mains €10-23; ⊘10am-1am Mon-Thu, to 3am Fri, 9am-3am Sat, 11am-11pm Sun) Traditional Westphalian fare is served to hordes of appreciative locals in the very centre of the city. Pray to the gods of digestion at one of the nearby churches. Seating is inside among loads of quirky knick-knacks or on the terrace that's perfect for keeping an eye on passers-by.

🍸 Drinking & Entertainment

Dortmund's centres of after-dark action include the lively Brückstrassenviertel around the Konzerthaus, the area between Alter Markt and Kleppingstrasse, and Lindemannstrasse in the hip Kreuzviertel (U42 to Möllerbrücke).

Balke COCKTAIL BAR

(☑ 0231-280 8944; www.fussballermodelszivilisten. de; Hohe Strasse 127; ⊘6pm-late Thu-Sat &

2½ hours before Borussia Dortmund games; [U]Polizeipräsidium) Balke is really a civilised cocktail bar, but on Borussia Dortmund game days, the black-and-white floors are flooded by a sea of yellow and black, the team colours. At other times, Balke is invaded by fans of quality tipples, including the homemade gin turned into creative potions by the resident barmeisters.

★ **Borussia Dortmund**   FOOTBALL
([✏]01805-309 000; www.bvb.de; Signal Iduna Park, Strobelallee 50; tickets €17-80; [U]Stadion) Dortmund's famous and massively popular and succesful Bundesliga soccer team plays its home games at the legendary Westfalenstadion, now branded as Signal Iduna Park. Cheering on the team with fans clad in the club's signature bumblebee-yellow and black can be a transporting experience.

Guided tours (in German, adult/concession €15/10) of the 80,000-seat stadium, Germany's largest, are popular. Check timings and book tickets online.

❶ Information

Dortmund Tourist Office ([✏]0231-189 990; www.dortmund-tourismus.de; Kampstrasse 80; ⊙10am-6pm Mon-Fri, to 3pm Sat) located on the main pedestrian drag. Provides maps, brochures and can make hotel reservations and book tickets.

❶ Getting There & Away

AIR
Dortmund Airport ([✏]0231-921 301; www. dortmund-airport.de; Flughafenring 2) is served by easyJet and Ryanair. It's about 12km east of the city centre. The AirportExpress bus to Dortmund's Hauptbahnhof leaves hourly from outside the terminal (€8.50, 25 minutes).

BUS
The **central bus station** (ZOB; Steinstrasse 54) is located on Steinstrasse, just outside the north exit of the Hauptbahnhof, and is served by Flixbus, Ouibus and a number of other bus companies.

TRAIN
There are frequent ICE and IC trains in all directions and RE and S-Bahn trains to other Ruhrgebiet cities departing every few minutes. The **Hauptbahnhof** (www.bahnhof.de/bahnhof-de/Dortmund_Hbf-1033426; Königswall 15) is on the northern edge of the partly pedestrianised city centre.

Bochum
[✏]0234 / POP 372,000
Wedged between Dortmund and Essen, Bochum doesn't have the football fame of the former or the urbanity of the latter, but it does have soul. Just listen to the 1984 song 'Bochum', a heartfelt anthem penned by acclaimed German singer-songwriter Herbert Grönemeyer about his home town.

Though indeed no beauty, as one of Grönemeyer's lyrics says, Bochum is a Ruhrgebiet nightlife hub with a huge university and an extensive green belt hugging the Ruhr River.

◉ Sights

Deutsches Bergbau-Museum   MUSEUM
(DBM, German Mining Museum; [✏]0234-587 70; www.bergbaumuseum.de; Am Bergbaumuseum 28; adult/concession €5/2; ⊙8.30am-5pm Tue-Fri, 10am-5pm Sat & Sun; [U]Bergbaumuseum) This hugely popular museum will remain closed until 2020 while getting a much needed refurb and completely updated permanent exhibition. It's still worth visiting, though, for a chance to descend into the earth's belly for a spin around a demonstration mine and to ride the lift up the landmark winding tower for commanding views.

Eisenbahnmuseum Bochum   MUSEUM
(Train Museum; [✏]0234-492 516; www.eisenbahn-museum-bochum.de; Dr-C-Otto-Strasse 191; adult/concession €8/4; ⊙10am-5pm Tue-Fri & Sun Mar–mid-Nov, last entry 4pm; 🚌345 Bahnhof Dahlhausen, 🚌318 Bahnhof Dahlhausen) Fans of historical trains have plenty to admire at this vast museum, which displays around 120 steam locomotives (many puffing away), coaches and wagons dating back as far as 1853. A highlight is the meticulously restored *Salonwagen* (parlour car) from 1937, which transported everyone from Nazi politicians and American generals to Queen Elizabeth II and the Shah of Iran.

The museum is located about 12km southwest of the centre in the suburb of Dahlhausen. From Bahnhof Dahlhausen, it's a 1.4km walk or a ride on the historical shuttle (Sundays only) to get to the museum.

✕ Eating

Bratwursthaus   GERMAN €
([✏]0234-684 270; www.facebook.com/pg/brat wursthaus; Kortumstrasse 18; snacks €2-8.50; ⊙10am-midnight Mon-Thu, to 4am Fri & Sat,

11am-midnight Sun) This famous sausage kitchen makes a mean *Currywurst* (slivered sausage in tomato sauce drizzled with curry powder) and enjoys cult status among locals and Bermuda Dreieck pub crawlers seeking to balance their brain.

Butterbrotbar　　　　　　　　CAFE €
(📞 0234-9158 6868; www.butterbrotbar.de; Hans-Ehrenberg-Platz 1; mains €4.50-7.80; ⊙9am-5pm Mon-Fri; 📮308/318 Schauspielhaus) In the hip Ehrenfeld quarter near the municipal theatre, Butterbrotbar is an easy-vibe cafe that dishes up made-with-love sandwiches (*Butterbrot*) on crusty home-baked bread, as well as daily lunch specials, fabulous cakes and coffee.

❶ Information

Bochum Tourist Office (📞 0234-963 020; www.bochum-tourismus.de; Huestrasse 9; ⊙9am-6pm Mon-Fri, 10am-4pm Sat)

❶ Getting There & Away

The station is on the southeastern edge of the largely pedestrianised city centre.

Duisburg

📞 0203 / POP 500,000

Duisburg, about 25km west of Essen, is home to Europe's largest inland port, the immensity of which is best appreciated on a boat tour (p680). Embarkation is at the Schwanentor, which is also the gateway to the Innenhafen Duisburg (inner harbour), an urban quarter with a mix of modern and restored buildings infused with museums, restaurants, bars, clubs and attractions set up in the old storage silos.

◉ Sights

★ **Landschaftspark**
Duisburg-Nord　　　　　　　　　PARK
(Landscape Park Duisburg-Nord; 📞 0203-429 1942; www.landschaftspark.de; Emscherstrasse 71; admission free, activities vary; ⊙park 24hr, visitor centre 9am-6pm Mon-Fri, 11am-6pm Sat & Sun; 🅿; 📮903 Landschaftspark Nord) Molten iron used to flow 24/7 from the fiery furnaces of this decommissioned ironworks that is now an urban oasis, performance space and all-ages adventure playground. You can free-climb its ore bunkers, dive in the former gas tank and climb to the top of the blast furnace. Visit at dusk from Friday to Sunday to witness the stunning light show created by British art-

LOCAL KNOWLEDGE

BOCHUM'S BERMUDA TRIANGLE

Every weekend thousands of revelers descend upon the Bermuda Dreieck (Bermuda Triangle, www.bermuda3eck. de), Bochum's famous hub of bars, clubs and restaurants. The three streets – the pedestrianised Kortumstrasse, Viktoriastrasse and Brüderstrasse – are all within five minutes of the Hauptbahnhof. For a more local crowd, head about 400m south to the boho-hip Ehrenfeld quarter near the municipal theatre (around Alte Hattinger Strasse).

ist Jonathan Park. The visitors centre by the park entrance has maps and organises tours.

The park is about 7km north of the city centre and is served by tram 903 from Duisburg train station. The entrance is about 700m from the Landschaftspark-Nord stop.

MKM Museum Küppersmühle für
Moderne Kunst　　　　　　　　MUSEUM
(📞 0203-3019 4811; www.museum-kueppers muehle.de; Philosophenweg 55; adult/concession €9/4.50; ⊙2-6pm Wed, 11am-6pm Thu-Sun; 📮934 Hansegracht) One of the biggest collections of German art created after 1945 is on display at this humongous historical mill and grain storage silo in the Inner Harbour district. It was converted by Swiss Pritzker Prize–winning architects Herzog & de Meuron, who are building a new extension due to open in 2019. From Baselitz and Kiefer to Richter, all the big names are showcased beneath the lofty ceilings; there are up to six international art exhibits annually.

Lehmbruck Museum　　　　　　MUSEUM
(📞 0203-283 3294; www.lehmbruckmuseum.de; Friedrich-Wilhelm-Strasse 40; adult/concession/ under 15yr €9/5/free; ⊙noon-5pm Tue-Fri, from 11am Sat & Sun) This museum is famous for its vast collection of modern international sculpture by artists including Archipenko, Giacometti, Kollwitz, Ernst and Chillida. The works are presented in a vast and impressive glass-fronted cube, while a second building showcases the works of Duisburg-born sculptor Wilhelm Lehmbruck, for whom the museum is named. More than three dozen sculptures are planted throughout the lovely surrounding park.

The museum is in a park about 500m from the Hauptbahnhof.

☞ Tours

Weisse Flotte Hafenrundfahrt　　CRUISE
(Harbour Tour; ☑ 0203-713 9667; www.wf-duisburg.
de; Schwanentor, Calaisplatz 3; adult/concession
€15/7.50; ⊙ 11am, 1.15pm & 3.30pm Apr-Oct;
🚌 901 Rathaus, Ⓤ U79 Steinsche Strasse) Explore the labyrinthine workings of Europe's
busiest inland port on a two-hour cruise.
The dock at Schwanentor is a 1.3km walk
through the centre from the train station;
it's also well served by public transport.

ⓘ Getting There & Away

The Hauptbahnhof is about 500m east of the
city centre.

Flixbus and other operators stop at the new
central bus station (Mercatorstrasse 90) about
700m southwest of the Hauptbahnhof.

MÜNSTER & OSNABRÜCK

Catholic Münster and Protestant Osnabrück
are forever linked – at least in the minds of
suffering high-school history students – as
the dual sites chosen to sign the Peace of
Westphalia, the series of treaties that ended the Thirty Years' War in 1648 (one of the
longest and comparatively most destructive
wars in history). Today you can find echoes
of the event in both towns, which have plenty to please visitors beyond memories of the
treaty.

ⓘ Getting There & Away

The two cities share the **Münster-Osnabrück
airport** (FMO; ☑ 02571-943 360; www.fmo.de;
Airportallee, Greven) which is about halfway
between them. Both are on a main train line with
regular links to points north (including Hamburg) and south (including Cologne).

Münster

☑ 0251 / POP 312,000
There are some 500,000 bicycles in Münster
– and that's just one example of the exuberance found in this captivating city, one of
the most appealing between Cologne and
Hamburg. Its historical centre was rebuilt
after WWII and features many architectural
gems. Yet Münster is not mired in nostalgia.
Its 50,000 students keep the cobwebs out
and civic pride is great – the town's main
cultural treasures have enjoyed ambitious
renovations and enhancements. Sampling

the slew of lively pubs and restaurants alone
warrants at least an overnight stop here.

◉ Sights

Münster is very walkable with most sights
clustering in the Altstadt, which is encircled
by the 4.8km Promenade, a car-free ring
trail built through parkland on top of the
former city fortifications. It's popular with
cyclists, joggers, lovers and walkers.

◉ Altstadt

St-Paulus-Dom　　CATHEDRAL
(☑ 0251-495 6700; www.paulusdom.de; Domplatz;
⊙ 6.30am-7pm Mon-Sat, to 7.30pm Sun) The two
massive towers of Münster's cathedral match
the proportions of this 110m-long structure
and the vast square it overlooks. It's a three-
nave construction built in the 13th century,
when Gothic architecture began overtaking
the Romanesque style in popularity. Enter
from Domplatz via the porch (called the
'Paradise'), richly festooned with sculptures
of the apostles. Inside, pay your respects to
the statue of St Christopher, the patron saint
of travellers.

Make your way to the southern ambulatory
with its astronomical clock. This marvel of
16th-century ingenuity indicates the time,
the position of the sun, the movement of the
planets, and the calendar. Crowds gather
daily at noon (12.30pm Sunday) when the
carillon starts up.

The Dom reopened in 2013 after a massive renovation that included a new roof
among other improvements (work was delayed after the first new roof's copper was
found to have the wrong shade of green).
Archaeological excavations at the same time
found parts of previous cathedrals on the
site, pre-dating the current structure. Note
how the aggressively restored golden-hued
stones on the west facade glow at sunset.

**★ LWL-Museum für
Kunst und Kultur**　　MUSEUM
(Museum for Art and Culture; ☑ 0251-590 701;
www.lwl-museum-kunst-kultur.de; Domplatz 10;
adult/concession €8/4, with special exhibit €12/6;
⊙ 10am-6pm Tue-Sat) After a harmonious fusion of the 1908 neo-Renaissance original
with an airy postmodern wing, Münster's
main museum for art and culture now has
the proper digs to match its prized collection of works from the Middle Ages to our
times. The undisputed highlight is the
collection of boldly pigmented German

expressionist paintings, most notably by August Macke, but also by such colleagues as Ernst Ludwig Kirchner and Franz Marc.

Historisches Rathaus
& Friedenssaal
HISTORIC BUILDING

(Historic City Hall & Peace Hall; ☑0251-492 2724; Prinzipalmarkt 8-9; adult/child €2/1.50; ☉Friedenssaal 10am-5pm Tue-Fri, to 4pm Sat & Sun) Dominating Prinzipalmarkt, Münster's city hall played a key role in ending the calamitous Thirty Years' War when an important sub-treaty of the Peace of Westphalia was signed here in 1648. You can visit the place of the signing, the splendidly wood-carved Friedenssaal.

St Lambertikirche
CHURCH

(☑0251-448 93; www.st-lamberti.de; Lambertikirchplatz; ☉8am-7pm Mon-Sat, from 9am Sun) One of Münster's finest churches, the late-Gothic St Lambertikirche was built in 1450. It's filled with wonderful treasures but the most fascinating attraction is the three wrought-iron cages dangling from the openwork spire. They once displayed the corpses

of Anabaptist ringleader Jan van Leyden and two of his cohorts who were executed in 1535 after their failed attempt to establish an Anabaptist kingdom.

Before their execution, the trio was publicly tortured with red-hot tongs.

Kunstmuseum Picasso
MUSEUM

(☑0251-414 4710; www.kunstmuseum-picasso-muenster.de; Königsstrasse 5; adult/concession/under 18yr €10/8/4; ☉10am-6pm Tue-Sun) A treat for fans of Pablo Picasso, one of the 20th century's seminal artists, in this 18th-century neoclassical mansion whose changing exhibits are drawn from a prized collection of around 800 lithographic works. The museum also owns graphics by Georges Braque, Marc Chagall and Henri Matisse.

Überwasserkirche
CHURCH

(www.liebfrauen-muenster.de/gemeinden/liebfrauen.html; Überwasserkirchplatz) The Überwasserkirche (officially known as Liebfrauenkirche) is a 14th-century Gothic hall church with handsome stained-glass windows in the apse. The nickname translates as 'church

---

WORTH A TRIP

CASTLE-HOPPING IN THE MÜNSTERLAND

Münster is surrounded by the Münsterland, a flat and rural region dotted with about 100 castles and palaces, some of which are still owned and inhabited by the landed gentry. Many are protected by water-filled moats, which today offer little protection from tax assessors. The region is a dream for cyclists.

The following trio of castles offer the greatest tourist appeal and are relatively accessible from Münster.

Burg Hülshoff (☑02534-1052; www.burg-huelshoff.de; Schonebeck 6, Havixbeck; castle grounds & park free, museum adult/concession incl audioguide €5/3.50, combined ticket incl Haus Rüschhaus €8/6; ☉11am-6.30pm daily Apr-Sep, 11.30am-5pm Wed-Sun, mid-Mar–late Mar, Oct & Nov, closed Dec–mid-Mar; [P]) Catch a glimpse of the life and times of Annette von Droste-Hülshoff, a seminal 19th-century German poet at the red-brick chateau where she was born. Lovely gardens to boot. It's 10km west in Havixbeck and can be visited in a half day.

Burg Vischering (☑02591-799 00; www.burg-vischering.de; Berenbrok 1, Lüdinghausen; adult/concession/child Vorburg €3.50/2/1.50, Hauptburg & Vorburg €7.50/5/3.50; ☉10am-6pm Tue-Sun) Westphalia's oldest castle, medieval Burg Vischering is surrounded by ramparts and moats and conjures romantic images of knights and damsels. A museum provides insights into medieval lifestyles. It's 30km southwest in Berenbrok and can be visited in a half day.

Haus Rüschhaus (☑02534-1052; http://haus-rueschhaus.de; Am Rüschhaus 81, Nienberge; park & castle free, adult/concession tours €5/3.50, combined ticket incl Burg Hülshoff €8/6; ☉tours hourly 11am-noon & 2-4pm Tue-Sun May-Sep, 11am, noon, 2pm & 3pm Tue-Sun Apr & Oct, garden 24hr; ◻5 Schonebeck) Pick up literary vibes in the baroque mansion – with original furnishings – where Annette von Droste-Hülshoff penned some of her finest work. It's surrounded by inspiring gardens. It's 8km northwest in Schonebeck and can be visited in a half day.

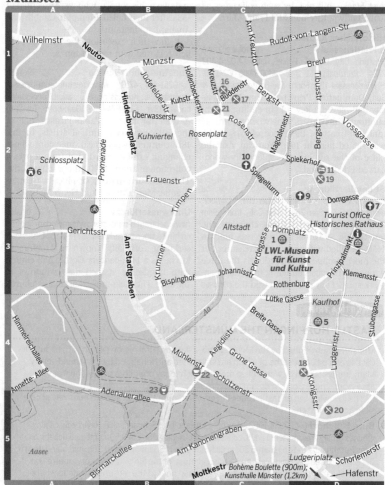

COLOGNE & NORTHERN RHINELAND MÜNSTER

across the water' and was inspired by its former location outside the city walls, beyond the wee river Aa.

Stadtmuseum MUSEUM
(City Museum; ☎0251-492 4503; www.stadt-muenster.de/museum; Salzstrasse 28; ⏱10am-6pm Tue-Fri, 11am-6pm Sat & Sun) FREE This sometimes engaging chronicle of 1200 years of Münster milestones includes a room on the Anabaptist rebellion where you can see the once-red-hot tongs used to torture Jan van Leyden and his unlucky colleagues before their execution. Another highlight is the collection of town models showing how the city grew and changed from the 16th century onward.

⊙ Hafen

A 10-minute walk southeast of the Hauptbahnhof (p687) takes you to the Hafen, Münster's partly revitalised old harbour on the Dortmund-Ems Canal. On the north end, once derelict halls and brick warehouses have been updated with avant-garde

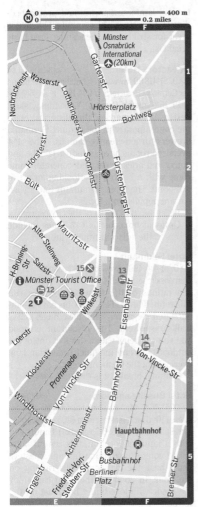

Münster

◎ Top Sights
1 LWL-Museum für Kunst und
  Kultur C3

◎ Sights
2 Clemenskirche E3
3 Erbdrostenhof E3
4 Historisches Rathaus &
  Friedenssaal D3
5 Kunstmuseum Picasso D4
6 Schloss A2
7 St Lambertikirche D3
8 Stadtmuseum E3
9 St-Paulus-Dom D2
10 Überwasserkirche C2

⌂ Sleeping
11 Hotel Busche am Dom D2
12 Hotel Feldmann E3
13 Hotel Mauritzhof F3
14 Sleep Station F4

✕ Eating
15 Altes Gasthaus Leve E3
16 Cavete C1
17 Drübbelken C1
18 Herr Sonnenschein D4
19 Holstein's Bistro D2
20 Krawummel D5
21 Pinkus Müller C2

◎ Drinking & Nightlife
22 Cafe Gasolin C4
23 Kruse-Baimken B4
  Pension Schmidt .... (see 15)

Kunsthalle Münster   MUSEUM
(☏ 0251-674 4675; www.kunsthalle.muenster.de;
Hafenweg 28; ⊙2-7pm Tue-Fri, noon-6pm Sat &
Sun; ☐6, 8, 17 Stadtwerke) **FREE** On the top
floor of Speicher II, an old warehouse in the
rebooted harbour, this gallery presents cutting-edge art by international artists. Admission is free, so there's no harm in popping in
while roaming around the Kreativkai.

◎ Aasee

Southwest of the Altstadt, the Aasee lake is
a beloved recreational getaway. Come for a
picnic, a stroll along its promenade or go for
a spin on the water itself. Family-friendly attractions abound.

Mühlenhof-Freilichtmuseum   MUSEUM
(Mühlenhof Open Air Museum; ☏ 0251-981 200;
www.muehlenhof-muenster.org; Theo-Breider-
Weg 1; adult/concession €5/3; ⊙10am-6pm, last
entry 5pm; ☐14 Mühlenhof) A fun open-air

architectural elements and now house artists' studios, creative offices, a theatre and a
contemporary art gallery in a string of buildings called the **Kreativkai**. It's also become
a popular area for hanging out and enjoying
coffee, cocktails and music. In good weather,
it's fun to promenade along the waterfront
and watch cargo barges cutting along the
canal.

To get to the Hafen, exit the Hauptbahnhof to the east via Bremer Platz, follow
Bremer Strasse south, cross Hansaring
and it will be on your left. It's about a
500m walk.

BAROQUE BEAUTIES BY JOHANN CONRAD SCHLAUN

The architect who left his mark on Münster more than any other was Johann Conrad Schlaun (1695–1773). He was a master of the Westphalian baroque, a more subdued expression of the baroque style than in southern Germany. A most exquisite example of Schlaun's vision is the 1757 **Erbdrostenhof** (☑0251-591 5553; www.erbdrostenhof.de; Salzstrasse 38; ☉8.30am-4.30pm Mon-Thu, to 3pm Fri) **FREE**, a lavish private mansion. Nearby, the equally stunning 1753 **Clemenskirche** (An der Clemenskirche 14; ☉9am-5.15pm Apr-Oct, to 4pm Nov-Mar) boasts a domed ceiling fresco supported by turquoise pillars. Less pristinely preserved is the 1773 **Schloss** (Schlossplatz), erstwhile residence of prince-bishops; today it's the seat of the university.

museum where you can stroll among historical Westphalian buildings, including a mill and bakery.

LWL-Museum für Naturkunde MUSEUM
(Natural History Museum; ☑0251-591 05; www.lwl-naturkundemuseum-muenster.de; Sentruper Strasse 285; museum adult/child €6.50/4, planetarium €5.50/3, both €10.50/6; ☉9am-6pm Tue-Sun; ☑14 Zoo/LWL-Naturkundemuseum) Dinosaurs and the universe are the stars at this large state-run nature museum, which also has a popular planetarium (programs in German only).

🛏 Sleeping

Münster has a good selection of small, family-run hotels but only a few are in the Altstadt. Places near the train station are within walking distance of all the sights. Hotels levy a 4.5% city tax on top of their rates (business travellers are exempt).

Sleep Station HOSTEL €
(☑0251-482 8155; www.sleep-station.de; Wolbecker Strasse 1; dm/d with bath €24/54, shared bath €17/50; ☉reception 8am-12.30pm & 5-9pm; ☻@🛜) This popular hostel is 200m from the Hauptbahnhof (p687) and caters to all needs and tastes, from women-only dorms to doubles with own bath and eight-bed dorms with shared baths. All have quality furniture (including beds with reading lamps), laminate flooring and proper bedding (€3 per stay). The communal kitchen is great for striking up friendships. Free basic breakfast.

★**Factory Hotel** DESIGN HOTEL €€
(☑0251-418 80; www.factoryhotel-muenster.de; An der Germania Brauerei 5; d €94-164; ᴾ☻❋🛜🏊; ☑15, 16 Germania Campus) This funky, sleek design hotel marries the historical with the contemporary in the defunct Germania brewery-turned-creative-campus. The 144 oversized rooms have an industrial vibe and marry red-brick, steel and concrete; some come with a balcony overlooking an artificial pond. The three restaurants and stylish bar are popular with locals.

It's about 2km north of the city centre.

Optional breakfast is €17. Rates include access to the adjacent fitness club.

Hotel Feldmann HOTEL €€
(☑0251-414 490; www.hotel-feldmann.de; An der Clemenskirche 14; d €125-147; ᴾ☻🛜) Four generations of the same family have run this refined hotel. The 20 rooms have an understated elegance; some have huge, glassy walk-in showers. The restaurant is good and you can relax with a drink at one of the outdoor tables on the quiet pedestrian lane overlooking the Clemenskirche.

Optional breakfast is €6.50.

Hotel Busche am Dom HOTEL €€
(☑0251-464 44; www.hotel-busche.de; Bogenstrasse 10; d incl breakfast from €105; ☉reception 7am-9pm; @🛜; ☑5, 6 Spiekerhof) Family-run with a fantastic location, this central hotel has 13 comfortable rooms in muted pastels. You'll hear the cathedral bells ringing on the hour. In good weather, you can enjoy the made-with-love buffet breakfast on the terrace.

Hotel Mauritzhof DESIGN HOTEL €€€
(☑0251-417 20; www.mauritzhof.de; Eisenbahnstrasse 17; d from €159-199; ☻❋🛜) Elegant hues, a harmonious interplay of glass and wood, and extravagant designer furniture (Vitra, Driade, Kartell) give this 52-room property a mod, cosmopolitan edge. Those in the smallest category are a tad wee while others come with balconies facing the promenade. Wind down the day in the restaurant, the bar or the reading room.

🍴 Eating

As befits a university town, Münster is hip to all the food trends from street food to avo toast and vegan bowls, but also has plenty of trad places dishing up Westphalian fare such as *Töttchen* (veal ragout) and *Pfefferpotthast* (pepper beef stew)

Herr Sonnenschein
CAFE €

(☑0251-8570 0288; www.facebook.com/herr sonnenschein1; Königsstrasse 43; ⊙9am-midnight Mon-Sat, 10am-6pm Sun) Stay on the sunny side at this feel-good cafe that's worth a stop no matter where the hands of the clock are. Highlights on the small but handmade menu (snacks €4 to €9) are the avo toast, porridge and the mysterious KoGuTo sandwich (carrot, cucumber, tomato). Excellent coffee, friendly folks and even a kiddie play corner.

Krawummel
VEGAN €

(☑0251-7478 8117; www.krawummel.de; Ludgeristrasse 62; mains €6-11; ⊙11.30am-10pm Mon-Fri, 11am-10pm Sat, noon-9pm Sun; 🖥☑) This darling cafe gets plenty of eco-cred for using only organic and sustainably grown ingredients and turning them into a rotating menu of super-tasty plant-based bowls, burgers, salads, curries and sandwiches. Pick your favourite from the blackboard, order at the counter, grab a white table in the cosy yet stylish room and start salivating.

★Altes Gasthaus Leve
GERMAN €€

(☑0251-455 95; www.gasthaus-leve.de; Alter Steinweg 37; mains €7.50-24; ⊙noon-midnight Mon-Sat) Münster's oldest inn (since 1607) has painted tiles, oil paintings and copper etchings that form a suitably rustic backdrop to the hearty Westphalian and German fare. Besides seasonal specials, try stalwart dishes such as lima bean stew and sweet-and-sour beef.

It all goes down well with a beer, including the local Pinkus Müller and eight others on tap.

★Holstein's Bistro
EUROPEAN €€

(☑0251-449 44; www.butterhandlung-holstein. de; Horsteberg 1; mains €10-25; ⊙11.30am-7pm Tue-Fri, 11am-5pm Sat; ☑) Münster's slow-food outpost has been raising the bar of inventive seasonal fare for almost 20 years. The ever-changing menu reflects what's fresh, but there's usually a variety of soups, salads, pastas and more on offer. Snare one of the tables in the shadow of the Dom (p680) along the alley.

Drübbelken
GERMAN €€

(☑0251-421 15; www.druebbelken.de; Buddenstrasse 14; mains €10-27; ⊙11.30am-2.30pm & 5.30pm-midnight Mon-Fri, 11.30am-midnight Sat & Sun) This locally beloved restaurant in a half-timbered house has been churning out top-notch earthy Westphalian fry-ups forever. Of course, the beer is Pinkus; watch for their many seasonal specials.

RADICAL REFORMERS: THE ANABAPTISTS

Anabaptism was a religious movement that swept through Europe in the early 16th century. Starting in Zurich, Anabaptists spread through much of Germany and beyond. But like many cultish groups, their true believers had sharp disagreements among themselves. The name alone was cause for strife as it referred to the core tenet that adults should be 'rebaptised' into the faith. However, many claimed that any original baptism as an infant hadn't counted because non-Anabaptist religions were not valid, thus your Anabaptist baptism was the first. And so it went. They did like to argue.

Other beliefs included polygamy and community ownership of goods. The movement reached its apex at Münster in 1534, when a Dutchman named Jan van Leyden and a crew of followers managed to take over the town. Soon they had baptised more than 1000 new followers.

Some rather extreme personalities also emerged: Jan Matthys marched out to confront a vast army of besiegers from the Catholic church who planned to retake the city. He was promptly beheaded and his genitals nailed to a town gate. Meanwhile, van Leyden proclaimed himself king and took 16 wives, which worked out to be about one for each month he was in power; besiegers overran Münster in 1535 and had van Leyden and many Anabaptists tortured and killed. Three of the bodies ended up in the cages you can still see today in St Lambertikirche (p681).

After the defeat at Münster, the movement was never the same. It had managed to bring both Catholics and Protestants together as both mercilessly tortured and killed Anabaptists. Splinters of the old faith eventually formed what later became the Amish and Mennonite faiths, among others.

For wine lovers, there's a good selection of vintages from the Baden region in southern Germany.

Pinkus Müller
PUB FOOD €€

(☑0251-451 51; www.pinkus.de; Kreuzstrasse 4; mains €9-24.50; ☺noon-midnight Mon-Sat) One of Germany's best small brewers, Pinkus Müller has a namesake pub and restaurant in the heart of the Kuhviertel nightlife zone. Nab an outdoor table under a big tree or get cosy in a warren of timeless carved-wood rooms. The menu has all the regional classics that go so well with delicious beers such as the very hoppy Extra.

Cavete
GERMAN €€

(☑0251-414 3516; www.muenster-cavete.de; Kreuzstrasse 38; mains €9-13; ☺6pm-2am) For a relaxed pint, steer to the Kuhviertel, the traditional student quarter north of the Dom (p680). Cavete has been a late-night classic for generations. Find a seat at one of the battered old wooden tables and enjoy a schnitzel or try their famous homemade green noodles.

Drinking & Entertainment

Expect plenty of watering holes to keep the the party-happy student population lubricated. The classic drinking quarter is the Kuhviertel, where you'll find the brewpub Pinkus Müller; its suds are poured throughout town.

★Kruse-Baimken
BEER GARDEN

(☑0251-463 87; www.kruse-baimken.de; Am Stadtgraben 52; ☺noon-1am) Huge trees soar over the passel of tables at this lovely beer garden right off the Promenade near the Aasee. Unsurprisingly it gets very crowded, especially as the food (mains €10 to €20) is just that much better than average beer garden fare – the sausages smokier, the salads fresher.

In cold months, the action moves inside, where there's an ambitious modern German menu.

Bohème Boulette
BAR

(☑0251-3963 0736; www.boheme-boulette.de; Hansaring 26; ☺6pm-2am Mon-Thu, to 3am Fri, 1pm-3am Sat, 1pm-midnight Sun; 🚌6, 8, 17 Hansaring) Friendly bar that reboots a 1920s vibe for the 21st century with good burgers, beers, football on the big screen, quiz nights and other events that bring out the party animals. En route to the Hafen. Service could be better.

Pension Schmidt
CAFE

(☑0251-9795 7050; www.pensionschmidt.se; Alter Steinweg 37; ☺10am-1am or later) This hip cultural cafe has top-quality coffee and comfortable sofas for lounging on. Join convivial locals at such events as poetry readings, a pub quiz, live bands and the Sunday jazz 'breakfast' that starts at noon.

Cafe Gasolin
CAFE

(☑0251-890 7843; www.cafe-gasolin.de; Aegidistrasse 45; ☺10am-1am or later Mon-Fri, 11am-2am or later Sat & Sun) This cleverly converted 1950s gas station has blissful cakes, light snacks and strong coffee. At night, different DJs keep the place busy after everything else has closed. Prices are low, quality is not; huge patio.

★Hot Jazz Club
LIVE MUSIC

(☑0251-6866 7909; www.hotjazzclub.de; Hafenweg 26b; tickets free-€35; ☺6pm-late Mon-Sat, from 3pm Sun May-Aug, 7pm-late Mon-Sat, from 3pm Sun Sep-Apr; 🚌6, 8, 17 Stadtwerke, 🚌33 Emdener Strasse) A fine reason to head out to the Hafen, this subterranean bar keeps it real with live music of nearly all stripes – despite the name. Many concerts are free, and comedy and improv nights also make calendar appearances.

❶ Information

You can find more info on many of Münster's sites at www.muenster.de.

Münster Tourist Office (☑0251-492 2710; www.tourismus.muenster.de; Heinrich-Brüning-Strasse 9; ☺10am-6pm Mon-Fri, to 1pm Sat) Plenty of info (much in English).

Tourist Office Historisches Rathaus (☑0251-492 2724; Prinzipalmarkt 10; ☺10am-5pm Tue-Fri, to 4pm Sat & Sun) A good source of information.

❶ Getting There & Away

AIR

The Münster-Osnabrück Airport (p680) is about 27km north of the city centre and has mostly domestic flights and charters to southern European holiday destinations. Bus S50 connects the airport and the Hauptbahnhof (€7.50, 30 minutes).

BUS

Flixbus and other coaches stop on **Berliner Platz** (Berliner Platz) outside the **Hauptbahnhof**.

TRAIN

Münster is on a main train line with regular links to points north including Hamburg (€60, 2¼ hours) and south to Cologne (€35, 1¾ hours) from its **Hauptbahnhof** (www.bahnhof.de/bahnhof-de/Münster__Westf__Hbf-1023308; Berliner Platz).

Flixtrain stops here on its Hamburg–Cologne route.

ⓘ Getting Around

Münster has a comprehensive bus route network. Single rides are €3.10 if bought from drivers or €2.70 from vending machines; day passes valid after 9am are €6.20 (€5.20 from machines).

Rent bikes from **Radstation** (☑0251-484 0177; www.radstation.de; Berliner Platz 27a; 1/3 days €8/20; ☺5.30am-11pm Mon-Fri, 7am-11pm Sat & Sun) right by the Hauptbahnhof.

Osnabrück

☑0541 / POP 164,000

Osnabrück is easily visited on a day trip from Münster or as a stopover en route to points north. Like Münster, it played a pivotal role in ending the Thirty Years' War (1618–48) by hosting the diplomatic negotiations leading to the Peace of Westphalia. Known as the 'City of Peace', it's apt that Osnabrück was the birthplace of Erich Maria Remarque, author of *All Quiet on the Western Front*, one of the seminal anti-war novels of the 20th century. Osnabrück is also where the painter Felix Nussbaum was born; his work can be admired in a striking museum by Daniel Libeskind.

◉ Sights

The compact and often charmless centre is easily explored on foot. Osnabrück's small but appealing old quarter eddies around Dom St Peter and Marienkirche. The Felix Nussbaum Haus is about 500m further west.

★ **Felix Nussbaum Haus**   MUSEUM
(☑0541-323 2237; www.osnabrueck.de/fnh; Lotter Strasse 2; adult/concession/under 18yr €5/3/free; ☺11am-6pm Tue-Fri, 10am-6pm Sat & Sun) Osnabrück-born Jewish painter Felix Nussbaum (1904–44), who emigrated to Belgium and was murdered at Auschwitz, hauntingly documented life, exile, persecution and death under Nazi occupation in much of his work. This museum presents works from all phases of his professional life, including visceral key pieces such as *Self-Portrait with Jewish Pass* and his last work *Triumph of Death*. The museum building, shaped like

an interconnected series of concrete shards, is a 1998 masterpiece by Daniel Libeskind.

Dom St Peter   CATHEDRAL
(☑0541-184 90; www.dom-osnabrueck.de; Domplatz; ☺6.30am-7.45pm Mon-Fri, 7.30am-7pm Sat, 7.30am-8pm Sun) The unbalanced towers are just one of the idiosyncratic architectural features that make Osnabrück's cathedral an intriguing place. Parts date to 1100, and given that the holy complex got rough treatment in WWII, it's fascinating to explore the surviving labyrinth, finding the cloister and discovering golden relics in the **Domschatzkammer** (Treasury; ☑0541-318 481; https://bistum-osnabrueck.de; Domhof 12; adult/concession/under 18 €5/3.50/free; ☺10am-6pm Tue-Sun).

Rathaus   HISTORIC BUILDING
(Markt; ☺9am-8pm Mon-Fri, to 4pm Sat, 10am-4pm Sun) **FREE** It was on the Rathaus steps that the Peace of Westphalia was proclaimed on 25 October 1648, ending the Thirty Years' War. The preceding peace negotiations were conducted partly in Münster, about 60km south, and partly in the Rathaus' Friedenssaal (Peace Hall). On the left as you enter the Rathaus are portraits of the negotiators. Also look around the Schatzkammer (Treasure Chamber) opposite, especially for the 13th-century *Kaiserpokal* (Kaiser goblet).

Erich Maria Remarque
Friedenszentrum   MUSEUM
(Erich Maria Remarque Peace Centre; ☑0541-323 2109; www.remarque.uos.de; Markt 6; ☺10am-1pm & 3-5pm Tue-Fri, 11am-5pm Sat & Sun) **FREE** The novelist Erich Maria Remarque, whose most famous work *All Quiet on the Western Front* deals with the horrors of WWI, was born in Osnabrück in 1898. This small museum uses photos and documents to chronicle his life and work.

Marienkirche   CHURCH
(☑0541-283 93; www.marien-osnabrueck.de; Markt; ☺10am-noon & 3-5pm Apr-Sep, 10.30am-noon & 2.30-4pm Oct-Mar) It took two centuries to complete this beautiful Gothic hall church whose four gables overlook the market square. Rebuilt after burning down during WWII, its interior is punctuated with religious eye candy such as a triumphal cross from the late 13th century and a panelled three-winged altar with paintings at the front and back.

COLOGNE & NORTHERN RHINELAND OSNABRÜCK

VARUS & THE BATTLEFIELD AT KALKRIESE

You don't need to be a history buff (or even a fan of Russell Crowe in *Gladiator*) to come to this **Varusschlacht Museum & Park Kalkriese** (☑ 05468-920 4200; www.kalkriese-varusschlacht.de; Venner Strasse 69 (B218), Bramsche-Kalkriese; adult/child €7.50/4.50; ☺ 10am-6pm daily Apr-Oct, to 5pm Tue-Sun Nov-Mar), although by the time you leave you'll have a fine idea about how rebellious Germanic tribes won a major victory over their Roman occupiers somewhere in the Osnabrück region in AD 9 – defeating three of military commander Publius Quinctilius Varus' legions. The site is about 22km north of Osnabrück.

Only in 1987 was this likely candidate for the site of the so-called Battle of Teutoburg Forest uncovered. In 2000, the battlefield was opened as an archaeological park to display the Germans' dirt ramparts and explain how they beat the Romans. Since then, facilities have expanded steadily and you'll find exhibits on the artefacts dug up so far, as well as high-tech displays and re-enactments. Enjoy a grand view of the landscape from the top of the tower at the end of the exhibit. Rent an audioguide for a more in-depth experience.

🛏 Sleeping & Eating

Not far west of the Markt, the Heger-Tor-Viertel area around the namesake old tower is a fine place to scout out a good meal and a drink.

Intour Hotel
HOTEL €€

(☑ 0541-963 860; www.intourhotel.de; Maschstrasse 10; d €98-104; P ⊛ ☎; ☒ 31, 32, 33 Weissenburgstrasse) Situated just west of the old quarter and handy to Felix Nussbaum Haus (p687), this hotel looks unprepossessing from the outside but inside is modern, with unfussy decor.

Barösta Kaffeehaus
CAFE €

(☑ 0541-7706 6946; www.baroesta.de; Redlingerstrasse 1; mains €4-9; ☺ 8am-7pm Mon-Sat, 11am-6.30pm Sun; ☒) Follow your nose to the source of the tempting java aroma at this upbeat, contemporary cafe-cum-roastery. It's good for just grabbing a quick cuppa but better if you stick around for homemade breakfast (great muesli!) or a fresh sandwich or salad made with hand-picked ingredients from the region. Yummy cakes too.

Cafe Läer
CAFE €

(☑ 0541-222 44; www.facebook.com/cafe.Laeer; Krahnstrasse 4; treats from €3; ☺ 8am-6pm Mon-Fri, 7.30am-4pm Sat) This charming cafe has plied loyal locals with freshly baked goods and gooey pastries and cakes for well over a century. Current owner Ulrich Läer, grandson of the founder, may retire soon, so hurry over for a last taste of old-fashioned goodness.

The setting in the city's prettiest half-timbered townhouse is a bonus.

Hausbrauerei Rampendahl
GERMAN €€

(☑ 0541-245 35; www.rampendahl.de; Hasestrasse 35; mains €8-20; ☺ 11am-11pm Mon-Thu, to midnight Fri & Sat, to 10.30pm Sun) This restaurant and microbrewery near the Dom (p687) is about as traditional as they come, serving substantial hearty dishes to accompany the house beers such as a delicious unfiltered lager. Soak up the suds along with the olde-worlde feel of this historical building with its fine baroque gable.

❶ Information

Osnabrück Tourist Information (☑ 0541-323 2202; www.osnabrueck.de; Bierstrasse 22/23; ☺ 9.30am-6pm Mon-Fri, 10am-4pm Sat) Close to the Rathaus (p687); has more gifts than info.

❶ Getting There & Around

Münster-Osnabrück Airport (p680) is about 33km southwest of town. It's connected to the city centre by bus X150; the journey takes about 40 minutes.

Trains from Münster (from €13.20, 36 minutes) leave several times hourly. ICE trains and the mamba-green Flixtrain running between Cologne and Hamburg also stop in Osnabrück.

The long-distance bus station is at the Hauptbahnhof, which is just west of the city centre.

Sights in the centre are easily explored on foot. Alternatively, take bus 584 from the Hauptbahnhof to the Theater stop (10 minutes, €2.80).

OSTWESTFALEN

The rolling hills and foliage of the Teutoburg Forest make for pleasant and scenic driving in largely rural Ostwestfalen (Eastern Westphalia). Both terrain and elevations get more dramatic in the Sauerland, where there are winter sports. The main towns are Soest and Paderborn, which are both filled with ancient and beautifully restored churches.

ℹ Getting There & Away

Eastern Westphalia is traversed by the east–west A2, A30 and A44 autobahns and the north–south A1 and A7. Regional trains come through from Münster and the Ruhrgebiet cities. Tiny Paderborn–Lippstadt airport has domestic and intra-Europe flights.

Soest

☑ 02921 / POP 47,500

One of eastern Westphalia's most appealing towns, Soest is a tranquil place of half-timbered houses and a clutch of treasure-filled churches that reflect the wealth it enjoyed during its Hanseatic League days. Although bombed in WWII, this maze of idyllic, crooked lanes has been beautifully rebuilt and preserves much of its medieval character. The little channels of water that course through it are utterly charming.

Among Soest's distinctive features is its stone: a shimmering greenish local sandstone used in building the town wall, churches and other public structures.

Only 45km southeast of Münster, Soest is compact enough to be explored on a day trip or as a side trip en route to somewhere else.

◎ Sights

Much of Soest's historical centre lies within a moated defensive wall, which today has a park-like appearance and is great for strolling and picnicking. Some of Westphalia's most important churches are near the Markt where the Rathaus, a baroque confection with an arched portico, looms on the western side.

★ St Maria zur Wiese   CHURCH

(Wiesenkirche; ☑ 02921-132 51; www.wiesenkirche.de; Wiesenstrasse; ⊙11am-6pm Mon-Sat, noon-6pm Sun Apr-Sep, to 4pm Oct-Mar) Close to the train station, this exquisite late-Gothic church is easily recognised by its neo-Gothic twin spires, which are undergoing restoration. One is complete and aglow with green, while the other is under wraps until at least 2020. The interior is bathed in colours from stained-glass windows, including one from 1520 showing Jesus and his disciples enjoy-

ing a Westphalian Last Supper of ham, beer and native pumpernickel bread.

St Maria zur Höhe   CHURCH

(Hohnekirche; ☑ 02921-2253; www.hohnegemeinde.de; Hohe Gasse; ⊙10am-5.30pm Apr-Sep, to 4pm Oct-Mar) St Maria zur Höhe is a squat 13th-century hall church that's less architecturally refined than others in town. Its sombreness is brightened by beautiful ceiling frescoes, an altar ascribed to the Westphalian painter known as the Master of Liesborn, and the *Scheibenkreuz*, a huge wooden cross on a circular board more typically found in Scandinavian churches; it's the only such cross in Germany.

Look for the light switch on your left as you enter to shed some light on the matter.

St Patrokli   CHURCH

(☑ 02921-671 0660; www.sankt-patrokli.de; Propst-Nübel-Strasse 2; ⊙10am-5.45pm) Ponder the balance and beauty of the soaring and dignified tower of St Patrokli, a three-nave 10th-century Romanesque structure partly adorned with delicate frescoes. Inside, note especially the muralled high choir and the statue of Patroclus, the church's name patron, who was martyred by the Romans in AD 275. On the outside, the west facade is especially elaborate.

Petrikirche   CHURCH

(☑ 02921-130 00; www.petri-pauli.de; Petrikirchhof 10; ⊙9.30am-5.30pm Tue-Fri, to 4.30pm Sat, 2-5.30pm Sun) Petrikirche has Romanesque origins in the 8th century and a choir from Gothic times, all topped by a baroque onion dome. It's adorned with wall murals and features an unusual modern altar made from the local green sandstone, glass and brushed stainless steel.

Nikolaikapelle   CHURCH

(☑ 02921-671 0660; Thomästrasse; ⊙11am-noon Tue-Thu & Sun Apr-Oct) The tiny Nikolaikapelle enjoys mystical simplicity enlivened by a masterful altar painting attributed to 15th-century master Conrad von Soest (who, despite the name, was actually born in Dortmund).

🛏 Sleeping

Deck 8 Designhotel Soest   HOTEL €€

(☑ 02921-339 4040; www.deck8-hotel.de; Werkstrasse 8; d €90-120; ⓟ❄✳🛜) Close to the train station, this contemporary hotel is in a hulk of a building, but rooms meet all the design and amenity expectations of modern nomads. All have floor-to-ceiling windows, minimalist furnishings, stylish bathrooms and city views from the upper floors. Spend a little more if you want a free-standing tub, a patio or a kitchenette. Optional breakfast €9.90.

Hotel Im Wilden Mann
HOTEL €€

(☑ 02921-150 71; www.im-wilden-mann.de; Am Markt 11; d incl breakfast €90; P @ 🛜 🛂) This central landmark in a portly half-timbered townhouse offers the opportunity to connect to the magic of yesteryear in a dozen comfortable rooms furnished in uncluttered country style.

✖ Eating

Local specialities include the Soester pumpernickel, a rough-textured rye bread made entirely without salt, and the *Bullenauge* (bull's eye), a creamy mocha liqueur.

★ Brauhaus Zwiebel
GERMAN €€

(☑ 02921-4424; http://brauhaus-zwiebel.de; Ulricherstrasse 24; mains €10-17.50; ⊘11am-midnight) A one-stop shop for myriad forms of pleasure in Soest, this long-running brewery produces a bevy of excellent seasonal beers throughout the year. The food is predictably hearty, ample (yes, many dishes come with *Zwiebel* – onion) and enjoyed either in the rustic half-timbered restaurant, in the winter garden or in the leafy beer garden in summer.

Restaurant Im Wilden Mann
GERMAN €€

(☑ 02921-150 71; www.im-wilden-mann.de; Am Markt 11; mains €10-30; ⊘noon-11pm Mon-Sat, to 10pm Sun; 🛜) This characterful restaurant shares a gorgeous double half-timbered building from the 15th century with a hotel of the same name. The kitchen turns out robust classics, some of them with an ambitious bent such as red-wine braised pork cheeks from Soest sows, and pan-fried pikeperch in lemon butter.

Brauerei Christ
GERMAN €€

(☑ 02921-155 15; www.brauerei-christ.com; Walburgerstrasse 36; mains €11-25; ⊘noon-1am) Dating from 1584, history oozes from every nook and cranny of this warren of living-room-style rooms stuffed with musical instruments, oil paintings and unique knick-knacks. Hunker down at polished tables for Westphalian specialities, schnitzel variations or marinated beef carpaccio. Nice beer garden.

❶ Information

Soest Tourist Office (☑ 02921-103 6110; www.soest.de; Teichsmühlengasse 3; ⊘9.30am-4.30pm Mon-Fri, 10am-3pm Sat year-round, 11am-1pm Sun Apr-Oct; 🛜) In an old water mill next to a placid duck pond and park.

❶ Getting There & Away

Soest's regular train connections include Dortmund (from €13.20, 45 minutes), Paderborn (from €13.20, 30 minutes) and Münster (€17.30, 50 minutes). The train station is on the north side of the ring road enclosing Soest's historical centre.

Paderborn

🗐 05251 / POP 150,500

The largest city in eastern Westphalia, Paderborn is a nice stopover, offering an intriguing blend of medieval marvels and a hi-tech vibe. It derives its name from the 4km Pader, Germany's shortest river. It's fed by about 200 springs surfacing in the Paderquellgebiet, a landscaped park currently undergoing partial ecological restoration.

Charlemagne used Paderborn as a power base to defeat the Saxons and convert them to Christianity, giving him the momentum needed to rise to greater things. A visit by Pope Leo III in 799 led to the establishment of the Western Roman Empire, a precursor to the Holy Roman Empire, and Charlemagne's coronation as its emperor the following year.

Paderborn remains a pious place to this day – churches abound, and religious sculpture and motifs adorn facades, fountains and parks. Many of Paderborn's 20,000 students are involved in theological studies (mathematics and computer science are other major fields).

◉ Sights

Most sights cluster in the largely pedestrianised Altstadt, which is easily explored on foot. It's about 500m east of the Hauptbahnhof via Westernstrasse, the main shopping street.

★ Museum in der Kaiserpfalz
MUSEUM

(☑ 05251-105 110; www.kaiserpfalz-paderborn.de; Am Ikenberg; adult/concession €3.50/2; ⊘10am-6pm Tue-Sun) In the 1960s, archaeologists stumbled upon remnants of the Carolingian palace where Charlemagne met with Pope Leo III, as well as the much better

SAUERLAND

Soest is considered the gateway to the Sauerland, a hilly forested region popular as an easy getaway for nature-craving Ruhrgebiet residents and hill-craving Dutch tourists. There are a few museums and castles sprinkled about, but the Sauerland's primary appeal lies in the outdoors. Thousands of kilometres of marked hiking trails weave through the terrain, mostly through beech and fir forest, spread across four nature parks. Cyclists and mountain bikers can pick their favourites from dozens of routes. In winter some of the steeper slopes around Winterberg come alive with downhill skiers.

The Sauerland is also home to the world's first hostel, which is now part of the museum at **Burg Altena** (☑02352-966 7033; www.burg-altena.de; Fritz-Thomée-Strasse 80, Altena; adult/concession €6/3.50; ☉9.30am-5pm Tue-Fri, 11am-6pm Sat & Sun), a fairy-tale medieval castle in the town of the same name.

The Sauerland is best explored with your own wheels; you can get loads of info from the regional tourist office website (www.sauerland.com).

preserved foundations of the 11th-century palace of Heinrich II. The latter has been reconstructed as faithfully as possible and now showcases excavated items from both residences, from weapons and jewellery to vessels and tools. Other galleries provide insights into daily life in the Middle Ages and highlight various phases in the city's history.

Dom
CATHEDRAL

(☑05251-125 1287; www.dom-paderborn.de; Markt 17; ☉6.30am-6.30pm) **FREE** Enter Paderborn's massive (104m long!) Gothic Dom through the southern portal (called 'Paradise') adorned with delicate carved figures. Inside, turn your attention to the high altar and the pompous memorial tomb of Dietrich von Fürstenberg, a 17th-century prince-bishop. Signs point the way to the Dom's most endearing feature, the *Dreihasenfenster*, a trompe l'oeil window in the cloister with tracery depicting three hares, ingeniously arranged so that each has two ears, even though there are only three ears in all.

Erzbischöfliches Diözesanmuseum
MUSEUM

(Archbishop's Diocesan Museum; ☑05251-125 1400; www.dioezesanmuseum-paderborn.de; Markt 17; adult/concession €4/2; ☉10am-6pm Tue-Sun) Outside the Dom, an incongruously modernist structure by Gottfried Böhm stands atop vestiges of a medieval bishop's palace and shelters prized church treasures from the 11th right through to the 20th centuries. Head into the vaulted basement to ogle the most precious pieces, including the gilded Liborius shrine and a portable altar crafted by master goldsmith Rogerus von Helmarshausen.

Bartholomäuskapelle
CHURCH

(Am Ikenberg; ☉8.30am-7.30pm) Paderborn's most important house of worship is also its smallest. The twee Bartholomäuskapelle was consecrated in 1017 and is considered the oldest hall church in Germany. It has otherworldly acoustics.

Attached to the Ottonian-Salian palace of Heinrich II, it was used by the emperor to get dressed before entering the cathedral.

Schloss Neuhaus
PALACE

(☑05251-801 92; www.schlosspark-paderborn.de; Im Schlosspark 10; park free, museums adult/concession €2.50/2; ☉park 24hr, museums 10am-6pm Tue-Sun, event hours vary; ℗; ☐1, 8, 11 Thuner Siedlung) Schloss Neuhaus, a moated palace with an expansive park, once served as the residence of the Paderborn prince-bishops. A new museum inside the palace illustrates their fanciful lifestyle through a series of period rooms, while additional exhibits in the stables train the spotlight on glass and ceramics, natural history, and 20th-century art. A potpourri of events takes place year-round.

If you have time, the nicest approach is on foot by following the river for about 4km northwest of the Paderquellgebiet.

Heinz Nixdorf Museumsforum
MUSEUM

(HNF; ☑05251-306 600; www.hnf.de; Fürstenallee 7; adult/concession €8/5; ☉9am-6pm Tue-Fri, 10am-6pm Sat & Sun; ☐11 Museumsforum) You don't have to be a techie to enjoy this museum, a high-tech romp through 5000 years of information technology from cuneiform to cyberspace. Established by the local founder of Nixdorf computers (since swallowed by bigger corporations), it displays all manner of once-high-tech gadgets from the predigital age; most memorable is the replica of Eniac, a room-sized vacuum-tube computer developed for the US Army in the 1940s.

It's about 3km north of the main train station.

Marienplatz
SQUARE

Rathausplatz blends into Marienplatz with its delicate Mariensäule (St Mary's Column) and Heising'sche Haus, an elaborate 17th-century patrician mansion that shares a wall with the tourist office. A modern addition is the Marienpassage with its central atrium.

Carolingian Kaiserpfalz
HISTORIC SITE

(Am Ikenberg) Remnants of the foundation of Charlemagne's palace, built in the late 8th century, have been unearthed north of the Dom.

Rathaus
HISTORIC BUILDING

(Rathausplatz) Paderborn's proud Rathaus (1616) with ornate gables, oriels and other decorative touches, is typical of the Weser Renaissance architectural style.

Marktkirche
CHURCH

(Market Church; Kamp 8; ⊙9am-6pm) One of the finest baroque buildings in Paderborn, the Marktkirche was founded by Jesuits and consecrated in 1692. Inside this galleried basilica, your gaze is immediately drawn to the dizzyingly detailed baroque high altar. A soaring symphony of wood and gold, this exact replica of the 17th-century original destroyed in WWII was completed in 2003.

Abdinghofkirche
CHURCH

(Am Abdinghof; ⊙11am-6pm) The Abdinghofkirche is easily recognised by its twin towers. The foundation stone was laid in the 11th century as part of a Benedictine monastery in business until its secularisation in 1803; it became a Protestant church in 1866. Its interior exudes serene austerity with its whitewashed and unadorned arches and flat wooden ceiling.

🍴 Sleeping & Eating

Near the Rathaus, the Rathauspassage has delis and markets where you can assemble a fine picnic to enjoy in the Paderquellgebiet.

Galerie-Hotel
BOUTIQUE HOTEL €€

(☑05251-122 40; www.galerie-hotel.de; Bachstrasse 1; s/d €80/100; 🅿☺🛜) Offering Paderborn's most ambient digs, this private boutique hotel is in a 1563 stone building

overlooking the Paderquellgebiet. The 11 rooms reflect the artist-owner's classy style and come with great beds, beautiful light and a tasteful vanilla-pistachio-chocolate colour scheme. Original art graces the downstairs cafe-restaurant, which also serves optional breakfasts (€12 per person).

Paderborner Brauhaus
GERMAN €€

(☑05251-282 554; http://bono-gastronomie.de/gastronomie/paderborner-brauhaus; Kisau 2; mains €10-25; ⊙5pm-1am Mon-Thu, to 2am Fri, 11.30am-2am Sat, to 1am Sun) When Paderborn locals arrange to meet at 'the' beer garden, they mean this sprawling gem sheltered by a grove of old trees hugging the little Pader river. The kitchen caters mostly to carnivores and includes some super-tasty schnitzel and steaks tickled on the lava grill.

In bad weather you'll find much of the same at the affiliated Deutsches Haus across the street.

🍷 Drinking & Nightlife

Paderborn has a good range of bars and pubs, from traditional haunts to lively student taverns and trendy cafes. The local brew, Paderborner Pilsner, has a sweet-bitter aroma that may not be to everyone's taste.

Sputnik
PUB

(☑017 0935 1830; www.sputnik-pb.de; Imadstrasse 7; ⊙7pm-1am Mon-Thu, to 3am Fri & Sat) If you're looking for a fun night out with a relaxed crowd, beam yourself up to the legendary Sputnik, home of cold beers and eclectic entertainment – from concerts to quiz nights and song and poetry slams – conducive to making new friends.

ℹ Information

Paderborn Tourist Office (☑05251-882 980; www.paderborn.de; Marienplatz 2a; ⊙10am-6pm Mon-Fri, to 4pm Sat Apr-Oct, 10am-5pm Mon-Fri, to 2pm Sat Nov-Mar)

ℹ Getting There & Around

Getting to Paderborn by train often involves a change in Hamm, although there are some direct connections from Dortmund and Kassel-Wilhelmshöhe. Trains to Soest (€13.20, 30 minutes) and Münster (€22.80, 90 minutes) leave several times hourly.

Radstation (☑05251-870 740; Bahnhofstrasse 29; per day from €10; ⊙6.30am-7pm Mon-Fri, to 3pm Sat) at the train station rents bicycles.

Lower Saxony & Bremen

POP 7,926,599 (LOWER SAXONY), 671,489 (BREMEN)

Best Places to Eat

➡ Seesteg (p741)

➡ Basil (p702)

➡ Natusch (p729)

➡ Schlegels Weinstuben (p712)

➡ Zum Schwejk (p708)

Best Places to Stay

➡ Althoff Hotel Fürstenhof (p707)

➡ Atlantic Grand (p723)

➡ Van der Valk Hotel Hildesheim (p711)

➡ Central Hotel Kaiserhof (p701)

Why Go?

Lower Saxony (Niedersachsen) is the largest German state after Bavaria. West to east, it stretches from the World Heritage–listed Wattenmeer tidal flats and the East Frisian Islands to Wolfsburg, global HQ of Volkswagen. Its green and liveable capital, Hanover, was named Unesco City of Music in 2014, but is better known for its annual CeBit and Messe technology trade shows. Between the state's patchwork of vibrant small towns and villages is a diverse landscape of forests, farmlands, river plains, heath and moors.

Bremen, the smallest of the German states, packs a punch for its size. Bremen City has a wealth of fine architecture and cobblestone streets; engaging, educational museums; a vibrant waterfront and a happening, modern, multicultural vibe that keeps things interesting. At the mouth of the Weser, its port city Bremerhaven upholds a rich seafaring tradition and is home to two of Germany's most original and entertaining museums.

When to Go

Spring heralds a welcome explosion of colour in endless fields of golden yellow canola and manicured floral gardens. It's warm enough to dine alfresco, picnic, cycle and hike comfortably, walk the Wattenmeer tidal flats and sojourn on the white sands of the East Frisian Islands.

Summer sees long days, social beer gardens and breathtaking late-hour sunsets on the North Sea coast.

There are few outdoor advantages to travelling in this lowlands area in winter: expect grey, windy weather and double-digit subzero temperatures in a harsh year. Fortunately, the region's museums, galleries, concert halls and theatres provide a packed calendar of indoor pursuits.

Lower Saxony & Bremen Highlights

1 **Gedenkstätte Bergen-Belsen** (p709) Contemplating the atrocities of war and paying respects at this Holocaust memorial.

2 **Deutsches Auswandererhaus** (p728)

Feeling moved by the experiences of millions of immigrants who passed through Bremerhaven's port.

3 **Böttcherstrasse** (p718) Admiring the golden archangel and red-brick angles of

Bremen's uniquely designed expressionist street.

4 **East Frisian Islands** (p736) Hiking across tidal mudflats or cycling to a deserted beach on these North Sea islands.

HANOVER & THE EAST

State capital Hanover is the urban heart of Lower Saxony, with a wealth of cultural events and attractions, picturesque parks and gardens and an active dining and night-life scene.

Many towns are within easy striking distance of the capital, by road or rail. To its south, you'll find Hildesheim, one of northern Germany's oldest towns, plus the historic Fagus Werk factory and impressive Schloss Marienburg. East of Hildesheim is the picturesque town of Wolfenbüttel and its intimate big brother, medieval Braunschweig, the 'Lion City'. Continuing north is Wolfsburg, headquarters of Volkswagen, and charming Celle, with its many pre-served half-timbered houses. North of Celle is the thought-provoking Bergen-Belsen memorial.

Further east is Brandenburg, and be-yond that Berlin, just under two hours away by high-speed train. The states of Hessen, Thuringia and Saxony-Anhalt, along with their castles, palaces, forests and gardens, lie to the south.

🛏 Sleeping

Hanover is a major convention town and has numerous options for accommodation, which go up in price around trade-fair time; Hildesheim is only 30 minutes away by train and can be a good alternative. Centrally lo-cated Braunschweig also makes a good base for this area.

❶ Getting There & Away

The main airport in this area is **Hanover Airport** (HAJ; www.hannover-airport.de), which is 12km north of Hanover's town centre. For those driv-ing, the A2 runs to this area from just outside Berlin. The region is well served by Deutsche Bahn trains.

Hanover

📞 0511 / POP 532,864

Locals love Hanover (spelt 'Hannover' in German) for the low cost of living; good pub-lic transport; wealth of museums, theatre, live music and other arts and cultural events; and the city's proximity to green spaces. The spectacularly Baroque Herrenhäuser Gärten, the constructed Lake Maschsee and the Ei-lenriede, Europe's largest urban forest, are all close at hand. That said, most Germans groan at the first mention of Hanover, whose dialect is regarded as the closest tongue to High German. Perhaps it's a complex socio-linguistic thing – or perhaps they're just jeal-ous of the laid-back lifestyle.

Hanover lacks the high profile of neigh-bouring Hanse city-states Hamburg and Bremen, and first appearances admittedly mightn't knock you off your feet, but spend a little time here and you'll soon be charmed.

The city swells in April and June, when its mammoth computer and technology trade fairs CeBit and Hannover Messe each attract more than 200,000 visitors.

History

Hanover was established around 1100 and became the residence of Heinrich der Löwe (Henry the Lion) later that century. An early Hanseatic city, by the Reformation it had de-veloped into a prosperous seat of royalty and a power unto itself.

A link was created with the monarchy of Britain in 1714, when the eldest son of Elec-tress Sophie of Hanover (a granddaughter of James I of England – James VI of Scot-land), ascended the British throne as George I while simultaneously ruling Hanover. This British–German union lasted until 1837.

In 1943, up to 80% of the centre and 50% of the entire city was destroyed by Allied bombing. The rebuilding plan included cre-ating sections of reconstructed half-timbered houses and painstakingly rebuilding the city's prewar gems, such as the Opernhaus (Opera House), the Marktkirche church and Neues Rathaus (New Town Hall). A scale model of the wartime destruction can be seen in the lobby of Neues Rathaus.

◎ Sights

The majority of Hanover's sights are conven-iently located in and around the Altstadt, which is just a few minutes' walk from the main train station. You can follow the red line embedded in the pavement to find many of them.

Of Hanover's many neighbourhoods, two of the most interesting and worthy of a visit are the northern section of formerly working-class **Linden-Limmer** (known as Linden), now popular with students and the tragically hip, and the upmarket **Ost-stadt** (also called List), particularly in the side streets around the pedestrianised sec-tion of Lister Meile and those fronting the Eilenriede, where you'll find some beautiful heritage architecture that survived WWII.

Both areas are quickly and easily reached by public transport.

◉ Altstadt & Around

Despite WWII bombing, Hanover's restored old town remains appealingly quaint. In the market square, the red-brick, Gothic Marktkirche has original elements, as do both the **Altes Rathaus** (Old Town Hall; U 3, 7, 9, 10 to Markthalle/Landtag), begun 1455, and the nearby **Ballhof** (Ballhofplatz; U 3, 7, 9, 10 to Markthalle/Landtag), a hall originally built (1649–64) for 17th-century badminton-type games and now used as a theatrical venue. An entire row of half-timbered houses has been re-created along Kramerstrasse and Burgstrasse near the Marktkirche, and here you also find **Leibnizhaus** (Holzmarkt 4; U 3, 7, 9, 10 to Markthalle/Landtag), once the home of mathematician and philosopher Gottfried Wilhelm Leibniz (1646–1716), with its reconstructed Renaissance facade. In front of the Leibnizhaus is the **Oskar-Winter-Brunnen** (Oskar Winter Fountain; Holzmarkt 4; U 3, 7, 9, 10 to Markthalle/Landtag); if you make a wish and turn the small brass ring embedded in the ironwork three times, local lore has it that your wish will come true.

★**Sprengel Museum**   MUSEUM
(📞0511-438 75; www.sprengel-museum.com; Kurt-Schwitters-Platz; adult/child €7/free, Fri free; ☺10am-6pm Wed-Sun, to 8pm Tue; 🚌100 to Maschsee/Sprengel Museum) The Sprengel Museum is held in extremely high esteem, both for the design of the building as well as for the art housed inside. Its huge interior spaces are perfectly suited to displaying its modern figurative, abstract and conceptual art, including works by Picasso, Léger, Alexander Calder and Louise Bourgeois. At the core of the collection are 300 works by Niki de Saint Phalle, creator of Die Nanas (p699); a selection is usually on show. Check the website for visiting exhibitions.

★**Neues Rathaus**   HISTORIC BUILDING, VIEWPOINT
(Trammplatz 2; elevator adult/child €3.50/2; ☺9am-6pm Mon-Fri, from 10am Sat & Sun, elevator closed mid-Nov–Mar; U Aegidientorplatz) **FREE**
An excellent way to get your bearings in Hanover is to visit the Neues Rathaus (built 1901–13) and ascend 98m in the curved elevator (the only one of its kind). It's shaped to travel to the top of the building's green dome, where there are four open-air observation platforms offering panoramic views

WALKING THE RED LINE

The city has painted a *Roter Faden* (red line) on pavements around the centre for a 4.2km, do-it-yourself loop of 36 city highlights. Follow it with the help of the multilingual *Red Thread Guide*, available from the tourist office (p705) or online at www.hannover.de; or download the iPhone app (€0.89). The route is barrier-free.

as far as the Deister hills. The cabin can take only five people at a time so expect queues.

Kestner Gesellschaft   GALLERY
(Kestner Society; www.kestnergesellschaft.de; Goseriede 11; adult/child €7/free; ☺11am-6pm Tue, Wed & Fri-Sun, to 8pm Thu; U 10, 17 to Steintor) It's always worth checking listings for the Kestner Gesellschaft. Founded in 1916 to bring innovative artworks from international artists to Hanover, the society exhibited works by Otto Dix, Georg Grosz, Wassily Kandinsky and Paul Klee before they became famous; today this renowned gallery still curates shows that later tour Europe. Its wonderfully light, high-ceilinged premises were once a bathhouse.

Aegidienkirche   RUINS, MEMORIAL
(Aegidius Church; 📞0511-3018 6611; cnr Breite Strasse & Osterstrasse, Altstadt; ☺carillon 9.05am, 12.05pm, 3.05pm & 6.05pm; U Aegidientorplatz) This former Gothic church (dating from 1347) was never repaired or reconstructed after it was bombed in 1943, and today stands as a reminder of the horrors of war. Inside the ruin is the **Peace Bell**, donated by sister city Hiroshima. Every 6 August at 8.15am, the date and time of the atomic detonation at Hiroshima, a delegation from both cities meets here to ring the bell.

Marktkirche   CHURCH
(www.marktkirche-hannover.de; Hanns-Lilje-Platz 2, Altstadt; tours €3; ☺10am-6pm; U 3, 7, 9, 10 to Markthalle/Landtag) The red-brick Gothic Marktkirche St Georgii et Jacobi (1349–59), located in the Market Sq, is Hanover's largest Lutheran church. Its foundations date back to a Romanesque predecessor from around 1125; it was heavily damaged during WWII and rebuilt in 1952. The linden-wood altar, which displays the Passion of Christ in 21 scenes, was carved around 1480. Public tours (with English availability) are offered

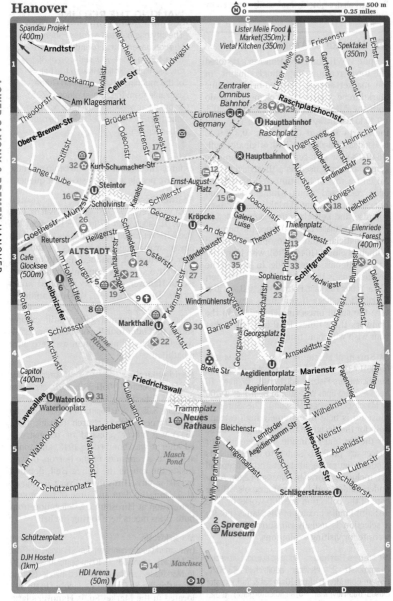

Map labels:

0 | 500 m
0 | 0.25 miles

Spandau Projekt (400m)
Arndtstr
Postkamp
Celler Str
Theodorstr
Am Klagesmarkt
Obere-Brenner-Str
Stiftstr
🏛 7
32 ★ Kurt-Schumacher-Str
Lange Laube
16 🚇 **Steintor**
Scholvinstr
Münzstr
26
Goethestr
Reuterstr
Heiligerstr
ALTSTADT
Cafe Glocksee (500m)
Am Hohen Ufer
🚇 6 **Leibnizufer**
Rote Reihe
5 Knöck 21
24
19 🚇
9 🛈
8 🏛
Markthalle 🚇
22
Burgstr
Schlossstr
Leine River
Archivstr
Capitol (400m)
Lavesallee 🚇 **Waterloo** 31
Waterlooplatz
Hardenbergstr
Am Waterlooplatz
Am Schützenplatz
Schützenplatz
DJH Hostel (1km)
HDI Arena (50m)

Herschelstr
Ludwigstr
Brüderstr
Odeonstr
Herrenstr
Herschelstr
17
Schillerstr
Georgstr
Schmiedestr
Osterstr
Ständehausstr
Kanalstr
Karmarschstr
Kramerstr
Markstr
14 🚇
10 ⊙
Breite Str
3
30
Friedrichswall
Culemannstr
Trammplatz
1 🏛 **Neues Rathaus**
Bleichenstr
Masch Pond
Langensalzastr
Willy-Brandt-Allee
Maschsee
2 🏛 **Sprengel Museum**

Lister Meile Food Market (350m); Vietal Kitchen (350m)
Friesenstr
Spektakel (350m)
Gartenstr
Sedanstr
Eichstr
★ 34
Zentraler Omnibus Bahnhof
28 🚌 29
Raschplatzhochstr
Eurolines Germany
🚇 **Hauptbahnhof**
Raschplatz
Volgersweg
Roscherstr
Heinrichstr
🚇 **Hauptbahnhof**
Augustenstr
Hinüberstr
Ferdinandstr
25
Königstr
Veilchenstr
🍴 18
Ernst-August-Platz
12
🍴 11
15 🛈
Joachimstr
Galerie Luise
An der Börse
Theaterstr
Thielenplatz
Lavesstr
13
Eilenriede Forest (400m)
Prinzenstr
33 **Schiffgraben**
Hedwigstr
Sophienstr
23
Kröpcke 🚇
35
Windmühlenstr
Georgstr
Landschaftstr
Baringstr
Georgswall
Georgsplatz
3
Aegidientorplatz 🚇
Arnswaldtstr
Prinzenstr
Marienstr
Aegidientorplatz
Lemförder Str
Aegidiendamm Str
Maschstr
Hildescheimer Str
Weinstr
Adelhidstr
Lutherstr
Schlägerstr
Schlägerstrasse 🚇
Blumenstr
20
Dieterichsstr
Ubbenstr
Warmbüchenstr
Papenstieg
Höltystr
Wilhelmstr
Baumstr

every Saturday at noon, January through November.

Maschsee   **LAKE**
(Rudolf-von-Bennigsen-Ufer; ☐ 100 to Maschsee/Sprengel Museum) This artificial lake, built by the unemployed in one of the earliest Nazi-led public-works projects, is now a favourite spot for boating and swimming. It's certainly the most central, at just 30 minutes' walk from the Hauptbahnhof and directly alongside the HDI Arena (p705), Hanover's football

Hanover

LOWER SAXONY & BREMEN HANOVER

stadium. Ferries – some solar-powered – ply the lake from Easter to October in good weather, and there are sailing, pedal and rowing boats for hire.

Die Nanas   SCULPTURE, PUBLIC ART
(Leibnizufer; Ⓤ 10, 17 to Clevertor) When these three earth-mama sculptures were first installed beside the Leine River in 1974, Hanover's city fathers and mothers were inundated with nearly 20,000 letters of complaint. Now, the voluptuous and fluorescent-coloured 'Sophie', 'Charlotte' and 'Caroline' are among the city's most recognisable, and most loved, landmarks. Their creator, the French artist Niki de Saint Phalle, was made an honorary citizen of Hanover in 2000; in gratitude she donated 300 of her artworks to the Sprengel Museum (p697).

⊙ Outside the Altstadt

★ **Herrenhäuser Gärten**   GARDENS
(☑ 0511-1683 4000; www.herrenhaeuser-gaerten. de; Herrenhäuser Strasse 4; combination ticket adult/child €8/free Apr-Oct, €6/free Nov-Mar; ☉ 9am-6pm Apr-Oct, to 4.30pm Nov-Mar, grotto to 5.30pm Apr-Oct, to 4pm Nov-Mar; Ⓤ 4, 5 to Herrenhäuser Gärten) 🆓 Proof that Hanover is not all buttoned-down business are the grandiose Baroque Royal Gardens of Herrenhausen, about 5km north of the city cen-

tre, which are considered one of the most important historic garden landscapes in Europe. Inspired by the gardens at Versailles, they're a great place to slow down and smell the roses for a couple of hours, especially on a blue-sky day. Two of the four gardens are free admission; visit the other two with a combination ticket.

The oldest, the Baroque Grosser Garten and Berggarten (p700), have paid admission; **Georgeangarten** (George Garden) and **Welfengarten** (Guelph Garden) are free and open to the public day and night. An on-site **museum** (☑ 0511-1684 4543; ☉ 11am-6pm Apr-Oct, to 4pm Nov-Mar) recounts the history of the Hanoverian rulers who created the gardens. East of the Grosser Garten, beyond a small canal, the lake-dotted Georgengarten counts the Wilhelm Busch Museum (p700) among its treasures.

➡ Grosser Garten

(combination ticket adult/child €8/free Apr-Oct, €6/free Nov-Mar; ☉ 9am-6pm, later in summer) The jewel in the crown of the Herrenhäuser Gärten is grand both in format and history, having been laid out as a Baroque garden in 1714 under the tutelage of the French landscape gardener Martin Charbonnier. The garden contains statues, fountains, a maze and the coloured tile walls of the Niki de Saint Phalle Grotto, creator of the city's much-loved Die Nanas (p699) sculptures. The Grosse Fontäne is Europe's tallest fountain, jetting water up to 80m.

In summer the synchronised **Wasserspiele** (Fountain Display; ⊙11am-noon & 3-5pm Mon-Fri, 11am-noon & 2-5pm Sat & Sun Apr-Oct) water fountains always pull a crowd, as do nightly garden illuminations, summer concerts and fireworks competitions. Dates and times vary: check the 'Events' section of the website for details.

The combination ticket entry includes admission to Berggarten and Museum Schloss Herrenhäusen (p699).

➡ **Berggarten**

(combination ticket adult/child €8/free Apr-Oct, €6/free Nov-Mar; ⊙9am-6pm, later in summer) The oldest botanical garden in Germany is redolent with a mind-boggling assortment of global flora – including glasshouses for orchids, cacti and tropical plants – and features 300-year-old lime trees lining an avenue leading to a mausoleum holding the remains of George I of England.

Eilenriede Forest   FOREST

(www.hannover-park.de; Fritz-Behrens-Allee; 🚊200 to Emmichplatz/Musikhochschule) More than 640 hectares (almost twice the size of NYC's Central Park), Europe's largest city forest, Eilenriede, is also known as Hanover's *grüne Lunge* (green lung). Beginning about 1km northeast of the Hauptbahnhof, it's well frequented and beloved by locals, who picnic, play and cycle through the enchanting woods, luminous green in the summertime. Here, it's easy to imagine you're not in the middle of a city of half a million people.

Wilhelm Busch Museum   MUSEUM

(☑0511-1699 9911; www.karikatur-museum.de; Georgengarten; adult/child €6/4; ⊙11am-6pm Tue-Sun; 🚇4, 5 to Schneiderberg/Wilhelm-Busch-Museum) Contains a wealth of caricature and cartoon art, including works by greats Busch, Honoré Daumier and William Hogarth, as well as British artist Ronald Searle and pieces by Francisco de Goya. No English signage.

⭐ Festivals & Events

International Fireworks Competition   FIREWORKS

(www.hannover.de; adult/child €21/18) Held over five evenings from May to September in the skies above the Herrenhäuser Garten (p699), this prestigious spectacle of light and sound attracts the world's most accomplished pyrotechnicians.

Maschseefest   CULTURAL

(www.maschseefest.de; ⊙Aug) This large annual festival by the lake extends over two and a half weeks and features a packed calendar of events and plenty of food and drink offerings in, on and around the Maschsee (p698), including a range of musical performances and fun activities for all ages.

🛏 Sleeping

During trade shows, accommodation rates can increase dramatically. Check the city website (www.hannover.de) to ensure your travel dates don't unintentionally coincide with one of these events. The tourist office (p705) books accommodation, including an inventory of private rooms, for a €5 fee.

HANOVER'S TRADE FAIRS

Trade fairs in Hanover are a time-honoured tradition. The first export fair was held in August 1947 in the midst of all the rubble from WWII. As most hotels had been destroyed, the mayor made an appeal to citizens to provide beds for foreign guests. The people did, the money came and to this day about a third more beds are available in private flats at fair time than in hotels, which book out months in advance at elevated rates.

There are two 'world's biggest' trade fairs held in Hanover each year. The pre-eminent fair today is CeBIT (www.cebit.de), a business IT and computer expo in mid-June. During its glory days of the late '90s, the fair recorded as many as 800,000 attendees. The other one is Hannover Messe (www.hannovermesse.de, an industrial technology trade show in late April.

The Messegelände fairgrounds are in the city's southeast, served by tram/U-Bahn 8 (and 18 during fair times) to Entrance Nord, as well as the S4 S-Bahn, IC and ICE trains. U-Bahn lines 6 and 16 serve the eastern part of the fairgrounds.

During major fairs there's a full-service tourist office at the airport and an information pavilion at the fairgrounds, in addition to the main tourist office outside the Hauptbahnhof.

DJH Hostel
HOSTEL €

(☑ 0511-131 7674; www.jugendherberge.de/jh/hannover; Ferdinand-Wilhelm-Fricke-Weg 1; dm from €26, d €70; P @ ?; 🚌 100 to Luise-Finke-Weg, Ⓤ 3, 7, 17 to Bahnhof Linden/Fischerhof) This huge structure houses a modern hostel with breakfast room and terrace-bar overlooking the river. Four-bed dorms all have sinks; some have private bathrooms (from €32). Non-HI members pay an extra fee. It's a short walk from here to the Maschsee (p698). Bed linens and breakfast are included.

Hotel City Panorama
HOTEL €

(☑ 0511-8970 6015; www.hannover-city-panorama.de; Münzstrasse 5; s/d from €60/70; P ⊕ ?; Ⓤ 4, 5, 6, 10, 11, 17 to Steintor) This small hotel offers 30 simple rooms, both singles and doubles, with basic amenities and free wi-fi. The decor is nothing to write home about and its Steintor location puts you near the red-light district – but it also means you're walking distance to the Hauptbahnhof and the Altstadt. A breakfast buffet is available for €8 extra.

★ Courtyard
Hannover Maschsee
HOTEL €€

(☑ 0511-366 000; www.marriott.com; Arthur-Menge-Ufer 3; r weekday/weekend from €105/171; P ⊕ ✱; 🚌 100 to HDI-Arena) The boxy '70s exterior of this hotel belies its ultra-modern, stylish interior; all common areas and guest rooms have been fully renovated. Standard rooms are comfortable, good-looking and functional. Perhaps its best feature is the lakefront location boasting a wonderful outlook from the shores of the shimmering Maschsee (p698); lake-view rooms cost a bit more. The 100/200 bus line stops outside.

★ Central Hotel Kaiserhof
HOTEL €€

(☑ 0511-368 3114; www.centralhotel.de; Ernst-August-Platz 4; d/ste from €100/120) With a lovely terrace bar-restaurant overlooking Ernst-August-Platz, this small but well-maintained independently owned hotel (family-owned for three generations) has neutrally decorated rooms of varying sizes, comfortable bedding, an excellent breakfast buffet and friendly, helpful staff. It's directly opposite Hanover's handsome, historic Hauptbahnhof.

Loccumer Hof
BOUTIQUE HOTEL €€

(☑ 0511-126 40; www.loccumerhof.de; Kurt-Schumacher-Strasse 14-16; s/d from €79/99; P @ ?; Ⓤ 10, 17 to Hauptbahnhof/Rosenstrasse)

Some of the stylish and well-decorated rooms here are themed by nations ('Australia'), elements ('air') and feng shui. Others are low-allergy. Rates are often lower for advance or internet bookings. The 'four elements' theme is carried over into the dinner menu of the stylish on-site restaurant.

City Hotel am Thielenplatz
HOTEL €€

(☑ 0511-327 691; www.smartcityhotel-thielenplatz.de; Thielenplatz 2; s/d from €80/90; P ?) This very central 'budget boutique' beauty has a reception and bar (open until 5am) restyled with leather seating, black-and-white leaf-patterned wallpaper and lots of wood laminate. All rooms have been renovated, mostly in a minimalist style. It's a block from the Hauptbahnhof.

Grand Hotel Mussmann
HOTEL €€€

(☑ 0511-365 60; www.grandhotel.de; Ernst-Aug-Platz 7; s/d Mon-Thu from €129/159, Fri-Sun from €99/129; ✱ @ ?) The central, four-star Mussmann is one of Hanover's old dames that has been revamped into a stylish, modern hotel with rooms named after famous city landmarks. Rooms and suites are spacious and well appointed, though the rates seem a little steep – stay at the weekend for discounts.

✗ Eating

✗ Altstadt & Around

Markthalle
MARKET €

(www.markthalle-in-hannover.de; Kamarschstrasse 49; dishes €3.50-10; ⊙ 7am-8pm Mon-Wed, to 10pm Thu & Fri, to 4pm Sat; ✎; Ⓤ 3, 7, 9, 10 to Markthalle/Landtag) This huge, indoor market of cafe stalls and gourmet delicatessens is popular at lunchtime and great for a quick bite, both carnivorous and vegetarian. There's a good range of cuisines – including Italian, Thai, German and Spanish tapas – and you can even take a break over a beer or cocktail.

★ Al-Dar
MIDDLE EASTERN €€

(☑ 0511-898-4994; www.aldar-hannover.de; Konigstrasse 3; mains €14-23; ⊙ noon-3pm & 6-11pm; ✎) This popular Syrian restaurant a stone's throw from the Hauptbahnhof features hushed, candlelit dining and attentive service within a pleasant, minimalist Middle Eastern decor. Besides the normal menu of warm and cold mezze and mains, Al-Dar offers set meals for two, either a vegetarian or vegan version (€31.50 per person) or with grilled lamb and fish (€34.50).

LOWER SAXONY & BREMEN HANNOVER

★ **Kilimanjaro** AFRICAN €€

(📞0151 5108 3093; www.kilimanjaro-hannover.de; Knochenhauerstrasse 23, Altstadt; mains €11-23; ⏰5pm-midnight Mon-Fri, from 1pm Sat; 🖤; 🚇3, 7, 9, 10 to Markthalle/Landtag) Feast on zebra steak (yes, really), *thieboudienne* (a traditional Senegalese fish dish) and other African specialities at this little restaurant in the Altstadt. Service can be slow but the food is delicious. Try one of the homemade juices: tamarind, ginger, even baobab. There are several vegetarian and vegan dishes, too.

Weinstube

Ristorante Leonardo ITALIAN €€

(📞0511-321 033; www.weinstube-leonardo.de; Sophienstrasse 6; mains €14-37; ⏰noon-2.30pm & 6-10pm Mon-Fri, 6-10pm Sat) This delightfully old-fashioned restaurant serves primarily Italian fare of the masterfully crafted variety. Tucked away in a side street behind the Hauptbahnhof, the restaurant itself is quite small and has been something of a local secret; book ahead if you can.

Hiller VEGAN €€

(📞0511-321 288; www.restaurant-hiller.de; Blumenstrasse 3; mains €9.50-12.50, buffet €10-17; ⏰noon-11pm Mon-Sat; 🖤) Germany's oldest vegetarian restaurant – in business since 1955, though now exclusively vegan since 2012 – is a tad hushed, but the interior, with colourful hanging lamps and wildflowers in jars, is cheery. Food is well prepared and excellent value (the daily lunch and dinner buffets even more so). Gluten-free options available, too.

✖️ Outside the Altstadt

★ **Spandau Projekt** INTERNATIONAL €

(📞0511-1235 7095; www.spandauprojekt.de; Engelbosteler Damm 30, Nordstadt; mains €8-12; ⏰noon-1am Mon-Fri, 10am-late Sat & Sun, kitchen to 10pm; 🖤🖤; 🚇6, 11 to Christuskirche) 🌿 Retro-'70s Spandau in Hanover's Nordstadt is more like a place in Berlin's Kreuzberg neighbourhood – students from nearby Leibniz University and the local Turkish community rub shoulders here. The varied menu (with plenty of vegetarian and vegan options) features curries, burgers, salads, soups and pastas, and there's a full bar with beer, wine and cocktails. Great for weekend breakfasts and people-watching anytime.

Street Kitchen VIETNAMESE €

(📞0511-9863 8834; www.streetkitchen-viet-cuisine.de; Limmerstrasse 26, Linden; mains

€5.50; ⏰noon-10pm Sun-Thu, to 11pm Fri & Sat; 🚇10 to Leinaustrasse) Simple wooden tables and benches are enhanced by colourful lanterns at this little cafe serving up fresh, fast and cheap Vietnamese specialities with beef, chicken and tofu, such as *bun bo xao sa* (thinly sliced marinated beef over rice noodles). The *lassi* fruit-yogurt drinks in mango, pineapple or papaya hit the spot.

Fischers MEXICAN €

(📞0511-441 404; www.estrella-gastro.de; Limmerstrasse 49, Linden; mains €8.50-15; ⏰5pm-2am Sun-Thu, to 3am Fri & Sat, kitchen to 11pm; 🖤; 🚇10 to Leinaustrasse) In the hip, arty suburb of Linden you'll find this spicy little number that will awaken your senses to the flavours of Mexico. There's a broad menu of small plates, plenty of vegetarian options and all the favourites – tacos, fajitas, margaritas – served up in a smart and stylish setting.

Cafe Mezzo CAFE €

(📞0511-314 966; www.cafe-mezzo.de; Lister Meile 4; dishes €3.50-9; ⏰9am-2am Tue-Thu, to 3am Fri & Sat, to midnight Sun & Mon; 🕿) This classic bar and cafe beyond the Hauptbahnhof used to be a student hang-out, but today attracts a balance of ages. It's popular any time of day (including for breakfast), but doubles as a place to warm up in the evening before moving on to a club or performance at Pavillon (p704).

★ **Vietal Kitchen** ASIAN €€

(📞0511-3887 7888; www.vietal-kitchen.de; Lister Meile 46, Oststadt; mains €11-19; ⏰11.30am-11pm Sun-Thu, to 11.30pm Fri & Sat; 🖤; 🚇3, 7, 9 to Sedanstrasse/Liester Meile) Pale-green louvres and bamboo lanterns set a French-colonial vibe for this trendy new Oststadt restaurant offering a modern-fusion take on traditional Vietnamese flavours, such as the 'dragon bowl' (grilled prawns in honey-garlic marinade on steamed rice noodles with shiso leaves) or *pho* in both meat and meatless options (almost half of the menu is vegan). It's popular, so book ahead.

★ **Basil** EUROPEAN €€

(📞0511-622 636; www.basil.de; Dragonerstrasse 30; set-course menus €35-58, mains €15-30; ⏰6-10pm Mon-Sat; 🚇1, 2 to Dragonerstrasse) These former stables to the north of town now house a hip fusion restaurant, with a high arched ceiling, pressed tablecloths and memorable, creative modern European cuisine with regional influences. The wine list is almost intimidatingly comprehensive. Dress to be seen. Various menus of different set courses offer the best value.

Choi's KOREAN €€

(📞 0511-313 132; www.restaurant-chois.de; Lister Meile 61; mains €14-30; ⊙ noon-2.30pm & 6-9.30pm Mon-Sat; ⓤ 3, 7, 9 to Sedanstrasse/Lister Meile) You can smell the traditional Korean cooking as you climb the stairs to this spotless family affair on the Lister Meile. Traditional Korean meals and some hybrid German-Chinese dishes are served. The Korean dumplings (fried or steamed) are hard to resist. The special lunch menu offers great value.

🍷 Drinking & Nightlife

Hanover has two main clusters of clubs and bars (though others are also dotted about town). One is the red-light district of Steintor, a former strip- and sex-club stronghold; the other is around the revamped Raschplatz, behind the Hauptbahnhof. Hanover's cultural centres, clubs and music venues are also good places for a drink.

⭐**Bukowski's** COCKTAIL BAR

(📞 0511-8664 1950; www.facebook.com/bukowskis.hannover; Königstrasse 45; ⊙ 6pm-late Tue-Sat; 🚊 100 to Königstrasse) One of the newest cocktail bars on the Hanover scene, sleek Bukowski's mixes leather couches with exposed brick walls and industrial-style stools. Spirits are taken seriously here, as evidenced by the huge collection of bottles and the menu of carefully designed bespoke cocktails. Ingredients like syrups are made from scratch in-house and drinks are poured with skill.

Holländische Kakao-Stube CAFE

(📞 0511-30 41 00; www.hollaendische-kakao-stube.de; Ständehausstrasse 2-3; ⊙ 9am-7.30pm Mon-Fri, to 6.30pm Sat; ⓤ Kröpcke) With the blue-and-white square-patterned floor matching the Delft pottery, and a curved ship's staircase and maritime paintings creating a subtle nautical feel, this historic Dutch coffeehouse – in operation since 1895 – has many fans, young and old. Try not to drool at the glass cases full of cakes, pastries, slices and all sorts of sweets (some come pre-packaged).

Brauhaus Ernst August PUB

(www.brauhaus.net; Schmiedestrasse 13, Altstadt; ⊙ 8am-2am Mon-Thu, to 5am Fri & Sat, 9am-3pm Sun; ⓤ 3, 7, 9, 10 to Markthalle/Landtag) A

LOWER SAXONY & BREMEN HANOVER

LGBT HANOVER

With Berlin so close at hand, Hanover's gay scene isn't huge but there's a handful of friendly establishments here. The best sources for listings are www.gaypers.de/Hanover and www.gay-szene.net.

Cafe Konrad (📞 0511-323 666; www.facebook.com/CafeKonrad; Knochenhauerstrasse 34, Altstadt; dishes €6-11; ⊙ 9am-11pm Mon-Thu, to midnight Fri & Sat, to 9pm Sun; 📶; ⓤ 3, 7, 9, 10 to Markthalle/Landtag) This convivial LGBT cafe has a changing menu of weekly specials and is the epicentre of Hanover's gay grapevine. Go for one of the breakfast dishes named after legendary gay icons: Bette Midler, Barbra Streisand, Edith Piaf et al.

Schwule Sau (www.schwulesauhannover.de; Schaufelder Strasse 30a; ⓤ 6, 11 to Kopernikusstrasse) This alternative gay and lesbian centre, refitted in 2015, regularly hosts concerts, theatre, karaoke and club nights.

Hanover institution, this sprawling brewpub makes a refreshing unfiltered pilsner called *Hannöversch*. A party atmosphere reigns nightly, helped along by a varied roster of live bands and DJs. There's also a daytime bistro serving coffee, light meals and desserts.

Spektakel PUB

(www.das-spektakel.de; Flüggestrasse 12, Oststadt; ⊙ 6pm-2am Sun-Thu, to 3am Fri & Sat; ⓤ 3, 7, 9 to Sedanstrasse/Lister Meile) Deep-red walls, wood panelling and candlelight give this side-street Oststadt pub a cosy feel. Order a pint of Guinness or Newcastle Brown Ale and something from the pub-food menu and settle in for a while.

Cafe Bar CAFE

(Limmerstrasse 25, Linden; ⊙ 8am-7pm Mon-Fri, from 10am Sat & Sun; ⓤ 10 to Leinaustrasse) Have a seat at the whitewashed communal table or sink into a leather armchair at this chill neighborhood cafe in artsy Linden and while away some time over a cappuccino and baked sweets. The *Apfelkuchen* (apple cake) – moist, dense and filled with apples, raisins and walnuts – is not to be missed.

Schöne Aussichten 360°
BAR

(✒ 0511-982 6833; http://beach.sceneevents.de; Parkdeck level 6, Röselerstrasse 7; ⊙ from 11am Apr-Sep; 🚍; ⓤ 3, 7, 9, 10 to Markthalle/Landtag) Putting a beach club atop a car park (with deckchairs and sand) is a very Berlin thing to do and it works here, too, bringing out that sense of fun in people. It's open in the warmer months, though daily openings are weather-dependent; check the website for the current event details.

Osho Diskothek
CLUB

(Baggi; ✒ 0511-6049 9172; www.osho-disco.de; Raschplatz 7l; ⊙ 10pm-6am Fri & Sat) Fondly nicknamed 'Baggi' by the Hanoverians, Osho offers classic disco hits for the over-25s. It runs mainly at weekends but occasionally a pre-holiday weeknight will find itself on the schedule. It's right behind the Hauptbahnhof.

Palo Palo
CLUB

(✒ 79 02 02 10; www.palopalo.de; Raschplatz 8a; ⊙ 11pm-6am Fri, Sat & Mon) On Hanover's nightlife calendars for more than two decades, this club behind the main train station spins dance classics, soul, R&B and hip-hop, with a high see-and-be-seen factor.

Waterloo
BEER GARDEN

(✒ 0511-156 43; www.waterloo-biergarten.de; Waterloostrasse 1; ⊙ 11am-1am; ⓤ 3, 7, 9 to Waterloo) Hanover's most popular beer garden has a lovely stand of trees, low prices and a large screen that shows German football matches – and always the Hannover 96 game.

Eve Klub
CLUB

(✒ 0511-262 5151; www.eve-klub.de; Reuterstrasse 3-4; ⊙ mostly Fri & Sat; ⓤ 10, 17 to Clevertor) This former striptease bar in the red-light district has kept the red lamps over the tables and red corduroy sofas. DJs play at the Friday- and Saturday-night parties (occasionally Thursday, too). Check the website for the schedule.

☆ Entertainment

Hochhaus-Lichtspiele
CINEMA

(✒ 0511-144 54; www.filmkunstkinos-hannover.de; Goseriede 9; tickets Tue €6, Mon, Wed, Thu & Sun €8, Fri & Sat €9; ⓤ 10, 17 to Steintor) This spacious art-house cinema is on the top floor of a magnificent expressionist building designed by Fritz Höger, the architect of Hamburg's Chilehaus. Check listing times, as the box office only opens just before screenings. Some English-language movies are shown in the original version with German subtitles.

Staatsoper Hannover
PERFORMING ARTS

(✒ 0511-9999 1111; www.oper-hannover.de; Opernplatz 1; ⓤ Kröpcke) Housed in the 19th-century opera house that was lovingly restored after suffering WWII damage. Classical music as well as ballet and opera are performed here.

Musiktheater Bad
PERFORMING ARTS

(✒ 0511-169 4138; www.musiktheater-hannover.de; Am Grossen Garten 60; ⊙ office 10.30am-3pm Mon-Fri; ⓤ 4, 5 to Schaumburgstrasse) In this large old building and its surrounding grounds, you'll find a mixed bag of live music, music theatre and dance offerings. It's great in summer when there's an outdoor stage. On event days there's a free shuttle from the U-Bahn stop at Schaumburgstrasse.

Marlene Bar & Bühne
PERFORMING ARTS

(✒ 0511-368 1687; www.marlene-hannover.de; Prinzenstrasse 10, cnr Alexanderstrasse; free-€15) Hanover's popular cabaret venue hosts everything from drag performers and French chanteuses to swing, jazz and blues bands. It's a couple of blocks east of the Hauptbahnhof.

★ Kulturzentrum Faust
PERFORMING ARTS

(✒ 0511-455 001; www.kulturzentrum-faust.de; Zur Bettfedernfabrik 1-3, Linden; ⊙ box office 10am-noon & 2-5pm Mon-Fri; ⓤ 10 to Leinaustrasse) Ska from Uruguay, Chinese new-year festivals, disco, reggae, heavy-metal gigs, hip-hop, multimedia installations, quiz evenings, book readings and film nights – all this, and more, happens in this former factory complex. The 1960s concert hall is complemented by the pub-bar Mephisto, a beer garden and cafe.

Jazz Club Hannover
JAZZ

(✒ 0511-454 455; www.jazz-club.de; Am Lindener Berg 38; tickets €15-20; 🚌 200 to Zur Sternwarte, ⓤ 9 to Nieschlagstrasse) Hanover's premier jazz club features top acts from Germany and abroad.

Pavillon
PERFORMING ARTS

(✒ 0511-235 5550; www.pavillon-hannover.de; Lister Meile 4; box office 10am-6pm) This huge circular venue beyond the Hauptbahnhof has a buzzing cafe-bar (p702), theatres and various rooms used as venues where you can catch a wide program of jazz, off-beat rock, world music, comedy and a range of other live performances.

Capitol
LIVE MUSIC

(✒ 0511-444 066; www.capitol-hannover.de; Schwarzer Bär 2; ⊙ box office 9.30am-6.30pm

Mon-Fri; Ⓤ 9, 17 to Schwarzer Bär) This former movie theatre features rock, pop, house, soul and more on weekends and frequently during the week, with both local and international acts. Tickets are available at several ticket outlets around town; check the website for locations.

Cafe Glocksee
CLUB

(Ⓙ 0511-161 4712; www.cafe-glocksee.de; Glockseestrasse 35; cover free–€5; ⊙ 8.30pm-5am Tue, 11pm-6am Fri & Sat; Ⓤ 10, 17 to Goetheplatz) Part live-music venue, part club, the Glocksee has everything from techno and trance DJs to grungy gigs – mainly on Tuesday, Friday and Saturday, with a Thursday thrown into the mix occasionally. Check the website for event listings.

HDI Arena
SPECTATOR SPORT

(www.hannover96.de; Robert-Enke-Strasse 3; Ⓤ 3, 7, 9 to Waterloo) This 49,000-capacity football stadium is home turf for the Hannover 96 football club. You can pick up available tickets at the ground on the same day for league matches or anytime from the DB service point inside the Hauptbahnhof. Those with extra tickets (scalpers if it's a big match) sell them on the tree-lined alley leading to the ground.

🔒 Shopping

Hanover's compact city centre contains a pedestrianised zone full of shops extending south from the Hauptbahnhof. To the northeast, Lister Meile also has some great shops.

In Linden, the main stretch of Limmerstrasse has a number of cute little shops for gifts, accessories and homewares, as well as a few hip clothing boutiques and a couple of thrift stores.

Contigo Fairtrade Shop
JEWELRY, HOMEWARES

(Ⓙ 0511-5696 0683; http://hannover.contigo.de; Lister Meile 74; ⊙ 10am-7pm Mon-Fri, to 6pm Sat; Ⓤ 3, 7, 9 to Lister Platz) Buy gifts with a good conscience at this fair-trade shop featuring the work of craftspeople from around the world – India, Thailand, Colombia, Chile and more. There's jewellery, leather and cloth goods and accessories, handmade bowls and mugs and even fair-trade chocolate and coffee (the staff can brew you a cup of the latter on the spot).

Lister Meile Food Market
FOOD

(Lister Meile, betw Gretchenstrasse & Celler Strasse; ⊙ noon-6pm Thu; Ⓤ 3, 7, 9 to Sedanstrasse/Lister Meile) Every Thursday afternoon numerous stalls set up along either side of the pedestrian Lister Meile just north of the Sedanstrasse U-Bahn stop, selling fresh fruit and veg, cheese, sausages, fish, bread, pastries – you name it. Perfect for those self-catering.

❶ Information

ACCESSIBLE TRAVEL

Hanover's tourism website (www.hannover.de/service) has information on barrier-free travel in the city, including a database of accessible hotels. Look under 'Barrierefrei'.

EMERGENCY

Diakoniekrankenhaus Friederikenstift
(Ⓙ 0511-304 31; www.diakoniekranken-haus-friederikenstift.de; Marienstrasse 37; Ⓤ 4, 5, 6, 11 to Marienstrasse)
Police (Ⓙ 110; Raschplatz)

MONEY

Reisebank (www.reisebank.de; Hauptbahnhof; ⊙ 8am-10pm Mon-Sat, from 9am Sun) Has ATMs plus currency exchange services. Inside the main train station.

POST

Post Office (Ernst-August-Galerie, Ernst-August-Platz 2; ⊙ 9am-7.30pm Mon-Fri, to 3pm Sat) Inside the Ernst-August-Galerie shopping centre, across from the Hauptbahnhof.

TOURIST INFORMATION

Information and brochures are available from a staffed desk at the **Neues Rathaus** (p697).
Hanover Tourist Office (Ⓙ information 0511-1234 5111, room reservations 12 34 55 55; www.hannover.de/tourismus; Ernst-August-Platz 8; ⊙ 9am-6pm Mon-Fri, 10am-3pm Sat year-round, plus 10am-5pm Sat, to 3pm Sun Apr-Oct; 🐦) One of Germany's most multilingual tourist bureaus.

❶ Getting There & Away

BUS

Long-distance and international services leave from the full-service **Zentraler Omnibus Bahnhof** (ZOB; Central Bus Station; www.hannover-zob.de/en; Rundestrasse 12), making coach travel to/from Hanover more convenient than ever before.
Eurolines Germany (Ⓙ 0511-940 4269; www.eurolines.de/en/home; Rundestraße 12; ⊙ 9am-8.30pm Mon-Fri, to 2pm Sat & Sun) serves long-distance routes in Europe.

TRAIN

Hanover is a major rail hub for European and national services, with frequent ICE trains to/from Hamburg Hauptbahnhof (€48, 1¼ hours),

HANNOVERCARD

Available at the airport (p696), the tourist office (p705) and the DB service point inside the main train station, the HannoverCard (1/2/3 days €9.50/15/18) offers unlimited public transport and discounted admission to museums. (A *gruppe* card good for up to five people together is also available for €20/27/35.)

Bremen (€35, one hour), Munich (€138, 4¼ hours), Cologne (€75, 2¾ hours) and Berlin (€72, 1¾ hours), among others. Left-luggage lockers are accessible 24 hours.

Getting Around

BICYCLE

Fahrradstation am Bahnhof (☑ 0511-3539 640; www.step-hannover.de/startseite/ angebote/radstation; Fernroder Strasse 2; bicycle per day €9.50; ⊘ 6am-11pm Mon-Fri, from 8am Sat & Sun) Rents out bikes, helmets and other accessories. It's around the corner to the left when you exit the Hauptbahnhof.

PUBLIC TRANSPORT

Getting around Hanover by public transit is fast and easy. The transit system of buses and tram/ U-Bahn lines (so-called *Stadtbahn* or 'city rail' because some are trams on lines underground) is run by **Üstra** (☑ 0511-166 80; ⊘ information 6am-11pm Mon-Fri, to 8pm Sat, 7am-8pm Sun). Board most U-Bahn lines, including U-Bahn 8 to the Messe (fairgrounds; €2.70, 19 minutes) from inside the Hauptbahnhof; all of the lines meet up at the main central U-Bahn station, Kröpcke.

U-Bahn lines 10 and 17 are the exception. These are overground trams leaving from behind the Hauptbahnhof, right near the ZOB main bus station, and they don't run to Kröpcke. (The late-night service of the 10 does, however, and starts from inside the station.)

Most visitors only travel in the central 'Cardzone Hannover 1' zone, where single tickets are €2.70 and good-value day passes cost €5.40. If you wish to travel in zones two/three, single tickets cost €3.50/4.40, while day passes cost €7/8.60.

Celle

☑ 05141 / POP 69,748

Celle is graced with a picture-book medieval town centre that is among the most attractive in the region, with 400 half-timbered houses and a ducal palace dating back to the 13th century. The white-and-pink Schloss, Celle's centrepiece set in small gardens, contrasts with the ultramodern Kunstmuseum across the road, which is illuminated at night into a '24-hour' museum, creating an interesting juxtaposition of old and new.

⊙ Sights

Schloss Celle
PALACE

(Ducal Palace; ☑ 05141-909 0850; www.residenz museum.de; Schlossplatz 1; adult/child €8/free, incl Bomann-Museum & Kunstmuseum €12/free; ⊘ 10am-5pm Tue-Sun May-Oct, 11am-4pm Nov-Apr) Celle's wedding-cake Schloss was built in 1292 by Otto Der Strenge (Otto the Strict) as a town fortification; in 1378 it was expanded and turned into a residence. Today it houses administrative offices, a theatre and the ResidenzMuseum, which lets you walk through various former state apartments and rooms to see clothing, weaponry and other historical items on display. There's some English signage throughout.

From May to October, one-hour guided tours in German (adult/child €9/free) depart at 11am, 1pm and 3pm from Tuesday to Friday and Sunday, and hourly from 11am to 3pm on Saturday. (From November to April there are fewer; see the website for more information.) These tours take you into sections of the palace you can't otherwise visit, such as the Renaissance Schlosskapelle (Palace Chapel), the 19th-century Schloss-küche (Palace Kitchen) and – rehearsals permitting – the Baroque Schlosstheater (Palace Theatre). You can also purchase a great-value combination ticket that allows you to visit the Schloss, the Kunstmuseum and the Bomann-Museum; it's good for two consecutive days.

The last duke in residence here was Georg Wilhelm (1624–1705), while the last royal was Queen Caroline-Mathilde of Denmark, who was exiled here after having an affair with a court physician and died in 1775 from scarlet fever at the tender age of 23. You'll see some of her clothing and personal effects in the museum.

Don't miss a stroll around the lovely grounds, where weeping willows stand guard over a meandering circular moat populated by ducks and geese.

Bomann-Museum Celle
MUSEUM

(☑ 05141-125 44; www.bomann-museum.de; Schlossplatz 7; adult/child €8/free, incl Kunstmuseum & Schloss Celle €12/free, Sat from 1pm free; ⊙11am-5pm Tue-Sun, last entry 4.15pm) This museum for cultural history houses a broad historic collection on the work, lives and times of ordinary people in the region. There are Bronze Age archaeological finds, a re-created farmhouse illustrating local rural life, and a section on the changing life of the bourgeoise in the 19th century. There's also a timely exhibit on foreign migration to the region, from 17th-century Hugenots to 20th-century Kurdish refugees. There's no English signage but the artefacts are still interesting.

Kunstmuseum Celle   GALLERY

(☑05141-125 44; www.kunst.celle.de; Schlossplatz 7; adult/child €8/free, incl Bomann-Museum & Schloss Celle €12/free, Sat from 1pm free; ⊙11am-5pm Tue-Sun) Billed as the world's first '24-hour art gallery', Celle's sexy cubed Kunstmuseum isn't actually open around the clock. During regular opening hours, you can admire the indoor collection of modern art, including the illuminated *Light Room* by Otto Piene. As night descends, the 'nocturnal museum' glows and oozes different colours as the actual building morphs into an artwork to be observed, with light and a few sounds.

Celle Synagogue   SYNAGOGUE

(Im Kreise 24; ⊙noon-5pm Tue-Thu, 10am-3pm Fri, noon-7pm Sun) FREE Dating back to 1740, Celle's synagogue is the oldest in northern Germany. It was partially destroyed during Kristallnacht and looks just like any other half-timbered house from the outside. Once a new Jewish congregation formed in 1997, services began to be held here regularly. Changing exhibitions on Jewish history take place in their small gallery next door. The synagogue is at the southeastern end of the Altstadt, in the town's former ghetto.

🛏 Sleeping

DJH Hostel   HOSTEL €

(☑05141-532 08; www.jugendherberge.de/jh/celle; Weghausstrasse 2; dm from €22.40; P 🐾) This rambling youth hostel inside a former school building caters mostly to school groups in its four- to six-bed dorms. It's a 25-minute walk from the train station, or take bus 9 to Jugendherberge from the top of Bahnhofstrasse, opposite the station. Linen is included.

Hotel Celler Hof   HOTEL €€

(☑05141-911 960; www.cellerhof.de; Stechbahn 11; s/d €85/124; P 🐾 @ 🛜) The friendly staff, Finnish sauna, tasteful furnishings and central location make this a good all-round option. All rooms have a writing desk and a minibar, and there's a small lobby bar for relaxing. The breakfast buffet is excellent. Parking is €13 per night.

★ Althoff Hotel Fürstenhof   HOTEL €€€

(☑05141-2010; www.fuerstenhof.de; Hannoversche Strasse 55/56; d from €140; P ❄ 🛜 ⛲) In a converted Baroque palace, much of this luxury hotel has been extensively refurbished to the highest modern standard. Executive double rooms exude style, sophistication and comfort. The hotel's two restaurants offer a gourmet fine-dining experience: dress to impress. Of course, there's a pool and day-spa for guests.

🍴 Eating

You can find numerous eating and drinking options along the streets Schuhstrasse and Neue Strasse, as well as on Am Heiligen Kreuz.

LOWER SAXONY & BREMEN CELLE

EXPLORING CELLE'S ALTSTADT

A good way to experience Celle is to take a stroll around the Altstadt to look at its beautifully restored 17th-century houses, many with gilt lettering proclaiming the year it was built (and often when it was rebuilt) as well as Bible verses or other proverbs, such as *man sieht nur mit dem herzen gut* ('one sees clearly only with the heart').

First, pop into the tourist office (p708) in the Weser Renaissance–style **Altes Rathaus** (from 1561–79) for an 'ex(Celle)nt' English walking map. One block south, on the corner of Poststrasse and Rundestrasse, is the ornate **Hoppener Haus** (1532). If you backtrack north past the tourist office and turn right into Neue Strasse, highlights include the **Green House** (1478) with the crooked beam at No 32 and the somewhat oddly decorated **Fairy-Tale House** at No 11 (across the street and down a few houses) – look for the troll sitting on a pile of gold.

★**Cafe Kiess**   DESSERTS €

(Grosser Plan 16/17; cake slices €2-3; ☺9am-6pm Mon-Sat, from 2pm Sat & Sun) Head upstairs to a window table overlooking a picturesque square of medieval houses and dig into a thick slice of one of Cafe Kiess' desserts: a strawberry-and-whipped-cream slice, some apple strudel or chocolate mousse cake – or try the regional speciality *Buchweizentorte*, a buckwheat cake with whipped cream and cranberry jam. Serves locally roasted Huth's coffee, too.

★**Zum Schwejk**   CZECH €€

(☑05141-233 53; http://zumschwejk.wordpress.com; Kanzleistasse 7; mains €14-23; ☺noon-2.30pm & 6-10pm Fri-Tue) Primarily hearty Czech meals with some German twists are served up in this wonderful historic *haus* with an excellent balcony dining area. Try the Svicková, marinated roast beef with cream sauce and bread dumplings (it's practically the Czech national dish). Come for comfort food, old-school Eu-romantic ambience and cold beer...you'll leave very slowly and need a nap. Highly recommended.

Restaurant Bier Akademie   GERMAN €€

(☑05141-234 50; www.bier-akademie-celle.de; Weisser Wall 6; mains €10-31; ☺noon-2pm & 5-10pm Mon-Thu, 5-10pm Fri, 6-10pm Sat) This family-run restaurant serves an excellent range of beef, poultry and lamb as well as pork, but its speciality is a local roulade made of beef and pork with a distinctive combination of spices, which you can order as a starter or main course. It's to the northeast of Schlossplatz.

▼ Drinking & Nightlife

Winklers   BAR, LOUNGE

(Schuhstrasse 44; ☺5pm-late Wed-Sat) Dim pendant lights, low couches and laid-back music give this bar-lounge a sleek, upmarket feel. Browse through a comprehensive menu of cocktails: whether you're after a Manhattan or a martini – or even a grasshopper – you'll find it here. Happy hour goes until 8pm. Unlike many of the other Altstadt bars, Winklers remains blessedly smoke-free inside.

Coffee Shop   CAFE

(☑05141-993 0690; Schuhstrasse 21; milkshakes & coffee drinks €3-4; ☺9am-6pm Mon-Fri, to 5pm Sat) This friendly, popular cafe in the northeastern corner of the Altstadt has a huge selection of espresso-based coffee drinks, both hot and cold, plus a range of delicious milkshakes.

🛍 Shopping

★**Huth's Kaffee**   FOOD & DRINKS

(☑05141-6008; www.huthskaffee.de; Grosser Plan 7; ☺9am-6pm Mon-Fri, to 5pm Sat) Huth's has been roasting its coffee in-house daily, in small batches, since 1851. But there's much more to browse here: two counters filled with gourmet chocolates; old wooden shelves groaning under the weight of locally made jams, sauces and honeys; cheese and smoked salmon in the cold case. Spirits, wines and locally brewed Celler beer are available, too.

Dannhus Keramik   CERAMICS

(www.dannhuskeramik.de; Schuhstrasse 27; ☺noon-6pm Mon-Fri, 10am-3pm Sat) This pocket-sized shop sells a range of ceramic housewares in pleasant blues and greens, all handmade by potter Annette Dannhus in her studio out back: bowls, mugs, candle holders, wine-bottle toppers, butter trays, ramekins, egg holders (some with cosies) and teapots, to name a few. Look for the *Töpferei* ('pottery') sign hanging out front.

❶ Information

Celle Tourist Office (☑05141-909 080; www.celle.travel; Markt 14-16; ☺9am-6pm Mon-Fri, 10am-4pm Sat, 11am-2pm Sun May-Sep, 9am-5pm Mon-Fri, 10am-1pm Sat Oct-Apr) There's a wealth of English-language information on offer here, as well as a touchscreen information kiosk outside that's available at all hours.

❶ Getting There & Away

CAR & MOTORCYCLE

The B3 from Hanover goes straight into the centre of town. Much of the Altstadt is a pedestrian zone, however, so you're better off parking at one of the car parks surrounding it. The **Parkhaus Karstadt** (Südwall; per day €4; ☺24hr) is a bit dingy but the all-day €4 parking fee is the cheapest in town.

TRAIN

Several trains each hour to Hanover take from 25 minutes (IC; €13) to 45 minutes (S-Bahn; €10). There are also IC services to Hamburg (€34, 1¼ hours).

To reach the centre from the train station, follow Bahnhofstrasse and turn left at the end of the street; it's a 1.2km walk.

❶ Getting Around

City buses 9, 100, 800 and 900 run between the Hauptbahnhof and Schlossplatz (the main central stop); these lines allow you to buy a cheaper *Innenstadthüpfer* ticket (adult/child €1.50/0.80) for the 'downtown hop' between the two. Otherwise single-trip tickets are €2.30 and day passes €5.80; buy them from the driver as you board. For more information on bus lines see www.cebus-celle.de.

Bergen-Belsen

The Nazi-built camp at Bergen-Belsen began its existence in 1940 as a POW camp, but became a concentration camp after being taken over by the SS in 1943, initially to imprison Jews as hostages in exchange for German POWs held abroad. In all, 70,000 prisoners perished here, most famously young diarist Anne Frank. The modern **Documentation Centre museum** (Bergen-Belsen Memorial Site; ☏ 05051-475 90; www.bergen-belsen.de; Anne-Frank-Platz, Lohheide; ☉ Documentation Centre 10am-6pm Apr-Sep, to 5pm Oct-Mar, grounds until dusk) poignantly chronicles the fates of the people who passed through here.

Unlike Auschwitz in Poland, none of the original buildings remain from the most infamous concentration camp on German soil. Yet the large, initially peaceful-looking lumps of grassy earth – covered in beautiful purple heather in summer – soon reveal their true identity as mass graves. Signs indicate approximately how many people lie in each – 1000, 2000, 5000, an unknown number...

Tens of thousands of prisoners from other camps near the front line were brought to Bergen-Belsen in the last months of WWII, causing overcrowding, an outbreak of disease and even more deaths. Despite attempts by the SS to hide evidence of their inhumane practices, by destroying documents and forcing prisoners to bury or incinerate their deceased fellow inmates, thousands of corpses still littered the compound when British troops liberated the camp on 15 April 1945.

After WWII, Allied forces used the troop barracks here as a displaced persons camp, for those waiting to emigrate to a third country (including many Jews who went to Israel after its establishment in 1948). This camp was closed in September 1950.

The Documentation Centre today is one of the best of its kind and deals sensitively with the lives of the camp prisoners – before, during and after incarceration. The exhibition is designed to be viewed chronologically, and part of it focuses on the role of Bergen-Belsen in its early years as a POW camp for mostly Soviet prisoners of war. About 40,000 POWs died here from 1939 to 1942, largely due to atrocious conditions. As you move through the exhibition you can listen to original-language descriptions through headphones (also subtitled on the screens), read documents and explanations, and watch a 25-minute documentary about the camp. This film includes a moving testimony from one of the British cameramen who filmed the liberation. Subtitled screenings rotate between different languages.

In the several hectares of cemetery within the gates is a large stone obelisk and memorial, with inscriptions to all victims; a cross on the spot of a memorial initially raised by Polish prisoners; and the Haus der Stille, where you can retreat for quiet contemplation.

A gravestone for Anne Frank and her sister, Margot, has also been erected (not too far from the cemetery gates, on the way to the obelisk). The entire family was initially sent to Auschwitz when their hiding place in Amsterdam was betrayed to police, but the sisters were later transferred to Bergen-Belsen. Although no one knows exactly where Anne lies, many pay tribute to their 15-year-old heroine at this gravestone.

Other monuments to various victim groups, including a Soviet memorial, are dotted across the complex.

ⓘ Information

The documentation centre's exhibition, cafeteria, library and toilets are barrier-free. Wheelchairs and stools are available on loan. All videos in the exhibit have subtitles in English and German.

ⓘ Getting There & Away

BUS

Getting to the memorial by bus is possible but difficult: your best bet is to either have your own transport or find people to share a taxi.

Travelling by bus takes about an hour, starting on the 900 bus to Winsen, then switching to the 110 to the memorial; on weekends you take line 100 to Winsen. The tourist office in Celle has a timetable sheet with a sketch map, and you can also find a timetable on the Bergen-Belsen website. Check www.efa.de for bus info.

CAR & MOTORCYCLE

Driving from Celle, take Hehlentorstrasse north over the Aller River and follow Harburger Strasse north out of the city. This is the B3; continue northwest to the town of Bergen and follow the signs to Belsen.

TAXI

Call ☑ 05051-55 55 or book at www.bettertaxi. de/en. Expect to pay €19 one way from the village of Bergen to the camp or €50 one way from Celle.

Hildesheim

☑ 05121 / POP 101,667

One of the oldest cities in Northern Germany, Hildesheim celebrated its 1200th birthday in 2015. Walking around its pretty, medieval-looking Altstadt area you may find it hard to believe that the old town was razed by bombing on 22 March 1945 – you're looking at a post-WWII reconstruction.

There are two Unesco World Heritage Sites in Hildesheim and history buffs will find it worth considering an overnight stop here. If you're visiting Hanover for a trade fair and find no rooms in the capital, Hildesheim makes an excellent alternative base with some decent modern hotels.

◉ Sights

One of the many tragedies of Hitler's excursion into megalomania was the horrendous damage inflicted upon once-magnificent architectural gems such as Hildesheim. After WWII, key parts of the old town such as the Marktplatz were lovingly reconstructed in their former style. Here you'll find, (clockwise from north) the Rokokohaus, Wollenweberhaus, Wedekindhaus, Knochenhauerhaus and Bäckeramtshaus.

The Marktbrunnen fountain in front of the Rathaus has a carillon of bells that play folk songs at noon, 1pm and 5pm daily.

★ **Dommuseum**   MUSEUM
(☑ 05121-307 760; www.dommuseum-hildesheim. de/en; Domhof; adult/child €6/free; ⊙10am-5pm Tue-Sun) This engaging museum showcases 1000 years of church history in the cloisters of World Heritage–listed Mariendom Cathedral. Its permanent exhibition *From the Middle Ages to the Modern* explores church life and religious history, including a rare and priceless collection of treasures, reliquaries and artefacts.

Mariendom   CHURCH
(St Mary's Cathedral; ☑ 05121-179 1646; www. dom-hildesheim.de/en; Domhof 17; ⊙10am-6pm Mon-Fri, to 4.30pm Sat, noon-5.30pm Sun) FREE

Hildesheim's Unesco World Heritage–listed cathedral took its present form in 1061 and was virtually rebuilt after its WWII bombing, then reopened in 2014 after a painstaking renovation and restoration process. It's famous for the almost 5m-high Bernwardstüren, bronze doors with bas-reliefs dating from 1015. These depict scenes from the Bible's Old and New Testaments. The church's wheel-shaped chandelier and the Christussäule (Column of Christ) are also from the original cathedral.

Go out through the rear doors to the cloister to see the giant Tausend-Jähriger Rosenstock (1000-year-old rosebush) climbing up the cathedral wall. Thought to date from the mid-800s, the rosebush served as a powerful symbol for Hildesheim when the cathedral was destroyed in 1945 and new shoots appeared from a root buried by debris.

To reach the Dom from Hauptbahnhof, take bus 1 to Bohlweg.

Fachwerkviertel   AREA
Hildesheim's 'Half-Timbered Quarter' is but a shadow of its former self – before WWII some 1900 of these buildings stood here – but it's still a great place to see typical old German architecture; start from around Bruhl and Neue Strasse. The Armourer's House (Gelber Stern 21) is Hildesheim's oldest, dating from 1548. Werner's House (Godehardsplatz 12), from 1606, has 29 elaborately decorated exterior panels. The Kehrwiederturm (off Kesslerstrasse) is the last remaining tower from the former city wall.

St Michaeliskirche   CHURCH
(☑ 05121-344 10; http://michaelis-hildesheim. wir-e.de; Michaelisplatz 2; ⊙8am-6pm Apr-Oct, 9am-4pm Nov-Mar, Tue from 10am) FREE The Unesco-protected Church of St Michael was built in the Romanesque style in 1022 and reconstructed after war damage. Unusual features inside include the alternation of round columns and square pillars as supports, the painted wooden ceiling, a late-12th-century chancel barrier decorated with angels, the cloisters and a crypt containing Bernward, the bishop of Hildesheim from 993 to 1022, who commissioned many artists and strove to make the city a cultural centre in his day.

Roemer-und-Pelizaeus Museum   MUSEUM
(☑ 05121-936 90; www.rpmuseum.de; Am Steine 1-2; adult/child €10/5; ⊙10am-6pm Tue-Sun) This museum houses one of Europe's best collections of Egyptian and Peruvian art and

DON'T MISS

SCHLOSS MARIENBURG

Perched grandly above the Leine River, the neo-Gothic **Schloss Marienburg** (☑ 05069-348 000; www.schloss-marienburg.de; Pattensen; tour adult/child €9/6.50; ⊙ 10am-6pm Jun-Aug, closed Mon Mar-May, Sep & Oct, 10am-4pm Sat & Sun Jan & Feb) was built from 1858–67 and was a present from Hanover's King George V to his wife Marie, who longed for a country refuge away from court life. She and her two daughters spent only a year in residence before going into exile after the dissolution of the Kingdom of Hanover. On a guided tour you can see the grand hall, the queen's apartments, the princesses' rooms, the huge kitchen and the chapel.

Though the tours are held in German, you can follow along with a free audioguide in English, French, Polish, Russian, Spanish or Swedish (bring a passport or driving licence as deposit). You can book in advance by phone or by email at office@schloss-marienburg. de or rock up on the day and try your luck.

Driving from Hanover, take the B3 28km south or the A7 south and exit 62 to Hildesheim. Take the B1 out of Hildesheim and continue 7km until you come to Mahlehrten. Turn right for Nordstemmen and you'll see signs for the castle. Admission is free for children under the age of six.

By public transport, the best way is to take Hanover's bus 300 (adult/child €4.40/1.30) to the stop 'Pattensen', then take line 310 (which often uses the same bus) headed for Eldagsen and get off at the stop 'Marienburg Abzweig Nord'; from there it's 1.5km (uphill) to the castle. From early March through early November, line 310 runs directly to the castle's gates twice a day on weekdays and four times each on Saturday and Sunday; you'll find the timetable at www.regiobus.de/service/ausflugstipps.

artefacts. There are dozens of mummies, scrolls, statues and wall hangings, but the life-size re-creation of an Egyptian tomb (of Sennefer) is a particular highlight. Take bus 1 from Hauptbahnhof to Museum.

🏃 Activities

JoWiese SWIMMING
(☑ 05121-281 5112; www.jowiese.de; Lucienvörder Allee 1; adult/child €4.40/2.20; ⊙ 6am-8pm Mon-Fri, from 7am Sat & Sun mid-May–Oct) This attractive swimming complex in landscaped parklands features outdoor splash, swimming and diving pools and its own 'beach' on a private lake. It's a great spot to cool down on a hot summer's day. It's 1km southwest of the Mariendom on foot, or a five-minute walk from the Vier Linden stop on bus 5.

🛏 Sleeping

★ **Van der Valk**
Hotel Hildesheim HOTEL €€
(☑ 05121-3000; www.vandervalk.de; Markt 4; s/d from €69/89; @ 🛜 🏊) Behind its historic frontage on the central market place, this luxury hotel reveals a surprisingly large interior, with a flagstone-floored atrium entrance giving way to tasteful rooms in subtle tones. The pool and wellness areas (Finnish sauna) are a bonus.

Novotel HOTEL €€
(☑ 05121-171 70; www.accorhotels.com; Bahnhofsallee 38; s/d from €88/108; 🅿 @ 🛜) Hildesheim's classy Novotel features exposed stone walls, gentle tones and cosy designer-chic style. It's set back from the street in a large, mid-19th century building on quiet grounds and has excellent dining and bar facilities.

1891 Hildesheim
Boutique Hotel BOUTIQUE HOTEL €€
(☑ 05121-281 3357; www.1891hildesheim.com; Leuinsstrasse 16; s/d from €84/99; 🅿 🛜) This boutique hotel offers friendly, attentive service for its 14 modern rooms set in a beautiful red-brick 1891 building. Superior rooms are larger; one even has a balcony. It's located right behind (and about five minutes' walk from) the Hauptbahnhof.

🍴 Eating

There are a handful of bars along and around Friesenstrasse.

Nil im Museum INTERNATIONAL €
(☑ 05121-408 595; www.nil-museum.de; Am Steine 1; mains €8-19; ⊙ 10am-6pm Tue-Sun; 🛜) This relaxed restaurant inside the Roemer-und-Pelizaeus Museum serves delicious antipasti, pasta and salads, along with poultry and red-meat main courses.

WORTH A TRIP

WOLFBURG'S AUTOSTADT

A hit with car buffs of all ages, Autostadt (Car City; ☑ 05361-400; Stadtbrücke; adult/child €15/6, car tower with discovery tour adult/concession €8/6; ⊗ 9am-6pm; ▣ 201, 202, 213 to Autostadt) is a celebration of all things automobile, spread across 25 hectares. A visit to this theme park and museum kicks off with a broad view of automotive design and engineering in the Konzernforum, then breaks off into exhibits relating to a bunch of European car makers, from Volkswagen, Porsche and Audi to Bentley, Lamborghini and Škoda.

Many exhibits are interactive and most have signage in German and English. Included in the tour is a 45-minute return Maritime Panorama Tour along the Aller River to the outlying district of Fallersleben. (Unfortunately, you can't get off the boat.)

For a pure, competitive adrenaline rush, ring ahead to organise an English-speaking instructor for the park's obstacle courses and safety training driving experiences (costing between €25 and €35). You'll need a valid licence, of course, and to be comfortable with a left-hand-drive car. The park even has a mini-course, with toy models that can be driven by kids.

You can get to Autostadt by walking over the pedestrian bridge right next to the Phaeno museum (next to the Hauptbahnhof), or by taking one of several bus lines. If you're driving, park at Designer Outlets (☑ 05361-893 500; www.designeroutlets-wolfsburg.de/en; An der Vorburg 1; ⊗ 10am-7pm Mon-Thu, to 8pm Fri & Sat) and then walk over the bridge – the parking's much cheaper there than at the Autostadt lots.

Frequent IC train services go to Wolfsburg from Berlin (from €20, 1½ hours) and Hanover (€20, 30 minutes). ICE trains are slightly faster and more expensive. Regional trains run from Braunschweig (€5.50, 19 minutes).

Venezia ICE CREAM €

(Rathausstrasse 2; sundaes €5-7; ⊗ 8am-11pm) This cafe right on the main square features tables outside plus a rustic-styled upstairs dining room decorated with old-fashioned coffee mills. There's a regular food menu but the main attractions are the numerous towering sundaes, which fill large glass goblets with ice cream, a wealth of toppings and a mountain of whipped cream, topped off with a biscuit.

Da Filippo ITALIAN €€

(☑ 05121-376 71; www.dafilippo-hildesheim.de; Dammstrasse 10; pizzas €8-12, mains €8-€28; ⊗ noon-3pm & 6pm-midnight) A casually elegant Italian restaurant directly across from the Roemer-und-Pelizaeus Museum, Da Filippo serves up a variety of pizzas, huge bowls of delicious pastas and other favourites such as chicken piccata, veal scallopini and calamari. Good service, too.

Dionysos GREEK €€

(☑ 05121-334 67; www.altstadt-dionysos.de; Wollenweberstrasse 26; mains €10-19; ⊗ 5.30-10pm, plus noon-2.30pm Sun) The inside may look more like a medieval German pub but it's actually the oldest Greek restaurant in Hildesheim, which has been serving up favourites like grilled lamb, moussaka, gyros, souvlaki and more for over 30 years.

★ **Schlegels Weinstuben** INTERNATIONAL €€€

(☑ 05121-331 33; www.schlegels-weinstuben.de; Am Steine 4-6; mains €17-27; ⊗ 5-11pm Mon-Fri, from 6pm Sat) The lopsided walls of this rose-covered, 500-year-old house add to its charm. Inside are historic rooms and, in one corner, a round, glass-topped table fashioned from a well, where you can dine overlooking the water. On offer is changing seasonal and regional cuisine that you'll select from the blackboard brought to your table. Book ahead.

❶ Information

Hildesheim Tourist Office (☑ 05121-179 80; www.hildesheim.de; Rathausstrasse 20; ⊗ 9.30am-6pm Mon-Fri, 10am-3pm Sat year-round, plus 10am-3pm Sun Apr-Oct) Helpful staff can provide a range of bilingual information and make accommodation reservations. Pick up the handy map that shows all of the sights.

❶ Getting There & Around

BUS

Most of the sights in Hildesheim are within walking distance of the centre, but from the Hauptbahnhof, bus 1 is useful as it passes Schuhstrasse (for Marktplatz and the tourist office), Bohlweg (for the cathedral sights) and Museum (for the Roemer-und-Pelizaeus Museum). Single tickets cost €2.50 (good for 60 minutes); day tickets cost €5.40.

CAR & MOTORCYCLE
The A7 runs right by town from Hanover, while the B1 goes to Hamelin.

TRAIN
Frequent regional and suburban train services operate between Hildesheim and Hanover (€8.90, 30 minutes), while ICE trains to/from Braunschweig (€16, 25 minutes) and Göttingen (€27, 30 minutes) stop here on the way to/from Berlin (€67, 1¾ hours).

Braunschweig

☑ 0531 / POP 251,364

In past centuries Braunschweig (Brunswick) was an important centre of trade and a member of the Hanseatic League; today its significance has lessened but it's still the largest town between Hanover and Berlin. About 90% of the city's buildings were destroyed in WWII, including its large Altstadt, but the medieval town centre has been since reconstructed. A number of museums and impressive buildings make Braunschweig an interesting place to while away a day or two, or perhaps throw in a day trip to nearby Wolfenbüttel.

Braunschweig was the capital of Duke Heinrich der Löwe (Henry the Lion), a 12th-century Guelph prince who was one of the most powerful people of his time, and you'll see his namesake lions popping up everywhere as the city's heraldic animal, not the least as a giant bronze sculpture atop a tall pillar in front of Heinrich's former castle.

⊙ Sights

★**Herzog Anton Ulrich Museum** GALLERY
(☑ 0531-122 50; www.3landesmuseen.de; Museumstrasse 1; adult/child €9/2; ⊙ 11am-6pm Tue-Sun) One of Europe's oldest museums, the Anton Ulrich has a world-class art collection, with about 1400 paintings, several hundred bronze and stone sculptures, one of the world's largest collections of Limoges porcelain and over 100,000 prints – and more. It's particularly strong on Dutch Old Masters, with works by Holbein, Dürer, Van Dyck, Rubens and Rembrandt, as well as a single Vermeer. The building was renovated in 2016 and is barrier-free. Its medieval collection can be seen at the **Burg Dankwarderode** (☑ 0531-1215 2618; Burgplatz 4; adult/child €5/2; ⊙ 10am-5pm Tue-Sun).

Städtisches Museum MUSEUM
(☑ 0531-470 4521; www.braunschweig.de/museum; Steintorwall 14; adult/child €5/2; ⊙ 10am-5pm Tue-Sun) Braunschweig's municipal museum is set in a beautiful 1906 building and holds a large and varied collection, with medieval religious art; arts and crafts such as faience, porcelain, silver and lacquerware; art and artefacts from Native Americans (including some rare pieces from the 18th century) and various peoples of Polynesia, Indonesia and Africa; and a large collection of historical musical instruments dating back to the 1600s, courtesy of Theodor Steinweg (whose father founded Steinway Pianos).

Dom St Blasii CHURCH
(St Blasius Cathedral; ☑ 0531-243 350; www.braunschweigerdom.de; Domplatz 5; crypt €1; ⊙ 10am-5pm) The tomb of Heinrich der Löwe, the powerful duke who made Braunschweig his capital in the 12th century, lies alongside that of his wife Mathilde in the crypt of Dom St Blasii. The Nazis decided to co-opt his image and in 1935 exhumed Heinrich's tomb to conduct an 'archaeological investigation'. The corpse found inside had one short leg and dark hair, which threw the master-race propagandists into a spin and raised doubt as to whether it's really Heinrich entombed here.

Magniviertel AREA
This little area is known for its handsome, half-timbered houses, especially in the streets just around the **St Magni church**. With a variety of shops, cafes and bars, this is a great place to have a wander. It's just southeast of Schlossplatz, behind the Schlossmuseum (p714) building.

Landesmuseum MUSEUM
(State Museum; ☑ 0531-121 50; www.3landesmuseen.de; Burgplatz 1; adult/child €4/2; ⊙ 10am-5pm Tue-Sun, to 8pm 1st Thu of every month) This chronologically ordered museum features engaging exhibits, starting with a large Foucault pendulum illustrating the principle of the earth's rotation, leading to artefacts narrating Germany's past, including eclectic objects like the strands of hair allegedly belonging to Duke Heinrich der Löwe and his wife Mathilde. They are in cases of silver, gold and marble, specially constructed in 1935 as part of Hitler's propaganda offensive to present Heinrich's many conquests as a predecessor to his own *Lebensraum* policy.

LOWER SAXONY & BREMEN BRAUNSCHWEIG

Braunschweiger Löwe MONUMENT
(Burgplatz) The Brunswick lion statue is based on the original lion Duke Heinrich der Löwe (Henry the Lion) ordered to be made in 1166 as a symbol of his power and jurisdiction. Today it's the symbol of the city, whose identity is intricately tied up with that of the duke, who was responsible for colonising the eastern regions of Germany beyond the Elbe and Saale. You can see the original statue at Burg Dankwarderode (p713).

Schlossmuseum MUSEUM
(☑ 0531-470 4876; www.schlossmuseum-braun schweig.de; Schlossplatz 1; adult/child incl audioguide €4/free; ⊙ 10am-5pm Tue & Thu-Sun, 1-8pm Wed) An impressive reconstruction using original elements of Braunschweig's Ducal Palace, which was badly damaged in WWII and demolished in 1960. Its palace museum uses multilingual, interactive technology – including a handy audioguide, available in English – to explain the region's rulers and history, and features a series of rooms with original furnishings from the 19th century, including a beautiful 1820 pianoforte with mother-of-pearl keys, the only palace instrument to survive.

🛏 Sleeping

DJH Hostel HOSTEL €
(☑ 0531-866 8850; http://braunschweig.jugend herberge.de/en; Wendenstrasse 30; dm from €31.90, s/d from €47.90/79.80; 🛜) This sparkling jewel in the crown of the DJH hostel network was opened in 2015 and offers the newest, cheapest digs in town: four-bed rooms with private bathroom, an en suite single or double, and family rooms. Breakfast and bed linen are included. Half- and full-board are also available for €5.80 or €11.60 extra, respectively.

★ Fourside Hotel HOTEL €€
(☑ 0531-707 200; www.fourside-hotels.com; Jöddenstrasse 3; s/d from €79/89; ✳🛜) In a great location around the corner from Burgplatz, the Fourside is one of Braunschweig's newest accommodation options, with 174 rooms done up in a relaxed, modern style, with tasteful splashes of colour. Showers are big enough for two and even come with a towel warmer. There's a fitness room and a sauna on-site. Breakfast is €10 extra.

Penta Hotel DESIGN HOTEL €€
(☑ 0531-481 4708; www.pentahotels.com; Auguststrasse 6; r from €68; 🛜) This contemporary design hotel 500m south of Schlossplatz is fresh off an on-trend renovation of its 130-odd rooms and chill lobby space, with distressed carpeting and gleaming subway tiles in the bathrooms. The whole vibe is young and cool, with employees casually dressed in Diesel shirts and there are even free PlayStation hand-helds available for guests to use. Breakfast will cost you an additional €17.

Frühlings-Hotel HOTEL €€
(☑ 0531-243 210; www.fruehlingshotel.de; Bankplatz 7; s/d from €59/79; 🅿@🛜) Friendly, good-humoured staff, a central location and varying categories of comfortable rooms make this a good choice. Its very popular bar-restaurant, Vielharmonie, offers gastropub takes on German cuisine. Parking is available for €7 per night at a car park across the street.

🍴 Eating

Belly Button Food VEGAN €
(☑ 0531-6128 5218; www.facebook.com/Belly buttonfood; Kleine Burg 15; 4-/5-salad plates €4.10/5.90, soup, salad & juice combo €8; ⊙ 11am-6pm Mon-Wed, to 9pm Thu-Sat; 🛜🍴) This little beaut of a cafe down a passageway beside the tourist office offers up 20 or so delicious salads (available in mixed platters) and four soups, all vegan and all made fresh daily from local, organic produce, plus fresh juices, coffee, tea and vegan and raw desserts. We liked the eclectic decor – especially the grove of actual tree trunks.

★ Mutter Habenicht GERMAN €€
(☑ 0531-459 56; www.mutter-habenicht.de; Papenstieg 3; mains €9-23; ⊙ noon-2.30pm & 6-10pm) This 'Mother Hubbard' dishes up filling portions of schnitzels, potatoes, steaks, spare ribs and the occasional Balkan dish in the dimly lit, bric-a-brac-filled front room, or in the small beer garden out the back.

Restaurant Brodocz BISTRO €€
(☑ 0531-422 36; www.restaurant-brodocz.de; Stephanstrasse 2; mains €6-28; ⊙ 11.30am-10.30pm; 🍴) All-organic food is on the menu at this pocket-sized restaurant, with fish, lamb, beef and turkey but plenty of options for vegetarians and vegans; gluten- and lactose-free customers are also catered for. It's tucked inside the stone-walled courtyard of a handsome, half-timbered building – on warm days you can sit outside and feel hidden away from the world.

Ox

STEAK €€€

0531-243 900; www.oxsteakhouse.com; Güldenstrasse 7; steaks €28-90; ⊗noon-2.30pm & 6-11pm) Ox bills itself as the best steakhouse in town, and there can be little doubt about this with its prime and choice steaks from the USA, Argentina and Australia (other options include grilled salmon and rack of lamb). Connoisseurs of schnapps will soon be hailing the waiter for the trolley, filled with excellent, often lesser-known local and international varieties.

🍸 Drinking & Nightlife

The Magniviertel has a smattering of traditional pubs, while Kalenwall has a string of nightclubs that are mostly open on Friday and Saturday (sometimes Thursdays). Useful listings can be found at the tourist office in the publications *Braunschweig Bietet* and the quarterly *Hin & Weg*.

Eulenglück

LOUNGE

(www.disko-kolchose.de; Gieseler 3; ⊗11pm-8am Thu-Sat) 'Owl's Luck' has everything you might want for a night out – it's part club, part lounge and part beer garden, with DJs or live bands every Thursday, Friday and Saturday night. Part of the same 'disco collective' as the Lindbergh Palace.

Brain Klub

CLUB

(🖉0531-6149 4255; www.yourpersonalklub.de; Bruchtorwall 12; ⊗from 11pm Fri & Sat) The best place in Braunschweig to go for dancing to drum 'n' bass, house and other electronic music. It's set behind a grey strip of office buildings on Bruchtorwall – look for the marquee and colourfully painted walls leading you to it.

Lindbergh Palace

CLUB

(www.disko-kolchose.de; Kalenwall 3; ⊗10pm-late Thu, from 11pm Fri & Sat) One of Braunschweig's premier clubs, playing mainly different kinds of rock, including metal and punk. Every Thursday features indie, hip-hop and alternative. Same owners as Eulenglück, down the road.

☆ Entertainment

Staatstheater
Braunschweig

PERFORMING ARTS

(🖉ticket office 0531-123 4567; www.staatstheater-braunschweig.de; Am Theater/Steinweg) This historic venue is used for classical music, theatre, dance and opera. The tourist office

WORTH A TRIP

FAGUS WERK

Designed and built by Bauhaus founder Walter Gropius in 1911, this factory (Fagus Factory; 🖉05181-7914; www.fagus-werk.com/en; Hannoversche Strasse 58, Alfeld; adult/child €7/5; ⊗10am-5pm Mar-Oct, to 4pm Nov-Feb), which has been producing shoe lasts for over 100 years, is regarded as the world's first modernist factory building (it was given Unesco World Heritage status in 2011). Sections of the building have been turned into a gallery that focuses on Gropius' life, the Bauhaus movement, the history of the Fagus company and footwear in general. Guided factory tours are recommended, but you can also go solo.

It's just over a five-minute walk to the factory from Alfeld station, serviced regularly by regional trains from Hanover (€11.40, 30 minutes), or a 30-minute drive from Hildesheim.

sells tickets, or turn up an hour before the event for rush tickets.

🛍 Shopping

Raum 23

HATS

(🖉0531-444 66; www.aufdenkopf.de; Ritterstrasse 23; ⊗noon-6pm Tue-Fri, 11am-4pm Sat) Put a lid on it at this cute little hat shop in the Magniviertel area. Designer Margret Porwoll makes headgear for both men and women by hand – everything from wool beanies and flat caps to cloches and fascinators. Contact her to enquire about bespoke designs.

Glückskinder

CHILDREN'S CLOTHING

(🖉0531-6149 9903; www.glueckskinder-bs.de; Ölschlägern 29; ⊗10am-6pm Mon-Sat) It's 'lucky children' indeed who end up with something from this fashion-forward kids clothing shop, which carries fun, trendy stuff for children, from babies to tweens, plus shoes, toys and accessories. Check out the adorable animal backpacks – you may want one for yourself.

ℹ Information

Braunschweig Tourist Office (🖉0531-470 2040; www.braunschweig.de; Kleine Burg 14; ⊗10am-6.30pm Mon-Fri, to 4pm Sat, plus 10am-noon Sun May-Sep) Helpful staff offer an array of English-language literature and maps.

ⓘ Getting There & Away

CAR & MOTORCYCLE

The A2 runs east–west between Hanover and Magdeburg across the northern end of the city. This connects with the A39 about 25km east of the city, which heads north to Wolfsburg. The A39 also heads south from the city.

TRAIN

There are regular RE services to Hanover (€13.60, 45 minutes) and IC trains to Leipzig (€47, two hours). ICE trains go to Berlin (€60, 90 minutes) and Frankfurt (€95, 2¾ hours). The **Hauptbahnhof** (Willy-Brandt-Platz 1) is southeast of the centre of town.

ⓘ Getting Around

Braunschweig is at the heart of an integrated transport network that extends throughout the region and as far south as the Harz Mountains. Ninety-minute bus and tram tickets cost €2.50; 24-hour tickets are €5.50; you can buy tickets at service centres at the Hauptbahnhof and near the Rathaus and then validate them on the tram.

Any bus or tram going to 'Rathaus' from the Hauptbahnhof (such as tram 1 and bus 420) will get you to the centre in 10 minutes; these leave from just outside the Hauptbahnhof. Tram 5 is useful, connecting the train station with Friedrich-Wilhelm-Platz via Am Magnitor and passing the Herzog Anton Ulrich Museum. More information is available at www.verkehr-bs.de.

If driving, be aware that there are one-way systems all around the Altstadt. Alternatively, there's parking by the train station.

Wolfenbüttel

☎ 05331 / POP 52,269

This friendly, charming little town is a true delight, only about 10 minutes by train

---

EXPLORING WOLFENBÜTTEL
•••••••••••••••••••••••••••••••••••••
Wolfenbüttel's **tourist office** has some excellent resources to help you explore town. The free brochure *A Walk Through Historic Wolfenbüttel* takes you on a walk through town lasting around one hour (2km), excluding visits.

You can also access an MP3 audio guide right on your smartphone from the website www.wolfenbuettel.tomis.mobi; audio is available in English, French or German.

---

from Braunschweig – practically a suburb, though worlds away in terms of its feel and architecture. Stadtmarkt, the town centre, is a five-minute walk northeast of the Hauptbahnhof.

'Alles mit Bedacht' ('Everything with prudence') was the expression favoured by Duke August II (1579–1666), who founded Wolfenbüttel's famous library and turned the town into a cultural centre in the mid-17th century.

First mentioned in records in 1118, Wolfenbüttel was virtually untouched by WWII, and it's almost a time capsule of half-timbered houses: there are more than 600 of them, almost all beautifully restored. It's also the home of the potent, herb-flavoured liqueur Jägermeister, which was invented here in 1934.

◎ Sights & Activities

Schloss Museum   MUSEUM

(☎ 05331-924 60; www.schlosswolfenbuettel.de; Schlossplatz 13; adult/child €5/free; ◷10am-5pm Tue-Sun) Wolfenbüttel's pretty Palace Museum showcases the living quarters of the Braunschweig-Lüneburg dukes, which have been preserved in all their glory of intricate inlaid wood, damask-covered walls, brocade curtains and lush furniture. A highlight is the large dining room, set with silver plates and a food-laden table fit for a ducal feast. A free audioguide is included with admission, available in German or English. The museum entrance is on the far side of the courtyard.

Herzog August Bibliothek   MUSEUM, LIBRARY

(Herzog August Library; ☎ 05331-8080; www.hab.de; Lessingplatz 1; adult/child €5/free; ◷10am-5pm Tue-Sun) This hushed building is one of the world's best reference libraries for 17th-century books. Its exhibition spaces feature two changing curated exhibits of antiquarian books and a permanent installation on the typography of Hermann Zapf (the inventor of the font Palatino and others), plus a collection of huge medieval globes. Type nerds and bibliophiles will be in heaven.

Bürger Museum   MUSEUM

(☎ 05331-863 77; www.schlosswolfenbuettel.de; Prof-Paul-Raabe-Platz 1; ◷10am-5pm Tue-Sun) **FREE** Wolfenbüttel's newest sight, this small 'citizens museum', which opened in 2017, relates the life of Wolfenbüttelers over the past five centuries through a hodgepodge of unique historical artefacts on display, such as canning machines, tin toy soldiers, a rather uncomfortable-looking chair made from stag antlers, Nazi propaganda from WWII and an absolutely gorgeous TV-stereo cabinet from 1959. While you're there you can pick up a little bag of tasty cookies made at a local confectionary school.

Klein Venedig   AREA
(Stobenstrasse) In the late 16th century, Dutch workers came to Wolfenbüttel and built an extensive canal system, remnants of which today survive in an area of town called Klein Venedig (Little Venice). The bridge across Stobenstrasse looks out onto a serene collection of half-timbered houses and is a popular spot for couples to attach a lock symbolising their steadfast love. To reach it from Schlossplatz, walk towards the town centre along Löwenstrasse, onto Krambuden and take a left at Mühlenstrasse.

Tours

Jägermeister Factory Tour   DISTILLERY
(☑ 05331-810; www.jagermeister.com/en/factory-tour; Jägermeisterstrasse 7) **FREE** The herbal liqueur beloved by party animals, Jägermeister was originally created in Wolfenbüttel in 1934, and the company is still headquartered here. Free 90-minute tours of the production process are offered Monday through Friday, in German or English (participants must be over 18). Advance booking is required; email tours@jaegermeister.de or contact the tourist office.

Eating

Unfortunately the eating options around the centre of town are less than inspired. You'll find a few options just off the Stadtmarkt; there are also pizza and burgers at the end of Grosser Zimmerhof and a delicious falafel and gyro place on Okerstrasse.

Information

Wolfenbüttel Tourist Office (☑ 05331-862 80; www.wolfenbuettel.de/Tourismus; Stadtmarkt 7; ☺10am-6pm Mon-Fri, to 2pm Sat & Sun) English-speaking staff can help out with maps, informational brochures and booking various tour packages.

Getting There & Away

Trains (€4, 9 minutes) connect Wolfenbüttel with Braunschweig's Hauptbahnhof. Bus 420 also runs between Braunschweig's Rathaus (€4, 24 minutes) and Wolfenbüttel's main bus interchange on Kornmarkt.

BREMEN & THE EAST FRISIAN COAST

Heading towards the northwestern edges of the country you'll find Bremen, an outward-looking, cultural and industrial capital of its own city-state enclave and a charming town that rewards urban exploration – it's a highlight of any visit to the region. Its port city Bremerhaven, further up the River Weser, offers harbourside history museums and wonderful seafood.

Other Lower Saxony towns of interest here include Worpswede, a century-old artists colony on the moors; Oldenburg and Jever, historic cities with scenic castles and old town centres; and friendly little Emden, near the Dutch border and gateway to the northern coast. If you like tidal flats, birdlife and blustery bike rides by the sea, you'll especially enjoy visiting any of the seven East Frisian Islands, which are ideally suited to slowing down the pace and immersing yourself in nature.

Sleeping

With the most variety across a range of budgets, Bremen City is the obvious choice as a base here, as Oldenburg and Worpswede can both be done as day trips, and even Bremerhaven is a short train ride away. As popular resort destinations, the East Frisian islands have plenty of accommodation.

Information

ACCESSIBLE TRAVEL
Contact tourist offices in the towns you want to visit for more information on accessible travel there. Some information is also available at www.barrierefreie-nordsee.de, and there's a searchable database of accessible museums, hotels, restaurants and more available at www.reisen-fuer-alle.de.

Getting There & Around

While rail connections to and around Bremen are excellent, you'll find a combination of buses, boats and trains necessary for exploring outlying regions and the islands. Renting a vehicle can help to keep things simple and let you go by your own schedule.

More information on regional transport is available at the Verkehrsverbund Bremen/Niedersachsen (http://en.vbn.de) website.

Bremen City

☑ 0421 / POP 565,719

Bremen, one of Germany's three city-states (along with Berlin and Hamburg), is known for being one of Germany's most outward-looking and hospitable places, with a vibe that strikes a good balance between style, earthiness and good living. Nature is never far away here, but Bremen is better known for its fairy-tale character, unique Expressionist quarter and one of Germany's most exciting football teams. It's also one of Europe's leaders in science and technology, home to the Airbus Defence and Space headquarters and a major Mercedes Benz plant.

More populous than Hanover, Bremen scrapes in as Germany's 11th largest city, but feels quite the contrary, offering a relaxed, unhurried lifestyle. Closer inspection reveals some vibrant districts with fine restaurants and fun bars, a lively entertainment calendar, a selection of excellent museums and a beautiful Altstadt.

History

Bremen's origins go back to a string of settlements that developed near today's centre from about AD 100, and one settlement in particular that in 787 was given its own bishop's seat by Charlemagne. In its earliest days, it was known as the 'Rome of the North' and developed as a base for Christianising Scandinavia. Despite this, it gradually shed its religious character, enjoying the greater freedom of being an imperial city from 1186, joining the Hanseatic League in 1260, and in 1646 coming directly under the wing of the Kaiser as a free imperial city; today it is a 'Free Hanseatic City', which includes Bremerhaven ('Bremen's Harbour'), and is the smallest of Germany's 16 states. In 1979 Bremen was the first to elect Green Party candidates to its state parliament, unwittingly becoming the cradle of a Green movement worldwide.

◉ Sights

Most of Bremen's major sights are in the centre, but its many neighbourhoods each have a different feel. The centre is compact and easy to walk around (or take a short tram ride); areas to the north and east of the centre have a sprinkling of sights that are usually best reached by tram or bus.

◉ Markt & Böttcherstrasse

★ **Böttcherstrasse**   STREET

(www.boettcherstrasse.de) The charming medieval coopers lane was transformed into a prime example of mostly expressionist architecture in the 1920s at the instigation of coffee merchant Ludwig Roselius. Its redbrick houses sport unique facades, whimsical fountains, statues and a carillon; many house artisanal shops and art museums. Its most striking feature is Bernhard Hoetger's golden Lichtbringer relief (Bringer of Light), which keeps an eye on the north entrance.

Paula Modersohn-Becker
Haus Museum   MUSEUM

(☑ 0421-336 5077; www.museen-boettcherstrasse.de; Böttcherstrasse 6-10; combined ticket adult/child €8/free; ⊙ 11am-6pm Tue-Sun) Showcasing the art of the eponymous artist Paula Modersohn-Becker (1876–1907), an early expressionist and member of the Worpswede (p730) artists colony, this is the first museum in the world dedicated to the works of a female painter. The building is the work of Bernhard Hoetger, the creative mind behind much of Böttcherstrasse. The combined ticket also includes admission to the Roselius-Haus Museum.

Dom St Petri   CHURCH

(St Petri Cathedral; ☑ 0421-334 7142; www.stpetridom.de; Sandstrasse 10-12; tower adult/child €2/1, museum free; ⊙ 10am-5pm Mon-Fri, to 2pm Sat, 2-5pm Sun Oct-May, Mon-Fri & Sun to 6pm Jun-Sep) Bremen's Protestant main church has origins in the 8th century, though its ribbed vaulting, chapels and two high towers date to the 13th century. Aside from the imposing architecture, the intricately carved pulpit and the baptismal font in the western crypt deserve a closer look. For panoramic views, climb the 265 steps to the top of the south tower (April to October). The Dom museum displays religious artefacts and treasures found here in a 1970s archaeological dig.

Roselius-Haus Museum   MUSEUM

(☑ 0421-336 5077; www.museen-boettcherstrasse.de; Böttcherstrasse 6-10; combined ticket adult/child €8/free; ⊙ 11am-6pm Tue-Sun) This 16th-century house contains a private collection of art from medieval times to the baroque era. It belonged to none other than Ludwig Roselius, the man who gave the world decaffeinated coffee and used the money from his beans and other ventures to bankroll the Expressionist Böttcherstrasse in the 1930s. The combined ticket includes admission to the museum's neighbour, the Paula Modersohn-Becker Haus Museum.

Bleikeller CRYPT
(Lead Cellar; www.stpetridom.de; Am Dom 1; adult/child €2/1; ⊙10am-5pm Wed-Fri, to 2pm Sat, noon-5pm Sun Apr-Oct) Located inside Dom St Petri, but accessed via a separate entrance south of the main door, the Lead Cellar was formerly the cathedral's cellar and today is a crypt, housing eight preserved corpses that mummified in the cathedral crypt's dry air. They include a Swedish countess, a soldier with his mouth opened in a silent scream and a student who died in a duel in 1705. It's more than a little creepy.

Rathaus HISTORIC BUILDING
(Marktplatz) Bremen's landmark and Unesco-listed Rathaus (city hall) dates to 1400 but was a work in progress for centuries, as succeeding generations each tried to leave their own mark on the ever-growing complex. Much of the most lavish detail was added in the 17th century. It's the only town hall in Germany from the late Middle Ages that has survived the centuries intact.

**Town Musicians of
Bremen Statue** STATUE
(Stadtmusikanten; Marktplaz) Local artist Gerhard Marcks cast this 1951 statute of the famous quartet in their most famous pose – scaring the robbers who invaded their house, with the rooster atop the cat, perched on the dog, on the shoulders of the donkey. On Sun-

days at noon between May and September a re-enactment of the story is staged for kids.

⊙ Schnoor

This maze of narrow, winding alleys was once the fishermen's quarter and later a red-light district. Today its tiny cottages house boutiques, restaurants, cafes and galleries. Though geared to tourists, Schnoor is a pretty place for a stroll (and a fun word to say out loud). Its restaurants are popular with locals in the evenings.

⊙ Schlachte & the Weser

**Weserburg Museum für
Moderne Kunst** GALLERY
(Weserburg Museum of Modern Art; ☑0421-598 390; www.weserburg.de; Teerhof 20; adult/child €9/free; ⊙11am-6pm Tue-Wed & Fri-Sun, to 8pm Thu; ⊡1, 2, 3 to Am Brill) Situated on an island in the Weser River across from the Schlachte promenade, this museum showcases works by German and international artists from private collections. Changing, hot-off-the-press exhibitions over five floors feature painting, sculpture, photography and video art.

⊙ Kulturmeile & Das Viertel

★**Kunsthalle** GALLERY
(☑0421-329 080; www.kunsthalle-bremen.de; Am Wall 207; adult/child €9/free; ⊙10am-5pm Wed-Sun, to 9pm Tue; ⊡2, 3 to Theater am Goetheplatz) For art lovers, the highlight of Bremen's *Kulturmeile* (Cultural Mile) is the Kunsthalle, which presents a large permanent collection of paintings, sculpture and copperplate

LOWER SAXONY & BREMEN BREMEN CITY

THE FANTASTIC FOUR

In the Brothers Grimm fairy tale, the Bremer Stadtmusikanten (Town Musicians of Bremen) never actually make it to Bremen, though you'll see statues and other references to them all over town. Starting with a donkey, four overworked and ageing animals – fearing the knacker's yard or the Sunday roasting pan – run away from their owners. They head for Bremen, intending, like many young dreamers, to make their fortune as musicians.

On their first night on the road, they decide to shelter in a house. It turns out to be occupied by robbers, as our heroes discover when they climb on the donkey to peer through the window. The sight of a rooster atop a cat, perched on a dog, which is sitting on a donkey – and the 'musical' accompaniment of braying, barking, meowing and crowing – startles the robbers so much, they flee. The animals remain and make their home 'where you'll probably still find them today'.

On Sunday from May to September, this story is charmingly re-enacted at noon in Bremen's Marktplatz.

Bremen City

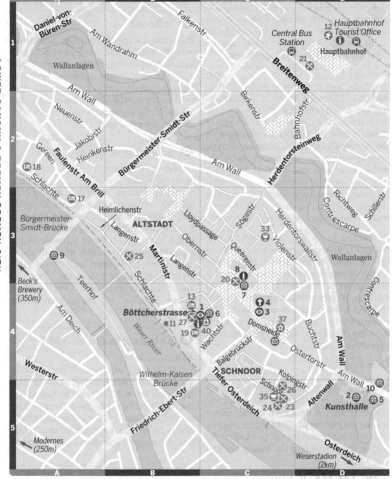

engraving from the Middle Ages into the modern era – some of the masterpieces here are more than 600 years old. The collection includes work by van Dyck, Rubens, Monet, Van Gogh and Picasso, as well as 10 sculptures by Rodin. Rotating exhibitions display both classical and contemporary art.

Gerhard Marcks Haus GALLERY
(☎0421-989 75 20; www.marcks.de; Am Wall 208; adult/child €5/free, 1st Thu of month free; ☺10am-6pm Tue-Wed & Fri-Sun, to 9pm Thu; ☒2, 3 to Theater am Goetheplatz) Among Germany's greatest sculptors, Gerhard Marcks (1889–1981) is the

man responsible for Bremen's famous Stadtmusikanten sculpture (p719) on Markt. Born in Berlin, he was condemned as a 'degenerate' artist by the Nazis in the 1930s and forbidden from exhibiting his work until after WWII. In 1966 he transferred much of his work into a foundation in Bremen, culminating in this excellent museum with exhibits of his own works as well as those of modern and contemporary sculptors.

Wilhelm Wagenfeld Haus MUSEUM
(☎0421-339 9933; www.wwh-bremen.de; Am Wall 209; adult/concession €5/3.50; ☺3-9pm Tue,

---

Bremen City

◉ Top Sights
1	Böttcherstrasse	C4
2	Kunsthalle	D5

◉ Sights
3	Bleikeller	C4
4	Dom St Petri	C4
5	Gerhard Marcks Haus	D5
6	Paula Modersohn-Becker Haus Museum	C4
7	Rathaus	C4
	Roselius-Haus Museum	(see 6)
8	Town Musicians of Bremen Statue	C3
9	Weserburg Museum für Moderne Kunst	A3
10	Wilhelm Wagenfeld Haus	D5

◉ Activities, Courses & Tours
11	Hal Över Schreiber Reederei	B4
12	Radstation	D1

◉ Sleeping
13	Atlantic Grand	B4
14	Dorint Park Hotel Bremen	E1
15	Hotel Bölts am Park	F1
16	Hotel Residence	E1
17	Hotel Überfluss	A3
18	Jugendherberge Bremen	A2
19	Radisson Blu	B4

◉ Eating
20	Bremer Ratskeller	C3
21	Edel Weiss	D1
22	Engel Weincafe	E5
23	Katzen Cafe	C5
24	Kleiner Olymp	C5
	Loui & Jules	(see 17)
25	Luv	B3
26	Schröter's	C5
27	Ständige Vertretung	B4
28	Tarte	F5
29	Vengo	F5

◉ Drinking & Nightlife
30	Cafe Kweer	E5
	Feldmann's Bierhaus	(see 25)
31	Harbour Coffee	F4
32	Lagerhaus	F5
33	NFF Club	C3
34	Queens	F2
35	Teestübchen in Schnoor	C5
36	Wohnzimmer	F5

◉ Entertainment
37	Die Glocke	C4
38	Lila Eule	F5
39	Theater Bremen	E5

◉ Shopping
40	Bremer Bonbon Manufaktur	C4
	Michael Falk Goldschmiede	(see 40)

10am-6pm Wed-Sun; ⊠2, 3 to Theater am Goetheplatz) Wilhelm Wagenfeld (1900–90) was a Bauhaus luminary whose foundation today promotes contemporary design in its many facets and forms in special exhibitions, including everything from industrial design to photography. It's housed in an 1828 former guardhouse and jail.

◉ Outside the Centre

★ Universum Science Centre   MUSEUM
(🖥0421-334 60; www.universum-bremen.de; Wiener Strasse 1a; adult/child €16/11; ⊗9am-6pm Mon-Fri,

WORTH A TRIP

DENKORT BUNKER VALENTIN

In 1943, the Nazis started construction of a massive concrete bunker (☎0421-6967 3670; www.denkort-bunker-valentin.de; Rekumer Siel, Farge; ☺10am-4pm Tue-Fri & Sun; ☐90 to Rekumer Siel, ☒RS1 to Farge) FREE to build submarines in. At a planned production rate of 12 subs per month it was meant to be the German war machine's most important naval project. The largest free-standing bunker in Germany – around 426m long and 97m wide, up to 27m high and with 4.5m-thick walls – it was built by up to 12,000 slave-labourers from POW and concentration camps, under intensely cruel conditions; thousands died at the site.

Allied bombing badly damaged the bunker when it was 90% completed, just a month before the Germans surrendered; not a single submarine was ever built there, and today it stands as a symbol of the futility of war. It's an eerie, ruined place, with rainwater and sunlight leaking in through the bomb craters in the ceiling; it's made all the more haunting by the stories of survivors, which you can read about and listen to in a free audioguide, available in English (ID deposit required). A 1.5km-long path runs through and around the bunker, with the audioguide and English signage providing information at 25 stops.

To get there from Bremen, take the Regio-S-Bahn train RS1 to Farge (€2.80, 44 minutes, every 30 minutes), the last stop; from the station, cross the road and walk to the right to the bus stop. Take bus 90 four stops to Rekumer Siel and follow the sign down a side street.

from 10am Sat & Sun; ☐6 to Universität-Süd) Bremen has a strong aerospace industry, and space buffs will enjoy the eye-catching, oyster-shaped Universum Science Centre, where you can make virtual trips to the stars, as well as to the ocean floor or the centre of the earth. Previous exhibits focused on astronomy and exploration, with a special display on women astronauts. Great for kids.

Botanika   GARDENS
(☎0421-427 066; www.botanika.net; Deliusweg, Rhododendron-Park; adult/child €10.50/5; ☺9am-6pm Mon-Fri, from 10am Sat & Sun; ☐31 to Rhododendronpark, ☐4 to Bürgermeister-Spitta-Allee) If you're a plant lover, don't miss a trip to Botanika and its replicated Asiatic landscapes ranging from the Himalayas to New Guinea. Admission to the rhododendron park, where you'll find more than 2000 rhododendron and azaleas, is free. Take the tram from Hauptbahnhof and then transfer to the bus.

⌖ Tours

★ **Beck's Brewery Factory Tour**   BREWERY
(☎0421-5094 5555; www.becks.de/besucher zentrum; Am Deich 18/19; tours €12.90; ☺tours 1pm, 3pm & 4.30pm Mon-Wed, 10am, 11.30am, 1pm, 3pm, 4.30pm & 6pm Thu-Sat; ☐1, 2, 3 to Am Brill) Two-hour tours of one of Germany's most internationally famous breweries

must be booked online through either the Beck's or tourist office websites. Expect a tasting at the end. The 3pm tour is also in English. Minimum age 16. Meet at the brewery's visitor centre; take the tram to Am Brill, cross the river, then turn right onto Am Deich.

Airbus Defence & Space Tour   SCIENCE & TECHNOLOGY
(www.bremen-tourism.de/airbus; adult/child €18.50/15.50; ☺2pm & 4pm Sat) Truly unique, these fascinating two-hour tours of the Airbus Defence & Space facility, which built major sections of the International Space Station, must be booked at least five days in advance, online or through the tourist office. For security, you must carry your passport with you at all times. Tours are in German only.

Hal Över Schreiber Reederei   CRUISE
(☎0421-338 989; www.hal-oever.de; Schlachte 2 & Martinianleger; ☺office 9am-5pm Mon-Fri) Operates a 75-minute Weser and harbour tour three to five times daily from April to October (plus two per weekend in February and March) as well as trips along the Weser to Bremerhaven from May through September, with various stops. Check the website for schedules and pricing. The office is at Schlacte 2; cruises depart from Martinianleger, a bit south.

LOWER SAXONY & BREMEN BREMEN CITY

✮✮ Festivals & Events

Karneval
STREET CARNIVAL

(www.bremer-karneval.de) As weird as it sounds, Bremen's popular carnival has become the largest samba festival in Europe. OK, so the competition isn't exactly enormous, but you can expect about 10,000 people to take to the streets every year in January or February for annual merrymaking that all began when the first Bremer Samba Group swung into action in 1986.

Breminale
CULTURAL

(www.breminale-festival.de; ⊙ Jul) This beloved free, five-day outdoor festival has been held on the banks of the Weser for over 30 years, with hundreds of musical acts from around the world, as well as food stalls, beer gardens and music and activities just for kids.

Bremer Weihnachtsmarkt
CHRISTMAS MARKET

(Marktplatz; ⊙ late Nov–23 Dec) December comes alive with this month-long Christmas market held in Bremen's picturesque central square. Sip on warm *Glühwein* (mulled wine) and nibble on traditional gingerbread cakes beneath thousands of magical white lights while browsing over 150 stalls of food, crafts, sweets and other holiday goodies.

🛏 Sleeping

Prizeotel Bremen City
HOTEL €

(☑ 0421-222 2100; www.prizeotel.com/bremen; Theodor-Heuss-Allee 12; s/d from €59/64; P ❄ 🕏) This funky, fresh and fluorescent-coloured design hotel won't be everyone's cup of tea, but if you like it, you'll love it. Ultra-modern, compact rooms are quiet despite their proximity to the rail lines: the hotel is a five-minute walk from the train station. All rooms feature 32-inch TVs, 'mega beds' and 'maxi showers'. Breakfast is €11.

Jugendherberge Bremen
HOSTEL €

(☑ 0421-163 820; http://bremer.jugendherberge. de; Kalkstrasse 6; dm/s/d from €29.50/34.50/73; @ 🕏; 🚊 2 to Radio Bremen) Looking like a work of art from the outside, with a yellow-and-orange Plexiglas facade and slit windows, this hostel has comfortable rooms, a rooftop terrace and a bar-breakfast room with huge glass windows overlooking the Weser River. Linen and breakfast are included; lunch and dinner are available for extra (there's no guest kitchen).

Atlantic Grand
HOTEL €€

(☑ 0421-620 620; www.atlantic-hotels.de; Bredenstrasse 2; r from €119) The simple but effortlessly stylish, dark-wooded rooms pitched around a central courtyard and the topnotch service from attentive staff make this classy hotel an excellent choice. It's moments from Bremen's quirky Böttcherstrasse and steps from the riverside Schlachte.

Radisson Blu
HOTEL €€

(☑ 0421-369 60; www.radissonblu.com/hotelbremen; Böttcherstrasse 2; r from €120; P ❄ 🕏 🛉) The 235 guest rooms and suites in this sprawling, full-service international hotel have been renovated to a high standard. In a premium location by the Markt, the hotel has annexed what was formerly the Haus Atlantis building. Its striking Himmelssaal room is now an event space – tours (€5) are available each Sunday at 11.30am.

Hotel Überfluss
DESIGN HOTEL €€

(☑ 0421-322 860; www.designhotel-ueberfluss.de; Langenstrasse 72; s/d from €111/116; ❄ 🕏 🛉; 🚊 1, 2, 3 to Am Brill) Just metres above river level, this cutting-edge-cool hotel is a good choice for design-minded urban nomads. Black, white and chrome create a sleek, postmodern vibe that extends to the rooms (those with views are €15 more). There's one suite (from €328) with a river view and a private sauna and whirlpool – perfect for a honeymoon. Breakfast costs €14.50.

Hotel Residence
BOUTIQUE HOTEL €€

(☑ 0421-348 710; www.hotelresidence.de; Hohenlohestrasse 42; s/d/apt from €70/80/120; P @ 🕏 🛉) This century-old terrace, now a charming hotel, also boasts some funky apartments. The main building has rooms facing the street, while the newer extension backs onto the railway line but is still reasonably quiet. Friendly staff and a sauna, bar and dining room complete the package. Rooms and apartments are furnished in differing styles. The buffet breakfast costs €10.

Hotel Bölts am Park
HOTEL €€

(☑ 0421-34 61 10; www.hotel-boelts.de; Slevogtstrasse 23; s/d €72/92; P 🕏) This cosy familyrun hotel in a leafy neighbourhood filled with 1900s apartment buildings has real character, from the wonderfully old-fashioned breakfast hall to the well-proportioned double rooms. Lower priced rooms with shared bathrooms are also available.

★ **Dorint Park Hotel Bremen** HOTEL €€€
(☎0421-340 80; http://hotel-bremen.dorint.com; Im Bürgerpark; s/d from €80/160, ste per person from €185.50; P @ 🛜 🏊; 🚊6 to Am Stern) Although its exterior is certainly dated, this domed lakeside mansion surrounded by parkland impresses through its sheer extravagance and could be considered Bremen's only true five-star, grand hotel. It offers access to excellent spa, fitness and beauty facilities, a heated outdoor pool and views over the lake in a 'spa resort' ambience.

Eating

Head to riverside Schlacte for a long line of restaurants, many with outdoor seating overlooking the water. The artsy, student neighbourhood Das Viertel is a good pick for cheaper meals or simply a glass of wine or beer along with something tasty.

✖ Town Centre

★ **Bremer Ratskeller** GERMAN €€
(☎0421-321 676; www.ratskeller-bremen.de; Am Markt 11; mains €9-30; ⏰11am-midnight; 🛜) Ratskellers were traditionally built underneath the Rathaus (town hall) in every German town to keep the citizens and civil servants fed. Bremen's – in business since 1405! – is quite the experience, with high vaulted ceilings, private booths in little cubbies (the better to discuss town business), and good, heavy, no-fuss German food and beer. Service is attentive and friendly.

Ständige Vertretung GERMAN €€
(☎0421-320 995; www.staev.de; Böttcherstrasse 3-5; mains €9-20; ⏰noon-11.30pm Mon-Thu, to 12.30am Fri & Sat, to 10pm Sun) An offshoot of Berlin's best-known restaurant for homesick Rhineland public servants, this large, bustling place thrives on its political theme and solid cuisine, washed down with Rhenish wines and beer. Try one of the regional specialities, such as fried black pudding on mashed potatoes with fried apple slices and baked onion rings.

Edel Weiss AUSTRIAN €€
(☎0421-2427 8094; www.edelweiss-bremen.de; Bahnhofsplatz 8; mains €9-32; ⏰noon-midnight Mon-Fri, from 11am Sat, 11am-11pm Sun) Opposite the Hauptbahnhof, this friendly, rustically decorated haunt is famed for its hearty fare and friendly staff, as well as its schnitzel and, in season, *spargel* (white asparagus) galore. If you're just coming off a train it's

a good first foray into Bremen's tasty restaurant scene.

✖ Schnoor

★ **Kleiner Olymp** GERMAN €€
(☎0421-326 667; www.kleiner-olymp.de; Hinter der Holzpforte 20; mains €12.50-22.50; ⏰11am-11pm) This homely kitchen in Schnoor has a wonderful atmosphere, delicious (and not too heavy) North German cuisine and very reasonable prices. With a selection of mouthwatering soups and starters, fish and seafood (not pork, for a change) feature predominantly on the menu: bouillabaisse, North Sea crabs and plaice cooked in a variety of ways.

Schröter's INTERNATIONAL €€
(☎0421-326 677; www.schroeters-schnoor.de; Schnoor 13; mains €12-28; ⏰noon-10pm) A modern bistro with artful decoration, Schröter's is known for its antipasti and abundant mains, with options such as risotto, duck breast and snapper. It's a veritable warren of rooms, including a Toulouse-Lautrec room upstairs, decorated with plenty of copies of the painter's pictures. Multiple-course menus are available.

Katzen Cafe INTERNATIONAL €€
(☎0421-326 621; www.katzen-cafe.de; Schnoor 38; mains €8.50-26.50; ⏰noon-11pm; 🚉Domsheide) This popular Moulin Rouge–style restaurant opens out into a rear sunken terrace bedecked with flowers. The menu runs the gamut from Alsatian to Scandinavian, with classic German meat dishes and market-fresh fish mains such as North Sea plaice and Norwegian salmon.

✖ Schlachte & Around

Loui & Jules STEAK €€
(☎0421-3017 4443; www.loui-jules.com; Schlachte 36; mains €9-37; ⏰noon-11pm Mon-Fri, 6pm-midnight Sat) This surf 'n' turf place located inside Hotel Überfluss (p723) does excellent wood-coal grills, with steaks starting from €20, but it also has many cheaper dishes, including all-beef burgers in a variety of styles like the 'Italian Job' (with burrata and olives) or eggs Benedict.

Luv INTERNATIONAL €€
(☎0421-165 5599; www.restaurant-luv.de; Schlachte 15-18; mains €9.50-40; ⏰11am-late Mon-Fri, from 10am Sun; 🖊) This upbeat bistro has a lounge-bar feel and a menu strong on salads

and pasta complemented by mostly meaty mains, including a respectable 'Giant Texas' burger, a giant *Wiener Schnitzel* and locally caught fish. In good weather, sit beneath the twinkling lights at the outdoor *Biergarten* tables overlooking the Weser River. The kitchen closes at 11pm (10pm on Sunday).

✖ Das Viertel

★ Vengo
VEGAN €

(☑ 0421-8978 5243; www.vengo-bremen.de; Ostertorsteinweg 91; mains €8-10; ☺ 11am-9pm Mon-Wed, to 10pm Thu-Sat; ☑; ☐ 2, 6 to Wulwesstrasse) This bright little cafe-restaurant with natural-edge wood tables serves up a menu of delicious, filling vegan dishes, namely soups, salads, pastas (including a killer bolognese), curries and mains like stuffed eggplant or potato-and-vegetable casserole. Leave some room for one of the desserts, made fresh on the premises.

Tarte
ALSATIAN €

(☑ 0421-1612 1804; www.facebook.com/ElsasslmViertel; Siellwall 50; mains €8-10; ☺ 11.30am-2pm & 6-11pm Tue-Fri, 4.30-11pm Sat, 2.30-10pm Sun; ☑; ☐ 2, 10 to Siellwall) A little tucked-away Das Viertel restaurant with cool jazz music, Tarte is dedicated to the Alsatian speciality *Flammkuchen*. A large piece of flatbread is covered in crème fraîche and baked with delicious combinations of meat, cheese and vegetable toppings, such as bacon, onions and Emmentaler cheese. Vegan versions are available, too. There's a small list of French and German wines.

Engel Weincafe
CAFE €

(☑ 0421-6964 2390; www.engelweincafe-bremen. de; Ostertorsteinweg 31; dishes €4.50-15.60;

☺ 9am-1am Mon-Fri, from 10am Sat & Sun; 🛜 ☑; ☐ 2, 6 to Wulwesstrasse) Situated on a sunny corner in Das Viertel, this popular hang-out exudes the nostalgic vibe of the old-fashioned pharmacy it once was. The menu features breakfast, a hot lunch special, crispy *Flammkuchen* (Alsatian pizza), carpaccio, or just some cheese and a glass of wine from the international list.

Drinking & Nightlife

The waterfront Schlachte promenade has a respectably long line of bars catering to all tastes. For a slightly alternative feel or a student vibe, head to Das Viertel's main Ostertorsteinweg ('O-Weg'). Auf den Höfen, north of O-Weg, also has a good selection of bars. Check listings mags, such as *Mix*, *Bremen4U* or *NordBuzz*, for more details.

★ Wohnzimmer
BAR

(www.wohnzimmer-bremen.de; Ostertorsteinweg 99; ☺ noon-2am Mon-Thu, to 4am Fri & Sat, to 1am Sun; ☐ 2, 6 to Wulwesstrasse) This bar and lounge mostly gets a relaxed 20s and early-30s crowd, who hang out on the sofas – which explains the name 'Living Room' – or lounge around on the mezzanine levels.

Lagerhaus
BAR

(☑ 0421-701 0000; www.kulturzentrum-lagerhaus. de; Schildstrasse 12/19; ☺ from 6pm; ☐ 2, 6 to Wulwesstrasse) This once-dilapidated warehouse off Ostertorsteinweg was squatted by young revolutionaries in the 1970s and later became a cultural centre. Today it houses a pub with an alternative flavour downstairs and a disco for a 20- to 30-something crowd upstairs. Concerts and performance art are held here, too.

LGBT BREMEN

Bremen's gay and lesbian scene is, like the city itself, small and friendly. A handful of bars and clubs in An der Weide (east of the Hauptbahnhof) and its extension Ausser der Schleifmühle make up the main quarter for guys. The gay and lesbian centre also has a small cafe with weekly parties; find out more at www.ratundtat-bremen.de.

Cafe Kweer (☑ 0421-700 008; www.ratundtat-bremen.de; Theodor-Körner-Strasse 1, Rat & Tat Zentrum; ☺ 8pm-midnight Fri, 3-6pm Sun) Part of the local information centre for gay men and lesbians, this place turns into a dance club on Fridays featuring everything from 1920s sounds to urban lounge. On Sundays it's a place for coffee, cake and a chat, and whenever Werder Bremen plays it shows matches. There are also special events, so check the website.

Queens (☑ 0421-325 912; www.queens-bremen.de; Ausser der Schleifmühle 10; ☺ 8pm-late Sun-Thu, to 7am Fri & Sat) One of Bremen's longest-running gay bars has a cool '70s atmosphere and appeals to a mainstream crowd.

LOCAL KNOWLEDGE

HARBOUR COFFEE

A pocket-sized shop with a black-and-white nautical theme, **Harbour** (www.harbourcoffee.de; Auf den Häfen 4; ☉8.30am-5pm Mon-Fri, 10am-4pm Sat & Sun) knows its coffee. Grab a delicious cinnamon roll to go with your cappuccino or flat white.

Feldmann's Bierhaus   PUB

(☑0421-168 9212; www.feldmanns-bierhaus. de; Schlachte 19-20; ☉11am-11pm Sun-Thu, to 12.30am Fri, to 2am Sat) A slightly older crowd can be found chatting and lingering over the wide range of Haake-Beck beers in this modern *Bierhaus* on the Schlachte bar-and-restaurant drag, with tables and benches set up to take advantage of views over the Weser. There's also a food menu (dishes €5 to €17).

Modernes   CLUB

(www.modernes.de; Neustadtwall 28; ☉Tue-Sat; ☑1, 8 to Hochschule Bremen) South of the river in Neustadt, this club converted from an old movie theatre also hosts live-music concerts and remains Bremen's best dance club, bar none. The centrepiece is the domed roof that can be opened to let in some much-needed air towards the end of the evening.

NFF Club   CLUB

(www.nffclub.de; Katharinenstrasse 12-14; ☉from 11pm Fri & Sat) With a futuristic-looking bar, a chic dance floor and lots of cocktails, Nur Für Freunde (Just for Friends) is the place for house, dance and electro. It's also where famous German and international DJs come to spin tunes.

Teestübchen in Schnoor   TEAHOUSE

(www.teestuebchen-schnoor.de; Wüstestätte 1; ☉10am-5.30pm Sun-Thu, to 10pm Fri & Sat) Set in a medieval building in the Schnoor district, this teahouse serves its numerous varieties – black, green, chai, rooibos, sencha, Darjeeling, you name it – on blue-and-white china in a quaint setting with bright white walls set off by a half-timbered ceiling. On nice days you can sit outside in the courtyard.

Cafe Sand   CAFE

(☑0421-556 011; www.cafe-sand.de; Strandweg 106; ☉from noon Mon-Sat, from 10am Sun, closing hours vary) This beach cafe on an island in the Weser River feels light years away from the city. It's favoured by everyone from swimmers and families to fans of the Werder Bremen football club. Get here on foot (1.5km) via the Wilhelm-Kaisen-Brücke (bridge) or by quick ferry from the Osterdeich directly across the water (return €2.30, free with ErlebnisCARD).

☆ Entertainment

★ Lila Eule   LIVE MUSIC

(www.lilaeule.de; Bernhardstrasse 10; ☉from 8pm; ☑2, 6 to Wulwesstrasse) A decade or more is a long time to be a hot tip, but this Das Viertel gem has pulled it off. A student crowd gathers here for parties and events, but it's also a very alternative place to watch the Werder Bremen football team; most Werder matches are shown here. Thursday night is the legendary student bash.

Die Glocke   CONCERT VENUE

(☑0421-33 66 99; www.glocke.de; Domsheide) Bremen's concert hall stages classical concerts, opera and a large variety of special events, many by visiting performers, in a venue whose acoustics are considered to be among Europe's very best.

Theater Bremen   PERFORMING ARTS

(☑tickets 0421-365 3333; www.theaterbremen.de; Goetheplatz 1-3; ☉11am-6pm Mon-Fri, to 2pm Sat) Bremen's main company has several theatres in the one complex: Theater am Goetheplatz, where well-known 1970s film director Rainer Werner Fassbinder honed his craft with the company; the attached Neues Schauspielhaus offering new interpretations of classics and avant-garde drama; and the small and versatile Brauhauskeller (Brewery Cellar) featuring anything from Elvis musicals to Edward Albee.

Schlachthof   LIVE MUSIC

(☑0421-377 750; www.schlachthof-bremen.de; Findorffstrasse 51; ☉bar from 4pm Mon-Sat, from 10am Sun; ☑25 to Theodor-Heus-Allee) Ethnic and world-music concerts, jazz, theatre, cabaret and variety are all complemented here by parties, art exhibitions and a bar.

Weserstadion   SPECTATOR SPORT

(☑0421-43 45 90, ticket hotline 01805-937 337; www.werder.de; Franz-Böhmert-Strasse 1a; ☉ticket centre 9am-6pm Mon-Fri plus match days; ☑3 to Weserstadion or 2, 10 to St-Jürgen-Strasse) The local Bundesliga team Werder Bremen is less a football team than a sporting religion. Worship takes place at the Weserstadion, where a seat costs €35 to €70; call the ticket hotline or get down on your knees outside the stadium and beg. Take the tram to Weserstadion or St-Jürgen-Strasse, then follow the crowds.

Shopping

You'll find plenty of sweets and 'Town Musician (p719)' souvenirs in shops around Marktplatz. Both Böttcherstrasse and Schnoor are full of interesting jewellery, from antique silver to modern designer pieces. Ostertorsteinweg, in Das Viertel, is the place to look for funky streetwear. For more mainstream shops, head north of Marktplatz to the pedestrian shopping strip Sögestrasse and the surrounding area.

Michael Falk Goldschmiede　JEWELLERY
(☑0421-32 35 38; www.goldschmiede-falk.de; Böttcherstrasse 8; ⊙10am-1pm & 1.30-6pm Mon-Fri, 11am-4pm Sat) Watch this gold and silver jewellery being made right in the studio in the window. Choose from necklaces, rings, bracelets and earrings – in interesting geometric and natural patterns, with precious and semi-precious stones – and even a few watches.

Bremer Bonbon Manufaktur　FOOD
(www.bremer-bonbon-manufaktur.de; Böttcherstrasse 8; ⊙11am-6pm Mon-Sat, plus noon-5pm Sun Apr-Dec) Different varieties of fudge, peppermints and a wall of candies in every colour of the rainbow, all made with natural flavours right on site. A small jar makes for a very sweet souvenir, indeed. Located in a small inner courtyard off Bötcherstrasse.

Information

Tourist office branches include **Böttcherstrasse** (☑0421-308 0010; www.bremen-tourism.de; Böttcherstrasse 4; ⊙9.30am-6.30pm Mon-Fri, to 5pm Sat, 10am-4pm Sun; 🛜), a full-service tourist office with friendly staff near Marktplatz, and **Hauptbahnhof** (☑0421-308 0010; www.bremen-tourism.de; Hauptbahnhof; ⊙9am-6.30pm Mon-Fri, 9.30am-5pm Sat & Sun; 🛜), handily located at the main train station. These offices can help book tours and offer free wi-fi.

Bremen's tourism website (www.bremen-tourism.de) has a page devoted to information on barrier-free access around the city, including a list of accessible hotels, restaurants, museums and theatres, with a comprehensive database at www.bremen.de/barrierefrei. You can also borrow a wheelchair free of charge (€50 deposit required) from the **tourist office**.

Krankenhaus St Joseph-Stift Bremen (☑0421-3470; www.sjs-bremen.de; Schwa-

chhauser Heerstrasse 54; ⊙24hr; 🚊1, 4 to St-Joseph-Stift)

Police (☑3621; Am Wall 200)

Post Office (Domsheide 15; ⊙9am-7pm Mon-Fri, 9.30am-1.30pm Sat)

Getting There & Away

AIR

Bremen Airport (BRE; ☑0421-559 50; www.airport-bremen.de) is about 3.5km south of the city centre and well-connected to the city by the line 6 tram (€2.80, 15 minutes). Fly from here to destinations in Germany and Europe. Airline offices here include Lufthansa Airlines (www.lufthansa.com). Low-cost carrier RyanAir (www.ryanair.com) flies to Dublin, Edinburgh and London Stansted.

BUS

Long-distance services depart from and arrive at the **central bus station** (ZOB; Breitenweg) on Breitenweg, in front of Übersee Museum. **FlixBus** (☑030-300 137 300; www.flixbus.com) runs regular service on wi-fi-enabled buses to various European destinations.

CAR & MOTORCYCLE

The A1 (from Hamburg to Osnabrück) and the A27/A7 (Bremerhaven to Hanover) intersect in Bremen. The city is also on the B6 and B75. All major car-rental agencies have branches at the airport; **Sixt** (☑0180-666 6666; www.sixt.de; An der Weide 50a, Bahnhofsplatz) and **Europcar** (☑0421-557 440; www.europcar.com; Breitenweg 32) also have offices near the Hauptbahnhof.

TRAIN

Frequent IC trains go to Hamburg (€30, one hour), Hanover (€31, one hour) and Cologne (€69, three hours). Less frequent IC trains go to Berlin (€93, three hours).

Getting Around

BICYCLE

Radstation (☑0421-169 0100; www.1-2-3rad.de; per day from €13.50, per weekend €22; ⊙8am-7pm Mon-Fri, 9am-2pm Sat & Sun) For bike rental, try the Radstation just outside the Hauptbahnhof (bring your passport).

> ## BREMEN'S ERLEBNISCARD
>
> Get the excellent-value **ErlebnisCARD** (adult and up to two children for one/two/three days €9.50/13/18.50, up to five adults €20.50/26.50/33) for free public transport and discounts on sights. It's available from tourist offices.

PUBLIC TRANSPORT

The city's public transport is operated by Bremer Strassenbahn AG (BSAG; 0421-559 60; www.bsag.de). Main hubs are in front of the **Hauptbahnhof** (p727) and at Domsheide near the Rathaus. A €2.80 single fare (Einzelkarte) covers most of the Bremen city area, while a day pass (Tageskarte) costs €8. You can also buy a four-pack of discounted single fares for €10.20.

TAXI

A taxi from the airport should cost €10 to €15. Call ☑0421-144 33 or 0421-140 14 or try www. bettertaxi.com.

Bremerhaven

☑0471 / POP 114,025

Anyone who has dreamt of running away to sea will love Bremerhaven's waterfront Havenwelten (Harbour Worlds) area, with its old ships, rusty docks and glistening modern buildings pointing to a recent re-imagining of the city's harbour as a place to play and learn.

Founded in 1827 as a North Sea harbour for Bremen, Bremerhaven has long been a conduit that gathered the 'huddled masses' from the verdant but poor countryside and poured them into the world outside. (Today it's the fourth-largest container port in Europe.) Of the millions who landed at New York's Ellis Island, a large proportion sailed from here, and an enticing exhibition at the German Emigration Centre shares their history. Continuing on this global theme, the neighbouring Klimahaus museum takes visitors on a fascinating journey around the world and its changing climes. If you have an inquisitive mind, both museums are reason enough to come to town.

◉ Sights

★ **Deutsches Auswandererhaus**   MUSEUM
(German Emigration Centre; ☑0471-902 200; www.dah-bremerhaven.de; Columbusstrasse 65; adult/child €14.80/8.80; ◷10am-6pm Mar-Oct, to 5pm Nov-Feb) This spectacular museum stands on the spot where more than 7.2 million emigrants set sail for the US, South America and Australia between 1830 and 1942, and does a superb job commemorating some of their stories. The visitor relives stages of their journey through high-quality re-creations, beginning at the wharf where passengers huddle together before boarding the ship, clutching the biographical details

of one particular traveller and heading towards their new life. Everything is available in both German and English.

★ **Klimahaus**
Bremerhaven 8° Ost   MUSEUM
(Climate House; ☑0471-902 0300; www.klima haus-bremerhaven.de; Am Längengrad 8; adult/ concession/family €16/11.50/48; ◷9am-7pm Mon-Fri, from 10am Sat & Sun Apr-Aug, 10am-6pm Sep-Mar) This shiny, space-age museum offers a journey around the world along the longitudinal meridian 8° east, through climate zones in Switzerland, Italy, Niger, Cameroon, Antarctica, Samoa, Alaska and Germany. The educational displays are aimed at kids but are adult-friendly, too. Temperatures soar and plummet accordingly, so along with sensible shoes to scale Swiss mountains and cross African rope bridges, bring a light jacket. Allow yourself at least three hours to get the most from the experience.

Technikmuseum U-Boot
Wilhelm Bauer   SHIP
(☑0471-482 0710; www.u-boot-wilhelm-bauer.de; Hans-Scharoun-Platz 1; adult/child €3.50/2.50; ◷10am-6pm Sep-May, to 7pm Jun-Aug) An innovative diesel-electric submarine built in early 1945 as part of the Nazi war machine, this *Unterseeboot* never saw combat action and was scuttled at the end of the war. It was later raised and recommissioned, but is now a fascinating museum – the only floating Type XXI submarine in existence. You can walk through to understand just how cramped life could be for the 57 men who served on it; English signage explains all the technical details.

Aussichts Platform   VIEWPOINT
(Am Strom 1; adult/child €3/2; ◷9am-8.30pm Apr-Sep, 10am-4.30pm Oct-Mar) Atop the Sail City hotel, this 86m-high two-floor outdoor observation deck affords 360-degree views of Bremerhaven, the Weser, the North Sea and miles around the region. Access is behind and around the corner from the hotel entrance, near the entrance to the Klimahaus building.

Kunstmuseum & Kunsthalle
Bremerhaven   GALLERY
(Art Museum & Art Hall; ☑0471-468 38; www. kunstverein-bremerhaven.de; Karlsburg 1 & 4; Kunstmuseum adult/concession €6/4, Kunsthalle €4/2, combined €8/5, Tue free; ◷11am-6pm Tue-Fri, to 5pm Sat & Sun) The permanent exhibition

of paintings in the Kunstmuseum focuses on Weser artists; changing exhibitions are staged in the adjacent Kunsthalle. Located just a couple of blocks east of the **Schiffahrtsmuseum** (German Maritime Museum; www.dsm.museum; Hans-Scharoun-Platz 1), on the other side of Columbusstrasse.

Schaufenster Fischereihafen HARBOUR

(☑0471-932 330; www.schaufenster-fischereihafen.de; An der Packhalle IV 12; ☑505, 506 to Schaufenster Fischereihafen) Situated a few kilometres south of Bremerhaven's train station, this so-called 'shop window to the fishing harbour' is a former fish-packaging hall that's been converted into a retail precinct filled with fish restaurants, bars and small shops. It's a nice place for a seafood lunch or to pick up some trinkets and souvenirs.

Sleeping

Bremerhaven is easy to do on a short trip – it's not a nightlife capital of Germany, so most people take in the city while based in Bremen. That said, there are quite a few midrange and upscale options on and around the harbour in the city centre.

Havenhostel Bremerhaven HOSTEL €

(☑0471-309 6690; www.havenhostel-bremerhaven.de; Bürgermeister-Smidt-Strasse 209; dm €24, s €45-57, d €69-77; P✆; ☑505, 506 to Rotersand) This smart hostel with 24-hour reception has modern six-bed dorms and private rooms with high ceilings and large windows. Located in a former maritime police barracks, it's a little away from the sights but there's a bus stop on the corner, plus supermarkets nearby. You'll find bars and restaurants just a few blocks south on Bürgermeister-Smidt-Strasse. Breakfast is €7.50.

Liberty HOTEL €€

(☑0471-902 240; www.libertybremerhaven.de; Columbusstrasse 67; s/d from €108/123; P✆) Bremerhaven's newest accommodation option is a harbourside four-star hotel with understated elegance. Rooms have midcentury styling with walnut set off by mustard and grey accents. All come with a minibar and safe. On site is a spa with two saunas and an excellent top-floor cocktail bar (p730) with perfect sunset views. It's right next to the Auswandererhaus museum.

Im Jaich Hotel HOTEL €€

(☑0471-9716 6330; www.im-jaich.de; Am Neuen Hafen 19; s/d €89/111; P✆) Floor-to-ceiling windows give you harbour or river views from every room in this hotel, each of which is supplied with a pair of binoculars, too. Oak floors and wall panelling lend a contemporary-rustic look. It's an easy walking distance to the main sights and right next to the riverside promenade.

× Eating

Unsurprisingly, fresh fish and seafood figure prominently on most menus here. There are a number of casual eateries along the main pedestrian shopping strip, Bürgermeister-Smidt-Strasse, and in the Mediterraneo shopping centre at Alter Hafen. Some finer dining can be found in the hotel restaurants around the harbour.

B – Burger Bar BURGERS €

(☑0471-8099 5696; Theodor-Heuss-Platz 10; burgers €7-15.50; ☺noon-midnight Sun-Thu, to 2am Fri & Sat; ✆) Choose from a dozen towering burgers in different styles at this upmarket-casual place. Menu options range from a classic bacon-cheeseburger to a 'surf & turf' with shrimp and a garlic-herb sauce made in-house from scratch; there are a number of vegetarian and vegan versions, as well. There's a full bar and beers on tap. Cash only.

Restaurant-Schiff Seute Deern SEAFOOD €€

(☑0471-416 264; www.seutedeern.de; Hans-Scharoun-Platz 1; mains €17-24.50; ☺11am-3pm & 6-11pm, kitchen to 9pm) The lower deck of a giant, three-masted barque (sailing ship) built in 1919 has been converted into a floating seafood restaurant with understated elegance. The deep wood tones and blue-cushioned captain's chairs give off a suitably old-fashioned nautical vibe, and the menu offers fish dishes ranging from sea bass on pasta in white-wine sauce to steamed cod or fried dab.

★Natusch SEAFOOD €€€

(☑0471-710 21; www.natusch.de; Am Fischbahnhof 1; mains €20.50-28.50; ☺11.30am-3pm & 5.30-10pm Tue-Sun; ☑505, 506 to Schaufenster Fischereihafen) This wonderful seafood restaurant is spread out over several dining rooms with distinct nautical styling (including one that purports to be a copy of Hollywood star Errol Flynn's yacht) and offers expertly prepared, mouthwatering fish fresh from the boat. Priced accordingly. It's located a few blocks from the main Schaufenster Fischereihafen plaza.

Drinking & Nightlife

New York Bar
COCKTAIL BAR

(Liberty, Columbusstrasse 67; ☺ 5pm-midnight Sun-Thu, to 2am Fri & Sat) This cocktail lounge features midcentury-modern decor, dark-wood panelling and dim lights, as well as a comprehensive cocktail menu. The pièce de résistance is the large harbour-view terrace that lets you see clear across the Weser – perfect for sunset drinks. It's on the 5th floor of the Liberty hotel (p729); ask at the lobby desk for an elevator card for access.

Cafe de Fiets
BAR

(Bürgermeister-Smidt-Strasse 155; ☺ from 7pm Wed-Sat) Decorated with old bike frames ('fiets' is the Dutch word for bicycle), this chill bar is a favoured local hang-out and a cosy place to unwind with a drink, with with amiable bartenders and Guinness, Jever and Czech brew Staropramen on tap. There's live music weekly, too.

 Information

Main Tourist Office (☏ 0471-41 41 41; www.bremerhaven.de/tourism; H-H-Meier-Strasse 6; ☺ 8am-6pm May-Sep, 9.30am-5pm Oct-Apr) Cross from the bridge behind the Auswanderhaus; it's located inside the building just ahead.

Schaufenster Fischereihafen Tourist Office (☏ 0471-41 41 41; www.bremerhaven.de/tourism; Am Schaufenster 6; ☺ 9.30am-6pm Apr-Sep, to 5pm Oct-Mar) Located at the Fischereihafen, near the FMS *Gera* ship.

 Getting There & Around

BUS

The **bus ticket office** (www.bremerhavenbus.de; Friedrich-Ebert-Strasse 73; ☺ 7am-6pm Mon-Fri, 8am-1pm Sat) outside Bremerhaven's train station has free maps of town, as do the tourist offices. Within Bremerhaven, single bus tickets/day passes cost €2.50/7.10. From the train station, buses 502, 506 and 509 stop at Havenwelten, near the Alter Hafen (Old Harbour) and Neuer Hafen (New Harbour). Buses 505 and 506 go to Schaufenster Fischereihafen, in the other direction.

CAR & MOTORCYCLE

Bremerhaven is quickly reached via the A27 from Bremen; get off at the Bremerhaven-Mitte exit.

TRAIN

Frequent trains connect Bremen and Bremerhaven (€12.95, 40 minutes).

Worpswede

☏ 04792 / POP 9285

Worpswede was originally a settlement of peat farmers, but in 1894 an artists colony was established here by a number of architects and painters who would later become associated with Bremen's Böttcherstrasse. Today it's a cute artisans town that provides lovely walking paths between a number of fine art museums and galleries.

The most famous international artist associated with Worpswede was the poet Rainer Maria Rilke, who dedicated several books to this pretty Niedersachsen village. Other major names involved include Paula Modersohn-Becker, whose works can be seen at her museum (p718) in Bremen, and her husband, the painter Otto Modersohn; the future designer of Böttcherstrasse, Bernhard Hoetger; architect and painter Heinrich Vogeler; and painter Fritz Mackensen, who was the first to move here. A visit to Worpswede on a sunny day makes for an excellent day trip from Bremen.

Sights

Haus im Schluh
MUSEUM

(☏ 04792-522; www.vogeler-worpswede.de; Im Schluh 35-37; adult/child €6/free, with Museum Card free; ☺ 2-6pm Mon-Fri, from 10am Sat & Sun Mar-Oct, 11am-5pm Tue-Sun Nov-Feb) This handsome, half-timbered thatched-roof house is where artist Heinrich Vogeler's first wife, Martha, moved with their three daughters after the couple divorced. It's still furnished with paintings by Heinrich and furniture he designed. Another building holds a gallery of more of his works, and a weaving studio with several large looms (you can buy handmade textiles at the museum shop). A third house has five apartments and rooms that can be booked for accommodation (rooms/apartments for three nights from €60/85)

Grosse Kunstschau
MUSEUM

(☏ 04792-4792 1302; www.worpswede-museen.de; Lindenallee 5; adult/child €8/free, with Museum Card free; ☺ 10am-6pm Mar-Oct, 11am-5pm Tue-Sun Nov-Feb) This beautiful brick building designed by Bernhard Hoetger in 1927 houses a permanent exhibition of some of the artists colony's greatest painters, with a giant round skylight that complements the wooden floors. A particular highlight is Heinrich Vogeler's *Sommerabend* (Summer

Evening), which depicts the artists relaxing on a summer's night but hints at the end of the idyll that was to come. There's a regularly changing exhibition of new art, too. The building also houses Kaffee Worpswede.

Barkenhoff MUSEUM
(☑04792-4972 3968; www.worpswede-museen. de/barkenhoff; Ostendorfer Strasse 10; adult/child €7/free, with Museum Card free; ☺10am-6pm Mar-Oct, 11am-5pm Tue-Sun Nov-Feb) The creative heart of the Worpswede artists colony was this half-timbered home remodelled in the art nouveau style by its owner, painter and designer Heinrich Vogeler. Today it houses the **Heinrich-Vogeler-Museum**, with exhibitions of his paintings and murals and even some furniture he designed; there's some English signage throughout. It's about a 10-minute walk from the tourist office via pleasant forest trails.

Niedersachsenstein MONUMENT
A highlight of a visit to Worpswede is the stroll to the 55m-tall Weyerberg dune, less than a kilometre from the centre, where you find the Niedersachsenstein, a contentious sculpture looming like a giant eagle. This is the work of Bernhard Hoetger, the man responsible for much of Bremen's Böttcherstrasse (p718). Follow Lindenallee from the tourist office and then follow the trails off to the right.

🍴 Sleeping & Eating

With Worpswede being such an easy day trip from Bremen, there's little reason to stay overnight, though the tourist office can help with accommodation booking. The Haus im Schluh also has a few rooms and apartments available.

Various cafes can be found up and down Bergstrasse, the main street, with a few others on Hembergstrasse. Most open around noon for lunching day-trippers.

Kaffee Worpswede INTERNATIONAL €€
(☑04792-1028; www.kaffee-worpswede.de; Lindenallee 5; mains €12.50-25.50; ☺11.30am-2.15pm & 6-9.30pm Wed-Sun) Worpswede's top restaurant serves up a seasonal menu of soups, salads, pasta, fish and meat dishes (such as lamb and duck) in a genteel dining room. It's set in the original brick building of the Grosse Kuntschau, which was designed in 1927 by Bernhard Hoetger.

ℹ️ Information

Worpswede Tourist Office (☑04792-935 820; www.worpswede-touristik.de; Bergstrasse 13; ☺10am-5pm Mon-Sat, to 3pm Sun Apr-Oct, 10am-3pm Nov-Mar) Sells the new Museum Card (adult/child €19/free) providing admission to Worpswede's four main museums, as well as a town brochure with map (€1). Can also assist with accommodation bookings.

ℹ️ Getting There & Around

BICYCLE

Fahrradladen Eckhard Eyl (☑04792-2323; www.fahrradladen-worpswede.de; Finddorfstrasse 28; bike rental per day €8) Hire out bikes at this outfit, a 10-minute walk from the tourist office via the path between the bank and the Village Hotel am Weyerberg; turn right at Finddorfstrasse. It's just before and across the street from the ALDI supermarket.

BUS

From the bus platforms outside Bremen's central train station, bus 670 (one way €4.70) makes the 45-minute trip 17 times a day during the week and every two hours on weekends. See www.fahrplaner.de or check the timetable at the departure point (platform G) in Bremen; ask the driver to drop you near the tourist office (stop 'Worpswede Insel').

TRAIN

The vintage **Moor Express** (☑04761-993 116; www.evb-elbe-weser.de; one way adult/child/family €8/4/20) runs between Worpswede and Bremen (and on to Stade) four times each way every Saturday and Sunday from May to October. First and last services from Worpswede to Bremen are 8.04am and 6.01pm. First and last services to Worpswede from Bremen are 9.07am and 7.07pm. The **train station** (www.freunde-worpswedes.de; Bahnhofstrasse) is about 1km north of the **tourist office** on Bahnhofstrasse (follow Strassentor or Bauernreihe north).

Oldenburg

☑0441 / POP 163,830
Being shuffled between Danish and German rule has left the relaxed capital of the Weser-Ems region with a somewhat difficult-to-pin-down identity. Most of its medieval buildings were destroyed in a huge fire in 1676, while others were later refashioned at various stages according to the prevailing architectural style of the time. Today it's principally a business des-

LOWER SAXONY & BREMEN OLDENBURG

THE LIFE & ART OF PAULA MODERSOHN-BECKER

One of Worpswede's most notable artists, Paula Modersohn-Becker (1876–1907) was an early expressionist painter (and the first woman artist to paint a nude self-portrait). Raised in an upper-middle-class Bremen family, Paula Becker began studying art at 16 but two years later defied her parents and moved to Worpswede when a lucky inheritance came her way. There she met respected painter Otto Modersohn, 11 years older and married. She later moved to Paris to study at the Académie Colarossi, one of the few art schools to accept female students. In 1900 Modersohn's wife died after a long illness, and the next year Paula married Otto and returned to Worpswede, becoming stepmother to his two-year-old daughter and continuing to paint.

Eschewing classical subjects, Modersohn-Becker depicted women of all ages in frank, everyday poses – often nude, or at tasks like breast-feeding or tending livestock – using bold, rough strokes, with simple forms and deep colours. Strong-willed and ambitious – and frustrated with society's constrictions on women – she was determined to be a painter, and over the next several years made more trips back to Paris, leaving Otto to settle there again in 1906. That year, working with a ferocity unmatched by most artists, she completed 80 canvases, an average of one every 4½ days.

In 1907 she reconciled with Otto and moved back to Worpswede, pregnant with their first child. In November she gave birth to a daughter, but died just 18 days later of an embolism when she stood up after her enforced bed-rest was over; her last words were 'Wie schade!' ('What a pity!'). Only 31 at her death, she left an exceptionally large body of work – over 700 pieces, many of which can be seen at galleries around Worpswede and at the Paula Modersohn-Becker Haus Museum (p718) in Bremen, the world's first museum devoted to the works of a woman artist. Though unrecognised in her lifetime (she sold only three paintings), today she's considered an important pioneer of German art. We'll never know how much more she could have contributed to the art world had she lived longer – wie schade indeed.

tination, but it makes a good day trip from Bremen or stopover on the way to the East Frisian Islands, with an attractive pedestrianised, canal-fringed Altstadt (old town) and a few interesting museums.

◉ Sights

Augusteum MUSEUM
(☑ 0441-220 7300; www.landesmuseum-ol.de; Elisabethstrasse 1; combined ticket adult/child €6/1.50; ⊘ 10am-6pm Tue-Sun) The Augusteum showcases European paintings – with a strong focus on Italian and Dutch masters – from the 15th to the 18th century. It opened in 1867 in a custom-designed Italian Renaissance building as Oldenburg's first art gallery to show off Grand Duke Nikolaus Friedrich Peter's collection. There's English signage throughout. The gallery also features changing exhibitions. It's part of the Museum of Art & Cultural History, all three buildings of which can be visited on a combined Landesmuseum ticket.

Prinzenpalais MUSEUM
(☑ 0441-220 7300; www.landesmuseum-ol.de; Damm 1; combined ticket adult/child €6/1.50; ⊘ 10am-6pm Tue-Sun) This branch of Oldenburg's Museum of Art & Cultural History focuses on German artists, beginning with romanticism and neoclassicism of the mid-19th century and culminating in post-1945 artworks. Included in the collection are a number of works by artists from the Worpswede (p730) colony, such as Paula Modersohn-Becker, Otto Modersohn, Fritz Mackensen and Heinreich Vogeler.

Landesmuseum für Kunst und Kulturgeschichte MUSEUM
(Museum of Art & Cultural History; ☑ 0441-220 7300; www.landesmuseum-ol.de; Schlossplatz 1; combined ticket adult/child €6/1.50; ⊘ 10am-6pm Tue-Sun) This museum chronicles the area's history from the Middle Ages to modern times with an entertaining hodgepodge of artefacts: a grand carriage, a penny-farthing bicycle, royal and military clothing, antique furniture, medieval documents and more. Ducal rooms of state have been retained with regal decor. On the 1st floor you'll find the Idyllenzimmer, with 44 paintings by court artist Heinrich Wilhelm Tischbein. It's housed inside the pale-yellow Renais-

sance-Baroque Schloss (1607) at the southern end of the Altstadt shopping district.

Sleeping & Eating

Oldenburg can be done as a day trip from Bremen, but if you want to stay overnight there are several options north of the Altstadt. The tourist office website can help with accommodation booking.

Eating options are dotted around the Altstadt, including a number of them right around the central Rathausmarkt. Slightly north of there is a nice little strip along Mottenstrasse and a few choices on pedestrianised Wallstrasse.

Der Schwan PUB FOOD €€
(☑0441-261 89; www.schwan-oldenburg.de; Stau 34; mains €8-23; ⊙9am-midnight Sun-Thu, to 1am Fri & Sat) A decent all-rounder, the Swan has a great spot on the water where you can drink and dine in the sunshine (weather permitting). Things get livelier in the evenings.

ⓘ Information

Tourist Office (☑0441-3616 1366; www. oldenburg-tourist.de; Schlossplatz 16; ⊙9.30am-6pm Mon-Fri, 10am-4pm Sat) Has maps and accommodation guides that are also available from the DB Service Point inside the train station.

ⓘ Getting There & Around

BICYCLE

Fahrrad Station Oldenburg Süd (☑0441-218 8250; www.fzol.de; Bahnhofplatz 14; bike rental per day from €10, per 4/5 days from €30/40; ⊙6.30am-8pm Mon-Sat) Rents out bikes for one day or multiple days. Located in front of the Hauptbahnhof on the south (Stadtmitte) side. Security deposit costs €50; a passport is required for ID.

BUS

Many buses, including bus 315, run to the Landesmuseum on Schlossplatz from Hauptbahnhof. Bus 315 to Am Festungsgraben is the best one for Augusteum and Prinzenpalais; take bus 315, 270 or 280 to Staatsarchive for the Landesmuseum Natur und Mensch. Single bus tickets (valid for 90 minutes) for the entire city cost €2.45 and day passes €7.

CAR & MOTORCYLE

Oldenburg is 50km from Bremen, at the crossroads of the A29 to/from Wilhelmshaven and the A28 (from Bremen to Leer, near the Dutch border).

TRAIN

There are trains at least once an hour to Bremen (€8.85, 35 minutes), Emden (€21.50, one hour) and beyond.

Emden

☑04921 / POP 50,694

You're almost in the Netherlands here, and it shows, from the flat landscape, dykes and windmills outside Emden to the lackadaisical manner in which locals pedal their bikes across the town's canal bridges. The Dutch, as well as Germans, have shaped Emden, and the local Plattdütsch dialect sounds like a combination of both languages.

While in most senses Emden stoically defies the adjective 'spectacular', the Kunsthalle and Ostfriesisches Landesmuseum (both closed Mondays) and the pretty coastal landscape of its environs – especially enjoyable via a cruise or kayaking tour of the canals – do make it a worthwhile stop in East Frisia.

ⓞ Sights

★**Kunsthalle** GALLERY
(☑04921-975 050; www.kunsthalle-emden. de; Hinter dem Rahmen 13; adult/child €9/free; ⊙10am-5pm Tue-Fri, from 11am Sat & Sun) Emden's art gallery shows off a range of big, bold canvases, focusing on 20th-century art, in its light-flooded, white-and-exposed-timber rooms. Every few months it closes for about a week as its exhibitions are completely changed; some shows rotate in from its collection while others cover topics such as American realism or the works of Paul Klee. You can purchase a combination ticket with the Ostfriesisches Landesmuseum for €14 to save some money.

Ostfriesisches Landesmuseum MUSEUM
(Regional History Museum; ☑04921-872 058; www. landesmuseum-emden.de; Brückstrasse 1, Rathaus; adult/child €8/free; ⊙10am-5pm Tue-Sun) This award-winning museum has an interesting and varied collection illustrating themes of local history and life in the region. Not surprisingly, its picture gallery has a strong focus on Dutch artists, as well as the works of Emden-born painter Ludolf Backhuysen. There's also a section on a centuries-old body and its clothing that was found preserved in an East Frisian bog. There's some English signage throughout.

🏃 Activities

The tourist offices have information on canal and harbour tours – or try the ticket office for EMS – and canoe/kayak hire, and can give tips on cycling, a favourite East Frisian pastime.

Paddel-und-Pedalstation
Emden   KAYAKING, CYCLING
(📞 0160-369 2739, 04921-890 7219; www.paddel undpedal.de; Marienwehrster Zwinger 13; bicycle/kayak/canoe rental from €7/15/36; ⏰ 8am-5pm Mon-Fri, 9am-6pm Sat & Sun mid-Apr–mid-Oct) Rent out kayaks or canoes and tour Emden via the city's canals. There are numerous 'Paddle & Pedal' stations – on a combination trip (€22) you can paddle to one, then ride back on a bicycle. You can also rent out stand-up paddle (SUP) boards (€10 per hour).

EMS   CRUISE
(📞 04921-890 70; www.ag-ems.de; harbour cruises adult/child €8/3.50; ⏰ ticket office 11.30am-4pm Mon-Sun) One-hour harbour cruises are offered five times daily between early April and late October, leaving from the northern end of the Ratsdelft harbour (near the EMS ticket kiosk). Also offers canal cruises (adult/child €11/5.50, 1¾ hours) at noon five days a week, and runs services to the East Frisian Island of Borkum and North Frisian Island of Helgoland.

🛏 Sleeping & Eating

Accommodation options here are not abundant, so it pays to use the walk-in and advance room-booking service at the well-run tourist office at the train station.

DJH Hostel   HOSTEL €
(📞 04921-237 97; www.jugendherberge.de/jh/emden; Thorner Strasse 3; dm from €25; ⏰ closed Nov-Feb; 🅿️ @ 🛜) This hostel has a canal-side location and offers bicycle and canoe rental. If you're not a member of HI or DJH there's a nightly surcharge, and over-27s pay higher rates. Dorm rooms have shared or en suite bathrooms; single and double rooms have bunk beds. Linen and breakfast included; half- and full-board rates available.

Hotel am Boltentor   HOTEL €€
(📞 04921-972 70; www.hotel-am-boltentor.de; Hinter dem Rahmen 10; s/d/tr €80/110/155; 🅿️) Hidden by trees from the main road nearby and next door to the Kunsthalle, this homey red-brick hotel has the quietest location in town, plus comfy and well-equipped rooms.

Hafenhaus   SEAFOOD €€
(📞 04921-689 5690; www.hafenhaus.com; Promenade Am Alten Binnenhafen 8; mains €10-28) This fancy, modern seafood restaurant has a wonderful outdoor deck and pontoon in the warmer months. Besides fish and shrimp, the menu features burgers, steaks and pork and chicken dishes. It's set right on the promenade south of the main square,

🍷 Drinking

Emden is not really the kind of place for an outrageous night, but Cafe Einstein (www.einstein-emden.de; Bollwerkstrasse 24; ⏰ 11am-2am Mon-Thu, to 3am Fri & Sat, 2-10pm Sun; 🛜) gets lively in the evenings. You'll also find a few bars along and around Neuer Markt.

ℹ Information

Emden's main tourist office (📞 04921-974 00; www.emden-touristik.de; Bahnhofsplatz 11; ⏰ 9am-5pm Mon-Fri, 10am-1pm Sat) is in the train station. There's another branch (📞 04921-974 00; www.emden-touristik.de; Alter Markt 2a; ⏰ 9am-6pm Mon-Fri, 10am-2pm Sat) on the main square.

ℹ Getting There & Around

Emden is connected by rail to Oldenburg (€21.50, 70 minutes) and Bremen (€27, 1¾ hours). Despite its relative remoteness, the town is easily and quickly reached via the A31, which connects with the A28 from Oldenburg and Bremen. The B70/B210 runs north from Emden to other towns in Friesland and to the coast.

Emden is small enough to be navigated on foot but also has a bus system (€1.60 per trip). The best transport method is bicycle, which you can rent at the Paddel-und-Pedalstation.

Jever
📞 04461 / POP 14,020

With its Russian-looking castle set in picturesque grounds and an interesting brewery tour, Jever is worth a brief visit, if only en route to the East Frisian Islands.

Famous for its eponymous pilsner beer, the capital of the Friesland region is also known for 'Fräulein Maria', who peers out from attractions and shop windows in Jever and is memorialised in a statue just outside the Schloss.

Maria was the last of the so-called *Häuptlinge* (chieftains) to rule the town in the Middle Ages, and Jever flourished during her nearly five decades in power. She never married and died without an heir, leaving Jever to her cousin, Count Johann VII of Oldenburg. Through the intricate royal family trees of Europe, official control passed 200 years later to Catherine the Great of Russia, where it stayed until Napoleon's armies occupied Jever in 1807.

◉ Sights

Schloss Museum Jever PALACE

(☑04461-969 350; www.schlossmuseum.de; Schlossplatz 1; adult/child €6/free, incl tower climb €7.50/4; ⊙10am-6pm Tue-Sun, plus Mon mid-May–mid-Oct) An onion-shaped dome is (literally) the crowning feature of Jever's 14th-century Schloss (palace). The town's 18th-century Russian rulers added it to the palace that was built by Fräulein Maria's grandfather, chieftain Edo Wiemken the Elder. Today it houses the Kulturhistorische Museum des Jeverlandes, with objects chronicling the daily life and craft of the Frieslanders, and a series of re-created period rooms. The pièce de résistance is the magnificent audience hall from 1560, with an intricately carved, coffered oak ceiling and leather wallpaper.

Stadtkirche CHURCH

(www.kirche-jever.de; Am Kirchplatz 13; ⊙10.30am-6pm summer, to 5pm winter) Many of Jever's sights are in some way connected to Fräulein Maria, the last of Jever's chieftains. The most spectacular is the lavish memorial tomb of her father, Edo Wiemken (1468-1511), found in the central Stadtkirche. The tomb is another opus by Cornelis Floris and miraculously survived eight fires. The church itself succumbed to the flames and was rebuilt in a rather modern way in the 1960s; the main nave is opposite the tomb, which is now behind glass.

☞ Tours

Friesisches Brauhaus zu Jever BREWERY

(☑04461-137 11; www.jever.de; Elisabethufer 18; tours adult/child €9.50/3.50; ⊙11am-4pm Mon-Fri, to noon Sat) This regional brewery has been producing beer since 1848. Two-hour weekday tours allow you a peek behind the scenes, travelling through the brewery's production and bottling facilities and a small museum (1½-hour Saturday tours only include the museum). Visitors over 16 get to taste the wares as well. Reservations are essential and can be made online.

🛏 Sleeping

DJH Hostel HOSTEL €

(☑04461-909 202; http://jever.jugendherberge.de; Dr-Fritz-Blume-Weg 4; r from €30.50; ⊙closed Dec–mid-Jan; P@🖘) Jever's cute *Jugendherberge* (youth hostel) is like a little village, with green-and-red-brick bungalows grouped around the reception, about 1km from the Altstadt. Two-, four- or six-bed rooms are clean, modern and comfortable, with en suites. Room prices are per person; singles pay €10 more per night, or doubles €5 per person. Half- and full-board plans available.

Stadt Hotel Jever BOUTIQUE HOTEL €€

(☑04461-917 7923; www.stadthotel-jever.de; Schlachte 3; s/d from €59/94; P🖘) Located on the edge of the Altstadt, Stadt Hotel Jever offers smart, modern rooms with spacious bathrooms and comfortable furnishings. For a few euros more, 'Comfort' rooms are a bit larger and snazzier than the 'Classic' rooms, and come with a pod coffee maker. An excellent breakfast buffet is served in the very popular restaurant downstairs.

Am Elisabethufer HOTEL €€

(☑04461-949 640; www.jever-hotel-pension.de; Elisabethufer 9a; s/d from €56/88; P@🖘) Frilly lampshades, floral duvet covers and an assortment of knick-knacks are par for the course in Jever's *Pensionen,* and exactly what you'll find in this attractive and comfortable place with free wi-fi and renovated bathrooms. New owners bought it in early 2018 and redecoration works are planned. From the tourist office, it's a short walk north along Von-Thünen-Ufer.

🍴 Eating & Drinking

An Der Schlachte GERMAN €€

(☑04461-917 7923; www.stadthotel-jever.de; Stadt Hotel Jever, Schlachte 3; mains €14-23; ⊙7am-11pm, kitchen to 9.30pm Apr-Oct, to 9pm Nov-Mar; 🍴) This popular restaurant with friendly service specialises in local fish and seafood – North Sea crab, perch, plaice and salmon, to name a few – but also has modern takes on classic German recipes for chicken, pork and beef. There's a small menu section for vegetarians, as well (which the cooks will make vegan on request).

Haus der Getreuen GERMAN €€

(☑04461-748 5949; www.hausdergetreuen.de; Schlachtstrasse 1; mains €11-24; ⊙11am-11pm Tue-Sun, kitchen noon-2pm & 5.30-9pm Tue-Thu & Sun, noon-2pm & 5.30-9.30pm Fri & Sat) Set in an historic building with a pleasant atmosphere, Haus der Getreuen is well known for its tasty regional dishes, especially fish. In warm weather there's outdoor seating in the *Biergarten*.

★ **Altstadtbrauerei**
Marienbräu MICROBREWERY
(☑04461-744 990; www.marienbraeu.com; Apothekerstrasse 1; ⊘5.30-10pm) Brick dividing walls and a blue-and-white-tiled fireplace give this microbrew-pub, named for beloved ruler Fraülein Maria, a homey feel. For an alternative to the ever-present Jever pilsener, try one of the four main Marienbräu beers or the seasonal special, all made with fresh regional ingredients and no preservatives. Can't decide? Get a flight of all five.

🛍 Shopping

Blaudruckerei TEXTILES
(☑04461-713 88; www.blaudruckerei.de; Kattrepel 3; ⊘11am-5pm Mon-Fri, 10am-2pm Sat) Craftspeople in East Frisia have been using indigo dye to make patterned white-and-blue batik cloth for centuries; this little workshop on a back lane continues the tradition with cloth hand-dyed on the premises, which you can buy made into lavender sachets, scarves, shirts, ties, handkerchiefs, pillowcases and more. Every Wednesday at 3pm there's a 45-minute demonstration (€4).

❶ Information

Tourist Office (☑04461-710 10; www.stadt-jever.de; Alter Markt 18; ⊘9am-5pm Mon-Fri, plus 10am-1pm Sat mid-May–mid-Sep) Located near the Schloss.

❶ Getting There & Around

The train trip to Jever from Bremen (€22, 1¾ to two hours) involves at least one change, in Sande, and sometimes one in Oldenburg too. By road, take the exit to the B210 from the A29 (direction: Wilhelmshaven).

Jever's compact, mainly pedestrian Altstadt (old town) is small enough to explore on foot.

East Frisian Islands

Lined up in an archipelago off the northern coast of Lower Saxony like diamonds in a tiara, the seven East Frisian Islands, with their long sandy beaches, open spaces and sea air, are both a nature-lovers' paradise and a perfect retreat for those escaping the stresses of the world.

Trying to remember the islands' sequence, Germans – with a wink of the eye – recite the following mnemonic device: 'Welcher Seemann liegt bei Nanni im Bett?' (which translates rather saucily as 'Which seaman is lying in bed with Nanni?'). The islands are (from east to west): Wangerooge, Spiekeroog, Langeoog, Baltrum, Norderney, Juist and Borkum.

Like their North Frisian cousins Sylt, Amrum and Föhr, the East Frisian Islands are part of the Wattenmeer (Wadden Sea) National Park. Along with coastal areas of the Netherlands, Germany's Wadden Sea is a Unesco World Heritage Site.

🛌 Sleeping & Eating

These islands are all popular resort destinations, so there's a lot of accommodation available, especially in the form of holiday apartments. If you want to go in high season (April through September, but especially July and August), make sure you book in advance. Many of the islands' tourism websites let you book directly online.

As resort destinations, the islands have plenty of beachside dining and ice-cream shops. Many hotels have their own restaurant; other options are usually found in each island's town centre. Many eateries serve right-off-the-boat fish and seafood in German or Italian dishes, though you'll also find regional East Frisian specialities. Kitchens often close earlier (around 9pm) than on the mainland.

❶ Information

Be aware that the opening hours of tourist offices in coastal towns change frequently and without notice. Call ahead if possible but note that you might not always be able to reach an English speaker and not all relevant websites have English pages.

❶ Getting There & Away

Most ferries sail according to tide times, rather than on a regular schedule, so it's best to call the local ferry operator or visit the Deutsche Bahn website (www.bahn.de/nordseeinseln) for information on departure times on a certain day. Tickets are generally offered either as returns – sometimes valid for up to two months – or cheaper same-day returns.

In most cases (apart from Borkum, Norderney and Juist), you will need to change from the train to a bus at some point to reach the harbour from where the ferry leaves. Sometimes these are shuttle buses operated by the ferry company, or scheduled services from Weser-Ems Bus (📞 0421-308 970; www.weser-ems-bus.de). For planning bus connections from Norden and Esens to ferry harbours, the tourist office in Emden has useful transport information.

Light aircraft also fly to every island except Spiekeroog and Wangerooge, leaving from Norddeich and Harle, and between the islands themselves. Contact **Luftverkehr Friesland Harle** (📞 in Harle 04464-948 10, in Norddeich 04931-933 20; www.inselflieger.de).

ℹ️ Getting Around

Only Borkum and Norderney allow cars, so heading elsewhere means you'll need to leave your vehicle in a car park near the ferry pier, which usually costs about €5 per day.

Wangerooge

📞 04469 / POP 1304

Car-free Wangerooge, the second-smallest of the East Frisian Islands (after Baltrum) is the easternmost of the group, lying about 7km off the coast in the region north of Jever. Its laid-back attitude can be summed up by the sign that greets you at the harbour: *Gott schuf die Zeit, von Eile hat er nichts gesagt* ('God created time; he said nothing about haste').

◉ Sights

Lighthouse LIGHTHOUSE
(www.leuchtturm-wangerooge.de; Zedeliusstrasse 3; adult/child €3/1.5; ⏰10am-1pm & 2-5pm Mon-Thu, 2-5pm Fri, 10am-noon Sat, 10am-noon & 2-5pm Sun May-Oct) If you're feeling active, you can climb the 161 steps of Wangerooge's 39m-tall lighthouse, which dates from 1855. A small

museum on site tells the history of the island through various artefacts.

Nationalparkhaus INFORMATION
(www.nationalparkhaus-wattenmeer.de/national-park-haus-wangerooge; Friedrich-August-Strasse 18; ⏰9am-1pm & 2-6pm Tue-Fri, 10am-noon & 2-5pm Sat & Sun mid-Mar–Oct, 10am-1pm & 3-5pm Tue-Fri, 2-5pm Sat & Sun Nov–mid-Mar) **FREE** An aquarium, exhibits and short films at this national parks office explain more about the varieties of plant, bird and sea life that call the Wattenmeer (Wadden Sea) home.

🏃 Activities

Bicycles are a great way to explore flat, car-free Wangerooge; bike rental is available from several places in town. The island's excellent winds make surfing, windsurfing and kitesurfing popular activities here. From May to September you can rent gear and organise lessons from Surfschule Wangerooge (www.windsurfing-wangerooge.de).

ℹ️ Information

Bahnhof Tourist Office (📞 04469-948 80; www.wangerooge.de; Bahnhofstrasse 6; ⏰8am-noon & 1-4pm Mon-Fri Easter-Oct, 9am-noon Mon-Fri rest of year) This tourist office at the train station can help you book lodgings. It's also open before and after each scheduled ferry service.

ℹ️ Getting There & Away

The **DB** (📞 in Harlesiel 04464-949 411, on Wangerooge 04469-947 411; www.siw-wangerooge.de) ferry to Wangerooge leaves from Harlesiel two to six times daily (1½ hours), depending on the tides.

 LOWER SAXONY & BREMEN EAST FRISIAN ISLANDS

OFF THE BEATEN TRACK

SLOW TRAVEL IN EAST FRISIA

One of the pleasures of travelling around East Frisia is that – intentionally or not – you can really slow down and enjoy the ride. A good way of taking advantage of the bike paths and waterways is by using the so-called Paddel-und-Pedalstations (www.paddel-und-pedal.de). These allow you to combine kayaking or canoeing with cycling, using some of the 21 stations scattered around the countryside. You can paddle to one, hire another kayak there, or switch to bicycle, then choose your next destination/station and set off again.

One option is a combination paddle/pedal trip (€22; advance booking required): from Emden (p734) you can hire a kayak, paddle about 11km (three hours) to the shallow quarry lake Grosses Meer (📞 04942-576 838; www.paddelundpedal.de; Langer Weg 25, Südbrookmerland), parts of which are a nature reserve, then change to a bicycle and ride back. Local tourist offices can help with planning.

To reach Harlesiel, take bus 211 from Jever train/bus station (adult/child €3.50/2.10, 40 minutes).

Spiekeroog

🕿 04976 / POP 768

It's the tranquillity of this rustic island that draws people – rolling dunes dominate the landscape of little Spiekeroog, with about two-thirds of its 18.25 sq km taken up by these sandy hills. Near the western end is the island's eponymous village. There are also plenty of places for swimming, but if you're looking to just hit the beach, another island might be a better bet: all that sand and all those dunes mean it can be a fair hike before you reach the water's edge – though you do have a 15km stretch of soft white sand to roam.

Spiekeroog is not only car-free but discourages bicycles, too.

◉ Sights & Activities

Inselmuseum MUSEUM

(www.inselmuseum-spiekeroog.de; Noorderloog 1; adult/child €2/1; ⊙ 3-5.30pm Tue-Sun Apr-Oct) A volunteer-run museum exhibiting all manner of things associated with the history of the island, from stuffed wildlife found on and around it to 19th-century clothing and objects, including a spinning wheel, old-fashioned skates, sextants, a butter churn and photographs of the village and its people. A huge colour-coordinated poster shows the interconnected family trees of Spiekeroog's inhabitants from 1700 to 1910. If you're waiting for the ferry back, it's a good way to kill some time.

Islandhof Spiekeroog HORSE RIDING

(🕿 04976-219; www.islandhof-spiekeroog.de; Up De Höcht 5; trail rides €22-35) In the saddle is a great way to explore the island. Beginner rides are offered at 2pm and 4pm on Tuesday and Thursday, and at 9am on Wednesday and Friday for those with previous riding experience. There's also an evening ride that's for adults and includes a wine-and-cheese break on the beach, every Tuesday at 6pm.

☞ Tours

Pferdebahn RAIL

(www.inselmuseum-spiekeroog.de; return adult/child €6/4; ⊙ hourly 1-4pm mid-Apr–mid-Oct, from noon Jun-Aug) The must-do activity on the island is to ride that horse-drawn train that runs on rails and dates back to 1885. The 15-minute ride takes you 1.1km to the western end of the island; the return trip departs after a 15-minute break.

🍴 Sleeping & Eating

Hotel Inselfriede HOTEL €€€

(🕿 04976-919 20; www.inselfriede.de; Süderloog 12; s €80-120, d €125-190; 🛜 ⊛) One of the nicest hotels on Spiekeroog, with sizable, comfortable double rooms that come with a small couch. There's a full restaurant onsite, and a spa with indoor swimming pool and sauna.

Capitäns Haus TAPAS, SEAFOOD €€

(🕿 04976-990 016; www.capitaenshaus-spiekeroog.de; Noorderloog 11; tapas €6.80-9.50, mains €13.50-25; ⊙ 11.30am-10pm, tapas to 5pm, kitchen to 9pm) This stylish restaurant is an excellent choice for seafood tapas and fresh grilled fish, such as perch, Norwegian salmon or sea bass.

GivtBude ITALIAN €€

(🕿 04976-959 8875; www.givtbude-spiekeroog.de; Noorderloog 3; pizzas €7.50-14.50, pastas €8-16.50; ⊙ noon-10pm, kitchen to 9pm) This small Italian restaurant turns out tasty pizzas and pastas, with modern twists such as pizza with scampi, spinach and cherry tomatoes or penne with organic beef strips and grilled vegetables. There's a little front terrace with outdoor seating. If you'd like to have dinner there, it's a good idea to pop in beforehand and make a booking.

🍷 Drinking & Nightlife

Cafe Teetied TEAHOUSE

(🕿 04976-1593; www.teetied-spiekeroog.de; Süderloog 1; ⊙ 10am-10pm) Snug little rooms with low, half-beamed ceilings, and a small tree-shaded patio out front. The menu has a variety of teas, coffees and other beverages – hot chocolate with whipped cream, *Glühwein* (mulled wine) – and a case full of cakes made in-house to enjoy them with. It's the first cafe you'll see after walking up from the harbour. Cash only.

Sir George's Pub PUB

(🕿 04976-919 2500; www.inselfriede.de/genuss/sir-georges-pub; Südermenss 1; ⊙ 6pm-midnight Mon-Fri, from 3.15pm Sat & Sun) Spiekeroog's version of an Irish pub has a cosy Victorian-era feel, with dark-wood trim, leather armchairs, shiny brass beer taps and a crackling fireplace in winter. There's a range of single-malt

Scotch whiskies and Guinness and Kilkenny on tap.

❶ Information

Spiekeroog Tourist Office (🖰 04976-919 3101; www.spiekeroog.de; Haus Kogge, Noorderpad 18; ⊗9am-12.30pm & 2-5pm Mon-Fri, 9am-12.30pm Sat & Sun; 🕾) The friendly folk in 'Haus Kogge' will let you know what's open on Spiekeroog in terms of food, lodging and activities.

❶ Getting There & Away

From the ferry departure point in Neuharlingersiel, it takes about 45 minutes to reach Spiekeroog. The **ferry** (🖰 in Neuharlingersiel 04976-919 3145, in Spiekeroog 04976-919 3133; www.spiekeroog.de) runs two to five times per day, depending on the season, and departures depend on the tides, so same-day returns aren't always possible. Find the latest schedules on www.spiekeroog.de.

From Jever, catch a train to Esens and change to a bus to Neuharlingersiel (€11.30, 50 minutes). From Emden, take a train to Norden and change there for a bus to Neuharlingersiel (€21.90, 1¾ hours). Check connections on www.bahn.de before setting out.

Langeoog

🖰 04972 / POP 1790

Floods and pirates feature prominently in the story of Langeoog, whose population was reduced to a grand total of two following a horrendous storm in 1721. By 1830 it had recovered sufficiently to become a resort town.

The island boasts the highest elevation in East Frisia – the 20m-high Melkhörndüne – and the grave of Lale Anderson, famous for being the first singer to record the WWII song 'Lili Marlene'. On a sunny day, however, the most popular thing to do is to stroll along the 14km-long beach. Langeoog is your best bet if you're looking for a quiet, day-return beach trip.

◉ Sights & Activities

The eastern tip of the island is a seal breeding ground in summer. Check with the tourist office for information on seal-watching trips.

Water Tower   TOWER, VIEWPOINT

(An der Kaapdüne; ⊗10am-noon Mon-Fri Easter-Oct, 10.30am-noon Sat rest of year) FREE The symbol of Langeoog has a ground-floor exhibition on drinking water and an observation deck 33m above sea level upstairs. Entrance is free but donations are appreciated.

Information

Langeoog Tourist Office (🖰 04972-6930; www.langeoog.de; Hauptstrasse 28; ⊗8am-noon & 2-4.30pm Mon-Thu, 8am-noon Fri Nov-Mar, plus 10am-noon Sat & Sun Apr-Oct) You'll find the friendly staff of this welcoming tourist office inside the Rathaus.

❶ Getting There & Away

The nearest mainland port is Bensersiel. From Jever, take the train to Esens and change to a bus for Bensersiel (€10.20, 45 minutes). From Emden, take the train to Norden and change to a bus for Bensersiel (€16.70, 1½ hours). Check connections on www.bahn.de before setting out.

The **Langeoog ferry** (🖰 04971-928 90; www.schiffahrt-langeoog.de) shuttles between Bensersiel and Langeoog around five times daily.

Baltrum

🖰 04939 / POP 610

The smallest inhabited East Frisian Island, delightful Baltrum is just 1km wide and 5km long, and peppered with dunes and salty marshland. It's so tiny that villagers don't bother with street names but make do with house numbers instead. Numbers have been allocated on a chronological basis; houses No 1 to 4 no longer exist so the oldest is now No 5.

As the island closest to the mainland, Baltrum is the most popular destination for Wattwanderungen guided tours (p740).

◉ Sights

Nationalpark Haus-Gezeitenhaus   MUSEUM

(National Park House-Tide House; 🖰 04939-469; www.nationalparkhaus-wattenmeer.de/nationalpark-haus-baltrum; house No 177; ⊗9.30am-1pm & 3-6pm Tue-Fri, 10am-noon & 3-6pm Sat & Sun) FREE If you just can't stand lying on the pristine white sand a moment longer, head here to this little exhibition on wildlife and the Wattenmeer (Wadden Sea).

❶ Information

Baltrum Tourist Office (🖰 04939-800; www.baltrum.de; house No 130; ⊗9am-noon Mon-Fri, from 10am Sat, plus 2-4pm Mon-Fri in summer)

❶ Getting There & Away

The closest mainland port is Nessmersiel. From Emden, you take a train to Norden (€7.10, 45

WALKING TO THE ISLANDS

When the tide recedes on Germany's North Sea coast, it exposes the mudflats connecting the mainland to the East Frisian Islands, and that's when hikers and nature-lovers make their way on foot to islands such as Baltrum and Norderney. This involves wallowing in mud or wading knee-deep in seawater, but it's one of the most popular outdoor activities in this flat, mountainless region. The Wadden Sea in the Netherlands and Germany became a Unesco World Heritage Site in 2009.

Wattwanderungen, as such trekking through the Wadden Sea National Park is called, can be dangerous. The tide follows channels that will cut you off from the mainland unless you have a guide who knows the tide times and routes. Tourist offices in Jever and Emden can provide details of state-approved guides, including **Martin Rieken** (☎04942-204 160, 0175 986 4974; www.wattfuehrung-rieken.de; adult/child €12/8; ☺Mar-Oct) and **Johann Behrends** (☎04944-913 875; www.wattwandern-johann.de; ☺Apr-Oct).

Coastal tours cost from €12 to €23 per person, which doesn't include the cost of taking a ferry back to the mainland. Necessary gear includes shorts or short trousers and possibly socks or trainers that you don't mind getting seriously muddy (although some people prefer going barefoot). In winter, wet-weather footwear and very warm gear is necessary.

---

minutes) and change to a bus to Nessmersiel (€7.50 same-day return, 30 minutes), where you catch the **Baltrum Linie** (☎in Baltrum 04939-913 00, in Nessmersiel 04933-991 606; www.baltrum-linie.de; one way €15.50, day trip €21.50) ferry.

Deutsche Bahn offers a combination ticket for the whole trip covering the train, bus and ferry ride (€29.10 each way, 2½ hours).

Norderney

☎04932 / POP 5935

Considered the 'Queen of the East Frisian Islands', Norderney was Germany's first North Sea resort. Of all the islands, it has the largest town with the best amenities for tourism, including plenty of restaurants.

Founded in 1797 by Friedrich Wilhelm II of Prussia, Norderney became one of the most famous bathing destinations in Europe, after Crown Prince George V of Hanover made it his summer residence, and personalities such as Chancellor Otto von Bismarck and composer Robert Schumann visited in the 19th century. Islanders call it 'Lüttje Welt' ('Little World') for the way fog makes it seem like it's the only place on earth.

⊙ Sights & Activities

Nationalpark-
Haus-Wattenmeer   VISITOR CENTRE
(☎04932-2001; www.nationalparkhaus-norderney.de; Am Hafen 1; adult/child €5/2.50; ☺9am-6pm Mar-Sep, 10am-5pm Oct-Feb) This visitor centre on the harbourfront has an interactive ex-

hibit all about the science and ecology of Unesco World Heritage-listed Wattenmeer (Wadden Sea), as well as the opportunity for guided walks onto the mudflats (check the website during the summer season for dates, times and prices).

★**Bade:haus**   SPA
(☎04932-891 400; www.badehaus-norderney.de; Am Kurplatz 3; per 4hr pool & sauna €28, pool only €20; ☺9.30am-9.30pm, women only from 5.30pm Wed) In the former art nouveau seawater baths, this sleek stone-and-glass complex is now an enormous thalassotherapy centre, with warm and cold swimming pools, a rooftop sauna with views over the island, relaxation areas where you can lie back on loungers and drink Frisian tea, and much more. The 'Wasserebene' (Water Level) holds the pools, the 'Feuerebene' (Fire Level) the saunas.

Happy Surfschule   WATER SPORTS
(☎04932-648; www.surfschule-norderney.de; Am Hafen 17) This top outfit offers a range of courses, rentals and tours for surfing, stand-up paddle-surfing, windsurfing, kitesurfing and kayaking. Activities are run according to the tides, so contact the office or check the website for more information.

⬡ Tours

Reitschule Junkmann   HORSE RIDING
(☎04932-924 10; www.reitschule-junkmann.de; Lippestrasse 23; group rides per person €50, pony rides €12; ☺7.30am-1pm & 3-6pm Mon-Sat)

Ride on horseback along the beach or on the dunes, on guided group rides aimed at both beginner and advanced riders. Advance booking recommended. Children up to 10 years old can go on pony rides (15 to 20 minutes).

🛏 Sleeping & Eating

Haus am Meer HOTEL €€
(☑ 04932-8930; www.hotel-haus-am-meer.de; Damenpfad 35; d from €95) This is a great option if you can get a good rate, with wonderful, tastefully furnished ocean-facing rooms and day-spa facilities.

deLeckerbeck GERMAN, SEAFOOD €€
(☑ 04932-990 753; www.leckerbeck-norderney. de; Schmiedestrasse 6; mains €13-26; ⏲ 11.30am-2pm & 5.30-9.30pm Tue-Sat, closes 9pm Sun) This friendly restaurant specialises in fresh North Sea fish and seafood dishes, as well as East Frisian regional dishes such as *Ostfriesische Dicke Bohnen,* a broad-bean stew with roast pork, potatoes and onions. Located in the building that until 1933 housed the island's synagogue, it has an upstairs terrace for alfresco dining.

★ Seesteg EUROPEAN €€€
(☑ 4932-893 600; www.seesteg-norderney.de; Damenpfad 36a; 3-/4-/5-course dinner €60/76/88; ⏲ noon-10pm, dinner from 6pm; ☑) Norderney's Michelin-starred restaurant offers à la carte and multicourse dinners using fresh seasonal ingredients, such as monkfish with fennel and pancetta, pigeon au jus with artichoke, and Scottish roast lamb (there's a vegetarian menu as well). You can have dinner overlooking the sunset on the terrace. Reservations highly recommended.

🍷 Drinking & Nightlife

Cafe Marienhohe CAFE
(☑ 04932-935 0153; www.marienhoehe-norderney. de; Damenpfad 42a; ⏲ 10am-10pm Wed-Mon) Set high atop a sand dune overlooking the sea on the western tip of the island, this octagonal 19th-century cafe has been redone on the inside with a modern Nordic interior, and is a terrific place to admire the view over some tea or coffee and cake, or a glass of wine or an apertif.

Milchbar am Meer LOUNGE
(☑ 04932-927 344; www.milchbar-norderney.de; Damenpfad 33; ⏲ 10am-11pm) This all-day bar-lounge-cafe has one of the best locations on the island, and people flock to its wrap-around windows and lounger-filled terrace to gaze out over the beach and the North Sea. It's the perfect place for a sundowner.

ℹ Information

Norderney Tourist Office (☑ 04932-891 900, room reservations 04932-891 300; www. norderney.de; Conversationshaus, Am Kurplatz 1; ⏲ 9am-5pm Mon-Fri, 10am-1pm Sat & Sun) Norderney's main tourist office can provide information or book rooms.

ℹ Getting There & Away

There are trains (€8.30, 35 minutes) from Emden to Norddeich Mole, the ferry landing stage. If you're driving there, you can park in the lots near the ferry for €5 for the day.

It's a 55-minute trip to the island on the **Reederei Frisia** (☑ 04931-98 70; www. reederei-frisia.de; return adult/child €19.80/8.40, bikes €11) ferry service from Norddeich.

ℹ Getting Around

You can rent a bicycle from plenty of places once you're in town, or from the **rental shop** (Gorch-Fock-Weg 22; bike rental per day €7; ⏲ 9.30am-6pm) right on the harbour.

Public buses run around Norderney. Line 1 (adult/child €2/1.40) meets incoming ferries and goes directly to the town centre. Get off at 'Rosengarten' for the tourist office. There's more information at www.inselbus-norderney.de.

Juist

☑ 04935 / POP 1596

On Juist, you're often alone with the screeching seagulls, the wild sea and the howling winds. Forest, brambles and elderberry bushes blanket large sections of the snake-shaped island, which is 17km long and only 500m wide. The only ways to travel around are by bike, horse-drawn carriage or on your own two feet.

> ## ℹ RESORT TAXES
>
> Each of the islands charges a resort tax (*Kurtaxe* or *Kurbeitrag*), allowing beach entry and offering small discounts for museums, transport etc. Typically around €2 to €3 per day, it's simply added to your hotel bill. For day trips, it may (or may not) be included with your ferry ticket – look on each island's tourist information website for more details.

One peculiarity of Juist is the idyllic Hammersee, a bird sanctuary and the only freshwater lake on all the islands (no swimming allowed). In 1651 Juist was torn in two by a storm tide, but in the early 20th century it was decided to close off the channel with dunes, eventually creating a freshwater lake.

The little Juister Küstenmuseum (Coastal Museum; ☑ 04935-1488; Loogster Pad 29; adult/child €3/1.50; ⊗ 9.30am-1pm Mon, 9.30am-1pm & 2.30-5.30pm Tue-Fri, 2.30-5pm Sun Apr-Oct, Tue & Sat 2.30-5pm only Nov-Mar) has exhibits on life on Juist, covering the island's geology, flora and fauna, and human history.

ⓘ Information

Juist Tourist Office (☑ information 04935-809 800, room reservations 04935-809 810; www.juist.de; Strandstrasse 5; ⊗ 9am-12.30pm & 3-6pm Mon-Fri, 10am-12.30pm Sat May-Sep, plus 10am-12.30pm Sun Jul & Aug, shorter hours rest of year) Friendly staff are found here, in the Rathaus. They can help with accommodation booking. Someone also meets all ferry arrivals, regardless of time.

ⓘ Getting There & Away

Trains from Emden (€8.30, 35 minutes) travel straight to the ferry landing in Norddeich Mole. **Reederei Frisia** (☑ 04931-9870; www. reederei-frisia.de) operates the ferries from Norddeich to Juist.

Borkum

☑ 04922 / POP 5473

The largest of the East Frisian Islands – which was once even larger before it was ripped apart by a flood in the 12th century – Borkum has a tough seafaring and whaling history. Reminders of those frontier times are the whalebones that you'll occasionally see, stacked up side by side or as unusual garden fences. In 1830, however, locals realised that reinventing the island as a 'seaside' resort was a safer way to earn a living, and today many of its inhabitants are involved in the tourism industry in one way or another. Borkum is popular with German and Dutch families who rent houses here for their summer holidays.

⊙ Sights

Heimatmuseum   MUSEUM

(Local History Museum; ☑ 04922-4860; www. heimatverein-borkum.de; Roelof-Gerritz-Meyer Strasse; adult/child €4/1.50; ⊗ 10am-5pm Tue-Sun Apr-Oct, from 2pm Sat & Sun Nov-Mar) To learn about the whaling era and other stages in the life of Borkum, visit this museum near the Old Lighthouse. Don't miss the giant sperm whale skeleton on display in one of the rooms.

Borkumriff   MUSEUM

(☑ 04922-2030; www.feuerschiff-borkumriff.de; Am Neuen Hafen; adult/child €3.50/2.50, incl tour €5/2.50; ⊗ 9.45am-5.15pm Tue-Sun mid-Mar-Nov) This decommissioned lightship-turned-museum is anchored at Borkum and has an exhibition on the Wadden Sea National Park. Tours are available Tuesday to Saturday at 10.45am, 11.45am and 2.45pm.

ⓘ Information

Borkum Tourist Office (☑ 04922-9330; www.borkum.de; Am Georg-Schütte-Platz 5; ⊗ 9am-5pm Mon-Fri, 10am-1pm Sat & Sun mid-Mar–Oct, 10am-5pm Mon-Fri, to noon Sat Nov–mid-Mar) Also handles room reservations.

ⓘ Getting There & Away

All-year boats to Borkum depart twice to six times daily from Emden. **AG-Ems** (☑ 01805-180 182; www.ag-ems.de) runs car ferries and faster catamarans.

Understand Germany

Germany Today

Germany has always been hard to ignore. Today, Europe's most populous nation is also its biggest economic power and consequently has – albeit reluctantly – taken on a more active role in global politics, especially in the Greek debt and Syria refugee crises. A founding member of the European Union, it is solidly committed to preserving the alliance and making sure it is poised to deal with the political, social and military challenges of this increasingly uncertain and complex world.

Best in Print

The Sorrows of Young Werther (Johann Wolfgang von Goethe; 1774) An influential work in the Romantic movement.

Grimms' Fairy Tales (Jacob & Wilhelm Grimm; 1812) The classic!

The Rise & Fall of the Third Reich (William L Shirer; 1960) 1000-plus pages of powerful reportage.

Berlin Alexanderplatz (Alfred Döblin; 1929) Berlin in the 1920s.

The Tin Drum (Günter Grass; 1959) WWII seen through the eyes of a boy who refuses to grow up.

The Reader (Bernhard Schlink; 1995) Boy has affair with an older woman, who later is put on trial for war crimes.

Best on Film

The Lives of Others (2006) The East German secret police (Stasi) unmasked.

Downfall (2004) The final days of Hitler, holed up in his Berlin bunker.

Das Boot (1981) WWII submarine drama.

Wings of Desire (1987) An angel in love with a mortal.

Metropolis (1927) Seminal sci-fi silent movie about a proletarian revolt.

Run Lola Run (1998) Time-resetting thriller set in Berlin.

Land of Immigration

Immigration remains at the centre of public debate and was a major bone of contention in the run-up to the September 2017 federal elections. By the end of 2017, Germany's foreign population had reached a record high at 10.6 million, an increase of 5.8% compared to the previous year. While Germany has seen a drop in the arrival of refugees and asylum seekers from war-torn countries such as Syria, Afghanistan and Iraq, immigration from EU countries including Poland, Bulgaria and Romania has risen sharply.

In response to the migrant crisis in 2015, Germany set a precedent with its open border policy, opening the floodgates to around a million refugees, with Chancellor Angela Merkel encouraging other EU nations to show solidarity and follow suit. The influx has been startling: Hamburg, for instance, accepted 40,000 refugees in 2016, more than the UK government committed to over a five-year period.

Despite Merkel's admirable intentions and '*Wir schaffen das*' (we can do it) attitude, there have been many hurdles to overcome. Immigration has been largely to areas where housing is plentiful but unemployment is higher, making integration more difficult. There has been a spike in violence, as well as a spate of terrorist attacks, ostensibly stoking far-right, anti-immigration sentiment.

Federal Elections 2017

Though admitting that responding to the refugee crisis had been 'as challenging as reunifying Germany', Merkel stood her ground in the run-up to the 2017 federal elections, defending her decisions as 'humane' and saying that faced with a similar crisis she would do the same again. Not all Germans agreed. Though Merkel emerged triumphant – being re-elected for her fourth term in a grand coalition between the country's two largest parties, the centre-left SPD and the centre-right CDU/CSU – her conservative party received its worst result since 1949, taking just 33% of the vote (down from 41.5% in 2013).

The SDP suffered a major blow in the elections, securing only 20% of the vote. It lost ground largely in areas with high unemployment, as support shifted to smaller parties such as the right-wing nationalist Alternative for Germany (AfD), which latched onto the growing undercurrent of discontent regarding issues such as immigration, asylum, 'Islamification' and national security. The AfD gained 13% of the vote, enough to secure access to the Bundestag; it's the first far-right nationalist party to enter German parliament in more than half a century. A major AfD stronghold is the eastern state of Saxony-Anhalt, one of Germany's poorest states.

Rise of the Right

The growing popularity of the AfD sent shock waves throughout Germany, with many Germans expressing deep concern about its place in parliament (as of 2017 it's the third-largest party in the Bundestag). The rapid change in Germany's demographics since the massive influx of migrants and refugees has sparked a backlash that has added fuel to the fire of the far-right and has brought national identity into question. Issues long considered taboo are now being openly debated.

In many towns and cities, particularly in the eastern states, locals have clashed with migrants, resulting in spates of xenophobic attacks and violence. In 2018, members of the far-right Freital group were found guilty of terror crimes and attempted murder, after propagating a 'climate of fear' with explosives attacks on refugee homes. In 2015, 18,000 supporters of the anti-Islam group PEGIDA marched in Dresden, the biggest protest of its kind. Some 30,000 counter-demonstrators protested in other German cities. Cologne expressed its outrage at the anti-Muslim march by turning off its cathedral lights.

Anti-immigrant sentiments are running strong in eastern Saxony. The AfD stronghold is home to the town of Bautzen, which made headlines in February 2016 when a mob cheered as a future refugee shelter was set on fire, then again that November when neo-Nazis attacked migrants with bottles and stones.

Even Berlin's hip, multicultural Neukölln neighbourhood has seen a rise in hate crimes and arson attacks targeting migrants and political activists.

AREA: **357,672 SQ KM**

POPULATION: **82.3 MILLION**

GDP: **€3.68 TRILLION**

INFLATION: **1.4%**

UNEMPLOYMENT: **3.5%**

LIFE EXPECTANCY: **WOMEN 83.4 YEARS, MEN 78.7 YEARS**

if Germany were 100 people

81 would be German
4 would be Polish
3 would be Turkish
2 would be Russian
10 would be other

belief systems
(% of population)

Roman Catholic   Protestant

5   2   37

Muslim   Orthodox   unaffiliated or other

population per sq km

GERMANY   FRANCE   USA

≈ 35 people

History

For most of its history, Germany was a patchwork of semi-independent principalities and city-states, becoming a nation-state only in 1871. Yet movements and events associated with its territory – from the Hanseatic League to the Reformation and the Holocaust – have shaped the history of Europe since the early Middle Ages. The impact of figures including Charlemagne, Martin Luther, Otto von Bismarck and Adolf Hitler resonates today, when Germany is inextricably bound up within – and a leading proponent of – European unity.

**Best
Roman
Sites**
....
Trier
....
Xanten
....
Cologne
....
Aachen
....
Regensburg
....
Bingen
....
Mainz

For more on
Germany's Roman
ruins log on to
www.historvius.
com.

Tribes & The Romans

The early inhabitants of present-day Germany were Celts and later nomadic German tribes. Under Emperor Augustus, the Romans began conquering the German lands from around 12 BC, pushing as far as the Rhine and the Danube. Attempts to expand their territory further east were thwarted in AD 9, when Roman general Varus lost three legions – about 20,000 men – in the bloody Battle of the Teutoburg Forest. The Germanic forces were led by Arminius, the son of a local chief who had been captured and brought to Rome as a hostage. Here he adopted Roman citizenship and received a military education, which proved invaluable in outwitting Varus.

For many years, Mount Grotenburg near Detmold in North Rhine–Westphalia was thought to have been the setting of the epic Teutoburg Forest battle, but no one can really say for sure where it happened. The most likely candidate is Kalkriese, north of Osnabrück, where in the 1990s archaeologists found face helmets, breast shields, bone deposits and other grisly battle remains. Today the site is a museum and park.

After Arminius' victory, the Romans never again attempted to conquer Germanic lands east of the Rhine, accepting the Rhine and the Danube as natural boundaries and consolidating their power by founding such colonies as Trier, Cologne, Mainz and Regensburg. They remained the dominant force in the region until 476.

TIMELINE	800–300 BC	100 BC–AD 9	4th Century
	Germanic tribes and Celts inhabit large parts of northern and central Germany, but by around 300 BC the Celts have been driven back to regions south of the Main River.	The Romans clash with Germanic tribes until defeat at the Battle of the Teutoburg Forest halts Rome's expansion eastwards. The Romans consolidate territory south of the Limes.	The arrival of Hun horsemen triggers the Great Migration. Germanic tribes are displaced and flee to various parts of the Western Roman Empire. The Lombards settle in northern Italy.

ROMAN FRONTIER LINES

In AD 83 the Romans started building what is today central Europe's largest archaeological site – a wall running 568km from Koblenz on the Rhine to Regensburg on the Danube. Some 900 watchtowers and 60 forts studded this frontier line, dubbed Der Limes (The Limes). The 800km-long Deutsche Limes-Strasse (German Limes Road) cycling route runs between Regensburg in the south and Bad Hönningen in the north (near Koblenz), largely tracing the tower- and fortress-studded fortification. See www.limesstrasse.de for more about the Limes and routes along the wall. A 280km-long cycling route links Detmold with Xanten (where there's an archaeological park), taking cyclists past various Roman remains and monuments.

The Frankish Reich

Based on the Rhine's western bank, the Frankish Reich (Empire) existed from the 5th to the 9th centuries and was the successor state of the Western Roman Empire, which had crumbled in 476. Under the leadership of the Merovingian and later the Carolingian dynasties, it became Europe's most important political power in those early medieval times. In its heyday, the Reich included present-day France, Germany, the Low Countries (Netherlands, Belgium and Luxembourg) and half the Italian peninsula.

Its most powerful ruler was Charlemagne (r 768–814), a Carolingian. From his grandiose residence in Aachen, he conquered Lombardy, won territory in Bavaria, waged a 30-year war against the Saxons in the north and was crowned kaiser by the pope in 800, an act that was regarded as a revival of the Roman empire. Charlemagne's burial in Aachen Dom (Aachen Cathedral) turned the court chapel into a major pilgrimage site.

After Charlemagne's death, fighting between his son and three grandsons ultimately led to the dissolution of the Frankish Reich in 843. The Treaty of Verdun split the territory into three kingdoms: the Westfrankenreich (West Francia), which evolved into today's France; the Ostfrankenreich (East Francia), the origin of today's Germany; and the Mittlere Frankenreich (Middle Francia), which encompassed the Low Countries and areas in present-day France and northern Italy.

> Throughout most of history, Germany was not a single country but a loose federation of fiefdoms known as the Holy Roman Empire of the German Nation. A proper nation-state did not emerge until 1871.

The Middle Ages

Germany's strong regionalism has its roots in the early Middle Ages, when dynasties squabbled and intrigued over territorial spoils. The symbolic heart of power in the early Middle Ages was Charlemagne's burial place, the cathedral in Aachen. It hosted the coronation of 31 German kings from 936 until 1531, starting with Otto I (aka Otto the Great). Otto proved himself on the battlefield, first by defeating Hungarian troops and then

482	716–54	732	773–800
Clovis becomes king of the Franks and unites diverse populations, laying the foundations for a Frankish Reich that begins conquering lands in Western Europe ruled by the crumbling Roman Empire.	The English Benedictine monk St Boniface undertakes a journey to preach Christianity in Frisia, Hesse, Thuringia and Bavaria. His missionary activities end when he is killed in Frisia.	Charles Martel, king of the Franks, wins the decisive Battle of Tours and stops the progress of Muslims from the Iberian Peninsula into Western Europe, preserving Christianity in the Frankish Reich.	The Carolingian Charlemagne, grandson of the king Charles Martel, answers a call for help from the pope. In return, he is crowned kaiser by the pope.

The Holy Roman Empire was also known as the First Reich. The Second Reich refers to the German Empire (1871–1914) under Kaisers Wilhelm I and II, and the Third Reich, of course, to Adolf Hitler's rule from 1933 to 1945.

by conquering the Kingdom of Italy. In 962, he renewed Charlemagne's pledge to protect the papacy, and the pope reciprocated by crowning him emperor and marking the birth of the Holy Roman Empire. For the next 800 years the Kaiser and the pope were strange, and often uneasy, bedfellows.

Power struggles between popes and emperors, the latter of which also had to contend with local princes and prince-bishops, were behind many of the upheavals in the early Middle Ages. A milestone was the Investiture Conflict between Heinrich IV (r 1056–1106) and Pope Gregory VI over whether the pope or the monarch was entitled to appoint bishops, abbots and other high church officials. The pope responded by excommunicating Heinrich in 1076. Heinrich then embarked on a walk of penance to the castle of Canossa in Italy, where the pope was in residence. Contrite, he reportedly stood barefoot in the snow for three days begging for the excommunication to be lifted. He was eventually absolved but the investiture question held the Reich in the grip of civil war, until a treaty signed in 1122 granted the emperor limited rights in selecting bishops.

Heinrich IV was a member of the Salians, one of several powerful dynasties that shaped the politics of the early Middle Ages. Others included the rival Hohenstaufen and Welf houses. One of the most powerful Welfs of the time was Heinrich der Löwe (Henry the Lion), who reigned over

WHAT WAS THE HOLY ROMAN EMPIRE?

The Holy Roman Empire was a political union of feudal states that greatly influenced the history and evolution of Europe for more than 800 years. Some historians peg its origins to Frankish king Charlemagne, who, in 800, was crowned emperor by Pope Leo III in Rome. It was the first time such a title had been bestowed in western Europe since the collapse of the Roman Empire in the 5th century. However, not until the crowning of Otto I in 962 did the territory truly fall under German rule; it would remain so almost exclusively until the abdication of Holy Roman Emperor Franz II in 1806.

The empire sometimes included Italy, as far south as Rome. Sometimes it didn't – the pope usually had a say in that. It variously encompassed present-day Netherlands, Belgium, Switzerland, Lorraine and Burgundy (in France), Sicily, Austria and an eastern swathe of land that lies in today's Czech Republic, Poland and Hungary. As such it was a decentralised, multi-ethnic mosaic with many languages. Unlike France, Spain or England, it was not a hereditary monarchy. Instead, emperors were selected by a small group of electors drawn from the ecclesiastical and political nobility, although the new king was usually – however distantly – related to the outgoing one. Since there was no capital city, rulers constantly moved from one city to the next.

Incidentally, the term 'Holy Roman Empire' was not used until the 13th century. In the 15th century, the words 'of the German nation' were added.

911	919–1125	1165	1241
Louis the Child dies without an heir at 18, and Frankish dukes in the eastern Reich bypass Charles the Simple in favour of their own monarch, electing the first truly German ruler.	Saxon and Salian emperors rule Germany, creating the Holy Roman Empire in 962, when Otto I is crowned Holy Roman Emperor by the pope, reaffirming the precedent established by Charlemagne.	Friedrich I Barbarossa is crowned in Aachen. He canonises Charlemagne and, while co-leading the Third Crusade, drowns while bathing in a river in present-day Turkey.	Hamburg and Lübeck sign an agreement to protect each other's ships and trading routes, creating the basis for the powerful Hanseatic League, which dominates politics and trade across much of Europe.

THE HANSEATIC LEAGUE

The origins of the Hanseatic League go back to various guilds and associations established from about the mid-12th century by out-of-town merchants to protect their interests. After Hamburg and Lübeck signed an agreement in 1241 to protect their ships and trading routes, they were joined in their league by Lüneburg, Kiel and a string of Baltic Sea cities stretching east to Greifswald. By 1356 this had grown into the Hanseatic League, encompassing half a dozen other large alliances of cities, with Lübeck playing the lead role.

At its zenith, the league had about 200 member cities. It earned a say in the choice of Danish kings after fighting two wars against the Danes between 1361 and 1369. The resulting Treaty of Stralsund in 1370 turned it into northern Europe's most powerful economic and political entity. Some 70 inland and coastal cities – mostly German – formed the core of the Hanseatic League, but another 130 beyond the Reich maintained a loose association, making it truly international. During a period of endless feudal squabbles in Germany, it was a bastion of political and social stability.

By the 15th century, however, competition from Dutch and English shipping companies, internal disputes and a shift in the centre of world trade (from the North and Baltic seas to the Atlantic) had caused decline. The ruin and chaos of the Thirty Years' War in the 17th century delivered the final blow, although Hamburg, Bremen and Lübeck retained the 'Hanse City' title. The latter's Europäisches Hansemuseum is a great place to learn more about this fascinating chapter in European history.

HISTORY THE MIDDLE AGES

the duchies of Saxony and Bavaria, while also extending influence eastwards in campaigns to Germanise and convert the Slavs.

Heinrich, who was very well connected (his second, English wife Mathilde was Richard the Lionheart's sister), founded not only Braunschweig (where his grave is), but Munich, Lübeck and Lüneburg, too. At the height of his reign, his domain stretched from the north and Baltic coasts to the Alps, and from Westphalia to Pomerania (in Poland). Eventually, though, the Hohenstaufen under Friedrich I Barbarossa (r 1152–90) would regain the upper hand and take Saxony and Bavaria away from him.

In 1254, after the death of the last Hohenstaufen emperor, Friedrich II, the Reich plunged into an era called the Great Interregnum, when no potential successor could gain sufficient support, leaving the Reich rudderless until the election of Rudolf I in 1273. Rudolf was the first of 19 emperors of the Habsburg dynasty that mastered the art of politically expedient marriage and dominated Continental affairs until the early 20th century.

In the 14th century, the basic structure of the Holy Roman Empire solidified. A key document was the Golden Bull of 1356 (so named for its golden seal), a decree issued by Emperor Charles IV that was essentially an early form of an imperial constitution. Most importantly, it set out precise rules for elections by specifying the seven *Kurfürsten* (prince-electors) entitled to choose the next king to be crowned Holy Roman Emperor by the pope.

Heinrich the Fowler: Father of the Ottonian Empire (2005), by Mirella Patzer, brings 10th-century Germany to life in a heady blend of history and fiction.

1245	1273	1338	1356
The chaotic period of the Great Interregnum begins when Pope Innocent IV deposes Friedrich II and a string of anti-kings are elected. Local bishops and dukes subsequently grab more power, weakening central rule.	The Great Interregnum ends when the House of Habsburg takes the reins of the Reich and begins its rise to become Europe's most powerful dynasty.	The Declaration of Rhense ends the need for the pope to confirm the Reich's elected kaiser, abolishing the dependence whereby the pope crowned the kaiser, in exchange for loyalty and protection.	The Golden Bull formalises the election of the kaiser. The archbishops of Cologne, Trier and Mainz, the rulers of Bohemia, Saxony and Brandenburg, and the count of Palatinate, become prince-electors.

What's in a name? Past German monarchs include Karl the Fat (r 881–87), Arnulf the Evil and Friedrich the Handsome (both medieval anti-kings), and the righteous Heinrich the Holy (r 1014–24).

The privilege fell to the rulers of Bohemia, Brandenburg, Saxony and the Palatinate, as well as to the archbishops of Trier, Mainz and Cologne. A simple majority was sufficient in electing the next king.

As the importance of the minor nobility declined, the economic power of the towns increased, especially after many joined forces in a strategic trading alliance called the Hanseatic League. The most powerful towns, such as Cologne, Hamburg, Nuremberg and Frankfurt, were granted Free Imperial City status, which made them beholden directly to the emperor (as opposed to 'non-free' towns that were subordinate to a local ruler).

For ordinary Germans, times were difficult. They battled with panic lynchings, pogroms against Jews and labour shortages – all sparked by the plague (1348–50) that wiped out at least 25% of Europe's population. While death gripped ordinary Germans, universities were being established all over the country around this time, with Heidelberg's the first, in 1386.

Reformation & the Thirty Years' War

In the 16th century, the Renaissance and humanist ideas generated criticism of rampant church abuses, most famously the practice of selling indulgences to exonerate sins. In the university town of Wittenberg in 1517, German monk and theology professor Martin Luther (1483–1546) made public his *Ninety-Five Theses,* which criticised not only indulgences but also questioned papal infallibility, clerical celibacy and other elements of Catholic doctrine. This was the spark that lit the Reformation.

Threatened with excommunication, Luther refused to recant, broke from the Catholic Church and was banned by the Reich, only to be hidden in the Wartburg, a castle outside Eisenach in Thuringia, where he translated the New Testament into German.

It wasn't until 1555 that the Catholic and Lutheran churches were ranked as equals, thanks to Emperor Karl V (r 1520–58), who signed the Peace of Augsburg, allowing princes to decide the religion of their principality. The more secular northern principalities adopted Lutheran teachings, while the clerical lords in the south, southwest and Austria stuck with Catholicism.

The religious issue refused to die. In 1618 it degenerated into the Thirty Years' War, which Sweden and France joined by 1635. Calm was restored with the Peace of Westphalia (1648), signed in Münster and Osnabrück, but it left the Reich – embracing more than 300 states and about 1000 smaller territories – a nominal, impotent state. Switzerland and the Netherlands gained formal independence, France won chunks of Alsace and Lorraine, and Sweden helped itself to the mouths of the Elbe, Oder and Weser rivers.

Napoleon & Revolutions

In the aftermath of the 1789 French Revolution, a diminutive Frenchman named Napoleon Bonaparte (Napoleon I) took control of Europe

1455	1517	1524–25	1555
Johannes Gutenberg of Mainz prints 180 copies of the *Gutenberg Bible* in Latin, using a moveable type system that revolutionises book printing and allows books to be published in large quantities.	Martin Luther makes public his *Ninety-Five Theses* in the town of Wittenberg. His ideas challenge the selling of indulgences, capturing a mood of disillusionment with the Church and among the clergy.	Inspired by the Reformation, peasants in southern and central Germany rise up against their masters, demanding the end of bonded labour. Luther at first supports the peasants, but later switches sides.	The Peace of Augsburg allows princes to decide their principality's religion, putting Catholicism and Protestantism on an equal footing. Around 80% of Germany's population at this time is Protestant.

and significantly altered its fate through a series of wars. The defeat of Austrian and Russian troops in the Battle of Austerlitz in 1805 led to the 1806 collapse of the Holy Roman Empire, the abdication of Kaiser Franz II and a variety of administrative and judicial reforms.

Most German kingdoms, duchies and principalities aligned themselves with Napoleon in the Confederation of the Rhine. In his restructure of the map of the Europe, Bavaria fared especially well, nearly doubling its size and being elevated to kingdom in 1806. It was to be a short-lived confederation, though, for many of its members switched allegiance again after Napoleon got trounced by Prussian, Russian, Austrian and Swedish troops in the bloody 1813 Battle of Leipzig.

In 1815, at the Congress of Vienna, Germany was reorganised into the Deutscher Bund, a confederation of 39 states with a central legislative assembly, the Reichstag, established in Frankfurt. Austria and Prussia dominated this alliance, until a series of bourgeois democratic revolutions swept

> The first potato was planted in Germany in 1621, the Gregorian calendar was adopted in 1700 and Germany's first cuckoo clock started ticking in 1730.

PRUSSIA ON THE RISE

As the power of the Holy Roman Empire waned, a new force to be reckoned with appeared on the horizon: Brandenburg-Prussia. Since 1411, the eastern duchy of Brandenburg had been under the rule of the Hohenzollern family, but remained pretty much on the fringes of power within the Reich. This changed in the 17th century under Friedrich Wilhelm (r 1640–88). Also known as the Great Elector, he took several steps that helped chart Brandenburg's rise to the status of a European powerhouse. He turned Berlin into a garrison town, levied a new sales tax, established the city as a trading hub by building a canal linking the Oder and Spree rivers, and encouraged the settlement of French refugees. Between 1680 and 1710, Berlin saw its population nearly triple to 56,000, making it one of the largest cities in the Holy Roman Empire. Seizing the opportunity, his son, Friedrich III, promoted himself to King Friedrich I (elector 1688–1701, king 1701–13) of Prussia, making Berlin a royal residence and capital of Brandenburg-Prussia.

Friedrich's son, Friedrich Wilhelm I (r 1713–40) laid the groundwork for Prussian military might. Soldiers were this king's main obsession and he dedicated much of his life to building an army of 80,000, partly by instituting the draft (highly unpopular even then, and eventually repealed) and by persuading his fellow rulers to trade him men for treasure. History quite appropriately knows him as the *Soldatenkönig* (soldier king).

Ironically, these soldiers didn't see action until his son and successor Friedrich II (aka Frederick the Great; r 1740–86) came to power. Friedrich fought tooth and nail for two decades to wrest Silesia (in today's Poland) from Austria and Saxony. He also embraced the ideas of the Enlightenment, abolishing torture, guaranteeing religious freedom and introducing legal reforms. With some of the leading thinkers in town (Moses Mendelssohn, Voltaire and Gotthold Ephraim Lessing among them), Berlin blossomed into a great cultural capital and came to be known as 'Athens on the Spree'.

1618–48	1648	1740–86	1789–1815
The Thirty Years' War sweeps through Germany, leaving its population depleted and vast regions reduced to wasteland. The Reich disintegrates into more than 300 states.	The Treaty of Westphalia ends the Thirty Years' War and formalises the independence of Switzerland, and of the Netherlands, which had been ruled by Spain since the early 16th century.	Brandenburg–Prussia becomes a mighty power under Friedrich the Great. Berlin becomes 'Athens on the Spree', as Absolutism in Europe gives way to the Enlightenment, heralding a cultural explosion.	The French Revolution and, from 1803, the Napoleonic Wars sweep away the last remnants of the Middle Ages in Europe. Napoleon Bonaparte takes Berlin in 1806.

through German cities in 1848, resulting in Germany's first ever freely elected parliamentary delegation convening in Frankfurt's Paulskirche. Austria, meanwhile, broke away from Germany, came up with its own constitution and promptly relapsed into monarchism. As revolution fizzled in 1850, the confederation resumed, with Prussia and Austria as dominant members.

In Bavaria, meanwhile, revolutionary rumblings brought out King Ludwig I's reactionary streak. An arch Catholic, he restored the monasteries, introduced press censorship and authorised the arrest of students, journalists and university professors whom he judged to be subversive. Bavaria was becoming restrictive even as French and American democratic ideals flourished elsewhere in Germany.

On 22 March 1848 Ludwig I abdicated in favour of his son, Maximilian II (r 1848–64), who put into place many of the constitutional reforms his father had ignored, such as abolishing censorship and introducing the right to assemble. His son Ludwig II (r 1864–86) introduced further progressive measures (welfare for the poor, liberalised marriage laws and free trade) early in his reign but ultimately became caught up in a world inspired by mythology, focusing on building grand palaces such as Schloss Neuschwanstein instead of running a kingdom. His death by drowning in shallow water in Lake Starnberg continues to spur conspiracy theories to this day.

Bismarck & the Birth of an Empire

The creation of a unified Germany with Prussia at the helm was the glorious ambition of Otto von Bismarck (1815–98), who had been appointed as Prussian prime minister by King Wilhelm I in 1862. An old-guard militarist, he used intricate diplomacy and a series of wars with neighbouring Denmark and France to achieve his aims. By 1871 Berlin stood as the proud capital of the Deutsches Reich (German Empire), a bicameral, constitutional monarchy. On 18 January the Prussian king was crowned kaiser at Versailles, with Bismarck as his 'Iron Chancellor'.

Bismarck's power was based on the support of merchants and the Junker, a noble class of non-knighted landowners. An ever-skilful diplomat and power broker, Bismarck achieved much through a dubious 'honest broker' policy, whereby he brokered deals between European powers and encouraged colonial vanities in order to distract others from his own deeds. He belatedly graced the Reich with a few African jewels after 1880, acquiring colonies in central, southwest and east Africa, as well as in numerous Pacific paradises, such as Papua New Guinea.

The early years of the German empire – a period called *Gründerzeit* (foundation years) – were marked by major economic growth, fuelled in part by a steady flow of French reparation payments. Hundreds of thousands of people poured into the cities in search of work in factories. New political parties gave a voice to the proletariat, especially the Socialist

---

One of the definitive histories on Prussia, Christopher Clark's *Iron Kingdom: The Rise and Downfall of Prussia* covers the period from 1600 to 1947, and shows the central role this powerhouse played in shaping modern Europe.

Bismarck to the Weimar Republic is the focus of Hans-Ulrich Wehler's *The German Empire 1871–1918*, a translation of an authoritative German work. For a revealing study of the Iron Chancellor himself, read *Bismarck, the Man and the Statesman* by AJP Taylor.

1806–13	1813 & 1815	1814–15	1834
The Holy Roman Empire collapses and Napoleon creates the 16-member Confederation of the Rhine after defeating Austrian and Russian troops in the Battle of Austerlitz.	Napoleon suffers defeat near Leipzig in 1813. He subsequently abdicates and is exiled to Elba. He returns to power in 1815 but is defeated at Waterloo that same year.	The post-Napoleon Congress of Vienna redraws the map of Europe, creating in the former Reich the German Alliance, with 35 states.	The German Customs Union is formed under the leadership of Prussia, making much of Germany a free-trade area and edging it closer to unification; the Union reinforces the idea of a Germany without Austria.

Workers' Party (SAP), the forerunner of the Sozialdemokratische Partei Deutschlands (Social Democratic Party of Germany; SPD).

Bismarck tried to make the party illegal but, when pressed, made concessions to the growing and increasingly antagonistic socialist movement, enacting Germany's first modern social reforms, though contrary to his true nature. When Wilhelm II (r 1888–1918) came to power, he wanted to extend social reform, while Bismarck envisioned stricter anti-socialist laws. By March 1890, the kaiser had had enough and excised his renegade chancellor from the political scene. Bismarck's legacy as a brilliant diplomat unravelled as a wealthy, unified and industrially powerful Germany embarked upon a new century.

World War I & its Aftermath

The assassination on 28 June 1914 of Archduke Franz Ferdinand, heir to the Austro-Hungarian throne, triggered a series of diplomatic decisions that led to WWI, the bloodiest European conflict since the Thirty Years' War. Initial euphoria and faith in a quick victory soon gave way to despair, as casualties piled up in the battlefield trenches and stomachs grumbled on the home front. When defeat came in 1918, it ushered in a period of turmoil and violence. On 9 November 1918, Kaiser Wilhelm II abdicated, bringing an inglorious end to the monarchy.

The seeds of acrimony and humiliation that later led to WWII were sown in the peace conditions of WWI. Germany, militarily broken, teetering on the verge of revolution and caught in a no man's land between monarchy and modern democracy, signed the Treaty of Versailles (1919), which made it responsible for all losses inflicted upon its enemies. Its borders were trimmed and it was forced to pay high reparations.

The Weimar Republic

In July 1919 the federalist constitution of the fledgling republic was adopted in the town of Weimar, where the constituent assembly had sought refuge from the chaos of Berlin. Germany's first serious experiment with democracy gave women the vote and established basic human rights, but it also gave the chancellor the right to rule by decree – a concession that would later prove critical in Hitler's rise to power.

The Weimar Republic (1919–33) was governed by a coalition of left and centre parties, but pleased neither communists nor monarchists. In fact, the 1920s began as anything but 'golden', marked by the humiliation of a lost war, hyperinflation, mass unemployment, hunger and disease.

Economic stability gradually returned after a new currency, the Rentenmark, was introduced in 1923 and with the Dawes Plan in 1924, which limited the crippling reparation payments imposed on Germany after WWI. But the tide turned again when the US stock market crashed in 1929,

After abdicating, Kaiser Wilhelm II was allowed to settle in Utrecht (the Netherlands) on the condition that he didn't engage in political activity. One of his final acts was to send a telegram to Hitler, congratulating him on the occupation of Paris.

Did you know that 9 November is Germany's 'date with destiny'? It was the end of the monarchy in 1918, the day of Hitler's Munich Putsch in 1923, the Night of Broken Glass in 1938, and the day the Wall fell in 1989.

1835	1848	1866	1870–71
Germany's first railway line opens between the Bavarian towns of Nuremberg and Fürth. Thanks to the Customs Union, the network quickly expands.	The March Revolution breaks out mainly in the Rhineland and southwest German provinces. Nationalists and reformers call for far-reaching changes; a first parliamentary delegation meets in Frankfurt.	Following a successful war against Denmark, Prussia defeats Austria in the Austro-Prussian War, and chancellor Otto von Bismarck creates a North German Confederation that excludes Austria.	Through diplomacy and the Franco-Prussian War, Bismarck creates a unified Germany, with Prussia at its helm and Berlin as its capital. Wilhelm I, king of Prussia, becomes Kaiser Wilhelm I.

JEWS IN GERMANY

The first Jews arrived in present-day Germany with the conquering Romans, settling in important Roman cities on or near the Rhine. As non-Christians, Jews had a separate political status. Highly valued for their trade connections, they were formally invited to settle in Speyer in 1084 and granted trading privileges and the right to build a wall around their quarter. A charter of rights granted to the Jews of Worms in 1090 by Henry IV allowed local Jews to be judged according to their own laws.

The First Crusade (1095–99) brought pogroms in 1096, usually against the will of local rulers and townspeople. Many Jews resisted, before committing suicide once their situation became hopeless. This, the *Kiddush ha-shem* (martyr's death), established a precedent of martyrdom that became a tenet of European Judaism in the Middle Ages.

In the 13th century, Jews were declared crown property by Frederick II, an act that afforded protection but exposed them to royal whim. Rabbi Meir of Rothenburg fell foul of King Rudolph I in 1293 for leading a group of would-be emigrants to Palestine; he died in prison. The Church also prescribed distinctive clothing for Jews at this time, which later meant that in some towns Jews had to wear badges.

Things deteriorated with the arrival of the plague in the mid-14th century, when Jews were persecuted and libellous notions circulated throughout the Christian population. The 'blood libel' accused Jews of using the blood of Christians in rituals.

Money lending was the main source of income for Jews in the 15th century. Expulsions remained commonplace, however, with large numbers emigrating to Poland, where the Yiddish language developed. The Reformation (including a hostile Martin Luther) and the Thirty Years' War brought difficult times for Jewish populations, but by the 17th century they were again valued for their economic contacts.

Napoleon granted Germany's Jews equal rights, but the reforms were repealed by the 1815 Congress of Vienna. Anti-Jewish feelings in the early 19th century coincided with German nationalism and a more vigorous Christianity, producing a large number of influential assimilated Jews.

By the late 19th century, Jews had equal status in most respects and Germany had become a world centre of Jewish cultural and historical studies. There was a shift to large cities, such as Leipzig, Cologne, Breslau (now Wrocław in Poland), Hamburg, Frankfurt am Main and the capital, Berlin, where a third of German Jews lived.

Germany became an important centre for Hebrew literature after Russian writers and academics fled the revolution of 1917. The Weimar Republic brought emancipation for the 500,000-strong Jewish community, but by 1943 Hitler had declared Germany *Judenrein* ('clean of Jews'). This ignored the hundreds of thousands of Eastern European Jews incarcerated on 'German' soil. Around six million Jews died in Europe as a direct result of Nazism.

The number of Jews affiliated with the Jewish community in Germany is currently around 100,000 – the third largest in Europe – but there are many more who are not affiliated with a synagogue. Among them are many of the 250,000 Russian Jews who arrived in Germany between 1989 and 2005 to escape economic and political turmoil, as well as perceived widespread anti-Semitism.

1880s	1914–18	1918–19	1918–19
The new German Reich demands its place in the sun in the form of colonies. This causes increasing friction with established colonial powers Britain and France.	WWI: Germany, Austria-Hungary and Turkey go to war against Britain, France, Italy and Russia. Germany is defeated. Some 10 million soldiers and 7 million civilians perish.	Sailors' revolts spread across Germany, Kaiser Wilhelm II abdicates, and a democratic Weimar Republic is founded. Women receive suffrage and human rights are enshrined in law.	The 'war guilt' clause in the Treaty of Versailles, holding Germany and its allies financially responsible for loss and damage suffered by its enemies, puts the new republic on an unstable footing.

plunging the world into economic depression. Within weeks, millions of German were jobless, and riots and demonstrations again filled the streets.

Hitler's Rise to Power

The volatile, increasingly polarised political climate led to clashes between communists and members of a party that had been patiently waiting in the wings – the Nationalsozialistische Deutsche Arbeiterpartei (National Socialist German Workers' Party, NSDAP, or Nazi Party), led by a failed Austrian artist and WWI corporal named Adolf Hitler. Soon jackboots, brown shirts, oppression and fear would dominate daily life in Germany.

Hitler's NSDAP gained 18% of the national vote in the 1930 elections. In the 1932 presidential election, Hitler challenged incumbent Reichspräsident (President of the Reich) Paul von Hindenburg, but only managed to win 37% of the second-round vote. However, a year later, on 30 January 1933, faced with failed economic reforms and persuasive right-wing advisors, Hindenburg appointed Hitler chancellor.

Hitler moved quickly to consolidate absolute power and to turn the nation's democracy into a one-party dictatorship. He used Berlin's Reichstag fire as a pretext to push through the Enabling Act, allowing him to decree laws and change the constitution without consulting parliament. When Hindenburg died a year later, Hitler merged the offices of president and chancellor to become Führer of the Third Reich.

The rise of the Nazis had instant, far-reaching consequences. Within three months of Hitler's power grab, all non-Nazi parties, organisations and labour unions ceased to exist. Political opponents, intellectuals and artists were rounded up and detained without trial; many went underground or into exile. There was a burgeoning culture of terror and denunciation, and the terrorisation of Jews began to escalate.

Hitler won much support among the middle and lower-middle classes by pumping large sums of money into employment programs, many involving rearmament and heavy industry. In Wolfsburg, Lower Saxony, affordable cars started rolling out of the first Volkswagen factory, founded in 1938.

That same year, Hitler's troops were welcomed into Austria. Foreign powers, in an attempt to avoid another bloody war, accepted this *Anschluss* (annexation) of Austria. Following this same policy of appeasement, the leaders of Italy, Great Britain and France ceded the largely ethnic-German Sudetenland of Czechoslovakia to Hitler in the Munich Agreement, signed in September 1938. By March 1939, he had also annexed Bohemia and Moravia.

Jewish Persecution

Jews were a Nazi target from the start. In April 1933 Joseph Goebbels, *Gauleiter* (district leader) of Berlin and head of the well-oiled Ministry of

---

Due to hyper-inflation, in 1923 a postage stamp cost 50 billion marks, a loaf of bread 140 billion marks and US$1 was worth 4.2 trillion marks. In November, the new Rentenmark was traded in for one trillion old marks.

HISTORY HITLER'S RISE TO POWER

In 1923, Adolf Hitler tried to kick off a revolution from a beer hall in what became known as the Munich Putsch. He wound up in Landsberg Prison, where he penned *Mein Kampf*.

Mid-1920s	1933	1933–34	1935
Amid the troubles of the Weimar Republic, Germans discover flamboyant pursuits. Cinemas attract two million viewers daily and cabaret and the arts flourish, but ideological differences increase.	Hitler becomes chancellor of Germany and creates a dictatorship through the Enabling Act. Only the 94 SPD Reichstag representatives present – those not in prison or exile – oppose the act.	The Nazi *Gleichschaltung* (enforced conformity) begins, signalling the death of tolerance and pluralism. The federal states become powerless, opposition parties and free-trade unions are banned.	The Nuremberg Laws are enacted. A law for the 'protection of German blood and honour' forbids marriage between 'Aryans' and 'non-Aryans'. Another law deprives Jews and other 'non-Aryans' of German nationality.

Propaganda, announced a boycott of Jewish businesses. Soon after, Jews were expelled from public service and banned from many professions, trades and industries. The Nuremberg Laws of 1935 deprived 'non-Aryans' of German citizenship and many other rights.

The international community, meanwhile, turned a blind eye to the situation, perhaps because many leaders were keen to see some order restored to the country after decades of political upheaval. Hitler's success at stabilising the shaky economy – largely by pumping public money into employment programs – was widely admired. The 1936 Olympic summer games in Berlin were a public-relations triumph, as Hitler launched a charm offensive. Terror and persecution resumed soon after the closing ceremony.

For Jews, the horror escalated on 9 November 1938, with the Reichspogromnacht (often called Kristallnacht, or Night of Broken Glass). Using the assassination of a German consular official by a Polish Jew in Paris as a pretext, Nazi thugs desecrated, burned and demolished synagogues and Jewish cemeteries, property and businesses across the country. Jews had begun to emigrate after 1933, but this event set off a stampede.

The fate of those Jews who stayed behind deteriorated after the outbreak of WWII in 1939. At Hitler's request, a conference in January 1942 in Berlin's Wannsee came up with the *Endlösung* (Final Solution): the systematic, bureaucratic and meticulously documented annihilation of European Jews. Sinti and Roma, political opponents, priests, homosexuals and habitual criminals were targeted as well. Of the roughly seven million people who were sent to concentration camps, only 500,000 survived.

Of the dozens of books covering Nazi concentration camps, *I Never Saw Another Butterfly: Children's Drawings and Poems from Terezin Concentration Camp 1942–1944*, edited by Hana Volavková, says it all. *This Way for the Gas, Ladies and Gentlemen*, by Tadeusz Borowski, is equally chilling.

World War II

WWII began on 1 September 1939 with the Nazi attack on Poland. France and Britain declared war on Germany two days later, but even this could not prevent the quick defeat of Poland, Belgium, the Netherlands and France. Other countries, including Denmark and Norway, were also soon brought into the Nazi fold.

In June 1941 Germany broke its nonaggression pact with Stalin by attacking the USSR. Though successful at first, Operation Barbarossa quickly ran into problems, culminating in the defeat at Stalingrad (today Volgograd) the following winter, forcing the Germans to retreat.

With the Normandy invasion of June 1944, Allied troops arrived in formidable force on the European mainland, supported by unrelenting air raids that reduced Germany's cities to rubble and the country's population by 10%. The final Battle of Berlin began in mid-April 1945. More than 1.5 million Soviet soldiers barrelled towards the capital from the east, reaching Berlin on 21 April and encircling it on 25 April. Two days later they were in the city centre, fighting running street battles with the remaining troops, many of them boys and elderly men.

1936	1938	1939	1939–45
Berlin hosts the Olympic Games. Embarrassingly for Hitler, who originally wanted to ban all black and Jewish athletes, African American Jesse Owens wins four gold medals in athletics.	The Munich Agreement allows Hitler to annex the Sudetenland, an ethnic-German region of Czechoslovakia. British Prime Minister Neville Chamberlain declares there will be 'peace in our time'.	WWII: Hitler invades Poland on 1 September. Two days later France and Britain declare war on Germany.	Millions of Jews are murdered during the Holocaust and 62 million civilians and soldiers die – 27 million in the Soviet Union alone.

Germany's Changing Borders

HOLY ROMAN EMPIRE AT THE END OF THE THIRTY YEARS' WAR (PEACE OF WESTPHALIA, 1648)

Past borders
Swedish possession
Present borders

GERMAN EMPIRE 1871–1918

Past borders
Present borders

GERMANY AFTER THE TREATY OF VERSAILLES (1919–38)

Past borders
Present borders

WEST GERMANY AND EAST GERMANY 1949–90

East Germany
West Germany
Present borders

On 30 April the fighting reached the government quarter where Hitler was holed up in his bunker with his long-time mistress Eva Braun, whom he'd married just a day earlier. Finally accepting the inevitability of defeat, the couple killed themselves. As their bodies were burning in the chancellery courtyard, Red Army soldiers raised the Soviet flag above the Reichstag.

On 7 May 1945, Germany surrendered unconditionally. Peace was signed at the US military headquarters in Reims (France) and at the Soviet military headquarters in Berlin. On 8 May 1945, WWII in Europe officially came to an end.

The Big Chill

At conferences in Yalta and Potsdam in February and July 1945, respectively, the Allies (the USA, the UK, the Soviet Union and France) redrew Germany's borders and carved up the country into four occupied zones.

One of a clutch of fabulous films by Germany's best-known female director, Margarethe von Trotta, *Rosenstrasse* (2003) is a portrayal of the 1943 protest by a group of non-Jewish women against the deportation of their Jewish husbands.

1940	1941–43	1945	1948–49
The German Luftwaffe is defeated by the Spitfires of the RAF in the Battle of Britain, a major turning point in WWII. Hitler gives up on plans to invade Great Britain.	Nazi Germany invades the USSR in June 1941, but the campaign falters almost from the outset and defeat in the Battle of Stalingrad in 1942–43 drains valuable resources.	Hitler commits suicide in a Berlin bunker while a defeated Germany surrenders. Germany is split into Allied- and Soviet-occupied zones; Berlin has its own British, French, US and Soviet zones.	The USSR blocks land routes to Allied sectors of Berlin when cooperation between the Allies and the Soviets breaks down. More than 260,000 US and British flights supply West Berlin during the Berlin airlift.

THE BERLIN AIRLIFT

The Berlin Airlift was a triumph of determination and a glorious chapter in Berlin's post-war history. On 24 June 1948, the Soviets cut off all rail and road traffic into the city to force the Western Allies to give up their sectors and bring the entire city under Soviet control.

Faced with such provocation, many in the Allied camp urged responses that would have become the opening barrages of WWIII. In the end wiser heads prevailed, and a mere day after the blockade began the US Air Force launched 'Operation Vittles'. The British followed suit on 28 June with 'Operation Plane Fare'.

For the next 11 months Allied planes flew in food, coal, machinery and other supplies to the now-closed Tempelhof Airport in West Berlin. By the time the Soviets backed down, the Allies had made 278,000 flights, logged a distance equivalent to 250 round trips to the moon and delivered 2.5 million tonnes of cargo. The Luftbrückendenkmal (Berlin Airlift Memorial) outside the airport honours the effort and those who died carrying it out.

It was a monumental achievement that profoundly changed the relationship between Germany and the Western Allies, who were no longer regarded merely as occupying forces but as Schutzmächte (protective powers).

Best GDR-themed Museums

DDR Museum (p72), Berlin

Zeitgeschichtliches Forum (p316), Leipzig

Stasi Museum (p316), Leipzig

DDR Museum (p308), Pirna

Haus der Geschichte (p416), Lutherstadt Wittenberg

Friction between the Western Allies and the Soviets quickly emerged. While the Western Allies focused on helping Germany get back on its feet by kick-starting the devastated economy, the Soviets insisted on massive reparations and began brutalising and exploiting their own zone of occupation. Tens of thousands of able-bodied men and POWs ended up in *gulags* (labour camps) deep in the Soviet Union. Inflation still strained local economies, food shortages affected the population, and the Communist Party of Germany (KPD) and Social Democratic Party of Germany (SPD) were forced to unite as the Sozialistische Einheitspartei Deutschlands (SED; Socialist Unity Party). In the Allied zones, meanwhile, democracy was beginning to take root, as Germany elected state parliaments (1946–47).

The showdown came in June 1948, when the Allies introduced the Deutschmark in their zones. The USSR regarded this as a breach of the Potsdam Agreement, under which the powers had agreed to treat Germany as one economic zone. The Soviets issued their own currency, the Ostmark, and announced a full-scale economic blockade of West Berlin. The Allies responded with the remarkable Berlin airlift. For 11 months, American and British air crews flew in food, coal, machinery and other essential supplies to Tempelhof Airport in West Berlin. By the time the Soviets backed down, the Allies had made 278,000 flights, logged a distance equivalent to 250 round trips to the moon and delivered 2.5 million tonnes of cargo.

1949	1950	1951–61	1953
Allied-occupied West Germany becomes the FRG (Federal Republic of Germany); Bonn is capital. A separate East Germany (German Democratic Republic, GDR) is established in the Soviet-occupied zone; Berlin is capital.	The Christian Democratic Union (CDU) is founded at federal level in West Germany. Adenauer, known for supporting strong relationships with France and the US, is elected its first national chairman.	The economic vision of Ludwig Erhard unleashes West Germany's *Wirtschaftswunder* (economic miracle). The economy averages an annual growth rate of 8%.	Following the death of Stalin and unfulfilled hopes for better conditions in the GDR, workers and farmers rise up, strike or demonstrate in 560 towns and cities. Soviet troops quash the uprising.

Two German States

In 1949 the division of Germany – and Berlin – was formalised. The western zones evolved into the Bundesrepublik Deutschland (BRD, Federal Republic of Germany or FRG) with Konrad Adenauer as its first chancellor and Bonn, as its capital. An economic aid package, dubbed the Marshall Plan, created the basis for West Germany's *Wirtschaftswunder* (economic miracle), which saw the economy grow at an average 8% per year between 1951 and 1961. The recovery was largely engineered by economics minister Ludwig Erhard, who dealt with an acute labour shortage by inviting about 2.3 million foreign workers, mainly from Turkey, Yugoslavia and Italy, to Germany, thereby laying the foundation for today's multicultural society.

The Soviet zone, meanwhile, grew into the Deutsche Demokratische Republik (DDR, German Democratic Republic or GDR) with East Berlin as its capital and Wilhelm Pieck as its first president. A single party, the Sozialistische Einheitspartei Deutschlands (SED, Socialist Unity Party of Germany), led by party boss Walter Ulbricht, dominated economic, judicial and security policy. In order to suppress any opposition, the Ministry for State Security, or Stasi, was established in 1950.

Economically, East Germany stagnated, in large part because of the Soviets' continued policy of asset stripping and reparation payments. Stalin's death in 1953 raised hopes for reform but only spurred the GDR government to raise production goals even higher. Smouldering discontent erupted in violence on 17 June 1953, when 10% of GDR workers took to the streets. Soviet troops quashed the uprising, with scores of deaths and the arrest of about 1200 people.

The Wall: What Goes Up...

Through the 1950s the economic gulf between East and West Germany widened, prompting 3.6 million East Germans – mostly young and well educated – to seek a future in the West, thus putting the GDR on the brink of economic and political collapse. Eventually, this sustained brain and brawn drain prompted the East German government – with Soviet consent – to build a wall to keep its citizens in. Construction of the Berlin Wall, the Cold War's most potent symbol, began on the night of 13 August 1961.

This stealthy act left Berliners stunned. Formal protests from the Western Allies, as well as massive demonstrations in West Berlin, were ignored. Tense times followed. In October 1961, US and Soviet tanks faced off at the Berlin border crossing Checkpoint Charlie in a display of brinksmanship.

The appointment of Erich Honecker (1912–94) as leader of East Germany in 1971, combined with the *Ostpolitik* (East-friendly policy) of West German Chancellor Willy Brandt (1913–92), allowed for an easier political relationship between the East and the West. In September that year all four Allies signed a Four Power Accord that regulated access between

HISTORY TWO GERMAN STATES

Interviews with former Stasi men in the mid-1990s form the basis of Australian journalist Anna Funder's *Stasiland* (2003) – crammed with fresh and alternative insights into what the men of the Stasi did after it was disbanded.

1954	1955	Early 1960s	1961
West Germany wins the FIFA World Cup, a famous victory that will become known as 'the miracle of Bern'.	In a sign of increasing divisions between the two states, West Germany joins NATO while East Germany puts its name to the Warsaw Pact.	Thousands of *Gastarbeiter* (guest workers) from Turkey, Yugoslavia, Italy, Greece and Spain are invited to take up jobs in the booming West German economy.	On the night of 13 August, the GDR government begins building the Berlin Wall, a 155km-long barrier surrounding West Berlin.

After the Wall (1995), by Marc Fisher, is an account of German society, with emphasis on life after die Wende (fall of the Berlin Wall and reunification). Fisher was bureau chief for the *Washington Post* in Bonn and presents some perceptive social insights.

West Berlin and West Germany, guaranteed West Berliners the right to visit East Berlin and the GDR, and even granted GDR citizens permission to travel to West Germany in cases of family emergency.

The accord also paved the way for the *Grundlagenvertrag* (Basic Treaty), signed a year later, in which the two countries recognised each other's sovereignty and borders and committed to setting up 'permanent missions' in Bonn and East Berlin.

In 1975 West Germany joined the G6 group of industrial nations. But the 1970s were also a time of terrorism, and several prominent business and political figures were assassinated by the anti-capitalist Red Army Faction (RAF). In the same decade, antinuclear and green issues appeared on the agenda, which ultimately lead to the founding of Die Grünen (the Green Party) in 1980.

...Must Come Down

Hearts and minds in Eastern Europe had long been restless for change, but German reunification caught even the most insightful political observers by surprise. The so-called die Wende (falling of the Berlin Wall and reunification) came about as a gradual development that ended in a big bang – the fall of the Berlin Wall on 9 November 1989.

Prior to the Wall's collapse, East Germans were, once again, leaving their country in droves, this time via Hungary, which had opened its borders with Austria. The SED was helpless to stop the flow of people wanting to leave, some of whom sought refuge in the West German embassy in Prague. Meanwhile, mass demonstrations in Leipzig spread to other cities, including East Berlin.

As the situation escalated, Erich Honecker relinquished leadership to Egon Krenz (b 1937). And then the floodgates opened: on the fateful night of 9 November 1989, party functionary Günter Schabowski informed GDR citizens they could travel directly to the West, effective immediately. The announcement itself was correct but it was not supposed to be made until the following day, leaving border guards overwhelmed. Tens of thousands of East Germans jubilantly rushed through border points in Berlin and elsewhere in the country, bringing to an end the long, chilly phase of German division.

The Post-Unification Years

The Germany of today, with 16 unified states, was hammered out after a volatile political debate and a series of treaties to end post-WWII occupation zones. The reunited city of Berlin became a city-state. A common currency and economic union became realities in July 1990 and a mere month later the Unification Treaty was signed in Berlin. In September that year, representatives of East and West Germany, the USSR, France,

1963	1972	1972	1974
US President John F Kennedy professes his solidarity with the people of Berlin when giving his famous 'Ich bin ein Berliner' speech at the main town hall in West Berlin.	Social Democrat chancellor Willy Brandt's *Ostpolitik* thaws relations between the two Germanys. The Basic Treaty is signed in East Berlin, paving the way for both countries to join the UN.	Munich hosts the Olympic Games, which end in tragedy when Palestinian terrorists murder two Israeli competitors and take nine hostage. A botched rescue operation kills all nine.	West Germany wins the FIFA World Cup. The final is played at Munich's Olympic Stadium.

the UK and the US met in Moscow to sign the Two-Plus-Four Treaty, ending postwar occupation zones and paving the way for formal German reunification. One month later, the East German state was dissolved; in December Germany held its first unified post-WWII elections.

The single most dominant figure throughout reunification and the 1990s was Helmut Kohl, whose Christlich Demokratische Union Deutschlands (Christian Democratic Union; CDU)/Christlich-Soziale Union (Christian Social Union; CSU) and Freie Demokratische Partei (Free Democratic Party; FDP) coalition was re-elected to office in December 1990 in Germany's first post-reunification election.

Under Kohl's leadership, East German assets were privatised; oversubsidised state industries were radically trimmed back, sold or wound up completely; and infrastructure was modernised to create a unification boom that saw the former East Germany grow by up to 10% each year until 1995.

Growth slowed dramatically from the mid-1990s, however, creating an eastern Germany that consisted of unification winners and losers. Those who had jobs did well, but unemployment was high and the lack of opportunities in a number of eastern regions was still causing many young people to try their luck in western Germany or in boom towns, such as Leipzig. Berlin, although economically shaky, was the exception. Many public servants relocated there from Bonn to staff the ministries, and young people from all over Germany were attracted by its vibrant cultural scene.

Kohl's involvement in a party slush-fund scandal in the late 1990s financially burdened his own party and resulted in the CDU stripping him of his position as lifelong honorary chairman. In 1998, a coalition of the SPD and Bündnis 90/Die Grünen (Alliance 90/The Greens) parties defeated the CDU/CSU and FDP coalition.

> **Top Insights into German History**
>
> *Deutsches Historisches Museum (p59),* Berlin
>
> *Haus der Geschichte (p647),* Bonn
>
> *Zeitgeschichtliches Forum (p316),* Leipzig
>
> *Jüdisches Museum (p85),* Berlin
>
> *Römisch-Germanisches Museum (p632),* Cologne

HISTORY THE NEW MILLENNIUM

The New Millennium

With the formation of a coalition government of SPD and Alliance 90/The Greens in 1998, Germany reached a new milestone. It marked the first time an environmentalist party had governed nationally – in Germany or elsewhere in the world. Two figures dominated the seven-year rule of the coalition: Chancellor Gerhard Schröder (b 1944) and the Green Party vice-chancellor and foreign minister Joschka Fischer (b 1948). Despite the latter's left-wing house-squatting roots in 1970s Frankfurt am Main, he enjoyed respect abroad and widespread popularity among Germans of all political stripes.

Under Schröder, Germany began to take a more independent approach to foreign policy, refusing military involvement in Iraq but supporting the USA, historically its closest ally, in Afghanistan and the war in Kosovo. Its stance on Iraq, which reflected the feelings of

1977	1985	1989	1989
The *Deutscher Herbst* (German Autumn) envelops West Germany, when a second generation of the left-wing Red Army Faction (RAF) murders key business and state figures.	Teenage sensation Boris Becker wins the Wimbledon tennis tournament. At the age of 17, he is the youngest player and first German to do so.	Demonstrations are held in Leipzig and other East German cities. Hungary opens its border with Austria, and East Germans are able to travel to the West.	The Berlin Wall comes down, causing communist regimes across Eastern Europe to fall like dominoes. East Germans flood into West Germany.

ANGELA MERKEL: THE ENIGMATIC CHANCELLOR

Some say that she's enigmatic; others, that she likes to keep a low profile when political dissonance breaks out, especially within her own party. Indisputable, however, is that Angela Merkel's rise to become German chancellor in 2005 brought about a number of firsts. She was Germany's first woman and first former East German in the job and, because of the latter, she also became the first Russian-speaking German chancellor.

Merkel was born in Hamburg in 1954 but grew up in the boondocks – in the Uckermark region (in Brandenburg, near the Polish border), where her father had a posting as a pastor in East Germany. She studied physics in Leipzig (and later earned a doctorate in quantum chemistry from the Academy of Sciences of the German Democratic Republic), entering politics as the GDR was falling apart. Soon she was honing her political skills in the ministries of a reunified Germany (Women and Youth was one ministry; Environment, Natural Protection and Reactor Safety was another) under Helmut Kohl, which is why she's sometimes called 'Kohl's foster child'. Her breakthrough came in the late 1990s when the reputations of several CDU high-flyers suffered as a result of a party slush fund.

While political commentators outside Germany have often compared her to the former UK prime minister Margaret Thatcher, Merkel's leadership style rarely has the bite of Britain's 'Iron Lady'. What Thatcher and Merkel do have in common, though, is that both have ranked among the *Forbes* list of the 100 most powerful women in the world – Angela Merkel has topped every list (bar the one in 2010 when she dropped to No 4) since 2006.

the majority of Germans, strained relations with the George W Bush administration.

The rise of the Greens and, more recently, the democratic socialist Die Linke (The Left), has changed the political landscape of Germany dramatically, making absolute majorities by the 'big two' (ie CDU/CSU and SPD) all the more difficult to achieve. The 2005 election brought a grand coalition of CDU/CSU and SPD with Angela Merkel (b 1954) as chancellor – the first woman, former East German, Russian speaker and quantum chemist in the job. While many Germans hoped this would resolve a political stalemate that had existed between an opposition-led *Bundesrat* (upper house) and the government, political horse trading shifted away from the political limelight and was mostly carried out behind closed doors.

When the financial crisis struck in 2008, the German government pumped hundreds of billions of euros into the financial system to prop up the banks. Other measures allowed companies to put workers on shorter shifts without loss of pay and such incentive schemes as encouraging Germans to trade older cars for new ones.

The election of 2009 confirmed the trend towards smaller parties and a five-party political system in Germany. Both CDU/CSU and SPD lost a considerable number of votes to the FDP, Left and Green parties. Support for the Left had been consistently strong in eastern Germany,

1990	2005	2006	2008
Berlin becomes the capital of reunified Germany. Helmut Kohl's conservative coalition promises East–West economic integration, creating unrealistic expectations of a blossoming economic landscape in the east.	Angela Merkel becomes Germany's first female chancellor, leading a grand coalition of major parties after the election results in neither the SPD nor the CDU/CSU being able to form its own government.	Germans proudly fly their flag as the country hosts the FIFA World Cup for the first time as a unified nation.	The economic crisis bites deeply into German export industries. German banks are propped up by state funds as unemployment and state debt rise again.

but success in 2009 allowed it to establish itself at the federal level. The 2013 election slightly reversed the trend, with the big parties gaining back some of the votes. The biggest loser that year was the FDP, which garnered a mere 4.8% (9.8% less than in 2009), thus falling below the 5% required for representation in the Bundestag.

The 2013 election also saw the meteoric rise of a new conservative party, the Euro-skeptic Alternative für Deutschland (AfD, Alternative for Germany). Founded in April 2013, it scooped up 4.7% of the vote, with a platform advocating a return to the Deutschmark and other national currencies, a flat tax of 25% and tighter immigration laws. Voters were drawn from across the political spectrum but shared a general disillusionment with existing parties.

Although narrowly missing the 5% Bundestag threshold, the AfD has since gained representation in the European Parliament and in the state parliaments of Brandenburg, Saxony, Thuringia, Hamburg and Bremen. However, the election of the national conservative Frauke Petry as party leader at the AfD convention in July 2015 prompted thousands of more moderate members, including co-founder Bernd Lucke, to leave the party. A couple of weeks later, Lucke founded a new party, called Alfa.

In her convention speech, Petry garnered some of the biggest applause for her Islamophobic stance, which reflects her popularity among sympathisers of the anti-Islam, anti-immigrant PEGIDA ('Patriotic Europeans against the Islamisation of the West'), a populist movement founded in Dresden in October 2014. Although subject to strong criticism for its ties to the far right, PEGIDA quickly managed to attract thousands of followers and made headlines throughout the winter of 2014–15 with weekly demonstrations that peaked with 25,000 participants in January 2015. This sparked numerous, even bigger counter-rallies, as well as public condemnation by senior politicians, including Angela Merkel, and celebrities.

The issue fuelling support for both AfD and PEGIDA is the wave of political and economic refugees trying to enter Europe. In 2017, Germany handled more asylum applications than the rest of the EU combined; as many as 524,185 applications for asylum were processed, an increase of 5.8% compared to the previous year. Xenophobia and frustration with existing immigration laws and policies have led to a number of arson attacks on shelters built for asylum seekers to live in while their applications grind through Germany's complex bureaucratic process.

Amid all these serious developments came a moment of levity in 2014, when the German national soccer team won the FIFA World Cup for the fourth time. The title had previously been bestowed in 1954, 1974 and 1990.

In early 2012 the tombstone on Hitler's parents' grave was removed from the Austrian village of Leonding, to prevent it becoming a shrine for neo-Nazis.

Two of the best websites for current reports and facts about Germany are *The Economist* magazine's country profile at www.economist.com/countries/germany and the BBC News website, www.bbc.com/news/world/europe (search for 'Germany' in the search bar).

2009	2014	2015	2017
The CDU/CSU and FDP achieve a majority in the federal election. Angela Merkel is re-elected as chancellor.	Germany's national football team wins the FIFA World Cup in Brazil, with a score of 1-0 against Argentina thanks to an extra-time goal by Mario Götze.	Germany is affected by the migrant crisis and welcomes around one million refugees. Numbers of asylum seekers continue to climb in subsequent years.	The country marks the 500th anniversary of the Reformation with festivals, concerts and special exhibitions across the country.

The German People

When a 2017 BBC Worldwide poll found that Germany was considered the most positively viewed nation in the world, it surprised many people, most of all the Germans themselves – having long been called arrogant, aggressive and humourless, they were hardly used to such positive feedback. But the poll shows that times are a-changing, proving that modern leadership, a belief in the power of diplomacy and, let's not forget, a pretty good national soccer team can ultimately make a difference.

The National Psyche

The German state of mind has long attracted speculation; two 20th-century wars and the memory of the Jewish Holocaust alone provide ample reason to consider the German psyche. Throw in Cold War division, a juggernaut-like economy that draws half of Europe in its wake and pumps tons of goods into the world economy, plus a crucial position at the crossroads of Europe, and this fascination is even more understandable.

Often, though, it pays to ignore the stereotypes, jingoism and headlines describing Germany in military terms – and maybe even forgive Germans for the systematic way they clog up a football field or conduct jagged discussion. It also helps to see the country through its regional nuances. Germany was very slow to become a nation; if you look closely, you'll notice many different local cultures within the one set of borders (somewhat similar to Italy). You'll also discover one of Europe's most multicultural countries, with Turkish, Greek, Italian, Russian and Balkan influences.

Around 15 million people live in the former GDR, a part of Germany where, until 1989, travel was restricted, the state was almighty and life was secure – albeit highly regulated – from the cradle to grave. Unsurprisingly, many former East Germans are still coming to terms with a more competitive, unified Germany. Many 'easterners' still maintain that the GDR had its good qualities, and some elderly former East German citizens say they were happier or lived better at that time. More than a quarter-century after reunification the eastern states continue to lose brains and skills to the west.

Germans as a whole fall within the mental topography of northern Europe and are sometimes described as culturally 'low context'. That means, as opposed to the French or Italians, Germans like to pack what they mean into the words they use, rather than hint or suggest. Facing each other squarely in conversation, giving firm handshakes and hugs or kisses on the cheek among friends are also par for the course.

Many Germans are very much fans of their own folk culture. Even a young Bavarian from, say, the finance department of a large company, might don the Dirndl (traditional Bavarian skirt and blouse) around Oktoberfest time and swill like a hearty, rollicking peasant. On Monday she'll be back at the desk, soberly crunching numbers.

The Deutscher Frauenrat (German Women's Council; www. frauenrat.de) lobbies for women's issues.

Lifestyle

The German household fits into the general mould of those in other Western European countries. However, a closer look reveals some distinctly German quirks, including a compulsion for sorting and recycling rubbish, a taste for fizzy mineral water and a springtime obsession with asparagus.

Although tradition is valued and grandmother's heirlooms may still occupy pride of place in many a house, 3D smart TVs babble away in living rooms across the land, and Germany boasts 71 million internet surfers (88% of the population), roughly 30 million of whom also have a Facebook account. Eight in 10 Germans own a bike, but there's a car in almost every driveway, embodying the German belief that true freedom comes on four wheels and is best expressed by tearing along the autobahn at 200km/h or more. For many outsiders this high level of car use is incongruous with the Germans' green credentials.

One aspect of life many visitors can't help but notice is the high number of smokers, although levels are declining. Almost 29% of German men and 20% of women smoke, despite various smoking bans (which are different in each state). Alcohol consumption is also high and on the increase.

Smoking is the least of the problems continuing to plague the east of the country, where unemployment and a brain drain to the west dog the economy. Even when in employment, eastern Germans can expect to earn around 20% less than they would in the western states.

Birth rates are among the lowest in the world (8.6 babies per 1000 inhabitants) and have fallen steadily over the last decade, prompting fears that future labour market shortages will damage the economy. Although the traditional nuclear family is still the most common model, there is no social stigma attached to other family forms. Since one in three marriages end in divorce, many families today are so-called 'patchwork families', composed of divorced new partners and their children from a previous relationship.

Controversially, abortion is still illegal (except when a medical or criminal indication exists), but it is unpunishable if carried out within

GREEN GERMANY

Germans are the original Greens. They cannot claim to have invented environmentalism, but they were there at the outset and it was they who coined the word to describe the movement. A few 'values' and 'ecology' parties were knocking around beforehand, but it was the group of politicians associated with Rudi Dutschke, Petra Kelly and artist Joseph Beuys who first hit on the name The Greens (Die Grünen) when contesting local and national elections in 1979 and 1980. They gained a strong foothold in Bremen, and other political groups across the world decided they quite liked the moniker.

The Greens' concern for the health of the planet and their strong opposition to nuclear power certainly struck a chord with the local populace. Contemporary Germans recycle vigilantly, often prefer to ride bicycles rather than catch buses, and carry their groceries in reusable cloth shopping bags; all of this is simply second nature here.

Green ideology has also wielded an enormous influence on the political agenda. In the 1990s, Greenpeace Germany made international news attempting to stop nuclear-waste transports in Lower Saxony and heavily populated North Rhine–Westphalia. German Greenpeace members also helped scuttle Shell's controversial plans to sink the Brent Spar oil platform in the North Sea.

Even more tellingly, the Greens were in government between 1998 and 2005, as the junior partner in Gerhard Schröder's coalition. Under the leadership of Joschka Fischer, the party had a major say in decisions to cut carbon emissions and to wind down the nuclear industry. In 2011, Germany announced the decision to phase out nuclear energy by 2022. In the 2017 federal elections, the Greens scooped 8.9% of the votes and 67 out of 709 seats in the Bundestag.

> Some 15% of German beach tourists say they have sunbathed in the nude, more than any other nation.

12 weeks of conception and after compulsory counselling. Same-sex marriage has been legal since 1 October 2017, when the Bundestag passed legislation allowing gay couples full marital rights. Gays and lesbians walk with ease in most cities, especially Berlin, Hamburg, Cologne and Frankfurt am Main, although LGBT folk do encounter discrimination in certain eastern German areas.

German school hours, which are usually from 8am to 1pm (until 4pm for the less common 'all day' schools), and the underfunding of child care make combining career and children difficult for German women. On the plus side, parents enjoy equal rights for maternity and paternity leave.

On the whole, the number of women in employment is increasing. About 74% of working-age women are employed – high for an EU country – but lower than neighbours Switzerland, the Netherlands and the Scandinavian countries. Almost half of these women work part-time, and in eastern Germany women tend to have more of a presence at managerial level.

The official retirement age is 67, but changes may see this gradually increase to 69 in the coming decades.

Sport

Always a keen sporting nation, Germany has hosted the summer Olympics and football World Cup twice each. The Germans, it seems, are dastardly good at most sporting disciplines, and if your country has a national game, the Germans probably thrashed you at it a long time ago.

Football

Football ignites the passion of Germans everywhere and has contributed to building Germany's self-confidence as a nation. Its national side has won the World Cup four times: in 1954, 1974, 1990 and 2014. West Germany's first victory against Hungary in Bern, Switzerland, was unexpected and quite miraculous for a country mired deeply in post-WWII depression. The 'miracle of Bern' – as the victory was dubbed – sent national morale soaring.

During the early stages of the World Cup in June 2018, the country fell into a state of deep shock following the surprise exit of the team after just three group-stage games in a 2-0 loss to South Korea. It was the first time Germany had been knocked out in the first round since 1938.

Germany has hosted the World Cup twice, in 1974 and 2006. The first occasion was particularly special, as West Germany beat Holland 2-1 in the final, held at Munich's Olympic stadium.

Domestically, Germany's Bundesliga has fallen behind other European leagues, such as Spain's La Liga and England's Premier League, but still throws up some exciting duels. On the European stage, Germany's most successful club is FC Bayern Munich, which has been *Deutscher Meister* (national champion) 28 times and has won the UEFA Champions League five times, the last time in 2012-13. A current star layer is Manuel Neuer, who has regularly been hailed the world's best goalkeeper.

Women's football is growing in popularity, partly because of the success of the women's national team. Germany has won the FIFA Women's World Cup twice (in 2003 and 2007) and hosted the event in 2011.

Tennis

Tennis was a minor sport in Germany until 1985, when the unseeded 17-year-old Boris Becker (b 1967), became the youngest ever men's singles champion. Suddenly every German kid aspired to be the next Becker. The red-headed net-diver, from Leimen near Heidelberg, went on to win five more Grand Slam titles in his career. Even more successful was Steffi Graf (b 1969), who is among the few women to have won all four Grand Slam events in one year, and in 1988 – after also winning the gold in Seoul at the Olympics – the 'golden slam'. A current player with the potential to follow in Becker's footsteps is Alexander Zverev, who clinched the No.4 ranking in men's singles in 2017, a career best on the ATP World Tour.

Other Sports
Though a relatively minor sport in Germany, basketball is gaining in popularity. Cycling boomed after Jan Ullrich (b 1973) became the first German to win the Tour de France in 1997. With seven world championships and a record 91 Grand Prix wins, Michael Schumacher (b 1969) was the most successful Formula One driver of all time, before suffering a major head injury in a skiing accident in 2013. After months in an induced coma, he returned to his home in September 2014, but remains paralysed and wheelchair-bound.

Multiculturalism
Germany has always attracted immigrants, be it French Huguenots escaping religious persecution (about 30% of Berlin's population in 1700 was Huguenot), 19th-century Polish miners who settled in the Ruhr region, post-WWII asylum seekers or foreign *Gastarbeiter* (guest workers) during the 1950s and 1960s to resolve labour shortages.

After reunification, the foreign population soared, as emigrants from the imploding USSR and the then war-ravaged Yugoslavia sought refuge. Between 1990 and 2011, Germany also accommodated around 1.4 million *Spätaussiedler* (people of German heritage), mainly from Russia, Poland and Kazakhstan.

In 2015 and 2016, a large influx of migrants, refugees and asylum seekers from the Middle East, Africa and elsewhere bolstered the number of people with an immigrant background in Germany to a record 18.6 million. A little over a fifth (22.5%) of the population were first- or second-generation immigrants, meaning that at least one parent was born without German citizenship.

The growth of the immigrant population has triggered a rise in extreme right-wing movements, which oppose such a huge non-native presence in the country. Ironically, the problem is worst in the eastern states, where there are fewer immigrants. As across Europe, the debate as to whether Germany should promote a German *Leitkultur* (lead culture), as opposed to multiculturalism, polarises opinion.

Religion
The constitution guarantees religious freedom; the main religions are Catholicism and Protestantism, with 23.6 million and 21.9 million members respectively. Religion has a stronger footing in western Germany, especially Catholic Bavaria.

Unlike the Jewish community, which has grown since the early 1990s due to immigration from the former Soviet Union, the Catholic and Protestant churches are losing worshippers. This is attributed partly to the obligatory church tax (8% or 9% of total income tax paid) forked out by those registered with a recognised denomination. Most German Protestants are Lutheran, headed by the Evangelische Kirche (Protestant Church), an official grouping of a couple of dozen Lutheran churches, with headquarters in Hanover. In 2005, for the first time in almost five centuries, a German, Joseph Ratzinger (b 1927), became pope, taking the name Pope Benedict XVI. He resigned in 2013.

The largest Jewish communities are in Berlin, Frankfurt am Main and Munich. Countrywide, 108 congregations are represented by the Zentralrat der Juden in Deutschland (Central Council of Jews in Germany). Around four million Muslims live in Germany, most of Turkish heritage.

Food & Drink

You probably didn't choose Germany for its food, right? But the culinary revolution that's been simmering for years under the sausage-cabbage-and-carbs layers is finally bubbling to the surface. Up and down the country you'll find chefs playing up local, seasonal produce and making healthy, creative street food. There are exciting riffs on vegetarian and vegan food, and organic everything. Some wines these days can rival the French and Italian old-timers. Dig in and drink up – you might just be surprised.

Local & Lighter

Above Golden chante-relle mushrooms, the Black Forest (p490)

The German love of nature and eye for quality is reflected in what lands on the table. Long before 'seasonal' and 'local' were buzzwords, Germans made the most of locally grown produce. Menus burst with *Spargel* (as-paragus) in spring and *Pfifferlinge* (chanterelles) in summer. In autumn the earthy delights of game, pumpkins and wild mushrooms enchant.

Regional food at its best is about perfect timing, top-quality ingredients and dishes with natural, integral flavours.

Cheap frankfurters, frozen Black Forest gateau and Liebfraumilch (a sweet white wine) may have tarnished Germany's culinary image in the past, but things are swiftly changing, with dishes getting lighter, healthier and more imaginative. Vegetarians, vegans and people with food allergies are well catered for, especially in big towns and cities. Germans like to shop at *Bauernmärkte* (farmers markets) and *Biomärkte* (organic markets and supermarkets), where they can put a face and place to a product.

Germany is also raising the bar in the street-food stakes, where you can now find a world beyond the ubiquitous wurst and kebab. The rest of the country, as always, is hot on the heels of Berlin, where food trucks and stands dish out everything from quirky takes on ceviche to *jiaozi* (Chinese dumplings), gourmet burgers made with 100% local beef and organic frozen yoghurt.

German Classics

Metre-long bratwursts with litres of foamy wheat beer in Munich, snowball-sized dumplings with an avalanche of sauerkraut and roast pork in the Alps, salads swimming in dressing and cakes drowning in cream – every traveller has a tale of German food excess.

On paper, Germany's best-known specialities appear deceptively simple: wurst, *Brot, Kartoffeln* and sauerkraut (sausage, bread, potatoes and pickled cabbage). But, as any local will tell you, the devil is in the detail. Where else will you find so many kinds of sausage, such a cornucopia of bread and potatoes in so many guises? Elevated to near art forms, these staples both unite and divide the country: ingredients are often similar but regional recipes interpret them in totally different ways.

Sausage Country

In the Middle Ages, German peasants found a way to package and disguise animals' less appetising bits and the humble Wurst (sausage) was born. Today, it's a noble and highly respected element of German cuisine, with strict rules determining varietal authenticity. In some cases, as with the finger-sized Nuremberg sausage, regulations even ensure offal no longer enters the equation.

SWEET TREATS

Unleash your sweet tooth on these German favourites:

Schwarzwälderkirschtorte (Black Forest gateau) A multilayered chocolate sponge, cream and kirsch confection, topped with morello cherries and chocolate shavings.

Nürnberg Lebkuchen Totally moreish gingerbread from Nuremberg made with nuts, fruit peel, honey and spices.

Lübecker Leckerli Honey-flavoured ginger biscuits. Also try the fabulous Lübeck marzipan.

Dresden Stollen Christmas wouldn't be the same without this spiced cake, loaded with sultanas and candied peel, sprinkled with icing sugar and spruced up with a ball of marzipan.

Leipziger Lerche As its name suggests, it was made with lark until songbird hunting was banned in 1876. Today it's a shortcrust pastry filled with almonds, nuts and a cherry or spoon of jam.

Aachener Printen Aachen's riff on traditional *Lebkuchen* (gingerbread), these spicy, moreish biscuits are sweetened with beet syrup.

Dresden Stollen

There are more than 1500 sausage types, all commonly served with bread and a sweet *(süss)* or spicy *(scharf)* mustard *(Senf)*.

Bratwurst, served countrywide, is made from minced pork, veal and spices, and is cooked in different ways: boiled in beer, baked with apples and cabbage, stewed in a casserole, grilled or barbecued.

The availability of other sausages differs regionally. A *Thüringer* is long, thin and spiced. *Blutwurst* is blood sausage (not to be confused with black pudding, which is *Rotwurst*), *Leberwurst* is liver sausage and *Knackwurst* is lightly tickled with garlic.

Saxony has brain sausage *(Bregenwurst)* and Bavaria sells the white, rubbery *Weisswurst,* made from veal. Hamburg, Berlin and the Ruhrgebiet all claim to have invented the takeaway *Currywurst* (slices of sausage topped with curry powder and ketchup).

Daily Bread

In exile in California in 1941, German playwright Bertolt Brecht confessed that what he missed most about his homeland was the bread. Tasty and textured, often mixing wheat and rye flours, and available in 300 varieties, German bread is a world-beater. A visit to an old-fashioned *Bäckerei* (bakery), with yeasty smells wafting from ovens, bakers elbow-deep in dough and staff who remember customers by name, is a treat.

'Black' rye bread *(Schwarzbrot)* is actually brown, but a much darker shade than the slightly sour *Bauernbrot* – divine with a slab of butter. Pumpernickel bread is steamed instead of baked, making it extra moist, and actually *is* black. *Vollkorn* means wholemeal, while bread coated in sunflower seeds is *Sonnenblumenbrot*. If you insist on white bread *(Weissbrot),* the Germans have that, too.

Fresh bread rolls *(Brötchen* in the north, *Semmel* in Bavaria, *Wecken* in southern Germany) can be covered in poppy seeds *(Mohnbrötchen),*

Pork knuckle with sauerkraut at Zur Letzten Instanz (p110), Berlin

cooked with sweet raisins *(Rosinenbrötchen)* or sprinkled with salt *(Salzstangel)*.

King Kartoffel

Chipped, boiled, baked, mashed, fried: Germans are almost as keen as Russians about the potato. The *Kartoffel* is not only the *Vegetable Nummer Eins* (first-choice vegetable) in any meat-and-three-veg dish; it can also be incorporated into any course of a meal, including potato soup *(Kartoffelsuppe)* as a starter, potato salad *(Kartoffelsalat)* with smoked fish as a main, or potato pancakes *(Reibekuchen* or *Kartoffelpuffer)* as a sweet, sugar-sprinkled treat.

In between, you can try *Himmel und Erde* (Heaven and Earth) – mashed potatoes and stewed apples served with black pudding – or potato-based *Klösse* dumplings. *Pellkartoffeln* or *Ofenkartoffeln* are jacket potatoes, usually capped with a dollop of *Quark* (a yoghurt-like curd cheese).

> *Quark* accounts for 50% of domestic cheese consumption in Germany. It is used in everything from potato dips to salad dressings and sauces to cheesecake.

Pickled Cabbage

It's the quintessential German side dish that many outside the country find impossible to fathom: sauerkraut. Bluntly put, it's shredded cabbage, doused in white-wine vinegar and slowly simmered. But if you haven't at least tried *Rotkohl* (the red-cabbage version of the white-cabbage sauerkraut), you don't know what you're missing. Braising the cabbage with sliced apples and wine turns it into *Bayrischkraut* or *Weinkraut*.

Regional Flavours

Berlin

Alongside Hamburg, Berlin has one of the country's most dynamic and swiftly evolving restaurant scenes, but it can still lay claim to local delicacies. First up is *Eisbein* (ham hock with sauerkraut), then *Kohlsuppe* (cabbage soup) and *Erbsensuppe* (pea soup). Then there's the classic meaty treat eaten on the hoof: the *Boulette,* a German-style hamburger, eaten with a dry bun and ketchup or mustard. Don't bypass the chance to give *Königsberger Klopse* (veal dumplings in caper sauce) a whirl, either.

Berlin is also where you'll find the country's highest concentration of Turkish *Döner Kebab* (doner kebab) spots, an essential end to any drink-fuelled night on the town. Germany's Turkish population invented the modern doner, adding salad and garlicky yoghurt sauce to spit-roasted lamb, veal or chicken in pita bread.

Bavaria

The Chinese say you can eat every part of the pig except the oink, and Bavarian chefs seem to be in full agreement. No part of the animal is spared their attention: they cook up its knuckles *(Schweinshax'n),* ribs *(Rippchen),* tongue *(Züngerl)* and belly *(Wammerl).* Pork also appears as *Schweinebraten* (a roast) and the misleadingly named *Leberkäse* (liver cheese), where it's combined with beef in a dish that contains no cheese – and in Bavaria at least – no liver. The Bavarians are also quite fond of veal *(Kalb).*

Dumplings are another staple, from the potato-based *Klösse* and *Leberknödel* (liver dumplings) to the sweet *Senfknödel,* made from *Quark,* flour and eggs, then dunked in milk. Dumplings also make a major appearance in the Franconian *Hochzeitssuppe* (wedding soup), a clear meat broth garnished with bread dumplings, liver dumplings and pancakes.

Music to the ears of Bavarian *Biergarten* (beer garden) fans is that the Bavarian *Brezel* (pretzel) and *Obazda* (Bavarian cheese) were given Protected Geographical Indication by the EU in 2014 and 2015, respectively.

Stuttgart & the Black Forest

The food here, in the country's southwestern crook, is rich and earthy. Black Forest musts include *Bachforelle* (brook trout), fished from crystal-clear streams, *Schwarzwälderschinken* (dry-cured ham with a smoky aroma) and the world-famous, off-the-calorie-charts *Schwarzwälderkirschtorte* (Black Forest gateau). Seasonal additions to local menus include asparagus in spring/early summer, and mushrooms and pumpkins in autumn. Another autumnal treat is *Zwiebelkuchen,* a deep-filled onion tart, made with cream, egg, bacon and onions.

A BELOVED TRADITION: KAFFEE & KUCHEN

Anyone who has spent any length of time in Germany knows the reverence bestowed on the 3pm ritual of *Kaffee und Kuchen* (coffee and cake). More than just a chance to devour delectable cakes and tortes, Germans see it as a social event. You'll find *Cafe-Konditoreien* (cafe-cake shops) pretty much everywhere – in castles, in the middle of the forest, even plopped on top of mountains. Track down the best by asking sweet-toothed locals where the cake is *hausgemacht* (homemade).

While coffee in Germany is not as strong as that served in France or Italy, you can expect a decent cup. All the usual varieties are on offer, including cappuccinos and lattes, although you'll still frequently see French-style bowls of milky coffee *(Milchkaffee).* Order a *Kanne* (pot) or *Tasse* (cup) of *Kaffee* and what you will get is filter coffee, usually with a portion of *Kaffeesahne* (condensed milk).

East Frisians in Bremen and Lower Saxony are the country's biggest consumers of tea, and have dozens of their own varieties, which they traditionally drink with cream and *Kluntje* (rock sugar). Tea frequently comes as a glass or pot of hot water, with the tea bag served to the side.

Käsespätzle (egg based pasta-like dish with cheese)

Swabian folk around Stuttgart are mad about *Spätzle*, egg-based noodles served as a main with cheese *(Käsespätzle)*, or as a side dish with meat or fish. *Zwiebelrostbraten* (roast beef with onions and gravy) and *Maultaschen* (ravioli-like pockets stuffed with ground meat, onion and spinach) are other favourites.

Frankfurt & the Southern Rhineland

Two former chancellors named dishes from Rhineland-Palatinate as their favourite: Helmut Kohl nominated *Saumagen*, stuffed pork belly with pickled cabbage (vaguely resembling Scottish haggis), while post-WWII chancellor Konrad Adenauer preferred *Reibekuchen* (potato pancakes served with blueberry or apple sauce). Despite this, *Rheinischer Sauerbraten* (roast beef marinated in spiced vinegar and braised) is the region's signature dish.

Hesse produces outstanding cured and smoked hams, typically smoking them over juniper berries. Another regional favourite is pig in the form of *Sulperknochen,* a dish from trotters, ears and tails, served with mushy peas and pickled cabbage.

Saarland borders France and it shows. Fried goose liver and coq au vin are common, as is *Budeng mit Gellenewemutsch,* hot black pudding served with carrot and potato mash. When it comes to the crunch, though, Saarlanders revert to true German form, and *Schwenkbraten* (marinated pork grilled on a spit) is probably their most popular dish.

Sanddorn (sea buckthorn), nicknamed 'the Mecklenburg lemon', is a shrub berry with a subtle citrus flavour, used to great effect in teas, ice creams and other dishes.

Central Germany

Saxony and Thuringia are slightly less meat-obsessed than some of their cousins. *Kartoffelsuppe* (potato soup) is a favourite, and *Leipziger Allerlei* (Leipzig hotpot) often comes in vegetarian versions. There are even lentils to be found in dishes such as *Linsensuppe mit Thüringer Rotwurst* (lentil soup with long, thin, spiced sausages).

Hamburg & the North

No two dishes better sum up northern Germany's warming, seafaring fodder than *Labskaus* and *Grünkohl mit Pinkel*. There are variations, but traditional *Labskaus* from Hamburg is a minced dish of salt herring, corned beef, pig lard, potato and beetroot, topped with gherkins and a fried egg. *Grünkohl mit Pinkel* combines steamed kale with pork belly, bacon and *Pinkelwurst* (a spicy pork, beef, oat and onion sausage from Bremen). *Aalsuppe* (eel soup) is sweet and sour – it's garnished with bacon and vegetables, and spiced with apricots, pears or prunes.

As you move towards Scandinavia, the German diet begins to encompass Nordic staples, such as rollmops and *Hering* (herring) in all its other guises (raw, smoked, pickled or rolled in sour cream).

Mecklenburg–Western Pomerania has a quite distinctive cuisine, with locals famed for liking things sweet and sour. Take *Mecklenburger Rippenbraten* (rolled pork stuffed with lemons, apples, plums and raisins), for example, or *Mecklenburgische Buttermilchsuppe* (a sweet buttermilk soup flavoured with spices and jam), or the Russian-style *Soljanka* (sour soup with sausage or fish, garnished with lemon and sour cream). Other typical mixes include raisins with cabbage, honey with pork, and plums with duck. Even the typical *Eintopf* (stew, often a potato version) is served with sugar and vinegar on the side.

Here's to Beer!

Few things are as deeply ingrained in the German psyche as the love of beer. *'Hopfen und Malz – Gott erhalt's!'* (Hops and malt are in God's hands) goes the saying, which is fitting, given the almost religious intensity with which beer is brewed, consumed and celebrated – not least at the world's biggest beer festival, Oktoberfest (p360). Brewing here

Thanks to the tradition of the *Reinheitsgebot* (purity law), German beer is supposed to be unique in not giving you a *Katzenjammer* or *Kater* (hangover).

Around 6.9 million litres of beer, give or take a stein, were downed by party-goers at Munich's Oktoberfest in 2017.

Beer tasting at Altes Mädchen (p172), Hamburg

JONATHAN STOKES/LONELY PLANET ©

A PRIMER ON GERMAN BEERS

Pils (Pilsner) This bottom-fermented pale lager, with a pronounced hop flavour and creamy head, has an alcohol content around 4.8%.

Weizenbier/Weissbier (wheat/white beer) Predominant in the south, especially in Bavaria, this contains 5.4% alcohol. A *Hefeweizen* has a stronger shot of yeast, whereas *Kristallweizen* is clearer, with more fizz. These beers are fruity and spicy, often recalling bananas and cloves. Decline offers of lemon as it ruins the head and – beer purists say – the flavour.

Dunkles (dark lager) Brewed throughout Germany, but especially in Bavaria. With a light use of hops, it's full-bodied with strong malty aromas.

Helles (pale lager) *Helles* (pale or light) refers to the colour, not the alcohol content, which is still 4.6% to 5%. Brewing strongholds are Bavaria, Baden-Württemberg and the Ruhr region. It has strong malt aromas and is slightly sweet.

Altbier A dark, full beer with malted barley, from the Düsseldorf area.

Berliner Weisse Berlin's top-fermented beer, which comes *rot* (red) or *grün* (green), with a *Schuss* (dash) of raspberry or woodruff syrup, respectively. A cool, fruity summer choice.

Bockbier Strong beers with 7% alcohol. There's a '*Bock*' for every occasion, such as *Maibock* (for May/spring) and *Weihnachtsbock* (brewed for Christmas). *Eisbock* is dark and aromatic. *Bock* beers originate from Einbeck, near Hanover.

Kölsch By law, this top-fermented beer can only be brewed in or around Cologne. It has about 4.8% alcohol, a solid hop flavour and a pale colour; it's served in small glasses (0.2L) called *Stangen* (literally 'sticks').

Leipziger Gose Flavoured with salt and coriander, this contrives to have a stingingly refreshing taste, with some plummy overtones. Tart like Berliner Weisse, it's often served with sweeteners, such as cherry *(Kirsch)* liqueur or the almond-flavoured *Allasch*.

Schwarzbier (black beer) Slightly stronger, this dark, full beer has an alcohol content of 4.8% to 5%. It's fermented using roasted malt.

goes back to Germanic tribes, and later monks, so it follows a hallowed tradition.

The 'secret' of the country's golden nectar dates back to the 1516 *Reinheitsgebot* (purity law) passed in Bavaria, demanding breweries use just four ingredients – malt, yeast, hops and water. Though it stopped being a legal requirement in 1987, when the EU struck it down as uncompetitive, many German brewers still conform to it anyway, seeing it as a good marketing tool against mass-market, chemical-happy competitors.

Kloster Weltenburg (near Kelheim, north of Munich), is the world's oldest monastery brewery; its Weltenburger Kloster Barock Dunkel was presented with silver at the World Beer Cup in 2018. This light, smooth beer has a malty, toasty finish. Other connoisseurs believe the earthy Andechser Doppelbock Dunkel, produced by the Benedictines in Andechs near Munich, to be among the world's best.

The craft beer movement has also arrived in Germany, especially in the major cities. Berlin, as per usual, is leading the way, with places such as Hops & Barley (p123) – which taps unfiltered Pilsner, dark and wheat beer in a former butcher's shop – and **Hopfenreich** (Map p86; ☏030-8806 1080; www.hopfenreich.de; Sorauer Strasse 31; ⊙4pm-2am Mon-Thu, to 3am Fri-Sun; Ⓤ Schlesisches Tor), the capital's first dedicated craft beer bar.

Some 1300 German breweries keep great beer-making traditions alive and turn out 5000 different beers. Eleven monasteries continue to produce beer today; these are known as *Klosterbrauerein*.

DOS & DON'TS
··

➜ Do say *'Guten Appetit'* (good appetite) before eating, and *'Prost!'* when drinking a toast.

➜ Do offer to help wash up afterwards if you're a guest – locals tend to be quite punctilious about housework.

➜ Do specify if you don't want your restaurant dishes slathered in mayonnaise, *Quark* (a type of creamy cheese) or dressing. Germans are generous in this department.

➜ Don't expect a glass of tap water at a restaurant or cafe; although things are changing, especially in cities, it's still an uncommon request that may not be understood or honoured.

➜ Don't plonk yourself down at the *Stammtisch* table. Empty or not, these are reserved for regulars only.

The Rise of German Wine

For decades the name of German wine was sullied by the cloyingly sweet Liebfraumilch and the naff image of Blue Nun. What a difference a decade makes. Thanks to rebranding campaigns, a new generation of winegrowers, and an overall rise in quality, German wine is staging a 21st-century comeback.

Even discerning wine critics have been pouring praise on German winemakers of late. According to British Master of Wine Tim Atkin (www.timatkin.com), 'Germany makes the best Rieslings of all', and, waxing lyrical on the country's Pinot Noirs, he muses, 'if only the Germans didn't keep most of them to themselves'.

Wine Regions

There are 13 official wine growing areas in Germany, the best being the Mosel-Saar-Ruwer region. It boasts some of the world's steepest vineyards, where the predominantly Riesling grapes are still hand-picked. Slate soil on the hillsides gives the wines a flinty taste. Chalkier riverside soils are planted with the Elbling grape, an ancient Roman variety.

East of the Moselle, the Nahe region produces fragrant, fruity and full-bodied wines using Müller-Thurgau and Silvaner grapes, as well as Riesling.

Riesling grapes are also the mainstay in Rheingau and Mittelrhein (Middle Rhine), two other highly respected wine-growing pockets. Rheinhessen, south of Rheingau, is responsible for Liebfraumilch, but also some top Rieslings.

Other wine regions include Ahr, Pfalz (both in Rhineland-Palatinate), Hessische Bergstrasse (Hesse), Baden (Baden-Württemberg), Würzburg (Bavaria) and Elbtal (Saxony).

The Württemberg region, around Stuttgart, produces some of the country's best reds, while Saxony-Anhalt's Saale-Unstrut region is home to Rotkäppchen (Little Red Riding Hood) sparkling wine, a former GDR brand that's been a big hit in the new Germany.

Literature, Theatre & Film

Germany, with a centuries-old literary tradition, is a nation of avid readers. Some 94,000 new books are released annually and Frankfurt's International Book Fair is the publishing world's most important gathering. Theatre, too, is a mainstay of the cultural scene, with hundreds of stages around the country; Germany produced famous playwrights including Lessing, Goethe and Brecht. In film, Germany is not only a pioneer of the genre but, in the new millennium, has gained international recognition with boundary-pushing movies.

Literature

Early Writing

Early forms of literary expression originated during the reign of Charlemagne (c 800); the most famous surviving work of this early period is the heroic epic poem *Hildebrandslied*. Medieval literature flourished in the 12th century, with *Minnesänger* – lyric poetry performed by bards, such as Walther von der Vogelweide – and more heroic poems, including the *Nibelungenlied*. A key figure in German writing was Protestant reformer Martin Luther, whose 1522 translation of the New Testament created a unified standard version of the German language.

A major work of the baroque period is Grimmelshausen's novel *Simplicissimus* (1668), which follows the adventures of a young ne'er-do-well in the Thirty Years' War. Another landmark is Christoph Martin Wieland's *Geschichte des Agathon* (Agathon; 1766–67), which is considered the first *Bildungsroman* (a novel showing the development of the hero) and an important piece of Enlightenment lit.

The rationality of the Enlightenment was followed by the *Sturm und Drang* (Storm and Stress) phase, which was characterised by emotional and subjective writing. The style was dominated by Germany's literary lion Johann Wolfgang von Goethe (eg *The Sorrows of Young Werther,* 1774) and his friend Friedrich Schiller (eg *The Robbers,* 1781). Both Goethe and Schiller later distanced themselves from the movement and ushered in what would become known as Weimar Classicism, with its emphasis on humanist ideals.

Though serious academics (they wrote *German Grammar* and *History of the German Language*), the Grimm brothers – Jacob and Wilhelm – are best known for their collection of fairy tales, myths and legends, published between 1812 and 1858. Heinrich Heine produced one of Germany's finest collections of poems, *Buch der Lieder* (Book of Songs) in 1827, but it was his more political writings that contributed to his work being banned under Prussian censorship laws in 1835.

Grimms' Fairy Tales by Jacob and Wilhelm Grimm is a beautiful collection of 210 yarns, passed orally between generations before being collected by German literature's most magical brothers.

Into the 20th Century

In the 1920s, Berlin became a literary hotbed, drawing writers including Alfred Döblin, whose *Berlin Alexanderplatz* (1929) is a stylised meander through the seamy 1920s, and Anglo-American import Christopher

Isherwood, whose semiautobiographical *Berlin Stories* formed the basis of the musical and film *Cabaret*. A key figure was Thomas Mann, recipient of the 1929 Nobel Prize for Literature, whose greatest novels focus on social forms of the day. Mann's older brother, Heinrich, adopted a stronger political stance in his work; his *Professor Unrat* (1905) inspired the 1930 Marlene Dietrich film *Der blaue Engel* (The Blue Angel). Erich Maria Remarque's antiwar novel *All Quiet on the Western Front* (1929) was banned (and burned) by the Nazis but today remains a widely read German book.

The postwar literary revival was led by *The Tin Drum* (1959), by Nobel Prize winner Günter Grass, tracing 20th-century German history through the eyes of a child who refuses to grow up. One of the first anti-Nazi novels published after WWII was Hans Fallada's *Alone in Berlin* (1947), based on a true story of a couple's entanglement in the German resistance. The book became a huge hit in the UK and the US after being translated into English in 2009.

Among East German writers, Christa Wolf is one of the best and most controversial, while Heiner Müller had the distinction of being unpalatable in both Germanys. His dense, difficult works include the *Germania* trilogy of plays.

Literature in Reunified Germany

In the 1990s, a slew of novels dealt with German reunification. Many of them are set in Berlin, including Thomas Brussig's tongue-in-cheek *Helden wie Wir* (Heroes Like Us; 1998) and Jana Hensel's *Zonenkinder* (After the Wall; 2002), which reflects upon the loss of identity and the challenge of adapting to a new society. Günter Grass' *Ein weites Feld* (Too Far Afield; 1992) addresses 'unification without unity' after the fall of the Wall.

The late novelist WG Sebald assured his place as one of Germany's best writers with his powerful portrayal of four exiles in *Die Ausgewanderten* (Emigrants; 1992). Russian-born author Wladimir Kaminer, whose *Russendisko* (Russian Disco; 2000) is made up of amusing, stranger-than-fiction vignettes, has been wildly successful and widely translated. Foreign authors also continue to be inspired by Berlin. Ian McEwan's *The Innocent* (1990) is an old-fashioned spy story set in the 1950s, while the *Berlin Noir* trilogy (1989–91), by British author Philip Kerr, features a private detective solving crimes in Nazi Germany.

Find reviews of the latest contemporary German books to be translated into English at www.new-books-in-german.com.

The Deutscher Buchpreis (German Book Award), the equivalent of Britain's Man Booker Prize and the US National Book Awards (in fiction), is a good guide to what's new each year. Search for shortlisted and winning authors at www.deutscher-buchpreis.de.

Theatre

Germany has around 300 state, municipal, travelling and private theatres, most of them heavily government subsidised. In fact, box office takings account for only 10% to 15% of production costs on average.

Germany's theatre history begins in the Enlightenment; a key piece of this period is Gotthold Ephraim Lessing's *Nathan the Wise* (1779), which is a strong plea for religious tolerance. The Thuringian town of Weimar was a cultural hotspot in the 18th century, home to both Friedrich Schiller *(Don Carlos, Wallenstein, The Robbers)* and his even more famous friend Johann Wolfgang von Goethe, whose two-part *Faust* is a powerfully enduring drama about the human condition.

Woyzeck, by Georg Büchner, is another popular piece and, having anticipated Theatre of the Absurd, lends itself to innovative staging. In the early 20th century, Max Reinhardt became German theatre's most influential expressionist director, working briefly with dramatist Bertolt

Brecht, whose *Threepenny Opera* (1928) enjoys international success to this day.

Like many others, Brecht went into exile under the Nazis but returned in 1949 to establish the Berliner Ensemble, which remains one of Germany's seminal stages. Others include Berlin's Deutsches Theater and the Volksbühne Berlin, the Thalia Theater and the Deutsches Schauspielhaus in Hamburg, the Kammerspiele München, the Staatsschauspiel Stuttgart and Schauspiel Hannover. Productions from these venue are regularly represented at the Deutsches Theatertreffen, a showcase of new plays held in Berlin every May. Contemporary playwrights to watch out for include Frank Castorf, Elfriede Jelinek, Rene Pollesch, Moritz Rinke, Botho Strauss, Rainald Goetz and Roland Schimmelpfennig.

Read up-to-date reviews of the latest plays by German playwrights and other cultural offerings at www.goethe.de/enindex.htm.

Film

Before 1945

The legendary UFA (Universum Film AG), one of the first film studios in the world, began shooting in Potsdam, near Berlin, in 1912 and evolved into one of the world's most famous dream factories in the 1920s and early '30s, As early as 1919, Ernst Lubitsch produced historical films and comedies such as *Madame Dubarry,* starring Pola Negri and Emil Jannings; the latter went on to win the Best Actor Award at the very first Academy Awards ceremony in Hollywood in 1929. In 1927 Walter Ruttmann's classic *Berlin: Symphony of a City* was released; it's a fascinating silent documentary that captures a day in the life of 1920s Berlin.

Other 1920s movies were heavily expressionistic, using stark contrast, sharp angles, heavy shadows and other distorting elements. Well-known flicks employing these techniques include *Nosferatu* (a 1922 Dracula adaptation by FW Murnau) and the groundbreaking *Metropolis* (1927), by Fritz Lang. One of the earliest seminal talkies was Josef von Sternberg's *The Blue Angel* (1930), starring Marlene Dietrich. After 1933, though, film-makers found their artistic freedom (not to mention funding) increasingly curtailed, and by 1939 practically the entire industry had fled to Hollywood.

Films made in Germany under the Nazis were mostly of the propaganda variety, with the brilliant, if controversial, director Leni Riefenstahl greatly pushing the genre's creative envelope. Her most famous film, *Triumph of the Will,* documents the 1934 Nuremberg Nazi party rally.

Read what the critics say about 500-plus German films at www.german-cinema.de.

THE MYSTIQUE OF MARLENE

Marlene Dietrich (1901–92) was born Marie Magdalena von Losch into a good middle-class Berlin family. After acting school, she first captivated audiences as a hard-living, libertine flapper in 1920s silent movies, but quickly carved a niche as the dangerously seductive femme fatale. The 1930 talkie *The Blue Angel* turned her into a Hollywood star and launched a five-year collaboration with director Josef von Sternberg. Dietrich built on her image of erotic opulence – dominant and severe but always with a touch of self-irony.

Dietrich stayed in Hollywood after the Nazi rise to power, though Hitler, not immune to her charms, reportedly promised perks and the red-carpet treatment if she moved back to Germany. She responded with an empty offer to return if she could bring along Sternberg – a Jew and no Nazi favourite. She took US citizenship in 1937 and entertained Allied soldiers on the front.

After the war, Dietrich retreated slowly from the public eye, making occasional appearances in films but mostly cutting records and performing live cabaret. Her final years were spent in Paris, bedridden and accepting few visitors, immortal in spirit as mortality caught up with her.

Berlin Alexanderplatz: The Story of Franz Biberkopf, by Alfred Döblin, is a masterful epic set in 1920s Berlin (film-maker Rainer Fassbinder made a 15-hour film adaptation).

Olympia, which chronicles the 1936 Berlin Olympic Games, was another influential work.

Some of the best films about the Nazi era include Wolfgang Staudte's *Die Mörder sind unter uns* (Murderers among Us; 1946); Fassbinder's *Die Ehe der Maria Braun* (The Marriage of Maria Braun; 1979); Margarethe von Trotta's *Rosenstrasse* (2003), and Oliver Hirschbiegel's Oscar-nominated *Der Untergang* (Downfall; 2004), depicting Hitler's final days, with the extraordinary Bruno Ganz in the role of the Führer.

After 1945

In the 1960s German film entered a new era with the *Neuer Deutscher Film* (New German Film) period – also known as *Junger Deutscher Film* (Young German Film) – which brought directors Rainer Werner Fassbinder, Wim Wenders, Volker Schlöndorff, Werner Herzog and Margarethe von Trotta to the fore. The impact of Fassbinder's *Die Sehnsucht der Veronika Voss* (Longing of Veronica Voss; 1981), Wenders' *Der Himmel über Berlin* (Wings of Desire; 1987), Herzog's *Aguirre, der Zorn Gottes* (Aguirre, the Wrath of God; 1972), Schlöndorff's film version of Günter Grass' *Die Blechtrommel* (The Tin Drum; 1979) and the Schlöndorff-von Trotta co-production *Die Verlorene Ehre der Katharina Blum* (The Lost Honour of Katharina Blum; 1975) can still be felt on screens today.

The '70s also saw Wolfgang Petersen's first major release, the psychological thriller *Einer von uns beiden* (One or the Other of Us; 1974), starring Jürgen Prochnow. Prochnow returned as the lead character in Petersen's WWII submarine epic *Das Boot* (1981), which became a huge international success and was nominated for six Oscars.

The first round of postreunification flicks were light-hearted comedy dramas, but towards the end of the 1990s filmic fare began to mature in terms of depth and quality, inspiring international critics to hail the birth of a new 'German Cinema'. A breakthrough film was *Lola rennt* (Run Lola Run; 1998), which helped Tom Tykwer establish his reputation as one of Germany's best contemporary directors.

Another international runaway hit was *Good Bye, Lenin!,* Wolfgang Becker's witty and heart-warming tale of a son trying to recreate life in East Germany to save his sick mother. It was released in 2003, the same year Caroline Link won the Oscar for Best Foreign Language Film for *Nowhere in Africa.* In 2007 Florian von Donnersmarck was bestowed the same honour with *The Lives of Others* (2006), a ruthless portrayal of the stranglehold the East German secret police (Stasi) had on ordinary citizens. Also Oscar-nominated was Uli Edel's *Baader Meinhof Komplex* (Baader Meinhof Complex; 2008), which addresses a dark chapter in West German history: the terrorist group Red Army Faction in the late 1960s and early 1970s. Another important director with a finger on the pulse of contemporary Germany is Turkish-German Fatih Akin. His breakthrough movie *Gegen die Wand* (Head-On; 2004) is a story about love and the cultural conflicts encountered by two Turks brought up in Germany.

These days, 'Germany's Hollywood' is once again in Potsdam, where an average of 300 German and international productions are filmed on location and at the UFA successor Studio Babelsberg each year. Movies that were at least partially shot here include *The Reader, Valkyrie, Inglourious Basterds, The Ghost Writer, Anonymous, Cloud Atlas, The Monuments Men, The Grand Budapest Hotel, The Book Thief* and *Hunger Games* (parts 3 and 4).

Music

Germany's reputation as a musical powerhouse is fuelled by such world-famous composers as Beethoven, Bach and Brahms. Today the country boasts 80 publicly financed concert halls, including internationally prestigious ones in Hamburg, Berlin, Dresden and Munich. But Germany has also punched well above its weight in the popular music arena and is one of the few countries outside the English-speaking world to have influenced rock, pop and electronic music in a significant way.

Classical Music

Middle Ages –20th century

Medieval German music is closely associated with Walther von der Vogelweide (c 1170–1230), who achieved renown with love ballads. A more formalised troubadour tradition followed, but it was baroque composer and organist Johann Sebastian Bach (1685–1750) who most influenced early European music. His legacy can be explored in Bach museums in his birth town of Eisenach and in Leipzig, where he died.

Bach contemporary Georg Friedrich Händel (1685–1759) hailed from Halle in Saxony-Anhalt (his house is now a museum) but lived and worked almost exclusively in London from 1714, where he wrote operas and choral music. Händel's music found favour in the circle of Vienna's classical composers, which included Joseph Haydn (1732–1809), a teacher of Bonn-born Ludwig van Beethoven (1770–1827), who paved the way for Romanticism. Struck with deafness later in life, Beethoven's most famous works are his nine symphonies, which he composed along with piano sonatas, string quartets and choral works.

Among the Romantic composers, Felix Mendelssohn-Bartholdy (1809–47) is hailed as a genius. He penned his first overture at the age of 17 and later rediscovered works by JS Bach; the revival gave Bach enduring fame.

Born in Leipzig, Richard Wagner (1813–83) lords it over 19th-century German music. With his operas based on German mythology (most famously *The Ring of the Nibelung*), he became Bavarian King Ludwig II's favourite composer. Hitler, who picked up on an anti-Semitic essay by Wagner and some late-life ramblings on German virtues, famously turned the composer into a postmortem Nazi icon. An annual summer music festival in Bayreuth celebrates Wagner's life and works.

Hamburg brought forth Johannes Brahms (1833–97) and his influential symphonies, plus chamber and piano works. Two figures whose legacies are tied to Bonn, Leipzig and Zwickau are composer Robert Schumann (1810–56) and his gifted pianist-spouse Clara Wieck (1819–96). Schumann (born in Zwickau) and Wieck (born in Leipzig) are buried in Bonn's Alter Friedhof.

For more information, both practical and historical, on the Berlin Philharmonic Orchestra, visit www.berliner-philharmoniker.de.

The 1920s – Post WWII

The pulsating 1920s drew numerous classical musicians to Berlin, including Arnold Schönberg (1874–1951), whose atonal compositions turned music on its head, as did his experimentation with noise and sound effects. One of Schönberg's pupils, Hanns Eisler (1898–1962), went into exile in 1933, like Schönberg, but returned to East Berlin to teach in 1950. Among Eisler's works was the East German national anthem, Auferstanden aus Ruinen (Resurrected from Ruins), lyric-less from 1961, when its pro-reunification words fell out of favour with party honchos.

Also working in Berlin, Paul Hindemith (1895–1963) explored the new medium of radio and taught a seminar on film music. He too was banned by the Nazis and composed his most important orchestral compositions in exile.

Perhaps better known is Dessau-born Kurt Weill (1900–50), another composer who fled the Nazi terror. He teamed up with Bertolt Brecht in the 1920s and wrote the music for the *The Threepenny Opera*, which premiered in 1928 with such famous songs as 'Mack the Knife'. Weill ended up writing successful Broadway musicals in New York.

The 1920s also gave birth to Schlager – light-hearted songs with titles such as 'Mein Papagei frisst keine harten Eier' ('My Parrot Doesn't Eat Hard-Boiled Eggs'), which teetered on the silly and surreal.

After WWII, the southwestern towns of Darmstadt and Donaueschingen emerged as hubs of contemporary classical music based on constructivist compositional techniques and modal methods, with Karlheinz Stockhausen emerging as a key figure. The arrival of American experimental composer John Cage, a pioneer of chance composition, electro-acoustic music and noise-as-music at the International Music Institute Darmstadt is widely considered a turning point in the European post-WWII musical scene.

> No song is more evocative of wartime Germany than Marlene Dietrich's haunting, dreamy *Lili Marleen*, released in 1944 to demoralise enemy soldiers.

Contemporary Sounds

Since the 1960s, Berlin has spearheaded many of Germany's popular music innovations. Riding the New Age wave of the late '60s, Tangerine Dream helped to propagate the psychedelic sound, while a decade later Kreuzberg's subculture launched the punk movement at SO36 and other famous clubs. Regulars included David Bowie and Iggy Pop, who were Berlin flatmates in the 1970s. Bowie partly wrote and recorded his Berlin Trilogy (Low, Heroes, Lodger) at the city's famous Hansa Studios.

Music in East Germany

In East Germany, access to Western rock and other popular music was restricted, while Eastern artists' artistic freedom was greatly compromised, as all lyrics had to be approved and performances were routinely monitored. Nevertheless, a slew of home-grown Ostrock (Eastern rock) bands emerged. Some major bands including The Puhdys, Karat, Silly, City and Keimzeit managed to get around the censors by disguising criticism in seemingly innocuous metaphors or by deliberately inserting provocative lyrics they fully expected to be deleted. All built up huge followings in both Germanys.

Many nonconformists were placed under an occupational ban and prohibited from performing. Singer-songwriter Wolf Biermann became a cause célèbre when, in 1976, he was not allowed to return to the GDR from a concert series in the West, despite being an avid – albeit regime-critical – socialist. When other artists rallied to his support, they too were expatriated, including Biermann's stepdaughter Nina Hagen, an East Berlin pop singer who later became a West Berlin punk pioneer. The small but vital East German punk scene produced Sandow and Feeling B, members of which went on to form the industrial metal band Rammstein in 1994. Known for provocative lyrics and intense sounds, the band is still Germany's top musical export today.

> Thomas Jerome Seabrook's *Bowie in Berlin: A New Career in a New Town* (2008) offers cool insights into the heady years the 'Thin White Duke' spent in Berlin.

The 1980s: Neue Deutsche Welle

Once in West Berlin, Nina Hagen helped chart the course for Neue Deutsche Welle (NDW; German New Wave). This early '80s sound produced such bands as D.A.F., Trio, Neonbabies and Ideal, as well as Rockhaus in East Berlin. The same decade also saw the birth of Die Ärzte, Die Toten Hosen and the seminal Einstürzende Neubauten, who pioneered a proto-industrial sound. Düsseldorf-based Kraftwerk, meanwhile, created the musical foundations for techno, the club sound that would sweep across Germany after 1989, spawning Berlin's legendary Love Parade.

Members of the Neue Deutsche Welle always sang in German, an exception being the singer Nena, who successfully recorded her hit single '99 Red Balloons' in English, too. The NDW movement spawned the Hamburg School of musicians, with recognised acts such as Blumfeld, Die Sterne and the Tocotronic.

The 1990s: Electronic Sounds

Dominated by disco in the 1970s and rap and hip-hop in the 1980s, the club scene in the 1990s moved strongly towards electronic music, taking the impulses of Tangerine Dream and Kraftwerk to new heights.

The seed was sown in dark and dank cellar club UFO on Köpenicker Strasse in 1988. The 'godfathers' of the Berlin sound, Dr Motte, Westbam and Kid Paul, played their first gigs here, mostly sweat-driven acid house all-night raves. It was Motte who came up with the idea to take the party to the street with a truck, loud beats and a bunch of friends dancing behind it – and the Love Parade was born (it peaked in 1999 with 1.5 million people swarming Berlin's streets).

The Berlin Wall's demise, and the artistic freedom it created, catapulted techno out of the underground. The associated euphoria, sudden access to derelict and abandoned spaces in eastern Berlin and lack of control by the authorities were all defining factors in making Berlin a techno epicentre. In 1991, the techno-sonic gang followed UFO founder Dimitri Hegemann to Tresor, which launched camouflage-sporting DJ Tanith, along with trance pioneer Paul van Dyk. Today, the Tresor label is still a seminal brand, representing Jeff Mills, Blake Baxter and Cristian Vogel, among many others.

Key label BPitch Control, founded by Ellen Allien in 1999, launched the careers of Modeselektor, Apparat (aka Sascha Ring), Sascha Funke, and Paul Kalkbrenner. Another heavyweight is the collective Get Physical, which includes the dynamic duo M.A.N.D.Y., who fuse house and electro with minimal and funk to create a highly danceable sound. The charmingly named Shitkatapult, founded in 1997 by Marco Haas (aka T.Raumschmiere), is focused on minimalist styles and counts Apparat and Daniel Meteo among its artists.

Anyone into electro will want to plug into bands currently having their moment to shine, such as Howling, Susanne Blech, Moderat and Hundreds.

Other Sounds

Other fine German music originates from a jazz/breaks angle such as electrojazz and breakbeats that favour lush grooves, obscure samples and chilled rhythms. Remix masters Jazzanova are top dogs of the downtempo scene. Their Sonar Kollektiv label also champions similar artists, including Micatone. Reggae-dancehall made a splash with Seeed, whose frontman Peter Fox's solo album Stadtaffe (2008) was one of the best-selling albums in Germany of the same year. Also commercially-successful is Culcha Candela, who have essentially pop-ified the Seeed sound. Home-grown rap and hip hop has a huge following, thanks to Sido, Fler, Bushido and Kool Savas. Also hugely successful are Berlin-based Casper and Marteria. K.I.Z., meanwhile, are more of a gangsta rap parody.

Foreign artists have also influenced the Berlin scene, including the provocative Canadian songster and performance artist Peaches, UK–Canadian techno innovator Richie Hawtin and Chilean minimalist master Ricardo Villalobos.

One of Germany's most famous pop duos in the 1980s, Modern Talking, had a string of hit singles in many countries, including You're My Heart, You're My Soul; Cheri, Cheri Lady; and Brother Louie.

MUSIC CONTEMPORARY SOUNDS

ALLA KHANANASHVILI/SHUTTERSTOCK ©

Visual Arts

From 1200-year-old church frescos to cutting-edge street art, you're never far from creative expression in Germany. While religious themes dominated the Middle Ages, the scope widened around the time of the Enlightenment and burst into a full spectrum of creativity in the 20th century, especially with seminal Weimar-era movements such as the Bauhaus and expressionism. With scores of museums, galleries, public artworks, art colonies and festivals, Germany's artistic world today continues to be vibrant, influential and reflective of the zeitgeist.

Middle Ages to the 19th Century

Above Stiftskirche St Georg, Reichenau (p523)

The origins of German medieval art can be traced to the Frankish Empire of Charlemagne (c 800). Frescos from that period still grace the Stiftskirche St Georg on Reichenau Island, while those from Trier's St Maximin crypt are now on display at the city's Bischöfliches Dom- und

Diözesanmuseum. Stained-glass enthusiasts will find colourful religious motifs lighting up Augsburg and Cologne cathedrals. By the 15th century, Cologne artists were putting landscapes on religious panels, some of which are on display in Hamburg's Kunsthalle.

The heavyweight of German Renaissance art, which flourished in the 15th century, is the Nuremberg-born Albrecht Dürer, the first artist to seriously compete with the Italian masters. Munich's Alte Pinakothek is one place showing several famous works, while his Nuremberg house is now a museum. In Wittenberg, Dürer influenced the court painter Lucas Cranach the Elder, whose *Apollo and Diana in a Forest Landscape* (1530) forms part of the collection at Berlin's Gemäldegalerie.

Two centuries later, during the baroque period, sculpture was integrated into Germany's buildings and gardens. A key work is Andreas Schlüter's *Great Elector on Horseback* in front of Berlin's Schloss Charlottenburg. Around the same time, it became fashionable to decorate palace walls and ceiling with trompe l'oeil frescos to create the illusion of generous space. The one by Tiepolo gracing Balthasar Neumann's grand staircase in Würzburg's Residenz is a standout.

In the early 19th century, neoclassicism emerged as a dominant sculptural style. Leading the artistic pack was Johann Gottfried Schadow, whose *Quadriga* – the horse-drawn chariot atop Berlin's Brandenburg Gate – ranks among his finest works. In painting, neoclassicism ushered in a return to the human figure and an emphasis on Roman and Greek mythology. Johann Heinrich Tischbein's *Goethe in der Campagna* (1787), which depicts the famous writer in a classical landscape surrounded by antique objects, hangs in the Städel Museum in Frankfurt am Main.

Heart-on-your-sleeve romanticism, which drew heavily on emotion and a dreamy idealism, dominated the later 19th century, spurred by the awakening of a nationalist spirit after the Napoleonic Wars (1803–15). Caspar David Friedrich, best known for his moody, allegorical landscapes, was a key practitioner. Both Hamburg's Kunsthalle and Berlin's Alte Nationalgalerie have sizeable collections of his works, along with canvases by Philipp Otto Runge, intensely religious works by the Nazarenes and some later realistic paintings by Wilhelm Leibl.

Impressionism did not flourish nearly as much in Germany as it did in France. Key representatives include Max Liebermann, whose work was often slammed as 'ugly' and 'socialist', Fritz von Uhde and Lovis Corinth, whose later work, *Childhood of Zeus* (1905) – a richly coloured frolic in nature with intoxicated, grotesque elements – can be admired in Bremen's Kunsthalle.

An art form popping up briefly in the final decade of the 19th century was *Jugendstil* (art nouveau), a florid, ornamental aesthetic inspired by printmaking that found expression less in visual art than in crafts and design. It was a reaction against the pompous eclecticism in vogue after the founding of the German Reich in 1871. In Munich, the Neue Pinakothek is the place to head for some fine examples of this most elegant of styles; in Berlin, check out the Bröhan Museum.

Birth of Modernism

In the last decade of the 19th century, a number of artists banded together to reject the traditional teachings of the arts academics that stifled any new forms of expression. This led to the Munich Secession in 1892 and to the Berlin Secession in 1898. This new generation of artists preferred scenes from daily life over historical and religious themes, shunned studios in favour of natural outdoor light and inspired a proliferation of new styles. Famous secession members included Max Liebermann, Lovis

---

Peter Vischer the Elder, Veit Stoss and Tilman Riemenschneider are regarded as the greatest German sculptors of the late Gothic and early Renaissance period.

Jugendstil – an alternative name in German for art nouveau – takes its name from the arts magazine *Jugend* (literally 'Youth'), first published in Munich in 1896.

Corinth, Max Slevogt, Max Beckmann, Käthe Kollwitz and Ernst Ludwig Kirchner.

Kirchner went on to found, along with Erich Heckel and Karl Schmidt-Rottluff, the artist group Die Brücke (The Bridge) in 1905 in Dresden. It turned the art world on its head with groundbreaking visions considered the dawn of German expressionism. As opposed to impressionism, which focuses on passively depicting light and nature, expressionism is imbued with an emotional quality. Abstract forms, a flattened perspective and bright, emotional colours that the artists believed exuded a spiritual quality characterised this new aesthetic. Die Brücke moved to Berlin in 1911 and disbanded in 1913. The small Brücke Museum in Berlin has a fantastic collection of these influential artists.

In 1911, another seminal group of German expressionists banded together in Munich. Calling themselves Der Blaue Reiter (The Blue Rider), this loose association of painters centred on Wassily Kandinsky, Gabriele Münter, Paul Klee and Franz Marc, and remained active until 1914. Munich's Städtische Galerie im Lenbachhaus has a superb collection of Blaue Reiter paintings. Klee fans should also make a beeline to Düsseldorf's K20 Grabbeplatz and the Museum Berggruen in Berlin. A pilgrimage site for Marc aficionados is the Franz Marc Museum in Kochel am See in the Bavarian Alps, where the artist lived after 1908.

The most important woman painter of the period was Käthe Kollwitz, whose social and political awareness lent a tortured power to her lithographs, graphics, woodcuts, sculptures and drawings. Among her many famous works is *A Weavers' Revolt* (1897). There are museums dedicated to this extraordinary artist in Berlin and Cologne.

Artist Joseph Beuys was a radio operator in a fighter plane shot down over the Crimea during WWII. He claims to have been nursed back to health by local Tartars, who covered him in tallow and wrapped him in felt, two materials which featured prominently in his later artworks.

Art in the 1920s

The 1920s was one of the most prolific and creative periods in Germany's artistic history. Many different forms of expression flourished in this decade, a diversity fuelled by the monarchy's demise, political and economic instability and the memory of the horrors of WWI.

One artist especially haunted by his wartime experience was Otto Dix, who, in the early 1920s, produced a series of dark and sombre paintings depicting war scenes – disfigured and dying soldiers, decomposing bodies, skulls in gas masks – in graphic detail. Dix was greatly influenced by Dada, an avant-garde art movement formed in Zürich in 1916 as a reaction to the

DEGENERATE ART

Abstract expressionism, surrealism, Dadaism and other forms of modern art were considered 'Jewish subversion' and 'artistic Bolshevism' in the eyes of the Nazis and classified as *entartet* (degenerate). The art promoted instead looked back to a classical Greek and Roman aesthetic and favoured the depicting of racial purity and the use of epic styles.

In 1937, 650 paintings by 112 artists, including Klee, Beckmann, Dix, Kirchner, Marc and Grosz, were put on display in the *Degenerate Art* exhibition in Munich. It was to serve as a counterpoint to the simultaneous *Great German Art* exhibition at Munich's palatial Haus der Deutschen Kunst, which showcased Nazi-approved art by such artists as the sculptors Arno Breker and Georg Kolbe and painters Thomas Baumgartner and Ivo Saliger. With only 600,000 visitors, interest was low compared with the degenerate art show, which drew over two million people.

A year later, a law was passed allowing for the forced removal of degenerate works from private collections. While some art collectors saved their prized art from Nazi hands, many pieces were sold abroad for foreign currency. In 1939, about 4000 paintings were publicly burned in Berlin.

Brandenburger Tor (p70), Berlin

brutality of WWI. The Kunstmuseum Stuttgart shelters one of the world's most important collections of Dix's works.

Dada artists had an irrational, satirical and often absurdist outlook that was often imbued with a political undercurrent and a tendency to shock and provoke. Aside from Dix, artists associated with this movement included Kurt Schwitters, Hannah Höch and George Grosz. Along with Max Beckmann, Dix and Grosz went on to become key figures of the Neue Sachlichkeit (New Objectivity), an offshoot of expressionism that emerged later in the 1920s and was distinguished by an unsentimental, practical and objective look at reality.

After a creative surge in the 1920s, the big chill of Nazi conformity sent Germany into an artistic deep freeze in the 1930s and 1940s. Many artists were classified as degenerate and forced into exile, leading to a creative explosion among the Bauhaus movement protagonists who settled in the USA. Other artists were murdered, retreated from public life or put away their brushes and paints forever. In Quedlinburg a fine collection of works by Lyonel Feininger survived thanks to a local citizen, who hid them from the Nazis.

Developments after WWII

After WWII, Germany's art scene was as fragmented as the country itself. In the East, artists were forced to toe the socialist realism line, at least until the late 1960s, when artists of the so-called Berliner Schule (Berlin School), including Manfred Böttcher and Harald Metzkes, sought to embrace a more interpretative and emotional form of expression, inspired by the colours and aesthetic of Beckmann, Matisse, Picasso and other classical modernists. In the 1970s, when conflicts of the individual in society became a prominent theme, underground galleries flourished in East Berlin and art became a collective endeavour. The Museum Junge

In 2017, Potsdam welcomed the arrival of Germany's most exciting new gallery – the Museum Barberini, built around the collection of billionaire software magnate Hasso Plattner. So far its outstanding exhibitions have ranged from impressionism (Monet, Renoir and the like) to abstract works by Gerhard Richter and artists in the GDR.

Kunst in Frankfurt (Oder) presents a thorough survey of art created in the GDR.

In West Germany, the creative influence of expressionists such as Emil Nolde, Schmidt-Rottluff and Kandinsky was revived, as a new abstract expressionism took root in the work of Stuttgart's Willi Baumeister and Ernst Wilhelm Nay in Berlin. Soon, however, artists eagerly embraced abstract art. Pioneers included Zone 5, which revolved around Hans Thiemann, and surrealists Heinz Trökes and Mac Zimmermann. In the 1950s and 1960s, Düsseldorf-based Gruppe Zero (Group Zero) plugged into Bauhaus, using light and space as a creative basis. The 'light ballets' of Otto Piene, relying on projection techniques, were among the best-known works. Celle's Kunstmuseum uses some of his light works for stunning effect.

In the 1960s social and political upheaval was a primary concern and a new style called 'critical realism' emerged, propagated by artists including Ulrich Baehr, Hans-Jürgen Diehl and Wolfgang Petrick. The 1973 movement Schule der Neuen Prächtigkeit (School of New Magnificence) had a similar approach. In the late 1970s and early 1980s, expressionism found its way back onto the canvasses of Salomé, Helmut Middendorf and Rainer Fetting, a group known as the Junge Wilde (Young Wild Ones). One of the best-known German neo-expressionist painters is Georg Baselitz, who became internationally famous in the 1970s, thanks to his 'upside-down' works.

Another top contemporary German artist is Anselm Kiefer, some of whose works are in Berlin's Hamburger Bahnhof – Museum of Contemporary Art. A standout is his monumental *Census* (1967), which consists of massive lead folios arranged on shelves as a protest against a 1967 census in Germany.

The same museum also has a large permanent display of works by Düsseldorf's Joseph Beuys (1921–86), the enfant terrible of the post-WWII German art world and yet one of the most influential artists of the period. Beuys created a huge body of work that ranges from drawing, sculpture and installations to print-making and performance. His personal and provocative style created controversy wherever he lay his trademark hat and ultimately led to his dismissal from the Düsseldorf Art Academy, where he had been a professor. Other places with sizeable Beuys holdings include Darmstadt's Hessisches Landesmuseum (including his ground-breaking *Stuhl mit Fett;* Chair with Fat; 1963), the K20 Grabbeplatz in Düsseldorf and Schloss Moyland, near Kalkar, in North Rhine–Westphalia.

Other icons of contemporary German painting include Gerhard Richter and Sigmar Polke. Richter, who was born in Dresden and fled to West Germany in the early 1960s, made a huge splash in 2007 with a mesmerising stained-glass window in Cologne's cathedral. Polke, along with Richter and others, relied heavily on pop art and what they dubbed 'capitalist realism,' which they used to describe a counterbalance in the West to socialist realism. Another heavy hitter, albeit from a younger generation, is Rosemarie Trockel, whose diverse and experimental works include drawings, sculpture, painting and video art. The Museum Ludwig in Cologne has works by her, as well as by Richter and Polke.

In the 1990s, the Neue Leipziger Schule (New Leipzig School) of artists emerged, achieving success at home and abroad with such superstar painters as Neo Rauch. Its return to representational painting may be regarded as a reaction to the dominance of conceptual art in previous decades.

These days, abstraction has again become a focus, with a particular nod to its roots in modernism. There is no particular style but a diversity

Museum Barberini (p141), Potsdam

of expression and an idiosyncratic, personal approach to art. Underlying themes include the commercialisation of art and critical awareness of the impact of technology. Artists to keep an eye on include André Butzer, Isa Genzken, Thomas Zipp, Georg Herold, Alexandra Bircken, Jutta Köther, Max Frisinger and Corinne Wasmuht.

Photography is another area where Germany has long made a splash. In the 1920s and '30s, German photographers took two very different directions. Influenced by the Hungarian László Maholy-Nagy, some adopted a playful approach to light, figure, form and how they developed the resulting images in the darkroom. The other direction was a documentary-style New Objectivity, whose main protagonists were Albert Renger-Patzsch, August Sander and Werner Mantz.

Key contemporary photographers Andreas Gursky and Candida Höfer honed their skills under Bernd Becher at Düsseldorf's Art Academy. Gursky's work, which can be seen in Cologne's Museum Ludwig (among others), encompasses superb images of architecture, landscapes and interiors, sometimes reworked digitally. Works by Höfer and other Becher students graces Hamburg's Kunsthalle, along with the often provocative images of Wolfgang Tillmans.

For the comprehensive low-down on Germany's contemporary art scene and events, see www.art-in.de.

Architecture

The bombs of WWII may have blasted away a considerable share of Germany's architectural heritage, but a painstaking post-war rebuilding program and a wealth of sites that survived with nary a shrapnel wound make Germany an architectural wonderland. Building styles from Roman amphitheatres to 21st-century skyscrapers dot townscapes across the country. Of special interest are the many Unesco-listed gems, including Bauhaus buildings in Dessau-Rosslau, the rococo Wieskirche pilgrimage church in southern Bavaria and the Zollverein coal mine in Essen.

Roman & Carolingian

Above Zeche Zollverein (p671), Essen

While traces of the Roman Empire are perhaps not as visible as in southern European countries, Germany has a handful of Roman sites of note. Trier, which sits on the banks of the Moselle in southwest Germany close to the border with Luxembourg, is particularly noteworthy. The city has a staggering ensemble of well-preserved Roman monuments, many of which are Unesco World Heritage-listed. Among them are the sturdy Porta Nigra gate, an amphitheatre, thermal baths, an imperial throne room, and the country's oldest bishop's church, which is Roman in part.

In Weiden on the fringes of Cologne, it's possible to take a fascinating peek inside a Roman burial chamber (the Römergrab Köln-Weiden), discovered by accident during excavations in 1843. Built from tuff (a light, porous rock), the rectangular chamber grave has niches lined with coloured marble.

Several centuries after the power of the Roman Empire fizzled out, the architectural styles they had evolved were still in vogue. Among the grand buildings of the north European, pre-Romanesque Carolingian period, Aachen's Charlemagne-built cathedral stands out, with its extraordinary octagonal Palatine Chapel, supported by antique Italian pillars. In Paderborn in the Northern Rhineland, remnants of one of Charlemagne's palaces, built in the late 8th century, have been unearthed north of the Dom.

Fulda in central Germany is home to the Michaelskirche, an early 9th-century masterpiece that was once the cemetery chapel for the Benedictine monastery. With its witch's hat towers, Carolingian rotunda and crypt, it's one of the finest surviving early-medieval churches in the country. Close to Heidelberg is an earlier example of the Carolingian style: Lorsch Abbey. A Unesco World Heritage site founded around AD 760, its beautifully preserved medieval buildings include the Königshalle and the Altenmünster.

Romanesque

As Carolingian, Roman and Byzantine influences slowly flowed together to create more proportional interiors, with round arches and integrated columns, Romanesque was born. A standout Romanesque building is the elegant Stiftskirche St Cyriakus in Gernrode, Quedlinburg. Construction on the cruciform basilica, with its early use of alternating columns and pillars (later a common hallmark of Romanesque), began in 959.

Other stellar examples of the Romanesque period in Germany are Cologne's 12 Romanesque churches, which shine a light on the importance of the city during the Middle Ages. The town of Speyer in the Southern Rhineland is crowned by the Kaiserdom, an immense Romanesque cathedral with square red towers and a green copper dome. Built from around 1030, the cathedral was once the largest in Christendom. The cathedrals in Worms and Mainz are also Romanesque stunners.

Gothic

Germany excels in Gothic architecture, which flourished during the Middle Ages. You'll find some magnificent examples of the style up and down the country.

Early Gothic architecture kept many Romanesque elements, as the cathedral in Magdeburg illustrates; the twin-steepled Dom is Germany's oldest Gothic cathedral. To the southwest, the Unesco-listed Kloster Maulbronn, built in 1147 and considered among Europe's best-preserved medieval monastery complexes, combines Romanesque and Gothic elements. Another early example is the Liebfrauenkirche in Trier, Germany's oldest Gothic church. Dating to around 1200, it has distinctive cross-shaped vaulting and a floor plan resembling a 12-petalled rose.

Later churches sported purely Gothic traits, such as ribbed vaults, pointed arches, tracery windows and flying buttresses, which allowed for greater height and larger windows – many of them shining like jewels with brightly coloured stained glass. There are many fine examples scattered across the country, including the cathedrals in Cologne (Kölner Dom), Marburg (Elisabethkirche), Freiburg (Münster) and Lübeck

Must-See Palaces & Castles

Schloss Neuschwanstein (p388)

Wartburg Castle (p254)

Schloss Sanssouci (p138)

Burg Eltz (p610)

Würzburg Residenz (p407)

Hohenzollern Castle (p482)

(Marienkirche). The highest of the high, however is Ulm's spirit-lifting Münster, with a 161.5m-high steeple – the world's tallest. The colossal cathedral took 500 years to build from the first stone laid in 1377.

Brick Gothic, or *Backsteingotik,* is prevalent in the north of the country, particularly around the Baltic. Red brickwork, ornate facades and step gables are emblematic of the style. Some classic examples can be seen in towns and cities such as Stralsund, Lübeck, Rostock and Wismar.

After the 15th century, elaborately patterned vaults and hall churches emerged. Munich's Frauenkirche, with its onion-domed twin towers, is typical of this late-Gothic style.

Renaissance to Neoclassical

The Renaissance rumbled into Germany around the mid-16th century, bestowing Heidelberg and other southern cities with buildings bearing ornate leaf-work decoration and columns. In central Germany, the secular Weser Renaissance style resulted in such gems as Celle's ducal palace.

As the representational needs of feudal rulers grew in the 17th and 18th centuries, they invested heavily in grand residences. This was the age of baroque, a style that merged architecture, sculpture, ornamentation and painting. In northern Germany it retained a more formal and precise bent (as exemplified by the work of Johann Conrad Schlaun in Münster), never quite reaching the exuberance favoured in the south in such buildings as the Wieskirche or Munich's Schloss Nymphenburg. One of the finest baroque churches, Dresden's Frauenkirche, built in 1743, was destroyed in the 1945 firebombing of the city, but reconstructed and reopened in 2005.

Erich Mendelsohn and the Architecture of German Modernism, by Kathleen James, zooms in on Mendelsohn's expressionist buildings in Berlin and Frankfurt.

Berlin's Brandenburg Gate, based on a Greek design, is an exquisite example of neoclassicism. Turning away from baroque flourishes, this style drew upon columns, pediments, domes and other design elements that had been popular throughout antiquity. A leading architect of the era was Berlin-based Karl Friedrich Schinkel, whose colonnaded Altes Museum (Old Museum), Neue Wache (New Guardhouse) and the Konzerthaus (Concert Hall) still grace the capital. In Bavaria, Leo von Klenze chiselled his way through virtually every ancient civilisation, with eclectic creations such as the Glyptothek and Propyläen on Munich's Königsplatz.

The architecture in vogue after the creation of the German Empire in 1871 reflects the representational needs of the united Germany and tends towards the pompous. No new style as such emerged, as architects essentially recycled earlier ones (eg Romanesque, Renaissance, baroque, and sometimes all three woven together) in an approach dubbed *Historismus* (Historicism). As a result, many buildings look much older than they actually are. Berlin's Reichstag, Schloss Neuschwanstein in Füssen and the palace in Schwerin in northern Germany are all prominent examples.

Modern & Contemporary

20th Century

No architectural movement has had greater influence on modern design than the Bauhaus (p278), an architecture, art and design institute founded in 1919 in Weimar by Walter Gropius. Based on practical, anti-elitist principles bringing form and function together, it united architecture, painting, furniture design and sculpture. The school had its most fruitful period after moving to Dessau in 1925. Its school building, which is considered a landmark of modern functionalist architecture, is open to visitors, as are the *Meisterhäuser* (private homes) of such Bauhaus teachers as Gropius, Wassily Kandinsky and Paul Klee. In Berlin, the Bauhaus Archive, designed by Gropius in 1964, is a must-see.

Bauhausgebäude (p277), Dessau-Rosslau

The Bauhaus moved to Berlin in 1932, only to be shut down by the Nazis a year later. Hitler, who was a big fan of architectural monumentalism, put Albert Speer in charge of turning Berlin into *Welthauptstadt Germania* (World Capital Germania), the future capital of the Reich. Today only a few buildings, including the Olympic Stadium and Tempelhof Airport, offer a hint of what Berlin might have looked like had history taken a different turn.

After WWII, East Germany found inspiration in Stalin-era pomposity, impressively reflected in East Berlin's showcase boulevard Karl-Marx-Allee. The city's main square, Alexanderplatz, also got a socialist makeover in the 1960s, culminating in the construction of its 368m-high TV Tower (still Germany's tallest building) in 1969. Another (in)famous structure – the Berlin Wall – survives only in fragments.

By contrast, in West Germany urban planners sought to eradicate any hint of monumentalism, instead embracing the 'less is more' glass-and-steel aesthetic of the Bauhaus tradition. Ludwig Mies van der Rohe's Neue Nationalgalerie (New National Gallery) is a masterpiece, as is Hubert Petschnigg's slender Thyssenhaus (1960) in Düsseldorf. In 1972 Munich was graced with its splendid tent-roofed Olympiastadion.

> Dresden was delisted as a Unesco World Heritage Site in 2009, when local authorities insisted on building a modern bridge across the Elbe River.

21st Century

After reunification, Berlin became the epicentre of contemporary building projects. On Potsdamer Platz, Italian architect Renzo Piano designed Daimler City (1998), while German-born (but Chicago-based) Helmut Jahn turned a playful hand to the glass-and-steel Sony Center (2000). Another notable Jahn creation in Berlin is the edgy Neues Kranzler Eck (2000).

Three spectacular successes in Germany by US star architect Daniel Libeskind are Osnabrück's Felix-Nussbaum-Haus (1998), Dresden's updated Militärhistorisches Museum (Military History Museum; 2011) and, most famously, the zinc-clad zigzag Jüdisches Museum (Jewish Museum; 2001) in Berlin. Also in Berlin, the haunting Holocaust Memorial (2005) is the work of New York-based Peter Eisenman, while the Hamburg-based architectural firm of Gerkan, Marg und Partner took glass-and-steel station architecture to new limits with the city's Hauptbahnhof (2006).

Frank Gehry has left his mark on German cities over the past two decades, first through the 1989 Vitra Design Museum in Weil am Rhein and later with his characteristically warped 1999 Neue Zollhof (New Customs House) in Düsseldorf's Medienhafen (Media Harbour), the Gehry-Tower (2001) in Hanover and the 1999 DZ Bank on Berlin's Pariser Platz.

The contrast of old and new in the extension of Cologne's Wallraf-Richartz-Museum (2001) by the late Oswald Mathias Ungers is a worthy addition to a city with one of the world's most beautiful cathedrals. In 2003 Axel Schultes and Charlotte Frank won the German Architecture Prize for their design of the Bundeskanzleramt (New Chancellery; 2001), which forms part of Berlin's new post-reunification Government Quarter. Its historic anchor the Reichstag, home of Germany's parliament, got a modern landmark addition with its sparkling glass cupola (1999), part of Norman Foster's building makeover.

Munich architect Stephan Braunfels masterminded his city's modernist Pinakothek der Moderne (2002), while the Berlin firm of Sauerbruch Hutton designed the nearby Museum Brandhorst, whose facade consists of 36,000 colourful ceramic square tubes. In 2006, Munich's famous football team, FC Bayern Munich, moved into its sparkling Allianz Arena, a remarkable rubber-dinghy-like translucent object that pleases football and architecture fans alike. Not to be outdone, Stuttgart added the futuristic Porsche Museum to its cityscape in 2009.

In Hamburg, an old docklands area has been revamped into the HafenCity, a new city quarter with futuristic architecture such as Herzog & de Meuron's startling Elbphilharmonie concert hall, a crystalline creation topped off with a tent-like roof, which opened in 2017. In terms of sustainable construction, an award-winning standout is Hamburg's Unilever building, which makes clever use of innovative LED lighting, a cooling double-layered outer shell and rooftop heat

Freiburg in the Black Forest is, architecturally speaking, one of the most sustainable cities in Europe. The city's Vauban district is a shining example of environmental planning and ecofriendly living. Its Solar Settlement is the world's first community with energy-plus houses that produce more energy from renewable sources than they use.

TOP UNESCO WORLD HERITAGE SITES IN GERMANY

Trier's Roman monuments (p616) The finest collection of Roman heritage in Germany.

Aachen Cathedral (p655) Begun in the 8th century, this blockbuster building is the final resting place of Charlemagne.

Kaiserdom (p580) Speyer's magnificent 11th-century cathedral holds the tombs of eight medieval German emperors.

Regensburg (p449) An Altstadt (old town) crammed with Romanesque and Gothic edifices.

Kölner Dom (p629) Cologne's 13th-century cathedral was completed over six centuries.

Potsdam's parks and palaces (p138) Includes 500 hectares of parks and 150 buildings raised between 1730 and 1916.

Würzburg Residenz (p407) This baroque 18th-century palace is perhaps Balthasar Neumann's finest creation.

Bauhaus sites If you're interested in the early 20th-century Bauhaus movement, Weimar's **Bauhaus Museum** (Map p246; www.klassik-stiftung.de; Theaterplatz 1) and Dessau's **Bauhausgebäude** (p277) are key.

Bundeskanzleramt, Berlin

exchangers. Architecture and urban planning aficionados should also flock to the nearby island of Hamburg-Wilhelmburg, a showcase of innovative, eco-sensitive buildings, including the striking home of the State Ministry for Urban Development and the Environment.

Not all new construction has to be cutting edge, as shown by the rebuilding of the Berlin City Palace, scheduled for completion in 2019. Although planned to be a modern repository of museums and cultural institutions on the inside, its facade will be an exact replica of the baroque-style palace that was blown up by the East German government in 1951. Nearby Potsdam has also created a replica of its Prussian city palace, which opened in 2014 as the new home of the Brandenburg state parliament.

Landscapes & Wildlife

For centuries the epic beauty of Germany's landscapes has inspired artists and writers toward the lyrical and profound. The sprightly Rhine coursing through emerald vines, the wave-lashed Baltic coast, the glacier-licked summits of the Bavarian Alps – all have been immortalised by Romantic painters and literary legends including Thomas Mann, Bertolt Brecht and Mark Twain. And, of course, the Brothers Grimm, who found in Germany's dark forests the perfect air of mystery for gingerbready tales of wicked witches and lost-in-the-woods children.

The Land

For all that it has been publicised, much of Germany's loveliness remains unsung beyond its borders. Take Mecklenburg–Western Pomerania's beech forests, poppy-flecked meadows and lakes; or the East Frisian Islands' briny breezes and shifting sands; Saxon Switzerland's wonderland of sandstone pinnacles; or the Bavarian forest's primordial woodlands tinged with Bohemian melancholy. Who has heard of them? Bar the odd intrepid traveller, only the Germans.

The good news is that the national passion for outdoor pursuits and obsessive efficiency has made such landscapes brilliantly accessible. Every inch of the country has been mapped, cycling and hiking trails thread to its remotest corners, and farmhouses and mountain huts offer travellers shelter and sustenance. Life here is close to nature, and nature here is on a truly grand scale.

Across its 357,021 sq km, Europe's seventh-largest country embraces moors and heaths, mudflats and chalk cliffs, glacial lakes, river wetlands and dense forests. Hugged by Poland, the Czech Republic, Austria, Switzerland, France, Belgium, the Netherlands, Luxembourg and Denmark, the land is mountainous in the south but flat in the north. Many visitors are surprised to learn Germany even possesses low-lying islands and sandy beaches.

Sidling up to Austria in the southeast are the Bavarian Alps, where Germany's highest peak – the 2962m Zugspitze – crowns the spine of the Northern Limestone Alps, and jewel-coloured lakes scatter the Berchtesgaden National Park. Rolling almost to the Swiss border in the southwest, the Black Forest presents a sylvan tableau of round-topped hills (the highest being 1493m Feldberg), thick fir forests and open countryside.

Starting its journey in Switzerland and travelling through Lake Constance (Germany's largest lake), the Rhine winds its 1320km-long way around the Black Forest, before crawling up the western border to drain into the North Sea. The Elbe, Oder and other German rivers likewise flow north, except for the Danube, which flows east.

Moving towards the central belt, you'll find memorable vineyards and hiking areas in the warmer valleys around the Moselle River. The land just north was formed by volcanic activity. To the east is the holiday area of the Spreewald, a picturesque wetland with narrow, navigable waterways.

Where Germany meets Holland in the northwest and Denmark in the north, the land is flat; the westerly North Sea coast consists partly of drained land and dykes. To the east, the Baltic coast is riddled with bays and fjords in Schleswig-Holstein but gives way to sandy inlets and beaches. At the northeastern tip is Germany's largest island, Rügen, renowned for its chalk cliffs.

The Wildlife

Animals

Snow hares, marmots and wild goats scamper around the Alps. The chamois is also fairly common here, as well as in pockets of the Black Forest, the Swabian Alps and Saxon Switzerland, south of Dresden.

A rare but wonderful Alpine treat for patient birdwatchers is a sighting of the golden eagle; Berchtesgaden National Park staff might be able to help you find one. The jay, with its darting flight patterns and calls imitating other species, is easy to spot in the Alpine foothills. Look for the flashes of blue on its wings.

Pesky but sociable racoons, a common non-native species, scoot about eastern Germany, and soon let hikers know if they have been disturbed with a shrill whistle. Beavers can be found in wetlands near the Elbe River. Seals are common on the North Sea and Baltic Sea coasts.

The north coast lures migratory birds. From March to May and August to October they stop over in Schleswig-Holstein's Wadden Sea National Park and the Vorpommersche Boddenlandschaft National Park while travelling to and from southerly regions. Forests everywhere provide a habitat for songbirds and woodpeckers.

Best Wildlife Spotting

North Sea common seals, harbour porpoises

Black Forest red deer, red squirrels

Bavarian Alps chamois, marmots, ibex

Mecklenburg Lake Plains otters

Lüneburger Heide Heidschnucken (moorland sheep)

Vital Statistics

Highest peak Zugspitze (2962m) in the Bavarian Alps

Major rivers Rhine, Danube, Elbe, Moselle, Main

Biggest lake Lake Constance (536 sq km)

Tallest waterfall Triberger Wasserfälle (163m)

Largest nature park Black Forest (12,000 sq km)

NATIONAL PARKS

Germany's vast and varied landscapes are protected to varying degrees by 105 nature parks, 15 biosphere reserves and 16 national parks. The Upper Middle Rhine Valley, the Wadden Sea and the beech forest of the Jasmund National Park are safeguarded as Unesco World Heritage Areas.

PARK & WEBSITE	FEATURES	ACTIVITIES	BEST TIME TO VISIT	PAGE
Bavarian Forest (www.nationalpark-bayerischer-wald.de)	mountain forest & upland moors (243 sq km); deer, hazel grouse, foxes, otters, eagle owls, Eurasian pygmy owls; botany	walking, mountain biking, cross-country skiing	winter, spring	p463
Berchtesgaden (www.nationalpark-berchtesgaden.de)	lakes, subalpine spruce, salt mines and ice caves (210 sq km); golden eagles, marmots, blue hares	wildlife spotting, walking, skiing	winter, spring	p404
Black Forest National Park (www.schwarz wald-nationalpark.de)	meadows, mountains, spruce, pine and beech forests, valleys, moors and lakes (100 sq km)	walking, birdwatching, cycling, nature trails	spring through autumn	p490
Eifel (www.national-park-eifel.de)	beech forest (110 sq km); wild cats, beavers, kingfishers; wild yellow narcissus	wildlife and flora spotting, hiking, hydrotherapy, spa treatments	spring, summer	p654
Hainich (www.national-park-hainich.de)	mixed deciduous forest (76 sq km), beech trees; black storks, wild cats, rare bats	walking	spring	p253
Hamburg Wadden Sea (www.nationalpark-wattenmeer.de)	mudflats, meadows and sand dunes (345 sq km); sea swallows, terns	birdwatching, mudflat walking	spring, autumn	See website
Harz (www.national-park-harz.de)	rock formations, caves (247 sq km); black woodpeckers, wild cats, deer	climbing, walking	spring, summer, autumn; avoid weekends (busy)	p260

Some animals are staging a comeback. Sea eagles, practically disappeared from western Germany, are becoming more plentiful in the east, as are falcons, white storks and cranes. The east also sees wolves, which regularly cross the Oder River from Poland, and Eurasian elk (moose), which occasionally appear on moors and in mixed forests.

Germany's 15 Unesco Biosphere Reserves include the Bavarian Forest, the Berchtesgaden Alps, the Spreewald and Rügen. For the low-down, visit www.unesco.org.

The wild cat has returned to the Harz Mountains and other forested regions, but don't expect to see the related lynx. Having died out here in the 19th century, lynxes were reintroduced in the 1980s, only to be illegally hunted to the point of extinction again. Today, a few populate the Bavarian Forest National Park, although chances of seeing one in the wild are virtually zero.

Deer are still around, although with dwindling natural habitats and a shrinking gene pool, the Deutsche Wildtier Stiftung (www.deutschewildtierstiftung.de) has expressed concern for their future.

Plants

Despite environmental pressures, German forests remain beautiful places to wander away from crowds and get back to nature. At lower altitudes, they're usually a potpourri of beech, oak, birch, chestnut, linden, maple and ash trees that erupt into a kaleidoscope of colour in autumn.

PARK & WEBSITE	FEATURES	ACTIVITIES	BEST TIME TO VISIT	PAGE
Hunsrück-Hochwald (www.nationalpark-hunsrueck-hochwald.de)	upland forests and fields (100 sq km); red deer, wild boar, black storks, wild cats	ranger tours, hiking, cycling	spring through autumn	See website
Jasmund (www.national park-jasmund.de)	chalk cliffs, forest, creeks and moors (30 sq km); white-tailed eagles	walking, cycling	avoid summer (paths like ant trails)	p217
Kellerwald Edersee (www.nationalpark-kellerwald-edersee.de)	beech and other deciduous trees, lake (57 sq km); black storks, wild cats, rare bats, stags	walking, wildlife spotting	spring, summer, autumn	p228
Lower Oder Valley (www.nationalpark-unteres-odertal.eu)	river plain (165 sq km); black storks, sea eagles, beavers, aquatic warblers, cranes	walking, cycling, birdwatching	winter (bird-watching), spring (other activities)	See website
Lower Saxony Wadden Sea (www.national park-wattenmeer.de)	salt-marsh and bog landscape (2780 sq km); seals, shell ducks	swimming, walking, birdwatching	late spring, early autumn	p740
Müritz (www.national park-mueritz.de)	beech, bogs and lakes (318 sq km); sea eagles, fish hawks, cranes, white-tailed eagles, Gotland sheep	cycling, canoeing, birdwatching, hiking	spring, summer, autumn	p203
Saxon Switzerland (www.nationalpark-saechsische-schweiz.de)	sandstone and basalt rock formations (93 sq km); eagle owls, otters, fat dormice	walking, climbing, rock climbing	avoid summer (throngs with day trippers)	p309
Schleswig-Holstein Wadden Sea (www.national park-wattenmeer.de)	seascape of dunes, salt marshes & mudflats (4410 sq km); sea life, migratory birds	mudflat walking, birdwatching, swimming	spring, autumn	See website
Vorpommersche Boddenlandschaft (www.nationalpark-vorpommersche-boddenlandschaft.de)	Baltic seascape (805 sq km); cranes, red deer, wild boar	birdwatching, water sports, walking	autumn (cranes), summer (water sports)	See website

At higher elevations, fir, pine, spruce and other conifers are prevalent. Canopies often shade low-growing ferns, heather, clover and foxglove. Mixed deciduous forests carpet river valleys at lower altitudes.

In spring, Alpine regions burst with wildflowers – orchid, cyclamen, gentian, pulsatilla, Alpine roses, edelweiss and buttercups. Great care is taken not to cut pastures until plants have seeded; you can minimise your impact by sticking to paths, especially in Alpine areas and coastal dunes where ecosystems are fragile. In late August, heather blossom is the particular lure of Lüneburger Heide, northeast of Hanover.

Environmental Issues

Germans are the original Greens. They cannot claim to have invented environmentalism, but they were there at the outset and coined the word to describe the movement. Recycling, cycling, carrying groceries in reusable bags, shopping at *Biomärkte* (organic supermarkets) – it's all second nature here.

Nuclear power and its demise is still a hot topic. In the wake of the 2011 Fukushima disaster, Angela Merkel made the bold move to abandon nuclear power and shut down all of Germany's 17 nuclear plants by 2022 (nine have already closed).

For the inside scoop on Germany's 105 nature parks and 16 national parks, visit www.naturparke.de, www.deutsche-nationalparks.com, www.germany.travel and the conservation-focused www.bfn.de.

LANDSCAPES & WILDLIFE ENVIRONMENTAL ISSUES

PlusEnergy Solar Settlement, Freiburg (p506)

In Frankfurt and the Southern Rhineland, environmental concerns delayed the construction of the Hochmoselbrücke (High Moselle Bridge) linking Ürzig and Zeltingen-Rachtig, but it was completed in late 2018.

Travelling across Germany, you'll be struck by the number of wind turbines dotting the landscape, especially in the windswept north. In the EU, Germany 'blows away' most of the competition, with some 23,000 wind turbines in action. In 2017 alone the country blazed ahead with a staggering 55,550 MW of installed wind capacity. While other countries debate pros and cons, Germany has long embraced the technology to become Europe's leading producer of wind energy. These turbines generate roughly 12% of German electricity and there are big plans to build more offshore.

The country is setting a shining example when it comes to solar power, too. There are more than 1.5 million solar PV systems across Germany, which makes it the world leader in photovoltaics, with solar energy accounting for an estimated 7.2% of its electricity generation in 2014. If eco-cities such as Freiburg, home to the 59-house PlusEnergy Solar Settlement, are anything to go by, Germany's future looks bright indeed.

In 2017, the country notched up its proportion of power produced by renewables to 35%, and on sunny, windy days, this figure rose to as much as 85%.

Südlink, the new part of the national grid linked to green energy distribution, plans to put cables for Germany's longest power link underground, with a ballpark date of 2025 for completion.

Germany's Green Goals

....

Cut 40% of greenhouse gas emissions from 1990 levels by 2020

....

Renewables to produce 35% of electricity by 2020

....

80% of electricity generated by renewables by 2050

Survival Guide

Directory A–Z

Accessible Travel

Download Lonely Planet's free Accessible Travel guides from http://lptravel.to/AccessibleTravel.

➡ Germany is fairly progressive when it comes to barrier-free travel. Access ramps and/or lifts are available in many public buildings, including train stations, museums, concert halls and cinemas. In historical towns, though, cobblestone streets make getting around difficult.

➡ Trains, trams, underground trains and buses are increasingly accessible. Some stations also have grooved platform borders to assist blind passengers in navigating. Seeing-eye dogs are allowed on all forms of public transport. For the hearing impaired, upcoming station names are often displayed electronically on public transport.

➡ Newer hotels have lifts and rooms with extra-wide doors and spacious bathrooms.

➡ Some car rental agencies offer hand-controlled vehicles and vans with wheelchair lifts at no charge, but you must reserve them well in advance. In parking lots and garages, look for designated spots marked with a wheelchair symbol.

➡ Many local and regional tourist offices have special brochures (usually in German) for people with disabilities.

Useful Resources

Deutsche Bahn Mobility Service Centre (01806-996 633, ext 9 for English; www.bahn.com) Train access information and route planning assistance. The website has useful information in English (search for 'barrier-free travel').

German National Tourist Office (www.germany.travel) Search for 'barrier free' for helpful info on accessible travel in Germany, including details on sights and attractions, bookings and transport.

Accommodation

Germany has all types of places to unpack your suitcase. Outside of high season, around holidays and during major trade shows it's generally not necessary to book your accommodation in advance.

Costs

Accommodation costs vary wildly between regions, and between cities and rural areas. What gets you a romantic suite in a countryside inn in the Bavarian Forest may only be worth a two-star room in Munich. City hotels geared to the suit brigade often lure leisure travellers with lower rates on weekends. Seasonal variations are common in holiday regions, less so in the cities.

PRACTICALITIES

Newspapers Major national newspapers include daily broadsheet *Frankfurter Allgemeine Zeitung* (www.faz.net), the *Süddeutsche Zeitung* (www.sueddeutsche.de) and weekly *Die Zeit* (www.zeit.de).

Magazines Popular news weeklies include *Der Spiegel* (www.spiegel.de) and *Focus* (www.focus.de).

Radio National radio stations include Deutsche Welle (www.dw.com). Regional stations feature a mixed format of news, talk and music.

Sizes For women's clothing sizes, a German size 36 equals a size 6 in the US and a size 10 in the UK, then increases in increments of two, making size 38 a US 8 and UK 12, and so on.

Weights & Measures The metric system is used.

Reservations

Most tourist offices and properties now have an online booking function with a best-price guarantee. If you've arrived in town and don't have reservations or online access, swing by the tourist office, where staff can assist you in finding last-minute lodgings. After hours, vacancies with contact details and addresses may be posted in the window or in a display case.

Categories

Budget stays will generally have you checking in at hostels, *Gasthöfe* (country inns), *Pensionen* (B&Bs or small hotels), simple family hotels or properties found via the usual home-sharing services. Facilities may be shared. Midrange properties offer extra creature comforts, such as cable TV, wi-fi and private bathrooms. Overall, these constitute the best value for money. Top-end places come with luxurious amenities, perhaps scenic locations, special decor or historical ambience. Many also have pools, saunas and business centres.

AGRITOURISM

Family-friendly farm holidays are a terrific (and inexpensive) back-to-nature choice. Kids get to run free and interact with barnyard animals. Accommodation ranges from bare-bones digs with shared facilities to fully furnished holiday apartments. Minimum stays are common, as is an *Endreinigungsgebühr* (final cleaning fee). Properties swing from organic, dairy and equestrian farms to wine estates. Note that places advertising *Landurlaub* (country holiday) no longer actively work their farms.

CAMPING

Camping grounds are generally well kept but many get jam-packed in summer. Book early or show up before noon to snap up a spot. The core camping season runs from May to September, but some sites are open year-round.

Given the remote location of many sites, having your own wheels is a definite asset. Camping on public land is not permitted. If you want to pitch a tent on private property, ask the landowner first.

Fees are broken down per person (between €3 and €10), tent (€6 to €16) and car or caravan (€3 to €20), plus additional fees for hot showers, resort tax and electricity. A Camping Card International (www.camping-cardinternational.com) often yields discounts.

See www.germany.travel/camping for an excellent searchable database with detailed information on 750 sites, as well as a downloadable version of its *Camping in Germany* brochure.

DJH HOSTELS

Germany's 500 Hostelling International-affiliated *Jugendherbergen* (hostels) are run by the Deutsches Jugendherbergswerk (DJH; www.jugendherberge.de). Although open to all ages, they're especially popular with school and youth groups, families and sports clubs.

In addition to gender-segregated dorms, most hostels have private rooms for families and couples, often with bathrooms. If space is tight, hostels may give priority to people under 27, except for those travelling as a family. People aged over 27 are charged an extra €4 per night.

If you don't have an HI membership card from your home country, buy an annual Hostelling International Card for €22.50 (€7 for those under 27), available at any DJH hostel.

INDEPENDENT HOSTELS

Independent hostels cater primarily for individual travellers and attract a mixed, international crowd. They're

---

PRICE RANGES

The following price ranges refer to the cost of a double room with private bathroom (any combination of toilet, bathtub, shower and washbasin), including 7% VAT, but not resort taxes and city taxes levied by some communities.

€ less than €80

€€ €80– €160

€€€ more than €160

MY HOME IS MY CASTLE

If you're the romantic type, consider a fairy-tale getaway in a castle, palace or country manor dripping with character and history. They're typically in the countryside, strategically perched atop a crag, perhaps overlooking a river or rolling hills. And it doesn't take a king's ransom to stay in one; even wallet-watchers can fancy themselves knight or damsel when staying in a castle converted into a youth hostel. More typically, though, properties are luxury affairs, blending mod cons with baronial ambience and old-fashioned trappings such as four-poster beds, antique armoires and heavy drapes. Sometimes your hosts are even descendants of the original castle builders – often some local baron, count or prince.

WHICH FLOOR?

In Germany, as elsewhere in Europe, 'ground floor' refers to the floor at street level. The 1st floor (what would be called the 2nd floor in the US) is the floor above that. Lonely Planet follows German usage.

most prevalent in big cities such as Berlin, Cologne and Hamburg, but there are now dozens in smaller towns throughout the country.

Hostels range from classic backpacker pads with large dorms and a communal spirit to more glam 'flashpacker' properties that can rival budget hotels. Many have private quarters with bathrooms and/or apartments with kitchens. Dorms tend to be mixed, although some hostels offer women-only units. Indie hostels have no curfew and staff tend to be savvy, multilingual and keen to help with tips and advice. Some charge a linen fee of around €3 per stay.

HOTELS

You'll find a hotel to suit every mood, moment and budget in Germany, including small family-run places; good old-fashioned *Gasthöfe* (inns) in the countryside, full of history and creaking charm; five-star spa hotels; and boutique city sleeps geared towards lifestyle-savvy travellers.

Cheaper rooms may have shared facilities (*WC und*

Dusche auf der Etage). Increasingly, city hotels are not including breakfast in their room rates, so always check for the price of *Frühstück* first.

CHAIN HOTELS

Hotel chains stretch from cookie-cutter anonymity to central five-star properties with historical flair and top-notch facilities (air-con, wi-fi, 24-hour check-in etc.). Most offer last-minute and/or weekend deals. Rivalling the big international chains are home-grown contenders such as **Dorint** (www.dorint. com), the luxury **Kempinski** (www.kempinski.com) group, city hotel chain **Leonardo** (www.leonardo-hotels.com) and **Steigenberger** (www. steigenberger.com), offering five-star luxury often in historic buildings.

PENSIONS, INNS & PRIVATE ROOMS

The German equivalent of B&Bs, *Pensionen* are small and informal and an excellent low-cost alternative to hotels. *Gasthöfe/Gasthäuser* (inns) are similar, but usually have restaurants serving regional and German food to a local clientele. *Privatzimmer* are guest rooms in private homes, though privacy seekers may find these places a bit too intimate.

Amenities, room size and decor vary. The cheapest rooms may have shared facilities. What they lack in amenities, though, they often make up for in charm and authenticity, with friendly hosts who take a personal interest in ensuring that you enjoy your stay.

Some tourist offices keep lists of available rooms; you can also look around for '*Zimmer Frei*' (rooms available) signs in house or shop windows. They're usually quite cheap, with per-person rates generally topping out at €30, including breakfast.

FURNISHED FLATS

Renting a furnished flat is a hugely popular – and economical – option. The benefit of space, privacy and independence makes them especially attractive to families, self-caterers and small groups. Peer-to-peer rental communities such as Airbnb or its German competitors Wimdu and 9flats have made enormous inroads.

Local tourist offices have lists of holiday flats/apartments (*Ferienwohnungen* or *Ferien-Appartements*) or holiday homes (*Ferienhäuser*). *Pensionen*, inns, hotels and even farmhouses also rent out apartments.

Stays under a week usually incur a surcharge, and there's almost always a 'cleaning fee' of €20 or €30 added to the total.

You could also consider a home exchange, where you swap homes and live like a local for free; see www. homeexchange.com for more on how it's done.

Booking Services

Bauernhof Urlaub (www.bauern hofurlaub.de) Farmstay central.

Bed and Breakfast (www.bed-and-breakfast.de) Solid selection of B&Bs and private rentals all over the country.

BVCD Camping Guide (www. bvcd.de) Handy resource for finding a campground.

Deutsches Jugendherbergswerk (DJH; www. jugendherberge.de) Hostelling International-affiliated digs.

Germany Travel (www.germany. travel) Accommodation searchable by region and theme.

Independent Hostels of Germany (www.german-hostels.de)

BOOK YOUR STAY ONLINE

For more accommodation reviews by Lonely Planet authors, check out http://lonelyplanet.com/germany/hotels. You'll find independent reviews, as well as recommendations on the best places to stay. Best of all, you can book online.

Wide range of indie hostels across the country.

Land Reise (www.landreise.de) Rural picks from mountain huts and farmstays to campgrounds, working wineries and *Heuhotels* (hay hotels).

Lonely Planet (www.lonely planet.com/germany/hotels) Recommendations and bookings.

Romantik Hotels (www.romantik hotels.com) Hotels with a high romance factor.

Customs Regulations

Goods brought in and out of countries within the EU incur no additional taxes, provided duty has been paid somewhere within the EU and the goods are for personal use. Duty-free shopping is only available if you're leaving the EU.

Duty-free allowances (for anyone over 17) arriving from non-EU countries:

➡ 200 cigarettes or 100 cigarillos or 50 cigars or 250g of loose tobacco or a proportional combination of these goods.

➡ 1L of strong liquor or 2L of less than 22% alcohol by volume, plus 4L of wine, plus 16L of beer.

➡ other goods up to the value of €300 if arriving by land, or €430 if arriving by sea or air (€175 for under 15 years).

Discount Cards

Concession discounts are widely available for senior citizens, children and students. In some cases, you may be asked to show ID or prove your age. Tourist offices in many cities sell Welcome Cards, which entitle visitors to discounts on museums, sights and tours, plus unlimited trips on local public transport. They can be good value if you plan on taking advantage of most of the benefits and don't qual-

Climate
Berlin

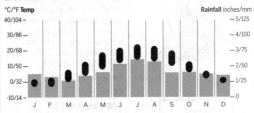

Munich

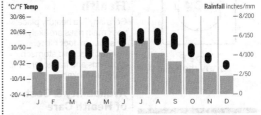

Frankfurt Am Main

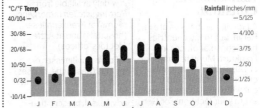

ify for any of the standard discounts.

If you qualify for one of the following discount cards, you can reap additional benefits on travel, shopping, attractions or entertainment:

Camping Card International (www.campingcardinternational. com) Up to 25% savings in camping fees; cardholders have third-party liability insurance while on the campground.

International Student Identity Card (www.isic.org) The most popular discount card, but only for full-time students. Available at ISIC points (see website) and online. Cost vary by country and range from US$15 to US$30.

International Youth Travel Card (www.isic.org) Similar to ISIC but for non-students under 30 years of age. Available at ISIC points.

Electricity

Type C
230V/50Hz

Type F
230V/50Hz

Embassies & Consulates

All foreign embassies are in Berlin, but many countries have consular offices in Frankfurt, Munich, Hamburg or Düsseldorf. Check online or call the embassy to find out which consulate is closest to your location. For German missions around the world and foreign missions in Germany, go to www.auswaertiges-amt.de.

Food

German eating options (p768) match all tastes and travel budgets. The following price ranges refer to a standard main course. Unless otherwise stated, 19% tax is included in the price.

€ less than €12
€€ €12–€22
€€€ more than €22

Health

Germany is a healthy place; your main risks are likely to be sunburn, foot blisters, insect bites, mild stomach problems and hangovers. Tap water is drinkable.

Availability & Cost of Health Care

➜ Excellent health care is widely available from *Rettungsstellen* (emergency rooms) at *Krankenhäuser* (hospitals) and at *Ärzte* (doctors' offices).

➜ For minor illnesses or injuries (headache, bruises, diarrhoea), trained staff in pharmacies can provide advice, sell prescription-free medications and make doctors' referrals if further help is needed.

➜ Condoms are widely available in drugstores, pharmacies and supermarkets. Birth control pills require a doctor's prescription.

Medical Services

➜ German *Drogerien* (chemists, drugstores) do not sell any kind of medication, not even aspirin. Even *rezeptfrei* (over-the-counter) medications for minor health concerns, such as a cold or upset stomach, are only available at an *Apotheke* (pharmacy).

➜ For more serious conditions, you will need to produce a *Rezept* (prescription) from a licensed physician. If you take regular medication, be sure to bring a supply for your entire trip, as the same brand may not be available in Germany.

➜ The names and addresses of pharmacies open after hours (these rotate) are posted in every pharmacy window, or call ☎01141.

Insurance

➜ Comprehensive travel insurance to cover theft, loss and medical problems is highly recommended.

➜ Some policies specifically exclude dangerous activities, such as motorcycling, scuba diving and even trekking; read the fine print.

➜ Check that the policy covers ambulance or an emergency flight home.

➜ Before you leave, find out if your insurance plan makes payments directly to providers or reimburses you for health expenditures.

➜ Paying for your airline ticket with a credit card sometimes provides limited travel accident insurance – ask your credit card company what it is prepared to cover.

➜ If you have to make a claim, be sure to keep all necessary documents and bills.

EUROPEAN HEALTH INSURANCE CARD (EHIC)

Citizens of the EU, Switzerland, Iceland, Norway and Liechtenstein receive free or reduced-cost, state-provided (not private) health-care coverage with the European Health Insurance Card (EHIC) for medical treatment that becomes necessary while in Germany. It does not cover emergency repatriation home. Each family member needs a separate card. UK residents can find information on how to obtain the card at www.ehic.org.uk.

You will need to pay directly and fill in a treatment form; keep the form to claim any refunds. In general you can claim back around 70% of the standard treatment cost.

Citizens of other countries need to check whether there is a reciprocal arrangement for free medical care between their country and Germany.

→ Consider coverage for luggage theft or loss. If you already have a homeowner's or renter's policy, check what it will cover and only get supplemental insurance to protect against the rest.

→ If you have prepaid a large portion of your holiday, trip cancellation insurance is worthwhile.

→ Worldwide travel insurance is available at www. lonelyplanet.com/travel-insurance. You can buy, extend and claim online any time – even if you're already on the road.

Internet Access

→ Some cafes and bars have wi-fi hot spots that let customers hook up for free, although you usually need to ask for a password.

→ Many hotels have an internet corner for their guests, often at no charge. Note that in some properties, wi-fi access may be limited to certain rooms and/or public areas; if you need in-room access be sure to specify at the time of booking.

→ Wi-fi is available for a fee on select ICE train routes, including Berlin to Cologne and Frankfurt to Munich and in DB Lounges (free in 1st class). Around 135 stations, including those in Berlin, Munich, Hamburg and Frankfurt, offer 30 minutes of free wi-fi with registration via DeutscheTelekom.

→ Locate wi-fi hot spots at www.hotspot-locations.com.

Legal Matters

→ The permissible blood alcohol content is 0.05%; drivers caught exceeding this are subject to stiff fines, a confiscated licence and even jail time. Drinking in public is not illegal, but be discreet.

→ Cannabis *consumption* is not illegal, but the possession, acquisition, sale and cultivation of it is considered a criminal offence. There is usually no prosecution for possessing 'small quantities', although the definition of 'small' varies by state, ranging from 6 to 20 grams. Dealers face far stiffer penalties, as do people caught with any other recreational drugs.

→ If arrested, you have the right to make a phone call and are presumed innocent until proven guilty, although you may be held in custody until trial. If you don't know a lawyer, contact your embassy.

LGBTIQ+ Travellers

Germany is a magnet for *schwule* (gay) and *lesbische* (lesbian) travellers, with the rainbow flag flying especially proudly in Berlin and Cologne. There are also sizeable communities in Hamburg, Frankfurt and Munich.

→ Legal stuff: Homosexuality has been legal since the late 1960s. Same-sex marriage is legal.

→ Attitudes tend to be more conservative in the countryside, among older people and in the eastern states.

→ As elsewhere, Germany's lesbian scene is less public than its male counterpart and is centred mainly on women's cafes and bars.

→ Gay pride marches are held throughout Germany in springtime; the largest, in Cologne and Berlin, draw hundreds of thousands of rainbow revellers and friends.

Publications

Blu (www.blu.fm) Free print and online magazine with searchable, up-to-the-minute location and event listings.

L-Mag (www.l-mag.de) Bi-monthly magazine for lesbians. Available at newsagents.

Spartacus International Gay Guide (https://spartacus.gay guide.travel) Annual English-language travel guide for men. Available online, in bookstores and as an app.

Websites & Apps

German National Tourist Office (www.germany.travel/en/ms/ lgbt/home/home.html?et_rp=1) Dedicated LGBT pages.

Spartacus World (www.spart acusworld.com) Hip hotel, style and event guide.

Patroc Gay Travel Guide (www. patroc.com) Travel information to 25 European destinations.

Maps

Most tourist offices distribute free (but often very basic) maps. For driving around Germany, however, you'll need a detailed road map or atlas such as those published by Falk, RV Verlag or **ADAC** (Allgemeiner Deutscher Automobil-Club; ☑for information 0800 510 1112, for roadside assistance from mobile 222 2222; www.adac.de). Look for them at bookshops, tourist offices, newsagents and petrol stations. Find downloadable maps and driving directions at www.google.de/ maps, www.stadtplandienst. de or www.viamichelin.de.

Money

The unit of currency in Germany is the euro (€). Euros come in seven notes (€5, €10, €20, €50, €100, €200 and €500) and eight coins (€0.01, €0.02, €0.05, €0.10, €0.20, €0.50, €1 and €2).

ATMs & Debit Cards

→ The easiest and quickest way to obtain cash is by using your debit (bank) card at a *Geldautomat* (ATM) linked to international networks such as Cirrus, Plus, Star and Maestro.

→ ATMs are plentiful in towns and cities and usually accessible 24/7.

→ ATM cards often double as debit cards, and many shops, hotels, restaurants and other businesses accept them for payment. Most cards use the 'chip and PIN' system; instead of signing, you enter your PIN. If your card isn't chip-and-PIN enabled, you may be able to sign the receipt, but ask first.

➡ Deutsche Bahn ticket vending machines at train stations and local public transport may not accept non-chip-and-PIN cards.

Cash

Cash is king in Germany. Always carry some with you, and plan to pay cash almost everywhere. It's also a good idea to set aside a small amount of euros as an emergency stash.

Credit Cards

➡ Credit cards are becoming more widely accepted, but it's best not to assume you'll be able to use one – ask first. Sometimes a minimum purchase amount applies. Even so, a piece of plastic is vital in emergencies and also useful for phone or internet bookings. Visa and Mastercard are more commonly accepted than American Express or Diners Club.

➡ Avoid getting cash advances on your credit card via ATMs, as fees are steep and you'll be charged interest immediately (in other words, there's no grace period as with purchases).

➡ Report lost or stolen cards to the central number ☏116 116 or the following:

American Express ☏069-9797 1000

Mastercard ☏0800-819 1040

Visa ☏0800-811 8440

Exchange Rates

Australia	A$1	€0.65
Canada	C$1	€0.65
Japan	¥100	€0.74
New Zealand	NZ$1	€0.60
UK	UK£1	€1.15
US	US$1	€0.81

For current exchange rates see www.xe.com.

Moneychanging

➡ Commercial banks usually charge a stiff fee (€5 to €10) per foreign-currency transaction, no matter the amount, if they offer exchange services at all.

➡ *Wechselstuben* (currency exchange offices) at airports, train stations and in bigger towns usually charge lower fees. Traveller-geared Reisebank (www.reisebank. de) branches are ubiquitous in Germany and are usually found at train stations. They keep longer hours than banks and are usually open on weekends.

➡ Exchange facilities in rural areas are rare.

Opening Hours

The following are typical opening hours; these may vary seasonally and between cities and villages. We've provided those applicable in high season. For specifics, see individual listings.

Banks 9am–4pm Monday to Friday, extended hours usually Tuesday and Thursday, some open Saturday

Bars 6pm–1am

Cafes 8am–8pm

Clubs 11pm to early morning

Post offices 9am–6pm Monday to Friday, 9am–1pm Saturday

Restaurants 11am–11pm (food service often stops at 9pm in rural areas)

Major stores and supermarkets 9.30am–8pm Monday to Saturday (shorter hours outside city centres)

Photography

Germany is a photographer's dream. A good general reference guide is *Lonely Planet's Guide to Travel Photography*.

➡ Germans tend to be deferential around photographers and will make a point of not walking in front of your camera, even if you want them to.

➡ No one seems to mind being photographed in the context of an overall scene, but if you want a close-up shot, you should ask first.

➡ Many museums, palaces and some churches charge a separate 'photography fee' (usually €2 or €3) if you want to take (non-commercial) pictures.

Post

Sending letters up to 20g to destinations within Germany costs €0.70; it's €0.90 to anywhere else in the world. For letters up to 50g, the rates are €0.85 and €1.50, respectively. For other rates, see www.deutschepost.de.

Mail within Germany takes one to two days for delivery; to other European countries or the USA it takes three to five days, and to Australia five to seven days.

Public Holidays

Germany observes three secular and eight religious public holidays. Banks, shops, post offices and public services close on these days. States with predominantly Catholic populations, such as Bavaria and Baden-Württemberg, also celebrate Epiphany (6 January), Corpus Christi (10 days after Pentecost), Assumption Day (15 August) and All Saints' Day (1 November). Reformation Day (31 October) is only observed in eastern Germany (but not in Berlin).

The following are *gesetzliche Feiertage* (public holidays):

Neujahrstag (New Year's Day) 1 January

Ostern (Easter) March/April; Good Friday, Easter Sunday and Easter Monday

Christi Himmelfahrt (Ascension Day) Forty days after Easter

Maifeiertag/Tag der Arbeit (Labour Day) 1 May

Pfingsten (Whit/Pentecost Sunday & Monday) Fifty days after Easter

Tag der Deutschen Einheit (Day of German Unity) 3 October

Weihnachtstag (Christmas Day) 25 December

Zweiter Weihnachtstag (Boxing Day) 26 December

Safe Travel

Germany is a very safe country in which to live and travel, with crime rates that are quite low by international standards. Though theft and other crimes against travellers occur rarely, you should still take all the usual precautions:

➡ Lock hotel rooms and cars, not leaving valuables unattended.

➡ Keep an eye out for pickpockets in crowded places; don't take midnight strolls in city parks.

➡ Many hostels provide lockers, but you need your own padlock.

➡ Train stations tend to be magnets for people who might harass you or make you feel otherwise uncomfortable, especially at night.

Government Travel Advice

The following government websites offer travel advisories and information on current hot spots:

Australian Department of Foreign Affairs (http://dfat.gov.au)

British Foreign Office (www.gov.uk)

Canadian Department of Foreign Affairs (www.international.gc.ca)

US State Department (http://travel.state.gov)

SCHOOL HOLIDAYS

Each state sets its own school holidays but, in general, German children have six weeks off in summer and two weeks each around Christmas, Easter and October. Traffic is worse at the beginning of school holidays in population-rich states such as North Rhine–Westphalia and can become a nightmare if several states let out their schools at the same time.

Germans are big fans of miniholidays around public holidays, which are especially common in spring, when many holidays fall on a Thursday or Monday. On those 'long weekends' you can expect heavy crowds on the roads, in the towns and everywhere else. Lodging is at a premium at these times.

Telephone

German phone numbers consist of an area code, starting with 0, and the local number. Area codes are between three and six digits long; local numbers are between three and nine digits. If dialling from a landline within the same city, you don't need to dial the area code. You must dial it if using a mobile.

Calling Germany from abroad Dial your country's international access code, then ☎49 (Germany's country code), then the area code (dropping the initial 0) and the local number.

Calling internationally from Germany Dial ☎00 (the international access code), then the country code, the area code (without the zero if there is one) and the local number.

Mobile Phones

➡ German mobile numbers begin with a four-digit prefix, such as 0151, 0157, 0170, 0178.

➡ Mobile (cell) phones are called 'Handys' and work on GSM 900/1800. If your home country uses a different standard, you'll need a multiband GSM phone while in Germany.

➡ Data roaming charges were scrapped in the EU as of 2017, but callers from other countries should check costs with their provider.

➡ If you have an unlocked phone that works in Germany, you may be able to save money by buying a prepaid, rechargeable local SIM card for €10 (including calling time).

➡ The cheapest and least complicated of these are sold at discount supermarkets, such as Aldi, Netto and Lidl. Telecommunications stores (eg Deutsche Telekom, O₂ and Vodafone) also sell SIMs. Top-up cards are widely available in kiosks and supermarkets.

➡ If you want to purchase an inexpensive unlocked phone, try the electronics chains Media Markt and Saturn. Prices start at €20.

➡ Calls made to a mobile phone are more expensive than those to a landline, but incoming calls are free.

➡ The use of mobile phones while driving is *verboten* (forbidden), unless you're using a headset.

Time

Clocks in Germany are set to Central European Time (GMT/UTC plus one hour). Daylight saving time kicks in at 2am on the last Sunday in March and ends on the last Sunday in October. Use of the 24-hour clock (eg 6.30pm is 18.30) is the norm. As daylight saving times vary across regions, the following time differences are indicative only.

CITY	NOON IN BERLIN
Auckland	11pm
Cape Town	1pm
London	11am
New York	6am
San Francisco	3am
Sydney	9pm
Tokyo	8pm

Toilets

➡ German toilets are sit-down affairs. Men are expected to sit down when peeing.

➡ Free-standing 24-hour self-cleaning toilet pods have become quite common. The cost is €0.50 and you have 15 minutes. Most are wheelchair-accessible.

➡ Toilets in malls, clubs, beer gardens etc often have an attendant who expects a tip of between €0.20 and €0.50.

➡ Toilets in airports are usually free, but in main train stations they are often maintained by private companies like McClean,

which charge as much as €1.50 for the privilege.

➡ Along autobahns, rest stops with facilities are spaced about 20km to 30km apart.

Tourist Information

German National Tourist Office (www.germany.travel) Should be your first port of call for travel in Germany.

Berlin Tourist Office (Map p66; ☑030-250 025; www.visitberlin.de; Hauptbahnhof, Europaplatz entrance, ground fl; ⊗8am-10pm; ⑤Hauptbahnhof, ⑧Hauptbahnhof) Useful tourist office on arrival at Berlin's **Hauptbahnhof** (Main Train Station; Europaplatz, Washingtonplatz; ⑤Hauptbahnhof, ⑪Hauptbahnhof).

Visas

➡ EU nationals only need their passport or national identity card to enter, stay and work in Germany for three months. If you plan to stay longer, you must register with the authorities at the *Bürgeramt* (Citizens' Registration Office) within two weeks of your arrival.

➡ Citizens of Australia, Canada, Israel, Japan, New Zealand, Poland, Switzerland and the US only need a valid passport (no visa) if entering Germany as tourists for up to three months within a six-month period. Passports must be valid for another four months beyond the intended departure date. For stays exceeding 90 days, contact your nearest German embassy or consulate, and begin your visa application well in advance.

➡ Nationals from other countries need a Schengen Visa, named for the 1995 Schengen Agreement that abolished international border controls between many European countries. Applications for a Schengen Visa must be filed with the embassy or consulate of the country that is your primary destination. It is valid for stays of up to 90 days. Legal residency in any Schengen country makes a visa unnecessary, regardless of your nationality.

➡ For full details, see www.auswaertiges-amt.de and check with a German consulate in your country.

Volunteering

Websites such as www.goabroad.com and www.transitionsabroad.com throw up a wide spectrum of opportunities for volunteering in Germany. Helping out on a family farm in the Alps, restoring a medieval castle in eastern Germany, helping kids or the elderly in Dresden, or teaching English to the long-term unemployed in Berlin are just some of the experiences awaiting those keen to volunteer their time and skills.

Here's a small selection of volunteer organisations:

Conversation Corps (www.geovisions.org) Volunteer 15 hours a week to teach a German

---

SMOKING REGULATIONS

➡ Germany was one of the last countries in Europe to legislate smoking. However, there is no nationwide law, with regulations left to each of the 16 states, creating a rather confusing patchwork of anti-smoking laws.

➡ Generally, smoking is a no-no in schools, hospitals, airports, train stations and other public facilities. But when it comes to bars, pubs, cafes and restaurants, every state does it just a little differently.

➡ Since 2011, Bavaria bans smoking practically everywhere, even in Oktoberfest tents. However, in most other states, lighting up is allowed in designated smoking rooms in restaurants and clubs.

➡ One-room establishments smaller than 75 sq m may allow smoking, provided they serve no food and only admit patrons over 18. The venue must be clearly designated as a *Raucherbar* (smokers' bar).

family English in exchange for room and board.

Volunteers for Peace (www.vfp.org) USA-based nonprofit offers a potpourri of opportunities, from construction to farm work or social work.

WWOOF (www.wwoof.de) Help out on a small organic farm harvesting, tending animals, bringing in the hay or gardening.

Work

➸ Non-EU citizens cannot work legally in Germany without a residence permit (Aufenthaltserlaubnis) and a work permit (Arbeitserlaubnis).

➸ EU citizens don't need a work permit. Since regulations change from time to time, it's best to contact the German embassy in your country for the latest information.

➸ If you're not in the market for a full-time job but simply need some cash to replenish your travel budget, options include babysitting, English tutoring, operating tours and bartending. You won't get rich, but neither will you need a high skill level, much training, or fluent German.

➸ Start by placing a classified ad in a local newspaper or listings guide. Other places to advertise include noticeboards at universities, photocopy shops and supermarkets.

➸ Au pair work is relatively easy to find and can be done legally even by non-EU citizens. Fluent German is not expected, although you should have some basic language skills.

➸ To read the full story, pick up Lonely Planet's The Big Trip, or the latest edition of The Au Pair and Nanny's Guide to Working Abroad by Susan Griffith and Sharon Legg. The website www.au-pair-agenturen.de (in German) provides links to numerous agencies in Germany.

➸ Citizens of Australia, New Zealand, Japan, South Korea and Hong Kong between the ages of 18 and 30 may apply for a Working Holiday Visa, which entitles them to work in Germany for up to 90 days in a 12-month period. A similar scheme is available for Canadians up to age 35. Contact the German embassy in your country for details.

➸ Also check out the 'Living & Working Abroad' thread on the Thorn Tree forum at www.lonelyplanet.com/thorntree.

Transport

GETTING THERE & AWAY

Most travellers arrive in Germany by air, or by rail and road connections from neighbouring countries.

Entering the Country

Entering Germany is usually a very straightforward procedure. If you're arriving from any of the 25 other Schengen countries, such as the Netherlands, Poland, Austria or the Czech Republic, you no longer have to show your passport or go through customs, no matter which nationality you are. If you're coming in from non-Schengen countries, full border procedures apply.

Air

Airports & Airlines

Lufthansa (www.lufthansa. com), Germany's national flagship carrier and a Star Alliance member, operates a vast network of domestic and international flights and has one of the world's best safety records. Practically every other national carrier from around the world serves Germany, along with budget airlines easyJet (www. easyjet.com), Flybe (www. flybe.com), airBaltic (www. airbaltic.com), Ryanair (www. ryanair.com) and Eurowings (www.eurowings.com).

Airports include:

Berlin-Schönefeld (SXF; ☎030-6091 1150; www.berlin-airport. de; 🚉Airport-Express, RE7 & RB14, 🚇S9, S45)

Berlin-Tegel (TXL; ☎030-6091 1150; www.berlin-airport.de; 🚌Flughafen Tegel)

Bremen (BRE; ☎0421-559 50; www.airport-bremen.de)

Cologne-Bonn (CGN; Cologne-Bonn Airport; ☎02203-404 001; www. koeln-bonn-airport.de; Kennedystrasse; 🚉Köln/Bonn Flughafen)

Düsseldorf (DUS; ☎0211-4210; www.dus.com; 🚉Düsseldorf Flughafen)

Frankfurt am Main (FRA; www.frankfurt-airport.com; Hugo-Eckener-Ring; ☎; 🚉Flughafen Regionalbahnhof)

Friedrichshafen (☎07541-2840; www.bodensee-airport. eu; Am Flugplatz 64)

Karlsruhe-Baden-Baden (Baden Airpark; ☎07229-662 000; www.badenairpark.de)

Hamburg (Flughafen Hamburg Helmut Schmidt; HAM; ☎040-507 50; www.hamburg-airport. de; Flughafenstrasse; 🚉Hamburg Airport)

Hanover (HAJ; www. hannover-airport.de)

Leipzig-Halle (LEJ; ☎0341-2240; www.leipzig-halle-airport.de)

Munich (MUC; ☎089-975 00; www.munich-airport.de)

Münster-Osnabrück (FMO; ☎02571-943 360; www.fmo.de; Airportallee, Greven)

CLIMATE CHANGE & TRAVEL

Every form of transport that relies on carbon-based fuel generates CO_2, the main cause of human-induced climate change. Modern travel is dependent on aeroplanes, which might use less fuel per kilometre per person than most cars but travel much greater distances. The altitude at which aircraft emit gases (including CO_2) and particles also contributes to their climate change impact. Many websites offer 'carbon calculators' that allow people to estimate the carbon emissions generated by their journey and, for those who wish to do so, to offset the impact of the greenhouse gases emitted with contributions to portfolios of climate-friendly initiatives throughout the world. Lonely Planet offsets the carbon footprint of all staff and author travel.

Nuremberg (NUE; ☎0911 93
700; www.airport-nuernberg.de;
Flughafenstrasse)

Stuttgart (SGT; ☎0711-9480;
www.stuttgart-airport.com)

Tickets

Timing is key when it comes
to snapping up cheap air-
fares. You can generally save
a bundle by booking early,
travelling midweek (Tuesday
to Thursday) or in low season
(October to March/April in
the case of Germany), or
flying in the late evening or
early morning.

If you're coming from Australia or New Zealand, round-
the-world (RTW) tickets may
work out cheaper than regular return fares, especially if
you're planning to visit other
countries besides Germany.
They're of most value for
trips that combine Germany
with Asia or North America.

Land

Germany's excellent road, rail
and bus connections make
for easy overland travel. The
country is very well connected to the rest of Europe.

Bicycle

Bringing a bike to Germany is
much cheaper and less complicated than you might think.

**Eurotunnel bike shuttle
service** (☎in the UK 0344 822
5822; www.eurotunnel.com)
through the Channel Tunnel
charges £25 to £30 one way
for a bike and its rider. Book
at least 48 hours in advance
to ensure your bike travels on
the same train as you.

A dismantled bike under
85cm tucked into a bike bag
may be carried on board a
Eurostar train (☎from outside the UK +44 1233 617 575,
in the UK 03432 186 186; www.
eurostar.com) as part of your
luggage allowance. During
peak travel periods, make
sure there is sufficient space
on the train before you complete your booking.

Deutsche Bahn (Germany
Railways; ☎0180-699 66 33;
www.bahn.de) charges €10 for

LOW-EMISSION STICKERS

To decrease air pollution caused by fine particles, most
German cities now have low-emissions environmental
zones that may only be entered by cars displaying an
Umweltplakette (emissions sticker, sometimes also
called *Feinstaubplakette*). And yes, this includes foreign
vehicles. No stickers are needed for motorcycles.

The easiest way to obtain the sticker is by ordering it
online from www.umwelt-plakette.de, a handy website
in many languages. The cost is €31.90. You can cut this
amount in half if you order from the TÜV (Technical
Inspection Authority) at www.tuev-sued.de or www.
tuev-nord.de, both of which provide easy instructions
in English. Once in Germany, stickers are also available
from designated repair centres, vehicle-licensing offices and car dealers. Drivers caught without one will be
fined €80.

transporting a bike internationally. You need to buy an
Internationale Fahrradkarte
and make reservations at
least one day ahead.

On ferries, foot passengers
can usually bring a bicycle,
sometimes free of charge.

Bus

Long-distance coach travel
to Germany from such cities
as Milan, Vienna, Amsterdam
and Copenhagen has be-
come a viable option thanks
to a new crop of companies
offering good-value connections aboard comfortable
buses with snack bars and
free wi-fi. Major operators include **MeinFernbus** (☎030-
300 137 300; www.meinfernbus.
de), **Flixbus** (☎030-300 137
300; https://global.flixbus.
com), **Megabus** (☎in the UK
0900 1600 900; www.megabus.
com) and **Eurolines** (☎in
the UK 08717-818177; www.
eurolines.com). For routes,
times and prices, check
www.busliniensuche.de (also
in English).

BUSABOUT

A backpacker-geared
hop-on, hop-off service,
Busabout (☎in the UK 0808
281 1114; www.busabout.com)
runs coaches along three
interlocking European loops
between May and October.

Passes are sold online and
through travel agents.

Germany is part of the
north loop. Service stops in
Berlin, Dresden, Munich and
Stuttgart.

You can opt for a Stop
Pass, offering the best value
for short trips, which lets you
select three to 15 cities to
visit (ticket prices begin at
£299), or the Unlimited Pass
(£949), giving access to all
routes and 46 cities over a
six-month period.

Car & Motorcycle

When bringing your own
vehicle to Germany, you
need a valid driving licence,
car registration and proof
of third-party insurance.
Foreign cars must display
a nationality sticker unless
they have official European
plates. You also need to carry
a warning (hazard) triangle
and a first-aid kit.

There are no special re-
quirements for crossing the
border into Germany by car.
Under the Schengen Agree-
ment there are no passport
controls if entering the country from the Netherlands, Belgium, Luxembourg, Denmark,
Austria, Switzerland, the
Czech Republic and Poland.

VIA EUROTUNNEL

Coming from the UK, the
fastest way to the Continent

USEFUL WEBSITES

www.raileurope.com Detailed train information and ticket and train-pass sales from Rail Europe.

www.railteam.eu Journey planner provided by an alliance of seven European railways, including Eurostar, Deutsche Bahn and France's SNCF. No booking function yet.

www.seat61.com Comprehensive trip-planning information, including ferry details from the UK.

is via the **Eurotunnel** (☎in Germany 01805-000 248, in the UK 08443 35 35 35; www.eurotunnel.com). These shuttle trains whisk cars, motorbikes, bicycles and coaches from Folkestone in England through the Channel Tunnel to Coquelles (near Calais, France) in about 35 minutes. From there, you can be in Germany in about three hours. Loading and unloading takes about one hour.

Shuttles run daily round the clock, with up to four departures hourly during peak periods. Fares are calculated per vehicle, including up to nine passengers, and depend on such factors as time of day, season and length of stay. Standard one-way tickets start at £30. The website and travel agents have full details.

Train

Rail services link Germany with virtually every country in Europe. In Germany ticketing is handled by **Deutsche Bahn** (Germany Railways; ☎0180-699 66 33; www.bahn. de). Long-distance trains connecting major German cities with those in other countries are called EuroCity (EC) trains. Seat reservations are essential during the peak summer season and around major holidays, and are recommended at other times.

Deutsche Bahn work in cooperation with ÖBB (www.oebb.at) to provide a night rail service to major European cities, such as Basel, Zürich, Vienna, Milan, Venice, Zagreb and Budapest. There are three different levels of comfort:

Schlafwagen (sleeping car) Private, air-conditioned compartment for up to three passengers; the deluxe version (1. Klasse) has a shower and toilet.

Liegewagen (couchette) Sleeps up to six people; when you book an individual berth, you must share the compartment with others; women may ask for a single-sex couchette at the time of booking but are advised to book early.

Sitzwagen (seat carriage) Roomy reclining seat.

EUROSTAR

Thanks to the Channel Tunnel, travelling by train between the UK and Germany is a fast and enjoyable option. High-speed **Eurostar** (☎from outside the UK +44 1233 617 575, in the UK 03432 186 186; www.eurostar.com) passenger trains hurtle at least 10 times daily between London and Paris (the journey takes 2¼ hours) or Brussels (1¾ hours). In either city you can change to regular or other high-speed trains to destinations in Germany.

Eurostar fares depend on carriage class, time of day, season and destination. Children, rail-pass holders and those aged between 12 and 25 and over 60 qualify for discounts. For the latest fare information, including promotions and special packages, check the website.

RAIL PASSES

If you want to cover lots of territory in and around Germany within a specific time, a rail pass is a convenient and good-value option. Passes cover unlimited travel during

their period of validity on national railways as well as on some private lines, ferries and riverboat services.

There are two types: the Eurail Pass, for people living outside Europe, and the InterRail Pass, for residents of Europe, including residents of Russia and Turkey.

EURAIL PASS

Eurail Passes (www.eurail.com) are valid for travel in up to 28 countries and need to be purchased – on the website, through a travel agent or at www.raileurope.com – before you leave your home country. Various passes are available (prices quoted are for 2nd class):

Global Pass Unlimited travel for 15 or 22 consecutive days, or one, two or three months. There are also versions that give you five days of travel within a 10-day period or 10 or 15 days of travel within a two-month period. The 15-day continuous version costs €480.

Select Pass Five, six, eight or 10 days of travel within two months in up to four bordering countries in 1st or 2nd class; a 2nd-class five-day pass in four countries costs €344.

Regional Pass Gets you around two neighbouring countries on four, five, six, eight or 10 days within two months. The Germany–Austria Pass for five days costs €247 in 2nd class.

Groups of two to five people travelling together save 15% off the regular adult fares. If you're under 26, prices drop 35%, but you must travel in 2nd class. Children aged between four and 11 get a 50% discount on the adult fare. Children under four travel free.

The website has details, as well as a ticket-purchasing function allowing you to pay in several currencies.

INTERRAIL PASS

InterRail Passes (www.interrail.eu) are valid for unlimited travel in 30 countries. As with the Eurail Pass, you can choose from several schemes.

Global Pass Unlimited travel in 30 countries, available for 15 days (€472), 22 days (€493) or one month (€637) of continuous travel; for five travel days within a 15-day period (€269) or for 10 travel days within a one-month period (€381).

Germany Pass Buys three/ four/six/eight days of travel within a one-month period for €192/218/262/297. This pass is not available if you are a resident of Germany.

Prices quoted are for one adult travelling in 2nd class. Different prices apply to 1st-class tickets and for travellers under 26 or over 60. Children under four travel for free and do not need a pass. Up to two children under 11 travel free with a child pass if accompanied by at least one person with an adult pass.

Sea

Germany's main ferry ports are Kiel (p188) and Travemünde (p188; near Lübeck) in Schleswig-Holstein, and Rostock (p204) and Sassnitz (p218; on Rügen Island (p214) in Mecklenburg–Western Pomerania. All have services to Scandinavia. From Kiel, there are also services to Klaipėda in Lithuania, and from Travemünde you can reach Liepāja and Ventspils in Latvia (saving much time on the roads in eastern Poland).

Timetables change from season to season.

Return tickets are often cheaper than two one-way tickets. Some ferry companies now set fares the way budget airlines do: the earlier you book, the less you pay. Seasonal demand is a crucial factor (school holidays and July and August are especially busy), as is the time of day (an early-evening ferry can cost much more than one at 4am). For overnight ferries, cabin size, location and amenities affect the price. Book well in advance if you're bringing a car.

People under 25 and over 60 may qualify for discounts. To get the best fares, check out the booking service offered by Ferry Savers (www. ferrysavers.com).

Lake Ferry

The Romanshorn–Friedrichshafen car ferry provides the quickest way across Lake Constance between Switzerland and Germany. It's operated year-round by **Schweizerische Bodensee Schifffahrt** (☐in Switzerland 071-466 7888; www.sbsag.ch) and takes 40 minutes.

GETTING AROUND

Air

Most large and many smaller German cities have their own airports, and numerous

carriers operate domestic flights within Germany. Unless you're flying from one end of the country to the other, say Berlin to Munich or Hamburg to Munich, planes are only marginally quicker than trains once you factor in the time it takes to get to and from airports.

Lufthansa (www.lufthansa. com) has the densest route network. The other main airline offering domestic flights is Eurowings (www.eurowings. com). Destination cities are Berlin-Tegel, Cologne-Bonn, Dortmund, Dresden, Düsseldorf, Hamburg, Hanover, Karlsruhe-Baden-Baden, Leipzig-Halle, Nuremberg, Sylt, Stuttgart, Usedom.

Bicycle

Cycling is allowed on all roads and highways but not on the autobahns (motorways). Cyclists must follow the same rules of the road as cars and motorcycles. Helmets are not compulsory (not even for children), but wearing one is common sense. Dedicated bike lanes are common in bigger cities.

On Public Transport

Bicycles may be taken on most trains but require a separate ticket (*Fahrradkarte*), costing €9 per trip on long-distance trains (IC and EC and night trains), or €10 on international routes. You need to reserve a space at least one day ahead and leave

INTERNATIONAL FERRY COMPANIES

COUNTRY	COMPANY	CONNECTION	WEBSITE
Denmark	Scandlines	Gedser–Rostock, Rødby-Puttgarden	www.scandlines.com
	Faergen	Rønne–Sassnitz	www.faergen.dk
Finland	Finnlines	Helsinki–Travemünde, Helsinki-Rostock	www.finnlines.com
Lithuania	DFDS Seaways	Klaipėda–Kiel	www.dfdsseaways.com
Norway	Color Line	Oslo–Kiel	www.colorline.com
Sweden	Stena Line	Trelleborg–Rostock, Trelleborg-Sassnitz	www.stenaline.com
	Finnlines	Malmö–Travemünde	www.finnlines.com
	TT-Line	Trelleborg–Rostock, Trelleborg–Travemünde	www.ttline.com

your bike in the bike compartment, which is usually at the beginning or end of the train. Bicycles are not allowed on high-speed ICE trains.

The fee on local and regional trains (IRE, RB, RE, S-Bahn) is €5.50 per day. There is no charge at all on some local trains. For full details, enquire at a local station or call ☑01805-99 66 33.

Many regional bus companies have vehicles with special bike racks. Bicycles are also allowed on practically all boat and ferry services.

Rental

Most towns and cities have some sort of bicycle-hire station, often at or near the train station. Hire costs range from €7 to €20 per day and from €35 to €85 per week, depending on the model of bicycle. A minimum deposit of €30 (more for fancier bikes) and/or ID are required. Some outfits also offer a repair service or bicycle-storage facilities.

Hotels, especially in resort areas, sometimes keep a stable of bicycles for their guests, often at no charge.

Call a Bike (www. callabike-interaktiv.de) is an automated cycle-hire scheme operated by Deutsche Bahn (German Rail) in some 50 German towns and cities. In order to use it, you need a credit card to pre-register for free online or at one of the dozens of docking stations scattered around the central districts. There are English instructions at the docking stations. Once you're set up, select a bike and call the phone number marked on it in order to release the lock. When you're done, you must drop the bike at another docking station. The base fee for renting a bike is €1 for 30 minutes to a maximum of €15 per 24 hours. Fees are charged to your credit card.

In around 45 German cities, competition for Call a Bike comes from **Nextbike** (☑030-6920 5046; www.next bike.de/en), which charges €1 per 30 minutes or €9 for 24 hours. Register for free via its website or smartphone app, by phone or at rental terminals. You'll need a credit or debit card.

Boat

Considering that Germany abuts two seas and has a lake- and river-filled interior, don't be surprised to find yourself in a boat at some point. For basic transport, ferry boats are primarily used when travelling to or between the East Frisian Islands in Lower Saxony; the North Frisian Islands in Schleswig-Holstein; Helgoland, which also belongs to Schleswig-Holstein; and the islands of Poel, Rügen and Hiddensee in Mecklenburg–Western Pomerania.

Scheduled boat services operate along sections of the Rhine, the Elbe and the Danube. There are also ferry services in river sections with no or only a few bridges, as well as on major lakes such as the Chiemsee and Lake Starnberg in Bavaria and Lake Constance in Baden-Württemberg.

From around April to October, local operators run scenic river or lake cruises lasting from one hour to a full day.

Bus

Local & Regional

Buses are generally slower, less dependable and more polluting than trains, but in some rural areas they may be your only option for getting around without your own vehicle. This is especially true of the Harz Mountains, sections of the Bavarian Forest and the Alpine foothills. Separate bus companies, each with their own tariffs and schedules, operate in the different regions.

The frequency of services varies from 'rarely' to 'constantly'. Commuter-geared routes offer limited or no service in the evenings and at weekends, so keep this in mind or risk finding yourself stuck in a remote place on a Saturday night. Make it a habit to ask about special fare deals, such as daily or weekly passes or tourist tickets.

PORT CONNECTIONS

There are no direct ferry services between Germany and the UK, but you can go via the Netherlands, Belgium or France and drive or train it from there. For fare details and to book tickets, check the ferry websites or go to www.aferry.co.uk or www.ferrysavers.com.

COUNTRY	COMPANY	CONNECTION	WEBSITE
Via France	P&O Ferries	Dover–Calais	www.poferries.com
	DFDS Seaways	Dover–Dunkirk	www.dfdsseaways.com
Via Belgium	P&O Ferries	Hull–Zeebrugge	www.poferries.com
Via the Netherlands	P&O Ferries	Hull–Rotterdam	www.poferries.com
	DFDS Seaways	Newcastle–Amsterdam	www.dfdsseaways.com
	Stena Line	Harwich–Hoek van Holland	www.stenaline.com

In cities, buses generally converge at the Busbahnhof (bus terminal) or Zentraler Omnibus Bahnhof (ZOB; central bus station), which is often near the Hauptbahnhof (central train station).

Long Distance

The route network has grown enormously in recent years, making exploring Germany by coach easy, inexpensive and popular. Buses are modern, clean, comfortable and air-conditioned. Most companies offer snacks and beverages as well as free on-board wi-fi.

Fierce competition has kept prices extremely low. A trip from Berlin to Hamburg costs as little as €8, while the fare from Frankfurt to Munich averages €15.

Flixbus (☑030-300 137 300; https://global.flixbus.com) and **Eurolines** (☑in the UK 08717-818177; www.eurolines. com) are the biggest operators, but there are dozens of smaller, regional options as well. A handy site for finding out which operator goes where, when and for how much is www.buslinien suche.de.

From April to October, special tourist-geared service the **Romantic Road Coach** (☑09851-551 387; www.romantic-road.com) runs one coach daily in each direction between Frankfurt and Füssen (for Schloss Neuschwanstein) via Munich; the entire trip takes around 12 hours. There's no charge for breaking the journey and continuing the next day. Note that buses get incredibly crowded in summer. Tickets are available for the entire route or for short segments. Buy them online or from travel agents, **EurAide** (www.euraide.de; Desk 1, Reisezentrum, Hauptbahnhof; ◷10am-7pm Mon-Fri Mar-Apr & Aug-Dec, 9.30am-8pm May-Jul; ▣Hauptbahnhof, ⓤHauptbahnhof, ⓢHauptbahnhof) in Munich or Reisezentrum (travel centre) offices in larger train stations.

Car & Motorcycle

German roads are excellent and motoring around the country can be a lot of fun. The country's pride and joy is its 11,000km network of autobahns (motorways, freeways). Every 40km to 60km, you'll find elaborate service areas with petrol stations, toilet facilities and restaurants; many are open 24 hours. In between are rest stops (Rastplatz), which usually have picnic tables and toilet facilities. Orange emergency call boxes are spaced about 2km apart.

Autobahns are supplemented by an extensive network of Bundesstrassen (secondary 'B' roads, highways) and smaller Landstrassen (country roads). No tolls are charged on any public roads.

If your car is not equipped with a navigational system, having a good map or road atlas is essential, especially when negotiating the tangle of country roads. Navigating in Germany is not done by the points of the compass. That is to say that you'll find no signs saying 'north' or 'west'. Rather, you'll see signs pointing you in the direction of a city, so you'd best make sure you have a map. Maps cost a few euros and are sold at bookstores, train stations, airports and petrol stations. The best are published by Freytag & Berndt, **ADAC** (Allgemeiner Deutscher Automobil-Club; ☑for information 0800 510 1112, for roadside assistance from mobile 222 2222; www.adac.de), Falk and Euromap.

Driving in the cities can be stressful thanks to congestion and the expense and scarcity of parking. In city centres, parking is usually limited to parking lots and garages charging between €0.50 and €2.50 per hour. Note that some parking lots (Parkplatz) and garages (Parkhaus) close at night and charge an overnight fee. Many have special parking slots for women that are especially well lit and close to exits.

Many cities have electronic parking-guidance systems directing you to the nearest garage and indicating the number of available spaces. Street parking usually works on the pay-and-display system and tends to be short term (one or two hours) only. For low-cost or free long-term and overnight parking, consider leaving your car outside the centre in a Park & Ride (P+R) lot.

Automobile Associations

Germany's main motoring organisation, the **ADAC** (Allgemeiner Deutscher Automobil-Club; ☑for information 0800 510 1112, for roadside assistance from mobile 222 2222; www. adac.de), has offices in all major cities and many smaller ones. Its roadside-assistance program is also available to members of its affiliates, including British (AA), American (AAA) and Canadian (CAA) associations.

Driving Licence

Drivers need a valid driving licence. International Driving Permits (IDP) are not compulsory, but having one may help German police make sense of your home licence (always carry that, too) and may simplify the car- or motorcycle-hire process.

Car Hire

As anywhere, rates for car hire vary considerably, but you should be able to get an economy-size vehicle from about €40 to €60 per day, plus insurance and taxes. Expect surcharges for rentals originating at airports and train stations, additional drivers and one-way hire. Child or infant safety seats may be hired for about €5 per day and should be reserved at the time of booking.

Rental cars with automatic transmission are rare in Germany and will usually need to be ordered well in advance.

German Autobahns

To hire your own wheels, you'll need to be at least 25 years old and possess a valid driving licence and a major credit card. Some companies lease to drivers between the ages of 21 and 24 for an additional charge (about €12 to €20 per day). Younger people or those without a credit card are usually out of luck. For insurance reasons, driving into an Eastern European country, such as the Czech Republic or Poland, is often a no-no.

All the main international companies maintain branches at airports, major train stations and towns. These include the following:

Alamo (0800-723 9253; www.alamo.de)

Avis (069-500 700 20; www. avis.de)

Europcar (040-520 188 000; www.europcar.de)

Hertz (01806-333 535; www. hertz.de)

National (0800-121 8303; www.nationalcar.de)

Sixt (01806-25 25 25; www. sixt.de)

Pre-booked and prepaid packages arranged in your home country usually work out much cheaper than on-the-spot rentals. The same is true of fly/drive packages. Deals can be found on the internet and through companies including **Auto Europe** (in Germany 0800-560 0333; www.autoeurope.com), **Holiday**

Autos (☐in the UK 020 3740 9859; www.holidayautos.co.uk), and **DriveAway Holidays** (☐in Australia 1300 363 500; www.driveaway.com.au).

PEER-TO-PEER RENTALS

Peer-to-peer car rental is still in its infancy in Germany. The main service is Drivy (www.drivy.de). You need to sign up on its website, find a car you'd like to rent, contact the owner and sign the rental agreement at the time you're handed the keys. Renters need to be at least 21 and to have had a driving licence for at least two years. If your licence was not issued in an EU member country, Norway, Iceland or Liechtenstein, you need to have an International Drivers' License. Payment is by credit card or PayPal. Rentals include full insurance and roadside assistance. For full details, see the website.

Fuel & Spare Parts

Petrol stations, nearly all of which are self-service, are ubiquitous except in sparsely populated rural areas. Petrol is sold in litres.

Finding spare parts should not be a problem, especially in the cities, although availability depends on the age and model of your car. Be sure to have some sort of emergency roadside-assistance plan in case your car breaks down.

Insurance

German law requires that all registered vehicles, including those brought in from abroad, carry third-party-liability insurance. You could face huge costs by driving uninsured or underinsured. Germans are very fussy about their cars; even nudging someone's bumper when jostling out of a tight parking space may well result in your having to pay for an entirely new one.

Normally, private cars registered and insured in another European country do not require additional insurance, but do check this with your insurance provider before leaving home. Also

keep a record of who to contact in case of a breakdown or accident.

When hiring a vehicle, make sure your contract includes adequate liability insurance at the very minimum. Rental agencies almost never include insurance that covers damage to the vehicle itself, called Collision Damage Waiver (CDW) or Loss Damage Waiver (LDW). It's optional, but driving without it is not recommended. Some credit card companies cover CDW/LDW for a certain period if you charge the entire rental to your card; always confirm with your card issuer what it covers in Germany. Note that some local agencies may refuse to accept your credit card coverage as proof of insurance.

Road Rules

Driving is on the right-hand side of the road and standard international signs are in use. If you're unfamiliar with these, pick up a pamphlet at your local motoring organisation or visit the **ADAC** (Allgemeiner Deutscher Automobil-Club; ☐for information 0800 510 1112, for roadside assistance from mobile 222 2222; www.adac.de) website (search for 'traffic signs'). Obey the road rules and speed limits carefully.

Speed- and red-light cameras as well as radar traps are common, and notices are sent to the car's registration address, wherever that may be. If you're renting a car, the police will obtain your home address from the rental agency. There's a long list of fineable actions, including some perhaps surprising ones such as using abusive language or gestures, and running out of petrol on the autobahn.

The usual speed limits are 50km/h on main city streets and 100km/h outside built-up areas, unless otherwise marked. Limits drop to 30km/h in residential streets. And yes, it's true: there really are no speed limits on autobahns...in theory. In fact, there are many stretches

where slower speeds must be observed (near towns, road construction), so be sure to keep an eye out for those signs or risk getting ticketed. And, obviously, the higher the speed, the higher the fuel consumption and emissions.

Other important driving rules:

➡ The highest permissible blood alcohol level for drivers is 0.05%, which for most people equates to one glass of wine or two small beers.

➡ Seat belts are mandatory for all passengers, including those in the back seat. There's a €30 fine if you get caught not wearing one. If you're in an accident, not wearing a seat belt may invalidate your insurance. Children need a child seat if under four years and a seat cushion if under 12; they may not ride in the front until age 12.

➡ Motorcyclists must wear a helmet.

➡ Mobile phones may be used only if they are equipped with a hands-free kit or speakerphone.

➡ Pedestrians at crossings have absolute right of way over all motor vehicles.

➡ Always watch out for cyclists when turning right; they have the right of way.

➡ Right turns at a red light are only legal if there's a green arrow pointing to the right.

➡ Winter tyres are mandatory for snow- and ice-covered roads during the winter months (generally November to March, but check the specific regional legislation).

Hitching & Ride-Sharing

Hitching (*trampen*) is never entirely safe in any country, and we don't recommend it. That said, in some rural areas in Germany that are poorly served by public transport – such as sections of the Alpine foothills and the Bavarian Forest – it is not

WATCH YOUR SPEED

If you've decided to rent a car to experience the thrill of autobahn driving or to get off the beaten track, you're well advised to pay attention to your speed. Although you're free to (safely) burn rubber on designated stretches of major autobahns, speed limits apply everywhere else. On regional highways and roads in the Harz, it's common for the speed limit to drop from 100km/h to 70km/h, then to 50km/h, and 30km/h when approaching villages. Coming off an autobahn at 150km/h onto a sparsely trafficked rural highway, there's a natural tendency to keep driving a little faster than you should. Don't.

Mobile police patrols and fixed position speed cameras (Radarkontrole) are commonplace and pop up without warning. While you won't lose points on your home licence, you will be fined: the faster you're driving over the limit, the higher the fine, so driving 45km/h in a 30km/h zone is considered the same as doing 115km/h in a 100km/h zone. Rental car companies process speed camera fines and automatically deduct the amount from your credit card.

uncommon to see people thumbing for a ride. If you do decide to hitch, understand that you are taking a small but potentially serious risk. Remember that it's safer to travel in pairs, and be sure to let someone know where you are planning to go. It's illegal to hitchhike on autobahns and from their entry or exit ramps.

A safer, inexpensive and eco-conscious form of travelling is ride-sharing, where you travel as a passenger in a private car in exchange for some petrol money. Most arrangements are now set up via free online ride boards, such as www.blablacar.de and www.mitfahren.de. You can advertise a ride yourself or link up with a driver going to your destination.

Local Transport

Germany's cities and larger towns have efficient public-transport systems. Bigger cities, such as Berlin and Munich, integrate buses, trams, U-Bahn (underground, subway) trains and S-Bahn (suburban) trains into a single network.

Fares are determined by zones or time travelled, sometimes by both. A multi-ticket strip (Streifenkarte or 4-Fahrtenkarte) or day pass (Tageskarte) generally offers better value than a single-ride ticket. Normally, tickets must be stamped upon boarding in order to be valid. Fines are levied if you're caught without a valid ticket.

Bicycle

Germans love to cycle, be it for errands, commuting, fitness or pleasure. Many cities have dedicated bike lanes, which must be used unless obstructed. There's no helmet law, not even for children, although using one is recommended. Bikes must be equipped with a white light at the front, a red one at the back and yellow reflectors on the wheels and pedals.

Bus & Tram

Buses are a ubiquitous form of public transport, and practically all towns have their own comprehensive network. Buses run at regular intervals, with restricted services in the evenings and at weekends. Some cities operate night buses along popular routes to get night owls safely home.

Occasionally, buses are supplemented by trams (Strassenbahnen), which are usually faster because they travel on their own tracks, largely independent of other traffic. In city centres they sometimes run underground. Bus and tram drivers generally sell single tickets and day passes only.

S-Bahn

Metropolitan areas, such as Berlin and Munich, have a system of suburban trains called the S-Bahn. They are faster and cover a wider area than buses or trams but tend to be less frequent. S-Bahn lines are often linked to the national rail network and sometimes connect urban centres. Rail passes are generally valid on these services. Specific S-Bahn lines are abbreviated with 'S' followed by the number (eg S1, S7).

Taxi

Taxis are expensive and, given the excellent public transport systems, not recommended unless you're in a real hurry. (They can actually be slower than trains or trams if you're stuck in traffic.) Cabs are metered and charged at a base rate (flagfall) plus a per-kilometre fee. These charges are fixed but vary from city to city. Some drivers charge extra for bulky luggage or night-time rides. It's rarely possible to flag down a taxi; more typical is to order one by phone (look up Taxiruf in the phone book) or board at a taxi rank. If you're at a hotel or restaurant, ask staff to call one for you. Taxis also often wait outside theatres or performance venues. Smartphone owners can order a taxi via the Mytaxi app (downloadable for free via iTunes or Google Play) in more than 30 German cities.

Uber (www.uber.com), an app that allows private drivers to connect with potential passengers, is not widely used in Germany after a court ruled in 2015 that the services UberPop and UberBlack violate German transportation laws. Uber reacted by creating UberX, which uses only professionally licensed drivers and is available in Berlin, Düsseldorf and Munich. Trip costs tend to be between 3% and 12% less than regular taxi fares. Exclusive to Berlin at the time of writing is Uber-Taxi, which hooks passengers up with regular taxis. Normal rates apply.

U-Bahn

Underground (subway) trains are known as *U-Bahn* in Germany and are the fastest form of travel in big cities. Route maps are posted in all stations, and at many you'll be able to pick up a printed copy from the stationmaster or ticket office. The frequency of trains usually fluctuates with demand, meaning there are more trains during commuter rush hours than in the middle of the day. Tickets bought from vending machines must usually be validated before the start of your journey. Specific *U-Bahn* lines are abbreviated with 'U' followed by the number (eg U1, U7).

Train

Germany's rail system is operated almost entirely by **Deutsche Bahn** (Germany Railways; ☏0180-699 66 33; www.bahn.de), with a variety of train types serving just about every corner of the country. The DB website has detailed information (in English and other languages), as well as a ticket-purchasing function with detailed instructions.

There is a growing number of routes operated by private companies – such as Ostdeutsche Eisenbahn in Saxony and Bayerische Oberlandbahn in Bavaria – but integrated into the DB network.

Tickets may be bought using a credit card up to 10 minutes before departure at no surcharge. You will

need to present a printout of your ticket, as well as the credit card used to buy it, to the conductor. Smartphone users can register with Deutsche Bahn and download the ticket via the free DB Navigator app.

Tickets are also available from vending machines and agents at the *Reisezentrum* (travel centre) in train stations. The latter charge a service fee but are useful if you need assistance with planning your itinerary (if necessary, ask for an English-speaking clerk).

Children under 15 travel for free if accompanied by at least one parent or grandparent. The only proviso is that the names of children aged between six and 14 must be registered on your ticket at the time of purchase. Children under six always travel free and without a ticket.

Smaller stations have only a few ticket windows, and the smallest ones are equipped with vending machines only. English instructions are usually provided.

Tickets sold on board incur a surcharge and are not available on regional trains (RE, RB, IRE) or the *S-Bahn*. Agents, conductors and machines usually accept debit cards and major credit cards. With few exceptions (station unstaffed, vending machine broken), you will be fined if caught without a ticket.

Most train stations have coin-operated lockers (*Schliessfach*) costing from €1 to €4 per 24-hour period. Larger stations have staffed left-luggage offices (*Gepäckaufbewahrung*), which are a bit more expensive than lockers. If you leave your suitcase overnight, you'll be charged for two full days.

Reservations

➜ Seat reservations for long-distance travel are highly recommended, especially if you're travelling any time on Friday, on a Sunday afternoon, during holiday periods or in summer.

Choose from window or aisle seats, row or facing seats, or seats with a fixed table.

➜ Reservations are €4.50 (free if travelling 1st class) and can be made online and at ticket counters until 10 minutes before departure. You need to claim your seat within 15 minutes of boarding the train.

Classes

German trains have 1st- and 2nd-class cars, both of them modern and comfortable. If you're not too fussy, paying extra for 1st class is usually not worth it, except perhaps on busy travel days, when 2nd-class cars can get very crowded. Seating is either in compartments of up to six people or in open-plan carriages with panoramic windows. On ICE trains you'll also enjoy reclining seats, tables and audio systems in your armrest. Newer-generation ICE trains also have individual laptop outlets, mobile-phone reception in 1st class and, on some routes, wi-fi access.

Trains and stations are nonsmoking. ICE, IC and EC trains are air-conditioned and have a restaurant or self-service bistro.

Tickets

Standard, non-discounted train tickets tend to be quite expensive. On specific trains, a limited number of tickets are available at the discounted *Sparpreis* (saver fare). You need to book early or be lucky to snag one of these tickets, though. There's a €5 service charge if tickets are purchased by phone, from a travel agent or in the station ticket office. Other promotions, discounted tickets and special offers become available all the time. Check www.bahn.com for the latest deals.

BAHNCARD

The BahnCard is geared towards residents but may be worth considering if you plan extensive travel or return trips to Germany within one year.

Cards are available at all major train stations and **online** (Germany Railways; ☎0180-699 66 33; www.bahn.de).

BahnCard 25 Entitles you to 25% off regular and saver fares and costs €62/125 in 2nd/1st class. Partners, children, students under 27 and adults over 60 pay €39/81.

BahnCard 50 Gives you a 50% discount on regular and saver fares and costs €255/515 in 2nd/1st class. The cost drops to €69/252 for children, partners, students and adults over 60.

Special Tickets

Deutsche Bahn (Germany Railways; ☎0180-699 66 33; www.bahn.de) offers a trio of fabulous permanent rail deals: the *Schönes-Wochenende-Ticket* (Nice Weekend Ticket) the *Quer-durchs-Land-Ticket* (Around Germany Ticket) and the *Länder-Tickets* (Regional Tickets). As with regular tickets, children under 15 travel for free if accompanied by at least one parent or grandparent. Tickets can be purchased online, from vending machines or, for a €2 surcharge, from station ticket offices.

LÄNDER-TICKETS

➡ One day of unlimited travel on regional trains and local public transport within one of the German states (in some cases, also in two adjacent states) for up to five people travelling together.

➡ Available for travel in 1st and 2nd class.

➡ Tickets are valid for travel Monday to Friday from 9am to 3am the following day and on weekends from midnight until 3am the following day.

➡ Some passes are priced as a flat rate for up to five people travelling together (eg the Brandenburg-Berlin-Ticket costs €29).

➡ Other passes have staggered pricing: the first person buys the main ticket and up to four people may join for a just few euros more per ticket (eg in Bavaria, the first person pays €25; additional tickets cost €5).

➡ Some states, including Brandenburg-Berlin, offer cheaper *Nacht-Tickets* (night passes), usually valid from 6pm until 6am the following day.

QUER-DURCHS-LAND-TICKET

A weekday variation of the useful *Schönes-Wochenende-Ticket*.

➡ One day of unlimited 2nd-class travel on regional trains (IRE, RE, RB, *S-Bahn*).

➡ Available Monday to Friday 9am to 3am the following day (from midnight on national holidays) and all day on weekends.

➡ Up to five people may travel together.

➡ Costs €44 for the first ticket and €8 each for up to four additional tickets.

SCHÖNES-WOCHENENDE-TICKET

➡ One day of unlimited 2nd-class travel on regional trains (IRE, RE, RB, *S-Bahn*), plus local public transport.

➡ Available from midnight Saturday or Sunday until 3am the next day.

➡ Costs €44 for the first person and €6 for each additional person up to five in total.

German Rail Pass

If your permanent residence is outside Europe (which for this purpose includes Turkey and Russia), you qualify for the German Rail Pass (GRP). Tickets are sold through www.germanrailpasses.com and www.raileurope.com and by agents in your home country.

➡ The **GRP Flexi** allows for three, four, five, seven, 10 or 15 days of travel within one month.

➡ The **GRP Consecutive** is available for five, 10 or 15 consecutive days.

➡ Passes are valid on all trains within Germany, including ICE trains, and IC buses to Strasbourg, Prague, Krakow, Antwerp, Brussels, London, Zagreb and Copenhagen; and

---

A PRIMER ON TRAIN TYPES

Here's the low-down on the alphabet soup of trains operated by Deutsche Bahn (DB):

InterCity Express (ICE) Long-distance, high-speed trains that stop at major cities only and run at one- or two-hour intervals.

InterCity (IC), EuroCity (EC) Long-distance trains that are fast, but slower than the ICE; also run at one- and two-hour intervals and stop in major cities. EC trains run to major cities in neighbouring countries.

InterRegio-Express (IRE) Regional trains connecting cities with few intermediary stops.

City Night Line (CNL) Night trains with sleeper cars and couchettes.

RegionalBahn (RB) Local trains, mostly in rural areas, with frequent stops; the slowest in the system.

Regional Express (RE) Local trains with limited stops that link rural areas with metropolitan centres and the *S-Bahn*.

S-Bahn Local trains operating within a city and its suburban area.

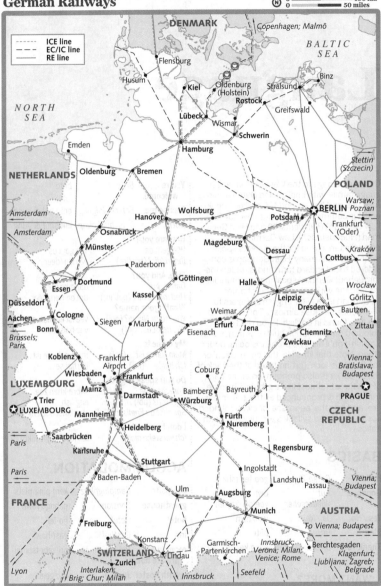

German Railways

0 — 100 km
0 — 50 miles

Legend:
- ICE line
- EC/IC line
- RE line

DENMARK
Copenhagen; Malmö
BALTIC SEA
Flensburg
Husum
Kiel
Binz
Oldenburg (Holstein)
Stralsund
Rostock
Greifswald
Lübeck
Wismar
Schwerin
NORTH SEA
Emden
Hamburg
Stettin (Szczecin)
NETHERLANDS
Oldenburg
Bremen
POLAND
Amsterdam
Amsterdam
Hanover
Wolfsburg
BERLIN
Warsaw; Poznan
Osnabrück
Potsdam
Frankfurt (Oder)
Münster
Magdeburg
Dessau
Kraków
Paderborn
Göttingen
Halle
Cottbus
Essen
Dortmund
Kassel
Leipzig
Dresden
Wrocław
Görlitz
Düsseldorf
Weimar
Bautzen
Aachen
Cologne
Siegen
Marburg
Erfurt
Jena
Chemnitz
Zittau
Bonn
Eisenach
Zwickau
Brussels; Paris
Koblenz
Frankfurt Airport
Coburg
Vienna; Bratislava; Budapest
Wiesbaden
Frankfurt
PRAGUE
LUXEMBOURG
Mainz
Bamberg
Bayreuth
CZECH REPUBLIC
Trier
LUXEMBOURG
Darmstadt
Würzburg
Mannheim
Fürth
Nuremberg
Heidelberg
Saarbrücken
Regensburg
Paris
Karlsruhe
Stuttgart
Ingolstadt
Landshut
Passau
Vienna; Budapest
Paris
Baden-Baden
Ulm
Augsburg
AUSTRIA
FRANCE
Freiburg
Munich
To Vienna; Budapest
Konstanz
Garmisch-Partenkirchen
Innsbruck; Verona; Milan; Venice; Rome
Berchtesgaden
Klagenfurt; Ljubljana; Zagreb; Belgrade
SWITZERLAND
Lindau
Zurich
Lyon
Interlaken; Brig; Chur; Milan
Innsbruck
Seefeld

---

on EuroCity trains to Kufstein, Innsbruck, Bolzano, Trento, Verona, Bologna, Liège and Brussels.

➡ Sample fares with GRP Flexi in 2nd class: three-day pass €207, seven-day pass €290. Children between six and 11 pay half fare. Children under six travel free.

➡ Those aged 12 to 25 qualify for the **German Rail Youth Pass**, starting at €166 in 2nd class for three days of travel within one month.

➡ Two adults travelling together can use the **German Rail Twin Pass**, starting at €311 in 2nd class for three days of travel within one month.

Language

German belongs to the West Germanic language family, with English and Dutch as close relatives, and has around 100 million speakers. It is commonly divided into two forms – Low German (Plattdeutsch) and High German (Hochdeutsch). Low German is an umbrella term used for the dialects spoken in Northern Germany. High German is considered the standard form and is understood throughout German-speaking communities; it's also the variety used in this chapter.

German is easy for English speakers to pronounce because almost all of its sounds are also found in English. If you read our coloured pronunciation guides as if they were English, you'll have no problems being understood. Note that kh is like the 'ch' in 'Bach' or the Scottish 'loch' (pronounced at the back of the throat), r is also pronounced at the back of the throat (almost like a g, but with some friction), zh is pronounced as the 's' in 'measure', and ü as the 'ee' in 'see' but with rounded lips. The stressed syllables are indicated with italics.

BASICS

Hello.	Guten Tag.	goo·ten tahk
Goodbye.	Auf Wiedersehen.	owf vee·der·zay·en
Yes./No.	Ja./Nein.	yah/nain
Please.	Bitte.	bi·te
Thank you.	Danke.	dang·ke

WANT MORE?

For in-depth language information and handy phrases, check out Lonely Planet's German Phrasebook. You'll find them at **shop.lonelyplanet.com**, or you can buy Lonely Planet's iPhone phrasebooks at the Apple App Store.

You're welcome.	Bitte.	bi·te
Excuse me.	Entschuldigung.	ent·shul·di·gung
Sorry.	Entschuldigung.	ent·shul·di·gung

How are you?
| Wie geht es Ihnen/dir? (pol/inf) | vee gayt es ee·nen/deer |

Fine. And you?
| Danke, gut. | dang·ke goot |
| Und Ihnen/dir? (pol/inf) | unt ee·nen/deer |

What's your name?
| Wie ist Ihr Name? (pol) | vee ist eer nah·me |
| Wie heißt du? (inf) | vee haist doo |

My name is ...
| Mein Name ist ... (pol) | main nah·me ist ... |
| Ich heiße ... (inf) | ikh hai·se ... |

Do you speak English?
| Sprechen Sie Englisch? (pol) | shpre·khen zee eng·lish |
| Sprichst du Englisch? (inf) | shprikhst doo eng·lish |

I don't understand.
| Ich verstehe nicht. | ikh fer·shtay·e nikht |

ACCOMMODATION

campsite	Campingplatz	kem·ping·plats
guesthouse	Pension	pahng·zyawn
hotel	Hotel	ho·tel
inn	Gasthof	gast·hawf
room in a private home	Privatzimmer	pri·vaht·tsi·mer
youth hostel	Jugend-herberge	yoo·gent·her·ber·ge

Do you have a ... room?	Haben Sie ein ...?	hah·ben zee ain ...
double	Doppelzimmer	do·pel·tsi·mer
single	Einzelzimmer	ain·tsel·tsi·mer

How much is it per ...?	Wie viel kostet es pro ...?	vee feel kos·tet es praw ...
night	Nacht	nakht
person	Person	per·zawn

Is breakfast included?
Ist das Frühstück inklusive? — ist das frü·shtük in·kloo·zee·ve

DIRECTIONS

Where's ...?
Wo ist ...? — vaw ist ...

What's the address?
Wie ist die Adresse? — vee ist dee a·dre·se

How far is it?
Wie weit ist es? — vee vait ist es

Can you show me (on the map)?
Können Sie es mir (auf der Karte) zeigen? — ker·nen zee es meer (owf dair kar·te) tsai·gen

How can I get there?
Wie kann ich da hinkommen? — vee kan ikh dah hin·ko·men

Turn ...	Biegen Sie ... ab.	bee·gen zee ... ab
at the corner	an der Ecke	an dair e·ke
at the traffic lights	bei der Ampel	bai dair am·pel
left	links	lingks
right	rechts	rekhts

EATING & DRINKING

I'd like to reserve a table for ...	Ich möchte einen Tisch für ... reservieren.	ikh merkh·te ai·nen tish für ... re·zer·vee·ren
(eight) o'clock	(acht) Uhr	(akht) oor
(two) people	(zwei) Personen	(tsvai) per·zaw·nen

I'd like the menu, please.
Ich hätte gern die Speisekarte, bitte. — ikh he·te gern dee shpai·ze·kar·te bi·te

What would you recommend?
Was empfehlen Sie? — vas emp·fay·len zee

What's in that dish?
Was ist in diesem Gericht? — vas ist in dee·zem

I'm a vegetarian.
Ich bin Vegetarier/ Vegetarierin. (m/f) — ikh bin ve·ge·tah·ri·er/ ve·ge·tah·ri·e·rin

That was delicious.
Das hat hervorragend geschmeckt. — das hat her·fawr·rah·gent ge·shmekt

QUESTION WORDS

How?	Wie?	vee
What?	Was?	vas
When?	Wann?	van
Where?	Wo?	vaw
Who?	Wer?	vair
Why?	Warum?	va·rum

Cheers!
Prost! — prawst

Please bring the bill.
Bitte bringen Sie die Rechnung. — bi·te bring·en zee dee rekh·nung

Key Words

bar (pub)	Kneipe	knai·pe
bottle	Flasche	fla·she
bowl	Schüssel	shü·sel
breakfast	Frühstück	frü·shtük
cold	kalt	kalt
cup	Tasse	ta·se
daily special	Gericht des Tages	ge·rikht des tah·ges
delicatessen	Feinkost-geschäft	fain·kost-ge·sheft
desserts	Nachspeisen	nakh·shpai·zen
dinner	Abendessen	ah·bent·e·sen
drink list	Getränke-karte	ge·treng·ke-kar·te
fork	Gabel	gah·bel
glass	Glas	glahs
grocery store	Lebensmittel-laden	lay·bens·mi·tel-lah·den
hot (warm)	warm	warm
knife	Messer	me·ser
lunch	Mittagessen	mi·tahk·e·sen
market	Markt	markt
plate	Teller	te·ler
restaurant	Restaurant	res·to·rahng
set menu	Menü	may·nü
spicy	würzig	vür·tsikh
spoon	Löffel	ler·fel
with/without	mit/ohne	mit/aw·ne

Meat & Fish

| beef | Rindfleisch | rint·flaish |
| carp | Karpfen | karp·fen |

NUMBERS

1	eins	ains
2	zwei	tsvai
3	drei	drai
4	vier	feer
5	fünf	fünf
6	sechs	zeks
7	sieben	zee·ben
8	acht	akht
9	neun	noyn
10	zehn	tsayn
20	zwanzig	tsvan·tsikh
30	dreißig	drai·tsikh
40	vierzig	feer·tsikh
50	fünfzig	fünf·tsikh
60	sechzig	zekh·tsikh
70	siebzig	zeep·tsikh
80	achtzig	akht·tsikh
90	neunzig	noyn·tsikh
100	hundert	hun·dert
1000	tausend	tow·sent

fish	Fisch	fish
herring	Hering	hay·ring
lamb	Lammfleisch	lam·flaish
meat	Fleisch	flaish
pork	Schweinefleisch	shvai·ne·flaish
poultry	Geflügelfleisch	ge·flü·gel·flaish
salmon	Lachs	laks
sausage	Wurst	vurst
seafood	Meeresfrüchte	mair·res·frükh·te
shellfish	Schaltiere	shahl·tee·re
trout	Forelle	fo·re·le
veal	Kalbfleisch	kalp·flaish

Fruit & Vegetables

apple	Apfel	ap·fel
banana	Banane	ba·nah·ne
bean	Bohne	baw·ne
cabbage	Kraut	krowt
capsicum	Paprika	pap·ri·kah
carrot	Mohrrübe	mawr·rü·be
cucumber	Gurke	gur·ke

fruit	Frucht/Obst	frukht/awpst
grapes	Weintrauben	vain·trow·ben
lemon	Zitrone	tsi·traw·ne
lentil	Linse	lin·ze
lettuce	Kopfsalat	kopf·za·laht
mushroom	Pilz	pilts
nuts	Nüsse	nü·se
onion	Zwiebel	tsvee·bel
orange	Orange	o·rahng·zhe
pea	Erbse	erp·se
plum	Pflaume	pflow·me
potato	Kartoffel	kar·to·fel
spinach	Spinat	shpi·naht
strawberry	Erdbeere	ert·bair·re
tomato	Tomate	to·mah·te
vegetable	Gemüse	ge·mü·ze
watermelon	Wasser-melone	va·ser-me·law·ne

Other

bread	Brot	brawt
butter	Butter	bu·ter
cheese	Käse	kay·ze
egg/eggs	Ei/Eier	ai/ai·er
honey	Honig	haw·nikh
jam	Marmelade	mar·me·lah·de
pasta	Nudeln	noo·deln
pepper	Pfeffer	pfe·fer
rice	Reis	rais
salt	Salz	zalts
soup	Suppe	zu·pe
sugar	Zucker	tsu·ker

Drinks

beer	Bier	beer
coffee	Kaffee	ka·fay
juice	Saft	zaft
milk	Milch	milkh
orange juice	Orangensaft	o·rang·zhen·zaft
red wine	Rotwein	rawt·vain
sparkling wine	Sekt	zekt
tea	Tee	tay
water	Wasser	va·ser
white wine	Weißwein	vais·vain

EMERGENCIES

Help!
Hilfe! hil·fe

Go away!
Gehen Sie weg! gay·en zee vek

Call the police!
Rufen Sie die Polizei! roo·fen zee dee po·li·tsai

Call a doctor!
Rufen Sie einen Arzt! roo·fen zee ai·nen artst

Where are the toilets?
Wo ist die Toilette? vo ist dee to·a·le·te

I'm lost.
Ich habe mich verirrt. ikh hah·be mikh fer·irt

I'm sick.
Ich bin krank. ikh bin krangk

It hurts here.
Es tut hier weh. es toot heer vay

I'm allergic to ...
Ich bin allergisch ikh bin a·lair·gish
gegen ... gay·gen ...

SHOPPING & SERVICES

I'd like to buy ...
Ich möchte ... kaufen. ikh merkh·te ... kow·fen

I'm just looking.
Ich schaue mich nur um. ikh show·e mikh noor um

Can I look at it?
Können Sie es mir ker·nen zee es meer
zeigen? tsai·gen

How much is this?
Wie viel kostet das? vee feel kos·tet das

That's too expensive.
Das ist zu teuer. das ist tsoo toy·er

Can you lower the price?
Können Sie mit dem ker·nen zee mit dem
Preis heruntergehen? prais he·run·ter·gay·en

There's a mistake in the bill.
Da ist ein Fehler dah ist ain fay·ler
in der Rechnung. in dair rekh·nung

ATM	Geldautomat	gelt·ow·to·maht
post office	Postamt	post·amt
tourist office	Fremden- verkehrsbüro	frem·den· fer·kairs·bü·raw

TIME & DATES

What time is it? *Wie spät ist es?* vee shpayt ist es

It's (10) o'clock. *Es ist (zehn) Uhr.* es ist (tsayn) oor

At what time? *Um wie viel Uhr?* um vee feel oor

At ... *Um ...* um ...

morning	Morgen	mor·gen
afternoon	Nachmittag	nahkh·mi·tahk
evening	Abend	ah·bent

yesterday	gestern	ges·tern
today	heute	hoy·te
tomorrow	morgen	mor·gen
Monday	Montag	mawn·tahk
Tuesday	Dienstag	deens·tahk
Wednesday	Mittwoch	mit·vokh
Thursday	Donnerstag	do·ners·tahk
Friday	Freitag	frai·tahk
Saturday	Samstag	zams·tahk
Sunday	Sonntag	zon·tahk

January	Januar	yan·u·ahr
February	Februar	fay·bru·ahr
March	März	merts
April	April	a·pril
May	Mai	mai
June	Juni	yoo·ni
July	Juli	yoo·li
August	August	ow·gust
September	September	zep·tem·ber
October	Oktober	ok·taw·ber
November	November	no·vem·ber
December	Dezember	de·tsem·ber

TRANSPORT

Public Transport

boat	Boot	bawt
bus	Bus	bus
metro	U-Bahn	oo·bahn
plane	Flugzeug	flook·tsoyk
train	Zug	tsook

At what time's	Wann fährt	van fairt
the ... bus?	der ... Bus?	dair... bus
first	erste	ers·te
last	letzte	lets·te
A ... to (Berlin).	Eine ... nach (Berlin).	ai·ne ... nahkh (ber·leen)
1st-class ticket	Fahrkarte erster Klasse	fahr·kar·te ers·ter kla·se
2nd-class ticket	Fahrkarte zweiter Klasse	fahr·kar·te tsvai·ter kla·se
one-way	einfache	ain·fa·khe

ticket	Fahrkarte	fahr·kar·te
return ticket	Rückfahrkarte	rük·fahr·kar·te

At what time does it arrive?
Wann kommt es an?   van komt es an

Is it a direct route?
Ist es eine direkte   ist es ai·ne di·rek·te
Verbindung?   fer·bin·dung

Does it stop at (Freiburg)?
Hält es in (Freiburg)?   helt es in (frai·boorg)

What station is this?
Welcher Bahnhof   vel·kher bahn·hawf
ist das?   ist das

What's the next stop?
Welches ist der   vel·khes ist dair
nächste Halt?   naykh·ste halt

I want to get off here.
Ich möchte hier   ikh merkh·te heer
aussteigen.   ows·shtai·gen

Please tell me when we get to (Kiel).
Könnten Sie mir bitte   kern·ten zee meer bi·te
sagen, wann wir in   zah·gen van veer in
(Kiel) ankommen?   (keel) an·ko·men

Please take me to (this address).
Bitte bringen Sie mich   bi·te bring·en zee mikh
zu (dieser Adresse).   tsoo (dee·zer a·dre·se)

platform	Bahnsteig	bahn·shtaik
ticket office	Fahrkarten-verkauf	fahr·kar·ten-fer·kowf
timetable	Fahrplan	fahr·plan

Driving & Cycling

I'd like to hire a ...	Ich möchte ein ... mieten.	ikh merkh·te ain ... mee·ten
4WD	Allrad-fahrzeug	al·raht-fahr·tsoyk
bicycle	Fahrrad	fahr·raht
car	Auto	ow·to

motorbike	Motorrad	maw·tor·raht

How much   *Wie viel kostet*   vee feel kos·tet
is it per ...?   *es pro ...?*   es praw ...

day	Tag	tahk
week	Woche	vo·khe

bicycle pump	Fahrradpumpe	fahr·raht·pum·pe
child seat	Kindersitz	kin·der·zits
helmet	Helm	helm
petrol	Benzin	ben·tseen

Does this road go to ...?
Führt diese Straße   fürt dee·ze shtrah·se
nach ...?   nahkh ...

(How long) Can I park here?
(Wie lange) Kann ich   (vee lang·e) kan ikh
hier parken?   heer par·ken

Where's a petrol station?
Wo ist eine Tankstelle?   vaw ist ai·ne tangk·shte·le

I need a mechanic.
Ich brauche einen   ikh brow·khe ai·nen
Mechaniker.   me·khah·ni·ker

My car/motorbike has broken down (at ...).
Ich habe (in ...) eine   ikh hah·be (in ...) ai·ne
Panne mit meinem   pa·ne mit mai·nem
Auto/Motorrad.   ow·to/maw·tor·raht

I've run out of petrol.
Ich habe kein   ikh hah·be kain
Benzin mehr.   ben·tseen mair

I have a flat tyre.
Ich habe eine   ikh hah·be ai·ne
Reifenpanne.   rai·fen·pa·ne

Are there cycling paths?
Gibt es Fahrradwege?   geept es fahr·raht·vay·ge

Is there bicycle parking?
Gibt es Fahrrad-   geept es fahr·raht·
Parkplätze?   park·ple·tse

GLOSSARY

(pl) indicates plural

Abtei – abbey
ADAC – Allgemeiner Deutscher Automobil Club; German Automobile Association
Allee – avenue
Altstadt – old town
Apotheke – pharmacy
Ärztehaus – medical clinic
Ärztlicher Notfalldienst – emergency medical service
Autobahn – motorway, freeway
Autofähre – car ferry

Bad – spa, bath
Bahnhof – train station
Bau – building
Bedienung – service; service charge
Berg – mountain
Besenwirtschaft – seasonal wine restaurant indicated by a broom above the doorway
Bibliothek – library
Bierkeller – cellar pub
Bierstube – traditional beer pub
BRD – Bundesrepublik Deutschland or, in English, FRG (Federal Republic of Germany); the name for Germany today; before reunification it applied to West Germany
Brücke – bridge
Brunnen – fountain, well
Bundesliga – Germany's premier football (soccer) league
Bundesrat – upper house of the German parliament
Bundestag – lower house of the German parliament
Burg – castle
Busbahnhof – bus station

CDU – Christlich Demokratische Union Deutschlands; Christian Democratic Union
Christkindlmarkt – Christmas market; also called *Weihnachtsmarkt*
CSU – Christlich-Soziale Union; Christian Social Union; Bavarian offshoot of CDU

DDR – Deutsche Demokratische Republik or, in English, GDR (German Democratic Republic); the name for former East Germany
Denkmal – memorial
Dirndl – traditional women's dress (Bavaria only)
Dom – cathedral
Dorf – village

Eiscafé – ice-cream parlour

Fahrplan – timetable
Fahrrad – bicycle
FDP – Freie Demokratische Partei; Free Democratic Party
Ferienwohnung, Ferienwohnungen (pl) – holiday flat or apartment
Fest – festival
Fleete – canals in Hamburg
Flohmarkt – flea market
Flughafen – airport
Forstweg – forestry track
FRG – see *BRD*

Garten – garden
Gasse – lane, alley
Gästehaus – guesthouse
Gaststätte, Gasthaus – informal restaurant, inn
GDR – see *DDR*
Gedenkstätte – memorial site
Gepäckaufbewahrung – left-luggage office

Hafen – harbour, port
Hauptbahnhof – central train station
Heide – heath
Hof, Höfe (pl) – courtyard
Höhle – cave
Hotel Garni – hotel without a restaurant that only serves breakfast

Imbiss – stand-up food stall; also called *Schnellimbiss*
Insel – island

Jugendherberge – youth hostel

Kanal – canal
Kapelle – chapel
Karte – ticket
Kartenvorverkauf – ticket booking office
Kino – cinema
Kirche – church
Kletterwand – climbing wall
Kloster – monastery, convent
Kneipe – pub
Konditorei – cake shop
KPD – Kommunistische Partei Deutschlands; German Communist Party
Krankenhaus – hospital
Kreuzgang – cloister
Kunst – art
Kurhaus – literally 'spa house', but usually a spa town's central building, used for events and often a casino
Kurtaxe – resort tax
Kurverwaltung – spa resort administration
Kurzentrum – spa centre

Land, Länder (pl) – state
Landtag – state parliament
Lederhosen – traditional leather trousers with braces (Bavaria only)
Lesbe, Lesben (pl) – lesbian (n)
lesbisch – lesbian (adj)

Markt – market; often used for *Marktplatz*
Marktplatz – marketplace or square; abbreviated to *Markt*
Mass – 1L tankard or stein of beer
Meer – sea
Mensa – university cafeteria
Mitwohnzentrale – accommodation-finding service for long-term stays
Münster – minster, large church, cathedral

Neustadt – new town
Nord – north
NSDAP – Nationalsozialistische Deutsche Arbeiterpartei; National Socialist German Workers' Party

Ost – east

Palais, Palast – palace, residential quarters of a castle
Paradies – literally 'paradise'; architectural term for a church vestibule or anteroom
Parkhaus – car park
Passage – shopping arcade
Pension, Pensionen (pl) – relatively cheap boarding house
Pfarrkirche – parish church
Platz – square
Putsch – revolt

Radwandern – bicycle touring
Radweg – bicycle path
Rathaus – town hall
Ratskeller – town hall restaurant
Reich – empire
Reisezentrum – travel centre in train or bus stations
Rundgang – tour, route

Saal, Säle (pl) – hall, room
Sammlung – collection
Säule – column, pillar
S-Bahn – suburban-metropolitan trains; Schnellbahn
Schatzkammer – treasury room
Schiff – ship

Schiffahrt – shipping, navigation
Schloss – palace, castle
Schnellimbiss – see *Imbiss*
schwul – gay (adj)
Schwuler, Schwule (pl) – gay (n)
SED – Sozialistische Einheitspartei Deutschlands; Socialist Unity Party
See – lake
Sesselbahn – chairlift
SPD – Sozialdemokratische Partei Deutschlands; Social Democratic Party
Stadt – city, town
Stehcafé – stand-up cafe
Strand – beach
Strasse – street; abbreviated to Str
Strausswirtschaft – seasonal wine pub indicated by wreath above the doorway
Süd – south

Tageskarte – daily menu; day ticket on public transport
Tal – valley
Teich – pond
Tor – gate
Trampen – hitchhike
Turm – tower

U-Bahn – underground train system
Ufer – bank (of river etc)
Verboten – forbidden
Verkehr – traffic
Verkehrsamt/ Verkehrsverein – tourist office
Viertel – quarter, district

Wald – forest
Wattenmeer – tidal flats on the North Sea coast
Weg – way, path
Weihnachtsmarkt – *see Christkindlmarkt*
Weingut – wine-growing estate
Weinkeller – wine cellar
Weinprobe – wine tasting
Weinstube – traditional wine bar or tavern
Wende – 'change' of 1989, ie the fall of communism that led to the collapse of the GDR and German reunification
West – west
Wiese – meadow
Wurst – sausage

Zahnradbahn – cogwheel railway
Zimmer frei – rooms available
ZOB – Zentraler Omnibusbahnhof; central bus station

Behind the Scenes

SEND US YOUR FEEDBACK

We love to hear from travellers – your comments keep us on our toes and help make our books better. Our well-travelled team reads every word on what you loved or loathed about this book. Although we cannot reply individually to your submissions, we always guarantee that your feedback goes straight to the appropriate authors, in time for the next edition. Each person who sends us information is thanked in the next edition – the most useful submissions are rewarded with a selection of digital PDF chapters.

Visit **lonelyplanet.com/contact** to submit your updates and suggestions or to ask for help. Our award-winning website also features inspirational travel stories, news and discussions.

Note: We may edit, reproduce and incorporate your comments in Lonely Planet products such as guidebooks, websites and digital products, so let us know if you don't want your comments reproduced or your name acknowledged. For a copy of our privacy policy visit lonelyplanet.com/privacy.

OUR READERS

Many thanks to the travellers who used the last edition and wrote to us with helpful hints, useful advice and interesting anecdotes.

Alessandra F Furlan, Barend Steyn, Christian Gansen, Colin Steward, David Shira, Richard McClelland, Fabian Matzerath, Florian Hahn, Heather Gilbert, Helen Rainger, Huib Derks, Lucy Stirland, Marcelo Tacuchian, Maria Luisa Colledani, Meghan Kirner, Nicolas Combremont, Patricia Rouiller, Roger Fisken, Rolf Wrelf, Tracey Burkinshaw, Valerie Alexander, William Ballantine

WRITER THANKS

Marc Di Duca

Huge thanks goes out to Robert Leckel of München Tourismus for his invaluable assistance and great ideas. I'd also like to thank all the staff of Bavaria's excellent tourist offices for their help, especially those in Landsberg, Nuremberg, Bamberg, Augsburg and Bayreuth. Finally many thanks to my wife for holding the fort while I was away in Bavaria.

Anthony Ham

I was greeted warmly wherever I went across northern Germany – there are too many people to thank them all individually. Special thanks to Thomas, Heike and Anouk Süssenbach in Flensburg. At Lonely Planet, I am grateful to my editor Niamh O'Brien for sending me to such wonderful places. To Ron

and Elaine Pumpa for such inspiration. And to my family – Marina, Carlota, Valentina and Jan: *con todo mi amor.*

Catherine Le Nevez

Vielen Dank first and foremost to Julian, and to all of the locals, fellow travellers and tourism professionals en route for insights, information and good times. Huge thanks also to Destination Editor Niamh O'Brien and the Germany team, and everyone at LP. As ever, *merci encore* to my parents, brother, *belle-sœur, neveu* and *nièce.*

Ali Lemer

A big *vielen Dank* to my editor Niamh O'Brien and fellow author Kerry Christiani; to Mara Voorhees and Mari Klement for their advice; to Low Maim and Joanna Wright for holding down the fort; to Pam Mandel, Krystyn Wells and Mark Batt for comms and morale; and to the lovely employees of the tourist offices of Lower Saxony & Bremen. Many thanks also to the numerous editors and cartographers who worked on this book.

Andrea Schulte-Peevers

Big heartfelt thanks to all these wonderful people who have plied me with tips, insights, information, ideas and encouragement (in no particular order): Henrik Tidefjärd, Barbara Woolsey, Tina Engler, Kerstin Riedel, Regine Schneider, Shaul Margulies, Frank Engster, Heiner & Claudia Schuster, Bernd Olsson, Tina Schürmann, Claudia Scheffler, Kirsten Schmidt, Renate Freiling, Tatjana Debel-Smykalla, David Eckel,

Shachar & Doreen Elkanati, Nora Durstewitz and, of course, David Peevers.

Benedict Walker

A huge, heartfelt thanks to my friends in Berlin: Matthieu, Anna, Robert & Kira, Chuck and Stefano; to Maxy, wherever you are; to the ever-lovely and patient Niamh at Lonely Planet, for keeping the good ship Ben sailing toward calmer waters; to Mum, for never giving up on me, and to my brother Andy and sister Pauline for stepping up when I needed you most.

Kerry Christiani

I'd like to say *vielen Dank* to all of the locals, travellers and tourism pros who made the road to research a pleasure. Particular thanks go to Andrea Mauch in Konstanz, Maren Schullerus in Baden-Baden, Anna Beyrer in Ulm, Yvonne Halmich in Karlsruhe, Christine Strecker in Freiburg, Sandra Nörpel in Stuttgart, and Stephanie Staudhammer in Salzburg.

Hugh McNaughtan

As always, I must thank Tasmin, Maise and Willa, my endlessly patient family, plus Niamh, the support team at Lonely Planet, and the many kind people in Thuringia who made this project a success and a pleasure.

Leonid Ragozin

I'd like to thank my wife, Masha Makeeva, for enduring my long absences and sharing some of my adventures in Saxony. Also, many thanks to all the kind and extremely helpful hotel receptionists, tourist office employees and random passersby who helped me find my bearings and overcome uncertainty on numerous occasions.

ACKNOWLEDGEMENTS

Climate map data adapted from Peel MC, Finlayson BL & McMahon TA (2007) 'Updated World Map of the Köppen-Geiger Climate Classification', *Hydrology and Earth System Sciences*, 11, 163344.

Cover photograph: Schloss Neuschwanstein, Olimpio Fantuz/4Corners ©

THIS BOOK

This 9th edition of Lonely Planet's *Germany* guide was curated by Marc Di Duca, Anthony Ham, Catherine Le Nevez, Ali Lemer, Andrea Schulte-Peevers and Benedict Walker, and researched and written by Kerry Christiani, Marc Di Duca, Anthony Ham, Catherine Le Nevez, Ali Lemer, Hugh McNaughtan, Leonid Ragozin, Andrea Schulte-Peevers and Benedict Walker. The previous edition was researched and written by Andrea Schulte-Peevers, Kerry Christiani, Marc Di Duca, Catherine Le Nevez, Tom Masters, Ryan Ver Berkmoes and Benedict Walker. This guidebook was produced by the following:

Destination Editor Niamh O'Brien

Senior Product Editor Genna Patterson

Product Editors Shona Gray, Sandie Kestell

Senior Cartographer Valentina Kremenchutskaya

Book Designer Gwen Cotter

Assisting Editors James Bainbridge, Michelle Coxall, Samantha Forge, Jennifer Hattam, Victoria Harrison, Gabrielle Innes, Rosie Nicholson, Susan Paterson, Tamara Sheward, Sam Wheeler, Simon Williamson

Cover Researcher Naomi Parker

Thanks to Ronan Abayawickrema, Catherine Naghten, Kirsten Rawlings, Kathryn Rowan, Angela Tinson, Alison Ridgway, Amanda Williamson

Index

Map Pages **000**
Photo Pages **000**

Map Pages **000**
Photo Pages **000**

Map Legend

Sights
- Beach
- Bird Sanctuary
- Buddhist
- Castle/Palace
- Christian
- Confucian
- Hindu
- Islamic
- Jain
- Jewish
- Monument
- Museum/Gallery/Historic Building
- Ruin
- Shinto
- Sikh
- Taoist
- Winery/Vineyard
- Zoo/Wildlife Sanctuary
- Other Sight

Activities, Courses & Tours
- Bodysurfing
- Diving
- Canoeing/Kayaking
- Course/Tour
- Sento Hot Baths/Onsen
- Skiing
- Snorkelling
- Surfing
- Swimming/Pool
- Walking
- Windsurfing
- Other Activity

Sleeping
- Sleeping
- Camping
- Hut/Shelter

Eating
- Eating

Drinking & Nightlife
- Drinking & Nightlife
- Cafe

Entertainment
- Entertainment

Shopping
- Shopping

Information
- Bank
- Embassy/Consulate
- Hospital/Medical
- Internet
- Police
- Post Office
- Telephone
- Toilet
- Tourist Information
- Other Information

Geographic
- Beach
- Gate
- Hut/Shelter
- Lighthouse
- Lookout
- Mountain/Volcano
- Oasis
- Park
- Pass
- Picnic Area
- Waterfall

Population
- Capital (National)
- Capital (State/Province)
- City/Large Town
- Town/Village

Transport
- Airport
- Border crossing
- Bus
- Cable car/Funicular
- Cycling
- Ferry
- Metro station
- Monorail
- Parking
- Petrol station
- S-Bahn/Subway station
- Taxi
- T-bane/Tunnelbana station
- Train station/Railway
- Tram
- Tube station
- U-Bahn/Underground station
- Other Transport

Routes
- Tollway
- Freeway
- Primary
- Secondary
- Tertiary
- Lane
- Unsealed road
- Road under construction
- Plaza/Mall
- Steps
- Tunnel
- Pedestrian overpass
- Walking Tour
- Walking Tour detour
- Path/Walking Trail

Boundaries
- International
- State/Province
- Disputed
- Regional/Suburb
- Marine Park
- Cliff
- Wall

Hydrography
- River, Creek
- Intermittent River
- Canal
- Water
- Dry/Salt/Intermittent Lake
- Reef

Areas
- Airport/Runway
- Beach/Desert
- Cemetery (Christian)
- Cemetery (Other)
- Glacier
- Mudflat
- Park/Forest
- Sight (Building)
- Sportsground
- Swamp/Mangrove

Note: Not all symbols displayed above appear on the maps in this book

Andrea Schulte-Peevers

Curator, Berlin, Around Berlin Born and raised in Germany and educated in London and at UCLA, Andrea has travelled the distance to the moon and back in her visits to some 75 countries. She has earned her living as a professional travel writer for over two decades and authored or contributed to nearly 100 Lonely Planet titles as well as to newspapers, magazines and websites around the world. She also works as a travel consultant, translator and editor. Andrea's destination expertise is especially strong when it comes to Germany, Dubai and the UAE, Crete and the Caribbean Islands. She makes her home in Berlin and tweets @ASchultePeevers.

Benedict Walker

Curator, Central Germany A beach baby from Newcastle, Australia, Benedict turned 40 in 2017 and decided to start a new life in Leipzig, Germany. Writing for Lonely Planet was a childhood dream come true, and Benedict grew up to cover big chunks of Australia, Canada, Germany, Japan, USA, Switzerland, Sweden and Japan. Benedict is on instagram @wordsandjourneys.

Kerry Christiani

Stuttgart & the Black Forest Kerry is an award-winning travel writer, photographer and Lonely Planet author, specialising in Central and Southern Europe. Based in Wales, she has authored/co-authored more than a dozen Lonely Planet titles. An adventure addict, she loves mountains, cold places and true wilderness. She features her latest work at https://its-a-small-world.com and tweets @kerrychristiani. Kerry also wrote the Plan Your Trip, Understand and Survival Guide sections.

Hugh McNaughtan

Cologne & Northern Rhineland A former English lecturer, Hugh swapped grant applications for visa applications, and turned his love of travel intro a full-time thing. Having done a bit of restaurant-reviewing in his home town (Melbourne) he's now eaten his way across four continents. He's never happier than when on the road with his two daughters. Except perhaps on the cricket field.

Leonid Ragozin

Saxony Leonid Ragozin studied beach dynamics at the Moscow State University, but for want of decent beaches in Russia, he switched to journalism and spent 12 years voyaging through different parts of the BBC, with a break for a four-year stint as a foreign correspondent for the Russian Newsweek. Leonid is currently a freelance journalist focusing largely on the conflict between Russia and Ukraine (both his Lonely Planet destinations), which prompted him to leave Moscow and find a new home in Rīga. He tweets @leonidragozin.

OUR STORY

A beat-up old car, a few dollars in the pocket and a sense of adventure. In 1972 that's all Tony and Maureen Wheeler needed for the trip of a lifetime – across Europe and Asia overland to Australia. It took several months, and at the end – broke but inspired – they sat at their kitchen table writing and stapling together their first travel guide, *Across Asia on the Cheap*. Within a week they'd sold 1500 copies. Lonely Planet was born.

Today, Lonely Planet has offices in Franklin, London, Melbourne, Oakland, Dublin, Beijing and Delhi, with more than 600 staff and writers. We share Tony's belief that 'a great guidebook should do three things: inform, educate and amuse'.

OUR WRITERS

Marc Di Duca

Curator, Munich, Bavaria A travel author for over a decade, Marc has worked for Lonely Planet in Siberia, Slovakia, Bavaria, England, Ukraine, Austria, Poland, Croatia, Portugal, Madeira and on the Trans-Siberian Railway, as well as writing and updating tens of other guides for other publishers. When not on the road, Marc lives near Mariánské Lázně in the Czech Republic with his wife and two sons.

Anthony Ham

Curator, Hamburg & the North Anthony is a freelance writer and photographer who specialises in Spain, East and Southern Africa, the Arctic and the Middle East. When he's not writing for Lonely Planet, Anthony writes about and photographs Spain, Africa and the Middle East for newspapers and magazines in Australia, the UK and US. Anthony tweets @AnthonyHamWrite.

Catherine Le Nevez

Curator, Frankfurt & Southern Rhineland Catherine's wanderlust kicked in when she roadtripped across Europe from her Parisian base aged four, and she's been hitting the road at every opportunity since, travelling to around 60 countries and completing her Doctorate of Creative Arts in Writing, Masters in Professional Writing, and postgrad qualifications in Editing and Publishing along the way. Over the past dozen-plus years she's written scores of Lonely Planet guides and articles covering Paris, France, Europe and far beyond.

Ali Lemer

Curator, Lower Saxony & Bremen Ali has been a Lonely Planet writer and editor since 2007, and has authored guidebooks and travel articles on Russia, Germany, NYC, Los Angeles, Melbourne, Bali, Hawaii, Japan and Scotland. A native New Yorker and naturalised Melburnian, Ali has also lived in Chicago, Prague and England, and has traveled extensively around Europe and North America. Ali is on instagram @alilemer.

OVER PAGE | MORE WRITERS

Published by Lonely Planet Global Limited
CRN 554153
9th edition – March 2019
ISBN 978 1 78657 376 6
© Lonely Planet 2019   Photographs © as indicated 2019
10 9 8 7 6 5 4 3 2 1
Printed in Singapore

Although the authors and Lonely Planet have taken all reasonable care in preparing this book, we make no warranty about the accuracy or completeness of its content and, to the maximum extent permitted, disclaim all liability arising from its use.

All rights reserved. No part of this publication may be copied, stored in a retrieval system, or transmitted in any form by any means, electronic, mechanical, recording or otherwise, except brief extracts for the purpose of review, and no part of this publication may be sold or hired, without the written permission of the publisher. Lonely Planet and the Lonely Planet logo are trademarks of Lonely Planet and are registered in the US Patent and Trademark Office and in other countries. Lonely Planet does not allow its name or logo to be appropriated by commercial establishments, such as retailers, restaurants or hotels. Please let us know of any misuses: lonelyplanet.com/ip.